Manx Bird Atlas

Dedicated to the memory of Mrs Mona Sharpe
– provider of excellent pies and cakes and known to the fieldworkers as 'mother'

Directors of the Manx Bird Atlas Charity
Dr J. P. Cullen, R. A. Jeavons, Dr J. P. Thorpe, C. M. Sharpe

Editing
C. M. Sharpe (principal editor), Dr J. P. Cullen and Dr J. P. Thorpe

Mapping
All maps included within this publication are reproduced from the Isle of Man Survey map with the permission of the Department of Local Government and the Environment, © Crown Copyright. The reproduction of these maps for other use is not permitted under the terms of the licence that Manx Bird Atlas has with the Department of Local Government and the Environment. Maps depicting habitat types have been derived from Phase I habitat data provided by the Isle of Man Department of Agriculture, Fisheries and Forestry.

Computing
Database design: A. C. Laidlaw
Database maintenance and development: J. P. Bishop

Artwork
Colour artwork: Dr Jeremy Paul
Anyone wishing to see more of Dr. Paul's artwork can visit his web site at www.natureartists.com/paulj.htm or contact him direct on 01624 832980 or by email: jpaul@manx.net
Logo design: Ms Jenny Kissack
Line drawings:
Alan Harris (principal contributor)
David Cook
Norman McCanch
Andrew MacKay
Simon Patient
Paul Roper
Gerard Russell
Michael Webb

Manx Bird Atlas

An Atlas of breeding and wintering birds on the Isle of Man
April 1998 to March 2003

Christopher Martyn Sharpe
Jason Paul Bishop
Dr James Patrick Cullen
Peter George Giovannini
Dr John Peter Thorpe
Peter Weaver

Liverpool University Press

First published 2007 by
Liverpool University Press
4 Cambridge Street
Liverpool L69 7ZU

British Library Cataloguing-in-Publication data
A British Library CIP record is available

ISBN 978-1-84631-039-3 cased
ISBN 978-1-84631-040-9 special edition

Typeset by Northern Phototypesetting Co. Ltd., Bolton and BBR Solutions Ltd., Chesterfield
Line drawings scanned by Mannin Media Group
Printed and bound in Slovenia by Compass Press, London

Contents

Preface

There is some debate about when the first bird atlas was produced, as it rather depends on your definition. In 1960, C. A. Norris published a series of maps showing the distribution – and indeed abundance – of thirty bird species across Britain and Ireland. Norris chose to plot this information on a 50km square grid, with data obtained in 1952 from a network of correspondents around Britain and Ireland. These correspondents had been asked to guess how many pairs of each species there were per 5km square, categorised into simple order of magnitude estimates. The resulting maps were hand-drawn and published in the scientific journal *Bird Study*. They showed, very crudely, areas where particular species were common or rare across Britain and Ireland.

The first systematic national atlas, however, wasn't published until more than a decade later, in 1976, and mapped the distributions of all of Britain and Ireland's breeding birds at a 10km square resolution, following a model adopted by botanists when mapping plant distributions. The information for the first British and Irish Atlas was collected by several thousand volunteer birdwatchers, following five years of fieldwork, and was a landmark in ornithology.

Since then, there has been a proliferation of bird atlases – more than 400 in total – around the world, though still largely restricted to North America and Europe. Within Europe, it seems that Italians, Germans, Brits, Spaniards and the French have a particular predilection for atlassing, as it is in these countries that most atlases have been published. Most have been of breeding bird distributions, with a smaller number considering wintering or year-round distributions. These atlases have varied enormously in the grid square size they have chosen to adopt (from 0.25km x 0.25km to 120km x 120km) and the area they have covered (from about 10km^2 in San Donà di Piave, Italy, to 10 million km^2 in North America). While most atlases map bird distributions, somewhat less than a third have also mapped patterns of abundance (i.e. how many birds, or an index of how many, in each grid square). Increasingly, new atlases are repeats of earlier ones, allowing changes in distribution to be revealed. Over time, the methods of data collection and presentation in the final published atlases have become increasingly sophisticated. Colour density maps produced with GIS software have replaced automated dot distribution mapping, which in turn have replaced hand drawn maps. How far we have come from the methods – though not the spirit – of Norris's attempts half a century ago.

Into this growing band of atlases comes *The Manx Bird Atlas*. How does this atlas measure up with those that have gone before? The only possible answer to this question is 'fantastically'. More than that, in fact, as it is beginning to set new standards. *The Manx Bird Atlas* maps patterns of bird abundance – estimated using a rigorous quantitative method – at a 1km square resolution during both breeding and wintering seasons. It is the first atlas in the world to do this. It is also (as far as I am aware) the only atlas to have recorded the precise locations of every bird found during fieldwork. The final maps are not only informative and attractive, but the data underlying them are enormously valuable; it is very rare for such fine resolution data to be captured so comprehensively. Because the method for determining abundance in each grid square was mostly based on counts during a set time-period, the method is entirely repeatable, allowing precise measures of the future change in numbers and range of Manx birds.

The Manx Bird Atlas was unusual in another way – much of the fieldwork was undertaken by a team of dedicated professional ornithologists. Most atlases use volunteer birdwatchers to collect field data, and while this has advantages, one downside is that areas with few people tend to receive scant coverage. Because of the level of professional input into this atlas, we can be confident that the distribution patterns obtained are a true reflection of those of Manx birds; this is not always the case for many other published atlases. Notwithstanding this, however, in the closing years of fieldwork members of the public and volunteer birdwatchers submitted about 400,000 supplementary records. This is an astonishing amount of additional information, and shows how Manx people embraced their bird atlas.

I could not finish this preface without congratulating Chris Sharpe, his co-directors and his fieldwork team for such an astonishing achievement. This atlas is more than just data and maps. It is an authoritative statement of the status of Manx birds at the turn of the millennium and will underpin their conservation in the coming decades.

Dr David W Gibbons
Sandy, June 2006
Head of Conservation Science, RSPB
Chair, European Birds Census Council 1998–2004
Author, *The New Atlas of Breeding Birds in Britain and Ireland: 1988–1991*

Abbreviations

1km square	1km x 1km square of the British grid
5km square	5km x 5km square of the British grid
10km square	10km x 10km square of the British grid
AMSL	above mean sea level
AON	apparently occupied nest
AOS	apparently occupied site
BBRC	British Birds Rarities Committee
bp	breeding pairs
BTO	British Trust for Ornithology
GDP	Gross Domestic Product
GIS	Geographical Information System
ha	Hectare
IA	individual adult
JNCC	Joint Nature Conservation Committee
MBA	Manx Bird Atlas
MWT	Manx Wildlife Trust
RSPB	Royal Society for the Protection of Birds
tetrad	2km x 2km square of the British grid
TT	Tourist Trophy

Frequently cited references

During the writing of the species accounts frequent reference was made to Calf of Man Bird Observatory reports and to the journal *Peregrine* which contains the annual Manx bird reports. Where references within an account are specific to a particular record or article these are cited. In cases where references are not specific to a particular record, or refer to trends over a number of years, obtained from an examination of records from either source, references are not included.

Instead, acknowledgement is given here to Manx National Heritage and to the Manx Ornithological Society, who respectively produce the Calf reports and *Peregrine*.

The following references have been frequently cited and have been referred to by an abbreviated title shown in parentheses.

Cramp, S. and Perrins, C.M. (eds) (1977–94). *Handbook of the Birds of Europe, the Middle East and North Africa, Birds of the Western Palearctic*, vols I–IX. Oxford University Press, Oxford. (BWP)

Cullen, J.P. and Jennings, P.P. (1986). *Birds of the Isle of Man*. Bridgeen Publications, Douglas, Isle of Man. (C&J)

Gibbons, D.W., Reid, J.B. and Chapman, R.A. (1993). *The New Atlas of Breeding Birds in Britain and Ireland 1988–1991*. T. and A.D. Poyser, London. (1988–91 Atlas)

Hagemeijer, W.J.M. and Blair, M.J. (1997). *The EBCC Atlas of European Breeding Birds*. T. and A.D. Poyser, London. (EBA)

Holloway, S. (1996). *The Historical Atlas of Breeding Birds in Britain and Ireland: 1875–1900*. T. and A.D. Poyser, London. (HA)

Kermode, P.M.C. (1901) *List of Birds of the Isle of Man with notes*. Brown and Sons, Douglas. (Kermode)

Lack, P.C. (1986). *The Atlas of Wintering Birds in Britain and Ireland*. T. and A.D. Poyser, Calton, Staffordshire. (WA)

Madoc, H.W. (1934). *Bird-life in the Isle of Man*. H.F. and G. Witherby, London. (Madoc)

Mead, C. (2000). *The State of the Nation's Birds*. Whittet Books, Stowmarket, Suffolk. (Mead)

Mitchell, P.I., Newton, S.F., Ratcliffe, N. and Dunn, T.E. (2004). *Seabird Populations of Britain and Ireland*. T. and A.D. Poyser, London. (Seabird 2000)

Ralfe, P.G. (1905). *The Birds of the Isle of Man*. D. Douglas, Edinburgh. (Ralfe)

Sharrock, J.T.R. (1976). *The Atlas of Breeding Birds in Britain and Ireland*. T. and A.D. Poyser, Berkhamsted, Hertfordshire. (1968–72 Atlas)

Wernham, C.V., Toms, M.P., Marchant, J.H., Clark. J.A., Sirwardena, G.M. and Baillie, S.R. (2002). *The Migration Atlas, movements of the birds of Britain and Ireland*. T. and A.D. Poyser, London. (MA)

Introduction

In 1996 the idea of undertaking an atlas of Manx birds took its first tentative steps. At that time the Island was in a period of prolonged economic and population growth, bringing associated social benefits, but increasing pressure on the natural environment. Though some major proposed developments included environmental impact assessments, others did not. For those schemes where local ornithologists were asked to provide information, we were often poorly placed to do so. Though some areas of the Island were regularly watched they tended to be areas of known interest, with little or no attention paid to other areas. Even for regularly watched areas the focus for record keeping was primarily on the rare or unusual rather than a structured assessment of the full suite of species.

It was considered, therefore, that the time was right to undertake a structured survey of the Island's birdlife, both during the breeding period and during the winter months. This would ensure that the Island would have up-to-date information on the status of all bird species present during those periods and this, in turn, would provide a clearer understanding of the relative significance attributed to different parts of the Island for various bird species. In addition, important baseline information would be provided which would enable future changes in bird populations to be assessed.

Much had been published already about Manx birds, most recently *Birds of the Isle of Man* by Cullen and Jennings (1986). This very readable work reported on the state of knowledge at the time of publication and also distilled much of what had been published previously. The authors also reported on the findings of a survey of the Island, undertaken from 1977 to 1981, showing in which 5km squares each breeding species was recorded. With few exceptions, however, they did not provide population estimates, or show where a given species was most commonly found. If our efforts were to increase knowledge, rather than simply update it, it was important that our methods should provide such information. In addition, the 1977–81 survey did not embrace the winter period, a gap which we were keen to fill.

We were also particularly keen to ensure as comprehensive a coverage of the Island as possible. Some atlas works in other areas of the British Isles had, by necessity of the large area they were covering, undertaken sample coverage of areas and extrapolated those results to the rest of their region of study. Others, while surveying the whole region, had used 5km squares to define survey plots, giving only a fairly broad view of the area as a whole. If our survey was to meet the goal of providing information that could be used for planning, conservation or development purposes, full coverage to a fine scale was needed. The sheer volume of fieldwork required to achieve those goals soon elevated the 'idea' into a major project that had to be completed in a relatively concise time period. This in turn led to the decision to employ staff to undertake the field research rather than to rely on volunteers.

By mid-1997 the proposed project had evolved into a five-year breeding bird survey and winter survey of the Isle of Man running between April 1998 and March 2003. Each 1km square of the Isle of Man was to be surveyed in the summer and each tetrad (2km x 2km square) in the winter. Staff would undertake the bulk of the research, with additional records being provided by members of the public. In September 1997 a charity, the 'Manx Bird Atlas', was formed as the vehicle to carry forward the research and by April 1998 sufficient funds had been raised to start work. By March 2003 all the fieldwork had been completed, despite losing an entire breeding season and much of a winter period in 2001 as a result of access restrictions imposed to prevent foot and mouth disease spreading onto the Island.

Those of us closely involved with the charity feel that we have successfully achieved our aim. Our hope is that those looking at the results will feel the same way. Its success is down to the enthusiasm and hard work of the few staff and directors of the charity and the invaluable support given by many individuals and organisations who supported our efforts.

Having started with the simple concept of a survey of the Island's breeding and wintering birds we have arrived at a point where, in addition to achieving that aim, we have

- developed highly repeatable survey methods that will allow future surveys to accurately measure change against our 'baseline' data;
- allowed for some measure of change in distribution to be identified for a range of species, by comparison with data from *Birds of the Isle of Man* (Cullen and Jennings, 1986);

- provided detailed information that can be used to aid future decision making on planning and conservation;
- provided information from which species in need of targeted conservation can be identified;
- created a quantifiable measure of each species, from which future research can study topics such as relationships between species and habitats, changing status and the success of conservation initiatives;
- enhanced the information available for people to enjoy the rich bird life that our Island has to offer.

Our research demonstrates the extraordinary variety of birdlife sustained by the range of habitats occurring on the Isle of Man. It is hard to imagine anywhere else in the British Isles where this diversity can be seen in so small a geographic area. That diversity is fragile, however, and sustained by a delicate ecological balance which remains only partially understood. We hope that our research will provide a significant resource to those shaping future policies for the Island and a benchmark for our own and future generations.

The following chapters include background information on the Isle of Man, a description of its climate and describe in full the methods employed during our work and discuss our findings. The directors and staff of the Manx Bird Atlas charity, past and present, hope you find it an enjoyable, informative and thought provoking read.

Our hope is that the charity, initially formed solely to undertake the five years research, will continue to work into the future for the benefit of Manx birdlife.

Chris Sharpe
Project Manager

The Isle of Man

The Isle of Man lies in the northern part of the Irish Sea, roughly equidistant from both Cumbria and County Down and a mere 29km from Burrow Head on the Galloway coast. Anglesey is 70km due south. Lying between latitude 54°4′ N and 54°22 ′N and longitude 4°20′W and 4°50′W, it is 51km long and reaches a maximum of 21km in width. At 572 sq. km, it is 20% smaller than Anglesey and, in European terms, almost identical in area to both Ibiza and Bornholm. It has a coastline circumference of around 120km.

Topography

A relief map of the Island shows a club-shaped range of hills running from Maughold in the north-east to Bradda Hill in the south-west and topped by a flat plain, shaped like a Phrygian cap, to the north, while a smaller lowland area occupies the south-east of the Island. The hill mass consists of three parts, the northernmost and largest rises steeply to North Barrule and then by Clagh Ouyr to Snaefell, whose summit at 621m is the highest point on the Island. The main range continues south-west for a further 11.5km where the slopes of Greeba (422m) descend to the central valley. This range, together with the Michael hills, reaching 488m in the west and those of Lonan to the east (up to 469m), accounts for 19 peaks in excess of 400m. These hill groups are cut by the long deep Sulby Glen and by the

Typical central farmland

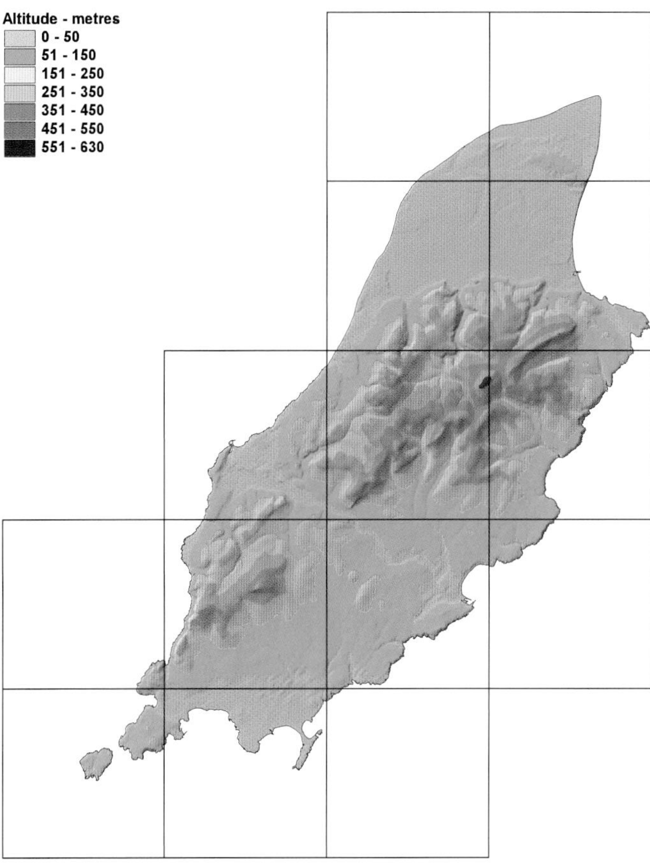

Topographical map of the Isle of Man

lesser valleys of the Glen Auldyn, Cornaa, Laxey, Glass and Rhenass rivers. The rivers Dhoo and Neb form the central valley and enter the sea respectively at Douglas and Peel.

South of this valley, the uplands are confined to the west and begin with the steep northern slopes of Slieau Whallian (333m), continuing over South Barrule (483m) to Cronk ny Arrey Laa (437m) and Lhiattee ny Beinnee, both of which fall away quite impressively to the sea. The tiny Fleshwick valley separates this upland zone from the smallest piece of high ground – Bradda Hill, only 233m high but possessing some dramatic cliff scenery, as does the coast from Port Erin round to Port St Mary. The Sound separates the main island from the Calf of Man, a rock-girt islet of 250ha rising to 128m. A further kilometre to the south-west is the Chicken Rock surmounted by its lighthouse.

Geology and the glacial period

The majority of the Island consists of hard slates and grits of the Primary Era, making up not only the hill country, but also the coastal plateaux. Small areas of igneous rocks, mainly granite, are found at Dhoon, Stoney Mountain and Oatlands. Earth movements have twisted the sheets of slate into unusual shapes, best seen at Whing on the coast to the south of Douglas. Red sandstone features on the German coast, going north from Peel, and typifies buildings in the city, while Carboniferous Limestone underlies the lowlands of Malew, the beautiful grey stone appearing in the fine buildings of Castletown. A curiosity is the basement conglomerate or pudding stone, occurring on Langness and also dating from the Carboniferous period.

Interestingly, both limestone and sandstone are found beneath the northern lowlands, but are now covered by deposits of glacial drift up to 50m deep and made up of soft clays, sands and gravel. The Ice Age ended some 20,000 years ago, having lasted several thousand years. Three phases are recognised as having affected the Island, during the first of which the upper slopes of the hills were entirely covered in ice. After a milder inter-glacial period, another general glaciation saw the ice rise to about 400m. This was responsible for the smooth blanket of drift now covering the foothills up to about 300m, the tops being almost devoid of soil. As this second glaciation retreated, so an ice-front moved south from Ulster, Galloway and Cumbria, depositing boulders on the northern plain and carrying pieces of granite south from Stoney Mountain. It has been suggested that some of the many small dubs (ponds) which are dotted across the northern plain may have resulted from large pieces of residual ice melting and leaving a depression in which water collected. Many of the, albeit stony and rather poor, agricultural soils are derived from the glacial period.

In the extreme north of the Island there is a barren strip of shingle, up to 2km broad, now forming a raised beach some 3-4m above high-water mark, although formerly below it. It provides evidence of an uplift in the level of the land in post-glacial times. In similar context, increased rates of uplift in the north Irish Sea led to the development of a land bridge embracing north-west England, the Isle of Man and south-west Scotland. This existed up to about 8,500 BC, after which global eustatic sea level rise outstripped local uplift and as sea levels rose over the next 4,500 years, so the land bridge was breached (Roberts 2004). The sea between the Island and Cumbria remains shallow and does not exceed 40m in depth, in fact several of the banks between Ramsey Bay and St Bees Head lie less than 10m below the surface. To the west however, a deep channel in excess of 100m separates the Island from Ireland.

Human factors

Little is known about the earliest human inhabitants of Mann, prior to the Celtic incursion, which occurred around 500 BC. Celtic relics can be seen all over the Island and this civilization is, to this day, the basis of Manx culture (Stenning 1958). The ninth century AD saw the arrival of the Scandinavians, and their kings were to rule the Island until the thirteenth century when Magnus was obliged to accept the overlordship of Alexander III of Scotland. During the Scandinavian period a form of legislature was established, which remains in use at the start of the twenty-first century. After an unsettled era, when the Island was ruled variously by Scottish kings and by nominees of the King of England, the Island was given to John Stanley in perpetuity, the lordship passing to the Dukes of Atholl in 1736. Towards the end of the seventeenth century a lucrative smuggling trade was established, causing the British government much irritation. The Atholls were notable beneficiaries and as a result Parliament demanded a change in the Island's constitution, which led to the Revestment Act of 1765, the Lordship of Mann passing to the Sovereign for a sum of £70,000. One hundred years later a further Act of Parliament saw Manx revenues separated from those of the United Kingdom, on condition that Tynwald (the Manx Parliament dating from 979 AD) became an elective chamber.

Agriculture and fishing had long been the basis of the Manx economy, but in 1819 the first regular steamship service was established, reducing the Island's isolation. From the mid-eighteenth century mining had become increasingly profitable, reaching its peak around 1850. Meanwhile the industrial revolution resulted in the Island becoming a popular holiday destination, with Douglas expanding considerably with the establishment of hotels and boarding houses along its great curving promenade and, in the 1870s, the creation of a railway system. Mining ceased early in the twentieth century, but it has left its mark with its wheel-cases, towers and shafts, which still provide nest sites for various corvids. The middle part of the twentieth century was a period of relative economic stagnation with, in particular, the tourist industry going into serious decline. Inexpensive package holidays to warmer destinations have taken their toll, but the TT motor cycle races, started in 1907, continue to attract considerable numbers of visitors in the late spring, as indeed do the Manx Grand Prix motor cycle races at the end of August. But prosperity has since revived, with favourable taxation encouraging new residents (and therefore a flourishing construction industry) and the establishment of the Isle of Man as an important offshore finance centre, indeed financial services now account for 36% of the GDP. A recent and important addition to the Manx economy has been the development of an increasingly buoyant film industry. The Isle of Man now has a population of 76,000.

Fauna and flora

The Isle of Man is deficient in many species which occur in the larger adjacent islands. Prominent absentees among the avifauna are such species as the woodpeckers, Dipper, Redstart, Ring Ouzel, Pied

Flycatcher, Nuthatch and Bullfinch, while, as in many other parts of Britain, the formerly plentiful Corn Bunting is now extinct. Of increasing interest is the Red-winged Laughingthrush, which has established an apparently self-sustaining population in the Ballaugh area. Notable mammalian absentees are deer, badgers, squirrels, all the mustelids, with the exception of stoats and a large population of polecat ferrets, moles and (probably) voles. Until 1987 foxes were also absent. Then an anonymous introduction took place and it was suggested that by 1990 their numbers had reached three figures. While such an estimate seems to have been a gross exaggeration, there is no doubt that a few do exist (Pooley 1997). As in Ireland, the common shrew is missing (although pygmy shrews are plentiful). There is a question mark over voles, insofar as skeletal remnants of the short-tailed vole have been found in the pellets of both *Asio* owls, yet the animal has never been found in any other situation on the Island. The brown rat is far too plentiful and both house and wood mice are abundant. Rabbits are common (melanistic forms being unusually plentiful) and there are good populations of both brown and mountain hare. The all too common occurrence of roadside corpses is testimony to the abundance of the hedgehog, bats are represented by seven species, while grey seals are plentiful. Mention should also be made of that most celebrated of all the Island's mammals, albeit domesticated – the Manx Cat. This unusual animal has no tail and rather long hind limbs; it is known as a rumpy, while the incomplete form, with a seriously abbreviated tail, is a stumpy. Another peculiarly Manx mammal is the Loaghtan sheep, a long-legged, rather goat-like, sheep with a modest covering of brown wool and one or two pairs of horns. This rare breed is farmed in increasing numbers and is now a quite familiar feature of the rural scene. Another oddity is the red-necked wallaby, an escapee from the Wildlife Park some 40 years ago, which now has a self-sustaining feral population in the curraghs of Ballaugh. A flock of feral goats frequents the fields to the south of Bulgham Bay. Freshwater fishes are very limited. Brown trout occur naturally in all the Island's streams and there are fair runs of both seatrout and salmon. Eels are abundant, flounders penetrate the lower stretches of some of the rivers, but both minnows (present in the Glass and at Kerrowdhoo) and sticklebacks are rather scarce. A variety of coarse fish have been introduced to some of the northern dubs, and perch are present in the River Neb. As in Ireland, there are no snakes (a feature attributed to St Patrick!) and the common toad is another absentee. Although we have a rather disappointing variety of Lepidoptera and Odonata, Langness is the only site in the British Isles for the lesser mottled grasshopper. Fine roadside hedges of fuchsia are a memorable feature around Ballamodha and Dalby, but the highlight of a somewhat limited flora is the dense-flowered orchid, otherwise known only from some areas of limestone pavement and dunes in the west of Ireland, but occurring on the dunes of the Ayres.

Habitats

Agricultural land

Improved farmland is a feature largely of the lowlands of the north and the south-east of the Isle of Man, with rough grazing extending into the hills from their landward margins. Mixed farming has long been practised, but although the total area of farmland has altered little since 1945, its utilization has changed considerably, with a significant increase in grassland and an even greater reduction in arable land. By 2000 arable land had decreased by 50%, the most notable fall being in land under potatoes (85%), but cereal crops also declined significantly. This decline is principally due to the area under oats dropping to only 6% of the 1945 figure, the export for porridge manufacture having ceased and popularity as an animal food greatly reduced. In contrast, barley production has increased more than thirteenfold, that of wheat has almost tripled and, since the mid-1990s maize has been gaining in popularity as a stock-feed. The majority of barley on the Island is spring-sown, creating a more wildlife-friendly environment than that sown in winter. Fodder roots, notably turnips accounting for almost 20% of the total arable area in 1945 – declined markedly and ceased to appear in the Agricultural Returns after 1990.

Roughly three-quarters of the grassland is now used for grazing, the remainder being saved as hay or silage. In the mid-1970s grass used for hay accounted for almost three times the area from which silage was being made, but by 2000 the major proportion was used for silage. Hay meadows are cut in July, but grass for silage is cut in early May, very probably contributing to the decline of ground-nesting birds such as Grey Partridge and Corncrake. In this context, it should be pointed out that the Manx Wildlife Trust (MWT) has been preserving hay meadows in its reserves in Ballaugh Curragh and this initiative was rewarded in 1999, when Corncrakes successfully nested there. Cattle have increased by almost 50% since 1945, while sheep, which utilize rough grazing, have increased by two and a half times during this period. Grazing of the coastal margins by sheep (and rabbits) is particularly beneficial for the rather specialized feeding habits of the Chough, while the increased population of sheep is regarded as a contributory factor to the success of the Raven on the Island.

In 1945, 63% of Manx farms were of less than 40ha and in 2000, although the number of farms had been reduced by about one quarter, the smaller farms still predominated, one third being of less than 8ha. Conversely, 1945 boasted only one farm of more than 120ha, yet there were 11 establishments of this size in 2000. Nevertheless the overall impression of the countryside has altered little with small fields bordered by great hedges of stones and sods, overgrown with brambles, bracken or gorse and often topped with hawthorn, fuchsia or ash. These hedges remain a valuable nesting habitat for Pied Wagtails, Wrens, Robins, Whitethroats and the declining Yellowhammer. Farm buildings provide nest sites for Swallows, while the pigeonholes, which so often occupy a gable end, accommodate Jackdaws, Starlings and House Sparrows.

In winter, the relatively large fields of the northern plain regularly attract a herd of Whooper Swans, which are often joined by Greylag Geese. Flocks of Golden Plovers, Curlews, and to a lesser extent Lapwings, also frequent these northern grasslands. Choughs are a typical feature of the fields above the Calf Sound, while gulls still follow the plough and Rooks and Jackdaws are drawn to recently seeded ploughed land. Winter stubble and the weedy field margins attract seedeaters such as Tree Sparrows, Goldfinches, Linnets and Twites. Chattering flocks of Fieldfares, often combined with Redwings, feed along the hawthorn hedges. Hen Harriers and Sparrowhawks hunt the margins of the great sod hedges. Once such a common feature of farmland in winter, the Grey Partridge is now

View over northern agricultural land

rarely seen, but the Red-legged Partridge is prospering and Pheasants can be found throughout the lowlands.

Organo-chlorine pesticides were widely used by Manx farmers resulting, notably, in the decimation of the Peregrine population. Although prior to 1988 there was no legislation on the Isle of Man controlling the import of pesticides, their use had been hugely reduced, due partly to non-availability of supplies from the United Kingdom and to practices adopted on the Island by Manx farmers on a voluntary basis (Williams 1989).

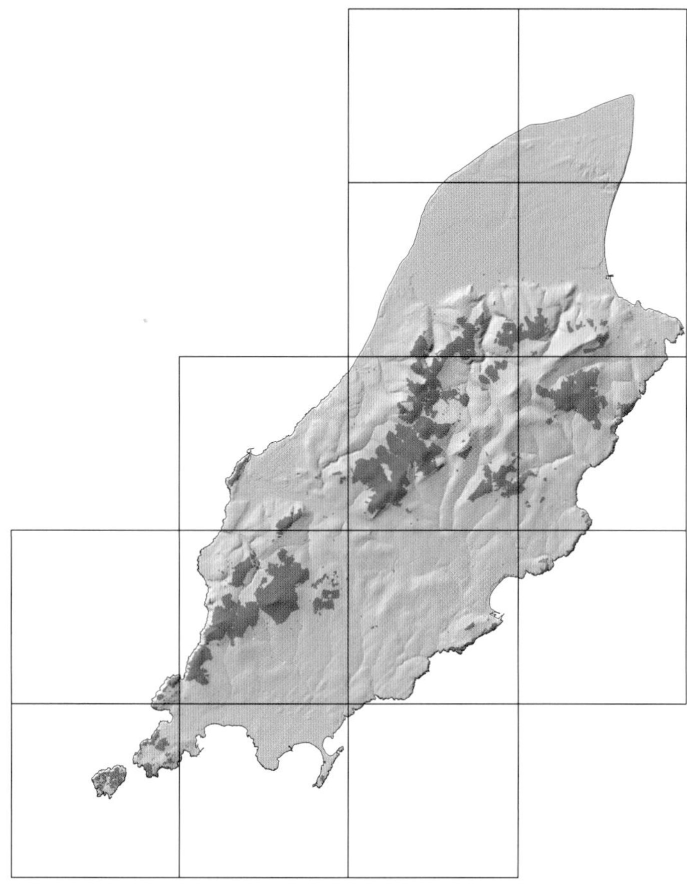

Areas of dry dwarf shrub heath (acid)

Uplands

Heather moorland

The Manx hills are typically smooth and rounded in outline and are clad in dry heath or acid grassland. Dry heath is most extensive on the southern hills, covering an area of almost 1,250ha, while on the much larger northern massif it covers over 2,800ha, especially from Greeba over Slieau Ruy and Colden to the Michael hills and, in the east, on Slieau Lhean and Slieau Ouyr, the principal species being ling heather and bell heather. Preservation of extensive tracts of heather moorland is vital for the prosperity of the Red Grouse and its area has been eroded to a considerable extent by afforestation, but also, at lower altitudes, by changes in hill-land management, resulting in the spread of bracken and gorse and the intrusion of grasses and rushes. In the 1970s and 1980s landowners, including the Government, planted large areas of conifers of very questionable economic value, while over-grazing by sheep and careless burning, as distinct from the essential, disciplined, rotational burning, have also taken their toll. Recent decisions to cease planting conifers on upland heath and the introduction of heather-burning regulations are both designed to protect this valuable habitat.

Grassy uplands

Acid grassland covers 2,400ha of the northern hills, including North Barrule and the ridge to Clagh Ouyr, Snaefell, Mullagh Ouyr, Beinn y Phott and much of Carraghan, but is of negligible extent in the south. Overall, the proportion of acid grassland to dry heath is approximately 5:8. Sometimes, for example on the north-eastern slopes of Snaefell, where the grass is short there is a struggling growth of cowberry. Sheep graze up to the summits of the highest hills and their corpses provide carrion for Ravens and Hooded Crows. Herring

Grassy uplands at Mt Karrin

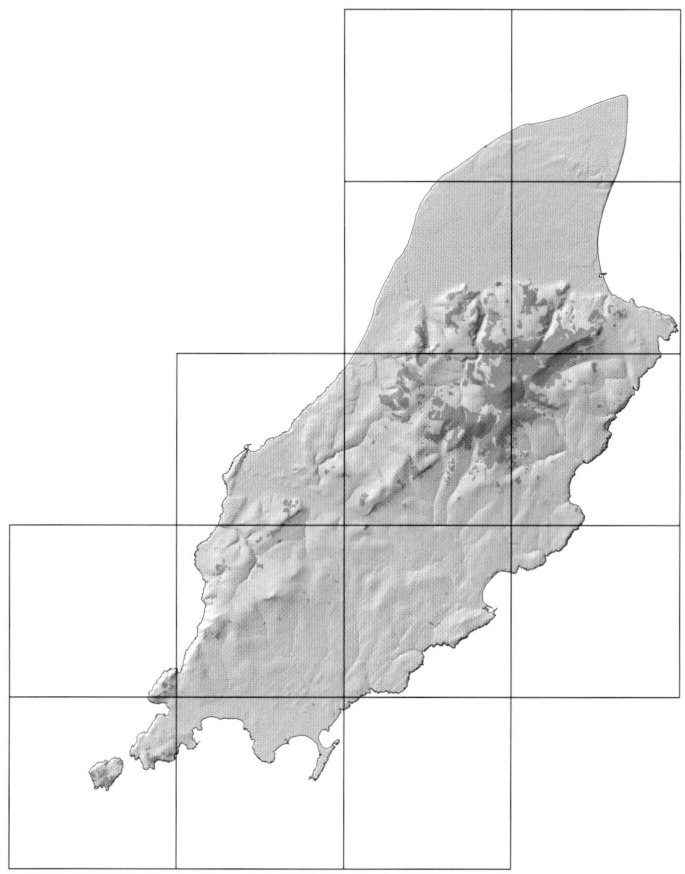

Areas of improved and semi-improved acid grassland

Upper Laxey valley

Gulls nest on the peculiarly bare summit of Sartfell at 450m and also on the north side of Slieau Freoghane.

Lower hill country

Descending a little from the rather bleak moorland to about 300m, one comes across the upper limit of enclosure by stone walls and there are, in places, considerable forests of bracken. Here there is a fine change of colours as the seasons progress: in spring bluebells flower in profusion to be replaced by the bright green bracken, which, in autumn becomes a rich red-brown. This is a particular feature of the sides of Sulby Glen, and of the Corrany and Laxey valleys. Quite luxuriant growths of bilberry cover many of the sod hedges and banks and survive within the moorland plantations at, for example, South Barrule. Crofters, who had smallholdings in the hills, deserted their properties many decades ago, leaving the tholtans, their collapsed walls and quite often a lone tramman tree (elder) as a lasting reminder. Relics of the mining industry still remain, better built and in a much better state of repair than these old farm buildings, their wheel cases, engine houses and shafts providing occasional nest sites for Choughs.

Bare rock

Bare rock, occurring naturally, is very sparse on the Island. There are modest rocky outcrops high on the eastern slopes of North Barrule, on the Carrick overlooking Sulby Glen and on the south-east side of Greeba, now concealed by plantation; but vertical inland cliffs are only found in quarries.

The Manx hill country is particularly the domain of the Raven, which, having occupied all the natural rocky sites mentioned above, as well as many quarries, is now nesting to an increasing extent in trees. It provides excellent hunting ground for the substantial population of Hen Harriers and, outside the summer months, the Merlin. The most abundant passerine is the Meadow Pipit, and Skylarks are also plentiful. Stonechats, typical moorland birds, occur sparingly (in comparison with their coastal abundance) and Wheatears frequent the stone walls – plentiful on passage, a few stay to breed. Wrens also penetrate well into the hills and are found in the bracken and among the overgrown rocky gorges characterizing the headwaters of many of the streams.

Woodlands

By 5000 BC the Island was heavily wooded, oak being the dominant species. However, the arrival of Neolithic man around 1500 BC heralded the gradual destruction of the forest, as it was felled to provide building material and cleared for agriculture. Even so, by the end of the eleventh century, there was still reasonably extensive woodland, but 300 years later the Island was effectively treeless, except perhaps for some surviving trees, notably on some of the coastal cliffs of Lonan and Maughold. It is reasonable to suppose that this period of treelessness deprived the Island of likely former woodland residents such as Jay and Bullfinch. The same may also be true of Tawny Owls, the woodpeckers and the Nuthatch, although these species are also missing from Ireland.

Reafforestation began in the mid-seventeenth century and one hundred years later planting began at Bishopscourt, to be followed by plantings around such country mansions as Ballamoar (Patrick), Ballachurry (Andreas) and Injebreck. Other great houses such as Billown Mooar, the Nunnery, Kirby, Milntown, Ballakillingan and (especially) Ballamoar (Jurby) still have quite extensive parkland, together with areas of denser mixed woodland with a fair shrub layer. All have at some time held large rookeries and some have also accommodated heronries.

Coniferous plantations

During the 1880s the first major plantations were established at Archallagan, South Barrule and Greeba. Much felling took place during both the First and Second World Wars and it was not until the early 1950s that replanting and the establishment of new plantations began in earnest. By 1987 there were 50 conifer plantations ranging in size from just 1ha (the Ayres) to 611ha (South Barrule, which is continuous with Stoney Mountain to the east, and Corlea and Cringle to the west). In all, coniferous plantation accounts for 2,400ha of the Island's surface. Mature conifer plantation is a poor ornithological habitat in which the principal species are the Coal Tit and Goldcrest, although Long-eared Owls, Siskins and, sometimes, Crossbills can be found in the smaller stands. From an economical point of view much of the planting can now be seen in retrospect to have been ill-advised, resulting in substantial areas of failure, notably at Glen Rushen (poor drainage), Archallagan (excessive exposure and heather check), Stoney Mountain (boulder-strewn granite with thin soils), Eairy Beg and the higher rocky parts of Greeba (too high and exposed) (Williams 1989). By 1977 Glen Rushen had an extensive area of long heather scattered with struggling conifers and it was here that the Hen Harrier first bred on the Island. Other beneficiaries have been Stonechats and Lesser Redpolls. Failed parts of the Stoney Mountain Plantation have attracted roosting Hen Harriers and breeding Short-eared Owls. South Barrule plantation has been cleared patchily and gradually replanted with an attractive mix of tree species of differing ages, attracting particularly Woodcock and Sparrowhawks. In their infancy the new plantations provide good hunting for Hen Harriers, Kestrels and owls.

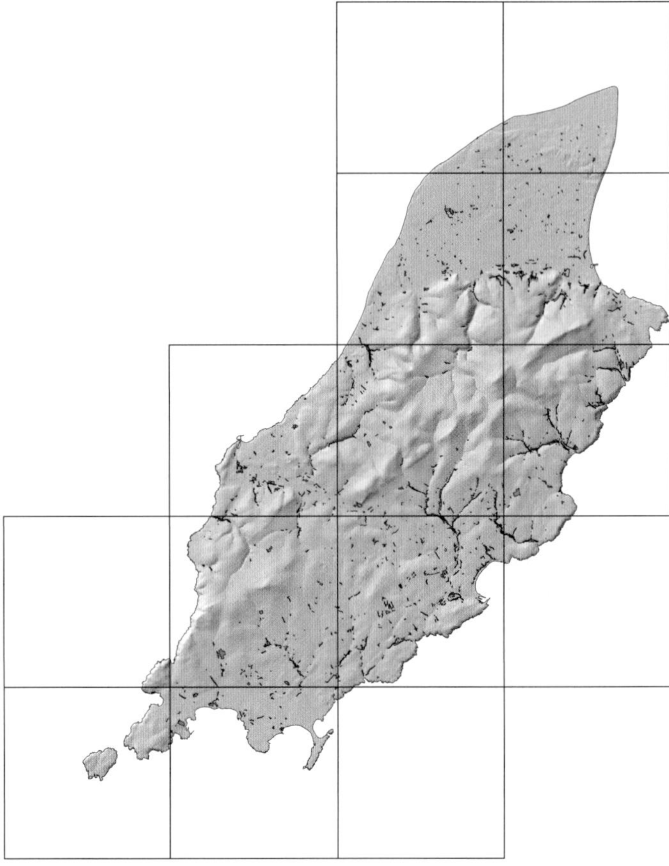

Broad-leaved woodland

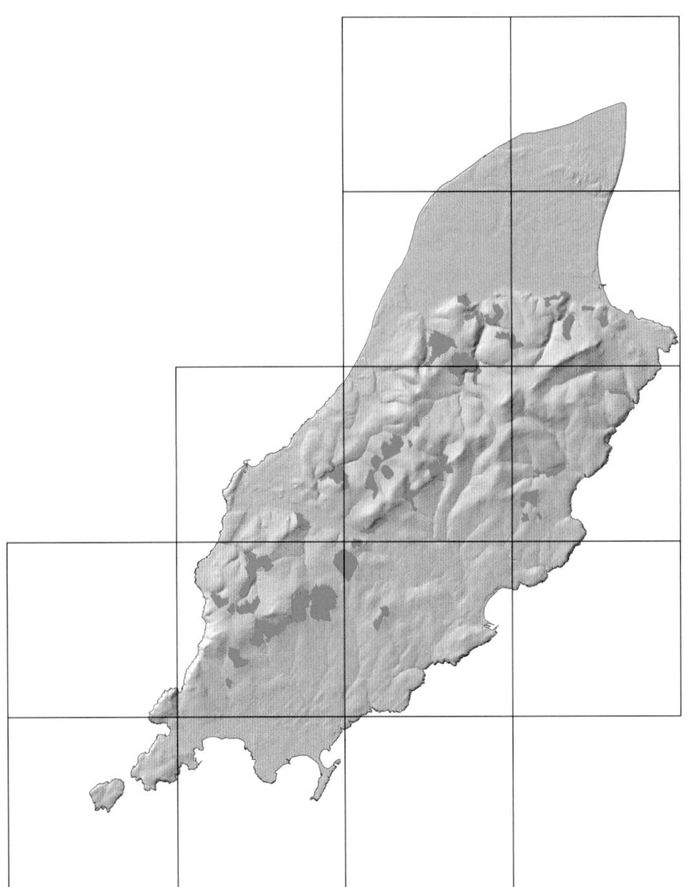

Conifer plantations

The voracious appetite of foresters has been a contentious subject throughout Britain owing to large scale destruction of heather moorland. Plans in 1985 to increase the area of afforestation by a further 2,800ha were later revised downwards to around 2,000ha and it is to be hoped that this figure might be further reduced. The main species planted are Sitka spruce, Japanese and European larch, and lodgepole, Scots and Corsican Pine.

Broad-leaved woodland

Only covering about 800ha, broad-leaved woodland is an all too scarce commodity on the Island. Towards the end of the nineteenth century planting of hardwoods took place extensively, notably in the Manx National Glens, now maintained by the Forestry Division of the Department of Agriculture, Fisheries and Forestry (DAFF). At Tholt y Will, Ballaglass, Dhoon, Molly Quirk's, Groudle and Glen Helen there are very fine stands of mature beeches, while a mixed population of tree species characterizes Laxey, Bishopscourt, Glen

Laxey valley woodlands

Maye and Silverdale, all of which have developed semi-natural characteristics and boast a good shrub layer. Of these, Silverdale has by far the most varied bird population including Blackcaps, Goldcrests, Spotted Flycatchers and Treecreepers. Oaks are disappointingly scarce, but are a feature of the Lezayre hillsides overlooking the northern plain – unfortunately they do not attract Pied Flycatchers, and Wood Warblers only nest sporadically. An unusual beech plantation is Montpelier in upper Druidale, where Ravens sometimes nest and the Island's highest rookery is found. To the south of Montpelier, the Forestry Division has recently carried out a major plantation of the hillside with broad-leaved saplings. Some of the best assortments of mixed broad-leaved trees are found bordering long-established conifer plantations such as Ballaugh, while the edge of Greeba has a patch of birches which attract Siskins and Lesser Redpolls in winter. Many of the broad-leaved woods have breeding Sparrowhawks.

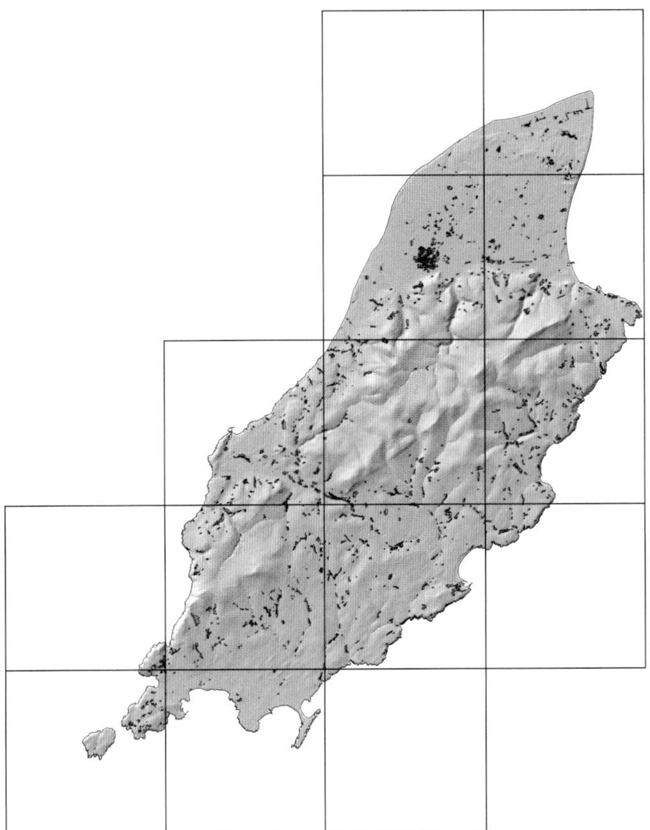

Dense Scrub

Dense scrub

Dense scrub is classified under woodland and consists of shrubs, usually less than 5m tall, forming a link between grassland and proper woodland. On the Island, the most prevalent species is European Gorse, which is particularly dense in a number of valleys such as the Baldwins and Glen Rushen and on such steep slopes as those above the quarries overlooking Douglas harbour. Other shrubs falling into this category are bramble, hawthorn, blackthorn, broom and willows. Remarkably, dense scrub covers over 1,000ha of the Island, but this figure includes the curraghs of Ballaugh and Greeba which are described elsewhere. The coastal mix of gorse, bramble and blackthorn is the prime habitat of Stonechats, Whitethroats, Dunnocks and Linnets and is also favoured by Robins and the ubiquitous Wren.

Water bodies

On the Isle of Man there are numerous rivers, streams, several reservoirs, a scatter of small dubs in the north and several areas of marshland.

Running water

Manx rivers are typically small streams, having their origins in moorland, from which they tumble via small rocky gorges through a succession of deep pools to the valley below. Their courses do not become sedate, but the waters continue to hurry over stony bottoms to the sea. Even in their latter stages they sometimes pass through rocky gorges with a succession of fine waterfalls as at Glen Maye, Cornaa, Dhoon and Santon. Weirs and salmon passes are a feature of most of the larger rivers, while their headwaters in several cases are dammed to create reservoirs. The Island's streams have long been renowned for their population of brown trout and migratory salmonids. Eels are also widespread.

The Sulby River is the longest, being 19km in length and draining the central part of the northern hills. After passing through the Claddagh below Sulby Glen, it follows a relatively sedate course, passing vertical clay banks (a potential Kingfisher site), then cutting through reed beds and, after being joined by the Glen Auldyn stream, reaches the small tidal saltmarsh at Poyll Dhooie and enters the sea through Ramsey harbour. Draining the east side of the northern hills are the Cornaa and Laxey Rivers, both about 7-8km long – the Cornaa tumbling spectacularly through Ballaglass Glen and forming a tidal lagoon prior to entering the sea, the Laxey passing through an atypical, long U-shaped valley, before being joined by the Glen Roy stream. The Laxey River receives on its northern side three significant streams the Foss, dropping in a protracted waterfall to Laggan Agneash, the Agneash stream and the Glen Drink stream, which together service the great Laxey water wheel. These little streams supported a small resident population of Dippers at the end of the nineteenth century. Most of the southern watershed supplies the Glass and the Dhoo (both over 12km in length), which join to form the Douglas River, a small contribution also being made by the 7km long Lower Sulby/ Groudle River. When it first enters the central valley, the Dhoo is little more than a sluggish drain as it passes through Greeba Curragh and, even though it gathers pace downstream, it continues to flow, unusually, over a sandy bottom. (These features are shared by the two small streams of the northern plain – the Lhen and the Killane, which drain Ballaugh Curragh.) The dominant river of the western side is the Neb (15.5km), which, like the Glass, has a good run of migrant salmonids, and is joined below St Johns by the Foxdale River (a stream on which a juvenile Dipper was found some years ago), some 5km before entering the sea at Peel.

The southern hills are drained on the eastern and southern sides by the Santon Burn and the Silverburn, both about 10km in length, although the latter gains significantly in size by its acquisition of the Awin Ruy above Ballasalla. The Silverburn and, to a lesser extent, the Santon have the best stock of wild brown trout in the Island. Finally the valley between Cronk ny Arrey Laa and South Barrule is occupied by the Glen Rushen River (7km), which empties through a long gorge into the sea at Glen Maye on the west coast.

The most typical bird of the fast flowing streams is the Grey Wagtail, while in their lower reaches most of the rivers have a good population of Mallard and Moorhen. Of particular interest recently has been the repeated occurrence of two or three Goosanders on the Glass and Sulby. Although Grey Herons regularly fish along both the Dhoo and the Glass, probably owing to the proximity of the large heronry at Kirby, in the south-east they seem to prefer the seashore.

During the mining era, the Laxey, Foxdale and Glen Rushen rivers were all seriously polluted, but recovered well in the last half of the twentieth century. More serious as we enter the twenty-first century is the acidification and raised aluminium levels of Manx watercourses. Acid rain, derived from the burning of fossil fuels, causes increased surface water acidity and a rainfall monitoring station on Beinn y Phott at an altitude of 411m has shown that rainfall on the Island is, on average, at least five times more acidic than unpolluted rainwater. In areas with acid grassland, lime is used to raise the pH and improve the quality of grazing. In the Isle of Man, reduced government subsidies have made liming more expensive, as a result of which the buffering capacity of water is eroded, resulting in increased acidity and, with it, increased concentrations of dissolved aluminium, which is highly toxic to many forms of aquatic life (Griffiths and Lamb 1995). This effect on the food chain of water birds may be critical. Water quality is affected also by effluents from farmland and, in some places, by discharge of raw sewage. These problems are being addressed by the recently formed Manx Rivers Improvement Association.

Stillwaters

The largest areas of open water are the reservoirs. First to be created were Clypse and Kerrowdhoo (1876-93) followed by West Baldwin (1904), for eighty years the Island's largest at 17ha, then Cringle, a small reservoir of 1.6ha created in 1940 and finally the most recently built and largest, the Sulby Reservoir (22ha). There is in addition a handful of very small reservoirs, which are of no ornithological

West Baldwin Reservoir

interest. Best of all are in fact the two small Foxdale dams, Eairy and Kionslieu. The two are separated by a marshy area of garey and their shallow waters attract an interesting assortment of wildfowl – fair numbers of Teal in the autumn and Pochard, Tufted Duck and the occasional Goldeneye through winter. Ruddy Duck first appeared here in 1996 and both Scaup and Gadwall are now regular visitors. Tufted Duck breed at Kionslieu. Of the larger reservoirs, Kerrowdhoo is the best, with good numbers of Mallard along with a few Wigeon and Tufted Duck in winter.

The northern plain is pockmarked with small dubs, three in particular deserving mention – Glascoe, Ballacain, and the Bishop's Dub. Just 1km from the sea, Glascoe attracts increasing numbers of Pink-footed Geese and good numbers of Wigeon and Teal, and is the best site for Shoveler. Ballacain is noted particularly for its annual visitation by Whooper Swans, which use both the dubs and the adjacent

Glascoe Dub

meadows, but it also has good riparian vegetation, making it an excellent site for Sedge Warblers and Reed Buntings. Despite its roadside situation, the small Bishop's Dub, with its rich growth of bog bean, is one of the few places where Little Grebes have nested, while during the winter months it often has a dozen or more Whooper Swans, fair numbers of Teal and up to 70 Snipe. There are other more recently established small lakes such as the dam at Shenvalla (Patrick), Port e Chee Lake and Billown House Dam, which are attracting a variety of wildfowl, but flooded quarries are less appealing, those at Scarlett and by the road at Billown being the only ones of any interest.

Without doubt the finest stillwater site on the Island is the Point of Ayre Gravel Pits. During the 1980s there were pits on either side of the road to the lighthouse. The eastern pits were rather featureless and had a little shallow water. Here there were colonies of Black-headed Gulls and Arctic Terns and in successive years a pair of Red-breasted Mergansers nested in marram grass tunnels overlooking the pits. These pits have since become a landfill site, where 70 or more Ravens now congregate. The western pits had considerably more water, with the occasional island, and also some shrub growth. They were also tenanted by Arctic Terns and Black-headed Gulls and, one year, held a nesting colony of Sandwich Terns. Sand and gravel extraction from the two large pits on the western side of the complex has now ceased and emergent vegetation is becoming established around their gravelly margins, which also have many small muddy areas, rich in invertebrates. The pits themselves are sheltered by high banks of gorse and bramble and within the complex are well established patches of willow scrub. In the south-east pit there is a good-sized well-vegetated island. In the larger north-west pit there are two further islands – one heavily vegetated, the other bare and gravelly – and it is planned to create a reed-bed in the eastern arm of this pit. August 2004 saw the signing of a tripartite agreement between the owners of the site (Island Aggregates Limited), the Isle of Man Government's Department of Agriculture, Fisheries and Forestry, and Manx Bird Atlas to form a partnership with the aim of restoring and conserving the site as a wetland nature reserve, with controlled public access and on-site education. Further pits to the south are still being worked, but a sizeable Sand Martin colony has already been established here and they will doubtless become attractive in the future.

The Gravel Pits are now being energetically monitored, with 2-3 hour birding visits nearly every day, so that more than 120 species are being recorded annually. Hitherto unheard of numbers of Pochard, Tufted Duck and Coot can now be seen, as well as good numbers of Wigeon and Goldeneye, underlining the site's value for both dabbling and diving wildfowl. Although the flock of feral Greylag Geese, now several hundred strong, can be a noisy and unwelcome intrusion, it does have the merit of pulling in increasing numbers of Pink-footed Geese, while small herds of Whooper Swans are frequent during passage periods. Breeding wildfowl include Shelduck and Eider, in addition to Greylag, Mallard and Tufted Duck. The pits also attract up to 20 varieties of wader annually, although only Lapwings (2-3 pairs) and Oystercatcher (up to 20 pairs) currently nest there. Common Sandpipers can be quite numerous on spring passage, while Ruff, Greenshank, Spotted Redshank and Green Sandpiper may occur during the return movement in autumn. Gulls dominate the bird scene around the Gravel Pits and landfill during the breeding

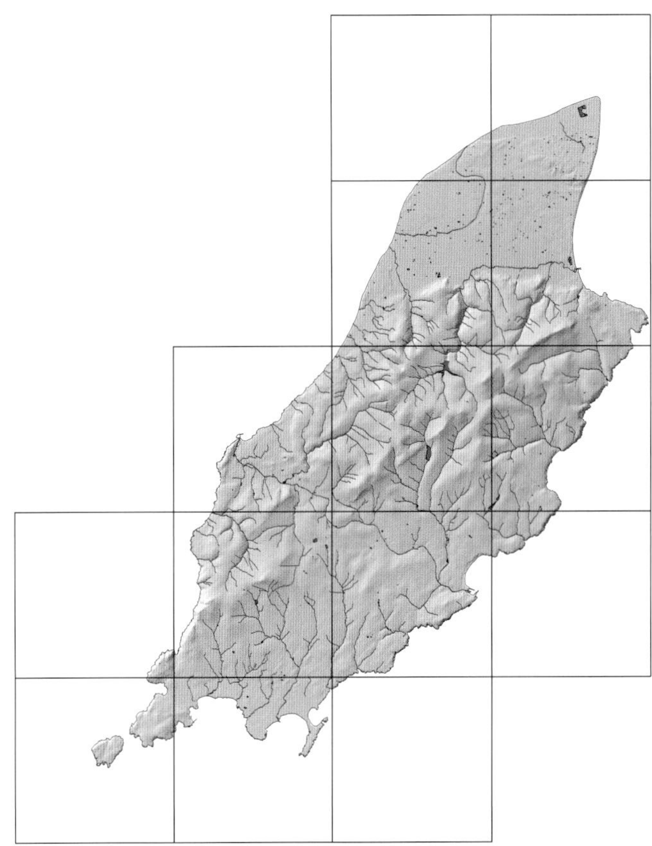

Rivers and main bodies of stillwater

season. This area now holds the largest colony of Lesser Black-backed Gulls, Herring Gulls nest in even greater number, a few pairs of Great Black-backed Gulls nest on the larger pit and a few, mostly unsuccessful, breeding attempts are made most years by Black-headed and Common Gulls. Terns no longer breed, but very small numbers of both Arctic and Sandwich do occur frequently in summer. The scrubby margins hold a thriving population of breeding Whitethroats, together with smaller numbers of Reed Bunting and Sedge Warbler around the damper areas. The most interesting passerine is the Twite, with a wintering flock of up to one hundred birds from November to March.

Marshland

Manx marshland is essentially of two types, Curragh or willow carr and garey, the rather patchy boggy land containing willow scrub, which is usable for grazing.

Ballaugh Curragh in the south-west part of the northern plain is the Island's most extensive wetland, the surviving 75ha being a relic of Lake Andreas, which had appeared at the end of the Ice Age. From the early sixteenth century the marshes were drained, but this was largely balanced by mills on the Killane and Lhen rivers, which required the maintenance of good water levels for their operation.

Ballaugh Curragh

Towards the end of the nineteenth century, following the closure of the mills, further drainage took place, significantly reducing the area of marshland. It seems likely that the Bittern was a resident of the Curragh up to this point. During the twentieth century drainage has continued to reduce the area of marshland, but the Manx Wildlife Trust has acquired a number of parcels of land, and hopefully will continue to do so, thus securing the future of this important wetland. The area is traversed by the canal-like Killane River and contains extensive areas of bog, one notable shallow pond, the Pollies, and a dense growth of willow, much of which grows in shallow water to the east of the river. Here the royal fern is a spectacular waterside plant. There is also a fair growth of birch, while in the drier areas creeping willow and bog myrtle are very prominent. Several lanes traverse the marshes and access has been further facilitated by the MWT's creation of some excellent paths, including board walks where necessary, beside and to the east of the river. This is the Island's premier site for Water Rail throughout the year, roding Woodcock are regularly seen, Long-eared Owls are resident and Teal occasionally nest. Here the call of the Curlew is every bit as evocative as the squeal of the Water Rail. Among the passerines, Grasshopper and Sedge Warbler are fairly plentiful, Reed Buntings and Lesser Redpolls are present in all seasons and parties of Siskins are prominent at times. A significant event in 1999 was the breeding of the Corncrake in one of the MWT's hay meadows on the edge of the Curragh in the Close Sartfield Reserve. Currently however, the Curragh is best known for its communal Hen Harrier roost. First identified in 1986, it soon became clear that this was the largest roost in Western Europe and in two of the years of the MBA survey over 100 birds were seen going to roost during autumn evenings. The arrival of the harriers can be watched from the MWT's viewing platform at Close Sartfield.

Other marshy areas in the north are at Lough Cranstal and the Dog Mills Lough, where there is a small *Phragmites* bed. In the central valley, there is a further narrow stretch of Curragh flanking the River Dhoo, characterized by dense willow thicket and damp overgrown areas, but no open water. Here Woodcock breed in good numbers. Garey is quite a common feature, especially in the upper parts of Santon, Malew and Arbory, at the Congary beside the lower Neb, at Cronk y Voddy and Ballacoine (Michael) and, in the east, at Ballacreetch (Onchan).

The coast

Approximately one third of the Manx coastline, beginning at Glen Mooar in the west and stretching northward to the Point of Ayre and then south to Ramsey, is made up of sand cliffs and dunes, while the remainder is rocky.

Sand cliffs and dunes

Soft sand cliffs start at Glen Mooar, continuing as far as Sartfield and interrupted at intervals by small streams entering the sea. For the most part these cliffs rarely exceed 20m in height, although at Orrisdale Head they climb to 50m and at Jurby Head 30m. There is a modest Sand Martin colony at Glen Mooar, a few Fulmars nest just to the north, one or two pairs of Shelduck nest along the Jurby coast and Wheatears are found in the sandy warren above Jurby Head. A little beyond Sartfield, the Lhen Trench runs parallel to the shore, from which it is separated by dunes which then continue almost to the Point of Ayre. This stretch of beach, shingly in its upper part and with sand exposed at low tide, is one of the Island's most important sites. Little Terns breed in several colonies, there is usually a scatter of Arctic Tern nests and both Ringed Plovers and Oystercatchers can be found nesting throughout its length. Stonechats are prominent on the scattered bushes along the dunes, within which Curlews also nest. The lower parts of the beach attract parties of Sandwich Terns during most of the summer, as well as good numbers of Kittiwakes from July onwards. Waders are plentiful, especially in autumn, when Oystercatcher, Ringed Plover, Sanderling and Dunlin can all exceed three figures. Offshore, Gannets can be seen fishing throughout the summer with often more than fifty in view at any one time, presumably birds breeding on the Scar Rocks, off the Galloway coast. Eiders, small rafts of Common Scoter and divers, mostly Red-throated, are frequently seen later in the year. At its eastern end, the beach becomes narrower and steeper, culminating in the desolate curve of the storm beach at the Point of Ayre. Behind the dunes to the east of Rue Point, in a shallow, overgrown, dry, gravel pit, a pair of Common Gulls nested for the first time in 1983. However, the principal habitat on the landward side of the dunes is the Ayres heath, made up of a carpet of lichens, burnet rose and wild thyme, together with heathers and, especially inland, gorse. The heath itself is the domain of Meadow Pipits and Skylarks, while Stonechats and Whitethroats are found in the denser peripheral vegetation. Flocks of Golden Plover are found in autumn and winter, when Short-eared Owls often hunt over the Ayres. Long-eared Owls nest in the small conifer plantation. Bordering the heath, to the west of Ballaghennie, and stretching for about 2km is a marshy strip with several permanent pools and a scatter of willow. These are the Back Slacks and are of historical interest as the first Manx nesting site of Shoveler, Redshank and Black-headed Gull. The slacks are subject to flooding in winter, as is the heathland bordering the Ballaghennie road. Behind the slacks is a further range of fixed dune, now heavily overgrown with gorse, bramble and bracken, a habitat favoured by the declining Yellowhammer. Approaching the Point of Ayre, the heath is interrupted by the Gravel Pits, described

The Ayres beach system

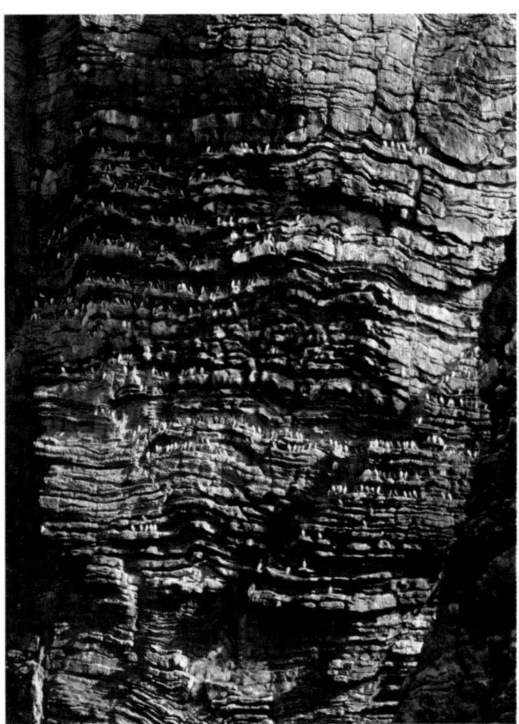

Guillemot ledges

in the Stillwaters section. After the Point, the narrow pebbly shore continues for 2-3km, then, as sand cliffs of increasing height develop, so the beach broadens. These cliffs achieve their highest point where the Bride Hills reach the coast at Shellag (70m). In 1987 there were cliff-nesting House Martins just south of Port Cranstal, while the higher cliffs, moving ever more westward due to erosion, have consistently accommodated a Ravens' nest as well as a few Fulmars'. Further south the cliffs become gradually lower and beyond the Dog Mills there is a substantial Sand Martin colony. Below the Vollan, up to fifty Goldeneye congregate about 200m offshore during the winter and around Ramsey extensive sands are exposed at low tide.

The rocky coast

At Ballure the coast becomes rocky, with cliffs and steep grassy brooghs beginning south of Port e Vullen. The slate cliffs become progressively higher as Maughold Head, the Island's most easterly point, is approached. The largest Cormorant colony is at Traie ny Feeyney and the vertical cliffs further east hold colonies of Guillemot and Kittiwake. Other breeding birds include Razorbills, Black Guillemots and occasionally Puffins. After Maughold Head, where there are sheer cliffs up to 50m high, the rocky coast continues, interrupted by two major sandy bays, backed by shingle, Laxey and Douglas and a number of small coves, Port Mooar, Dhoon, Onchan Harbour, Port Soderick, Port Grenaugh and Port Soldrick. There are several sections of high cliffs around Cornaa and Dhoon, at Bulgham Bay, Skerrip, Laxey Head and to the north of Groudle. Between Douglas and Port Soderick, spectacular cliffs over 100m high at Wallberry and Whing are easily accessible via the Marine Drive. The cliffs at Port Soderick support a colony of House Martins (14 nests in 2001). Last of the high cliffs of the east coast are around Pistol Castle, in fact the cliffs finally peter out at Cass ny Hawin.

There follows a series of low-lying promontories and bays, which continue to beyond Port St Mary. Pre-eminent in this region is the Derbyhaven/Langness complex. Derbyhaven Bay has a substantial area of intertidal mud, protected by a detached breakwater and by the rocky promontory of Fort Island. Langness is a rocky peninsula, the site of a golf course, beyond which is a picturesque area of heath, surmounted by the Herring Tower. Further on is the lighthouse and a succession of rocky humps forming the eastern border of Castletown Bay. On its western side Langness consists of wrack-covered rocks terminating at Sandwick, which marks the beginning of the broad sandy sweep of Castletown Bay. Below the ruins of Langness Farm, known as the Haunted House, is a small area of saltmarsh and just to the north is Poyll Breinn, often referred to as the Pool or the Stinking Dub, a tiny area of intertidal mud. This complex is the prime Manx site for a good variety of waders and for wildfowl, in particular Shelduck and increasing numbers of Brent Geese. Derbyhaven Bay is the Island's best site for grebes. The extensive wrack-covered rocks between the Haunted House and Sandwick support flocks of Oystercatcher and several hundred Golden Plover and Curlew. The sands of Castletown Bay give way to a rocky shore before the town, the rocks continuing around Scarlett Stack as far as Strandhall. Poyllvaaish is like a larger version of Langness Pool, Ghaw Gortagh is a rocky inlet and Strandhall has similar features to Sandwick – at low tide the Poyllvaaish to Strandhall section also has extensive wrack-covered rocks, the area being much favoured by Shelduck and Wigeon. The sands of Bay ny Carrickey are interrupted by the Kentraugh Black Rocks, but continue to Gansey Point and reappear in Port St Mary's sheltered Chapel Bay.

Just beyond the harbour, the flat rocks of Kallow Point attract a wintering flock of Purple Sandpipers and after Perwick Bay cliffs of increasing grandeur continue as far as Burroo Ned on the Calf Sound. The most interesting stretch embraces the Anvil, Sugar Loaf and Chasms, the ledges on the near vertical cliffs crowded with Guillemots and Kittiwakes. These colonies are particularly well seen from above the deeply fissured Chasms, a favourite site for Choughs, their calls ringing out above the seabird clamour. As the walker passes Black

Derbyhaven Bay

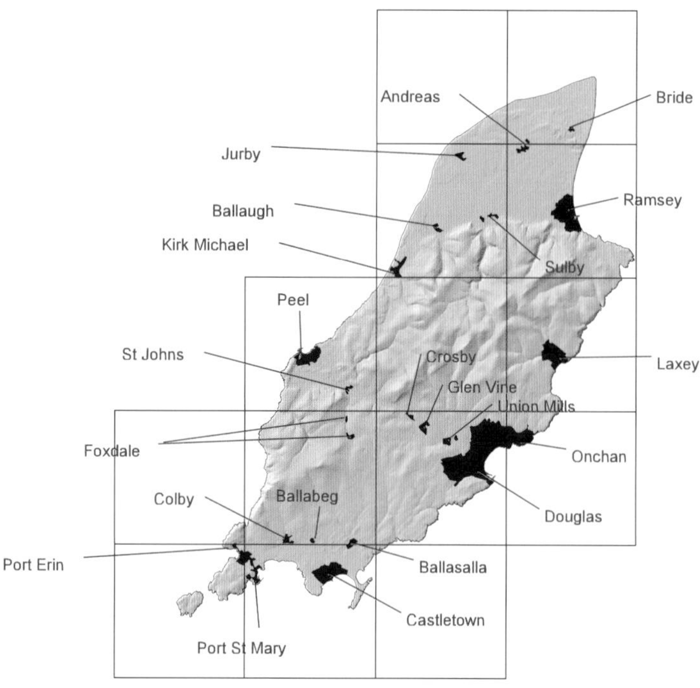

The main towns and villages on the Island

Head and approaches Spanish Head, a fine view of the Calf emerges. At the Sound Café the rocks are low and look out over the Kitterland to the Calf across the narrow strait. High cliffs again develop as the coast continues to Port Erin, a very fine sandy bay. From Bradda Head northward towards Peel several hilltops, namely Bradda Hill, Lhiattee ny Beinee and Cronk ny Arrey Laa are close to the coast, their steep western sides falling sharply to sea cliffs 30-40m in height. There are shingle beaches at Fleshwick and Traie Vane, and the low rocky promontory, Niarbyl, creates another pebbly cove. This picturesque stretch of coast was one of the first sites where Eiders started to breed in 1992 and sizeable family parties are now seen around Niarbyl each summer. There follows a stretch where farmland slopes gently to a much indented but low-lying rocky coast, then, just as the cliffs reappear they trace the Glen Rushen River inland for 500m before returning to the coast. This gorge usually has about fifteen Fulmars' nests. The final six kilometres north to Peel are characterized by a succession of fine cliffs and rocky bluffs, a favourite area for Black Guillemots, a few Puffins and, at Cashtal Mooar, Guillemots and Kittiwakes. The rocky St Patrick's Isle, the Island's most important site for Purple Sandpipers, is largely covered by Peel Castle, from which a breakwater stretches east, sheltering the harbour. Following the 700m sandy Peel Bay, the rocky coast resumes, now red sandstone rather than slate, with relatively low cliffs and a succession of small bays, continuing to Glen Mooar. The cliffs all around the Island support a good population of Peregrines and the entire rocky coastline is frequently penetrated by sea caves, which provide nest sites for Choughs.

Towns and villages

Built-up areas now cover about 4% of the Island. In the early eighteenth century only 17% of the Island's population of around 15,000 lived in the four main towns, but one hundred years later this proportion had increased to 28% of a population of 40,000 and by 1970, 73% were town dwellers. The last thirty years have witnessed expansion particularly on the fringes of Douglas and Onchan, but also around the smaller towns, including Port Erin, and villages such as Colby, Ballasalla, Kirk Michael, Ballaugh and Andreas. There are also several small industrial and business 'parks'. Swifts continue to nest in the Victorian buildings, which are a feature of the older residential areas of Douglas, while House Martins quickly colonise the contemporary housing estates. One of the features which may surprise the visitor is the relative abundance of cabbage palms, which adorn town parks and squares, as well as many gardens. There is a dwindling number of rookeries in some of the large gardens of town houses and Magpies and Hooded Crows are developing an increasing urban population. Winter brings such country-loving strangers as Grey Wagtail and Meadow Pipit to the streets of Douglas, while Oystercatchers and gulls gather in good numbers on playing fields. There are well-sheltered harbours utilizing river mouths at Douglas, Ramsey, Laxey, Castletown and Peel as well as at Port St Mary. Fishing boats are a characteristic feature, particularly at Peel and Port St Mary. Mute Swans nest in or just above several of these harbours and the principal herd of some 30 birds collects at Ramsey, together with a like number of Canada Geese.

The Calf of Man

The 250ha islet, administered by Manx National Heritage as a bird sanctuary and nature reserve, lies 700m off the south-western tip of the main island. Its rocky coastline is characterized by slate cliffs and steep bracken-clad brooghs, its principal residents being Shags, Kittiwakes, Razorbills and, more recently, Eiders, as well as Raven and Peregrine. Grant's and Cow Harbour look onto the Sound, while the bigger South Harbour provides an alternative landing site on the east coast.

Inland, much of the islet is covered in heath, with bracken particularly prominent. From the old Calf farmhouse, now a bird observatory, several fields, separated by stone walls, extend southward beside the willows of The Glen, below which is the millpond. The Mill Giau is a deep cleft leading to the sea. High above the west coast are two lighthouses, designed by Robert Stevenson and built in the early part of the nineteenth century. (They had been superseded in 1875 by the

Chicken Rock lighthouse and a new lighthouse came into use between the two old lights in 1968) (Bawden *et al.* 1972). Two hundred metres to the east of the lower lighthouse is the ruined smithy.

After an absence of about 200 years Manx Shearwaters have returned to breed in burrows on the Calf. Burrows are also visited by Storm Petrels, but there is no evidence yet of breeding. Short-eared Owls and Hen Harriers have nested on the heath and there is a small communal roost of the latter. There is a substantial flock of Loaghtan sheep and their grazing, together with that of rabbits, has been particularly beneficial to the Chough. No fewer than 14 pairs nested in 2002. Particularly successful has been a Chough nest box set up in the silo close to the Observatory and birds also regularly utilize the old lighthouses.

The Calf of Man Bird Observatory has had a warden, resident throughout the year except for a winter break, since 1959. The warden's principal ornithological activities are ringing and monitoring the breeding birds of the islet. By the end of 2002 over 197,000 birds had been ringed, with almost 2,500 recoveries.

Climate of the Isle of Man

The Isle of Man experiences a fairly typical mid-latitude, maritime, temperate climate. Along with other coastal regions of north-west Europe, temperatures are affected by the presence of the North Atlantic or Gulf Stream Drift. Winters are generally mild and summers, though pleasantly warm, are rarely hot. The weather is often humid and calm days are uncommon. The two main influences on the weather locally are the surrounding Irish Sea and the Island's own topography.

There are three main sites on the Island where long-term records have been kept. Ronaldsway (16m AMSL), where the Island's own meteorological office is situated, is on the eastern side of the Southern Plain. Douglas Borough Cemetery (85m AMSL) is on the coastal ledge in the upper part of the Island's capital, which is more or less mid-way along the east coast. Point of Ayre (9m AMSL) is at the northern tip of the Island on a raised beach on the edge of the northern Plain. In addition, the Island's Water Authority measures rainfall at a number of sites across the Island. Also, various data have been collected from other sites around the Island from time to time.

Temperature

Air temperatures tend to reflect the annual sea temperature cycle. It is usually coldest in February or perhaps early March, with average daily maximum temperatures between 7 and 8 Celsius and an average night minimum close to 3 Celsius. The warmest weather occurs in July and August with the average daily maximum between 17 and 18 Celsius at both Ronaldsway and Douglas but about one degree higher at the Point of Ayre. Air frost occurs on average some 20 times per annum at Ronaldsway, 16 times per annum in Douglas and 13 times per annum at Point of Ayre. It occurs most frequently during January and February with an average frequency of about 5 or 6 occasions for each of those months over much of the Island. It is likely to be more frequent over the higher hills (above about 300m) and also in some low-lying hollows. It should also be noted that there has been an observed decrease in the frequency of frosts since the early 1990s.

Rainfall

Rainfall varies across the Island, influenced to some extent by topography and to a larger extent by altitude.

Annual average rainfall (mm)

Southern Plain	850–900
Southern Uplands	1200–1500
Central (Peel to Douglas) Valley	1000–1300
Northern Uplands	1200–1800
Northern Plain	825–875

These figures suggest that orographic enhancement of precipitation is most effective in the hills themselves. However, where land at lower levels lies immediately to the lee of the hills, taking into account the prevailing south-westerlies, e.g. the central valley, there continues to be some orographic enhancement. This is also borne out by individual values for Ramsey where there is an annual average of about 1150mm, and the Cornaa area with about 1350mm. It should also be noted that these are average figures and individual annual totals can vary significantly. If we take Ronaldsway for example, in the driest calendar year on record (1995) there were just 683mm of rainfall and in the wettest year (1954) there was a total of 1086mm.

The driest months are April to July and the wettest months are October to January.

Snow

Prolonged and heavy snowfalls are rare, though most winters will see occasional snow showers with a little snow lying above about 300m from time to time.

Thunder

Thunderstorms are also rare. The relatively cool sea which surrounds the Island tends to attenuate the convective activity in the warm, moist, unstable, thundery plumes of air which sometimes drift across the British Isles from the south in summer. Conversely the sea is warm relative to the polar air in showery north-westerlies in winter and this can trigger the development of cumulonimbus cloud and the occasional thunderstorm.

Sunshine

Bright sunshine in coastal areas of the Island averages about 1560 hours per annum. The sunniest month is usually May with around 220 hours.

An Island or a coastal region will normally enjoy more sunshine than the inland areas of a larger land mass since daytime heating in summer will be tempered by the surrounding sea and this helps to limit the formation of fair weather cumulus clouds.

Wind

The prevailing wind direction over the Island is undoubtedly south-westerly. However, detailed examination of data shows an increase in winds between north-east and south-easterly between February and May, when the Island is less affected by cyclonic activity tracking across the North Atlantic.

Mean wind speeds for Ronaldsway (mph)

January	17.9
February	17.3
March	15.6
April	13.5
May	12.2
June	11.4
July	10.8
August	11.3
September	13.1
October	17.3
November	16.7
December	17.6

Distribution of speeds (%)

Calm	1
Less than 12mph (Force 1 to 3)	45
Between 12 and 24mph (Force 4 or 5)	43
Between 25 and 38mph (Force 6 or 7)	10
≥39mph (Gale Force 8 or more)	1

Extremes

Highest hourly mean speed	64mph
Highest gust	98mph

These data are for Ronaldsway where measurements are taken on a 10m mast on the airfield.

Higher speeds and gusts will occur over headlands and hills and where the air accelerates down into some of the Island's valleys. Known examples of locally strong winds are for instance where the north-westerlies funnel through the Fleshwick Gap and then accelerate across into Port St Mary Bay; where the south-easterlies accelerate off the hills into the Kirk Michael and Ballaugh areas and where south-westerlies accelerate and eddy off the Northern Uplands into the Ramsey area.

Typical characteristics of airstreams over the Island

North or north-easterly flows are usually Polar or Arctic in origin. Winds are seldom very strong from these directions and since the Island is effectively in the lee of Scotland and the Borders it is then usually dry and often mostly cloud free, though obviously often cold.

Airflows from the east and south-east are commonly associated with dry, continental air, cold in winter but producing the warmest days in summer. Visibility is often reduced by the haze caused by industrial activity over mainly England and sometimes from the industrial heartland of Europe.

Southerlies and south-westerlies often bring mild but moist air from the subtropical region of the North Atlantic. These winds are the ones usually associated with the frontal systems which bring bands of layered cloud and rain to the British Isles. As this moist air moves across the relatively cold waters of the Celtic and Irish Sea, condensation leads to the formation of the low cloud which envelops the Manx hills and sometimes also to sea fog banks which lap onto the Island's coasts, especially in the south and south-east. Sea fog is most common in spring and summer.

West and north-westerly winds often follow the passage of a frontal trough, bringing polar maritime air to the region. These are the flows most often associated with showers over the Isle of Man. Showers are most frequent in the north-westerlies which feed through the North Channel.

With thanks to all those people, both professional and private, who have collected data over the years and in particular to Dave Brown at Ronaldsway Meteorological Office for producing and maintaining the summaries from which this piece was written.

Historical background and methods

Ornithology on the Isle of Man has a rich history, the early years of which are beautifully distilled in C&J. From the depiction of Raven and Woodpigeon on the Scandinavian crosses of the tenth century, C&J lead us through to the time immediately prior to the publication of their work in 1986. In the years leading up to that point many eminent ornithologists, amateur enthusiasts and professional naturalists have added their knowledge to our understanding of Manx avifauna. Anyone wishing to learn more about the history of Manx birding should avail themselves of a copy of C&J and of those notable publications to which they refer.

In the time that has elapsed since the publication of C&J there have been a number of short reports on the status of individual species or groups of species. These provide a valuable insight into the changing status of those relatively few species that have been subject to a regular programme of monitoring. Most such reports are published in the volumes of *Peregrine*, a journal of Manx Natural History produced by the Manx Ornithological Society.

C&J was the first publication that, at least in part, drew information from data gathered during a systematic coverage of the Island. In the period 1977–81 each of the Island's 39 five-kilometre squares was surveyed during the summer months. For each square, species observed were given a breeding status of 'possible', 'probable' or 'confirmed', depending upon observed activity. These degrees of evidence of breeding were represented by C&J on species maps as small, medium and large dots respectively.

Although the research undertaken by C&J was valuable, developments since have changed forever the way in which atlas research is conducted. The 1977–81 research, which covered only the breeding season, simply recorded the maximum breeding status encountered for each species within each five-kilometre square. It did not quantify the numbers of each species observed, nor did it identify, more accurately than to a five-kilometre square, the locations at which species were observed. That research reflected best practice at the time and followed closely the aims of *The Atlas of Breeding Birds in Britain and Ireland* (Sharrock 1976), which presented the results of similar research conducted throughout the British Isles in the breeding seasons of 1968–72. That Atlas classified as 'possible', 'probable' or 'confirmed', the breeding status of each species recorded within each of the 3,858 ten-kilometre squares surveyed.

Unlike these earlier surveys, identifying the abundance of species now lies at the core of most modern atlas works both in the British Isles and further afield. *The Atlas of Wintering Birds in Britain and Ireland* (Lack 1986), drawing data from the winter periods 1981/82 to 1983/84 included information about the abundance of each species, citing the highest counts made of each species in each survey area on any one day. The first breeding atlas to include a measure of regional variation in abundance throughout its survey area was *The New Atlas of Breeding Birds in Britain and Ireland 1988–1991* (Gibbons *et al.* 1993). This 1988–91 atlas allowed for the measurement of abundance by standardising observation time; a method which works well, provided that the same level of observer effort is applied uniformly to each square over the entire area being surveyed. The 1988–91 atlas achieved this by dividing each ten-kilometre square in the British Isles into 25 tetrads (2×2 kilometre squares). Within each ten kilometre square at least 8 tetrads were surveyed, for two hours each. Although a large number of additional records were also gathered, it was only the timed fieldwork that was used to calculate abundance. All records were, however, used to evaluate distribution and breeding status.

Thus, a new layer of information, 'abundance', was added to the distribution and breeding status data gathered in previous surveys. The 1981–84 winter and 1988–91 breeding atlas works set the standard for all county and regional atlases that have followed since, and are the works that guided us as we planned our own Manx Atlas.

Given that the winter atlas of 1981/82 to 1983/84 and the breeding atlas of 1988–91 both included the Isle of Man in their survey area, one might wonder why a local atlas was necessary. Firstly, the passage of time since either of those pieces of research had been undertaken meant that an up-to-date review of our bird life held merit. Secondly, as a nation with its own unique cultural and natural heritage, it was appropriate for a Manx Atlas to be undertaken. Finally, though invaluable in providing information on distribution and abundance across the British Isles and Ireland as a whole, the 1981/82 to 1983/84 Winter Atlas and 1988–91 Breeding Atlas were less informative in identifying regional differences at a fine scale. They were therefore of limited value in examining distribution and abundance within the Isle of Man.

Rationale and methods

The need for up-to-date research on the Island's avifauna was first considered in 1996, partly in order to update knowledge reflected in C&J but primarily to fill important gaps in our understanding of the status of local birdlife. It was determined that the most appropriate means of doing this was to undertake breeding and wintering research, covering every one-kilometre square on the Island. Three clearly defined goals were identified to:

- establish the distribution of breeding and wintering birds;
- provide a measure of abundance; and
- produce population estimates for species breeding and wintering on the Isle of Man.

During the planning stage of the research a number of key points were agreed upon. Principal among these was the recognition that our work presented a unique opportunity to provide very detailed information on the Island's birdlife and that it was important that the most was made of that opportunity. It was determined, therefore, that the entire Island should be researched, rather than sample selected areas, the Island's relatively small geographic area making this a practical, though challenging proposition. We also strove to use information technology and mapping systems as constructively as possible, allowing the data to be analysed and presented in a variety of ways, ensuring that it is of use to as wide an audience as possible.

Breeding bird survey

Although some species start breeding early in the year, or have a prolonged breeding season, our breeding survey was undertaken from April to July in each year, the period when the majority of species are known to breed. Additional survey effort was applied to those few species known to regularly breed outside that core period. Fieldwork for the breeding bird survey commenced in April 1998 and was completed in July 2002, with staff employed by the charity surveying each 1km square of the Island that contained land above the high-water mark. During each year a number of 1km squares were selected for survey, approximately 20% of the Island being earmarked for survey in a given year. However, in 2001, no breeding surveys were possible as a result of foot-and-mouth disease access restrictions. Therefore, in 2002 approximately 40% of the Island was surveyed to make up for the lack of surveying in 2001. The survey period April–July was divided into two: April–May and June–July, with each square being surveyed twice, once in each period. This division ensured that birds that breed early, as well as migrants that breed later in the season, were likely to be recorded.

Operating singly, surveyors visited each 1km square during April–May for a standardised period of time. For squares consisting entirely of land above the high-tide mark each survey lasted two hours. For squares that comprised partly sea, survey times were reduced proportional to the amount of land that lay above the high-tide mark. Surveys were conducted only on dry mornings with wind speeds of Force 4 or less on the Beaufort Scale. This avoided under-recording as a result of birds being less mobile or not singing during adverse weather or being missed because song was masked by wind noise. Survey periods were confined to a time from just after dawn until mid-morning, that part of the day when the majority of species are most active and vocal. Typically, each surveyor conducted two full surveys each morning.

Within each 1km square the surveyor chose a route that ensured that the whole range of terrestrial habitats represented within the square were covered. The position of each bird seen or heard was plotted on a 1:4000 scale map of the 1km square, together with a code denoting its activity (see Table 1) and the route walked by the surveyor. Summary sheets were completed for each 1km square, indicating the total number of each species recorded together with the maximum breeding status for each species. The breeding status for each species was derived from the observed activity, with each bird seen or heard being assigned to one of four categories: 'non-breeding', 'possible', 'probable' or 'definite'.

Table 1 Activity codes and breeding status

These are based upon the standard BTO list with further codes added to suit our needs.

Code	Activity
'Non-breeding'	
F	Feeding flocks or individuals, where suitable breeding habitat is absent
FO, (FS etc.)	Flying over (flying south over) the 1km square and considered not to be using it
HT	Hunting, if no suitable breeding habitat present
IMM/JUV	Immature birds and juveniles
L	'Loafing' – e.g. flocks of gulls standing in fields
MI	Bird considered to be on active migration
NB/NS	Considered not to be breeding or not in suitable habitat
R	Roosting
X	Found dead
'Possible'	
H	Individual(s) seen in suitable habitat
IF	Bird(s) in flight, using the square and with suitable breeding habitat available
'Probable'	
AOS	Apparently occupied (nesting) site
D/PM	Bird(s) undertaking display or courtship, including pair observed mating
M	Bird(s) collecting or carrying nest material – unless seen to fly out of the square being surveyed
N	Bird(s) visiting a probable nest site
P	Pair in suitable habitat
SG	Singing males in suitable habitat – except migrant species heard before the cut-off date (see later)

'Definite'	
A	Agitated adult(s)
AF	Pair allo-feeding
AON	Apparently occupied nest
B	Observed nest building
CN/UN	Current nest or used nest from current year
DD	Distraction display
ES	Egg shell remains (hatched not predated)
FP	Food pass
FY	Adult carrying food (unless seen to fly from square) or faecal sac
NE/NY	Nests with eggs or young
ON	Adult indicating occupied nest
RF	Recently fledged young – including downy young of nidifugous species
SC	Soliciting call by adult
T	Adult(s) holding/defending territory

A second visit to each square was undertaken during June–July, in the same year as the first survey, a gap of at least six weeks being left between surveys. During this second visit the surveyor walked the same route as for the first visit, adopting the same recording protocol.

This approach worked well for the vast majority of species. However a different approach was needed for colonial species. Time spent counting large numbers of birds at seabird colonies or trying to identify occupied burrows at Sand Martin colonies would have significantly reduced the amount of time available to visit the rest of the square, resulting in an under-recording of other species. One option for overcoming this problem was to suspend the two-hour time period while counts of colonies were undertaken. However this would then have resulted in surveys being completed later in the morning, at a time when activity and song was less, again reducing the number of records obtained.

The preferred method of overcoming the problem was to undertake systematic counts of all seabirds and colonial nesting species outside the timed fieldwork. A census of seabirds was undertaken in 1999, as part of Seabird 2000, a census of seabirds throughout the British Isles, coordinated by the Joint Nature Conservation Committee (JNCC). A summary of the methods employed during that survey is presented later. Other colonial species were counted within the overall survey period of 1998–2003, with survey effort being timed to fit in with other workloads.

Using the data gathered during the timed visits to each 1km square the relative abundance of each species was calculated. These timed visits also provided the majority of the records from which distribution and breeding status were derived, though other records gathered by staff of the charity, volunteers and many members of the public added to our understanding of distribution and breeding status.

Though staff were asked to record every bird that they observed during their timed visits, not all of these records were used to calculate abundance. Only records of those birds deemed to be using the 1km square for breeding were used for that purpose, with birds attributed a 'non-breeding' status being excluded.

Inevitably, some subjectivity was necessary by surveyors in determining whether a given record was of a bird using the square or not. Training was given to standardise the approach adopted, with particular attention paid to how a range of summer migrants should be treated. As part of the planning process for the research a review of data from the Calf of Man Bird Observatory was undertaken. From that, each of a number of summer migrants was assigned a date, before which surveyors were asked to presume that birds of that species seen in suitable habitat or singing were still on active migration and therefore given a 'non-breeding' status. However, migrant species observed undertaking a probable (other than singing) or definite breeding activity, before the cut-off date, could be classed as breeding and therefore be included for the purpose of determining abundance.

During our research singing birds were given a 'probable' breeding status, an approach that was carefully considered before survey work commenced. Some atlas works categorised such records as 'possible' (e.g. 1988–91 Atlas), whereas others classed singing males as 'probable' only if they were heard to sing from the same place on more than one date (e.g. 1968–72 Atlas). Both approaches were designed to reduce the risk of over-stating abundance of migrants as they take account of the fact that birds do sing while still on active migration. Our approach of setting a cut-off date before which singing migrant species should be treated as 'non-breeding' largely overcomes that concern and therefore singing birds after the 'cut-off' date were treated as probably breeding, providing suitable habitat was present.

Winter atlas

Surveying for the winter period commenced from 15 November in each year and continued until the end of February the following year. These dates were chosen to minimise the risk of recording passage migrants. Originally planned for only the winters 1998–99 to 2000–01 this target proved to be too ambitious and surveying was not completed until the end of February 2003.

Though following similar principles to those adopted for the breeding bird survey, the winter research used tetrads (2km×2km) as the survey unit. During winter, many species are less tied to particular geographic areas, ranging more widely in search of food and moving larger distances to and from roosts. It was therefore considered more appropriate to use a larger survey unit for winter surveys than the 1km square used for the summer.

A total of 192 tetrads contained some area of land above the high-water mark. Tetrads comprising wholly land were surveyed for four hours, part tetrads being surveyed for a time proportional to the amount of land they contained. Surveys were undertaken only during dry days, with winds of Force 5 or less on the Beaufort Scale. Surveys did not start until at least one hour after dawn and were completed at least one hour before sunset. These time constraints were set to reduce the risk of failing to record birds that had either not arrived from, or which had already departed for, roosts.

Each tetrad was subject to a timed survey only once, during which the positions of all birds seen or heard, together with the route taken by the observer, were plotted on a 1:4000 scale map. Summary sheets were completed for each tetrad. As breeding was not taking place, fewer activity codes were necessary during the winter than for the summer. However, codes were used where appropriate to identify those birds that, in the opinion of the surveyor, were only observed flying over the tetrad and not considered to be using it. This distinction allowed such records to be ignored for the purpose of abundance calculations.

Surveying in only one winter for each tetrad ran the risk of under-recording species which visit the Island infrequently (e.g. Waxwing), or which are secretive (e.g. Woodcock). In order to optimise the recording of such species a second, untimed or 'additional', visit to each tetrad was conducted during the period, in a winter other than the one in which the timed visit took place. These visits were not constrained by time, but experience showed that they lasted approximately as long as a timed visit. They were undertaken at the same time of day as timed visits, but were sometimes undertaken in slightly stronger wind conditions. The majority of records gathered during 'additional visits' were not plotted on maps, but simply noted on a summary sheet with the record being assigned to the 1km square in which the birds were seen or heard.

Field maps and recording forms

Unlike many other atlas works the charity was fortunate in having available to it geographical information system (GIS) mapping software. This allowed for the generation of maps showing line detail of features such as roads, hedgerows, buildings, rivers and ponds. Using a scale of 1:4000 a copy of each 1km square was printed on a field map which surveyors used to plot sightings and the survey route taken. A high degree of plotting accuracy was usually possible, as a result of the detailed geographical information on each map. Less accuracy was possible for distant birds observed in flight, or in areas where geographical features were few, such as open moorland.

During the winter, mapping and recording on summary sheets followed the same principle as the summer research, with one key exception: all birds present except those considered not to be using the tetrad were included for the purposes of abundance calculation. Additional recording forms were available to staff to note records other than those from the core 'timed' fieldwork. On these, species name, date, activity, breeding status and six-figure grid references were noted. Members of the public who expressed an interest in becoming involved in the research were sent similar recording forms, or could submit records via the charity's web site. Many other records were obtained from telephone calls, emails and letters.

Organisation

With a large volume of work to be undertaken within a short time period, keeping track of progress was vital. Before each fieldwork season, a set of clear objectives was identified. These included the selection of the 1km squares or tetrads that were to be surveyed and agreeing a programme of 'species specific' surveys, tying these in, where possible, with surveys being undertaken in the rest of the British Isles. Overall survey objectives were then broken down into weekly targets, lead responsibility being given to various staff to suit skills and particular interests. Where necessary, new members of staff were given induction training in the methods being employed. A high level of continuity of approach was achieved as a result of having three members of staff who were with the project from start to finish.

As each survey period progressed, weekly meetings reviewed progress against targets, provided the opportunity to discuss concerns and ideas and enabled the following week's workload to be adjusted where necessary. On a daily basis a telephone call was made to the local meteorological office at Ronaldsway Airport, to obtain the following day's forecast. From this a decision was made about which (if any) areas would be surveyed the next day and all necessary landowners contacted to confirm that a staff member would be on their land.

Additional data

Though a significant proportion of staff time was absorbed by the systematic surveying of the Island, other work was also undertaken. This included a seabird census, surveys of Peregrines, Hen Harriers, Choughs, Cormorants, Rooks and Grey Herons, all linking with census work in the rest of the British Isles, as well as a range of other surveys targeting species in which we were particularly interested, such as Whinchats and Water Rails. All of these added greatly to our understanding of the species in question, often providing the bulk of the data for those species.

Mention has already been made of the important role played by volunteers and other members of the public. Initially contributions came from a relatively small band of enthusiasts drawn largely from the membership of the Manx Ornithological Society and the Manx Wildlife Trust. As time went by an increasing number of individuals became aware of the research, resulting in many more records being obtained.

In most cases it was possible to attribute accurate grid references to records from the public, though in some cases a centralised reference was given where only a general location was stated. Where no indication of breeding activity was given, records from the public were given a 'non-breeding' status. These records, however, added to our understanding of species' distributions in both summer and winter. Summer records that did include an indication of activity were assigned a breeding status commensurate with that activity.

On occasions records were obtained of species classed locally as rarities. The Manx Ornithological Society is the body that considers whether or not such records should be accepted on the Island, with some also being considered by the British Bird Rarities Committee (BBRC). When such records were obtained the observer was invited to submit a short description of the sighting, which was then forwarded to the County Recorder for eventual consideration by the appropriate committee. Records where no description was forthcoming, or which were rejected by either body, have not been included in this publication.

From April 1998 to March 2003 a total of 402,855 records were obtained from the public, an impressive contribution that has added greatly to the value of the work undertaken.

Seabird colonies

In 1999, a complete census of seabirds was undertaken, timed to coincide with the Seabird 2000 census, organised by the JNCC, which took place between 1998 and 2002. The method of recording followed those laid down by Walsh *et al.* (1995). Known inland colonies were surveyed, together with a survey of coastal towns, where, increasingly,

Herring Gulls are to be found breeding. The main survey effort was, however, applied to our coastline.

The entire length of coast was walked; the location of each nest site or individual adult (depending upon the species) being noted on maps. Surveyors plotted these sightings to a high degree of accuracy, noting to which side of a gully or promontory the record related, whether the nest was on bare rock or within vegetation and whether, in the opinion of the surveyor, the nest could be seen from sea level. The rocky coastline of the Island was similarly surveyed by small boat, during calm weather, with surveyors indicating whether or not they felt that a given nest could be seen from the cliff top.

Through comparing the results from sea and land it proved possible to arrive at an overall estimate of breeding numbers.

Data verification and data entry

On return to the office from timed fieldwork, surveyors transferred the information on their field maps to a neat copy, reconciling the information on that map to the summary sheet compiled in the field. Though this was time-consuming, experience revealed that field maps were often not sufficiently clear to the person subsequently entering the data onto the database.

On completion of this process the set of two maps and summary sheet were passed to another staff member for checking. The copy map was checked against the original and then to the summary sheet, with queries referred back to the surveyor for clarification. Checking of maps was mostly undertaken within three days of the survey having been undertaken, in order that the surveyor could remember the survey if any queries needed resolving. This process proved worthwhile as inevitably errors of omission occurred. Once the maps and summary sheet had been verified, they were put aside for data entry. This took place as soon after checking as the demands of fieldwork permitted.

Data for a given survey were entered at three levels. The first layer recorded the square surveyed, date, surveyor and a short report on the survey, including anything of interest. The short report was used to periodically update the Manx Bird Atlas web site.

The second layer contained the summary data for each species recorded, including maximum breeding status, total number of adults, juveniles and recently fledged young and the number of Apparently Occupied Nests/Sites.

The final layer contained the details of every sighting plotted on the map including activity codes, six-figure grid reference, number and gender of birds at each sighting.

Data for the first two layers were entered directly from the summary sheet, while the final layer was entered from the copy map. Records were given a six-figure grid reference, which placed the record at the bottom left hand corner of the 100m square in which the birds were observed.

Within the database, a system of automatic verification ensured that the total number of birds entered at the mid-layer matched the sum of those entered in the final layer. Further checks ensured that the maximum breeding status for each species was reflected by at least one of the activity codes in the final layer. Verification reports were run regularly to ensure that errors of data entry were kept to a minimum and that those that did occur could be readily identified and corrected.

Before being entered on the database, records from the public and miscellaneous records from staff were examined by a staff member to identify gaps in information and where possible resolve these with the observer.

Map production

Change maps from 1977–81 to 1998–2003

In C&J, accounts for those species that were known to breed in 1977–81 include a small-scale map indicating in which of the 39 5km squares on the Island breeding was known to occur. Three different sized dots were used to indicate 'possible', 'probable' and 'confirmed' status. For species where breeding took place during the most recent survey, those maps have been reproduced together with comparative maps for the 1998–2002 results.

These two maps provide a useful indication of changing status for a range of species. However, some caution does need to be applied when comparing the two. Changes over time in the breeding status attributed to certain activities mean that some species may have been classed as 'probably' breeding in 1977–81, while they would be classed as 'definitely' breeding in 1998–2002. These changes are few in number and are relatively unimportant. Of greater significance is the level of observer effort that was applied during the two surveys. The 1977–81 surveyors undertook their efforts as volunteers, visiting areas whenever time permitted. In 1998–2003, up to five staff per summer were able to dedicate their time to a structured survey that covered areas of the Island not visited in the earlier survey, spending at least four hours in each 1km square. In addition a large volume of records was obtained from the public. Significantly more observer effort was therefore applied to the 1998–2003 survey than was possible in 1977–81. The two maps are not therefore directly comparable, though they are a useful indicator of expansion or contraction in distribution for many of our breeding species in the twenty-plus years that have elapsed since the first survey.

A comparison of the 1977–81 and 1998–2002 maps for some auk species reveals an apparent reduction in breeding status for some coastal areas during the current research compared to that of C&J. This is a result of the count unit for auks in the most recent research being 'individual adult', which represents the number of adults observed on suitable nest ledges, omitting those seen in flight, on the sea nearby or on land away from the nest ledges. Use of 'individual adult' as the count unit gives only a 'possible' breeding status for those occupied colonies where no records of young were obtained.

Breeding status and summer distribution

Data for these maps are drawn, with only a few exceptions, from data gathered within the period 1 April to 31 July in each of the years 1998–2002. Exceptions relate to those species that are known to have a breeding season which starts before 1 April and those that have an extended breeding season. In such cases the relevant species account will mention the time period used. Though the main source of information used to compile these maps was derived from the timed visits to each 1km square, records from all sources are used, including those from members of the public.

Species presence, irrespective of breeding status, is indicated by a background shade of green. 'Possible', 'probable' and 'definite' breeding status are represented by one of three variably sized dots, running from small to large respectively. Squares where a species was present, but considered not to be breeding, are shown on the maps for a number of reasons. Firstly, though no evidence of breeding was found, the presence of a species in a square might be an early indication of future breeding effort. Secondly, while breeding evidence was not found in a square, the species might regularly use the area for foraging. For some species an understanding of foraging areas can be as important as knowing where they breed. Finally, many of the non-breeding records relate to birds considered to be on active migration. Including squares where such records were obtained adds to the overall picture of where migrants were recorded.

Winter distribution

Winter presence of a species is indicated on each map by the use of an orange shade, indicating in which 1km squares the species was observed during the period 15 November to end of February in each year from November 1998 to February 2003. Data from all sources were used, though the majority of records were obtained from the timed fieldwork. For most species the shading for presence is truncated at the coast. However, for those species that are largely coastal in distribution, the shading covers the whole 1km square, extending over the sea where necessary. This has been done to ensure that records of presence in squares containing only a small area of land are still capable of being seen at the mapped scale.

Abundance maps

With the exception of seabirds, the data used to generate summer abundance maps are derived from timed fieldwork only and are thereby corrected for survey effort. Breeding data were identified and mapped, each 1km square being given an abundance figure equal to the maximum count from the first or second timed visits. Records of non-breeding birds were omitted for this purpose. Using spatial analyst software donated by ESRI (UK) Ltd, interpolated (smoothed), kernel density maps were then produced, where the value for each 1km square was summed with those that fell within the search area (encompassing eight adjoining 1km squares), with weighting in favour of the central square. Abundance maps use a colour scale from light blue (low density) to red (high density), the same as was used in the 1988–91 Atlas.

Abundance data for seabird species are drawn from the seabird census rather than timed fieldwork. Depending upon the species, seabird breeding abundance maps use individual adults, apparently occupied site or apparently occupied nest as the count unit.

For the winter period abundance maps were produced in the same way as for the summer though using the maximum count from timed survey work and 'additional visits'. Records of birds that were not considered to be using the survey area were excluded for this purpose.

For each abundance map the intervals within the overall range are calculated by dividing the data into ten quantiles (i.e. deciles, Robinson *et al.* 1984), the same approach as used in the 1988–91 Atlas. Each interval represents one tenth of the overall value range for each species, resulting in each colour being represented on the maps as approximately 10% of the overall area of the colour range. The range and intervals vary for each species and these are shown adjacent to each map. Smoothed abundance maps have not been produced for those, relatively few, species that were not recorded on timed fieldwork, or which were not recorded with sufficient frequency to produce meaningful abundance maps.

Analysing the data using spatial software gave rise to practical considerations that needed to be addressed before the results for each species could be mapped. Firstly, the technique resulted in low densities being shown beyond the coast of the Island. This was addressed by masking values that fell beyond the outline of the Island, effectively blanking them off the finished maps. Secondly the process of smoothing the data resulted in low densities being assigned to areas, radiating out from centres of density. In most instances this is an appropriate means of demonstrating the results. However, it was recognised that this was undesirable when looking at density towards the uplands.

As an example, the draft map of summer abundance for Great Tits suggested that they occurred in low density in heather moorland, simply as an artifact of the mapping software. This problem was overcome by identifying the upper ten-metre altitude band, beyond which a given species ceased to be observed during timed research. For breeding and winter research periods, separate values were obtained for each species and a mask generated at the identified ten-metre altitude level, thereby more accurately reflecting the true abundance of each species.

Applying altitude masks to species that have a mainly coastal distribution resulted in values being represented by narrow bands of colour sandwiched between the coast and altitude masks. At the scale of map reproduction much of that detail was not clearly visible. Therefore, for a limited number of species, altitude masks have not been applied to the maps indicating breeding and/or wintering abundance. This approach has been adopted for the 'seabird' suite of species, though it was also appropriate for species such as Rock Pipit.

Treatment of sensitive species

Unfortunately there are a number of species that are susceptible to unlawful interference, either because they are valued by egg collectors, they have a commercial value for falconry or because they are seen as a threat to the commercial or other interests of a few.

Careful consideration has been given to the level of detail that is presented in the species accounts for those few species that are considered most at risk. For a limited number of species the decision has been taken to mask the accuracy of the mapped data. In such cases the breeding status map does not indicate presence or breeding status at 1km square resolution, but simply summarises the status for each 5km square.

Treatment of regularly occurring non-breeding and non-wintering species

With two exceptions, the main species accounts are confined to those species that bred on the Island and/or wintered here during the survey period. The exceptions are Gannets, which are considered an integral part of the offshore avifauna, and Storm Petrels, which are highly likely to breed on the Calf of Man, though efforts to prove this during the survey proved fruitless.

A large number of other species were also recorded during the period. Some were seen only on one or a small number of occasions and do not warrant a full account. Others, though occurring regularly, only do so on spring or autumn passage neither breeding nor over-wintering locally. All species recorded during the Atlas period that are not covered by a full account are included in Appendix A.

Relative merits of the approach adopted

Limiting the weather conditions and time of day during which surveying took place caused problems, due to the unpredictable nature of Island weather. Consequently, there were times when work plans fell behind schedule and it looked as if targets would not be met. Overall, however, there is no doubt that by surveying in dry conditions with light winds, the recording of species presence was optimised. This was illustrated clearly one morning when wind speeds were stronger than forecast. All surveyors separately took the decision to abandon their surveys, as song was being masked by the noise of wind in the trees.

Deciding to survey the entire Island, and doing so only during favourable weather conditions, resulted in the third main decision effectively being made for us, that of employing staff to undertake the main research effort. Most other atlas works have relied only upon a willing band of volunteers. While the Island does have a number of keen individuals who could have helped, it was recognised that the necessary survey work could not be achieved within the five-year target period without compromising either the level of coverage or the timing of visits, if reliance was placed solely on volunteers.

Employing surveyors had the advantage of ensuring that every suitable morning for surveying could be utilised and that further research effort could be applied to target species, at times when weather prevented timed fieldwork taking place. It also helped ensure a consistent approach was applied to the survey methods. Clearly though it significantly increased the cost of the research.

Thanks to the cooperation of the farming community access was granted to most of the Island, one of the cornerstones that made the research so successful. The alternative would have been to restrict routes walked to roads, lanes, footpaths and areas of public open space. While cheaper in terms of staff time, as considerable resources were applied to seeking permission, this would have resulted in a significant reduction in the quality of data gathered.

Setting a time constraint for each survey was important as it allowed relative abundance to be calculated. During the summer, the setting of a two-hour time constraint linked with early morning surveying did have some disadvantages. Rare, elusive or nocturnal species will have been under-recorded using this method. This was partly overcome, for some species, by applying survey effort on target species outside of the core survey times, though for such species abundance calculations were not always possible. For others, like some warblers for which the Island is at the limit of their range, most records were obtained outside of timed fieldwork.

During the winter the ideal approach would have been to adopt the same level of coverage as for the summer, surveying twice for 2 hours per 1km square. By this means, a direct comparison could have been made between winter and summer distribution and abundance for species that occur during both periods. This was not done, as resources were limited.

As already mentioned the programme of winter research took longer than anticipated. To achieve the same level of coverage for the winter as for the summer would have either significantly extended the length of the research or resulted in additional staff costs, neither option being practical. In hindsight there would have been greater merit in replacing the 'additional visits' with a second, timed, visit to each tetrad, with all records being mapped. At the time there was uncertainty about the level of staff resource that could be applied to winter research, with no certainty that all tetrads would be afforded a second visit. Future research of this kind should consider changing this approach.

The systematic coverage of the Island in a series of timed surveys provided comparable information for mapping the distribution and breeding status of the majority of common species. A further advantage, however, was that the methods employed are highly repeatable. Future atlas work on the Island using the same methods will be able to quantify changes in distribution, breeding status and abundance based upon the same level of observer effort, within standardised weather conditions, at the same time of day and following the same routes. This will be critical in identifying real change in the fortunes of each species covered by this atlas.

Interpreting the species accounts

During the period from 1 April 1998 to 31 March 2003, a total of 258 species were recorded. Of these, 150 bred and/or wintered on the Island and full accounts for each of these species are included in the following section. The remaining 108 species occurred either infrequently or only on spring/autumn passage. These species are covered in Appendix A.

In both the main account section and in Appendix A species are shown in taxonomic order, using the list published by the British Ornithologists Union (2004). The species name at the start of each account is that which has been in common usage for a number of years and with which most readers will be familiar. Recent proposed changes of name for a number of species are shown in parentheses after the common name. Scientific names are shown for each species and where there is one, the Manx name is also given, following C&J.

Annual presence

Within each species account a bar chart depicts the calendar year, divided into 24 increments corresponding to the first and second halves of each of the twelve months. A dark shade for a given half-month indicates that the species was observed in either four or five of the years of the recording period (April 1998 to March 2003). A medium shade indicates presence in two or three of the years, while the palest shade shows that the bird was observed in only one of the five years. For each species this provides a simple way of identifying whether it is a resident, a summer visitor or is only present for the winter. Additionally it demonstrates the likely first arrival and last departure periods for migrant species. Similar bar charts are included for some of the species covered in Appendix A, in order to give an indication of main passage periods. A sample bar chart is shown below.

The fact box

For each species a fact box is provided, summarising the local breeding and wintering status. For the Manx data the number of grid squares (for both breeding and wintering periods) refers to the number of 1km squares in which the species was observed during each of the two periods. The number in parentheses after each figure expresses that value as a percentage of the 665 1km squares surveyed, giving an indication of how widespread each species is.

For the majority of species the estimate of the breeding population on the Island is derived from an analysis of timed fieldwork data. From this the likely breeding population within each 1km square was estimated for each species. Additional records from non-timed sources were also included so that infrequent or secretive breeders were not excluded. The data from each 1km square were then summed to provide an overall population estimate. Using purely observational data to determine population estimates, rather than extrapolation, has the advantage of ensuring that future research can directly compare results and quantify change. It does however mean that all population figures should be recognised as minimum estimates.

For a limited number of species, the breeding population figure is derived from non-timed research undertaken during the survey period. For example, Raven estimates were drawn from a census of the species undertaken in 2002. Seabird data were derived from the seabird census of 1999. Unless otherwise stated the figures quoted for breeding populations relate to pairs.

Winter population estimates were derived partly from a review of timed data and, for flocking species particularly, a review of flock sizes reported during the winter months of the research. Given that numbers present in successive winters and within winters vary greatly for many species, the winter population estimates owe as much to informed opinion as they do to rigorous analysis of the data.

The fact boxes also include data for Britain and Ireland both for the breeding and wintering periods. For the breeding period the number of grid squares for Britain and Ireland are shown separately and are taken from Mead, who used data collected for the 1988–91 Atlas. The unit for this survey was the 10km square, so the number of squares in which a species was found is shown as a percentage of the total of 3,858 10km squares surveyed during 1988–91. Breeding population figures for Britain & Ireland are as cited in Mead, with the exception of seabirds, which are taken from *Seabird Populations of Britain & Ireland* (2004), referred to hereafter as 'Seabird 2000'. Seabird figures are rounded to the nearest 100, apart from those for the Irish population of Little Terns, which was so small that it was omitted.

The total population for Britain and Ireland (which for this purpose includes the Isle of Man) is also expressed as a percentage of the estimated European population, as given by Mead. Unfortunately the corresponding percentages quoted in the Seabird 2000 publication refer to such geographical units as the North Atlantic and are not therefore comparable with those in Mead. Therefore the percentages for seabird populations cited in Mead have been retained, though for seabird species where the populations have changed between the 1988–91 Atlas and Seabird 2000 such percentages may be significantly inaccurate. Unless otherwise stated, the British and Irish breeding population estimates refer to pairs.

For winter the number of grid squares for Britain and Ireland was taken from the Winter Atlas, in which the figures relate to 10km squares, but were not split between Britain and Ireland. Percentages of squares and wintering populations were also taken from the Winter Atlas and again refer to combined British and Irish totals. Winter population estimates refer to individual birds, unless otherwise stated.

Although more up-to-date data on UK or Irish populations are available for a range of species, in many cases these lack comparability regarding geographical units and recording methods. Therefore the decision was taken to use only Mead, Seabird 2000 and the Winter Atlas as source documents for comparative purposes.

Text

Each main species account commences with a brief introduction to the species, moving on to discuss favoured habitat, highlighting any notable differences locally, compared with other parts of the species' range. Commentary on breeding distribution follows, including reference to the European range, but more particularly the range in the British Isles and locally, referring to the maps accompanying each account to highlight local areas of note.

Reference to known migration patterns is included where appropriate, after which the findings of the winter research are summarised, again referring to accompanying maps and making mention of the British Isles situation where appropriate. Finally, information is given on the history of the species on the Isle of Man, as far as this is known.

Maps

The maps within each species account show the results of the research. In addition the main maps show a shaded relief of the Island's topography and the 10km grid. A detailed description of the methods used to produce the various maps that illustrate the species accounts is given in the section 'Map Production' in the previous chapter. Here it is sufficient to summarise the main types of map used.

Change maps

These small-scale maps indicate the breeding status and distribution for each 5km square, as indicated in C&J and as found during the current research, thus providing some level of comparison (but see Map production section of previous chapter).

Summer presence and breeding status map

This type of map is used for all the species which were given a full account and which occurred on the Island during the breeding season. Two types of information are shown. Species presence in a given 1km square is indicated by green shading of the squares in question, while the maximum level of breeding status is indicated by three variably sized dots.

Winter presence

For all species that were found to over-winter on the Island a simple map is included indicating, with the use of orange shading, each 1km square where the species was present.

Abundance map

For species that were recorded with sufficient frequency to provide meaningful data, abundance maps are produced covering the summer and/or winter survey periods. For the summer maps only those sightings of birds with a breeding status of 'possible' or higher are used and data are only drawn from timed fieldwork. An exception is seabirds, for which data are derived from the seabird survey of 1999. For the winter period, abundance maps use data from timed and additional visits. Records of birds that were seen only to fly over the survey area, and thereby not considered to be using it, are excluded.

Methods of referencing

All references are shown on pages 376–77, with frequently cited references being given an abbreviation, as shown on page viii.

Main species accounts

Mute Swan
Cygnus olor

Manx: *Ollay* = Swan

Among the most familiar of birds, the conspicuous and beautiful Mute Swan utters few sounds other than the odd snort or hiss, although flying birds produce a loud twanging noise with their wings. The Mute Swan of modern times is a product of domestication for food and ornament since the medieval period, followed by a partial return to the wild. Habits such as carrying small young on their backs may endear swans to the general public, but many people remain wary of this large and often aggressive species. Birdwatchers tend to ignore the Mute Swan because of its doubtful status as a wild bird, but it does have some points in its favour, being remarkably easy to census, so that in a small area like the Isle of Man an accurate idea of numbers present may be gained.

Any kind of water providing a decent supply of aquatic vegetation and sufficient space for its long pattering take-off is likely to suit the Mute Swan, including large and small lakes, rivers of a reasonable depth, coastal lagoons and sheltered inlets of the sea, while these versatile waterfowl also feed on land, not only around the margins of water bodies but sometimes in damp areas or even dry fields some distance from open waters. Their history of domestication has removed any fear of humans, and so urban areas and other much disturbed habitats pose few problems and offer advantages such as provision of food by the swan-loving public. Mute Swans are almost entirely vegetarian, feeding on many kinds of submerged plants, and often up-ending to take advantage of the long reach of their slender necks. When out of the water they eat grass and the leaves of a wide range of other plants.

In its natural state the Mute Swan breeds very discontinuously across Eurasia in middle latitudes from western Europe (where its original distribution is uncertain as a result of introductions by man) to the Far East. In Britain and Ireland most lowland areas have their Mute Swans, but food-rich (eutrophic) waters are rare in the highlands and so the species shows a marked concentration in southern and eastern England and the midlands of Ireland. As can be seen on both the summer and winter maps, this factor is also significant in the Isle of Man, with most records in the coastal lowlands and major inland valleys. The largest sheets of water on the Island, namely the upland reservoirs of Sulby and West Baldwin (Injebreck) are deep and sparsely vegetated, and so are of little interest to Mute Swans, which are consequently found on a range of smaller waters, with a slightly wider distribution outside the breeding season.

The summer map shows confirmed breeding at eleven sites, none of them further north than the central valley. One of these locations (Langness) is truly marine, and three others (the harbours at Peel and Castletown and the river beside Leigh Terrace in Douglas) are situated where flowing and salt water meets, the other seven sites consisting of inland lakes and ponds (for example Tromode Dam and the lakes at Billown). Except at Castletown, sites are usually occupied by single pairs, and the only one used in all five years of the MBA survey was at Leigh Terrace. Breeding attempts often fail for a variety of reasons, such as infertility of the eggs or flooding of the nest. Pairs and immature birds are seen on many additional waters and may show signs of breeding, sometimes doomed to certain failure, as with the nest built by two males at Port e Chee Lake in 2002, one attempting to incubate a drinks can! During the Atlas period swans were seen at Ramsey during the breeding season, with no evidence of nesting. Despite the existence of suitable waters the northern plain was largely ignored by this species though breeding has occurred previously at Ramsey and in the Point of Ayre gravel pits.

The nesting population of the Isle of Man is estimated to consist of 11 to 12 pairs, although the number of actual breeding attempts varied during the Atlas survey from three (in 1998) to eight (in 2001). Up to 30 or so birds may be present on the Island during summer, with young birds increasing the figure to 50 or more in winter. This feral population appears to have become established during the middle decades of the twentieth century, with C&J suggesting a slightly lower total than the MBA fieldwork. General observation, backed up by marking with numbered rings, shows a good deal of movement between waters, especially on the part of immatures and other non-breeders, and in winter gatherings of up to 36 birds (at Ramsey) have been reported although groups of just a few swans are more usual. While Manx birds do not normally move off the Island movements to northern Ireland and Lancashire are known to have occurred, and arrivals from elsewhere have been suspected on odd occasions.

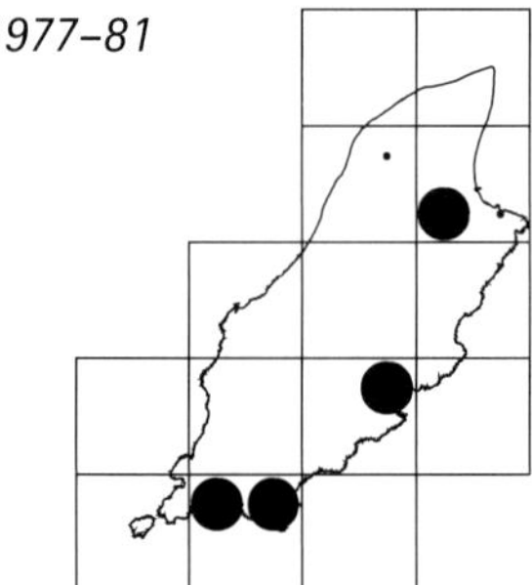

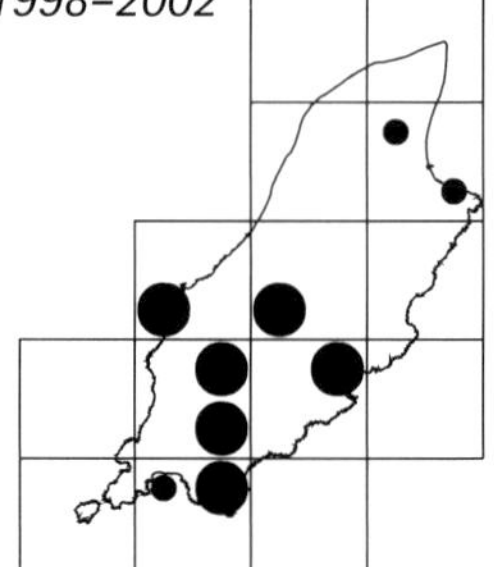

Breeding	Grid squares:	Isle of Man 35 (5.26%) Britain 1,579 Ireland 560 Total 2,139 (55%)
	Population:	Isle of Man 11-12 Britain 25,750+ Ireland 19,500 (48% of European)
Wintering	Grid squares:	Isle of Man 39 (5.86%) Britain and Ireland 2,238 (58%)
	Population:	Isle of Man 50+, including young birds Britain and Ireland 20,000

Jan	Feb	Mar	Apr	May	Jun	Jul	Aug	Sep	Oct	Nov	Dec

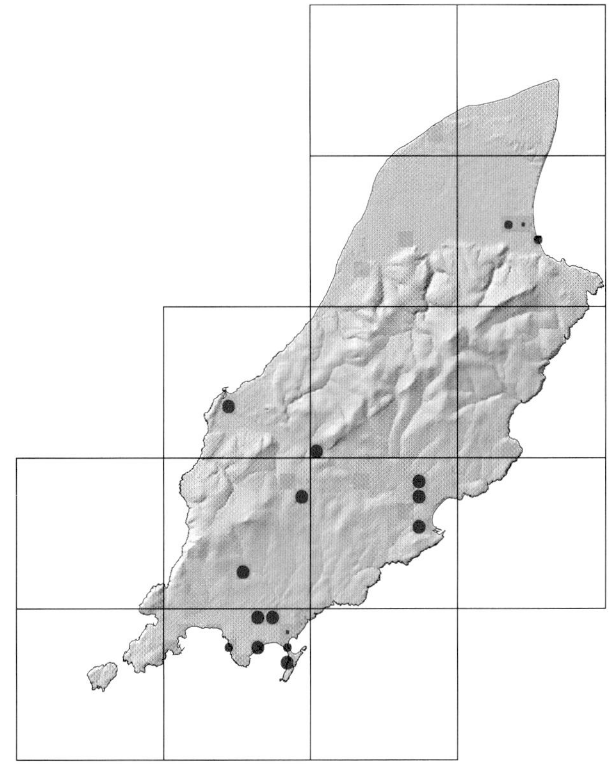

Summer presence and breeding status

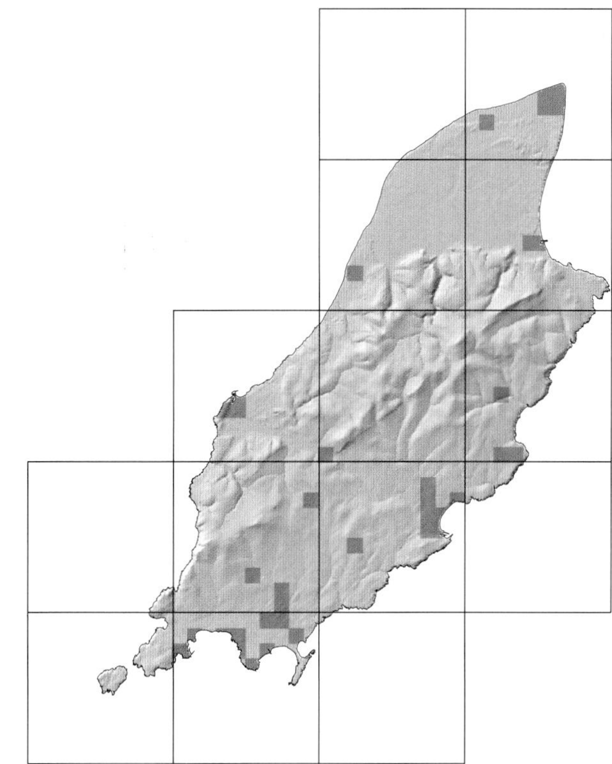

Winter presence

Individual Sponsors – Mr. & Mrs. Allsebrook

Whooper Swan
Cygnus cygnus

Manx: *Ollay Chiaullee*

In contrast to the Mute Swan, the Whooper has a loud voice which it is not afraid of using, and so the species is a noticeable bird in terms of sound as well as sight. Unlike its homely relative, this northern swan is truly wild, without any history of domestication. Within winter flocks birds tend to stay in family parties, and the numbers of smoky-grey juveniles accompanying their parents give a valuable indication of the success of the previous breeding season. Although very wary and susceptible to disturbance, if unmolested Whoopers may become quite approachable for careful birdwatchers, including in the Isle of Man.

The Whooper Swan frequents a wide range of waters, many of them quite small but others of considerable size, with associated marshes and reedbeds. Although overlapping to a great extent with Mute Swans with regard to habitat selection, Whoopers will accept lakes and ponds with relatively poor supplies of food, including some at comparatively high altitudes. In some areas, notably Scotland and the Isle of Man, they forage regularly on agricultural land, including both pasture and arable, and they may also be seen feeding on muddy intertidal areas, where they favour eelgrass (*Zostera*) (WA). The food of the Whooper resembles that of the Mute Swan, and consists mainly of aquatic plants, plus grass and crop material such as waste potatoes and spilt grain.

Despite their northerly distribution and unlike Bewick's Swans, breeding Whoopers are not really Arctic birds, preferring the forested and steppe zones to the south of the true tundra, and ranging from Iceland and Scandinavia right across Eurasia to its eastern extremities. This species does not normally breed in the British Isles, although some nesting has occurred, notably in Shetland in recent years. After the breeding season continental birds migrate southwards and westwards for the winter, some moving as far as the Mediterranean region but most stopping on Baltic coasts, and how many reach Britain is debatable. Most Whoopers wintering in Britain and Ireland originate in Iceland, where an annually varying proportion of the swans migrates, three-quarters of them to the British Isles (BWP), and the Whooper Swans which visit the Isle of Man are Icelandic birds. The bulk of those spending the winter in Britain occur in Scotland and northern England, and a similar northern bias is also apparent in Ireland (WA).

The first Whooper Swans of the autumn to arrive in the Isle of Man are likely to be seen in October, with numbers increasing during November, when some birds settle on the Island for the winter and others move on, presumably heading for wintering grounds in Ireland. Although Whoopers are by no means unknown in the south of the Island, occurring for example on Kionslieu Dam and seen flying over the Calf of Man, the main sites for this species lie on the northern plain, notably in the area between Ballaugh and Jurby. The dubs at Ballacain seem to act as a base for these birds, which roam around the district and are usually observed feeding on farmland, often frequenting the same fields for some weeks, as at Ballaugh Cronk and Ballacain itself. Other places include Bishop's Dub and the fields to the west, floodland south of Orrisdale and (farther south) fields north-west of Poortown. The habit of foraging on agricultural land is common in Scotland (WA), and may be a recent development in the Isle of Man, as this practice is not mentioned by C&J.

Numbers of Whooper Swans recorded in the Isle of Man vary greatly from year to year and within particular winters, perhaps to some extent reflecting the weather in Iceland. During the atlas period a figure of 60 or more birds could perhaps be regarded as an average wintering population, and the species was observed in 5% of the 1km grid squares on the Island. C&J suggest that this species has increased as a visitor to the Isle of Man during the twentieth century, and the Atlas data seem to indicate a further rise in numbers since these authors were writing (in the mid 1980s), especially during the late winter and early spring. Although groups of just a few birds (often parents with young) are not unusual, sizeable herds are also frequently seen nowadays, especially at the main sites. Thus fields east of Ballaugh Cronk held up to 67 Whoopers during the winter of 2000–01 and over 50 birds in the following season, this herd also being seen on farmland at nearby Ballacain. The largest flock reported to the MBA, however, contained 80 birds and was seen flying over Peel in mid-March 2001, at a time when Whooper Swans return to their Icelandic breeding grounds, and so presumably birds from elsewhere fly across the Island. By April sightings are few and numbers are small.

Wintering	Grid squares:	Isle of Man 33 (4.96%)
		Britain and Ireland 1,304 (34%)
	Population:	Isle of Man 60+ (variable year on year)
		Britain and Ireland 500,000

Jan Feb Mar Apr May Jun Jul Aug Sep Oct Nov Dec

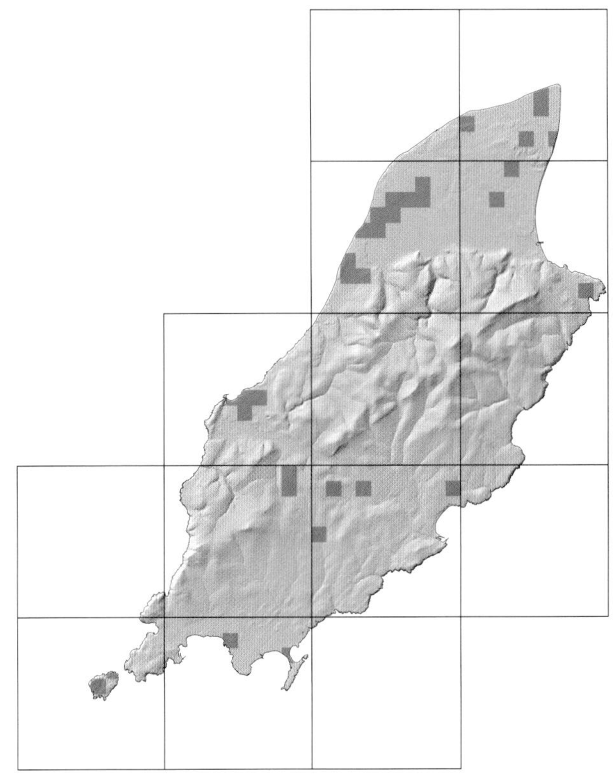

Winter presence

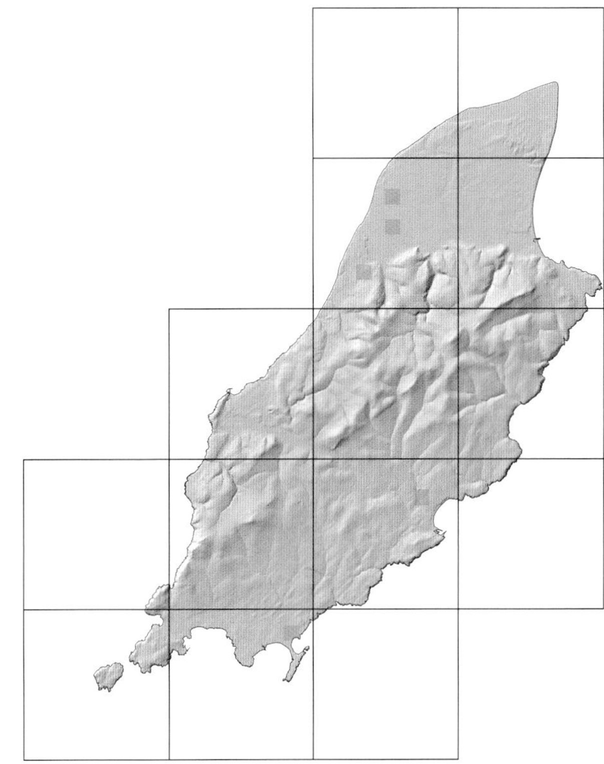

Summer presence

Pink-footed Goose
Anser brachyrhynchus

The Pink-footed Goose is a little smaller and neater than its better known relative the Greylag, with a less honking but still far-carrying voice. A large flock of Pinkfeet, scattered across a winter sky and accompanied by incessant wild calling, is not easily forgotten, although sadly the small numbers of this species visiting the Isle of Man are rather less spectacular. These attractive grey geese are delightful to watch as they 'whiffle' down to the ground, side-slipping and free-falling from a height with aerobatic skill and landing exactly where they want to be, displaying considerable agility not perhaps to be expected in a goose.

Foraging Pink-footed Geese are essentially birds of farmland during the winter, although they generally roost on lakes or estuaries, flighting at dawn and dusk to and from their feeding grounds. They prefer large fields with good all-round visibility, and the activities of wildfowlers influence the birds' choice of places for both feeding and roosting. None of these points, however, really apply to the Isle of Man, where sizeable flocks are rare and shooting is not a problem. On the Island Pinkfeet are attracted to water bodies with farmland around them, and they are sometimes observed on the coast. Outside the breeding season the diet of the Pinkfoot consists of a wide range of vegetable material, mainly based on agricultural crops, including grasses, spilt grain, waste potatoes and growing leaves of cereals and brassicas. These foods contrast markedly with the tundra plants, such as horsetails, sedges and the catkins of dwarf willow (BWP), consumed on its Arctic breeding grounds.

The Pink-footed Goose has a restricted breeding distribution, confined to east Greenland, Iceland and Spitsbergen, nesting in boggy areas and on grassy or heathery slopes or ridges, and somewhat remarkably on cliff ledges and rock exposures (presumably to avoid ground predators). The birds from Spitsbergen winter in continental Europe, mainly in Denmark, Germany and the Netherlands, whereas the Pinkfeet breeding in Greenland and Iceland migrate exclusively to Britain for the winter, this country therefore holding more than 75% of the world's Pink-footed Geese at that season (WA). Scotland hosts up to three-quarters of the British wintering birds, most of the rest being found in coastal areas of Lancashire, Lincolnshire and Norfolk. The faithfulness shown by these geese towards traditional areas and sites, coupled with the virtual absence of Pinkfeet in Ireland, reduces the potential for wandering to the Isle of Man to a tiny trickle, despite the proximity of the huge flocks on the Solway Firth and the Ribble Estuary.

Apart from a few summer records which presumably refer to escapes from wildfowl collections (as may also be the case with some of the winter reports), during the Atlas period Pink-footed Geese visited the Isle of Man between late September and March, with October the most usual month for the first records of the autumn, tying in with the main arrival across the water in Britain. Pinkfeet reported on the Island fall into two categories: those merely flying over and those choosing to stay for a while. Among the first group some considerable flocks are occasionally observed, and the largest one recorded by the MBA involved 160 birds east of Groudle on 1 March 2002. Only three other flocks containing more than 30 birds were logged, however, and many records refer to single figures or even single individuals. The only reliable locality is Glascoe Dub, where numbers often approach 30, but there is a scatter of records across the northern plain, including the gravel pits at the Point of Ayre. Further south, however, Pinkfeet are rarely reported, although C&J state that during the first half of the twentieth century Manx records were largely confined to the areas of Langness, Cregneash and the Calf of Man.

The Pink-footed Goose was not recorded in the Isle of Man until 1916 and there were only 17 reports between 1930 and 1982 (C&J), yet during the period 1997 to 2003 the MBA received dozens of records of this species. Bearing in mind the fact that many observations will refer to the same birds, and taking into consideration the variability of numbers from year to year, perhaps around 50 birds now frequent the Island during the winter months. In connection with this obvious rise in numbers visiting the Isle of Man, it is interesting to note that both the Icelandic population of Pinkfeet and the numbers wintering in Britain have increased markedly in recent years (BWP, WA).

Wintering	Grid squares:	Isle of Man 8 (1.20%)
		Britain and Ireland 529 (14%)
	Population:	Isle of Man 50+ (variable year on year)
		Britain and Ireland 101,000

Jan Feb Mar Apr May Jun Jul Aug Sep Oct Nov Dec

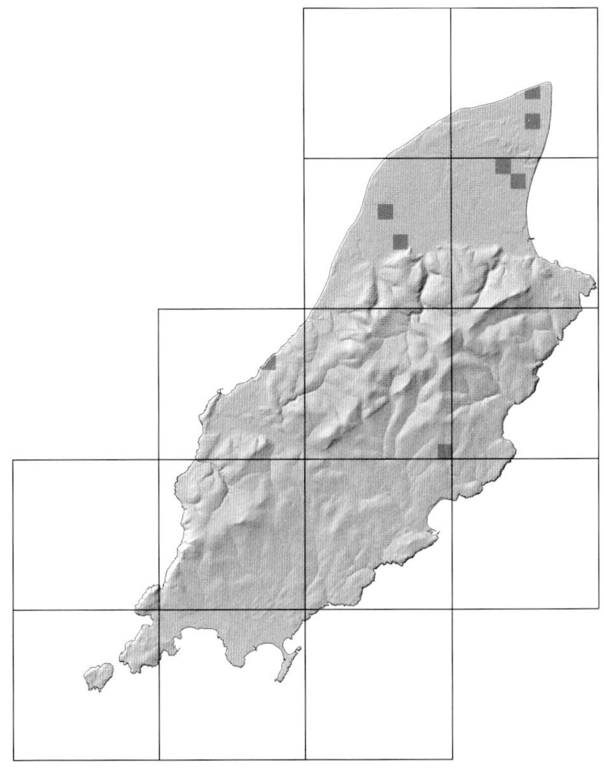

Winter presence

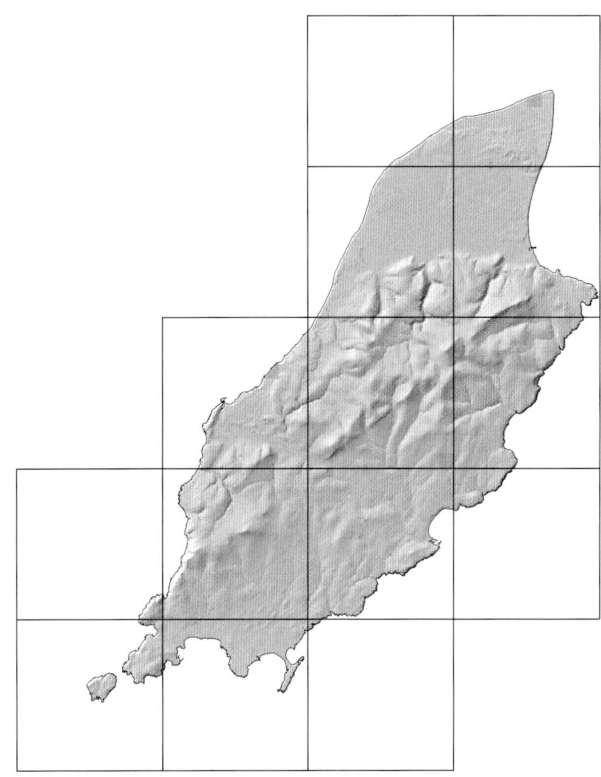

Summer presence

Greylag Goose
Anser anser

Manx: *Guiy feie* = Wild Goose

The large and weighty Greylag is the ancestor of the typical domestic goose, and is a solid-looking bird with a massive bill and a loud, deep honk. Most if not all Greylags seen in the Isle of Man are descended from birds that were introduced in various parts of Britain from the 1930s onwards, and they perhaps lack the romance of their smaller relatives, some being found in proximity to people or accompanying farmyard geese. Nevertheless most Greylags can be counted as wild (albeit feral) birds on the Island, and the flocks on the northern plain behave much as their wild ancestors would have done. Originally a native breeding bird in Britain, the Greylag may have received its name as the goose that lagged behind after the Pinkfeet and Whitefronts had departed for the Arctic in spring.

Water surrounded by open areas of grass or crops is the usual focus for Greylag Geese, preferably with islands or dense bankside vegetation for breeding. Foraging Greylags frequent freshwater margins of many types, from well-vegetated curraghs to the open banks of gravel pits and reservoirs, often using the same sites for roosting if undisturbed. Although sometimes found on the shore, Greylags are not particularly associated with the Manx coast. They are more aquatic than Pink-footed Geese, happily feeding while swimming and sometimes 'up-ending' where the water is deeper. Conversely, they habitually feed in fields away from wetlands, taking grass and cereal leaves, spilt grain, brassicas, root crops and potatoes. Relatively bold, they are unperturbed by closeness to buildings or livestock. Their natural food consists of the leaves, flower heads, fruits and tubers of a variety of plants of land and water.

The breeding distribution of the Greylag Goose extends from Iceland, the British Isles and Scandinavia across Eurasia to its eastern end, mainly within the north temperate zone and only marginally reaching the Arctic, thus lying generally further south than the breeding ranges of other geese. In western Europe the Greylag's distribution is markedly discontinuous, partly as a result of drainage of wetlands and other human factors, although introductions in some places have enabled the species to recover lost ground. The Greylag is a native of the northern half of Britain, but truly wild stock is now confined to the north of Scotland and the Outer Hebrides, all other birds being descended from introductions to various parts of Scotland and England since about 1930 (1968-72 Atlas). Additionally some feral groups have been established in Wales (mainly in Anglesey) and Ireland (notably around Strangford Lough).

The MBA estimates that up to 55 pairs of Greylags breed in the Isle of Man, but a significant increase since the Atlas survey is acknowledged. Ralfe knew of no definite records of this species at all on the Island, and Cullen and Jennings mention no reports of breeding. Their origin is obscure, but the Wildlife Park is a possibility (Manx Bird Report 1990), and they probably began nesting in the wild during the 1980s. They nest in the Ballaugh Curraghs and the Ayres, notably the gravel pits at the Point of Ayre, with the only MBA breeding record outside the northern plain referring to a small lake south-west of Glen Vine during 2002. It seems certain that the number of breeders in the Isle of Man will continue to increase, although with so much suitable habitat in the far north a southward spread is unlikely. The implications of the presence of large numbers on the Island, especially with regard to feeding on farm crops, trampling of agricultural grassland, and fouling of public places, are perhaps worthy of some consideration.

Although British populations of Greylag Geese, whether native or feral, are mostly resident, the majority of European Greylags are migratory, with Icelandic birds wintering in Britain and Scandinavian breeders flying south-westwards to the Netherlands, France and especially Spain. Most of the Greylags visiting Britain penetrate no further south than Scotland, but some reach northern England and perhaps a few straggle to the Isle of Man. When Cullen and Jennings were writing (1986), this species was observed mostly in midwinter, chiefly in groups of up to 8 birds, and most often at Langness, these occurrences suggesting visits by wild migrants. Nowadays, however, such birds would be swamped by the large numbers of feral Greylags, which could be local in origin, or some of which might themselves be arriving from off the Island. When compared with the single figures quoted by Cullen and Jennings, the size of the present-day midwinter flocks is striking, for example 250 birds in Ballaugh Curraghs in December 2000 and 175 at the Point of Ayre Gravel Pits in January 2004. The MBA estimate of a winter population of 600+ Greylags in the Isle of Man during the survey period is clearly already inadequate, with over 800 present in late 2005.

Breeding	Grid squares:	Isle of Man 47 (7.1%) Britain 718 Ireland 23 Total 741 (19%)
	Population:	Isle of Man 42-55 Britain 14,300 Ireland 700 (20% of European)
Wintering	Grid squares:	Isle of Man 27 (4.1%) Britain and Ireland 1,056 (27%)
	Population:	Isle of Man 600+ (comprising mostly feral birds) Britain and Ireland 100,000+ (excluding feral birds)

Jan	Feb	Mar	Apr	May	Jun	Jul	Aug	Sep	Oct	Nov	Dec

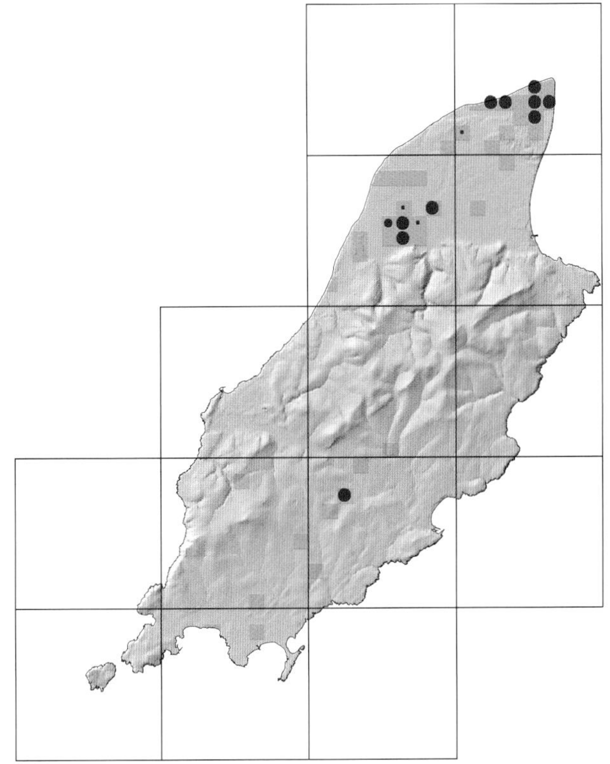
Summer presence and breeding status

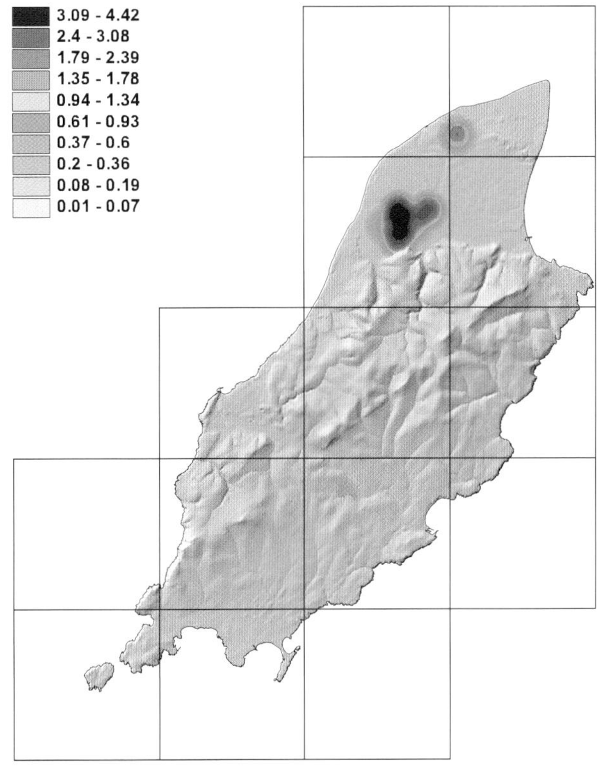

Breeding abundance

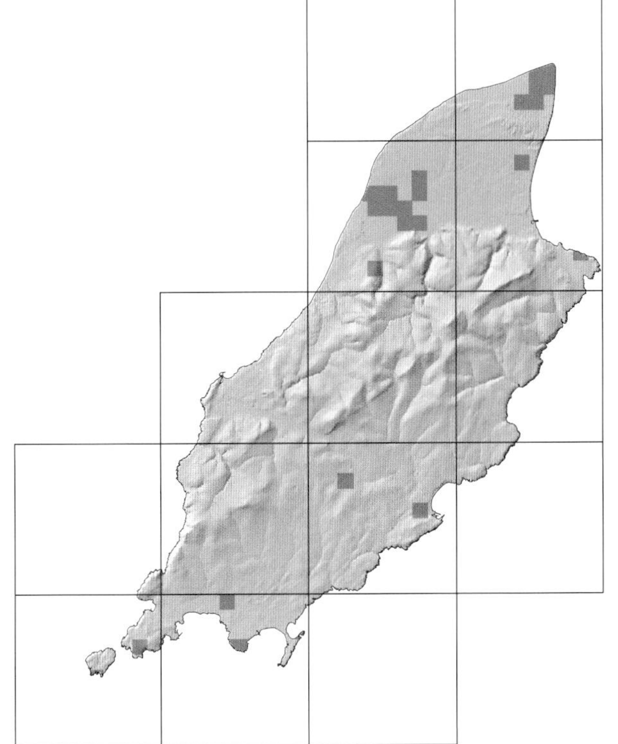
Winter presence

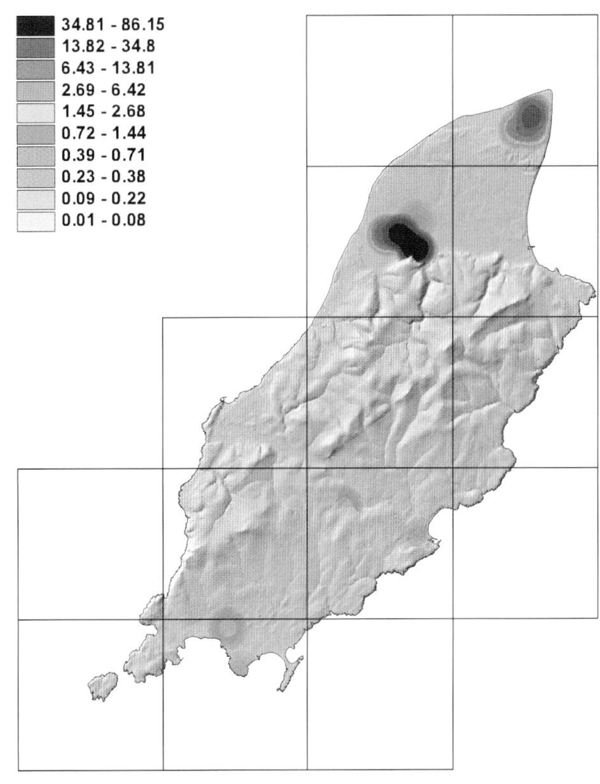

Winter abundance

Canada Goose (Greater Canada Goose) *Branta canadensis*

In its native North America the Canada Goose is a far-travelling bird of wild and lonely places, a far cry from its semi-tame and largely sedentary descendents on the man-made waters of the British Isles. This long-necked, distinctively marked goose could be regarded as an attractive addition to our native birdlife, but nowadays might equally be considered a pest, an aggressive and noisy mess-maker in public parks and a crop-consumer on agricultural land. Birdwatchers tend to ignore Canada Geese, so the history of the colonisation of Britain and Ireland by these birds is far from complete, but whether we like it or not, this species has now become an established part of the British avifauna.

The original releases of Canada Geese took place at ornamental waters on country estates in England, and the rural parkland habitat remains the stronghold of the species, with its artificial lakes surrounded by open areas of short grass and scattered trees, plus islands and patches of longer bankside vegetation suitable for nesting. Urban parks, however, are now also widely used by Canada Geese, along with a wide range of natural and man-made water bodies in lowland areas, including gravel pits, reservoirs, farm ponds, rivers and canals. Although not usually straying far from water, Canada Geese graze on nearby ornamental and agricultural grassland, and also frequent fields of young cereals, brassicas and root crops. They eat leaves, stems, roots, fruits and seeds of a variety of wild and cultivated plants, including grasses, clover, pondweed, wheat, barley, kale and root crops, foraging mainly on land but also in shallow water. In urban areas feeding by the public may be significant.

In its native North American range the Canada Goose breeds from Alaska through most of Canada southwards into northern parts of the USA. Introductions into Europe have established feral populations in the British Isles (from the seventeenth century) and in Scandinavia (from the 1930s), with much smaller numbers in the region between Denmark and France. Following undocumented releases or escapes in various parts of Britain the species was breeding in the wild by the 1780s, and is now a common nester over most of lowland England and in a few areas of Scotland, Wales and Ireland. The MBA estimates that some 30 pairs of Canada Geese are present in the Isle of Man during the breeding season, with the production of young raising the figure to more than 70 birds on the Island in winter, but the origins of these feral birds are unknown, although C&J record introductions at Ballasteen (south-west of Andreas), Glascoe and Crogga. While moving around in their local area (and in some cases undertaking moult migrations), British and Irish birds generally do not wander far, so it seems unlikely that Canada Geese have reached the Isle of Man from outside. Deliberate releases or escapes from captivity are presumably the sources of the Manx birds, and breeding in the wild seems to have begun by the end of the 1970s (Manx Bird Reports).

The Canada Goose is not a common species on the Island, being recorded by the Atlas survey in only 6% of grid squares during summer and in fewer than 4% in winter. The summer maps show a marked concentration of breeding birds on the northern plain, where the many pools and small lakes provide ideal conditions. The abundance map suggests the greatest numbers in the drainage areas of the Lhen Trench and Killane River (for example the districts of Jurby and Ballacain), extending southwards into the Curraghs, plus the country around Lough Cranstal and Glascoe near the north-east coast. Further south, Canada Geese breed in the inner harbour at Castletown and at nearby Billown lakes, also at the artificial pools at Ballanette. The winter map resembles that for the breeding season, but suggests a retreat to the main sites from the more peripheral areas, together with an obvious movement into the harbour at Ramsey, where Canada Geese are recorded throughout the year but do not seem to breed. Genuinely wild vagrants from North America, involving birds of smaller races than the introduced ones, have not been proved to visit the Island.

Although rather few Canada Geese inhabit the Isle of Man, in contrast to their feral relative the Greylags, it seems likely that numbers will increase, as is suggested by the establishment of a breeding population since Cullen and Jennings wrote in 1986. In view of the damage to agriculture caused by this species in some parts of Britain, it could be said that this addition to the Manx avifauna should not be welcomed on the Island.

Breeding	Grid squares:	Isle of Man 40 (6.0%) Britain 1196 Ireland 19 Total 1,215 (31%)
	Population:	Isle of Man 28–29 Britain 46,700 Ireland 650 (76% of European)
Wintering	Grid squares:	Isle of Man 23 (3.5%) Britain and Ireland 1,030 (27%)
	Population:	Isle of Man 70+ (comprising mostly feral birds) Britain and Ireland 30,000–35,000

Jan	Feb	Mar	Apr	May	Jun	Jul	Aug	Sep	Oct	Nov	Dec

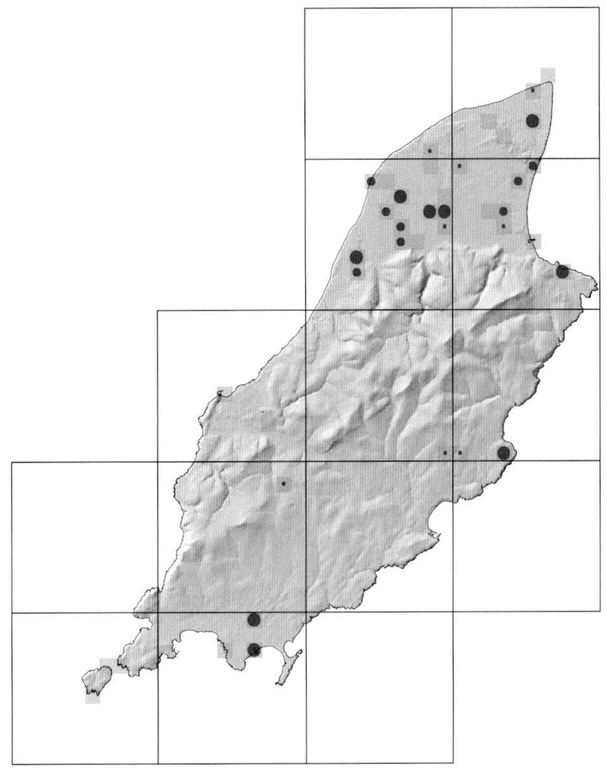

Summer presence and breeding status

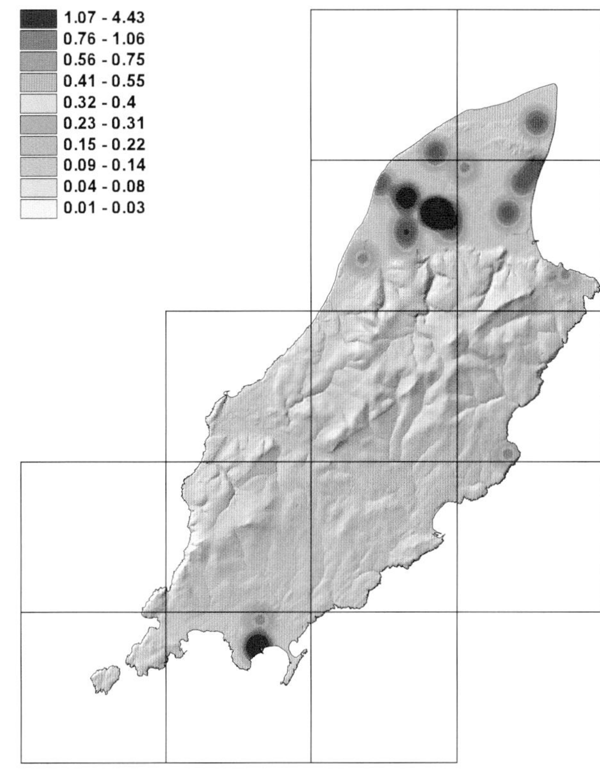

Breeding abundance

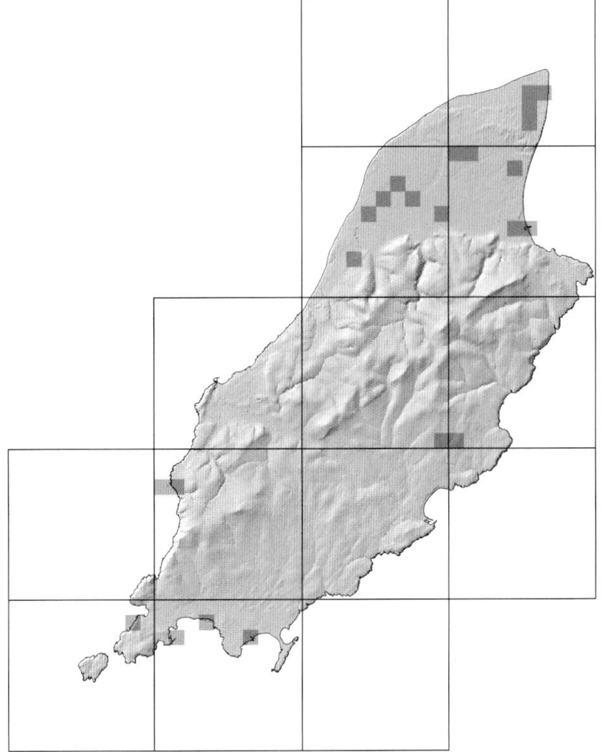

Winter presence

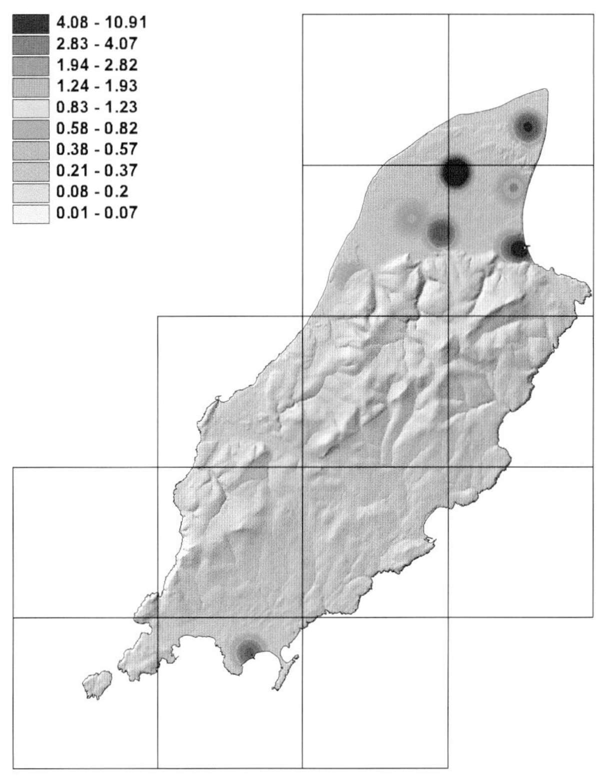

Winter abundance

Brent Goose
Branta bernicla

The attractive little Brent Goose is no bigger than a Mallard, and is rather duck-like in its flight, with quicker wing-beats and more agile manoeuvring than larger geese. Not a colourful bird in its black, white and grey plumage, and having a somewhat croaking voice, the Brent nevertheless is endowed with a considerable charm, and is much liked by birdwatchers. Two different subspecies migrate to the British Isles, light-bellied birds from the North American and European Arctic, and dark-bellied Brents from Siberia. This goose is one of the most northerly-breeding species of bird in the world, the harsh climate of its polar nesting grounds allowing the birds no more than 15 weeks or so to complete the breeding cycle and escape southwards with their young before the big freeze starts to bite.

Brent Geese tend to stay on or near the coast throughout their lives, nesting mainly on low pool-spattered tundra not far from the sea, and spending the winter particularly on shores and estuaries with wide intertidal areas and plenty of soft seaweed. They seek out mud and avoid rocky terrain, so they find little to attract them to the Isle of Man. Brents take to the sea itself for roosting, choosing sheltered waters close to the shore and habitually resorting to the same sites if undisturbed. Their natural food consists of grass, moss, pondweed and other plants on their northern breeding grounds, while in winter they exploit eelgrass (*Zostera*), green algae such as *Enteromorpha*, and other plants of shallow salty water and the intertidal zone. During the last thirty years or so Brents have increasingly joined other geese on coastal farmland, feeding on cultivated grasses, cereals and oilseed rape (WA).

Dark-bellied Brent Geese, belonging to the subspecies *Branta bernicla bernicla*, breed along the Arctic coasts of Asia and on neighbouring islands, while the other race, the Light-bellied Brent Goose *Branta bernicla hrota*, nests from Alaska through the maritime Canadian Arctic to Greenland and the European Arctic archipelagoes of Spitsbergen and Franz Josef Land. Dark-bellied birds winter from Denmark to western France, with many thousands using muddy coasts in south-east England, while light-bellied Brents from the European Arctic head for Denmark and Northumberland. Other light-bellied birds, breeding in Greenland and the eastern Canadian Arctic islands, spend the winter mainly in Ireland, especially on Strangford Lough, at North Bull island in Dublin Bay and in Tralee Bay (Co. Kerry). The small numbers of Brent Geese which reach the Isle of Man are (not surprisingly) chiefly light-bellied birds, and most of these visitors to the Island could be overshooters from Strangford Lough.

Although the Island has little to offer Brent Geese in terms of feeding grounds, every winter produces at least a few birds and in some years rather larger numbers. During the Atlas period single birds or groups of two or three were normal, with slightly larger parties sometimes seen, though counts into double figures of birds actually on the ground were unusual. Sizeable flocks, however, may be observed in flight, with 44 Brents heading north over Port St Mary at the beginning of March 2002, and the exceptional records of 160 birds over Port St Mary and 150 over the Laxey area (probably the same flock) in mid-January 2001. These geese were no doubt simply passing the Isle of Man on their way to somewhere else, and most of the Brents seen on the ground do not stay long, although birds were present at Derbyhaven from late February to mid-April 2005 in numbers that gradually increased to over 40.

The first Brent Geese of the autumn usually arrive between September and November, and this species may be seen at any time during the winter and spring until April or occasionally May. The south coast is the most favoured part of the island, notably at Derbyhaven, Langness and Strandhall, localities which provide reasonably suitable habitat for Brents, especially at Derbyhaven. Elsewhere the scatter of records shows no obvious pattern, although the gravel pits at the Point of Ayre have produced one or two birds in several years and odd Brents are sometimes seen from the Calf of Man. Overall numbers seen in the Isle of Man appear to have increased during the twentieth century, but some years still produce few records and there is considerable annual variation.

Wintering	Grid squares:	Isle of Man 10 (2%) Britain and Ireland 421 (11%)
	Population:	Isle of Man 6-40 (variable year on year) Britain and Ireland 93,000

Jan	Feb	Mar	Apr	May	Jun	Jul	Aug	Sep	Oct	Nov	Dec

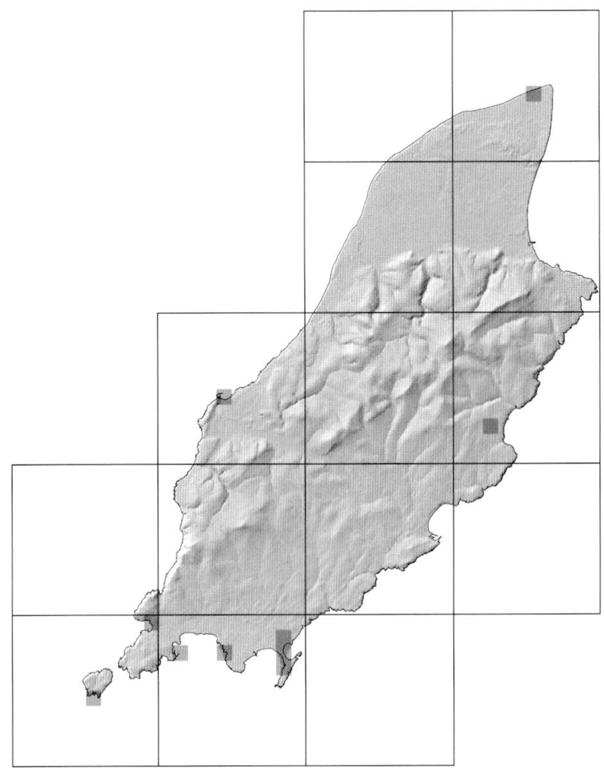

Winter presence

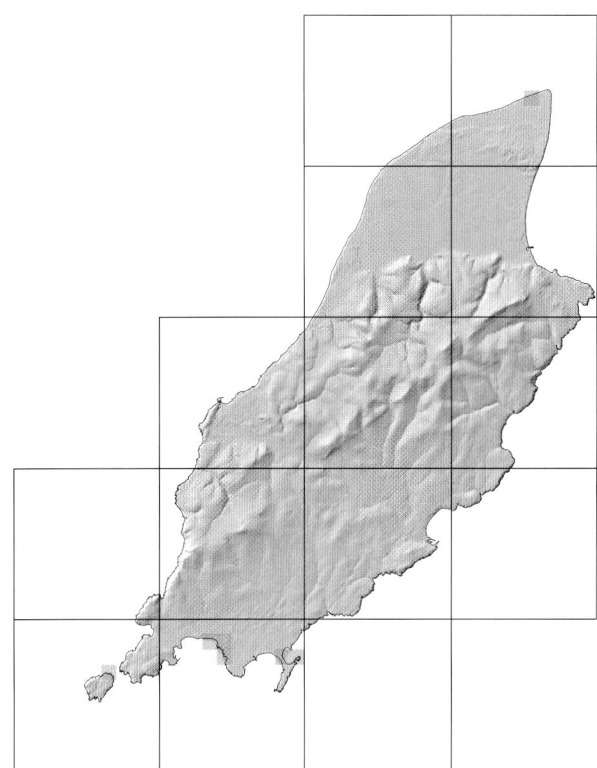

Summer presence

Shelduck (Common Shelduck)
Tadorna tadorna

Manx: *Thunnag y Scape*

The distinctive and conspicuous Shelduck is a member of a curious group of birds which to some extent seem to combine the features of both ducks and geese. Certainly Shelducks are quite at home on land and walk without a waddle, and in flight their speed and wing-beats are slower than those of more typical ducks. Their un-ducklike habits include perching on cliffs, roofs and other structures, nesting in burrows, and disappearing in summer on moult migrations, leaving their young in the care of 'aunties' which remain behind on the breeding grounds. Yet feeding Shelducks can be seen dabbling and up-ending in shallow water along with normal ducks, albeit keeping rather to themselves.

The Shelduck is essentially a bird of estuaries and muddy shores, most western European breeders spending their entire lives on lowland coasts, feeding in soft intertidal areas and nesting wherever there are suitable holes (notably rabbit burrows among sand dunes but including cavities in rocks, trees or even buildings) or patches of dense cover. As may be seen in the Isle of Man, a mixture of sandy and rocky shores is suitable for Shelducks, although numbers are smaller in such suboptimal habitats. Generally they do not penetrate far inland in western Europe, but further east a continental population is based on lakes and rivers remote from the sea, and since the late twentieth century a spread inland in parts of England has become apparent. Shelducks feed on animal matter, favouring the tiny marine snails called *Hydrobia*, but also taking other molluscs and crustaceans, plus insects and earthworms in drier habitats.

The breeding range of the Shelduck is peculiar in that it consists of two separate parts, namely a western European section stretching from the British Isles to Scandinavia and the countries from Germany to France, heavily concentrated on maritime regions, and an inland eastern part across the interior of Eurasia from the Black Sea to China. In Britain the species is generally distributed around the coasts, except in rocky and cliffbound areas, and now extending some way inland in eastern and southern England and around the Irish Sea. In Ireland suitable coastal districts are fairly well populated, but breeding away from the sea is not well developed. In the Isle of Man the Shelduck is almost entirely coastal, although Cullen and Jennings mention possible inland breeding on the northern plain and in the south-west of the Island.

The Manx breeding population of Shelducks is estimated by the MBA to consist of rather more than 100 pairs, although in view of the contention that in Britain rather less than half of adult Shelducks present in spring actually breed (1988-91 Atlas), the total number of birds on the Island during the breeding season is likely to be somewhat higher. The summer maps show two quite distinct breeding areas, one along virtually the whole coast of the northern plain (but not the Ramsey district), and the other taking in the south and south-east coast from the Calf of Man to Santon Head. The northern dunes, heaths and gravel pits provide plenty of suitable habitat, but the abundance map suggests that the stronghold of this species lies on the low but somewhat rocky coast of the south, around Carrick Bay and along the stretch from Langness to Santon Head. In the north, concentrations are apparent in the areas of the Point of Ayre, the Lhen and Jurby, while isolated groups are found at Port Mooar and Niarbyl. Comparison of the MBA map with that of Cullen and Jennings suggests some expansion in the range of the Shelduck in the Isle of Man, and the MBA estimate of the number of breeding pairs amounts to seven times that made by these earlier authors.

Shelducks largely abandon the Isle of Man by July, migrating to moulting grounds on the Heligoland Bight or perhaps in Bridgewater Bay, and in most years few birds are then recorded on the Island until November or even December. From November onwards numbers build up to a peak during the late winter, when flocks of up to 40 birds may be seen in favoured spots on the south coast such as Carrick Bay, Langness and Derbyhaven. By this time around 150 Shelducks are likely to be present in the Isle of Man, more than twice as many as implied by Cullen and Jennings, thus again indicating a considerable increase. The winter maps confirm the dominance of the southern shores of the Island at this season, with few birds returning to other areas until spring. Flocks of non-breeders, perhaps containing as many as 60 birds (C&J), remain in the south until June or July, when they depart for the moulting grounds ahead of the breeding birds.

1977–81

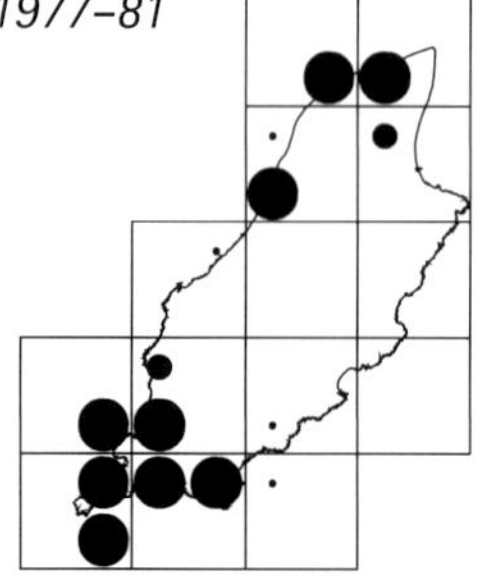

1998–2002

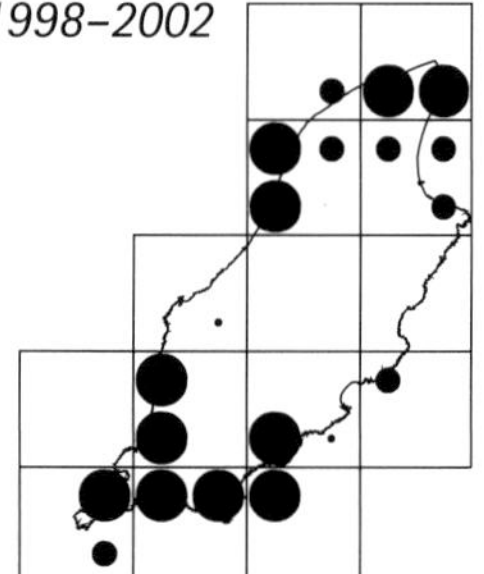

Breeding	Grid squares:	Isle of Man 87 (13%) Britain 959 Ireland 183 Total 1,142 (30%)
	Population:	Isle of Man 105-109 Britain 10,600 Ireland 1,100 (28% of European)
Wintering	Grid squares:	Isle of Man 28 (4%) Britain and Ireland 1,135 (29%)
	Population:	Isle of Man <150 Britain and Ireland 66,000-73,000

Jan	Feb	Mar	Apr	May	Jun	Jul	Aug	Sep	Oct	Nov	Dec

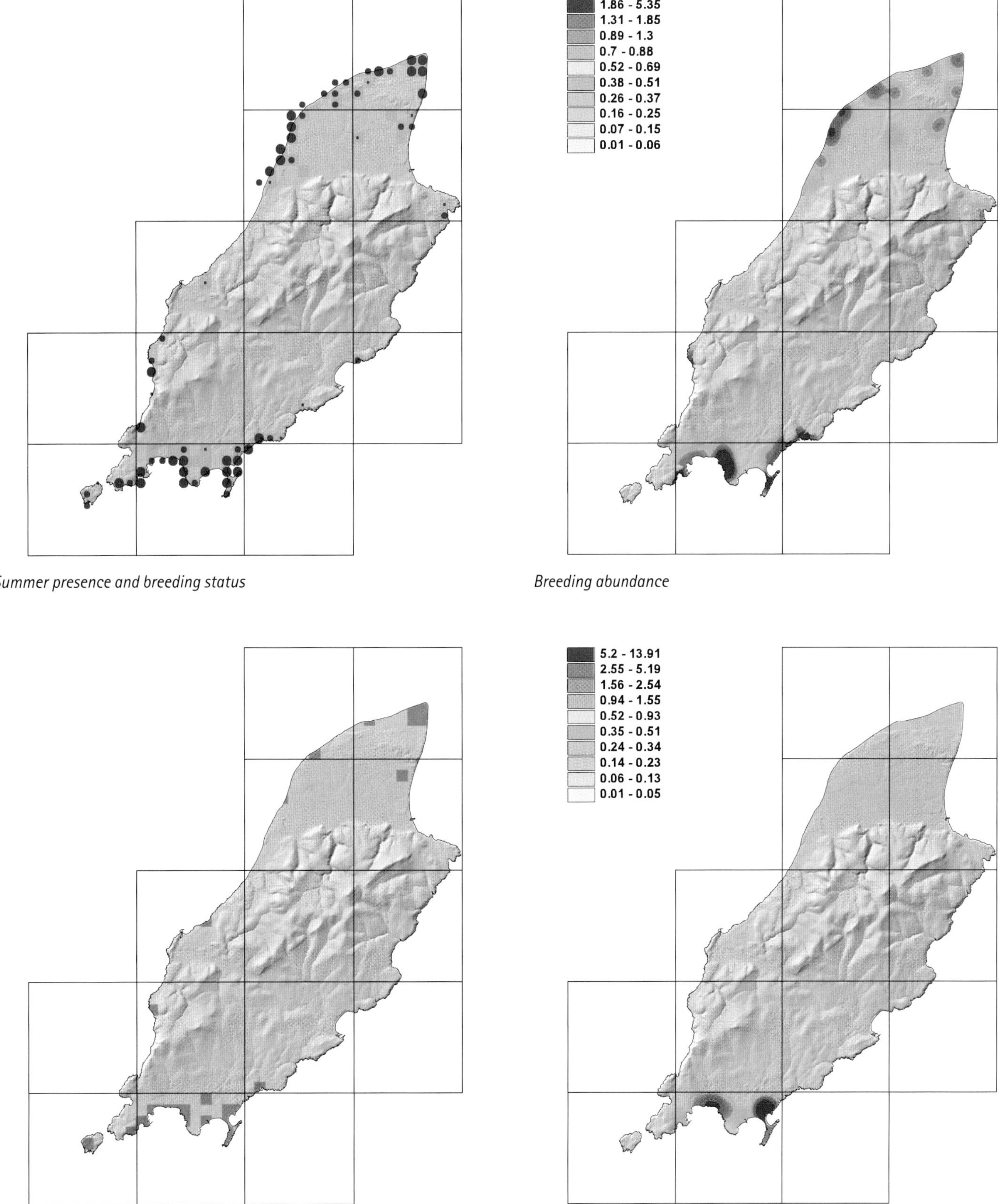

Summer presence and breeding status

Breeding abundance

Winter presence

Winter abundance

Individual Sponsors – Mr. G Craine, Mr. C & Mrs. M Crosland, Mr. & Mrs. R D Quine, Mrs. M F Sharpe, Dr. W R Walsh

Wigeon
Anas penelope

Manx: *Thunnag veg feie* = Little wild duck

The neatly proportioned Wigeon has its distinctive features, at least in the male bird, such as the reddish-brown head and the buffy-yellow forehead, but the real clincher is the pleasant but penetrating whistle given by the drake, sure to be heard if these gregarious birds are around. If a closely packed flock of ducks is seen busily grazing in a grassy area during the winter, they are almost sure to be Wigeon, as these birds habitually leave the water and feed on land. They also like to forage while swimming, but prefer to obtain their food from the surface rather than up-ending like other dabbling ducks. When they take to the air, the white forewings of the males catch the eye.

Although Wigeon breed mostly at fresh waters, where they prefer open lakes with plentiful plant life on and under the surface, as wintering birds they are particularly associated with the coast, ideally with shallow reasonably sheltered water and wide expanses of intertidal sand or mud. These requirements cause Wigeon to congregate particularly on estuaries, but modest numbers are also found on more exposed and even relatively rocky coasts, such as those in the Isle of Man. Saltmarshes and brackish lagoons attract this species, which also occurs increasingly inland in the British Isles, favouring lowland lakes and reservoirs with extensive shallows and gently sloping banks, and feeding additionally in grass and arable fields and on flooded land. The basic foods of Wigeon include eelgrass (*Zostera*) and algae on the coast, pondweed and other aquatic vegetation in fresh water, and grasses, herbs and crop material on land, the birds consuming most parts of the plants including leaves, roots and seeds.

The Wigeon breeds widely in Eurasia, from Iceland and Great Britain eastwards to the farthest extremity of the continent, mainly in the boreal zone between the Arctic and the temperate regions. There were no British breeding records until 1834 in Scotland and 1897 in England, but by the late twentieth century an estimated 300 to 500 pairs were nesting in Britain, mainly between Orkney and Yorkshire and particularly favouring lakes and pools in upland areas. The Wigeon, however, has not succeeded in colonising Ireland, where a great deal of apparently suitable breeding habitat exists. In the Isle of Man Wigeon are simply winter visitors and there are no breeding records, not surprisingly in view of the lack of attractive nesting places on the Island.

The majority of Wigeon migrate from their breeding areas for the winter, those from Scandinavia and further east moving to the British Isles and continental coastlands between Denmark and Iberia, and Britain and Ireland also receive birds from Iceland, while British breeders are either more or less resident or shift south-west to some extent. Large numbers winter in Ireland, where the species is less coastal in its distribution than in Britain (WA). The origins of the birds which visit the Isle of Man are unknown, but Scotland and Iceland seem to be likely sources. The earliest arrivals take place during August, though September and especially October comprise the main period of migration to and (presumably) through the Island, flocks of up to 150 birds being regularly recorded during the latter month. During the winter there is an increase in numbers until January or February, at which time flocks of over 200 birds are not unusual and 300 or even 400 may be exceeded, the MBA estimating that 1,000 Wigeon may be present on the Island in midwinter. During March flocks are smaller, although counts of over 100 birds may occur early in the month, and by April groups of single figures are normal, with odd ones recorded occasionally in the summer.

The localities in the Isle of Man which attract Wigeon are situated in the far north and the extreme south of the Island, reflecting the dearth of suitable habitat on the mainly cliffbound coasts in between these areas. Three sites stand out as favourites for Wigeon, namely the Glascoe area north of Ramsey and the southern shores at Langness and Strandhall. Glascoe Dub and the often flooded fields nearby produced flocks of up to 420 birds during the Atlas period, although numbers fluctuate according to the conditions there. The combination of mud, sand and seaweed-covered rocks at Langness and Derbyhaven is traditionally the most reliable haunt of Wigeon on the Island, regularly holding 200 or more birds, but the low rocky shore at Strandhall, also customarily hosting 200+ Wigeon, is now a clear rival. Sites with smaller numbers of this species include the gravel pits at the Point of Ayre and parts of Carrick Bay other than Strandhall. Cullen and Jennings highlight the same major sites for Wigeon as those identified from the MBA data, but the number of birds present on the Island may have increased somewhat since their book was published.

Breeding	Grid squares:	Isle of Man 14 (2%) – all non-breeding Britain 360 Ireland 25 Total 385 (10%)
	Population:	Isle of Man 0 Britain 400 Ireland 0 (<1% of European)
Wintering	Grid squares:	Isle of Man 44 (7%) Britain and Ireland 1,885 (49%)
	Population:	Isle of Man 1,000 Britain and Ireland 300,000+

Jan	Feb	Mar	Apr	May	Jun	Jul	Aug	Sep	Oct	Nov	Dec

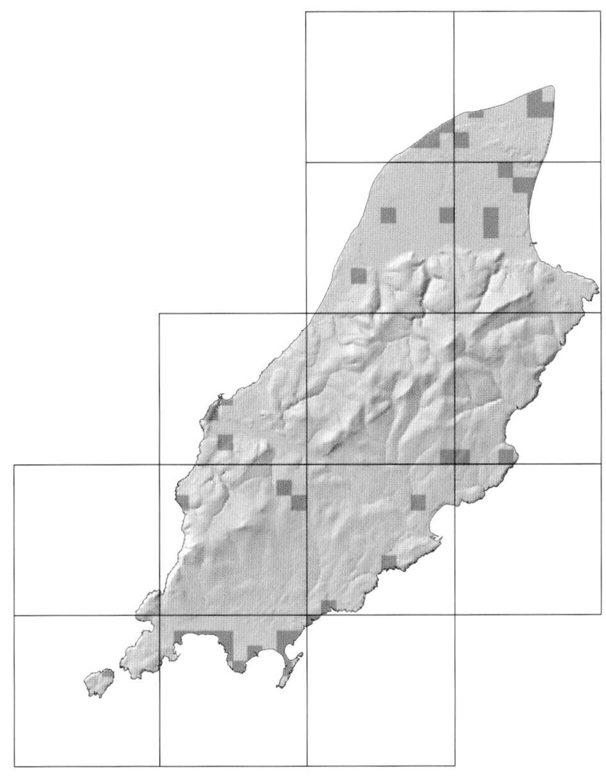

Winter presence

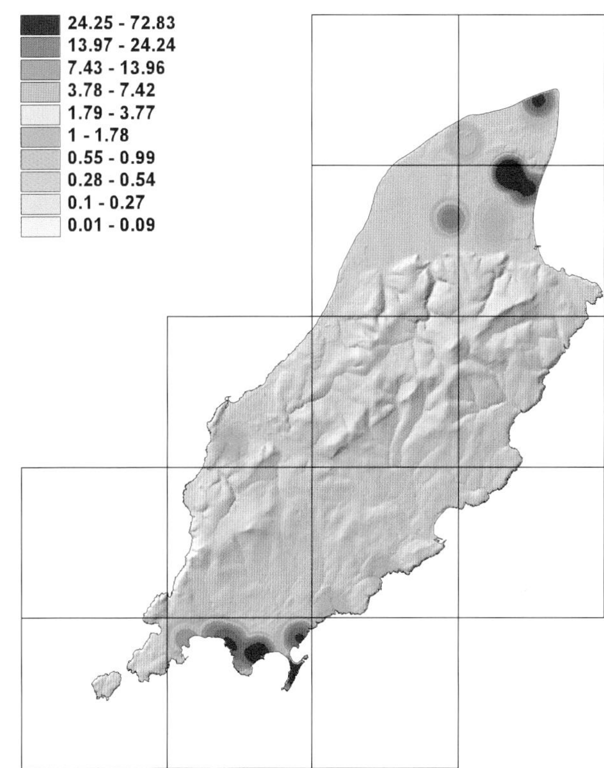

Winter abundance

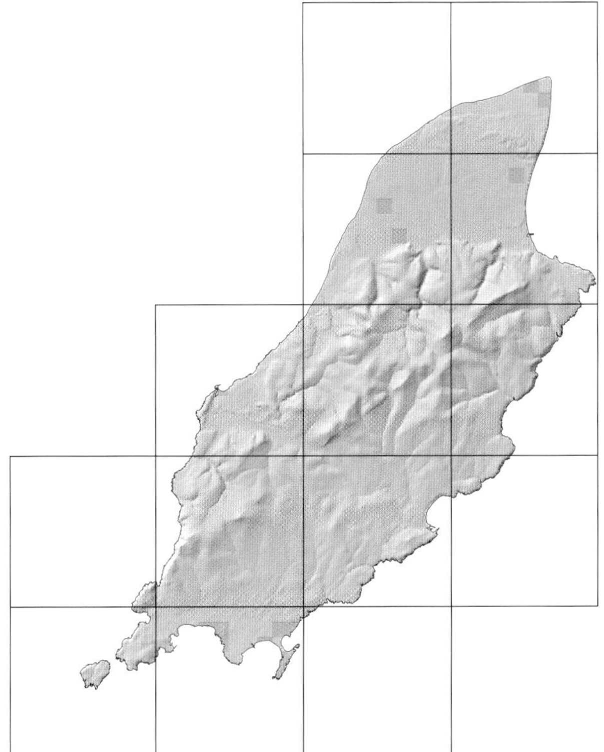

Summer presence

Individual Sponsor – Manx Game Preservation Society

Gadwall
Anas strepera

Manx: *Laagh ghlass*

At first sight the Gadwall (even the male) seems to be rather a drab bird by the standards of dabbling ducks, with grey, brown and black plumage relieved only by a white belly and a conspicuous white speculum on the wing. Seen closely in good light, however, Gadwalls are quietly attractive, their apparently dull colouring being made up of spots, crescents and freckles intricately superimposed on a paler background. This species does not stand out in a mass of ducks and is easily overlooked at a casual glance, but is worth searching for as a relatively uncommon bird in the Isle of Man whose numbers, however, appear to be on the increase.

Gadwalls are essentially freshwater birds, preferring reasonably shallow conditions with plentiful growth of emergent plants around the margins but also substantial open stretches of water surface and dry ground. In winter they congregate on larger water bodies than during the breeding season, favouring sizeable lakes, reservoirs and estuaries, a choice of habitat which suggests that the Isle of Man is unlikely to become a major resort for this species. On the other hand, as most of the Gadwalls nesting in England are thought to be descended from captive stock, tolerance of smaller sheets of water may be a feature of those visiting the Island. Like some of its relatives, the Gadwall is not averse to feeding on land, either on the banks of water bodies or in fields of grass and crops, notably cereals. Its basic food consists chiefly of leaves, roots, tubers and seeds of aquatic plants like pondweeds and sedges, obtained largely by head-dipping rather than by up-ending or by picking from the surface, and at times Gadwalls seem to feed on insects and other small invertebrates.

Although the Gadwall breeds right across Eurasia and North America in middle latitudes, its distribution in western Europe, eastern Asia and eastern North America is remarkably patchy, and it seems most at home in the continental interiors, far from the oceans. The British Isles form part of a scatter of breeding places between Iceland and the Black Sea, and the first record of nesting in Britain relates to wing-clipped captured birds breeding in Norfolk about 1850, since when a slow spread has taken place through eastern, midland and southern England. Small numbers breed in Wales, Scotland and Ireland, some of these birds perhaps being truly wild rather than feral in origin. The Gadwall seems to have become a regular visitor to the Isle of Man only since the 1980s (C&J), most often recorded in the autumn and early winter, although it has occurred in every month of the year. Numbers remain small, with no group of more than 7 birds reported to the MBA, although Madoc (writing in the early 1930s) mentions as many as 12 at Langness in August to September.

The origins of the Gadwalls seen on the Island are open to question. Most British breeders, perhaps in keeping with their introduced status, are more or less sedentary and winter in their breeding areas, while the birds recorded in Ireland and (the few) in Scotland in winter are probably genuinely wild visitors from Iceland. Gadwalls nesting in the more northerly and central parts of Europe generally migrate to the countries bordering the North Sea, including Britain, for the winter. The nearest significant breeding groups to the Isle of Man are those of Strangford Lough and Anglesey, and wanderers from these areas could easily reach Manx territory. The population of this species in the British Isles continues to increase, but the Isle of Man is situated well away from the main concentrations, and it seems unlikely that anything but a minor improvement in its status will take place on the Island during the foreseeable future. In early May 2001, however, a pair of Gadwalls were seen in what was considered to be suitable nesting habitat among pools on the heath of the Ayres, a rather unexpected record of 'probable breeding' which seems not to have been repeated.

During the Atlas period only five grid squares held Gadwalls in winter, containing the gravel pits at the Point of Ayre (two squares), the artificial pools at Ballanette, Kionslieu Dam, and the ornamental lakes at Billown. Reports at other seasons were scattered through all months between March and October and involved very few birds, including a total of about half a dozen over three years at Langness and the notable count of seven at the lake within Glen Truan Golf Course (on the Ayres), the latter record relating to mid-July 2002. Even at the most reliable sites, Gadwalls remain elusive quarry for the Manx birdwatcher.

Breeding	Grid squares:	Isle of Man 6 (1%) Britain 357 Ireland 25 Total 382 (10%)
	Population:	Isle of Man 1 Britain 770 Ireland 30 (3% of European)
Wintering	Grid squares:	Isle of Man 5 (1%) Britain and Ireland 645 (17%)
	Population:	Isle of Man 0-2 Britain and Ireland 4,000+

Jan	Feb	Mar	Apr	May	Jun	Jul	Aug	Sep	Oct	Nov	Dec

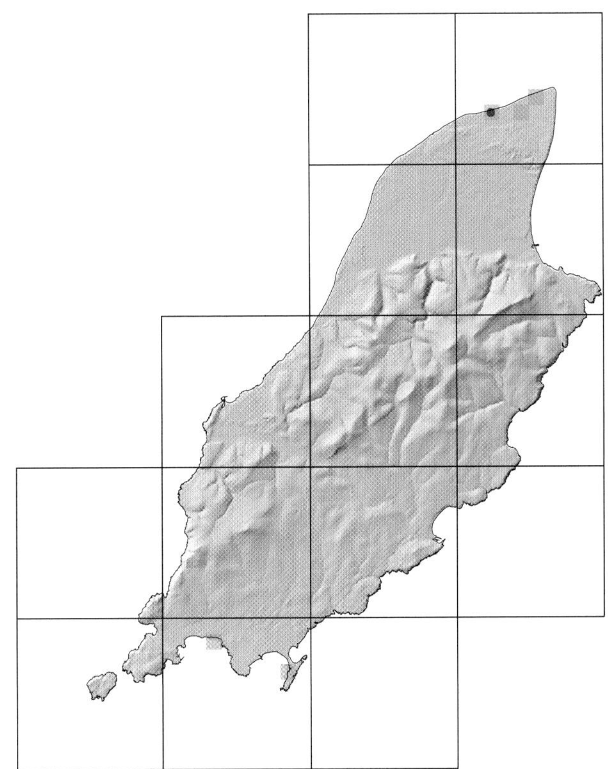

Summer presence and breeding status

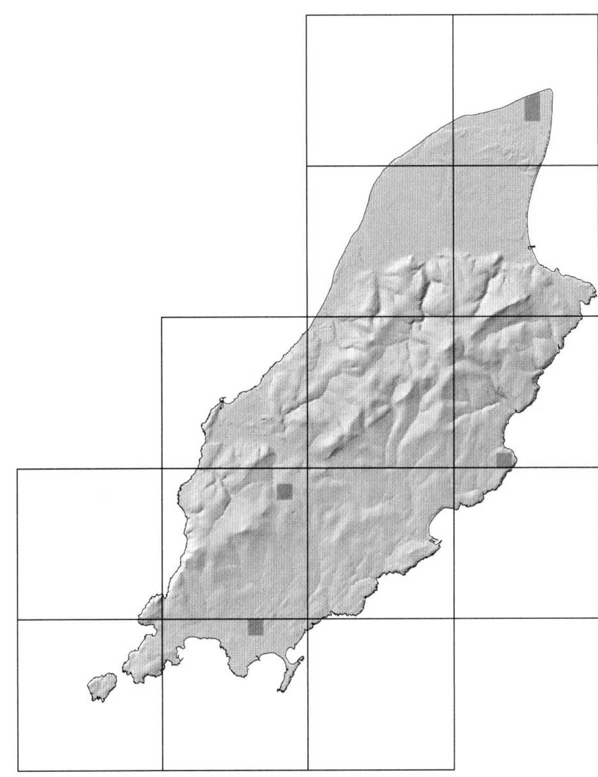

Winter presence

Teal (Eurasian Teal)
Anas crecca

Manx: *Laagh Laaghag*

With its diminutive size and narrow, pointed wings, the Teal in flight could at first glance be mistaken for a wader, an impression possible even on the ground, as this species sometimes forages by walking in very shallow water and filtering liquid mud through its bill. Among the other wader-like flying habits of these agile ducks are their almost vertical take-offs from both land and water and the synchronised manoeuvres in tightly packed flocks as they zip across a lake just above the surface. Teal swim rather delicately but they have a waddling gait typical of the dabbling ducks, as is the marked difference in plumage between the striking drake and unassuming female.

Almost any kind of water body may be frequented by Teal, including small ponds and pools, sometimes remote from other waters. Although preferring productive (eutrophic) conditions, this species is able to utilise relatively infertile (oligotrophic) upland bogs, much favoured for nesting in Britain, the main requirement being a zone of fringing vegetation providing adequate cover. In lowland areas Teal breed on all types of still or slow-flowing water with plentiful emergent plants, including pools and streams which are parts of large wetlands. In winter they are not averse to more open lakes and reservoirs, and they also occur on lagoons and saltmarshes along coasts, even appearing on the sea itself in shallow inlets and other sheltered spots. Although Teal will eat molluscs, crustaceans, insect larvae and other invertebrates, this animal food is mainly taken in summer, and at other seasons seeds, mainly those of aquatic plants such as sedges, pondweeds and bulrushes.

The Teal breeds in a broad band, mainly in middle latitudes, across Eurasia from Iceland, the British Isles and France all the way to the Pacific shores, being replaced in North America by the very similar Green-winged Teal *Anas carolinensis*, now regarded as a separate species. Although nesting over most of northern and central Europe, Teal tend to breed at low density even in favourable areas, a situation exemplified in Britain and Ireland, where considerably fewer pairs breed than might be suggested by the maps in the BTO atlases. They are scattered through the uplands of Scotland and northern England, extending into the Midlands and East Anglia and even reaching the south coast, but most of the English population is very thinly spread and breeding is sporadic in many areas. The Teal has been seriously declining in Britain since the mid-twentieth century, and even more so in Ireland, where the species breeds mainly in the north and west.

In the Isle of Man Teal have long been known to breed in very small numbers, and Cullen and Jennings mention nesting in the Ballaugh Curraghs and beside the pools along the inland edge of the Ayres heath. Teal are secretive when nesting, and they occur as odd pairs in overgrown watery places, so that the inconspicuousness of the birds and difficulties of access for observers seriously reduce the chances of finding evidence of breeding. The situation on the Island has not changed since the publication of Cullen and Jennings' book, and the MBA estimates a Manx breeding population of 10 to 15 pairs, with nesting confirmed on the Ayres east of Rue Point and counted as probable in twelve other northern grid squares, including five in the area of the Curraghs, two on the Ayres and one containing Lough Cranstal. A cluster of three squares near the centre of the Island refers to the dams at Kionslieu and the Eairy, and the central valley west of Crosby, breeding being confirmed at Kionslieu in 2002 (Cullen 2004).

Although Teal breeding in the British Isles and on the European continent from the Netherlands and France southwards are more or less resident, most populations of this species migrate south or south-west in the autumn, those from Scandinavia eastwards wintering around the North Sea (also south to the Mediterranean) and reaching the British Isles in large numbers, where they are joined by most of the Icelandic breeders. The Isle of Man plays host to perhaps 1,500 Teal in winter, the birds arriving mainly from October onwards and departing fairly suddenly in March and early April. Peak counts tend to occur between November and February, but Teal move to milder areas during hard weather in Britain and so numbers on the Island would be expected to fluctuate during the season. The Manx wintering population is widely scattered, the small waters of the northern plain holding the largest numbers overall, although Langness is the single most productive site, with maxima in recent years topping 200 or 300 and sometimes approaching 500. Other localities attracting significant flocks include Glascoe Dub, Bishop's Dub, Kionslieu Dam and Eairy Dam. With the obvious exception of Langness, Teal on the Island are not particularly associated with the coast.

1977–81

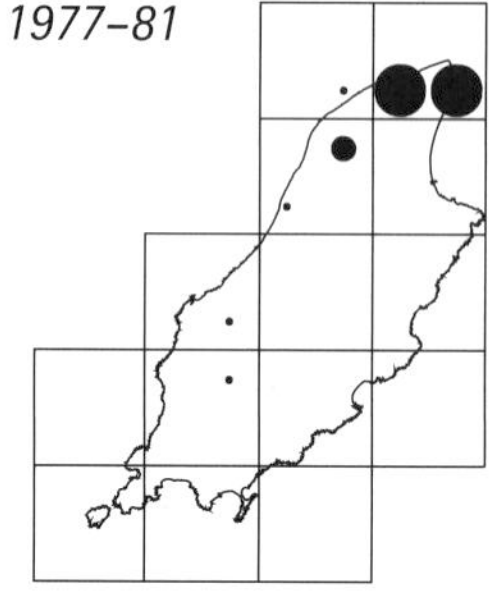

1998–2002

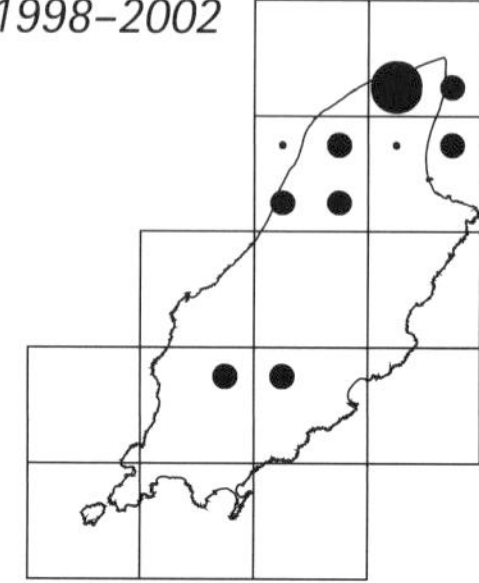

Breeding	Grid squares:	Isle of Man 50 (8%) Britain 1,147 Ireland 188 Total 1,335 (35%)
	Population:	Isle of Man 10-15 Britain 2,050 Ireland 550 (1% of European)
Wintering	Grid squares:	Isle of Man 66 (10%) Britain and Ireland 2,522 (65%)
	Population:	Isle of Man 1,500 Britain and Ireland 130,000-150,000

Jan	Feb	Mar	Apr	May	Jun	Jul	Aug	Sep	Oct	Nov	Dec

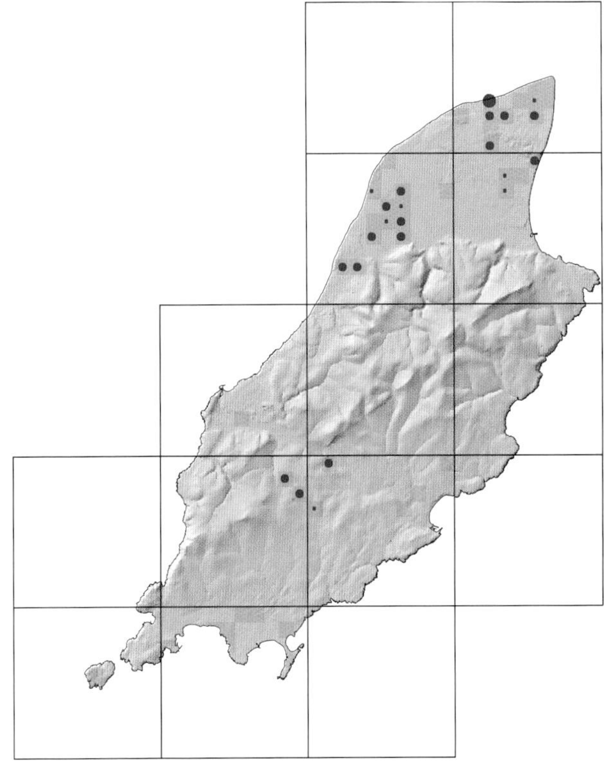

Summer presence and breeding status

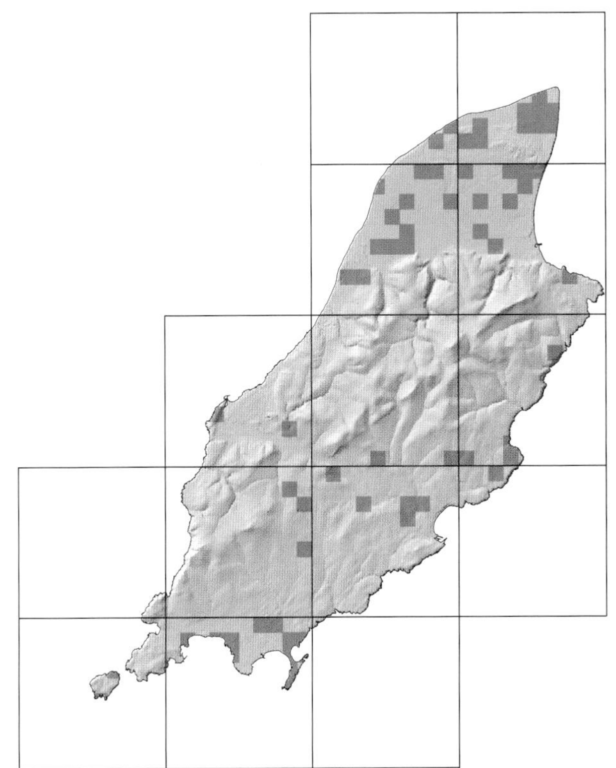

Winter presence

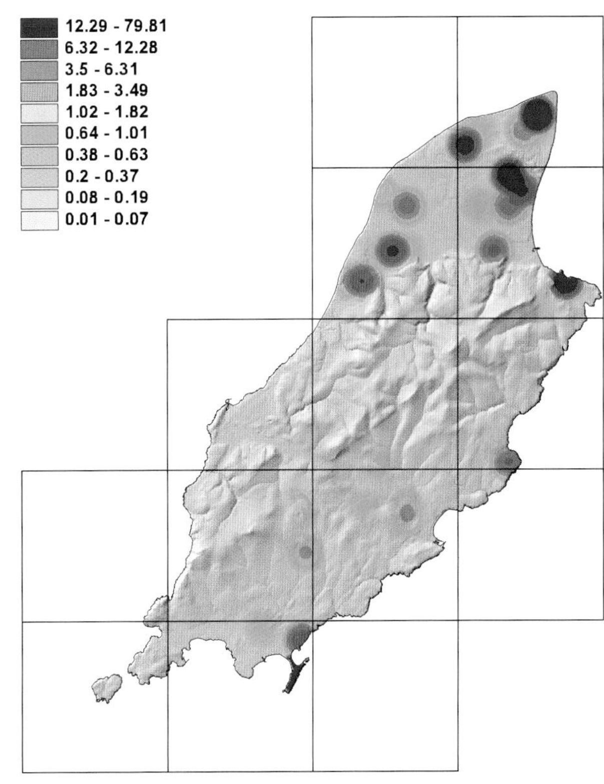

Winter abundance

Individual Sponsors – Crane of Cluny, Ms C M Moore

Mallard
Anas platyrhynchos

Manx: *Thunnag feie* = Wild Duck

By far the commonest and best known of the ducks, the familiar Mallard needs no introduction. A large and solid bird, the Mallard is regarded as the standard dabbling duck, showing all the normal features of such birds, including plumage details like a metallic speculum on the wing, feeding methods such as head-dipping and up-ending, and the quacking calls of the female birds. As the Mallard is the ancestor of most of the domestic types of ducks, wild Mallards often breed with farmyard varieties, producing a mixed array of colours and patterns, while some genuine-looking Mallards may not be truly wild. At lakes in town parks, in the grounds of wildfowl collections, and even on waters situated well away from sources of tame birds, the exact status of many Mallards is impossible to judge.

The Mallard occurs on virtually any type of water body, from the largest lakes to the smallest ponds, whether still or flowing, open or choked with vegetation, fresh, brackish or saline, natural or artificial, urban or rural. Even the apparently ubiquitous Mallard, however, has its limitations, generally avoiding deep or exposed sites, infertile (oligotrophic) waters, fast-flowing rivers and streams, and rocky or cliffbound coasts. Although basically a species of inland habitats, the Mallard often resorts to sheltered and shallow areas of sea, a habit particularly well seen in the Isle of Man. When breeding, plentiful growth of aquatic and bankside vegetation is preferred, although Mallards use a wide range of nest-sites, including hollow trees, nest boxes and recesses in buildings. This omnivorous species feeds on leaves, buds, seeds and other parts of a great variety of aquatic and terrestrial plants, including farm crops such as grass, cereals and potatoes, and many birds rely on artificial food provided by the public. Animals taken include insects, crustaceans, molluscs, worms and fish, with a concentration on the immobile or slower-moving types.

Mallards breed in a broad zone stretching from the Arctic fringes to the warm temperate regions, right across Eurasia and North America, including Greenland and Iceland. In the British Isles there are few districts without nesting Mallards, most of the gaps in the range corresponding to the loftier uplands, with the highest densities found on lower ground in southern Scotland and north-west, central and eastern England. A decrease is apparent in Ireland, where the distribution of this species became more patchy during the period between the two BTO atlases of 1968–72 and 1988–91. Presence of Mallards during the breeding season was recorded by the MBA in about half of the 1km grid squares of the Isle of Man, with the most obvious blanks on the map faithfully tracing the hilly backbone of the Island, where such waters as exist are acidic and therefore oligotrophic. Elsewhere Mallards are common breeders in suitable places, with their main strength, as shown by the abundance map, based on the northern plain, the central valley, and the south-east of the Island. The MBA estimates breeding numbers of Mallards in the Isle of Man at 600 or 700 pairs, but Ralfe, writing in 1905, considered that 'very few' nested in his day, and clearly a major increase and expansion took place during the twentieth century. Comparison of Cullen and Jennings' map of breeding distribution with its MBA equivalent suggests that consolidation is still occurring on the Island.

Mallards breeding in the maritime regions of western Europe are chiefly resident and reluctant to move far, even if freezing conditions develop in their home areas. Manx Mallards, therefore, may generally stay on the Island all their lives, although ducklings ringed in the Isle of Man have been recovered in Scotland, Yorkshire and Northern Ireland (C&J), suggesting some movement of young birds. Most of the Mallards of northern and eastern Europe move to the British Isles and the adjacent continent for the winter, and many Icelandic birds also migrate to Britain and Ireland. Numbers in the Isle of Man begin to increase in July and this trend usually continues until the end of the year, when peak numbers may top 2,000 (MBA estimate), followed by a decrease between January and April (C&J), leaving the locally nesting birds and a population of perhaps 100 non-breeders.

The winter map shows a similar distribution to that of the breeding season, although the map of abundance suggests some coastward movement in the east of the Island. Highest figures are recorded at Langness, where over 200 birds may occur, and other notable haunts include the Point of Ayre Gravel Pits, Bishop's Dub, Ballaugh Curraghs, the reservoirs of Kerrowdhoo and Kionslieu, some small waters like the lakes at Ballachrink (south of Baldwin) and Crogga (west of Port Soderick), together with the coasts at Garwick, Ballanayre Strand and Carrick Bay. Most of these sites hold good numbers of Mallards all year round, emphasising the relatively sedentary nature of this species.

1977–81

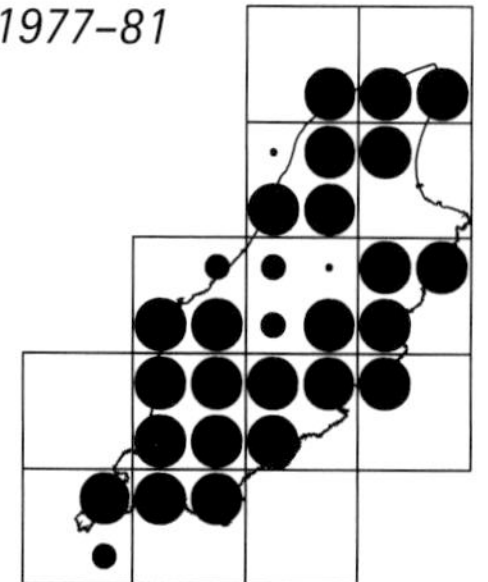

1998–2002

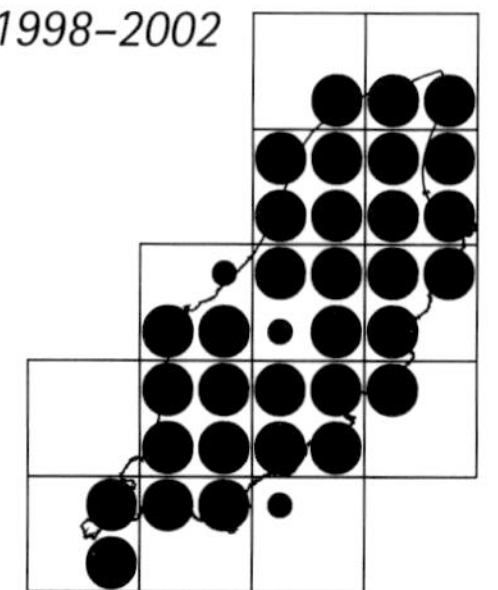

Breeding	Grid squares:	Isle of Man 355 (53%) Britain 2,596 Ireland 831 Total 3,427 (89%)
	Population:	Isle of Man 596-688 Britain 115,000 Ireland 23,000 (6% of European)
Wintering	Grid squares:	Isle of Man 221 (33%) Britain and Ireland 3,360 (87%)
	Population:	Isle of Man 2,000+ Britain and Ireland 550,000

Jan	Feb	Mar	Apr	May	Jun	Jul	Aug	Sep	Oct	Nov	Dec

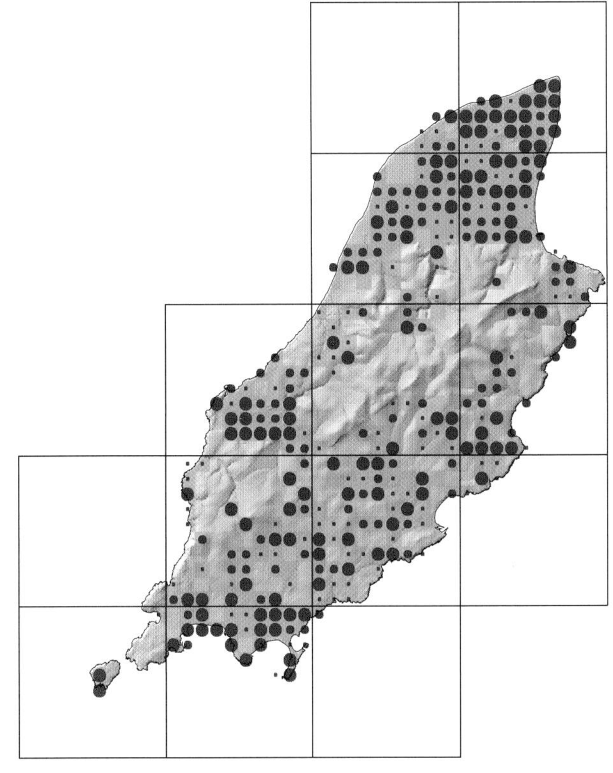

Summer presence and breeding status

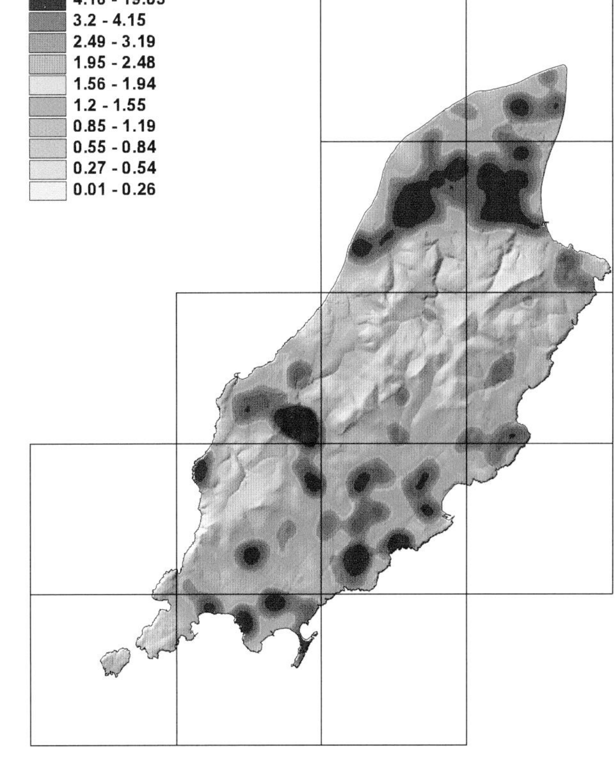

Breeding abundance

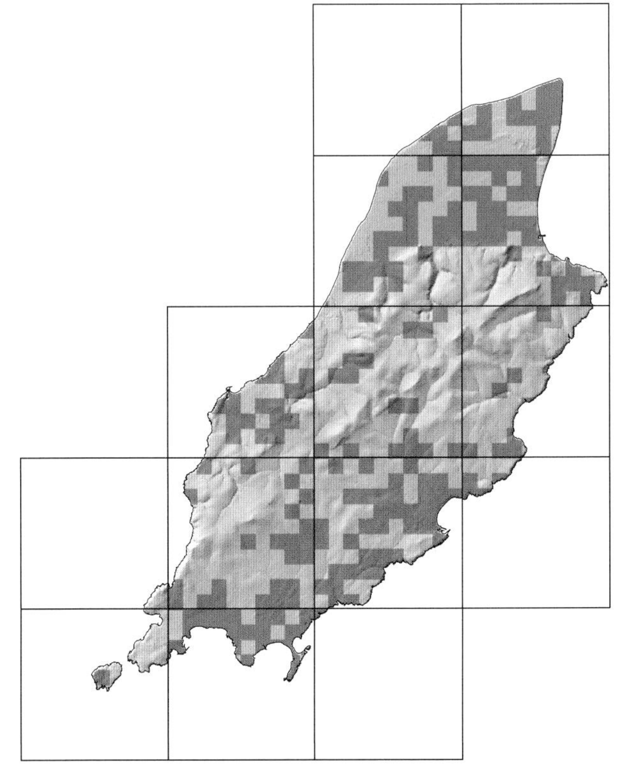

Winter presence

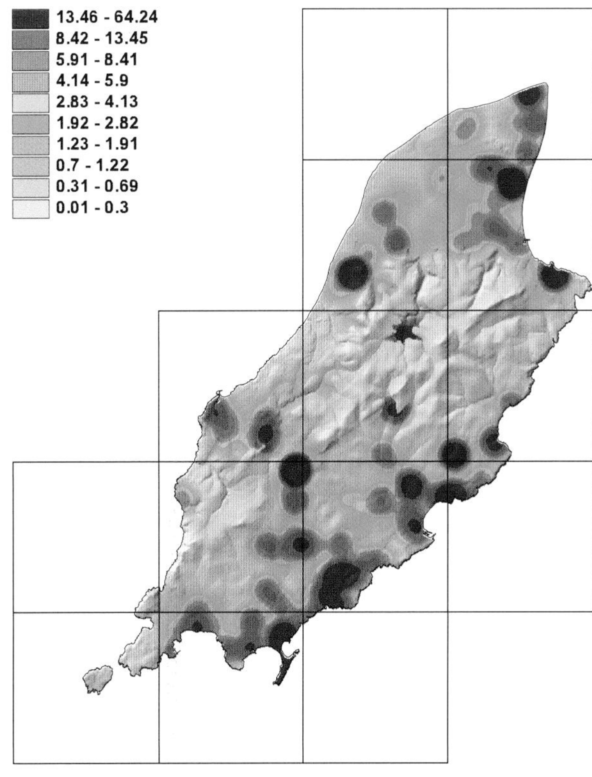

Winter abundance

Individual Sponsors – Mr. N & Mrs. L Keig

Shoveler (Northern Shoveler)
Anas clypeata

Manx: *Thunnag ny Sleryst*

The giant-sized spatulate bill of the Shoveler is usually easy to see, even when the bird is in flight, but the drake is also distinctively plumaged, with his bottle-green head, snow-white breast and bright chestnut sides and belly, and both sexes display rather surprising light blue forewings. Shovelers are not just dabbling ducks, but could almost be described as avian vacuum cleaners, sweeping the surface and sucking in water through the filters in their impressive bills. This highly specialised duck looks rather top-heavy when swimming, but in fact is nicely adapted for its particular way of feeding.

For both breeding and wintering the Shoveler favours fairly small, shallow and productive (eutrophic) waters, normally with no shortage of emergent vegetation round the edges. Shovelers are essentially birds of lowland fresh or brackish lakes and marshes, avoiding the infertile water bodies of the uplands and unsuited to feeding in marine conditions except where there are shallow pools or lagoons. They use their massive bills to take in considerable quantities of water, from which tiny food items are strained out by fine serrated structures in their mouths, a technique found in other dabbling ducks but taken to an extreme in the case of the Shoveler. Additionally this species uses other feeding methods typical of ducks, such as head dipping and up-ending, and sometimes even engages in shallow dives. Shovelers eat a wide variety of both animal and vegetable material, including small crustaceans and molluscs, aquatic insects and their larvae, and various parts of water plants, particularly seeds, many of these foods forming part of the freshwater plankton.

The breeding range of the Shoveler stretches virtually the whole way across Eurasia and North America east as far as the Great Lakes, almost entirely contained within temperate latitudes and mainly based in the continental interiors. In western Europe its distribution is decidedly patchy and extends from Iceland (fewer than 50 pairs), Norway, the British Isles and France eastwards. Shovelers are sparsely distributed in Britain, concentrated in the eastern and midland counties of England between Yorkshire and the Thames basin, and Ireland holds hardly more than 100 pairs, chiefly in the area of Lough Neagh and the middle Shannon system. In the Isle of Man the Shoveler is a winter visitor in very small numbers, but perhaps rather unexpectedly there have also been three definite instances of breeding on the Island, first proved with two nests at pools on the Ayres in 1947 after being suspected for at least 12 years (C&J). Further breeding records came from St Judes in 1964 and the Lagagh (north of Andreas) in 1979 (C&J), and during the Atlas surveys nesting was thought probable at Glascoe Dub in 1999 and possible at the Point of Ayre gravel pits in 1998 and 2000. Over the years breeding has been suspected at various sites in the north of the Island, where the numerous ponds and little lakes provide suitable habitat, but Shovelers in Britain are known to occur in early summer on waters where they apparently do not intend to nest.

The majority of Shovelers are migratory, including most British breeders, which winter mainly in the Mediterranean region, to be replaced in the British Isles by birds from Scandinavia, Russia and (presumably) Iceland. The birds reaching the Isle of Man arrive mainly in October, sometimes earlier, and fewer than ten birds are recorded through the winter, reports continuing during April and so on some occasions giving rise to suspicions of breeding. Cullen and Jennings suggest similar numbers to those recorded by the MBA, but Glascoe seems to have replaced Langness as the prime site for this species, being particularly reliable in autumn. Other haunts include the gravel pits at the Point of Ayre and a pond at Ballaghaue near Andreas, with odd records from elsewhere on the Island, chiefly on the northern plain and the south coast. The tendency of Shovelers to occur on small waters seldom visited by birdwatchers may cause some birds to be missed, but there can be no doubt that this species remains uncommon in the Isle of Man.

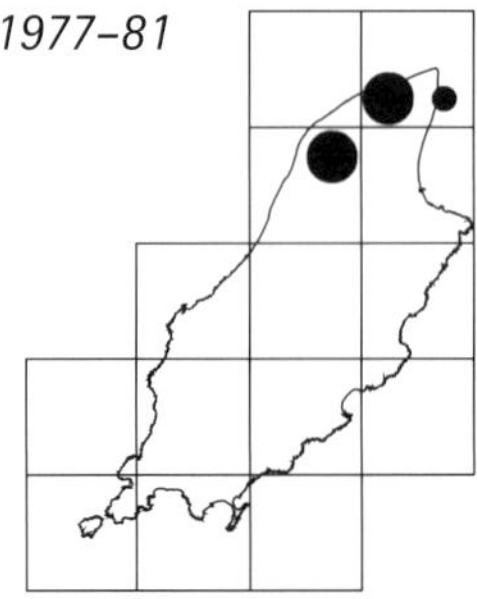

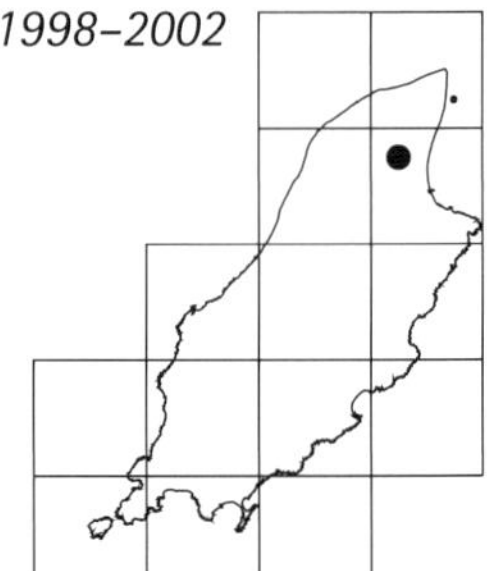

Breeding	Grid squares:	Isle of Man 8 (1%)
		Britain 454 Ireland 45 Total 499 (13%)
	Population:	Isle of Man 1-2
		Britain 1,250 Ireland <100 (4% of European)
Wintering	Grid squares:	Isle of Man 12 (2%)
		Britain and Ireland 909 (24%)
	Population:	Isle of Man <10
		Britain and Ireland 9,000-11,000

Jan Feb Mar Apr May Jun Jul Aug Sep Oct Nov Dec

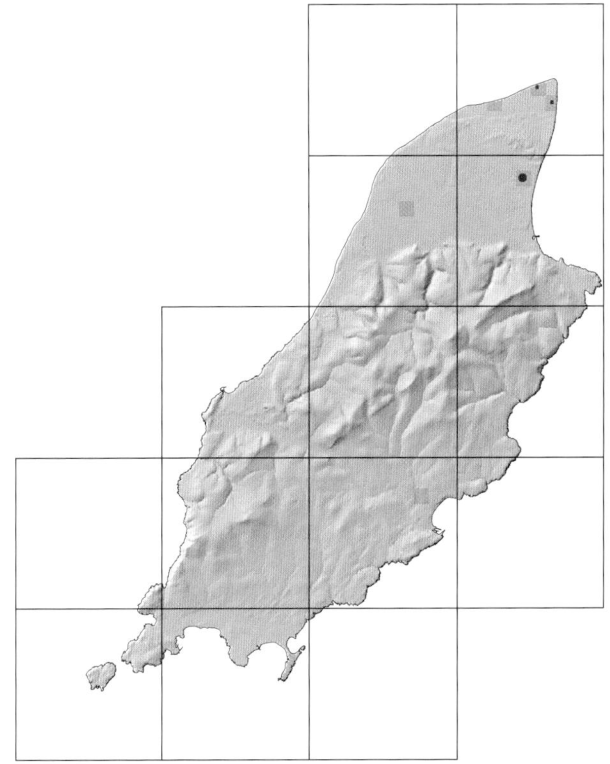

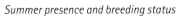

Summer presence and breeding status

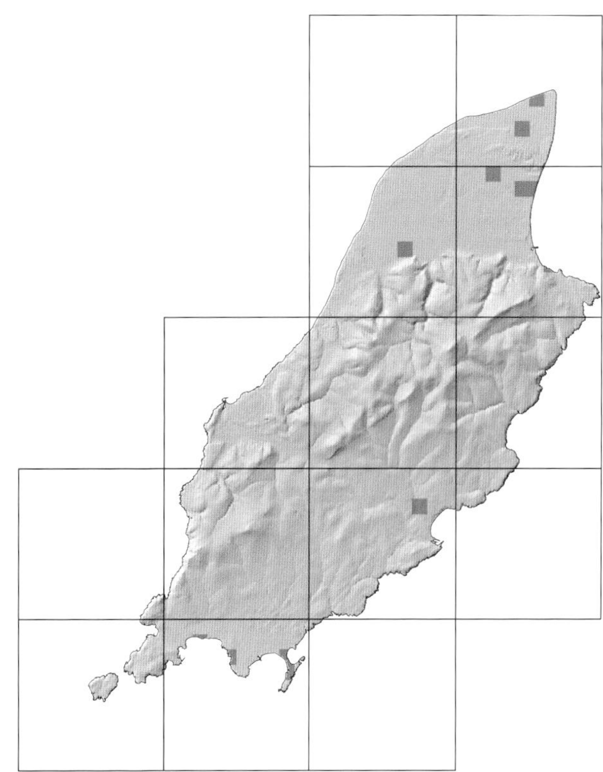
Winter presence

Pochard (Common Pochard)
Aythya ferina

Manx: *Kione Mollagh*

The rather dumpy Pochard is not brightly coloured, although the male does have a chestnut-red head and a quite conspicuous light grey body. In flight its somewhat inelegant appearance is emphasised by its relatively short wings, and like other diving ducks the Pochard needs to patter across the water surface to become airborne, in contrast to the near-vertical take-off seen in the dabbling ducks. Gatherings of this species may contain a predominance of either males or females, as the drakes flock up and leave the breeding grounds while their mates are still caring for the ducklings. Pochards and Tufted Ducks often associate, and members of this genus (*Aythya*) are prone to hybridisation with each other and consequent confusion of some unsuspecting birdwatchers when the resulting offspring are seen!

Pochards have somewhat strict habitat requirements, mainly as a result of their feeding methods, which involve diving to a depth of no more than about 2.5 metres (BWP) to collect mainly vegetable food from the bottom, so shallow and fertile (eutrophic) waters with plentiful submerged plants are sought. Pochards seem to be susceptible to disturbance while breeding, but at other seasons, though still wary by disposition, they are less fussy and visit a range of waters from large reservoirs through gravel pits to park lakes. Except in very sheltered situations, Pochards are not normally seen on the sea, as generally the conditions that they need are only provided by fresh waters. The diet of the Pochard includes all parts of aquatic plants such as pondweeds and sedges, and variable quantities of animal matter, chiefly small crustaceans and molluscs, annelid worms and water-based insects.

As a breeder the Pochard is confined to Eurasia, nesting in temperate latitudes across the continent from the British Isles as far east as central Siberia. The species breeds widely across the North European Plain and around the Baltic Sea, and scattered groups are found as far south as the Mediterranean region, with its density affected in many places by the relative scarcity of ideal habitat. In Britain Pochards were apparently rare breeders until the middle of the nineteenth century, since which time they have spread from a base in East Anglia to various parts of eastern and southern England, the Midlands and eastern Scotland, although breeding density tends to be low even in favoured areas. Some southern populations have originated from, or have been increased by, the presence of feral birds. Few Pochards breed in Ireland, and the Isle of Man, which largely lacks the substantial eutrophic waters preferred by the Pochard, counts the species merely as a scarce winter visitor.

Most Pochards leave their breeding areas for the winter, those from Scandinavia, northern Germany and further east moving to the countries around the North Sea, or flying on to reach Ireland, France, Iberia and even North Africa. British and Irish breeders may be resident, or they may simply move south or west to some extent. Whatever their origin, the birds visiting the Isle of Man begin to arrive in early August, the initial small parties reaching double figures by October or November and similar numbers being maintained or increased during the winter. Maxima at the Point of Ayre gravel pits recorded by the MBA stand at 23 for October, 46 in November, 42 during December, 56 in January, and 52 in February. The MBA estimate of a population of up to about 80 birds wintering on the Island as a whole represents a considerable increase since the 1980s (C&J), with counts since the completion of the MBA research topping 100 in the autumn of 2005. March sees numbers fall back to single figures, and odd birds are recorded during the later spring and summer, although no breeding is thought to have taken place during the Atlas period.

The winter map shows a wide but thin scatter of records around the Island, almost all on inland waters, albeit some of these close to the shore (presumably by chance). The development of the gravel pits at the Point of Ayre as an attraction for Pochards, as indeed for various other species, is responsible for a change in distribution (and perhaps an increase in numbers) on the Island since the time when Cullen and Jennings were writing (1986). These flooded pits are now by far the most important Manx resort for this species, with winter numbers there regularly topping 40 or even 50 birds. The former stronghold of the Foxdale dams (C&J) continues to play a part, however, with counts at the Eairy reaching double figures in midwinter and smaller numbers occurring at nearby Kionslieu Dam. The ornamental lakes at Billown may hold groups approaching ten birds, and other sites where at least one or two Pochards may be seen during winter include Bishop's Dub, Kerrowdhoo and Clypse Reservoirs, and the lake at Shenvalley (south of Patrick).

Breeding	Grid squares:	Isle of Man 7 (1%) Britain 511 Ireland 40 Total 551 (14%)
	Population:	Isle of Man 0 Britain 380 Ireland 30 (<1% of European)
Wintering	Grid squares:	Isle of Man 18 (3%) Britain and Ireland 1,800 (24%)
	Population:	Isle of Man <80 Britain and Ireland 80,000

Jan	Feb	Mar	Apr	May	Jun	Jul	Aug	Sep	Oct	Nov	Dec

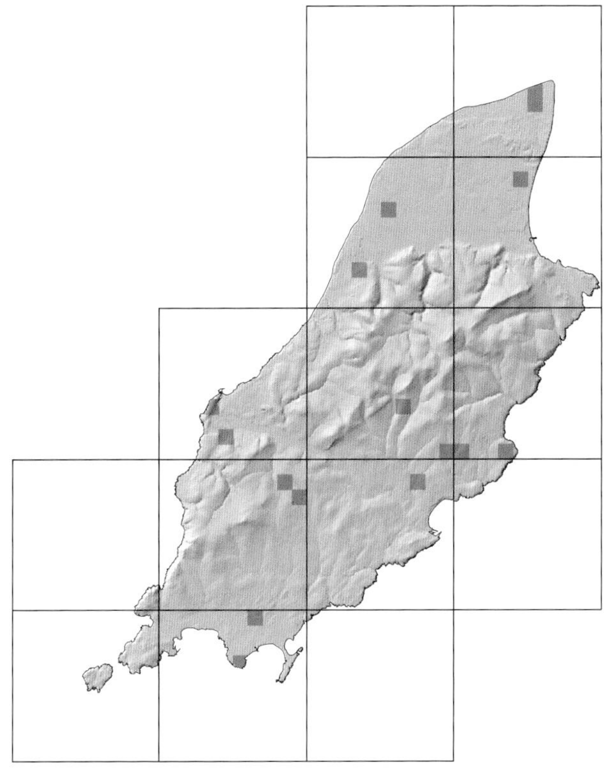

Winter presence

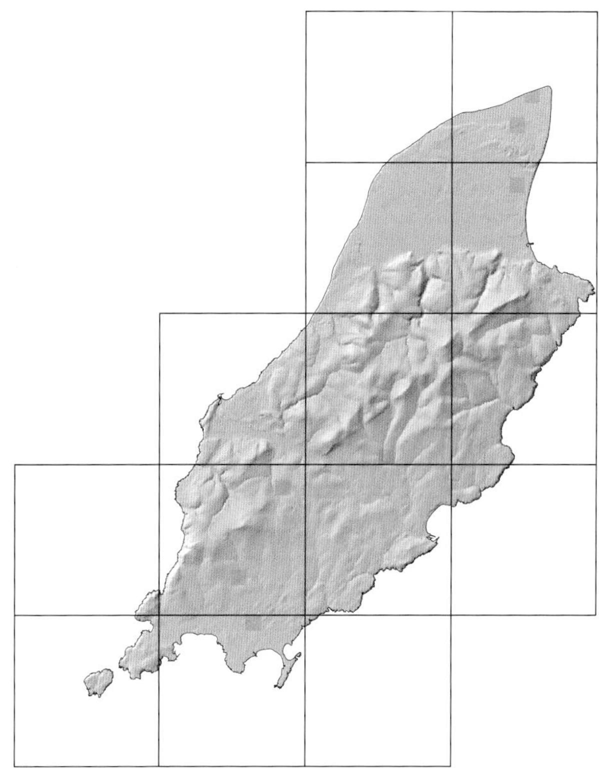

Summer presence

Tufted Duck
Aythya fuligula

Manx: *Thunnag Happagh*

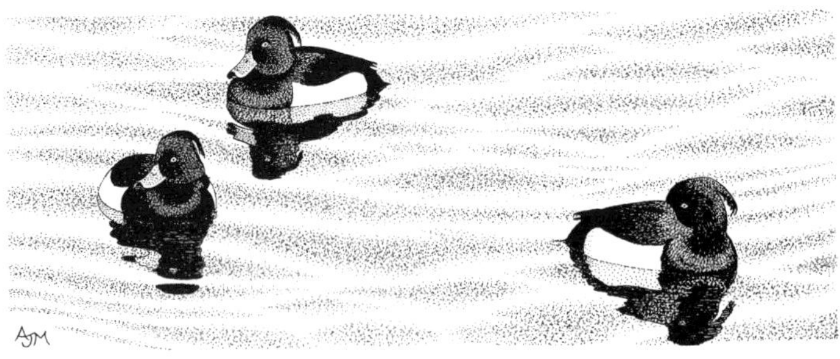

To the birdwatcher based in the British Isles the smart and compact Tufted Duck is one of the most familiar of wildfowl, and certainly the best known of the diving ducks. The drake's striking black and white plumage is a conspicuous sight on a wide range of inland waters, although the untidy drooping crest which gives the species its name may be harder to spot, and the shades-of-brown female may not catch the eye of the casual observer. The Tufted Duck is an opportunistic and successful bird which has taken advantage of new artificial habitats without the need for aid from deliberate or unintentional introductions by man.

As predominantly carnivorous diving ducks, Tufties need water with a depth of 3-14 metres (BWP) and a well-developed bottom fauna, requirements which largely confine them to productive (eutrophic) lakes and pools in lowland areas. They have shown a remarkable ability to colonise man-made stretches of water in the form of reservoirs, gravel pits and park lakes, now so much a part of the modern landscape, the birds often using islands for nesting and not being slow to accept food provided by the public. On the other hand, Tufted Ducks seem unsuited to marine conditions and tend to avoid all but the most sheltered salt water, unless freezing of their inland lakes forces them on to the coasts. Tufties eat molluscs such as freshwater mussels, crustaceans like freshwater shrimps, and aquatic insects such as the larvae of caddis flies, though seeds and other vegetable matter may also be important items in their diet.

The Tufted Duck breeds from Iceland, the British Isles and northern France eastwards across Eurasia to the Pacific coast, mostly in the more northerly parts of the temperate zone. Its solid-looking distribution in the oceanic areas of western Europe is largely a product of expansion and infilling during the last century and particularly in recent decades, this process being nowhere better illustrated than in Britain, where the species was not known to nest at all until 1849 but now boasts an estimated breeding population of up to 7,500 pairs and a range extending to almost all suitable regions of the country. Breeding was first reported in Ireland in 1877 and rapid colonisation of the north-western half of the island followed. Blank areas on the atlas maps, as in western Scotland, most of Wales, Devon and Cornwall, and south-east Ireland, reflect the lack of water bodies which satisfy the Tufted Duck's particular requirements. The success story of this species seems to have been based on climatic improvement, construction of new waters, and the spread of the zebra mussel (a major food source).

Inevitably in view of the increasing population across the water, Tufted Ducks began to appear in the Isle of Man on a regular basis during the 1920s, and breeding was first proved in the Ballaugh Curraghs in 1979 (C&J). Around 20 years later, the MBA estimates the breeding population of the Island at fewer than 20 pairs, although the late breeding of this species causes some problems in obtaining accurate counts. The gravel pits at the Point of Ayre form the Manx stronghold of the Tufted Duck, and up to six pairs have been proved to breed there, with plenty of potential for an increase as the pits gradually become more suitable for Tufties, although predation of ducklings by gulls and corvids could limit future numbers at this site. Elsewhere the species has definitely bred at seven other localities in the Isle of Man, most of these being small lakes or pools off the beaten track well inland in the south-central part of the Island. Additionally breeding has been suspected at a number of other waters, including Glascoe Dub, Kionslieu Dam, Tromode Dam and the lakes at Billown.

Tufted Ducks from Scandinavia and Germany eastwards migrate for the winter mainly to the British Isles and the Netherlands, while Icelandic breeders move particularly to Ireland, where some birds from northern Britain also winter (other British and Irish nesters being largely resident). The Isle of Man could receive visitors from any of these sources, and modest numbers of Tufties are present each year, with the wintering population perhaps no more than 50 birds (MBA). How many of these birds are incomers (as opposed to local residents) is impossible to judge, but counts at the Point of Ayre gravel pits may suggest some movement between July and September, and again during March and April. Typical numbers for this site amount to about 30 birds during the winter, and smaller numbers are scattered across the Isle of Man on various inland waters at this season, with double-figure counts regular at Kerrowdhoo Reservoir, Tromode Dam, Kionslieu Dam, Eairy Dam and the lakes at Billown. There seem to be few birds during winter in the north of the Island away from the gravel pits.

1977–81

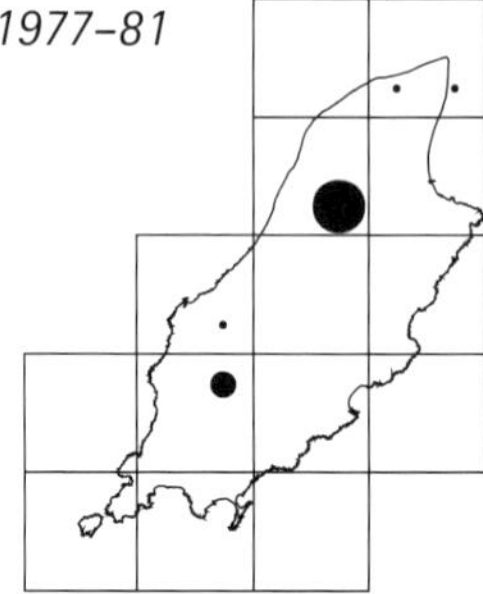

1998–2002

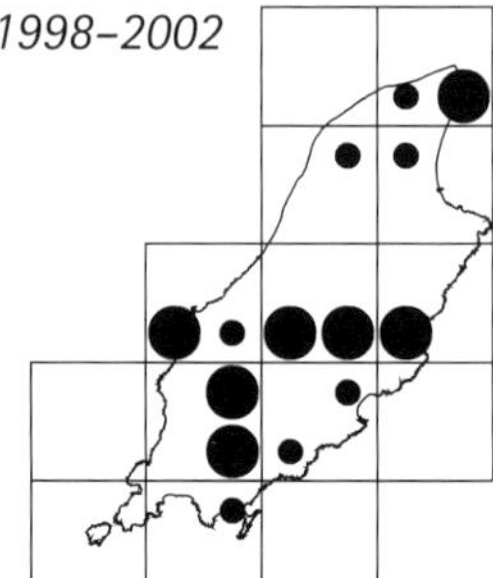

Breeding	Grid squares:	Isle of Man 34 (5%) Britain 1,484 Ireland 252 Total 1,736 (45%)
	Population:	Isle of Man <20 Britain 7,500 Ireland 1,800 (3% of European)
Wintering	Grid squares:	Isle of Man 25 (4%) Britain and Ireland 2,042 (53%)
	Population:	Isle of Man <50 Britain and Ireland 85,000

Jan	Feb	Mar	Apr	May	Jun	Jul	Aug	Sep	Oct	Nov	Dec

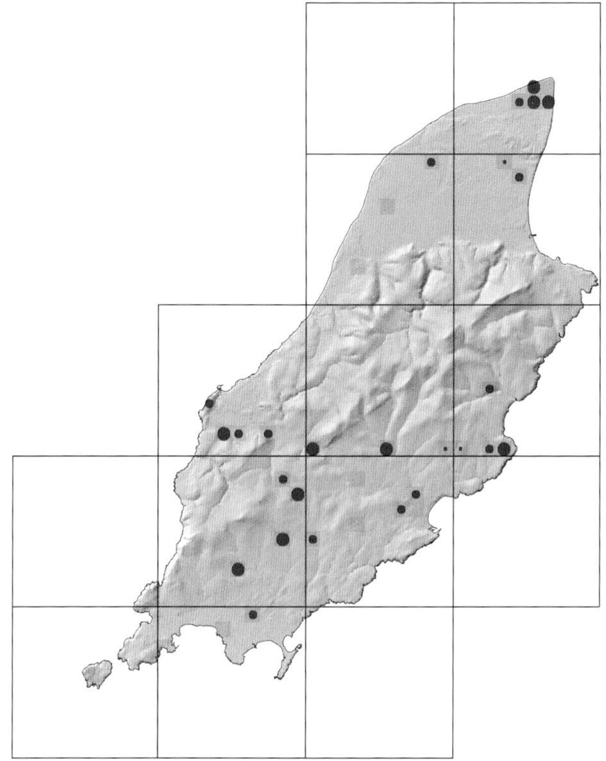

Summer presence and breeding status

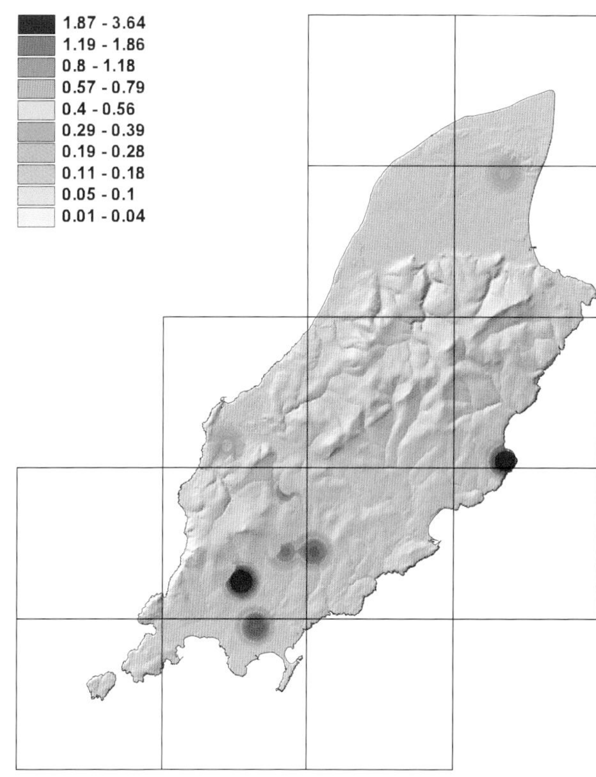

Breeding abundance

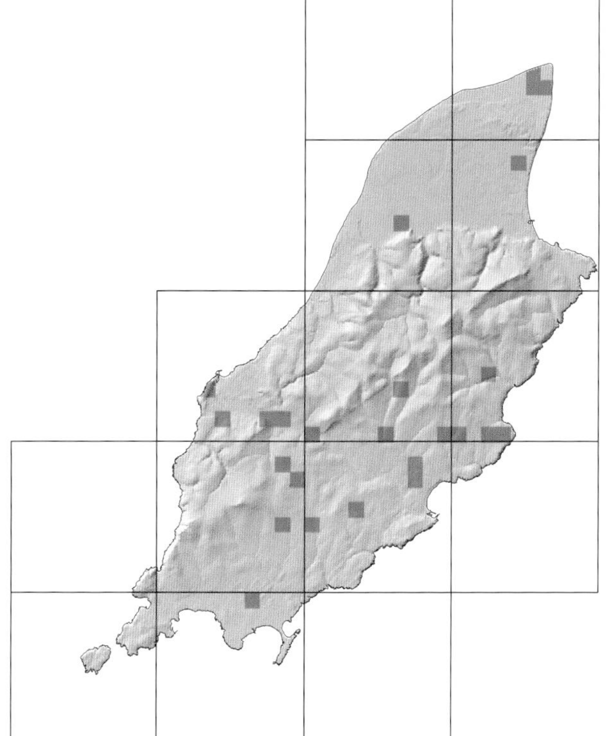

Winter presence

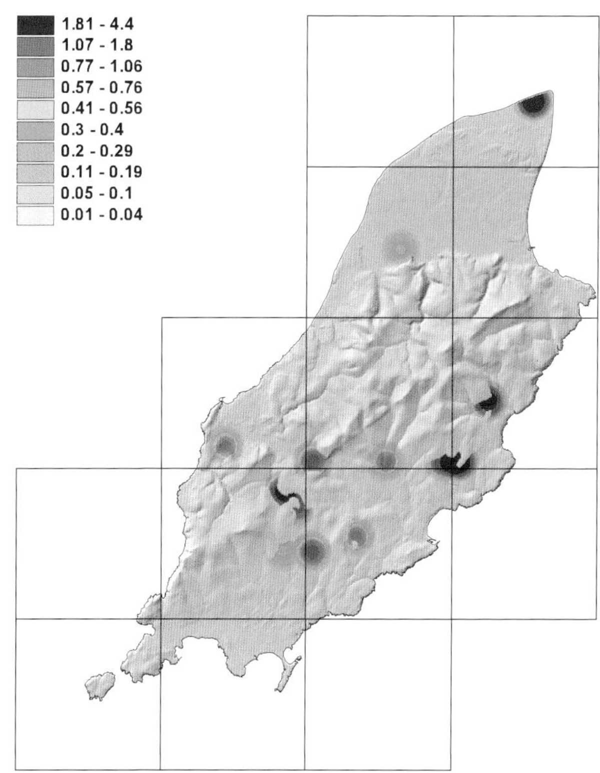

Winter abundance

Scaup (Greater Scaup)
Aythya marila

Manx: *Thunnag Varrey*

In some ways the solid-looking Scaup is a northern version of its close relative the Tufted Duck, but the two species differ completely in one respect: whereas the Tufty is undeniably a freshwater duck all year round, the hardy Scaup favours the sea in winter, happy enough even on exposed coasts with rough water, although the Scaup as a diving bird is said to be inferior to the Tufted Duck (BWP). As with Pochards and Tufted Ducks, flocks of Scaups may be dominated by one or other sex, with males commoner in the north, and females more numerous further south.

The Scaup breeds mainly inland, using waters of varying size from small pools to large lakes, but most birds select coastal habitats for the winter, favouring estuaries and other food-rich inlets of the sea, and gathering in flocks of a thousand or more in particularly advantageous localities like the Solway Firth and the Dee Estuary (WA). Sources of food such as sewer outlets may attract still larger numbers of Scaups, although modern developments in disposal of waste have reduced such opportunities for these and other ducks, notably in the Firth of Forth. Some Scaups are found on inland waters during the winter, particularly on those situated near the coast or on very large lakes such as Lough Neagh. Rocky or cliffbound coasts and infertile (oligotrophic) inland waters are avoided, so the Scaup is not a bird of highland regions. The diet consists of both animal and plant matter, but in marine feeding areas molluscs such as mussels and cockles tend to dominate, with crustaceans, worms and fish also significant. Inland, crustaceans and insects become more important, as do the seeds of pondweeds, bulrushes and other aquatic plants.

The breeding range of the Scaup is based on the tundra of the low Arctic, extending southwards into the coniferous forest zone in places, and stretching from Iceland along the northern edges of Eurasia and North America, but excluding Greenland. In continental Europe Scaups do not normally breed outside Scandinavia, Estonia and Russia, but nesting was first confirmed in Britain in 1897 and since that date there have been a number of instances of breeding, predominantly in Scotland. Almost all Scaups are migratory, Icelandic birds wintering in the British Isles and the Netherlands, and most of those from Scandinavia eastwards move only as far as the Baltic region.

Cullen and Jennings, writing in 1986, state that Scaups had been recorded in the Isle of Man mainly between October and March in about half of the preceding fifty years, the birds favouring the south coast although not always the same localities, with Port St. Mary, Carrick Bay and Langness/Derbyhaven all featuring in the reports. Other coastal haunts include Ramsey Harbour and Peel Bay, the latter site holding no fewer than 15 birds in mid-March 1947, and C&J also mention records from a number of inland waters, including Glascoe Dub, Kionslieu Dam, Eairy Dam and the lakes at Billown. The present situation appears to be broadly similar to that described by Cullen and Jennings, with the MBA estimating a winter population of up to four birds, although for most of the time there are probably none present on the Island at all. The first birds of the autumn tend to be seen in October, with odd ones recorded in September or even August, and December is probably the most reliable month. Following the turn of the year Scaups may be completely absent, with a few reports for January and hardly any in subsequent months. An unusual event was the occurrence of a late male Scaup at the Point of Ayre gravel pits between 7 and 18 May 2002.

Curiously, fewer Scaups reported to the MBA were seen on the sea than on fresh water, with most marine sightings coming from Peel Bay and the area of Derbyhaven and Langness. The best sites of all for this species would appear to be the Eairy Dam, the lakes at Billown and Glascoe Dub, but with so few records each year generalisation is difficult. The majority of reports concern either single birds or twosomes, the only larger groups during the Atlas period all being seen during 2001, namely four at Derbyhaven in late October, four in Peel Bay in late November, and a remarkable 13 Scaups at Rue Point in mid-November. It seems unlikely that this scarce winter visitor will change its status in the Isle of Man during the foreseeable future.

Wintering	Grid squares:	Isle of Man 8 (1%)
		Britain and Ireland 464 (12%)
	Population:	Isle of Man 0-4
		Britain and Ireland 5,000-10,000

Jan	Feb	Mar	Apr	May	Jun	Jul	Aug	Sep	Oct	Nov	Dec

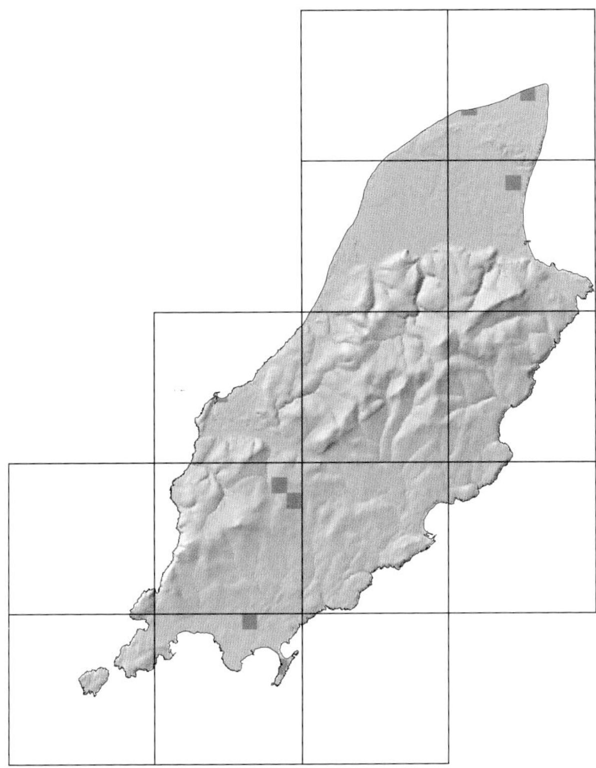

Winter presence

Eider (Common Eider)
Somateria mollissima

Manx: *Laagh Loughlinagh*

The large and powerful Eider is the ultimate sea-duck, hardly ever seen inland and thoroughly at home when being tossed about on the waves. The species shows a startling difference between the black and white drake and dark brown female, the latter to some extent reminiscent of a dabbling duck, despite her obvious prowess as a diver. Apart from the insulating qualities and former commercial value of the female's down feathers, the main claim to fame of the Eider is surely the seductive cooing call of the male, commonly heard during courtship in the winter flocks and contrasting with the harsh guttural rattling of the female birds.

Eiders are coastal birds, found on both sandy and rocky shores but avoiding completely cliffbound stretches, preferring fringing islands and skerries. Their requirements for feeding restrict them to reasonably sheltered waters with depths of less than three metres and a rich bottom-living fauna, but fortunately these conditions are plentiful. Eiders do not normally wander far from the water's edge, and roost either on the sea itself or on the shore if undisturbed. For nesting most Eiders select a site with some cover, whether provided by rocks or vegetation, although open positions are also used, often where the nests of this basically colonial species are closely packed. Molluscs, particularly mussels, provide the bulk of the food of the Eider, but crustaceans (notably crabs), starfish, sea urchins and other invertebrates are also taken, but not fish, as Eiders are not well suited to pursuing quick-moving prey. The birds nesting on the coasts of south-west Scotland, north-west England and north-east Ireland live literally within sight of the Isle of Man, and perhaps it was inevitable that eventually Eiders would take an interest in the Island.

The Eider is an Arctic-breeding species, nesting round the edges of the polar sea in both Eurasia and North America, with a curious gap along most of the Siberian shores, while in Europe a southward extension of its range reaches the British Isles and the Baltic region. Not surprisingly for a bird on the southern fringe of its world distribution, as a breeder the Eider is confined to the northern half of Britain, being found no further south than Cumbria on the west coast and Northumberland in the east. Its stronghold remains in the northern and western isles of Scotland, but since the mid-nineteenth century Eiders have been slowly spreading southwards, reaching Ireland by 1912 and Walney Island (Cumbria) in 1949.

Cullen and Jennings described the Eider as an 'irregular and transient visitor' to the Isle of Man, yet now the MBA estimates a breeding population approaching 50 pairs and the species is a common sight along much of the Manx coast. There were no records of the Eider at all on the Island until 1928, when a drake was seen off Peel Castle, and Cullen and Jennings could cite only 21 more reports between that date and their time of writing (1986). By the year 1990, however, there had been a rapid rise in the number of visitors, and the first breeding record came from the Calf of Man in 1992, Eiders having bred at this site in every year since (Calf Reports). The first nesting on the main island was reported from Niarbyl in 1995, and two broods were seen at the Point of Ayre Gravel Pits in 1996 (Manx Bird Reports). During the Atlas period, confirmed breeding took place in 12 grid squares, at (from north to south) Point of Ayre Gravel Pits (2000), Ballaghennie (2002), the Phurt (1999), the Dog Mills (2001), Peel Castle (2001), the Niarbyl district (all years), Port Erin Bay (2001), Strandhall (2002) and the Calf (all years).

In addition to the confirmed records listed above, breeding of Eiders was suspected in another 31 grid squares, and the summer map shows the north, west and south coasts of the Island to have a fairly general presence of the species at this time of year. The largely cliffbound east coast of the Island is clearly unattractive to Eiders, with few undisturbed potential nesting places. The abundance map well illustrates the sort of places favoured by these birds, suggesting nesting may take place in the future on Langness and in the little bays north of Peel. During autumn and winter the Eider population in the Isle of Man may rise to over 100 birds, but its distribution on the Island remains almost identical to that of the summer, reflecting reluctance to move far from their breeding grounds. Curiously the number of Eiders present round the coast seems to dip from mid-June to mid-July in some years, birds possibly moving to moulting grounds elsewhere. The source of the birds which have colonised the Island could be the thriving colony at Walney Island in Cumbria, or perhaps Northern Ireland and south-west Scotland. Whatever its actual origin, continued growth and expansion of the Manx population of this splendid duck seems to be assured in at least the immediate future.

Breeding	Grid squares:	Isle of Man 61 (9%) Britain 488 Ireland 45 Total 533 (14%)
	Population:	Isle of Man <50 Britain 31,500 Ireland 800 (4% of European)
Wintering	Grid squares:	Isle of Man 35 (5%) Britain and Ireland 704 (18%)
	Population:	Isle of Man 100 Britain and Ireland 72,400

Jan Feb Mar Apr May Jun Jul Aug Sep Oct Nov Dec

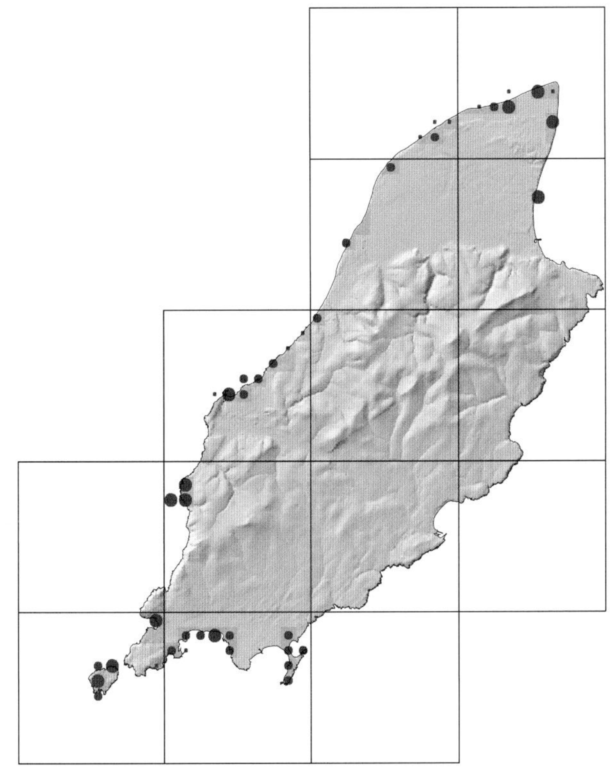
Summer presence and breeding status

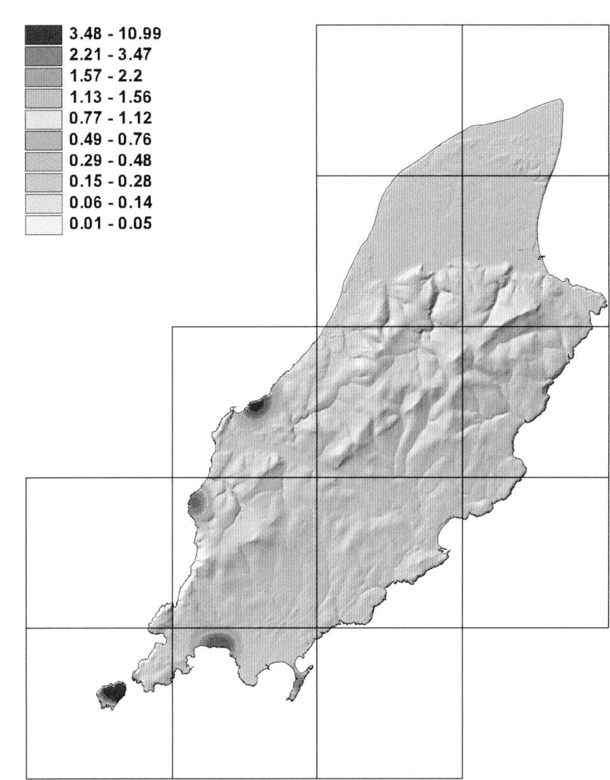

Breeding abundance

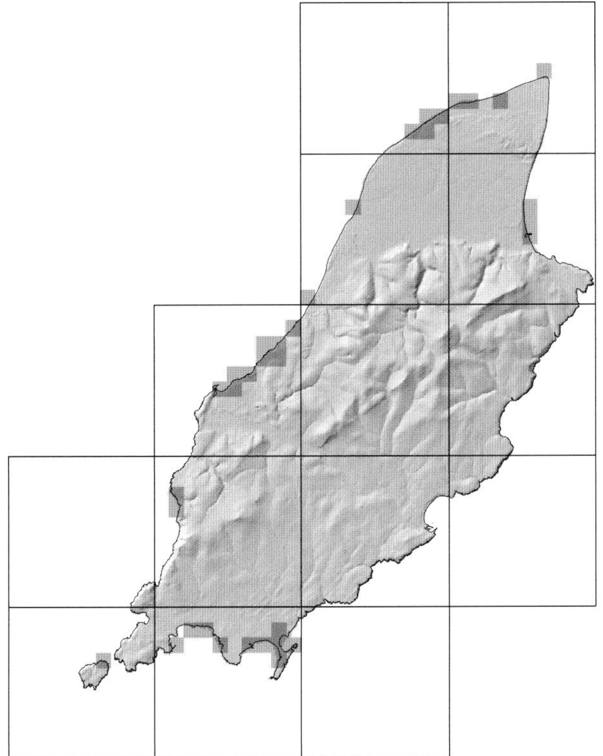
Winter presence

Individual Sponsors – Mrs. S Bolton, Mr. & Mrs. J Corlett, Mr. G Craine, Mrs. C Roper

Long-tailed Duck
Clangula hyemalis

Manx: *Laagh Lheeah*

The small Long-tailed Duck shows a bewildering array of plumages according to sex, age and season, the long tail being confined to the adult male and looking most unusual on a duck. Females and juveniles have a more ordinary appearance, but their brown and white colours, short bills and steep foreheads make them worth a second glance, if only to establish their identity! These are special birds for most observers, associated with cold seascapes and thoughts of the Arctic, and the glorious yodelling calls of the drakes heard in chorus provide a spine-tingling experience on a remote shore.

Long-tailed Ducks breed typically on tundra with a mixture of dry and wet patches, pools and boggy ground, ridges and hollows, often on islands and deltas along the coast, but also in uplands among the dwarf willows and birches of the arctic-alpine zone. Outside the breeding season Longtails effectively become seabirds, seldom appearing inland and spending much of their time well out from the shore where the water is sufficiently shallow, although they are also found along coastlines and among islands and inlets, preferring soft bottoms to rocky seabeds (WA). Although some winter flocks are very large, Long-tailed Ducks may also occur in smaller, more dispersed groups, even where they are present in an area in considerable numbers. A highly skilled diver, this species is capable of capturing both moving and immobile prey, concentrating on molluscs such as mussels and cockles, crustaceans like shrimps and crabs, marine worms and small fish, plus insects, leaves and seeds on inland breeding grounds.

The Long-tailed Duck is virtually confined to the Arctic as a nesting bird, extending right round the polar basin in both Eurasia and North America, including Greenland. In Europe this is a bird of the Arctic fringe, breeding in Iceland, Spitsbergen, northernmost Scandinavia and Russia, although penetrating southwards along the mountains of Norway and Sweden as far as the latitude of Shetland. After breeding there is a general southerly shift, taking Scandinavian and Russian birds to the Baltic region and the North Sea, with Icelandic birds either not migrating at all or moving to southern Greenland. In Britain wintering Longtails are concentrated in Shetland, Orkney, the Outer Hebrides and along the Scottish east coast, especially the Moray Firth. The main period of arrival is late in the season, often in December or even after the New Year, and spring movements have begun by March, so the birds may be present for a short time only.

Although Long-tailed Ducks are regularly recorded around much of the British and Irish coast, the Isle of Man is well south of their favoured wintering haunts, and the Irish Sea is not noted for this species, and so the Manx birdwatcher can expect odd birds only, and not necessarily in every year. The first ever record for the Island involved a female which spent three weeks at Derbyhaven during November 1928, eventually being shot, and since those days reports have been irregular, mostly referring to single birds at Derbyhaven or in Peel Bay and peaking in November (C&J). During the Atlas period, probably three birds were seen during 1999, there were no records at all in 2000 and only one bird was reported in 2001. Two were logged in 2002, plus a group of nine birds flying past the Point of Ayre in late October, the largest number yet recorded in the Isle of Man. In 2003 there were two new birds seen, with a long-stayer from the previous year still present. Long-tailed Ducks sometimes return to localities used in previous seasons, and so fewer individuals than the numbers listed above might have been involved in visits to the Island.

The earliest date of arrival documented by the Atlas was on 26 October at the Point of Ayre, and birds were present mainly in November, December and February. During March just a single bird was seen, although in 1999 a pair of Longtails was observed in the area north of the Phurt on the remarkably late date of 14 June. All Long-tailed Ducks reported to the MBA were seen either at Blue Point, Ballaghennie, the Point of Ayre or the Phurt in the north of the Island, or from the Calf of Man, in Port Erin Bay or at Derbyhaven in the south. Even without the flock of nine at Point of Ayre, the north coast slightly beats the south in terms of numbers of birds, and the dominance of Derbyhaven mentioned by Cullen and Jennings no longer holds. This species is known for its tendency to stay awhile in one spot, and a bird which first appeared in Derbyhaven on 29 October 2002 remained at this site until at least 5 April 2003.

Wintering	Grid squares:	Isle of Man 8 (1%)
		Britain and Ireland 496 (13%)
	Population:	Isle of Man 0-2
		Britain and Ireland 20,000

Jan	Feb	Mar	Apr	May	Jun	Jul	Aug	Sep	Oct	Nov	Dec

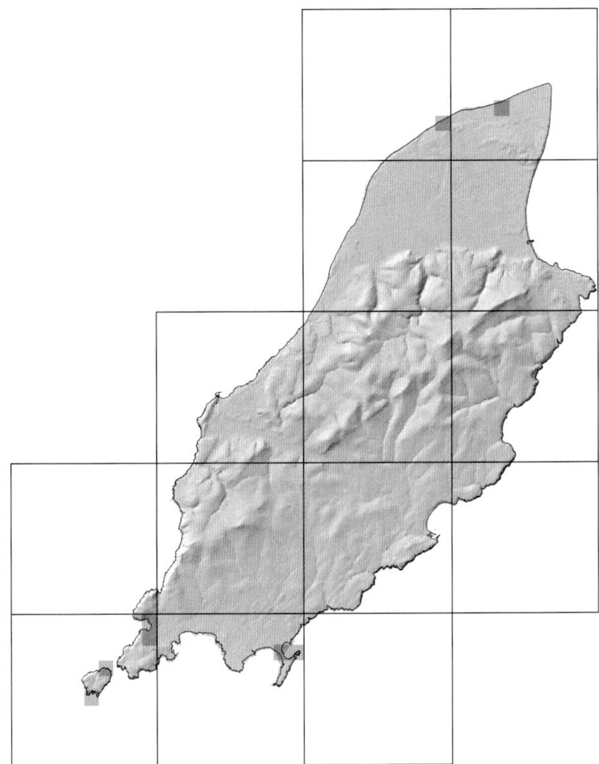

Winter presence

Common Scoter
Melanitta nigra

The black drakes and dark brown females ensure that the Common Scoter is one of the least noticeable of the ducks, and its habit of staying well offshore means that parties bobbing about on the waves or flying low over the sea often escape the attention of the casual birdwatcher, and seldom are these birds seen closely enough to appreciate the male's knobby bill with its yellow patches. The Common Scoter is hardly a beautiful duck, with a rather dumpy shape and a distinct lack of elegance, but this essentially Arctic species can still brighten up a cold birdwatching trip to a winter shore, or even a family visit to the beach on a hot day in August!

Common Scoters breed mainly on tundras and moors inland, using all sizes and types of waters, from small pools to large lakes, provided that tall vegetation provides adequate cover for the nest, and favouring islands and undisturbed promontories. From the late summer, however, the birds shift to the coast, seeking shallow conditions with a soft and food-rich sea bed, and generally they do not approach within about 500 metres of the shore (BWP). Although not much affected by rough water, scoters tend to avoid very rocky or cliffbound coasts, presumably because of a lack of food in such places, and major bays and the entrances to estuaries are particularly attractive to this species (WA). Common Scoters concentrate on molluscs, notably mussels, but will also take shrimps, crabs, worms and other invertebrates, while on their freshwater breeding grounds the larvae of aquatic insects are important in their diet.

The main breeding range of the Common Scoter stretches along the Arctic fringe of Eurasia from northern Scandinavia eastwards to Alaska, with extensions into Iceland, the mountains of southern Norway and Sweden, parts of Scotland and Ireland, and a few localities across Canada. The first confirmed breeding in Britain took place in Sutherland in 1855, and by the 1920s this species had spread to other areas of Scotland, north to Shetland and as far south as Argyll. In 1905 the first Irish nest was found, on Lower Lough Erne in Co. Fermanagh, and scoters then spread to other lakes in the north-west of Ireland. In recent years the Scottish population has shown an uncertain trend, while the Irish birds have seriously declined at some sites.

Common Scoters are virtually all migratory, although those breeding in the British Isles may not show much movement. Most of the birds wintering in Britain and Ireland originate in Iceland, Sweden, Finland and Arctic Russia, others from these populations wintering south to Iberia. Birds may reach the Isle of Man as early as July, when groups of up to 20 have been recorded, but the main time of arrival varies from one year to the next and may be as late as September or October. During the Atlas period maximum flock sizes amounted to nine in August, eleven in September, 21 in October, and 43 in November. Numbers were generally lower through the winter itself, and hardly any scoters were reported in March or April, but during May birds passing the Calf of Man peaked at 16 in 2000, and records for June (involving up to nine birds) occurred in four out of the five years of the Atlas survey. Thus although the Common Scoter is basically a passage migrant and winter visitor in the Isle of Man, in fact it may be seen in any month of the year.

The records suggest that the best places on the Island to look for Common Scoters are the north coast from the Lhen to Rue Point and the Calf of Man. In the former area most reports refer to the period from November to February, while birds were observed from the Calf chiefly between July and September. Flock size was greater on the north coast, with 20 to 30 birds sometimes recorded and no fewer than 43 counted at Blue Point in mid-November 2001. Elsewhere Common Scoters appear regularly off Peel Castle (mainly in single figures during autumn), and they may be seen at various other points along the west coast, with double-figure flocks reported from the Point of Ayre and Niarbyl. No records at all for the east coast of the Island were received by the MBA (other than odd ones from Derbyhaven in the extreme south), reflecting the unsuitability of the waters below tall cliffs for this species. Overall, the present position of the Common Scoter in the Isle of Man appears to be similar to that described by Cullen and Jennings in 1986, although the average size of flocks observed may have increased slightly since their time of writing.

Breeding	Grid squares:	Isle of Man 8 (1%) Britain 51 Ireland 16 Total 67 (2%)
	Population:	Isle of Man 0 Britain 100 Ireland 65 (2% of European)
Wintering	Grid squares:	Isle of Man 15 (2%) Britain and Ireland 457 (12%)
	Population:	Isle of Man 10-40 Britain and Ireland 25,000-30,000

Jan	Feb	Mar	Apr	May	Jun	Jul	Aug	Sep	Oct	Nov	Dec

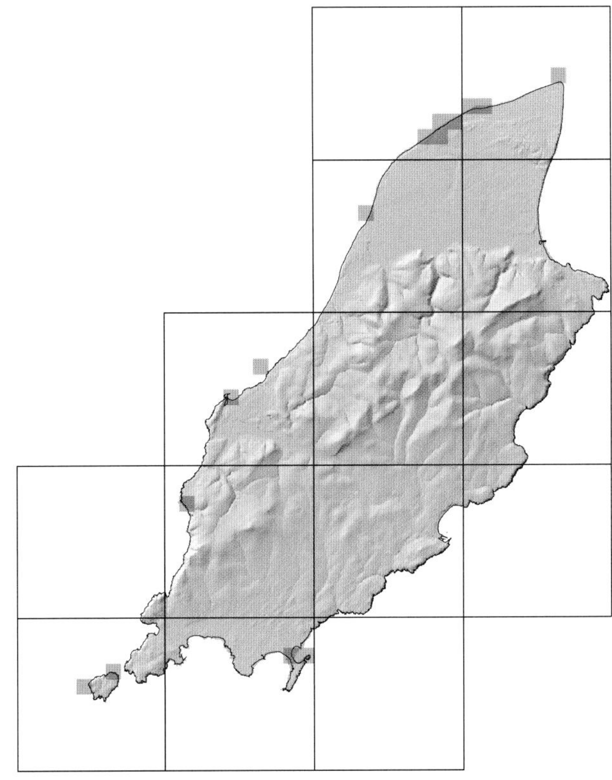

Winter presence

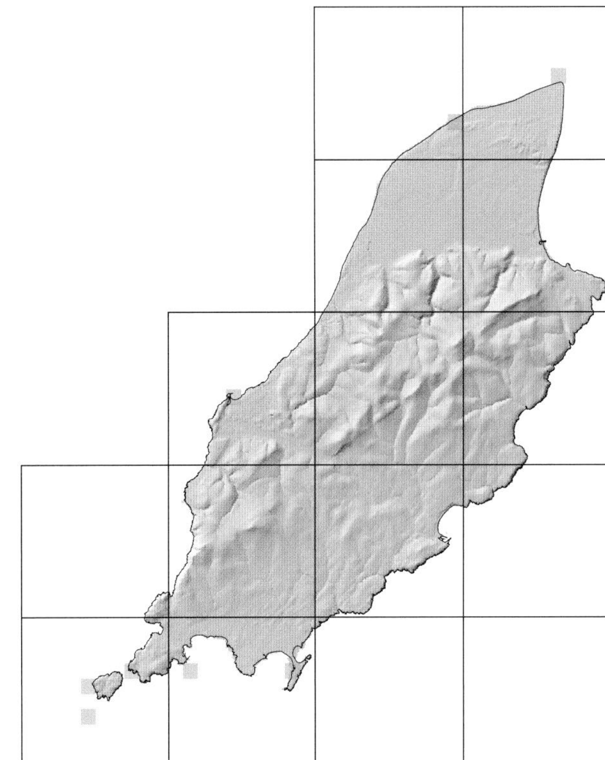

Summer presence

Velvet Scoter
Melanitta fusca

On the sea odd Velvet Scoters tend to be inconspicuous among flocks of Common Scoters, and so they can be easily missed even by careful observers, but once they fly Velvets stand out as a result of the white patches on their wings. The drake's orange bill, little white eye patch and red feet are not easily visible except at close range, and likewise the female looks nondescript from a distance. Although very similar to the Common Scoter in its general habits, even in areas where present in large numbers the Velvet Scoter normally occurs in parties of fewer than 20 birds, in contrast to the often large flocks of its more numerous relative. As with some other diving ducks, one sex may predominate in groups of this species, with drakes more prevalent than females in the north, including the British Isles.

The Velvet Scoter nests in varied habitats including tundra, mountains and forests, but essentially it breeds at fresh or brackish water bodies of various sizes, plus slow-flowing rivers and, around the Baltic Sea, shores with plenty of tree cover. Although stopping off at inland waters during migration, this species winters on the sea, often in company with Common Scoters, with which it shares a preference for shallow, sandy conditions such as are found in the mouths of estuaries. Velvet Scoters, however, are more often seen close to shore than Commons, and enter more enclosed waters around skerries and islands, while also not avoiding rough seas on open coasts. Within mixed flocks of scoters they may keep to themselves to some extent, and they are less wary than the commoner species. The diet of Velvet Scoters is usually based on molluscs, particularly mussels, with crustaceans (notably crabs and shrimps), starfish, worms and aquatic insects also taken, but their tastes are more varied than those of Common Scoters, and on the breeding grounds some vegetable matter may be eaten.

The breeding distribution of the Velvet Scoter extends from Scandinavia eastwards through Eurasia and into western North America, showing considerable overlap with the range of the Common Scoter but penetrating much further south into the boreal forest zone. In Europe the two species are rather similarly distributed, apart from the Velvet's curious southerly extension along the Baltic coasts and the breeding of the Common Scoter in Iceland and the British Isles (where nesting of the Velvet in Scotland has been suspected but not proved). In autumn the European populations of Velvet Scoters migrate mainly to the coasts of the countries surrounding the North Sea and English Channel, from Norway to France. Up to 5,000 birds are thought to winter in British waters (WA), the majority frequenting the east coast, all the way from Orkney to Kent but particularly in the Moray Firth.

In western Britain and Ireland the Velvet Scoter is something of a rarity, and the Isle of Man, therefore, is poorly placed to receive more than a smattering of this species in any given year. Cullen and Jennings, writing in 1986, state that after the first record in 1936 there had been twenty more reports referring to a total of 29 birds, and by the start of the Atlas period the number of records had reached 26. The MBA found Velvet Scoters on the coasts of the Island in every year of its survey, following complete blanks in four of the preceding six years, the improvement no doubt resulting from the increased efforts of observers at the time of the MBA fieldwork. There were perhaps minima of six birds present in 1998, three in 1999, six in 2000, two in 2001, one in 2002 and three in 2003, these figures providing some indication of the small numbers visiting the Island, and tying in with the MBA estimate of an average winter population of one to four birds in Manx waters each year. How many Velvets have been missed, however, is a moot point!

All of the Velvet Scoters reported to the Atlas were seen on northern coasts, except for records from Peel Bay in 1999 and the Calf of Man in 1998 and 2003, and the stretch between the Lhen and Rue Point accounted for the bulk of the sightings, producing birds in all years except for 1999, the largest group being three at the Lhen in early November 1998. Most Atlas reports concern October, November and December, with one in September and none at all in other months, although Cullen and Jennings cite occurrences in January, February and March and a bird was observed near Rue Point in February 1994 (Craine and Moore 1997). There has been one record of a Velvet Scoter since the end of the Atlas period, at Derbyhaven in late November 2004, and it seems unlikely that the status of this elusive species as a scarce visitor to the Island will change in the foreseeable future.

Wintering	Grid squares:	Isle of Man 7 (1%)
		Britain and Ireland 179 (5%)
	Population:	Isle of Man 1-4
		Britain and Ireland 2,500-5,000

Jan	Feb	Mar	Apr	May	Jun	Jul	Aug	Sep	Oct	Nov	Dec

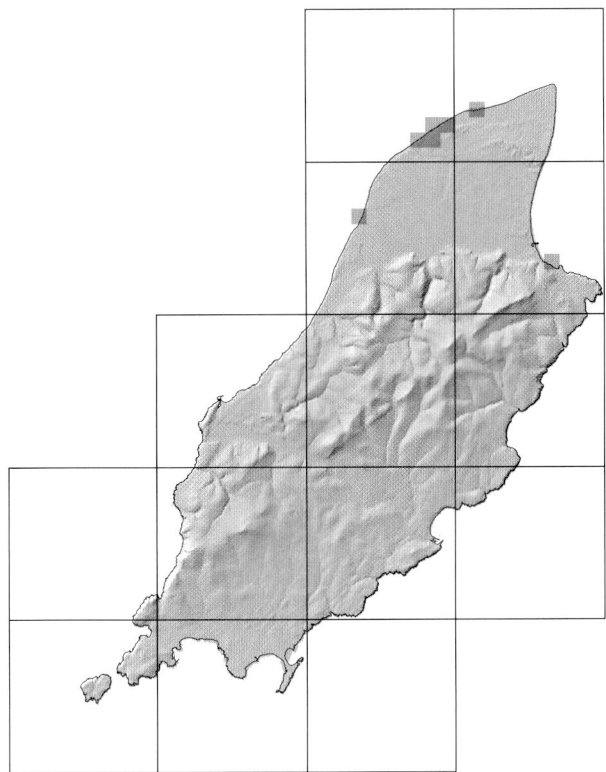

Winter presence

Goldeneye (Common Goldeneye) *Bucephala clangula*

Manx: *Laaghag Hooillagh*

Both sexes of the chunky but lively Goldeneye are pleasing in their different ways, whether the smartly pied drake with his oval white facial spot, or the charming grey female with her chocolate-brown head. It would seem that the high crown of this species results from the presence of large sinuses which fill with air and may aid buoyancy or lengthen diving times, while the short but deep bill is well suited to grasping prey (Ogilvie 1975). Goldeneyes sometimes dive in unison and as winter wears on they increasingly indulge in communal courtship displays, greatly adding to the interest and pleasure in watching flocks of these spirited and attractive ducks.

When breeding, Goldeneyes are unusual among ducks, in that they nest in holes in trees up to 15 metres above ground, so they are in one sense birds of forests. Their nest sites need to be situated within reach of lakes, pools or rivers of medium depth, with plenty of open water but also reasonably productive in terms of food supplies. Outside the breeding season, however, most types of water body may be visited by Goldeneyes, and although they prefer coastal habitats, notably shallow bays and inlets such as estuaries, they also occur in considerable numbers on inland waters, particularly large lakes and reservoirs. Goldeneyes concentrate on animal food, such as molluscs, crustaceans, insect larvae and small fish, using their highly developed diving skills to pick up immobile items or to catch moving prey, and they also feed on vegetable material, mainly the leaves, roots and seeds of aquatic plants. This species takes advantage of coastal sewer outlets, especially where grain or other vegetable products are discharged into the sea.

The Goldeneye breeds right across Eurasia and North America, following mainly the belt of coniferous forest in a broad band south of the tundra. In Europe this species nests from northern Scandinavia as far south as the edge of the Alps, but is missing from Iceland, where it is replaced by the very similar Barrow's Goldeneye *Bucephala islandica*. Goldeneyes have bred in a restricted area of the Scottish Highlands since 1970, greatly aided by the provision of nest boxes, and the population is now approaching 100 pairs (Ogilvie *et al.* 2004). The Goldeneye is almost entirely migratory, birds from its European range wintering chiefly in the southern Baltic region and the countries around the North Sea, though small numbers move on as far south as the Mediterranean. This species is a common and widespread winter visitor to Britain and the northern half of Ireland, being found generally along the coastline and on many inland waters, mainly in Scotland and sparsely in the south of England, Wales and central and southern Ireland.

The Goldeneye has apparently always been a fairly common but not very numerous winter visitor to the Isle of Man, and Cullen and Jennings suggest an increase during the 1930s and a further rise in numbers from the mid-1960s. The MBA estimate of 70 to 80 birds as the typical wintering population seems to be slightly higher than the totals implied by C&J, but does not signify a rapid increase overall. Migrant Goldeneyes are not usually seen on the Island until early October, with flocks of double figures achieved by the end of that month, followed by a rise through November to maximum flock sizes from December to February, with regular counts of 20–30+. The largest gathering reported during the Atlas years, at the Vollan near Ramsey in mid-January 2002, contained 50 birds. Numbers decline significantly in March, and by April only odd birds remain, although a flock of 17 was seen at Strandhall in late April 2001. During the summer occasional single Goldeneyes are observed.

As is well shown on the map, Goldeneyes are recorded at various points around the Manx coast and on a wide scatter of fresh waters. The principal saltwater sites for this species are found in the bays of Ramsey and Castletown, mainly around the sewer outlets at the Vollan and off Scarlett Road respectively. Numbers at the Vollan are mainly in double figures right through the winter, often topping 20 birds and regularly approaching 40, while at Scarlett Road counts of around 20 may be achieved in midwinter. Reorganisation and improvement of sewage treatment however, could threaten the future of these locations as attractions for Goldeneyes, as has already happened in similar circumstances in Britain and indeed at Port Jack at the northern edge of Douglas Bay. Langness, Derbyhaven and Carrick Bay hold small numbers of Goldeneyes in most years, while the gravel pits at the Point of Ayre (where flocks may reach double figures) record the highest inland totals. Odd birds may appear almost anywhere, however, especially Glascoe Dub, Bishop's Dub, Kerrowdhoo Reservoir and Kionslieu and Eairy Dams.

Breeding	Grid squares:	Isle of Man 10 (1%) Britain 173 Ireland 13 Total 186 (5%)
	Population:	Isle of Man 0 Britain 200 Ireland 0 (<1% of European)
Wintering	Grid squares:	Isle of Man 46 (7%) Britain and Ireland 1,923 (50%)
	Population:	Isle of Man 70-80 Britain and Ireland 10,000-15,000

Jan	Feb	Mar	Apr	May	Jun	Jul	Aug	Sep	Oct	Nov	Dec

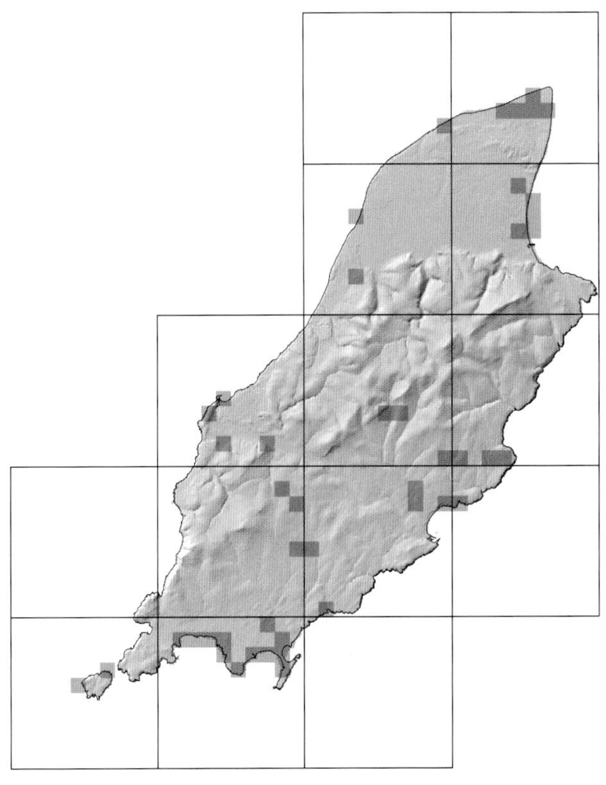

Winter presence

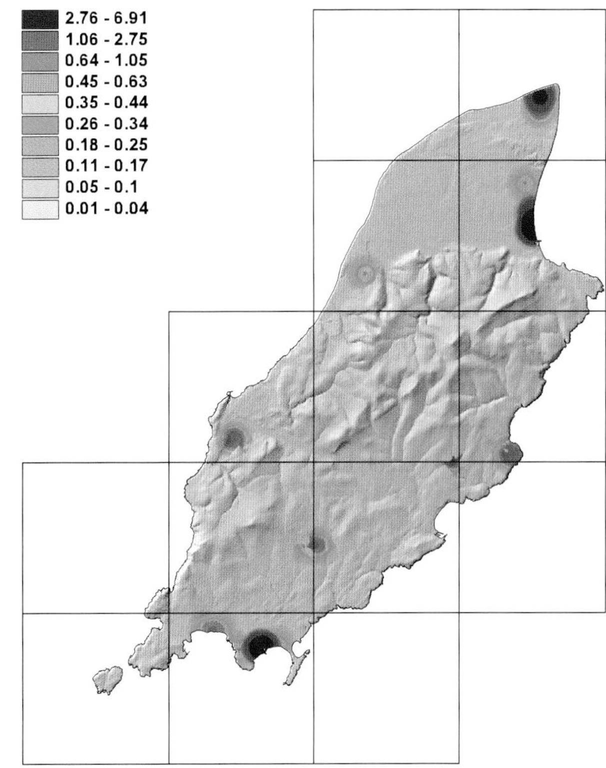

Winter abundance

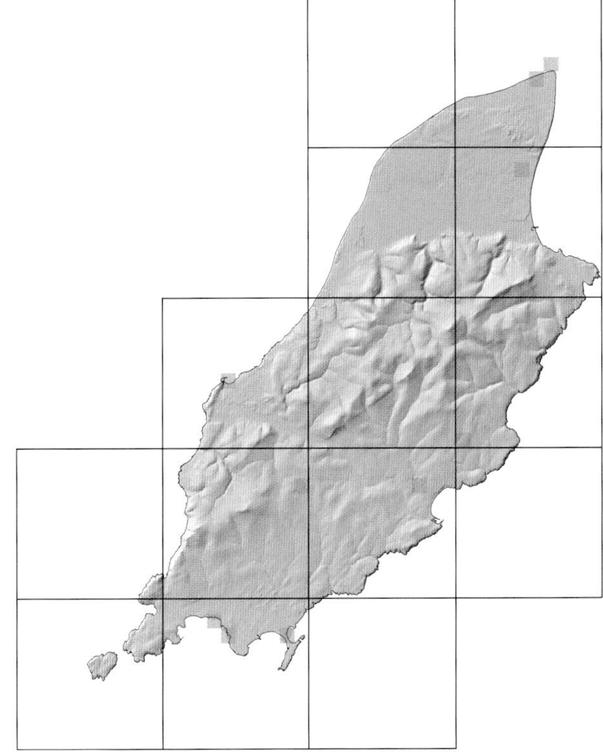

Summer presence

Red-breasted Merganser
Mergus serrator

Manx: *Thunnag Cleeau Yiarg*

For Manx birdwatchers the rakish and shaggy Red-breasted Merganser is the most familiar of the three sawbilled ducks found regularly in the British Isles, although the species is sufficiently uncommon on the Island to be regarded as a rather special bird to see. These fish-eating divers have slim grasping bills equipped with rear-facing serrations for securing their slippery prey, which they actively pursue underwater, deftly manipulate and then swallow head first. The so-called 'red' breast appears on the males only and actually looks somewhat brownish, covered with a fairly dense overlay of solid black spots.

Unlike its relative the Goosander, the Red-breasted Merganser shows a preference for coastal habitats, favouring sheltered and sandy-bottomed bays and inlets, especially those with spits and islands. Mergansers are also often found breeding far inland, not only beside lakes and pools but also along reasonably deep and slow-flowing rivers, and as a result of their requirement for nest sites with plentiful cover they tend to choose places with tall herbage, shrubs and trees. In winter this species becomes almost completely marine in its distribution, although still concentrated in the more sheltered and shallow waters, such as estuaries, sea lochs, and channels among islands and promontories. The Red-breasted Merganser is an animal feeder specialising in fish up to about 10cm in length (BWP), including salmon, trout, perch and sticklebacks in fresh water, and flounders, cod, herrings and sandeels in the sea. Some crustaceans, molluscs and insect larvae may also be taken.

Red-breasted Mergansers breed through the boreal forest zone of Eurasia and North America, with limited extensions northward on to the tundra and south into more temperate regions. In Europe they range from Iceland and the British Isles through Scandinavia into Russia, with a few small outliers in more southerly localities such as the Baltic-facing parts of Germany and Poland. Scotland has an old-established breeding population, with its stronghold in the Western Isles and on the adjacent mainland, but in Ireland occupied areas are more scattered, mainly in the west, and a serious decline has taken place there since the publication of the 1968-72 Atlas. In contrast, British mergansers have spread from Scotland southwards as far as the Lake District, the Peak District and mid-Wales. In the light of this expansion, the first breeding record in the Isle of Man, at the Point of Ayre Gravel Pits in 1985 (Cullen 1985), was perhaps not surprising, although apart from a repeat at the original site during the following year no further nesting is known on the Island.

The British and Irish populations of Red-breasted Mergansers probably spend the winter on coasts near their breeding grounds, while a number of Icelandic breeders migrate to the British Isles in the autumn. Some birds from southern Scandinavia and Germany move to the Norwegian seaboard, others combining with the more eastern European contingents to winter on Baltic shores and around the coasts of the Netherlands, Britain and Ireland. Among the localities within the British Isles most frequented by this species in winter are the major Scottish firths, the Northern and Western Isles, the English and Welsh estuaries and the many small bays of Ireland. In the Isle of Man odd mergansers are seen in October (sometimes earlier), and from November until March about four or more may be present on the Island, the largest group documented by the MBA consisting of eight birds at the Lhen in mid-March 2001. This count was equalled at the same site in early April of the same year, Red-breasted Mergansers being seen regularly at the Lhen from 10 March to 24 May, but between April and September numbers of this species normally involve one or two birds only. Cullen and Jennings note that during the early 1930s as many as 14 mergansers were observed on the south coast of the Island in winter and spring, but no such figure has been reached in recent years.

Virtually all Manx records of Red-breasted Mergansers are coastal, most relating to the northern and southern extremities of the Island, especially Langness/Derbyhaven, although during the Atlas period no more than two birds at once were reported there. Carrick Bay holds one or two mergansers in most years, notably at Strandhall and along the shores to the west. In the north of the Island, the coast between Jurby and Rue Point regularly attracts this species, but no single location stands out apart from the Lhen, which has produced records in March in three of the years of the Atlas survey, notably in 2001. Elsewhere the most reliable site is Peel Castle, where birds may be seen flying past over the sea. The scatter of records for the period April to September involves the same stretches of coast, with midsummer reports of single birds coming from the Ayres, Peel Castle, Niarbyl and Langness.

Breeding	Grid squares:	Isle of Man 16 (2%) Britain 674 Ireland 167 Total 841 (22%)
	Population:	Isle of Man 0 Britain 2,200 Ireland 700 (4% of European)
Wintering	Grid squares:	Isle of Man 22 (3%) Britain and Ireland 1,087 (28%)
	Population:	Isle of Man 0-4 Britain and Ireland 11,000

Jan	Feb	Mar	Apr	May	Jun	Jul	Aug	Sep	Oct	Nov	Dec

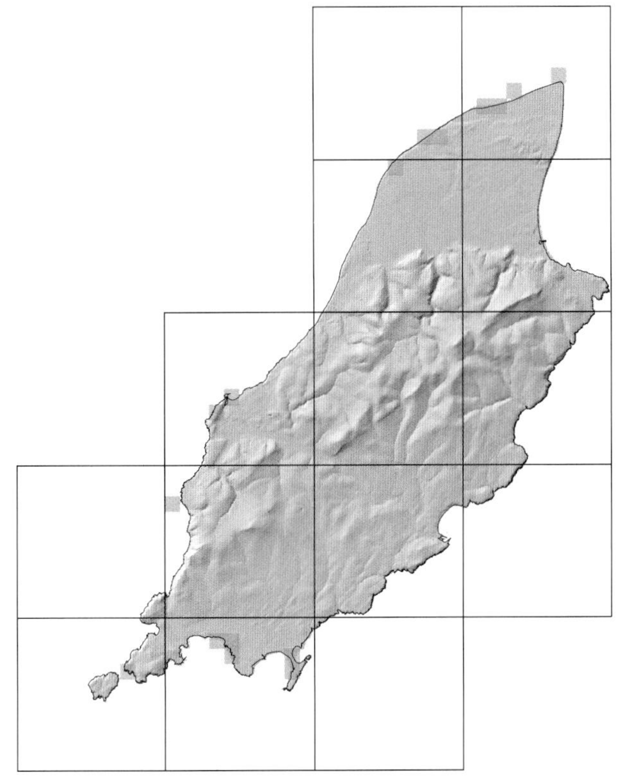

Summer presence

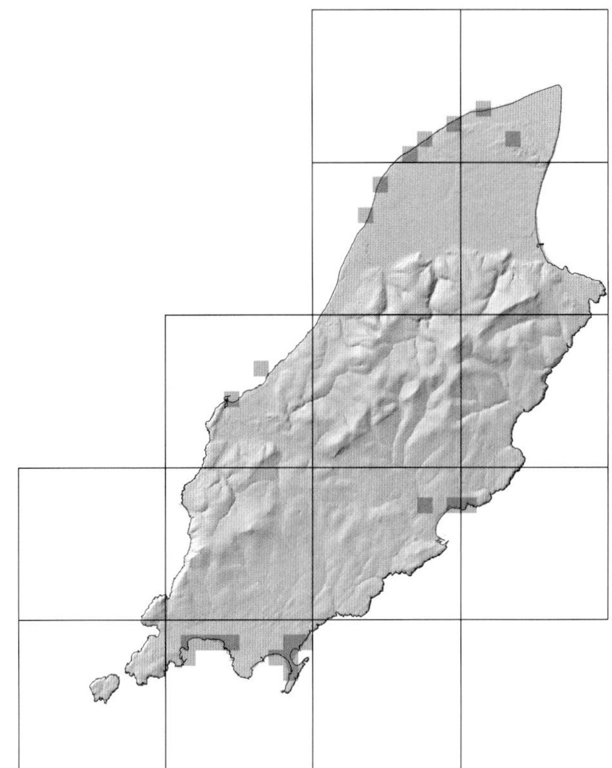

Winter presence

Goosander
Mergus merganser

Manx: *Laagh 'Eeacklagh*

The clean-cut Goosander has the appearance of a tidied-up version of the Red-breasted Merganser, with the latter's unkempt crest removed completely from the drake and replaced by a smarter one in the female, while the body plumage has apparently been simplified and smoothed. Both sexes of this impressive duck have their attractive features, whether the delicate pink flush on the breeding male's creamy-white underparts, or the dove-grey pencilling on the back and sides of the female. The drake's dark green head might suggest a dabbling duck, but the streamlined Goosander is purpose-built for diving and underwater pursuit, and its slim saw-edged bill belongs to a true fish-eater.

Although sometimes seen in marine habitats, Goosanders are essentially birds of fresh water, favouring large lakes and the upper reaches of rivers, but avoiding sites encumbered by prolific submerged or marginal vegetation. As the Goosander nests primarily in holes in trees, its breeding waters are usually situated in well wooded areas, although crevices in rocks or even buildings may be used and nest boxes are readily accepted. Wintering Goosanders prefer large open lakes and reservoirs, also resorting to rivers and sometimes coastal inlets and other sheltered stretches of salt water, though never aspiring to be seagoing ducks like Red-breasted Mergansers. The diet of the Goosander is based on fish, no more than 10cm long and not too bulky (BWP), notably salmon, trout, eels, perch and other common freshwater species, plus small aquatic animals such as insects and their larvae, crustaceans, molluscs and worms.

The Goosander has a similar breeding range to that of the Red-breasted Merganser, roughly coinciding with the boreal forest belt of Eurasia and North America, but it differs from its relative in its lack of a coastal bias and its extensions into mountainous terrain. In northern Europe the ranges of the two species largely overlap, but the Goosander penetrates slightly further south, with a small population breeding in the Alps and odd pairs nesting in the Balkan region. This species was not recorded as a breeder in Britain until 1871 (in Perthshire), but once established it spread through the upland areas of Scotland and reached northern England by the 1940s. Since the time of the 1968-72 Atlas, colonisation has extended down the Pennines to the Peak District, across most of the Welsh hills, and even on to Dartmoor, although there is an almost complete lack of Irish breeding records.

Goosanders breeding in Britain probably do not move far from their nesting grounds for the winter, and birds from Iceland, southern Scandinavia and areas further south are also unlikely to migrate any distance, so perhaps there is little potential for Goosanders to reach Manx territory. Many birds from northern Scandinavia and Russia spend the winter in Britain, but probably do not penetrate very far west, as is shown by the remarkable year-round absence of Goosanders from Ireland, again suggesting a lack of candidates for wandering to the Isle of Man. In any case, the Island lacks the sizeable lakes and rivers which are attractive to Goosanders, and for whatever reason they remain no more than scarce winter visitors. During the Atlas period the Goosander was recorded in every year, usually as single birds but occasionally in twos, and as this relatively prominent species is unlikely to be missed, these few reported birds were almost certainly the only ones on the Island at these times. The months from December to February are perhaps the most productive, but records are so few that generalisation is difficult.

Cullen and Jennings mention sightings at such inland sites as Kionslieu Dam and the Silverburn River, but coastal locations are also cited by these authors, at Ballaugh, Douglas, Langness, the Calf of Man and particularly Derbyhaven. Records collected by the MBA refer to single birds on the coast at the Lhen, the Calf and Langness/Derbyhaven, but otherwise Goosanders were reported from fresh water. Pairs were seen on the River Glass and the nearby pools at Tromode in 1998, 2002 and 2003, and two birds (sex not reported) on the lake at Ballachrink near Baldwin in 2002. Sites with single Goosanders during these years included the reservoir at Injebreck and Kionslieu Dam, the gravel pit at Peel, the Sulby River at Ramsey and the Santon River in its gorge north of Derbyhaven.

Breeding	Grid squares:	Isle of Man 1 (0.5%) Britain 674 Ireland 2 Total 676 (18%)
	Population:	Isle of Man 0 Britain 2,600 Ireland 1 (5% of European)
Wintering	Grid squares:	Isle of Man 11 (2%) Britain and Ireland 1,008 (26%)
	Population:	Isle of Man 0-2 Britain and Ireland 8,000

Jan	Feb	Mar	Apr	May	Jun	Jul	Aug	Sep	Oct	Nov	Dec

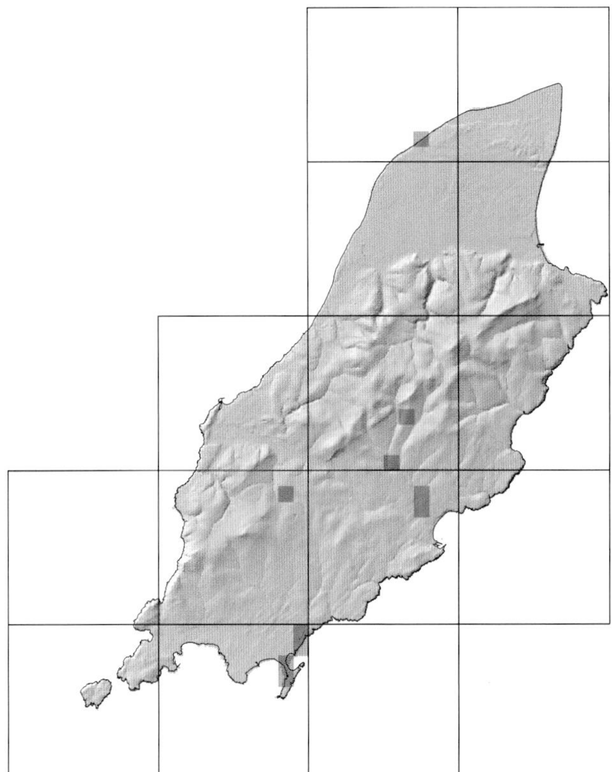

Winter presence

Ruddy Duck
Oxyura jamaicensis

The diminutive and perky Ruddy Duck seems to some extent more like a grebe than a duck in its appearance and habits, being so aquatic that it rarely ventures on to land, building a floating nest in dense emergent vegetation. This species is a member of the distinctive group of ducks known as the stiff-tails, expert divers which use their tails as rudders and are able to submerge without going through the movements of a dive. The drake is a handsome bird with his black crown, pure white cheeks and bright blue bill, but the brownish female is rather nondescript, albeit still very much a stifftail in her form and mannerisms.

The Ruddy Duck has fairly precise requirements with regard to habitat, with a need for productive (eutrophic) fresh waters with prolific plant growth, whether floating, submerged or marginal, although some open areas are also necessary to allow unobstructed dives and take-offs. During the breeding season its usual haunts are pools and small lakes in lowland regions, including artificial ones with sufficient underwater and fringing vegetation, but Ruddy Ducks generally dislike flowing water and they are seldom seen on the coast. In winter larger and more exposed waters may be frequented, flocks of several hundred birds gathering in favoured locations such as the reservoirs of the English Midlands. The standard feeding method used by the Ruddy Duck involves sieving soft sediment on the bed of the water body, extracting such items as midge larvae, beetles, tiny crustaceans and molluscs, aquatic worms, and plant material like seeds and tubers.

Ruddy Ducks are natives of North and South America, plus the West Indies, and they are present in Europe as a result of escapes from captivity. During the 1950s and 1960s perhaps as many as 70 young birds reared by the Wildfowl and Wetlands Trust at Slimbridge in Gloucestershire managed to avoid being pinioned and so were able to fly away, the first nesting in the wild being recorded in 1960 in Somerset. By 1975 at least 50 feral pairs were breeding, notably in the West Midlands (1968–72 Atlas), and the present English and Welsh total may exceed 1,000 pairs (Mead). The midland counties remain the stronghold of the Ruddy Duck, but a spread in all directions is evident, and both Scotland and Ireland have been colonised. Although the British population is largely resident, some birds must wander more widely, appearing in many parts of Europe, with subsequent breeding in (for example) Iceland, the Netherlands, Belgium, France and Spain. In the latter country, interbreeding with the native White-headed Duck *Oxyura leucocephala* is causing fear among conservationists that this rare European stifftail could be hybridised out of existence by the more dominant Ruddy Duck.

From late July until late August 1996 a pair of Ruddy Ducks was seen frequently on Kionslieu Dam, providing the first record of this species in the Isle of Man, and a bird was reported from Eairy Dam in mid-August of the same year. These two waters also held Ruddies in the late summer of 1997, with four birds additionally seen at Glen Truan Golf Course (Bride) in early August of that year. Remarkably, up to six ducklings were seen with various adults at Eairy Dam in July of 1998, and two juveniles were present there in early August. Although Ruddy Ducks have been regularly recorded at the Foxdale Dams and other waters in subsequent years, nesting has not been confirmed since this one record, although during the Atlas period probable breeding has been suggested at Kionslieu in 2000 and 2002, and possible breeding at this site in 2001 and at the Eairy in each of the years from 1999 to 2002. As the Ruddy Duck nests on small scattered pools, many potential breeding places exist on the Island, particularly on the northern plain, although the secretive behaviour of the birds, the concealment of their nests in thick aquatic vegetation, and the seclusion of the little nesting waters all cause difficulties in proving breeding.

The Foxdale dams (Kionslieu and the Eairy) have provided the bulk of the records of Ruddy Ducks in the Isle of Man (Manx Bird Reports and MBA data), with up to four birds present in every year since 1996. Other sites which have hosted this species are Glen Truan (four birds in 1997 and one in 2000), the Point of Ayre Gravel Pits (two records of singles in 2000), and Port St Mary (a single bird in 2002). This species is reported through most of the year, with peak numbers in spring, late summer and autumn, and few records between December and February (none at all during January). Kionslieu and Eairy Dams have held Ruddy Ducks in all seasons. Numbers are so small, however, that no conclusions can be drawn from lists of dates and places.

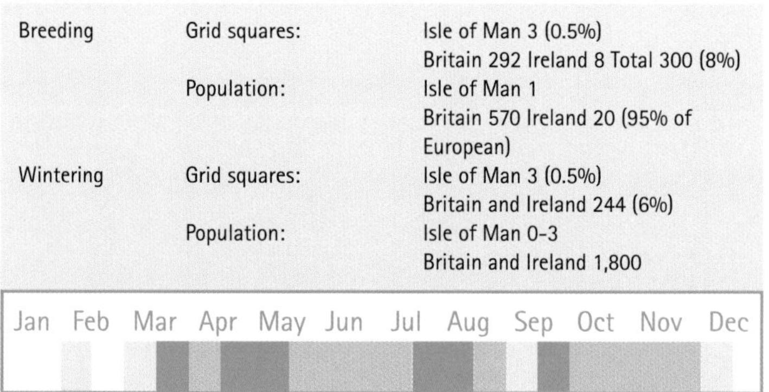

Breeding	Grid squares:	Isle of Man 3 (0.5%)
		Britain 292 Ireland 8 Total 300 (8%)
	Population:	Isle of Man 1
		Britain 570 Ireland 20 (95% of European)
Wintering	Grid squares:	Isle of Man 3 (0.5%)
		Britain and Ireland 244 (6%)
	Population:	Isle of Man 0-3
		Britain and Ireland 1,800

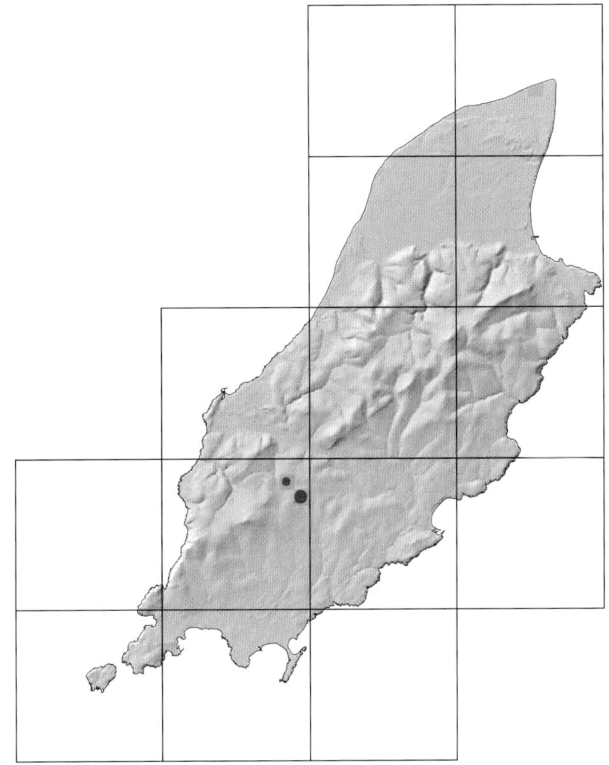

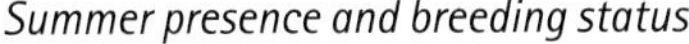

Summer presence and breeding status

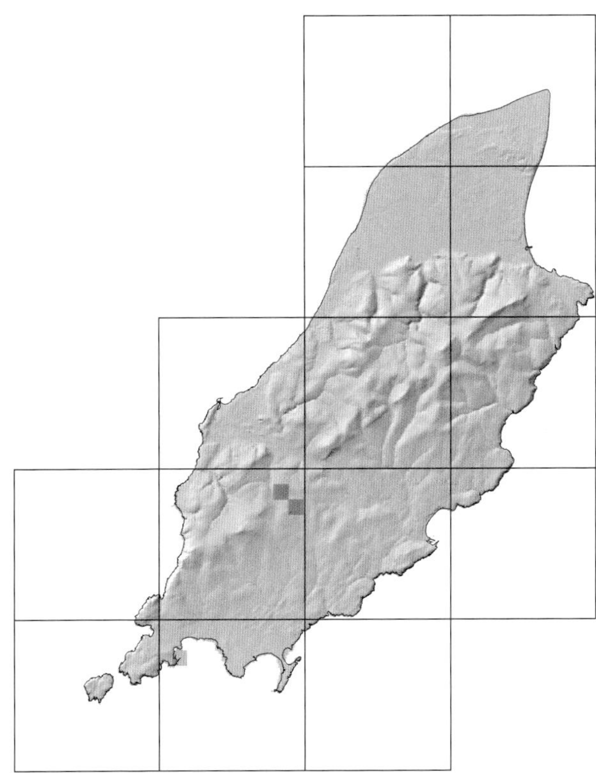

Winter presence

Red Grouse (Willow Ptarmigan) *Lagopus lagopus*

Manx: *Kellagh Ruy* = Red Cock. *Kiark Freoaie* = Heath Hen

The Red Grouse, *Lagopus lagopus scoticus*, is the British endemic subspecies of the Willow Grouse, now confusingly named Willow Ptarmigan. The plumage of the Red Grouse is essentially brown with a reddish tinge, the eye topped with a variable red comb. When flushed, it takes off with whirring wings and flies away with a mix of rapid wing beats and glides on bowed wings. The unmistakeable call is a barked 'go-back'. It is a bird of heather moorland, feeding almost exclusively on heather throughout the year.

The Willow Grouse has an arctic, subarctic and boreal distribution right across the Northern Hemisphere. Within Europe, the Willow Grouse occupies both open tundra and lowland areas forested especially with birch, but also willow and conifers. In contrast, the Red Grouse is a bird of heather moorland, being one of the most characteristic birds of that habitat.

The Red Grouse is present in its chosen habitat on the Pennines, most of Scotland, including its islands, and in Wales. There are only small numbers in the West Country, while in Ireland the distribution is very patchy, with a 66.4% decline there between 1968–72 and 1988–91. Much reduced in numbers and range, Red Grouse are still widely distributed over most of the heather moorland of the Isle of Man, mainly in the south. Prior to 1982 there had been no disciplined heather-burning, with block burning being the norm. The uplands supported a population of about 200 pairs until the early 1970s, although there was then about 33% more moorland than exists today. Walked-up shooting in the central hills could yield 50 brace in a season in the mid-1930s, and similar bags came from Lanagore and Colden in the early 1970s. The late 1970s saw a massive population crash, and poor breeding years up to 1984. In 1982 Bruce Walker and Denis Hughes began ordered heather burning and since 1985 they have kept details of the Manx grouse population particularly in the southern hills. An estimated 35 territorial cocks in 1985 had increased to 45–52 in 1987. Since 1993 there has been a voluntary shooting ban, yet there followed a steady decline to just 17 territorial males in 1996, recovering to 35–38 in 2000, the highest population in the southern hills during the MBA survey.

The intensive planting of conifers between 1955–69 reduced the area of moorland substantially but also resulted in fragmentation of the remaining heather ground, adversely affecting breeding density as well as overall numbers. More good grouse habitat was lost to a further planting programme begun in 1986, and to agricultural improvement. Predation too played a part, as Hen Harriers became established on the Island in the late 1970s and Peregrine numbers began to increase after the organo-chlorine induced poisoning of the 1960s. Peregrines are a traditional Manx predator, but the local grouse population was unprepared for harriers, which employ an entirely different hunting method. However, Walker and Hughes have noticed that grouse have learned to cope more effectively with the newcomers and fewer adult grouse are now taken by harriers.

Red Grouse nearly always nest on the margins of heather of different lengths allowing the shallow scrape to be well concealed. Laying of 8-10 (occasionally 7-11) eggs begins about the third week in April, incubation starting after the laying of the last or penultimate egg. Hatching takes place synchronously, usually during the last week of May (much later than on the Yorkshire hills), although during the summer of 2000 a hen was flushed from a clutch of 7 eggs on Cringle on 16 July.

Between 1992 and 1999, Walker and Hughes radio-tagged 120 birds, yielding valuable information about their movements. They showed that even when numbers are low some cocks have two hens, others none. Cocks are extremely sedentary, moving no more than a few hundred metres from their natal site, while hens move around in small groups from late autumn until they find territories. All hens surviving the winter attempt to breed. There have been three known instances of hens moving from the southern to the northern hills. Conversely, movement from north to south, though likely, is unproven. The winter survey did show two instances of unusual movement, with records from above Laxey Bay and from the southern slopes of the Carnanes, while between 1971 and 1991 there were three records from the Calf. Radio-tagging has shown that Manx grouse, like British birds are short-lived, very few breeding for a third season.

As grouse were plentiful until at least the mid-eighteenth century, it seems likely that they were indigenous to the Isle of Man. By 1835 however, they were extinct, but were re-introduced in Druidale in 1880 and were thereafter well distributed through the northern and southern hills (C&J). Bruce Walker disputes C&J's statement that grouse are regularly released in the Manx hills – it is unlikely that there were any introductions during the twentieth century, and almost certainly none since 1945.

1977–81

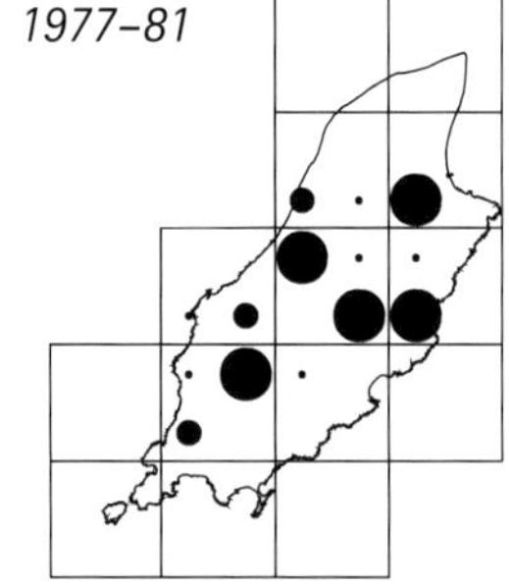

1998–2002

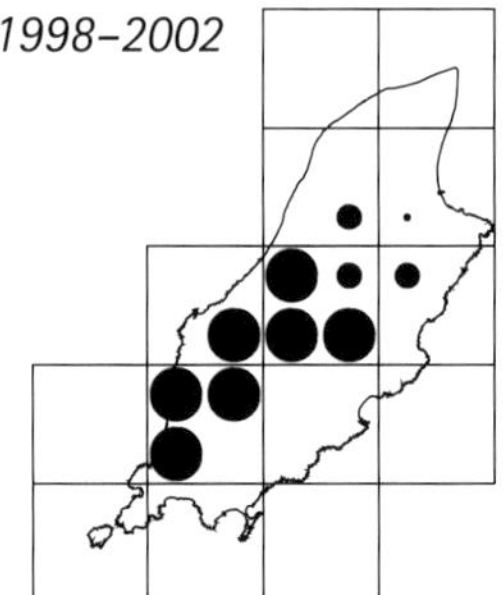

Breeding	Grid squares:	Isle of Man 35 (5%) Britain 945 Ireland 141 Total 1,086 (28%)
	Population:	Isle of Man 52-63 Britain 250,000 Ireland 3,000 (23% of European)
Wintering	Grid squares:	Isle of Man 26 (4%) Britain and Ireland 903 (23%)
	Population:	Isle of Man <100 Britain and Ireland c300,000-c800,000

Jan	Feb	Mar	Apr	May	Jun	Jul	Aug	Sep	Oct	Nov	Dec

Corporate Sponsor – The late Ms. P Gelling

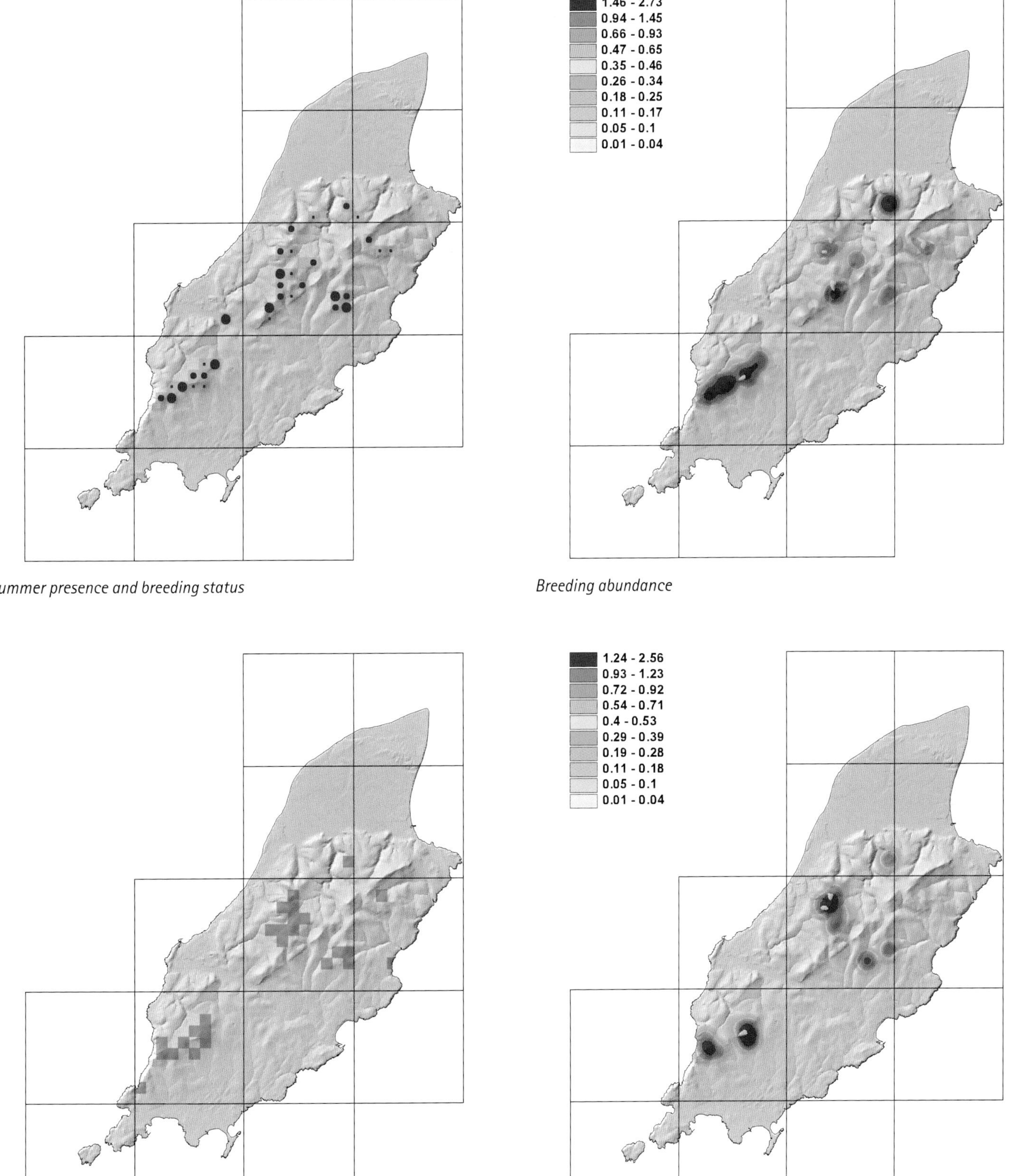

Summer presence and breeding status

Breeding abundance

Winter presence

Winter abundance

Individual Sponsors – Mr. I Bedey, Crane of Cluny, Mr. D Hughes, Manx Game Preservation Society, Mr. D Stott, Mr. B Walker

Red-legged Partridge
Alectoris rufa

The gaudily attired Red-leg is easily distinguishable from the Grey Partridge, when seen (usually running) on the ground, but if the first view is of the bird in flight, confusion can arise as both have rich chestnut on the tail and the purer grey of the Red-leg's lower back and rump is not particularly easy to distinguish. Seen from the side, the black-bordered white cheek and the heavily barred flank distinguish it from the Grey Partridge's orange bib and much more discrete flank markings.

In mainland Europe, the Red-legged Partridge has shown itself to be very adaptable, occupying arid mountain slopes and foothills, marginal cultivation, vineyards, open woodland and orchards as well as a range of farmland (BWP). In Britain it thrives best on areas of arable crops, in particular sugar beet (1988–91 Atlas), favouring areas of calcareous and sandy soils, where there is a relatively low rainfall, typified by East Anglia (1968–72 Atlas). Food is mainly vegetarian (seeds, leaves and roots), with the addition of insects in late spring and summer, when young are being fed (BWP).

The natural range of the Red-leg once embraced western Germany, France, Switzerland, northern Italy and Iberia, but over several centuries it has withdrawn from Germany, north-east France and Switzerland (EBA). Currently an overwhelming majority of the population is found in Spain. It was first introduced, unsuccessfully, to England in 1673 and there followed other failures before, in 1790, several thousand birds of French origin were released in Suffolk, where the species finally became established. Many further introductions followed and by 1930 their range extended north to the East Riding of Yorkshire, and westward to the Welsh Marches and Somerset. Nowadays they are most prosperous on the intensively cultivated farmland in the relatively drier and warmer counties of East Anglia and Lincolnshire. During the twenty-year period between the two British Atlas surveys, numbers increased within the existing range, but although records came from several hundred new squares, these were due entirely to introductions and it is doubtful if more than a very few would be self-sustaining.

First introductions took place in the Isle of Man sometime after 1967 and by 1972 Garrad was able to describe the species as 'introduced and apparently well-established'. This was certainly an over-optimistic statement as the only records during the next 16 years consisted of 1-2 at Balladoole, Arbory (1973 and 1974) and at Aust, Lezayre, where young were reared in 1980 and 1981. In 1988 however there was a good scatter of records from the north, reflecting fresh introductions and the period from then until the start of the Atlas survey saw increasing numbers of records from the northern plain and also from the Peel area and from Lonan parish. Breeding records came from Laxey in 1993, Dhoon in 1995 and Lonan Old Church in 1997.

At a shoot in Lonan, Red-legs have been released in July each year since 1995. During the Atlas period this amounted to 200 in 1998, 230 the following year, 300 in 2000 and 250 in 2002, between 32% and 50% being shot. Other releases have taken place in the north of the Island.

The Isle of Man is very much on the western limit of the Red-legged Partridge's range and neither the high rainfall nor most of the terrain are conducive to its prosperity. Having said that, the Ayres heath and adjacent farmland does have certain similarities, on a much smaller scale, to the Suffolk sandlings.

In large part, the distribution of Red-legged Partridge during the MBA matches areas of known releases, with breeding evidence across much of the northern plain, extending down the west coast towards Peel as well as in the area of Laxey and Glen Roy. Records south of the central valley were scattered and few in number. These may represent birds that have spread from known areas of release or might be the result of some small-scale, undocumented releases in the south of the Island. During the winter, distribution is largely the same as for the summer.

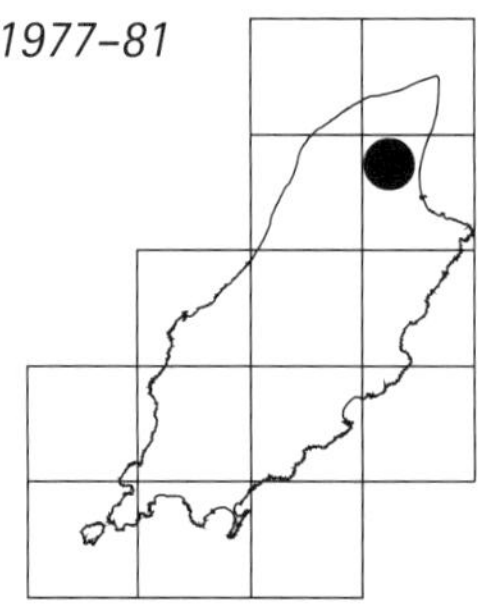

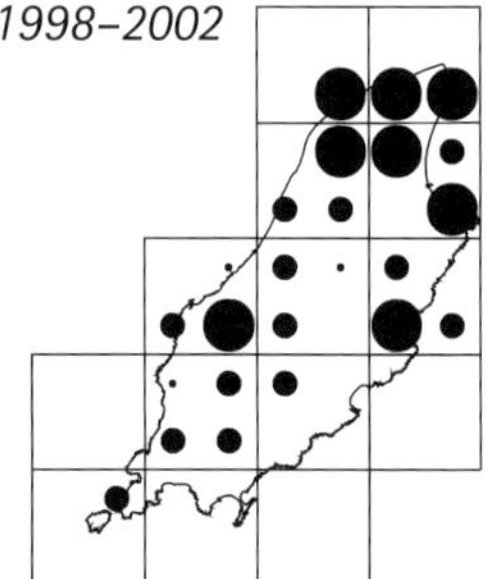

Breeding	Grid squares:	Isle of Man 108 (16%) Britain 1,214 Ireland 12 Total 1,226 (32%)
	Population:	Isle of Man 116-130 Britain 170,000 Ireland 0 (5% of European)
Wintering	Grid squares:	Isle of Man 43 (6%) Britain and Ireland 885 (23%)
	Population:	Isle of Man 400 Britain and Ireland c500,000

Jan	Feb	Mar	Apr	May	Jun	Jul	Aug	Sep	Oct	Nov	Dec

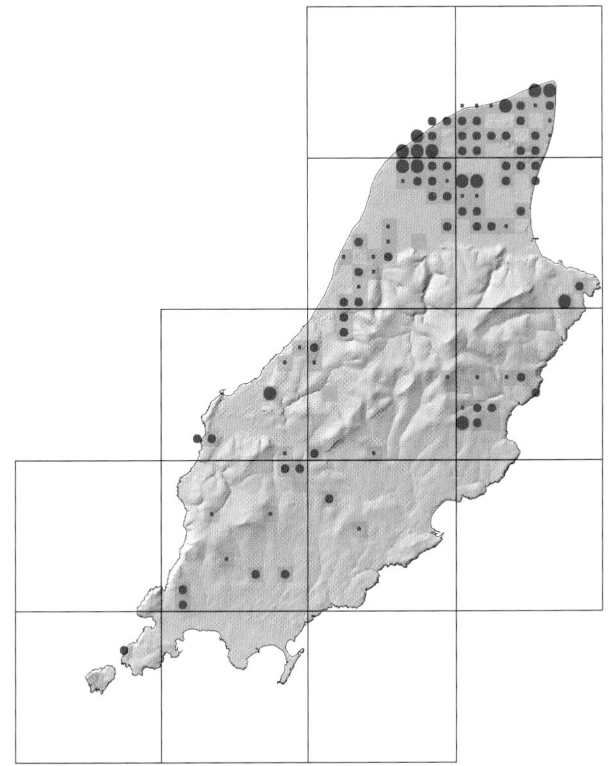

Summer presence and breeding status

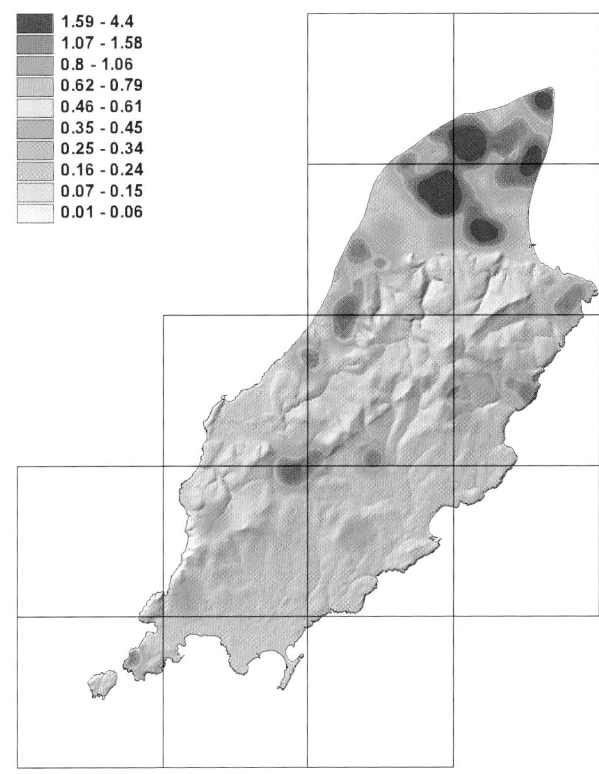

Breeding abundance

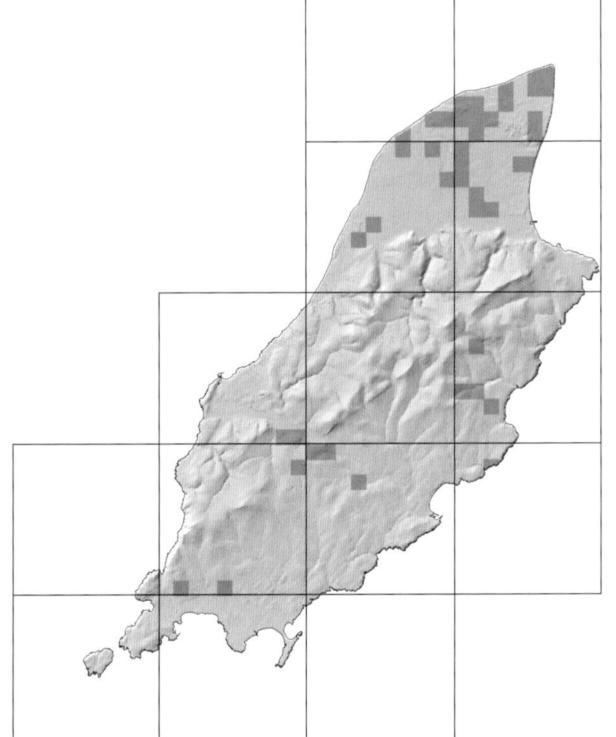

Winter presence

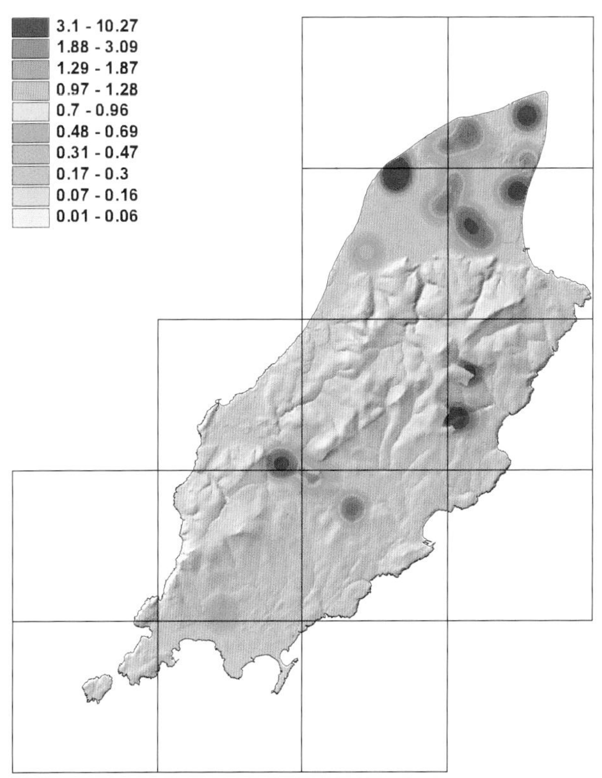

Winter abundance

Grey Partridge
Perdix perdix

Manx: *Kiark Rennee* = Fern Hen

The Grey Partridge is readily distinguishable when standing, by its orange face and a broad, dark brown patch on the belly, shaped like an inverted horseshoe. It is a bird of low-intensity mixed farmland, especially where hedges separate small fields (EBA). It feeds chiefly on plant materials, with insects being an important addition when small young are being fed (BWP). Pairing starts in mid-January and coveys, formerly numbering up to 40 birds, break up in early February. Laying starts during May or sometimes in late April, a typical clutch containing 16–22 eggs. Laying dates are not adjusted to compensate for inclement spring weather and this threat to chick survival is further augmented if the weather is cold and wet during June and July.

The Grey Partridge occurs across Europe from Ireland to the Urals (and further east in Asia, as far as Mongolia) and from the Mediterranean into southern Scandinavia, reaching 66°N in Finland. It has also been successfully introduced into North America (EBA). It is well distributed in Britain, showing an eastern bias in Scotland and has become scarce in south-west England, Wales and Ireland. Decline had been evident in Ireland during the nineteenth century and it was only because of restricting shooting, together with restocking, that the species was saved from extinction. This decline has been moving eastward and had become apparent in England during the 1960s and is likely to have involved the Isle of Man in a similar manner. The results of the 1988–91 Atlas showed that the Grey Partridge was on the verge of extinction in Ireland and there had been major losses in south-west Scotland and in Wales. These losses have been shared by many countries in Europe and only in parts of Poland and northern France have numbers remained reasonably high (EBA).

Although in the present survey breeding on the Isle of Man was confirmed in only one 10km square in the west, there were 'probables' in all but three of the 10km squares, suggesting a reasonable population. This is misleading, however, as compared to the 1980s, the northern hills have been almost completely deserted by Grey Partridge and there have also been notable losses in the centre of the Island. On the south-eastern margins of the southern hills there were records of probable breeding north of the Ronague at 260 and 220m, while single birds were seen at 240m near Kirkill and also at 230m just south of Conrhenny and 170m in Glen Roy. The only two winter records from high ground were in the south at minimum elevations of 200 and 150m. The scattered pockets of relative prosperity are well illustrated on the maps. The Grey Partridge is a bird of farmland and its uncultivated margins. In fact Manx farmland is ideal for the partridge; fields are, for the most part small, and hedges are clad in an untidy mix of gorse, bramble and bracken.

The Grey Partridge is not an indigenous Manx species, having been introduced during the second half of the seventeenth century. By the beginning of the twentieth century Grey Partridge were quite well distributed, but not abundant. Declines were first suspected in 1973, although the fine summers of 1975 and 1976 resulted in excellent breeding seasons, with at least 40 pairs being located in the spring of the latter year. During the next few years it was noticeable that few families were reported and winter coveys were smaller, not exceeding 12. There was a major crash in 1981, followed by gradual recovery, which probably peaked in 1990, to be followed by a further sustained decline. Attempts to reverse this trend have been made with introductions in the Andreas area and at Ellerslie, where 200 birds released into 21 acres of fodder beat in July 1999 had all fallen victim to raptors by the following January, though other factors may well have contributed to the losses.

The recent history of the Grey Partridge on the Calf is quite different to elsewhere. After first breeding in 1961, a peak of 11 pairs was achieved four years later. Between 1966 and 1969 there were 3–5 pairs, in 1970 and 1971 eight pairs and 16 pairs in both 1972 and 1973. Nine to ten pairs continued to nest up to 1977, but since six in the wet summer of 1978 and the very cold winter that followed, there have been no further breeding records, in fact the partridge is now just a very occasional transient visitor in spring. Langness was once an important stronghold, but with the exception of a single bird in 1989, they have not been seen there since 1981.

Analysing the causes of the decline in the 1988–91 Atlas, Potts states that 40% of the decline in the UK has been as a result of a decrease in chick survival rate, which is itself due to the use of herbicides reducing the amount of food available to the chicks. He goes on to state that this trend can be reversed by the use of 'selective unsprayed conservation headlands' or by returning to the undersowing of cereals with ley pasture, as sawflies, a favourite chick food, particularly benefit from this. Another factor which has compromised the sawfly is autumn ploughing.

1977–81

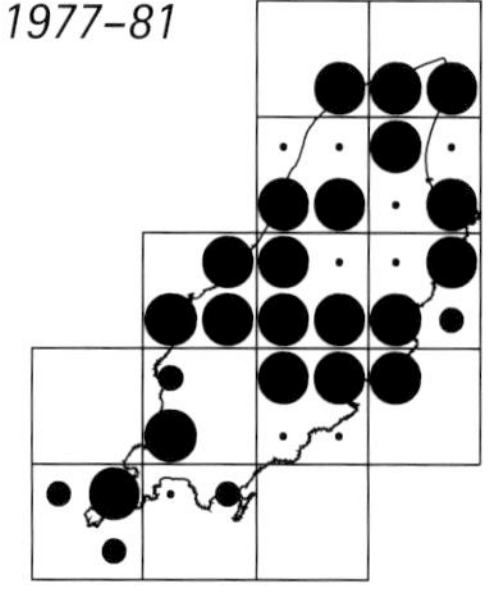

1998–2002

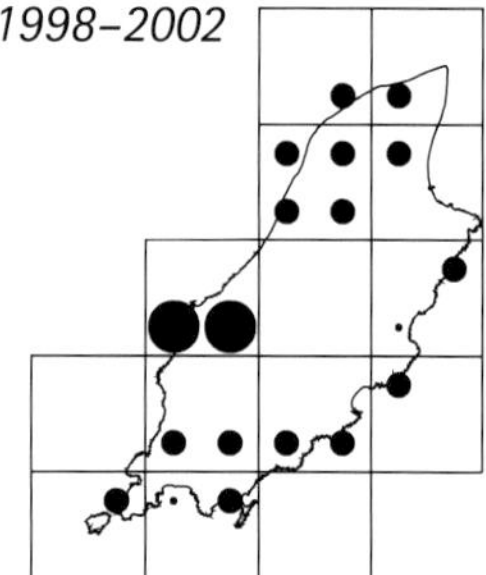

Breeding	Grid squares:	Isle of Man 55 (8%) Britain 1,629 Ireland 35 Total 1,664 (43%)
	Population:	Isle of Man 49 Britain 145,000 Ireland 50 (7% of European)
Wintering	Grid squares:	Isle of Man 21 (3%) Britain and Ireland 1,542 (40%)
	Population:	Isle of Man 100+ Britain and Ireland <1 million

Jan	Feb	Mar	Apr	May	Jun	Jul	Aug	Sep	Oct	Nov	Dec

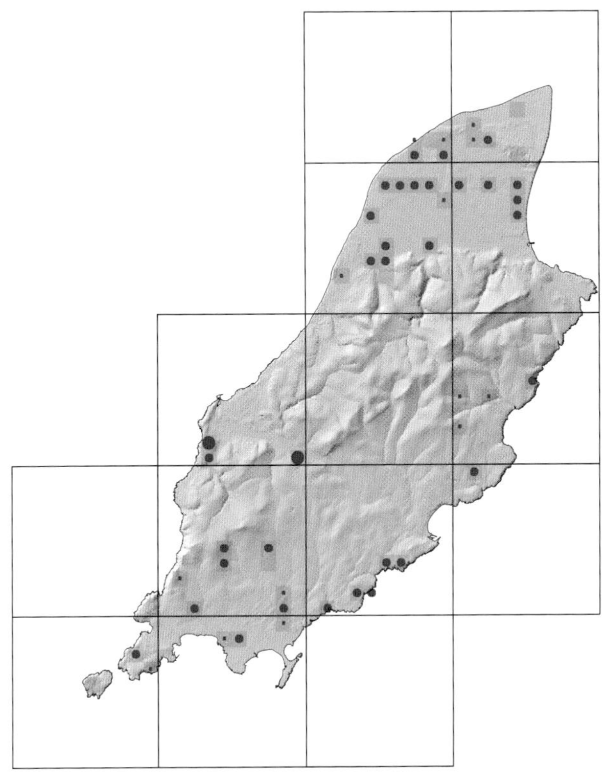

Summer presence and breeding status

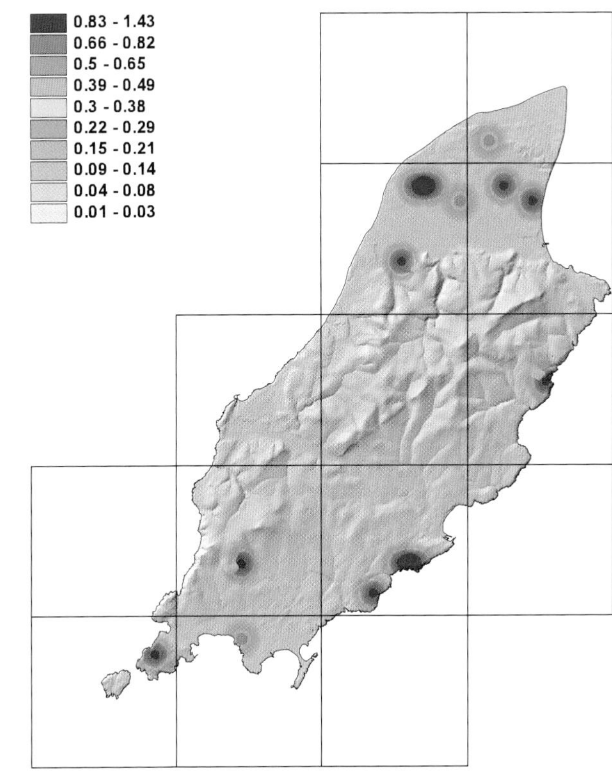

Breeding abundance

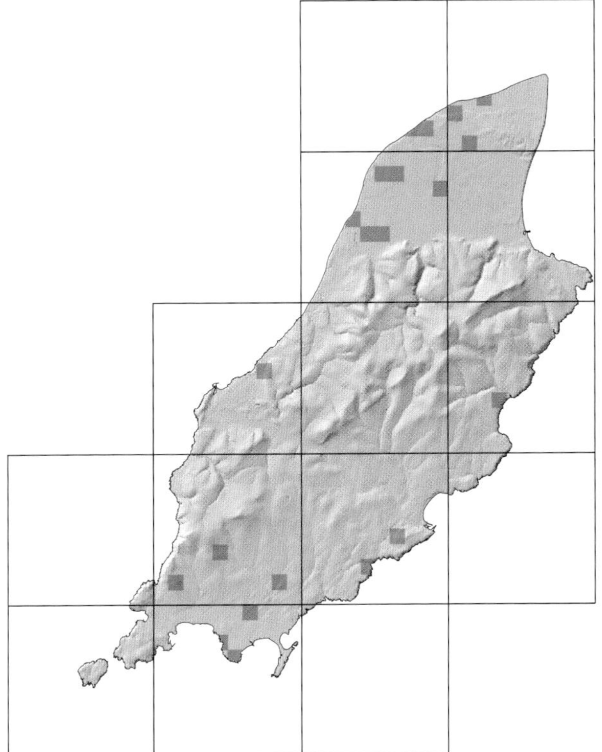

Winter presence

Individual Sponsors – The Anderson Trust, Crane of Cluny, Manx Game Preservation Society, Mr. R Stott, Mrs. W Kirkpatrick

Quail (Common Quail)
Coturnix coturnix

Manx: *Eean Feie*

No bigger than a Starling, the Quail is our smallest, and only migratory, game bird. Rarely seen, the male has a very distinct, far-carrying trisyllabic, liquid, whip-like song, expressed as 'wet-my-lips', with the stress on the 'wet'. It is repeated up to eight times at one-second intervals. In most surveys, records refer mainly to calling birds. This does not however constitute proof of breeding, as calling may go on for weeks if a male fails to find a partner, furthermore unmated males may travel up to 40km. Calling is thought to cease after pairing. If flushed, the Quail flies away with rapid wing beats, low and direct, before dropping into cover, and confusion with a young partridge is not impossible.

In most of its European breeding range, the Quail is a bird of wide open spaces, choosing dense, moist vegetation, tall enough to conceal its small frame. It nests in corn and hayfields and other crops such as flax, clover and rape. Omnivorous, its food consists mainly of seeds and insects (BWP).

The Quail occurs in the Western Palearctic, including the small islands of the north-west Atlantic, its range extending eastwards as far as northern China. Its breeding distribution lies very largely between 30 and 61°N. In Western Europe, Spain has by far the largest population, followed by France, while Denmark and Sweden receive only token appearances in some years. Quail breeding in Europe migrate to Africa, but are not thought to go south of the equator (BWP). In Britain, numbers are very variable, breeding occurring quite regularly in scattered parts of southern England, with periodic extensions into Scotland. To the Isle of Man it is an irregular visitor, having been recorded in 15 of the last 30 years. In years that they do occur, there are usually between one and three records, but on a few occasions there have been considerable invasions, perhaps initiated by warm, dry, spring weather in southern Europe. Perhaps the greatest Quail year on record was in 1893, but was rivalled by that of 1989, when at least 25 calling birds were located on the Island, especially around Andreas, but also in the Ballaugh neighbourhood and on the northern side of the central valley. In fact Andreas, and more precisely, the farmland just to the south, has been a chosen area for at least 70 years, and for 3–4 years in the early 1950s Quails were present at Ballavarry annually. The fields around Bride village have also been frequently favoured.

During the present survey birds were heard at just three sites: in 1998 in grass moorland east of Slieau Managh at 340m on 27 June, in farmland at Ballanea (Michael) on 6 July and, in 2000, at another moorland site (260m) south of Mount Karrin on 28 June. These records show that the Quail is quite catholic in its choice of habitat, although the majority of past records have been of birds calling from corn or hayfields.

Quail are heard most frequently in June and to a lesser extent in July, and there are a few records up to 11 August. Exceptionally, song has been heard from mid-May and in 1995 one was heard calling at Knockrushen on 1 September. In 1989 song records were confined to the period 14 June to 8 August. It is interesting to recall that Quails regularly over-wintered in Ireland during the nineteenth century and recently there have been two Manx records well outside the normal summer period. In 1983 one was seen near Bride on 27 March, while in 1989 one was caught alive by a cat in Port Erin on 12 December.

1977–81

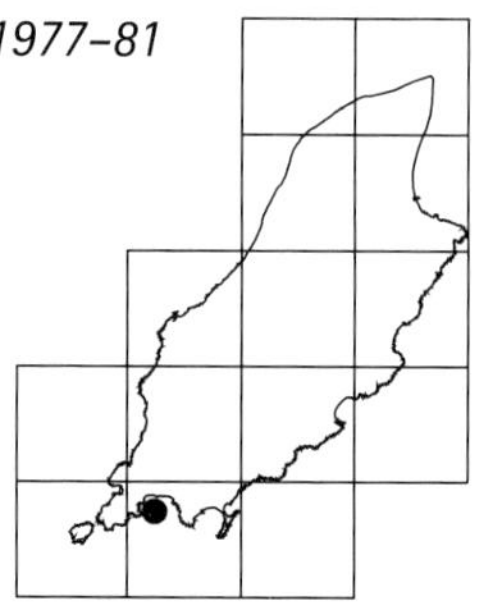

1998–2002

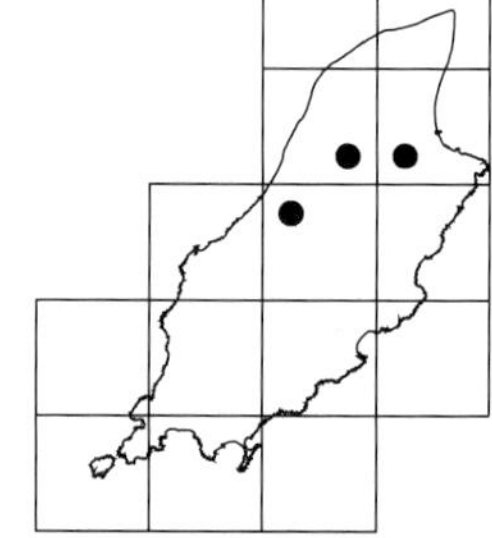

Breeding	Grid squares:	Isle of Man 3 (0.5%)
		Britain 804 Ireland 34 Total 838 (22%)
	Population:	Isle of Man 0-3
		Britain 300 Ireland 20 (0% of European)

Jan	Feb	Mar	Apr	May	Jun	Jul	Aug	Sep	Oct	Nov	Dec

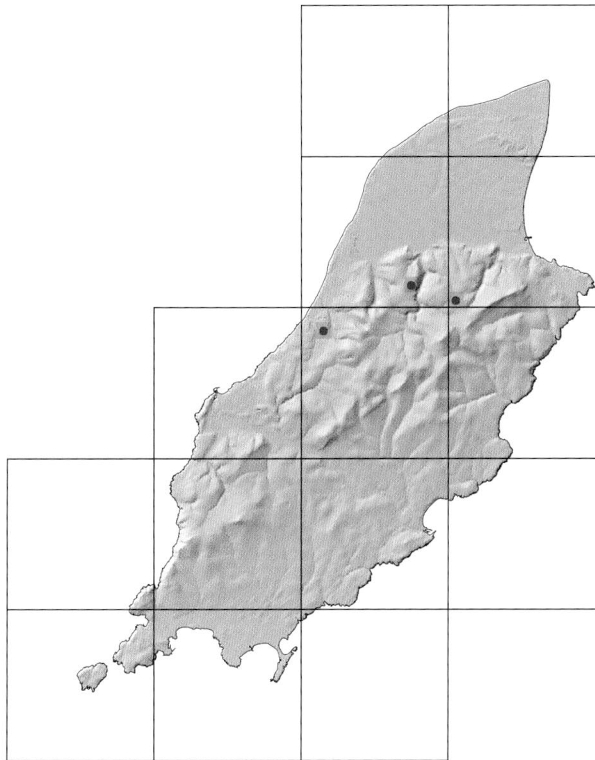

Summer presence and breeding status

Pheasant (Common Pheasant)
Phasianus colchicus

The cock Pheasant is a very large, long-tailed gamebird, with beautiful but very variable plumage, highlighted with splashes of iridescence. Two principal types predominate, but there is a whole range of variants, arising from crossing for sporting purposes. Perhaps the majority are of the white-collared Chinese *torquatus* type, the other common variety being the collarless Caucasian *colchicus* type. Common to all is the bare red face and dark green head. The hen is also a beautiful bird in an understated way, the soft brown plumage being strongly patterned. She also has a long tail, but has a small, unadorned partridge-like head. Flying young are short-tailed, brown birds, which can easily be confused with partridges.

Although principally inhabitants of farmland, Pheasants are also found in light broad-leaved woodland, and, on the Isle of Man, the curraghs of Greeba and Ballaugh and the bracken-covered margins of the coastal brooghs and the foothills. Pheasants are polygynous, a cock serving usually two or three hens. The nest, a scrape on the ground, is well concealed in thick cover, and the eight or more eggs are brooded exclusively by the female. Although the young are capable of flight at twelve days, they remain with the parent hen for 10-11 weeks. They are omnivorous ground feeders which favour grain predominantly but will take any seeds, nuts or fruit that are available. As garden visitors, their ability to locate and extract subterranean bulbs can be quite tiresome.

Except in the extreme south-east, the European stock is entirely derived from introduced birds. It ranges from the Bay of Biscay to the Black Sea and from the Mediterranean to the southern parts of Sweden and Finland. The most populous countries are the United Kingdom (where there are more than twice as many birds as in any other country), France, Hungary, Germany, Denmark and Romania (EBA). Both British breeding atlases have shown an absence of Pheasants from much of north-west Scotland, the Hebrides and parts of Donegal, Mayo and Galway. On the Isle of Man the Pheasant is abundant and widespread, being absent only from the centre of towns and from ground above about 300m. They are, in fact, rarely seen on moorland. They stray into the more peripheral urban gardens, attracted initially by food put out for passerines in winter, but not infrequently breeding if there is sufficient cover. Nowadays two or three can usually be found around Langness pool.

Given the status currently, it is hard to believe that all attempts to introduce Pheasants on the Isle of Man during the late nineteenth century met with failure, yet they had been well established in mainland Britain from the late sixteenth century, with stock originating from the Caucasus and China. Although large numbers were subsequently released on the Island, the population gradually dwindled, so that by 1934 there were none, and it is only during the last fifty years that they have really become established, aided by the release of many thousands of birds. A Baldrine farmer recalls how around 1965, the arrival of a Pheasant caused great excitement, such that it was caught and then kept on the farm. The 1968–72 survey showed definite breeding in eleven of the fourteen 10km squares, but in C&J's survey this figure had increased to thirteen and they were able to write 'there is now a well-established wild population, which is regularly fortified by introductions'. At that time large numbers were being released in Santon, and Pheasants appeared super-abundant in the parish. Comparing C&J's 5km data with the present survey there has effectively been no change. One odd feature is that in none of the three surveys has breeding been confirmed in the Castletown/Langness area.

In Britain, between 25 and 35 million Pheasants are released by game syndicates annually, 40% being shot, 40% dying from other causes and 20% surviving to face another season. On the Isle of Man a total of up to 10,000 birds are released annually by three syndicates in the north, while more modest numbers are released by a shoot in Lonan. Here 150 were put down in 1998, with 300 in both 1999 and 2000, and 350 in 2002. Although only 25% of Lonan released birds were shot in 1998, the tally since then has been nearer 50%. Prior to release, polecat predation of chicks has been a problem.

1977–81

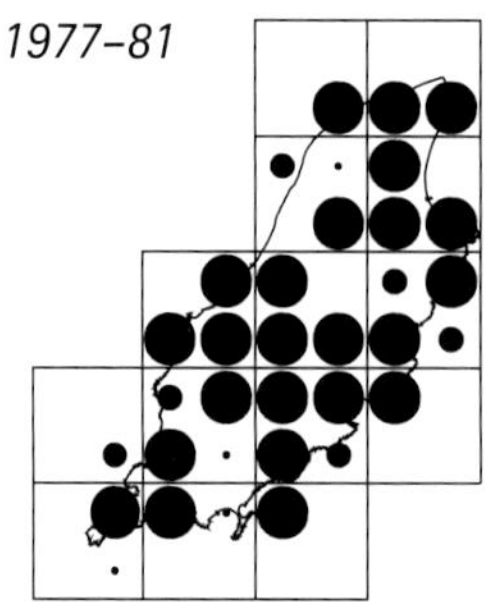

1998–2002

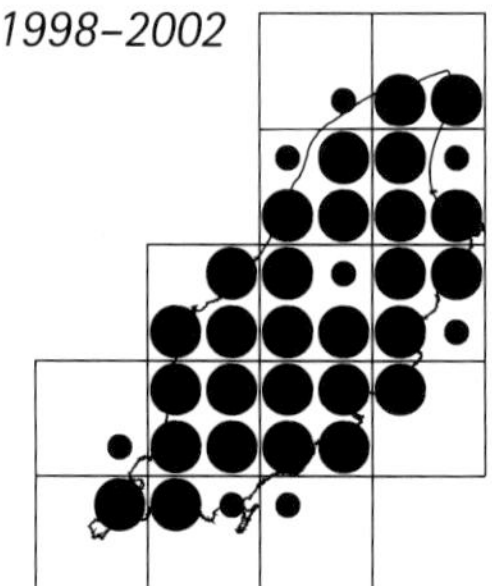

Breeding	Grid squares:	Isle of Man 516 (77%) Britain 2,269 Ireland 844 Total 3,113 (81%)
	Population:	Isle of Man 1,740-2,092 (females): Britain 1,550,000 Ireland 570,000 (7% of European)
Wintering	Grid squares:	Isle of Man 399 (60%) Britain and Ireland 2,829 (73%)
	Population:	Isle of Man 8,000+ Britain and Ireland 8 million

Jan	Feb	Mar	Apr	May	Jun	Jul	Aug	Sep	Oct	Nov	Dec

Corporate Sponsor – Marsh (Isle of Man) Limited

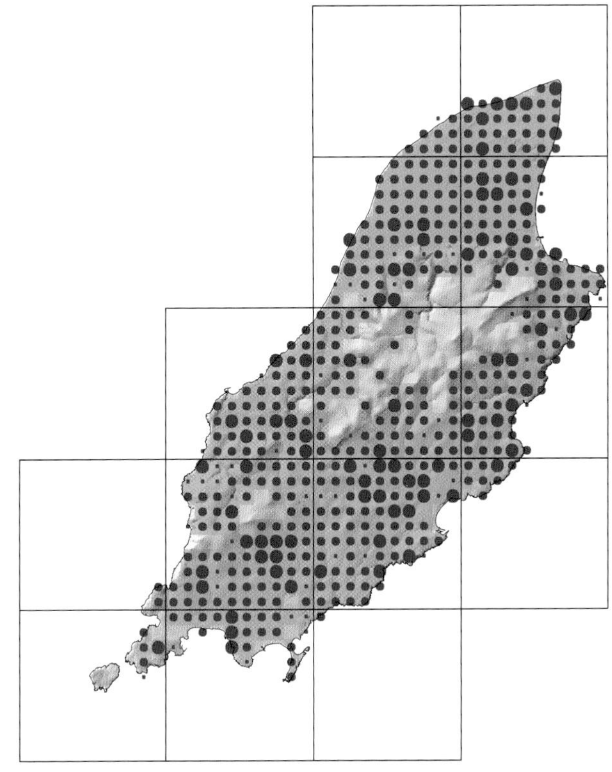

Summer presence and breeding status

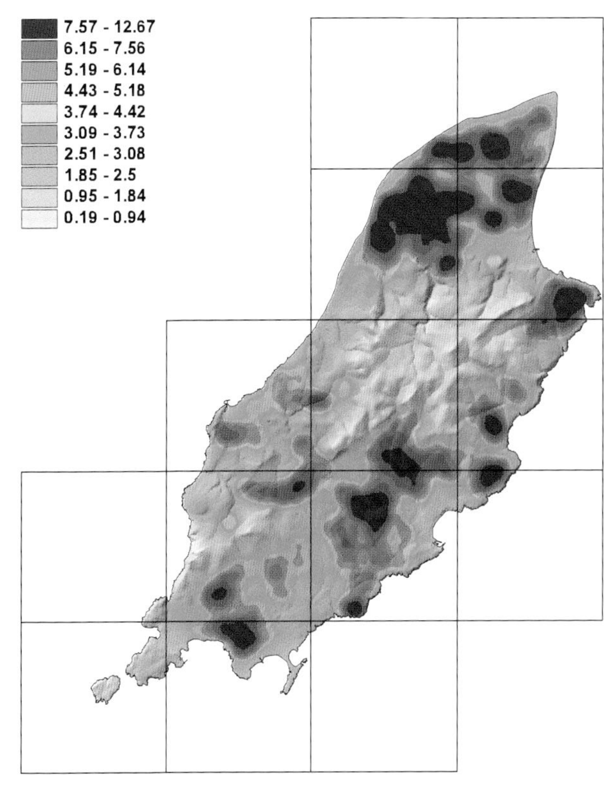

Breeding abundance

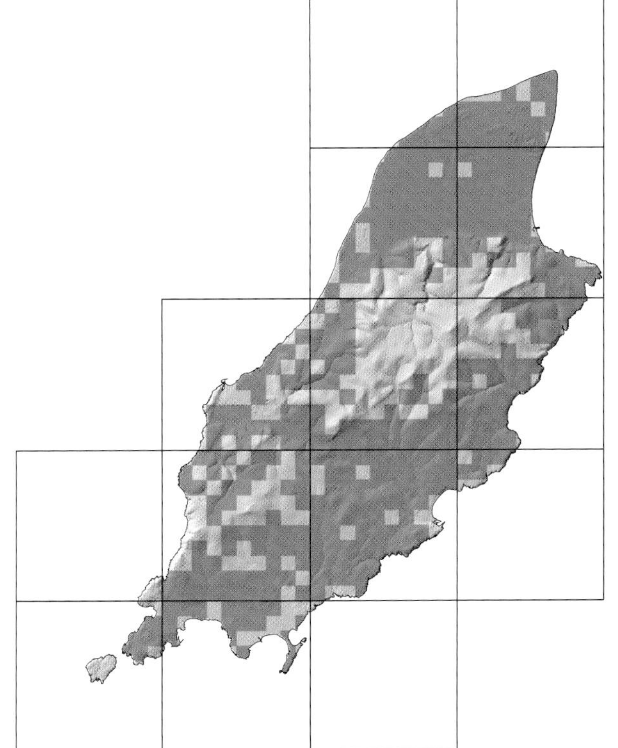

Winter presence

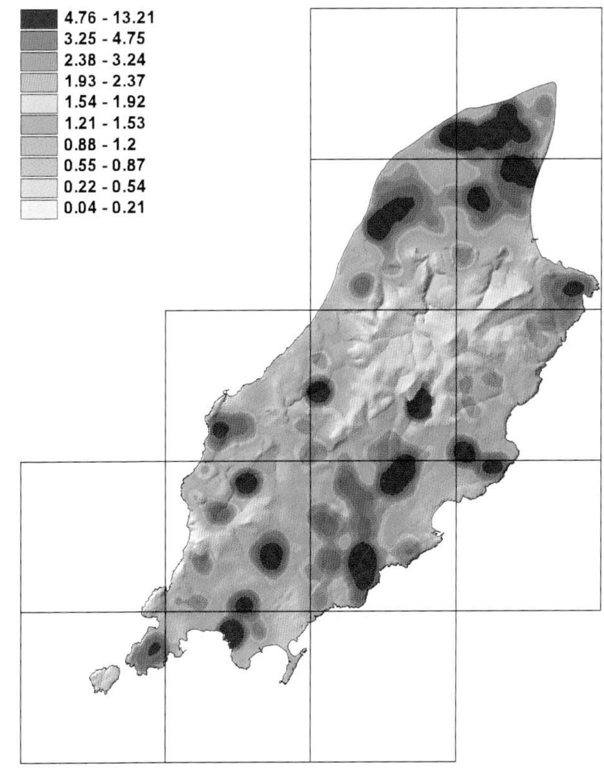

Winter abundance

Individual Sponsor – Miss S Goodwin

Red-throated Diver
Gavia stellata

Manx: *Lhargey Mooar*

This, the smallest of the divers, is also the most frequently observed and occurs as a winter visitor and passage migrant. Though most records are of birds in winter plumage, birds in full summer plumage do occur off the Manx coasts. In such plumage they are striking, especially in good sunlight, with the red throat reducing the chances of confusion with other diver species. At distance or in poor light, however, the red throat can look dark resulting in occasional confusion with Black-throated Divers. In winter plumage, risk of misidentification is increased, though the generally more slender build, extensive white on the neck and a slightly upward tilting bill combine to help the developing 'birder' in correctly identifying the species.

Breeding Red-throated Divers favour small stands of fresh water, of less than $100m^2$, and seldom breed on large lakes or lochs. Breeding ponds often lack fish so adults need to fly to larger lakes or the sea to find food (EBA). In the winter, birds abandon their breeding sites to inhabit shallow inshore waters, where they take a range of prey including sandeels and small crustaceans (WA).

Red-throated Divers have a circumpolar distribution and are among the most northerly of aquatic birds, the majority of the population breeding north of 60°N, in Greenland, Iceland, Scandinavia, Russia and North America (EBA, MA). Breeding in Britain and Ireland is confined largely to Shetland, Orkney, the Outer Hebrides, and the northern and western extremities of mainland Scotland. A few pairs breed in the north of Ireland (1988–91 Atlas). The species has never bred on the Isle of Man and, not surprisingly given the lack of suitable habitat, no evidence of breeding was obtained during our research. The summer distribution map demonstrates a clear preference for the north-west coastline of the Island, where shallow inshore waters offer plenty of feeding opportunities. Records during this period from the regularly watched Calf of Man, Langness and Peel Castle all relate to single birds in flight. The majority of summer records were in April, a few in May, only two in June and none in July.

Post-breeding migration occurs from August onwards, with the dispersal of birds moving south, though this is not usually evident on the Island until September when the number of sightings starts to increase. Many Scottish birds, along with birds from Iceland, the Faeroes and some from Greenland are thought to move down the west coast of Britain and the coasts of Ireland, though Shetland birds probably move down the east coast (WA). It is likely, therefore, that our initial autumn sightings relate to British birds, with birds from further afield adding to numbers as the autumn progresses. The number seen in any one year will vary, depending upon whether or not prevailing winds bring them close to our shores. From mid-September Scandinavian birds arrive, predominantly down the east coast of Britain.

Winter numbers are variable, year on year and within seasons, much depending upon prevailing weather conditions. Low numbers occur along the north-west coast of England, but there is a good distribution along the east coast of Ireland (WA). It is probable that the Manx wintering population is a combination of birds remaining in local waters and Irish coastal birds moving to the Island in response to local weather conditions. The winter distribution map reveals a very similar picture to that for the summer, with presence along much of the north-west coast, though Red-throated Divers are also sometimes to be seen in the Island's more sheltered bays, such as Derbyhaven, Port Erin and Ramsey.

Numbers present in any one winter are hard to determine with any accuracy. The shallow coastal waters of the Ayres are clearly an important feeding area, however, supporting the majority of our wintering birds. Return passage occurs in two distinct periods. Late February and early March marks the return of British breeding birds to their breeding grounds, with a further movement in April–May, presumed to comprise Scandinavian birds (WA). Though numbers involved were variable over the period, records obtained during the MBA research suggest evidence of passage past the Island during both periods.

Ralfe regarded Red-throated Divers as regular winter visitors, though he only mentioned 'several' wintering in Douglas Bay during 1891 and did not comment upon general distribution. C&J described the species as a 'regular passage migrant and rather scarce winter visitor to our shores', noting that since 1960 the species has been observed with increasing frequency, a view supported by the survey of 1998-2003, which provided records in all months except July.

Breeding	Grid squares:	Isle of Man 16 (2%) Britain 379 Ireland 10 Total 389 (10%)
	Population:	Isle of Man 0 Britain 935 Ireland <10 (16% of European)
Wintering	Grid squares:	Isle of Man 36 (5%) Britain and Ireland 695 (18%)
	Population:	Isle of Man 10-100 Britain and Ireland 12,000-15,000

Jan	Feb	Mar	Apr	May	Jun	Jul	Aug	Sep	Oct	Nov	Dec

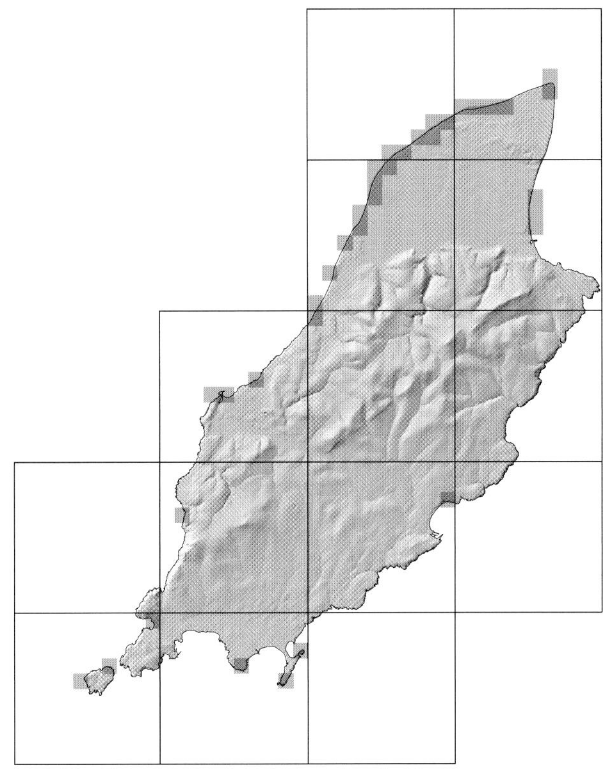

Winter presence

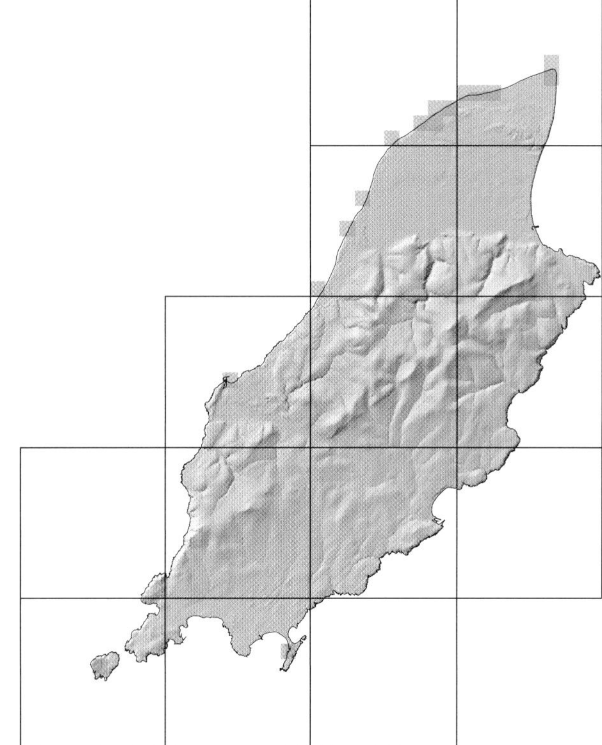

Summer presence

Black-throated Diver
Gavia arctica

Manx: *Lhargey*

Though the Black-throated Diver is larger than the Red-throated this is not always easy to determine when observing birds on the sea. In good light the darker mantle and white flank patch of the Black-throat in winter should be evident and are good identification features. In poor light, or in choppy seas, however, these features are less reliable and, on such occasions, the heavier set to the head and straighter bill can help to confirm identification. The species is rarely seen locally in its full summer breeding splendour, when the combination of pale grey crown and neck, black throat and black and white upper parts cause few identification problems.

Breeding territories are usually on the shores of lakes or lochs, with islands being particularly favoured (1988–91 Atlas). Wintering Black-throated Divers favour very similar locations to those chosen by Red-throats; shallow sandy coastal waters and bays, where they feed on a range of prey including sandeels, crustaceans and flatfish (WA).

Breeding Black-throated Divers are to be found throughout the Arctic and boreal zones in Europe, Asia and North America. The Russian population is in excess of 100,000 pairs and accounts for the majority of European breeding birds. Other significant populations are found in Finland, Sweden and Norway. The small population of the British Isles amounts to about 170 pairs, and is restricted to the Outer Hebrides and the mainland of north and west Scotland (EBA, Mead). There was a single record of possible breeding in Donegal (1988–91 Atlas, Mead). They have never been recorded breeding on the Isle of Man.

Birds from more northerly breeding populations move south during the autumn, the main wintering grounds being in the Baltic region. The extent to which British breeders move further south is not known. Autumn passage to or past the Island is not heavy, with the species only being noted during September to mid-November on eight days during the five autumns of the MBA research period. With the inshore seas of Britain and Ireland lying to the west of migration routes, they support only a small percentage of the overall wintering population. Winter distribution of the species in British waters indicates a marked east coast bias, probably involving Scandinavian birds, and it is possible that wintering birds in the west of Scotland are local breeders. In comparison with the rest of the British coast, the species is rare in the Irish Sea, numbers of birds possibly fluctuating in response to weather patterns further north (WA).

Unsurprisingly, therefore, the species is not common in Manx waters, the winter distribution map highlighting the preponderance of records in the shallow seas of the north-west coast, where ample food will be present. Most records are of single birds, though records of 2–3 birds are not uncommon. A remarkable record of about 20 individuals on 15 February 2002 off Glen Wyllin represents the largest gathering of the species ever noted in Manx waters. With the exception of this record it is unlikely that our coastal seas regularly support more than 1-5 individuals each winter.

The only 'inland' record was of a dead bird on the gravel pits at the Point of Ayre; the bird's general condition indicating that it had probably died of starvation.

The only reference to the species by Ralfe is of a male 'taken off the Vollan, Ramsey, 21 January 1886', and a female 'taken in Ramsey Harbour, February 1900', both records being attributed to Kermode. C&J classed it as a 'scarce passage migrant and winter visitor to coastal waters'. Though the species has, in recent years, been seen more frequently than had previously been the case, it is likely that this is due to increased observer effort and improved recording systems. It is unlikely that the local status of the species has changed recently and it may have been more frequent in Ralfe's time than is suggested.

Breeding	Grid squares:	Isle of Man 8 (1%) Britain 199 Ireland 0 Total 199 (5%)
	Population:	Isle of Man 0 Britain 170 Ireland ?1 (1% of European)
Wintering	Grid squares:	Isle of Man 18 (3%) Britain and Ireland 316 (8%)
	Population:	Isle of Man 0-20 Britain and Ireland 1,300

Jan	Feb	Mar	Apr	May	Jun	Jul	Aug	Sep	Oct	Nov	Dec

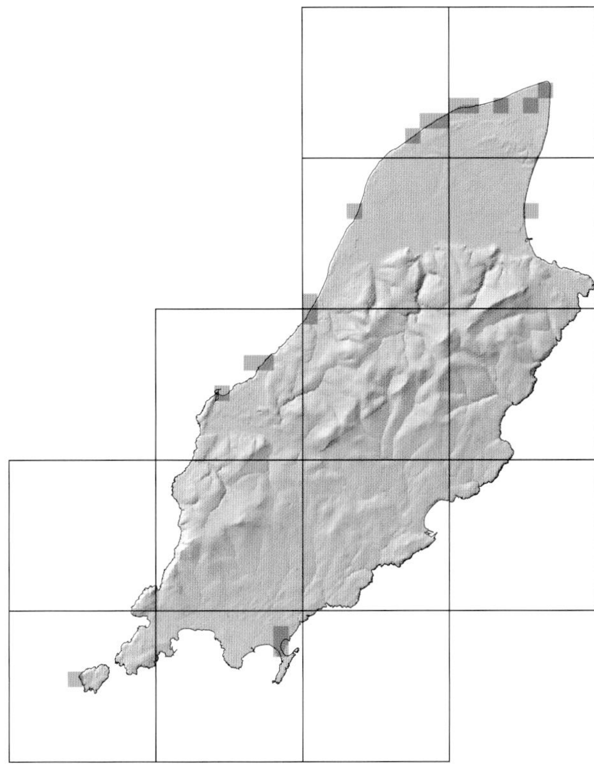

Winter presence

Great Northern Diver
Gavia immer

Manx: *Arrag Vooar* = Big Pullet. *Thummeyder*

Great Northern Divers are the largest of the three diver species seen regularly around the Manx coast. They are rather bulky in appearance with a thick neck and heavy straight bill, combining to make it a relatively straightforward species to identify. As always however, accurate identification becomes more of a challenge when the bird is seen at a distance, disappearing behind waves and while your binoculars are being covered in salt spray! In summer plumage, which is seldom observed locally, it is quite eye-catching, having an all black head, set off by a white striped patch on the neck and black and white chequered upperparts.

Breeding Great Northern Divers prefer large freshwater lakes that lack tall vegetation along the shore (BWP). Outside of the breeding season they are rarely seen inland, being primarily birds of the sea, occurring further offshore than either of the other two species of diver found locally (WA).

Within Europe, the species only breeds regularly in Iceland, with an estimated 300 pairs. The main breeding range is in the Aleutians, Alaska, Canada and the northern United States, and into Greenland, which has only a small population of between 200 and 2,000 pairs (EBA). The most recent record of breeding in the British Isles was of a pair with young in the Scottish Highland region in 1997 (Mead). The species has never been recorded as breeding on the Isle of Man. Summer presence around Manx coasts is sporadic and records were confined, during the research period, to the coast from Peel north to the Point of Ayre. Many of these records were obtained during April–May and are likely to be of birds returning to breeding territories, while the few June and July records probably relate to non-breeding birds, small numbers of which are known to remain in British waters in the summer (WA).

Breeding birds mainly leave their territories in Greenland and Iceland in September and October though some, probably failed breeders and immature birds, can arrive in wintering areas as early as August. Locally, the species is seldom seen in August and September, records only increasing during October and into November.

Winter distribution in Britain and Ireland demonstrates a marked Atlantic coast bias, with relatively few in the Irish Sea. With an estimated 3,500-4,500 birds wintering in Britain and Ireland it is suggested that birds from Greenland and even Canada might winter around Britain, adding to the Icelandic and British over-summering population (WA). Locally, most sightings of Great Northern Divers in winter relate to single birds. The highest count obtained during the Atlas period was on 31 December 1998, following a prolonged period of gales, when nine birds were present in Peel Bay, the location of the highest ever documented Manx count of 14 birds in December 1929 (C&J). Weather related peaks such as this give an indication of the numbers that go unrecorded, the species being known to winter as far as 10km offshore in suitable weather (WA). Winter distribution was more extensive than for the summer. With the exception of birds seen flying past the Island, winter records away from favoured summer areas were confined to various bays in which birds sought shelter from high seas.

Records away from the coast were rare. One was present on a lake at the Glen Truan Golf Course at the Ayres on 26 December 2002 and a first winter bird was present on the lower reaches of the River Neb from 28 October to 11 November 2001. Numbers gradually decrease during February with records on only three days in March during the research period.

Perhaps the most remarkable record was of a bird, stunned but otherwise unharmed, found below a window at Ronaldsway Airport on 30 December 1999. The bird was released in Derbyhaven Bay, where it remained for several days, actively feeding throughout its stay.

Kermode considered that Peel and Castletown Bays were especially frequented by the species, while Ralfe described it as far from rare on the Manx coast during winter months, though rarely observed in complete (summer) plumage. C&J described the species as a 'regular winter visitor and passage migrant', though it is likely that then, as now, the species was occasionally present as a non-breeding summer resident.

Wintering	Grid squares:	Isle of Man 33 (5%)
		Britain and Ireland 721 (19%)
	Population:	Isle of Man 0-10
		Britain and Ireland 3,500-4,500

Jan Feb Mar Apr May Jun Jul Aug Sep Oct Nov Dec

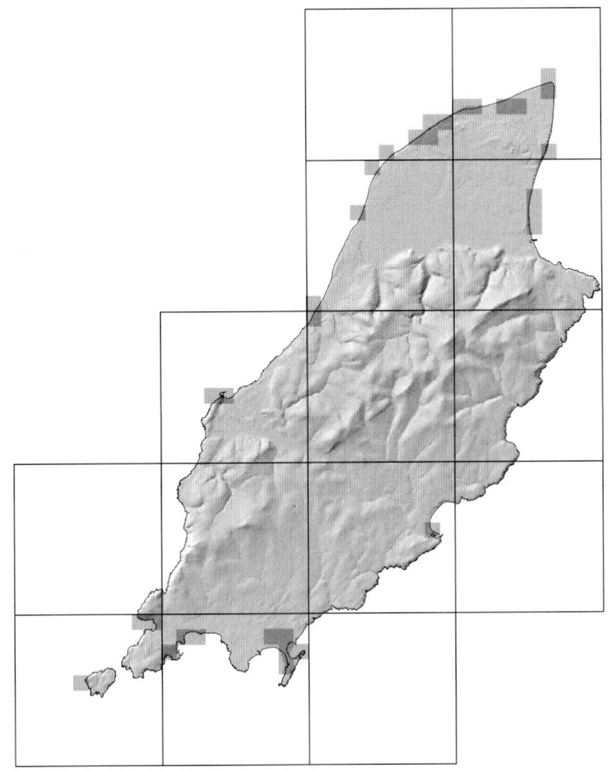

Winter presence

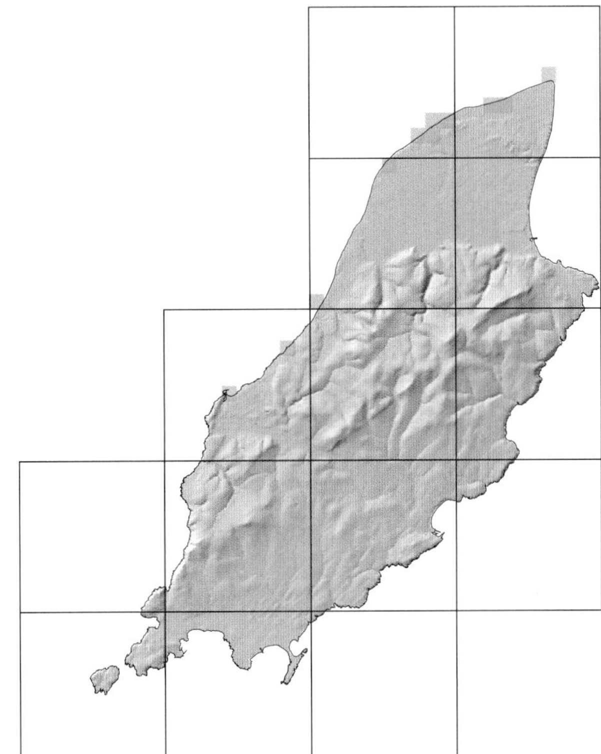

Summer presence

Little Grebe
Tachybaptus ruficollis

Manx: *Eean Kereen Beg*

Small, round, with a stout bill and a blunt-ended body, the Little Grebe has a distinctive shape that is fairly unmistakable. When actively feeding it dives from the surface, often with a small jump, before reappearing again a short while later, rather abruptly, almost like a fisherman's float after the bait has been nibbled. These features combine to make the Little Grebe, or Dabchick, an endearing bird that is always a welcome sight when out birding for the day.

Throughout their range Little Grebes breed on freshwater bodies with emergent and submerged vegetation. They prefer small ponds and lakes, though reservoirs and slow moving waters such as canals and rivers are also used. Locally, plenty of seemingly suitable habitat is available, especially in the north, with its numerous dubs. Food is varied, comprising insects, larvae, molluscs, crustaceans and small fish. Prey is taken chiefly by diving though they will also surface feed (BWP).

Within the British Isles only the subspecies *Tachybaptus ruficollis ruficollis* occurs, also breeding throughout temperate Europe as far as 60°N, north-west Africa, Turkey and Israel (EBA). Within Britain and Ireland it is confined to the lowlands, where suitable water bodies occur, with the highest counts being along major river valleys such as the Test, Hampshire Avon and Trent. The Central Lowlands represent its Scottish stronghold while it is widely distributed in the low-lying wetland areas of Ireland, occurring in greater densities per occupied 10km square there than in Britain (1988–91 Atlas). Given the presence of apparently suitable breeding habitat locally, and good densities in Ireland, the lack of a regular breeding population of Little Grebes on the Island is disappointing and might be due to the shortage of prey; coarse fish being largely absent. Breeding was suspected at only three locations during the survey period. Birds were present at the gravel pits in the north of the Island in four of the five summers, and on the Eairy Dam in two summers, though at neither site was more than one bird seen at a time. The only record of a pair was from Bishop's Dub, in May 1998, the location at which breeding was last confirmed on the Island when in June 1986, a nest with four eggs was found (Peregrine 1987).

Within Britain it is suggested that most Little Grebes disperse from breeding grounds to nearby coasts for the winter (Vinicombe 1982), though some birds are thought to remain on their breeding territories through the winter (WA). It is known that Britain and Ireland receive migrants from western Europe, birds moving west to avoid freezing conditions (MA).

In winter, Little Grebes occupy a wider range of habitats than in summer. Inland the winter distribution in Britain and Ireland is largely the same as the summer, though fewer birds are present. The species is found more frequently in sheltered coastal locations in winters than in summer and birds present will comprise immigrants as well as resident birds (WA). Locally very few birds are present in the winter and numbers are variable, year on year as well as within winters. The origin of our wintering population is unknown, but is likely to comprise mainly British and Irish birds that have left breeding territories, with possibly some European migrants.

Locations where wintering Little Grebes are most commonly seen on the Island are along the coast at Poyllvaaish and increasingly at the gravel pits at the Point of Ayre. The most reliable location in recent years (though not guaranteed) is the lower reaches of the Sulby River, from the Whitebridge above Ramsey, downstream to the upper harbour, where in some winters as many as five birds have been present. The winter distribution map reveals that a number of other inland waters have been used including Port-e-Chee Lake, Clypse Reservoir, Eairy Dam, and Billown Lakes, though many of these locations provided only single sightings. It is considered that fewer than ten birds may be present in any one winter.

Ralfe did not comment on the breeding status of the species, though he referred to a number of different nests, from which it is safe to assume that it formerly bred in greater numbers than it does currently. He considered that the species occurred more widely in winter than in summer, being found on both salt and fresh water. C&J described the Little Grebe as a scarce and irregular breeder and regular winter visitor. The current research indicates that the status has not changed in recent years.

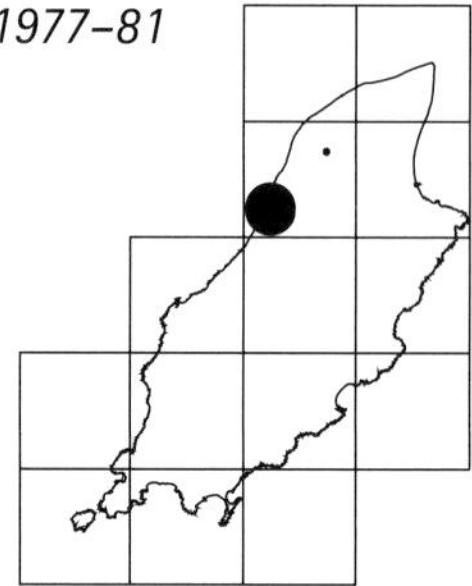

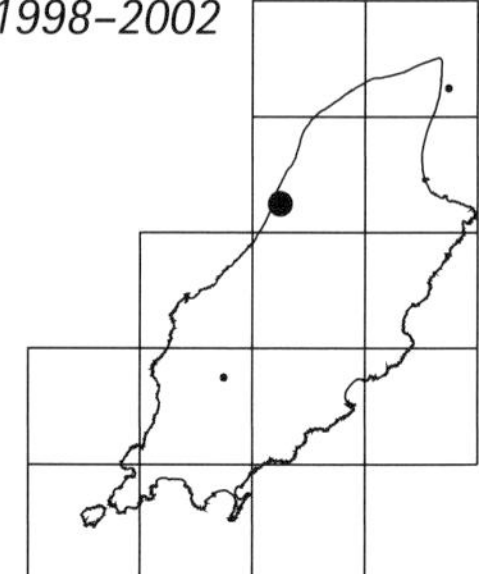

Breeding	Grid squares:	Isle of Man 5 (1%) Britain 1,275 Ireland 336 Total 1,611 (41%)
	Population:	Isle of Man 1-3 Britain 7,500 Ireland 4,500 (15% of European)
Wintering	Grid squares:	Isle of Man 15 (2%) Britain and Ireland 1,810 (47%)
	Population:	Isle of Man <10 Britain and Ireland 11,000

Jan Feb Mar Apr May Jun Jul Aug Sep Oct Nov Dec

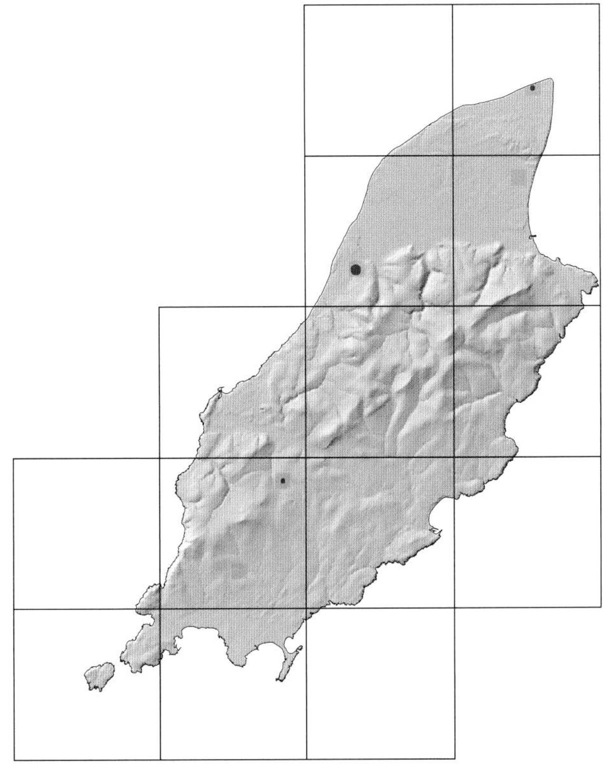

Summer presence and breeding status

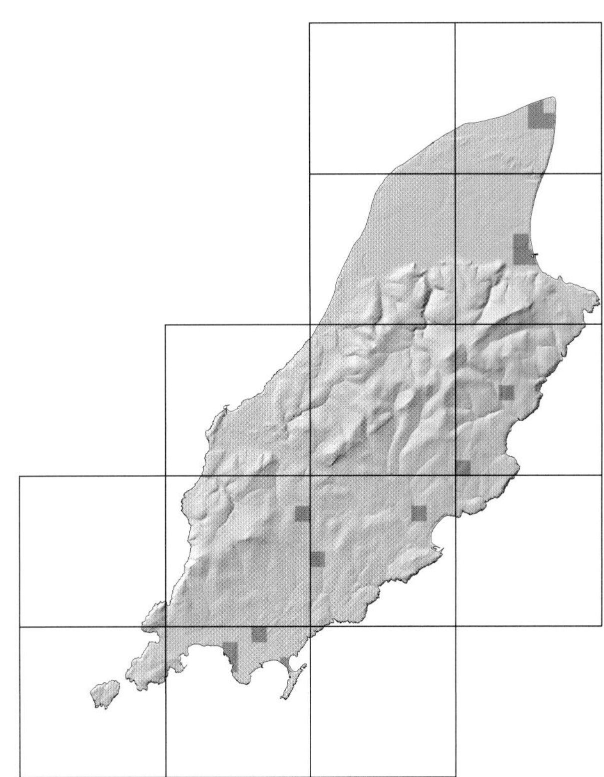

Winter presence

Slavonian Grebe
Podiceps auritus

Manx: *Eean Kereen Cleayshagh*

Unfortunately the Slavonian Grebe is never seen locally in its full summer plumage of golden ear tufts and chestnut neck and underparts. In fact, during the winter it is rather unremarkable, appearing generally black above and white below. On closer inspection it has a distinct small black cap, white cheeks and a narrow black line down the back of the neck. To the less experienced eye it can be hard to distinguish from the less frequently observed Black-necked Grebe. Despite the Slavonian Grebe's rather plain appearance it is always pleasing to see, reaffirming the belief that days of routine watching can be rewarded by the occasional local rarity.

Preferred breeding habitat is shallow, nutrient-rich lakes, though artificial sites such as gravel pits are used as well as brackish habitat (EBA). Within Britain breeding occurs predominantly on mesotrophic lakes (1988–91 Atlas). The species has never been recorded as breeding on the Isle of Man, as this is well to the south of the British Isles breeding range.

Within the Western Palearctic the Slavonian Grebe breeds most abundantly in Russia (5,000–10,000bp), with Finland, Sweden and Norway having 4,500-9,000bp between them. Smaller populations also exist in Iceland and the Baltic states (EBA). Breeding within Britain and Ireland is confined to Scotland, mainly within the Highland Region (1988–91 Atlas). Having first bred in 1908 it reached a peak in the late 1970s when up to 80 pairs were present. The latest figures available from the Rare Birds Breeding Panel indicate 46 pairs breeding in 2002, a welcome increase on the record low of 31 pairs in 2000 (Ogilvie 2004).

Slavonian Grebes are generally migratory, birds from Norway and Iceland wintering on the Norwegian coast, around the Faeroes and Britain and Ireland. Autumn movements occur from September to November (EBA, WA).

Wintering Slavonian Grebes in Britain and Ireland have an essentially coastal distribution and are comparatively infrequent on inland waters. Only approximately 450 birds are thought to winter in Britain and Ireland, with strongholds in the north of Scotland and southern England and only an estimated 30–40 in Ireland (WA). It is not surprising therefore that Manx wintering records are limited. Indeed with only four winter records during the survey period up until December 2002, each of single birds on single days, it appeared as if the species might not justify an account as a 'wintering bird'. However in the winter of 2002/03 up to two birds were present in Derbyhaven Bay throughout December and January, rescuing the species from the 'other species seen' Appendix.

The species has never been abundant or regular as a winter visitor to Manx coasts. Ralfe makes only two references to the species, one having been caught in a trammel net off Langness in 1893 and the other killed 'near Ramsey' in 1907. C&J describe it as an irregular winter visitor, commenting that nearly all records are from Derbyhaven Bay. An examination of Manx data for the 25 years from 1979 to spring 2003 suggests that 32 individual birds have been observed around the Island, with all but three being between November and February, with 20 of the birds having been seen in Derbyhaven Bay. Anyone wishing to see the species should concentrate their efforts in there, though it might be best to take a flask!

Breeding	Grid squares:	Isle of Man 0 (0%) Britain 24 Ireland 0 Total 24 (1%)
	Population:	Isle of Man 0 Britain 56 Ireland 0 (1% of European)
Wintering	Grid squares:	Isle of Man 5 (1%) Britain and Ireland 309 (8%)
	Population:	Isle of Man 0-2 Britain and Ireland 430-440

Jan	Feb	Mar	Apr	May	Jun	Jul	Aug	Sep	Oct	Nov	Dec

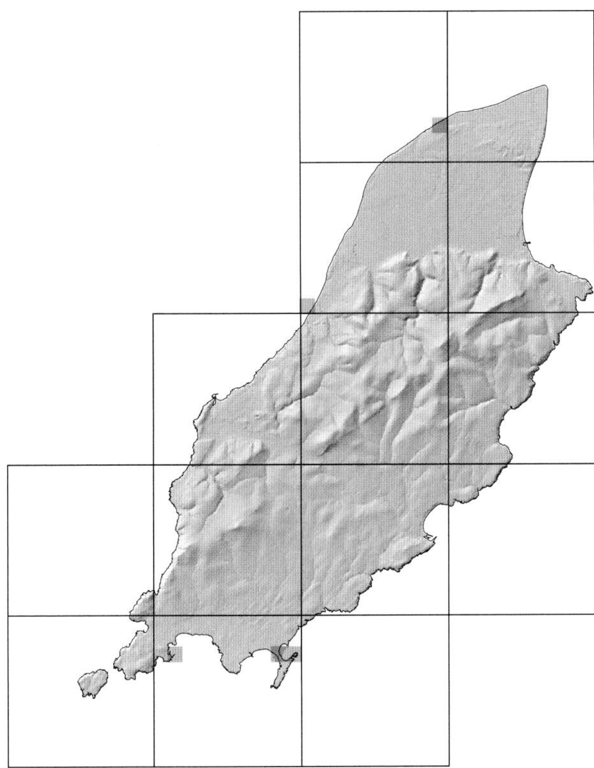

Winter presence

Fulmar (Northern Fulmar)
Fulmarus glacialis

Manx: *Eean Croymmagh*

Fulmars are always a pleasure to watch, whether soaring close over the wave tops or sitting on the sea behind a boat, waiting for scraps of bait, the gentle facial expression belying a fierce character. At nest sites Fulmars are vocal, a mixture of crooning and cackling, depending upon whether they are bonding with a partner or defending a nest ledge. If under threat they regurgitate a foul smelling oily substance that can render predators such as Peregrine flightless.

Fulmars will occupy a range of nest sites, their preferred location being steep sea cliffs with grass slopes. In some areas inland crags and quarries are used, as are both derelict and occupied buildings, while the lack of suitable rocky coasts in some parts of the range has resulted in some utilising low sand cliffs and banks (1988–91 Atlas, EBA). On the Isle of Man, high cliffs with grassy slopes and ledges are favoured, with some sand cliffs and one river gorge being used. Food is varied but is always taken at sea and includes zooplankton, the by-catch from fishing, fish offal, and waste from sewer outlets.

Fulmars are essentially birds of the high Arctic which over the last 250 years have undergone a considerable range expansion. Prior to the middle of the eighteenth century the species bred only on St Kilda and Iceland, after which they started to spread, with breeding on Shetland confirmed in 1878 (Seabird 2000). They now occur in Iceland, Faeroes, Britain and Ireland and are widespread on islands to the north of Norway and Russia, such as Svalbard. Small isolated colonies also occur in Brittany, Normandy, Heligoland, south-west Sweden and north-west Norway (EBA). Large populations also exist in Alaska and Canada. Within Britain and Ireland over 90% of the population is in Scotland and 7% in Ireland. They are present around much of the coast, being absent only from low-lying areas such as the Mersey north as far as St Bees Head and the coasts of Suffolk and Essex.

Within the Isle of Man the summer distribution map demonstrates the species' preference for high sea cliffs. Fulmars are absent from the larger bays, low-lying areas of rock such as Langness, the area around Niarbyl and the shingle and sandy beaches of the Ayres in the north. They nest, however, in small numbers on the sand cliffs of Bride and Jurby. The apparent reduction in breeding status suggested by comparing the two small maps of breeding distribution for 1977-81 and 1998-2002 is misleading. The 'count unit' used when assessing Fulmar numbers is the Apparently Occupied Site (AOS), as it is not always possible to see whether a nest is present. In the most recent survey, AOS is afforded a 'probable' breeding status, while in the presentation of the results from 1977-81, AOS was given a 'confirmed' status. Taking this difference into account there is little evidence of an expansion in range locally, although there has been a considerable increase in population (28%) since the seabird census of 1985–86 (Moore 1987). Fulmars are the latest of the seabirds to fledge their young, which are sometimes still present on nests until early September.

Fulmars, after leaving their territories as late as September, have usually returned by October, with almost full occupancy by December. Young birds, having fledged, are thought to spend the first four years of their life at sea, during which time they range widely through the Atlantic, birds from Britain and Ireland being recovered in Greenland and Newfoundland (MA). Although most breeding birds return to nest sites by December they can sometimes be absent for a number of days at a time, making accurate winter census counts more problematic. However, although numbers were generally lower in winter, the winter distribution and abundance maps demonstrate a high correlation with those of the summer. No birds were observed on the Jurby coast during winter research. The two inland records both relate to birds found dead in fields and were presumably the victims of storms.

The first Manx record of the Fulmar came in the winter of 1927 and breeding first occurred in 1936 (C&J). Since becoming established as a breeding species, Fulmars have continued to do well on the Island and, though the rate of growth has slowed, there is nothing to suggest that their future locally is anything but secure.

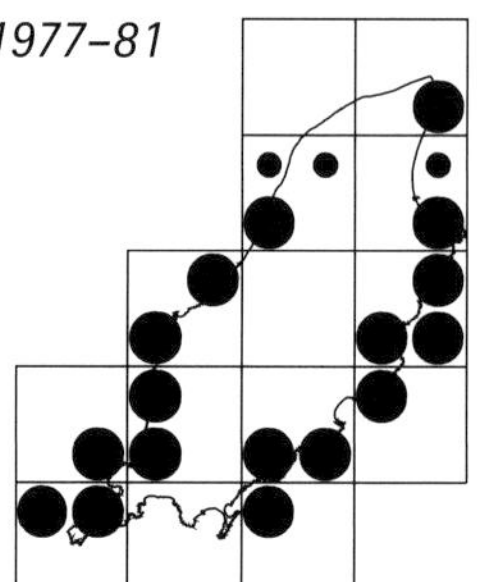

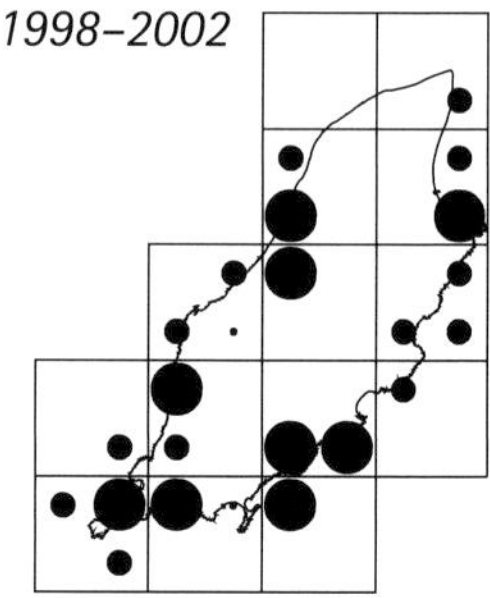

Breeding	Grid squares:	Isle of Man 121 (18%) Britain 550 Ireland 159 Total 709 (18%)
	Population:	Isle of Man 2,981-3,143 Britain 499,100 Ireland 38,900 (20% of European)
Wintering	Grid squares:	Isle of Man 66 (10%) Britain and Ireland 630 (16%)
	Population:	Isle of Man <8,000 Britain and Ireland 1.6-1.8 million

Jan Feb Mar Apr May Jun Jul Aug Sep Oct Nov Dec

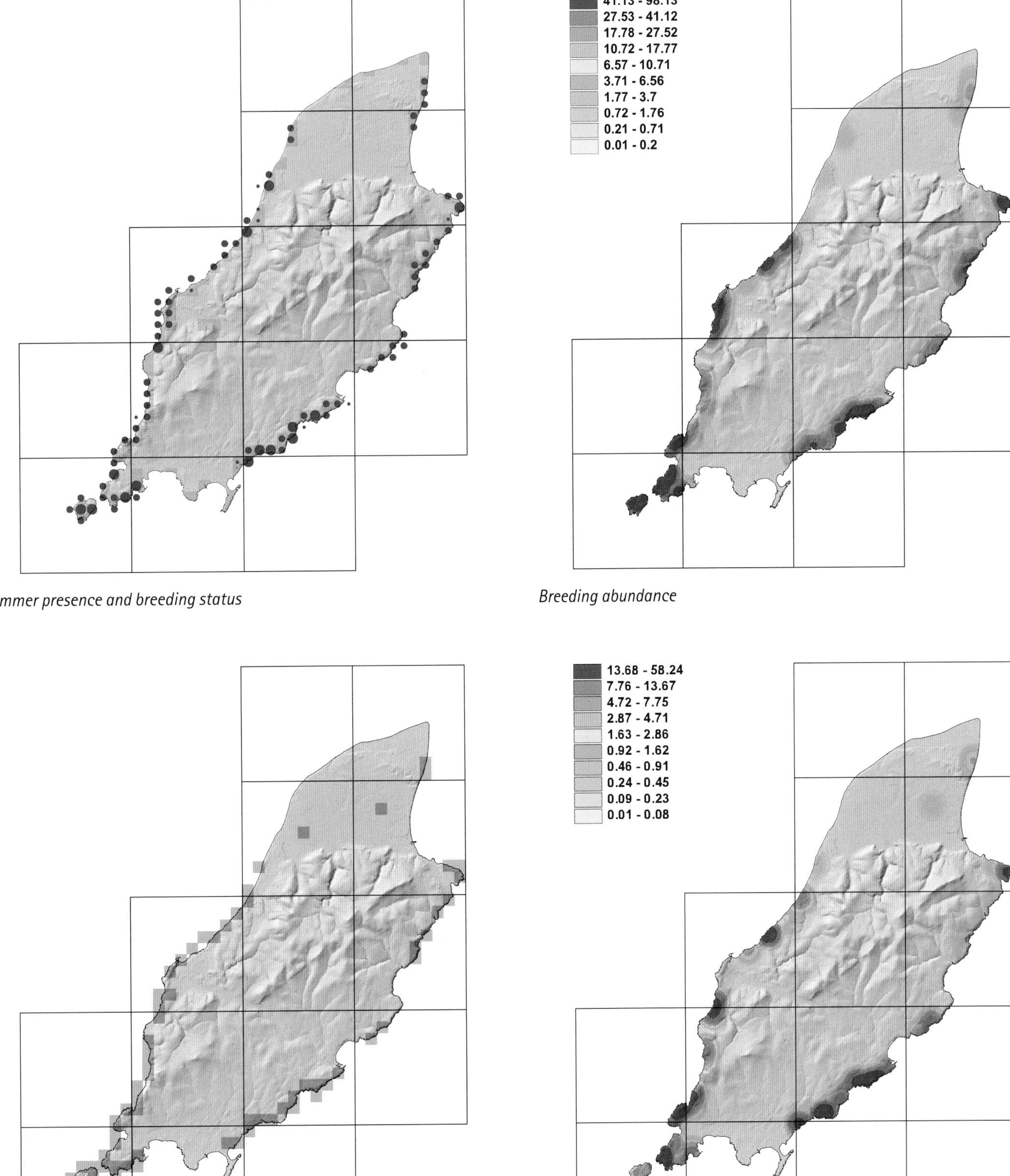

Summer presence and breeding status

Breeding abundance

Winter presence

Winter abundance

Individual Sponsors – Captain B Clark, Mr. P Weaver

Manx Shearwater
Puffinus puffinus

Manx: *Scraayl*

Watching Manx Shearwaters gliding effortlessly over a storm-tossed sea, one has to marvel at the resilience of these oceanic wanderers. Their distinctive black back and white underparts are revealed alternately as they fly over peaks and through troughs, catching the air pressure waves that push them along with hardly a flap of their long narrow wings.

Manx Shearwaters spend most of their lives at sea, only coming ashore during the breeding season, and then only at night, to incubate their single egg or tend the young. Nests are in burrows and the male and female bird share incubation, the incubating bird staying in the burrow for between five and seven days before being relieved by its partner. Manx Shearwaters breed in colonies and these can appear abandoned during the day, as incubating birds sit quietly in their burrows. Colonies become alive at night, when there is a constant noise of birds calling in the air and from their burrows as pairs swap parental duties. Feeding mainly on small fish, cephalopods, crustaceans and surface offal, Manx Shearwaters range widely for food and feed their young partially digested regurgitated remains (BWP).

The world population of Manx Shearwaters is estimated at 340,000–410,000 pairs, approximately 90% of which breed in Britain and Ireland. Sizeable colonies occur also in the Faeroes and Iceland, with colonies of less than 1,000 pairs in France, the Azores, Madeira and the Canaries. A colony of less than five pairs is present in Newfoundland (Seabird 2000). Of the 40 known colonies in Britain and Ireland, four (Rum, Skomer, Skokholm and Middleholm) account for 90% of the population. On the Isle of Man, breeding has only ever been documented on the Calf of Man, with no historic reference to breeding on the main island, and so it was with our research. Historically, the Manx Shearwater bred in large numbers on the Calf and, writing in 1940, Williamson described the Calf colony as 'probably in its hey-day the largest the world has ever known'. The colony is generally thought to have become extinct prior to 1789, following the arrival of brown rats on the Calf (C&J). After what appears to have been a long period with no Manx Shearwaters breeding on the Calf, the establishment of a Bird Observatory there, in 1959, allowed the status to be reassessed, with calling from a burrow that year suggesting that breeding birds might be present. Since then it has been assumed that they bred on the Calf in small numbers (C&J), with Lloyd *et al.* (1991), stating the population as 32 'Apparently Occupied Burrows'.

During the current research period a programme of surveying was undertaken, whereby a tape-recording of the call of Manx Shearwaters was played down suitable burrows. After unsuccessful work in 1999 there was success in 2000, when four responses were obtained from 970+ attempts. Later in that year, two of those burrows were found to contain young (Bagworth 2001), the first proof that the Manx Shearwater had definitely returned as a breeding bird to the Calf of Man. Similar work in further years revealed increased levels of occupancy, probably a combination of more focused survey effort and a real increase in breeding levels. By the summer of 2005, a total of 104 occupied burrows was found in five small colonies. The increase in nesting Manx Shearwaters probably followed from a sustained effort to reduce the numbers of rats on the Calf.

Though breeding is confined to the Calf, large numbers of Manx Shearwaters can be seen off the Ayres coast, from June onwards. Initially these congregations, which can number in excess of 2,000 birds, are likely to comprise breeding birds from colonies in Ireland and Wales that are gathering to feed in the rich coastal waters. On calm days they form large 'rafts' sitting on the water, making occasional short flights, whereas on windy days they can form a constant backdrop of movement low over the sea. As the summer progresses numbers increase as migration starts, peaking in late August, at which time many thousands can be seen in a day from favoured watch points such as Peel Castle, the Point of Ayre and the Calf.

Migration routes are little understood, but it is considered likely that birds leaving British and Irish waters head south to France and Spain, at least some following the Atlantic coast of the African continent before heading across to Brazil and Uruguay (MA).

The species is seldom seen off the Island in winter, with only two records in the survey period, in November and December 1999. Mention has already been made of the historic status of the species; the current research has added significantly to our understanding and may mark the start of a welcome return to former glories.

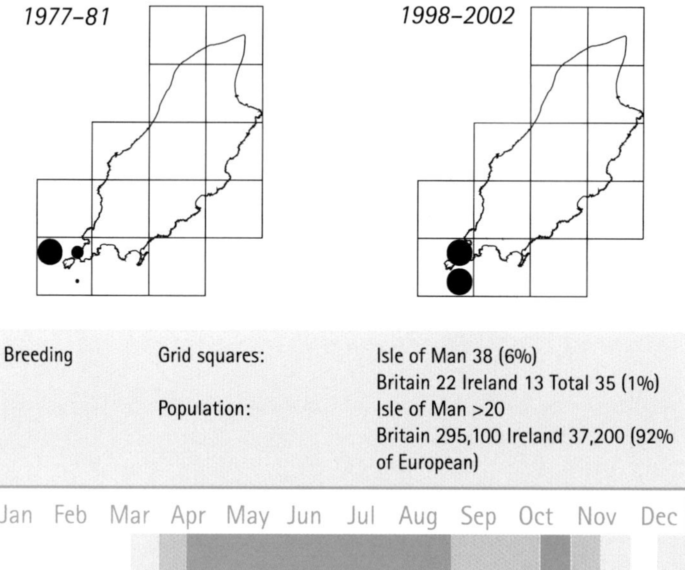

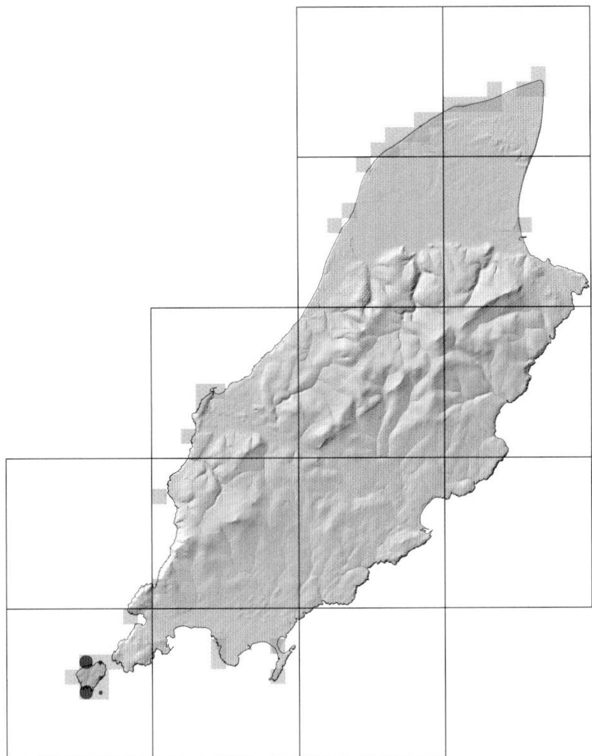

Summer presence and breeding status

Individual Sponsors – Mr. T W Cain, Mr. J Penn, Mrs. B Tomlinson

Storm Petrel (European Storm-petrel)
Hydrobates pelagicus

Manx: *Kitty Varrey* = Sea Kitty i.e. Wren

The Storm Petrel is the smallest of the seabirds that occur within Britain and Ireland, being not much bigger than the House Martin, a species with which most people are familiar. Like House Martins, Storm Petrels have distinctive white rumps, but otherwise appear uniformly dark, with a diagnostic broad white under-wing panel. As they spend most of their lives at sea and seldom come close to land in daylight, they are seen infrequently and present a worthwhile challenge to anyone wishing to watch their graceful flight as they flit through wave troughs searching for food.

Most Storm Petrels nest on remote offshore islands, usually in large colonies, using a variety of sites to lay their single egg. Nest sites can be in natural crevices, within boulder scree, in stone walls, in old rabbit burrows or in soil and hedge banks (BWP). Food includes small fish, cephalopods and medusae and is taken almost exclusively off or just below the surface of the water (BWP). Their preference for remote islands and inaccessible nest sites, coupled with the fact that they only come ashore at night, creates real problems when estimating breeding numbers throughout their range.

The world breeding distribution of Storm Petrels is restricted to the western Palearctic, ranging from Iceland, Faeroes, Norway, Britain and Ireland, parts of Iberia and extending into the Mediterranean as far as Malta (EBA). Within Britain and Ireland colonies are confined, with one mainland exception in Ireland, to remote islands in the Northern Isles, north west Scotland, south west Wales, the Isles of Scilly, Channel Islands and western Ireland, with around 80% of the population in Ireland (Seabird 2000). Despite effort being applied during MBA research to establish whether a colony exists on the Calf of Man, no evidence was found. It is strongly suspected, however, that breeding does take place, though with many parts of the islet not accessible in safety, this may be difficult to establish.

Successive wardens on the Calf, as well as other people on the main Island, have attempted to catch Storm Petrels at night, by playing a tape-recording of their call along the coast, luring birds into the area to be caught in nets. This method has been found to be a highly successful means of catching birds, with large numbers being caught annually. However, it is known from studies elsewhere that many of the birds attracted to tape-lures tend to be non-breeders or 'wanderers', often covering large distances in short periods (Seabird 2000). Evidence from captures locally supports that understanding, as there are numerous examples of birds netted on the Island having been ringed elsewhere within Britain and Ireland a few days previously, or in some cases earlier in the same night. Numbers of Storm Petrels caught on the Calf, or indeed elsewhere on the Isle of Man, do not therefore indicate local breeding.

Given the difficulties inherent in observing this small offshore species, the summer distribution map will certainly understate presence, most records being obtained from the regularly watched vantage points of the Ayres, Peel Castle, Langness and the Calf. Records of Storm Petrels seen from the coast during the early part of the summer are rare, with no records in April or May during the research period, and the majority of records being obtained in July. Sightings of single birds at this time may well relate to foraging breeding birds as well as 'wanderers'. As the summer progresses towards autumn, larger numbers can be seen in a day, with occasional sightings exceeding 100 birds. Initially these are likely to be non-breeding birds returning to wintering sites, with increasing numbers of breeding and young birds moving through in the autumn. Locally, few sightings are obtained beyond the middle of September, with only very occasional October records and none during the winter months. Storm Petrels appear to winter off south-west and South Africa, with some perhaps wintering north off Mauritania (MA).

Ralfe mentions small parties of Storm Petrels having been seen off Douglas Head, though no evidence of breeding was found. In 1863 Thwaites wrote that the species was still found on the Calf, whereas Ralfe described the species as rare, though not unfamiliar to fishermen on the fishing grounds, and supposed that it should not be considered impossible that it breeds locally. C&J regarded Storm Petrels as common summer visitors that probably breed on the Calf. Despite our most recent efforts, that summary remains valid today.

Breeding	Grid squares:	Isle of Man 16 (2%)
		Britain 48 Ireland 19 Total 67 (2%)
	Population:	Isle of Man 0
		Britain 25,700 Ireland 99,100 (33% of European)

Jan	Feb	Mar	Apr	May	Jun	Jul	Aug	Sep	Oct	Nov	Dec

Corporate Sponsor – Cain's Advocates

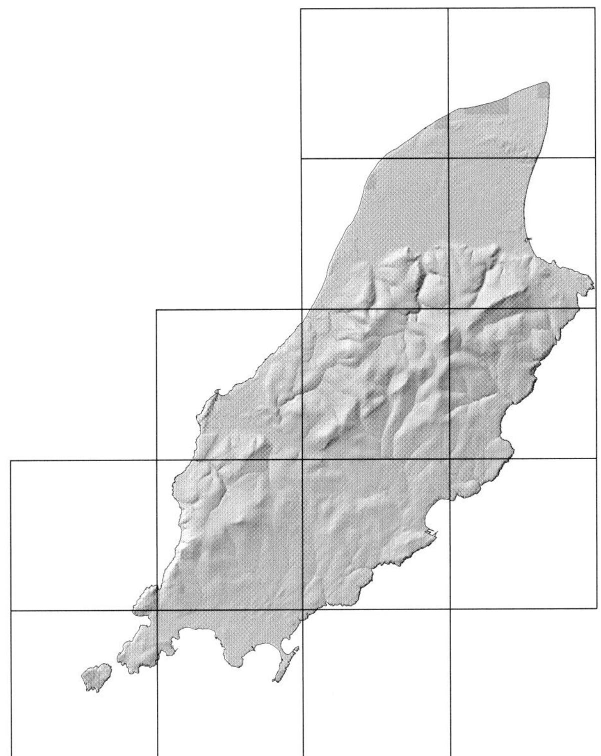

Summer presence

Individual Sponsors – Mr. J Bishop, Mr. G Craine, Miss M A Riley, Mr. J G Walmsley

Gannet (Northern Gannet)
Morus bassanus

Manx: *Gant*

Though not a species that breeds on the Island, nor one that could be classed as a winter visitor, the Gannet has nonetheless been afforded a full account as it is such an integral part of Manx ornithology. Whether Gannets are gliding effortlessly over the sea or plunging vertically into the water to catch fish, their white plumage, offset by black wing tips and a creamy orange crown and neck, always catches the eye and brightens up many a coastal walk.

Most gannetries are situated on cliffs or the upper slopes of islands, close to where the Gannet's main prey of herring, mackerel and sandeels are abundant (Nelson 1978). Gannets breed in Canada, Iceland, Norway, the Faeroes and France with small populations in Germany and Russia. The main centre of population, however, is within Britain and Ireland, where 21 gannetries hold 266,000 pairs (68% of the world breeding population). In 1968-70 the figure stood at about 137,000 pairs, the increases since then being attributed at least in part to reduced persecution (Nelson 2002). The closest gannetry to the Isle of Man is on Scar Rocks, Dumfries and Galloway (1,670 pairs). While some of the birds seen locally during the summer will be from this site, many are likely to be from further afield as Gannets are known to forage great distances for food (Hamer *et al.* 2001).

The summer distribution map reveals that the species is widespread off the Manx coasts, being seen off most of the west coast and off promontories and in bays along the east coast. The sightings obtained during the early part of the summer will initially comprise birds on passage to breeding sites further north, often seen flying 'line astern' low over the water or in small skeins. As the summer progresses most Gannets seen are either actively feeding or sitting on the water. At this time they can occur in large numbers, most often seen off the Ayres shore, where food is abundant. Counts of over 1,000 along small stretches of coast are not infrequent from late May onwards, with many thousand likely to be present along the Ayres coast on suitable days. Numbers are still high during August and into September and October, though as the autumn progresses there is greater evidence of birds being on active migration, with many records being of birds heading south.

As relatively few adult Gannets are ringed little is known about their preferred wintering location, though young birds are known to winter south of the Bay of Biscay, many as far as Morocco with some getting as far as Senegal (MA).

By November and through December relatively few Gannets are seen locally, with no December records in some years. By January birds are more regularly seen, with a high count of 131 off the Calf in late January 2002. The winter distribution map reflects the relative paucity of records at this time. A preponderance of records from the west might possibly be due to birds passing closer to that coast as they move through the Irish Sea than to the east coast.

Ralfe considered the Gannet to be common during the summer, but found no record of any breeding locally. Interestingly, he commented that immature birds (which are brown) were uncommon off the Manx coast, a fact that appears to hold true today. Given the size of colonies to the north of the Island, more young birds might be expected. It is possible that many young birds travel south past the west coast of Ireland. C&J refer to the Gannet as a common passage migrant, which feeds in good numbers in local coastal waters. In Camden's Britannia (1586), reference is made to 'Soland Goose' breeding on the Calf of Man, and this is almost certainly referring to Gannets (C&J). Given the increases in numbers of Gannets in Britain and Ireland in the last thirty years, including some new gannetries, perhaps in the future Gannets might start breeding on the Isle of Man.

Breeding	Grid squares:	Isle of Man 84 (13%) Britain 18 Ireland 5 Total 23 (1%)
	Population:	Isle of Man 0 (nests) Britain 226,600 Ireland 32,800 (79% of European)
Wintering	Grid squares:	Isle of Man 20 (3%) Britain and Ireland 414 (11%)
	Population:	Isle of Man not known Britain and Ireland not known

Jan	Feb	Mar	Apr	May	Jun	Jul	Aug	Sep	Oct	Nov	Dec

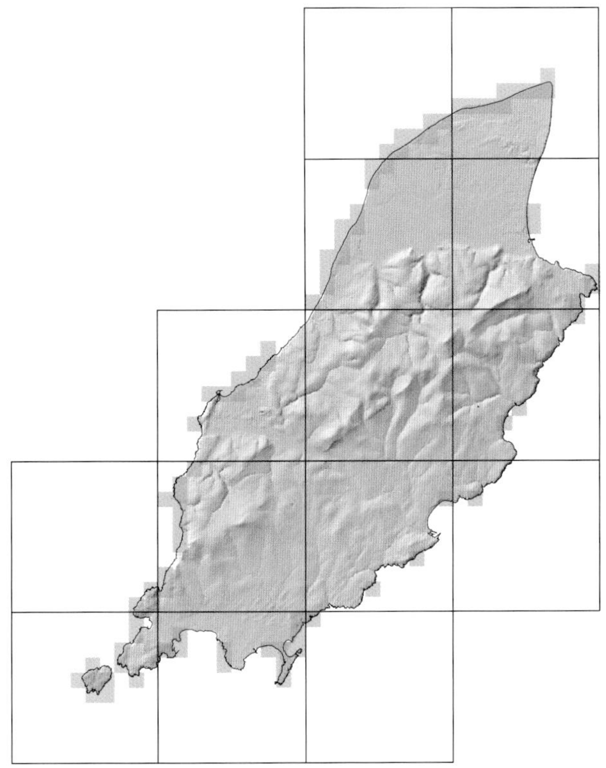

Summer presence

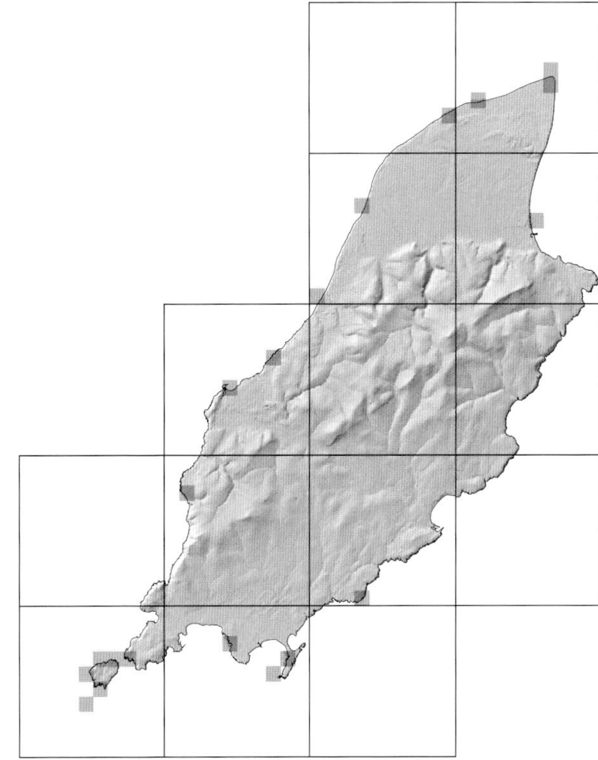

Winter presence

Cormorant (Great Cormorant)
Phalacrocorax carbo

Manx: *Shag. Fannag or Feeagh Varrey* = Sea Crow or Raven. *Arragh Vooar*

The Cormorant can be readily distinguished from the closely related Shag by its larger size, thicker neck and, during the early part of the breeding season, by an oval white thigh patch. Though not a cast-iron identification feature, Shags seldom fly over land, preferring to fly round a promontory rather than over it, while Cormorants frequently fly over land and unlike Shags are found on fresh water.

The endemic subspecies in Britain and Ireland *Phalacrocorax carbo carbo* selects predominantly coastal sites, located on rocky cliffs and offshore islands. Some inland colonies do exist, where trees adjacent to freshwater are utilised. Within the British Isles there are a small number of inland tree-nesting colonies, where increased occupancy by the subspecies *P.c. sinensis* from continental Europe has become evident over the last 40 years (Seabird 2000). Cormorants eat fish, caught by diving from the surface. Though a range of fish species is taken, flatfish are known to comprise a major percentage (BWP), while examination of regurgitated food in local colonies indicate that wrasse and gadoids (Coalfish and Pollack) are also taken in numbers.

The subspecies *P.c. carbo* is a bird of the Atlantic coasts, breeding in northern France, Britain, Ireland, Iceland, Norway, west Greenland and the Kola peninsula. The continental subspecies *P.c. sinensis* occurs throughout the rest of Europe and parts of Asia (EBA). Within Britain and Ireland, Seabird 2000 found a total of 13,628 apparently occupied nests (AONs), 85% of birds nesting in 232 coastal colonies with the remaining 15% being in 35 inland colonies. Coastal breeding colonies are found around most of Britain and Ireland, where habitat is suitable, though a westerly bias is evident (Seabird 2000). During the research period breeding within the Isle of Man was confined to just four coastal colonies, with no inland sites. During the local seabird survey of 1999 the number of apparently occupied nests stood at 134, though by 2002 that number had grown to 159.

The largest colony is at Maughold (109 AON) with colonies to the north-east of Peel, at Pistol Castle and at Howstrake having 24, 16 and 10 AONs respectively. The 2002 figure represents an increase of 194% over the 54 nests found during the seabird census of 1985-86 (Moore 1987). The summer distribution map reveals a mainly coastal distribution, though birds were often seen at inland waters, such as Sulby, Injebreck, Clypse and Kerrowdhoo Reservoirs, as well as smaller water bodies and some rivers. Inland records at the extreme north of the Island include those of birds flying over, cutting across the Island from one coast to the other. Away from colonies, most early summer records are of individual birds or groups of two or three, with numbers increasing as the summer progresses. Gatherings of up to about 30 individuals can be seen resting on the sandy beaches of the Ayres, near Rue Point.

The subspecies *P.c. carbo* is considered to be only partially migratory or dispersive. While the majority remain close to their breeding sites for the winter, ringing recoveries indicate that some move as far as France and Portugal. Autumn movements take place from July onwards, with return passage from November to May (MA).

The winter distribution map is very similar to that for the summer, demonstrating a primarily coastal distribution with inland records being on freshwater bodies or of birds observed flying to and from inland feeding sites. The winter abundance map demonstrates high numbers spread along the shallow coast north of Ramsey towards the Point of Ayre and round to the Ayres. Birds also frequented the gravel pits at the Point of Ayre, while Ramsey Harbour mouth, the Conister Rock in Douglas Bay, Langness and Perwick Bay all held small groups.

Cormorants have a long history on the Isle of Man, bones of the species having been found in the Perwick Bay midden deposit dated AD90 (Garrad 1972). Kermode considered that they bred around the coast in small numbers, though Ralfe mentioned only two breeding sites; on the Calf and on the west coast, each having around twelve pairs. C&J describe the Cormorant as a common resident and summer visitor. The species has demonstrated significant growth in numbers since the mid-1980s, with new colonies now well established on the east coast and one new nest site near Cashtal Mooar south of Peel in 2003 (Cullen 2004). Given the recent growth in numbers, both locally and within the wider British Isles, the future for the species looks favourable.

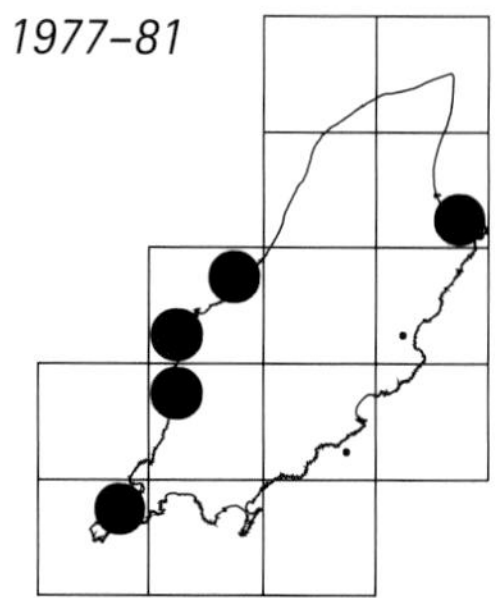

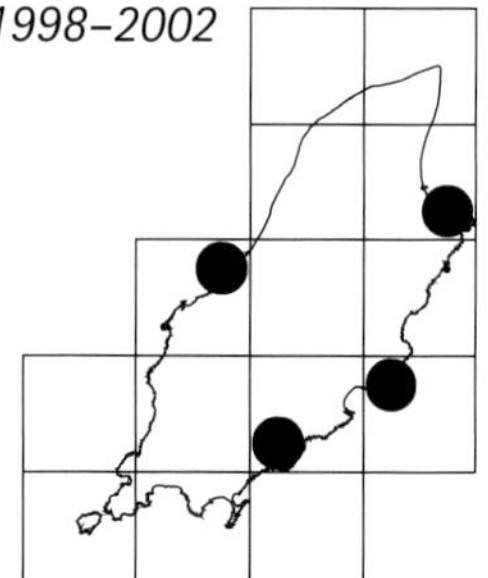

Breeding	Grid squares:	Isle of Man 131 (20%) Britain 174 Ireland 93 Total 267 (7%)
	Population:	Isle of Man 134 Britain 85,000 Ireland 5,200 (8% of European)
Wintering	Grid squares:	Isle of Man 106 (16%) Britain and Ireland 2,157 (56%)
	Population:	Isle of Man <300 Britain and Ireland 20,000-25,000

Jan	Feb	Mar	Apr	May	Jun	Jul	Aug	Sep	Oct	Nov	Dec

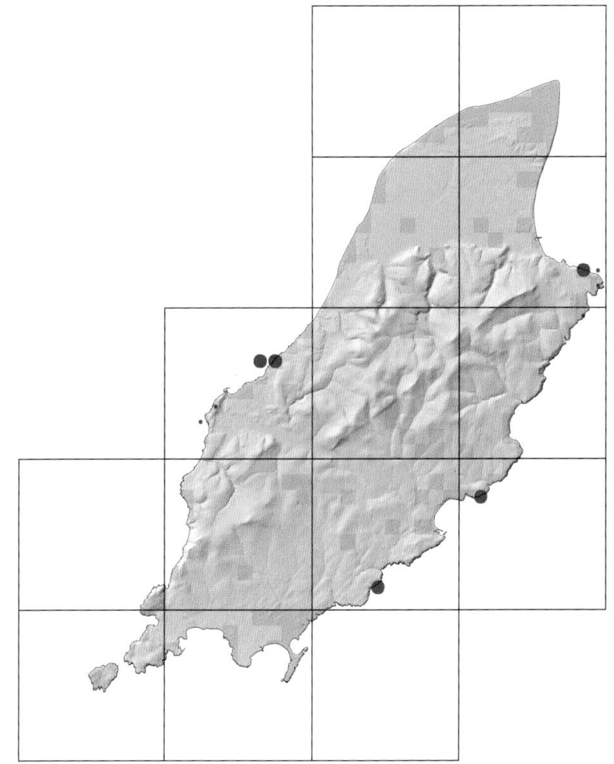

Summer presence and breeding status

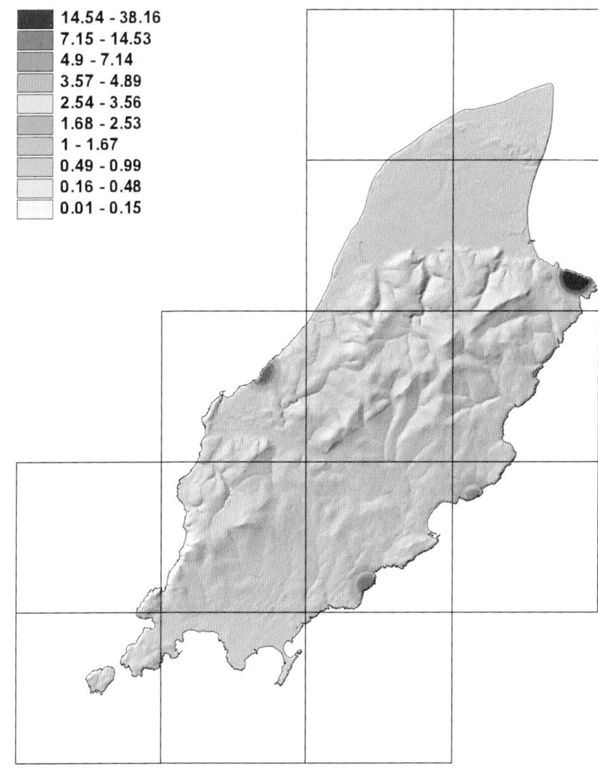

Breeding abundance

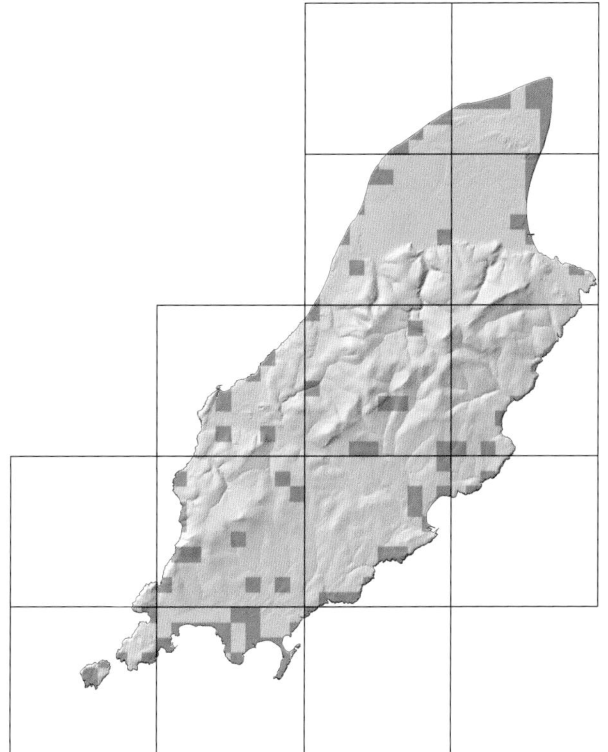

Winter presence

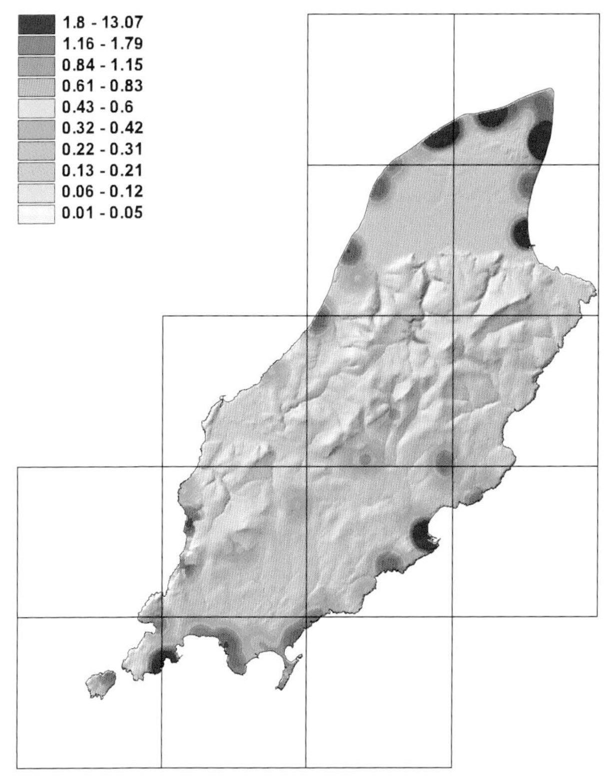

Winter abundance

Shag (European Shag)
Phalacrocorax aristotelis

Manx: as for Cormorant

This medium-sized colonial seabird appears dull black-brown at a distance, but seen closer to hand the breeding plumage is glossy dark green, with a purple hue to the wings. The combination of plumage, a pronounced forward-facing crest and bright green eyes make Shags an eye-catching sight, whether perched close to their nests or feeding in coastal waters. Historically Shags and Cormorants were seldom distinguished from each other, both being referred to as the 'Jinnie Diver' (Ralfe), a name that still persists locally.

Shags are predominantly colonial breeders, selecting steep sea cliffs, though in some areas nests within colonies can be quite scattered. Nest sites are varied, some being on suitable ledges that afford a level of shelter from rain, others being in areas of large boulder scree where nests are built in crevices or under boulders. Food is almost entirely fish, caught by surface diving for up to four minutes, though usually for less than one minute (BWP). One bird was observed at 30m depth chasing a shoal of poor cod on a shipwreck about 1km off the Island's east coast.

The subspecies of Shag that occurs in the British Isles *Phalacrocorax aristotelis aristotelis* also breeds in Iceland and the Faeroes and, on mainland Europe, the breeding range extends from the Kola peninsula, south along the Norwegian coast and along parts of the Atlantic coasts of France, Spain and Portugal (EBA). The British Isles population comprises between 45-50% of the world population of *P.a. aristotelis*. Within the British Isles the Seabird 2000 census estimated the population to be 32,306 apparently occupied nests, with breeding strongholds in the north and west, 66% of the population being in Scotland. It is absent from Flamborough Head to the Isle of Wight and from the Solway Firth down to Colwyn Bay, due largely to a lack of suitable nesting habitat (Seabird 2000).

Shags have a protracted breeding season, making a true assessment of breeding population more problematic than for many other seabirds. Adults have been observed taking nest material to ledges in December while young have still been present in nests as late as September. Within the Island the 1999 seabird census revealed Shags along most suitable stretches of coast. On the west coast breeding occurred along all rocky shores, except in Port Erin Bay and on the low rocks around Niarbyl. East coast breeding was also extensive, only the larger bays and low lying rocks being avoided. In the early summer non-breeding birds were commonly seen around much of the rest of the coast, as were birds hunting for food to take back to young. Young of the year and failed breeders become more evident away from colonies as the summer progresses. By the end of the summer large gatherings of Shags can be seen, particularly off the south and south-east coasts, with a maximum of 900 birds feeding in the rich waters off the Calf in late July. The breeding distribution is almost identical to that shown in C&J, though numbers have increased since the survey of 1985-86, during which an estimated 590–690 AONs were found (Moore 1987). The east coast colonies increased by 107% between the two periods, compared to an increase of 19% for the west coast, though such increases might in part be a result of more comprehensive coverage of the east coast in 1999 than was possible in 1985–86.

The British Isles' population is largely non-migratory, though dispersal from colonies after the breeding season is mainly southerly for adult as well as young birds (MA). Therefore many of the birds seen around our coast in the winter are likely to be from local colonies or from those in the near Irish Sea basin. In winter Shags are widely distributed around the Island's coast, with the lack of inland records emphasising the maritime preference of the species. Winter records divide into two broad categories. Many were of birds either roosting, often near breeding colonies, or feeding in shallow coastal waters. Others were of birds passing our coasts, observed from favoured sea watch points.

Kermode described the species as breeding all around the rocky coast, whereas Ralfe considered it largely confined to the west coast, though he mentions that a few bred at Maughold Head. C&J referred to the Shag as an abundant resident, a good description of its current status. With approximately 1% of the world population and 3% of the British Isles' population breeding on the Island, the number of Shags on the Isle of Man is of international significance.

1977–81

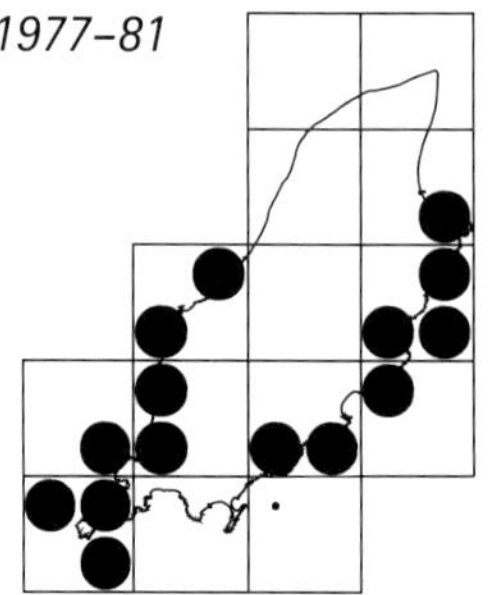

1998–2002

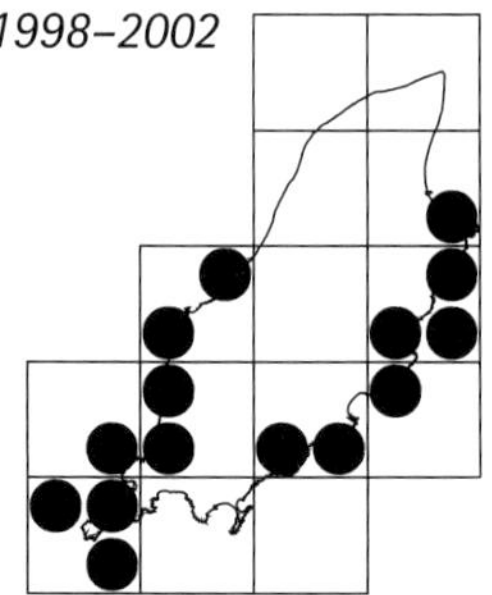

Breeding	Grid squares:	Isle of Man 116 (17%) Britain 386 Ireland 123 Total 509 (13%)
	Population:	Isle of Man 912 Britain 28,600 Ireland 3,700 (55% of European)
Wintering	Grid squares:	Isle of Man 114 (17%) Britain and Ireland 1,042 (27%)
	Population:	Isle of Man 2,000 Britain and Ireland 100,000-150,000

Jan	Feb	Mar	Apr	May	Jun	Jul	Aug	Sep	Oct	Nov	Dec

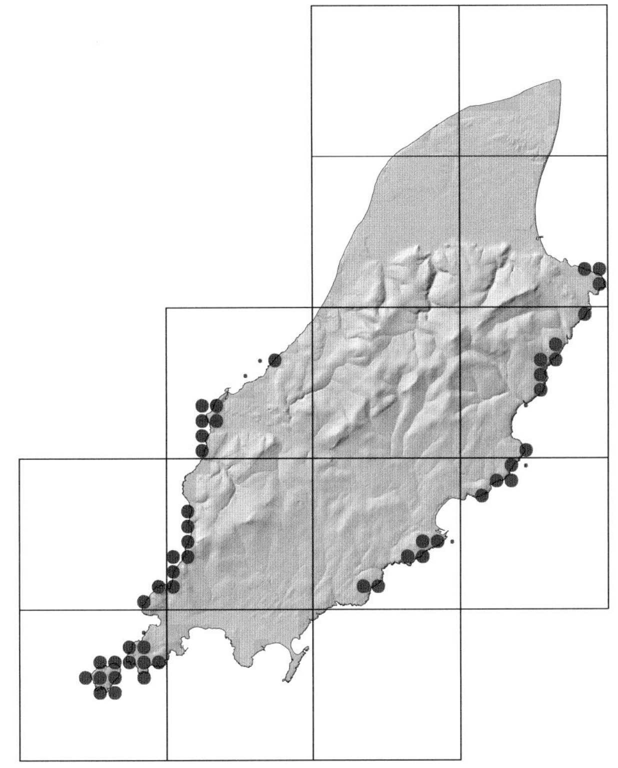

Summer presence and breeding status

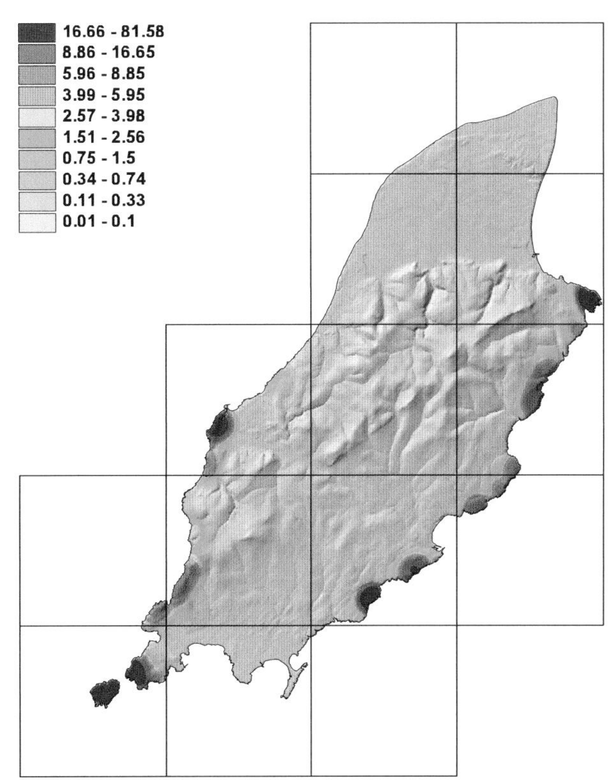

Breeding abundance

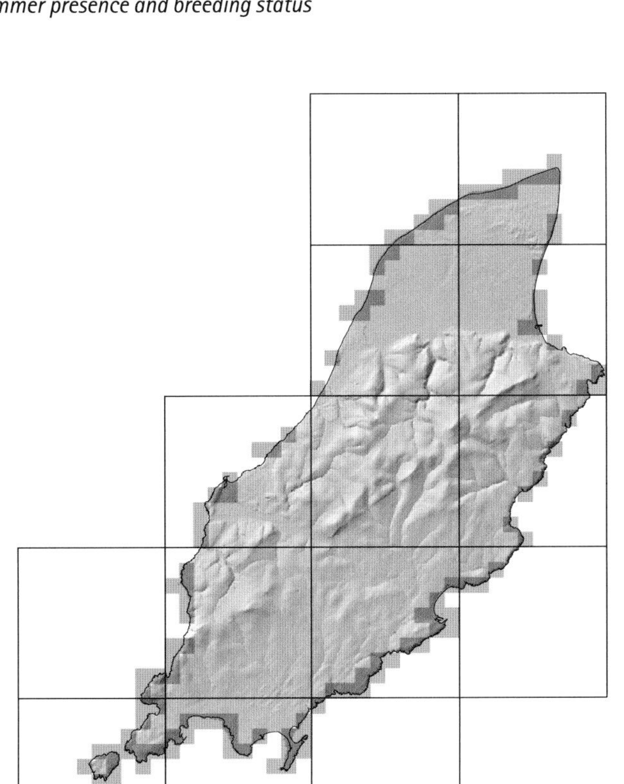

Winter presence

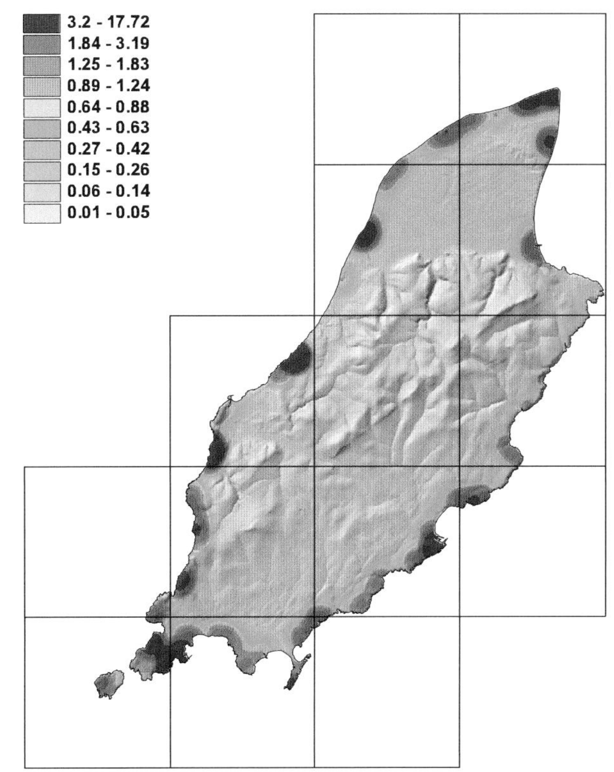

Winter abundance

Individual Sponsors – The late Mr. S Hudson, Mrs. S C Wright

Grey Heron
Ardea cinerea

Manx: *Coayr. Coayr ny Hastan* = Crane of the eel. *Coayr Glass* = Grey Crane

The Grey Heron (still known to many Manx people as the crane) is unmistakable. A very large grey bird, long-legged and with a straight, powerful bill it will most easily be seen on the rocky coast, either hunched in statuesque contemplation or stepping carefully through the pools, neck outstretched and perhaps striking at prey with lightning-like speed. It is then that the white head, adorned with a black line behind the eye, together with the discretely black-streaked neck can be seen. The flight is leisurely on bowed wings, the head drawn in, but legs outstretched.

Although primarily fish eaters, herons will extend their diet to include frogs, crustaceans, small mammals and birds. They are prepared to fly several kilometres to feed during the summer, which explains their scattered, but well distributed presence on the map. They feed, principally on trout and eels, along the less hasty stretches of the Island's rivers. In the south they particularly favour the rocky coasts between Gansey and Poyllvaaish and the west side of Langness, where they will take a variety of small marine fish. Similar feeding areas are favoured in winter and, while solitary along the watercourses and on the margins of still waters, they may congregate in groups of up to ten birds at coastal sites such as Langness.

The Grey Heron has an extensive breeding range over much of Eurasia, as well as east and southern Africa. Its rather patchy European range lies mostly between 44 and 59°N, with a notable Gulf Stream-aided extension up the Norwegian coast as far as the Lofoten Islands. It is widespread in Britain and Ireland, being absent only from the most mountainous regions. The 1988–91 Atlas revealed a 38.4% increase in Britain (but only 3% in Ireland) since the survey of 1968–72. There are currently five Manx heronries, tenanted every year, while single nests are occasionally built at a very few other sites. The Manx population reached a peak of 35 breeding pairs in the mid-1970s, followed by a decline and then a sustained recovery. The Atlas period saw a considerable increase, which is well illustrated in the table opposite.

With the exception of the isolated nesting in willows at the Garth, all nests are in conifers. Only at Ballachrink and the Garth are the heronries not in the extensive grounds of large mansion houses.

The nests vary considerably from a flimsy platform to a great mass of sticks, increasing in bulk year by year. In proving breeding early in the season, droppings splashed over the ground vegetation are the first clue and inspection of the nests above will reveal fresh whitewash covering much of the structure. Later, the presence of large pale blue broken eggshells below the nests and the incessant 'chacking' of the young provide further confirmation. At Kirby, herons gather in the trees from November and nesting activity starts in mid February. Herons breeding in Britain and Ireland constitute Europe's only non-migratory population (BWP). The few local ringing recoveries indicate that some dispersal to and from the Island does occur. The winter distribution and abundance maps reveal the close association with main rivers and the extensive areas of inter-tidal rocks at Douglas and on the south-east coast.

Numbers of occupied nests of Grey Heron 1998-2002

Location	1998	1999	2000	2002
Ballachrink, Santon	1	3	2	2
Ballachurry, Andreas	0	1	0	0
Balladoole, Arbory	2	1	0	0
Ballamoar Castle, Jurby	5	5	8	8
Great Meadow, Malew	5	10–11	14	15
Kentraugh, Arbory	8	4	9	7
Kirby Park, Braddan	16	13	15–18	14–16
The Garth, Marown				1
Total	37	37–38	48–51	47–49

Herons were first protected by law in 1422 and were clearly plentiful during the eighteenth century. By 1905, however, Ralfe knew of no heronries, though one did exist at Ballaskeig, Maughold in around 1910, but was deserted after a fire in the wood, and there was a nest at Injebreck in 1912. By 1986, C&J considered it to be a 'fairly common breeding bird' and by the start of the MBA research the breeding numbers approximated to those of the mid-1970s. It is not clear why the population has risen so markedly since 1998, but loss of nest trees as a result of storms in early 2005 may cause some reversal of fortune.

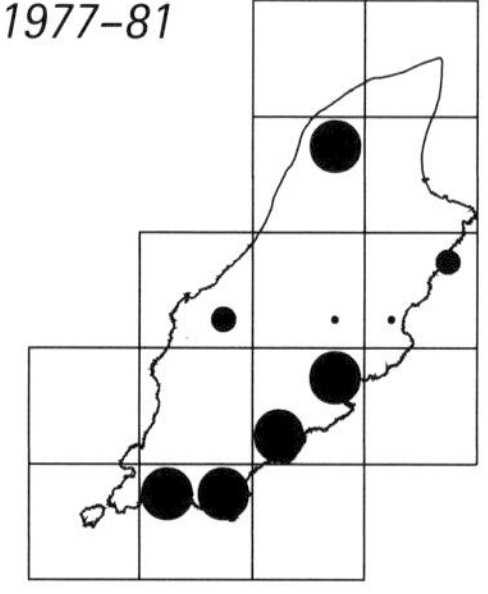

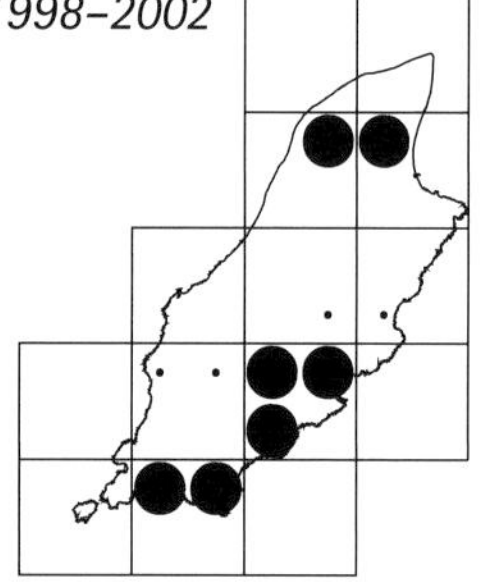

Breeding	Grid squares:	Isle of Man 204 (31%) Britain 2,335 Ireland 791 Total 3,126 (81%)
	Population:	Isle of Man 47–49 (nests) Britain 10,000 Ireland 3,650 (11% of European)
Wintering	Grid squares:	Isle of Man 140 (21%) Britain and Ireland 3,197 (83%)
	Population:	Isle of Man 150 Britain and Ireland 30,000

Jan	Feb	Mar	Apr	May	Jun	Jul	Aug	Sep	Oct	Nov	Dec

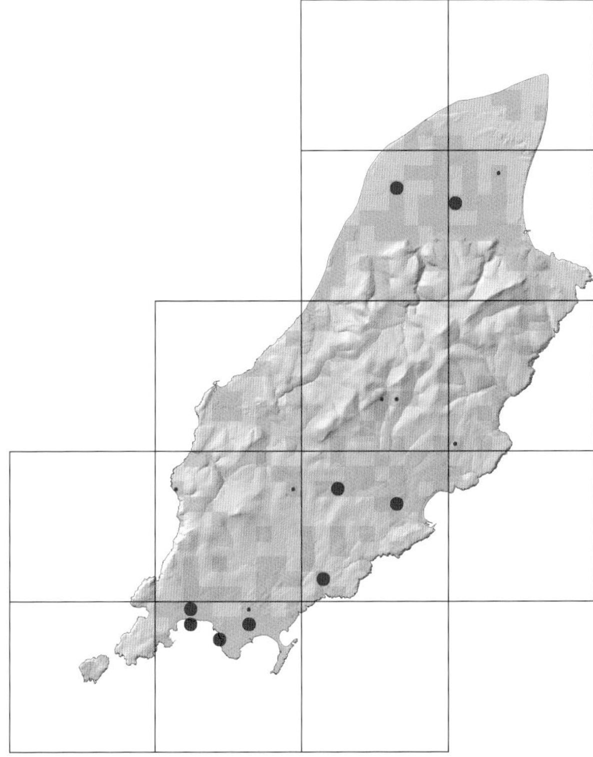

Summer presence and breeding status

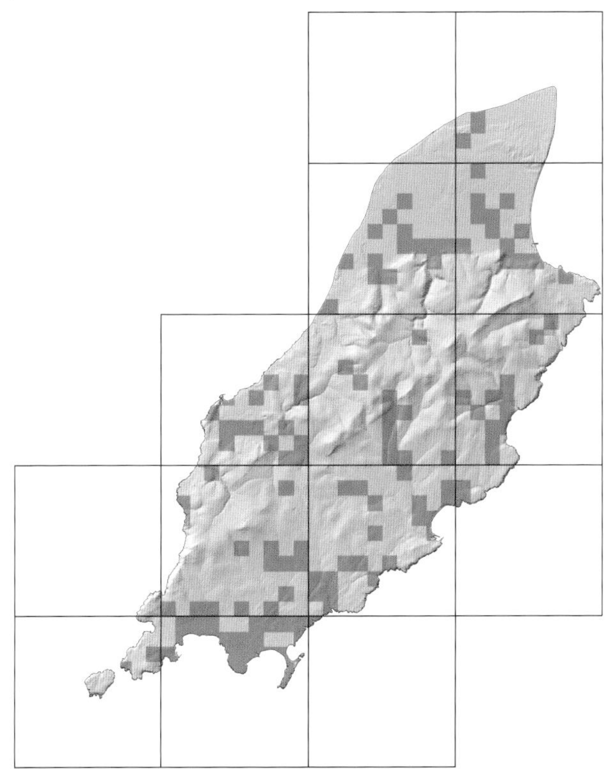

Winter presence

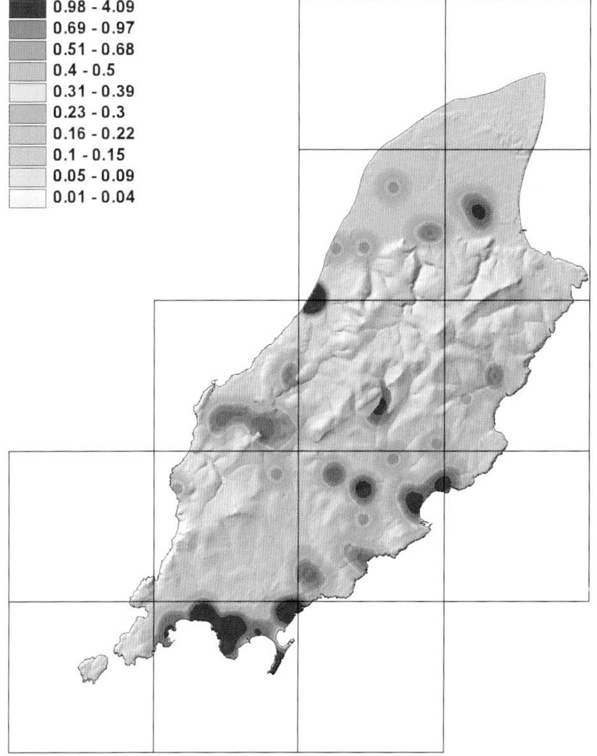

Winter abundance

Individual Sponsors – Miss S Carmichael, Mrs. J C Corlett, the late Mrs. C M Marshall

Hen Harrier
Circus cyaneus

Sitting quietly on the moors, watching a Hen Harrier quartering low over the land has to be one of the more enjoyable sights that the uplands have to offer. Adult males, with their pale grey bodies and black wing tips, contrast smartly with the heather backdrop, while the larger brown females merge into the landscape, movement rather than colour catching the observer's eye.

Despite their strong association with heather moorland, Hen Harriers utilise a range of other habitats for breeding including fen, marshes, forest clearings, young plantations and arable farmland (EBA). Locally, they demonstrate a preference for open heather moorland, though young plantations, clearings within mature plantations and rank stands of European Gorse are commonly used. On the Isle of Man, Campbell *et al.* (1994) noted 143 different prey items at nests, 54% of which were birds, mostly larks and pipits, with the remaining 46% mainly rabbits.

The breeding range of the Western Palearctic subspecies *C.c. cyaneus* is extensive, from Ireland in the west, as far as Kamchatka in Siberia in the east, being absent in Europe only in the Balkans, Italy, Switzerland and Austria (EBA). A survey of the species in the UK and Isle of Man undertaken in 1998 (Sim *et al.* 2001) estimated the population at 570 territorial pairs, 436 (76%) of which were in Scotland. The numbers and range of Hen Harriers in the UK is considered to be limited by human persecution (Sim *et al.* 2001). Persecution is widespread on grouse moors, with one study demonstrating that 11-15% of the total population of breeding females in Scotland, other than those in Orkney, were killed by gamekeepers each year (MA). There was no evidence of persecution of the species on the Isle of Man during the research period, the number of pairs in 1998 (49-51) being comparable to that in 1990 (44-46) (Campbell *et al.* 1994). To minimise the risk of persecution (e.g. from egg collectors), the breeding status map shows results at 5km resolution. It should be stressed, however, that those involved in managing the Manx moors for the benefit of Red Grouse are not considered to pose a threat to the wellbeing of the Hen Harrier population. Indeed many provided valuable information on the location of nests during the research period. The majority of breeding took place within or adjacent to areas of high ground, though breeding did occur in the lowlands. The breeding abundance map demonstrates the close association with upland habitats.

The pattern of post-breeding dispersal and migration of British Isles Hen Harriers is not clear. Evidence from recoveries and observations of marked birds suggest that many remain within the vicinity of the natal area. It is known that at least some young Scottish male birds move south in the autumn, into England, with sightings along the south coast in October and November, suggestive of movements to the continental mainland (MA). The extent to which Manx breeding birds migrate is not known, nor is it understood whether autumn dispersal from the uplands regularly takes birds to adjacent islands. A limited number of birds that have been wing-tagged in Scotland have been observed on the Isle of Man in some winters (J. Thorpe *pers. comm.*)

During the winter, birds range throughout most of the Island in search of food, though uplands are less used at this time, prey only being available there in low densities. The winter abundance map suggests a clear movement away from the uplands. In the lowlands, the largest known Manx roost of Hen Harriers is located in the Ballaugh Curragh, where counts in excess of 60 birds are not uncommon, making this one of the largest roosts within the west of Europe.

The first definite sighting on the Isle of Man was not until 1906 when a male was shot at Ballagarraghyn, after which there was a gap until the next two records, in 1921 (Ralfe 1923). In the next 40 years there were only 18 records, but there was a marked increase from 1963 (C&J). Breeding was first established in 1977, in Glen Rushen (McIntyre *et al.* 1978). Thereafter, breeding numbers increased steadily. C&J estimated 5-6 pairs breeding annually, though clearly the species has undergone significant change in status since then. The establishment of the Hen Harrier on the Island coincided with an expansion of its range in the British Isles, having been virtually eliminated from mainland Britain in the nineteenth century, through a mixture of persecution and changed land use (Sim *et al.* 2001). Despite the lack of voles, which comprise a significant proportion of its diet elsewhere, the Hen Harrier is faring well locally. Further study could usefully be applied to increase our understanding of the local ecology of this internationally important species.

1977–81

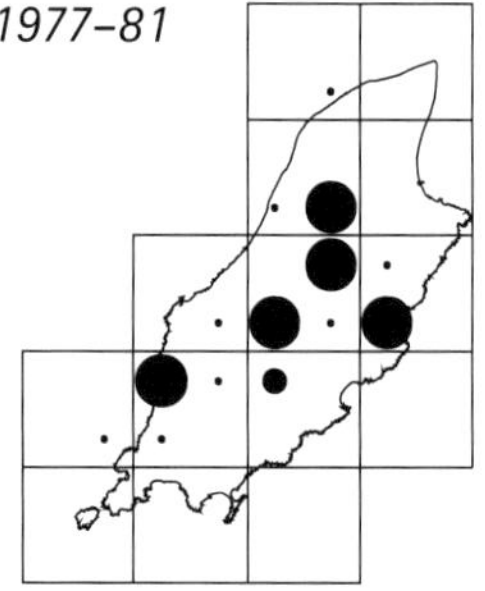

1998–2002

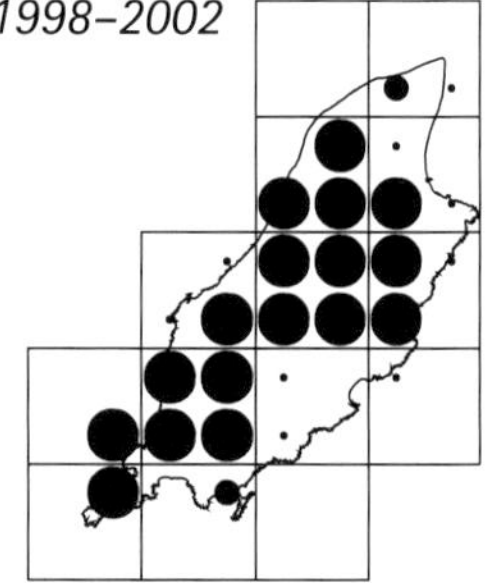

Breeding	Grid squares:	Isle of Man 346 (52%) Britain 498 Ireland 123 Total 621 (16%)
	Population:	Isle of Man 51 Britain 630 Ireland 180 (9% of European)
Wintering	Grid squares:	Isle of Man 268 (40%) Britain and Ireland 1,192 (31%)
	Population:	Isle of Man <150 Britain and Ireland 900

Jan Feb Mar Apr May Jun Jul Aug Sep Oct Nov Dec

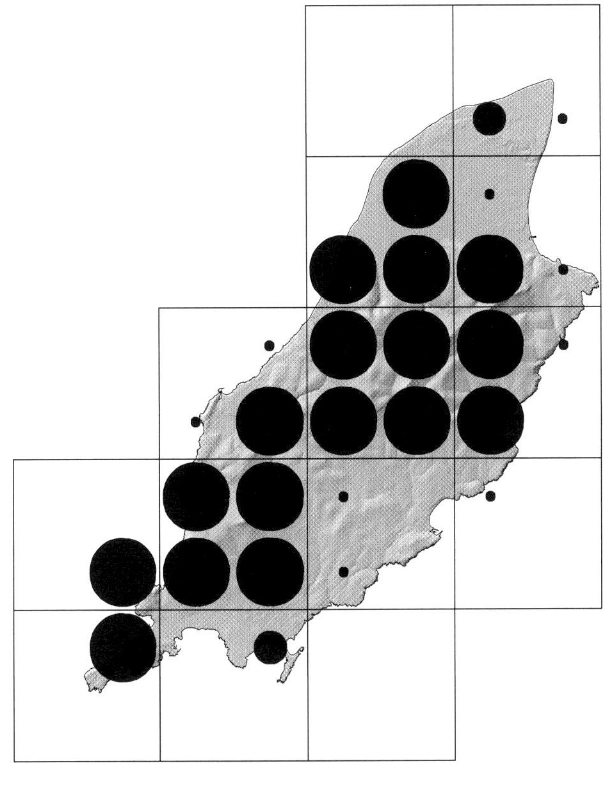

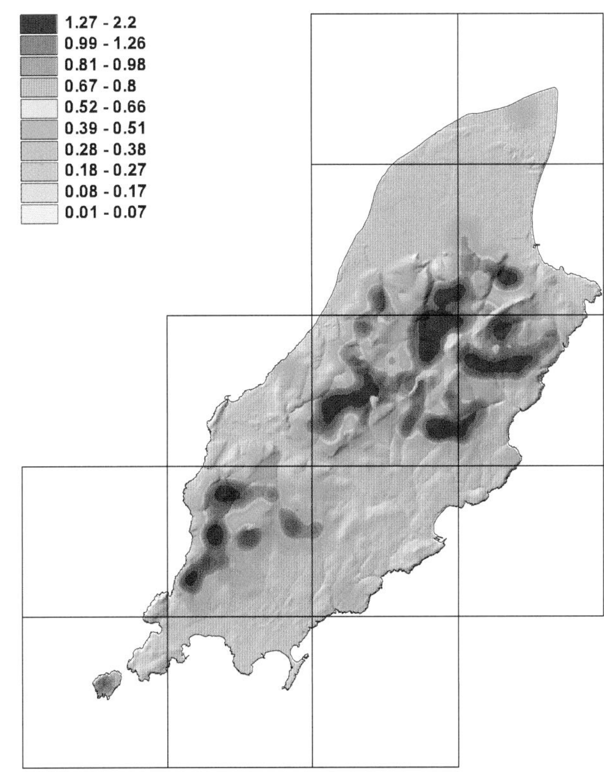

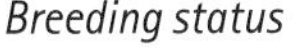
Breeding status

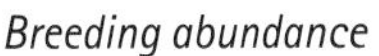
Breeding abundance

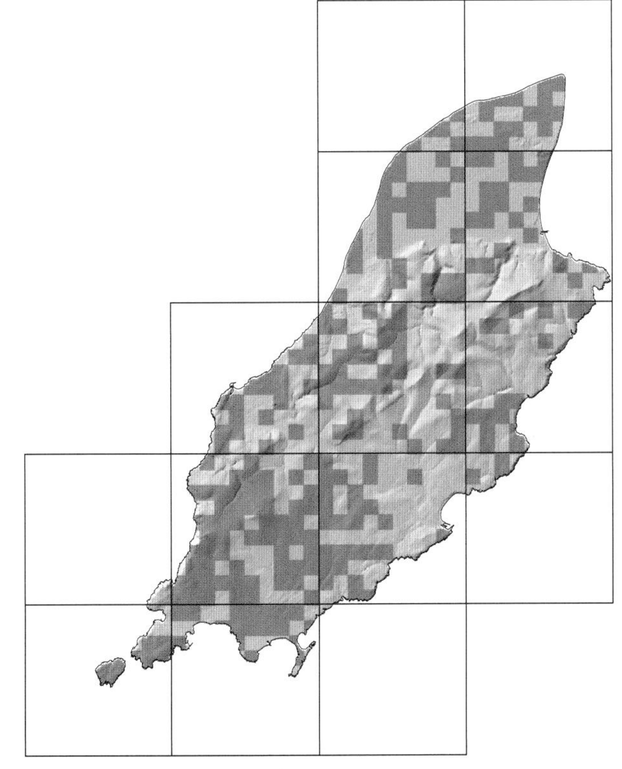

Winter presence

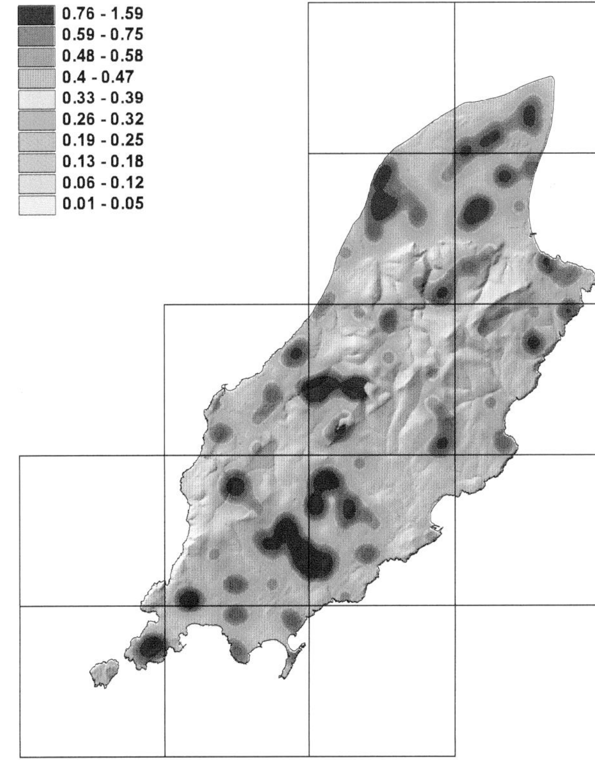

Winter abundance

Individual Sponsors – The late W T Callow, Mr. A Chase, Crane of Cluny, Mr. L Cowell, Mr. H K Larsen, Mr. D Marsden, Mrs. K Owens, Mr. T R Quayle, Mr. A & Mrs. J Sharpe

Sparrowhawk (Eurasian Sparrowhawk) *Accipiter nisus*

Manx: *Shawk, Shirragh* = Hawk, *Shirragh ny Giark* = Hen Searcher

Relatively short, broad wings coupled with a long tail give the Sparrowhawk the essential combination of speed and agility that makes it so effective when hunting. Its hunting strategy relies on surprise and stealth; the first indication of presence is usually marked by a frantic scattering of small birds with the Sparrowhawk already in their midst.

Sparrowhawks are a woodland species, preferring well-grown stands of coniferous or mixed trees. Breeding within dense, un-thinned mature plantations is confined to clearings, glades or rides, as these offer easy access to the nest. Where large stands of trees are absent Sparrowhawks will nest in sub-optimal areas including dense hedgerows, small copses and in riverbank trees (BWP, 1988–91 Atlas). Food taken is almost entirely birds, with female Sparrowhawks capable of taking larger prey items than the smaller males. They can be regular attendees in gardens with feeding stations, a practice that produces a mixed response from those providing the feed.

The Sparrowhawk has a wide breeding range, being present throughout Europe, with the exception of Iceland, and having a range that extends across Asia to Japan (EBA). Within the British Isles it breeds extensively, absences within the uplands of Scotland and some of the Northern and Western Isles being due to a lack of suitable habitat. Since the 1968-72 Atlas the British Isles population has increased, continuing the recovery from the impact of pesticides in the late 1950s (1988–91 Atlas).

Locally, estimating the breeding population of Sparrowhawks proved problematic. As indicated on the summer distribution map, the species was regularly encountered throughout the lowlands, where much suitable habitat exists. Based only upon a measure of species presence against available nesting habitat, one approach would have been to attribute a 'possible' breeding status to nearly every 1km square in which the species was observed. It is known, however, that the species rarely nests at such densities and that the hunting range can cover several kilometres. Adopting this approach would probably have resulted in an overestimate of the numbers breeding. Staff were therefore cautious about attributing a 'possible' breeding status to birds that were only observed hunting, albeit in habitat that could sustain a pair. It is possible therefore that the population is underestimated. Notwithstanding this caveat it is evident that the species is faring well locally, having previously suffered the same levels of decline in the mid-1950s as witnessed in the rest of the British Isles (C&J).

Sparrowhawks breeding within the British Isles are considered non-migratory and relatively sedentary, though some post-fledging dispersal is evident. In contrast, birds from northern Europe are migratory or partly so, moving generally south-west in autumn. Most continental Sparrowhawks that winter in the British Isles come from Norway and Denmark (MA). It is unlikely that many of these birds reach the Island. Analysis of Calf records suggests that there are three peaks of birds during autumn; late August, late September and mid-October, the first two comprising local (and possibly British) young with the later peak relating to Scandinavian birds (McCanch 1997).

The winter distribution of Sparrowhawks in the British Isles shows absence only from open mountain areas and parts of eastern England, the latter area yet to be recolonised from earlier declines (WA). The Manx wintering population of Sparrowhawks is likely to be made up of the same birds as the summer, though some young dispersing from adjacent coastal areas possibly reach the Island. The winter distribution and abundance maps both indicate almost complete absence from higher ground, where prey is only available at low densities and foraging habitat is largely unsuitable. Winter presence is evident in most towns and villages, underlining the opportunistic nature of the species, which will readily take to hunting in rural and suburban gardens, where the Sparrowhawks take birds at garden feeders.

Ralfe described the species as fairly abundant, while C&J considered that it had recovered from the decline caused by pesticides to become 'as abundant as at any time this century'. Despite the difficulties in accurately estimating breeding numbers during our research, there is nothing to suggest that the status of the species has changed since then. With legal protection against persecution in place, abundant nest sites available and a plentiful supply of food, the fortunes of this essential part of the food chain seems secure on the Island.

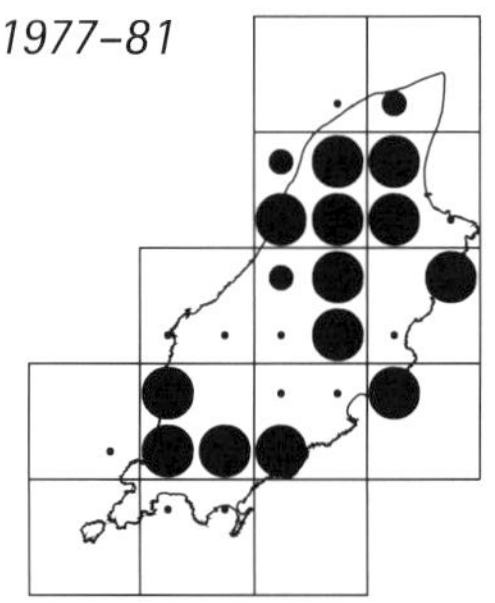

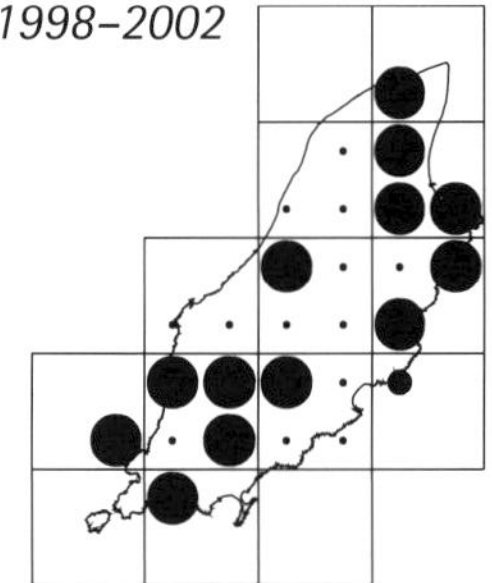

Breeding	Grid squares:	Isle of Man 213 (32%) Britain 2,178 Ireland 663 Total 2,841 (74%)
	Population:	Isle of Man 75-80 Britain 32,000 Ireland 11,000 (28% of European)
Wintering	Grid squares:	Isle of Man 214 (32%) Britain and Ireland 2,737 (71%)
	Population:	Isle of Man 200+ Britain and Ireland 120,000+

Jan Feb Mar Apr May Jun Jul Aug Sep Oct Nov Dec

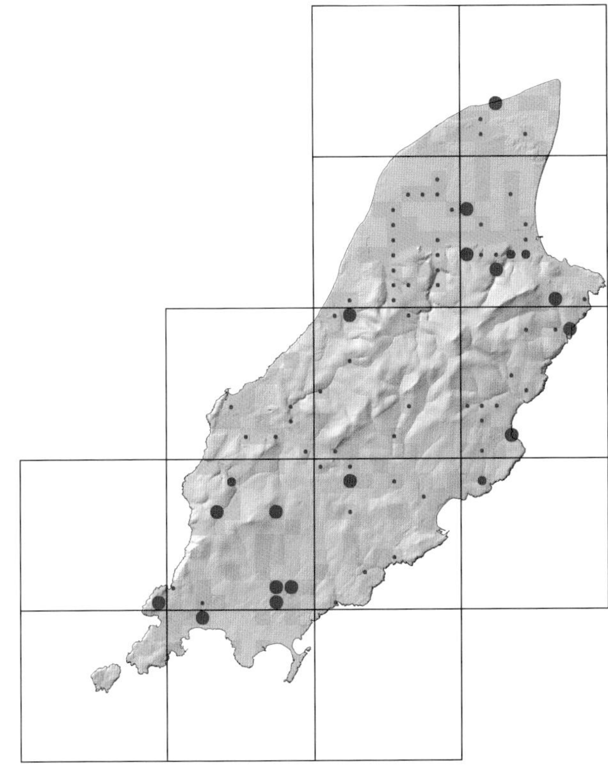

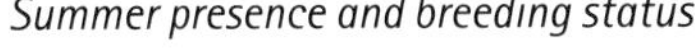

Summer presence and breeding status

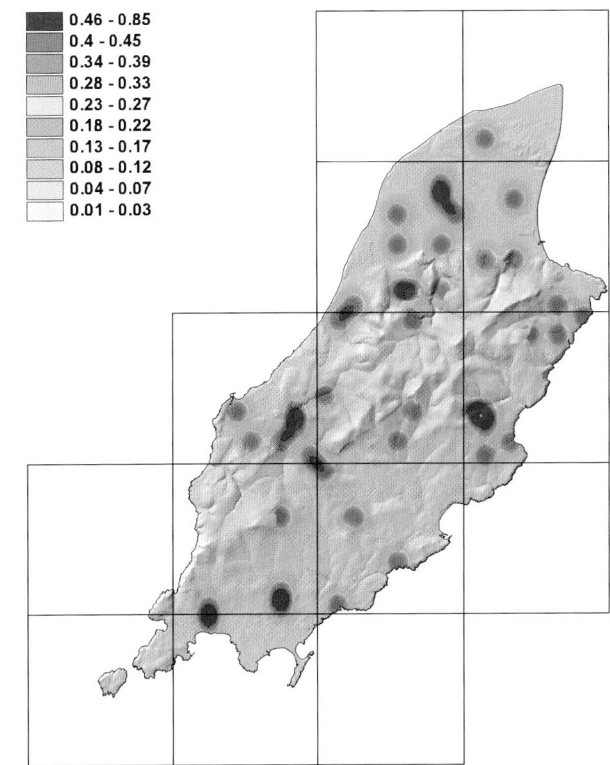

Breeding abundance

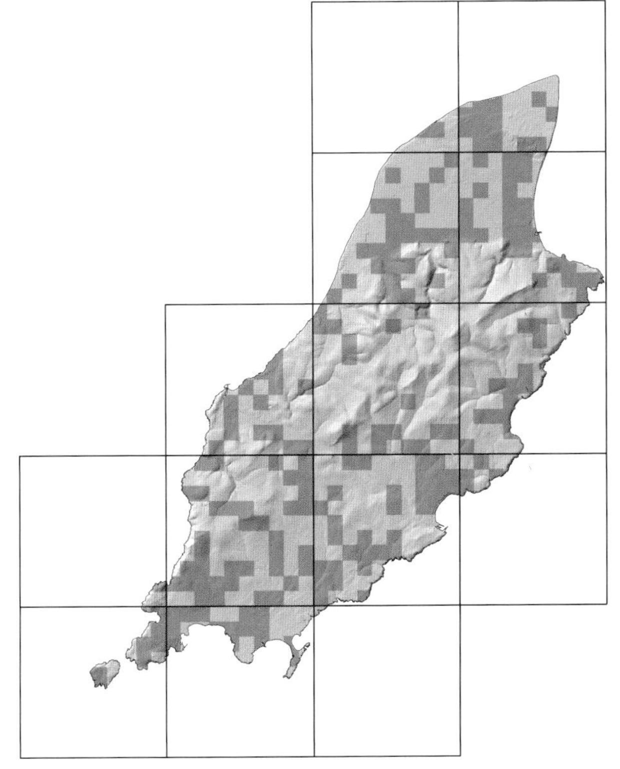

Winter presence

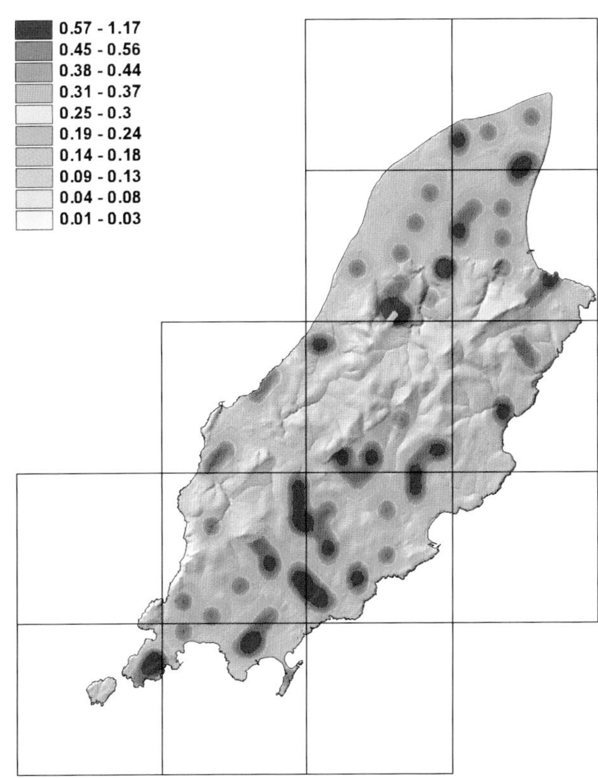

Winter abundance

Individual Sponsors – The late Mr. T Hopson, Mr. M Ibanez, Mr. P & Mrs. S Lille

Kestrel (Common Kestrel) *Falco tinnunculus*

Manx: *Stannair Ruy*

A hovering Kestrel is one of the easier birds of prey to identify. Even in the most blustery conditions constant changes to the angle of wings and fanned tail combine to keep the head almost motionless as it watches for movement below, suddenly dropping to the ground when prey is spotted. The height at which birds hover is variable, in some instances being only a few metres above the ground, giving spectacular views of their aerial prowess.

Kestrels breed in a wide range of habitats, including coastal cliffs, inland crags, rock outcrops, holes in trees, old stick nests of other species, nest boxes and even buildings within towns and cities, though dense forests are avoided and nests are seldom on the ground. Throughout most of its range voles are a main source of food for Kestrels, with numbers being highest in good vole years in upland grass areas including south Scotland and the Pennines (1988–91 Atlas). Other small mammals are taken, however, as are small birds, lizards and insects. With no voles on the Isle of Man local Kestrels need to rely upon a range of other foods, with small birds presumed to form a significant proportion of their diet.

Kestrels breed throughout Europe with the exception of Iceland, the Faeroes, the Arctic islands and the Azores (BWP). Within the British Isles they are widespread and common, however scarcity in the north-west of Scotland and some of the Scottish Isles is attributed to low food supplies (1988–91 Atlas). The 1988–91 Atlas indicates higher levels of abundance in the south-east of England; the area having recovered from the slump caused by pesticide use in the late 1950s. Densities are low in Ireland where, like the Isle of Man, there are no short-tailed voles (MA). On the Island the results of the current research indicate a very similar distribution to that indicated in C&J, the increase in breeding status in many 5km squares possibly being a result of increased survey effort. Coastal breeding occurred along sections of the east coast of the Island with records on the west coast confined to the rocky section south of Peel. Inland there was a noticeable shortage of summer records between the south-east coast and the start of the southern uplands, though the reasons for this are unclear. Absence across much of the northern plain might also be attributable to restricted nesting habitat. More Kestrels occur on the Ayres, where isolated stands of trees provide nesting habitat. Kestrels also breed in a line running along the western edge of the uplands, a combination of rock outcrops, old quarries and scattered deciduous woodland being used as nest sites. A mean density of 20 pairs per 100km² for the British Isles is suggested in the 1988–91 Atlas. Applied to the Isle of Man this would give a figure of 110 pairs, in line with the estimate of 121–123 pairs from our research, though both figures are higher than might be expected given the absence of voles.

Kestrels are partial migrants, birds from the northern reaches of the British Isles being more likely to move south than those from southern regions. Juveniles disperse from July onwards, movements away from nests appearing to be in random directions. Many such movements involve only short distances, though three first-winter birds from Manx nests have been recovered in Belgium, France and Spain (C&J). Long-distance migratory movement occurs from September onwards and is largely complete by November (MA), though the extent to which local adults leave the Island is unknown. The British Isles wintering population includes birds from Fenno-scandia, France, Belgium and the Netherlands. These continental birds are known to reach Ireland occasionally, so it is possible that the Manx wintering population might occasionally include a continental bird.

The winter distribution of Kestrels on the Isle of Man suggests a general movement out of the uplands, but an increase in abundance in the northern and south-eastern agricultural areas. It is likely that birds that spend much of the winter in the lowlands will travel the short distance to feed in the uplands during clear winter days. During the winter a slight bias away from eastern areas is still evident, as in the summer.

Ralfe considered the Kestrel as plentiful in coastal localities that suited it. He knew of a number of inland nestings, but had no records of tree nesting. C&J described the Kestrel as a 'well represented resident and passage migrant', but estimated that only 25–40 pairs bred on the Island, significantly fewer than suggested by our survey.

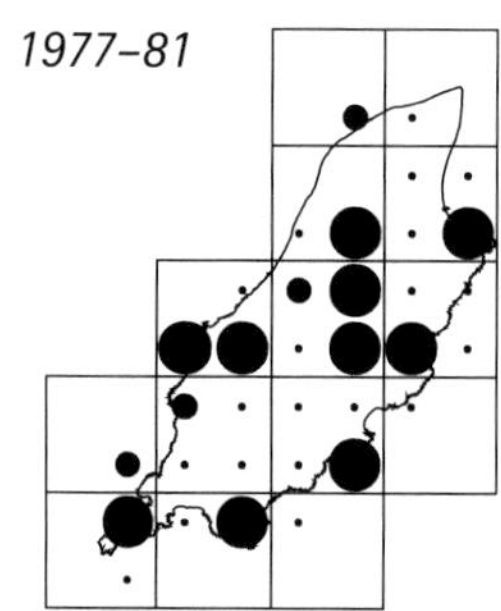

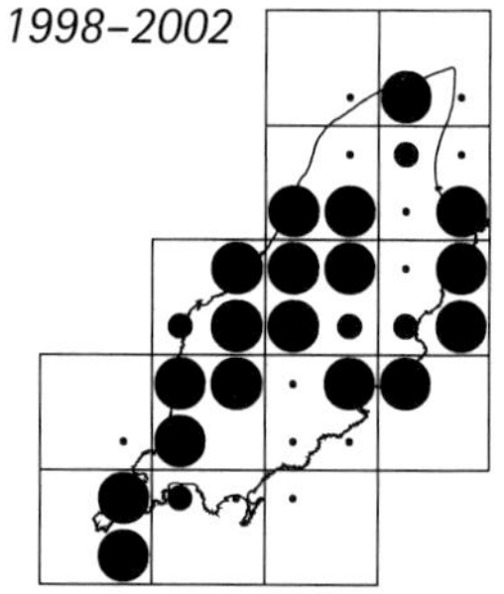

Breeding	Grid squares:	Isle of Man 216 (32%)
		Britain 2,481 Ireland 804 Total 3,285 (85%)
	Population:	Isle of Man 120
		Britain 50,000 Ireland 10,000 (21% of European)
Wintering	Grid squares:	Isle of Man 185 (28%)
		Britain and Ireland 3,142 (81%)
	Population:	Isle of Man 200
		Britain and Ireland 100,000

Jan	Feb	Mar	Apr	May	Jun	Jul	Aug	Sep	Oct	Nov	Dec

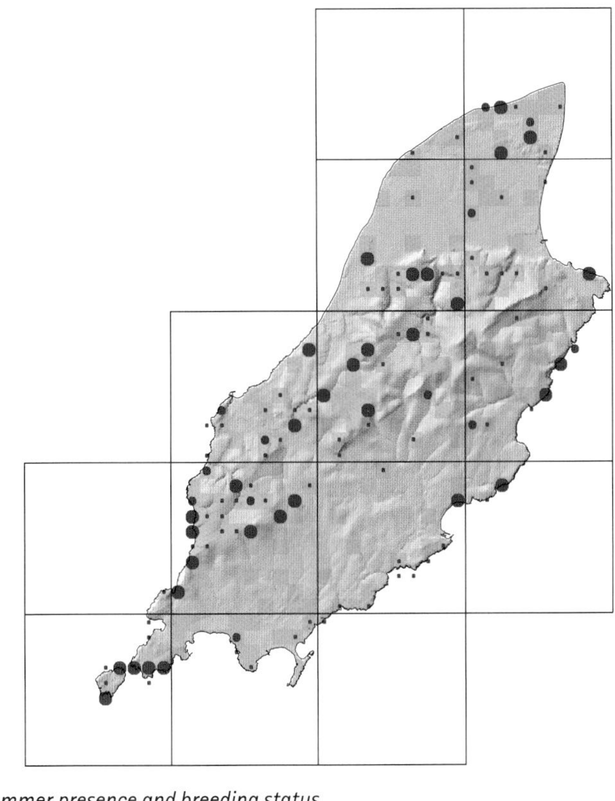

Summer presence and breeding status

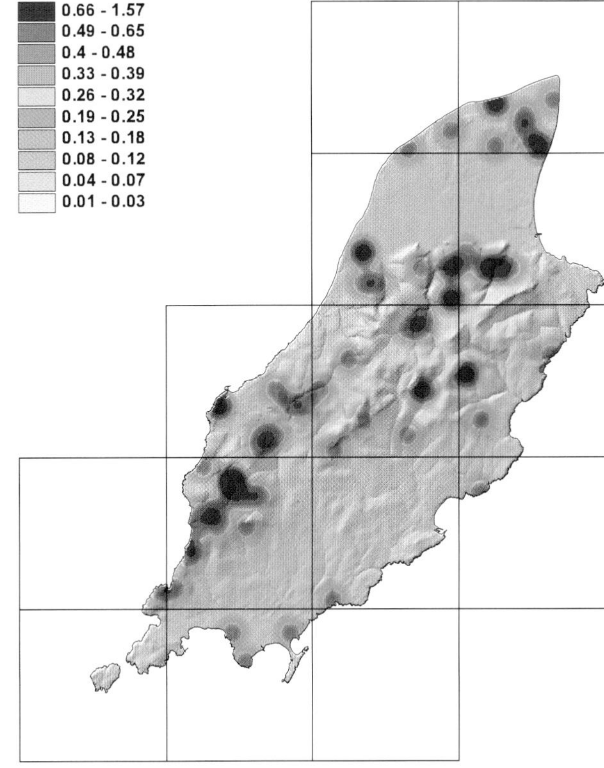

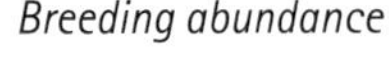

Breeding abundance

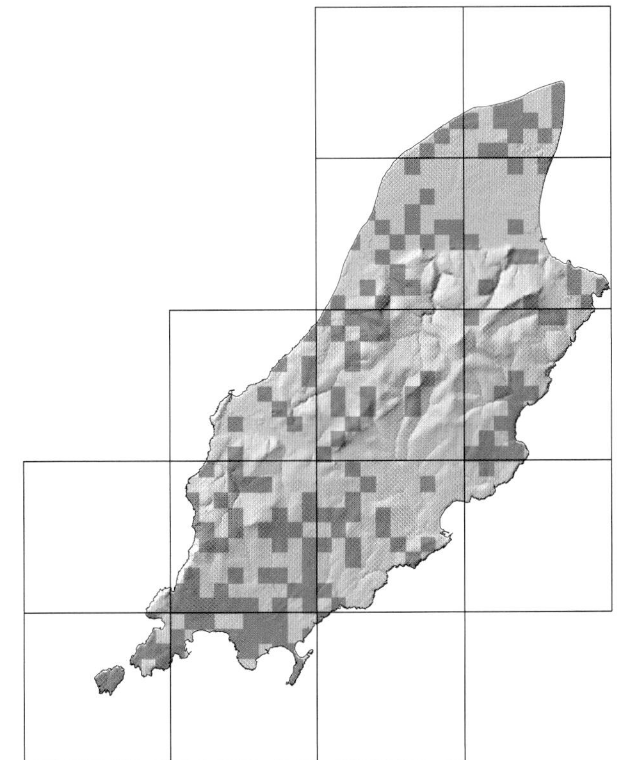

Winter presence

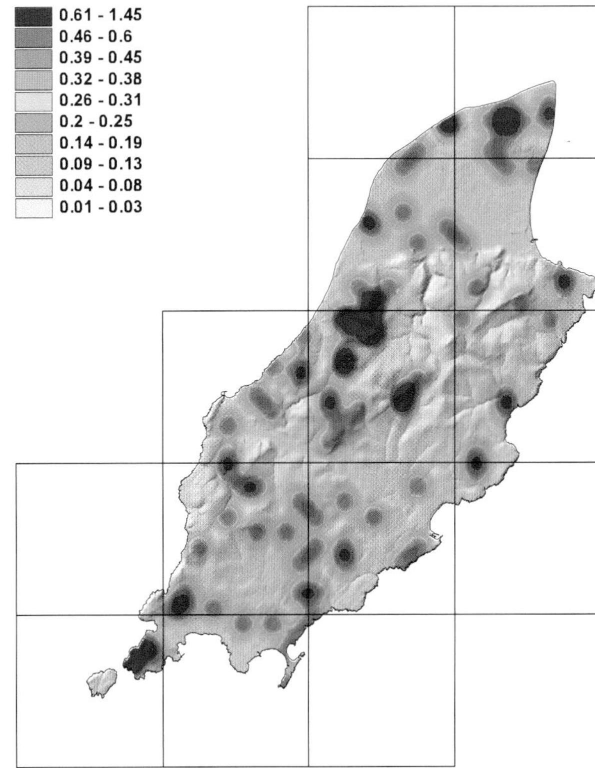

Winter abundance

Individual Sponsors – Mr. P Brackpool, Ms. L Pateman, Mr. G Craine

Merlin
Falco columbarius

Merlins are the smallest birds of prey that breed within the British Isles. Males, in common with most raptors, are smaller than females, and are not much larger than Blackbirds. Their habit of hunting low over the ground, coupled with a secretive nature and sparse distribution can make them difficult to see. When they are seen, however, observers can often be rewarded with good views of birds sitting on the ground or low perch, between hunting episodes.

Throughout their breeding range Merlins are birds of the uplands, nesting on rocky crags, in old nests of corvids or among ground vegetation. Within the British Isles they have historically demonstrated a preference for ground nesting among heather or bracken. With upland plantations maturing there is evidence that greater numbers of pairs within the British Isles are starting to use trees for nesting, such nests being more successful than those on the ground, due to lower levels of predation (EBA). Food taken is mainly small birds, with Meadow Pipits and Skylarks likely to form the bulk of the diet. Hunting usually takes the form of low flight about 1m over the ground, prey being taken by surprise, though prolonged pursuit does occur. One such episode lasted for approximately five minutes when a female was unsuccessful in an attempt to catch a Snipe over the Langness salt marsh.

Of nine subspecies, *Falco columbarius aesalon* has a breeding range that extends from Ireland to north-west Siberia. The subspecies *F.c. subaesalon* breeds in Iceland. Within the British Isles, breeding occurs throughout most upland areas, mainly within heather moorland. In Scotland they are more abundant in the eastern Highlands than in the west, possibly due to poorer land productivity in the wetter, colder, west (1988–91 Atlas). On the Isle of Man there were few records during the summer research period that suggested breeding. As indicated on the distribution map many of the records were from the coastal lowlands and, with 80% of all summer sightings being obtained during April and early May, the majority of records were judged to be of migrating birds on return passage. The Merlin, though possibly breeding on the Island in small numbers, is more common during spring and autumn migration, with some of those birds remaining for the winter.

Most young Merlins have fledged by late July, following which there is a dispersal to lower altitudes, the majority of young and adults from the British Isles population remaining within the British Isles, though small numbers appear to cross into continental Europe (MA). Birds from Iceland are known to migrate to the British Isles, mainly to Ireland and the west of Britain and were previously considered to be separable from *F.c. aesalon* due to their larger size. It is now known that birds from northern parts of Scotland have a size overlap with *F.c. subaesalon* (MA). It is likely, therefore, that the Isle of Man winter population includes larger birds from both Iceland and northern Scotland, which were previously considered to be only from Iceland, as well as the more typically sized birds from the rest of the British Isles.

On the Island, Merlins are seen with increasing frequency during October, though in some years records are infrequent and, during the winter period, birds can be encountered throughout much of the lowlands and, less often, at high altitudes, prey availability rather than climate being the governing factor. Despite an apparently widespread winter distribution, many locations had just single winter sightings during the five-year period, suggesting that some birds are overlooked or are not present at all most of the time. The Ayres heath, the south-east coast from Port St Mary to Langness and the Ballaugh Curragh produced the majority of winter records.

The historic status of breeding Merlins on the Island is unclear; summer records referred to by Chaloner in 1656 probably being of migrating birds (C&J). Nesting did take place in 1860, on the southern slopes of Peel Hill, with sporadic records thereafter, with C&J pointing out a 'notable increase in summer records' in the 10 years preceding their publication. It is certainly clear that the species has always been much more abundant in winter than in summer. The presence of ground predators may be a limiting factor as both suitable habitat and food are apparently present in some quantity. Efforts to improve the fortunes of the species locally could usefully include the erection of artificial nests in conifers bordering suitable moors as this would prevent most ground predators reaching the eggs.

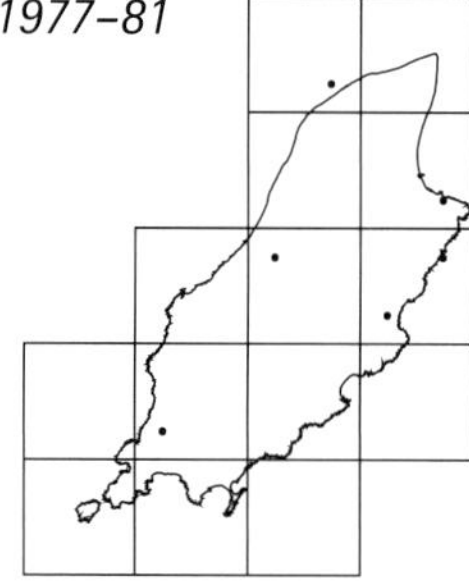

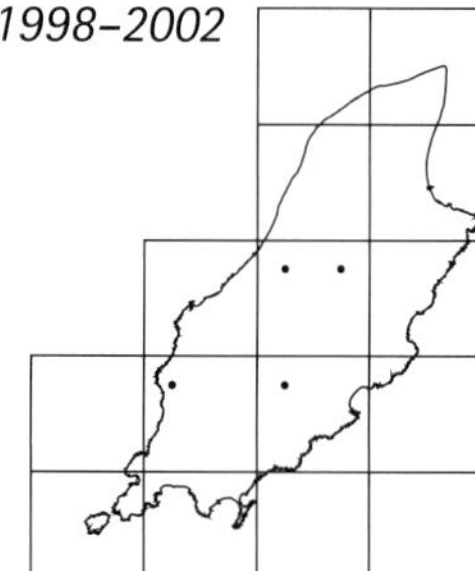

Breeding	Grid squares:	Isle of Man 34 (5%) Britain 693 Ireland 158 Total 851 (22%)
	Population:	Isle of Man 0–4 Britain 1,300 Ireland 120 (6% of European)
Wintering	Grid squares:	Isle of Man 72 (11%) Britain and Ireland 1,217 (32%)
	Population:	Isle of Man <30 Britain and Ireland 2,000–3,000

Jan Feb Mar Apr May Jun Jul Aug Sep Oct Nov Dec

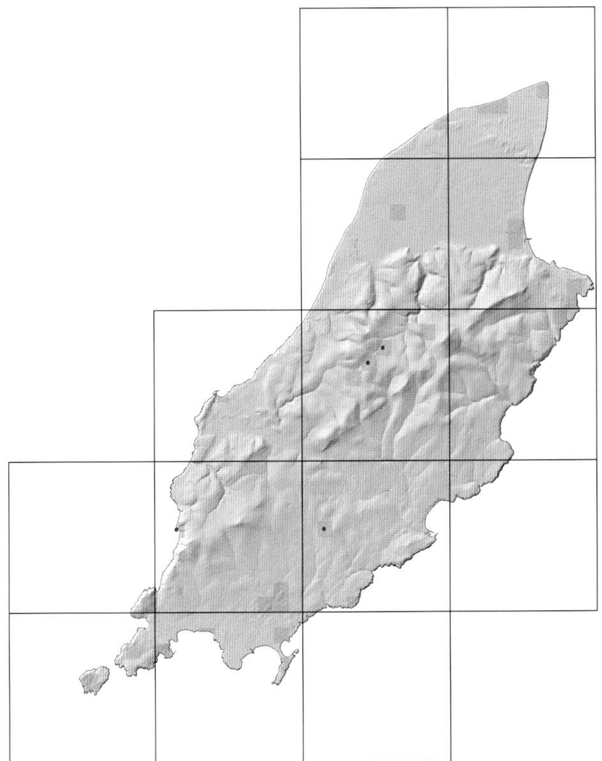

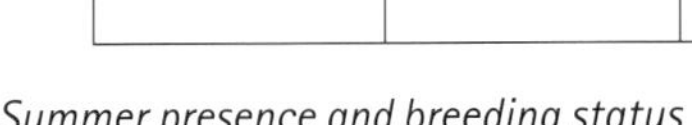

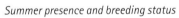

Summer presence and breeding status

Winter presence

Peregrine (Peregrine Falcon) *Falco peregrinus*

Manx: *Shirragh y Ree*

Peregrines are almost certainly the best known of our resident raptors, securing a high profile after the 1950s due to their drastic decline in numbers as a result of insecticides in the food chain causing widespread low productivity. This, together with their deserved reputation as one of the world's 'ultimate' predators, means that few people will not have heard of them. Anyone fortunate enough to watch a Peregrine in full hunting stoop must surely have marvelled at its speed and power.

Peregrines nest mainly in areas where cliffs provide suitable ledges, whether on rocky coasts or inland crags in upland areas. In parts of their breeding range, however, they take readily to quarries and a variety of other human sites including pylons, bridges, churches and tall urban buildings. Tree nesting is rare while there is greater evidence of ground, or 'walk-in' nests being used. Prey taken is primarily birds, C&J noting 41 different species as having been taken locally, ranging in size from Wren to Raven, with rabbit also being noted in the diet. Peregrines will hunt over a wide range of habitats, especially outside the breeding season, though heavily wooded areas are not favoured. Most prey is taken in the air, after rapid stoops, estimated as reaching 240km/h, which can involve paired birds hunting in unison. Local moorland managers have noted Peregrines 'hanging' in the air upwind to stoop on prey flushed by their activity.

Peregrines have a world-wide distribution, being absent from only a few regions, such as Iceland, Antarctica, New Zealand and parts of South America (EBA). Of 19 recognised subspecies, only four occur in Europe, with *Falco peregrinus peregrinus* occurring in the British Isles and Scandinavia. Within the British Isles the species suffered significant declines in breeding numbers during the early part of the twentieth century, a combination of insecticides in the food chain and illegal persecution leaving the population at less than half its former size by the 1960s. Since then the species has undergone a marked reversal of fortunes, first noted during the 1968–72 Atlas, with a census in the UK, including the Isle of Man, in 1991 estimating 1,283 breeding pairs, a 147% increase over the levels in 1930–39 (Crick & Ratcliffe 1995). By 2002 a repeat census found 1,402 pairs (Banks *et al.* 2003). The Manx element of that research was undertaken by the MBA, during which 29 occupied territories were found, in which there were 25 definite breeding attempts, the highest number of pairs ever recorded on the Island, increases being in line with those found elsewhere. In order to protect sites, which are at risk particularly from egg collectors, the breeding status map is at the 5km square level, while a summer abundance map has been omitted as sightings during summer fieldwork demonstrated a strong correlation with known nest sites. Comparison with the map from C&J underlines the local range expansion of the species during the intervening years.

Within the British Isles, established breeding pairs are considered sedentary, though non-breeders and juveniles will disperse more widely, while some Scottish Highland birds, breeding at high altitude, may move to lower levels in winter. Evidence from ringing recoveries indicates that some birds from the Scandinavian population move into the British Isles in winter (MA).

During the winter Peregrines are widely, though sparsely, distributed throughout the Island and can turn up almost anywhere, though the winter abundance map suggests that the uplands are not favoured, presumably due to a relative shortage of prey. The species occurs with greater frequency throughout the northern and, especially, southern lowlands.

In 1405 King Henry IV gave the Isle of Man to Sir John Stanley, on condition that he gave two falcons to him and every future King of England on his coronation day, a practice that continued until the coronation of George IV in 1821 (C&J). In the 1880s the species was heavily persecuted and by the time of Ralfe only ten or eleven sites were known, all coastal. The local effect of insecticides on Peregrines was particularly marked, resulting in there being no records of birds breeding between 1963 and 1972. A recovery was evident from that time with 18-20 occupied sites by the time of the last complete census of 1991. With further increase evident since then, the future of the Peregrine on the Island appears healthy. The risk of egg collection remains real, however, while increased recreational activity near nests, particularly those inland, may cause accidental disturbance.

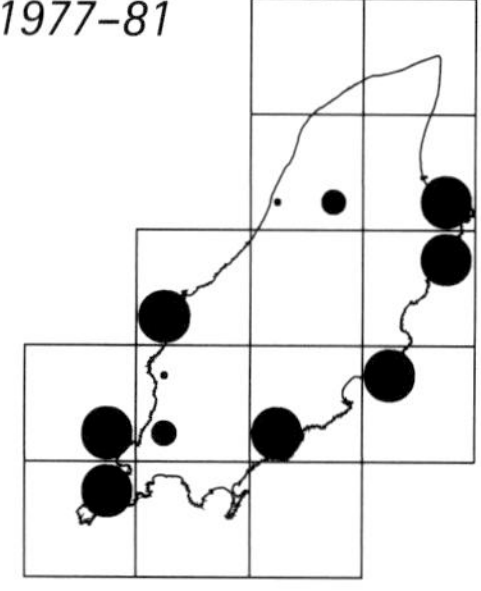

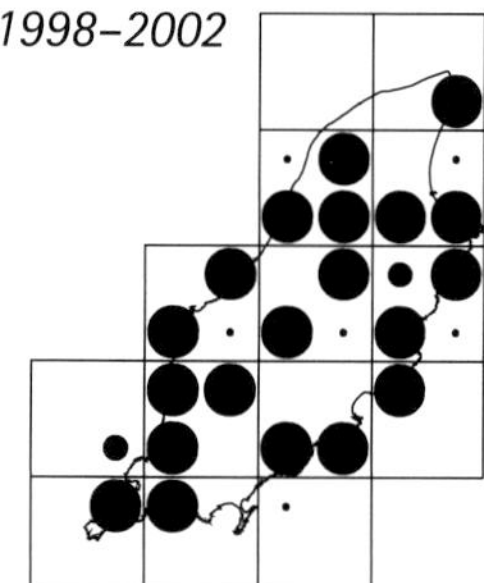

Breeding	Grid squares:	Isle of Man 202 (30%) Britain 1,048 Ireland 290 Total 1,338 (35%)
	Population:	Isle of Man 25–29 Britain 1,185 Ireland 365 (27% of European)
Wintering	Grid squares:	Isle of Man 144 (22%) Britain and Ireland 1,282 (33%)
	Population:	Isle of Man <100 Britain and Ireland 4,000+

Jan	Feb	Mar	Apr	May	Jun	Jul	Aug	Sep	Oct	Nov	Dec

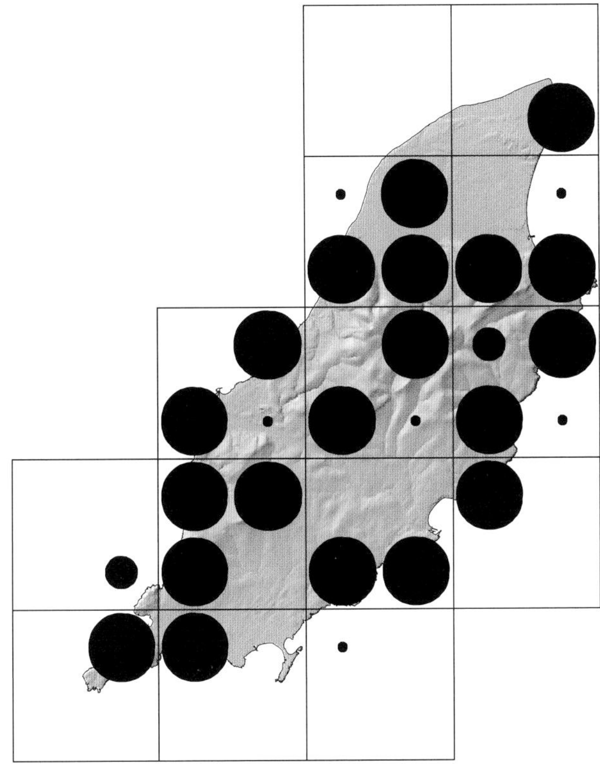

Breeding status

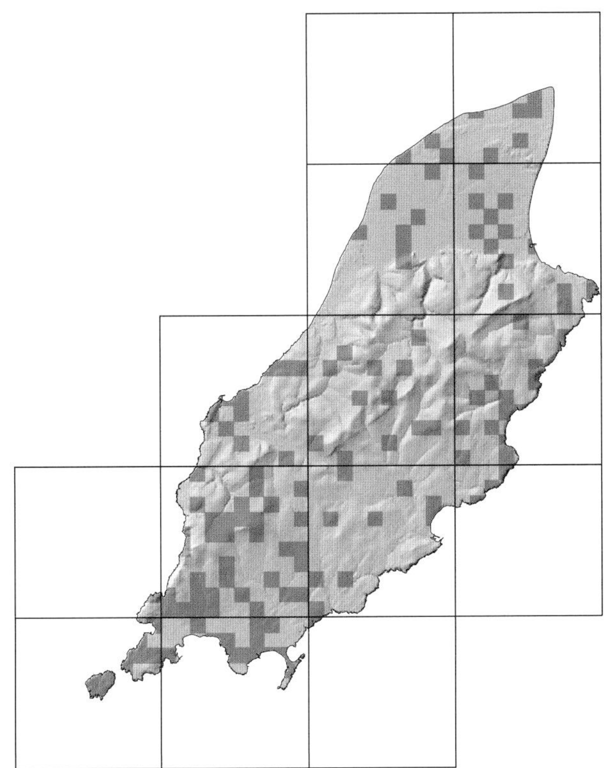

Winter presence

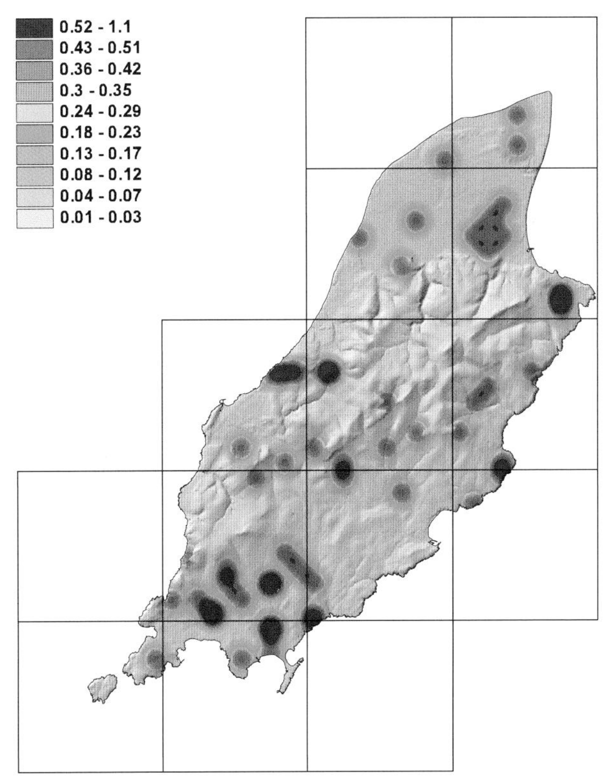

Winter abundance

Individual Sponsors – The Anderson Trust, Mrs. M J Bull, Mr. G Craine, Ms J. O'Neill, Possan Gaelgagh, Mr. M Rosevear, Ms. S Slatter, Mr. A Vokins

Water Rail
Rallus aquaticus

Manx: *Drean Ushtey* = Water Wren

Like the other small, and much rarer, members of the *Rallidae*, the Water Rail is more commonly heard than seen. Its body is about the same size as that of a Starling, but the long, slightly decurved red bill adds as much as 4.5cm to its overall length and it also has the long legs which characterise all members of the family. A chance sighting will reveal the generally dark grey face and underparts with brown back, spotted and streaked with black, as well as the black and white barring of the flanks. It steps warily and will hurry away into deeper cover if alarmed. Flight is usually rapid and brief with legs dangling. Water Rails have a considerable vocal repertoire, but the most distinctive call is very aptly likened to a pig squealing, terminating in a rapid diminuendo.

They are found in shallow and waterlogged, well-vegetated, areas such as marshes, swamps, ditches and sewage farms. Reedbeds, dense patches of sedge, horsetails and, especially on the Isle of Man, willow carr, provide cover for nesting. The diet consists mainly of insects and their larvae, supplemented, particularly in winter, by plant shoots and roots, especially watercress. It is an opportunistic feeder, taking carrion, fish, amphibians, birds, eggs and small mammals.

The breeding range extends from the Atlantic coasts across Europe and discontinuously east as far as Sakhalin and from the Mediterranean, north to southern Fennoscandia and to Iceland (BWP). Greatest populations are in Spain and France, but it is well-represented in Sweden and across much of north and central Europe (EBA). In the British Isles it breeds very patchily from the English Channel as far as Orkney and from County Kerry across to the Suffolk coast. A decline in population of 34.5% occurred between the breeding atlases of 1968–72 and 1988–91. Evidence of Water Rail breeding on the Island has always been extremely scanty. In the period 1940–85 C&J could only find records of confirmed breeding at Ballaugh Curragh, the Dog Mills Lough and the Congary, although they conceded that the marshland between the Foxdale Dams as well as other marshy areas on the northern plain were likely sites. During the period prior to the MBA survey, presumptive evidence of breeding on the main island came only from the Rule, in Ballaugh Curragh, and from the Congary. The great surprise was that between 1988 and 1994, two or three pairs bred annually on the Calf, using both the withy and the front field. Unaccountably there have been no breeding records from the islet since.

Because of this scanty knowledge, it was decided to target the species for survey in 2000. Potential breeding sites were identified during the winter, from staff knowledge and maps showing the Phase 1 habitat types. During visits to each site, tape-recording was played for 60 seconds, followed by 60 seconds of silence. If there was no response, the tape was replayed for a further 30 seconds, followed by 30-second period of listening. If there was still no response, it was assumed that no birds were present and the observers moved on 100m, or to the next chosen site, and repeated the procedure. If birds did respond, the location was recorded on a map, a distinction being made between pairs and single birds. It was found that established pairs usually responded more readily and moved quickly towards one another while calling. Single birds were less inclined to call and any response was usually brief. Visits were made to sites within 26 1km squares. About half the squares were, of necessity, surveyed a little earlier than the optimum recommended period. It is therefore possible that some responses came from winter visitors destined to migrate, while nil responses could result from breeding birds having not yet arrived. This may be overcritical, given that the breeding season extends from March to July. Responses were received from 29 different individuals, ten of which were outside the Ballaugh Curragh, and from eight pairs, all of which were within the Curragh. Utilising records from all sources, definite breeding also took place at Ballacain and Gansey sewage works and there were records of probable breeding at the Congary, the Dollagh Dub and near Ballaghaie. Sites in the 'possible' category were the Ayres back slacks, Lough Cranstal, the Dog Mills Lough, the neighbourhood of the Bishop's Dub, the Foxdale Dams and the Calf.

Water Rails are mainly resident in the west and south of Europe, but the remainder are migratory, Britain and Ireland receiving birds from Sweden, Central Europe and further east (BWP). During the winter, most of the summer sites on the Island remained tenanted, but distribution was scattered in the south. In winter, Water Rails are invariably heard at dusk from the hide at Close Sartfield, ten squealing birds being located one November evening in 1999. There is an old record of a Water Rail being ringed at Ballachurry (Andreas) in December and being recovered at Alkmaar, North Holland, in November two years later.

1977–81

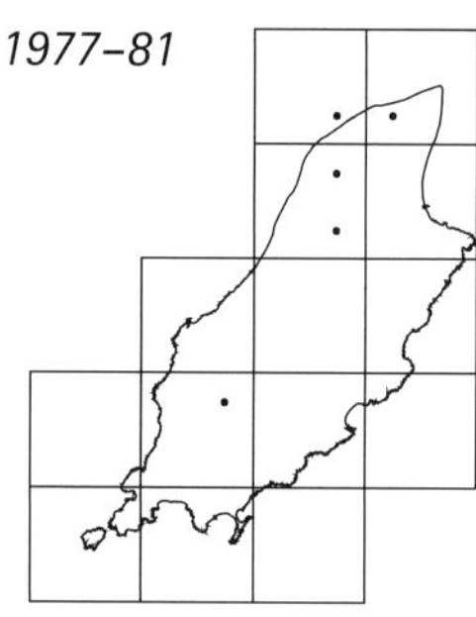

1998–2002

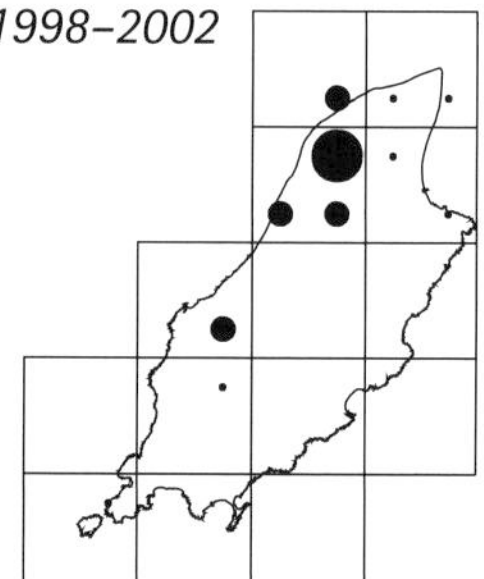

Breeding	Grid squares:	Isle of Man 24 (4%) Britain 420 Ireland 176 Total 596 (15%)
	Population:	Isle of Man 36–47 Britain 700 Ireland 1,300 (1% of European)
Wintering	Grid squares:	Isle of Man 18 (3%) Britain and Ireland 981 (25%)
	Population:	Isle of Man <100 Britain and Ireland 2,000-4,000+

Jan Feb Mar Apr May Jun Jul Aug Sep Oct Nov Dec

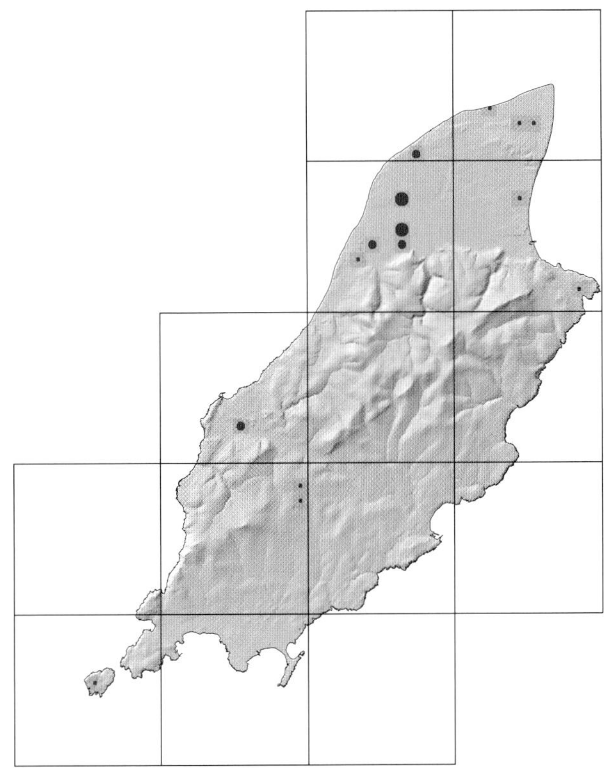

Summer presence and breeding status

Winter presence

Individual Sponsor – Mrs. A J Harrison

Corncrake (Corn Crake)
Crex crex

Manx: *Eean Raip* = the bird (which cries) 'raip'

Gone are the days when, in many parts of the Island, one's night-time sleep could be disturbed by the incessant, almost mechanical, hoarse 'raip-raip raip-raip' of the territorial male Corncrake. Delivered from long grass or thick vegetation, this was often the only evidence of a Corncrake's presence, although on occasions the display call might be delivered from an elevated position such as a wall. Rarely seen in its rather hesitant flight, the rich chestnut of the wings together with outstretched neck and legs, leave little room for confusion with any other bird.

Corncrakes breed in hayfields, and particularly in damp meadows and their well-vegetated margins. They are omnivorous, but most of the diet consists of a variety of insects, plant matter making up only a small proportion.

The breeding range extends from France eastward as far as western Siberia and lies mostly between 42°N and 62°N, although rather further north around the coastal margins of Norway and Sweden. The Corncrake is exclusively a summer visitor, wintering in eastern Africa from Uganda southward. Having declined alarmingly in the final three decades of the twentieth century, its main European stronghold is Belarus, with fair populations in Poland and the Baltic States. In the British Isles its main strongholds are Scotland's Western Isles and Ireland, where the Shannon callows, the Erne basin, County Mayo and the western parts of Ulster retain moderate populations. Once a very common inhabitant of farmland on the Isle of Man, numbers were probably falling towards the end of the nineteenth century, but remained high until a further slump in the mid-1930s. A further period of stability followed, favoured sites being occupied year after year for the next two decades, but then came an inexorable decline, such that in 1976 it is very likely that no Corncrakes bred on the Island. Subsequently there were sporadic records of birds calling, but never over a sustained period, although an adult was seen with a chick, inland from Rue Point, in June 1988. The period 1989–95 was particularly dire, with records in only two of the seven years.

Against this depressing background, the situation during the Atlas survey period gives cause for qualified optimism. In the summer of 1999 the Manx Wildlife Trust's preservation of hay meadows at its Close Sartfield Reserve was rewarded by the sight of an adult Corncrake with eight fluffy young on 10 July. Although there is no definite evidence that any other pairs bred, Corncrakes were seen in other parts of the Curragh later in the summer. Nesting again took place in Ballaugh Curragh the following year, but monitoring during 2001 was impossible owing to the embargo on farmland visits because of foot-and-mouth disease precautions. In 2002, however there was an impressive, and unexpected, invasion of an area covering four 1km squares astride the old railway line which runs by Ballacross Farm in German. Corncrakes called every day from 5 June to 26 July and at least three (possibly as many as five) clutches hatched. During the same summer a brood was seen on Jurby Airfield. In 2003, following completion of the fieldwork for this publication, Corncrakes returned to the area in German, song being heard from 5 May to 6 July and males also called for substantial periods in 2004 and 2005. There must therefore be guarded optimism that a significant revival is under way.

The decline of the Corncrake has been witnessed throughout the whole of the British Isles, indeed, with the exception of Sweden, the whole of Western Europe also. The cause of the decline is considered to be the replacement of manual by mechanical grass-cutting and the increasing preference for silage, for which grass is now cut as early as the first week of May in the Isle of Man. Mechanical grass-cutting of hayfields, which takes place much later in the year, puts nests and young at risk of destruction. C&J pointed out that on the Calf of Man the twelve-year period 1959-70 produced 43 records of migrants, while between 1971 and 1982 there were only nine. Pursuing this comparison further there were just three records between 1983 and 1994 and by 2003, there had been only one more.

When Corncrakes were relatively common, first calling was usually heard between 22 April and 4 May, rather earlier than at Ballacross, with unusually early birds being heard on 16 and 17 April, while the latest song date was 4 August. The earliest date on which young were seen was 5 June (1945) and conversely, a very late nest held 13 warm eggs on 10 August 1913. During the current survey period the last sight record was on 14 September, but there have in the past been records in every month of the year.

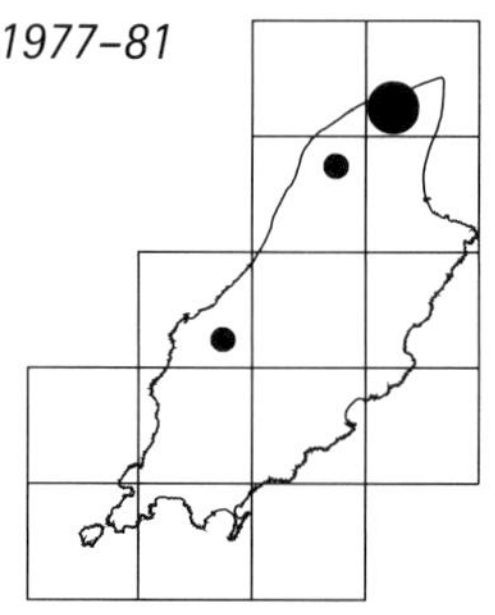

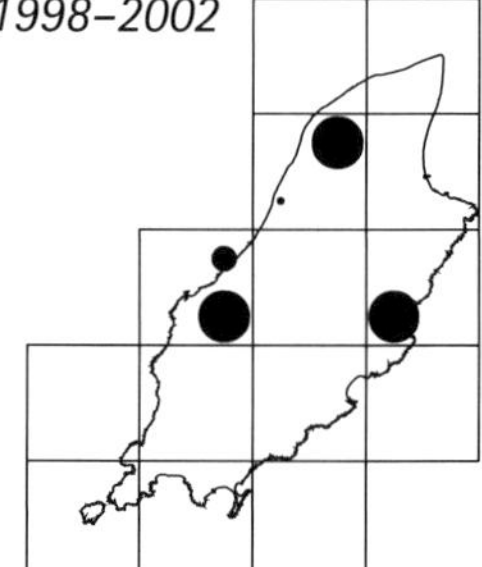

Breeding	Grid squares:	Isle of Man 13 (2%) Britain 161 Ireland 246 Total 407 (10%)
	Population:	Isle of Man <10 Britain 641 Ireland 158 (2% of European)

Jan Feb Mar Apr May Jun Jul Aug Sep Oct Nov Dec

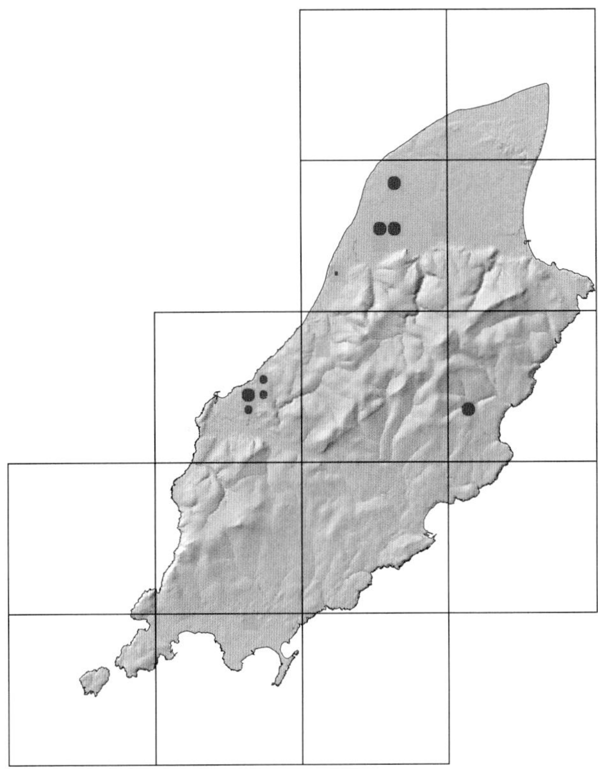

Summer presence and breeding status

Moorhen (Common Moorhen) *Gallinula chloropus*

Manx: *Kiark Ushtey* = Water Hen

The Moorhen has long been a familiar resident of the lower parts of the Island's rivers and most of the smaller ponds and dams. Its yellow-tipped, sealing-wax red bill and white sides to the under tail coverts clearly distinguish it from the larger Coot with its distinctive white shield. Both on land and when swimming, its progress is jerky. The downy young is a tiny bundle of black fluff with a distinctive red bill.

It is essentially a lowland species, so that the more rapid upper courses of streams, where they pass through acid moorland, are rarely tenanted. Nor is the Moorhen attracted by the larger reservoirs with little bankside vegetation, the Eairy Dam being about the largest piece of water with a resident population. Food is a mix of plant and animal matter. A great variety of leaves, stems, berries and fruit feature in the diet, which also includes an assortment of insects, spiders, molluscs and amphibians (BWP).

The Moorhen has an almost cosmopolitan distribution, with a substantial presence on all continents except Australasia. Although breeding in all European countries except Iceland, its distribution is uneven. Only along the coast of Norway does its range extend north of 61°N (EBA). In Britain it is absent from the higher ground of England, Wales and Scotland and now has a rather patchy distribution in Ireland. Its range has contracted in several western areas, notably in south-west England, Wales and north-west Scotland including the Hebrides. In Ireland this has been seen in several western counties, in fact, the period between 1968–72 and 1988–91 saw a 21% decline compared to just 9.2% in Britain (1988-91 Atlas). Despite this, Britain supports the largest Moorhen population of any European country, with the European Atlas estimating that the United Kingdom holds considerably more than twice the population of any other country with the exception of France.

It is interesting to compare the breeding distribution mapped by C&J with that derived from the present survey. According to the earlier work, Moorhens bred on some of the streams of the Snaefell watershed, while they were clearly absent from the MBA survey, and the same is true of the Glen Rushen River in the west. The apparent absence along the lower Sulby, shown in C&J, is an artefact arising from incomplete coverage. It would certainly appear that the last twenty years have seen a desertion of the faster-flowing streams. On the Calf, the Moorhen's status has fluctuated – one or two pairs bred annually up to 1978, it reappeared in 1984, breeding in 1985 and 1986, was absent from 1988 to 1990 and, after increasingly frequent appearances, bred successfully on the millpond from 1999 onwards.

The winter distribution closely follows that found in summer, with some contraction in both the north and the south produced by small gatherings on some ponds. Here again, perusal of the annual Manx Bird Reports suggests some decline in the overall population. Ballasteen (Andreas) had a flock of 52 in 1975, there were 31 at Ballacorey in September 1991 and the much-favoured Wildlife Park had as many as 84 in November 1995. Fifteen were also present on Port e Chee Lake in that same autumn of 1995. With the exception of the Wildlife Park, where winter numbers remain high, no double-figure gatherings have been reported since. The apparent decline had been evident in the 1988–91 Atlas, especially in the western parts of the British Isles, and it was suggested that land drainage and mink might have played a part. Mink are absent from the Island and while some land drainage has occurred it is considered not to be a significant factor.

On the Isle of Man, first clutches are usually laid in April (earliest known egg date is 11 March). Six is the commonest clutch size, followed equally by five and four eggs, with occasional records of up to eight. Nests are usually built on emergent or bankside vegetation, but have been found in trees up to 5m above the ground. They are particularly at risk from corvid predation and the high failure rate can result in as many as three repeats extending the breeding season to early August. There is no ringing evidence of movement away from or to the Island, although birds from Scandinavia do winter in Britain and Ireland and may well visit the Isle of Man.

1977–81

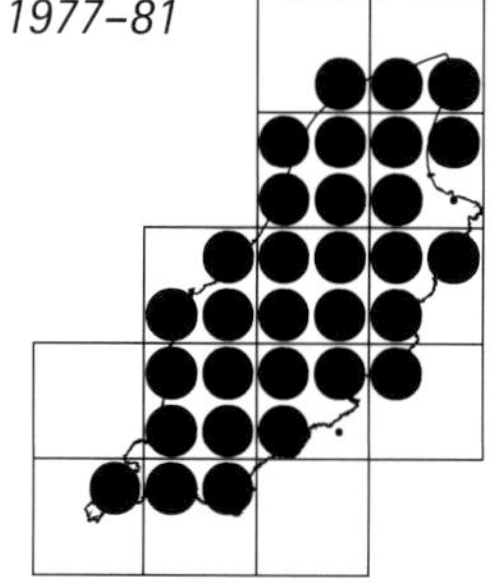

1998–2002

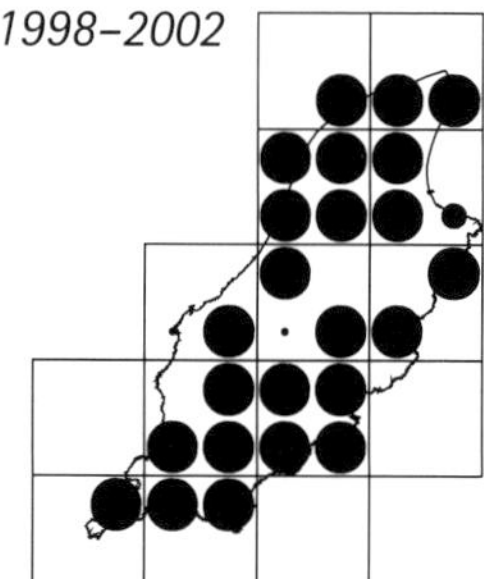

Breeding	Grid squares:	Isle of Man 169 (25%) Britain 2,032 Ireland 714 Total 2,746 (71%)
	Population:	Isle of Man 197–268 (territories) Britain 240,000 Ireland 75,000 (32% of European)
Wintering	Grid squares:	Isle of Man 127 (19%) Britain and Ireland 2,693 (70%)
	Population:	Isle of Man 1,000+ Britain and Ireland 1 million+

Jan	Feb	Mar	Apr	May	Jun	Jul	Aug	Sep	Oct	Nov	Dec

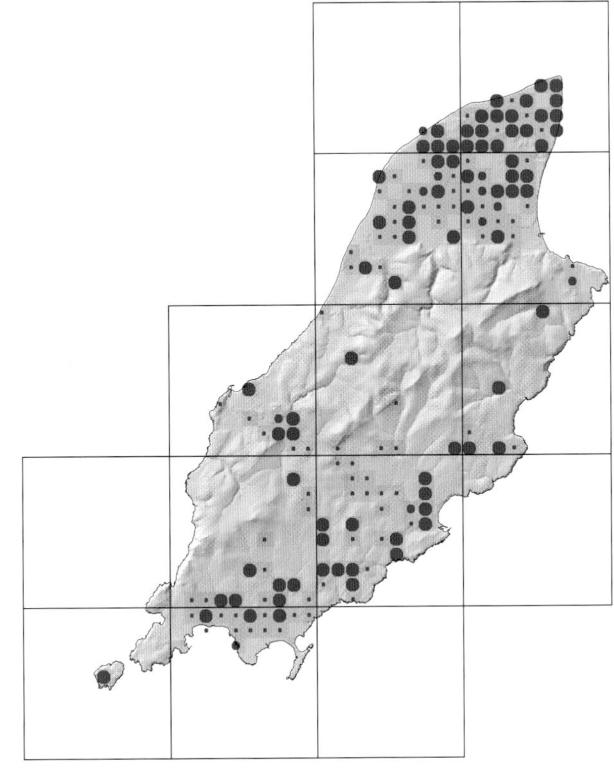
Summer presence and breeding status

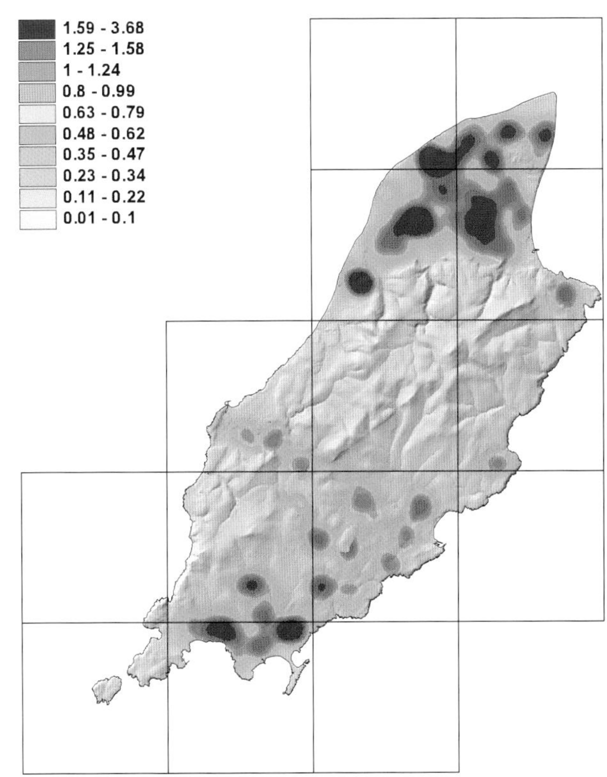

Breeding abundance

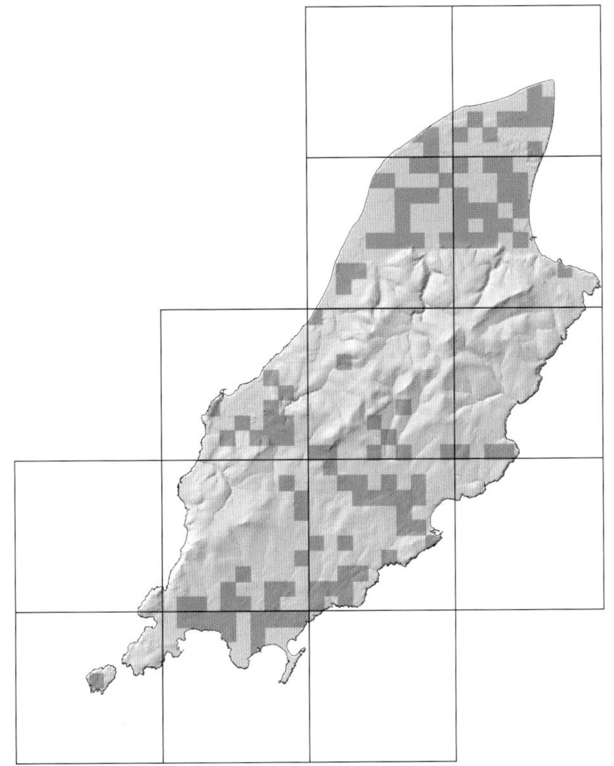
Winter presence

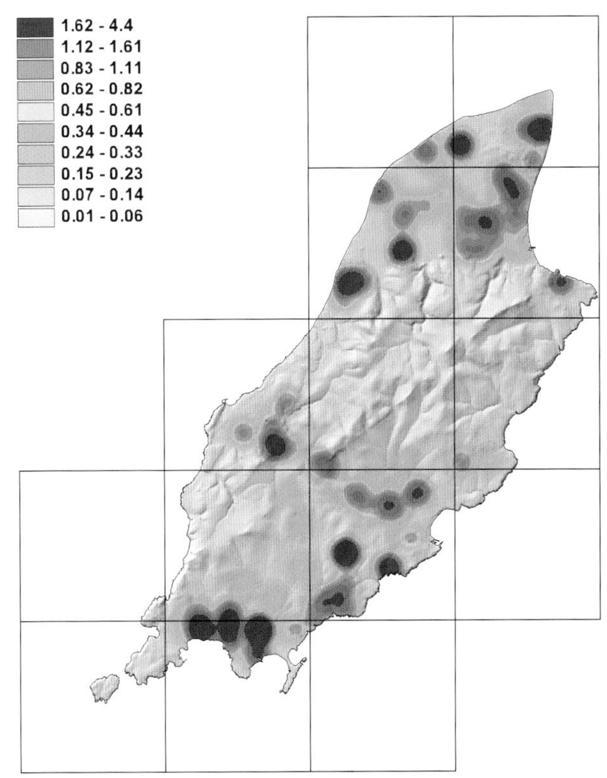

Winter abundance

Individual Sponsors – Ms. G Cowley, D E Salmon

Coot (Common Coot)
Fulica atra

The Coot is a solidly built dark grey water bird, distinguished by a white bill, surmounted by a similarly coloured shield. It dives with a little leap and reappears suddenly on the surface, cork-like. It takes off for flight by pattering along the surface. The downy young is black with red and blue on the head and a yellowish collar, which distinguishes it from the very similar Moorhen.

The Coot breeds on lakes and slow-moving rivers. It will utilize larger areas of stillwater than the Moorhen, although on the Isle of Man the two species often share small dubs and dams. Away from the Island, winter flocks gather on reservoirs, and in northern harbours and sheltered estuaries and bays. It has a plant-dominated omnivorous diet, feeding mostly on shoots and seeds of aquatic vegetation, but also on insects and molluscs. Nesting starts in April, but many such nests being pitifully exposed on barely emergent vegetation are heavily predated, especially by Hooded Crows. However, as the spring advances they become well concealed among such marginal plants as bog-bean and water horsetail.

The distribution of the Coot across Europe is very similar to that of the Moorhen, and extends across Asia rather more continuously as far as Sakhalin. It is present in Australasia, but absent from the New World and most of Africa. Although breeding in every European country except Iceland, distribution is very patchy around the Mediterranean countries and its range does not extend beyond 66°N. Representation is strongest from Holland eastward to Lithuania and south to Hungary (EBA). Less widespread than the Moorhen in the British Isles, the distribution quite nearly resembles that of its smaller relative. In Ireland a contraction in range has left a relatively poorly populated band between Sligo and Wexford (1988–91 Atlas).

On the Isle of Man, the twentieth century witnessed a gradual extension of the Coot's range over a number of small northern dubs, and to the Foxdale dams and Kerrowdhoo Reservoir. Apart from the gravel pits at the Point of Ayre, where there is a growing population, further expansion has taken place mostly in the south, where at least eight new sites have been colonised in the last twenty years. All these new sites are recently created dams such as those at Shenvalla (Patrick), Glen Vine and Port e Chee. Even allowing for the less thorough surveying of C&J, who suggested a population of just 15 breeding pairs, there seems little doubt that numbers have increased substantially. This is in contrast to the 1988–91 Atlas which showed a 5.1% diminution in the British population and a huge 37.2% decline in Ireland.

Outside the breeding season, by far the greatest congregation is at the Point of Ayre Gravel Pits. Here numbers have increased steadily year by year during the present survey, two peaks being identifiable – one in late summer and the other around midwinter. The surge in numbers occurring between July and September (97 birds in August 2002) is well in excess of the breeding population and is likely to be a moult assembly, such as is seen in some British fresh waters (BWP), while the December peak must include winter visitors from elsewhere. At the other main site, the Eairy Dam, numbers consistently peak in winter alone. During very cold weather one or two birds are occasionally seen on the sea, although this was not recorded in the survey period. The MBA survey showed very little difference in the occupation of water bodies in summer and winter.

1977–81

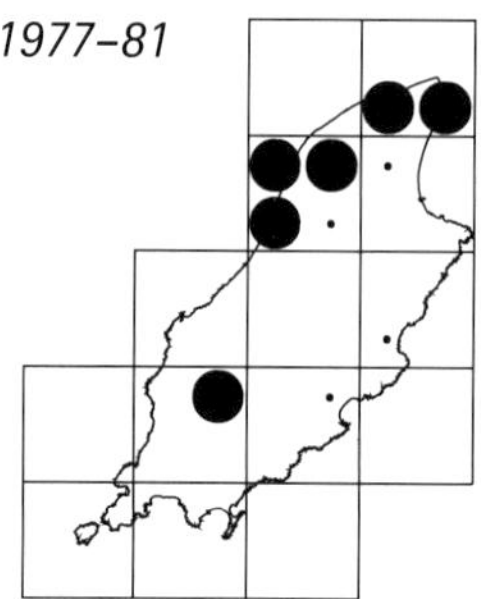

1998–2002

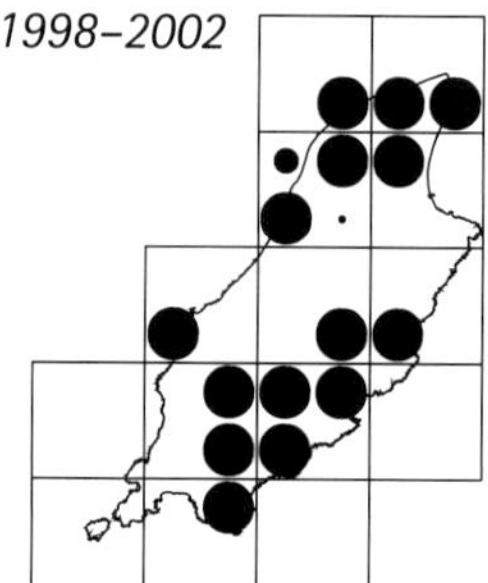

Breeding	Grid squares:	Isle of Man 42 (6%) Britain 1,603 Ireland 354 Total 1,957 (51%)
	Population:	Isle of Man 49–51 (adults) Britain 46,000 Ireland 8,600 (2% of European)
Wintering	Grid squares:	Isle of Man 33 (5%) Britain and Ireland 2,063 (53%)
	Population:	Isle of Man 200 Britain and Ireland 200,000

Jan	Feb	Mar	Apr	May	Jun	Jul	Aug	Sep	Oct	Nov	Dec

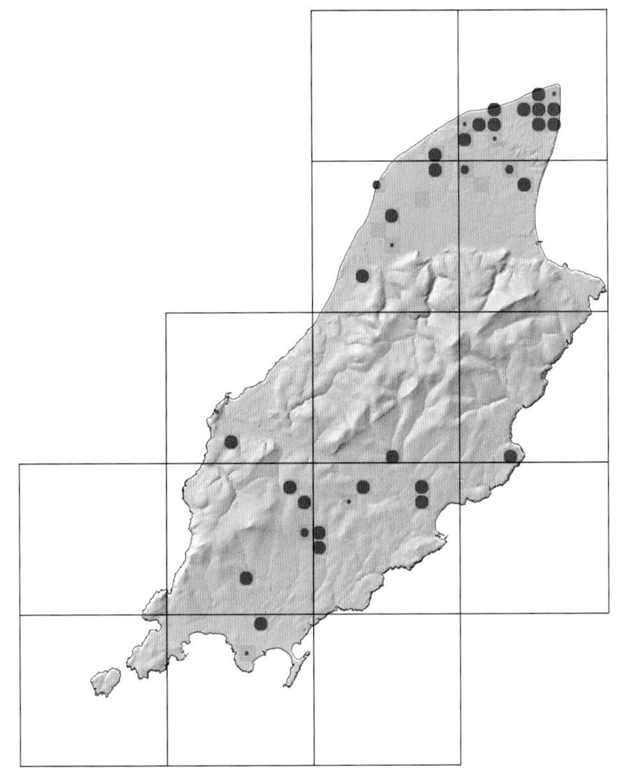

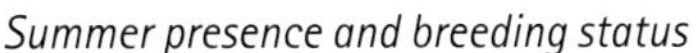

Summer presence and breeding status

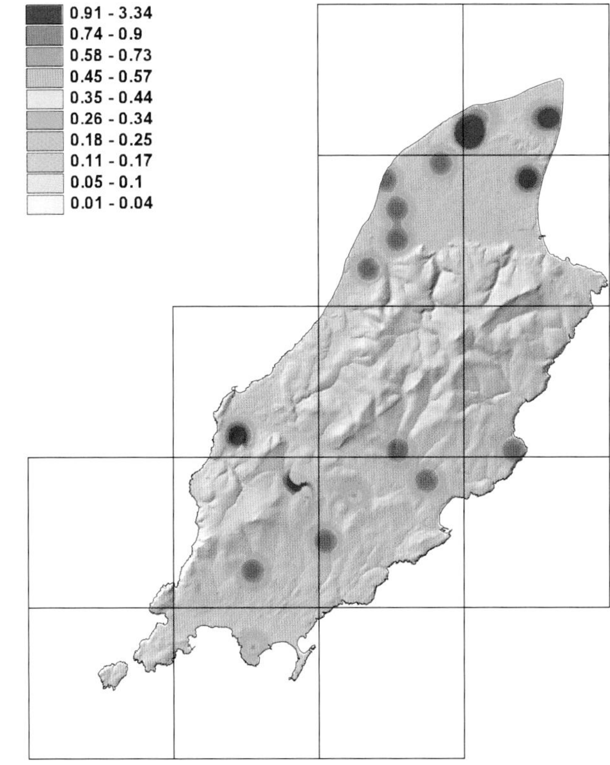

Breeding abundance

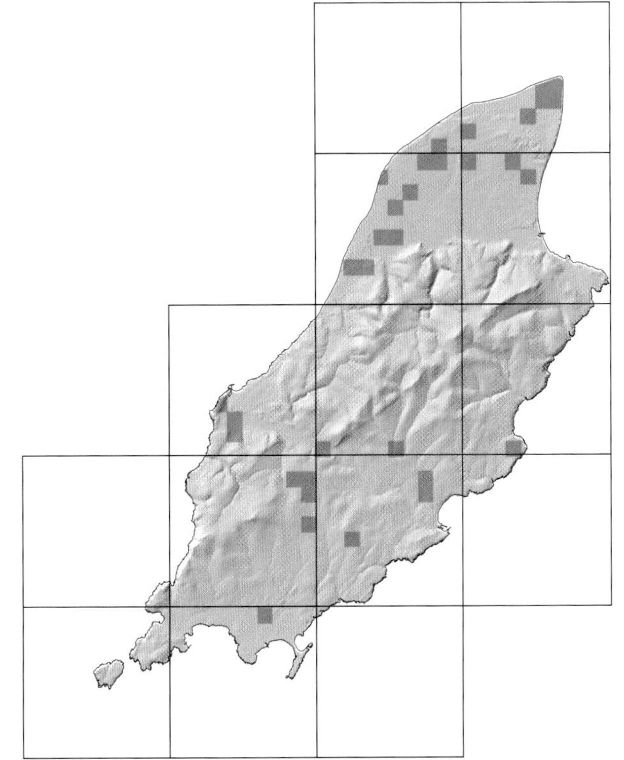

Winter presence

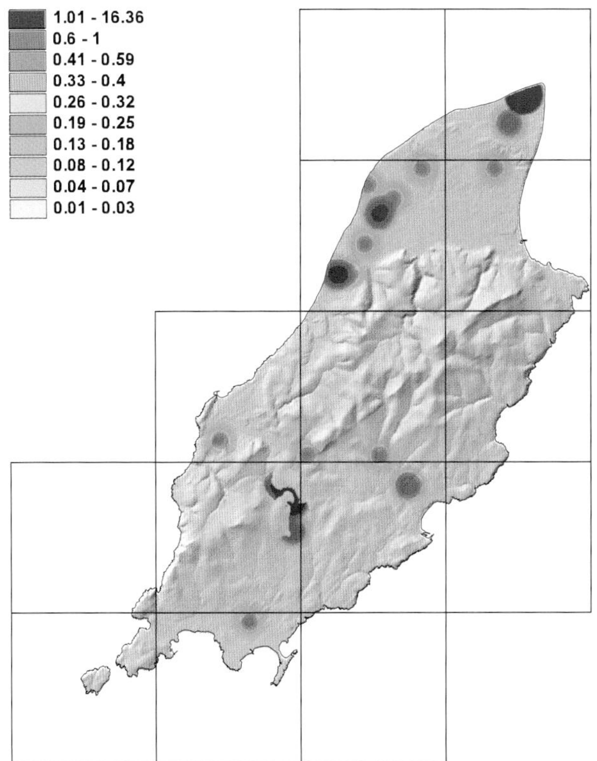

Winter abundance

Individual Sponsors – Mr. P & Mrs. A Fletcher, Miss J Maginn

Oystercatcher (Eurasian Oystercatcher) *Haematopus ostralegus*

Manx: *Garee breck* = Pied Creature (north). *Bridgeen* (south)

The extrovert of the shore, the distinctive Oystercatcher is conspicuous in both appearance and behaviour and literally cries out for attention with its shrill piping calls. The pied plumage and long orange bill catch the eye, and this numerous and widespread species is perhaps the most familiar wader in the Isle of Man. Oystercatchers are unusual among waders in that they generally lay clutches of three eggs rather than four, and they actually feed their young rather than leaving the chicks to provide their own meals.

Oystercatchers may be found on almost any kind of shore, whether rocky, sandy or muddy, although their most typical feeding grounds consist of sandy beaches. They are fond of coastal grassland, such as fields, parks and golf courses, and outside the Isle of Man they are also found far inland, frequenting river valleys, lakesides, marshy areas and even farmland. They nest on shingle ridges, among rocks and on various types of open land, including fields and the margins of water bodies. The staple food of the Oystercatcher consists of bivalve molluscs, such as cockles and mussels, and its powerful bill is able to break into the shells of these animals. Away from the shore, earthworms are the main attraction.

Oystercatchers breed from Iceland and the British Isles discontinuously across Eurasia, favouring coasts in most of western Europe (where they are sparse breeders south of the Netherlands), but nesting widely inland further east. In Britain and Ireland they breed round most of the coasts but also far from the sea in Scotland, northern England and to some extent elsewhere. The map of Manx breeding distribution shows almost complete occupation of the coast, plus considerable inland nesting on the northern plain. The only significant gaps along the coastline coincide with high cliffs, notably in the south-west, and the major bays (as at Douglas and Ramsey), where disturbance may be a limiting factor even for the aggressive Oystercatcher. The uplands are avoided completely, even the river courses and reservoir margins, probably because of a relative shortage of food. The abundance map reveals the densest populations along the shingle shores and on the coastal heaths of the far north, with concentrations also on the coast north of Kirk Michael and in the area south of Maughold Head, while inland breeding roughly marks out the drainage basin of the Killane River. In the south the most favoured localities lie along the coast from Santon Head to Langness, in the Scarlett area, and on the Calf of Man.

Although British and Irish populations are partly resident, most European Oystercatchers move south for the winter, and the British Isles receive many birds from further north, probably mainly Scottish and Icelandic breeders (WA). Some of these incomers undoubtedly reach the Isle of Man, either staying for the winter or moving on, and a proportion of Manx nesters may well leave the Island to winter elsewhere. Immigration (and presumably passage) reaches a peak in early autumn, with a subsequent fall in numbers in October and November indicating departures from the Island, and a second peak in midwinter suggesting further arrivals (C&J).

The winter map largely mirrors the summer distribution around the coast, with evidence of greater use of the larger bays, perhaps because outside the breeding season disturbance is less of a problem. The most obvious difference between the summer and winter maps is the desertion of the inland nesting areas of the northern plain after the breeding season, resembling the autumnal coastward movement of inland breeders in Britain. The map of winter abundance indicates striking concentrations at the northern and southern ends of the Island, with relatively few birds frequenting the areas in between. During winter an estimated 1,500 birds are present on the Island, though numbers are variable between winters. Spring movements may begin as early as January, and are completed by the end of April, leaving not only Manx nesters but fair numbers of non-breeders (C&J), presumably immature birds.

Cullen and Jennings suggest a breeding population of 350 to 400 pairs of Oystercatchers on the Island, a figure comparable with the 337 to 372 pairs estimated from the MBA surveys. An extension of the breeding range in the Isle of Man appears to have taken place during at least the early part of the twentieth century, with colonisation of Langness, for example, postdating the publication of Ralfe's book in 1905 (C&J). This development reflects the spread in Britain (but not in Ireland) that began during the late nineteenth century (1968–72 and 1988–91 Atlases), although Manx Oystercatchers seem to have been less willing to expand their range inland than their British counterparts, resembling the Irish birds in this respect.

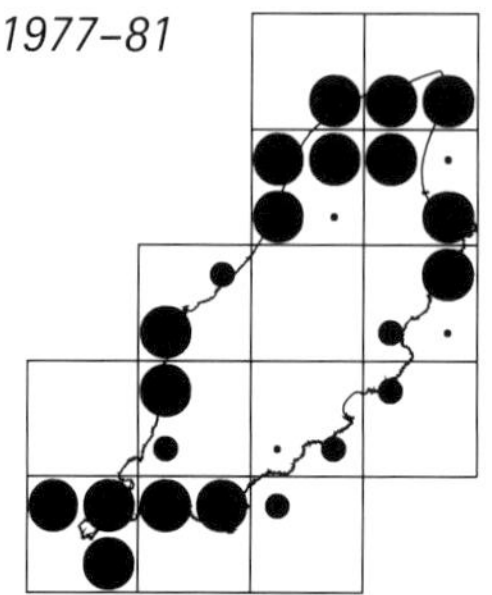

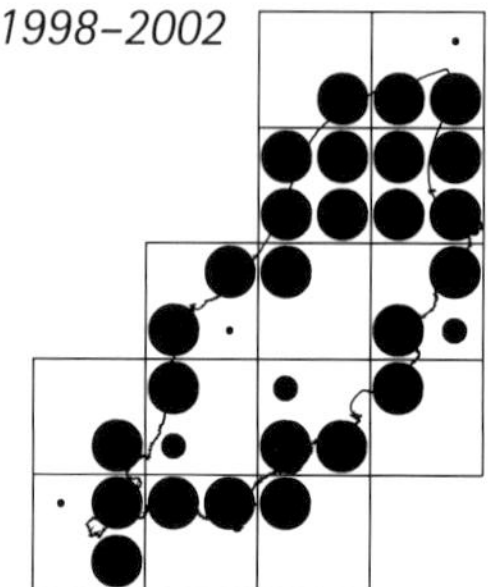

Breeding	Grid squares:	Isle of Man 191 (29%) Britain 1,702 Ireland 263 Total 1,965 (51%)
	Population:	Isle of Man 337–372 (adults) Britain 38,000 Ireland 3,500 (18% of European)
Wintering	Grid squares:	Isle of Man 116 (17%) Britain and Ireland 1,535 (40%)
	Population:	Isle of Man 1,500 Britain and Ireland 300,000

Jan Feb Mar Apr May Jun Jul Aug Sep Oct Nov Dec

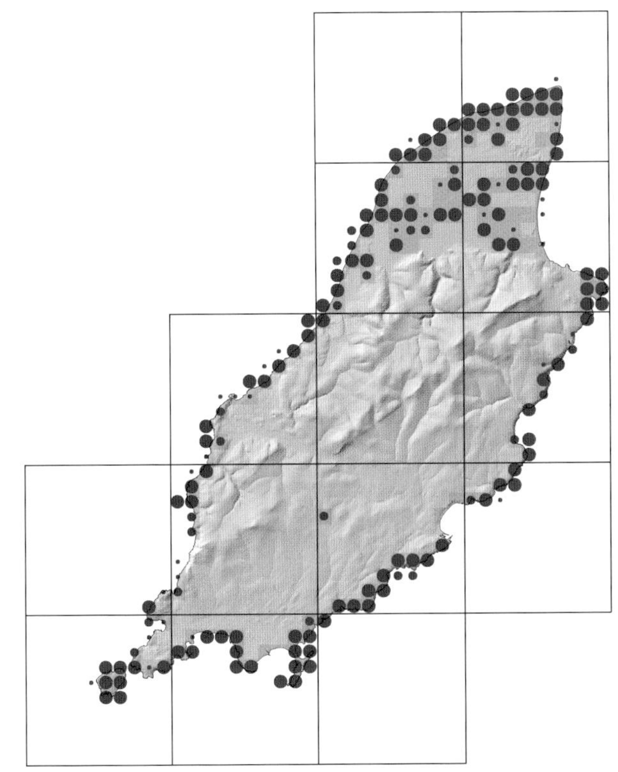

Summer presence and breeding status

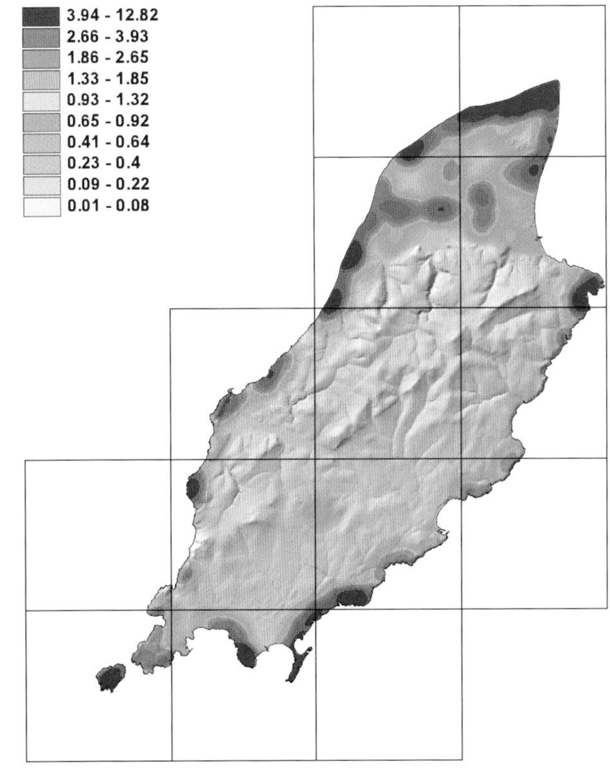

Breeding abundance

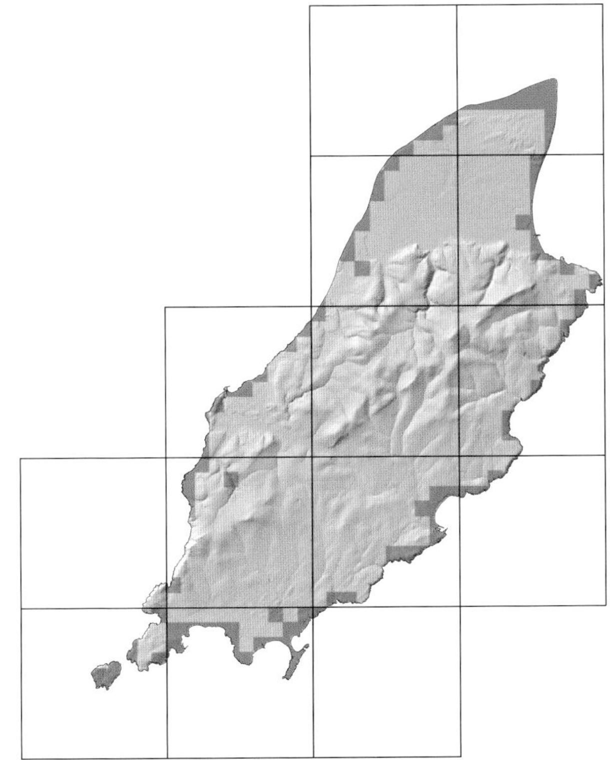

Winter presence

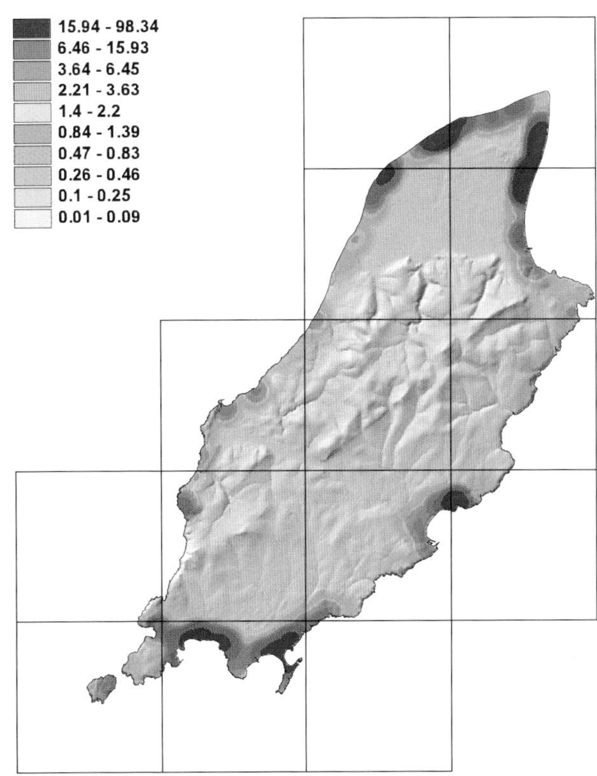

Winter abundance

Individual Sponsors – Mrs. J M Bowen, Mr. R Harper, Mrs. R Penn, in memory of Harry & Clare Sandiford, Mr. K Scott, the late Mr. T Whipp, Mrs. M Whipp

Ringed Plover
Charadrius hiaticula

Manx: *Feddag Ainnit*

The diminutive Ringed Plover shows up quite well on a sandy beach. It melts into the background, however, if it moves on to a shingle ridge, when the bold black and white bands on its head and breast serve to break up its outline among the pebbles and its generally brown and white plumage merges with the overall colour of the shore. Its eggs and chicks are similarly camouflaged, although the bird tends to give away its breeding area with its territorial song-flight. Despite a difference in feeding technique, Ringed Plovers often associate with Dunlins and other small waders in their busy search for food.

Ringed Plovers are birds of the shore but also occur far inland in some parts of their range. On the coast they usually occur on sand or shingle beaches, but they may also be found on patches of sand in otherwise rocky situations, and sometimes visit coastal grasslands or heaths and moors near the sea. Inland they frequent shallow rivers, stretches of gravel and sand, lakesides, tundra and similar terrain.

In the Isle of Man, however, Ringed Plovers are almost entirely birds of the coast, hardly penetrating inland at any time of year. They nest mainly on shingle but also on open ground among rocks and on short turf or in other low vegetation. The Ringed Plover feeds chiefly on small marine worms, crustaceans and molluscs, plus other invertebrates such as insects and spiders, using the typical plover foraging routine of a short run, a pause to eye up potential prey, and then a quick strike.

The breeding range of the Ringed Plover extends from Baffin Island and Greenland right across Eurasia to its eastern extremity, mainly along the Arctic fringes but penetrating south in western Europe as far as northern France. In Britain and Ireland they nest around most of the coastline, their strength lying mainly in the Scottish islands and on the shores of eastern England, with many birds breeding inland in northern and eastern Britain. The Manx distribution map shows breeding largely confined to the coasts of the northern plain and the bays of the south-east, with the strip from Ballaugh to the shore north of Ramsey almost continuously occupied. On the abundance map the greatest densities are apparent along the Ayres coast from the Point of Ayre to Blue Point, the Ballaugh shore, and the peninsula of Langness, with a few pairs also in the area of Strandhall and Poyllvaaish on the east side of Carrick Bay.

Most European Ringed Plovers leave their breeding areas in the autumn, many birds wintering in southern Europe and in Africa. British and Irish breeders are largely non-migratory, although they may move around within the British Isles, which also receive considerable numbers of visiting birds from the Baltic area and other parts of the continent (WA). In the Isle of Man movement first becomes obvious during August, when passage birds stop off on the Island on their way south, and by November the birds have settled into their wintering sites (C&J).

The map of winter distribution shows a rather sparse scatter around the Manx coast, with the beaches of the far north and the southern bays, as on the summer map, providing the main interest, along with the northern part of Douglas Bay and the district around Peel. The winter abundance map partly supports the statement by Cullen and Jennings that the windswept beaches of the Ayres are largely abandoned at this season, but Ringed Plovers clearly occur on the shores around Blue Point and Ballaugh Cronk. A clear concentration marks out the more sheltered eastern shore between Shellag Point and Ramsey, but the bulk of the winter population favours the south coast, especially the sandy beaches and low rocks at Port St Mary, Sandwick and Derbyhaven. Spring departure and passage take place mainly in April and May, though Manx breeders may return to their nesting grounds as early as February.

Cullen and Jennings note an apparent slight increase during the twentieth century, and an estimate of breeding numbers in the Isle of Man provided by Prater (1989) suggests about 70 pairs in 1984, rather lower than the MBA figure of 89 to 95 pairs. Perhaps fewer than 500 birds are present on the Island in winter, with up to 30 or 40 at each of Ramsey and Douglas Bays, Langness/Derbyhaven, and the shore around Strandhall.

1977–81

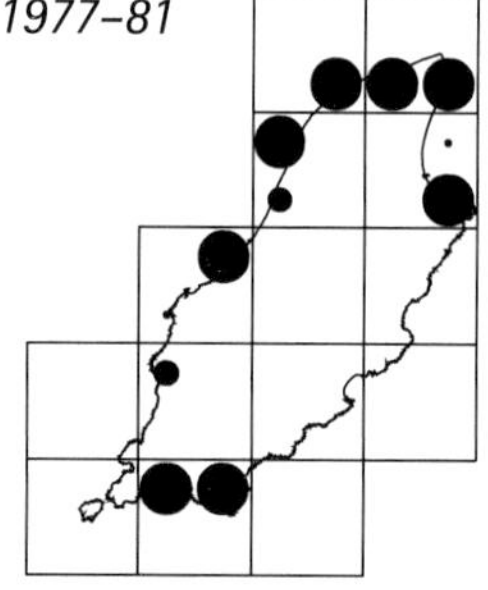

1998–2002

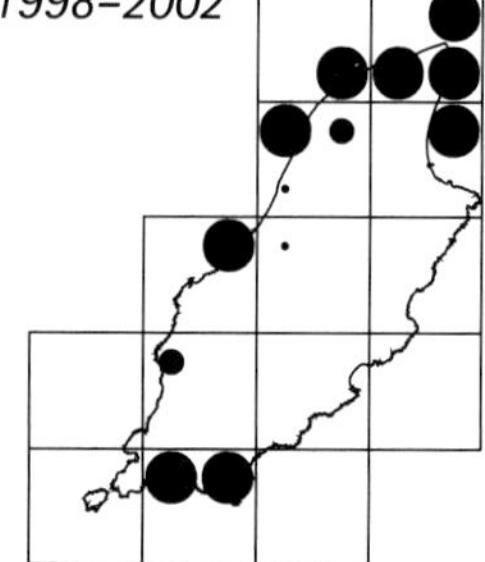

Breeding	Grid squares:	Isle of Man 52 (8%) Britain 1,025 Ireland 244 Total 1,269 (33%)
	Population:	Isle of Man 89-95 Britain 8,500 Ireland 1,250 (10% of European)
Wintering	Grid squares:	Isle of Man 44 (7%) Britain and Ireland 1,031 (27%)
	Population:	Isle of Man <500 Britain and Ireland 35,000

Jan Feb Mar Apr May Jun Jul Aug Sep Oct Nov Dec

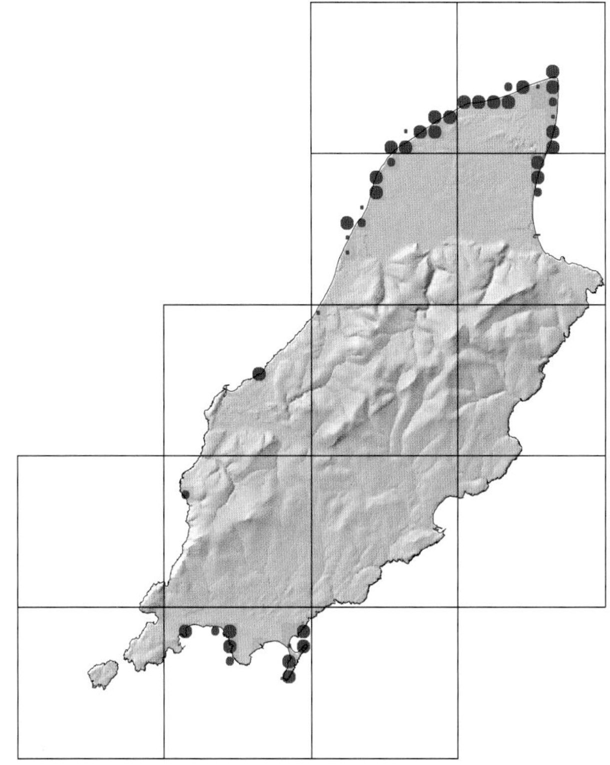

Summer presence and breeding status

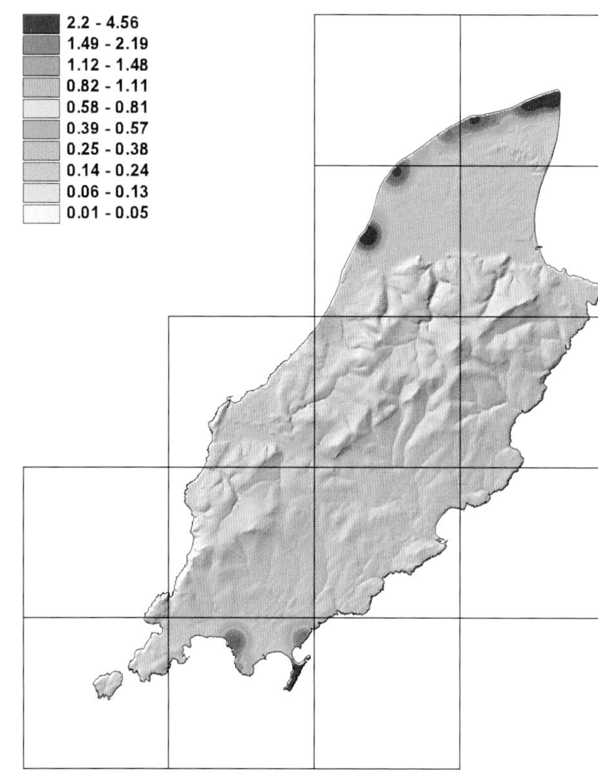

Breeding abundance

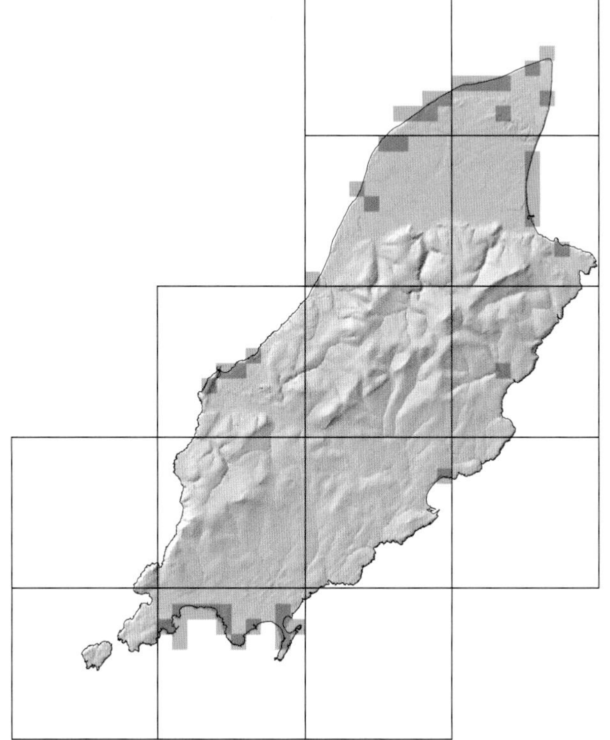

Winter presence

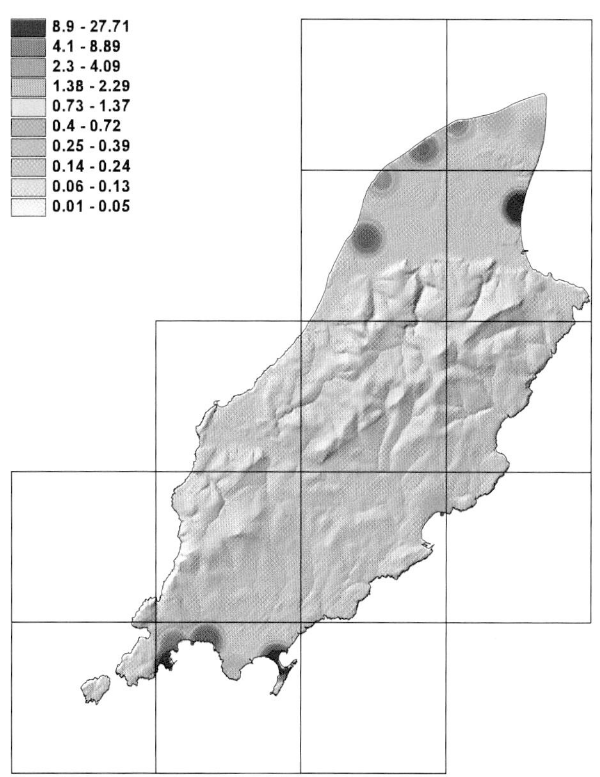

Winter abundance

Golden Plover (European Golden Plover)
Pluvialis apricaria

Manx: *Ushag Reeast* = Bird of the Waste. *Fedjag Reeast* = Whistler of the Waste

There are few more striking waders than the Golden Plover in its breeding plumage of gold-spangled upperparts and black underparts separated by a prominent white band. In the Isle of Man, however, we are more familiar with the vaguely golden-brown upperside and breast and whitish belly of the bird's more modest winter dress. A substantial flock of 'goldies' taking to the air and circling in rapid flight over the shore is always a thrilling sight, while observing the same individuals standing quietly on the low rocks or shingle at high tide is a pleasant and relaxing pastime, and equally the far-carrying whistling call of the Golden Plover stirs the imagination of the birdwatcher.

Golden Plovers are birds of the uplands and the Arctic tundra during the breeding season, but switch to low ground for the winter. They frequent both coasts and inland areas, and may be found roosting in a variety of places, including relatively rocky shores, sand and shingle beaches and agricultural land. They feed to some extent in the intertidal zone, although not in sandy or muddy spots, and favour grass fields with a short sward and similar places such as the airfields at Jurby and Ronaldsway (C&J). They eat a varied selection of invertebrates, but concentrate on terrestrial prey such as earthworms and insects rather than aquatic animals like crustaceans or molluscs, in line with their usual choice of habitats.

The Golden Plover breeds from east Greenland through the low Arctic zone of Europe into western Asia, with a marked southerly extension of its range as far as the Baltic region and the British Isles. Its distribution within Britain is based on Scotland and northern England, matching almost exactly the occurrence of moorland and mountains, and in Ireland virtually all Golden Plovers nest in the uplands near the north-western coasts. The moors of the Isle of Man would appear to be suitable for this species, and Cullen and Jennings suggest that Golden Plovers may have bred on the Island in the past, noting the existence of place-names including the word 'fedjag' ('plover' in Manx). In recent times, however, the only confirmed breeding records have come from Colden in July 1973 (C&J), and from the moors south of Sulby Reservoir, during an Atlas survey in late June 1999 (Bishop and Giovannini 2000). The summer map also shows the presence of birds on the north-west coast and at scattered points in the uplands, but these records will presumably refer to late migrants.

All European Golden Plovers are migratory except for those breeding in Britain and Ireland, most of which probably do not travel overseas. The southerly autumn movement within Europe brings many northern 'goldies' to the British Isles, some moving on as far as the Mediterranean. Those passing through or wintering in the Isle of Man may consist mainly of birds from northern Britain and Iceland, and (as with Lapwings) numbers may be higher during freezing weather in Britain, when these surface-feeding waders are vulnerable to starvation and move to the milder south and west. The first arrivals on the Island may take place as early as July, but the main passage is evident from late September and through October. Numbers build to a peak, normally in January, after which they gradually decrease. The maps of winter distribution and abundance emphasise the importance of the shores and their hinterlands in the far north and to a lesser extent those of the south-east. Although spring migration probably takes place chiefly during April, Golden Plovers may begin to move in February, and these early passage birds may explain the upland records which are apparent on the winter maps.

During January flocks of the highly gregarious Golden Plover in the Isle of Man may reach four figures in favoured localities such as the Jurby and Ballaugh areas and at Ronaldsway, but maxima of 600 to 800 are more usual and most flocks are much smaller. Cullen and Jennings suggest a midwinter total of about 3,550 birds, based on counts made in early January 1977, though the current research suggests a somewhat smaller figure ranging from 500 to 2,000, depending upon the weather in a given winter. Changes in the uplands appear to have caused continuing declines among most British and Irish breeding populations during the twentieth century, but whether these decreases will affect numbers of Golden Plovers wintering on the Island is unclear.

Breeding	Grid squares:	Isle of Man 34 (5%) Britain 784 Ireland 57 Total 841 (22%)
	Population:	Isle of Man 1 Britain 22,600 Ireland 400 (4% of European)
Wintering	Grid squares:	Isle of Man 66 (10%) Britain and Ireland 1,971 (51%)
	Population:	Isle of Man 500-2,000 Britain and Ireland 700,000

Jan	Feb	Mar	Apr	May	Jun	Jul	Aug	Sep	Oct	Nov	Dec

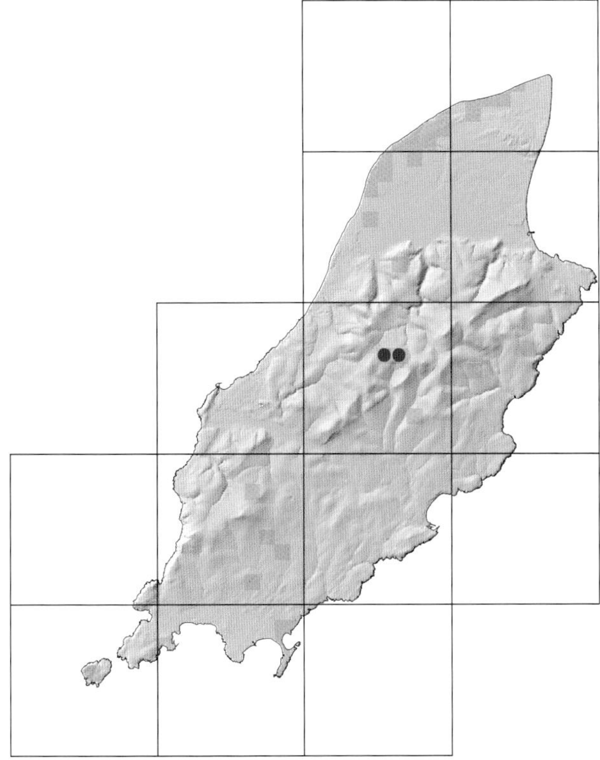

Summer presence and breeding status

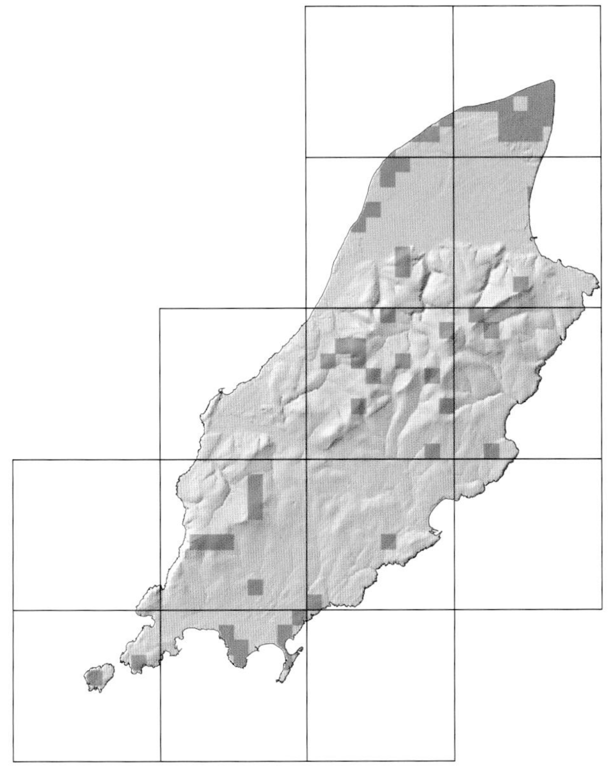

Winter presence

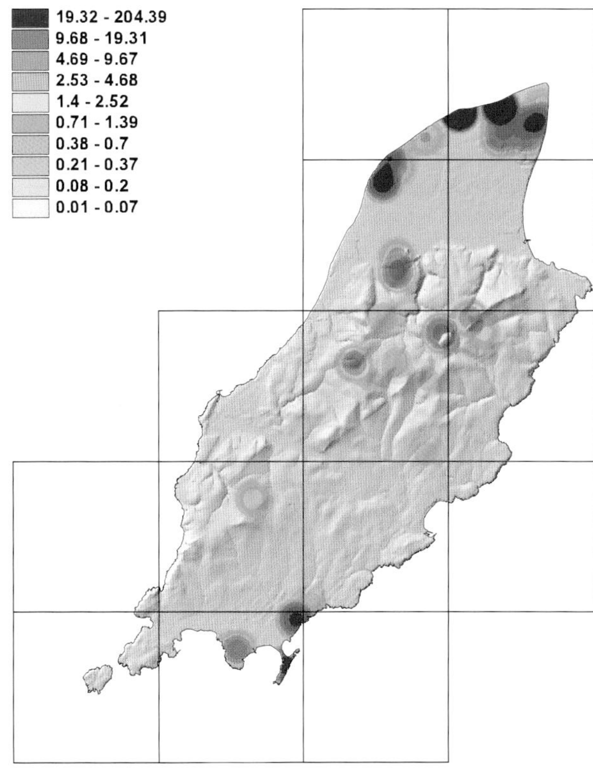

Winter abundance

Grey Plover
Pluvialis squatarola

A relatively large wader, the substantially built Grey Plover seems to spend a good deal of its time doing nothing in particular, standing on the shore or walking slowly around. It moves quickly enough, however, when it spots a prey animal, and its flight is rapid and strong. Somewhat solitary and rather detached, appearing longer-legged and heavier-billed than its near relative the more colourful Golden Plover, this not very common winter visitor is inconspicuous in its brownish-grey non-breeding plumage. After the spring moult, in contrast, Grey Plovers turn into rather smart black and white birds as they head off north for their nesting grounds on the Asiatic tundra.

During the winter the Grey Plover is a true bird of the shore, not normally occurring inland at all. It prefers wide sandy beaches, and it is happy enough with muddy stretches but not fond of shingle. In the Isle of Man it seems partial to intertidal areas where sand gives way to low rocks, and may also be seen foraging among the seaweed-covered rocks, as on the eastern side of Derbyhaven towards Fort Island. Unlike many waders, Grey Plovers feed relatively little along the tideline, and they are usually seen further up the shore, though still below the high-water mark. Their food outside the breeding season consists mainly of marine worms, small molluscs and crustaceans, caught in the classic plover manner of pause, dash and peck.

Grey Plovers breed right round the North Polar Basin except in Greenland, Iceland and Scandinavia, their only European population inhabiting the Russian Arctic in the far north-east corner of the continent. During winter they all move to warmer climes and become real world travellers, some birds reaching the southernmost extremities of South America, Africa and Australia, although many from the western Siberian population (from which our birds are drawn) fly no further than the British Isles, south-west Europe and West Africa. In Britain and Ireland large numbers are seen on passage, and wintering birds are well scattered round the coasts except in most of Scotland and the northern parts of Ireland. MBA data support the view of Cullen & Jennings that the first Grey Plovers of the autumn normally appear in the Isle of Man around the middle of September, reaching a peak during October. Records during this period will, no doubt, relate to birds passing through the Island as well as the arrival of winter residents. Numbers are variable through the winter, but Grey Plovers can usually be found in their favoured localities on the coast at any time until March, although their numbers never amount to more than a few birds in one particular spot.

The map showing winter distribution indicates the dearth of Grey Plovers along the major part of the Manx coast, explicable perhaps in the light of their preference for the limited number of relatively extensive beaches. Accordingly, the long shores of the far northern coast have their regular records, but Grey Plovers have their stronghold in the southern bays. Derbyhaven and the east side of Castletown Bay at Sandwick are pre-eminent sites for this species, plus odd birds on the beach at Strandhall and elsewhere in the eastern part of Carrick Bay. Except on large estuaries (notably the Wash) during passage periods, the Grey Plover is typically found singly or in small groups, and most sightings on the Island involve no more than three or four birds together, with the largest gathering recorded by the MBA containing ten individuals. Examination of the Atlas data suggests that the total number of Grey Plovers in the Isle of Man at any one time is unlikely to exceed 20 birds. Spring departure from the Island is virtually complete by the end of April, with a few birds lingering or passing in May.

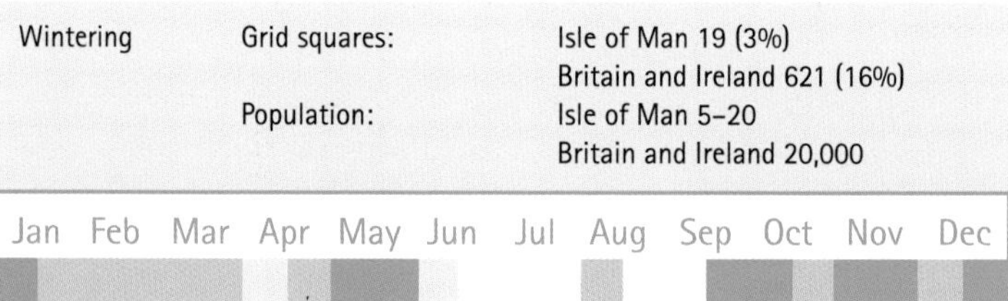

Wintering	Grid squares:	Isle of Man 19 (3%)
		Britain and Ireland 621 (16%)
	Population:	Isle of Man 5–20
		Britain and Ireland 20,000

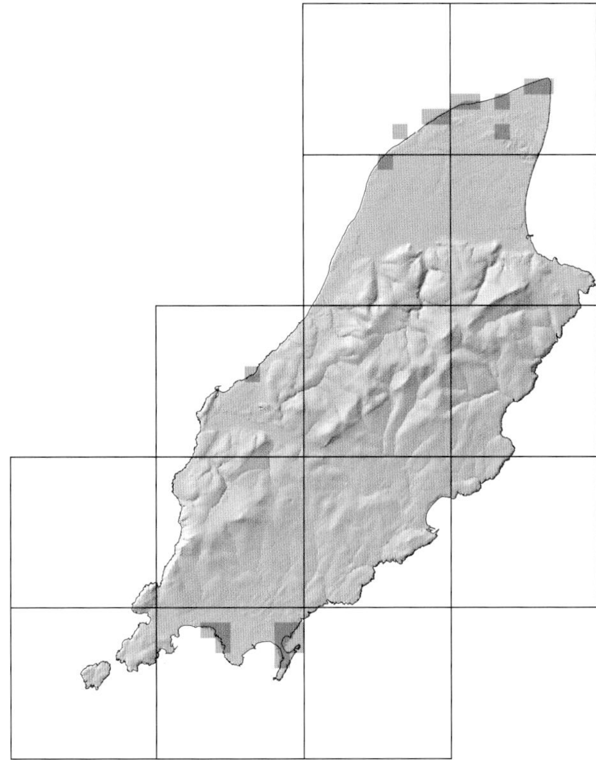

Winter presence

Lapwing (Northern Lapwing)
Vanellus vanellus

Manx: *Earkan*

The broad-winged and wispy-crested Lapwing is the most numerous and widespread of British breeding waders, and also the most familiar, mainly because of its unwaderlike habits as a species of farmland and other relatively dry countryside away from the shore. The attractive 'Peewit' is also a popular bird, whether scattered through the sky in ragged flocks, dotted across a field of grass or ploughed earth, or hurling itself around above its nesting territory while pouring out its rollicking song. In the past the Lapwing was liked for a different reason, its eggs being much esteemed for the table.

Lapwings are found in a variety of open habitats, both natural and man-made, with bare ground or short vegetation. In the Isle of Man damp fields of permanent pasture, often with rushy areas, are favoured for nesting, notably on the northern plain and on the lower slopes of the hills. Other pairs choose grassy patches within the maritime heaths of the Ayres (C&J), or the surroundings of the Point of Ayre Gravel Pits. Outside the breeding season Lapwings may be found mainly on pasture and arable fields and in comparable places such as the airfields at Jurby and Ronaldsway, also sometimes on the shore, where they roost and occasionally feed with other waders. The diet of Lapwings varies with habitat, ranging from earthworms and molluscs to insects and even small fish.

The map of Manx breeding distribution shows the predominance of the north of the Island, with few birds nesting elsewhere. The northern plain holds most of the population, with concentrations on the Ayres and in the fields east of Jurby and south of Andreas highlighted by the abundance map. The northern edge of the central Manx hills, south and south-east of Sulby, also has its breeding Lapwings, an interesting location as the area contains the place-name Park ne Earkan, incorporating the Manx word for Lapwing (C&J). A few other sites in the uplands are occupied, and in the far south Lapwings nest on the marsh at Langness and on the fields south of Cregneash.

The change map illustrates the contraction of the breeding range of the Lapwing on the Island since the publication of Cullen and Jennings' book in 1986. Of the 24 5km squares in which these authors reported confirmed breeding, the MBA could prove breeding in only eleven, the main losses affecting the central and southern hills. In the British Isles generally Lapwings have been decreasing since at least the late nineteenth century (Parslow 1973), although the 1968–72 Atlas maintains that only the southern part of Britain was affected, and that the species was actually increasing in the north. The maps in the 1988–91 Atlas show the continuing decline to be concentrated in western Britain and in Ireland. Although the latter point may be relevant to the situation in the Isle of Man, we have no means of knowing whether Manx Lapwings have been influenced by the causes suggested for the British and Irish declines. Factors implicated include the ploughing up of old pastures, switching from spring to autumn sowing of cereals and replacement of mixed farming by specialisations.

Almost all European Lapwings breeding north and east of the British Isles and the Netherlands migrate south or west in autumn, many travelling as far as the Mediterranean region. Some birds reach the Isle of Man as early as July, although most arrive in September or later. The winter flocks on the Island form a small part of the huge numbers spending the cold season in Britain and Ireland, and at any time more birds may move to or through the Isle of Man in response to freezing weather further east. The winter distribution and abundance maps show Lapwings well spread through the Manx lowlands, especially on the northern plain and in the far south, with the country from Point of Ayre to Glascoe, the Jurby area and the damp ground south of Ballabeg pre-eminent. Local birds may be back on their breeding territories by February, but March is the main month for spring passage.

A Manx breeding population of about 100 pairs of Lapwings is estimated from the MBA counts, with no comparable figures available from the past. This highly gregarious species occurred on the Island in flocks of up to 1,000 during the winter survey period. However, such flocks were rare and were probably linked to cold weather movements. In general flock sizes were smaller, often less than 100 strong, suggesting a decline in numbers compared to C&J. Perhaps milder winters further east have reduced the incentive for Lapwings to travel as far west as the Isle of Man.

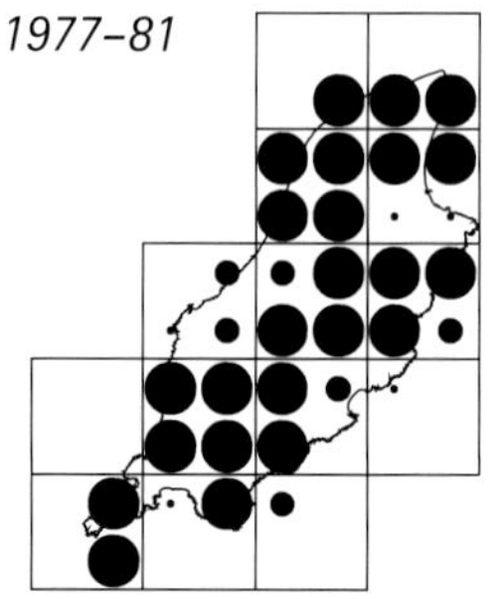

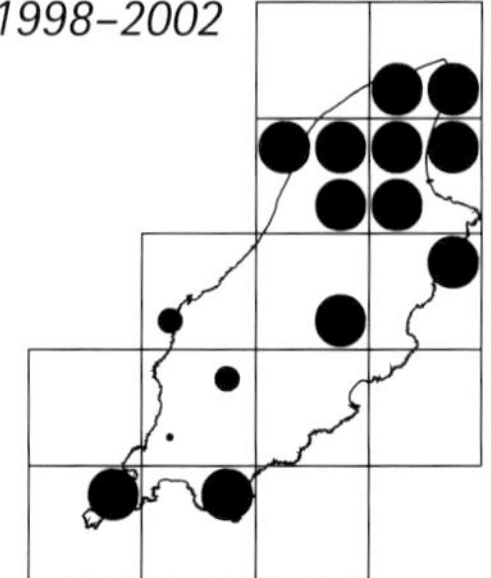

Breeding	Grid squares:	Isle of Man 62 (9%) Britain 2,340 Ireland 491 Total 2,831 (73%)
	Population:	Isle of Man 96–110 Britain 126,300 Ireland 21,500 (19% of European)
Wintering	Grid squares:	Isle of Man 94 (14%) Britain and Ireland 3,065 (79%)
	Population:	Isle of Man 500-1,500 Britain and Ireland 1 million+

Jan	Feb	Mar	Apr	May	Jun	Jul	Aug	Sep	Oct	Nov	Dec

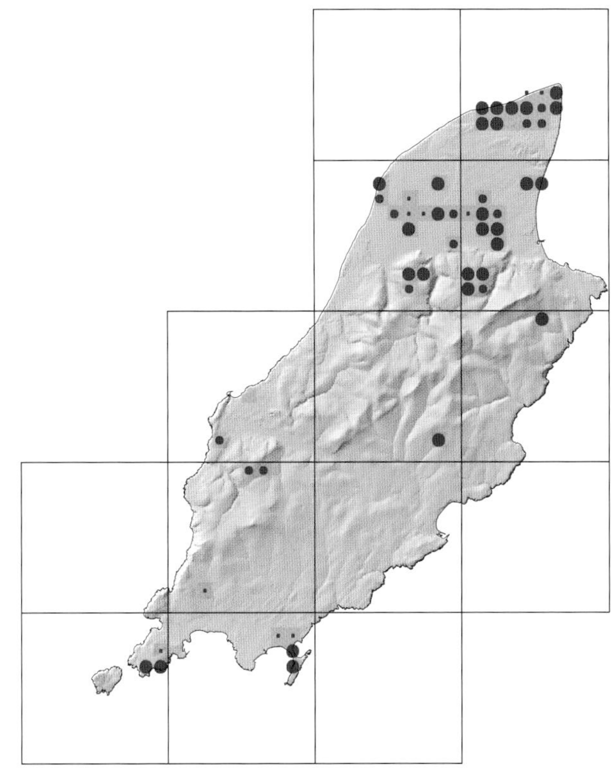

Summer presence and breeding status

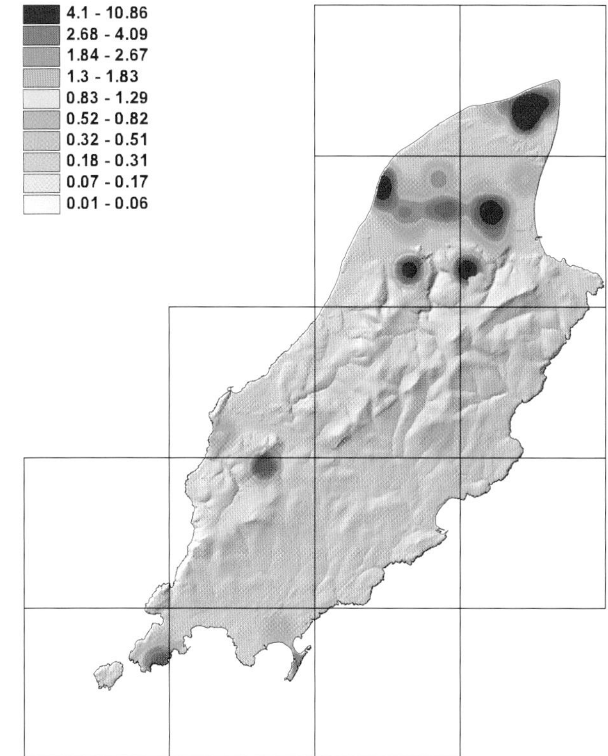

Breeding abundance

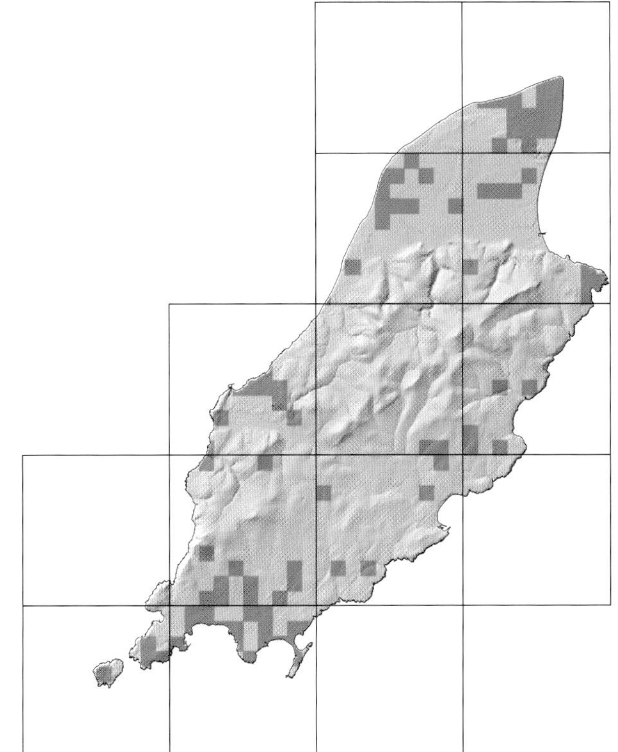

Winter presence

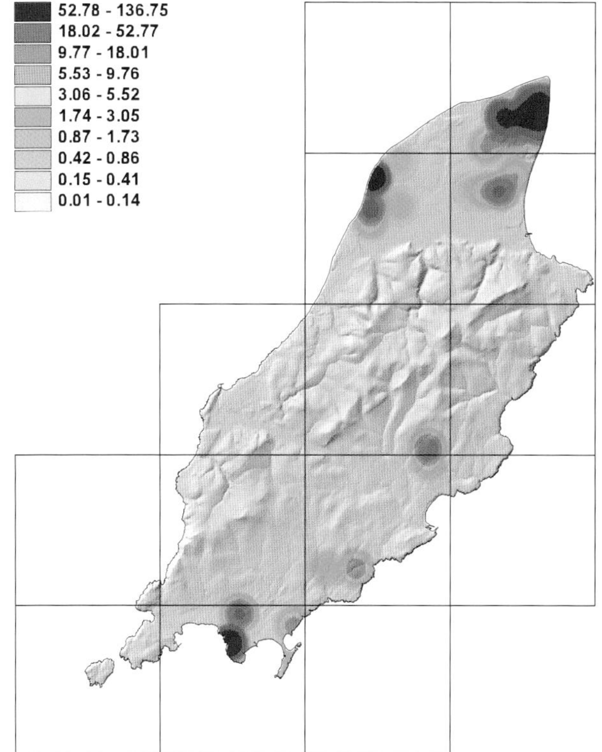

Winter abundance

Individual Sponsors – Mrs. M Anderson, Ms. L Charter, Mr. E Creer, Mrs. H Hannan MHK, Miss D Hughes, Mr. T Kennan

Knot (Red Knot)
Calidris canutus

A rather portly and somewhat short-legged wader, the unathletic-looking Knot feeds at a less frenetic pace than its smaller relatives, and seems altogether a more relaxed bird. The nondescript pale grey and white winter plumage is replaced in spring by conspicuous reddish-chestnut underparts and black and white mottling on the back and wings. Early autumn migrants retain this attractive breeding dress when they arrive in the Isle of Man. Unfortunately the scarcity of Knots visiting the Island deprives us of the thrilling sight of the dense roosting flocks and breathtaking mass aerobatics which form such spectacular features of major British estuaries.

Outside the breeding season Knots are characteristic of extensive mudflats and wide beaches of sand and shingle, although during the midwinter period they become more scattered and may then appear on smaller intertidal areas. In Britain and Ireland they are particularly drawn to the larger estuaries, whose wide expanses of muddy and sandy deposits, exposed at low tide, have no counterpart in the Isle of Man, where the birds use comparatively small stretches of beach and relatively rocky shores. During winter the Knot is almost exclusively marine wherever in the world it occurs, but when breeding it moves at least a little way inland, choosing marshy or stony ground with patchy vegetation far to the north of the Arctic Circle. The food of Knots on the shore is more specialised than that of many waders, consisting mainly of small molluscs such as the Baltic Tellin (*Macoma*), but crustaceans and marine worms are also taken, while in the nesting area the birds eat chiefly insects and plant matter.

The breeding distribution of the Knot is one of the most northerly among birds, confined to the High Arctic in Siberia, Canada and Greenland. For the winter, the population of eastern Canada and Greenland migrates to Europe, mainly the British Isles but also the Netherlands and France, while the birds from the western part of Siberia head for west Africa via continental Europe, in general missing the British Isles (WA). In Britain there are huge concentrations on the Wash, in Morecambe Bay, and on the estuaries of the Dee and the Ribble, with good numbers on some other estuaries like those of the Humber and the Thames. In Ireland the major focus is around Strangford Lough in the north-east of the island.

The Isle of Man, with its cliffs, rocks and narrow intertidal areas, is of little interest to Knots, and perhaps fewer than 100 birds visit the Island each year. The earliest autumn migrants arrive in late July, with August and September the main months for passage, which may continue into October in some years (C&J, MBA data). Even at this time of year, however, flock size seldom reaches double figures. Knots tend to move around a good deal during winter, and numbers fluctuate considerably, although most records refer to only one or two individuals together. Hardly any Knots are seen on the Island after February, except for a few passage birds, which occasionally form flocks of more than ten during May.

The Atlas maps indicate how restricted is the distribution of the Knot in the Isle of Man, although records outside the core winter period show that odd birds or small groups may occur in other places scattered around the Manx coast. The south-east corner of the Island, particularly the adjoining sites of Langness, Sandwick and Derbyhaven, provides the bulk of the reports of this species, with other birds nearby at such places as Strandhall and Kallow Point on Carrick Bay. In the north of the Island a few birds (up to 15 in recent years) may often be found on the Ayres coast, chiefly during spring and especially autumn passage. However, the beaches there do not seem particularly to suit Knots, perhaps because these birds require a more abundant food supply than such exposed shores can offer.

Wintering	Grid squares:	Isle of Man 9 (1%) Britain and Ireland 444 (12%)
	Population:	Isle of Man 0–10 Britain and Ireland 230,000

Jan	Feb	Mar	Apr	May	Jun	Jul	Aug	Sep	Oct	Nov	Dec

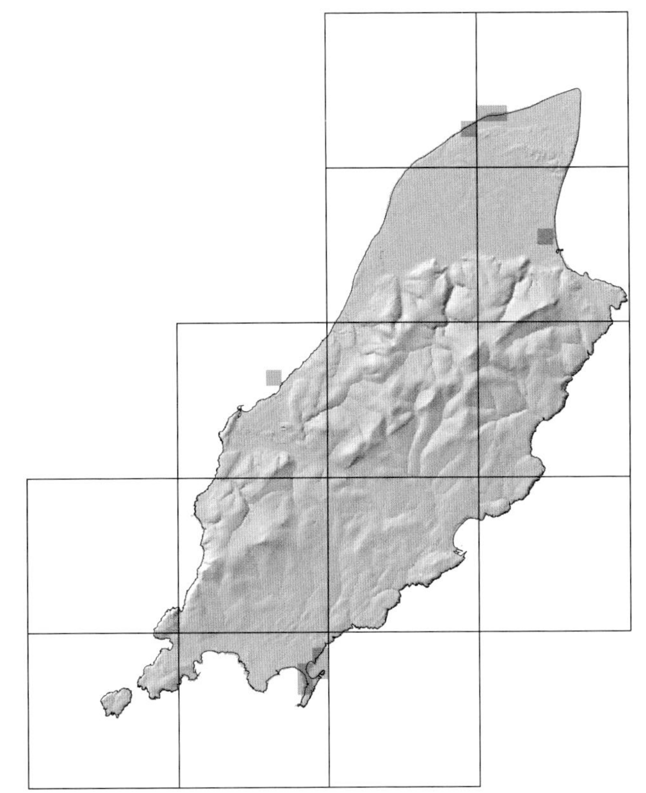

Winter presence

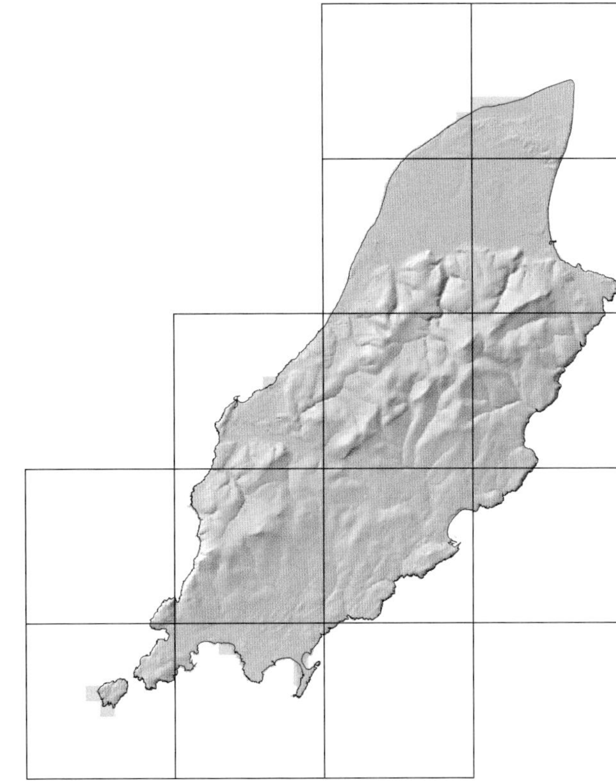

Summer presence

Sanderling
Calidris alba

The dashing Sanderling lives life at a fast pace, often running at such a speed that it seems to be travelling on wheels rather than legs as it moves across the flat, smooth shores which it prefers. In their winter plumage Sanderlings appear decidedly white, although their upperparts are actually light grey, with their black bills and legs setting them off smartly. These appealing little waders turn chestnut and black on their upperparts for the breeding season and these colours are shown by Sanderlings passing through the Isle of Man in spring and late summer. They are fascinating to watch as they rush seawards following the backwash of a wave and then rapidly reverse direction to avoid the swash of the next one, seemingly never making a misjudgement!

As its name suggests, the Sanderling is a bird of sandy beaches, particularly extensive ones in exposed situations with sizeable breakers and firm wet sand, while muddy shores and rocky coasts are normally avoided. A few birds also frequent smaller stretches of sand and lines of cast-up seaweed, pebbles and small rocks may also be present in such places. Although Sanderlings are almost entirely marine during winter, on their polar breeding grounds they may nest some distance inland, and they favour sites with a little short vegetation, in contrast to the bare terrain of the chosen winter habitat. Sanderlings feed by sprinting over the sand, stopping and probing or grabbing, then sprinting off again, often snatching prey being washed in by the waves. On the shore their food consists mostly of worms and small crustaceans, although the birds may work the strandline for flies and other small creatures (WA), while insects and plant material form the mainstay of the diet in their nesting areas.

Like its relative the Knot, the Sanderling is restricted to the High Arctic as a breeding bird, extending north as far as the land goes in Greenland, Siberia and parts of northern Canada, the only European representation being a few pairs in Spitsbergen. After breeding, their southward migrations take Sanderlings to most of the temperate and tropical coasts of the world, the species reaching the southern extremities of South America and Africa and many Australian shores. Fair numbers, however, travel no further than Europe, stopping mainly in the British Isles but also to some extent in the Netherlands, France and Iberia. In Britain the main concentrations are found on the coast of south Lancashire and the island beaches of Orkney and the southern Outer Hebrides, with a good scatter all the way down the east side of England.

In the Isle of Man the Sanderling is chiefly a passage migrant, though never very numerous, with a few birds present during the winter. The first autumn migrants appear in late July, when the largest numbers of the year occur, with flocks often approaching and sometimes exceeding 100, the largest so far recorded, at Rue Point in 1999, containing a remarkable 300 birds. As August progresses numbers decline markedly, with flock size falling below 50, and September shows a further fall, few gatherings rising above 20 birds. From October through the winter to April the population fluctuates, with most counts failing to reach double figures, the best record from the Atlas period concerning 40 birds at Rue Point in late December 1998. Spring passage seems to take place during May, when flocks of up to 40 or more are not unusual, and three figures may occasionally be reached, although autumn passage is usually heavier than that of spring. Cullen and Jennings imply that overall numbers of Sanderlings visiting the Island increased during the second half of the twentieth century, and certainly flock sizes recorded by the MBA are considerably larger than those mentioned by these authors.

As Sanderlings move around a good deal, it seems unlikely that there is ever a settled population on the Island, but some localities are reliable enough for this species, particularly the Ayres shore from the Lhen to Ballaghennie, as shown by the Atlas maps and noted by Cullen and Jennings. This stretch of coast can be regarded as classic Sanderling habitat, whereas elsewhere on the Island only small numbers could reasonably be expected. Nevertheless, the beach at Sandwick regularly holds a few birds during the passage months, and other possibilities include the shore at Ramsey, the north end of Douglas Bay, the beach at Strandhall, and Kallow Point at Port St Mary.

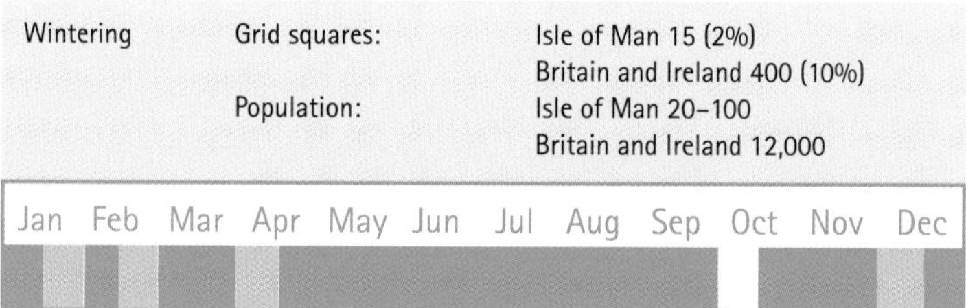

Wintering	Grid squares:	Isle of Man 15 (2%)
		Britain and Ireland 400 (10%)
	Population:	Isle of Man 20–100
		Britain and Ireland 12,000

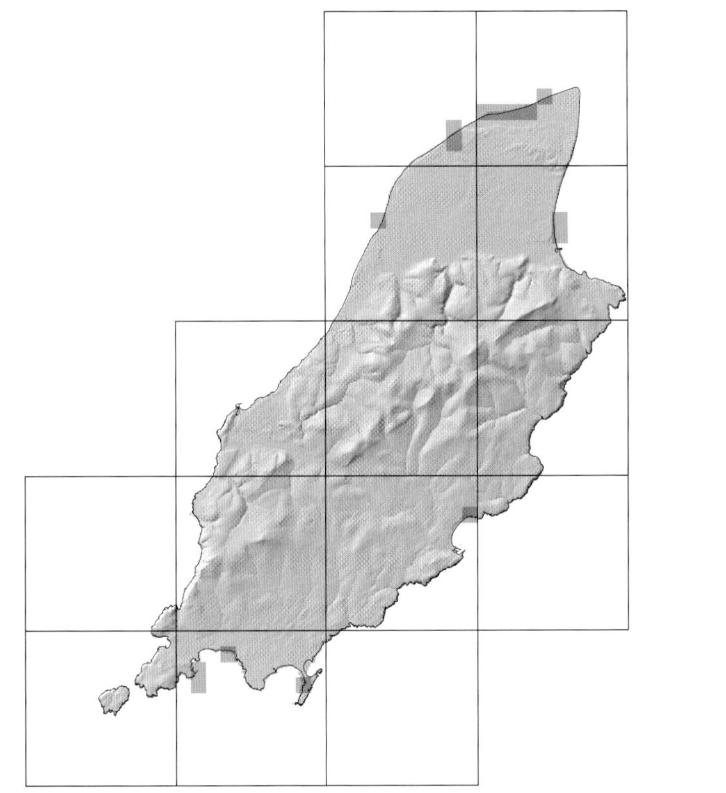

Winter presence

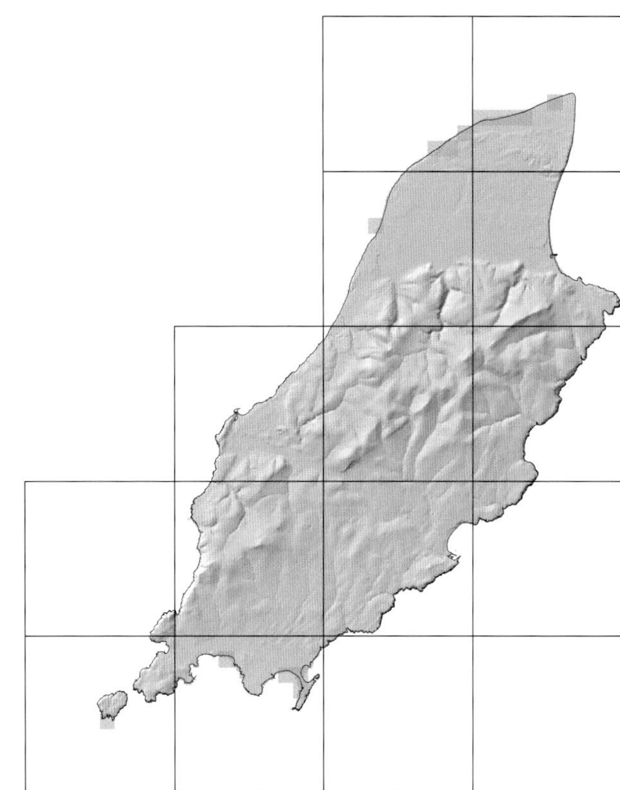

Summer presence

Purple Sandpiper
Calidris maritima

The dark-feathered Purple Sandpiper has much in common with its frequent companion the Turnstone: both species are rotund and short-legged, both haunt rocky areas rather than beaches or marshes, and both breed mainly in the high Arctic. Purple Sandpipers are more closely related to Dunlins, however, than to Turnstones, and they lack the latter's distinctive plumage patterns. Quite hard to find and rather mysterious, the Purple Sandpiper is nevertheless charmingly confiding and allows a close approach, while also fascinating to watch as it darts about among the rocks and seaweed, deftly dodging the waves and winkling out food items from the cracks and crannies.

Purple Sandpipers are almost confined to rocky stretches of coast, especially outside the breeding season, and these hardy birds may be found in exposed situations on headlands and islands where few other birds would venture. They are willing to accept artificial features of the coast in lieu of natural rocks, and so piers, jetties and breakwaters may attract them in otherwise unsuitable areas of sand or mud. Purple Sandpipers, however, are not unknown on beaches, and seem to occur regularly on passage on the sandy shores of the Ayres coast (C&J). During the breeding season they may nest near the sea, but hilly terrain far inland is also to their taste.

The breeding range of the Purple Sandpiper extends from the islands of north-east Canada through Greenland and Iceland to the Arctic coasts and archipelagoes of Europe and western Asia, with a southward extension along the Scandinavian mountains to southern Norway. In 1978 a pair of these birds bred in the Scottish Highlands, and up to four pairs may have nested in Scotland since that date. Otherwise Purple Sandpipers are passage migrants and winter visitors in the British Isles, which form one of the more southerly wintering areas for the species, with many birds penetrating no further south than Iceland and Norway. Their distribution in Britain is biased towards the north-east coast, between Shetland and Yorkshire, south of which rocky coasts are replaced by sandy and muddy shores. In the west of Britain and in Ireland numbers are smaller, and there are few birds south of Anglesey.

The first autumn arrivals in the Isle of Man take place as early as July, with numbers gradually building up until November or December, the lack of an earlier peak perhaps being an indication of the late passage which is typical of this species. The birds visiting the Island are likely to originate in Iceland, Greenland or even Canada, as Scandinavian migrants have been shown to favour the coast of eastern Britain. Like Turnstones, once they have arrived at their wintering grounds Purple Sandpipers tend to stay within a restricted area, and to return to that locality in subsequent years. The distribution map shows the species to be concentrated in a few regular haunts in the southern half of the Island, as the northern coasts are generally less rocky, although absence from the cliffbound coast between Maughold and Onchan is perhaps surprising.

Cullen and Jennings provide details of the occurrence of Purple Sandpipers at their main sites on the Island. The largest numbers are found on the rocks at Peel Castle, where 40 or even 50 birds may be counted in December, while up to 20 have been seen at both extremities of Douglas Bay (Onchan Head/Derby Castle and Douglas Head). The Calf of Man has a significant population, with 20 birds regularly recorded, and the nearby Chicken Rock may attract similar numbers at low tide. Kallow Point at Port St Mary also attracts up to 20, and a few birds may winter at Niarbyl, Black Head and Fort Island. MBA records suggest that these numbers have generally been maintained, the largest winter flock reported during the Atlas period amounting to 40 birds at Peel Castle rocks in December 2000. If these figures are summed and allowance is made for birds that may have been missed, a population in excess of 100 Purple Sandpipers wintering on the Manx coast might be suggested. They probably begin to depart in February, most leaving the Island during March (with 50 reported in mid-month from Peel Castle rocks, possibly indicating passage) and on through April, with a few birds lingering into May.

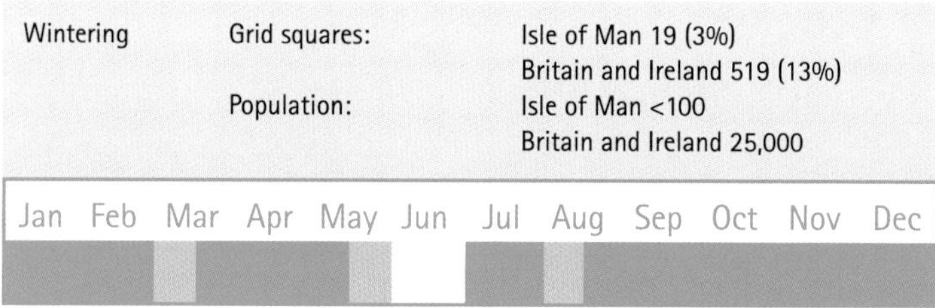

Wintering
Grid squares:
Isle of Man 19 (3%)
Britain and Ireland 519 (13%)
Population:
Isle of Man <100
Britain and Ireland 25,000
Jan Feb Mar Apr May Jun Jul Aug Sep Oct Nov Dec

Winter presence

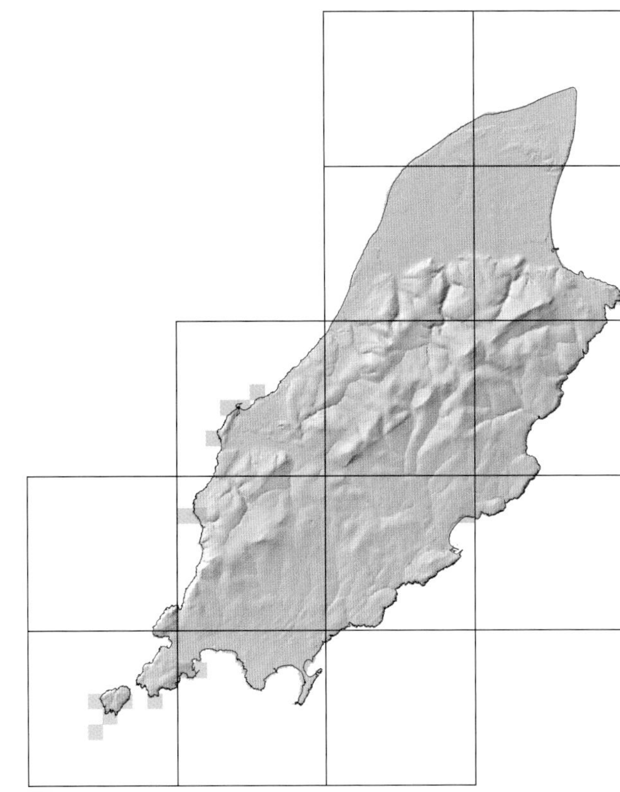

Summer presence

Dunlin
Calidris alpina

Manx: *Breck ny Traie*

If a little wader is spotted on the shore, the chances are that it will be a Dunlin, as this unassuming species is easily the most common of the small sandpipers in the British Isles. As a fair number of rarities may resemble Dunlins, the latter are much contemplated by twitchers, in the hope that they are not Dunlins at all, but something less ordinary. The Dunlin, however, is an interesting bird in its own right, highly variable in size, a master of aerobatic flight in fast-moving flocks, and often feeding by 'stitching' (rapidly jabbing its bill into mud many times in close succession).

Outside the breeding season Dunlins are essentially birds of the shore, with a particular liking for extensive mudflats and wide sandy beaches, but also using smaller patches of intertidal habitat and the edges of standing or flowing water. In the Isle of Man, as well as showing their preference for sand and mud, they may also be found among low rocks, on which they regularly roost, as at the northern end of Douglas Bay (C&J). Dunlins are often observed feeding and flying in the company of the similarly sized Ringed Plover, although the foraging techniques of the two species are completely different. For breeding the Dunlin favours boggy moorlands and marshy ground at various heights above sea level, together with coastal habitats like saltmarshes and lagoons and inland sites such as flood plains and the margins of water bodies. The diet of Dunlins includes marine worms, molluscs, crustaceans and insects, varying greatly with habitat and season.

The Dunlin breeds mainly in the Arctic, from Greenland through northern Europe and Asia to Alaska and parts of northern Canada, extending southwards in Europe to reach the British Isles and the Baltic region. In Britain most Dunlins nest in Scotland and northern England, with rather few breeding south of the Pennines, while Ireland has a sparse population largely confined to the north-west. Dunlins have shown a general decrease in recent decades, with extensive afforestation of their breeding moors probably the main factor. Despite birds being recorded in all months of the year in the Isle of Man, breeding on the Island has yet to be proved, though strongly suspected in 1931, 1942 and 1947 (C&J). The summer Atlas map shows no evidence of the presence of Dunlins in the uplands, where any potential breeders might be expected to occur.

All populations of the Dunlin appear to be migratory. British and Irish breeders may winter as far south as West Africa, being replaced in the British Isles at that season by large numbers of birds from northern Scandinavia and Russia. Those that have bred in Iceland and Greenland pass through Britain in autumn on their way further south (WA). The Isle of Man presumably receives Dunlins from all these populations, with the wintering birds having mainly continental origins. Movement first becomes apparent during late July and seems to continue until October or even November, with passage occurring mainly during August and September. Through the winter, numbers at particular sites may vary both within and between years. The Atlas map suggests that Dunlins depend on relatively few locations around the Manx coast, perhaps partly as a result of the birds being faithful to particular sites through the winter and in subsequent years. Ramsey, Douglas, Carrick, Castletown and Derbyhaven Bays (all large by Manx standards) hold the bulk of the population. Other birds occur along the Ayres coast, at Niarbyl and on the Calf of Man. Spring departure may take place by March, but numbers build up again in late April and May, suggesting further passage at that time.

Dunlins may be seen on the Island in flocks of all sizes from small groups to several hundred birds. The largest gatherings occur at Langness during autumn passage, with relatively few birds observed in spring. During winter numbers are smaller, with flocks of three figures less often observed. With so many birds coming and going, accurate estimation of a total Manx population is impossible even outside the passage periods, though it is unlikely to exceed 500 birds.

Breeding	Grid squares:	Isle of Man 34 (5%) Britain 569 Ireland 69 Total 638 (17%)
	Population:	Isle of Man 0 Britain 9,500 Ireland 175 (3% of European)
Wintering	Grid squares:	Isle of Man 27 (4%) Britain and Ireland 1,065 (28%)
	Population:	Isle of Man <500 Britain and Ireland 500,000

Jan	Feb	Mar	Apr	May	Jun	Jul	Aug	Sep	Oct	Nov	Dec

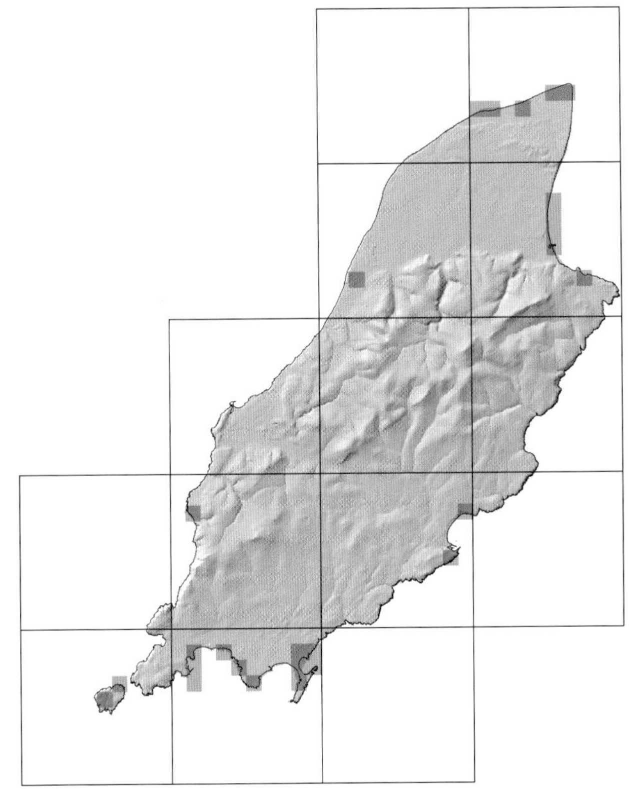

Winter presence

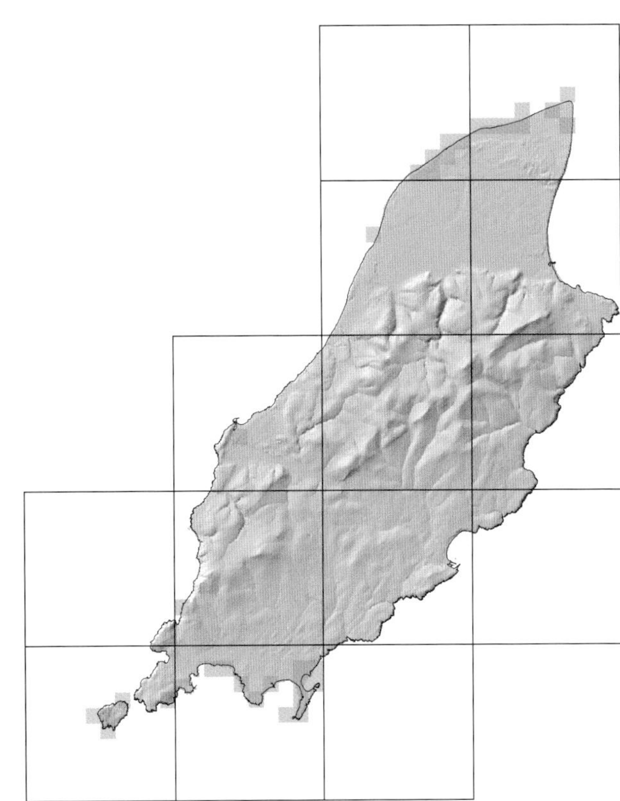

Summer presence

Jack Snipe
Lymnocryptes minimus

An elusive and little-known species, the Jack Snipe frustrates the birdwatcher with its crepuscular habits and liking for dense cover. Reluctant to fly until almost trodden upon, camouflaged by its brown, streaky plumage, and apparently solitary by preference, this is not a species that is easy to get to know. The Jack Snipe partly overlaps with its larger and commoner relative in its choice of habitat and its lifestyle, but the comparatively short bill and general failure to call when flushed mark it out as a different bird. Actively searching for Jack Snipe is largely a waste of time, and most sightings are simply the result of being in the right place and having a lucky day!

Jack Snipe occur in a variety of wet situations, but the presence of relatively thick vegetation is more or less compulsory and water must be shallow, with muddy areas where the birds can probe for food. Acid bogs on moorland, marshes and floods in the lowlands, water meadows and riverbanks are all utilised and small patches of suitable habitat are no less attractive than large expanses. In the Isle of Man the moors of the uplands seem to provide the preferred habitat, but this species is so inconspicuous that numbers of birds hidden away in damp spots anywhere could easily be missed. On their northern breeding grounds Jack Snipe typically nest in peaty places with considerable plant growth, fairly open but often with bushes or trees in the neighbourhood. Their diet consists largely of adult and larval insects, worms, molluscs and seeds, the latter food perhaps helping them survive during freezing weather in their winter quarters (WA).

The breeding distribution of the Jack Snipe extends from north-east Scandinavia eastwards through the coniferous forest belt and subarctic zone into eastern Asia. During autumn the more westerly populations migrate generally south-west to spend the winter in the milder conditions of western and southern Europe, notably the British Isles and the maritime continental countries from Norway to Spain, some birds moving on to north and tropical Africa. Wintering Jack Snipe are generally distributed in England apart from the far north, but they are sparsely scattered in Scotland, Wales and Ireland. Even allowing for birds that are overlooked, according to the figures included in the Winter Atlas it seems likely that few areas can boast high numbers of this species.

In the Isle of Man the Jack Snipe is a bird of passage and a winter visitor in rather small numbers. In the autumn the first birds are usually noted during October, with little variation in numbers from then through the winter to March. The majority of observations involve single birds, with some reports of two together, and during the Atlas period there were two records of three birds, two of four, and one of five (the latter on moorland south of Round Table in mid-February 2001). April produces few birds, with only two mentioned in the MBA data. Cullen and Jennings refer to passage through the Calf of Man in autumn, peaking in mid-October (with many fewer birds in spring), but since the 1980s numbers recorded there have tumbled, with none at all seen in some years (Calf Reports). Whether a similar decrease has taken place on the main island is impossible to say.

The distribution map shows a concentration of Jack Snipe in the southern hills, particularly in the vicinity of South Barrule, Glen Rushen, and the area to the east of Cronk ny Arree Laa. Obviously these moors represent an important area for Jack Snipe in the Isle of Man, but their true significance depends on how many birds might occur in other parts of the Island. Interestingly the map published in the Winter Atlas suggests that in Britain Jack Snipe actually avoid the uplands. Whereas the southern hills are regularly watched, many records from elsewhere refer to birds seen by chance on odd occasions. Two locations in the Manx lowlands, however, are clearly attractive to Jack Snipe, namely the gravel pits at the Point of Ayre in autumn, and Langness during the winter.

Wintering	Grid squares:	Isle of Man 29 (4%)
		Britain and Ireland 788 (20%)
	Population:	Isle of Man <50
		Britain and Ireland <100,000

Jan	Feb	Mar	Apr	May	Jun	Jul	Aug	Sep	Oct	Nov	Dec

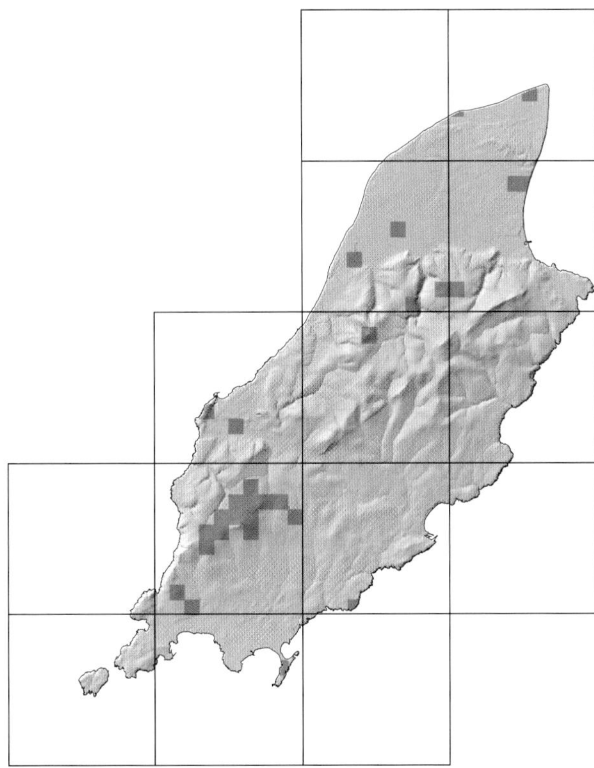

Winter presence

Snipe (Common Snipe)
Gallinago gallinago

Manx: *Coayr Heddagh* = Spear-face

A quarter of the length of a Snipe consists of the bill, a remarkable probing tool which can be thrust deep into soft mud. Snipe are not easy to spot on the ground because of their cryptic colours and patterns, their tendency to hide in cover, and their love of the dusk. They are, however, unmistakable when they fly, usually exploding from under the feet of the observer, zigzagging rapidly at low level, then swiftly rising, while uttering one or more rasping calls usually written as 'scaap'. On their breeding grounds they advertise their presence with territorial flights, during which they produce a so-called 'drumming' sound with their fanned tail feathers, a non-vocal version of song.

Any piece of wet ground with some vegetation could produce a Snipe, provided that the soil is soft and contains food. Upland bogs, wet fields, temporary floods and the margins of lakes and rivers are typical habitats all year round, while in winter Snipe may be found in saltmarshes and even on the shore, for example feeding or resting among small rocks. They nest on many types of waterlogged ground, choosing sites which are likely to remain wet during the summer, thus continuing to provide suitable feeding conditions. Although Snipe specialise in probing, they feed on a wide range of animals of mud and water, including adult and larval insects, worms, molluscs and crustaceans, with some seeds and pieces of vegetation.

The Snipe breeds in a broad zone of northern and middle latitudes right across Eurasia and North America, the major part of its European distribution covering Iceland, the British Isles, Scandinavia, and a belt from the Netherlands and Germany eastwards through Russia. In Britain the species is widespread but not necessarily common in the uplands of Scotland, northern England and Wales, and much scarcer in the English lowlands, with eastern areas holding the highest numbers (1988–91 Atlas).

The MBA map of the breeding distribution of the Snipe in the Isle of Man shows confirmed breeding in five 1km squares and probable or possible breeding in 18 more, amounting to only 3.5% of the squares on the Island. These figures might suggest that Snipe are rather rare Manx breeders, but their secretive nature means that nests will undoubtedly have been missed, so that their true status in the Isle of Man is not quantifiable. The change map suggests that Snipe may have decreased on the Island in recent years, as was the case during the period between the two BTO atlases.

The five squares where breeding was proved during the Atlas survey are all on upland moors, four of them in the area of South Barrule in the southern hills, and the other to the north of Slieau Ruy in the centre of the Island. The squares with suspected breeding are scattered through the high ground and its margins and across the northern plain, with most of the squares in which mere presence was recorded being on or near the coast. Although the map is inevitably incomplete, it does suggest that boggy moorlands, rough soggy fields and lowland marshes represent the typical breeding habitats of the Snipe in the Isle of Man.

Snipe from the British Isles, Denmark and the Low Countries are at least partly resident, but most birds from other populations migrate south and west to winter in Britain and Ireland, the Netherlands, France and Iberia, many moving on to Morocco and tropical Africa. Although the majority of Snipe wintering in Britain originate in the Baltic region (WA), it seems likely that the large Icelandic population provides at least some of the birds seen in the Isle of Man. As suggested by observations on the Calf of Man (C&J), autumn migration into the Island begins during July and rises to peaks in both August and October, with smaller numbers present over the winter. In winter Snipe may be seen on the coast, notably at Langness and Derbyhaven, as well as inland, for example in flooded fields, at the edges of water bodies like the Bishop's Dub and Glascoe Dub, and in wet parts of the moorlands. In favoured spots flock size may reach up to 70 birds at times, but most Snipe are seen in small groups (known as 'wisps' when seen in flight). Spring passage builds up to a maximum in April, and is more or less over by the end of that month.

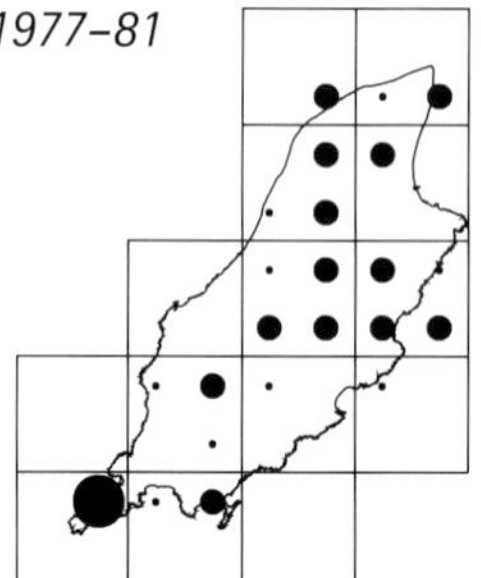

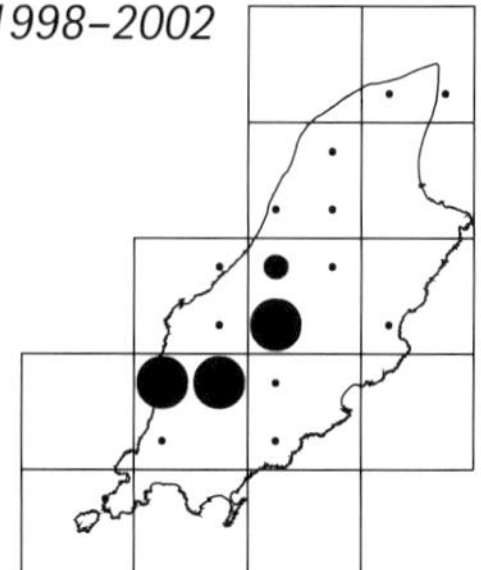

Breeding	Grid squares:	Isle of Man 49 (7%)
		Britain 1,806 Ireland 641 Total 2,447 (63%)
	Population:	Isle of Man 21–24
		Britain 55,000 Ireland 10,000 (8% of European)
Wintering	Grid squares:	Isle of Man 162 (24%)
		Britain and Ireland 2,929 (76%)
	Population:	Isle of Man <500
		Britain and Ireland "many hundreds of thousands"

Jan	Feb	Mar	Apr	May	Jun	Jul	Aug	Sep	Oct	Nov	Dec

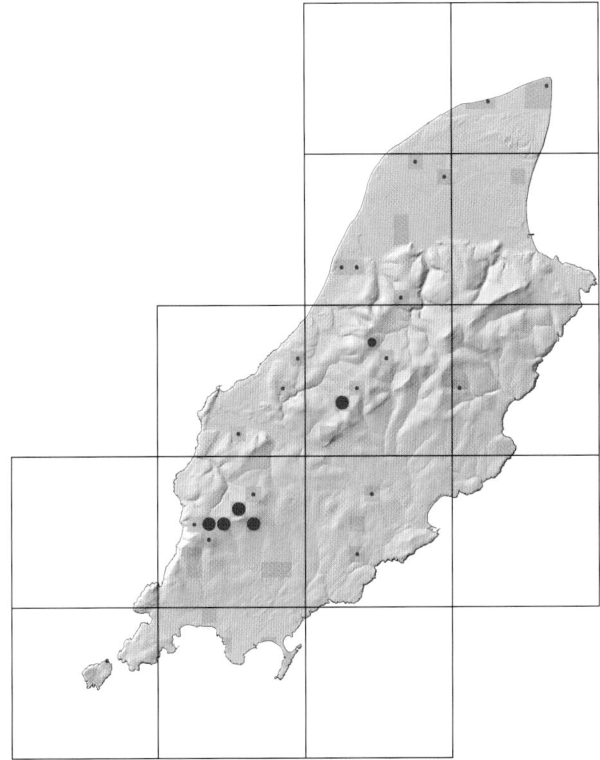

Summer presence and breeding status

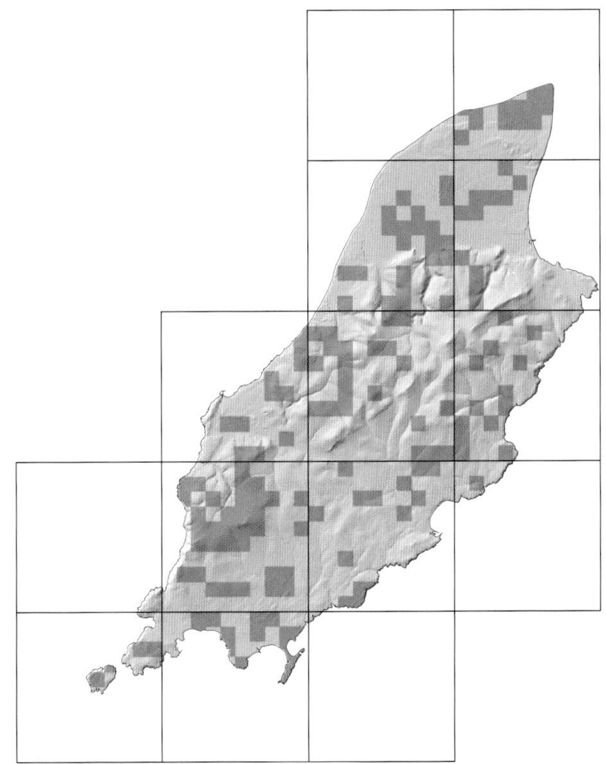

Winter presence

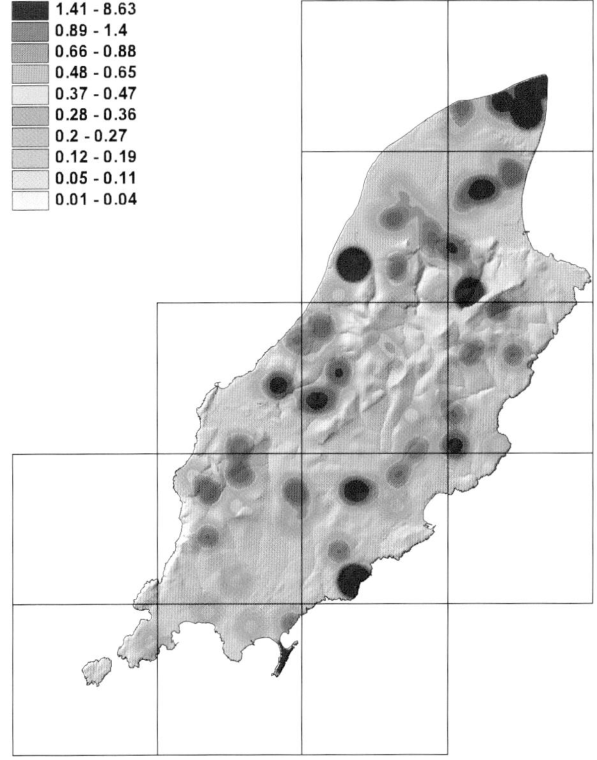

Winter abundance

Individual Sponsors – Sir R Goff, Manx Game Preservation Society, Rye Meads Ringing Group, Mr. J Walton

Woodcock (Eurasian Woodcock)
Scolopax rusticola

Manx: *Ushag Rennee* = Fern Bird

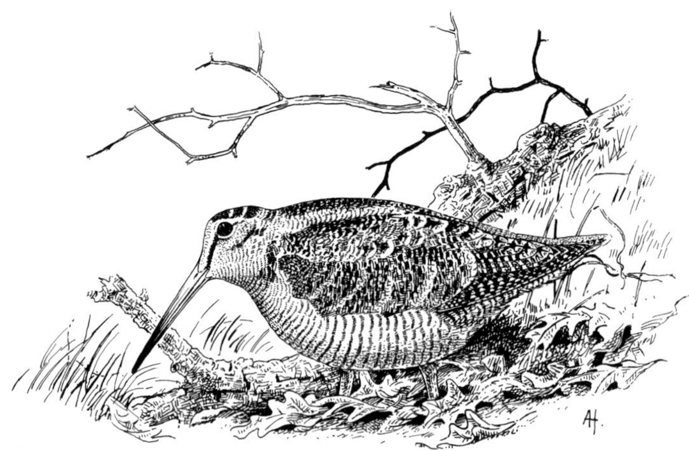

The forest-haunting Woodcock is an unusual, fascinating but frustrating wader, staying out of sight most of the time and active mainly under cover of darkness. Its beautifully barred and dappled russet and buff plumage provides perfect camouflage on the woodland floor, the bird sitting tight unless an intruder unwittingly wanders too close, when the Woodcock shoots into the air with a flurry of wings and twists and turns through the trees. In contrast, the male's 'roding' display flight over the breeding area in the dusk is executed in full view, accompanied by a curious mixture of snoring and sneezing sounds, the whole performance apparently intended to impress the local females rather than defining a territory.

Woodcocks may be found in most types of woods, whether broadleaved, coniferous or mixed, natural or planted, but they need substantial undergrowth and the soil should be neither too dry nor too wet. The species of trees and other plants are of little consequence, but thick foliage is not liked while bracken is a definite attraction. An overall mixture of trees, bushes and non-woody plants suits the Woodcock, which also favours more open areas such as rides and clearings. At any season, but particularly on migration and during winter, birds may also be found in fields, on moors, along hedgerows and at streamsides, and they do not invariably nest among trees, although a low vegetation cover is needed for concealment. Woodcocks eat worms, insect larvae and other animals obtained by probing in soft ground, plus adult insects and spiders taken from the surface or leaf litter.

The Woodcock is a Eurasian species, its breeding range stretching from the British Isles and the western seaboard of Europe, mainly in middle latitudes, to the Pacific coast of Asia and Japan. In Britain the species is generally distributed with some gaps, notably in Cornwall and the Scottish islands, while in Ireland the birds are thinly spread. The small number of breeding squares shown on the MBA summer map of the Isle of Man perhaps partly reflects the relative scarcity of woodland on the Island, but mainly results from the extreme difficulty of finding adults, nests and young of this species, leading to serious under-recording. The map suggests breeding centres in the Ballaugh Curraghs, the western section of the central valley, and the southern hills from Kerrowdhoo Plantation to Stoney Mountain. Wooded marshes and (in the uplands) conifer plantations provide ideal habitat for Woodcocks in these localities, and similar terrain elsewhere on the Island is likely to hold many more breeding birds.

Though long suspected, breeding of the Woodcock in the Isle of Man was not proved until the discovery of nests in Greeba Plantation in 1906 (C&J), at a time when colonisation of Britain and Ireland was virtually complete following over two centuries of expansion (1988–91 Atlas). It seems likely that the breeding population of the Island increased still further and its range was extended during the twentieth century, but unfortunately the difficulties involved in censusing this species cause assessment of its numbers and status to be impossible.

Although Woodcocks nesting in the British Isles and neighbouring parts of the European continent may be more or less resident, those from further north and east migrate south and west for the winter, arriving in Britain and Ireland in large numbers, especially during hard weather. Many of these birds from Scandinavia and perhaps Russia must reach the Isle of Man, passage becoming evident in October and continuing through November (C&J, using data from the Calf of Man). The winter map displays a remarkably general though somewhat sparse distribution, with the same areas of concentration as during the breeding season, together with apparent gaps which to some extent coincide with lack of major woodlands. The importance of conifer plantations in the hills and of curraghs and similar habitat on low ground is suggested by the map, together with an intriguing avoidance of most coastal areas, and yet again one wonders how many birds have been missed. Spring passage, lighter than that of autumn, lasts from mid-February to the middle of April.

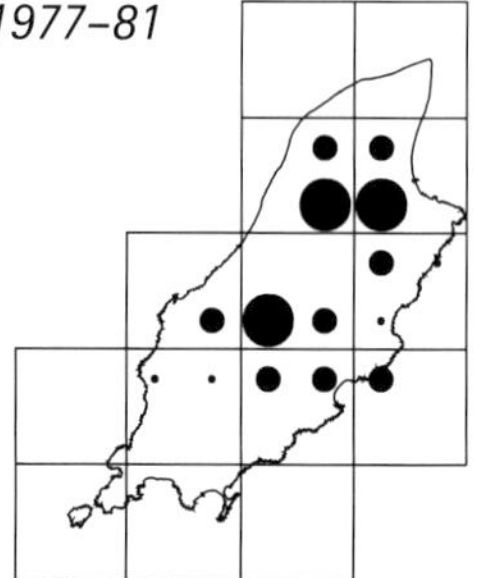

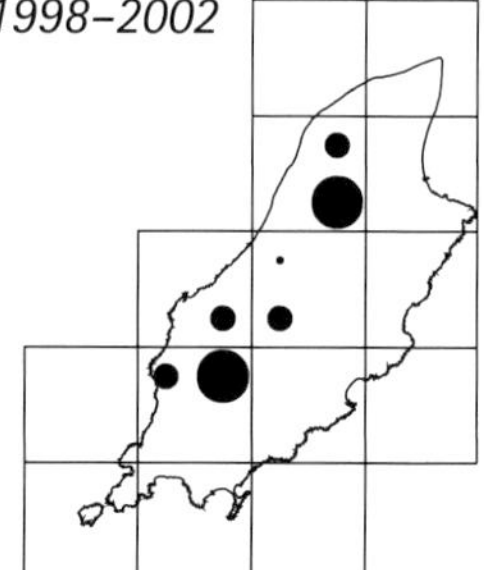

Breeding	Grid squares:	Isle of Man 13 (2%) Britain 1,204 Ireland 179 Total 1,383 (36%)
	Population:	Isle of Man <50 Britain 15,000 Ireland 3,000 (3% of European)
Wintering	Grid squares:	Isle of Man 109 (16%) Britain and Ireland 2,237 (58%)
	Population:	Isle of Man 100+ Britain and Ireland not known

Jan Feb Mar Apr May Jun Jul Aug Sep Oct Nov Dec

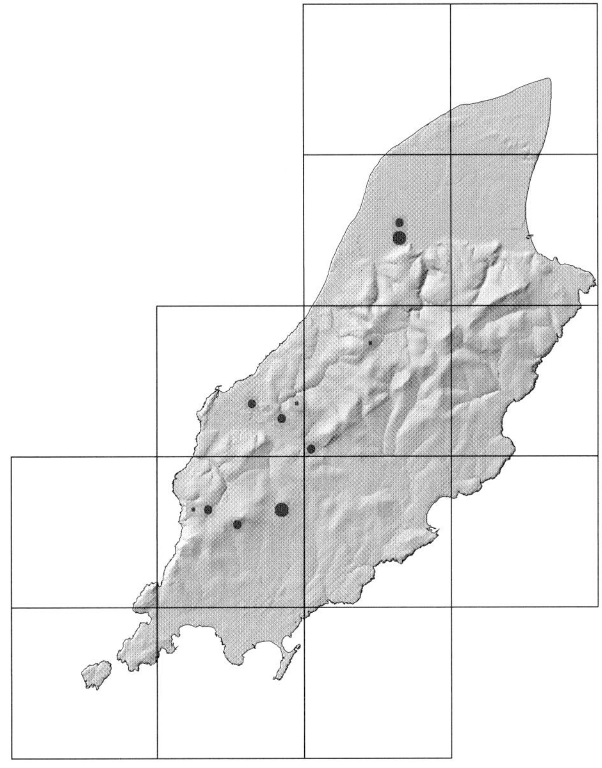

Summer presence and breeding status

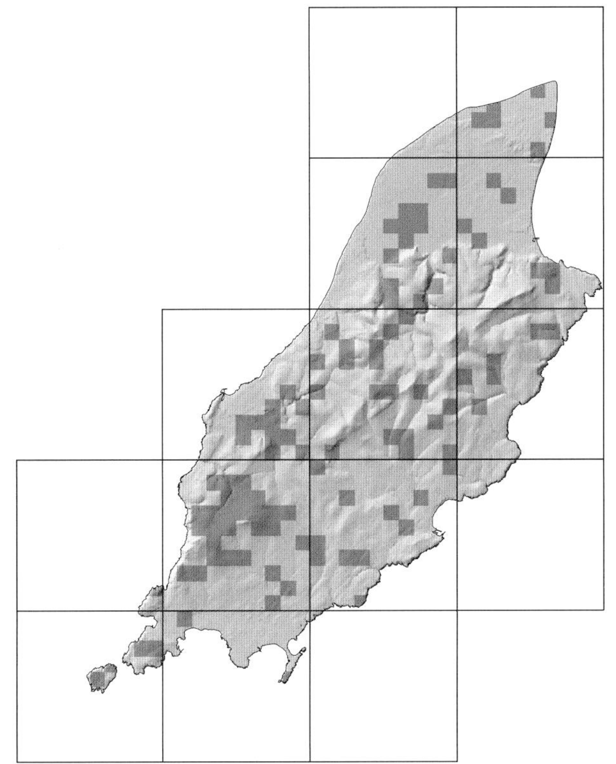

Winter presence

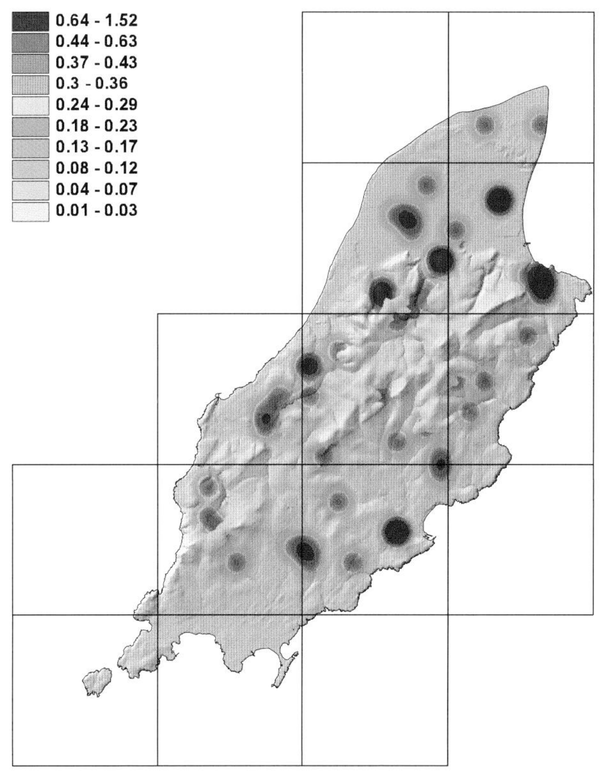

Winter abundance

Individual Sponsors – Mrs. J Clague, Mr. W J H Corlett, Mr. J H S Cowley, Manx Game Preservation Society, Mr. J Walton, Dr. G L Woodcock

Bar-tailed Godwit
Limosa lapponica

The elegant Bar-tailed Godwit is a relatively large wader with rather long neck and legs, plus a lengthy, slim and slightly upcurved bill. In contrast to the male's mainly chestnut breeding dress, the winter plumage of both sexes is a nondescript streaky greyish-brown, yet somehow this species has an appeal which gives the observer a cheery feeling on a cold shore. The flocks of hundreds or even thousands of birds that may be seen on certain British estuaries are sadly absent from the harder and less welcoming coasts of the Isle of Man. During the period between autumn and spring, however, at least a few of these quietly attractive Arctic sandpipers can usually be found on the Island.

Away from its breeding grounds the Bar-tailed Godwit is almost completely a coastal bird, feeding and roosting within or close to the intertidal area. Not fond of exposed shores, it prefers estuaries, bays and other inlets, happy on either sand or mud, but generally avoiding rocks. These godwits breed mostly on lowland tundra not far from the edges of the Arctic Ocean, but some nest inland on peat bogs and in marshlands. On the shore they feed chiefly along the water's edge, following the ebb and flow of the tide and probing or picking with their slim bills. Their food consists particularly of marine worms, especially the burrow-living lugworm, but they also take molluscs and crustaceans, while insects become important in their nesting areas.

Bar-tailed Godwits breed from the far north of Scandinavia, eastwards along the Arctic fringes of Eurasia into westernmost Alaska. After nesting is over they migrate all the way to the southern tips of Africa and Australasia, but most European and western Siberian birds travel no further than the British Isles, the continental seaboard from the Netherlands to Spain, and the Atlantic shores of north-west Africa. In Britain and Ireland most lowland coasts have their passing and wintering Bar-tails, especially where there are major estuaries such as the Ribble and the Wash, but the presence of cliffs excludes these birds of soft shores from much of the coastline in Scotland, Wales, Devon and Cornwall.

The Isle of Man, lacking estuaries and substantial sandy bays, with much of the coast rocky and cliffbound, is generally unattractive to Bar-tailed Godwits, and suitable areas for them are few in number and small in size. The long beach stretching round the north of the Island from Kirk Michael to Ramsey might seem to provide an exception, but relatively few Bar-tails are recorded there. The godwits may find this wide-open shore too windswept and wave-battered or perhaps lacking in the type and quantity of food that they require. At the northern extremity of the Island, the coast between Blue Point and Point of Ayre produces a few Bar-tailed Godwits every year, with some suggestion of passage during September and May. The vast majority of records, however, come from the two neighbouring localities of Sandwick (on Castletown Bay) and Derbyhaven, both having fair-sized exposures of sand (and, in the case of Derbyhaven, some mud) at low tide. The first autumn migrants arrive on the Island in late July, with numbers rising during August and especially in September (C&J). The largest flocks tend to be reported at this season, maximum numbers for the Atlas years reaching 14 (at the Point of Ayre in August 2002). Cullen and Jennings mention up to 31 birds at Sandwick in September 1979 and no fewer than 44 flying over the Calf of Man in August 1974.

It would seem that the Bar-tailed Godwit was known almost entirely as an autumn passage migrant in the Isle of Man at the time when Ralfe wrote his book, the habit of wintering on the Island apparently developing during the early twentieth century and passage in spring not truly becoming apparent until the 1970s (C&J). Although nowadays regularly observed in every month of the year except for June (when there are nevertheless occasional records), numbers have remained small, despite the highly gregarious nature of this species, and most sightings have involved no more than three or four birds together. Except perhaps for a brief period in autumn, the total of Bar-tailed Godwits present in the Isle of Man at any one time seems unlikely to exceed ten or so birds.

Wintering	Grid squares:	Isle of Man 9 (1%)
		Britain and Ireland 560 (15%)
	Population:	Isle of Man 1-10
		Britain and Ireland <60,000

Jan Feb Mar Apr May Jun Jul Aug Sep Oct Nov Dec

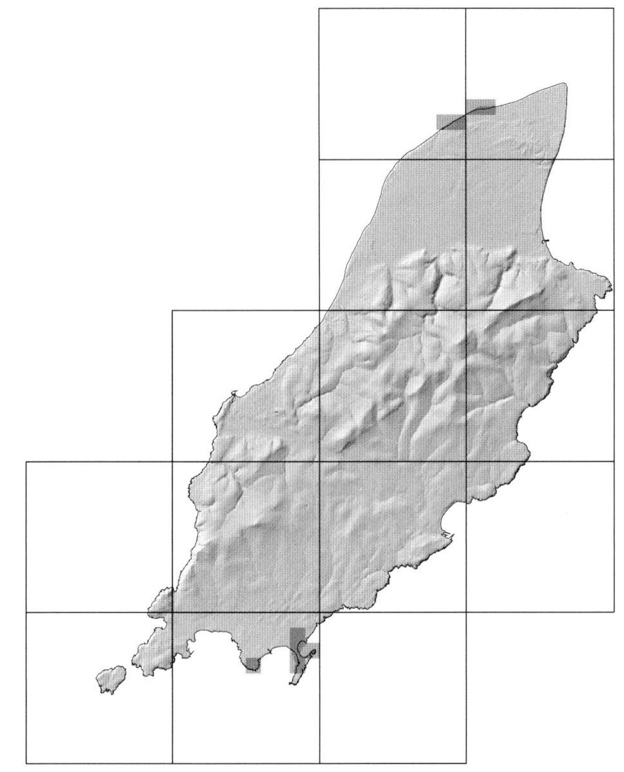

Winter presence

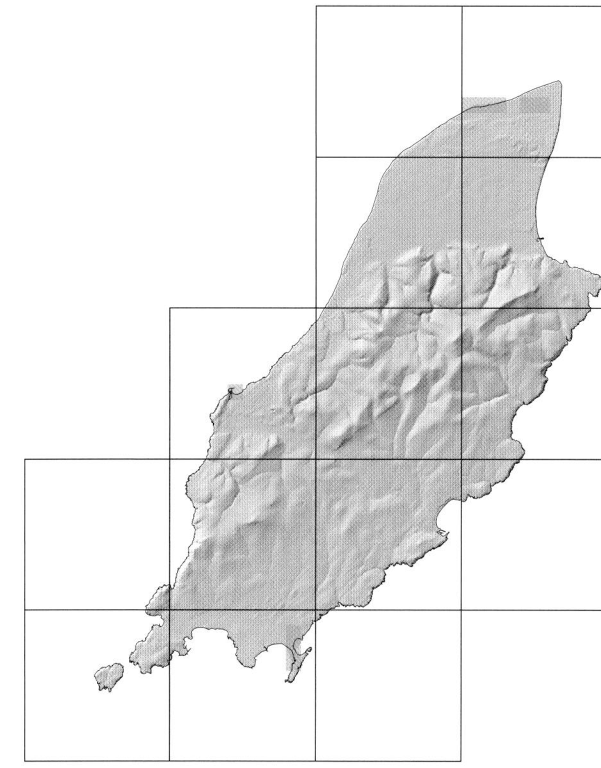

Summer presence

Curlew (Eurasian Curlew)
Numenius arquata

Manx: *Crottag* i.e. *Cruittagh* = Humped

Largest of the European waders, the familiar Curlew is famous for its remarkably long downcurved bill and its fluty bubbling voice, but not for its rather ordinary greyish-brown plumage, although a close view will show the beautiful streaking and barring on its feathers. Perhaps more than any other bird, in both sight and sound the Curlew is an integral part of the upland moors during the breeding season and the tidal flats of the coast in winter, being one of the few waders to make an impact on the non-birdwatching public.

When breeding, Curlews are particularly associated with moorland and adjoining rough fields, having plant cover such as heather, grass and rushes. They are also often found, however, in lowland agricultural areas, even nesting in fields of crops, although a preference for the more marginal sites is usually apparent (1988–91 Atlas). Some wetness in the terrain is essential, ranging from boggy or marshy patches to the margins of open water. After the breeding season, by contrast, most Curlews move to the coast, where they favour extensive stretches of mud and sand but may be encountered almost anywhere away from cliffs, including saltmarsh creeks, rock pools, flooded ground, and all sorts of grassland near the sea. Those which choose to remain inland chiefly frequent the edges of substantial bodies of water. The Curlew feeds by probing (more deeply than other waders) and by grabbing or picking, on marine worms, crustaceans and molluscs on the shore, and inland on earthworms and insects, plus many other types of mainly invertebrate food.

Curlews breed from the British Isles, Scandinavia and the western continental seaboard eastwards through Russia into eastern Asia, reaching no further south than France and central Europe. Their distribution in Britain has a markedly northern and western bias, clearly based on the uplands of Scotland, northern England and Wales, and despite some expansion during the last century the species remains sparse or absent in most of the English lowlands. Greater abundance in the north and west is also apparent in Ireland, but not quite so obviously as in Britain. The Curlew is a common breeding bird in the Isle of Man, present during the season in over half of the 1km squares on the Island, and a glance at the Atlas map will show its liking for the uplands and the northern plain. Nesting is well distributed across the moors and marginal lands of both the northern and southern hills. High densities (as seen on the abundance map) are evident on either side of the central spine, including the catchment of the Sulby River, the area between Snaefell and Laxey, and the Glen Mooar and Glen Rushen district further south.

Another centre of abundance occurs on lower ground, namely along the south-eastern edges of the southern hills and roughly centred on the Braaid area, where there are many boggy patches and unimproved pastures. On the northern plain Curlews breed widely (except in the well-drained Bride Hills and in the farmlands between Jurby and Ballaugh), the many damp pockets of ground evidently suiting these birds, particularly on the Ayres and in the Curraghs. The southern extremity of the Island, however, produced only a single record of confirmed breeding during the whole Atlas period, an unsuccessful nest being found on the Calf of Man in 2001. Cullen and Jennings report a steady spread of breeding Curlews on the Island during the twentieth century, but the change maps suggest that, as in Britain, this increase may not be continuing.

The majority of Curlews are migratory, most European birds wintering on the coasts of Europe or north-west Africa, although some carry on south and even reach Cape Province. British Curlews tend to move south-west, many travelling no further than the west coast of Britain or flying across to Ireland, while others move on to France or Iberia, and meanwhile large numbers arrive in Britain and Ireland from the northern half of the continent. The first signs of migration into the Isle of Man appear by the end of June, and passage continues until early October, with flocks of several hundred appearing especially on the Ayres coast and in the area of Langness and Derbyhaven. The largest numbers of Curlews are present during winter, when four-figure totals may be counted in the southern bays. Many others can be seen on coasts in the far north, around Douglas Bay, and along the west coast around Kirk Michael and the little bays towards Peel (C&J, MBA maps). Although many of these birds are found in coastal fields, few Curlews are seen inland at this season. By the end of March most visitors have departed and the Manx breeders are back on territory.

1977–81

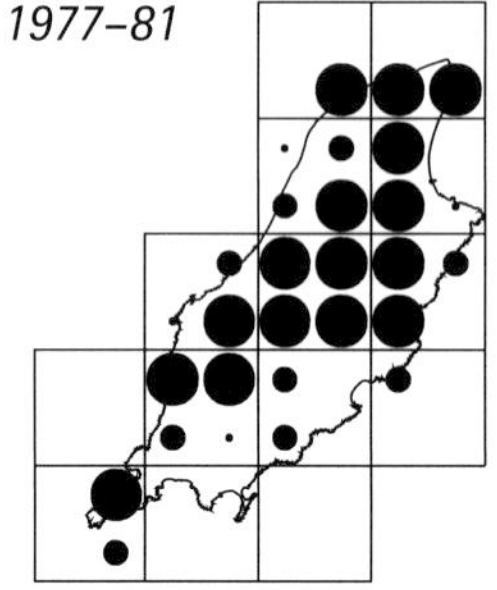

1998–2002

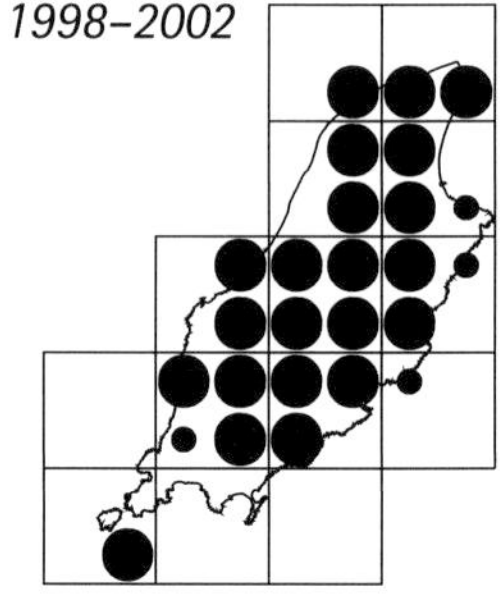

Breeding	Grid squares:	Isle of Man 348 (52%) Britain 1,893 Ireland 671 Total 2,564 (66%)
	Population:	Isle of Man 399–483 Britain 35,500 Ireland 12,000 (36% of European)
Wintering	Grid squares:	Isle of Man 97 (15%) Britain and Ireland 2,198 (57%)
	Population:	Isle of Man <2,000 Britain and Ireland 200,000

Jan Feb Mar Apr May Jun Jul Aug Sep Oct Nov Dec

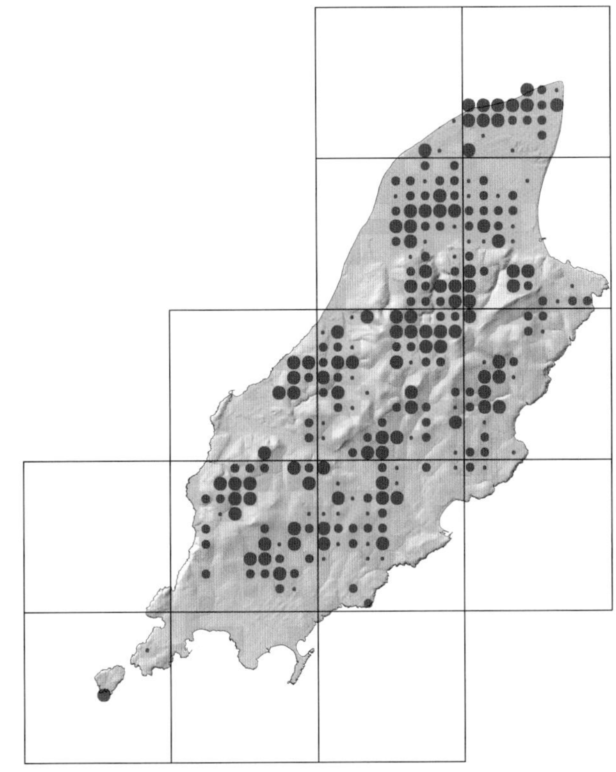

Summer presence and breeding status

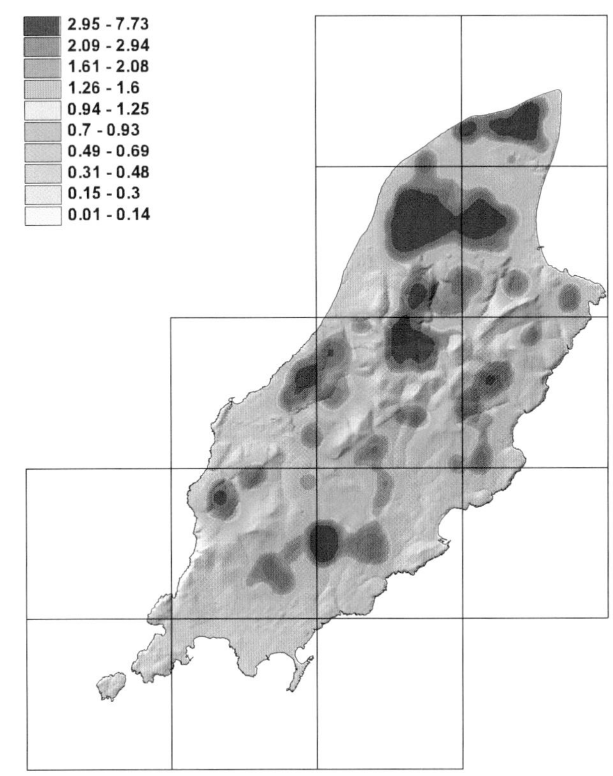

Breeding abundance

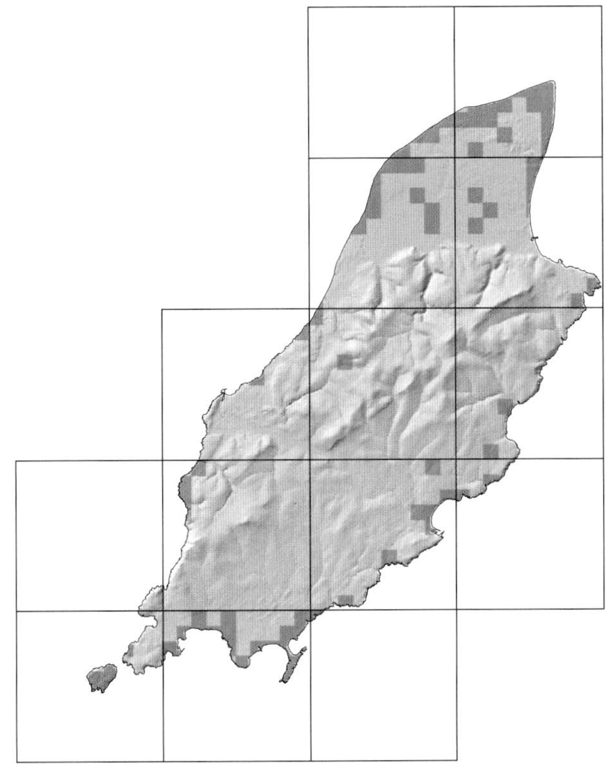

Winter presence

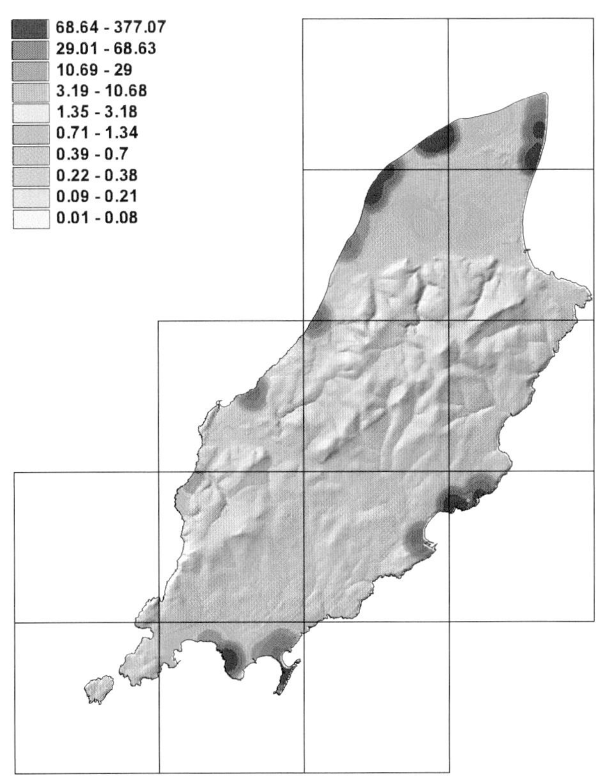

Winter abundance

Individual Sponsors – Mr. I Bedey, His Honour & Mrs. J W Corrin, Mr. J J Crellin, Mr. & Mrs. J C Fargher, Mrs. E van Genutchen, Mr. & Mrs. G Huntley, Mr. C Jelfs, Mrs. B Kelly, Mrs. J A Scowcroft, Mrs. J E Turner, the late Mr T Whipp and Mrs M Whipp

Redshank (Common Redshank)
Tringa totanus

Manx: *Goblan Marrey* = Beaked bird of the sea

If it were not for its orange-red legs and reddish base to its bill, the grey-brown Redshank would not be very noticeable until it flew, when the white trailing edges of the wings and the musical trisyllabic call would mark it out. Common on the shore in the Isle of Man, the Redshank is more or less absent for a few weeks in midsummer, but otherwise is quite easy to find in suitable places. This wary and noisy species has a reputation for easily taking alarm and alerting other birds around it, but on the Island Redshanks are relatively tame and seem able to tolerate people quite close to them.

Although favouring sandy and muddy shores, the Redshank also occurs in rocky areas, especially where there are masses of seaweed among which it can forage, but it tends to avoid cliffbound coasts and is not fond of shingle. Redshanks often use grassland near the sea, even feeding on the grass of Queen's Promenade in Douglas. They habitually perch on walls, posts and fences, and they may forage on hard surfaces such as promenades. In the Isle of Man Redshanks are very much birds of the coast, but elsewhere, particularly during the breeding season, they are also found in wetland habitats far from the sea. They are less gregarious than some other waders, scattering along the shore in small parties rather than forming substantial flocks. The diet of the Redshank varies widely but is usually based on crustaceans, small molluscs and marine worms when feeding on the shore and on earthworms and insect larvae at inland sites.

The Redshank breeds mainly in middle latitudes from Iceland and the British Isles right across Eurasia. It nests along coasts and inland throughout the British Isles, but is commoner in the north than in the south, and also shows an easterly bias outside northern England, with Ireland very thinly populated except in the midwestern wetlands. Redshanks were first proved to breed in the Isle of Man in 1928, when a nest was discovered near the Ayres coast, and since that date breeding has been recorded on the northern plain and elsewhere, with the Ayres and Langness to the fore (C&J). In any given year, however, only odd pairs have been present. During the MBA period breeding was proved only once, in the marsh at Langness in 2002. Therefore, despite the existence of apparently suitable habitat, such as the marshy areas on the northern plain and the rushy fields on the fringes of the uplands, the Isle of Man does not appeal to breeding Redshanks. This is also the case with other westerly regions such as much of the western Scottish mainland, most of Wales, and the major part of Ireland.

Virtually all European populations of Redshanks other than those of the British Isles are migratory, moving south and west for the winter and reaching as far as West Africa. Britain and Ireland host many birds from further north, especially Iceland, and by mid-July Redshanks begin to arrive in the Isle of Man, numbers increasing through the late summer and autumn and probably peaking in October/November. This level seems to be more or less maintained through the winter, and the distribution map shows a general scatter of Redshanks around the Manx coast, with obvious gaps coinciding with stretches of cliffs, but no real penetration inland. The northern beaches are perhaps less attractive to Redshanks than might be expected, possibly because these birds need muddier and more sheltered feeding areas. The appeal of the southern bays of Carrick, Castletown and Derbyhaven, on the other hand, is readily apparent, and the abundance map bears out their importance, other concentrations showing up in Ramsey and Douglas Bays and along the Jurby shore. The spring departure begins in March and by the end of May just a few birds are left on the Island.

Cullen and Jennings suggest that during winter the south coast holds perhaps 200+ Redshanks, with up to 80 birds in each of Douglas and Ramsey Bays and maybe a total of 100 or so elsewhere, indicating an all-Island total of about 400 birds, rather more than estimated currently. There may well have been a decrease in recent decades, possibly reflecting less need for movement to the milder conditions of the west as winters have become less severe during recent times.

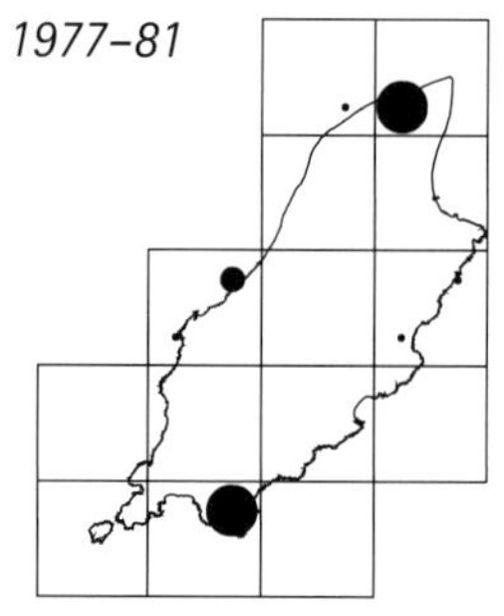

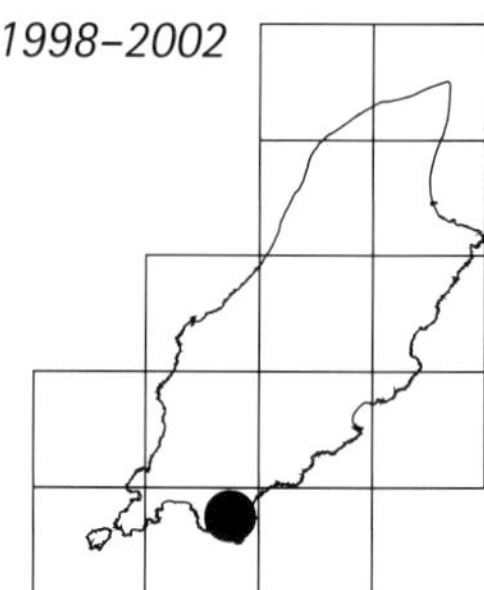

Breeding	Grid squares:	Isle of Man 34 (5%)
		Britain 1,473 Ireland 213 Total 1,686 (44%)
	Population:	Isle of Man 1
		Britain 32,100 Ireland 4,700 (11% of European)
Wintering	Grid squares:	Isle of Man 58 (9%)
		Britain and Ireland 1,607 (42%)
	Population:	Isle of Man 200
		Britain and Ireland 100,000+

Jan	Feb	Mar	Apr	May	Jun	Jul	Aug	Sep	Oct	Nov	Dec

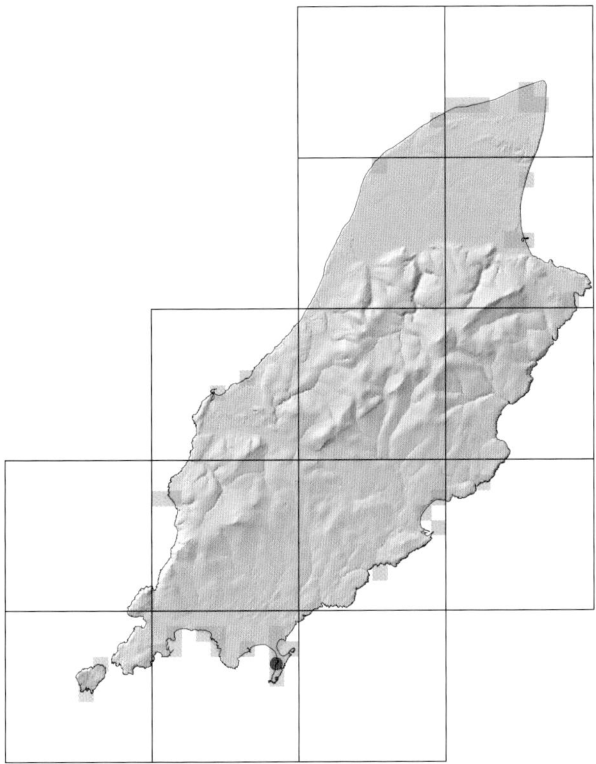

Summer presence and breeding status

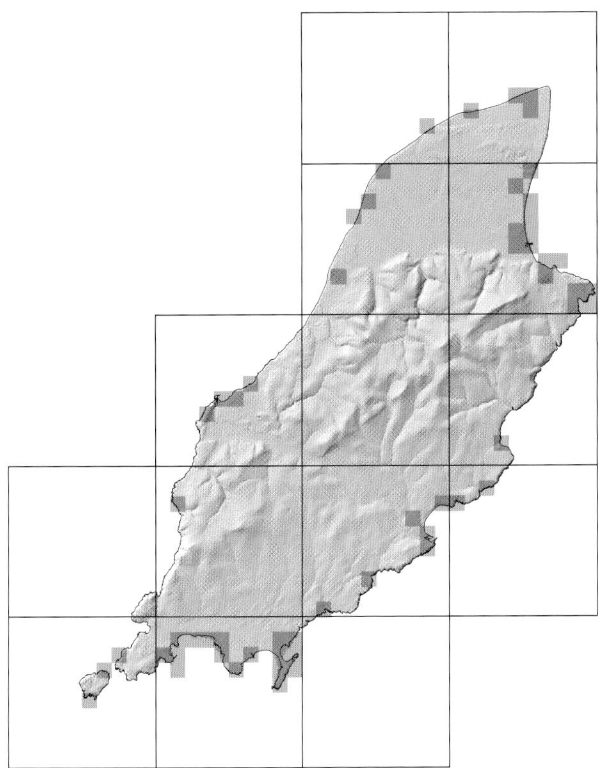

Winter presence

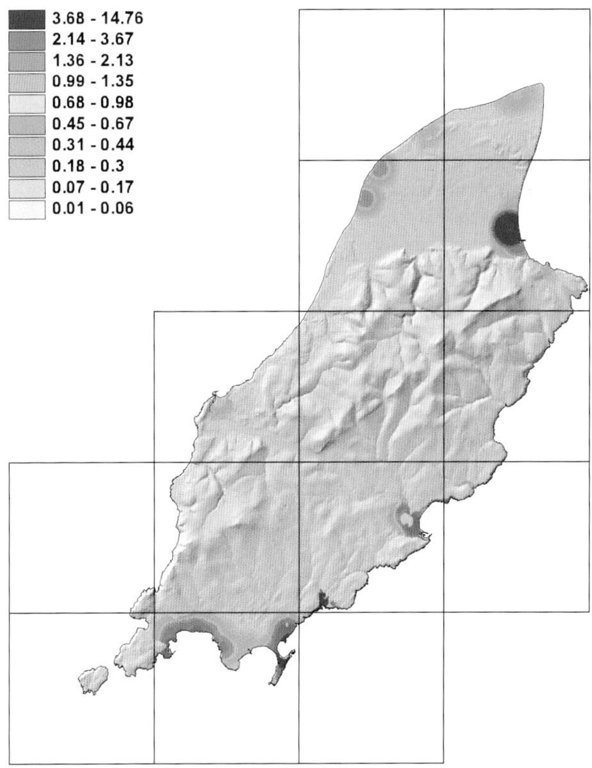

Winter abundance

Turnstone (Ruddy Turnstone)
Arenaria interpres

Manx: *Goblaghan*

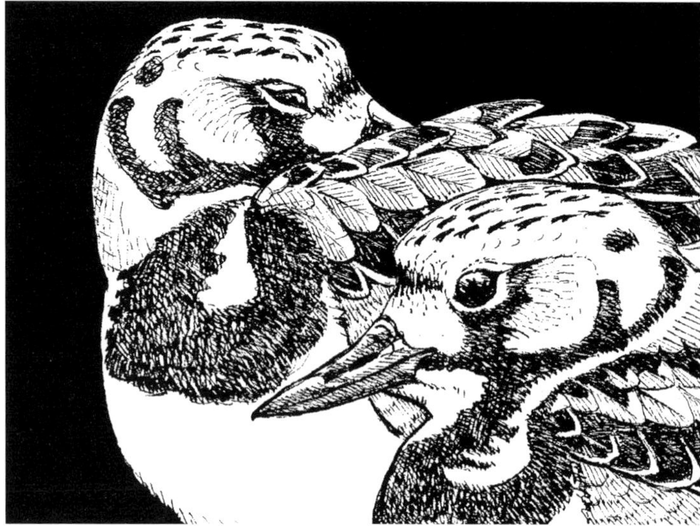

Turnstones are easy to miss among the intertidal rocks, but if one bird is spotted, a few others are likely to be found nearby, all carefully searching among the crevices and seaweed for anything edible. The full-bodied, thick-billed and short-legged Turnstone is designed to overturn pebbles, and has strong neck muscles to help with the task. Its black breast and pure white underside may suggest a plover, but in fact this unusual species is a sandpiper, an offshoot from the group that includes the Redshank.

The Turnstone is essentially a bird of rocky shores, and is often seen accompanying the similarly inclined Purple Sandpiper. Shingle is also frequented, as well as artificial structures such as harbour walls and breakwaters, and Turnstones may also appear on sandy beaches alongside more typical waders. The presence of abundant seaweed is an attraction, and the birds may be seen flipping over bunches of wrack to obtain prey lurking underneath. In winter the Turnstone is a highly maritime species, only observed inland on rare occasions, and even on its northern breeding grounds most nests are found within a few kilometres of the sea, mainly in open sites on rocky or pebbly ground with sparse vegetation. The food of Turnstones consists basically of crustaceans like shrimps and barnacles, small molluscs such as winkles, plus insects and other invertebrates, but Turnstones are not averse to scavenging on dead fish and other corpses.

The Turnstone is a high Arctic breeder, nesting in the northernmost parts of both Eurasia and North America, with a marked southerly extension into the Baltic region. Almost all birds migrate south in autumn to spend the winter on temperate and tropical shores virtually throughout the world, and large numbers arrive in the British Isles. Those originating in Scandinavia and the Russian Arctic mainly pass through on their way to winter quarters in West Africa, and the Turnstones actually wintering in Britain and Ireland breed mostly in Greenland and the Canadian Arctic (WA).

Although odd birds (probably first-years) may be observed on the Manx coast during summer, the main period of arrival on the Island falls in September and October. Some of these autumn migrants will undoubtedly fly on to destinations further south, and an impressive flock of about 300 birds reported at Rue Point in late September 1999 would presumably have contained such transients. Birds seen later in the year will probably be spending the winter on the Island, as Turnstones do not move around much once they have settled in a particular area (WA). They leave for their breeding grounds during April and May, when (as in autumn) passage is apparent on the Calf of Man (C&J).

The winter map shows Turnstones scattered generally around the Manx coast, with long gaps mainly reflecting the presence of cliffs. It should be borne in mind, however, that some stretches of shore that are likely to attract Turnstones are largely inaccessible and seldom visited by birdwatchers, so that some birds could be missed. Two localities are particularly favoured by Turnstones, one being the mixture of rock and sand around the southern bays (Carrick, Castletown and Derbyhaven), and the other covering the sandy and shingle shores of the Ayres in the far north. The abundance map emphasises the importance of the south coast between Port St Mary and Derbyhaven, while other noteworthy sites for this species include the shores around Ramsey, the Niarbyl district, and parts of Douglas Bay (especially the vicinity of Derby Castle).

Estimation of the number of Turnstones present in the Isle of Man during winter is somewhat hampered by the probability of birds being overlooked, but figures for individual sites given by Cullen and Jennings might suggest a total in excess of 300 individuals, current data supporting that view. These authors also state that an increase in the Manx population of Turnstones took place during the early 1960s, and they imply that numbers have been maintained since that time.

Wintering	Grid squares:	Isle of Man 41 (6%)
		Britain and Ireland 933 (24%)
	Population:	Isle of Man 300+
		Britain and Ireland 50,000

Jan	Feb	Mar	Apr	May	Jun	Jul	Aug	Sep	Oct	Nov	Dec

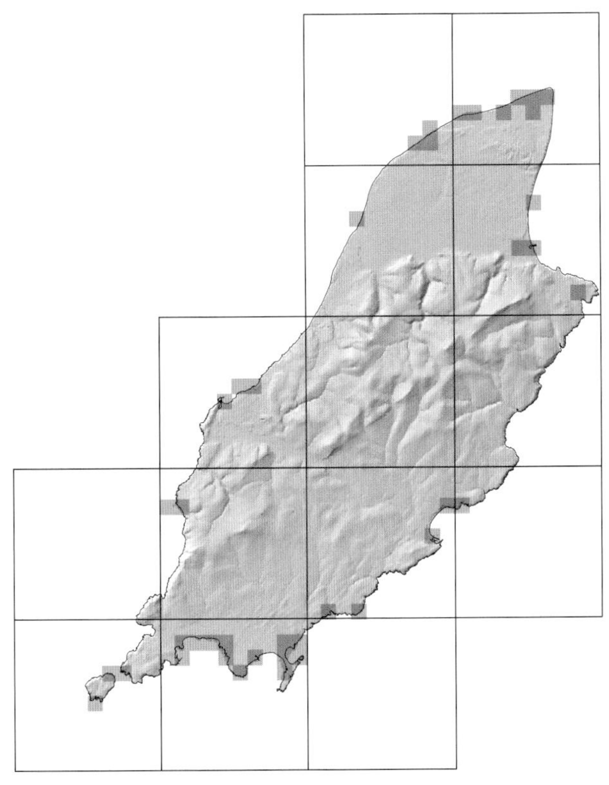
Winter presence

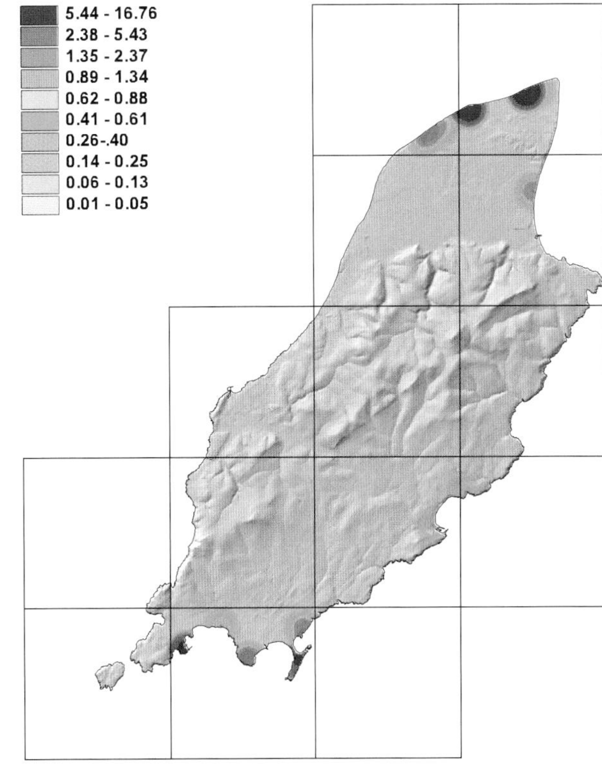

Winter abundance

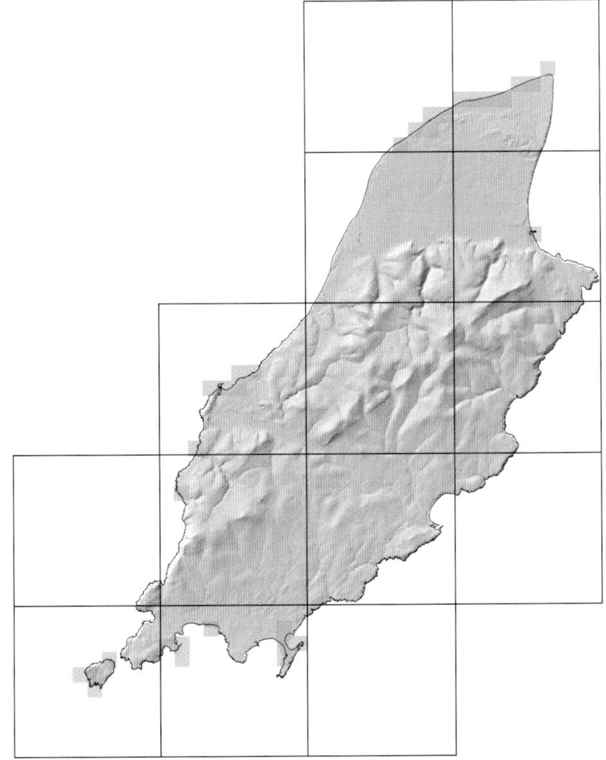
Summer presence

Black-headed Gull
Larus ridibundus

Manx: *Pirragh*

During the breeding season adult Black-headed Gulls are easy to identify, having dark brown heads, a white eye ring and red legs and bill. Out of their breeding plumage they lack the distinctive brown head but are only slightly more challenging to identify correctly, their delicate build setting them aside from larger members of the genus *Larus*.

Black-headed Gulls use a range of breeding habitats, wetlands, bogs and marshes being preferred, though drier sites close to water are also utilised, including sand dunes, heather moor and industrial waste dumps (EBA). When feeding, both during and outside the breeding season, habitats as diverse as farmland, shallow coastal waters and the centres of towns are used. With such a wide range of feeding habitats, it is unsurprising that the species has a diverse diet, though insects and earthworms comprise the main items. Small fish, crustaceans, eggs and young birds, fruit and berries have all been recorded as food (BWP). Late one summer, over Onchan, approximately 20 Black-headed Gulls were observed at a height of about 50m frantically feeding on an emergence of ants, feeding continuously for about 30 minutes, presumably until the emergence was complete.

The species has an extensive breeding range, extending from Kamchatka in the east, across the Palearctic to the Atlantic coast, with populations also present in Iceland, Greenland and Canada (EBA). A total world population of 2,800,000 pairs is estimated (Seabird 2000). Within the British Isles the majority (78%) of nests are located on the coast. The species has suffered a 16% fall in breeding numbers from the census of 1985-88. Reasons cited for this include an increase in the range of the American Mink, an aggressive predator, loss of habitat and changes in agricultural practice reducing the amount of spring tillage (and therefore food) which leaves birds in poor condition prior to breeding (Seabird 2000).

Locally, the species is faring badly, only two nests being found during the 1999 seabird survey and a maximum of six pairs breeding in 1998, all of which were unsuccessful. No young were thought to have fledged during the research period, and no breeding took place in 2004 or 2005. Breeding was confined to the gravel pits at the Point of Ayre and the adjacent restored landfill tips. The precise sites varied between years, resulting in four 1km squares having a breeding status, though only one was used in a given year. Summering non-breeding birds were observed around much of the Island's coastline, occurring inland rarely. During April numbers present in a given area could reach 50, though generally they were much lower than this, records often being of single birds. During May numbers were lower and distribution more restricted, rising again through June and into July, when larger flocks appeared at places like Langness, Strandhall and the shoreline north of Ramsey Harbour, the largest summer number being 170 on Port e Chee Lake, Douglas in July 2001.

Birds breeding in the British Isles are largely dispersive, rather than migratory, though some movement to France, Spain and Portugal is evident. Birds breeding in the north-west and south-west appear to move mainly west into Ireland (MA) and, presumably, also come to the Isle of Man. Such dispersal occurs from July onwards and probably accounts for the increased numbers locally. A large migratory influx into the British Isles from northern Europe is predominantly to the south and east of England and Scotland (MA), though some birds from those populations are also likely to reach Manx shores.

Winter distribution is not dissimilar to that of summer, though there is a greater incidence of birds inland, especially in the northern agricultural areas. As indicated by the winter abundance map, concentrations occur along the foreshore at Ramsey, when up to 500 birds can be present, Douglas Bay, with a maximum count of 580, and Langness Peninsula/Derbyhaven Bay, where up to 1,000 birds have been counted. It is likely that, though there are favoured feeding areas, some within winter movements occur, allowing birds to take advantage of local tidal and weather conditions, but making an accurate assessment of winter numbers difficult.

Ralfe found no evidence of breeding on the Island, describing Black-headed Gulls as abundant around the coast for most of the year. Breeding first occurred in 1947 at the Ayres (Ladds 1948), appearing to peak in 1976 when 170 pairs bred (C&J), declining by the seabird survey of 1985-86 to 74 pairs (Moore 1987), falling to only six pairs by 1998, with no pairs breeding in the period after the current research. It is likely that the local decline is due to the increase in the number of larger gulls breeding at the Ayres.

1977–81

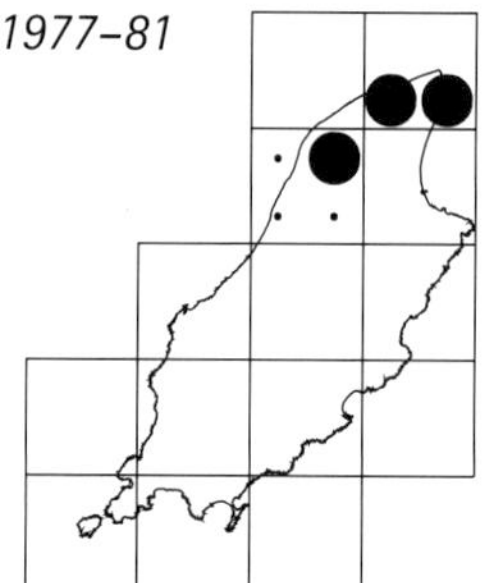

1998–2002

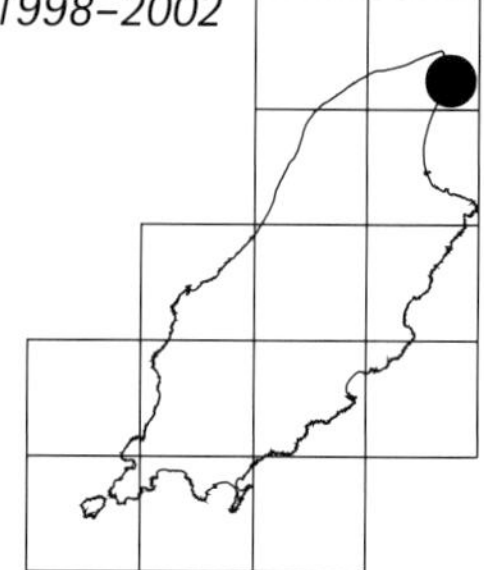

Breeding	Grid squares:	Isle of Man 76 (11%) Britain 671 Ireland 145 Total 816 (21%)
	Population:	Isle of Man 0-6 Britain 127,900 Ireland 14,000 (11% of European)
Wintering	Grid squares:	Isle of Man 118 (18%) Britain and Ireland 3,137 (81%)
	Population:	Isle of Man 2,000+ Britain and Ireland 3 million

Jan	Feb	Mar	Apr	May	Jun	Jul	Aug	Sep	Oct	Nov	Dec

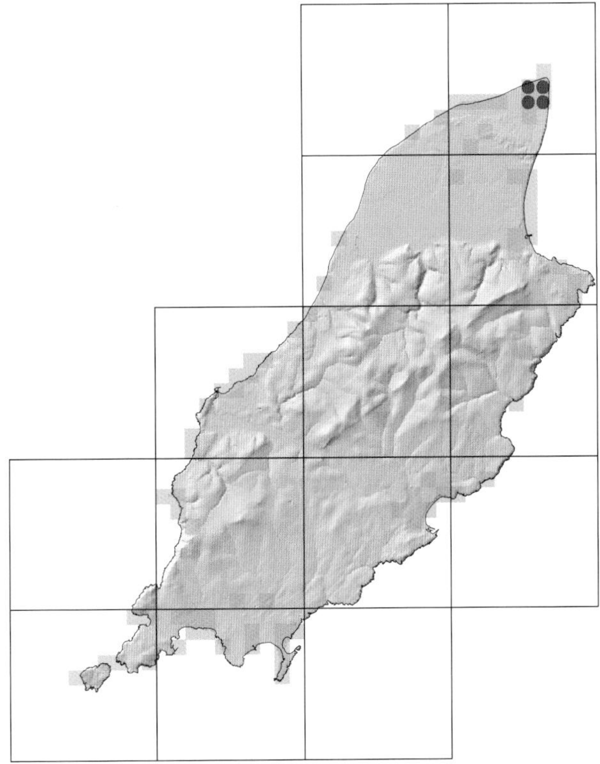

Summer presence and breeding status

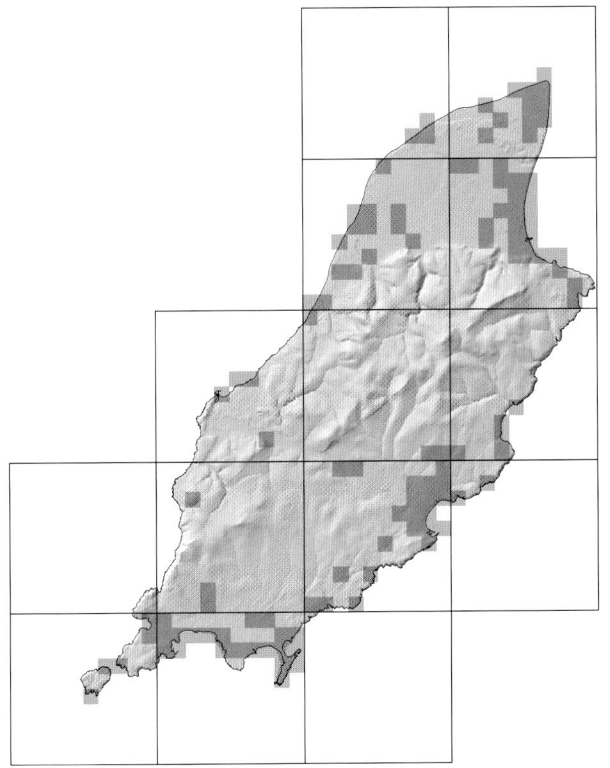

Winter presence

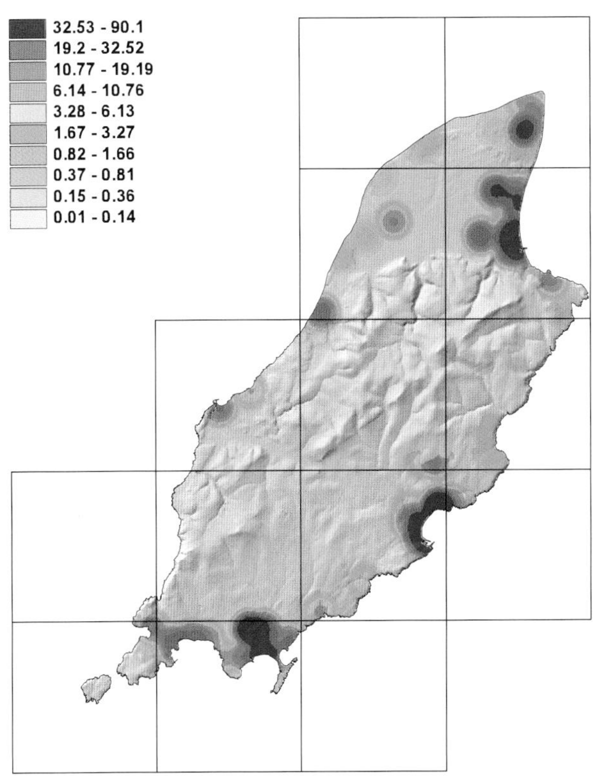

Winter abundance

Common Gull (Mew Gull)
Larus canus

Manx: *Foillan Vane*

At first glance the Common Gull appears very similar to the Herring Gull, having the classic gull plumage of pale grey wings, with black tips offset by otherwise white plumage. However, its smaller build and more compact appearance readily sets it aside, even at a distance, while the more slender bill, which lacks any red, and the yellow-green legs further aid identification.

In most cases Common Gulls nest near to water, often near the sea, but commonly inland, on islands on lakes, in marshes and bogs as well as in moorland and on heather slopes (EBA). Outside the breeding season they range more widely, demonstrating a preference for feeding on grass fields and coastal margins, often travelling some distance to communal roosts (WA). In fields earthworms and other invertebrates are primarily taken, either from within the soil or from the surface, while on the coast small fish, molluscs and other invertebrates are taken, with food often being selected from the debris stirred up by waves breaking on the shore.

The most abundant of the three subspecies of Common Gull, *Larus canus canus* breeds in Iceland, the Faeroes and northern Europe, the bulk of the population nesting in Fennoscandia, the British Isles and the Baltic States (EBA). Within the British Isles breeding is confined primarily to Scotland and the north and west of Ireland with a few records in England. There is no confirmed breeding in Wales and the Seabird 2000 census gave a total of 49,780 apparently occupied nests for the British Isles, of which 97% were in Scotland. This is a 39% increase since the census of 1985-88, though the number of 10km squares in which breeding was recorded fell by 32%, losses considered to be a consequence of habitat changes and predation (Seabird 2000). Locally, the breeding range of the species is restricted to the north, primarily the area of gravel pits and restored landfill at the Point of Ayre. The probable breeding record further west on the Ayres relates to a pair observed in May 2000. In 1999 six pairs bred, and eight pairs nested in both 2000 and 2001. Since then no more than six pairs have bred in any one year, though the true status is slightly masked by failed pairs re-laying in different areas. Fledging success is low with predation by larger gulls being the likely cause. Away from the breeding site, records in May and June are uncommon, and many of the records shown on the summer distribution map are from April and July and are of birds presumed to be on migration.

Post-breeding dispersal and migration is evident from July, when birds appear in suitable feeding areas on the coast, with up to 50 in some areas at this time. These Common Gulls are probably from breeding areas in Scotland. As the autumn progresses birds from the British Isles population, many of which do not migrate, are joined by large numbers of Common Gulls from continental Europe, including birds from Norway, Sweden, Denmark, the Baltic states and Russia (MA). In August 1995 a Common Gull ringed in Poland as a nestling in May 1993 was found dying at Rue Point, suggesting that the Island population of non-breeding birds may be partly derived from continental Europe.

Within the British Isles it is estimated that around 700,000 birds may be present in winter, making this the most important wintering area for the species in Europe (WA, MA). Winter distribution demonstrates a southerly bias, Common Gulls being relatively scarce away from the coast in both Scotland and Ireland, but much more common inland in England (WA). On the Island winter distribution is still mainly coastal, though the northern plain produces occasional records of feeding birds, while a few birds were seen at and near the roost on Clypse and Kerrowdhoo reservoirs, north of Douglas. Particular parts of the coast appear to be favoured, with the winter abundance map revealing concentrations near the Dog Mills, along Douglas beach and down the east coast to Langness/Derbyhaven, while the beaches around Kirk Michael and Jurby are apparently favoured in the west. Numbers present in any one area are small however, with no single winter count in excess of 80 birds.

Ralfe commented that the species appears in small numbers in autumn, winter and spring, referring to one nesting attempt, in 1904, when an egg was obtained from a nest, presumed to be that of Common Gull. C&J described it as common on autumn passage and as a winter visitor, having bred once, referring to a nest with eggs at Rue Point in 1983, and breeding has been confirmed annually since 1990. Though the species does not breed in large numbers, the breeding status of the Common Gull on the Island appears to be as healthy as it has ever been.

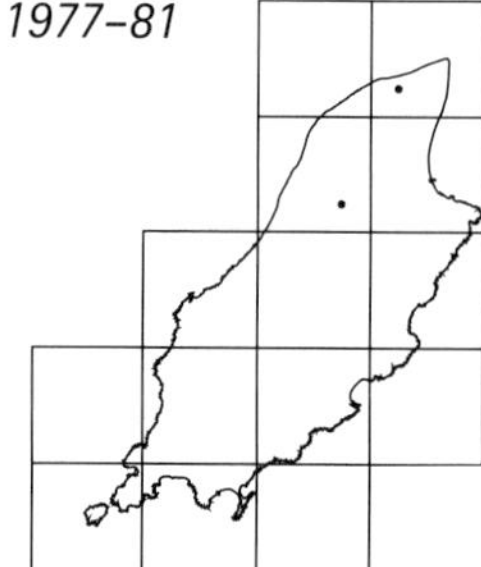

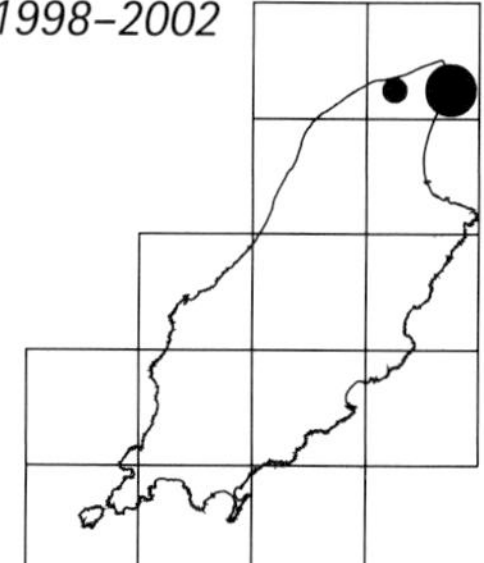

Breeding	Grid squares:	Isle of Man 20 (3%)
		Britain 577 Ireland 87 Total 664 (17%)
	Population:	Isle of Man 6–10
		Britain 48,200 Ireland 1,600 (15% of European)
Wintering	Grid squares:	Isle of Man 63 (10%)
		Britain and Ireland 2,741 (71%)
	Population:	Isle of Man <400
		Britain and Ireland 700,000

Jan	Feb	Mar	Apr	May	Jun	Jul	Aug	Sep	Oct	Nov	Dec

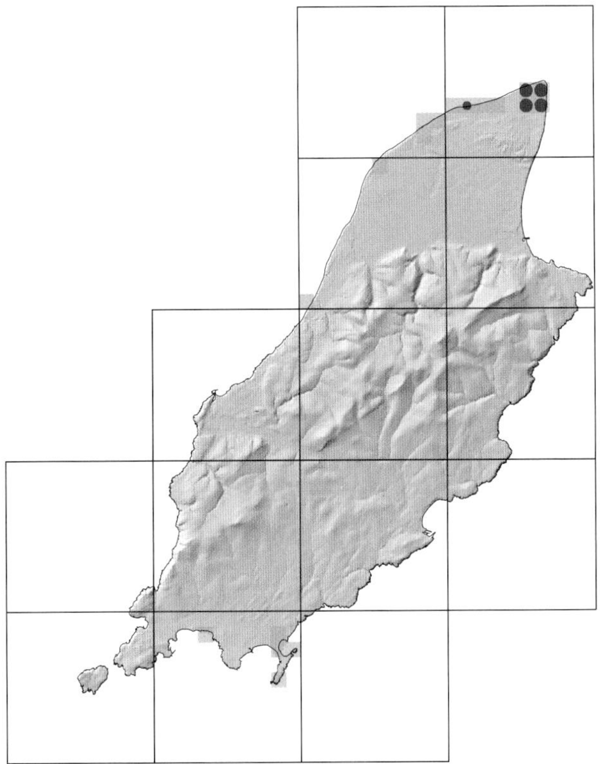
Summer presence and breeding status

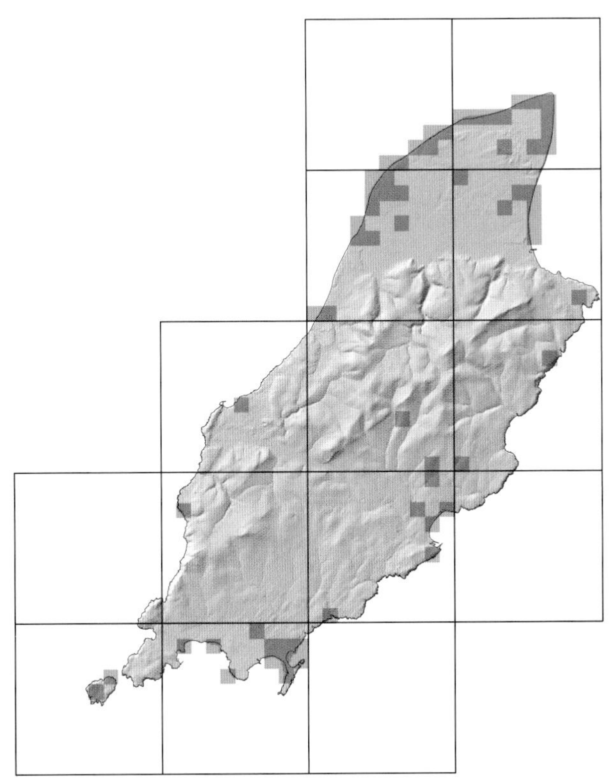
Winter presence

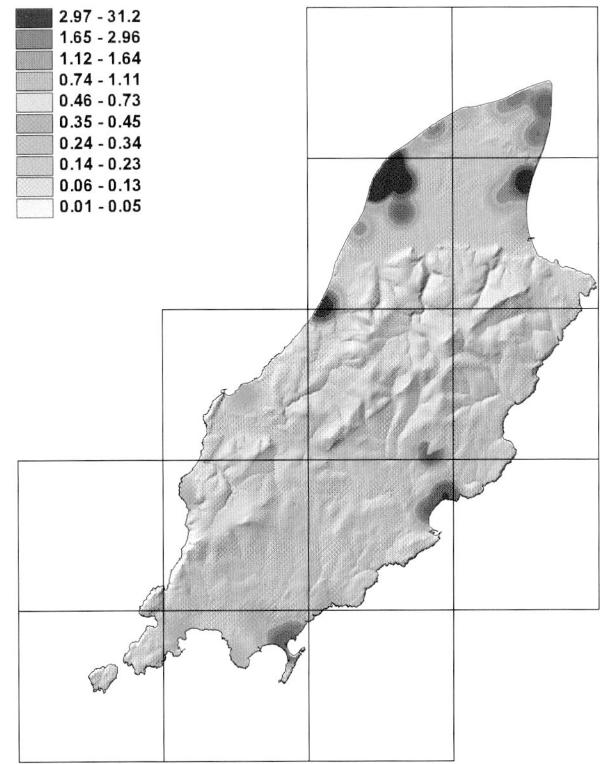

Winter abundance

Individual Sponsor – Mr. D J Sharpe

Lesser Black-backed Gull
Larus fuscus

Manx: *Foillan Saggyrt* = Priest Gull

The Lesser Black-backed Gull is approximately the same size as the more numerous Herring Gull, from which it can be distinguished by its slate-grey back and wings and yellow-orange legs. In bright sunlight, against a backdrop of vegetation, Lesser Black-backed Gulls stand out as the most attractive of the three larger gull species that occur regularly around Manx coasts and are always worth looking out for during a cliff-top walk.

In common with many gulls the Lesser Black-backed Gull is adaptable and uses a wide range of habitats for foraging, including agricultural land, where soil invertebrates are taken, rubbish tips, and at sea where fish are caught or obtained by piracy from other species (MA). Nest sites are typically on level or undulating ground, rather than rocky cliffs, and the species is less restricted to coastal areas than other large gulls, with some nesting in moorland (BWP).

It has a restricted breeding range, occurring only in north and west Europe, from Iceland east as far as the White Sea and south to Iberia. There are five subspecies within that range, with only the subspecies *Larus fuscus graellsii* breeding in the British Isles (Seabird 2000). Within the British Isles, breeding occurs around much of the coast, but is more sporadic along the east coasts of both Britain and Ireland. Over 80% of the estimated 116,684 pairs breeding were concentrated in just five broad areas – the Forth to the Clyde in Scotland, Morecambe Bay, West Wales, the Severn Estuary and East Anglia (Seabird 2000). Although the Seabird 2000 census found that 22% of the population nested inland, very few were further than 20 km from either the coast or an estuary.

Locally, breeding is confined almost entirely to coastal or near coastal locations. Inland nesting occurred in 1998, with two pairs on the slopes of South Barrule and a further pair to the east of Brandywell. During the seabird census of 1999, although 114 pairs were located, no birds were found nesting inland. The 1999 census reflected a modest increase compared to the 87-105 pairs located in 1986 (Moore 1987). A distinct east and south coast bias is evident, the generally less steep coastal slopes appearing to be favoured over the more rugged west coast. Three main colonies accounted for 73% of breeding pairs; the Point of Ayre restored landfill site (38 pairs), Maughold Head (19 pairs) and the Calf of Man (28 pairs). Of these colonies only the latter appeared in the seabird survey of 1985–86 (Moore 1987) when it was slightly larger, at 30-40 pairs.

It is likely that the Point of Ayre colony was under-counted in 1999. The flat terrain caused difficulty in counting birds on nests, while the presence of many Herring Gulls, which have very similar nests and eggs, created difficulties in accurately attributing nests to species when walking through the mixed colony. The growth of the Point of Ayre colony is attributed to the presence of open landfill in the area, providing an easy source of food. With landfill having ceased recently, it will be interesting to see whether numbers of breeding birds diminish. As demonstrated by the summer breeding status and distribution map, Lesser Black-backed Gulls were seen through much of the northern and south-eastern agricultural land and were probably a combination of non-breeding birds and foraging birds from nearby nest sites.

Through a combination of post-breeding dispersal and migration, numbers around Manx coasts decrease from mid-July onwards, though small numbers can still be present well into October or early November. Most of the Lesser Black-backed Gulls from the British Isles that migrate appear to move south to winter, mainly to Iberia (MA). Historically, Lesser Black-backed Gulls were considered to be complete migrants, only occasional birds being seen in winter. However, over the last 50 years Lesser Black-backed Gulls are increasingly remaining in the British Isles (WA), numbers being swollen by an influx of Icelandic, Faeroese and continental birds (MA).

Winter distribution in the British Isles demonstrates a strong inland bias, particularly favouring areas of dense human population, with their associated reservoirs and ample food supply (WA). Winter records are still rare on the Island, the species seldom being seen from late November through to January, and then usually only singly. Most of the winter records shown on the distribution map relate to sightings from the middle to the end of February, marking the first return of breeding birds to nest locations.

Kermode did not include the species in his 1888 list of breeding birds, while Ralfe mentions that it bred in good numbers on the Calf, with occasional nesting elsewhere, and also refers to 'one, two, or a small party' associating with Herring Gulls in summer and winter. C&J describe the species as a 'rather scarce summer visitor', noting also occasional winter records.

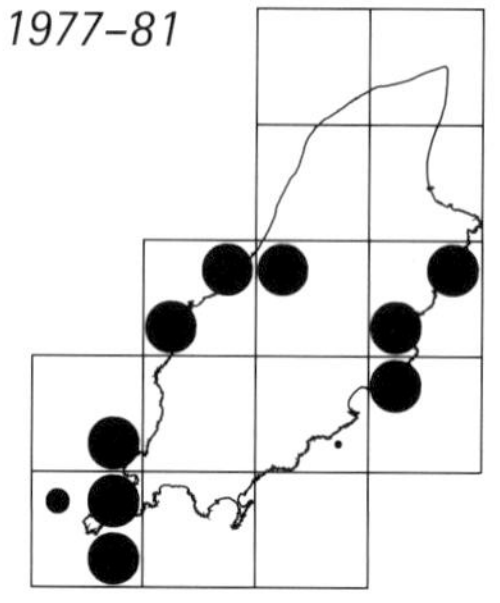

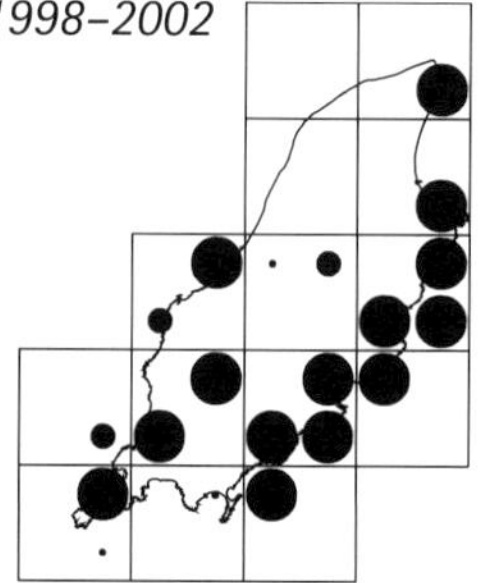

Breeding	Grid squares:	Isle of Man 176 (26%) Britain 434 Ireland 81 Total 515 (13%)
	Population:	Isle of Man 114 Britain 111,900 Ireland 4,800 (40% of European)
Wintering	Grid squares:	Isle of Man 30 (5%) Britain and Ireland 1,682 (44%)
	Population:	Isle of Man <100 Britain and Ireland 70,000

Jan	Feb	Mar	Apr	May	Jun	Jul	Aug	Sep	Oct	Nov	Dec

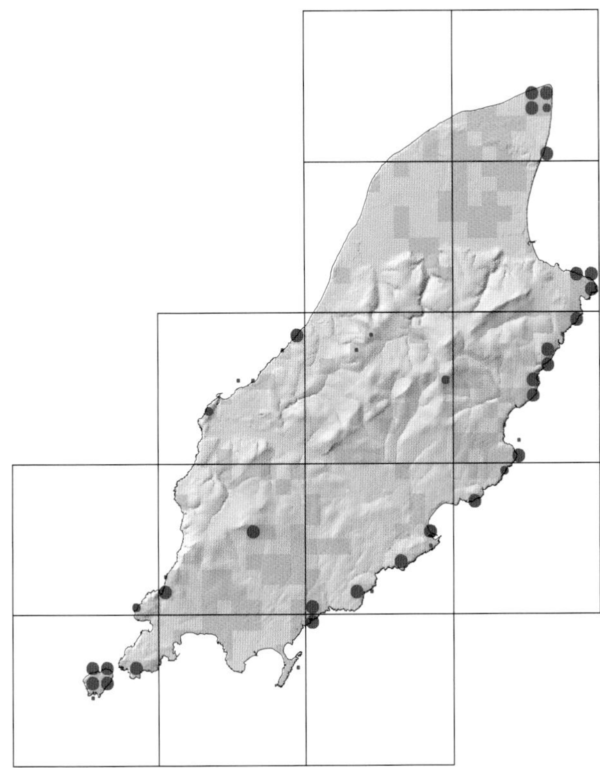
Summer presence and breeding status

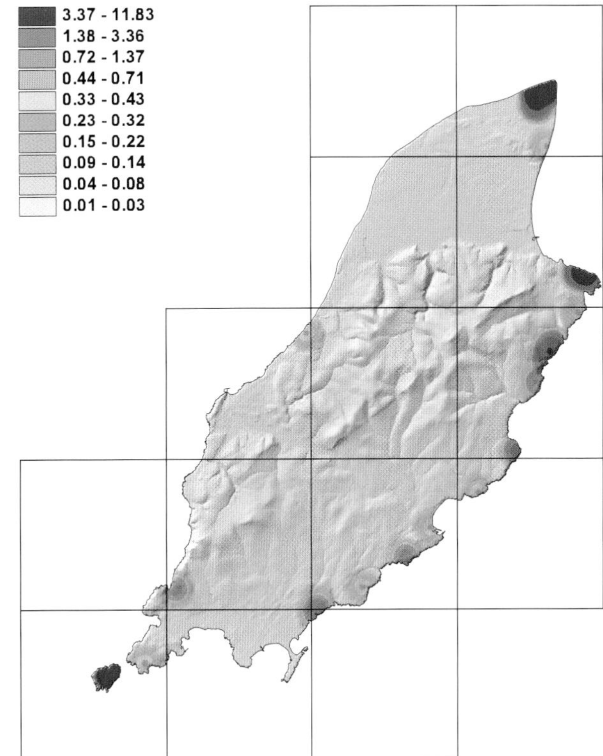

Breeding abundance

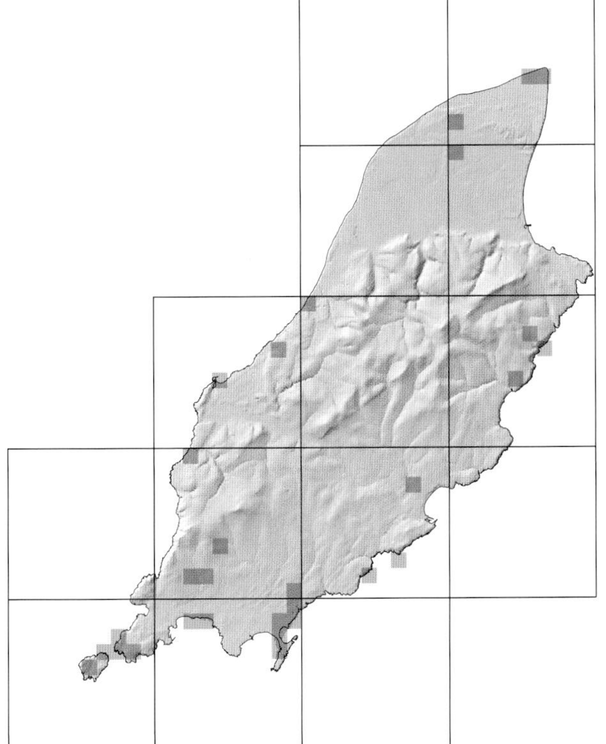
Winter presence

Herring Gull
Larus argentatus

Manx: *Foillan*

The Herring Gull is probably known to all, the stereotypical 'seagull', with pale grey back and wings, black wingtips and white head and under parts. The ultimate opportunists, Herring Gulls have learnt to good effect how to exploit the waste generated by humans, and their strident call is an almost constant feature of most towns and villages.

This adaptable species will utilise a wide range of habitats both for breeding and, especially, when foraging. Nesting occurs on steep coastal cliffs, shingle beaches, heather moorland and, increasingly, on buildings. A wide range of food is taken and 'pattering' for earthworms is commonly seen, as is more general foraging on fields and parks, while scavenging at tips and in towns provides rich rewards. At sea Herring Gulls will catch their own prey, pirate food from other birds or pick up waste from trawlers.

A number of different subspecies exist, classification seeming to be in a constant state of flux. The subspecies breeding within the British Isles *Larus argentatus argenteus*, also breeds in Iceland, the Faeroes, France, western Germany and Belgium (Seabird 2000). The total number of pairs breeding in the British Isles during the Seabird 2000 census was about 147,000, a decline of 57% from that of 340,000+ during the census of 1969-70 (Seabird 2000). The species is widely distributed around the coast of the British Isles, with absences or only intermittent presence on the eastern coasts of both England and Ireland, due largely to shortage of suitable natural nesting habitat (Seabird 2000). On the Isle of Man it nests primarily on rocky coasts, though sand cliffs are used near Jurby Head in the west and north of Shellag Point in the east. Natural inland breeding sites are confined to the slopes of Sartfell, where 144 pairs bred in 1999, nearby Slieau Freoghane, which had six nests in 2000, and Beary Mountain where six pairs were present in 1998. Buildings are used for breeding in most coastal towns, with the furthest from the sea being a nest in St Judes, 5km from the coast. Accurate counts of roof-nesting birds proved impossible, so the overall figure of 7,126 pairs obtained from our census of 1999 should be treated as a minimum. Despite breeding occurring throughout more of the Island than indicated in C&J (see comparative maps), numbers breeding fell by 21% in the period since the seabird survey of 1985-88. As in many other places in the British Isles, losses are probably directly attributable to avian botulism, with open landfill tips considered to be one of the primary sources through which birds can become infected (Seabird 2000). Summer distribution of Herring Gulls is almost complete, with absences from only a few of the Island's peaks. While some of these records will relate to non-breeding birds they will also include birds from the breeding population, which will range widely to obtain food.

Post-breeding movements are considered to be mainly dispersive, rather than migratory. Birds of the subspecies *L.a. argentatus*, which breeds in northern Europe, move to the British Isles to winter from September to February, though they mainly occur on the east coast (MA). The majority of Herring Gulls wintering on the Island are therefore likely to be from our summer population, with numbers increased by birds dispersing from nearby areas of the Irish Sea coast.

Although the winter distribution of Herring Gulls is extensive, their range covers less of the uplands than in summer. Winter abundance demonstrates an east coast bias, Port Erin and the coast from Peel north to Ladyport holding the only coastal concentration in the west. Pockets of higher density are evident at most towns, and on the Clypse and Kerrowdhoo Reservoirs north of Onchan. The landfill site at the Point of Ayre attracted many thousands of birds during the research period, with a conservative estimate of 10,000 birds present on some days. Since the completion of the research period tipping has ceased and, by the winter of 2005–06, counts of fewer than 100 birds were more typical.

Ralfe described the Herring Gull as 'perhaps the dominant bird of Man', with C&J defining it as an 'abundant resident'. Clearly the species is still common and widespread on the Island, though recent declines in breeding populations suggest that its fortunes may have peaked.

1977–81

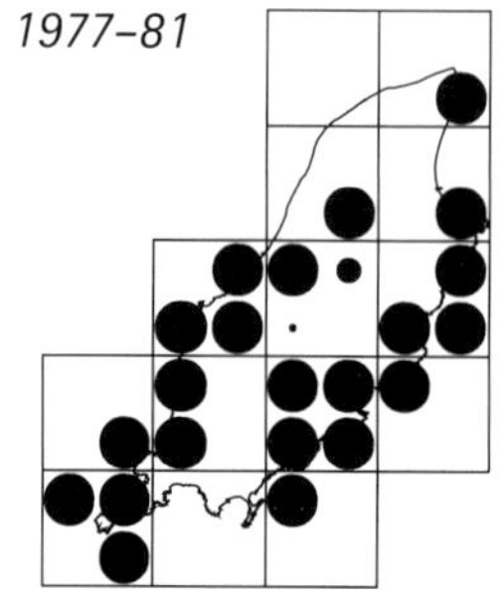

1998–2002

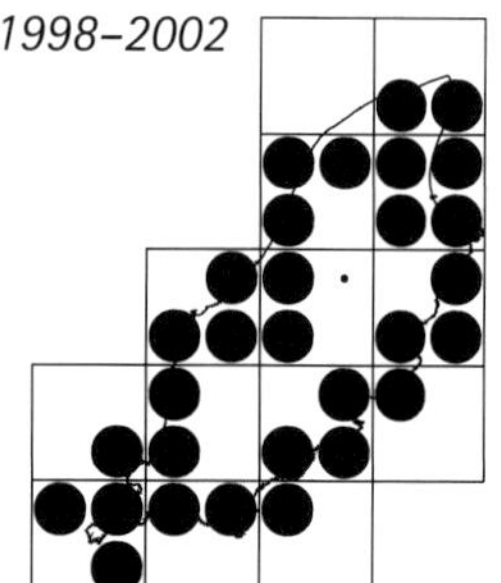

Breeding	Grid squares:	Isle of Man 615 (92%)
		Britain 729 Ireland 163 Total 892 (23%)
	Population:	Isle of Man 7,126
		Britain 142,900 Ireland 6,200 (26% of European)
Wintering	Grid squares:	Isle of Man 468 (70%)
		Britain and Ireland 3,032 (79%)
	Population:	Isle of Man 20,000-30,000
		Britain and Ireland 275,000

Jan	Feb	Mar	Apr	May	Jun	Jul	Aug	Sep	Oct	Nov	Dec

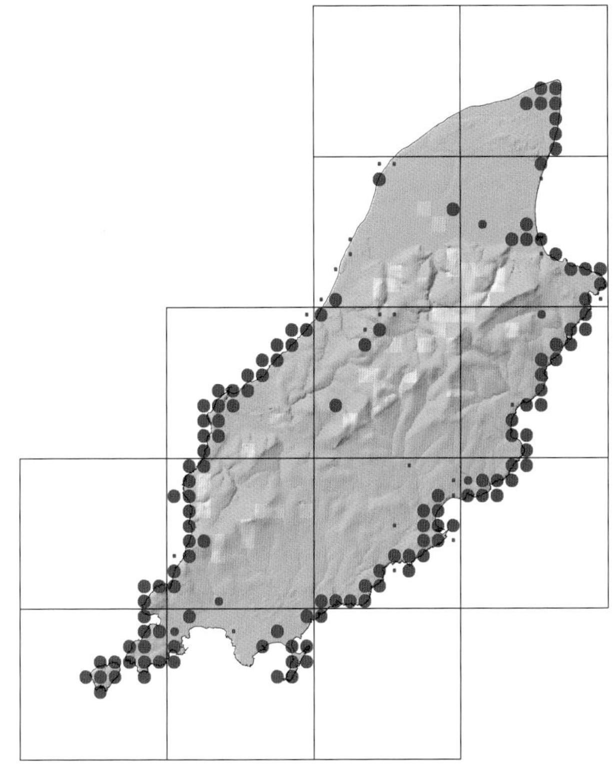

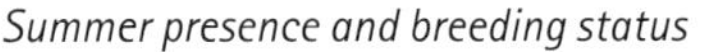

Summer presence and breeding status

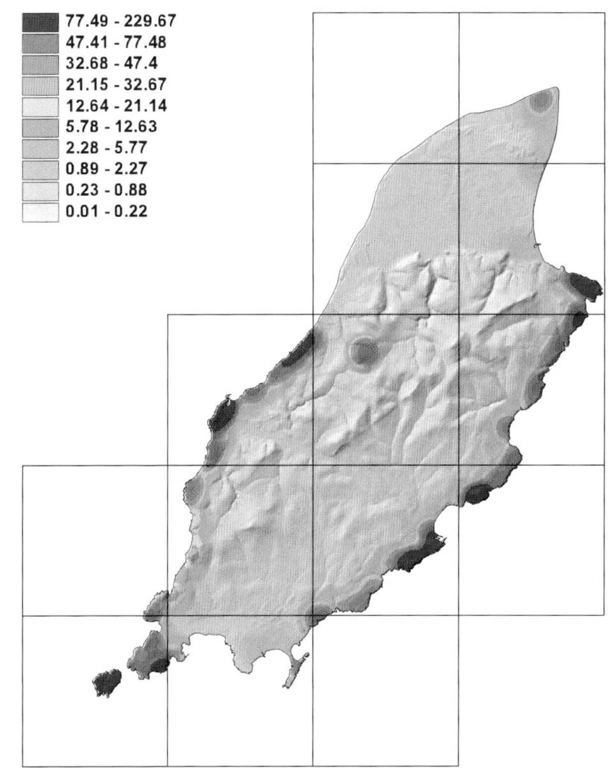

Breeding abundance

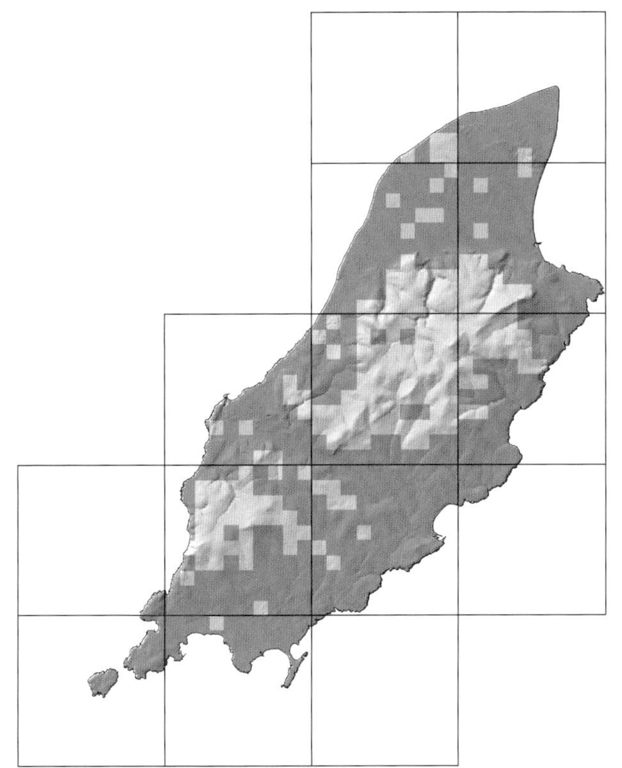

Winter presence

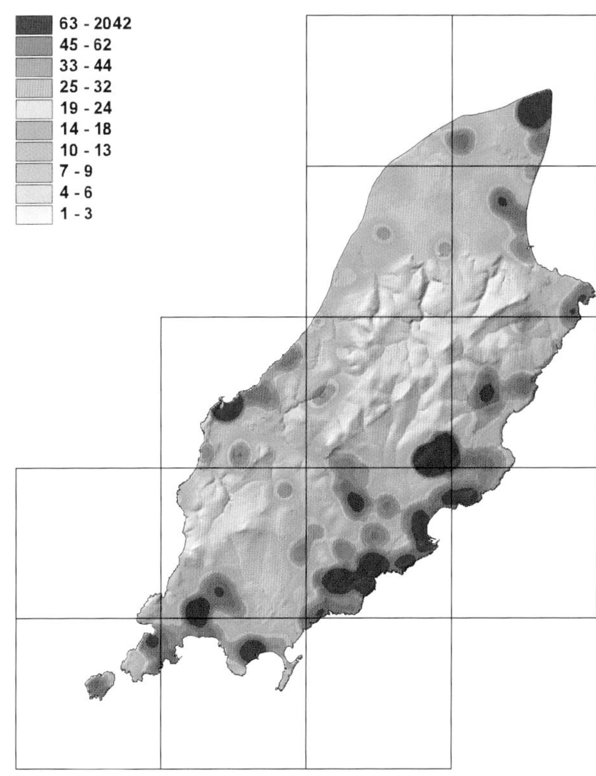

Winter abundance

Individual Sponsors – Dr. M Hannan, Mr. D J Slinn

Great Black-backed Gull
Larus marinus

Manx: *Juan Mooar* = Big John

This, the largest of our gulls, with a wingspan exceeding 1.5m, presents few identification challenges, its size, heavy-set appearance, dark black back and wings setting it aside from the similar Lesser Black-backed Gull. Unpopular with many, it is still persecuted by farmers to defend livestock and causes problems for conservationists as it will predate more vulnerable species. It is nonetheless a striking bird, the stark contrast of black and white plumage drawing the eye whenever it is seen.

Great Black-backed Gulls are essentially birds of the coast, with nest sites generally located on rocky outcrops and stacks (MA). In such places the species usually nests in scattered pairs, seldom in colonies. Great Black-backed Gull colonies tend to be situated on flatter grassy headlands or, to a more limited extent, at inland sites such as on lakes and moorland (EBA). They scavenge and will take a wide range of food sources. Pirating of eggs and young of a variety of species, as well as cannibalism, is commonplace, and live rabbits, sickly or newborn lambs and placentae are also taken. It is however the most marine of the large gulls, and in winter a high proportion of the British Isles population appears to forage mainly on natural marine foods (WA).

The breeding range is confined largely to the coasts of the North Atlantic and Baltic. Of about 180,000 breeding pairs worldwide approximately 66,000 are found in North America and Greenland. Norway has the largest number of European breeders at 40,000 pairs, with the population in the British Isles estimated at over 19,000 pairs (Seabird 2000). Scotland hosts 75% of the pairs in the British Isles. The species demonstrates a marked north and west coast bias in distribution, with absences along much of the east and south-east coasts of England and Ireland. Similarly, the west of England along the Irish Sea coast has only scattered pairs. Overall there has been little change in the population within the British Isles since the census of 1969-70, though some marked change in several areas and colonies is evident (Seabird 2000).

On the Isle of Man a total of 405 pairs was located in the census of 1999, an increase of 47% on 1969–70, but only an 8% increase on the 376 pairs found in 1985-86 (Seabird 2000). Comparison of the map included in C&J with that for the MBA research reveals that the species has also become more widely distributed. Breeding was primarily confined to rocky coasts with many pairs not breeding colonially. The colonies on the Calf of Man and Kitterland held a total of 180 pairs, a significant percentage of the overall population, with further concentrations along the east coast from Laxey north to Maughold Head and on the west coast both to the north and south of Peel. Inland, small numbers bred at Beary Mountain, Druidale and near Barregarrow. When foraging the species occurred widely throughout the Island during the summer although less commonly on the agricultural lowlands than the Herring Gull.

The British Isles population of breeding Great Black-backed Gulls is largely sedentary. Some localised dispersal does occur, but generally this involves movement of less than 100km (MA). There is, however, an influx of birds derived mainly from the Norwegian population, arriving from July to September. A few of these reach western Britain (MA), and presumably, the Isle of Man.

The Manx wintering population comprises local birds, augmented by variable numbers of birds from within the near geographic area. Throughout England the species is found more commonly inland in the winter than during the summer, though it retains a mainly coastal distribution in the rest of the British Isles (WA). On the Island too it occurred inland only rarely during the winter, such sightings often being of lone birds or small flocks either foraging or moving to and from roosts. Winter concentrations in the south and west of the Island largely reflect those found in summer, though rather fewer birds were evident along the coast north of Laxey. The Point of Ayre landfill site regularly hosted flocks of 200+ Great Black-backed Gulls with 1,000+ present in late February 2003. However, relatively few were present during the timed fieldwork from which our abundance data were derived.

Ralfe showed that the Great Black-backed Gull was only starting to become established as a breeding species on the Island in the late nineteenth or early twentieth century, the first definite nest being found in 1911 (Ralfe 1923). By the time of C&J they had become well established, described as a 'common resident with most of the population showing some dispersal. Fairly common winter visitor'. There is currently little to suggest that their status locally is under threat.

1977–81

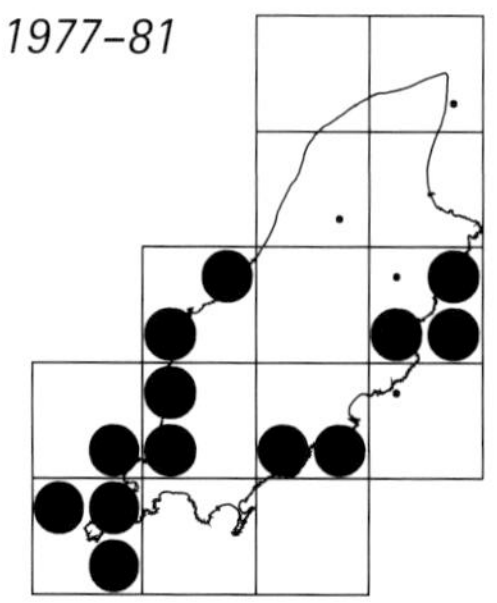

1998–2002

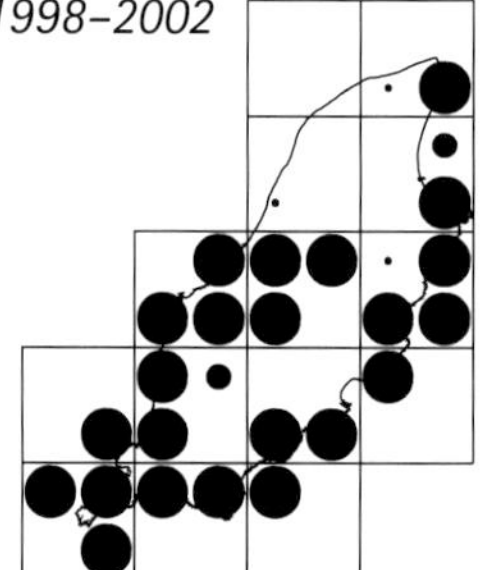

Breeding	Grid squares:	Isle of Man 377 (57%) Britain 486 Ireland 137 Total 623 (16%)
	Population:	Isle of Man 405 Britain 17,400 Ireland 2,300 (22% of European)
Wintering	Grid squares:	Isle of Man 176 (26%) Britain and Ireland 2,542 (66%)
	Population:	Isle of Man <1,000 Britain and Ireland 80,000

Jan	Feb	Mar	Apr	May	Jun	Jul	Aug	Sep	Oct	Nov	Dec

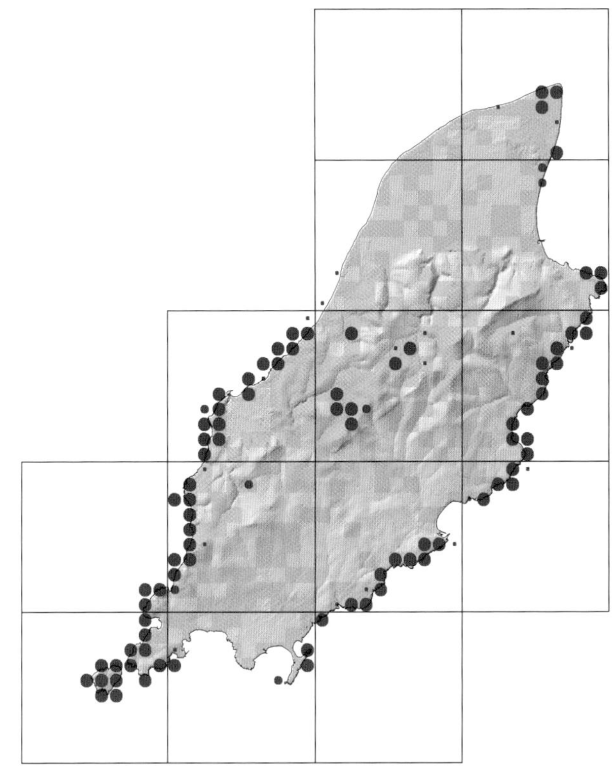

Summer presence and breeding status

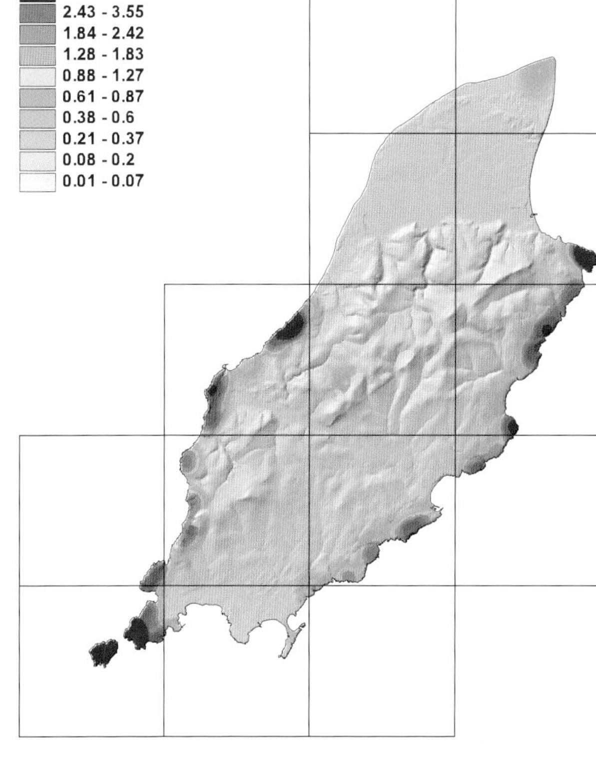

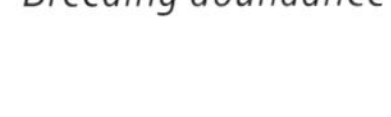

Breeding abundance

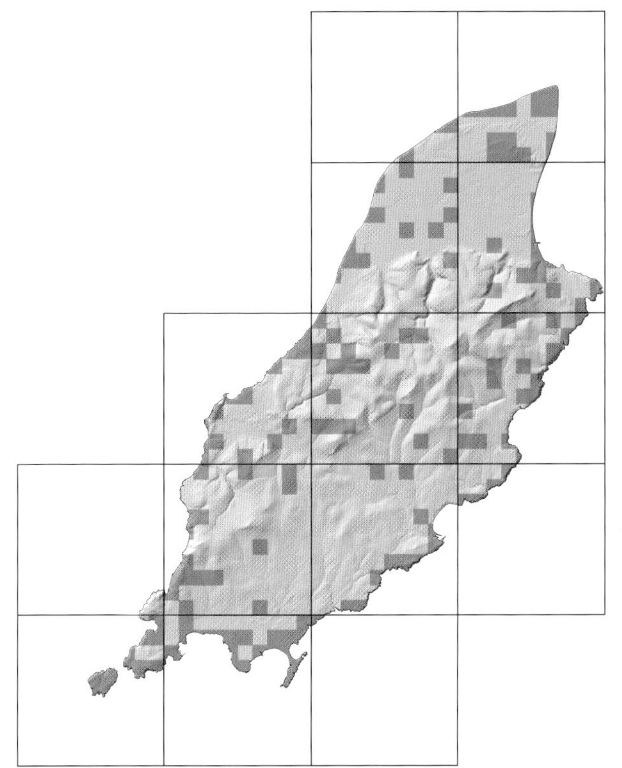

Winter presence

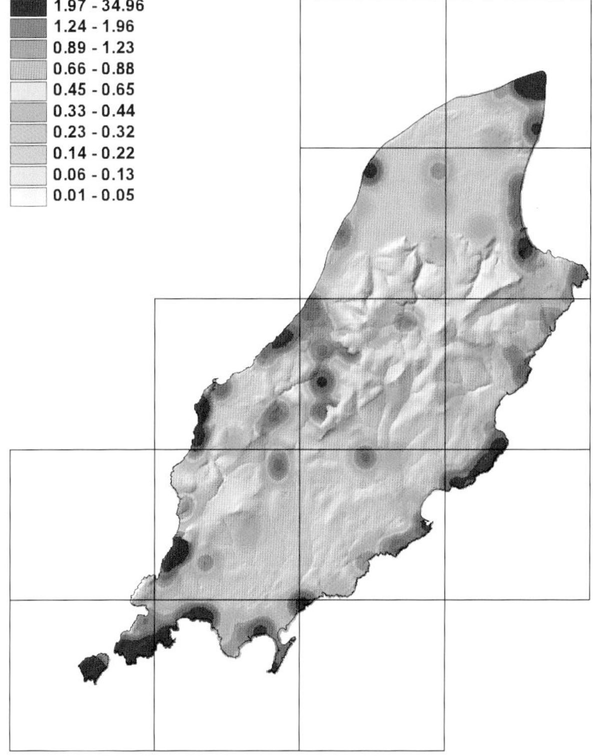

Winter abundance

Individual Sponsors – Mr. A Lang, Ms. M Masters

Kittiwake (Black-legged Kittiwake)
Rissa tridactyla

Manx: *Perragh*

'Dainty' and 'neat' are words that spring to mind when describing this small gull. Such words, however, do not do justice to this hardy oceanic species that graces our shores for a short time each year. The call, from which its name is derived, forms a continuous background clamour to the constant activity at colonies, the level of noise often reaching deafening proportions.

Precipitous sea cliffs provide the main nesting sites for Kittiwakes, though in some areas man-made structures are used, including buildings, bridges and offshore oil installations (Seabird 2000). Food is taken from the surface or near surface of the sea and comprises mainly small fish and planktonic crustaceans, though offal and discards from fishing boats are also sought (Seabird 2000).

There are two subspecies of Kittiwake, which combined make the species the most numerous gull in the world, with a population estimate of 4.3m to 5.2m pairs (Seabird 2000). The subspecies that occurs locally, *Rissa tridactyla tridactyla*, breeds along North Atlantic coastlines from Portugal to Russia, with main concentrations in Iceland, Norway, the British Isles, Svalbard and the Faeroes (EBA). Within the British Isles, the Seabird 2000 survey found 415,995 breeding pairs, 68% of which were in Scotland; the majority of colonies and greatest numbers of birds being on the northern and eastern coasts, including Shetland and Orkney. The species is less abundant down the west coast, with only small, scattered, colonies along the south coast of England. Overall, the British Isles breeding population fell by 23% between 1985–88 and 1998–2002, though there was considerable regional variation. The reduction probably resulted from a combination of adverse weather and variable food availability (Seabird 2000). On the Isle of Man breeding Kittiwakes are confined to only four locations; Calf of Man (131), Sugarloaf/Chasms (580), Maughold Head (205) and Peel Hill (129), these being the number of pairs breeding in 1999, giving a total of 1,045 pairs. This represents a decline of around 17% from that found in 1986 (Moore 1987), slightly less than the decline throughout the British Isles but comparable with Wales and Cumbria. Elsewhere around Manx coasts the Kittiwake can be seen throughout the summer; early season records including birds still returning to breeding sites. Breeding does sometimes not commence until early June if conditions are not suitable. Though June records away from colonies are rather scarce, in some years large numbers can be seen, for example 700 birds roosting along the Ayres foreshore in mid-June 2000, these possibly comprising failed breeders. More typically it is not until July that larger numbers are seen, including birds on passage, particularly along the Island's north-west coast.

By the end of July in most years Kittiwakes have finished breeding and have deserted their nesting ledges, the young not being fed by parents once they have fledged. Autumn movements past the Island, presumably of more northerly breeders, can be sizeable, with counts of over 5,000 in a day. For the winter the species is oceanic, and spreads across the North Atlantic south to about 30–35°N, often making extensive movements to avoid atmospheric depressions (MA).

Winter presence in the British Isles is evident around much of the coast, although only about 1% of birds present in the summer remain (WA). Some inland records are also obtained during the winter, many if not all relating to storm-blown birds most of which probably die within a few days (MA). Lack (1986) observed that, within the British Isles, observations of Kittiwakes in late November and December used to be rare, other than those of birds passing offshore, but more recently they were occurring in small numbers around harbours.

Around the coast of the Isle of Man winter records remain rare, mainly consisting of low numbers seen occasionally from the Ayres, Peel Castle and the Calf of Man. By late February, though sightings are still infrequent, the number of birds seen during observations increases, with counts of up to 100. Also birds occasionally visit breeding colonies. During the Atlas period the only inland record was of a dead bird.

By 1905 Ralfe knew of only one colony, numbering 30–40 pairs, on the Calf of Man, understood to have existed for at least 40 years. By 1921 he noted the colony had disappeared, being replaced by one where there were 'hundreds of pairs', near the south end of the main Island, at Spanish Head and Black Head; these areas had been abandoned by 1964 (C&J). The Calf colony appears to have been reoccupied around 1956, while breeding was first noted at Maughold in 1946, Peel Hill in 1947 and in the area of the Sugarloaf in 1969 (C&J). The four current colonies have therefore been in constant use since at least 1969. These sites are relatively secure from disturbance; threats to the future for the species locally are a combination of changing climate, and hence altered food availability at key stages of their life cycle.

1977–81

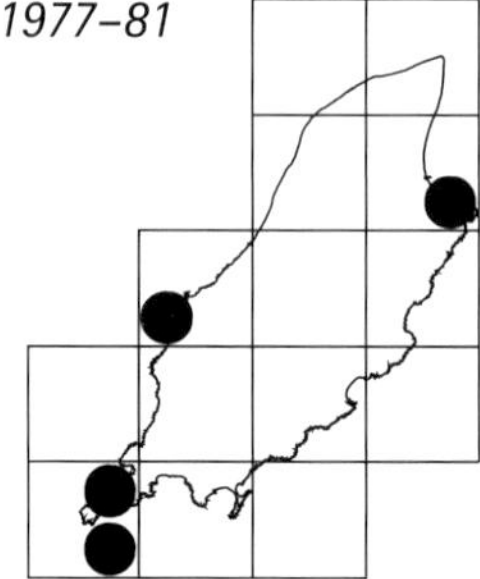

1998–2002

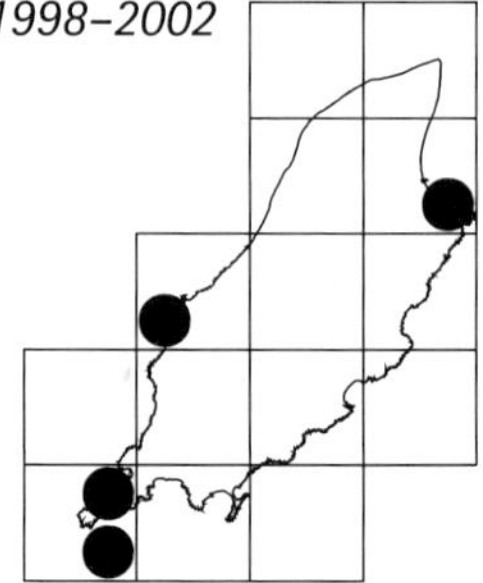

Breeding	Grid squares:	Isle of Man 45 (7%) Britain 252 Ireland 62 Total 314 (8%)
	Population:	Isle of Man 1,045 Britain 336,800 Ireland 49,200 (23% of European)
Wintering	Grid squares:	Isle of Man 15 (2%) Britain and Ireland 876 (23%)
	Population:	Isle of Man a few along coast Britain and Ireland 1,000 near coasts

Jan Feb Mar Apr May Jun Jul Aug Sep Oct Nov Dec

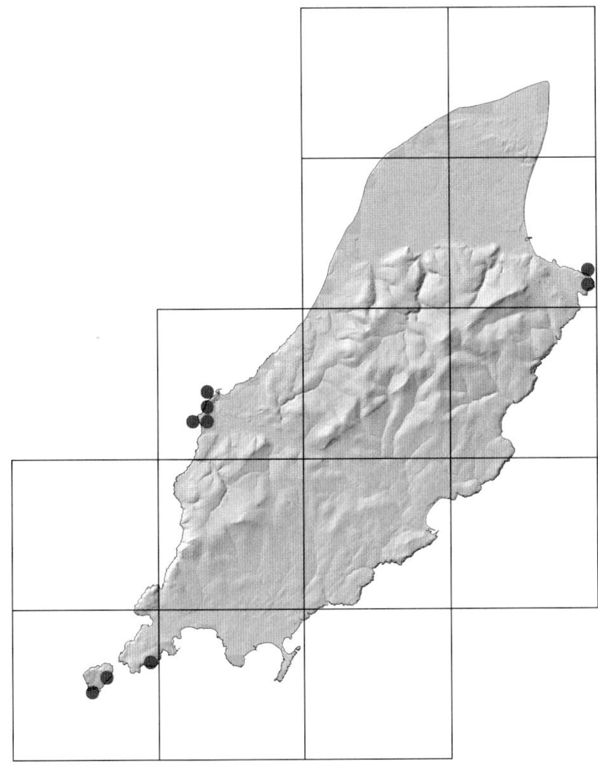
Summer presence and breeding status

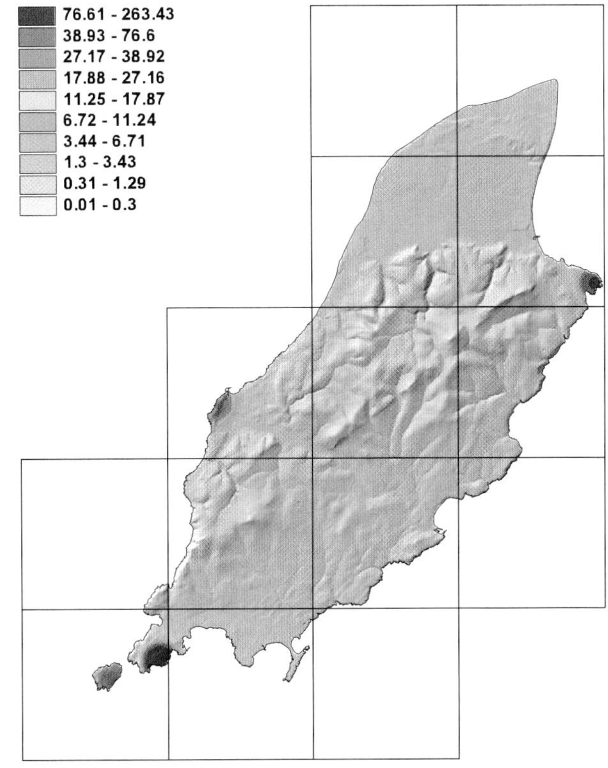

Breeding abundance

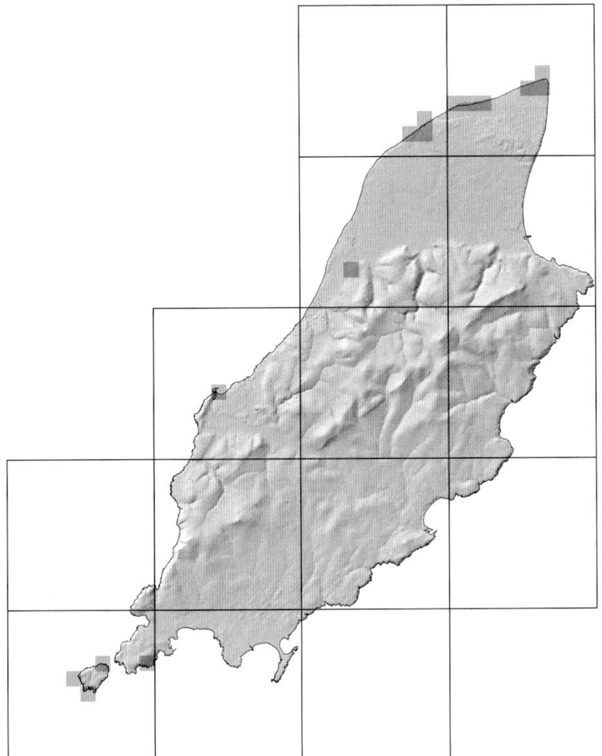
Winter presence

Individual Sponsors – The Fitzpatrick family

Little Tern
Sternula albifrons

Manx: *Gant Beg*

Locally, Little Terns present few identification challenges. They are easily separated from Arctic Terns by their small size, more rapid wing beats and black-tipped yellow bill, beneath a white forehead. In common with the Arctic Tern they will be fearless in their defence of nesting colonies, hovering low over human intruders, calling constantly and making repeated dives, though they are less prone to striking than the Arctic Tern, usually terminating their dive just above head height.

Little Terns nest in colonies on marine and lake shores and along inland rivers, often at considerable distances from the sea (EBA). Nest sites are on sand and shingle beaches and spits, the nests often consisting of no more than a shallow scrape, with or without pieces of vegetation. Throughout their range a variety of prey is taken, including invertebrates, although locally their diet consists almost entirely of fish, with sandeels dominating. Hunting consists of quartering over the shallows, head down, followed by a brief hover and then a plunge, either partially or completely submerging to catch prey from the surface or near surface of the sea.

Of the three subspecies of Little Tern, *Sternula albifrons albifrons* breeds throughout much of Europe, North Africa, the Middle East and India, with a population estimate of 34,000–59,000 pairs of which 17,000–22,000 occur in Europe (Seabird 2000). Within the British Isles, Seabird 2000 recorded occupancy at only 130 colonies, with a British Isles total of just 2,153 pairs and 21% of these in only three colonies. Colonies occur around much of the British Isles coast, though they are largely absent from Wales, with 70% of pairs situated on the east and south-east coasts of England. On the Isle of Man the species has a very restricted breeding range, occurring only along the coast from the Lhen to the Ballaghennie Ayres, with most breeding attempts in the Rue Point area. Throughout the research period numbers breeding were variable, with a maximum of 26 pairs in 2000 and a minimum of six pairs in 2002. Fledging success was also subject to sizeable annual variation, the best year being 1999, when 16 fledged young were seen, but only one fledged bird was observed in 2001. Human disturbance, predation by Herring Gulls, corvids and hedgehogs and adverse weather, combine to make the Little Tern one of our most vulnerable species. During the summer it is seldom seen away from the Ayres coast, the only other record during the research period being of a single bird off the Calf of Man in May 2002.

Although in some parts of the British Isles Little Terns can be present into September (MA), sightings beyond the end of July are rare on the Island. All of the later records during the period of research were confined to August, with only one sighting away from the Ayres beaches, that of two birds flying south off the Calf in 2000. Little is known of migration routes for the species, though most of the European population is thought to winter off the coast of western Africa (MA).

In 1898 Ralfe found a colony of about 20 nests, probably at Rue Point, constituting the first record of breeding of Little Terns on the Isle of Man. By 1938 there were 50 pairs at Rue Point and a further colony at Ballaghennie (C&J). In 1979 a complete census yielded 43 pairs (Cullen 1980), from the Lhen Trench area to Ballaghennie.

Moore (1987) undertook a complete survey of the Ayres coast and gravel pits in June 1985, resulting in a total of 57-60 pairs of Little Terns being located between the Lhen Trench and Ballaghennie, the majority at Rue Point. With only a small breeding population, centred on one or two colonies per year, continued protection from human disturbance and a greater understanding of the impact of predation are critical to the future of the species on the Isle of Man.

1977–81

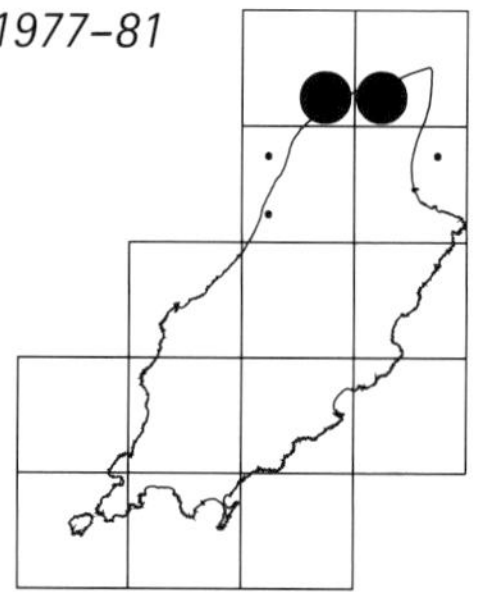

1998–2002

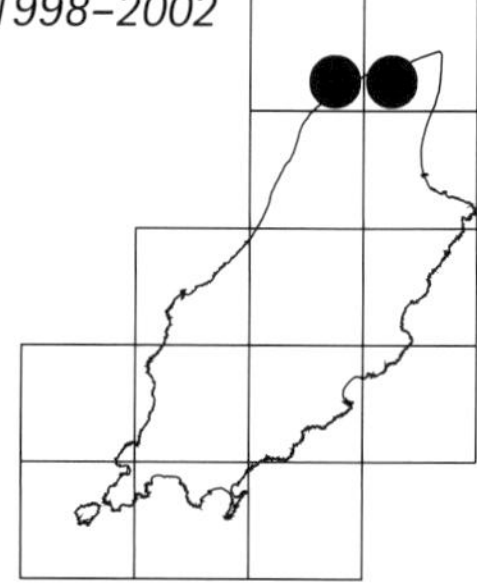

Breeding	Grid squares:	Isle of Man 15 (2%) Britain 110 Ireland 36 Total 146 (4%)
	Population:	Isle of Man 6–25 Britain 1,900 Ireland 206 (13% of European)

Jan	Feb	Mar	Apr	May	Jun	Jul	Aug	Sep	Oct	Nov	Dec

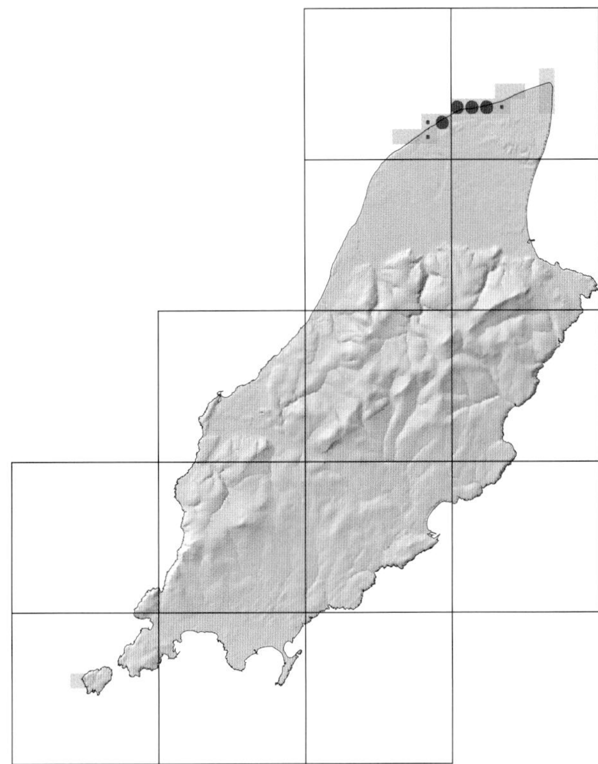

Summer presence and breeding status

Individual Sponsors – Ms. H E Park, Mr. D J Sharpe

Arctic Tern
Sterna paradisaea

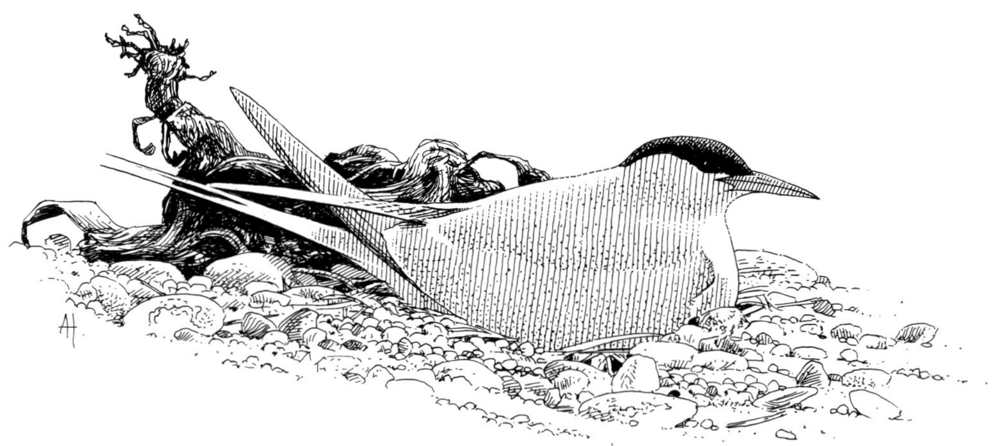

Anybody careless enough to wander into a colony of Arctic Terns will soon be made very aware of their mistake, as these delicately built summer visitors have an accurate eye and sharp bill, not hesitating to draw blood from any unprotected head. Their screeching call should be enough, however, to warn off intruders, who should then carefully retrace their steps to avoid trampling the beautifully camouflaged eggs and young. Watching the constant comings and goings of adults at a colony one has to marvel at their agile flight, giving the impression of birds 'bouncing' through the sky, at an instant turned to a direct meaningful stoop if danger threatens.

Throughout its breeding range the Arctic Tern is primarily a coastal breeding species; although breeding on the Isle of Man is confined to the coast, they will also nest inland, often along rivers and on islets within lakes, on flat grassed areas, shingle and on beaches. While a range of foods is taken, fish constitute the main bulk of their diet, with sandeels appearing to be the main prey taken locally. Feeding typically comprises a brief hover followed by a short plunge into the water, the bird disappearing beneath the surface only briefly before reappearing with a fish held crosswise in the bill.

The breeding range of the Arctic Tern is extensive, occurring on both the west and east coasts of North America as well as along the coasts of Greenland, Iceland, other Arctic Ocean islands and along the coast of Siberia to the Bering Strait. Within Europe, Iceland hosts the largest population with breeding also occurring in Scandinavia, the Baltic States, northern Germany, the Netherlands and the British Isles (EBA). Breeding within the British Isles is confined almost completely to coastal sites and demonstrates a distinct northerly bias, most colonies being in Shetland, Orkney and the Outer Hebrides. With the exception of small colonies in East Anglia, Arctic Terns are absent around the coast of England and Wales south of Northumberland and Anglesey, though they are more evenly spread around the coast of Ireland (Seabird 2000).

Locally, Arctic Terns have a very restricted breeding distribution, breeding only taking place in the extreme north of the Island. In 1998 and 1999 two and three pairs respectively bred on Ballaghennie Ayres, with a further pair in 1998 being unsuccessful in an attempt on the east coast, south of the Point of Ayre. Apart from these records breeding in each of the five years of the MBA survey was confined to the bare shingle ridges of the Point of Ayre, the maximum numbers in any year (2002) reaching 15 pairs. Moore (1987) found 13 pairs breeding in 1985, all within the Point of Ayre Gravel Pit complex, though a further 15 pairs of undifferentiated, Common or Arctic Terns were also present. The gravel pit site continued to be used by small numbers until 1997 when it was opened as a landfill site, work commencing at the height of the breeding season, causing total breeding failure. There were a few summer records away from the Ayres, being mainly at the start and end of the breeding season, and these were likely to be of birds on passage.

Arctic Terns commence migration as soon as breeding is complete. There are few local records in August and the species is only rarely reported in September or October. The Arctic Tern undertakes the most extensive migration of any bird, the winter quarters extending to reach the pack ice of the southern oceans (MA). A single migration that can extend from one Arctic region to another is a remarkable and exacting journey. Despite this, individuals can live for many years. In 1998, one of the adults nesting on the Isle of Man was found to have been ringed as a chick in 1980 on the south-east coast of Norway.

The Arctic Tern has enjoyed mixed fortunes on the Isle of Man. Numbers appear to have been at their highest in the middle of the nineteenth-century, when J. C. Crellin (1862) made reference to 'hundreds of birds of this kind' coming to breed. During the middle part of the twentieth century Arctic Terns bred in scattered colonies along the Ayres coast from Rue Point to the Point of Ayre, and part way down the east coast of the Ayres (C&J). Now, as then, the main colony is at the Point of Ayre, a popular walking spot for many residents and visitors to our Island. Though long-term climatic change will influence food availability and hence breeding success, the most immediate threat to our small population of Arctic Terns is human disturbance and destruction of nests.

1977–81

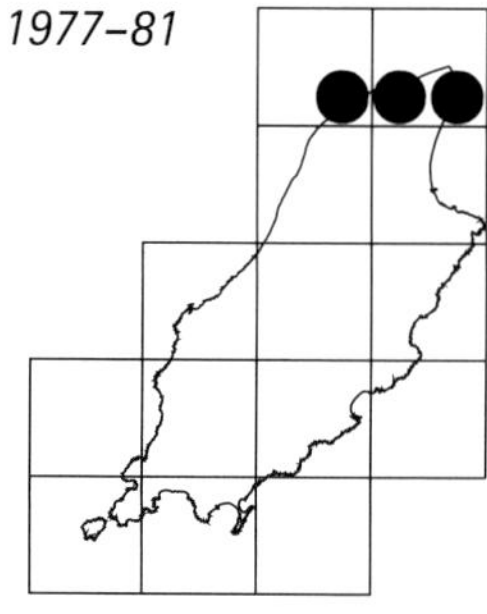

1998–2002

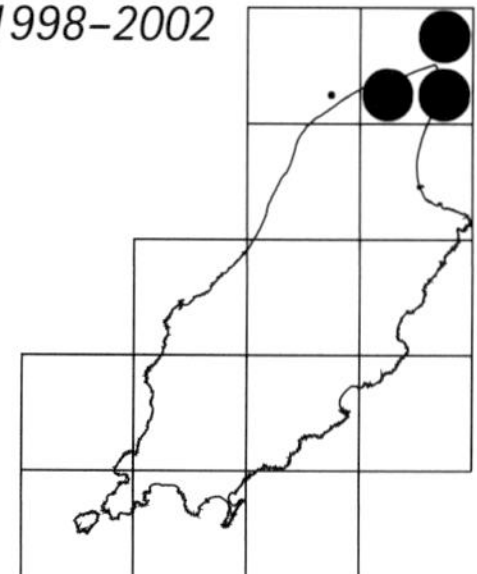

Breeding	Grid squares:	Isle of Man 17 (3%) Britain 303 Ireland 72 Total 375 (10%)
	Population:	Isle of Man 15 Britain 52,600 Ireland 3,500 (9% of European)

Jan Feb Mar Apr May Jun Jul Aug Sep Oct Nov Dec

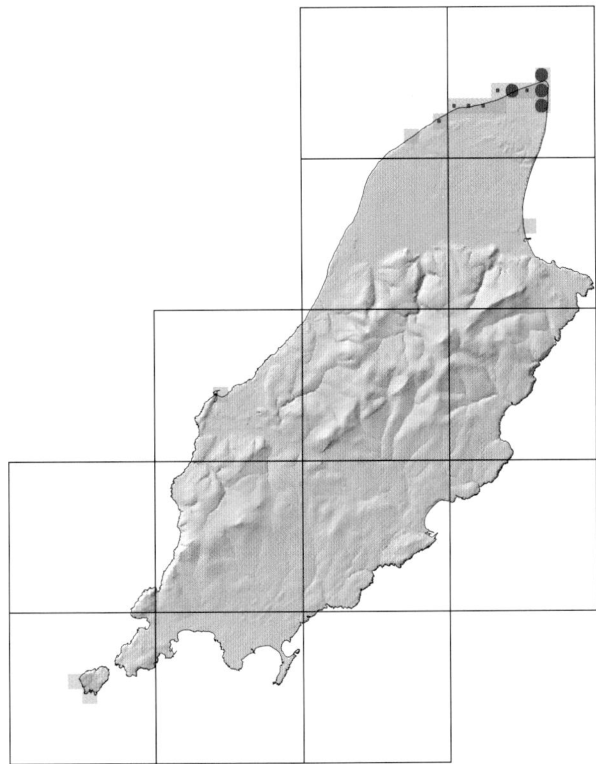

Summer presence and breeding status

Individual Sponsor – Mrs. M Masters

Guillemot (Common Guillemot)
Uria aalge

Manx: *Stronnag. Chennell*

Guillemot breeding colonies are spectacular, a combination of noise, movement and smell assaulting the senses. Birds arriving and departing constantly interrupt ranks of Guillemots lined up on ledges, their chocolate-brown backs and throats complementing the white underparts. Arriving birds often approach at speed, low over the water, before using a combination of height gain and spread feet and wings to slow down to alight on the narrowest of ledges, never seeming to dislodge their eggs. An underwater visit to the seabed beneath colonies indicates otherwise, however, with several complete eggs usually evident among the rocks during the incubation period.

Breeding sites are located on cliff ledges or flat rock outcrops or, occasionally in crevices. Nests are seldom built, most eggs being laid on bare rock, eggs being pointed at one end to minimise the risk of them rolling off the ledge. Throughout their range Guillemots take a variety of fish, obtained mainly by diving from the surface, often preceded by frequently immersing the head to look for prey. Locally, most of the fish brought to feed young at nest are sandeels, though small herring are also taken.

Guillemots are widely distributed throughout the northern Atlantic and Pacific Oceans and adjacent Arctic Ocean, the range in the north-east Atlantic extending from Portugal to Spitsbergen, including the Baltic. Within this area there are three subspecies. *U.a. aalge* occurs in most of coastal Europe including Scotland and possibly northern England, with the smaller *albionis* found in the rest of the British Isles (including the Isle of Man), Heligoland, France and Iberia. North of about 69°N *aalge* is replaced by *hyperborea* (MA, Seabird 2000). Seabird 2000 estimated the British Isles population at 1,559,484 birds, a 32% increase on that in the previous seabird census of 1985–88 when 1,182,791 birds were found. Scotland holds about 75% of the British Isles population, though breeding occurs around most of the rest of the coast, with the exception of much of the east and south-east coasts of England, where habitat is unsuitable.

Within the Isle of Man, breeding distribution is limited to areas of high steep cliffs, distribution being broadly as indicated on the map within C&J. A total of 4,566 individual adults was found during the seabird census of 1999, an increase of 108% over the 1985-88 figure of 2,195 (Seabird 2000). Four main breeding areas account for 96% of birds, the largest area being the coast from the Anvil to the Chasms, including the Sugar Loaf (2,139), followed by Peel Hill (1,438), the Calf (416) and Maughold Head (409). Among each of these main colonies small numbers of the bridled form of Guillemot were found, with their attractive white eye-ring and spectacle, this form occurring more frequently with increased latitude. Away from known colonies summer sightings along the coast are rare, many of these being in April of birds observed making passage.

By mid-July most nest ledges have been abandoned, the young gliding and tumbling down into the sea before they are fully fledged. Once the young are on the sea, adults take them offshore, away from predators, so few young are seen near local colonies. Guillemots are not considered migratory, but do disperse in the autumn, with fewer birds being seen near coasts during August and September, at which time they are moulting and flightless (MA). From October onwards Guillemots make frequent visits to nest ledges, though such visits are unpredictable, large numbers being present one day and none the next. Such large movements probably account for the flocks of up to several hundred birds that can be seen flying past watch points in the late autumn and early winter. During the winter research period, Guillemots were recorded around much of the coast, but generally in small numbers. The lack of records in some remote areas probably owes more to a combination of reduced observer effort and high vantage points, making birds harder to see, than it does to a true lack of birds. The largest winter count obtained was in January 2002 with over 1,000 birds centred on the Sugar Loaf colony.

The Guillemot has a long association with the Island, remains being identified in the Perwick midden deposit of approximately AD90 (Garrad 1972). Early observers wrote glowingly of the numbers present, Townley (1791), considering them 'beyond the art of numeration'. The first complete census, in 1969-70, gave a figure of 1,050 adults, numbers increasing since then, the most recent count being the highest recorded.

1977–81

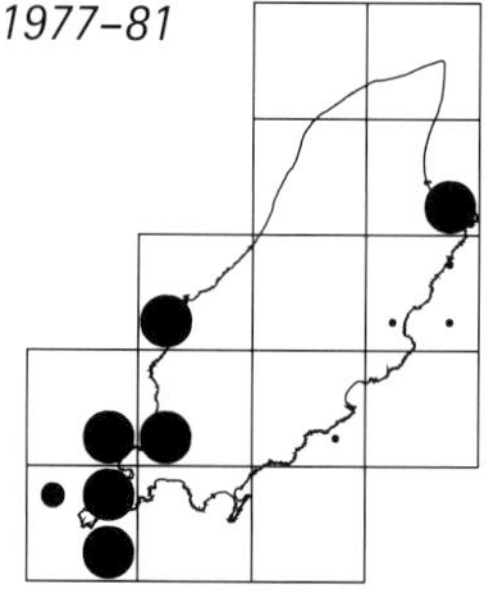

1998–2002

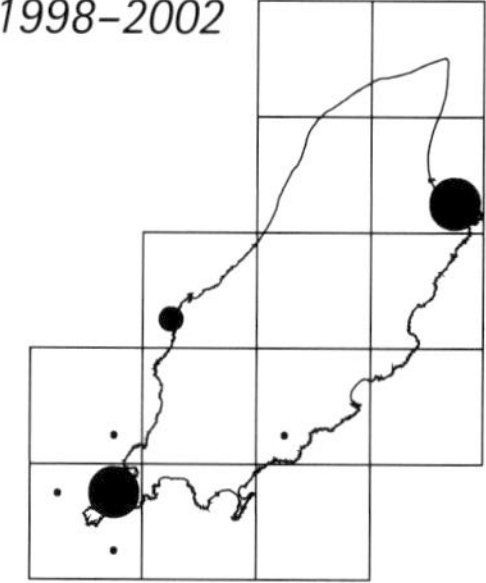

Breeding	Grid squares:	Isle of Man 34 (5%) Britain 212 Ireland 59 Total 271 (7%)
	Population:	Isle of Man 4,566 (adults) Britain 1,332,800 Ireland 236,700 (30% of European)
Wintering	Grid squares:	Isle of Man 19 (3%) Britain and Ireland 750 (19%)
	Population:	Isle of Man 0-1,500 Britain and Ireland not known

Jan Feb Mar Apr May Jun Jul Aug Sep Oct Nov Dec

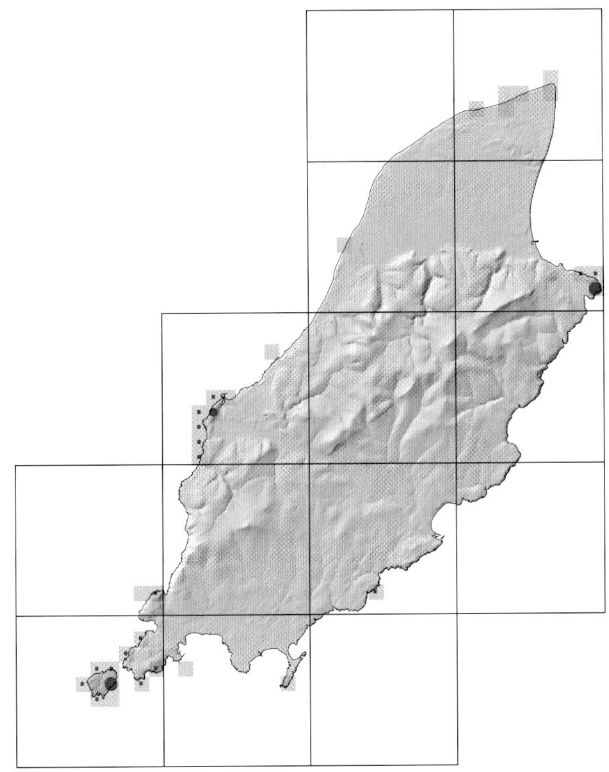
Summer presence and breeding status

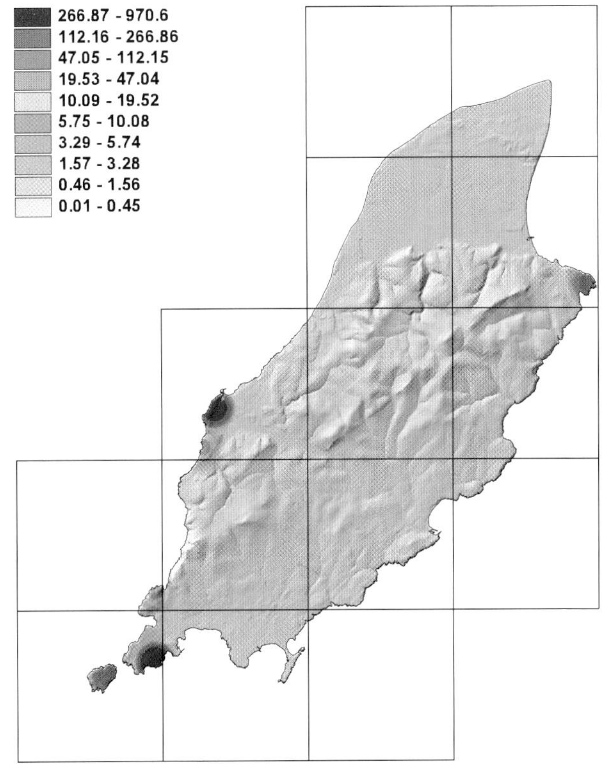

Breeding abundance

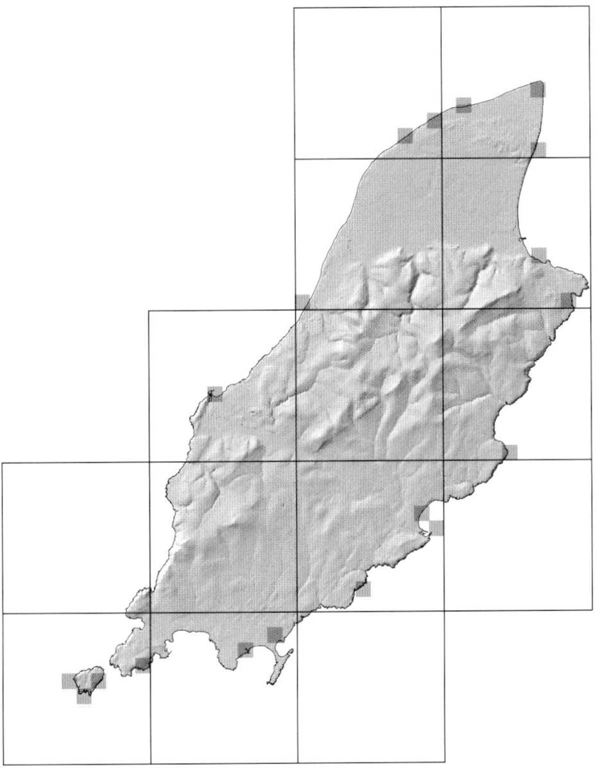
Winter presence

Individual Sponsor – Mr. R H Taylor

Razorbill
Alca torda

Manx: *Coltrag*

The upperparts of Razorbills are black, rather than the dark brown of their near relative and close associate the Guillemot. This feature, coupled with the Razorbill's larger, deeper, bill with thin white stripes, usually makes it easy to correctly identify the species, when seen well. At distance or in flight, however, they are less easy to differentiate, resulting in some counts of birds passing our coasts being attributed to 'auk species' rather than to either species specifically. Razorbills' facial markings give them an aggressive appearance, as they stand guard at nest sites, growling at intruders.

Although Razorbills nest among colonies of Guillemots and other seabirds, they are more dispersed, not forming the massed ranks for which Guillemots are noted, and can be overlooked within large mixed colonies. Razorbills also nest in more discrete colonies and in odd pairs, scattered among small ledges and in cracks on rock cliffs and among boulder scree (Seabird 2000). Fish make up the bulk of the diet and, like the Guillemot, they hunt mainly by surface diving, frequently immersing the head to look for prey before doing so. Sandeels and small herring form the majority of food taken to young at the nest, adults often bringing several fish at once, carried crosswise in the bill (BWP).

Razorbills are restricted to the North Atlantic and adjacent Arctic waters, from north-east North America to the White Sea and south as far as Brittany. Within this range, two subspecies exist, with *Alca torda islandica* breeding in Iceland, the Faeroes, the British Isles and, in small numbers, in France and Germany (Seabird 2000). Seabird 2000 estimated the world population of *islandica* to be 530,000 pairs, 27% of which occur in the British Isles. Within Britain and Ireland, they are absent from most of the east and south coasts of England, due to lack of suitable breeding sites, but are otherwise widely distributed around the coast. Of about 216,000 adults counted at suitable nest sites 64% were in Scotland (Seabird 2000). On the Island 1,524 adults were counted at nest sites during the 1999 seabird census compared to only 848 in 1985-87. Razorbills are absent from much of the east coast, with the notable exceptions of the steep cliffs of Maughold Head, Marine Drive and to the south of Port Soderick. The largest concentration is to be found along the cliffs from Port St Mary to Bradda Head, and on the Calf of Man. Razorbills occur in smaller numbers along the coast to the north of Bradda Head, as far as the most northerly west coast colony at Peel Hill. Away from known colonies summer distribution is rather restricted, being a mix of April records of birds presumably still on passage, and records of mainly single birds feeding in the shallow waters of the Ayres.

In the post-breeding period Razorbills leave colonies and move offshore, during which time young complete their growth and adults moult, becoming flightless for a period (BWP). Thereafter, a gradual movement south is evident, initially of young birds. They winter mainly off Iberia and Morocco, with some in the western Mediterranean, but other birds favour the North Sea and western Norway (MA). During September and particularly October, large numbers of Razorbills can be observed heading south past the Island, with single day counts in excess of 500 commonplace and counts exceeding 1,000 not unusual.

Winter records of Razorbills off Manx shores are relatively few with the winter distribution map showing that most are off the Ayres. Other records are a mix of birds passing favoured watch points, mainly during February, and storm-bound birds taking shelter in bays such as Ramsey and Derbyhaven.

The Razorbill has a long history on the Isle of Man, remains being present in the Perwick midden deposit dated AD90 (Garrad 1972). The species was recognised as 'plentiful' by Willughby in 1660 (C&J). In 1898 Ralfe described Razorbills as more widely distributed, if not more abundant, than Guillemots. The first full survey was conducted in 1969, when Slinn (1971) put the Manx Razorbill population at 576 pairs, with a comparable number found in the survey of 1985-87 (Moore 1987). The 1999 count was the highest recorded for the Island.

1977–81

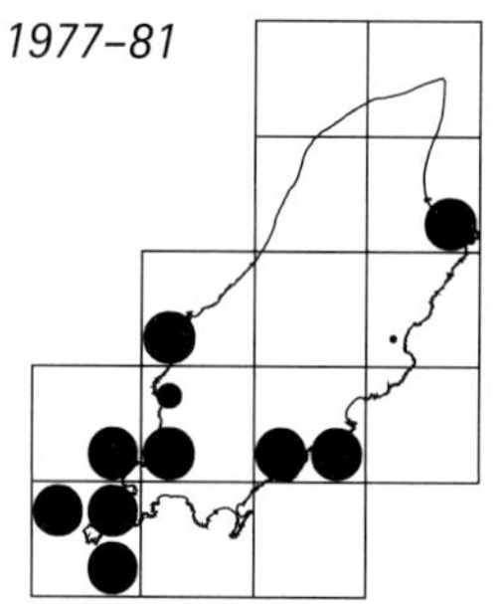

1998–2002

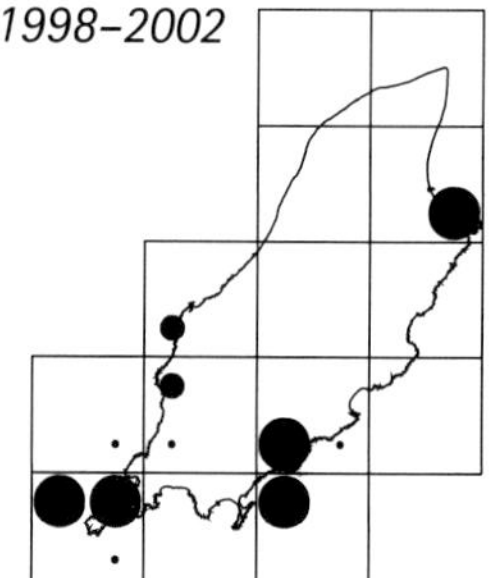

Breeding	Grid squares:	Isle of Man 53 (8%) Britain 233 Ireland 63 Total 296 (8%)
	Population:	(adults) Isle of Man 1,524 (adults) Britain 164,600 Ireland 51,500 (19% of European)
Wintering	Grid squares:	Isle of Man 30 (5%) Britain and Ireland 618 (16%)
	Population:	Isle of Man 100-200 Britain and Ireland not known

Jan	Feb	Mar	Apr	May	Jun	Jul	Aug	Sep	Oct	Nov	Dec

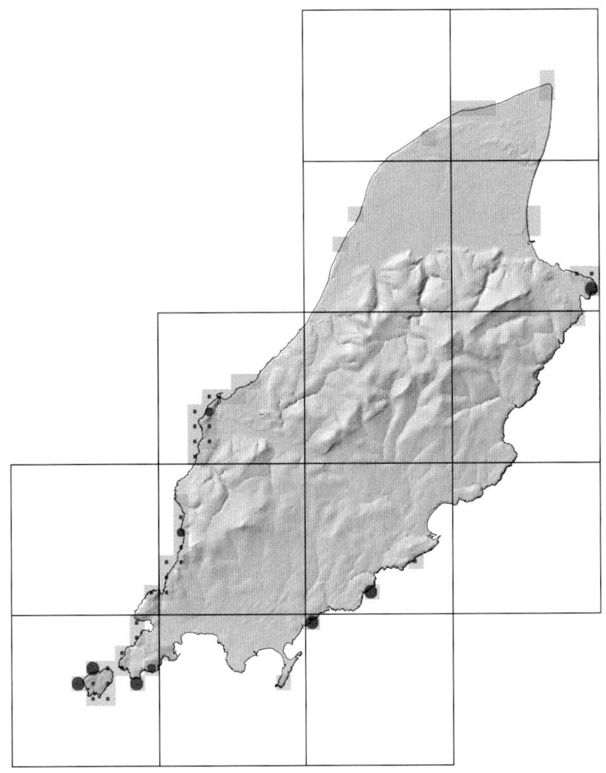

Summer presence and breeding status

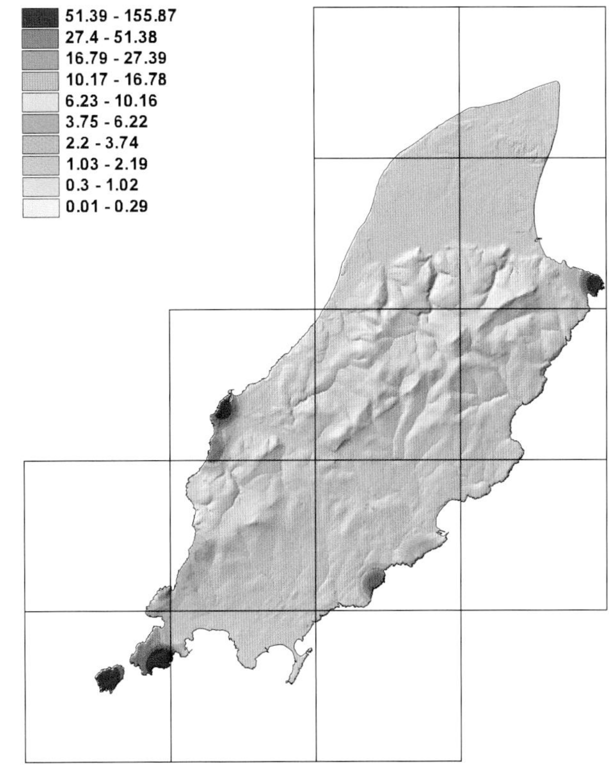

Breeding abundance

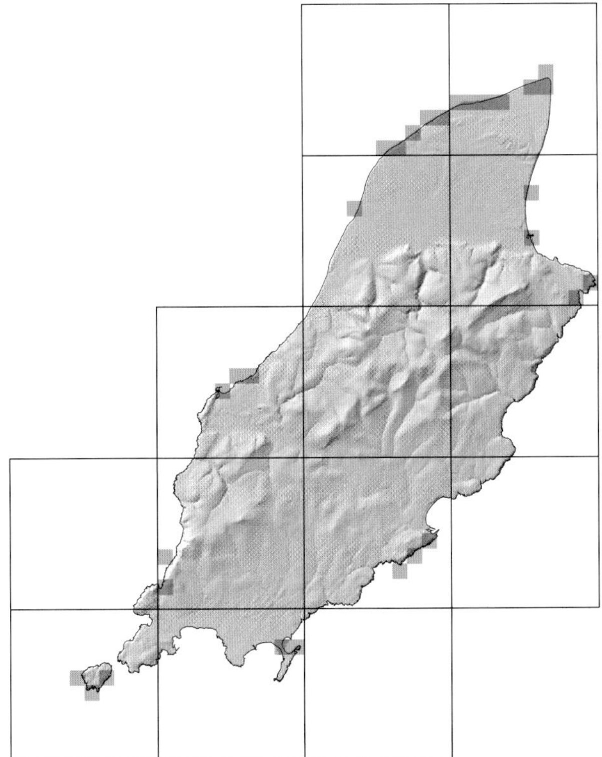

Winter presence

Individual Sponsors – Mr. G & Mrs. M Maggs

Black Guillemot
Cepphus grylle

Manx: *Caillagh Ghoo*

The Black Guillemot, or 'Tystie' as it is often called, is a charismatic species, the overall sooty black breeding plumage offset by startlingly white wing panels. In flight the rapid wing beats leave the impression of a white blur, rather than two patches. When seen close up on the water or perched upright on rocks, the bright red feet are clearly visible. The inside of the mouth is also red, though this is only usually seen when the bird is 'singing', a series of endearing high-pitched notes, not expected from an auk. In winter the plumage is markedly different, being largely white, with a variable amount of black and grey on the upperparts.

Black Guillemots breed on rocky coasts, nests always being in cavities, though utilising a range of habitats. In areas secure from ground predators they will nest in burrows and under boulders, while in more vulnerable areas cliff crevices and caves are selected. In recent years holes in harbour walls, buildings and wooden nest boxes have been used (EBA). A wide range of fish prey is taken, as well as small crustaceans. During the breeding season Black Guillemots feed much closer inshore than the other three auk species breeding locally, a different range of small fish are therefore taken, with butterfish commonly seen being brought ashore for young.

The Black Guillemot is widely distributed along Arctic and North Atlantic coasts, including the Baltic, with a world population estimate of 260,000-410,000 pairs. While all five subspecies breed in Europe, *Cepphus grylle arcticus* is the only one to breed in the British Isles (Seabird 2000). Within the British Isles the species is concentrated in the north and west, with only a tiny population in England (seven adults in Cumbria) and 28 birds in Gwynedd, Wales. They are more evenly distributed in Ireland, but it is nonetheless Scotland that hosts the highest population with 37,505 adults (87%) (Seabird 2000). Given its small size, the Isle of Man holds a significant percentage (1%) of the overall British Isles population, with 602 adults present during the census of 1999. This is almost double the numbers found in 1985–86 (Moore 1987). Concentrations are restricted to discrete sections of coast, with Maughold Head, Clay Head and Gob Lhiack south of Port Soderick containing most of the east coast population. In the south, concentrations of Black Guillemots are restricted mainly to the south-west side of Perwick Bay and the coast either side of Fleshwick Bay. The longest stretch of coast that attracts Black Guillemots is that from Glen Maye, north past Peel as far as Wood's Strand, the majority of birds being south of Fenella Beach. In 2003, a pair occupied a hole in the inside wall of Peel Breakwater, successfully raising at least one young. Black Guillemots are known to feed close to breeding areas, and it is therefore unsurprising that they are seldom seen away from nest areas in summer. Observations along the Ayres shoreline in the north and within Derbyhaven Bay in the south were primarily confined to the early summer, probably of birds still returning to more northerly colonies, as well as some local non-breeders. At both Derbyhaven and the Ayres records were also obtained from mid-July onwards and these were probably local birds that nested early or failed to breed successfully.

Once breeding is complete adults moult into their winter plumage, and become flightless for much of September (MA). At such times they can gather into large flocks, though during the research period such large gatherings were not reported. Within the British Isles the winter distribution mirrors that for the summer (WA), reinforcing the view that the population is sedentary, though small-scale movement occurs as a response to local weather conditions and food availability. On the Island, the winter distribution map shows a marked similarity to that for the summer, though mid winter numbers near colonies are much lower, only building up during the latter half of February. The inshore seas of the Ayres usually have a few birds through the winter, though the ability to count these is dependent upon the sea state. During and shortly after storms the Island's bays, particularly Derbyhaven, provide both shelter and feeding opportunity.

C&J record that breeding of Black Guillemots on the Isle of Man was confirmed in the late 1850s. In 1901 Black Guillemots were recorded as breeding in small numbers at Maughold, Clay Head, Peel and the south of the Island, and in 1905 Ralfe knew of four or five nesting localities on the west coast and at least two on the east side of the Island. With the 1999 census revealing a significant increase in numbers since the last complete census of 1985-86, it would appear that the future for the species locally is favourable.

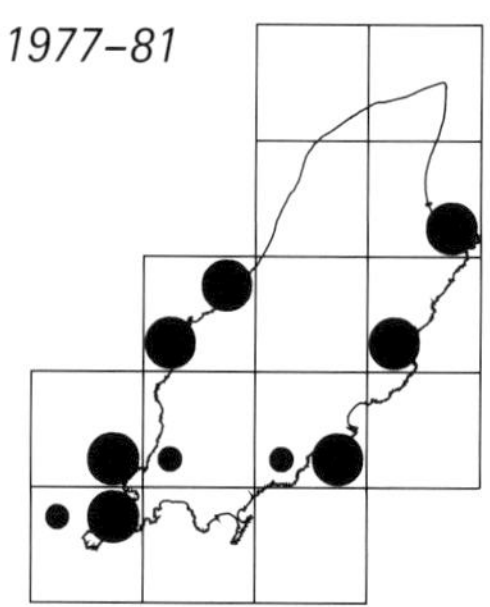

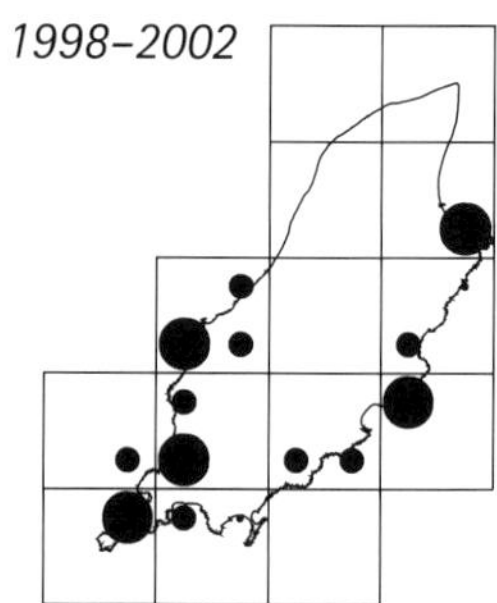

Breeding	Grid squares:	Isle of Man 57 (9%) Britain 283 Ireland 90 Total 373 (10%)
	Population:	(adults) Isle of Man 602 (adults) Britain 38,100 Ireland 4,500 (20% of European)
Wintering	Grid squares:	Isle of Man 37 (6%) Britain and Ireland 512 (13%)
	Population:	Isle of Man 100-200 Britain and Ireland 58,000-80,000

Jan Feb Mar Apr May Jun Jul Aug Sep Oct Nov Dec

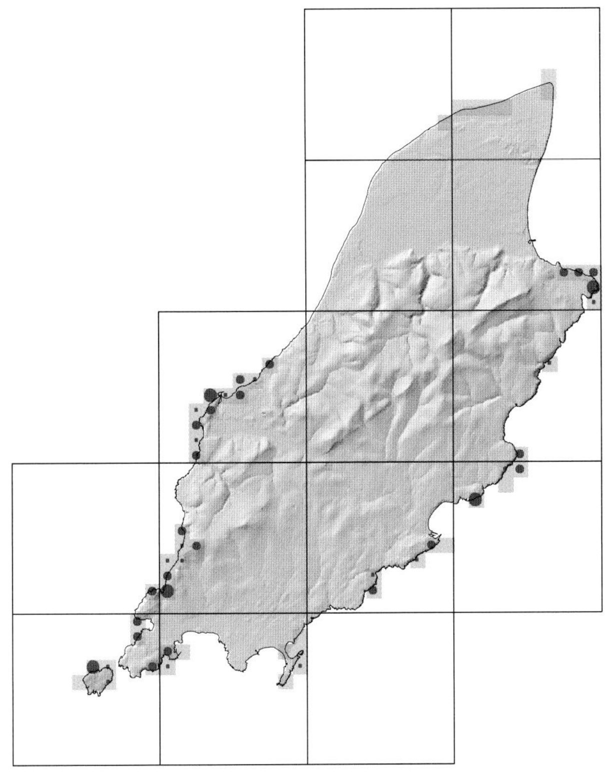
Summer presence and breeding status

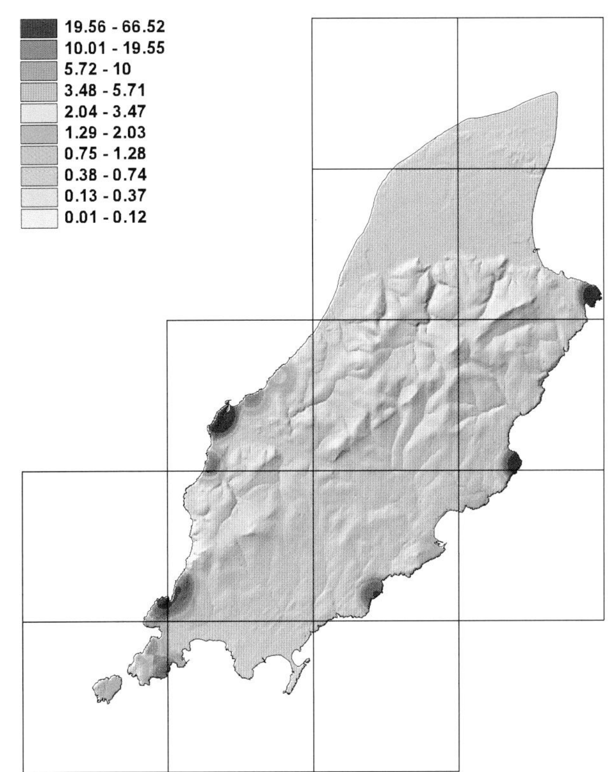

Breeding abundance

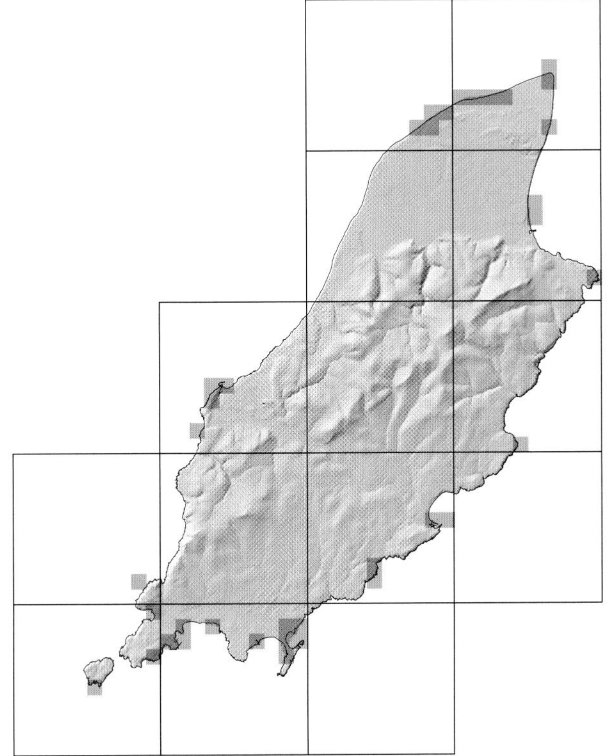
Winter presence

Individual Sponsors – Mr. G Craine, Mr. P & Mrs. K Etherton, Mrs. A C Kaye, Mr. P Speak

Puffin (Atlantic Puffin)
Fratercula arctica

Manx: *Pibbin. Poltrag*

On summer boat trips around Manx coasts, the Puffin, sometimes referred to as the 'sea parrot', is the species that most passengers wish to see. In full summer plumage it must surely rank as one of the best known and well liked of birds within the British Isles. The combination of large colourful bill and facial pattern give it a quizzical, comical appearance. Out of the breeding season, however, the bill is much less colourful, making it harder to distinguish from other members of the auk family when seen in distant flight.

Most Puffin colonies are situated on remote isolated islands, lacking mammalian predators, though they also occur on steep mainland cliffs. Nests are usually within burrows, though in some areas cavities under boulder scree are used (EBA). The main diet is fish, though small crustaceans are also taken. Sandeels are mainly taken locally, though a range of other small fish are caught with only those intended for young at the nest being carried back to colonies in the bill, often several at a time.

Puffins breed on the coasts surrounding the colder parts of the North Atlantic and adjacent Arctic Ocean. Their range extends from the east coast of the United States, through Canada, Greenland, Iceland, the Faeroes and Norway into western Russia in the north but reaching south only into the British Isles and France (EBA). The world population is estimated at between 5.5 and 6.5 million pairs, with over 620,000 pairs within the British Isles. As with other auk species, distribution within the British Isles is restricted to areas of suitable cliffs and islands, leading to concentrations in the north and west. Puffins are generally absent around much of the English coast south of Flamborough Head with the exception of a few small colonies in the south-west including the Channel Isles. Within the Irish Sea area, colonies are thinly scattered and mainly small (Seabird 2000). During the 1999 census only 85 individuals were found on the Island. Maughold Head had the largest number (37 birds), the area south of Peel having 29 birds and the south of the Island having a maximum of 19 birds. The location of Puffins in the south varied between visits, birds occasionally being seen off the Calf of Man and sometimes near the Sugarloaf, making an accurate assessment of breeding sites difficult. They were, however, consistently seen on the sea close under Spanish Head and occasionally on land there. In the years since 1999 fewer birds have been evident at both Maughold and in the south, suggesting a decline, though structured counts have not been undertaken. The figure of 85, while low, is comparable to the last Island-wide census in 1985–86 (Moore 1987), when 116 and 63 birds were counted in 1985 and 1986 respectively. Since that time, however, it is evident that the species no longer breeds on the Calf of Man.

Generally, all Puffins have left colonies and adjacent seas by the end of August (MA), though the scarcity of records locally during that month suggests that birds leave earlier on the Island. In the autumn, records of Puffins locally are mainly obtained from watch points, being counts of birds passing our coasts. Numbers sometimes exceed 100 in a day, but counts of fewer than 10 are more usual. Outside the breeding season Puffins are pelagic, seldom being seen near coasts, winter distribution extending from Norway south to the Canary Islands and from Newfoundland east to Italy, it being assumed that they also winter in the central North Atlantic (MA). Only one winter record was obtained during the research period, that of a single bird flying south off Peel in December 2000 (Cullen 2004).

The Perwick midden deposit dated AD90 provides the first evidence of Puffins on the Island, while Ralfe referred to them as 'numerous on the Calf', also making mention of breeding at the current colonies. Historically, they were commonly harvested for food, though that practice had long ceased when counts were made of 65 pairs on the Calf (1979), 60 pairs at Maughold (1941) and 14 pairs at Peel (1977-81) (C&J), ruling out local human persecution as the cause for more recent declines. Seasonal and longer term alterations to food supply influenced by changes in climate and oceanic currents and predation by brown rats make the future of Puffins on the Isle of Man less than secure.

1977–81

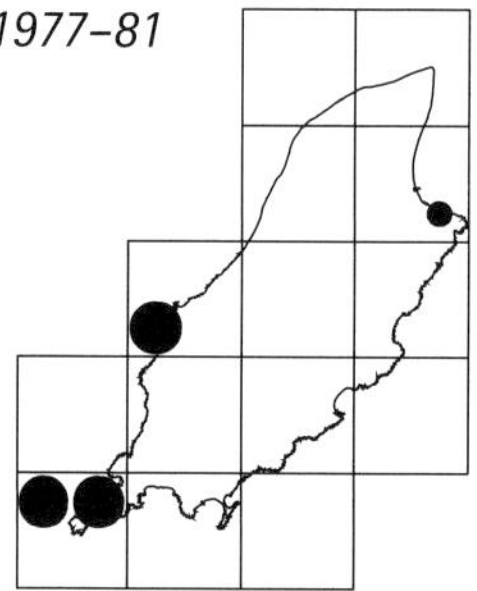

1998–2002

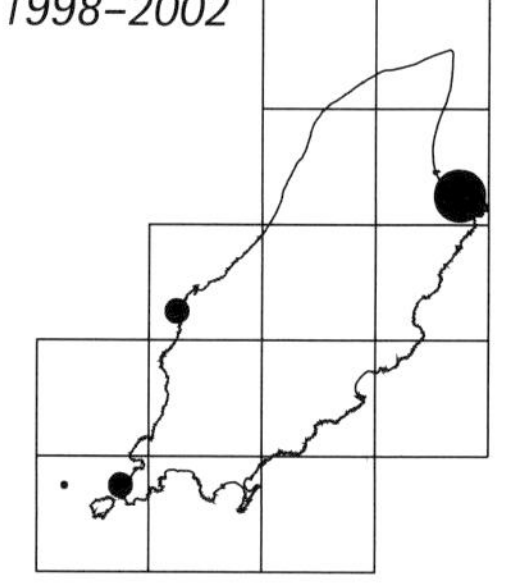

Breeding	Grid squares:	Isle of Man 17 (3%) Britain 151 Ireland 25 Total 176 (5%)
	Population:	(adults) Isle of Man 85 (adults) Britain 579,500 Ireland 21,300 (9% of European)
Wintering	Grid squares:	Isle of Man 1 (0.5%) Britain and Ireland 126 (3%)
	Population:	Isle of Man <10 Britain and Ireland not known

Jan Feb Mar Apr May Jun Jul Aug Sep Oct Nov Dec

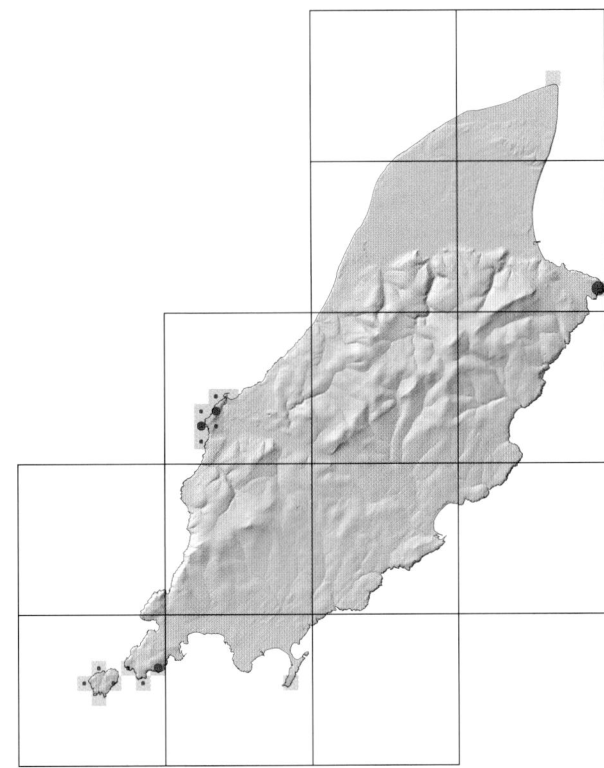

Summer presence and breeding status

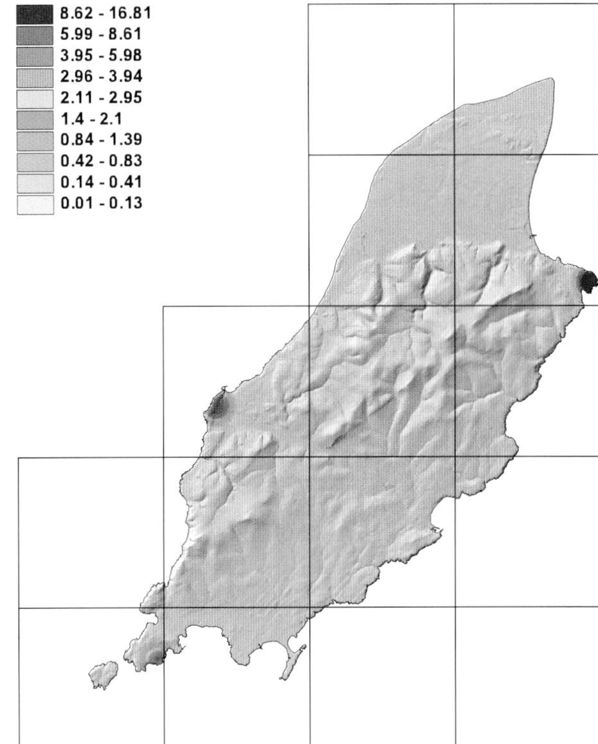

Breeding abundance

Individual Sponsors – Mrs. M Brierley, Mrs. M J Bull, Mrs. G Cowley, Mr. G Craine, Mrs. B Deakin, Rev. J L Guthrie, Mr. R Hogben, Mr. W D Kelly, Miss L Lane

Feral Pigeon/Rock Dove (Rock Pigeon)
Columba livia

Manx: *Calmane ny Creggey*

This account relates entirely to the Feral Pigeon, a bird of many quite widely differing plumages, which is derived from the Rock Dove. Feral Pigeons can almost exactly replicate the plumage of the Rock Dove with the diagnostic white rump, except that the bill is stouter and the cere rather florid. This is the so-called 'blue' and when such birds, which are often wild and shy, are encountered on coastal cliffs it is tempting to conclude that they really are Rock Doves, however, during the MBA research no evidence of 'pure' Rock Dove was found. Variations in plumage of Feral Pigeon are common, from nearly black, through many shades of grey with white, to brown. Many of these variants lack the white rump.

The Feral Pigeon is an urban species, relying on man for its nest sites in all manner of buildings and also for its food. It is however showing an increasing tendency to frequent cliffs, both coastal and inland. There is also a considerable population of racing/homing pigeons, free-flying, but kept in cages. Feral Pigeons feed mainly on grain, often in the company of Woodpigeons, both within towns and in parks and agricultural land.

The Feral Pigeon is now found worldwide, while the range of the true Rock Dove is poorly understood, due to the progressive dilution of the population by Feral Pigeons occupying the same habitat. There remains a shrinking population of Rock Doves occupying the coasts of northern and western Scotland, as well as some of the islands, and also the coasts of northern, western and southern Ireland. Feral Pigeons are most common in the Island's larger towns, especially Douglas and Ramsey. Both Peel and Ballasalla have modest flocks resident in the ancient buildings of the Castle and Rushen Abbey respectively. The virtual absence of proven breeding in farms may be due to the surveying method, as early morning investigations within farm buildings were often not possible. During MBA research surveyors tried to distinguish free-flying but captive birds from truly feral birds. Where distinction was possible, captive birds were not mapped.

In spite of the fact that racing pigeons have an enviable homing instinct, free-living Feral Pigeons are extremely sedentary, so that summer and winter distribution are very similar.

Formerly abundant along the coastal cliffs of the Isle of Man from Peel down to the Calf and also in Santon, Lonan and Maughold, Rock Doves were remorselessly hunted for food and became extinct sometime between 1860 and 1905. Feral Pigeons have never generated much interest among ornithologists and the best pointer to their former status is the presence of pigeon holes of brick construction in a very large proportion of the older farm buildings. Although 15-40 holes are usual, often making a triangle in a gable, East Lhergydhoo has 60 holes in a single line below the eaves, Ballachurry (Rushen) has 150 pigeon holes and Ballacoar (Lonan) 177. C&J wrote that 'nowadays flocks of up to 20 pigeons are resident in a number of farms, although they tend to nest in the rafters of Dutch barns – only at Ballachurry do they exist in their former numbers'. There, despite the culling of 200 birds the previous winter, there were well over 200 around the farm in the summer of 1984. Currently the species is undoubtedly prospering despite the fact that the Feral Pigeon is a favourite prey of the Peregrine.

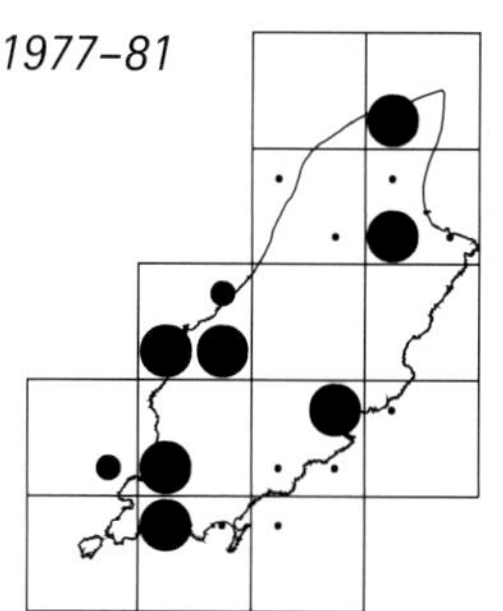

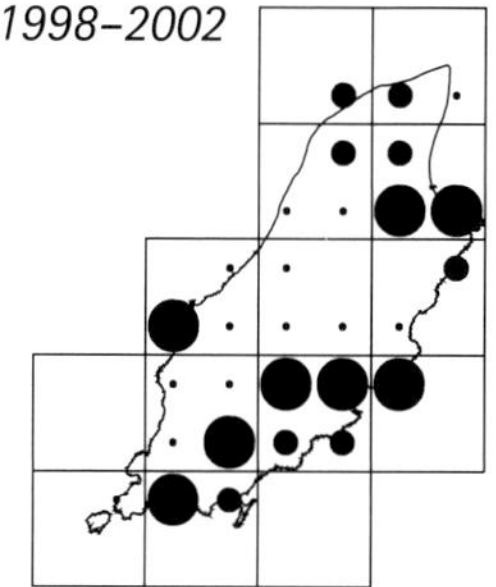

Breeding	Grid squares:	Isle of Man 155 (23%) Britain 2,086 Ireland 345 Total 2,431 (63%)
	Population:	Isle of Man 488–907 Britain c200,000 Ireland c50,000 (1% of European)
Wintering	Grid squares:	Isle of Man 88 (13%) Britain and Ireland 2,249 (58%)
	Population:	Isle of Man 2,000+ Britain and Ireland not known

Jan	Feb	Mar	Apr	May	Jun	Jul	Aug	Sep	Oct	Nov	Dec

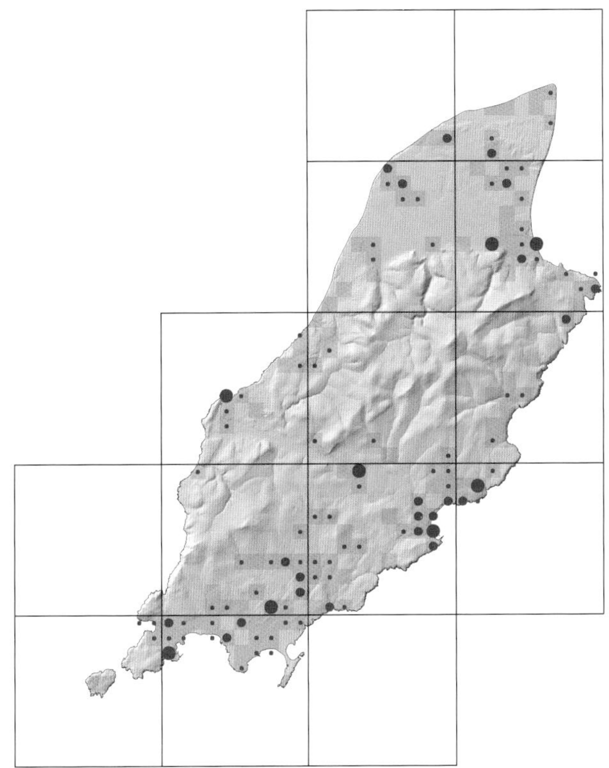
Summer presence and breeding status

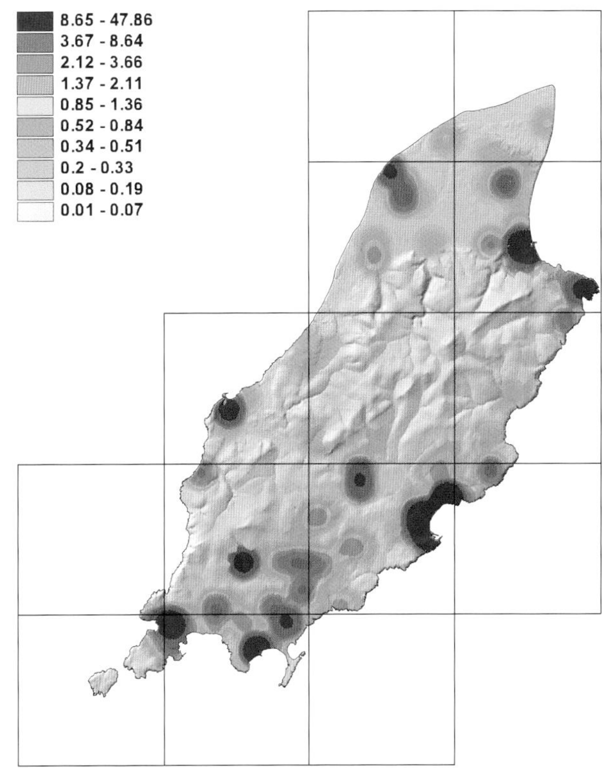

Breeding abundance

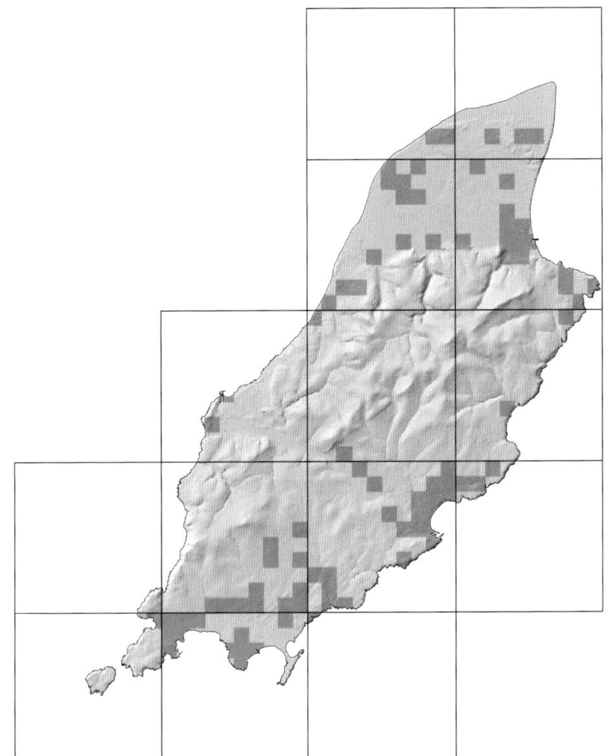
Winter presence

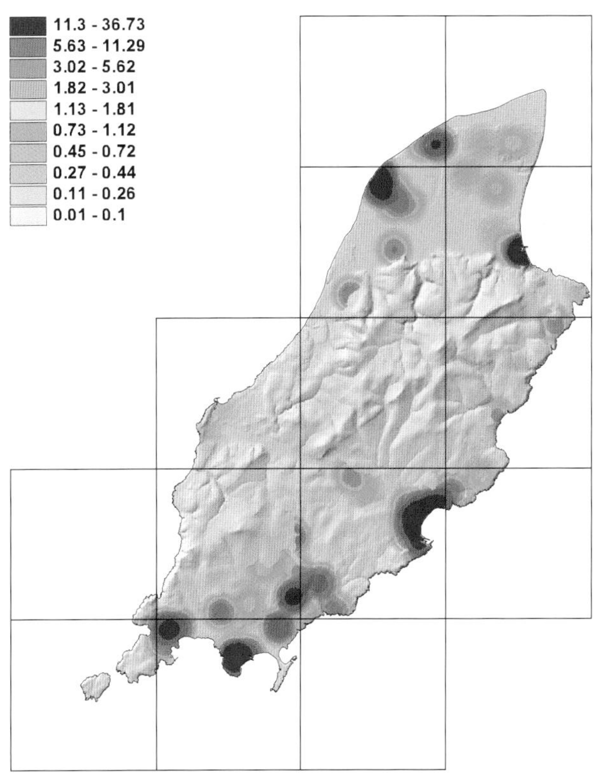

Winter abundance

Stock Dove (Stock Pigeon)
Columba oenas

Manx: *Calmane Gorrym*

Comfortably the scarcest of the Island's pigeons, the Stock Dove is rather shy and easily overlooked. It is similar in size to the Feral Pigeon and in flight may be separated from it by grey underwings, as distinct from the white of the Feral. At rest, the paired short, black, linear wing markings, together with an iridescent green neck patch, are diagnostic. It is distinguished from the adult Woodpigeon (a much bulkier bird) by its lack of a white neck patch, but the juvenile Woodpigeon, lacking this patch, may be confusing. Often, the first indication of a Stock Dove's presence in wooded areas is the unmistakable disyllabic song represented as 'ooo-uh', repeated several times with increasing vigour.

The Stock Dove breeds in wooded areas and in parkland such as at Ballakillingan. It also (at least, until recently) frequented coastal cliffs and quarries. It feeds on arable land, sometimes in the company of Woodpigeons, taking weed seeds and grain in fields of root crops and in stubble.

The Stock Dove breeds across much of Europe from the Atlantic coast eastwards as far as western Siberia and Kazakhstan (EBA). In Fennoscandia its range generally reaches 62°N, with further extensions almost to the head of the Gulf of Bothnia. Formerly confined to south-east England, Stock Doves extended their range markedly during the nineteenth century, reaching Ireland in 1875 and breeding in Kirkcudbrightshire the following year. Britain now has the largest population of any European country by a considerable margin. In the Isle of Man, breeding was confirmed in 1896 and, as in other areas of Britain, colonisation was rapid and flocks of 60 or more were commonplace in the early 1900s. It seems that numbers were well maintained until the mid-1930s, but there followed a decline, such that since the mid-1960s, with one exception, flocks have not exceeded 20. In fact, since 1984 only two flocks have exceeded ten (16 were in a kale field at Ballacain [Jurby] in February 1989 and 26 were seen near St Johns in January 1990). There was a significant decline in Britain during the 1950s due to toxic seed dressings and it seems that the Manx population suffered similarly, but rather later, between 1956 and 1964, with only a very modest recovery. The 1968–72 Atlas showed confirmed breeding in nine of the Island's 10km squares, with probable breeding in two others, while the 1988–91 Atlas shows confirmed breeding in only one square, with just four more 'possibles'. The local decline during that period is not dissimilar to the situation in Ireland and along the west coasts of England and southern Scotland. Manx Bird Atlas recorded probable breeding at 19 sites, involving six 10km squares, which does suggest an increasing population. C&J showed an exclusively coastal distribution, with a notable gap between Maughold and Douglas, whereas the present breeding survey presented a completely different picture, characterised by a sparse scatter along the central valley and in the southern lowlands and a relatively substantial presence over the northern plain. Records from the coastal cliffs were non-existent. The five-year survey period yielded only eleven parties of three to six birds and one, in mid-April, of ten.

The strangest feature of the winter survey was the occurrence of only two records, one involving three birds and the other four, in adjacent squares in Bride. Stock Doves are migratory in the eastern part of their range, but become progressively less so in Western Europe and are regarded as sedentary within the British Isles, yet the shortage of winter records does suggest movement away from the Island in winter. There are no ringing data to support this supposition, although there has been a suggestion of autumn passage, with Woodpigeons, through the Calf (C&J). The UK Winter Atlas presented evidence of a contraction in range in winter, compared to summer, in Ireland, Scotland, Cumbria, Wales and south-west England as well as the Isle of Man.

1977–81

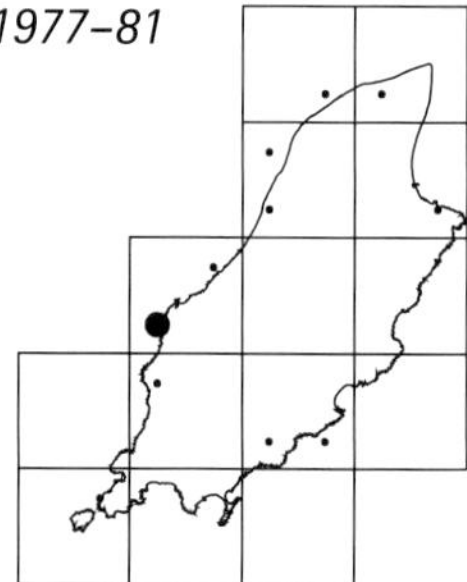

1998–2002

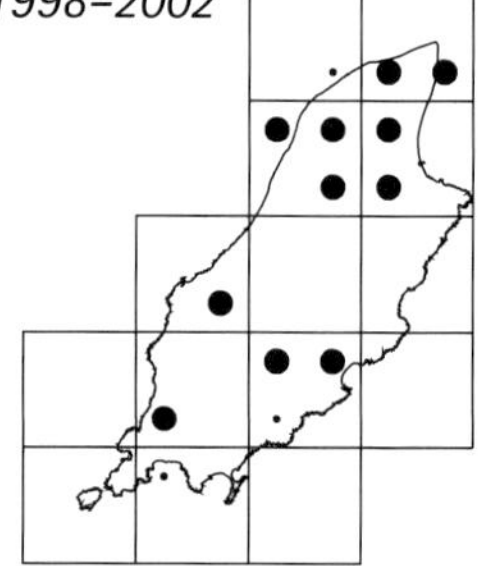

Breeding	Grid squares:	Isle of Man 45 (7%) Britain 1,821 Ireland 363 Total 2,184 (57%)
	Population:	Isle of Man 32–37 Britain 240,000 Ireland 30,000 (53% of European)
Wintering	Grid squares:	Isle of Man 2 (0.5%) Britain and Ireland 1,925 (50%)
	Population:	Isle of Man <10 Britain and Ireland 30,000-63,000+

Jan Feb Mar Apr May Jun Jul Aug Sep Oct Nov Dec

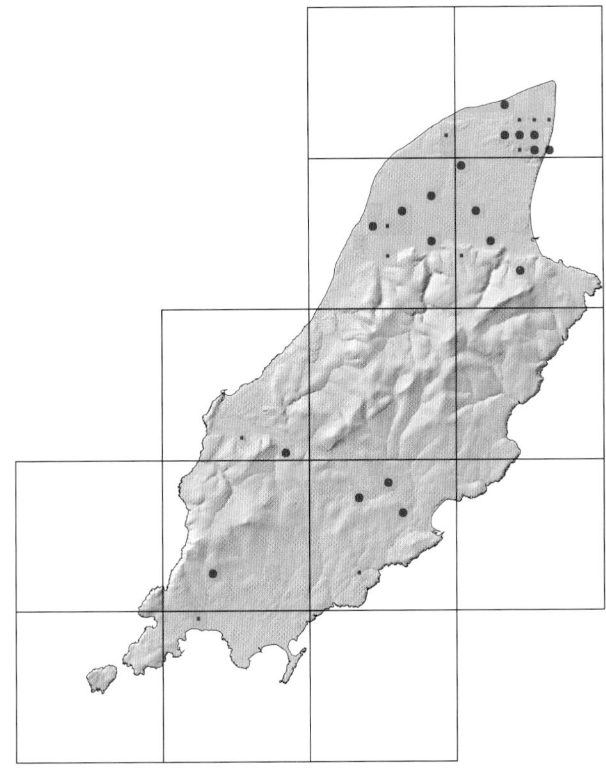

Summer presence and breeding status

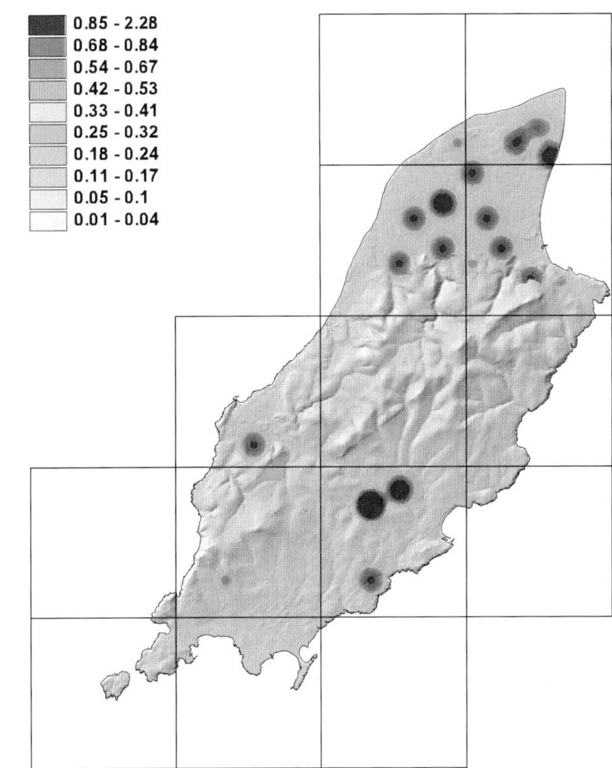

Breeding abundance

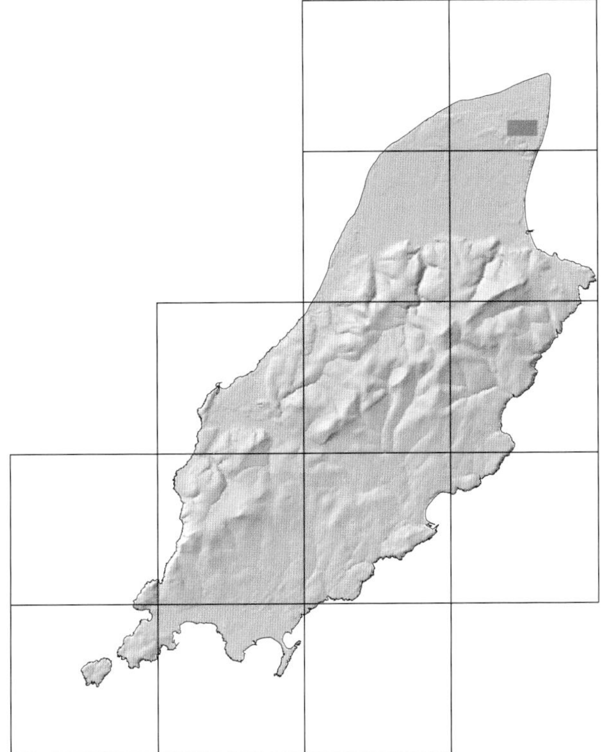

Winter prescence

Individual Sponsor – Crane of Cluny

Woodpigeon (Common Wood Pigeon)
Columba palumbus

Manx: *Calmane keylley*

The soothing cooing of the Woodpigeon is one of the most familiar sounds of spring and summer. The portly adult which waddles over our lawns, parks and playing fields needs no introduction, while in flight the white transverse marking on the upper wing prevents confusion with any other pigeon. The drab juvenile lacks the adult's white neck patch, but the absence of black markings on the wings separates it from the Stock Dove.

Woodpigeons are plentiful throughout the lowlands of Man, where they collect on cultivated land, feeding on grain (qualifying them as major avian pests) and all manner of other seeds. They also occur in most woodland habitats from the largest conifer plantation to the smallest spinney, as well as rural and urban gardens and town parks. Large numbers may collect in deciduous woods in autumn, attracted by beech mast and acorns, as well as ivy berries.

The Woodpigeon breeds in all countries within the European Palearctic, its range extending some way north of the Arctic Circle. Throughout Britain and Ireland, the Woodpigeon is represented in virtually every 10km square and only in the central and western highlands of Scotland, the Outer Hebrides and Shetland is it scarce or absent. In both England and Ireland, the population is densest in the south and east. The British and Irish population is considerably in excess of that of any other country. Abundance maps indicate the relative scarcity in mountainous regions and the same obtains in the Isle of Man, where no good evidence of breeding was found above 300m. Around the Manx coast Woodpigeons are notably absent from the Jurby coast and the majority of the promontories such as the Point of Ayre, Clay Head, Marine Drive, Langness, Scarlett and the southern tip of the Island. These areas are all treeless, but include suitable farmland for feeding.

In Britain, nesting has been recorded in every month, but Manx birds are more conventional, the extreme dates of nests with eggs being 9 April and 22 September. The nest is a sparse platform of sticks, usually close to the trunk of a tree and rarely at a height of more than 5m. Birds carrying twigs provide conspicuous evidence of breeding. In conifers the nests are often plentiful and easy to see, but in deciduous woodland they may be well concealed by ivy. From such hidden sites, birds fly away noisily when approached, thus revealing their unexpected presence. Two pure white eggs are laid and their neatly halved used shells on the forest floor provide further signs of nesting. Woodpigeons' nests seem to be particularly targeted by corvids, especially Magpies, so that replacement clutches are laid almost routinely. In treeless areas, less usual nest sites are used. On the Ayres, for example, ground nesting beneath a gorse bush has been recorded, while on the Calf, where 1-2 pairs bred annually in the early 1970s, they have also nested successfully under thick bracken and on a ledge near the Observatory – here a nest within one of the Heligoland traps failed.

The summer and winter maps are not significantly different. Flocking is very much a feature of winter, with all gatherings in excess of 100 (27 observations) falling between 18 November and 18 February. Largest by far was a flock of 1,500 near Ellerslie in November 1999, but there were also over 500 at Ballaspit to the west of St Johns in December 2001 and flocks of 300 were also present inland from Port Soderick, a consistently well populated area, near Ballavale and to the west of the Guilcagh.

Ringing recoveries show that a part of our population is migratory, while others are resident. Movement through the Calf used to be a frequent sight twenty years ago – nearly 2,000 birds flew west in November 1977 and flocks of around 400 were not uncommon. Nowadays autumn flocks as large as 100 are exceptional and very few birds were seen during this survey. Six January recoveries of birds ringed on the Island have come from Hereford, Shropshire, Cheshire, Anglesey, Antrim and the Isle of Man. Another was in County Down in its second winter, while two third winter birds were recovered on the Island. Three have been recovered in summer on the Isle of Man 1–3 years after ringing.

1977–81

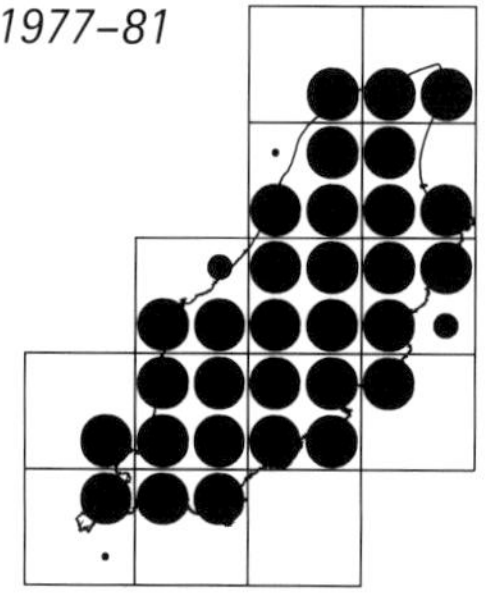

1998–2002

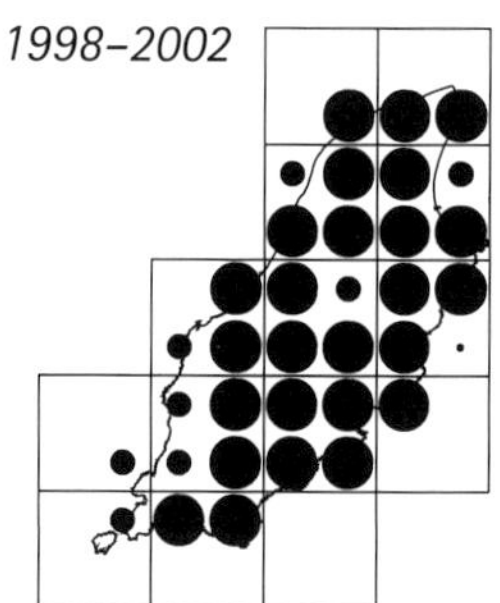

Breeding	Grid squares:	Isle of Man 449 (68%) Britain 2,510 Ireland 945 Total 3,455 (90%)
	Population:	Isle of Man 1,363–2,402 Britain 2,350,000 Ireland 900,000 (33% of European)
Wintering	Grid squares:	Isle of Man 290 (44%) Britain and Ireland 3,305 (86%)
	Population:	Isle of Man <3,000 Britain and Ireland 4.8 million (excluding Ireland)

Jan	Feb	Mar	Apr	May	Jun	Jul	Aug	Sep	Oct	Nov	Dec

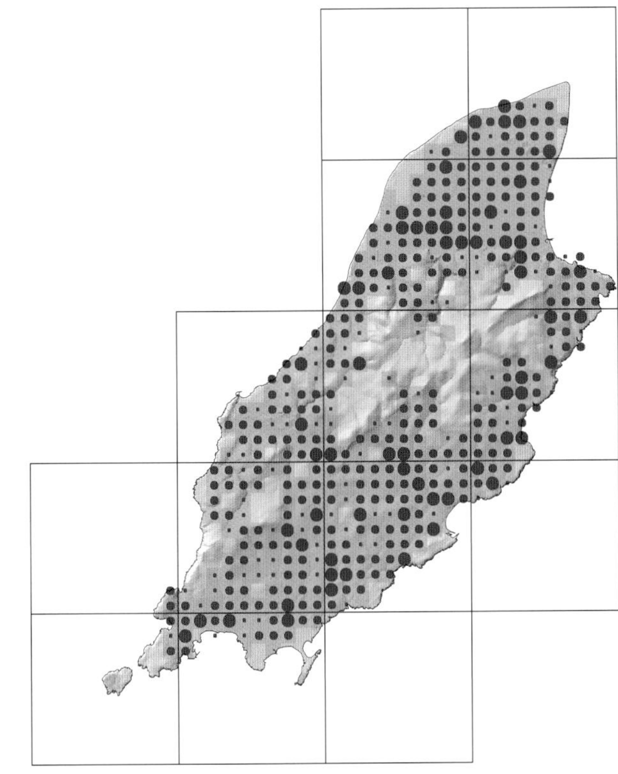

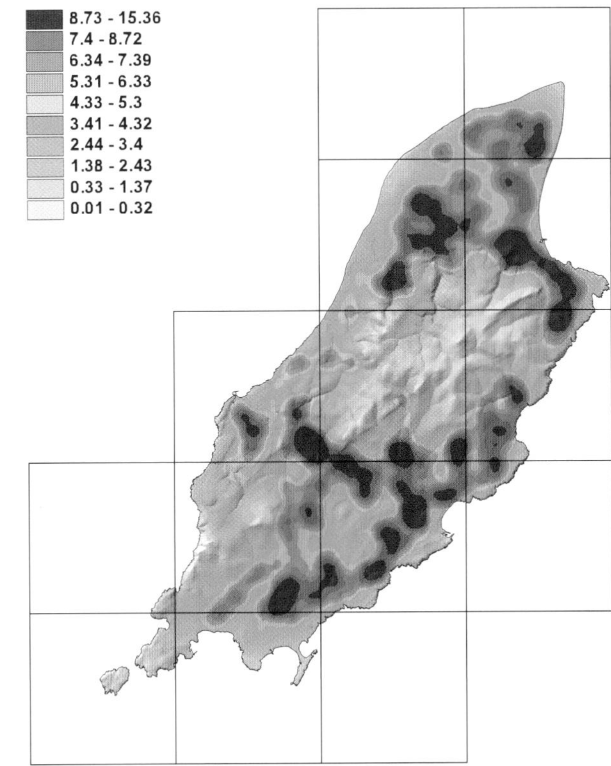

Summer presence and breeding status

Breeding abundance

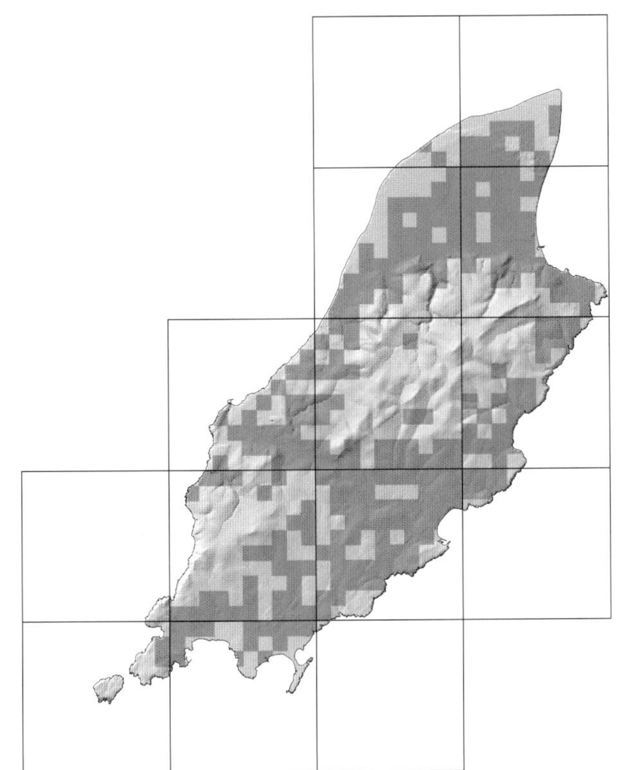

Winter presence

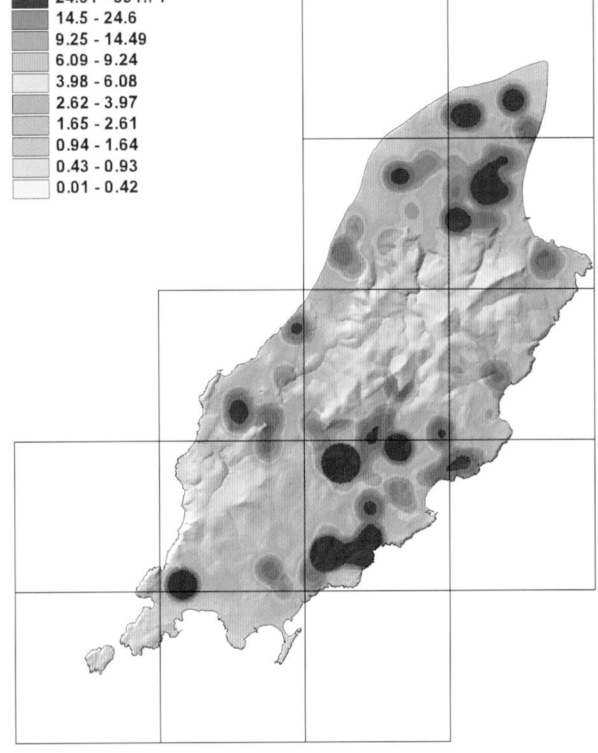

Winter abundance

Individual Sponsors – Mr. & Mrs. J D Kennan, Mr. A Stephenson, Mr. J Wood

Collared Dove (Eurasian Collared Dove)
Streptopelia decaocto

The Collared Dove is a light fawn bird with a distinctive narrow, black half collar, these two features combining to separate it from the much browner Turtle Dove. The distinctive song – 'coo-coo co' can be irritating if delivered repeatedly from the roof above a bedroom window. It is also frequently confused with that of the Cuckoo.

Of all the Columbidae, the Collared Dove is the most closely associated with human activity, occurring particularly in suburban gardens, villages and around farm buildings. It feeds largely on grain, but as a regular visitor to gardens, it readily takes other foods from bird tables.

Originally an Indian species, Collared Doves were breeding in Turkey by 1900, in fact in many European countries it is known as the Turkish Dove. By 1928 it had colonised much of the Balkans and a relentless extension of range to the north and west followed, reaching Austria in 1938, Holland in 1947 and Norfolk in 1955. By 1962 they were nesting in Denbighshire, but by this time they had also reached Ireland and were breeding in County Down (1960) and had been seen as far to the north-west as Tory Island off the Donegal coast (1961) (Hudson 1965). There was also a comparable eastward progression, which has now reached western Siberia (EBA). Prior to 1962 Collared Doves were unknown in the Isle of Man. The Calf provided the first Manx record, as well as three more in the spring of 1963, while breeding first took place north of Ramsey the following year. By 1975 Collared Doves were generally distributed in suitable habitats throughout the Island. During this period of colonisation a flock of 110 was present at the foot of Richmond Hill and flocks of 30 were seen in several gardens in the Douglas area. Subsequently Laxey flour mills regularly hosted a flock of up to 60 birds, increasing to 110 in 1985. Since 1989 flocks have rarely exceeded 30, exceptions being 70 at Ballamaddrell (Arbory) in 1991 and 46 in Peel in 1996. During the present survey, the largest flock contained 46 birds (at Saddlestone on the western fringe of Douglas), while 40 were recorded at both Ellerslie and Cranstal. The nine flocks of 20 or more birds were all found during the period 18 November to 24 January. The Manx Bird Atlas revealed that the range of the Collared Dove is probably unchanged since the late 1970s, but the undoubted reduction in flock size does suggest that the population has declined. The 1988–91 Atlas showed a small reduction in Ireland, although numbers in England and Wales had continued to increase. Away from the northern plain, where Collared Doves are widely distributed, the present survey shows a lowland distribution (up to about 160m AMSL), centred on the main towns and villages and, to some extent, following the main thoroughfares. The overall distribution in summer and winter is the same, but, particularly in the north, a number of summer sites are deserted in winter.

They have a long breeding season and as often as not will lay three clutches of two eggs. A pair mating and nest-building in January 2001 provides the earliest evidence of breeding and the latest calculated laying date was 28 August. Like Woodpigeons, they are the frequent victims of Magpie predation.

Established breeding adults are sedentary, but some of their offspring tend to disperse, especially westwards, during the late spring or early summer of their second calendar year (BWP). Up to 1969 small numbers, increasing year by year, would visit the Calf between April and June. During the next decade, there would usually be a peak day during April involving up to 17 birds in the early years, but increasing to 27 and 23 in 1976 and, the most ever, 60 on 14 May 1976. Peaks became progressively smaller thereafter and since 1987 have never exceeded four. There have been no ringing recoveries, so it is not known whether these were Manx birds or birds from the adjacent islands dispersing.

1977–81

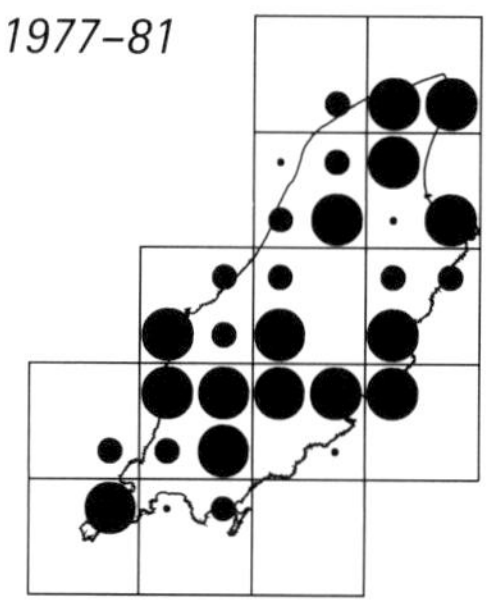

1998–2002

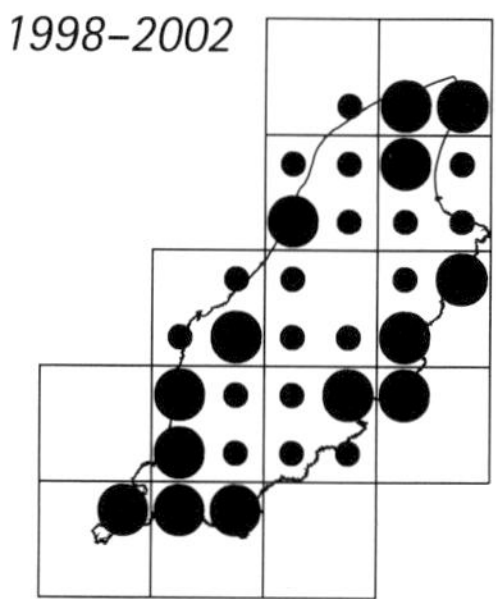

Breeding	Grid squares:	Isle of Man 259 (39%) Britain 2,210 Ireland 559 Total 2,769 (72%)
	Population:	Isle of Man 534–790 (territories) Britain 200,000 Ireland 30,000 (4% of European)
Wintering	Grid squares:	Isle of Man 183 (28%) Britain and Ireland 2,332 (60%)
	Population:	Isle of Man 2,000 Britain and Ireland 150,000+

Jan Feb Mar Apr May Jun Jul Aug Sep Oct Nov Dec

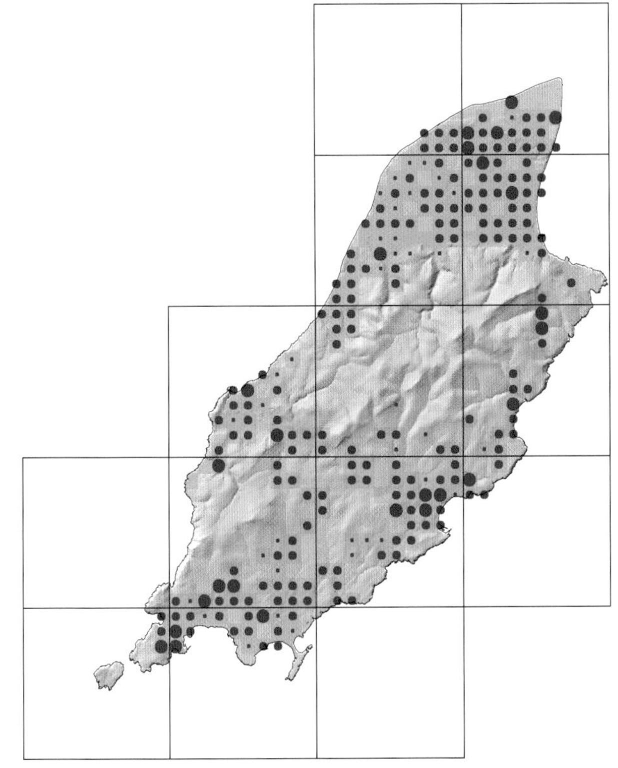
Summer presence and breeding status

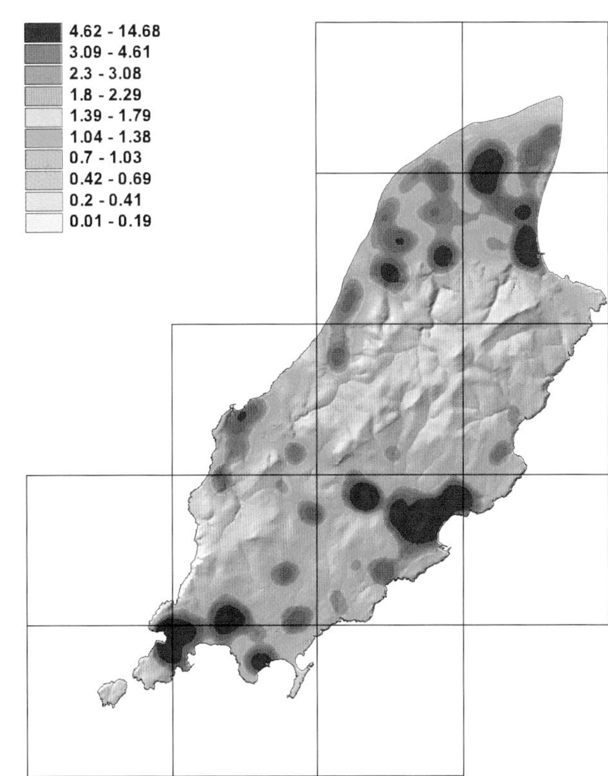

Breeding abundance

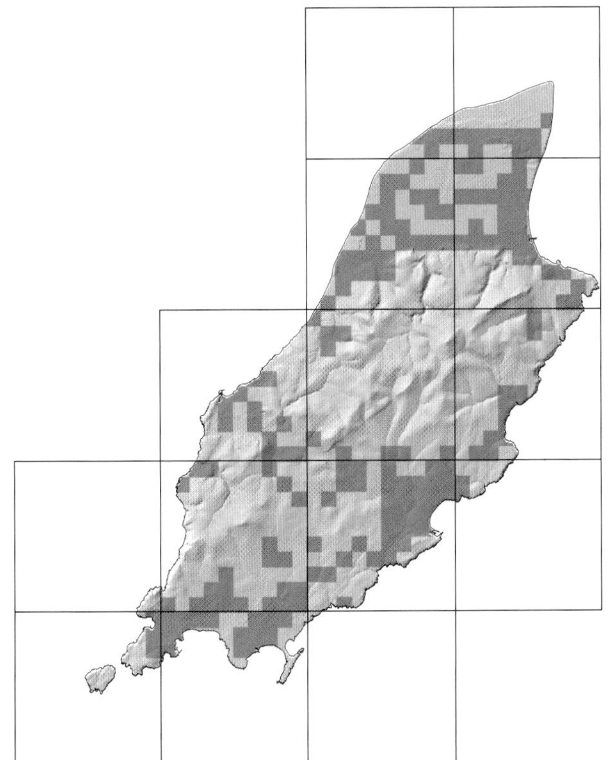
Winter presence

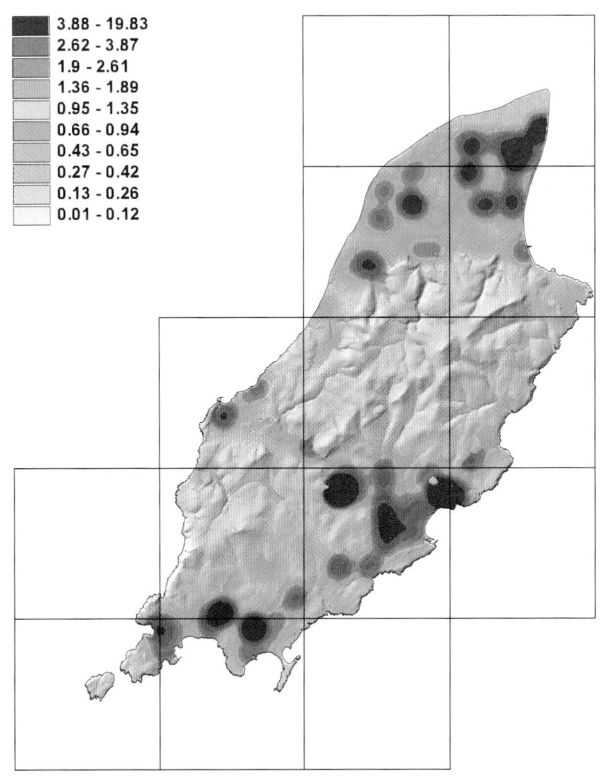

Winter abundance

Individual Sponsor – J D R Kewley

Cuckoo (Common Cuckoo)
Cuculus canorus

Manx: *Cooag*

The Cuckoo is of course best known for its call. It is a slim, long-tailed bird, the grey head and upperparts, combined with strongly barred belly suggesting a falcon. In a less common form, the grey is replaced by a rufous colouration. Either because of its raptorial appearance, or because of its known parasitic behaviour, it is often mobbed by small passerines. It is disappointing that on the Isle of Man the casual observer can easily go through a summer without hearing the familiar song of the male Cuckoo. This reflects a notable decline in the Cuckoo's fortunes on the Island which probably began in the third decade of the twentieth century and gathered momentum from the mid-1950s, a situation mirrored in Ireland.

Within its European breeding range most habitats are occupied, other than those lacking suitable hosts; urban areas, extensive dense forests, extreme deserts, bare mountains and small islands (EBA). C&J have described how, on the Isle of Man, the Cuckoo has withdrawn from such habitats as suburban gardens and cultivated farmland and is now a bird of curragh, lowland heath and moorland. The present survey suggests that this statement is now not entirely true, as one of only four definite breeding records came from a housing estate near the northern edge of Douglas, and farmland accounted for the majority of 'probable' records, which notably embraced adjacent squares just to the west of Port Erin. Probable breeding occurred near two upland farms at around 200m – Eary Farm (Michael) and Cronkgarroo (Lezayre). The lowland heath of the Ayres barely featured, although Cuckoos bred in the adjacent farmland. There were no records from moorland.

The Cuckoo has an extensive breeding range covering Europe, except Iceland, and most of Asia, extending east across Russia to China and Japan. Within the British Isles it is widespread, though areas of highest density are in southern and central England, and the west of both Scotland and Ireland (1988–91 Atlas). The 1988–91 Atlas calculated a 4.9% decline over 20 years in Britain, this figure increasing to 25.1% for Ireland, this latter reduction possibly being due to a reduction in numbers of Meadow Pipit which is the main host species in Ireland. As in Ireland, Meadow Pipits are the commonest hosts on the Isle of Man, but others recorded locally are Dunnock, Sedge Warbler, Yellowhammer, Robin, Skylark and (on the Calf, during the present survey) Rock Pipit. The majority of records of confirmed breeding relate to young Cuckoos being fed by the host.

Four local surveys during the last 34 years have shown a progressive depletion of occupied areas. During 1968-72 evidence of breeding was found in all 14 10km squares on the Island, falling to twelve (1977-81), eleven (1988-91) and only nine during 1998-2002. These figures are remarkable in view of the fact that Manx Bird Atlas achieved a much more complete coverage than any of its predecessors and also included records from the public. They present unequivocal evidence of a significant decline. Elsewhere numbers have decreased in Fennoscandia and across northern Europe, perhaps associated with habitat loss and agricultural intensification (EBA), factors which seem unlikely to apply to the Isle of Man.

Wintering in equatorial Africa, first arrivals in the Isle of Man are likely to be in late April. C&J gave a mean date for the period 1928-1982 as 25/26 April and could find no arrival date earlier than 28 March. Four records between 8 and 17 March in 2000 were therefore unprecedented. Excluding these atypical records (there were in fact no further records in 2000 until 1 May), during the five years of the present survey, the mean first arrival date was 17 April. Historically, there have been a few records in early October, with an unusually late bird on 12 November, but in the MBA's survey the latest of only ten autumn records was 18 August.

It is difficult to explain the considerable diminution of Cuckoos visiting the Island. Lack of availability of specific host species and non-availability of food are usually offered as the cause, these factors perhaps being secondary to habitat change. Of the three main host species in the British Isles, Meadow Pipit and Dunnock are abundant on the Island, while the third, the Reed Warbler, has historically been absent, only starting to breed in 2004. Cuckoos feed primarily on insect larvae, particularly those of moths, and there seems little doubt that numbers of moths throughout Britain have dropped in recent years, but these changes are not specific to the Isle of Man. Although over 100 Cuckoos have been ringed on the Calf, there has only been one recovery. This was an adult ringed in early May and found dead in Westphalia in late August, two years later.

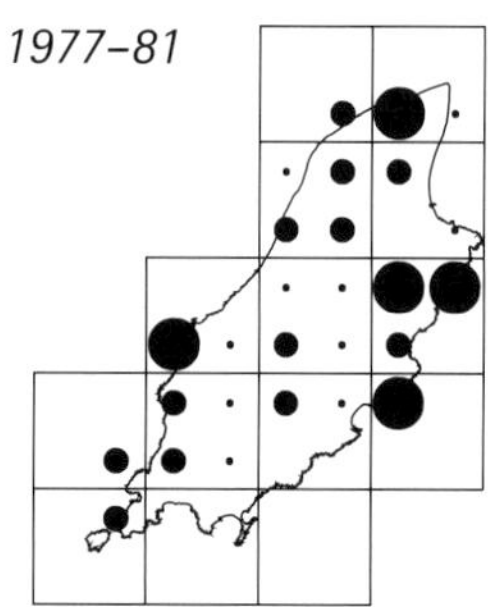

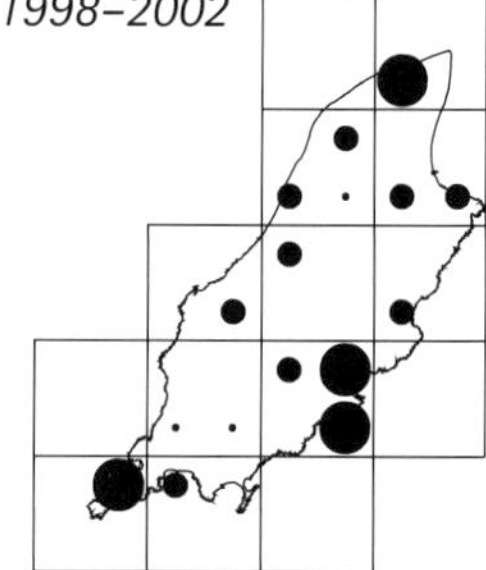

Breeding	Grid squares:	Isle of Man 73 (11%)
		Britain 2,418 Ireland 706 Total 3,124 (81%)
	Population:	Isle of Man 25
		Britain 19,500 Ireland 4,500 (2% of European)

Jan Feb Mar Apr May Jun Jul Aug Sep Oct Nov Dec

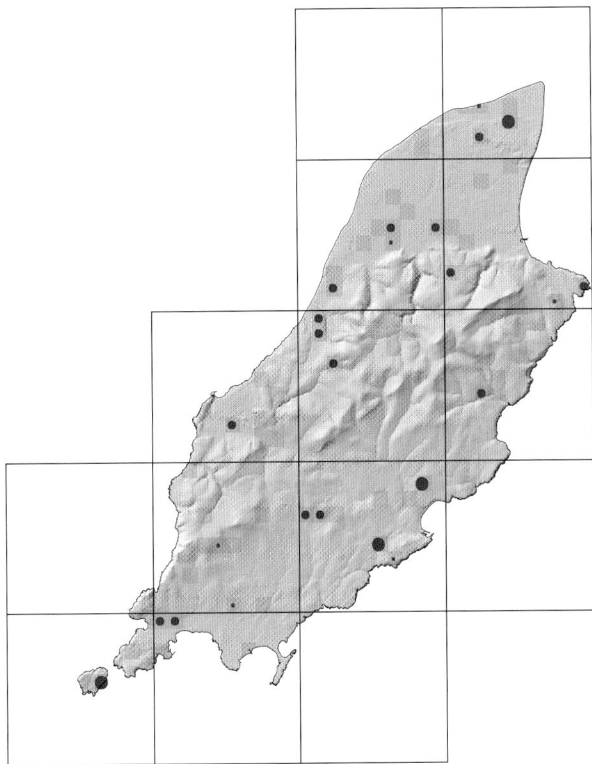

Summer presence and breeding status

Barn Owl
Tyto alba

Manx: *Screeaghag oie* = Night-screecher

The slow, hesitant flight of the ghostly white Barn Owl over farmland at dusk or dawn remains one of the most exciting sights, despite the huge reduction in population which has befallen the species. Its continuing popularity is evidenced by the fact that in this survey it has been sponsored by no fewer than 16 individuals. When seen perched, one is struck by the dark eyes in a white heart-shaped face. The upperparts are buff, heavily mottled with grey, the underparts and underwings almost pure white.

It is a bird of farmland, preferably well-hedged, with a scatter of spinneys, ponds and rough uncultivated ground, typical of the Island's northern plain. It has a closer relationship with man than other owls and typically roosts by day in farm buildings. Such buildings also provide nest sites as do church towers, chimneys and reasonably covered rural ruins, while hollow trees are also frequently used, as in the rest of Britain. They will use nest boxes set up in barns which lack suitable dark cavities – an ideal box would be closed and rectangular, with a width and depth of 45 cm, and 75cm or more in length, and with a suitable entrance hole (Bunn *et al.* 1982). In the final survey year a box put up eight years previously at a farm in the parish of German was visited for the first time during May, with successful breeding in the years thereafter. Barn Owls usually lay 4-6 eggs and while eggs have been found as early as 15 March, first clutches are not normally laid until the first half of May. Typically, only 2 young are likely to fledge, although 3 late young flew from a Bride nest at the end of November (Foulkes-Roberts 1949).

Small rodents are the usual food of the Barn Owl. In Britain mice, small voles and shrews are the most usual prey, while on the Isle of Man the absence of voles and common shrews means that the diet is almost entirely limited to wood and house mice and the pygmy shrew, perhaps supplemented by young rats (or, as the superstitious Manxman would insist, 'those long-tailed fellers').

The Barn Owl is one of the most widely distributed of all birds, breeding in every continent except Antarctica. In Europe its range extends westward from a line joining Lithuania and Crimea to the Atlantic seaboard as far north as Islay. It is only patchily distributed in Romania, Bulgaria and Greece and extends no further north than central Jutland, being absent from the rest of Fennoscandia, as well as the more mountainous regions. In Britain the distribution is patchy, with considerable areas such as north-east England and most of the northern half of Scotland having no Barn Owls. In Ireland, distribution becomes increasingly sparse away from the south and east. On the Isle of Man, scattered summer records were obtained from much of the agricultural lowlands, with the northern plain accounting for many of the sightings. Breeding was proven in just seven 1km squares, spread over five 10km squares, one more than in the 1988–91 Atlas survey. At the 5km resolution evidence of definite breeding in seven squares suggests an improvement on the four shown in C&J. However, there is at least one sanctuary on the Island from which captive birds have been released (still permissible under Manx Law) and, at other sites, free-flying released birds and their young have their diets regularly supplemented with dead hen chicks. It is thus difficult to evaluate the apparent increase in the Barn Owl's prosperity.

Within Europe Barn Owls are considered to be sedentary, and the MBA winter map shows a marked similarity to that for the summer. Interestingly, there were rather more winter records in the south of the Island than for the summer suggesting that breeding pairs in the area may have gone unrecorded.

Over much of its European range, and throughout Britain, the Barn Owl population has been in serious decline. Following two decades of prosperity, this first became apparent on the Isle of Man in the mid-1950s. Over the next 15 years there were increasing reports of corpses, accounting for up to 50% of records received. In two instances, lethal amounts of Dieldrin were found, but Warfarin has also been implicated, both directly and also by significantly reducing the rodent population and therefore the food supply. From 1987 there were definite signs of recovery, which have been sustained, echoing the situation in Britain as a whole. Bunn *et al.* regarded loss of suitable nest sites as the next most relevant factor after poisoning in the demise of the Barn Owl, citing the increasing dilapidation of previously suitable ruins or the replacement of stone farm buildings by modern prefabricated structures. Furthermore, the tidying up of farmland has involved the removal of many dead, hollow trees.

Unknown in the Isle of Man until 1880, Barn Owls are remarkably sedentary, and with eight recoveries of Manx-ringed birds revealing movement of no more than 18km, it is strange that spontaneous colonisation was possible in the first place. There is increasing evidence of a revival in this fine bird's fortunes and with a better understanding of its requirements and in the absence of toxic chemicals, this prosperity should be sustained.

1977–81

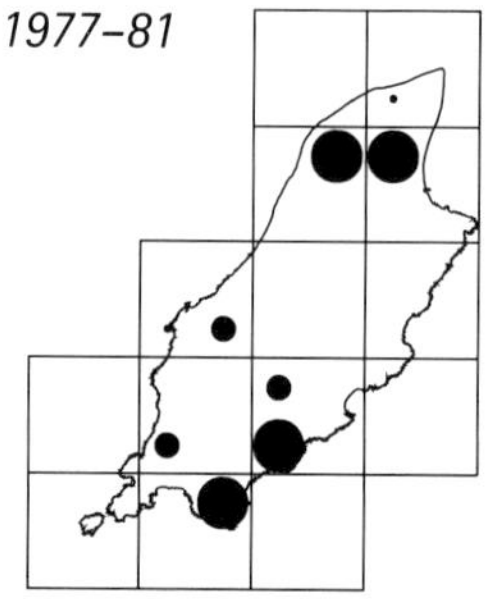

1998–2002

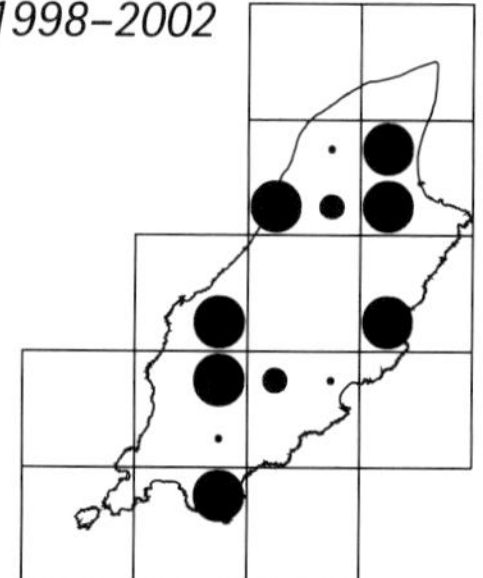

Breeding	Grid squares:	Isle of Man 48 (7%)
		Britain 1,110 Ireland 185 Total 1,295 (34%)
	Population:	Isle of Man <40
		Britain 4,400 Ireland 750 (4% of European)
Wintering	Grid squares:	Isle of Man 48 (7%)
		Britain and Ireland 1,278 (33%)
	Population:	Isle of Man <100
		Britain and Ireland 12,500-25,000

Jan Feb Mar Apr May Jun Jul Aug Sep Oct Nov Dec

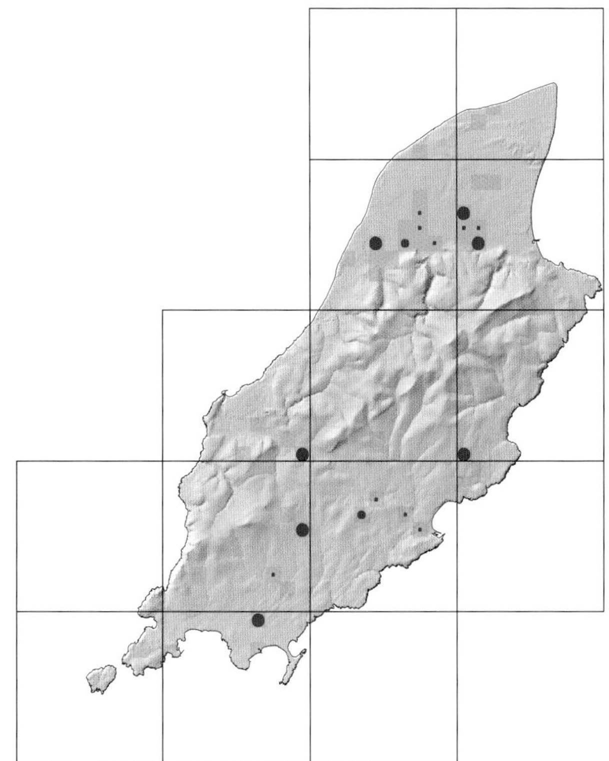

Summer presence and breeding status

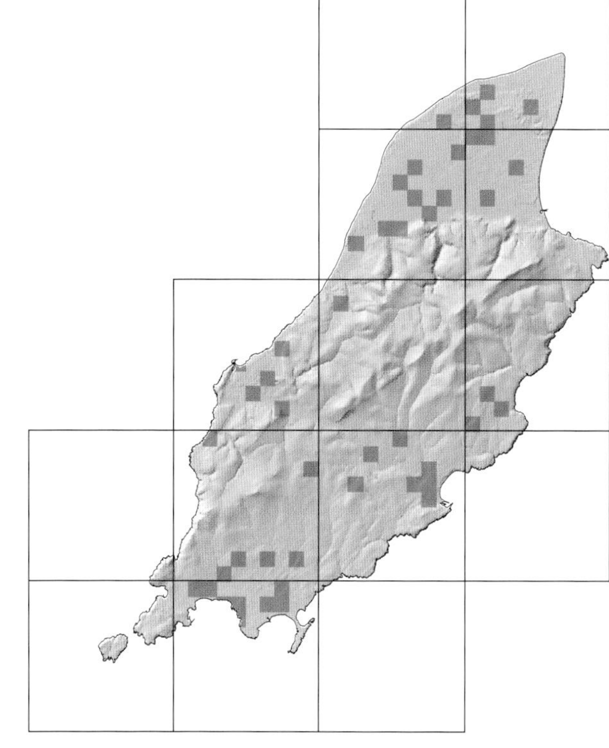

Winter presence

Individual Sponsors – The Anderson Trust, Mrs. S L Bird, Mrs. D M Cowley, Mr. G Craine, Mr. G R Crellin, Ms. E M Eaton, Mrs. R Fryer, Mr. H D N Hanson, Mrs. H E Hodgett, Mr. C Mitchell, Mrs. S M Morrey, Mrs. B Nelson, Mr. S & Mrs. J Prescott, Mr. R Sargent, Mrs. J Taylor, Mr. R A Watson

Tawny Owl
Strix aluco

The brown owl of children's books is a compact, rounded, large-headed bird. Black eyes look out from a brown face topped with a pair of fine white lines forming a 'V'. In flight, the short rounded wings distinguish the Tawny from the two, much more common, *Asio* owls found on the Island.

It is found typically in broad-leaved woodland and is not averse to wooded gardens, both rural and urban. Food is more varied than that of other owls, birds, beetles and amphibians being taken in addition to small mammals.

The Tawny Owl is found throughout most of mainland Europe, extending northwards into central Finland and Sweden and around the lowlands of Norway's southern bulge. It is widely distributed in Britain, although more patchily in northern Scotland, being absent in the Northern and Western Isles due to a lack of mature woodland. It is also absent from Ireland, probably due to it being a very sedentary species. Until quite recently, the only Manx record had been of one, which spent a week on the Calf in September 1961. Then in both 1982 and 1984, one was heard at Glen maye, on the edge of the Arrasy Plantation, while 1987 brought a sight record from Derbyhaven. The present story began in 1990, when feathers of a Tawny Owl were found in a barn at Upper Lhergydhoo (German), and it is little more than a kilometre away that at least one owl has been repeatedly heard since the autumn of 2000. Although outside the survey period, a Tawny Owl was heard on several occasions in the summer of 2003, while in 2004 at least two males and a female were present. Elsewhere, one was present at Close Sartfield (Ballaugh) in July 2001, followed by the observation of one being mobbed by Blackbirds at Brough Jairg, just 3km to the west. Further evidence of a sustained presence in the area came from a record of one hooting at Close Sartfield in the autumn of 2003. Finally, in the late summer of 2005, at least two recently fledged Tawny Owl chicks were present at a site near Andreas in the north. There are thus encouraging signs that the Tawny Owl is becoming properly established as a resident on the Isle of Man.

Breeding adult Tawny Owls are sedentary, but in temperate Europe juveniles disperse, usually a few kilometres, in their first autumn (BWP). One might perhaps postulate that the Ballaugh bird originated at the site in the parish of German.

Breeding	Grid squares:	Isle of Man 4 (1%) Britain 2,054 Ireland 0 Total 2,054 (53%)
	Population:	Isle of Man 1 Britain 20,000 Ireland 0 (4% of European)
Wintering	Grid squares:	Isle of Man 1 (0.5%) Britain and Ireland 1,683 (44%)
	Population:	Isle of Man <4 Britain and Ireland 35,000-350,000

Jan	Feb	Mar	Apr	May	Jun	Jul	Aug	Sep	Oct	Nov	Dec

Corporate Sponsor – Strix Ltd

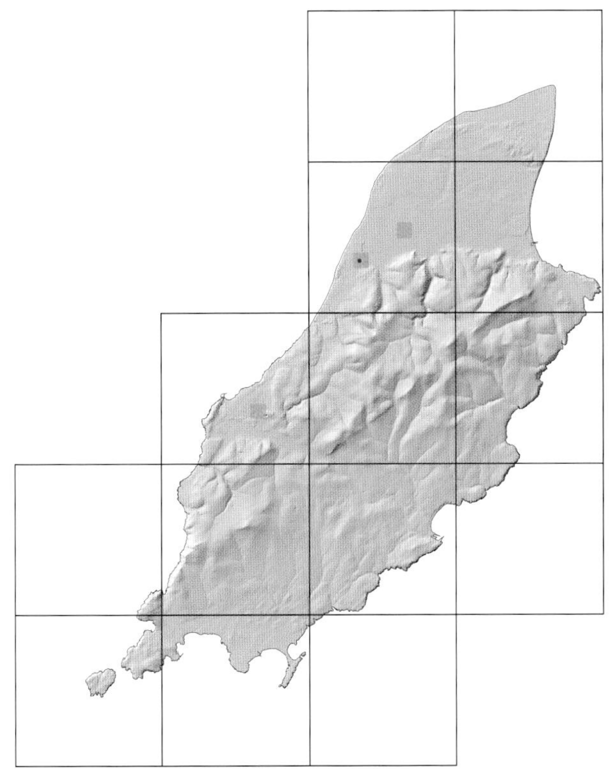

Summer presence and breeding status

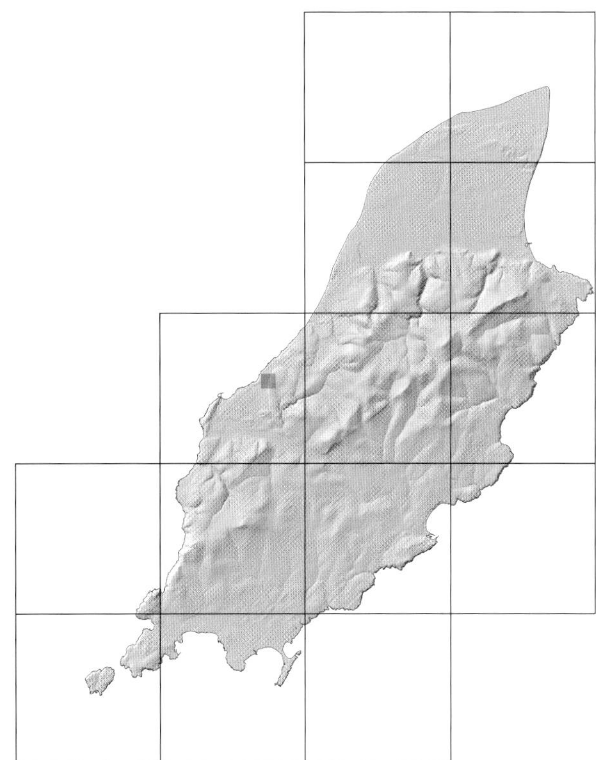

Winter presence

Long-eared Owl
Asio otus

Manx: *Hullad. Kione chayt* = Cat's Head

The Manx name, translated as Cat's Head, aptly describes the face of the Long-eared Owl, when seen perched upright, orange-eyed, with extended 'ears', close to the trunk of a conifer. In flight, separation from the Short-eared Owl is less easy, the best guides being the Long-eared's lack of black wing tips and white trailing edges to the wings. The wings of both species are long, although those of the Long-eared are somewhat broader, and it may be possible to pick out the fine barring on the tail. The call is a triple hoot, but the most easily recognised sound is the begging call of fledged young, suggestive of a poorly oiled bicycle.

Small blocks of conifers, both evergreen and larch, are the most frequent nesting habitat on the Island, but large wooded gardens, curragh, and scattered trees on the moorland fringe such as at Garey Mooar (north Arbory), also attract Long-eared Owls. They utilise the old nests of corvids, most commonly Magpies, but also nest occasionally on the ground. On the Island, eggs may be laid as early as the last week of February, although more usually during March or April. They hunt at night over adjacent farmland, rough grassland and moorland. The wood mouse takes precedence as a prey item, but house mice and rats are also taken. A short-tailed vole (a species absent from the Isle of Man) has been identified in pellets found in Glen Auldyn, and remains of small birds and beetles have also been found.

The Long-eared Owl is well distributed worldwide, breeding for the most part between latitudes 35° and 65°N, the more northerly populations being migratory. In Europe, distribution is patchy in Portugal, western France and Britain. Within the British Isles the 1988–91 Atlas found that it bred throughout most of mainland Scotland, but was absent from the Outer Hebrides and Shetland, while it was scarce over much of south-west Britain. It is generally regarded as the commonest owl in Ireland and the Isle of Man, due perhaps to lack of competition from the Tawny Owl. Its nocturnal habits and tendency to sit tight when roosting or on the nest, makes the Long-eared Owl a most difficult species to assess. The authors of the two breeding atlases of the British Isles readily admit to the incompleteness of their mapping. Observations within MBA timed survey work, not surprisingly, were nil! All records received were opportunistic, so it can reasonably be argued that the results of C&J and MBA can be compared without the inevitable bias of a more comprehensive study by the latter. Long-eared Owls were present in thirteen 5km squares in C&J and 15 in MBA, but the two maps are notably different, with C&J charting six squares not shown in MBA and MBA showing nine squares, where C&J failed to record birds. Overall the two maps suggest that the distribution is at least stable, and probably expanding in the south. The five years yielded 63 records for the periods March to July; three nests were found, the remaining eleven records of confirmed breeding referring to recently fledged young. Curragh, conifer plantation and large wooded gardens each accounted for three of these records. With the exception of fledged young seen in Druidale at 350m, all records came from lowland sites.

The breeding population in the British Isles is considered largely resident, and the only two ringing recoveries of locally ringed birds showed very short movement within the Isle of Man. Birds from Fennoscandia and to a lesser extent Russia are migratory, arriving in the British Isles mainly in October. Numbers vary greatly from year to year, probably related to food supply and breeding success, with numbers arriving biased in favour of females (MA). European migrants occur throughout the British Isles in winter, reaching as far as Ireland, thus numbers present in any given winter on the Isle of Man are likely to be influenced by the extent of migration from continental Europe. That the Island receives migrants from further north is suggested by the presence of vole remains in the Glen Auldyn pellet referred to earlier.

There is a significant correlation between numbers arriving in the British Isles in autumn and the number of communal roosts in the following winter (MA). C&J mentioned as many as eleven roosting communally at a Santon site in November, but in the present winter survey, only single birds were reported, mostly hunting. During the MBA research only 17 records were obtained, rather fewer than had been expected, reflecting the difficulties inherent in surveying a largely nocturnal species that is mainly silent outside the breeding season.

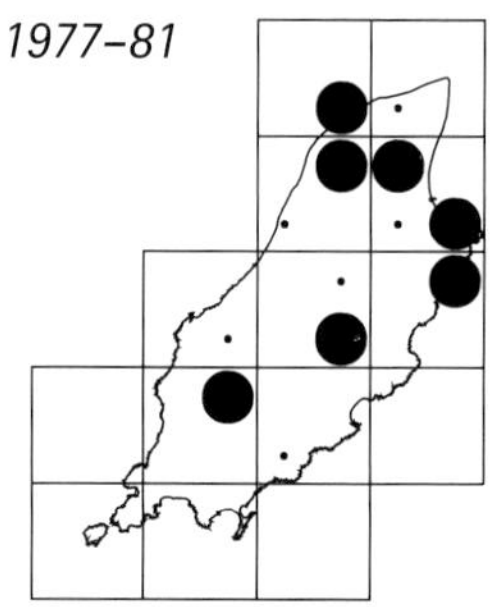

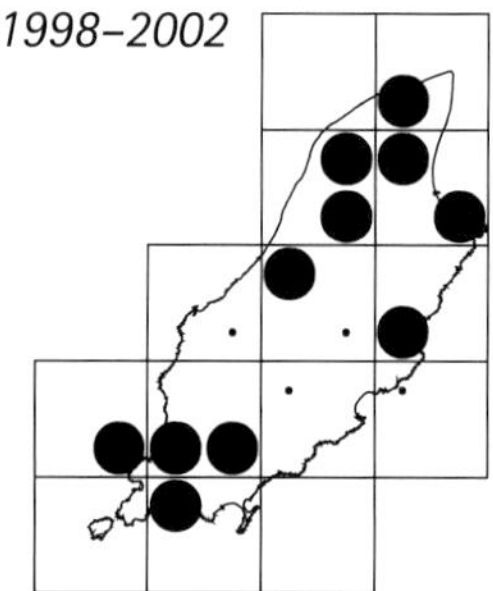

Breeding	Grid squares:	Isle of Man 38 (6%) Britain 445 Ireland 230 Total 675 (17%)
	Population:	Isle of Man 22 Britain 2,350 Ireland 2,350 (2% of European)
Wintering	Grid squares:	Isle of Man 14 (2%) Britain and Ireland 350 (9%)
	Population:	Isle of Man 100 Britain and Ireland 10,000-35,000

Jan	Feb	Mar	Apr	May	Jun	Jul	Aug	Sep	Oct	Nov	Dec

Corporate Sponsor – Strix Ltd

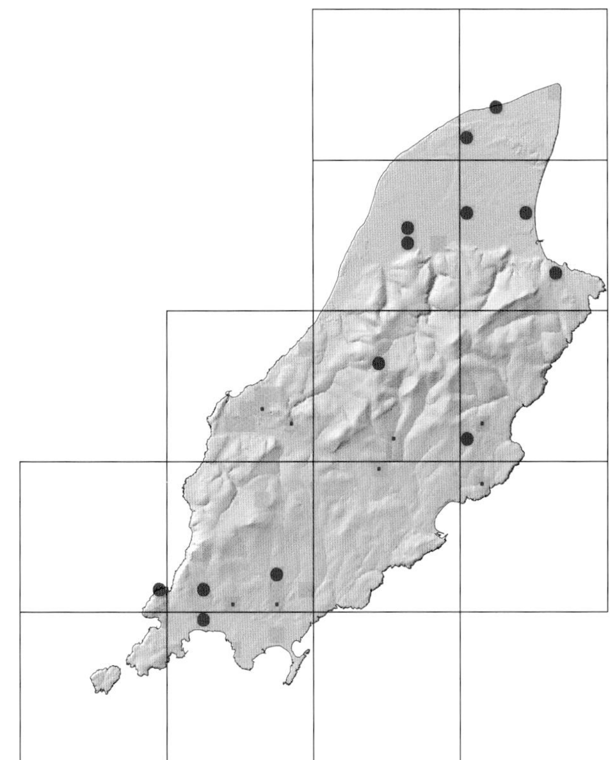
Summer presence and breeding status

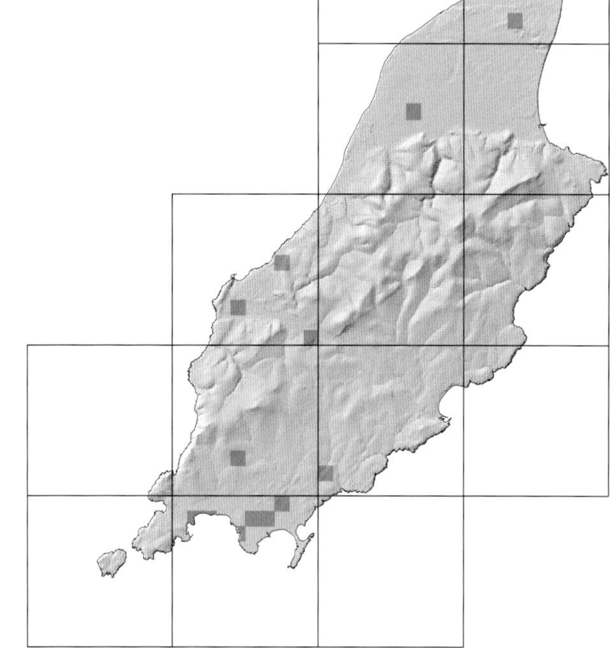
Winter presence

Individual Sponsors – Mr. G Craine, the late Mr. R Crellin

Short-eared Owl
Asio flammeus

To most people on the Isle of Man, the Short-eared is the most familiar of the owls, being a regular winter visitor to Langness. On an island where Hen Harriers are abundant, an initial distant sighting, with the naked eye, of the long-winged owl in graceful, buoyant, wavering flight can easily suggest a harrier. On closer inspection however, it is only from the Long-eared Owl that this species has to be distinguished. The black-tipped, narrow wings with white trailing edge, together with bold barring on the tail, characterise the Short-eared. Furthermore, an owl hunting in daytime will almost certainly be a Short-eared. At rest, the posture on the ground inclines towards the horizontal, the expression of the yellow eyes is glaring and the 'ears' are invisible.

This is an owl of heathland, infant conifer plantations, rough pasture, marshland and dunes, well away from human interference. Studies in the British Isles, France, Holland and Finland reveal that, when voles are available, they are the most commonly taken prey (BWP). As that food source is unavailable on the Island local birds need to utilise different prey. Haycock (1974) analysed the Short-eared Owl's prey from 243 pellets collected at nest sites on the Calf.

Prey species identified from 243 pellets collected on the Calf of Man in 1973 and 1974 (after Haycock)

Species	Total number of individuals	% of total
Pygmy Shrew	184	54.3
Natterer's Bat	1	0.3
Rabbit	17	5.0
Short-tailed Vole	1	0.3
Wood Mouse	9	2.7
Brown Rat	71	20.9
Bird spp.	56	16.5

The rabbits were all young animals and the birds included Meadow Pipit, Wren, Dunnock, Wheatear, Blackbird and Linnet. The most interesting feature of Haycock's analyses is the preponderance of Pygmy Shrew records, shrews barely featuring in other studies.

The Short-eared Owl breeds across North America from about 40°N latitude and across Russia from 50°N extending almost to the shores of the Arctic Ocean. There is also a South American population. The bulk of the European population is to be found in Finland, Sweden and Norway, there only being a scanty representation in the west of mainland Europe (mostly in north Germany and Holland), with a small Icelandic population established in 1958 (EBA). The British population is largely concentrated on Scotland and the Pennines, with breeding also recorded in parts of Wales, Hampshire, and sporadically down the east coast of England (1988–91 Atlas). Owls summering on the Isle of Man vary numerically from year to year, 1999 for example producing more than twice as many records as any other year within the survey period. In terms of proven breeding, it is likely that Short-eared Owls have nested in varying numbers every year since 1977 in the South Barrule/Glen Rushen/Cronk Fedjag area. Here, at least two pairs bred during the survey period, with one or two pairs on Stoney Mountain, a pair on Slieau Earystane and a pair close to the southernmost point of the Island (a hitherto untenanted area). Thus most records during the period were obtained from the southern hills, occasionally in the hills further north and rarely in the Ayres, where no evidence of breeding was obtained. Short-eared Owls nested on the Calf until 1981, but although a pair prospected there during the summers of 1995 and 1996, numbers visiting the islet have now become very small.

Within the British Isles the Short-eared Owl is a partial migrant, some birds travelling large distances (one recovered in Malta; MA), others undertaking only a local dispersal away from uplands to lower ground where prey is more abundant. A Calf-ringed nestling was recovered off the north Irish coast during its first August, indicating dispersal if not true migration from the Island. Birds from northern continental Europe are migratory, the British Isles receiving a substantial influx throughout autumn, many of which will remain for the winter (MA).

It is uncertain as to what extent the owls wintering on the Island are visitors or residents. The southern hills remain tenanted for much of the winter, but the birds breeding there may be the same as those regularly seen on Langness and in the general vicinity of Poyllvaaish. In common with other parts of the British Isles occasional communal roosts of Short-eared Owls occur on the Island, the largest during the MBA research being of nine birds at Scarlett, with a number of roosts of three or four birds, all in the south of the Island.

1977–81

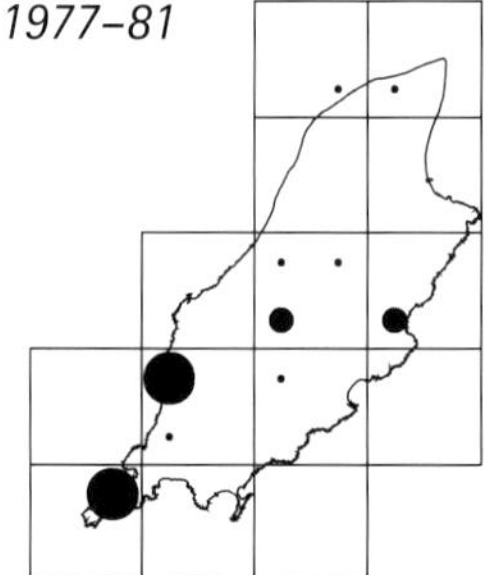

1998–2002

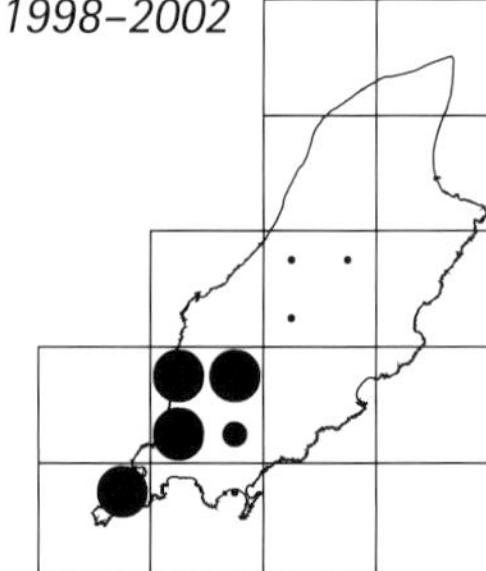

Breeding	Grid squares:	Isle of Man 38 (6%) Britain 679 Ireland 11 Total 690 (18%)
	Population:	Isle of Man 0-5 Britain 2,250 Ireland 0 (13% of European)
Wintering	Grid squares:	Isle of Man 28 (4%) Britain and Ireland 1,023 (27%)
	Population:	Isle of Man 10-20 Britain and Ireland 5,000-50,000

Jan Feb Mar Apr May Jun Jul Aug Sep Oct Nov Dec

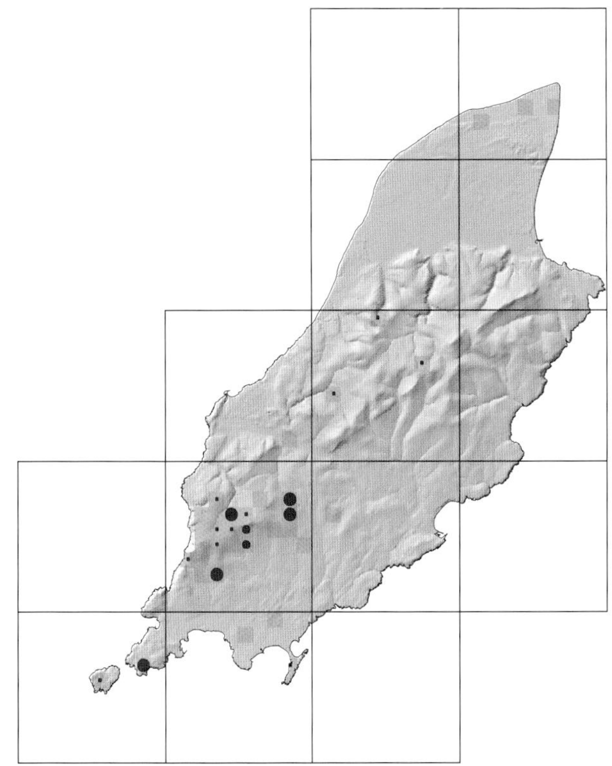

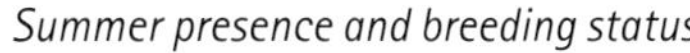

Summer presence and breeding status

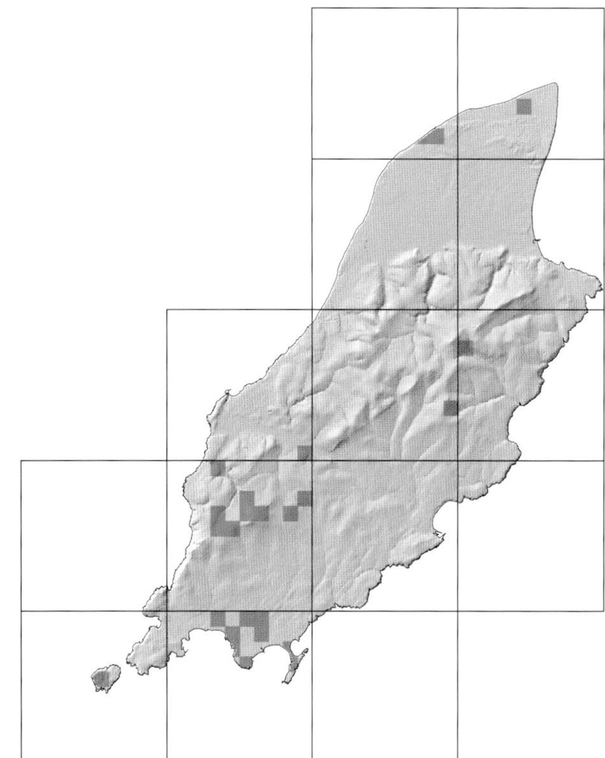

Winter presence

Individual Sponsors – Mr. G Craine, Mrs. R Fryer

Swift (Common Swift)
Apus apus

Manx: *Gollan ny Greg*

After the Sand Martins and Wheatears of mid-March and the Willow Warblers of early April, the noisy arrival of Swifts, usually during the first day or two of May, screaming as they chase one another at high speed over one of the Island's towns, is evidence that summer really is approaching. That is how one most usually sees Swifts, but equally they may mix with hirundines high overhead, their much longer, sickle-shaped wings clearly distinguishing them.

In the Isle of Man, Swifts breed primarily in towns, nesting under the eaves of long-established residential buildings and in church towers. More isolated groups of buildings are also used, while historically they have nested in the walls of Peel Castle, Ballamona Hospital at the Strang and possibly on the cliffs of Contrary Head. They are exclusively aerial feeders, taking insects and small spiders, often at some considerable distance from their nest sites.

The breeding range is confined to temperate Eurasia and the fringes of North Africa. They barely penetrate to the extreme north-west of both Scotland and Norway and are absent from Iceland, but reach the Murman coast on the Arctic Sea. Otherwise, the European distribution is virtually complete, with the exception of much of Romania. The French population is about ten times that of Britain and there are also very much greater populations in Italy, Spain, Germany and Sweden (EBA). The 1968–72 Atlas showed confirmed breeding in ten 10km squares on the Isle of Man, this figure being reduced to five in C&J, four in the 1988–91 Atlas and only three in the present survey. Closer inspection of these results suggests a progressive retreat to the larger centres of population – Douglas, Ramsey, Castletown and Port St Mary, but not Peel (absent as a breeding bird since 1995). In an attempt to gain more accurate information regarding the population, a number of volunteers took part in a coordinated count between 2000hrs and 2200hrs on 18 June 2000. Counts of individuals were: Port Erin 13, Port St Mary 9-11, Castletown 44-68 (a minimum of 11 pairs), Douglas 91-92 (minimum 8 pairs, with 5 visiting nest sites) and Ramsey 36-38 (a minimum of 2 pairs). Owing to the Swift's high-speed movements, duplication of recording, even by the same observer, could not be excluded. The map illustrates well how feeding Swifts can be found through much of the Island, in particular along many stretches of the coast, as well over the hills – notably Cronk ny Arrey Laa and the Carnanes. The 1988–91 Atlas estimated a 14.4% reduction in the Irish population since 1968-72, and flock sizes on the Isle of Man suggest that the species is also in decline here. With one or two exceptions numbers passing through the Calf have become progressively smaller.

Swifts migrate to Western Europe from wintering grounds in Zaire and Tanzania, and further south. Until recently the earliest arrival date on the Isle of Man had been 18 April, but in 1996 one was seen on 19 March and during the present survey, there were records on 3 April (1999) and 7 April (2002). The vanguard typically reaches the Isle of Man at the beginning of May, although it is often 2-3 weeks later that the main arrival takes place. As soon as the weather permits, laying begins (usually 2-3 eggs), and after 3 weeks' incubation the young hatch. They have an unusually long fledging period of about 6 weeks, but are then immediately self-sufficient and will migrate promptly, adults usually following a few days later. In most years Swifts become scarce after the first or second week of August. There were a few September records in four of the five MBA survey years and three in October (1999), but the latest ever remains 30 October in 1960 (C&J).

Ralfe considered the Swift to be a 'rather scarce species', but knew of breeding in both Douglas and Peel, with his notes of 1923 mentioning breeding in Ramsey from 1915. C&J knew of nesting in Douglas, Peel, Ramsey, Castletown, Port St Mary and the Strang. Based upon the evidence available it appears that the species fared well until the early 1980s, at which time it might have been at its peak, with clear indications of a decline since then. It is reasonable to suggest that declines might, at least in part, be due to property renovations reducing available nest sites. Artificial nest boxes, which are increasingly used elsewhere, would do much to arrest the decline in fortunes for this spectacular urban species.

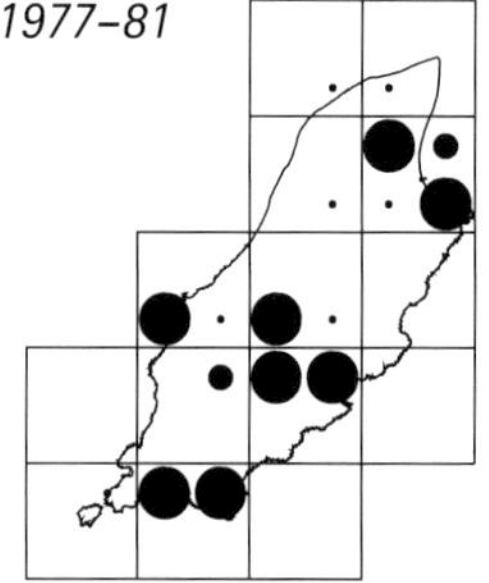

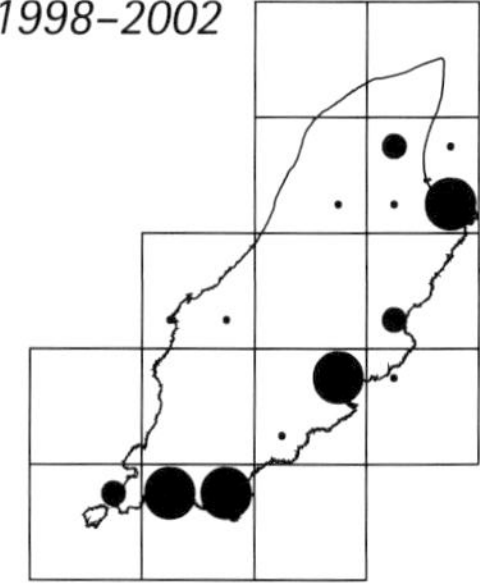

Breeding	Grid squares:	Isle of Man 170 (26%) Britain 2,215 Ireland 743 Total 2,958 (77%)
	Population:	(birds) Isle of Man 193-222 Britain 80,000 Ireland 20,000 (2% of European)

Jan Feb Mar Apr May Jun Jul Aug Sep Oct Nov Dec

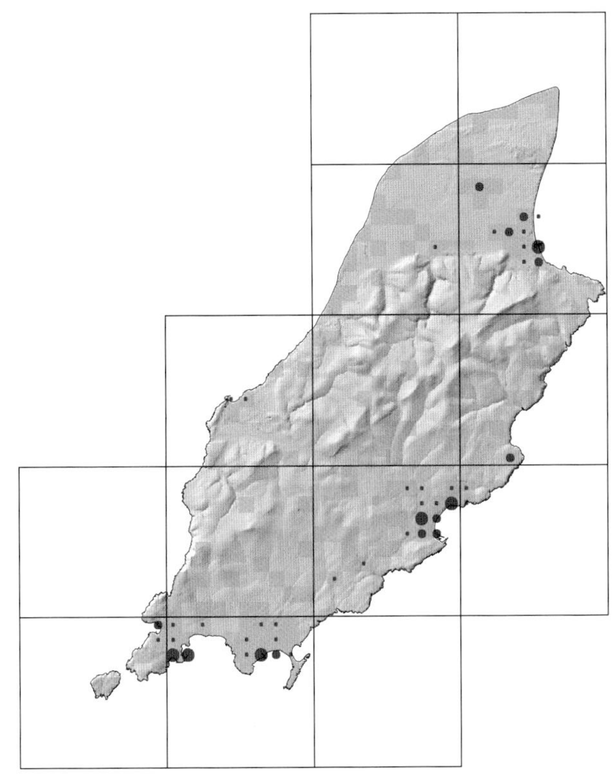

Summer presence and breeding status

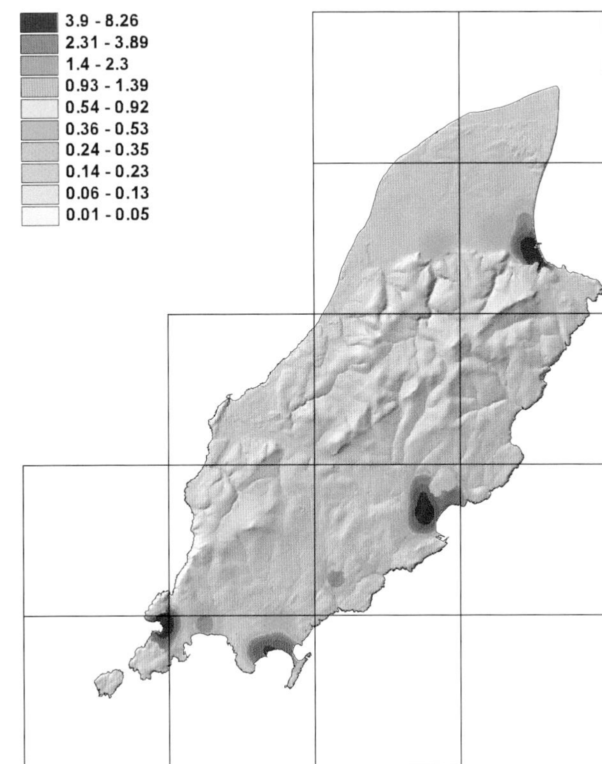

Breeding abundance

Individual Sponsors – Mr. I & Mrs. J Kelly, Mrs. P Morland, Mr. & Mrs. A J Sayle, Mrs. M E Woolams

Kingfisher (Common Kingfisher) *Alcedo atthis*

Manx: *Ushag Awiney* = River Bird

The short, high-pitched whistle, drawing attention to a stumpy form of unbelievably brilliant blue, flying at high speed, low over a quietly flowing stream, is a rare event on the Isle of Man. More usually a Kingfisher may be found during the winter months, perched by one of perhaps three favoured watercourses or on a rocky shore, when the rich orange breast, contrasting with the blue, together with the disproportionately heavy, dagger-shaped bill can be seen.

During the breeding season, the Kingfisher requires a slowly flowing stream, rich in small fish. The banks need to be at least lightly wooded, providing perches when fishing, and should in places be vertical and suitable for excavation of the nest hole. On the larger adjacent islands bullheads, minnows and sticklebacks are the most favoured prey, but on the Isle of Man, bullheads are absent and both minnows and sticklebacks scarce, so that for the occasional birds that do summer here, small salmonids are likely to form the bulk of the diet. Those birds seen on the rocky coast will feed mainly on shrimps.

Across Europe, Kingfishers are not found north of the 61st parallel. The north-eastern population is migratory, the extent of movement decreasing as one moves westward. In England and Wales it is resident, extending rather patchily into southern Scotland, while in Ireland, although widely distributed, numbers fell by an estimated 60% between the two national atlases of breeding birds. On the Isle of Man, Kingfishers are rare in summer (with only two during the MBA research period), but are regularly seen through the winter months, favouring particular sites over very many years. Foremost among the Island's rivers is the Sulby and in its course below Sulby Bridge it most nearly fulfils the Kingfisher's habitat requirements. Two birds probably summered near Ballakillingan in 1984, and during the present survey, individuals were seen there during May, October and December in 2000 and in March and July the following year. Further downstream one (possibly the same bird) was often seen between Poyll Dhooie and the stone bridge at Ramsey during the winter of 2000/01. Although outwith the survey period, one, and sometimes two Kingfishers were seen regularly from late September 2003 to the year's end, with an additional October record coming from Sulby Bridge. Surprisingly, a Kingfisher was seen twice in May 1999 on the Lagg, a tiny stream which tumbles quite precipitously for barely 2km off Dalby Mountain. One was seen on the River Neb below the Raggatt in March 2000 and again in August 2001 and October 2002, with further records coming from Ballaspit, 3km upstream, in both September and late October that same autumn. On the River Glass, one was at the Nunnery in late October 2000, January 2001 and September 2002, and further upstream in the Tromode area in October 2000 and in both January and March 2001. There have also been autumn records from both Kerrowdhoo Reservoir and Kionslieu Dam, but unusually, only one from the coast, at Port Jack in December. There is a possibility that one or more Kingfishers are resident in an inaccessible stretch of the Sulby, between Ballakillingan and Ramsey, but elsewhere records appear to relate to birds dispersing from outside the Island.

Writing at the beginning of the twentieth century, Ralfe implied that the Kingfisher was not scarce. He was unaware that Kingfishers had nested by the Sulby River to the west of Ramsey in 1893, and the same location was to yield an adult with two juveniles in 1920, while during the 1930s they possibly nested under the boathouse at the Mooragh Lake. This same period produced a number of reports from the Neb at Glenfaba and regular nesting was reputed to have occurred on the River Glass at Sir George's Bridge (C&J).

1977–81

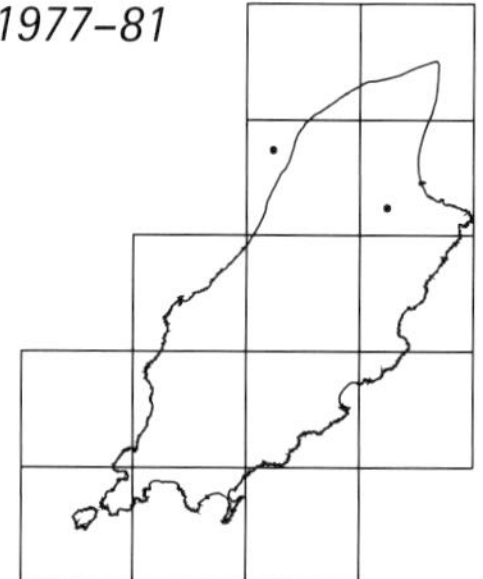

1998–2002

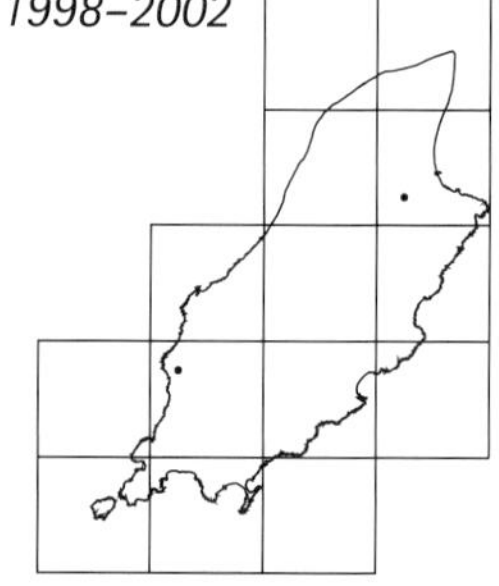

Breeding	Grid squares:	Isle of Man 2 (0.5%) Britain 1,224 Ireland 306 Total 1,530 (40%)
	Population:	Isle of Man 0-2 Britain 4,400 Ireland 1,700 (12% of European)
Wintering	Grid squares:	Isle of Man 7 (1%) Britain and Ireland 1,294 (34%)
	Population:	Isle of Man 0-4 Britain and Ireland 9,000-15,000

Jan Feb Mar Apr May Jun Jul Aug Sep Oct Nov Dec

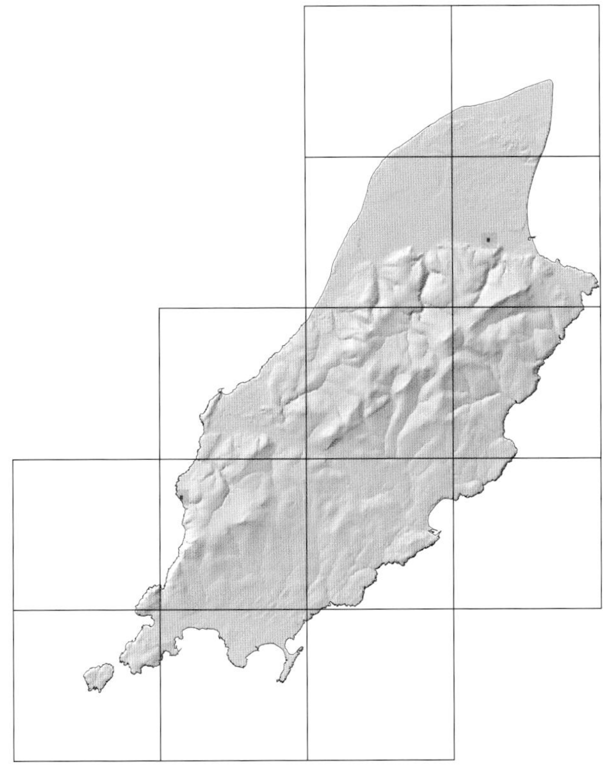

Summer presence and breeding status

Winter presence

Great Spotted Woodpecker
Dendrocopos major

Manx: *Snoggeyder*

The identification of the Great Spotted Woodpecker should present no problem on the Isle of Man, but it is particularly helpful to the analyst, confronted with just a handful of records in most years, if the sex can be established. Quite simply, the male has a square red nape patch, while in the female the black crown continues, uninterrupted over the nape. Juveniles on the other hand have a red crown. The British subspecies *Dendrocopos major anglicus*, shows a much less striking contrast between black and white than the subspecies *D.m. major*, which reaches Britain from Scandinavia in irruption years.

Trees of virtually any sort, whether in broad-leaved or mixed woodland, coniferous forest, parkland or gardens, are the sole requirement of the Great Spotted Woodpecker. It is omnivorous, the summer diet consisting mainly of wood-boring insects, but also eggs and nestlings of hole-nesting birds; in fact wooden nest boxes are often spoiled, either by enlarging the existing hole or creating an additional one. In winter, insects are still sought after, but it also resorts to tree seeds, in particular those of conifers, as well as beech mast, acorns and fruit pips. Seed is extracted by wedging a cone or nut into an 'anvil'. The Great Spotted Woodpecker readily visits garden feeding stations, where it will attack and easily spoil suspended nut feeders and also take items that have fallen on to the ground below.

The Great Spotted Woodpecker breeds over most of Iberia and across Europe, but excluding much of Greece and also a broad northern band bordering the Arctic Ocean. Highest densities are in the central European countries. It is now well distributed over most of England and Wales, but less thoroughly in Scotland, which was only recolonised towards the end of the nineteenth century. It remains scarce in northern Scotland and is absent from the northern and western island groups as well as the whole of Ireland. To the Isle of Man it is an irregular winter visitor, 1–3 birds being seen each year since 1994, although the species was absent during all of the ten previous years.

Sightings of Great Spotted Woodpecker during the MBA research split largely into three geographic areas. In the north, a male was often seen in the area of Lezayre Church between early August 2000 and 1 April the following year, an area where there is a long history of woodpeckers visiting the general vicinity. In 1994 one arrived in late December and lingered on until the following July or August, when it was killed by a cat or dog.

In the south, after one had been seen at Surby in late September 2001, a male was often seen in the Colby/Kentraugh area from mid-October until 12 May 2002. Finally, in the Douglas area one was seen at Anagh Coar on 31 January 2002 and it is likely that it was the same bird (a female) which visited Peel Road on 19 March and spent the period 31 March to 7 April in a Tromode garden, where it regularly came to a feeding station. This bird was a very distinctive example of the Scandinavian race. Outside these three areas, there was one at Monks' Bridge (Ballasalla) on 22 February 1999 and one (possibly the Colby bird) at Billown Farm on 4 December 2001. Although no evidence of breeding was found it is strongly suspected that nesting may have taken place in the summer of 2005.

Although essentially resident throughout its range, the Scandinavian race is subject to periodic eruptions, notably in the autumns of 1962 and 1968 when a minimum of four birds are thought to have wintered on the Isle of Man. Although there is some post-fledging dispersal of British-bred birds, this is rarely more than a few kilometres, so the origin of Manx visitors remains uncertain.

There seems little doubt that Great Spotted Woodpeckers have visited the Island more frequently since 1950. Ralfe could only list three nineteenth-century records (one being in the Lezayre Church area), while the first half of the twentieth century yielded only five more reports. They have, however, been seen in 22 of the last 53 years.

Breeding	Grid squares:	Isle of Man 4 (1%) Britain 1,959 Ireland 0 Total 1,959 (51%)
	Population:	Isle of Man 0–2 Britain 27,500 Ireland 0 (1% of European)
Wintering	Grid squares:	Isle of Man 8 (1%) Britain and Ireland 1,732 (45%)
	Population:	Isle of Man 2-4 Britain and Ireland 150,000-200,000

Jan Feb Mar Apr May Jun Jul Aug Sep Oct Nov Dec

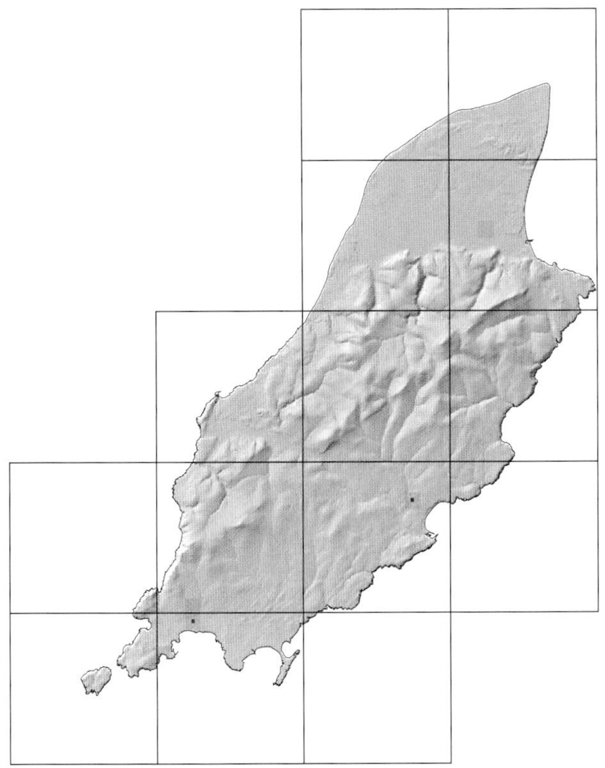

Summer presence and breeding status

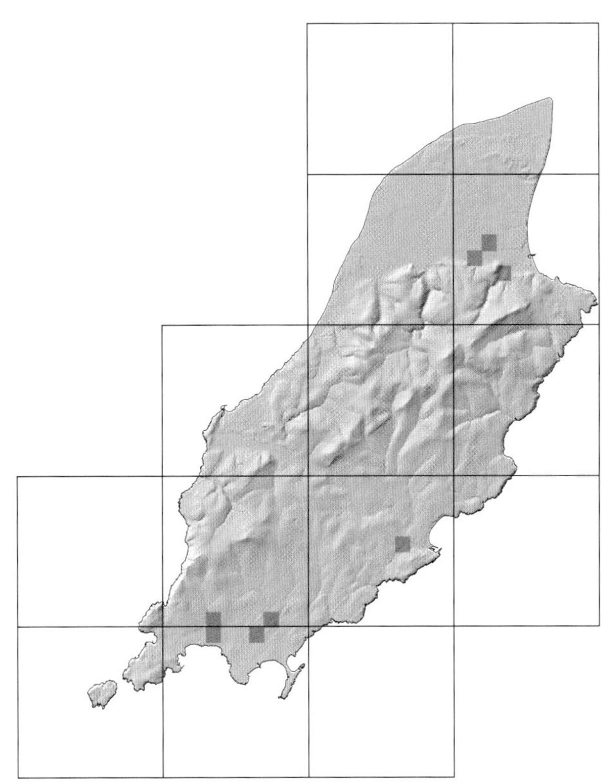

Winter presence

Skylark (Sky Lark)
Alauda arvensis

Manx: *Ushag Tappagh, Ushag y Tappee, Ushag Happagh* = Crested Bird. *Ushag Cabbagh* = Stammering Bird

There can be few finer sounds in the late spring than a Skylark singing from on high. It is almost impossible to resist the temptation to search the sky to find the bird, a tiny speck, proclaiming its territory before dropping back to earth.

Skylarks will utilise a wide range of habitats, including steppe grassland, farmland, sand dunes and rough upland pasture (EBA). In Britain, they will use a variety of open habitats, but favour areas of mixed or arable farmland. Locally, they are almost absent from the pasture and ley grasslands, preferring the permanent grass of the uplands and areas of low-lying grass and heath. The main food of the Skylark is weed and cereal seeds, obtained whilst foraging on the ground. It will take a range of foods, however, and during the summer insects form a greater proportion of its diet than at other times (BWP).

Absent from Iceland, Skylarks otherwise breed extensively throughout Europe, and are widespread in northern Asia extending east to north-east Russia and south to Iran and northern China (BWP). Within the British Isles the species is widespread, though concentrations are to be found in the arable heartland of the east of England as well as in the west of Ireland. MBA maps of breeding distribution and summer abundance highlight the importance of our upland habitats, particularly the central and northern hills, with few birds located in the more intensively farmed lowlands. On the coast, scattered populations are to be found on headlands where remnant heath or rough grass is present, with the Ayres heath and Langness being particularly important. Though the grassed areas on all three of the Island's airfields are subject to different cutting regimes, each is well used by breeding Skylarks. A reduction in range is evident, compared to C&J, suggesting a reduction in breeding numbers, probably as a result of changes from spring to autumn sowing, and increased silage production, though general declines in the British Isles population will also have an impact.

Monitoring at three coastal locations during autumn 1999 and 2000 indicated that Skylarks start to move through the Island in mid to late September, peaking in October, with relatively few being observed by November. These birds are probably mainly from the continent, though the extent to which British and Irish birds migrate is largely unknown. Nor is it clear whether the birds observed on passage during the autumn remain in Britain or continue their passage south (MA).

Manx winter data do, however, indicate that Skylarks largely abandon the uplands at this time, reflecting known altitudinal movements elsewhere. It appears likely that local birds remain on the Island through the winter, primarily using a combination of stubble fields, rough grassland, brassica crops and lowland heath. Winter flocks in excess of fifty birds are relatively rare, though notable gatherings do occur. For example, in January 1999, at least 350 birds were feeding in a number of stubble fields in the area of Clay Head. Cold weather movements do occur, during which large flocks seek out areas where the ground is not frozen. With our generally mild climate, which is relatively frost and snow free, it is likely that during cold spells the Island will receive an influx of the species from elsewhere.

Kermode considered the Skylark to be 'resident', and Ralfe described it as 'common on our open pastures and sandy wastes and even high on the mountain land'. He considered the species to be commoner in winter and was aware that it occurred at lighthouses on the Island. Madoc described the species as one of the commonest on the Island and C&J describe it as a 'common summer and winter visitor and passage migrant'. From these descriptions, and in the absence of numerical data, it is not possible to determine the level of change in abundance of Manx Skylarks over the last century or so. However, in the UK, and indeed over much of Europe, Skylark numbers have declined markedly in recent years (1988–91 Atlas, EBA). The changes are thought to follow intensification of agriculture and changes in land use. Thus there will probably be fewer Skylarks visiting the Island in winter and, following the European trend, a reduction in breeding numbers is also likely. C&J considered that the Skylark's breeding range had contracted, while compared with their distribution map our data indicate that further contraction in range has occurred since.

1977–81

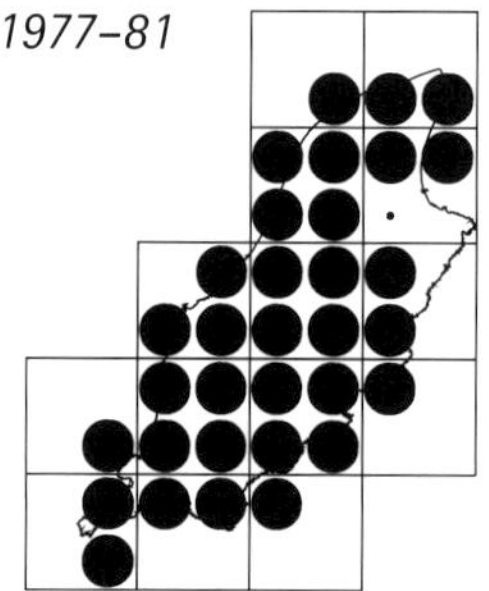

1998–2002

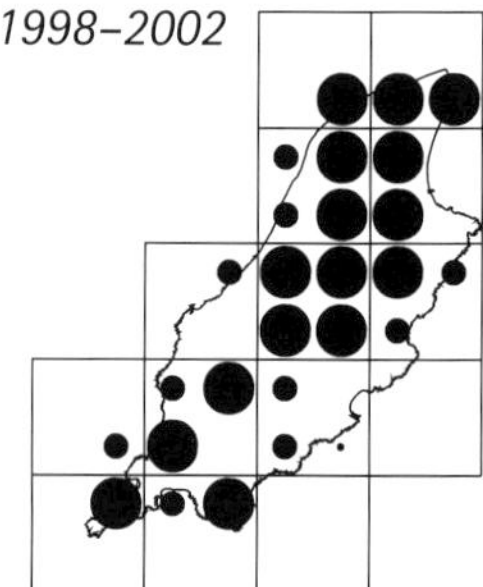

Breeding	Grid squares:	Isle of Man 204 (31%) Britain 2,729 Ireland 927 Total 3,656 (95%)
	Population:	Isle of Man 787-984 Britain 1,046,000 Ireland 570,000 (8% of European)
Wintering	Grid squares:	Isle of Man 141 (21%) Britain and Ireland 2,695 (70%)
	Population:	Isle of Man 1,000+ Britain and Ireland 2.5 million

Jan	Feb	Mar	Apr	May	Jun	Jul	Aug	Sep	Oct	Nov	Dec

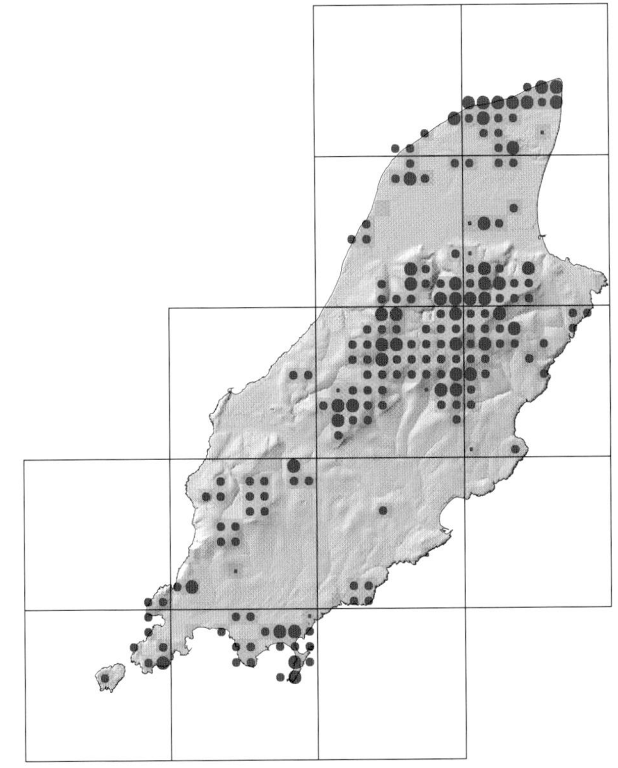

Summer presence and breeding status

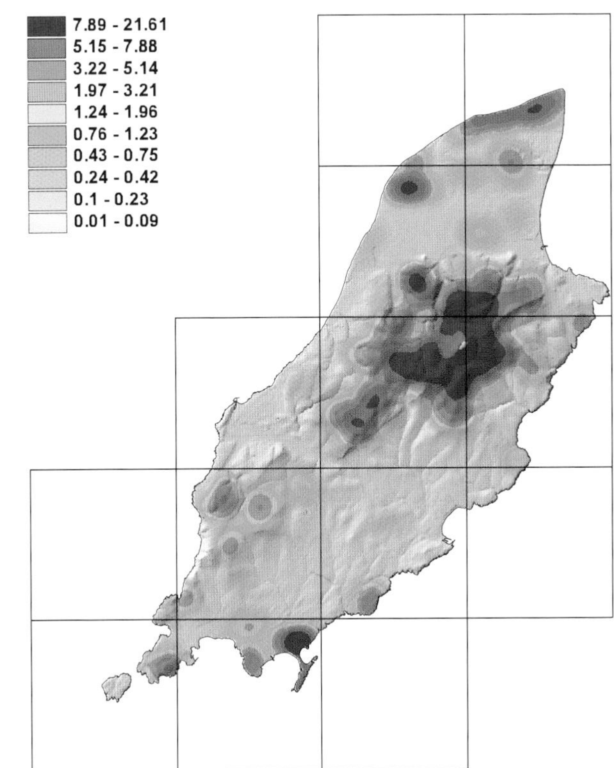

Breeding abundance

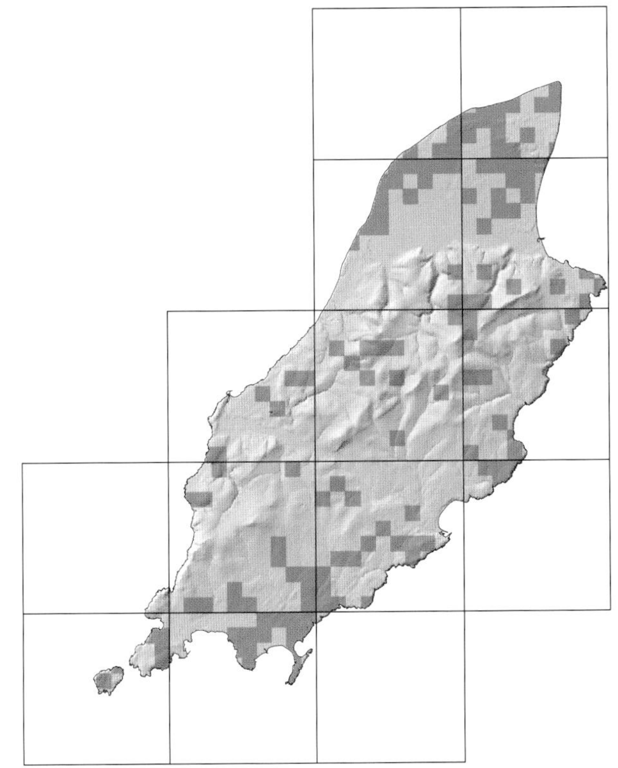

Winter presence

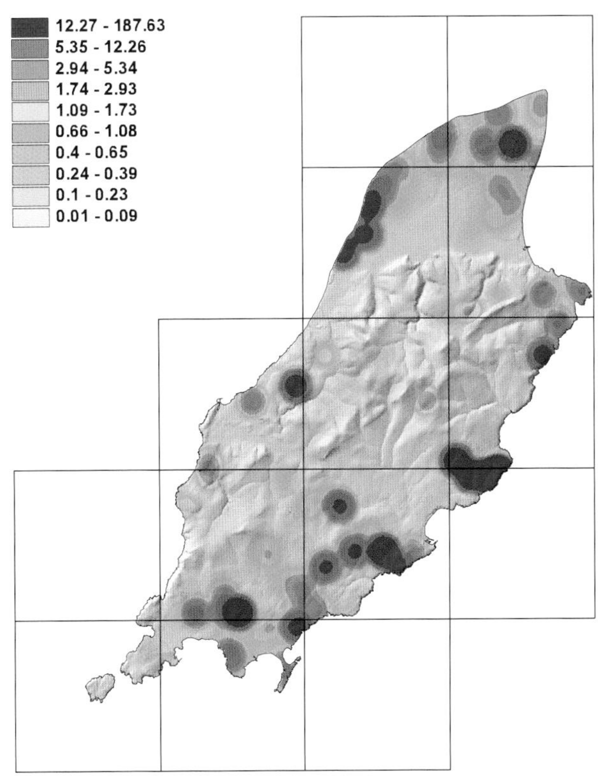

Winter abundance

Individual Sponsors – Mrs. L M Allan, Dr. Brownsden, Mrs. S Corlett, Mrs. P Crowe, Mr. T Flynn, Mrs. J Fryer, Mr. G Gardiner, Ms. G Hampton, Miss M Lucas, Mr. & Mrs. J B Phillips, the late Mrs. B Price, Mr. P A Turner

Sand Martin
Riparia riparia

Manx: *Gollan Geinnee*

One of the first summer migrants to return to the British Isles, the Sand Martin is often overlooked as a harbinger of spring, the more colourful and flamboyant Swallows or House Martins usually attracting more attention. It is a small-brown hirundine, lacking the House Martin's white rump, and sometimes appearing in the first half of March, though more usually towards the end of the month.

The first few records of the spring are often of ones and twos feeding along the coast, having just made landfall. Before settling into their breeding area they can be found wherever there are sufficient numbers of flying insects to attract them, with areas of sheltered water being preferred. On the Island, the first records are often from places like Langness, Glascoe Dub, Peel and the Calf of Man, though birds quickly leave these and settle into their breeding colonies.

The species breeds commonly throughout Europe and across Asia, as far as north India and south-east China, as well as over much of North America. Within Europe, breeding extends from Mediterranean regions through to the sub-arctic (EBA). The distribution of breeding in the British Isles is rather patchy, concentrations occurring in areas where suitable natural or man-made sheer sand cliffs occur. This is also the case locally, with the breeding distribution map clearly highlighting dependence on a limited number of inland quarries, and the soft substrate of the cliffs to the north of Peel on the west coast and north of Ramsey in the east. With the exception of a small colony at the mouth of the river at Glen Mooar, river banks are not used locally as they do not provide the soft vertical banks that are commonly exploited by Sand Martins. In 2001 a census of the species was carried out, in which counts of occupied burrows were used to evaluate breeding status. Over 1,000 pairs were considered to be breeding, approximately 33% of which were in quarries. Sheer faces of sand appear to be preferred, so areas of recent erosion on cliffs or the newly excavated faces of quarries are favoured.

In suitable summers Sand Martins can have two broods of young, the first brood usually staying within or near the colony for some time. By July return migration is underway; it reaches its peak during August and September, and is largely complete by the middle of the latter month. Rarely, small numbers are seen in October, the latest date during the survey period being 14 October 2002 when a single bird was seen in East Baldwin. British and Irish birds have their wintering quarters in Senegal, gradually spreading east into Mali as the winter progresses (MA). Return migration starts in March, comprising mainly older birds and continuing into May, when younger birds arrive at breeding colonies (MA).

Kermode considered the species a 'regular summer visitor', while Ralfe indicated that it was restricted by the paucity of nest sites. Madoc's view was similar to that of Ralfe. C&J described the Sand Martin as a 'common summer visitor and passage migrant'. As with many other species it is difficult, in the absence of detailed historical numerical data, to assess whether numbers have changed greatly. In the UK long-term trends may be downwards, but are difficult to assess because of periodic crashes and major fluctuations between years (1988–91 Atlas).

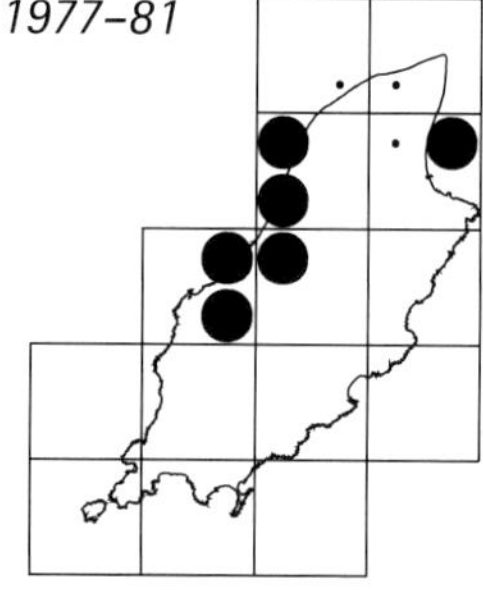

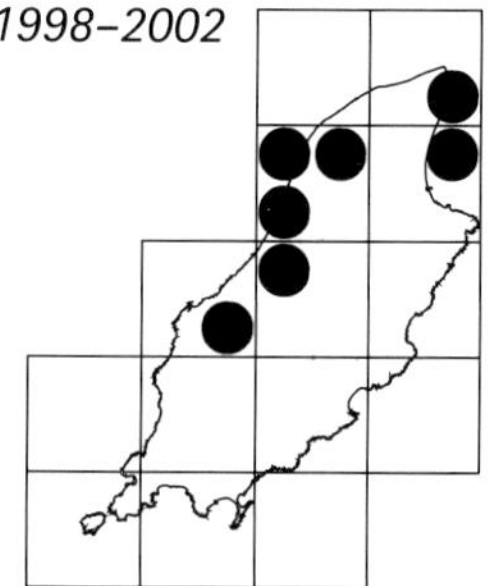

Breeding	Grid squares:	Isle of Man 111 (17%) Britain 1,559 Ireland 595 Total 2,154 (56%)
	Population:	Isle of Man 1,128 Britain 160,000 Ireland 100,000 (11% of European)

Jan Feb Mar Apr May Jun Jul Aug Sep Oct Nov Dec

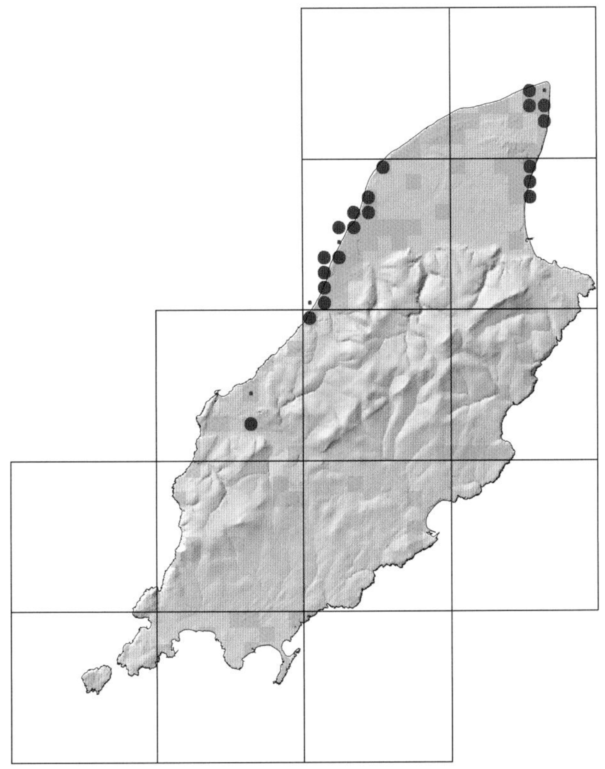

Summer presence and breeding status

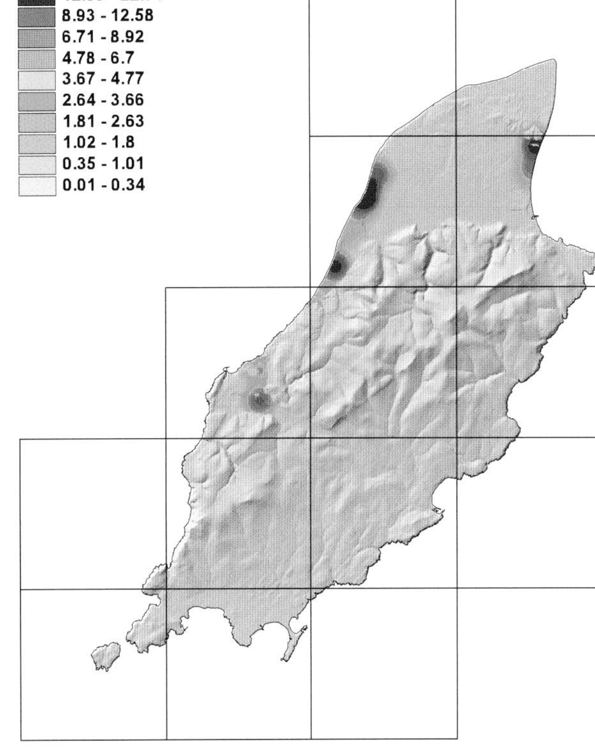

Breeding abundance

Individual Sponsors – Mr. & Mrs. M Ellis

Swallow (Barn Swallow)
Hirundo rustica

Manx: *Gollan geayee* = Fork of the Wind

Judging by the number of telephone calls about Swallows received by the MBA during the research period this is a very popular bird. Whether it was a report of the first sighting or expressions of concern that 'they seem late arriving this year', the early summer always resulted in a spate of calls about Swallows. Likewise, in the autumn 'last Swallow' records were common. These graceful, active and aerobatic long-distance migrants always attract attention, whether feeding low over fields or swooping with ease through narrow doorways and windows to gain access to their mud nests.

Wherever there are suitable nest sites, combined with sufficient quantities of food, Swallows can be found. They are particularly fond of farmland, most nest sites being associated with old outbuildings and barns with few new farm buildings being used. A range of other nest sites is also used, including derelict buildings, outhouses, sheds and the porches of private houses. The Swallow's prey consists almost entirely of insects such as hoverflies, horseflies, robberflies and bluebottles (1988–91 Atlas). Farming changes, such as increased pesticide use, limit the amount of aerial prey available and impact on the numbers of Swallows breeding; the increasing number of barns converted for residential use also limits the numbers of nesting sites.

With a Holarctic distribution, the Swallow breeds throughout most of Europe, though seldom in Iceland, and is absent from the Faeroes, the Arctic coast of Fennoscandia and northern Russia (EBA). It also breeds extensively in North America (MA). Within the British Isles the species is widespread, though it is absent or scarce in the upland areas of north-west Scotland, the Outer Hebrides and Shetland. It is more common in Ireland and parts of east England and less so in northern England and Scotland (1988–91 Atlas). The breeding status map illustrates the Swallow's extensive range on the Isle of Man. It is largely absent from the main towns, where lack of sufficient prey is likely to be the limiting factor. In the uplands, a combination of shortage of suitable nest sites and lower prey densities result in only scattered breeding, while the heath of the Ayres, though commonly used for feeding, is largely lacking in nest sites. The abundance map demonstrates reasonable densities extending along the coastal fringes, the lowlands of both the northern and southern agricultural areas and along the central valley.

Swallows are commonly double-brooded, with some pairs making a third breeding attempt. Later broods are still in the nest beyond the end of July and well into August. The young from each brood continue to be fed by the parents for a period, before dispersing within the general area to enter communal roosts, familiarising themselves with the area, to which they may return the following summer (Baker 1978). Migration starts in August, during which large flocks of birds may gather at roosts. Locally, the few beds of common reed are favoured, though maize fields are also utilised. The largest flock observed during the period was of an estimated 1,200 birds over Glen Vine in early September 1999. Migration seems to peak during September, with numbers tailing off during October, though later records are not uncommon. Records during the winter are rare, but during the life of the research, six December records were obtained, four of which were in 1998, the latest date being 15 December, when a single bird was seen in Port St Mary.

Many Swallows have been ringed on the Isle of Man, recoveries giving an insight into where local birds spend our winter. Two young birds were re-caught in South Africa during the February following fledging, one in Cape Province and the other in the Transvaal. Though some British birds are known to use the western coastal fringes of Africa on their way south, the majority are considered to cross the Sahara, having first built up fat reserves in, probably, Spain or North Africa (MA). Having spent the winter south of the Sahara, return migration starts in February (BWP), the first few records on the Island generally being obtained from mid-March onwards, depending on prevailing weather conditions. The earliest during the research period was 10 March 2001 when four were seen over Ballaugh Curragh.

Kermode considered the Swallow to be 'a regular summer visitor' and Ralfe thought it 'in summer … generally distributed'. Madoc gives no estimate of abundance and C&J considered it a 'common summer visitor and passage migrant'. There are no detailed numerical data from which to assess whether numbers have changed greatly. In the UK there seems to have been a moderate decline in recent decades (1988–91 Atlas) and this is likely to be the case locally, though no contraction in range is evident since C&J.

1977–81

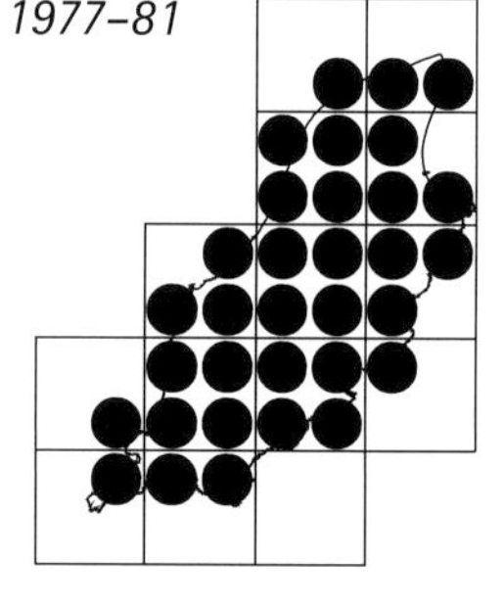

1998–2002

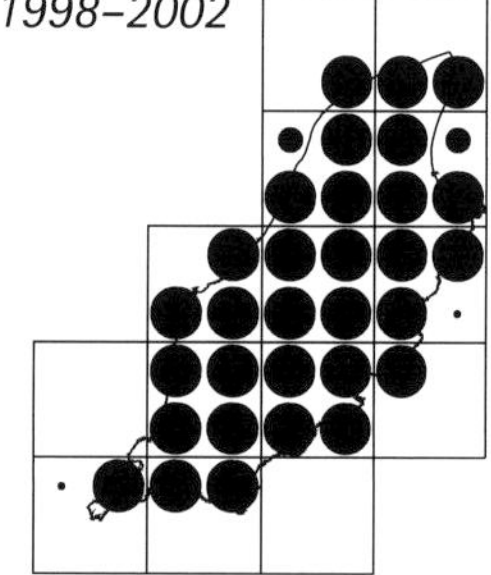

Breeding	Grid squares:	Isle of Man 539 (81%) Britain 2,626 Ireland 982 Total 3,608 (94%)
	Population:	Isle of Man 1,689–2,577 Britain 570,000 Ireland 250,000 (5% of European)

Jan	Feb	Mar	Apr	May	Jun	Jul	Aug	Sep	Oct	Nov	Dec

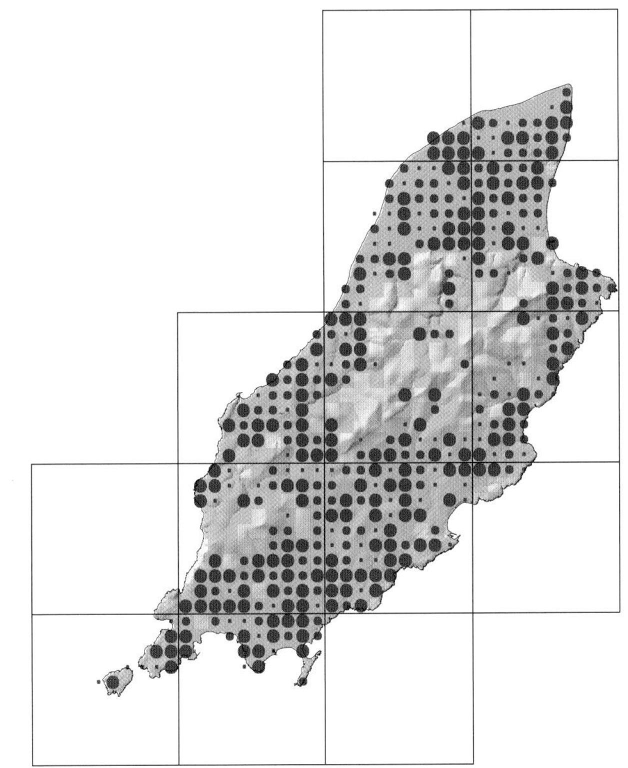

Summer presence and breeding status

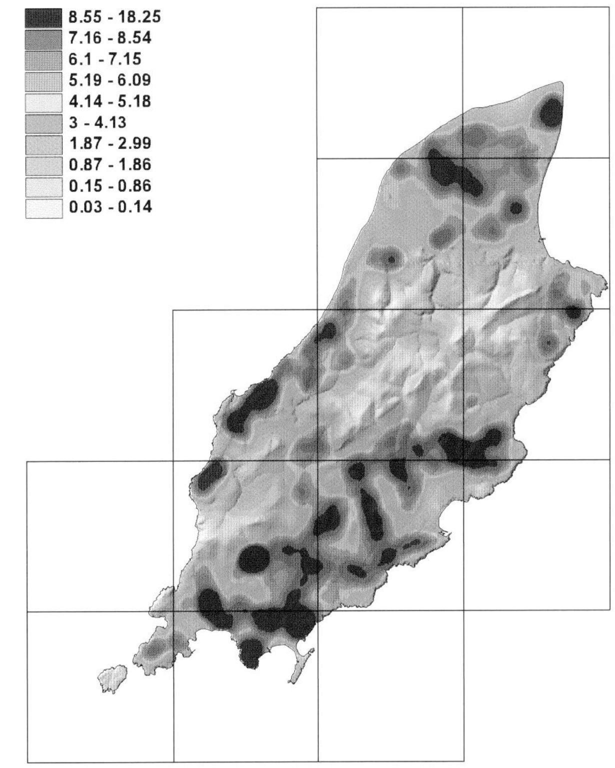

Breeding abundance

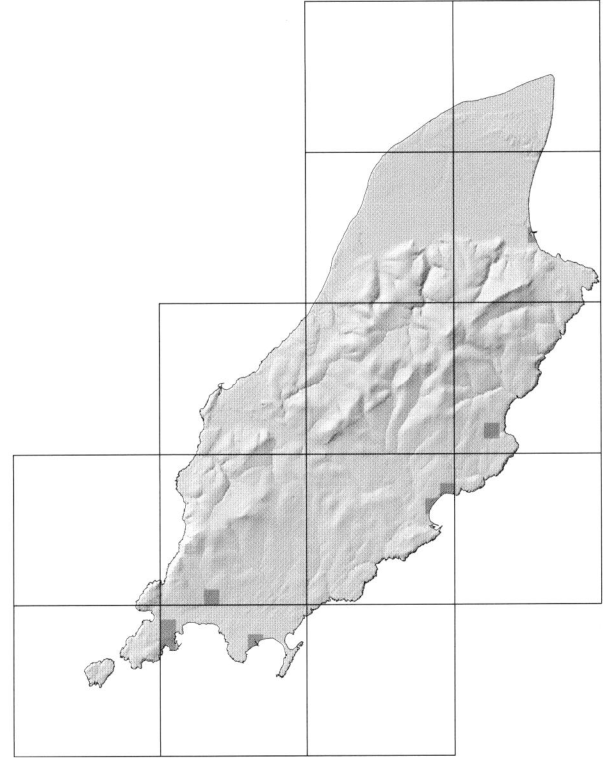

Winter presence

Individual Sponsors – Mrs. I Bedey, Mr. M Chadwick, the late Mrs. M A Collister, Edwards & Hartley, Mrs. M Hadwin, Mr. I & Mrs. J Kelly

House Martin
Delichon urbicum

Manx: *Gollan Thie*

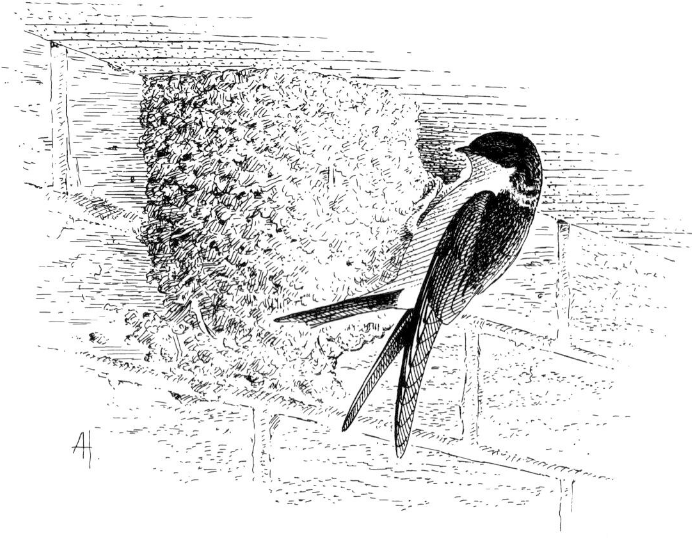

To those with only a passing interest in birds and those starting to develop their bird-watching skills, the House Martin is sometimes confused with the Swallow. Both have adapted well to human presence and the majority of nests of both species are built on or in properties. As a general guide, however, House Martin nests are almost invariably attached to the outside of a property, while those of the Swallow are usually inside, even if only in a porch. When seen well the distinctive white rump and short forked tail of the House Martin provide the necessary confirmation of identity.

Although the majority of nests are on buildings, House Martins still occasionally use natural nest sites such as coastal cliffs and, in some parts of their breeding range, inland rock faces. Food is almost entirely flying insects, caught by aerial pursuit, usually in higher airspace than that favoured by the Swallow (BWP).

House Martins have a considerable breeding distribution, extending from the British Isles in the west as far as Japan and China in the east, reaching north into Fennoscandia and south to the western Mediterranean coast of North Africa (EBA, MA). Within the British Isles they have a wide distribution, but they are localised in exposed and coastal areas in the west and north, and they are rare or absent from the west coast of Ireland, upland areas of England and Wales and the Scottish Highlands and Islands (1988–91 Atlas).

On the Isle of Man the House Martin is a common passage migrant and summer visitor. In most years, the first few birds are usually seen in the second half of March, though these are probably not part of the Manx breeding stock, most local nests not being re-occupied until the middle of April. On the Island, House Martins have an extensive lowland breeding distribution, which appears to be influenced by two main factors. The first is availability of nest sites, thus they are largely absent from upland areas, and also from the Ayres in the north and from the south-west coast. The second factor is availability of food, which probably accounts for the lack of breeding in the centres of the Island's larger towns, such as Douglas and Ramsey, where suitable nest sites appear to be available. Nests were found on only two natural sites, one on the cliffs south-west of Port Soderick at Gob Lhiack where 27 nests were found and the other further down the same coast at Port Soldrick, with only one nest located. This represents just over 1% of the estimated breeding population, a figure in line with that estimated as using cliff sites throughout their breeding range (MA).

Post-breeding migration is a protracted affair, extending from the end of August until mid-October, with occasional records beyond this into early November. Though the majority of birds seen on migration locally will be birds from the Island or from further north in the British Isles, it is known that some Scandinavian birds migrate through Britain (MA) and some of these birds may reach the Isle of Man. Despite the fact that over one million House Martins have been ringed in Europe, only 20 of these have been recovered south of the Sahara, so little is known about their wintering quarters in Africa.

Kermode considered the species to be a 'summer visitor in small numbers', whilst Ralfe described it as a 'somewhat scarce summer visitor' with the nests 'rarely attached to houses', making a number of references to cliff nest sites. Even as late as 1934 Madoc thought the species to be a 'regular nester', but 'in no great numbers', but by 1986 C&J describe the House Martin as a 'common passage migrant and summer visitor', though they knew of only three active cliff colonies. Thus the Atlas survey data support the earlier conclusion of C&J that there has been a great increase in breeding House Martins on the Isle of Man over the earlier part of the twentieth century. This increase seems to have followed a major change in the choice of breeding sites, from attaching the mud nests to cliffs and other natural sites to nesting under the eaves or overhangs of houses. It is difficult to determine whether there has been an increase in numbers in the time since C&J wrote their book. In the intervening period, however, the Island has witnessed significant increases in human population and consequent increases in housing numbers. New housing estates are often rapidly colonised by House Martins, in some cases birds taking over occupancy before the property's new owners have moved in. It is likely, therefore, that numbers of House Martins have increased since the mid-1980s.

1977–81

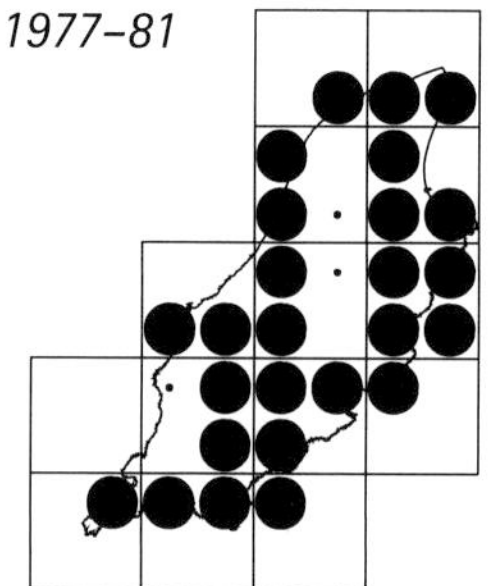

1998–2002

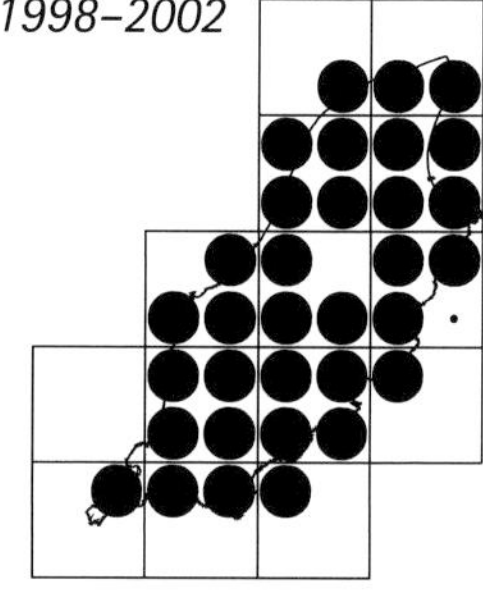

Breeding	Grid squares:	Isle of Man 305 (46%) Britain 2,393 Ireland 810 Total 3,203 (83%)
	Population:	Isle of Man 1,456–1,714 Britain 375,000 Ireland 105,000 (4% of European)

Jan	Feb	Mar	Apr	May	Jun	Jul	Aug	Sep	Oct	Nov	Dec

Summer presence and breeding status

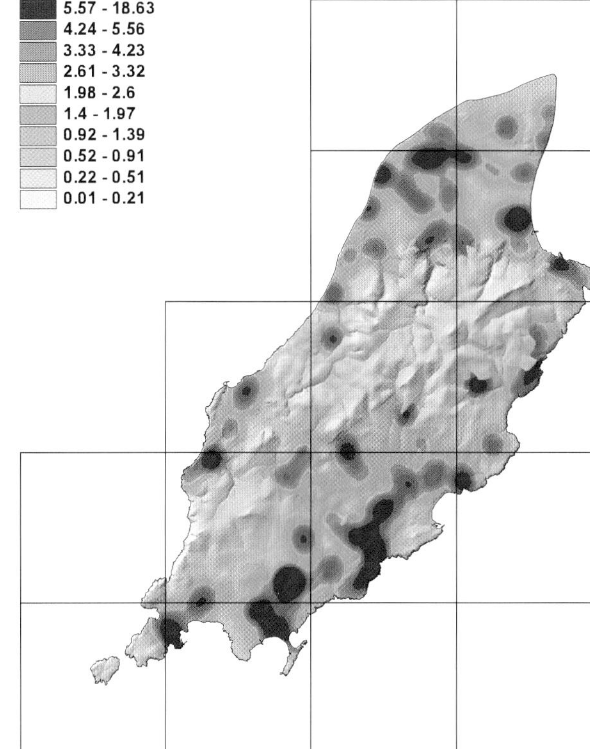

Breeding abundance

Individual Sponsors – Mr. R Fryer, Mr. I & Mrs. J Kelly, Mrs. T Steer

Tree Pipit
Anthus trivialis

Tree Pipits are regular but not very common passage migrants to the Island, which breed only rarely. In appearance they are very similar to the Meadow Pipit, from which they are most easily distinguished by their call.

Breeding habitat comprises open country containing scattered trees and bushes for song-posts, including heath and grasslands. Young conifer plantations provide additional breeding habitat (MA). Food is mainly insects obtained from the ground or low vegetation, though short pursuit flights are undertaken (BWP).

The species breeds across most of Europe and east across Asia to Central Siberia (EBA), but it does not breed in Iceland and is largely absent from Ireland and southern Iberia. Areas of high abundance of Tree Pipits in the British Isles occur mainly in upland regions, from Devon, through Wales and northern England into the central Highlands of Scotland, but they are largely absent from coastal fringes and areas of intensive arable farmland (1988-91 Atlas). The species is thought to have been fairly stable over most of Europe for the past few decades; changes in the UK are ascribed to regional variation in the planting of conifers (EBA). In the Isle of Man, over the period of the Atlas research, only a single pair of Tree Pipits was found breeding, in Glen Rushen in June 2002. Other than this single record, all other summer records were of birds considered to be on passage. It is likely that, with the species being unfamiliar to many local residents, some birds go unnoticed. The Isle of Man, however, like Ireland, is at the extreme western extremity of the species breeding range, so it is unsurprising that few birds breed here, despite the presence of much apparently suitable habitat.

The Tree Pipit is a long-distance migrant that winters mostly in tropical Africa, with a few birds being found around the Mediterranean (MA). Locally migration is evident during August and September and rarely into the first week of October. While more Tree Pipits are noted on the Island during autumn migration than during the spring they are still infrequent, with only 45 individuals seen over the five autumns of the MBA research. Rather few Tree Pipits ringed in the UK have been recovered abroad (none at all from Ireland), but of the modest number ringed on the Calf one was found in West Africa (C&J). UK ringing data suggest that a few Scandinavian Tree Pipits migrate through Britain in spring.

Neither Kermode nor Ralfe (1905) mentions the Tree Pipit, although a nest had been claimed to have been found in 1890 (C&J). Ralfe (1923) mentioned a bird at Injebreck for several days in early June 1911. Madoc was familiar with the species here, but knew it only as a passage migrant, and C&J described it as a 'fairly common passage migrant which has bred'. It appears that the Tree Pipit remains today, as it was during the twentieth century, an irregular breeder that is present in small numbers during both spring and autumn migration.

Breeding	Grid squares:	Isle of Man 11 (2%) Britain 1,524 Ireland 5 Total 1,529 (40%)
	Population:	Isle of Man 1 Britain 120,000 Ireland <1 (1% of European)

Jan Feb Mar Apr May Jun Jul Aug Sep Oct Nov Dec

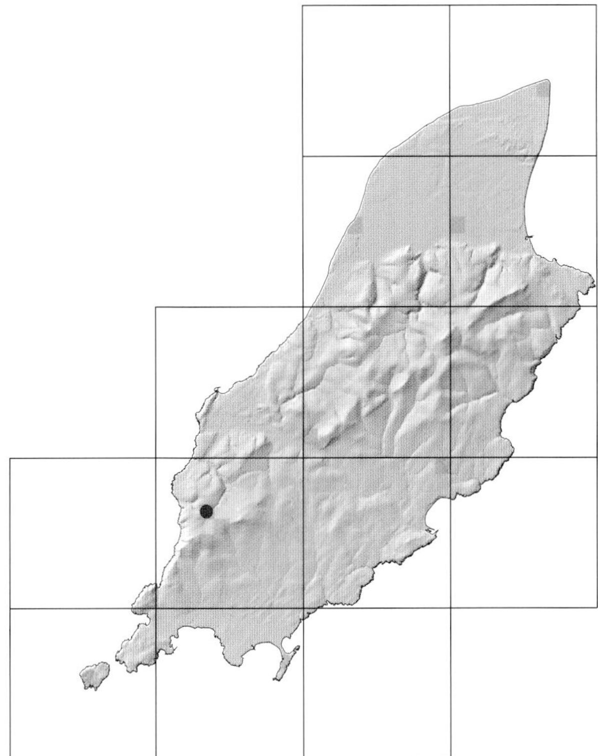

Summer presence and breeding status

Meadow Pipit
Anthus pratensis

Manx: *Tweet or Cheet. Ushag y Veet*

The Meadow Pipit is one of the commonest breeding birds on the Island and is likely to be encountered on almost any country walk, irrespective of the time of year. Despite this it is probably overlooked by birders and non-birders alike, its rather unremarkable streaky plumage and soft 'chip' call combining to make it the archetypal 'little brown job'. During the summer, however, its flight song is a welcome backdrop to the general quiet of the moors, while its 'parachuting' display at the end of the song is always a source of enjoyment.

Throughout its range the Meadow Pipit utilises a wide range of habitats including tundra, moorland, all types of grasslands, heaths, saltmarshes, fallow land and, to a degree, arable land (EBA). Food consists mainly of invertebrates, obtained almost always by walking and picking prey from foliage or the ground (BWP).

The Meadow Pipit is almost exclusively a European species, though its range extends from eastern Greenland through to western Siberia (EBA). It is widely distributed throughout the British Isles, though it is more thinly spread in the English lowlands, with highest densities evident in northern England, mid-Wales and the north and west of both Scotland and Ireland (1988–91 Atlas). On the Island Meadow Pipits breed from sea level to 600m, being absent or scarce in urban areas and in the most intensively farmed areas of arable and stock-grazed lowland of the northern plain, central valley and the south-east. Areas of highest density are evident in the upland heather and grass moorland, with other pockets of high abundance confined to lowland rough grassland and coastal heath.

Although Meadow Pipits are present throughout the year, the species is migratory, many birds passing through the Island during spring and autumn, others arriving for the winter and some remaining all year. Spring passage is evident in late March and April, while that for autumn occurs between late July and October. During this period large numbers of birds can be observed flying over the Island, most noticeable at coastal locations, or busily feeding near the coast or on suitable fields. Numbers range from ones and twos to loose flocks of hundreds of individuals. The majority of Meadow Pipits breeding in the British Isles will winter in the Iberian Peninsula, but many remain within Britain and Ireland throughout the year (MA). Birds from Greenland, Iceland, the Faeroes and Scandinavia are known to pass through the British Isles (including the Isle of Man) on migration, though there is no evidence to suggest that any over-winter here (MA). Thus, it is probable that the winter population on the Island consists mainly of local breeding birds and their young, together with some immigrants from elsewhere in the British Isles.

In winter fewer birds are present on the Island, an estimate of 2,000+ perhaps being slightly conservative. Though the species remains widespread, there is a noticeable shift in the pattern of distribution and abundance. Meadow Pipits are more thinly represented on higher ground, with none being found above 460m during MBA research, while the species was much more evident in lowland field systems. This changed pattern mirrors that within the British Isles where the uplands are generally deserted in winter (WA).

Kermode considered the Meadow Pipit to be 'resident' and Ralfe described it as 'very common'. Madoc noted it as 'one of the commonest birds in the Island' while C&J described it as a 'common summer visitor, passage migrant and winter visitor'. Thus there is nothing to suggest a change in abundance of Manx Meadow Pipits over the last century; it continues to be one of our commonest breeding birds. In the UK and Ireland the breeding population has suffered a 25–49% decline over the last 25 years (Anon 2002)

1977–81

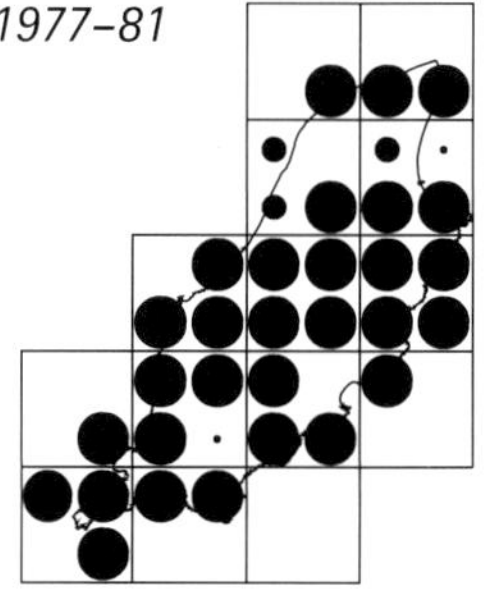

1998–2002

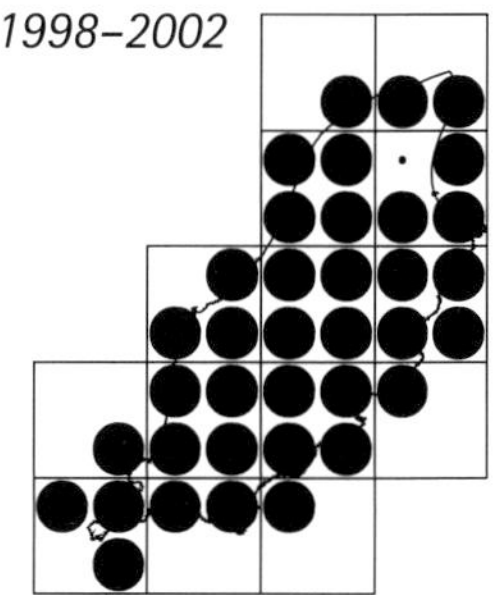

Breeding	Grid squares:	Isle of Man 545 (82%) Britain 2,539 Ireland 945 Total 3,484 (90%)
	Population:	Isle of Man 3,602–6,198 Britain 1,900,000 Ireland 900,000 (32% of European)
Wintering	Grid squares:	Isle of Man 384 (58%) Britain and Ireland 3,246 (84%)
	Population:	Isle of Man 2,000+ Britain and Ireland 1–2.5 million

Jan	Feb	Mar	Apr	May	Jun	Jul	Aug	Sep	Oct	Nov	Dec

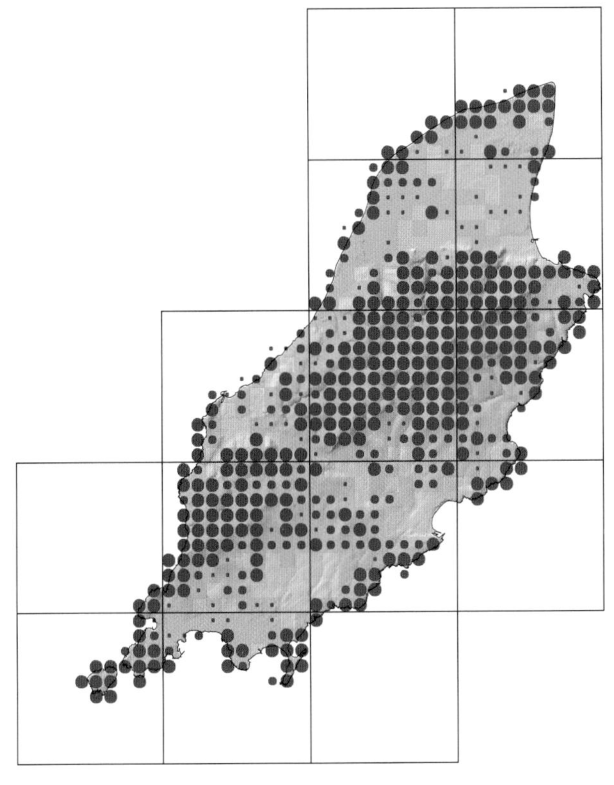

Summer presence and breeding status

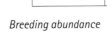

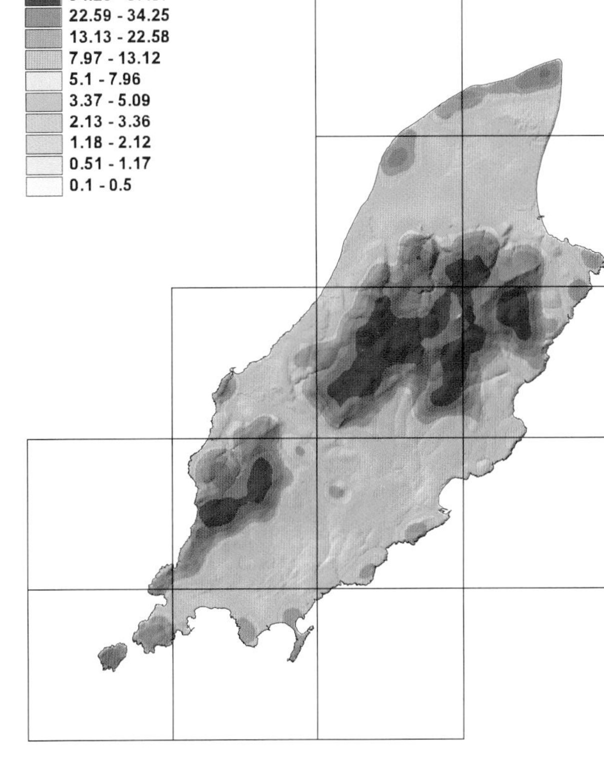

Breeding abundance

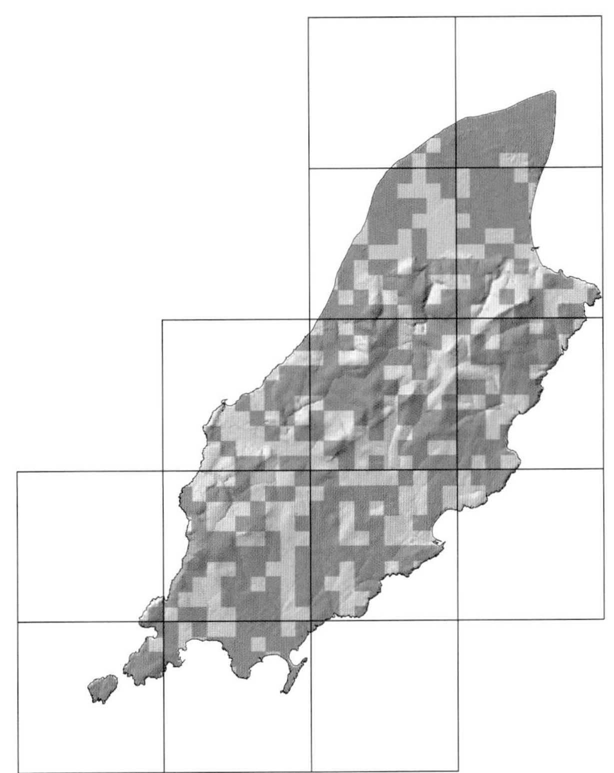

Winter presence

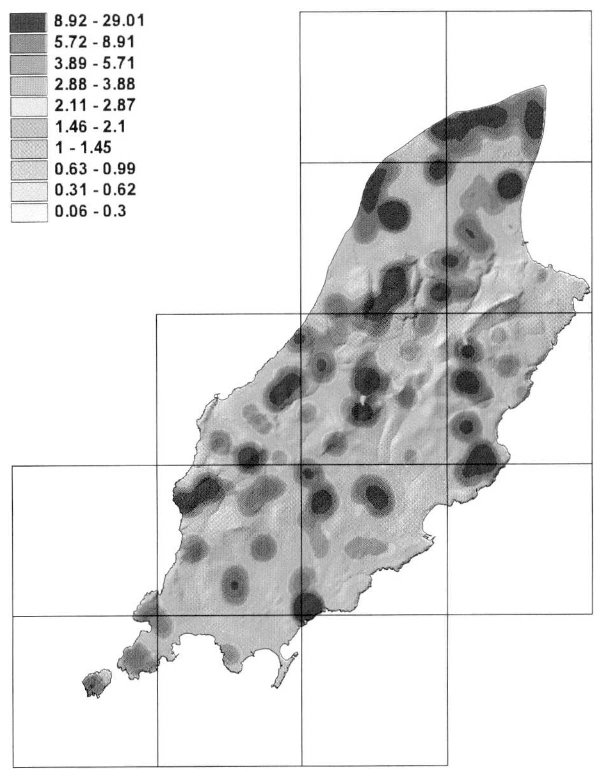

Winter abundance

Individual Sponsor – Mr. C M Sharpe

Rock Pipit
Anthus petrosus

Manx: *Fushag Varrey*

At first glance the Rock Pipit can be hard to differentiate from the more common and widespread Meadow Pipit. With good views, however, the Rock Pipit's dark legs, darker plumage and grey-white outer tail feathers become apparent. Like Meadow Pipits, perhaps their most eye-catching feature is the display flight and song, during which the males descend in a wide arc, wings outstretched and tail spread. Their song is delivered from shortly after take-off until the point of landing.

Rock Pipit breeding habitat is confined almost entirely to the rocky coast, though in some parts of their range they can occur inland (1988–91 Atlas). Outside the breeding season they remain largely territorial, though they will gather at productive feeding areas such as sand and shingle beaches, especially those having seaweed deposits, where they will forage for a range of invertebrates and, in particular, seaweed fly larvae. They do not feed exclusively in the intertidal zone, however, being equally at home foraging in the grass on coastal slopes and cliff tops.

Of the two main subspecies *Anthus petrosus petrosus* breeds throughout the British Isles and north-west France, while *A.p. littoralis* breeds in Fennoscandia and the Baltic countries (MA). Within Britain and Ireland Rock Pipits breed around all stretches of coast that contain suitable cliffs or rocky shorelines; thus in England they are largely absent from the west coast between the Wirral and the Solway Firth and between the Humber and the Solent in the east and south (1988–91 Atlas).

Rock Pipits are common residents on the Isle of Man, though it is unusual for them to venture more than a few hundred metres from the coast. The breeding status map reveals absence only from sandy bays and from Maughold Head north around the Point of Ayre as far as Glen Mooar on the west coast; all of this area comprising soft substrate. For this species the summer abundance map is slightly misleading. During the MBA structured survey, from which the map is derived, surveyors could only safely walk along the tops of cliffs. Rock Pipits were, therefore, under-recorded along stretches of high coastal cliffs such as those between Fleshwick Bay and Niarbyl in the south-west, and north of Laxey to Port Mooar in the north-east, as birds could not always be detected. The seabird survey of 1999, during which all rocky coasts were visited by boat, provided the bulk of the records from those coasts inaccessible from land.

Rock Pipits on the Isle of Man, as in the rest of the British Isles, are considered largely sedentary (MA), though some dispersal is likely at the end of the breeding season, including movements to nearby beach systems to take advantage of seasonally abundant food. The Fennoscandian subspecies *littoralis* occurs in the British Isles as a winter visitor (MA) and has been recorded on the Island. There is generally no obvious spring or autumn passage of Rock Pipits through the Calf of Man and the few ringed there have yielded no recoveries from elsewhere.

During the winter it is likely that all Rock Pipits on the Isle of Man are those present in summer, together with young of the year, though a few Scandinavian birds may reach here in some years. The distribution in winter largely reflects that of the summer. Absences along some of the steeper, inaccessible cliffs might be due to birds being missed. Gatherings of over 30 birds at beach systems adjacent to these areas, however, suggest that cliff sites might be abandoned in winter in favour of beaches. Gatherings exceeding 30 birds were noted at Port Mooar, Niarbyl and from Port Grenaugh, in the middle of the south-east cliff complex. The abundance map underlines the importance of suitable beach systems in winter, high densities of Rock Pipit occurring along Douglas Bay and from Langness through to Port St Mary.

Kermode and Ralfe both regarded the Rock Pipit as a common coastal species and C&J described it as a 'common resident which also occurs as a passage migrant', although subsequent national publications would suggest that the statement regarding migration is inaccurate. Thus there is no evidence of substantial population change on the Isle of Man over the last century. In the rest of the British Isles Gibbons *et al.* (1988–91 Atlas) considered the population of Rock Pipits to have declined slightly in recent decades. The reasons for this decline are not known. Elsewhere in Europe *A.p. littoralis* is expanding in both numbers and range (1988–91 Atlas).

1977–81

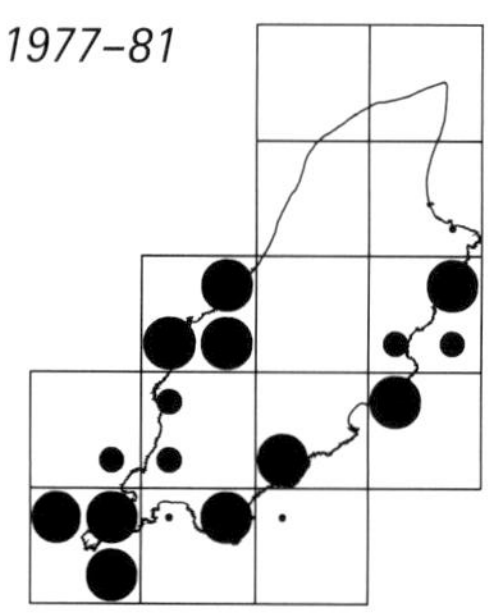

1998–2002

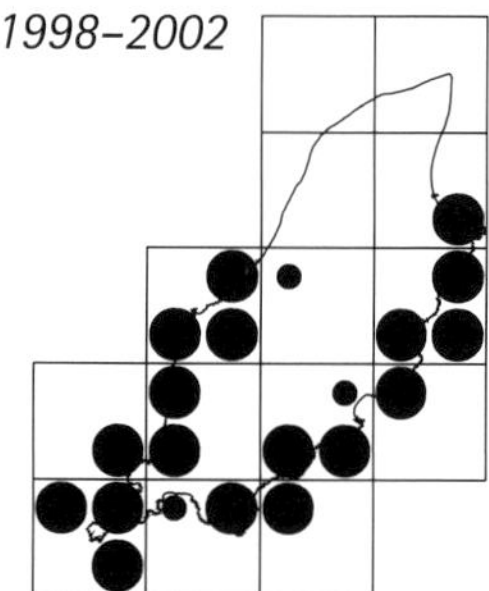

Breeding	Grid squares:	Isle of Man 103 (15%) Britain 654 Ireland 259 Total 913 (24%)
	Population:	Isle of Man 207-272 Britain 34,000 Ireland 12,500 (11% of European)
Wintering	Grid squares:	Isle of Man 66 (10%) Britain and Ireland 1,148 (30%)
	Population:	Isle of Man 500+ Britain and Ireland 100,000–150,000

Jan	Feb	Mar	Apr	May	Jun	Jul	Aug	Sep	Oct	Nov	Dec

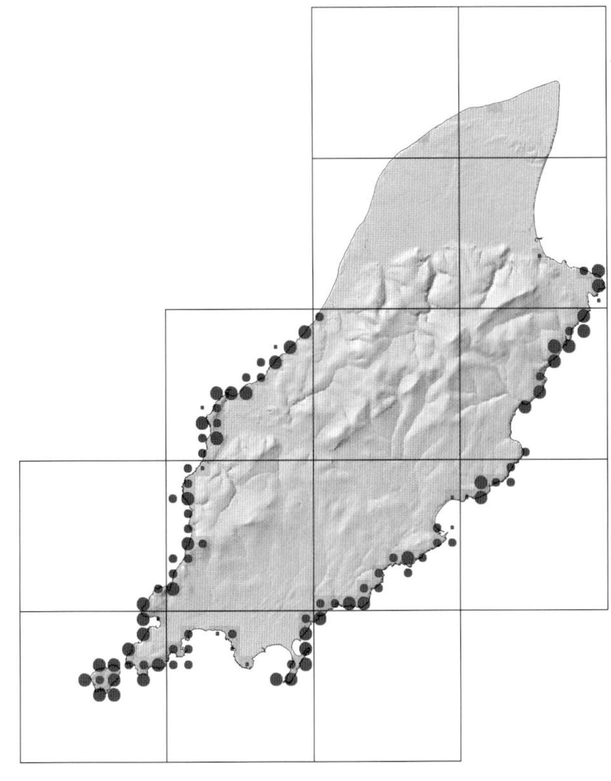

Summer presence and breeding status

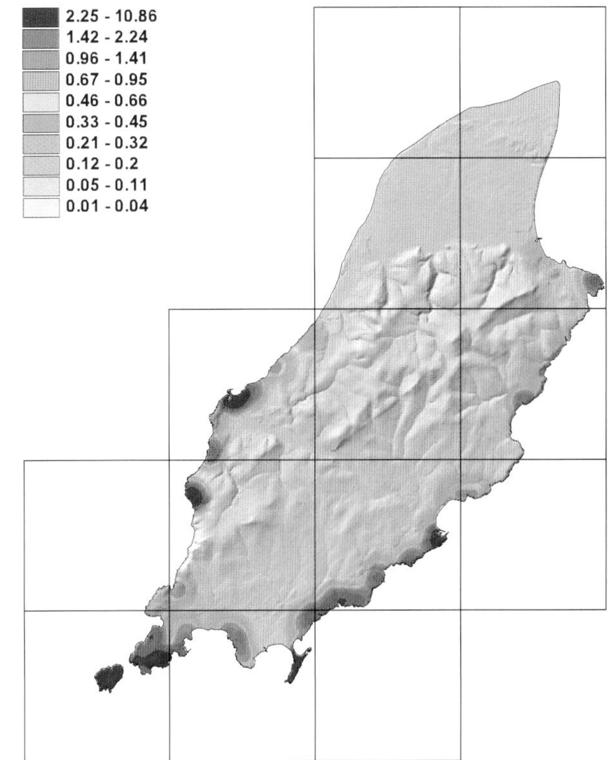

Breeding abundance

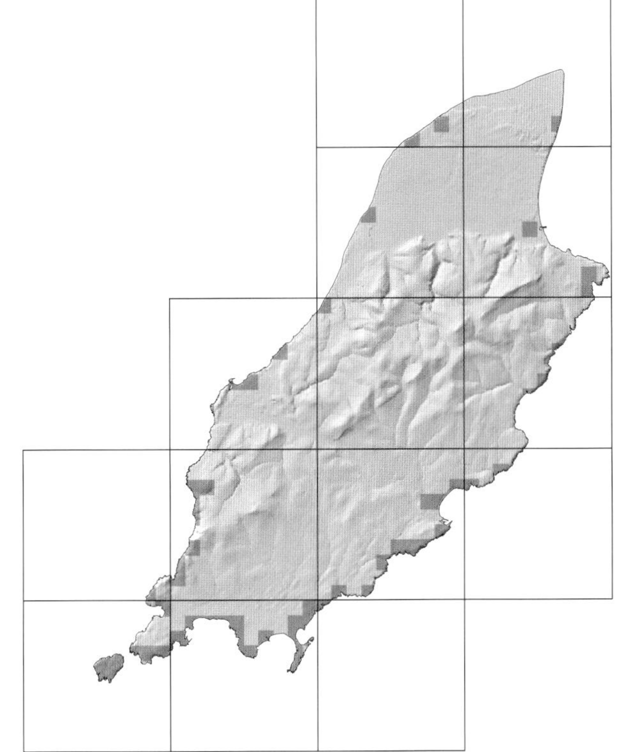

Winter presence

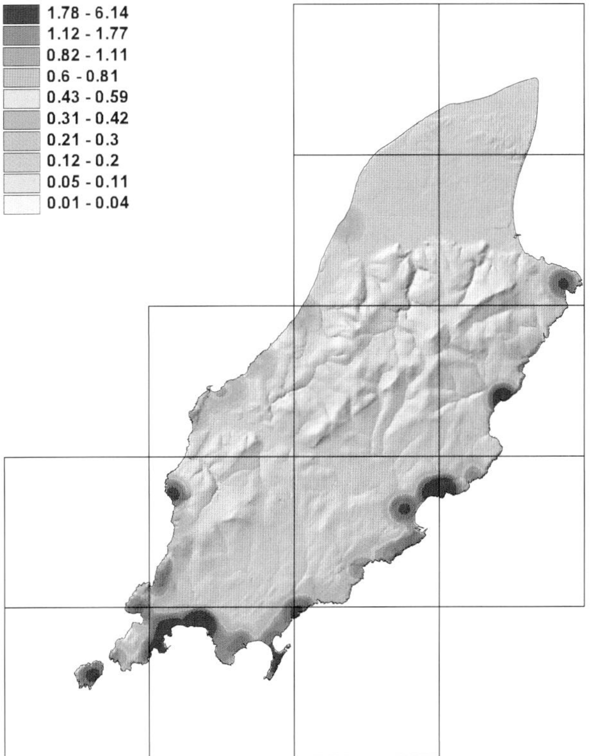

Winter abundance

Individual Sponsors – Ms. J Hinchliffe, in the memory of Allan Quillin

Grey Wagtail
Motacilla cinerea

Manx: *Ushag Ghlass*

Grey Wagtails have vibrant, bright yellow under-parts, usually paler on the flanks, and a dull slate-grey back, from which they derive their name. When seen well their smart plumage catches the eye and adds a splash of colour to the riverbanks on which they are typically seen. Locally, it is often reported as being a 'Yellow Wagtail', though that species is uncommon on the Island, the resultant unfamiliarity probably being the cause of the confusion.

During the breeding season Grey Wagtails are confined almost exclusively to fast-flowing streams and rivers. They use a range of nesting sites, including root systems in river banks and man-made structures such as bridges and walls. Seemingly suitable watercourses that lack bordering broad-leaved woodland are not favoured, as they lack sufficient food (1988–91 Atlas). Adult flies form the bulk of the diet, though spiders and caterpillars can be valuable in the diet of nestlings (1988–91 Atlas).

Grey Wagtails breed throughout the Palearctic, from Ireland south to Morocco and Algeria, and east to Japan and Sichuan, with resident races of the species present in the Atlantic Islands (Canaries, Madeira and Azores) and in Morocco (MA). Within the British Isles the species is well distributed, though scarce in the Outer Hebrides, Orkney, Shetland and the lowland eastern and central counties of England. Lack of suitable breeding habitat is likely to be the reason for scarcity in these areas. On the Island the species is seldom seen above 300m, though this will be influenced by habitat, rather than altitude, as it can be found nesting as high as 3,000m in some parts of the range (EBA). Most of the Island's rivers and streams seem to support at least one breeding pair. When conditions are suitable several pairs can be found along relatively short stretches, with at least three pairs breeding from the mouth of the Laxey River to the Laxey Fire Station, a distance of only 1.5km. Breeding was not found along the lower reaches of the Sulby River, though it did occur further upstream and on the faster-flowing feeder streams, such as the Auldyn River.

The summer abundance map supports the evidence of a wide breeding distribution, highlighting favoured areas such as Laxey River, and the Dhoo and Glass, near Douglas.

During August and September there is evidence of migration through and from the Island, with over 150 birds trapped and ringed during these months in recent years at a site near Kentraugh in the south of the Island, with over 50 birds present on some days. This indicates considerable movement, which is likely to include birds from Scotland and northern England. Grey Wagtails from these areas are known to winter in southern Britain or Ireland (MA). It is unknown what percentage of local birds remain for the winter; however, the winter distribution map reveals that the species is both well represented and well distributed throughout our lowlands during the winter months. Grey Wagtails largely abandon the uplands during the winter and are often to be found away from breeding habitats, ranging much more widely in search of food. As the abundance map indicates, they are common in the winter, with reasonable densities in many of the Island's main towns, birds often being observed in gardens, especially if ponds are present.

Kermode described the Grey Wagtail as being less numerous than the Pied Wagtail and 'confined to streams and glens, although I have seen it in the towns in autumn'. Ralfe considered it 'thinly scattered' and also mentioned that it 'frequents rapid streams', but is often found in villages in autumn and winter, while Madoc suggested that the species was 'by no means uncommon' and considered that it could be 'found on every or almost every stream'. C&J state that the Grey Wagtail is a fairly common breeding bird, and also discuss how the species moves away from water in winter. If the earlier accounts are taken at face value it could be suggested that numbers of Grey Wagtails are now greater than when Ralfe was writing, but possibly fewer than indicated by Madoc. However, as with many species, in the absence of numerical data it is difficult to draw conclusions.

1977–81

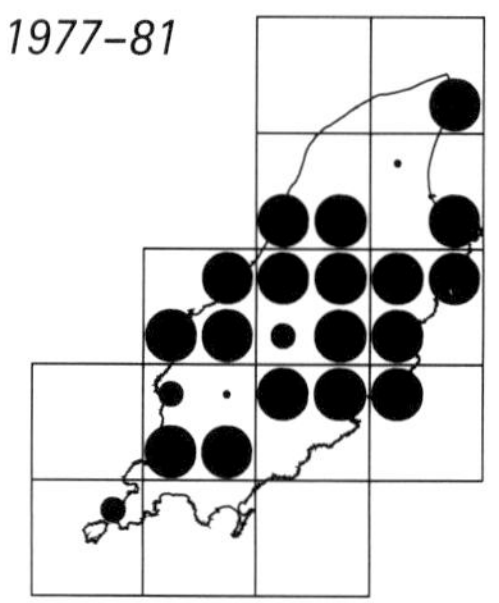

1998–2002

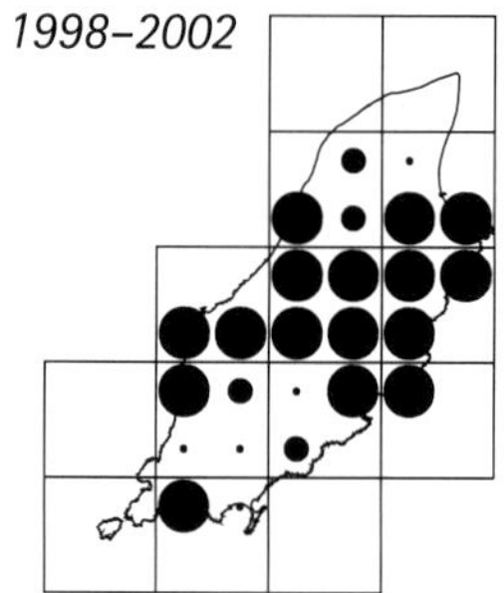

Breeding	Grid squares:	Isle of Man 174 (26%)
		Britain 1,979 Ireland 816 Total 2,795 (72%)
	Population:	Isle of Man 99–113
		Britain 34,000 Ireland 22,000 (8% of European)
Wintering	Grid squares:	Isle of Man 237 (36%)
		Britain and Ireland 2,155 (56%)
	Population:	Isle of Man <300
		Britain and Ireland 40,000

Jan	Feb	Mar	Apr	May	Jun	Jul	Aug	Sep	Oct	Nov	Dec

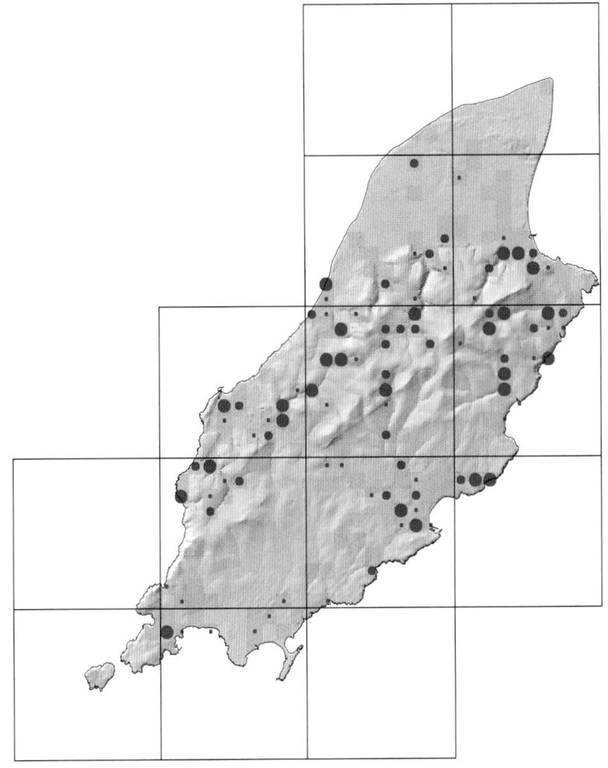

Summer presence and breeding status

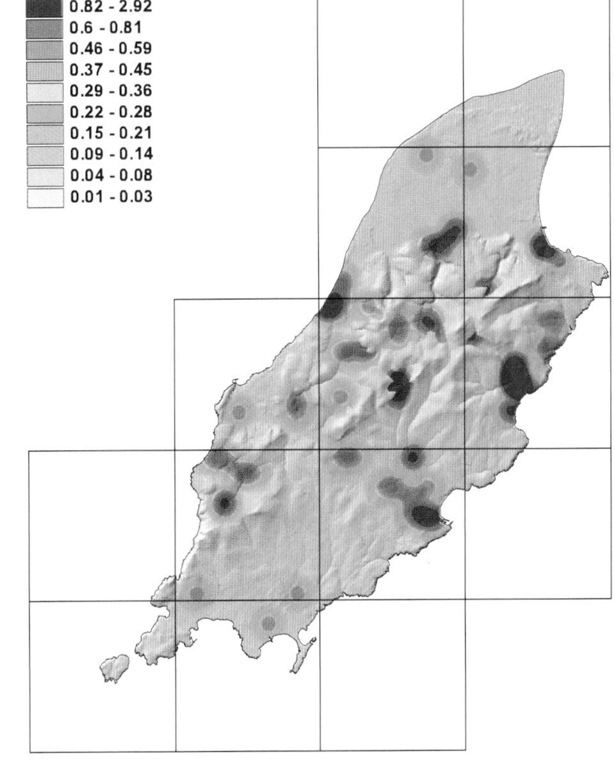

Breeding abundance

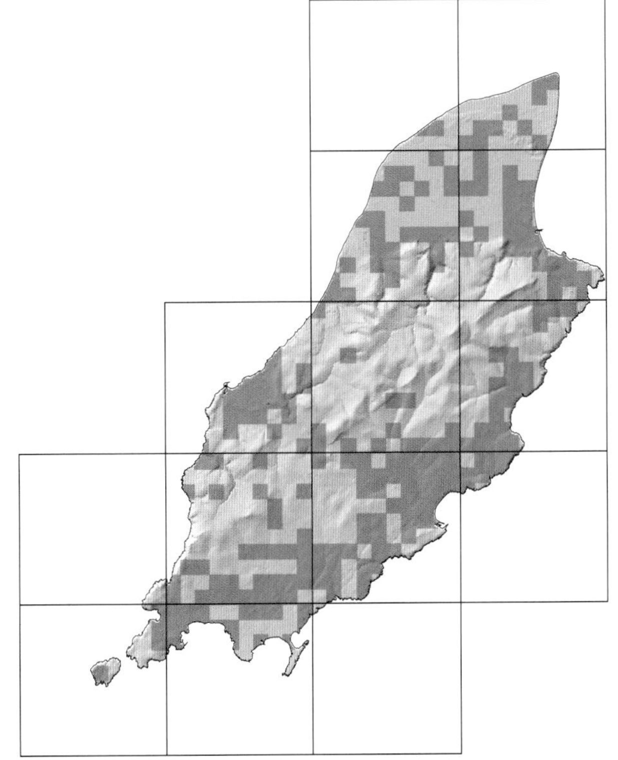

Winter presence

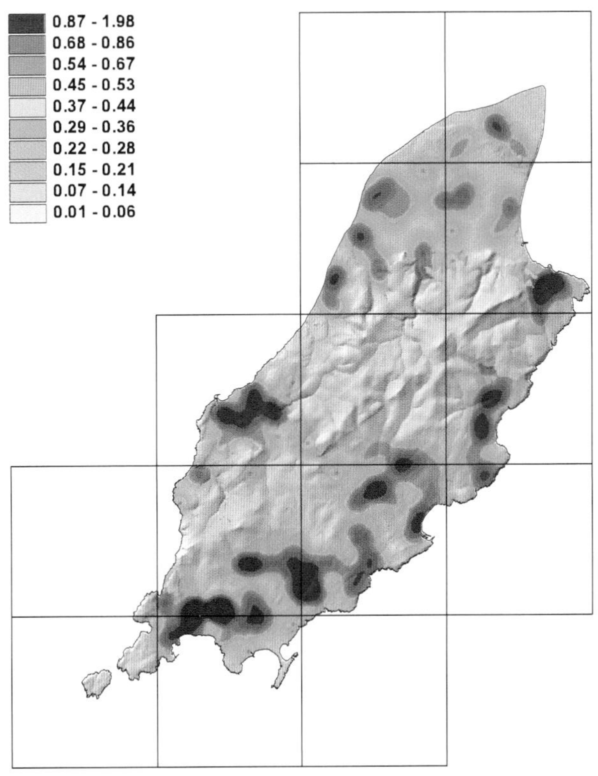

Winter abundance

Individual Sponsors – Miss H E Elliston, Master C Johnson

Pied Wagtail
Motacilla alba

Manx: *Ushag Vreck* = Pied Bird. *Ushag voltee* = Weather Bird

The Pied Wagtail is one of the most familiar and easily recognised birds on the Isle of Man. The distinctive black and white plumage, constantly wagging tail and tameness endears the 'Willy Wagtail' to all who encounter it.

The Pied Wagtail is an adaptable bird and occurs in a wide range of habitats, from remote rural areas to urban centres, though the presence of water nearby is usually a prerequisite. Pied Wagtails often breed in close proximity to humans, sometimes selecting unusual nest sites. During the MBA research one pair nested under the bonnet of a vehicle that regularly travelled over 9km, the owners ceasing to use it only when they discovered a full clutch of five eggs, all of which successfully hatched. Another successful nest was in a truck travelling daily through four different 1km squares, leading to some debate about where the nest should be plotted on our maps!

There are two subspecies of this wagtail in Europe. *Motacilla alba yarrellii*, our Pied Wagtail, breeds only in the British Isles and a few adjacent parts of the continent, while *M.a. alba* (White Wagtail) breeds over most of the rest of Europe (EBA). *M.a. alba* are also known to breed in the British Isles in small numbers, either as pure pairs or paired with *M.a. yarrellii* (1988–91 Atlas), though no evidence of such breeding locally was found during MBA research. In the British Isles Pied Wagtails are widespread and common during the breeding season, though they are relatively scarce in the Scottish Highlands and in lowland England. Declines in this latter area are attributed to reduced habitat diversity and hence more limited food supply, resulting from increased arable farming and a move away from mixed farming (1988–91 Atlas). Within the Island Pied Wagtails are widespread, breeding wherever there is suitable habitat, from the summit of Snaefell to the coasts. It is notable that some of the higher breeding densities are in built-up areas. Many of the Manx stone walls and sod hedges provide suitable nesting opportunities, as do the numerous old farm buildings and 'tholtans' or deserted crofts. It is these tholtans and their associated remnant stone-walled field systems that support scattered breeding pairs of Pied Wagtails in the uplands.

In autumn many British Pied Wagtails migrate south to France, Spain or North Africa for the winter, although others, particularly adults, are sedentary or travel only short distances (MA). Thus, while some Manx Pied Wagtails will winter on the European continent or in Africa, others probably stay on the Island or travel no further than the British mainland. It is also probable that some Pied Wagtails wintering on the Island will be birds that have migrated here from more northerly parts of the British Isles.

Conversely, White Wagtails do not winter in the British Isles (WA), but many from the northern parts of continental Europe move through in both spring and autumn. These also are heading to or from southern Europe or Africa (MA). White Wagtails occur on the Island only during spring and autumn passage, at which times significant numbers can be found. Sightings are mainly limited to coastal locations, particularly the Ayres, Langness, Baie ny Carrickey and the Calf of Man, though some birds are likely to go unrecorded at less frequently watched locations. The first few White Wagtails of spring are usually present from the second half of March, peaking by early May, with return migration being most evident during August and September.

In winter Pied Wagtails largely abandon upland areas, no records above 220m being found during MBA formal surveys. At this time they are much more evident in urban areas, and are plentiful along seafronts at Ramsey, Castletown and Douglas, numbers exceeding 200 birds on occasions. Pied Wagtails often roost communally in winter, most towns having at least one small roost, while the industrial properties near Ronaldsway Airport in the south host a sizeable roost, birds presumably taking advantage of the warm roofs.

Kermode, Ralfe and Madoc all regarded the Pied Wagtail as common, while C&J considered it to be common both as a breeding bird and a passage migrant. Thus there is no evidence of a change in abundance of Manx Pied Wagtails during the last 100 years. Within the UK, breeding numbers of Pied Wagtails are thought to have been approximately stable for some decades (1988–91 Atlas).

In contrast White Wagtails were not mentioned by Kermode, and Ralfe knew of very few records. However Madoc knew them as common passage migrants and described them similarly. It is possible that White Wagtails were far less common in the early twentieth century, but it is more likely that they were not generally identified.

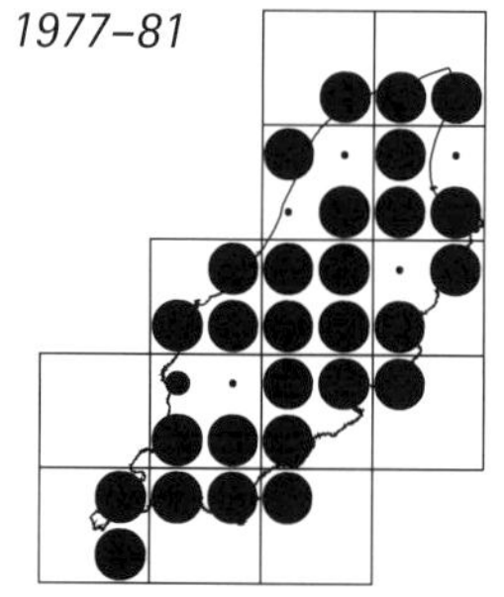

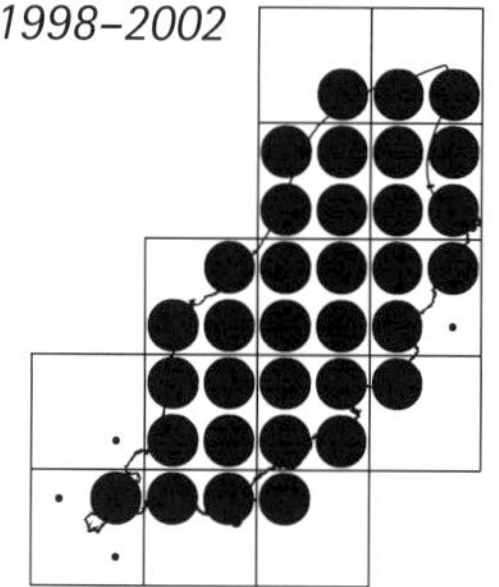

Breeding	Grid squares:	Isle of Man 493 (74%) Britain 2,669 Ireland 966 Total 3,635 (94%)
	Population:	Isle of Man 579–851 Britain 300,000 Ireland 130,000 (5% of European)
Wintering	Grid squares:	Isle of Man 332 (50%) Britain and Ireland 3,027 (78%)
	Population:	Isle of Man 2,000+ Britain and Ireland 750,000–2 million

Pied Wagtail

Jan Feb Mar Apr May Jun Jul Aug Sep Oct Nov Dec

White Wagtail

Jan Feb Mar Apr May Jun Jul Aug Sep Oct Nov Dec

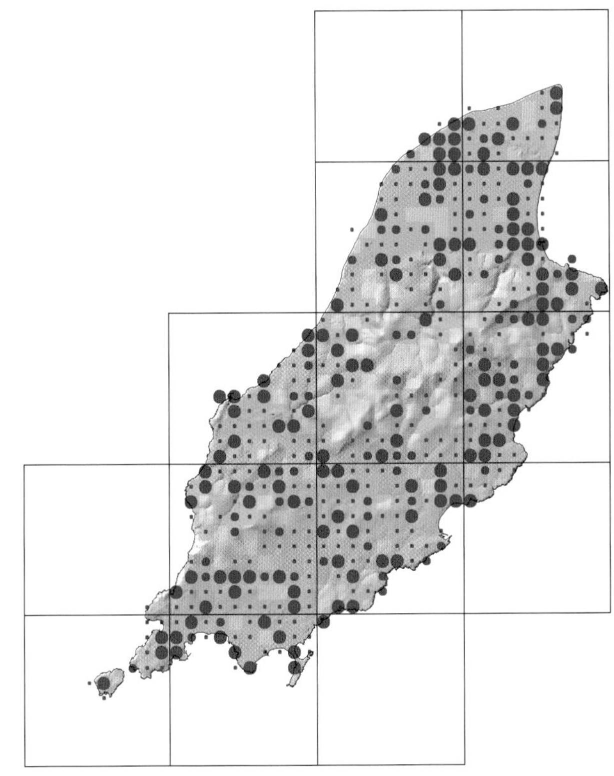

Summer presence and breeding status

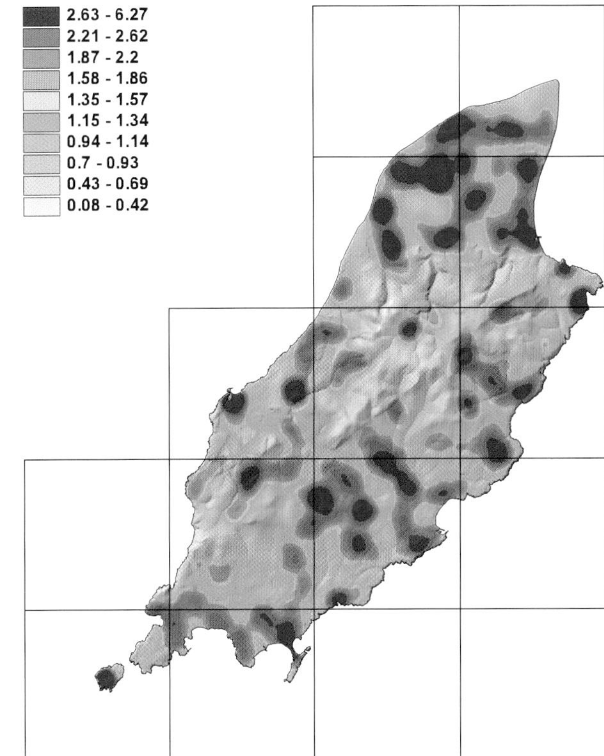

Breeding abundance

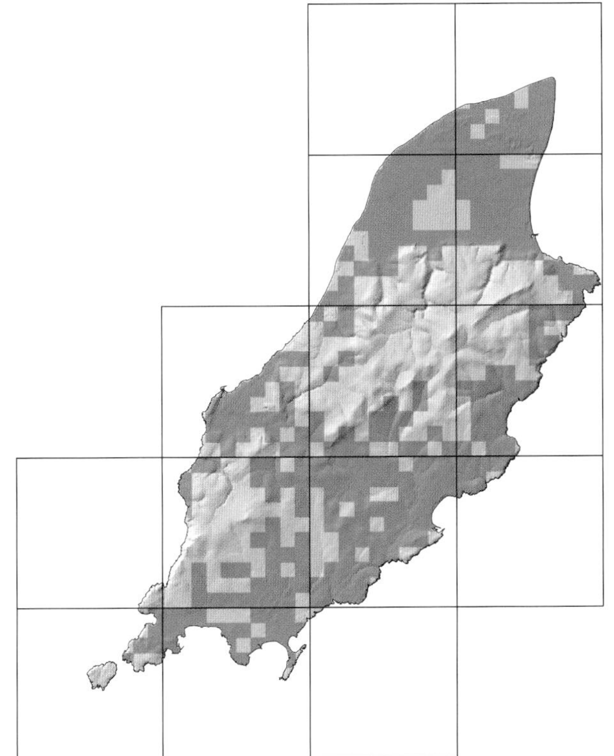

Winter presence

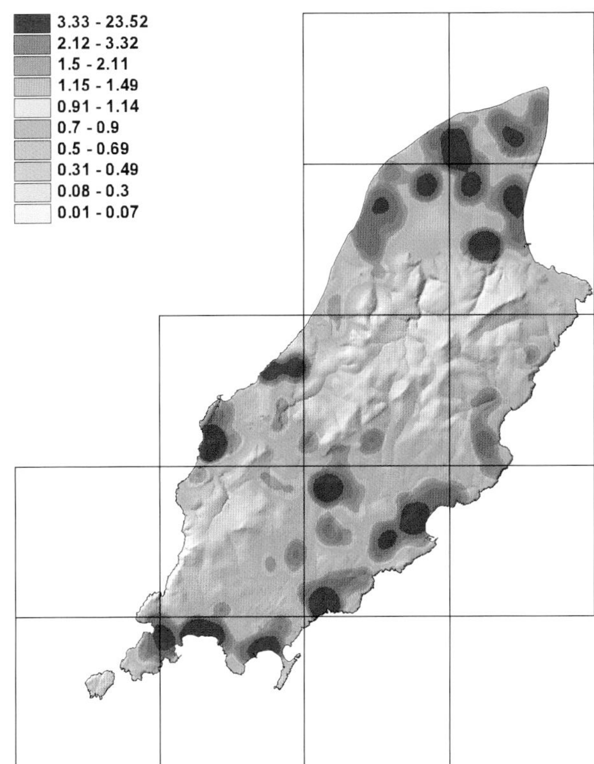

Winter abundance

Individual Sponsors – Mr. & Mrs. F Montgomerie, Dr. B Watterson

Waxwing (Bohemian Waxwing)
Bombycilla garrulus

Though many people are unfamiliar with Waxwings they are so distinctive that those who see them almost invariably report them, if only to ask what they are. It is likely therefore that few, if any, of these Starling-sized birds are overlooked. A combination of colourful plumage, crest, acrobatic feeding habits and confiding nature makes these winter visitors hard to ignore.

During the breeding season Waxwings favour mature or old stands of coniferous trees, where the main food taken is insects. In winter they occur in habitats dominated by trees and shrubs that bear fruit and berries, their food of choice at this time (EBA, BWP). Favoured sources include rowan, crab apples, apples and a variety of ornamental berries such as cotoneaster. It is unsurprising therefore that many sightings of Waxwings are from gardens and parks as well as urban areas, such as business parks and supermarket car parks, where ornamental berry-bearing shrubs are often planted to soften the otherwise harsh landscape.

Waxwings do not breed in Britain; the subspecies of Waxwing that occurs in the British Isles in winter breeds in boreal forests from north-eastern Fennoscandia to west Siberia (MA). Although the major part of the breeding range is deserted in winter, numbers reaching the British Isles each year are variable, influenced by post-breeding population size and the abundance of its favoured food, rowan berries, during autumn dispersal (MA). In years of high population and poor berry supply, large numbers can invade the British Isles, while in other years few birds arrive; perhaps as few as 100 in poor winters (WA). These periodic irruptions occasionally result in birds reaching the Isle of Man.

Over the Atlas survey period unusually large numbers of Waxwings were seen on the Island, birds being present in all winters except that of 2001-02. Flocks were mainly in single figures, although some were of up to 30 birds. Most records were between November and March, though in 2000 three birds were present in October. During the winter of 2000–01 a large-scale irruption reached the British Isles, many thousands of birds being present, while on the Island they were seen in many of the towns and villages, notably Port Erin, Douglas, Onchan and Ramsey. As is typical of the species, presence and duration in a given area were dictated by the abundance of food; consequently the flocks were very mobile, making it difficult to produce an accurate assessment of numbers present on the Island. While the largest flock seen in that winter was of 30 birds it is estimated that as many as 50 may have been on the Island at that time, probably being the largest number ever recorded. The last bird seen during that 'winter' was on the particularly late date of 1 May. In other years during the Atlas period numbers were as few as one or two individuals. The winter distribution map reveals the close association between Waxwings and human settlements. The winter population of up to 200 birds is largely meaningless for such an irruptive species and it is based on the fact that none occur in some years, while a flock of 152 birds, easily the largest ever on the Island, was seen in Onchan during November 2004, with other birds scattered elsewhere.

Kermode and Madoc do not mention the Waxwing, but Ralfe knew of a few records, and C&J describe the species as an 'irregular winter visitor in very small numbers'. The considerable numbers recorded over the Atlas period may herald an increase in the species on the Island, but are more likely to be an artefact of the unpredictable nature of the population and migration dynamics of the species. The years of the MBA survey period were generally good 'Waxwing years' in the UK also.

Wintering	Grid squares:	Isle of Man 27 (4%)
		Britain and Ireland 156 (4%)
	Population:	Isle of Man 0-200
		Britain and Ireland <100 + irruptions

Jan Feb Mar Apr May Jun Jul Aug Sep Oct Nov Dec

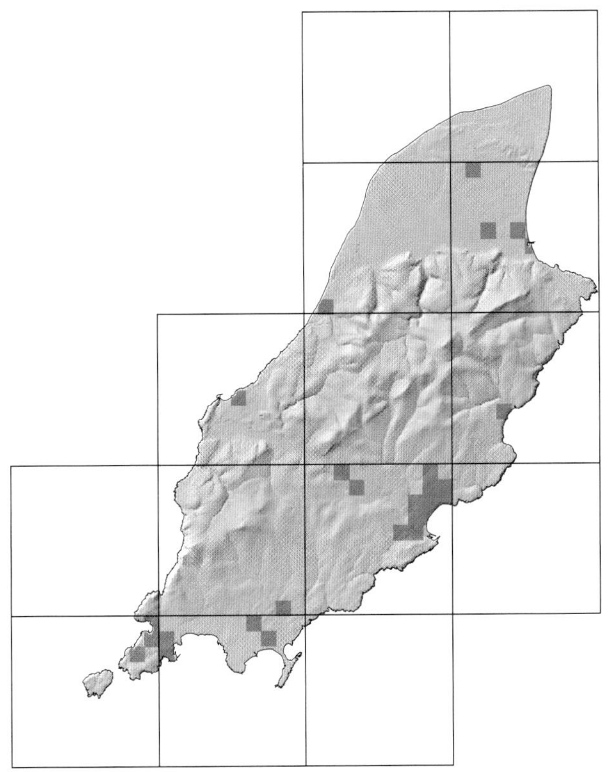

Winter presence

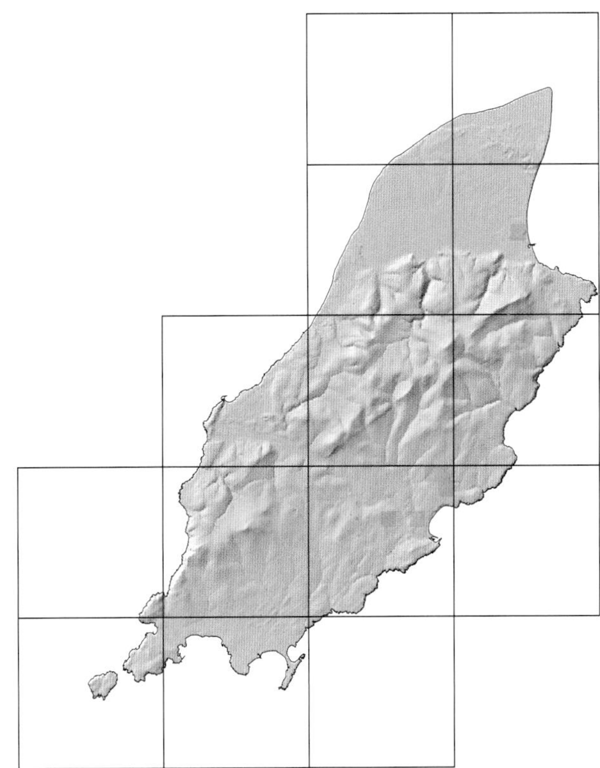

Summer presence

Wren (Winter Wren) *Troglodytes troglodytes*

Manx: *Drean*

More often heard than seen, the Wren certainly makes up for its diminutive size with a hearty song, delivered with gusto. Indeed, this is a very vocal species with a wide range of song and calls and will readily use its scolding call against perceived threats, including humans. This is an active species, always on the move searching for food or flitting through the undergrowth and seldom seen at rest.

The Wren will use a wide range of habitats both for breeding and to forage for food, though areas of dense low vegetation, particularly within woodland or along the banks of watercourses are preferred (BWP, 1988-91 Atlas). Feeding almost exclusively on insects, the Wren can be found almost anywhere on the Island where prey abundance is sufficient to support a pair and their young and it is among the most common and widespread of our resident birds.

It breeds throughout Europe, north-west Africa and through Asia as far as Japan. The Palearctic breeding range is continuous with that of continental North America. Indeed the Wren is one of the few passerine species that has successfully invaded the Palearctic from North America (EBA). Within the British Isles the Wren is widespread, though more numerous south of a line from the Mersey to the Humber, further north being mainly a bird of the lowlands (1988–91 Atlas). The breeding distribution map indicates how widespread the species is on the Island. During the seabird survey of 1999 it was not unusual to hear singing Wrens holding territory in small areas of vegetation near the base of high sea cliffs. Equally, Wrens were found high up the Island's hillsides, particularly among areas of thick undergrowth, in gullies or in rank heath. The summer abundance map shows reduced abundance in these, sub-optimal, habitats; the species not being found above the 420m level. Density is greatest in the lowlands, though suitable upland conifer plantations such as Tholt-y-Will support high numbers. The highest density was found during a two-hour visit to the 1km square that includes the Stoney Mountain plantation when 55 singing male Wrens were located.

In Britain and Ireland most Wrens are sedentary, though there is evidence to indicate that they will largely abandon higher ground to avoid the harshest of weather (WA). Movement away from breeding areas occurs mainly in September and October, the majority of long distance movements being southerly (MA). The majority of Wrens, however, are likely to stay in their breeding territories for the winter, with some local dispersal as a result of territorial competition in the autumn. There is no evidence to indicate the extent to which local birds move off the Island.

The winter distribution map reveals just how widespread the species is, being absent only from the highest ground. Broadly speaking, the pattern for winter density is similar to that of the summer, though showing a more coastal bias, particularly down the south-east coast. Fewer birds were evident along the central valley, an area prone to colder low-lying air, perhaps suggesting local movement of Wrens to avoid lower temperatures.

Kermode considered the species to be 'plentiful and generally distributed', whilst Ralfe described it as 'common and well distributed' but 'without being really numerous'. Madoc gave no information on abundance and C&J described the Wren as a 'very common resident'. As with many other species it is difficult, in the absence of detailed numerical data, to assess whether numbers have changed greatly. C&J concluded that the species had increased on the Island since the early twentieth century, but this conclusion was based on Ralfe's rather pessimistic assessment of numbers, which does not agree with that of Kermode only slightly earlier. In the UK the population probably shows little long-term change, but this is difficult to assess because of periodic crashes and major fluctuations between years (1988–91 Atlas). Wrens are known to be particularly susceptible to severe winters (1988–91 Atlas).

1977–81

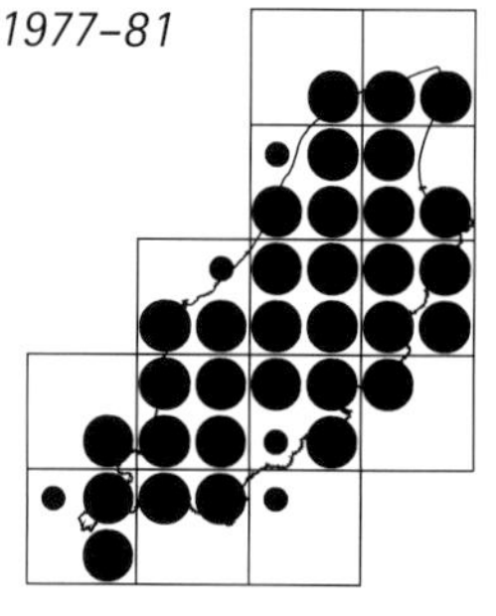

1998–2002

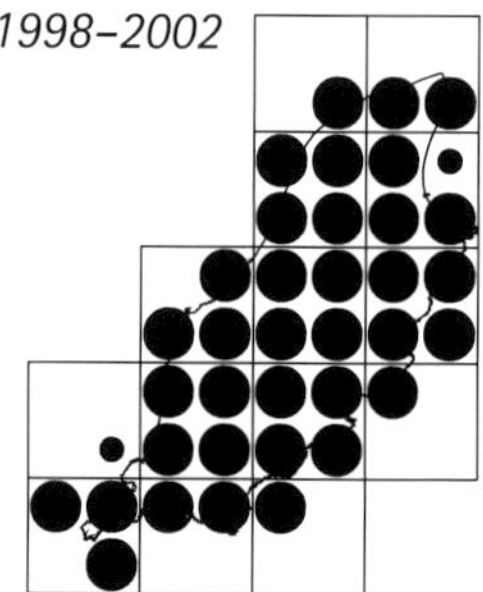

Breeding	Grid squares:	Isle of Man 616 (93%) Britain 2,747 Ireland 987 Total 3,734 (97%)
	Population:	Isle of Man 9,329–9,832 Britain 7,100,000 Ireland 2,800,000 (41% of European)
Wintering	Grid squares:	Isle of Man 599 (90%) Britain and Ireland 3,573 (93%)
	Population:	Isle of Man 25,000+ Britain and Ireland 12–20 million

Jan	Feb	Mar	Apr	May	Jun	Jul	Aug	Sep	Oct	Nov	Dec

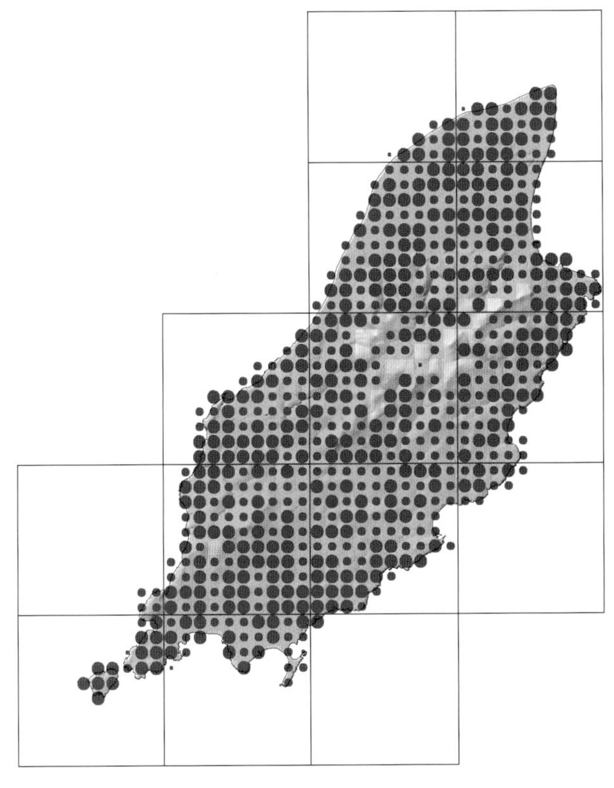

Summer presence and breeding status

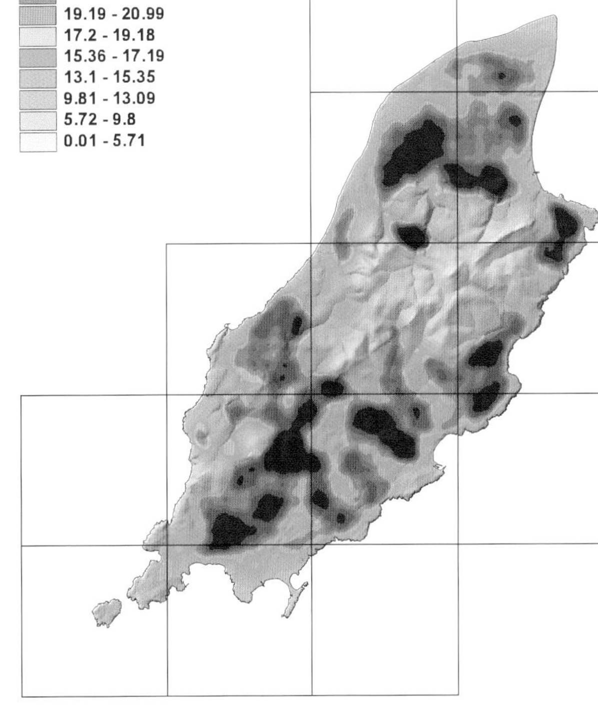

Breeding abundance

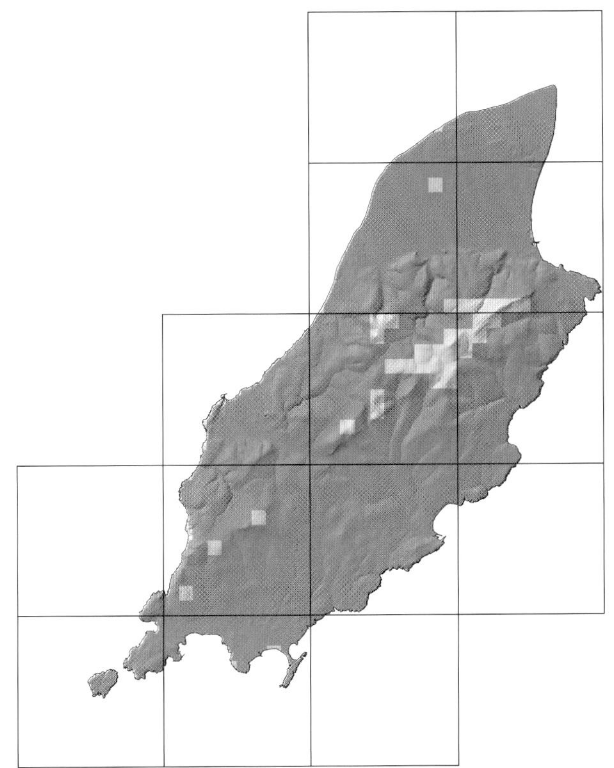

Winter presence

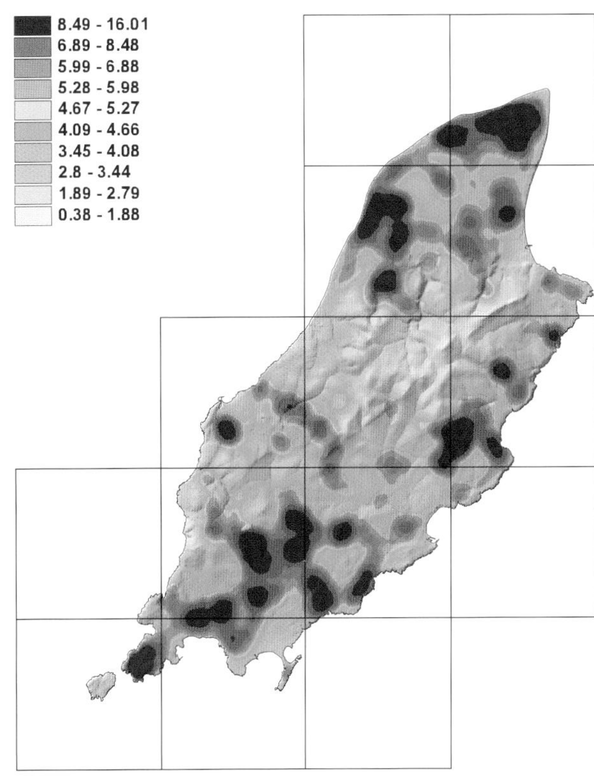

Winter abundance

Individual Sponsors – R & P Allan, Mrs. D Cowley, Mrs. M Irwin, Mr. I & Mrs. J Kelly, the late Mr. W J Killip, Mr. N Pinder, Dr. F M Rennie, E & H Stewart, the late Mrs. F Taggart, Ms. J Thompson, Mrs. J Wilson

Dunnock (Hedge Accentor)
Prunella modularis

Manx: *Drean mollagh* = Rough Wren. *Bogh Keeir* = Grey Poor One

'Skulking' is a word that captures the very essence of this overlooked bird. With its relatively drab appearance and secretive nature many people ignore it or simply do not see it, as it creeps around the garden, usually under the bushes or hedgerow, picking for food. When seen clearly, however, it is really rather a dapper little bird, with streaked brown and black upper parts, offset by a grey head. In polite society its sexual promiscuity would be spoken of only in hushed tones. While many Dunnocks are monogamous, it is common for one female to have two males, while regularly one male will have two or three females. Occasionally two or three males will share from two to four females (1988–91 Atlas).

Throughout Britain and Ireland the Dunnock will utilise a wide range of habitat types, though low thick growth is necessary as a nest site. In other parts of Europe, however, it prefers scrubby vegetation at altitudes not far below the tree-line (1988–91 Atlas). In the Isle of Man it demonstrates the same sort of habitat preference as for other parts of the British Isles. The main food source of the Dunnock is insects, though it will take a variety of small food items and can often be seen foraging for scraps under bird feed tables.

Save for small isolated populations in Turkey and Iran, the Dunnock is confined to Europe as a breeding species. It is, however, widely distributed, occurring from the high Arctic to the Mediterranean and the Caucasus, breeding in most countries other than Iceland (MA). Within the British Isles the species demonstrates a southern bias in density, being absent or scarce only in the Outer Hebrides and the highlands of Scotland (1988–91 Atlas). On the Island it is also evenly distributed, being absent only from the uplands and the Calf. The species' current breeding absence from the Calf, as with some other species, is thought to be a result of habitat loss caused by over grazing by sheep (McCanch 1999). Density is highest in the lowland agricultural areas of the main Island, especially where mature hedgerows provide the dense cover necessary for nest building. Plantations are also favoured, especially where rides or clearings support brambles and other thick cover. Mature, medium to large gardens might also support breeding birds, though density is clearly lower in urban areas.

Within the British Isles the Dunnock is highly sedentary, but the north European population is at least partly migratory, moving south-west in autumn and north-east in spring. Though mostly confined to the continent, suitable weather will result in these movements being noticeable down the east coast of Britain (MA). Data gathered on the Calf of Man during the research period demonstrated movement of Dunnocks both during spring and autumn, with many more birds during the autumn than spring. The vast majority of autumn birds were young of the year, while most birds in spring were in their first year. It is likely therefore that most of the birds moving through the Calf are young ones dispersing from their natal area and are likely to be mainly from the southern part of the Isle of Man rather than long-distance migrants.

During the winter there is nothing to suggest that Dunnocks are generally less widespread than in the summer. There does, however, appear to be some abandonment of the higher ground, as evidenced by the winter abundance map, with no birds being recorded above 310m compared to 360m in the summer. The more open field systems of the northern plain appeared to be less favoured during the winter, though this might have been a consequence of the species being less vocal at this time and therefore more easily overlooked.

Kermode considered Dunnocks to be 'common and resident' and Ralfe described them as 'abundant and familiar'. He considered the species to be commoner in winter and was aware that it occurred at lighthouses on the Island. Madoc gives no indication of abundance and C&J describe it as a 'common resident which also occurs as a passage migrant'. From these descriptions, and in the absence of numerical data, there is little from which to assess any change in abundance of Manx Dunnocks over the last century. In the British Isles there has been a slight decline in recent years but this is not the case over much of Europe (1988–91 Atlas, EBA). The decline in Britain is thought to follow intensification of agriculture and changes in land use.

1977–81

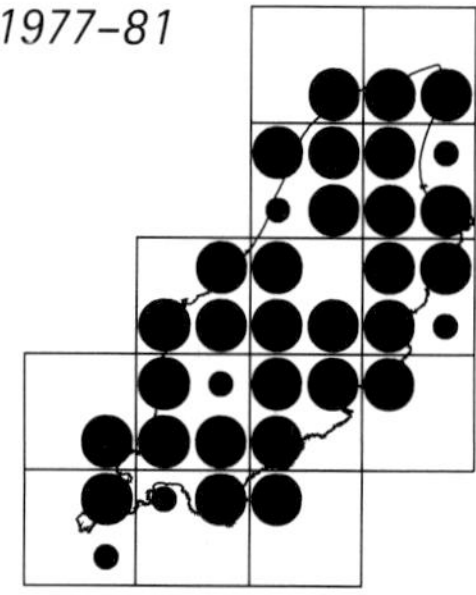

1998–2002

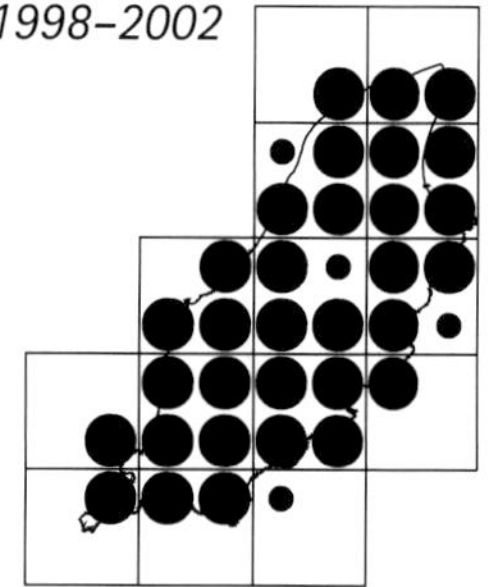

Breeding	Grid squares:	Isle of Man 543 (82%) Britain 2,511 Ireland 947 Total 3,458 (90%)
	Population:	Isle of Man 2,344–2,617 Britain 2,000,000 Ireland 810,000 (26% of European)
Wintering	Grid squares:	Isle of Man 466 (70%) Britain and Ireland 3,359 (87%)
	Population:	Isle of Man 10,000 Britain and Ireland 20 million

Jan	Feb	Mar	Apr	May	Jun	Jul	Aug	Sep	Oct	Nov	Dec

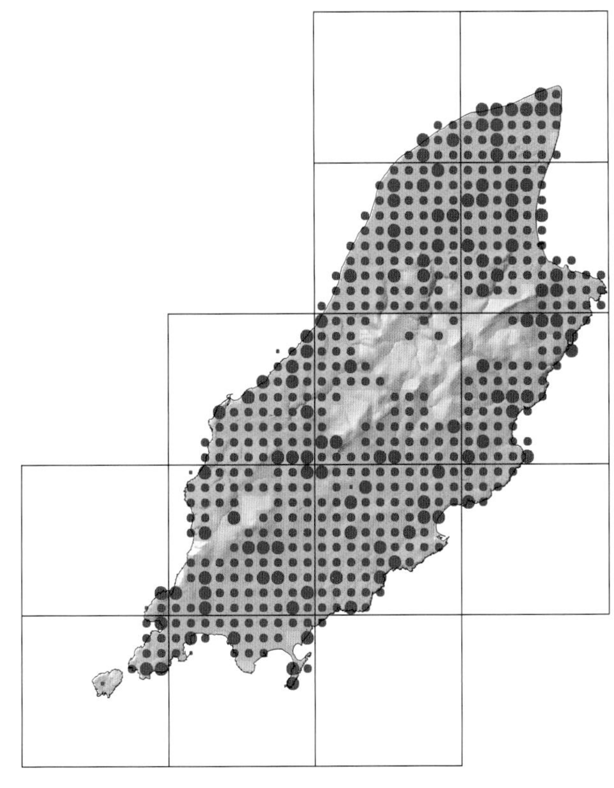

Summer presence and breeding status

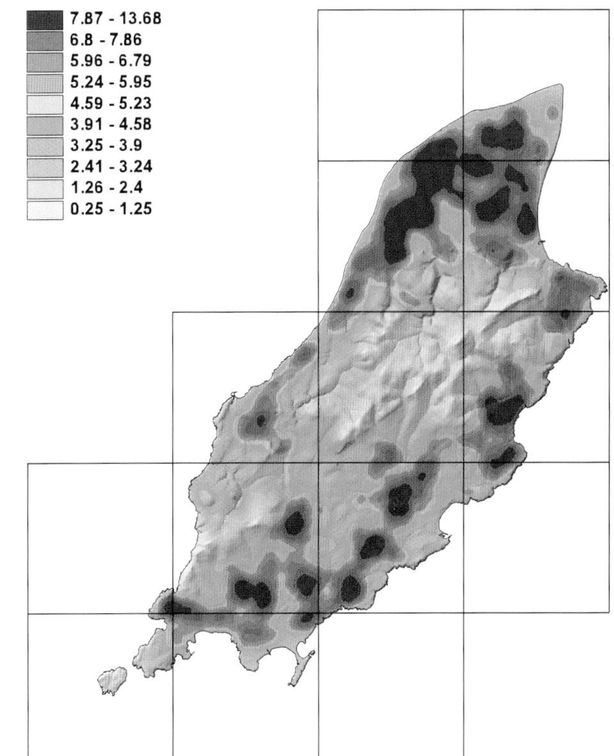

Breeding abundance

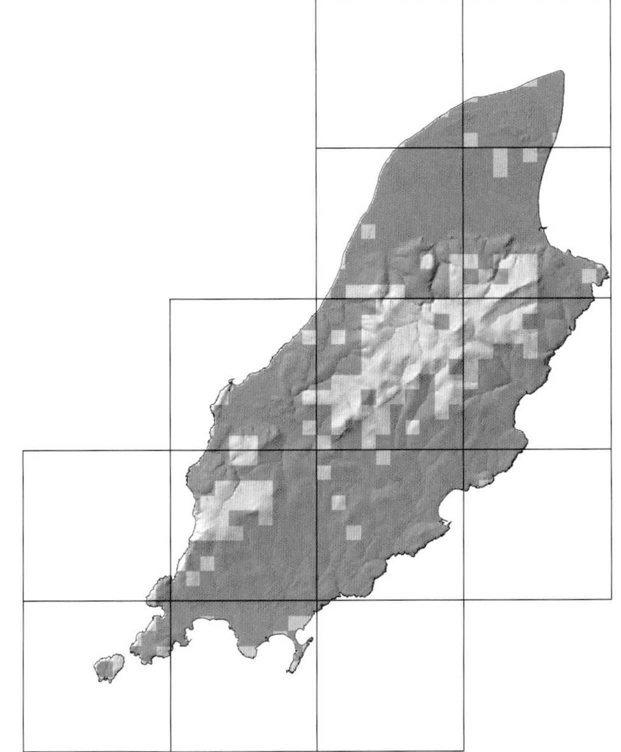

Winter presence

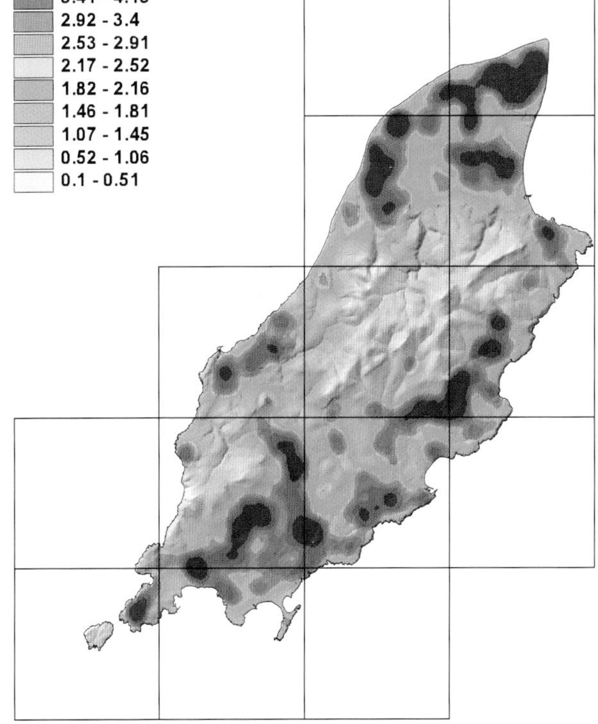

Winter abundance

Individual Sponsors – The late Miss W M Carine, Mrs. E Clucas, Mr. D J Evans

Robin (European Robin) *Erithacus rubecula*

Manx: *Cleean jiarg* = Redbreast. *Spittag*

Probably the most popular and most easily recognised bird on the Island, the Robin is always a pleasure to watch. Its tameness and smart appearance, coupled with the fact that it readily visits gardens, have combined to give a special fondness for the species, especially among those who welcome 'their' Robin. While the adult plumage is almost unmistakable to nearly all of us, fewer people might be aware that the juvenile plumage lacks the distinctive red breast, young birds having spotted brown underparts.

Robins prefer habitats that include moist areas of cool shade with cover of medium height and density and near patches or fringes of open ground. Within parts of the European range they occupy coniferous forest, but in other areas they are mainly attracted to broad-leaved or mixed woodland and, especially in Britain and parts of western Europe, to parks, gardens with trees and shrubs, road verges, cemeteries, and other humanly managed and disturbed habitats (BWP). With a diet that includes a wide range of invertebrate prey, supplemented by fruits and seeds, food availability is likely to be less influential in restricting breeding range than is habitat.

The species is common across most of Europe, where it breeds in almost all areas apart from Iceland and up around the Arctic Circle. It also breeds in western Siberia and parts of north Africa, including the Canary Islands (BWP). Within the British Isles the species occurs at higher density south of Chester and in Ireland than it does in Scotland and northern England, though pockets of low density are apparent where tree cover is limited, for example the East Anglia fens (1988–91 Atlas). The MBA breeding distribution map demonstrates widespread breeding, with the species only absent from higher ground, steep coastal slopes in the south-west and Scarlett and Langness. The abundance map reveals high densities throughout much of the lowlands, including the central valley. Marked increases in density are apparent where the northern hills give way to the flat agricultural land on the northern plain, with a similar effect noticeable where the southern hills give way to the flat low-lying Patrick and St Johns areas. Robins were absent above 390m.

Migration of Robins occurs after the breeding season, though the pattern and extent of migration is unclear. In Fennoscandia and eastern Europe they are almost totally migratory, while in southern Europe they are largely sedentary (MA). In Britain and Ireland most male and some female Robins winter on their breeding territory. Of those that move, it is suggested that many might move only short distances, occupying winter sites that are generally unsuitable for breeding, such as reed beds and urban areas (MA). Some British breeding Robins, including young, however, move further afield, having been recorded in Spain. The picture is further clouded by migration of birds, probably from Fennoscandia, moving through Britain and Ireland during August to November, with a peak in October. Most do not stay in the British Isles long before continuing to wintering grounds as far south as north Africa, though some are known to over-winter.

Locally, studies at three coastal sites during the autumns of 1999 and 2000 indicated increased numbers of Robins from mid-September to mid-October, suggesting passage at this time, while data from the Calf of Man also indicated peak movement at this time of year. It is likely that these are partly local and British birds undertaking short-distance, post-breeding, dispersal, as well as European birds moving through the Island. Return migration can occur from as early as December, continuing into May.

During the winter Robins occur throughout much of the Island, though they are absent from the uplands. The winter abundance map reveals that they were not found above 320m, some 70m lower than the breeding period, indicating abandonment of less favourable habitat. Apart from this the map demonstrates a similar pattern to that for summer abundance, unsurprisingly, as most male Robins stay on their breeding territories during the winter. Lower densities for the winter, as indicated on the map, will be at least partly due to birds being less vocal during winter and therefore more easily overlooked.

Kermode considered the Robin to be 'resident. Plentiful and widely distributed' and Ralfe described it as 'common at all seasons'. He considered the species to be resident, although he was aware that it occurred at lighthouses on the Island. Madoc makes it clear that the species was very familiar throughout the year and C&J describe it as a 'common resident, passage migrant and winter visitor'. Thus there is nothing to suggest a change in abundance of Manx Robins over the last century, although thanks to ringing work we now know that they are far more migratory than once thought.

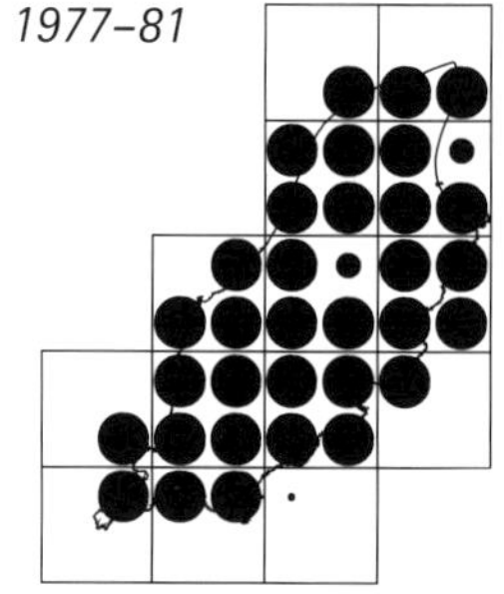

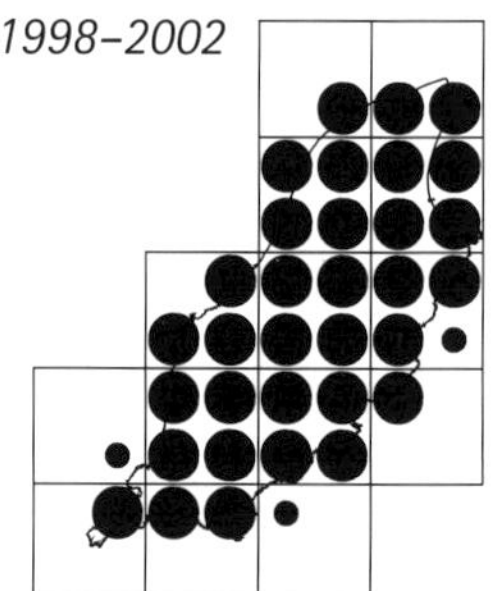

Breeding	Grid squares:	Isle of Man 542 (82%) Britain 2,629 Ireland 967 Total 3,596 (93%)
	Population:	Isle of Man 4,844–5,691 Britain 4,200,000 Ireland 1,900,000 (17% of European)
Wintering	Grid squares:	Isle of Man 553 (83%) Britain and Ireland 3,557 (92%)
	Population:	Isle of Man 20,000 Britain and Ireland 10 million+

Jan	Feb	Mar	Apr	May	Jun	Jul	Aug	Sep	Oct	Nov	Dec

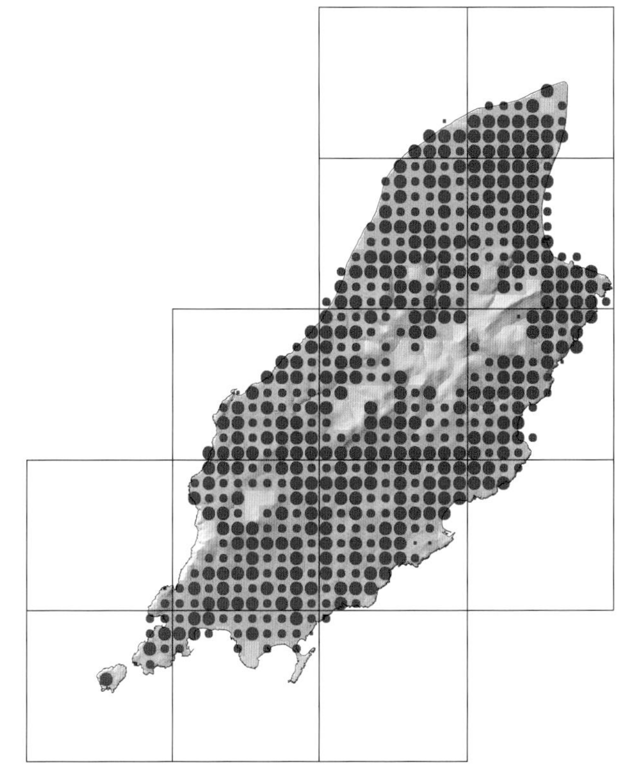

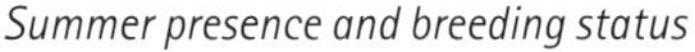
Summer presence and breeding status

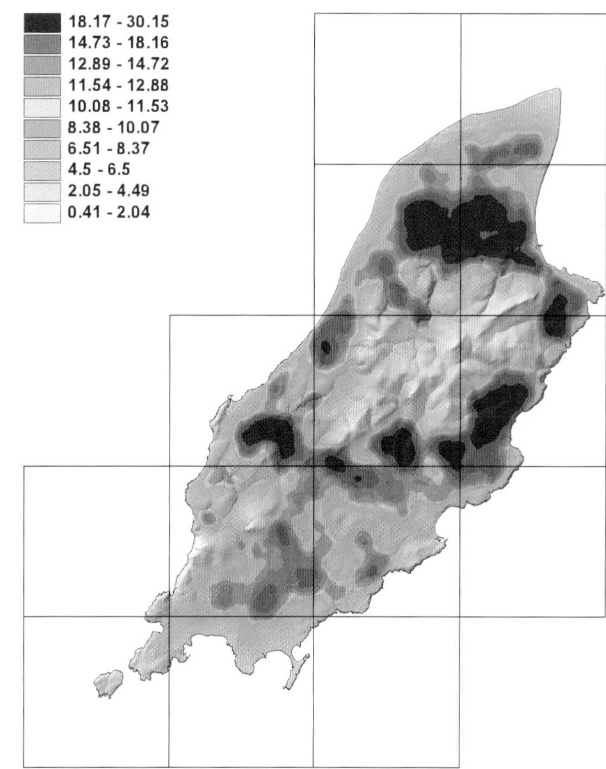

Breeding abundance

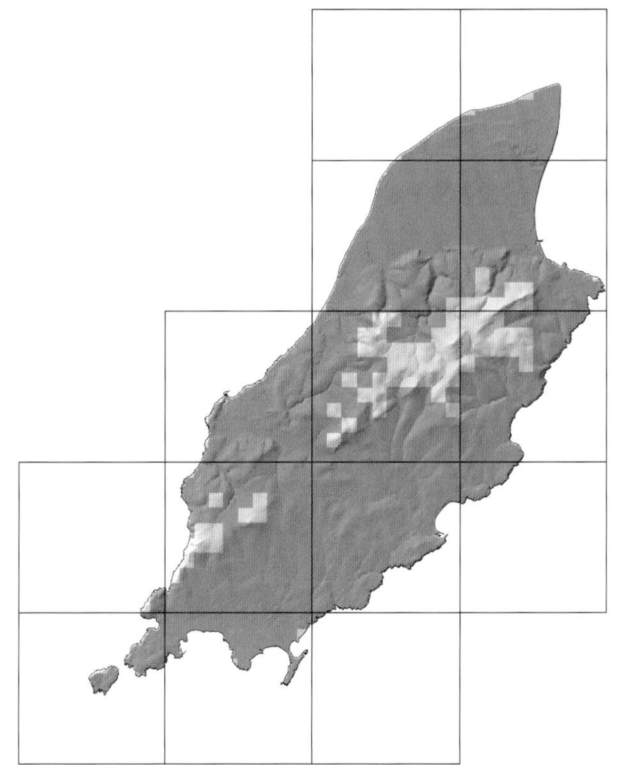

Winter presence

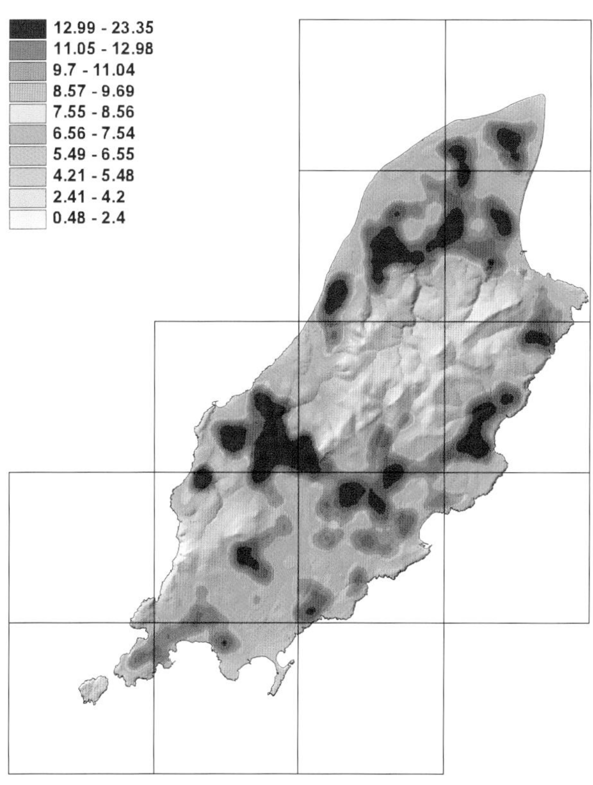

Winter abundance

Individual Sponsors – Mrs. L M Allan, Mr. S Beresford, Mrs. S Corlett, Mr. & Mrs. J C Fargher, Ms. W Ferrer, Mrs. A J Harrison, Mr. N C Kearney, the late R M Lamming, Mr. R Oake

Black Redstart
Phoenicurus ochruros

Unless observed well the Black Redstart can easily be overlooked by the casual observer. At first glance it appears drab and rather plain, but it is really quite smart in appearance. About the size of a Robin, the species share the same upright and bold stance, though Black Redstarts are more shy. Adult males have an overall dark grey to black plumage with a striking white wing patch. Females are duller grey-brown and lack the white wing patch. All ages and both sexes have orange tail feathers and rump, though these are generally more striking in adult males.

Within its European breeding range the Black Redstart prefers areas of exposed rock, pebbles or boulders, cliffs and crags as well as shaded ravines and rocky river banks (EBA). In the British Isles, breeding was first noted from 1923, initially on natural cliff sites in Sussex and Cornwall. Second World War bombsites were colonised during the 1940s, with a slow spread into other built up areas over the ensuing years (1988–91 Atlas). Williamson (1975) considered that continued colonisation after the 1940s was attributable to favourable microclimates in cities. During the winter Black Redstarts occur at some of their breeding sites, but are more frequently seen near or on the coast of Britain and Ireland, particularly on cliffs and beaches, as is the case in the Isle of Man.

The species is common across much of central Europe, but its disjunct breeding range covers most of western and central Europe and extends from Iberia to China and from the Baltic states to North Africa (BWP). The species does not breed in the Isle of Man, Ireland or Scotland and fewer than 100 pairs are known to breed in England, most of which are in the south-east, with 0–2 pairs in Lancashire and North Merseyside (Ogilvie *et al.* 2004). In winter the species has a wider distribution, though the west and south coasts of Wales, east coast of Ireland and the south coast of England account for most concentrations, records being thinly scattered elsewhere (WA). Only small numbers occur in any one location and this is certainly the case on the Island. Nearly all winter records are coastal, with sparsely vegetated areas being favoured. Peel Castle and Fenella Beach produce regular records, as does the south end of Ramsey's north Promenade. In the south, Port St Mary has had up to two birds present in recent years, with the Calf having the occasional wintering bird. Black Redstarts are not a species that can be 'guaranteed', however, some years producing more records than others, and many a search has proved fruitless. However, once a bird has settled into an area for the winter, it can usually be located, often actively searching for food, which consists mainly of insects and other invertebrates.

Autumn migration through and into Britain and Ireland peaks in late October and early November (WA). As British Black Redstarts are known to head south for the winter (MA) they are unlikely to reach the Isle of Man and those moving through or wintering here are almost certainly of continental origin. Spring passage of Black Redstart is slight, compared to the autumn, and it is suggested that it might comprise mainly birds that have drifted west from their normal migration route (MA).

Kermode and Ralfe knew of only one record of Black Redstarts on the Island (two at Ramsey Harbour on 31 January 1895). Madoc lists a handful of records, covering both spring and autumn passage and mid-winter. C&J describe the species as a 'regular passage migrant in small numbers, individuals wintering in some years'. The colonisation of parts of north-west Europe would be expected to have resulted in an increase in Black Redstarts on passage or wintering in the Island since the time of Kermode and Ralfe and this is probably the case. Calf records show considerable annual fluctuation, but, as pointed out by C&J, there is evidence of some increase in passage volume since the early 1970s. The situation is complicated by occasional invasions on the Calf, usually in autumn. Recent examples were 18 on 28 October 1975 and 35 on 31 October 1982, but by far the largest was about 250 over the period 24–28 November 1939 (Williamson 1940).

Breeding	Grid squares:	Isle of Man 6 (1%) Britain 103 Ireland 0 Total 103 (3%)
	Population:	Isle of Man 0 Britain 99 Ireland 0 (<1% of European)
Wintering	Grid squares:	Isle of Man 18 (3%) Britain and Ireland 406 (11%)
	Population:	Isle of Man <5 Britain and Ireland 500

Jan	Feb	Mar	Apr	May	Jun	Jul	Aug	Sep	Oct	Nov	Dec

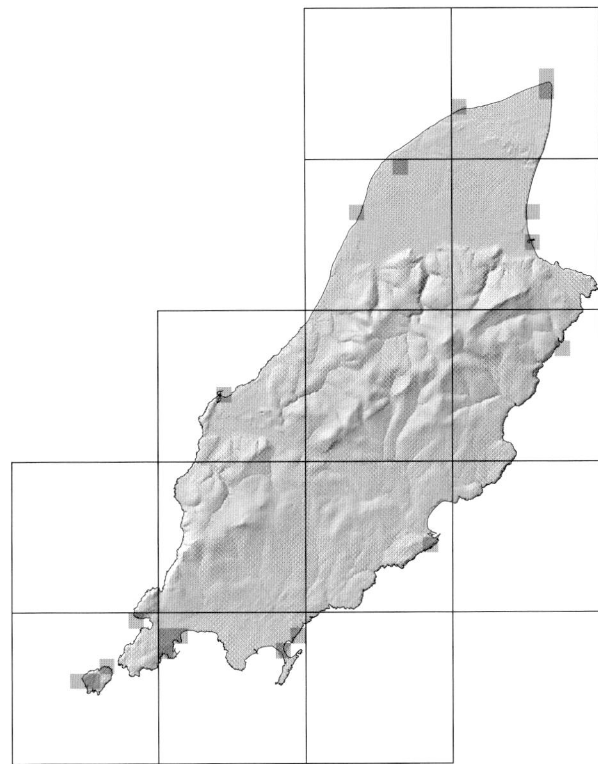

Winter presence

Whinchat
Saxicola rubetra

Not dissimilar in build and size to the more familiar Stonechat, the Whinchat is slightly slimmer, with longer wings and a less rounded head. Females are rather plain in appearance, while the males are less colourful than male Stonechats. Whinchats are quite striking and attractive birds however, with a red-ochre chest and a distinctive white supercilium, and are always a welcome addition to our Island's uplands.

Elsewhere within their range Whinchats favour wet meadows, pastures, bogs, upland grassland and heath (EBA), demonstrating a preference for the uplands in Britain and Ireland. On the Island they are confined to the uplands, with MBA research demonstrating a strong association with south-east to south-west facing valley slopes where banks of bracken are present.

The species breeds widely throughout Europe, but it is absent from Iceland, the Arctic coasts of continental Europe and some parts of the Mediterranean lowlands (MA). Within Britain and Ireland marked reductions in its range occurred in the period between the 1968–72 and 1988–91 atlas surveys. These reductions were evident mainly in Ireland, the English Midlands, the lower Thames valley, Suffolk and Kent and are probably linked to agricultural changes such as increased drainage, improved soil and the creation of monocultures (1988–91 Atlas). The breeding distribution map for the Island reveals that Whinchats are essentially birds of our central and northern uplands, occurring at coastal and lowland sites only during active migration. Although the bracken slopes of Snaefell/Agneash, Corrany and upper Sulby valleys represent the local stronghold for the species, nesting was also found further south within the relatively new plantation of Glion Gill. New conifer plantations are known to be exploited in the short term by Whinchats, though such sites are abandoned as the plantation matures. The abundance map defines the upper limit of known breeding by Whinchats at 300m, with 98% of the Island's dense bracken occurring below that height.

On the Island, autumn migration is confined almost entirely to August and September, only rarely being recorded into October. Whinchats appear to migrate in a south-easterly direction through Britain and Ireland and this may account for the relatively few records on the Calf of Man in the autumn, compared to the spring. Birds from the British Isles reach France and Iberia by late autumn (MA), but little is known of their wintering quarters, though it is generally accepted that they winter to the west of the species' general African range, which is mainly within a narrow band from Senegal to Uganda (BWP).

Spring passage is heavier than the autumn, starting after the third week of April. Numbers vary greatly between years, sometimes being as many as 50 in a day (e.g. McCanch 1999). With only around 60 pairs breeding on the Isle of Man the spring passage will include birds heading through the Island to breed in the west of Scotland, as well as local birds.

The small, but thriving, breeding population of c.60 pairs is far larger than previously suspected. Kermode considered the species to be 'an occasional, perhaps accidental, summer visitor', while Ralfe knew of only a handful of records. Neither thought the species bred on the Island. Madoc thought the species to be a regular passage migrant, although 'in no numbers', but suspected a pair had bred and that the species may breed 'in small numbers'. C&J list the small number of known records of breeding over the 20th Century and apparently considered that only over the previous ten years had breeding become regular (in the Laxey valley). However, by 1986 they were aware of the species as a regular passage migrant.

Against this background the finding of several pairs in various areas on the Island must be regarded as one of the more surprising revelations of the Manx Bird Atlas survey work. It is doubtful whether there has been a recent major increase in breeding here, as elsewhere in the British Isles the population is stable or declining and Calf records provide no clear evidence of change in passage volume over the past few decades. It is likely that, at least in part, the 'increase' relates to more comprehensive coverage during this survey than previously, though short-term increases are likely within young conifer plantations.

The almost complete lack of nineteenth century breeding records is also puzzling. The species is a common long-distance migrant, which at that time was more widespread and abundant in Britain than it is today (HA). It is difficult to see how it could not have been breeding, albeit, as now, in small numbers, in suitable habitat on the Island.

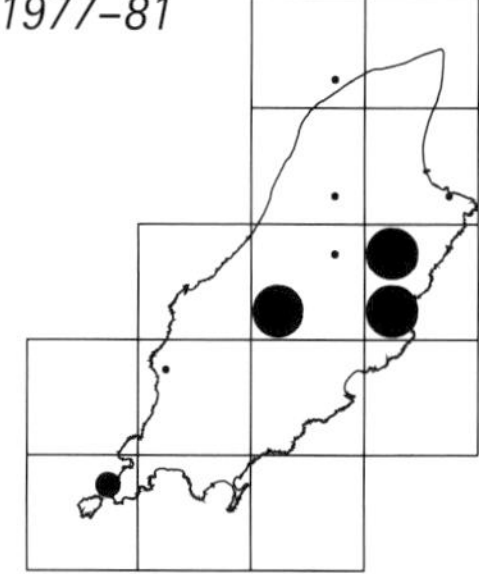

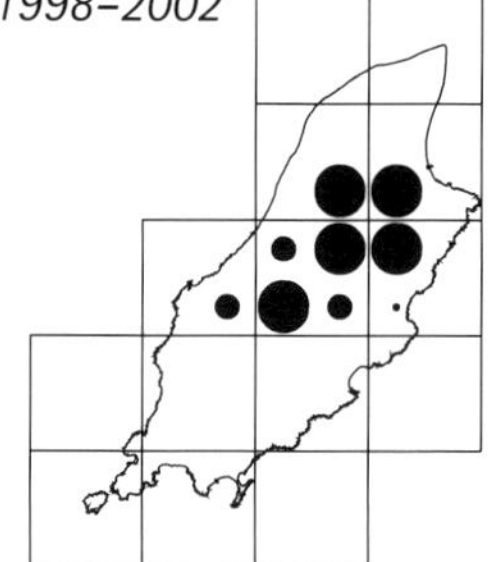

Breeding	Grid squares:	Isle of Man 52 (8%) Britain 1,404 Ireland 124 Total 1,528 (40%)
	Population:	Isle of Man 59-62 Britain 21,000 Ireland 1,900 (1% of European)

Jan Feb Mar Apr May Jun Jul Aug Sep Oct Nov Dec

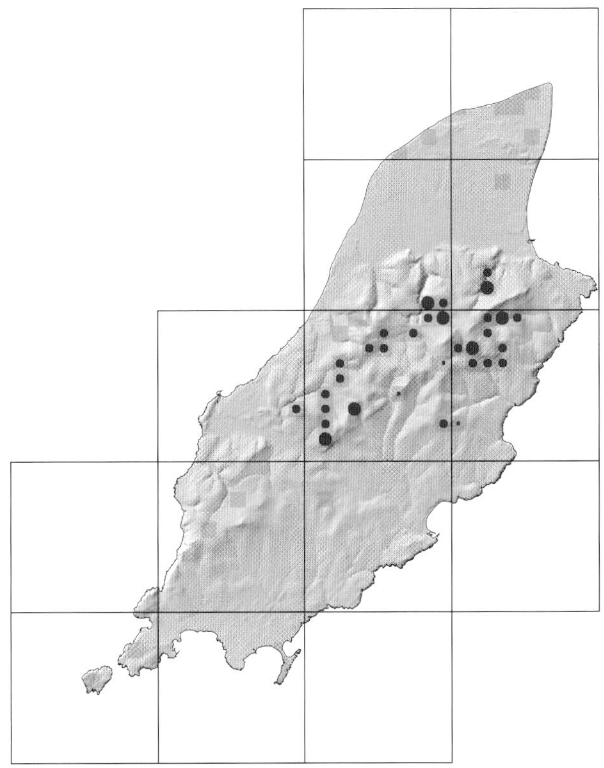

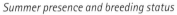

Summer presence and breeding status

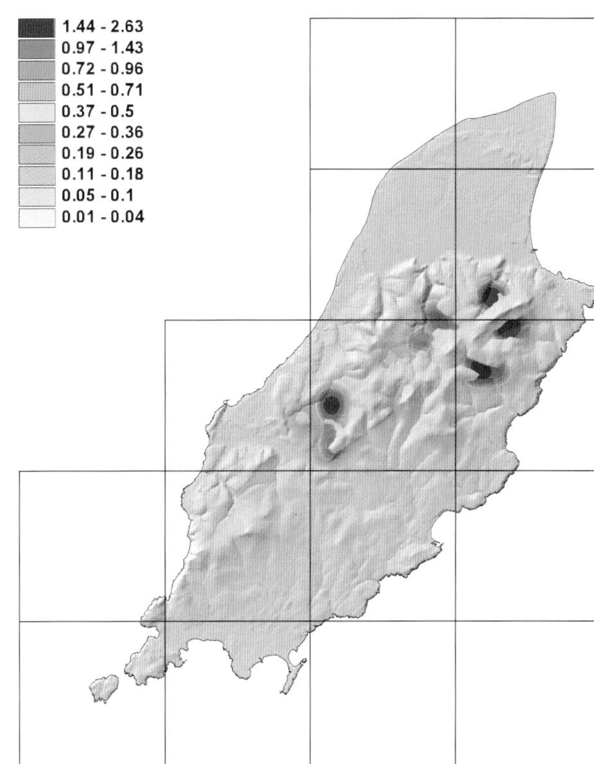

Breeding abundance

Stonechat
Saxicola torquata

Manx: *Boid y chonnee* = Point of the gorse. *Kione dhoo y eeigyn* = Black head of the stacks

This small charismatic bird is one of *the* birds of the Isle of Man. The male tends to catch the eye first, being more striking with a black head, white partial collar and orange underparts, while the female tends to merge more readily into the background. Often, however, Stonechats are most easily located by listening for the call, which is a repeated sound likened to two pebbles being banged together.

Throughout its European range the Stonechat primarily occurs from sea level up to around 500m, though in southern Europe it reaches 2,230m (EBA). Within each territory three key features are necessary: frequent perching points from which to sing and drop onto prey (predominantly insects), reasonably short vegetation in which to feed, and plentiful cover for nesting (1988–91 Atlas).

The subspecies of Stonechat that breeds in Britain and Ireland *Saxicola torquata hibernans*, also occurs in western France and Iberia. The subspecies *S.t. rubicola* occurs throughout most of Europe and north Africa, while the subspecies *S.t. maura* breeds in Finland and Siberia (EBA). Within Britain and Ireland the species has a distinctly north-west bias in both distribution and abundance, favouring the region's more temperate climate. The species is known to be prone to population crashes as a result of harsh winters, making comparison of numbers over time problematic, though a real decline appears to have occurred between the Atlases of 1968–72 and 1988–91. Locally, the species demonstrates a wider distribution than was found by C&J. This is probably a consequence of a number of mild winters in the years just prior to the MBA research period, together with increased coverage in the Atlas survey. Though breeding is widespread throughout the Island, there are notable gaps; the Stonechat is almost completely absent from the low farmland areas (probably due to lack of suitable nesting areas), creating marked 'coastal' and 'upland' centres of populations. Stonechats are absent also from the tops of our uplands; a combination of fewer insects, comparative lack of thick cover for nesting and more exposed conditions result in the species not being found above 390m.

On the coast, areas of high abundance are along the Marine Drive, south of Douglas, the slopes of the west coast from Niarbyl to the Calf of Man and the Ayres heath in the north. In the uplands Stonechats were found in valleys, presumably where vegetation was thicker, and were seldom on slopes of greater than 20°. A range of habitats is used, with upland and coastal heath appearing to be the most popular, though gorse, young conifer plantations, brambles, hedgerows and bracken slopes were also used. Stonechats start breeding early in the season, with young fledging during April. In favourable years a pair will typically have two broods, with three being not uncommon.

Young from early broods can start to move away from their natal area from June onwards, with adult passage taking place between mid-September and early November. Some of these birds may stay within Britain and Ireland, while others move further afield. Of around 2,000 Stonechats ringed on the Calf of Man, only eight have been recovered, with three of these being in France, Spain and Portugal, demonstrating that Manx Stonechats do form part of a more general movement out of the British Isles to known wintering areas in Iberia (MA). Some Stonechats from Cumbria and Scotland are likely to pass through the Island or arrive here as part of autumn movements. However, many Stonechats that breed in Britain and Ireland remain on, or near, their summer territories, often retaining a pair bond, even when not on their breeding site. This appears to be the case, at least partially, on the Island.

The winter distribution map indicates a fairly uniform coastal presence, but a marked reduction in the uplands. This seasonal abandonment of higher ground is particularly evident when the winter and summer abundance maps are compared, few areas in the uplands supporting more than the occasional bird in winter. Some of the upland records in February may be of birds returning early to re-establish breeding territories. In the south of the Island the winter abundance map reveals higher densities on the coast from Douglas round to the Calf, with none from Niarbyl south to Fleshwick. This may be due to occupied coastal slopes receiving significantly more winter sunshine, thus supporting higher densities of invertebrates, compared to the shaded steep coastal slopes from Niarbyl to Fleshwick.

Kermode considered the Stonechat to be a 'common resident', and Ralfe thought it 'very common'. Madoc described the species being present 'in big numbers … in some places it swarms', whilst C&J considered it a 'common resident, summer visitor and passage migrant'. Without detailed numerical data it is difficult to assess whether Stonechat numbers have changed greatly. It is hard to believe it was ever quite as abundant as suggested by Madoc, and if his description is disregarded there is no evidence of major change over the last hundred years.

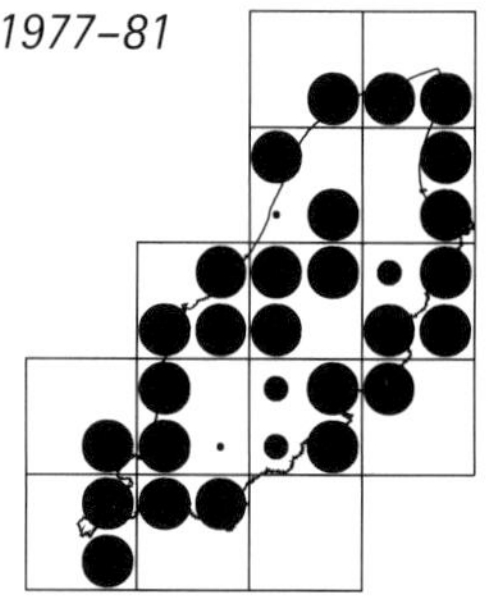

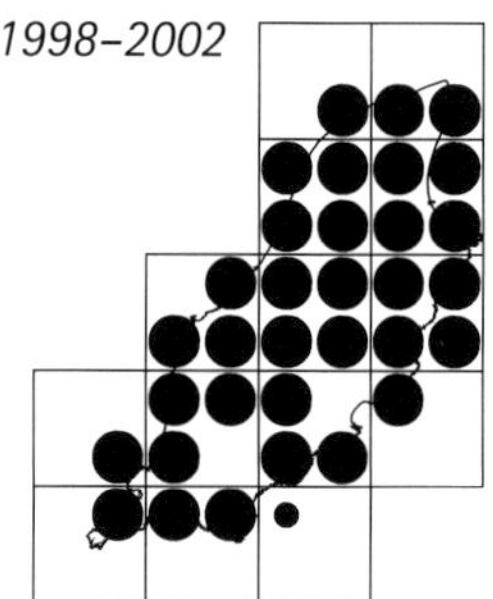

Breeding	Grid squares:	Isle of Man 285 (43%) Britain 1,034 Ireland 569 Total 1,603 (42%)
	Population:	Isle of Man 426–464 Britain 15,000 Ireland 13,000 (2% of European)
Wintering	Grid squares:	Isle of Man 198 (30%) Britain and Ireland 1,385 (36%)
	Population:	Isle of Man 1,000 Britain and Ireland 30,000–60,000

Jan	Feb	Mar	Apr	May	Jun	Jul	Aug	Sep	Oct	Nov	Dec

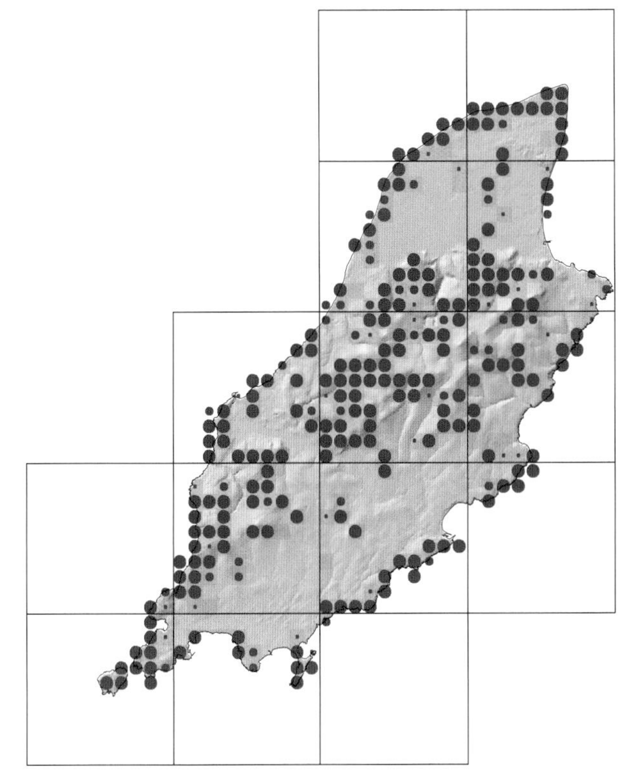

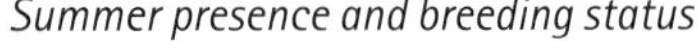
Summer presence and breeding status

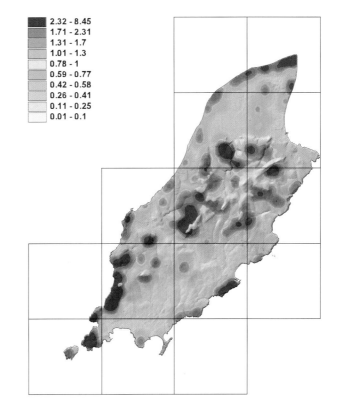

2.32 - 8.45
1.71 - 2.31
1.31 - 1.7
1.01 - 1.3
0.78 - 1
0.59 - 0.77
0.42 - 0.58
0.26 - 0.41
0.11 - 0.25
0.01 - 0.1

Breeding abundance

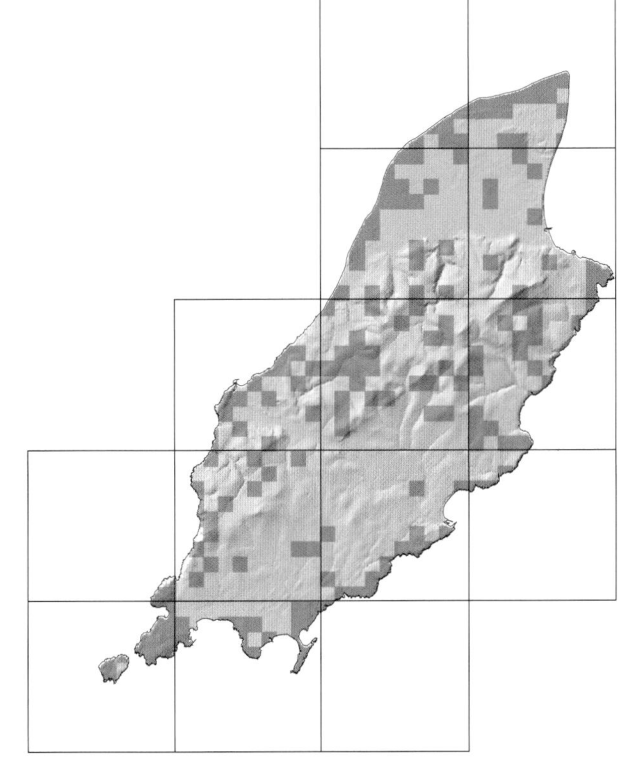

Winter presence

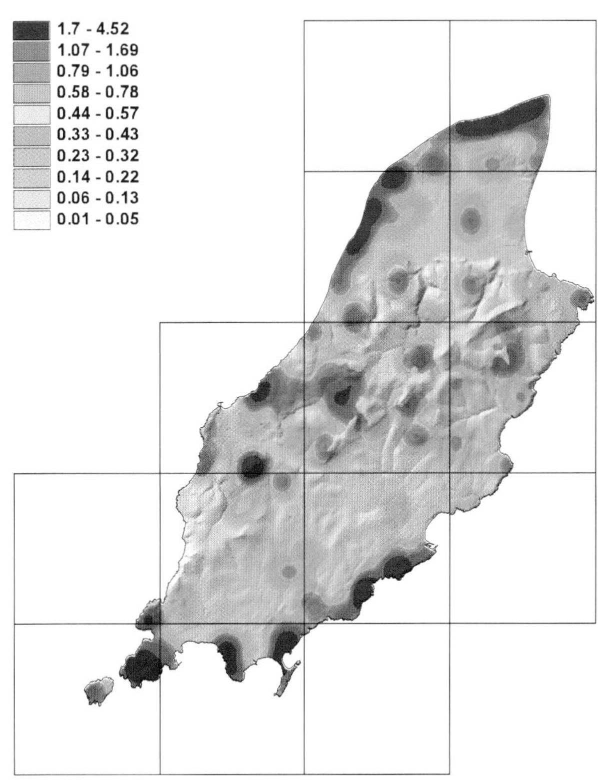

Winter abundance

Individual Sponsors – Mr. R M Barfoot, Mrs. F J Cain, Mr. P Giovannini, Ms. A Lee, Miss S Moxham, Mr. & Mrs. G Williams

Wheatear (Northern Wheatear)
Oenanthe oenanthe

Manx: *Claggan cloaie*

The Wheatear is a common passage migrant which also breeds in small numbers on the Island. It is one of the earliest migrants to appear after the winter; in some years the first bird arrives during the second half of February, becoming a true herald of spring. The striking black, grey and white plumage of the male is offset by a buff throat and breast, while in females the grey is largely replaced by brown. Both sexes share the species' most diagnostic feature, the white rump, this often being the first feature to draw attention – a sudden flash of white against the green of a spring coastal field.

In lowland nesting areas Wheatears breed mainly in holes in the ground and in particular rabbit burrows, though holes in stone walls are used when available. In upland areas holes within walls, under rocks or within boulder scree are preferred. Favoured nesting areas are within short grassland grazed by stock or rabbits. Food is mainly insects, also spiders and other invertebrates (BWP). Wheatears have two main foraging strategies. They will either run along the ground, pausing periodically to pick up food, or, if low perches are available, they will sit up or scan for movement before dropping onto prey.

Wheatears have an extensive breeding range from north-east Canada and Greenland, through the Palearctic, across the former USSR to Alaska and north-west Canada. Of the two subspecies that occur on the Isle of Man, *Oenanthe oenanthe oenanthe*, the northern European subspecies, breeds throughout most of Europe, including the British Isles, while *O.o. leucorhoa* (Greenland Wheatear) breeds in Iceland, Greenland and northern Canada. In spring, migration through the Island of *O.o. oenanthe* peaks in late March or early April, while the Greenland subspecies passes through rather later, peaking in late April to mid-May. Within the British Isles Wheatears have a mainly north and west distribution, areas of greatest abundance demonstrating a close relationship to land above 300m (1988–91 Atlas). On the Island, breeding occurs on the Ayres coastal heath in the north, though only in small numbers, and probably not annually, while the main breeding concentrations are within the northern and central hills and on the Calf of Man. These three areas share the common features of short grass/heath with abundant nesting holes.

All 'Greenland' Wheatears observed on the Island are on passage, as are many of the early *O.o. oenanthe* and, as can be seen on the distribution map, non-breeding, passage birds can be seen through much of the coastal and upland regions of the Island.

Return migration is evident from mid-July onwards, but, as with spring passage, it is a protracted affair, birds of both subspecies being common through September and into October, with occasional stragglers as late as mid-November in some years. It is thought that all the Wheatears that pass through the British Isles winter in Africa to the south of the Sahara (MA), and this will include those from the Island.

Kermode thought Wheatears 'not infrequent' on the Isle of Man. Ralfe considered the species common and plentiful as a migrant, but a scarce breeder. Madoc was clearly familiar with the species but gave no estimate of abundance, and C&J described it as a 'rather scarce but regular summer visitor and common passage migrant'. In the British Isles Wheatears are thought to have declined significantly since the 1968-72 Atlas period, partially as a result of habitat loss caused by ploughing and afforestation and partially due to myxomatosis reducing rabbit numbers, resulting in loss of burrows and the consequent growth of vegetation (1988–91 Atlas). In the absence of numerical data from the past it is difficult to assess whether breeding locally is in decline or on the increase.

1977–81

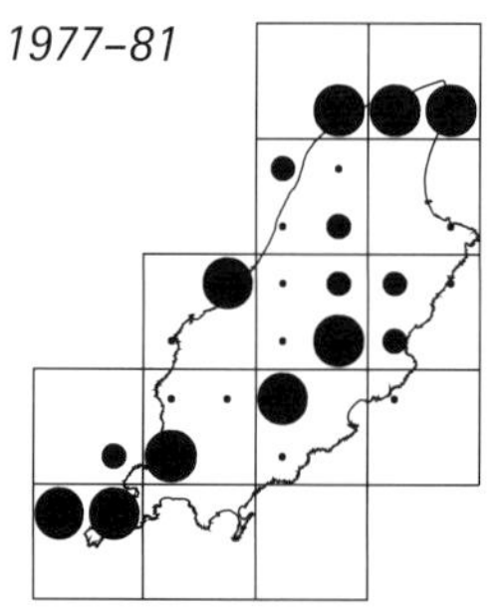

1998–2002

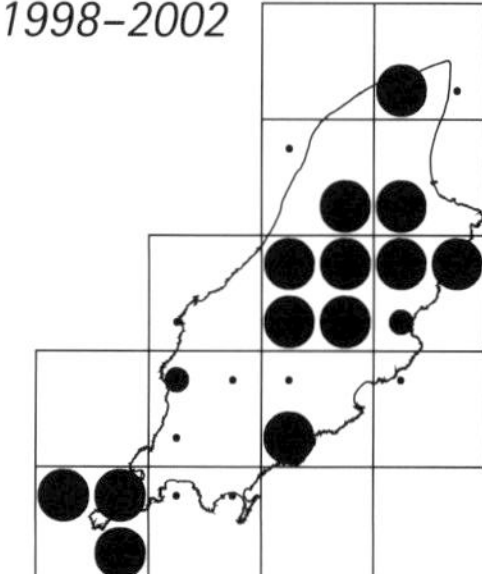

Breeding	Grid squares:	Isle of Man 269 (40%) Britain 1,738 Ireland 433 Total 2,171 (56%)
	Population:	Isle of Man 114-132 Britain 55,000 Ireland 12,000 (2% of European)

Jan	Feb	Mar	Apr	May	Jun	Jul	Aug	Sep	Oct	Nov	Dec

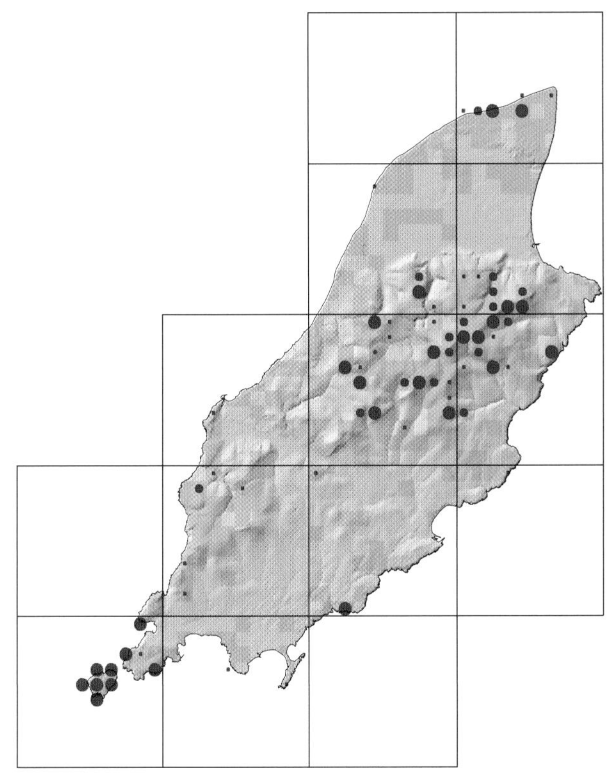

Summer presence and breeding status

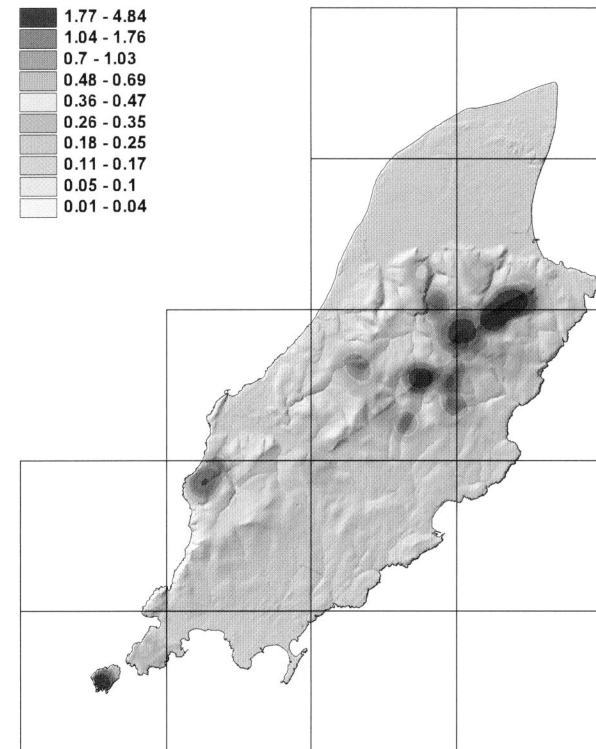

Breeding abundance

Individual Sponsors – Mr. J Fairhurst, Mrs. M Oates, Mr. C Spittal

Blackbird (Common Blackbird)
Turdus merula

Manx: *Lhondhoo*

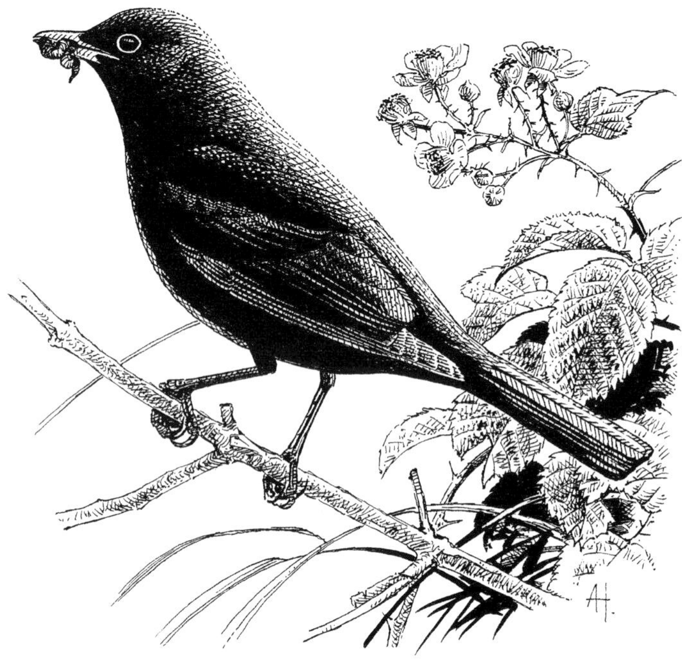

Some species have been particularly well named, though perhaps with a lack of imagination, and the Blackbird must be high on that list. The male is strikingly black, offset only by a bright yellow bill and eye-ring. The female is brown in colour with slightly paler underparts and a spotted breast. It is a common bird, frequently seen in gardens, hunting for food on the lawn or getting scraps from under the bird table.

Blackbirds are commonly associated with semi-open habitats such as farmland, gardens and woodland edges, though it is likely that they were originally birds of the forest, a habitat that is still their stronghold in parts of their European range (1988–91 Atlas). Diet is varied, though insects and earthworms form the staple, augmented by seasonally available fruit and berries, together with food put out in gardens by humans.

Other than in northernmost Fennoscandia, the Kola Peninsula and the Russian lowlands north-east of Moscow the Blackbird breeds throughout Europe, with a world range stretching from north Africa to south-east China. Introduced populations exist in Australia and New Zealand (EBA, MA). In Britain and Ireland increased use of man-made habitats from the nineteenth century onwards has led to an expansion of range and an increase in numbers, levelling off in the 1950s. Consequently, it is abundant throughout, with lower densities only apparent in highland and moorland areas (1988–91 Atlas). On the Island it is common and widespread as a breeding species, even in the centres of our main towns, and is absent only from higher ground, a combination of low-density food supplies and limited nesting opportunity making such areas unappealing. Breeding density is high on much of the northern plain, decreasing towards the Ayres heath. To a slightly lesser degree Blackbirds are also abundant in the southern lowlands, with higher density along the central valley, and north towards Laxey. Ramsey, Douglas and Onchan also support high densities, mature suburban gardens presumably affording better nesting opportunity than the older-style street systems in, for example, Peel and Castletown, where Blackbird density is markedly lower.

In autumn substantial numbers migrate through the Island, particularly noticeable on the Calf of Man, with numbers peaking from mid-October to mid-November. Some of these come from further north, with ringing returns indicating that some Calf-ringed Blackbirds travel from Denmark and Germany as well as Scandinavia, while others have travelled on as far as France and Spain for the winter. It is likely that the Manx wintering population includes a substantial proportion of these northern-breeding birds. Blackbirds from breeding territories in Scotland and northern England are more migratory than are those in southern England, though some northern birds are known to remain in their breeding territories for the winter (WA). It is likely, therefore, that some migration of Manx birds does occur, though many are likely to remain on the Island.

The winter distribution map reveals a very similar picture to that for the summer with only the uplands devoid of the species. The winter abundance map also demonstrates a remarkable similarity to that for the summer, though birds were generally found lower down the upland slopes in winter: a 320m upper limit compared to 390m in the summer. A reduction in abundance in the central valley is suggested, perhaps due to birds moving out of the colder valley where frosts are more prevalent. A slightly higher upper level of density is evident in the winter which, when differences in survey effort between the two seasons are taken into account, suggests that many more Blackbirds are present in the winter than in the summer. In suitable feeding areas they are extremely common, with many birds per field or stretch of hedgerow, all busily turning over decaying leaves in their search for food.

Ralfe describes the Blackbird as being 'extremely abundant and widely-spread' and notes that the species was 'even a hundred years ago remarkably common in Man', although Madoc does comment that the Blackbird 'gets more plentiful every year'. The species was described by C&J as a very common resident, passage migrant and winter visitor to the Island and little seems to have changed since then. Cullen and Jennings indicated that Blackbirds were present in all the 5km squares on the Island, but were unable to provide detailed population estimates.

1977–81

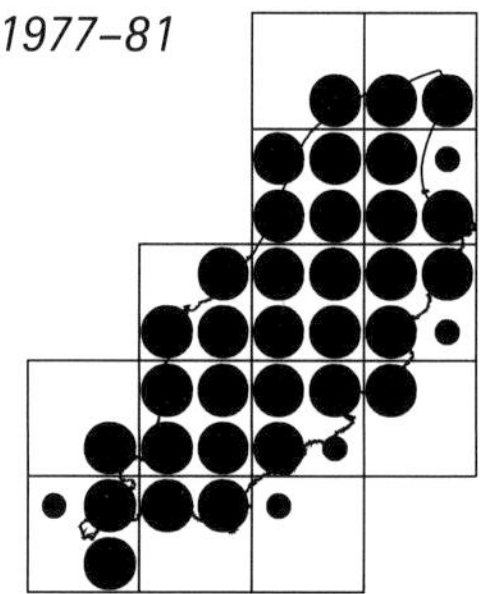

1998–2002

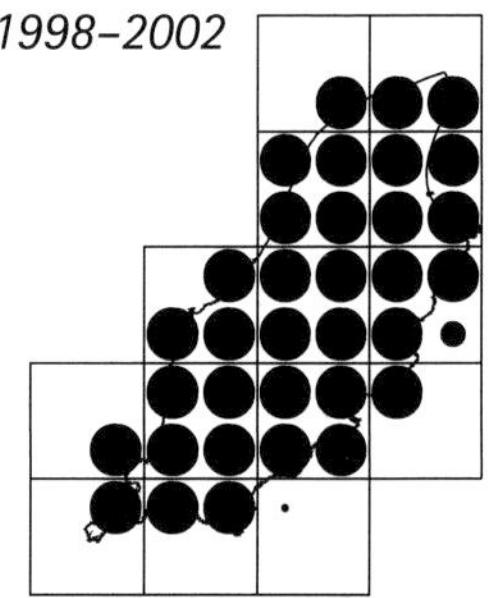

Breeding	Grid squares:	Isle of Man 536 (81%) Britain 2,664 Ireland 976 Total 3,640 (94%)
	Population:	Isle of Man 2,122–3,217 Britain 4,400,000 Ireland 1,800,000 (14% of European)
Wintering	Grid squares:	Isle of Man 508 (76%) Britain and Ireland 3,627 (94%)
	Population:	Isle of Man 10,000+ Britain and Ireland 14–20+ million

Jan	Feb	Mar	Apr	May	Jun	Jul	Aug	Sep	Oct	Nov	Dec

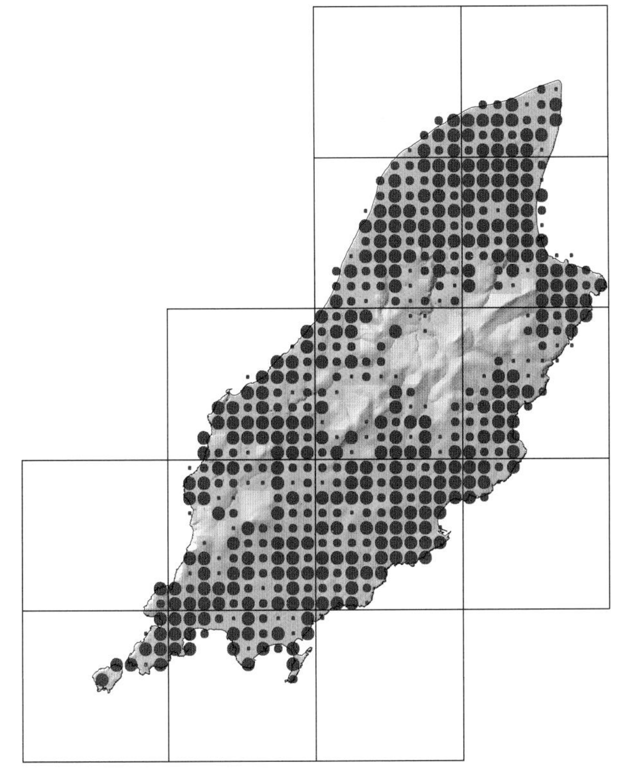

Summer presence and breeding status

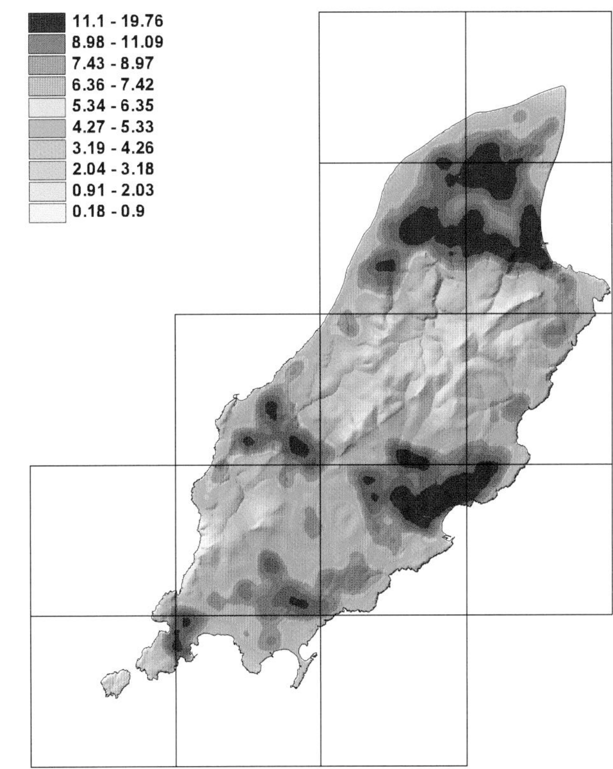

Breeding abundance

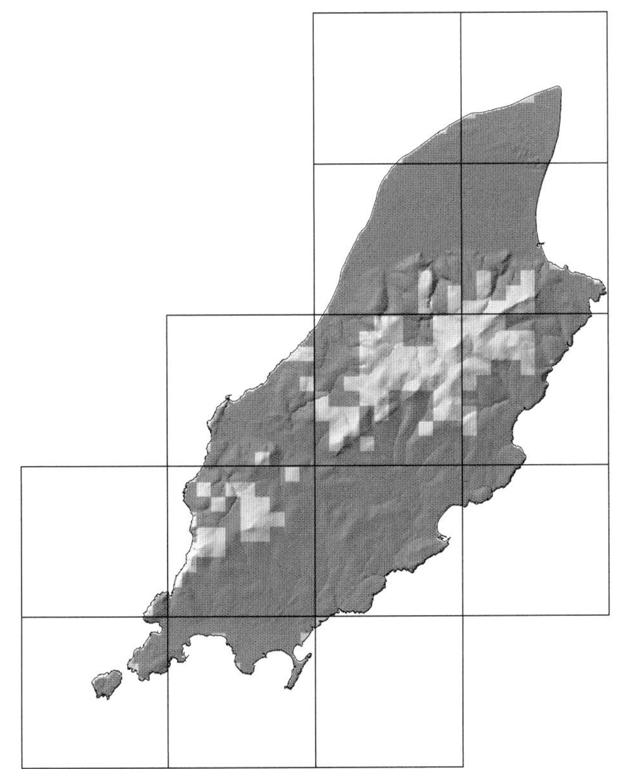

Winter presence

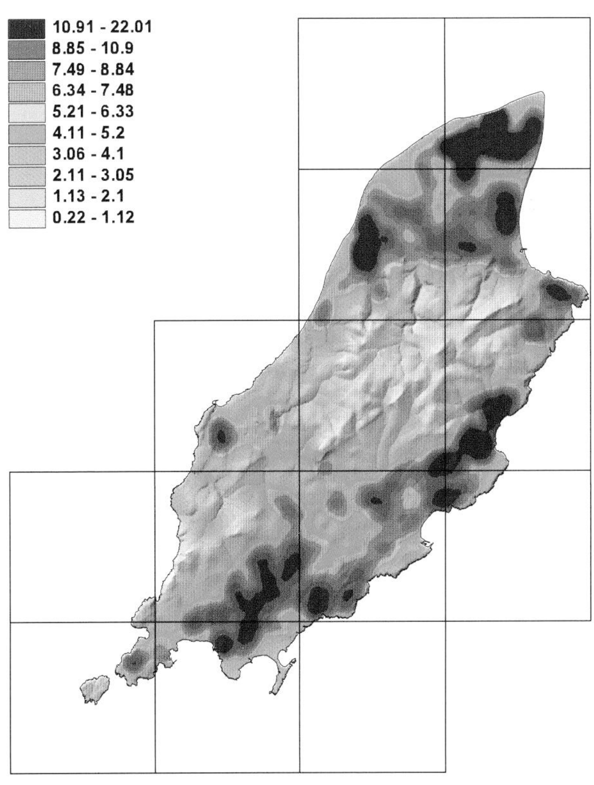

Winter abundance

Individual Sponsors – Mr. P & Mrs. A Green, Mrs. M Skelly

Fieldfare
Turdus pilaris

Manx: *Ushag sniaghtey* = Snow bird

After the Mistle Thrush, Fieldfares are the largest of the *Turdus* thrushes to be found on the Island. They are handsome birds with a chestnut brown mantle that contrasts smartly with the grey back, nape and crown and black tail. The breast is cinnamon, streaked with black, with paler flanks, which are streaked with black chevrons, while the belly is white. Attention is often drawn to these birds in flight by their chattering 'schack-schack-schack' call.

To the Isle of Man the Fieldfare is a passage migrant and winter visitor, frequenting farmland and other cultivated areas and feeding on berries (especially haws and rowan), fruit, earthworms and other soil invertebrates. It has a considerable breeding range from northern and central Europe across Siberia and on to north-west China. The European breeding population is probably about 6 million pairs (EBA). As with the Redwing there is also a very small breeding population in Britain, mainly in Scotland. The first breeding was in the 1960s, but the increase is slow (1988–91 Atlas), with only one or two pairs breeding in 2002 (Ogilvie *et al.* 2004). Fieldfares may have bred on the Island in 1989, when a male was seen giving agitated calls on 19 April and an apparent family party was seen in the same area of Glen Rushen on 27 July and nearby on 5 August (Moore and Thorpe 1990). On the Island, small wintering flocks on return passage can still be seen in most years during April, though later records are rare, with no evidence of breeding during the MBA research.

Fieldfares winter in central, western and southern Europe and adjacent areas of western Asia (BWP) and thus, as with Redwings, autumn migration is primarily to the west rather than south. In general Fieldfares wintering in the British Isles come from Scandinavia or adjacent parts of Russia (MA), and those intending to winter further south in Europe mostly do not move through Britain (BWP). Thus migrants passing through the Isle of Man are probably going no further than the UK or Ireland. In the British Isles as a whole the winter population is probably typically of the order of a million birds (WA), but fluctuates greatly, depending on factors including weather and food supply on the continent. Although a few records were obtained in September during the MBA research, it is not until October that the species becomes numerous locally, when flocks comprising several hundred birds can be seen, frequently accompanied by Redwings. As the Fieldfare is a common passage migrant as well as a winter visitor, many of these initial birds will not remain on the Island long, pausing only to take advantage of food supplies before continuing their migration. Numerous Fieldfares migrate through the Calf, where over 200 have been ringed, but, none have ever been recovered. During the winter months, however, they are sometimes widespread over much of the Island, as can be seen from the winter distribution map, although they mainly avoid uplands and coastal fringes, where both food and shelter are in short supply. As with Redwings the most favoured habitats are principally farmland and other open habitats, particularly with trees nearby to which the birds can retreat if disturbed, and in these habitats the two species often form mixed flocks in winter. In some years Fieldfares are decidedly scarce in comparison with the numbers seen on passage. The winter abundance map demonstrates a strong correlation between high densities and those lowland farming areas that have an abundance of hedgerows.

C&J described the Fieldfare as a 'common passage migrant and winter visitor' and MBA data support this view. Our research suggests that something in the order of 5,000 birds might be present in winter, though an accurate assessment is difficult, as numbers vary greatly between and within years, depending upon weather and food supplies. Kermode did not comment on the abundance or otherwise of the Fieldfare, but Ralfe describes it as being 'a fairly plentiful species with us in winter', thus its status was probably much the same as at present. C&J suggest that Fieldfares often occupy higher ground than Redwings and tend to penetrate higher into the hills on the Island, though the current survey data indicate that any difference in distribution between the two species is small.

Breeding	Grid squares:	Isle of Man 66 (10%) Britain 104 Ireland 0 Total 104 (3%)
	Population:	Isle of Man 0 Britain 2 Ireland 0 (<1% of European)
Wintering	Grid squares:	Isle of Man 243 (37%) Britain and Ireland 3,351 (87%)
	Population:	Isle of Man 500–1,500 Britain and Ireland 1 million

Jan Feb Mar Apr May Jun Jul Aug Sep Oct Nov Dec

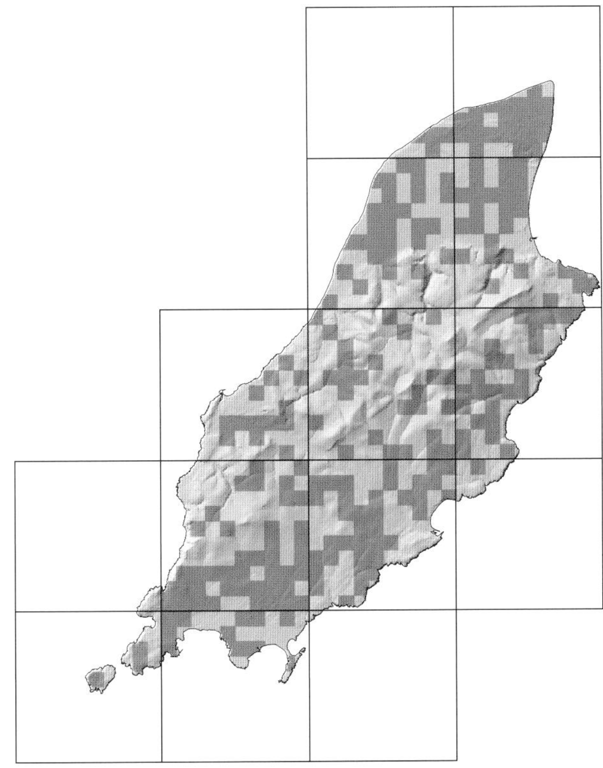

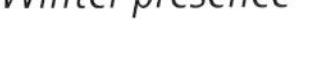

Winter presence

16.94 - 73.33
10.22 - 16.93
6.43 - 10.21
4.05 - 6.42
2.47 - 4.04
1.47 - 2.46
0.81 - 1.46
0.4 - 0.8
0.16 - 0.39
0.01 - 0.15

Winter abundance

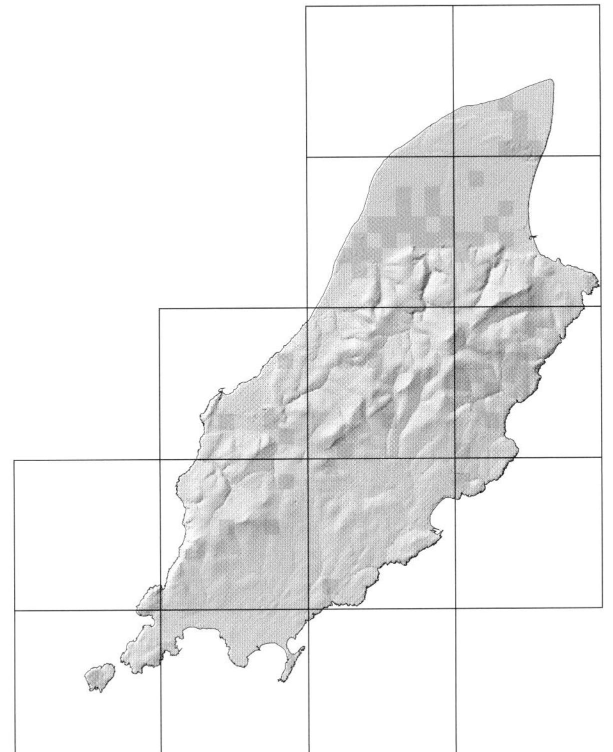

Summer presence

Song Thrush
Turdus philomelos

Manx: *Lhon. Thresh len*

At first glance the Song Thrush appears rather drab and uninteresting, but its brown upperparts have a pleasing warm tone, contrasting with the paler underparts and dense black spotting of the chest. They take readily to gardens, especially those with lawns and like the larger Blackbird, are constantly active, hopping around probing for worms or turning over leaf litter searching for food.

Song Thrushes are capable of living in a wide range of habitats which possess a combination of open ground, bushes and trees coupled with areas of dense undergrowth, favoured for nesting. The species is therefore common and widespread over most of the Isle of Man, both as a breeding bird and in winter. Song Thrushes eat mainly invertebrates, but as well as insects and worms they specialise in gastropod molluscs (slugs and snails). Snails are broken open by repeatedly hammering them against a particular stone until the shell breaks open and the body can be eaten.

The species has a large breeding range including most of Europe and extending into central Siberia (BWP). Most of this vast area is vacated in winter, the species concentrating in the British Isles, France, southern Europe and North Africa. Within the British Isles Song Thrushes are widely distributed, being recorded in most 10km squares in the summer, although they are largely absent from Shetland and parts of north-west Scotland. Concentrations within mainland Britain are evident in the south-east, but they are more evenly spread throughout Ireland (1988–91 Atlas). On the Isle of Man they breed widely throughout much of the lowlands, becoming scarce above 150m, where there is a relative shortage of nesting habitat, similarly causing absences along stretches of the coast. Where habitat is suitable they occur in reasonable densities, higher abundance being evident across the northern plain, in the central valley and through much of the eastern lowlands.

Within the British Isles the breeding population is thought to make short-distance movements, with a minority crossing the English Channel to France and the Iberian Peninsula. However, large numbers of continental Song Thrushes arrive in autumn, as passage migrants or winter visitors (WA, MA). Of the substantial numbers ringed on the Calf, particularly in autumn, a high proportion of recoveries are from the Isle of Man, suggesting that many of them may be resident here, while most others are from other parts of the British Isles. Flocks of migrating Song Thrushes, often with Redwings, are frequently to be heard flying low over the Island heading south, particularly on misty nights in October and November; the presence of Redwings suggesting that the birds probably originate in Scandinavia.

Within the British Isles the winter distribution demonstrates absences or only low numbers throughout much of Scotland as well as in the uplands of England and Wales. This enables Song Thrushes to avoid the effects of harsh winter weather, to which they are particularly susceptible. For example, the Shetland population was wiped out by the very severe winter of 1947, and in Britain as a whole, populations crashed after the harsh winter of 1962–63 (1988–91 Atlas). However, the species can also be resilient; after 1963, population levels were back to normal in 3–4 years (1988-91 Atlas).

On the Island the species demonstrates a similar distribution in winter to that of summer, underlining its essentially sedentary nature; there is however a greater level of occupancy along coastal areas. Here they are similarly absent from the uplands, survey work indicating that they occur at lower altitudes in the winter (290m maximum), than they do in the summer (350m maximum).

The Song Thrush was described by Cullen and Jennings as a 'common resident, summer and winter visitor and passage migrant' and this is probably still the case. They indicated that Song Thrushes were present in almost all the 5km squares on the Island, but could not give numerical estimates. Our surveys indicate about 1,300 breeding pairs, with perhaps in excess of 5,000 birds in winter, though birds on passage and cold weather movement of winter visitors make an accurate assessment difficult. Ralfe described the Song Thrush as being 'not an abundant bird' and suggested that it had declined since the late eighteenth century, while Kermode considered the species to be 'diminishing in numbers' and 'rarely seen' in the 'northern and westerly parishes'. Elsewhere in the British Isles Gibbons *et al.* (1993) considered the population to have been largely stable over the twentieth century, but since then there is evidence of a substantial decline in numbers, attributed to changes in land use and farming practice. However, a similar decline does not seem to have occurred on the Isle of Man and, given the rather pessimistic assessments of the early twentieth century, the population may well have increased since that time. As with most other species, there are no numerical data from which to assess change.

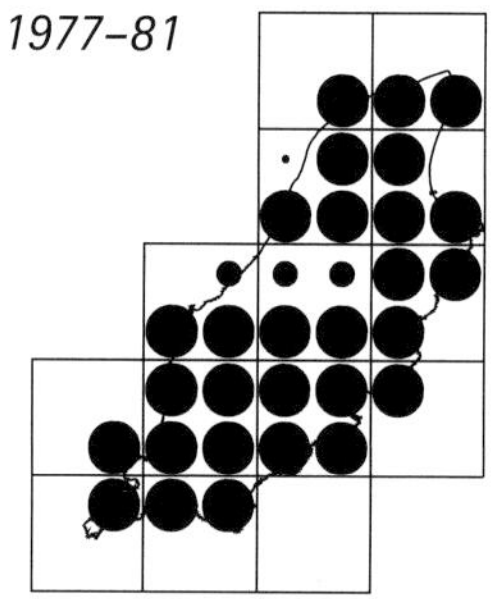

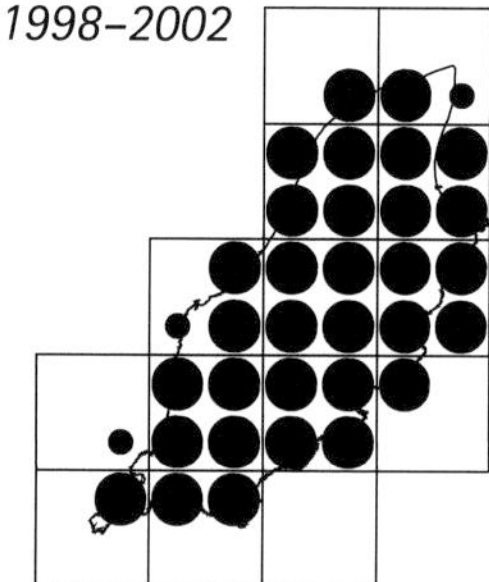

Breeding	Grid squares:	Isle of Man 462 (69%) Britain 2,620 Ireland 947 Total 3,567 (92%)
	Population:	Isle of Man 952–1,334 Britain 990,000 Ireland 390,000 (9% of European)
Wintering	Grid squares:	Isle of Man 470 (71%) Britain and Ireland 3,327 (86%)
	Population:	Isle of Man 5,000+ Britain and Ireland 6–10 million

Jan	Feb	Mar	Apr	May	Jun	Jul	Aug	Sep	Oct	Nov	Dec

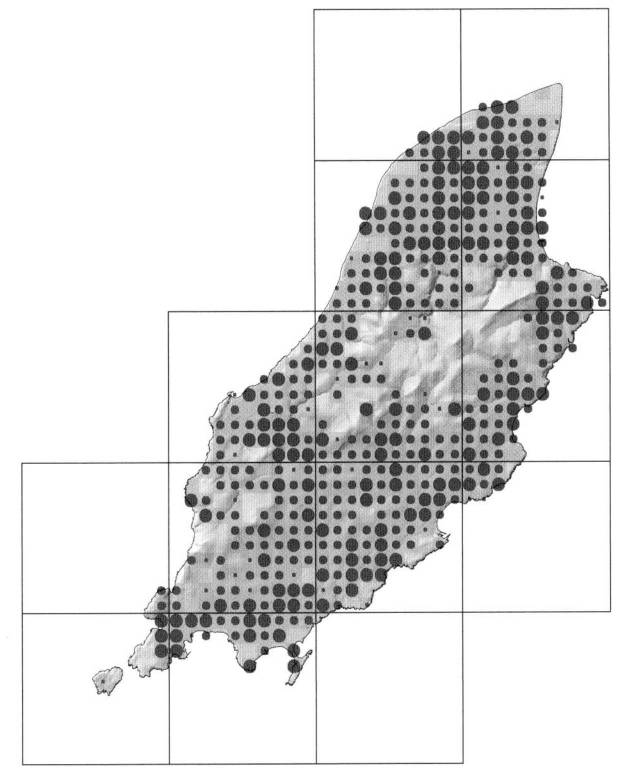

Summer presence and breeding status

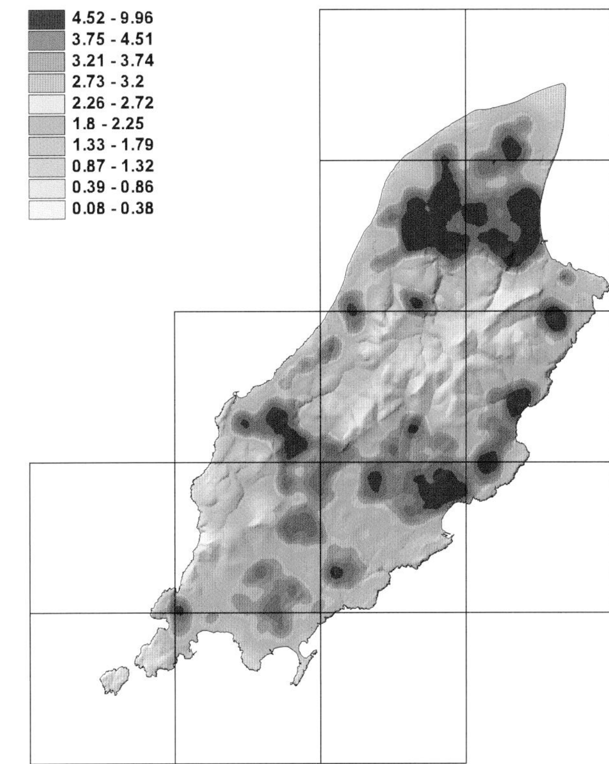

Breeding abundance

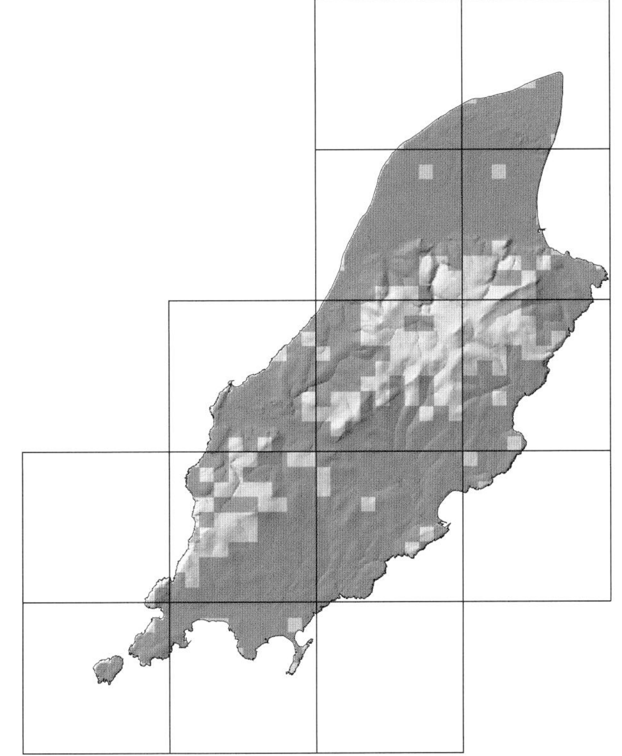

Winter presence

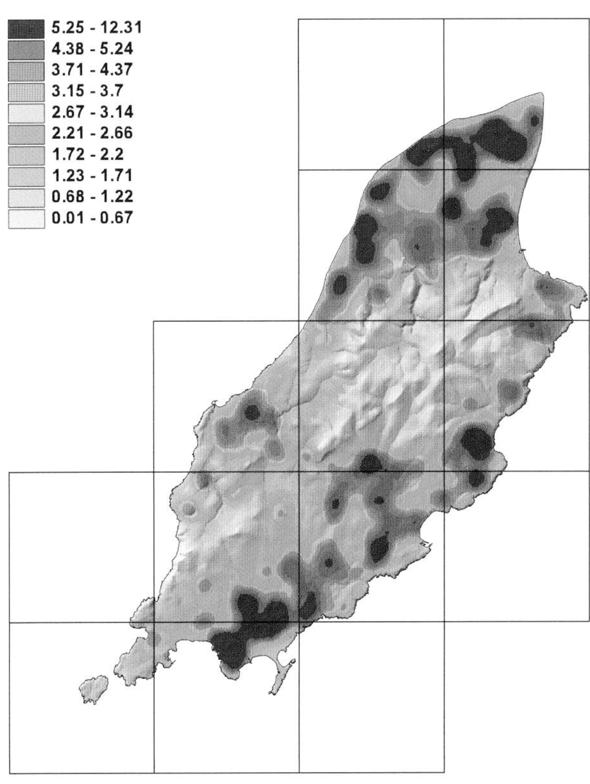

Winter abundance

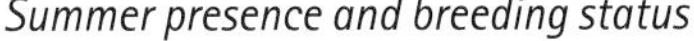

Individual Sponsors – The Anderson Trust, Mr. J & Mrs. M Cain, Mrs. D Cowley, Mr. C & Mrs. G Eaton, Mr. R Harris, the Helks family, Mr. S Sewell, Mrs. M Skelly, Mr. & Mrs. W Starkey, Mrs. M Turner, Mr. A E Wheatley

Redwing
Turdus iliacus

Manx: *Lhon Geayee*

Redwings are marginally smaller than Song Thrushes, to which they bear a superficial resemblance, but the combination of a bright chestnut/orange underwing and a distinct, striped facial pattern distinguishes the Redwing from any other thrush likely to be found on the Island. The chestnut underwing colour, which gives the bird its English name, extends onto the sides of the breast and flanks and is visible even when the bird is at rest. Gardens containing autumnal windfall fruit often attract small parties of Redwings, adding colour to a drab day.

Redwings are common winter visitors to the Isle of Man, with substantial numbers also passing through on migration, particularly in autumn. The species has a huge geographical breeding range extending from Iceland through Scandinavia across northern Europe and northern Russia into eastern Siberia. The European breeding population is probably about 5.5 million pairs (EBA). Within the British Isles the small breeding population is confined to northern Scotland, but with an estimate of only 2-21 pairs in 2002 (Ogilvie *et al.* 2004) breeding is unlikely to spread to the Isle of Man. The few summer records of Redwing obtained during the research period were all considered to be of birds on spring passage.

It appears that the entire breeding population of the continental race *Turdus iliacus iliacus* winters either in western Europe, or in areas adjoining the Mediterranean or the Black Sea (BWP), and thus autumn migration of this race is primarily to the west rather than south. The race *T.i. coburni* which breeds in Iceland, undertakes a south-easterly movement in autumn to winter mainly in Ireland, with some in Scotland, France and Iberia (MA). *T.i. iliacus* and *T.i. coburni* occur commonly on the Island. Although the first few migrants are sometimes seen in late September it is not until the first week of October that they arrive in any numbers, with loose flocks of several hundred birds sometimes being seen. Movement into and over the Island continues into November and is often marked by birds heard flying low over the Island, particularly on misty nights, frequently in the company of Song Thrushes. Numerous Redwings pass through the Calf, where some are ringed. The only recoveries were from southern France and Algeria, while one bird caught on the Calf had been ringed as a pullus in Finland.

The winter population in the British Isles as a whole is considered to have been largely stable over the course of the twentieth century, amounting to about 1 million birds, though it may be much greater (WA). In winter Redwings prefer low-lying open farmland habitat, where they forage for soil invertebrates and feed on berries and fruit, often in company with the other 'winter thrush', the Fieldfare. On the Island they may be found throughout the winter over most of the lowland, but are scarce above about 180m and also along coastal fringes where habitat is largely unsuitable. Thus, concentrations are evident throughout the northern and eastern lowland agricultural areas, through the central valley and on to the north-east of Peel towards Kirk Michael. Redwings are adversely affected by hard winters on the Island and will then enter towns and villages to feed in gardens.

The Redwing was described by C&J as a 'common passage migrant and winter visitor' and this is still the case. Our surveys suggest a population in the region of 5,000 birds in winter, though the number present will vary through each winter and in successive winters. Kermode considered the Redwing to be 'a regular winter visitor' and Ralfe described it as being 'a regular visitor', thus its status on the Island has probably not changed greatly over the past hundred years.

Breeding	Grid squares:	Isle of Man 21 (3%) Britain 136 Ireland 4 Total 140 (4%)
	Population:	Isle of Man 0 Britain 17 Ireland 0 (<1% of European)
Wintering	Grid squares:	Isle of Man 272 (41%) Britain and Ireland 3,316 (86%)
	Population:	Isle of Man 500–1,500 Britain and Ireland 1 million+

Jan	Feb	Mar	Apr	May	Jun	Jul	Aug	Sep	Oct	Nov	Dec

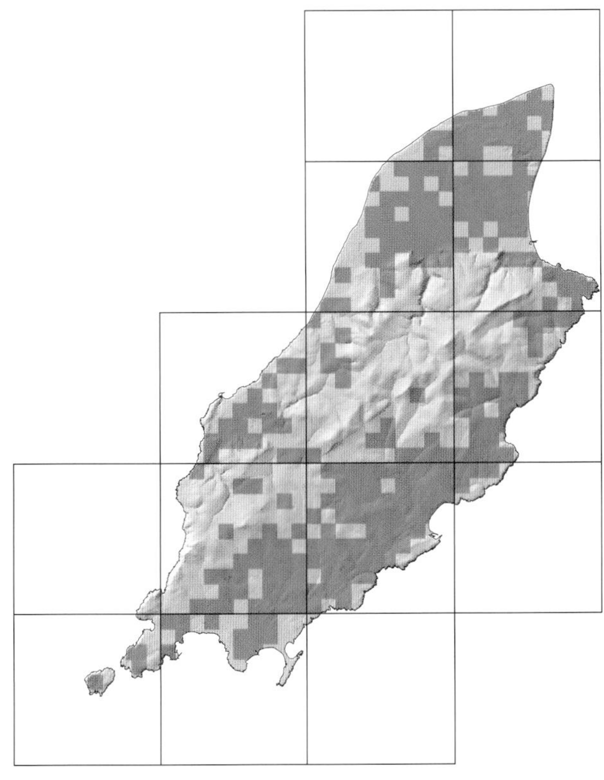

Winter presence

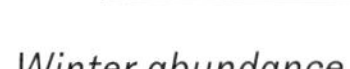

Winter abundance

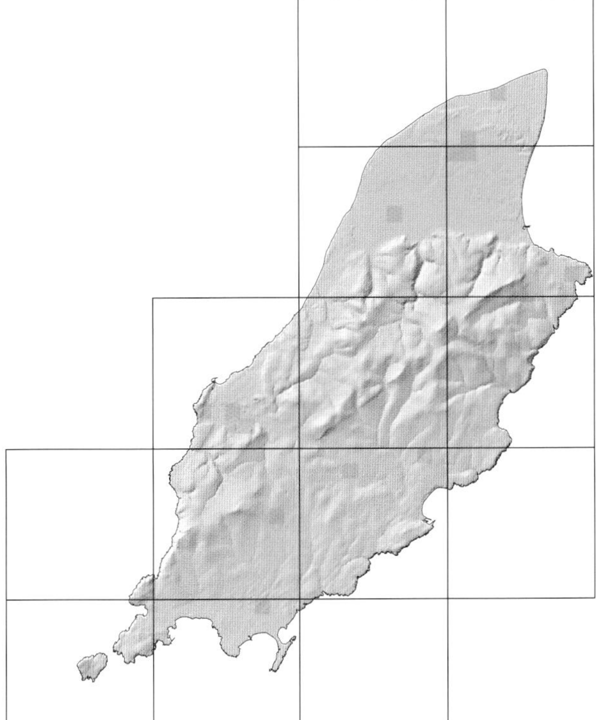

Summer presence

Mistle Thrush
Turdus viscivorus

Manx: *Lhon Keylley*

Mistle Thrushes are the largest of the Manx thrushes. They are sometimes confused with the smaller and more compact Song Thrush, which is superficially similar, though Mistle Thrushes are much greyer, the black spots on the belly are more rounded, and they appear relatively slimmer. They are also more wary, but when disturbed tend to fly up into trees rather than into bushes and undergrowth. Their distinctive song is usually delivered from the tops of trees, and has a melancholy almost mournful tone that is often heard before stormy spring weather, giving rise to the colloquial name of 'Storm cock'.

During the breeding season the species favours woodland glades and mature stands of broad-leaved woodland, adjacent to areas of grassland or recently cultivated soil, tending to avoid dense conifer plantations. Though woodland areas are strongly preferred, Mistle Thrushes will sometimes nest on ledges, both on cliffs and in buildings, with the result that occasional nests can be found away from trees. In 1927 a pair nested on a rocky ledge near the summit of Snaefell at about 600m (C&J).

The Mistle Thrush has an extensive breeding range across the Palearctic, avoiding the extreme north, but including most of Europe, parts of North Africa and much of Asia north of the Himalayas as far as eastern Siberia (BWP, EBA). It is common and widespread throughout much of the British Isles, being absent in Shetland and Orkney and in areas where suitable habitat is largely absent, such as on exposed coasts and in upland areas (1988–91 Atlas). Within the Isle of Man Mistle Thrushes breed rather sparsely over most of the lower ground, with isolated pairs nesting in upland valleys, but they are scarce above 200m and mostly avoid extensive open areas with few mature trees.

The majority of Mistle Thrushes in the British Isles are sedentary and, though some British ringed birds have been recovered in France, most came from south-east England (MA), suggesting post-breeding dispersal or cold weather movements, rather than migration. Although large numbers of continental Mistle Thrushes move from northern to western Europe in autumn, it appears that relatively few reach the British Isles either as winter visitors or passage migrants (WA, MA). Small numbers of Mistle Thrushes migrate through the Calf of Man, almost entirely in autumn, and moderate numbers have been ringed there since 1959. The few recoveries have all been on the Isle of Man, suggesting that many of them may be resident.

Given the largely sedentary nature of the species, it is unsurprising that the distribution on the Isle of Man in winter is broadly the same as in summer, with some dispersal from higher ground evident. The population is concentrated mainly on the northern plain, eastern areas from Laxey south to the Castletown area and in the central valley. Higher winter densities are probably a result of young birds joining the population, together with, possibly, some localised movement to the Isle of Man from adjacent islands.

Kermode stated that 'probably it has settled here, as in Ireland, since the beginning of the 19th century', while Ralfe considered it 'probable' that settlement was 'recent', describing it as a common resident. C&J described the Mistle Thrush as a common resident, probably also occurring as a passage migrant, with the species being indicated as breeding in most 5km squares, as was the case during the MBA research. Elsewhere in the British Isles the population was, until recently, considered to be stable, but it is now thought that it may be declining (MA), although the reasons for this are unknown. There is no clear evidence of any change in numbers on the Isle of Man and the species is still as described by Ralfe.

1977–81

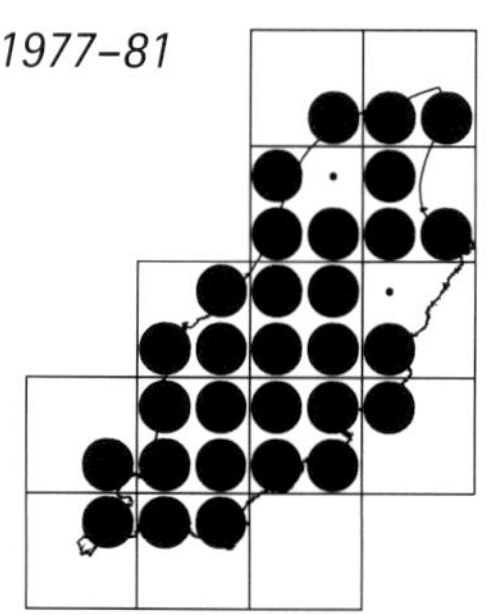

1998–2002

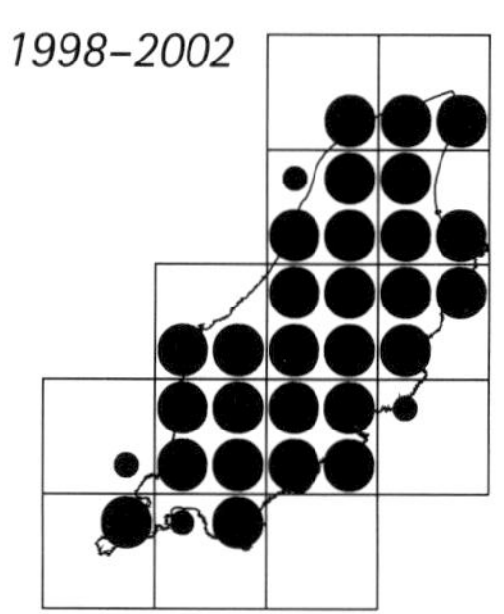

Breeding	Grid squares:	Isle of Man 321 (48%) Britain 2,397 Ireland 857 Total 3,254 (84%)
	Population:	Isle of Man 334–463 Britain 230,000 Ireland 90,000 (13% of European)
Wintering	Grid squares:	Isle of Man 288 (43%) Britain and Ireland 3,175 (82%)
	Population:	Isle of Man 1,000+ Britain and Ireland 400,000–800,000

Jan Feb Mar Apr May Jun Jul Aug Sep Oct Nov Dec

Summer presence and breeding status

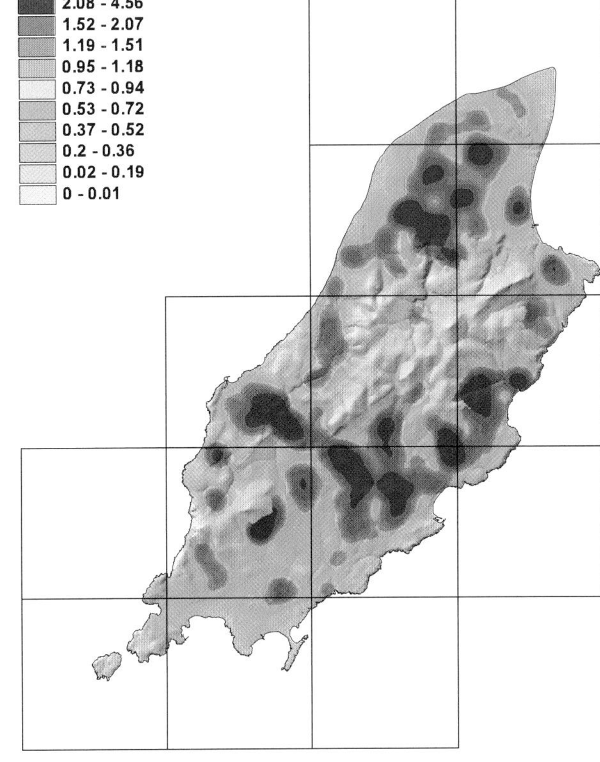

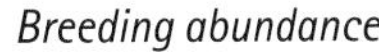

Breeding abundance

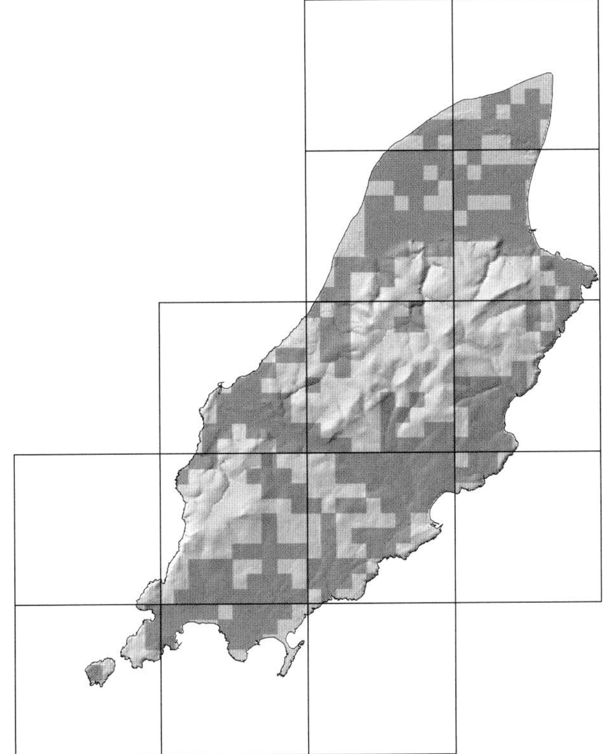

Winter presence

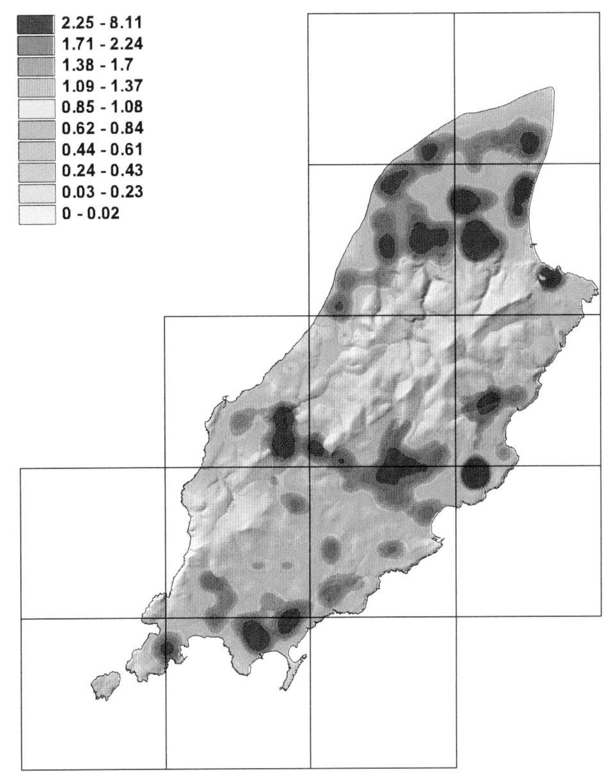

Winter abundance

Individual Sponsors – The Anderson Trust, Ms. C Bramall

Grasshopper Warbler (Common Grasshopper Warbler)
Locustella naevia

This shy, almost reclusive, summer visitor to the British Isles can easily be overlooked. The characteristic reeling song, which gives the species its name, is unmistakable, the sound rising and falling in volume as the male turns its head from side to side proclaiming his territory. The males will sing from elevated positions like posts or the tops of tussocks, but otherwise the species stays on or very close to the ground, often creeping mouse-like through thick vegetation (BWP).

The first few Grasshopper Warblers usually reach the Island in late April, although it is during the first half of May that most arrive. At first they are often heard close to the coast, though they will soon move to their breeding sites, or continue their migration. A range of habitats is used for nesting, provided that thick ground cover is present. These include the banks of ditches and small rivers or areas of bog or curragh and stands of young trees as well as coarse grasses or brambles in drier areas (BWP, 1988–91 Atlas). Suitable habitat is plentiful and widespread on the Island.

Outside the British Isles the breeding range of the species extends from western Europe across most of central and northern Europe to central Siberia and northwest China (BWP). Within the British Isles the distribution is widespread but sparse, a description that suits well the local situation, with only about 60 pairs during the MBA research period. This small and highly secretive warbler is likely to be under-recorded. An additional problem is that numbers reaching the British Isles are known to fluctuate greatly from year to year (C&J, MA); the reasons for this variation are unknown. Within the Island, Grasshopper Warblers bred in many of the wetter curragh areas where the hills give way to the northern plain, occurring also as isolated pairs in other similar habitats around the Island. The majority of records were obtained from the wet valleys and adjacent new plantations along the western edge of the central hills and the south-east facing lower slopes of South Barrule.

Young from early broods start their migration in July, with adults and later broods leaving mainly in August and September (MA). October records are rare and there were no winter records during the research period. Many Grasshopper Warblers have been ringed on the Island, mainly on the Calf, but there are no migration data from birds ringed or recovered here; indeed there are very few for the British Isles and not many more for Europe. The British Isles and European data suggest they winter in tropical West Africa (1988–91 Atlas, MA). Birds seen on passage may be local breeders or moving through the Island en route to or from breeding areas elsewhere in the British Isles. British data provide no direct evidence of birds moving through the British Isles from continental Europe (MA), although presumably this may also occur, since the species breeds in much of Scandinavia (EBA).

The species was apparently unknown to Kermode and had only recently been 'discovered' by Ralfe, although by then it was already known to be quite widely distributed. Madoc was clearly very familiar with the species and described it as being 'in some years … very plentiful'. C&J considered the species to be an 'irregular and locally distributed summer visitor and passage migrant in small numbers'. Assessing change in status since C&J is difficult, given the lack of numerical data, though the change maps suggest a wider distribution now than in the late 1970s. With a significant number of birds during this current survey being found associated with young plantations, it is anticipated that numbers might drop in the future as these plantations mature and become unsuitable.

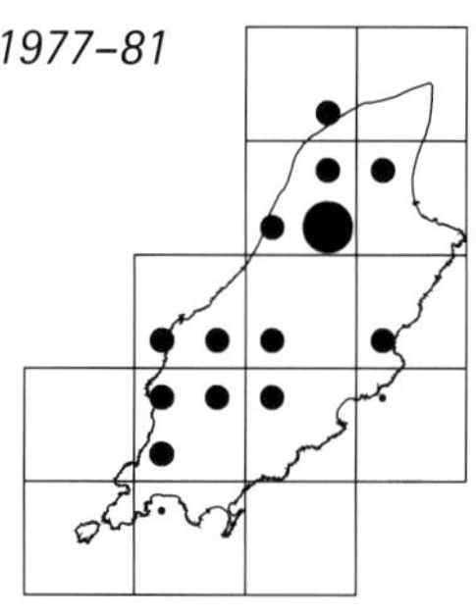
1977–81

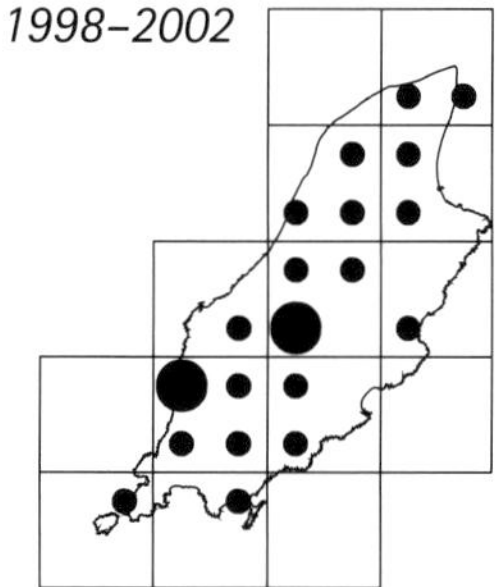
1998–2002

Breeding	Grid squares:	Isle of Man 106 (16%) Britain 1,189 Ireland 409 Total 1,598 (41%)
	Population:	Isle of Man 57 Britain 10,500 Ireland 5,500 (5% of European)

Jan Feb Mar Apr May Jun Jul Aug Sep Oct Nov Dec

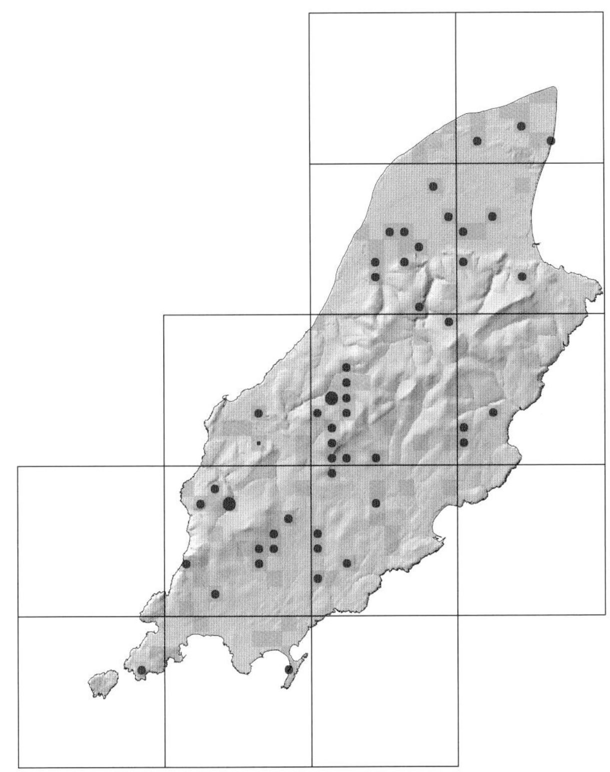

Summer presence and breeding status

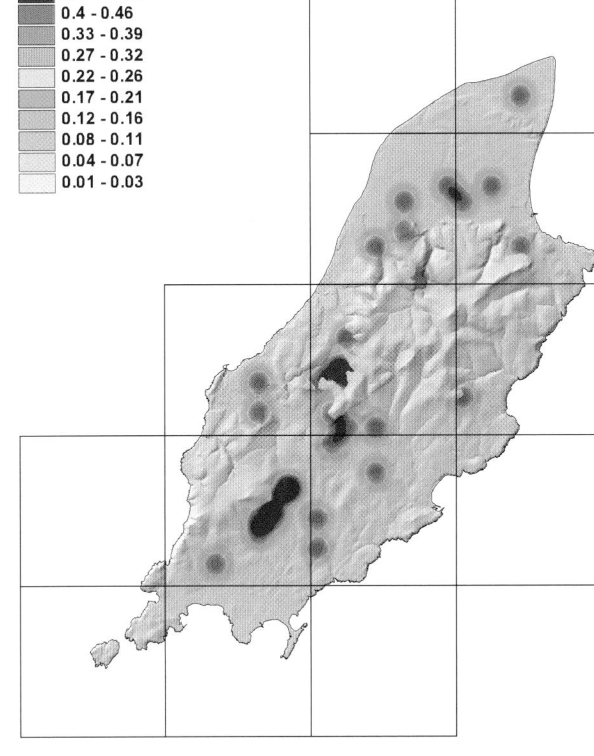

Breeding abundance

Individual Sponsors – Mrs. R Fryer, Mr. P Hargreaves

Sedge Warbler
Acrocephalus schoenobaenus

Male Sedge Warblers have a loud, cheerful, scratchy song and it is this that most often draws attention to their presence, rather than their smart buff-brown plumage offset by a bold pale supercilium.

Sedge Warblers will use a wide variety of low, dense vegetation in which to breed, often, though not exclusively, adjacent to water or wet areas. Areas of dry scrub, stands of young conifers and crops are also used (BWP, MA). Food taken is mostly insects, usually obtained by picking from vegetation as the bird moves through thick cover, though it will also catch flying insects. One bird, in the process of being ringed, caught a passing fly while being held by the ringer.

Sedge Warblers breed commonly throughout much of Europe, their range extending from the high Arctic to Greece and from Ireland in the west to central Siberia in the east (EBA). Within the British Isles the species is widely distributed throughout lowland areas, with losses evident in some parts, probably as a result of drainage of wetlands and agricultural intensification. Areas of high abundance occur in many of the counties of eastern England, the Scottish lowlands, central Ireland and the north of the Isle of Man (1988–91 Atlas).

On the Isle of Man the Sedge Warbler is a common passage migrant and summer visitor. The species does not usually arrive on the Island until the last week of April, the main bulk of birds arriving during the first half of May. The survey data indicate that breeding pairs are to be found commonly in damp or boggy areas, particularly in low-lying parts of the Island. Within suitable habitat the greatest concentrations occur over the northern plain and in the south and south-east of the Island. They also breed in other areas, including the central valley, though surprisingly few were found in this area. They are absent from the higher hills, rarely breeding above about 150m.

From late July pre-migration movement of Sedge Warblers is evident, migration taking place from August through to October, with most birds having left the Isle of Man by September. Considerable numbers migrate through the south of the Island, including the Calf of Man, with many of these being caught and ringed. On some days in late July in excess of 50 individuals have been caught at a small reed bed near the coast at Gansey. Similar numbers of unringed birds caught on following days give some indication of the large numbers moving through the area.

The few ringing returns indicate that Manx-ringed Sedge Warblers travel through Belgium, France, Holland and Spain as well as various parts of Britain and Ireland. However, it is thought that the main wintering area for Sedge Warblers from Britain is in Africa south of the Sahara, from Senegal to Ethiopia and south to South Africa (MA).

Kermode knew the Sedge Warbler as a summer visitor to a handful of localities, whilst Ralfe was aware of few records. By 1934, Madoc thought the species to be found 'in every suitable place' and C&J list the Sedge Warbler as a common summer visitor and passage migrant. The almost complete lack of nineteenth-century breeding records combined with the very small breeding numbers known to either Kermode or Ralfe would seem to indicate a major increase in breeding Sedge Warblers on the Isle of Man between the early twentieth century and the 1930s. This may be the case, but alternatively, since the species is a common long-distance migrant, which at that time was more widespread and abundant in Britain than it is today (HA), it is difficult to see how it could not have been breeding, albeit, as now, limited to suitable habitat on the Island. The apparent scarcity of Sedge Warblers on the Island in the nineteenth-century may therefore have been a consequence of a widespread failure to recognise the species. This becomes more likely if, as was apparently the case, the song was not generally known; according to Kermode (and Ralfe), the (often nocturnal) song may have been mistaken for that of the Nightingale.

1977–81

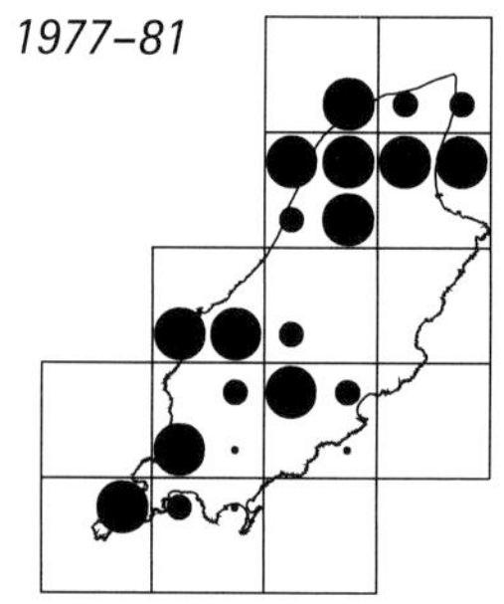

1998–2002

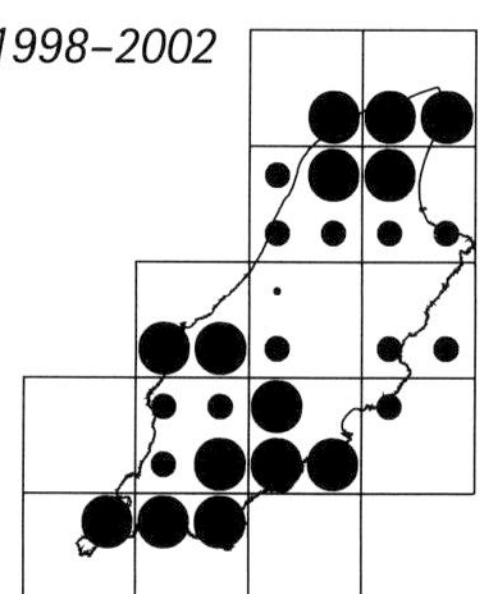

Breeding	Grid squares:	Isle of Man 165 (25%) Britain 1,887 Ireland 681 Total 2,568 (66%)
	Population:	Isle of Man 188-220 Britain 250,000 Ireland 110,000 (15% of European)

Jan	Feb	Mar	Apr	May	Jun	Jul	Aug	Sep	Oct	Nov	Dec

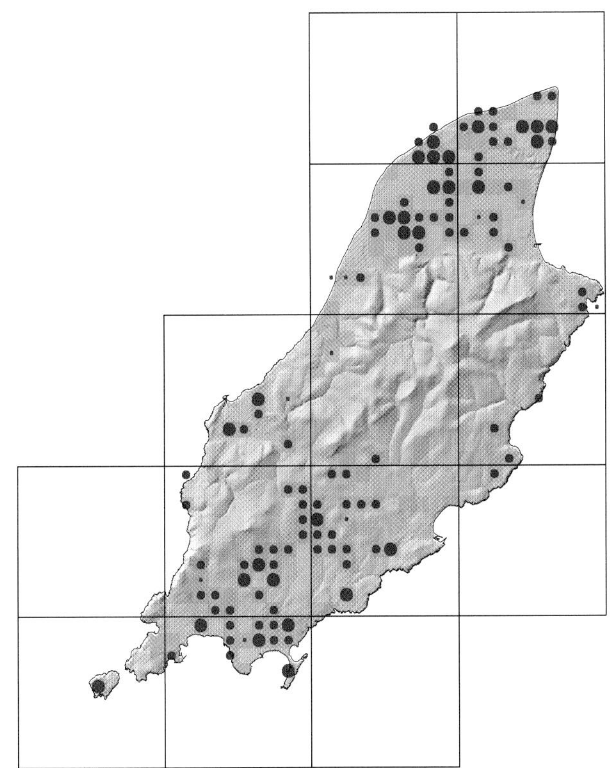

Summer presence and breeding status

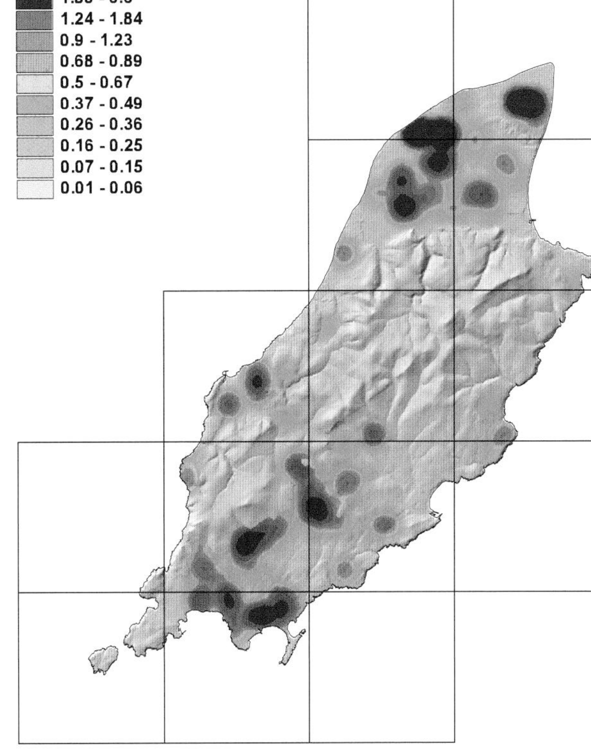

Breeding abundance

Individual Sponsors – Mr. & Mrs. I W Shields

Reed Warbler (Eurasian Reed Warbler)
Acrocephalus scirpaceus

The Reed Warbler is a rather secretive small brown bird, but its scratchy, rattling song, not unlike that of the closely related Sedge Warbler, is a characteristic sound of reed beds across southern England in early summer. It breeds almost entirely in stands of reed, particularly common reed. Within larger reed beds densities of breeding Reed Warbler are lower in the centre than near the edge, thus the species does not need extensive stands of reed in which to nest, with dense linear strips of reed along rivers and ditches suiting it well (EBA). The common reed is a habitat type in short supply on the Isle of Man; hence the Reed Warbler is not a common bird locally. Food consists mainly of insects and spiders, though some small snails are also taken (BWP).

The Reed Warbler has a breeding range that extends across the western and central Palearctic. The subspecies breeding in the British Isles, *Acrocephalus scirpaceus scirpaceus*, has a northern limit of approximately 65°N in Fennoscandia and reaching as far south as coastal north-west Africa (BWP, EBA). Within the British Isles its breeding distribution was largely limited to southern and central England, but in recent decades Reed Warblers have extended their range to the north and west, now nesting regularly in Ireland (1988–91 Atlas). On the Island, Reed Warblers are scarce, occurring largely in spring and autumn. These are presumably mainly birds which have overshot or strayed from their more southerly strongholds or birds which have undergone drift migration on their way to or from more northerly parts of Europe. In recent years records of Reed Warbler locally have increased in frequency, and they have been recorded in all years of the MBA research. With the exception of Calf records, all were from a small reed bed adjacent to a sewage treatment plant near Port St Mary. During the research period breeding there was suspected; a singing male was present in 1999 and a female with brood patch was caught later in the same year. It was not until 2004 that breeding was confirmed. Two females with well-developed brood patches were caught on a number of occasions, with three young birds from the same brood present between late July and early September, this representing the first known breeding of the species on the Isle of Man.

After the breeding season, Reed Warblers have a protracted migration period, single-brooded adults and their young starting to move south from late July, while adults having a second brood, together with their later young, may still be present into October. A small number of autumn records were obtained during the MBA research, all from the south of the Island, with one particularly late record from the Calf of Man on 17 November 1998 (Bagworth 1999). The Reed Warbler is a long-distance migrant that winters in tropical Africa, birds from western Europe including the British Isles probably wintering in West Africa (MA) with those from further east travelling to East Africa. It is thought that Reed Warblers return to the same areas in subsequent winters (MA).

The Reed Warbler was unknown to the earlier Manx authors and C&J considered it to be a scarce passage migrant. Since that time, and probably thanks to a range expansion within the UK, their status on the Island has changed considerably.

Breeding	Grid squares:	Isle of Man 2 (0.5%) Britain 790 Ireland 13 Total 803 (21%)
	Population:	Isle of Man 1–2 Britain 60,000+ Ireland c50 (2% of European)

Jan	Feb	Mar	Apr	May	Jun	Jul	Aug	Sep	Oct	Nov	Dec

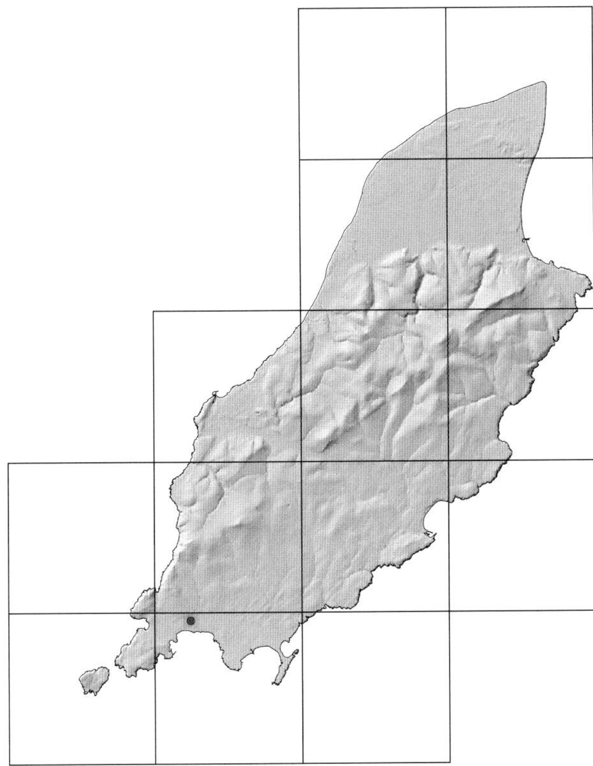

Summer presence and breeding status

Blackcap
Sylvia atricapilla

Manx: *Bayrn dhoo*

After the Whitethroat the Blackcap is the commonest of the various *Sylvia* warblers that occur or have occurred on the Island. Though the plumage appears somewhat drab, Blackcaps are attractive birds, their generally grey body offset by a neat black cap in the case of males, with a less obvious red-brown cap on females. Males have a rich, clear and often prolonged song, delivered with gusto, that brightens up many a spring morning walk.

Blackcaps prefer mature stands of deciduous lowland woodland in which to breed, including trees found along the banks of rivers, but will also utilise tall, dense, shrubby undergrowth. Conifer plantations are usually avoided (EBA). During the breeding season they take mainly insects, while at other times fruit forms a major proportion of their diet (BWP). The species is adaptable and is becoming an increasingly frequent visitor to garden feeding sites.

The overall breeding distribution of the species extends across most of Europe apart from Iceland and northern Fennoscandia (EBA). Within the British Isles Blackcaps are a widespread breeding species, being absent only from the high ground and areas of fenland, where suitable breeding habitat is absent. Areas of highest density are in southern England (1988–91 Atlas).

Within the Isle of Man the Blackcap is a fairly common and widespread breeding species that is mainly a summer visitor, with birds arriving from early to mid April, migration extending into the first half of May. Throughout the Island breeding Blackcaps were found to be associated with two main habitat types. The most widespread habitat was woodland adjacent to rivers and streams, primarily in lowlands but extending to 300m where suitable habitat existed. The second main habitat to support breeding Blackcaps was curragh, such as that found scattered along the southern edge of the northern plain and along the central valley. Within such habitat birds were often to be found in the slightly drier places, tending to avoid those areas where willows predominated. High densities were evident within the Ballaugh Curragh and Glen Auldyn in the north, Ballaglass Glen in the north-east, the Baldwin valleys near Douglas, around St Johns in the west and Glen Grenaugh in the south-east.

Blackcaps start migration rather later than some other warbler species, with few being caught on the Calf of Man prior to the start of September, and movement continuing well into October, with November records not being uncommon. Data for the British Isles suggest that the coastal areas of the western Mediterranean in both Europe and North Africa are the main wintering areas for the British population, though some may cross the Sahara (1988–91 Atlas, MA). Some birds from northern Europe also pass through Britain on passage (MA).

Blackcaps winter in the British Isles in small numbers, a curious feature of the wintering population being that probably none of these Blackcaps breed in Britain. All appear, from ringing data, to be northern European (mainly German) Blackcaps, which in recent decades have changed their migration pattern to winter in the British Isles (MA), where they are widespread, but rather more frequent in south-west England than elsewhere (WA). Within the Isle of Man they were present in greater numbers than had been anticipated. Many of the records obtained came from people participating in the Garden Birdwatch Scheme (GBW) run by MBA, with 27% (91) of the participating gardens recording the species as present at some time during the winter of 1999/2000. The winter distribution map for the Blackcap therefore partly reflects the distribution of Garden Birdwatch participants, with presence in all major towns and villages. While it is known that many Blackcaps will attend garden feeding sites during winter, it is assumed that others do not, so winter distribution is likely to be greater than that reflected on the map.

Kermode and Ralfe knew of no records of Blackcaps on the Island and Madoc had only a handful of records. C&J, with the benefit of information from the Calf, were able to list the species as a regular passage migrant, but regarded it as a scarce breeding bird, which had only recently colonised the Island. This ties in with Britain where a northward spread has seen Blackcap numbers increasing in northern England, southern Scotland and Northern Ireland (1988–91 Atlas). The reasons for this are not clear, but may be related to increased survival in the wintering areas around the western Mediterranean (1988–91 Atlas).

1977–81

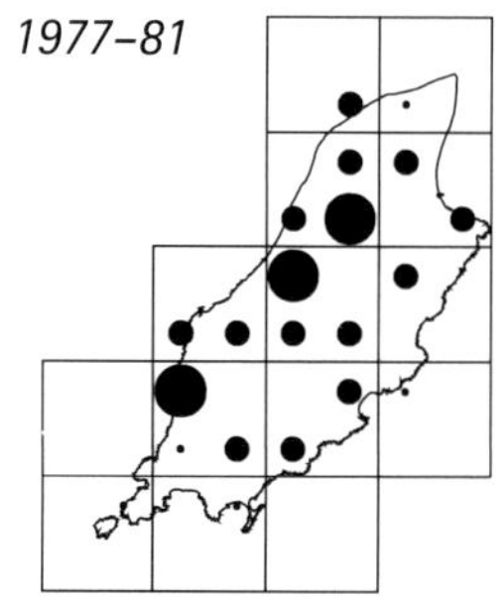

1998–2002

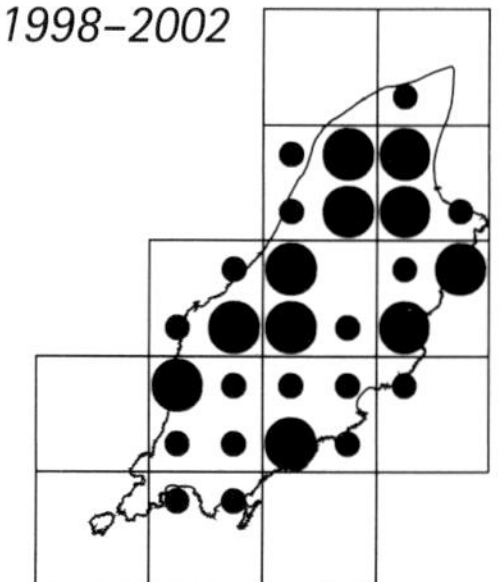

Breeding	Grid squares:	Isle of Man 235 (35%) Britain 2,048 Ireland 357 Total 2,405 (62%)
	Population:	Isle of Man 343-349 Britain 580,000 Ireland 40,000 (3% of European)
Wintering	Grid squares:	Isle of Man 80 (12%) Britain and Ireland 976 (25%)
	Population:	Isle of Man <100 Britain and Ireland 3,000

Jan	Feb	Mar	Apr	May	Jun	Jul	Aug	Sep	Oct	Nov	Dec

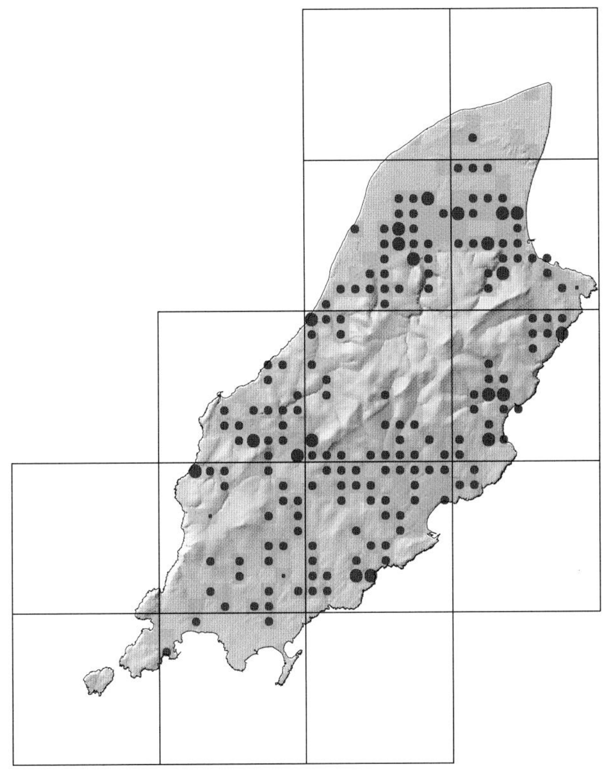
Summer presence and breeding status

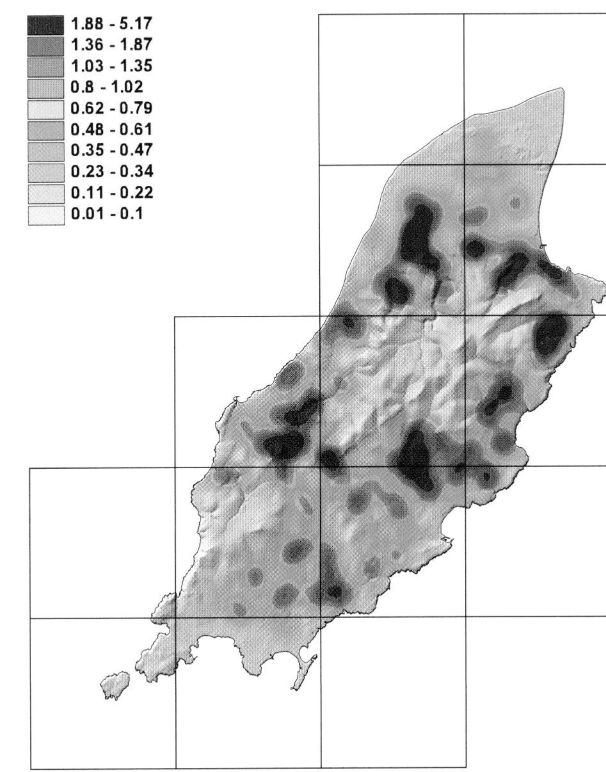

Breeding abundance

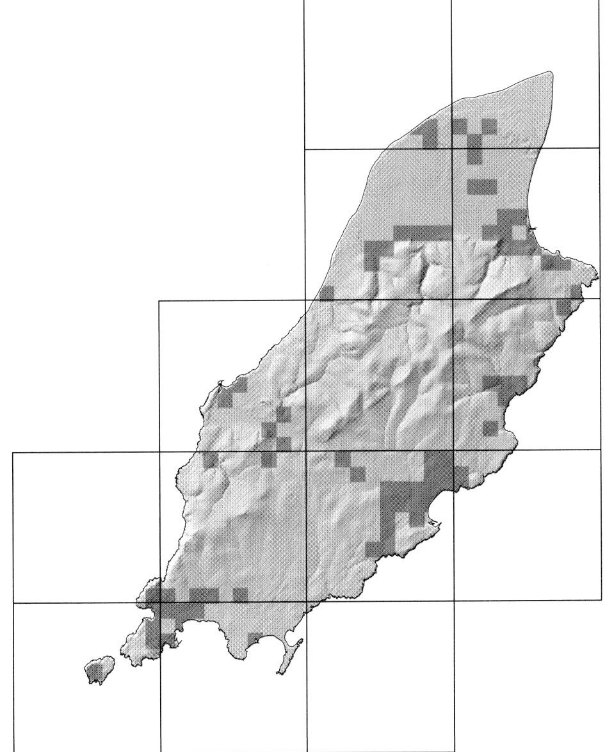
Winter presence

Individual Sponsors – Mrs. H C Cowell, Dr. J P Cullen, Mrs. J Kewley

Garden Warbler
Sylvia borin

Manx: *Kiaulleyder garee*

Garden Warblers are inconspicuous and shy birds that are difficult to detect even when breeding and, with no particular outstanding identification features, they can be hard to identify. This problem is exacerbated on the Isle of Man, where, because they are fairly uncommon summer visitors, many local residents may be unfamiliar with the species. Those of an unkind disposition may say that it is well suited to its scientific name of '*borin*' (sic), though the sweet, flowing song delivered in a rather understated fashion does much to redeem it.

Garden Warblers inhabit deciduous woodland and scrub, preferring a fairly open canopy with dense ground cover for nesting, most nests being less than 2m above the ground (EBA, BWP). In common with the Blackcap they take mainly insects during the breeding season, changing to fruit at other times, but, unlike the Blackcap, they have not developed the habit of supplementing their diet by visiting bird tables.

Outside the British Isles the Garden Warbler has a large breeding range extending across most of Europe from southern Spain and Ireland in the west, north as far as North Cape in Norway and east beyond Europe into western Siberia (BWP, EBA). Within the British Isles it is a common species throughout most of England, Wales and southern Scotland, with areas of high density evident in Wales and southern England, although northern Scotland and Ireland are largely unoccupied (1988–91 Atlas). Locally, Garden Warblers start to arrive in May, though occasionally birds are seen in late April. As shown on the accompanying map, summer records came from several 1km squares, but many of these were from the start or end of the breeding season and were thus attributed the status of 'passage migrants' and so were considered not to be breeding. Breeding records were few, with only seven males singing in the main breeding period, including one in scrub adjacent to the MBA office, with one further bird thought to be possibly breeding. As the Island is towards the western breeding limit of the species it is likely that numbers vary between years. With each 1km square being formally surveyed in only one of the five years, some birds may have gone unrecorded.

The migration period for Garden Warblers in the British Isles is rather protracted, extending from late July to early November. Peaks in late August or early September probably represent departing adults and young from the British and Irish populations, while peaks in late September or early October result from continental birds moving south (MA). During the MBA research period insufficient numbers were noted on migration to determine whether such peaks of movement were evident locally, though sporadic sightings from August through to early November, mostly from the Calf of Man, suggest that the Isle of Man does have continental migrants passing through in autumn. Ringing data from the UK indicate that all of those nesting in the British Isles winter in West Africa south of the Sahara, particularly in Nigeria and Ghana (1988–91 Atlas, MA)

Kermode did not include the Garden Warbler in his publication and by 1905 Ralfe knew of no definite records from the Island. In his notes of 1923, Ralfe mentions a record of one in a Lezayre garden in 1921 and comments that 'the species has several times been obtained at the Point of Ayre light'. Madoc knew the species as a spring visitor in very small numbers. C&J considered it a 'regular passage migrant in small numbers which has bred occasionally'. Against these assessments the Atlas surveys have shown the Garden Warbler to be more plentiful than previously supposed, although it is still an uncommon bird. It is surprising that more Garden Warblers are not present and presumably the Island's geographic position is the limiting factor rather than climate, food availability or shortage of habitat (1988–91 Atlas). In the UK the population seems to have been largely stable in recent decades.

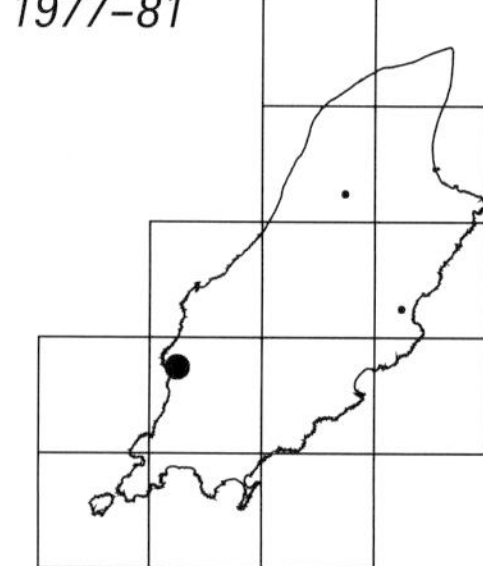

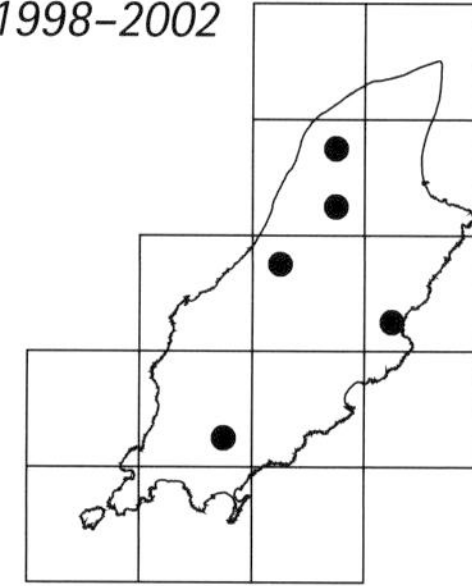

Breeding	Grid squares:	Isle of Man 24 (4%)
		Britain 1,867 Ireland 56 Total 1,923 (50%)
	Population:	Isle of Man 8
		Britain 200,000 Ireland 240 (2% of European)

Jan Feb Mar Apr May Jun Jul Aug Sep Oct Nov Dec

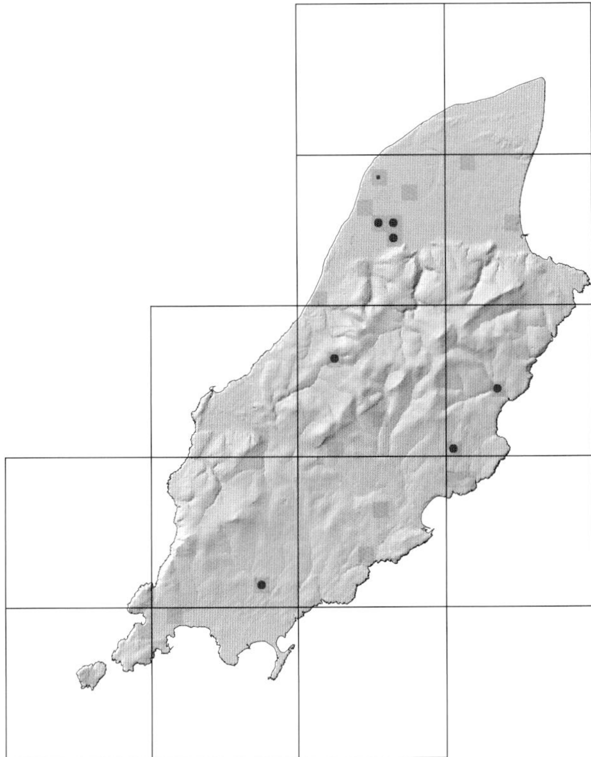

Summer presence and breeding status

Lesser Whitethroat
Sylvia curruca

Many residents of the Isle of Man will probably be unfamiliar with the Lesser Whitethroat, for the Island is at the extreme north-westerly limit of distribution for this summer visitor to the British Isles. It is therefore a rather scarce breeding bird that also occurs uncommonly on passage, though some individuals may go unrecorded due to their generally skulking habit and rather nondescript appearance, coupled with the probability that many local people will be unfamiliar with the song. Although resembling the larger Whitethroat superficially, the lack of brown on the wings, together with black legs, make identification relatively straightforward.

Throughout its extensive breeding range it is known to occupy a variety of habitats, though within the British Isles birds are generally to be found in areas of scrub, parkland or farmland with mature hedges, including those along grass-verged country roads (BWP). These habitat requirements are, in many ways, similar to those of the Whitethroat, which is abundant on the Island; thus the scarcity of Lesser Whitethroats is presumably a result of the Island being at the extreme edge of their range, rather than lack of suitable habitat. Food consists chiefly of invertebrates, together with berries during late summer and autumn (BWP).

The breeding range of the Lesser Whitethroat extends over much of the Palearctic, from western Europe to eastern Siberia and western China (BWP, EBA), but it is absent from Italy, Iberia and most of France and northern Scandinavia. Within the British Isles Lesser Whitethroats breed mainly in eastern parts of southern and central England, with few pairs in the south-west, Wales or to the north of Cheshire. In the east of England they breed commonly, their range extending into Yorkshire, with odd pairs along the east coast far into Scotland (1988–91 Atlas). They are absent or infrequent breeders in Ireland, for probably the same reason as on the Isle of Man. Before the Atlas period there were very few records for the main Island, with none at all in many years, but the more detailed fieldwork undertaken for the Atlas has revealed that Lesser Whitethroats are probably present annually in small numbers and breed in some years. During the MBA survey, breeding is thought to have occurred at several scattered locations, including the central valley, Hillberry to the north of Douglas and on the fringes of the Ballaugh Curraghs. Birds thought to be on passage have been seen mainly near the coast, for example on Langness and near Rue Point, as well as on the Calf, sightings at these locations coinciding with the known spring migration period of late April (rarely) and May. On the Calf of Man numbers arriving in spring vary from year to year, although this variation probably reflects local weather conditions, with individuals overshooting their usual breeding range, rather than major changes in numbers within the British Isles.

Lesser Whitethroats breeding in the British Isles start migrating from mid-July, on completion of moult. They follow a mainly southerly route, until reaching continental Europe, after which ringing recoveries reveal a south-easterly movement through Italy to reach wintering grounds in Sudan, Chad, Eritrea and north and central Ethiopia (MA). On the Isle of Man few Lesser Whitethroats are observed after September, although some are seen into October on the Calf, with one bird present from 23 October to 18 November in 1999 (Bagworth 2000).

Though the Lesser Whitethroat was not added to the Manx list until 1908 (C&J), Ralfe makes reference to the species having been seen at both Laxey and Peel prior to June 1893, adding that Kermode 'in his latest list states, "(it) is, I think, a regular visitor"'. Madoc considered the species to visit the Island in small numbers and knew of breeding records, and C&J described it as a 'scarce passage migrant, which has bred'. As with many other species it is difficult, in the absence of detailed numerical data, to assess whether numbers have changed greatly, particularly given annual fluctuations. As with the Whitethroat, the Manx population may have increased between the start of the twentieth century and the 1930s when Madoc was writing, but whether it has altered much in more recent years is unclear. The British breeding population shows no clear long-term trends in recent decades, although it fluctuates markedly in the short term. Whitethroats also undergo these fluctuations, which are probably the result of excessive mortality on migration. Even on the Calf, the Lesser Whitethroat cannot reliably be seen in spring, and elsewhere on the Island it can only be found with luck, a knowledge of its song, or through systematic surveys.

Breeding	Grid squares:	Isle of Man 14 (2%) Britain 1,271 Ireland 1 Total 1,272 (33%)
	Population:	Isle of Man 7–8 Britain 80,000 Ireland c1 (4% of European)

Jan Feb Mar Apr May Jun Jul Aug Sep Oct Nov Dec

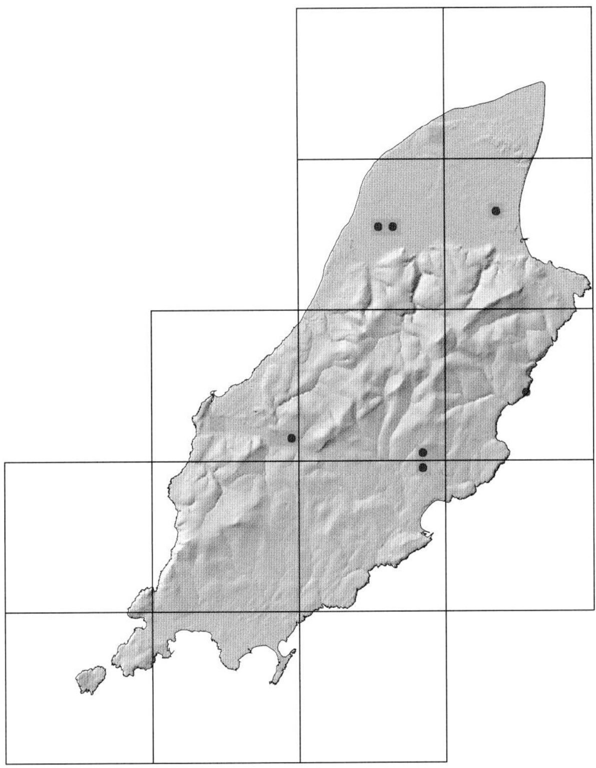

Summer presence and breeding status

Whitethroat (Common Whitethroat) *Sylvia communis*

Manx: *Fynnag ny Keylley*

Male Whitethroats have a characteristic scratchy song accompanied by a jerky display flight, which often gives the first indication of presence. The species is otherwise rather skulking in its habits and can be overlooked. Whether they are only heard or seen well enough to enjoy their perky, long-tailed stance and distinctive white throat, the first few records of each spring provide a welcome indication that summer is just around the corner.

For breeding, Whitethroats require fairly dense but patchy cover comprising a mix of tall herbage, low bushes and shrubs, usually on dry, almost level terrain with a sunny aspect. Thus, tall closed forests are avoided in favour of field hedgerows, ditches or road margins. Nests are often near the ground, in grasses, tall herbs or low bushes. Food taken during the breeding season consists mainly of insects, especially beetles, larvae and bugs, with fruit forming a greater proportion of the diet as autumn progresses (BWP).

The breeding range of the Whitethroat extends from western Europe to central Siberia and from north Africa to the Arctic Circle (EBA). Within the British Isles it is largely absent from high ground, the Outer Hebrides, Orkney and Shetland. Distribution in Ireland is patchy and abundance is typically higher in eastern England than elsewhere. Towards the north and west the species has a marked coastal distribution (1988–91 Atlas). The Whitethroat is a common summer visitor and passage migrant to the Isle of Man, the first few sightings usually being in late April with most birds not arriving until May. The survey data indicate that the species avoids open areas, including most of the high ground on the Island; it is also absent from the main towns. It is particularly abundant in the north, which is largely flat and generally more sunny than the rest of the Island and contains much suitable habitat. Further concentrations can be found in pockets of flatter agricultural land on the east and particularly the north-west coasts, with the southern lowland also being favoured. The central valley, though flat, is not favoured, presumably because it is too wooded and wet.

Despite the fact that many Whitethroats do not arrive on the Island to start breeding until May, some have started their return migration by mid to late July, with the main movement being evident through August, declining rapidly in September, during which there are only a few records in some years. There were no winter records over the Atlas period and indeed the species has hardly ever been recorded in winter within the British Isles (WA). Many Whitethroats have been ringed on the Island, mainly on the Calf, but there have been few recoveries. Ringing data from elsewhere suggest that all of those nesting in the British Isles winter in Africa south of the Sahara (1988-91 Atlas, MA). Some birds moving through the Island are presumably en route to or from breeding areas elsewhere in Britain and Ireland; UK data indicate that few birds move between there and continental Europe (MA).

Kermode considered the Whitethroat to be 'regular' and 'generally distributed, but in small numbers' and Ralfe thought it a 'fairly common summer visitor' and that it was 'probably increasing in numbers'. It seems likely that the Manx population increased between the very early twentieth century and the 1930s when Madoc described the species as 'one of the commonest migrants', while C&J considered it a 'common summer visitor and passage migrant'. The change maps demonstrate a similar distribution during the MBA research to that found by C&J. In the absence of detailed numerical data, however, it is difficult to assess whether numbers have changed greatly, particularly as the species is known to suffer from dramatic crashes in population as a result of climate-related changes in its African wintering quarters (1988–91 Atlas). The species appears to be faring well on the Isle of Man, though significant declines as a result of such climatic influences would clearly impact locally in subsequent summers. On the Island, threats to its future success include inappropriate and ill-timed hedge management, including the reduction of herb and grass cover at the base of hedges.

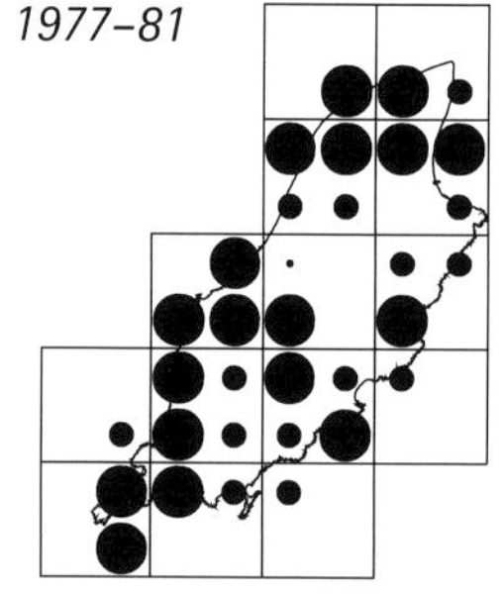

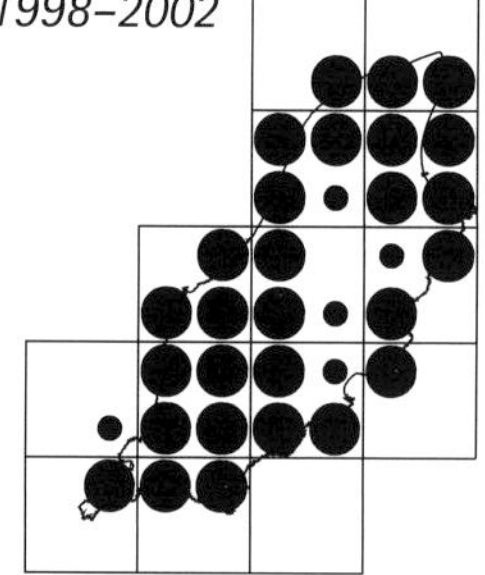

Breeding	Grid squares:	Isle of Man 380 (57%) Britain 2,186 Ireland 628 Total 2,814 (73%)
	Population:	Isle of Man 725–815 Britain 660,000 Ireland 120,000 (11% of European)

Jan Feb Mar Apr May Jun Jul Aug Sep Oct Nov Dec

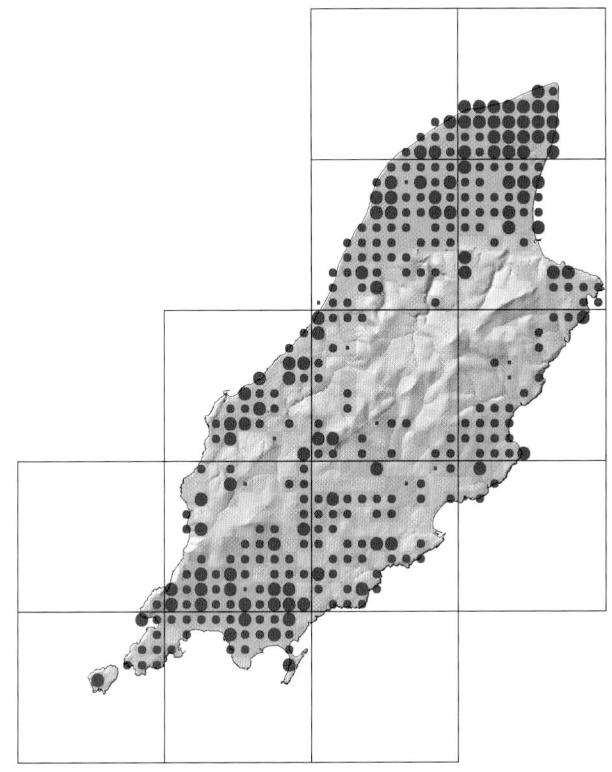
Summer presence and breeding status

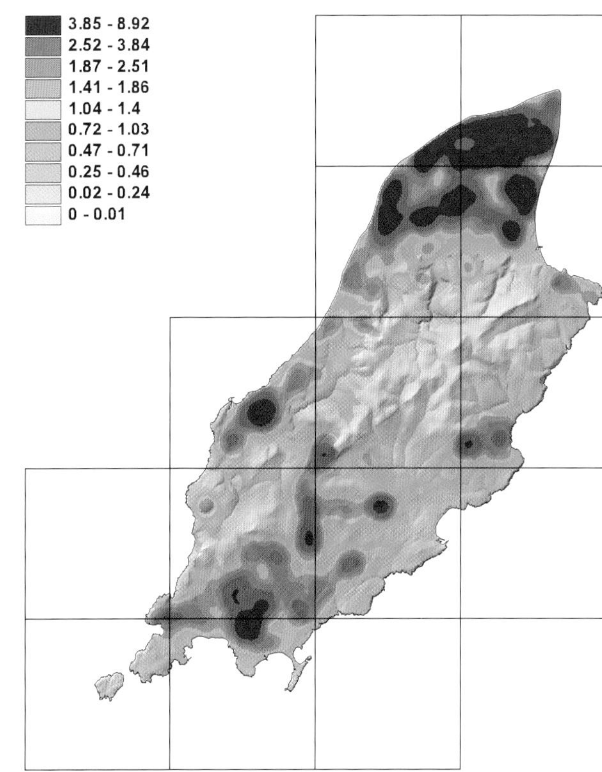

Breeding abundance

Wood Warbler
Phylloscopus sibilatrix

Manx: *Kiaulleyder Keylley*

On the Isle of Man Wood Warblers breed only rarely and are infrequently seen as passage migrants. Consequently many people on the Island are probably unfamiliar with the species and could mistake it for the very similar Willow Warbler. Wood Warblers are slightly larger, however, and have a brighter lemon-yellow throat and paler breast, which contrasts with the clean white of the belly.

The species favours mainly closed canopy, broad-leaved woodlands that have only a sparse, low ground cover in which it nests. It is particularly associated with beech woods and oak forests, this latter habitat preference also being shared by two other characteristic species, Redstart and Pied Flycatcher, which in common with Wood Warbler are also rare or absent as breeding birds on the Island. In common with most warblers food taken is almost entirely insects and other invertebrates.

The breeding distribution of Wood Warblers extends from the British Isles in the west, east to southern Siberia, reaching north as far as the Arctic Circle and south to northern Greece (MA). Within the British Isles only small numbers breed in Ireland, with concentrations in the upland oakwoods of Devon, Wales and the Marches, parts of western Scotland and the Great Glen (1988–91 Atlas). On the Isle of Man, it is apparent that Wood Warblers seldom breed, with only three of the eight records obtained during the summer research period thought to be of breeding birds: one in Glen Auldyn, one in Ballasalla and the other in Dhoon Glen, where the species has bred previously. The remaining five records were all of birds considered to be on migration.

The species is an uncommon passage migrant on the Calf and the main Island, most records being after the third week of April. Records after the breeding season are few, with none after the middle of September in the years of the MBA research. The breeding localities of Wood Warbler passing through the Island are unknown, but presumably most are going to or have come from northern England or Scotland. Birds from the British Isles population appear to migrate through Italy and from there are thought to cross the Sahara to winter in equatorial Africa (MA).

Kermode knew of no records of Wood Warblers, while Ralfe mentions individual birds at Rhenass Glen (1901), Ballamoar, Patrick, and 'a number in full song' in Elfin Glen in May 1905, on the same day as the Patrick record. Madoc had only a handful of records, but these indicated both spring and autumn passage and he also knew of breeding. C&J, with the benefit of information from the Calf, were able to list the species as a scarce, but regular, passage migrant, which has bred on the Isle of Man. Despite a considerable increase in observer effort during the MBA research period, the Wood Warbler remains a scarce passage migrant that only very occasionally breeds on the main Island.

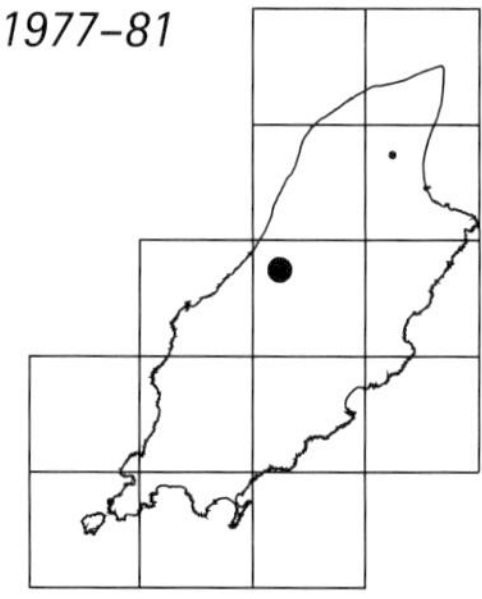

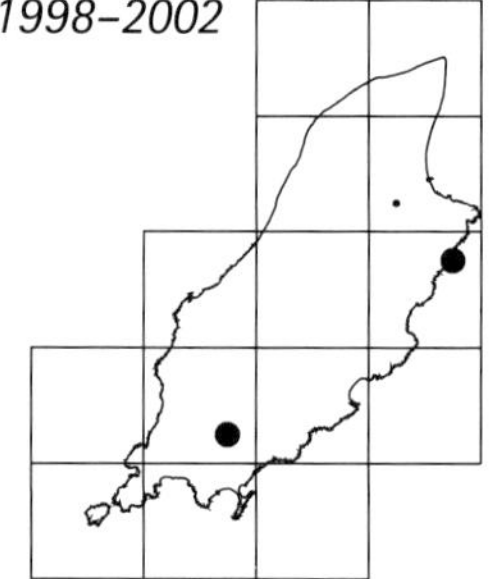

Breeding	Grid squares:	Isle of Man 7 (1%)
		Britain 1,270 Ireland 28 Total 1,298 (34%)
	Population:	Isle of Man 3
		Britain 17,200 Ireland 30 (<1% of European)

Jan	Feb	Mar	Apr	May	Jun	Jul	Aug	Sep	Oct	Nov	Dec

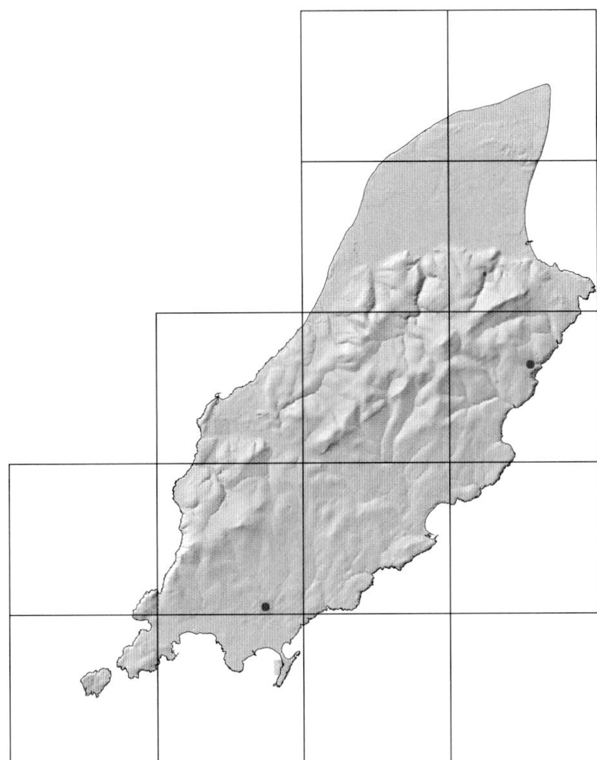

Summer presence and breeding status

Chiffchaff (Common Chiffchaff)
Phylloscopus collybita

Manx: *Beealerey*

Chiffchaffs are the smallest of the *Phylloscopus* warblers which breed on the Isle of Man. Though they are very similar in appearance to Willow Warblers they are overall more drab, with darker legs and shorter wings. The song is easily the most distinctive feature of Chiffchaff, the rather monotonous, often repeated, 'chiff-chaff' being unmistakable.

The Chiffchaff is a species of mature lowland woodland, preferably broad-leaved or mixed, and it can be found in parks and large gardens (BWP). Locally, it was found on the fringes of some conifer plantations, but only where some broad-leaved trees were present. Food is almost entirely insects, with some fruit taken in autumn (BWP).

The species' breeding range extends from north-west Africa, throughout most of Europe and as far east as about 155°E. Within the British Isles Chiff-chaffs are common throughout the south, including much of Ireland, becoming scarce in the English Midlands and sparse in Scotland. The British Isles population is considered stable, though it is subject to periodic fluctuations (1988–91 Atlas). On the Isle of Man the Chiffchaff is a common passage migrant and summer visitor. The first migrants of spring can be seen as early as February, with the main movement of birds through and to the Island occurring in March and April. The distribution of breeding birds is rather scattered, broadly reflecting the presence of preferred habitat, especially stands of riverine trees. Areas of relatively high abundance are generally associated with rivers and streams, allowing birds to extend into the uplands, where they are otherwise absent. The more or less continuous deciduous woodland and adjacent curragh that runs west from Ramsey along the foot of the northern hills clearly suits the species.

Chiffchaffs undertake return migration from August, with a peak of movement evident in the second half of September, though birds can still be passing through the Island during October and occasionally into November. It is likely that these migrants are a combination of Manx Chiffchaffs and others from northern Britain, although some continental Chiffchaffs are also known to enter the British Isles (MA). Ringing data from Britain suggest that the main wintering areas for British breeding Chiffchaffs are around the Mediterranean and south of the Sahara in tropical West Africa (MA).

Within the British Isles, Chiffchaffs are present in the winter, though it is unknown whether most of these birds have bred there (WA, MA) or whether, as with Blackcaps, they are migrants from northern Europe. It is possible, therefore, that some of the late observations of Chiffchaffs on migration in November may be of individuals arriving on the Island, rather than leaving it.

The majority of winter records within the British Isles are obtained south of a line from the Wash to the Mersey, though in some winters the species is seen as far north as Orkney (WA). On the Isle of Man Chiffchaffs were recorded in each of the five winter periods, though rather fewer were seen in the last two winters than in the earlier three. The species is known to show fluctuations in numbers between winters in the British Isles (WA). As they are less vocal outside the breeding season, it is likely that a greater proportion of birds go undetected in winter than in summer. All of the winter records locally were from low ground, many from near the coast, where higher temperatures will support the necessary insects to sustain birds, the species apparently retaining a wholly insectivorous diet even in winter (WA).

Kermode considered the species to be a 'regular summer visitor, but not numerous', while Ralfe knew of few records. Madoc thought the Chiffchaff to be a particularly early migrant, but gives no estimate of abundance, although he appears to consider it more common than did the earlier authors. C&J describe the Chiffchaff as a 'common summer visitor and passage migrant which sometimes winters in small numbers'. C&J concluded that there has been an increase in breeding Chiffchaffs on the Isle of Man since the earlier decades of the twentieth century. On the evidence of a wider breeding distribution during the current research, that increase appears to have continued since C&J.

1977–81

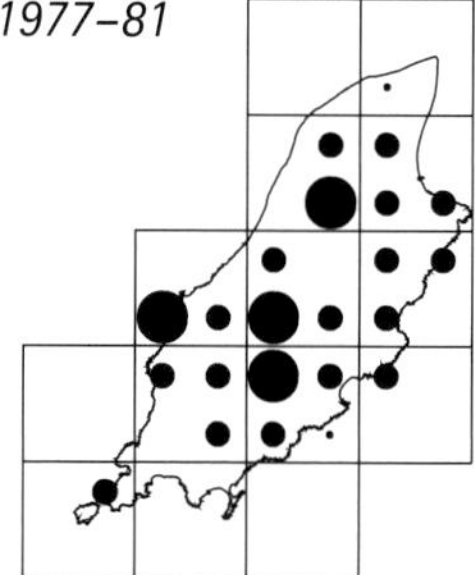

1998–2002

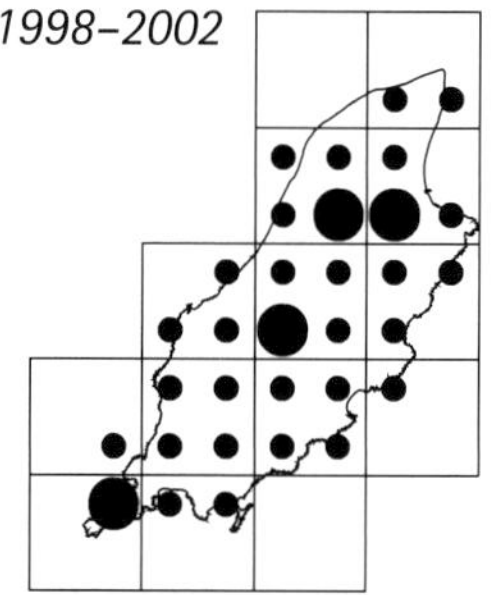

Breeding	Grid squares:	Isle of Man 212 (32%) Britain 2,100 Ireland 836 Total 2,936 (76%)
	Population:	Isle of Man 183–185 Britain 640,000 Ireland 290,000 (6% of European)
Wintering	Grid squares:	Isle of Man 23 (3%) Britain and Ireland 667 (17%)
	Population:	Isle of Man <50 Britain and Ireland 500+

Jan	Feb	Mar	Apr	May	Jun	Jul	Aug	Sep	Oct	Nov	Dec

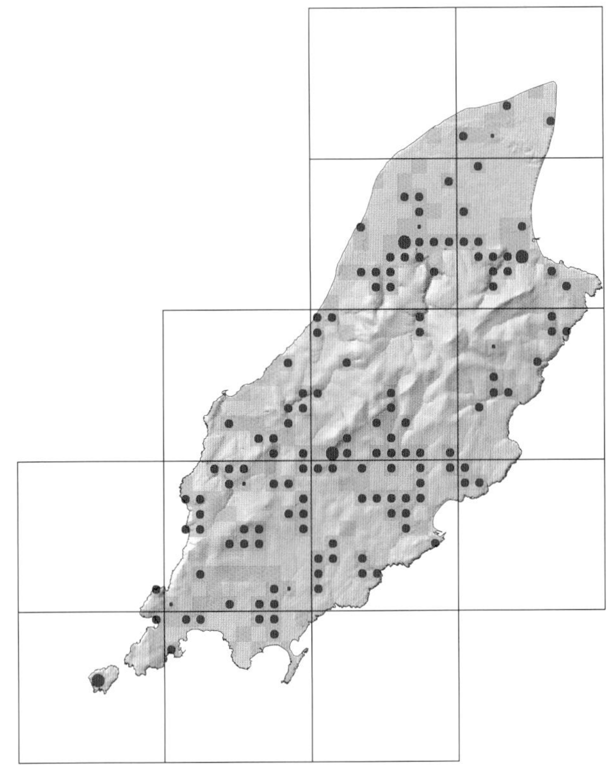

Summer presence and breeding status

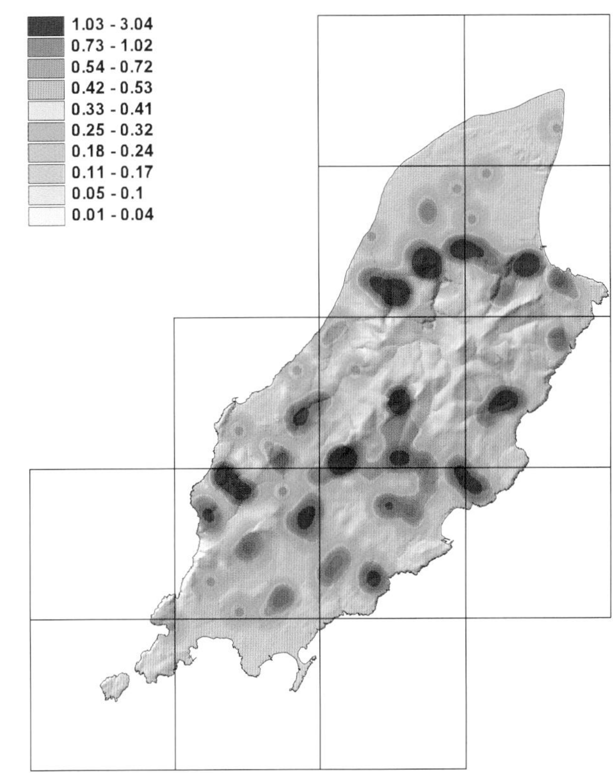

Breeding abundance

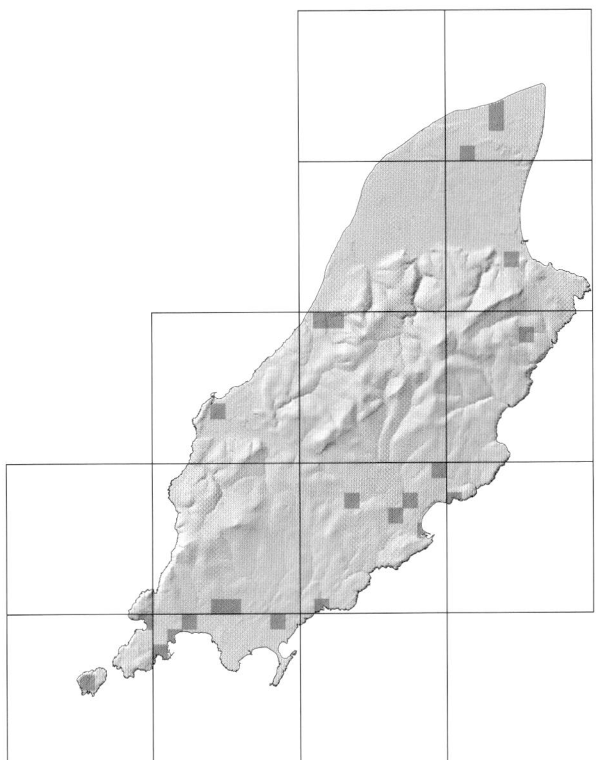

Winter presence

Individual Sponsors – Mrs. E Raynor, Mr. A Sapsford

Willow Warbler
Phylloscopus trochilus

Manx: *Drean vane* = White Wren

Despite being one of the commonest summer visitors and passage migrants on the Island, Willow Warblers are probably unknown to many non-bird-watchers. Their song, though distinctive and pleasing to the ear, is softly delivered and can be swamped by more vibrant songsters, while their greyish-brown-green upperparts and pale yellow underparts do not immediately catch the eye. When seen clearly, however, Willow Warblers prove to be attractive enough and in suitable habitat the combined song of a number of competing males can be almost continuous.

Provided shrub and scrub layers are available, Willow Warblers will utilise a wide range of habitats for breeding, the presence of trees not being a prerequisite. They will settle in wooded areas and make use of a range of tree species, preferring those with the most easily accessible insect life, which together with spiders, forms the bulk of the diet (BWP). The nest is usually low down in dense vegetation.

The Willow Warbler has an extensive breeding range, from Ireland in the west, east through Europe to eastern Siberia. It does not occur in Iceland and is rare or even absent as a breeding species south of 45°N. Within the British Isles it is widespread, being missing only from Shetland, from areas of high ground and from some lowland areas (1988–91 Atlas), where suitable habitat is lacking. On the Island, as in other parts of the British Isles, most Willow Warblers arrive during April, though in each of the five years of the MBA research, one or more birds were noted in the last week of March. Migration can continue until early May, the timing in each year influenced by prevailing weather. Willow Warblers are widespread on the Island, with breeding taking place in most suitable lowland areas. No evidence of breeding was obtained above 390m. The species is largely absent from most urban areas and is not frequent immediately adjacent to the coast, probably due to a shortage of suitable nest sites.

Most Willow Warblers have only one brood, young starting to migrate from mid-July onwards with adult movement evident from early August (MA). By mid-September migration from and through the Isle of Man is largely completed, though in some years birds occur in late September and, rarely, in early October. Ringing data from throughout the British Isles, including those from the Calf of Man, suggest that all Willow Warblers nesting in the British Isles winter in West Africa south of the Sahara, particularly the Ivory Coast and Ghana (1988–91 Atlas, MA). UK ringing data also indicate that some continental Willow Warblers migrate through the British Isles, presumably including the Isle of Man.

Kermode considered the Willow Warbler to be a 'regular summer visitor. Generally distributed and fairly abundant' while Ralfe thought it 'pretty plentiful' and Madoc 'immensely common throughout the Island'. C&J considered it a 'common summer visitor and passage migrant'. There are no detailed numerical data from which to assess whether numbers have changed greatly; the Willow Warbler is still clearly a common bird on the Island, with evidence of breeding throughout. In the British Isles the population seems to have been largely stable in recent decades (1988–91 Atlas) though decline has been noted since the MBA research period.

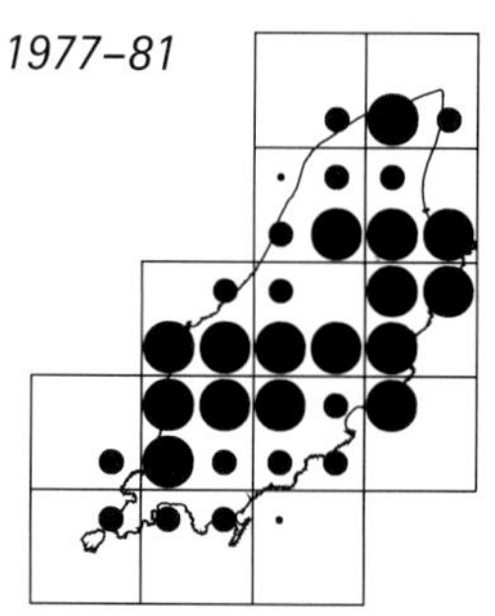

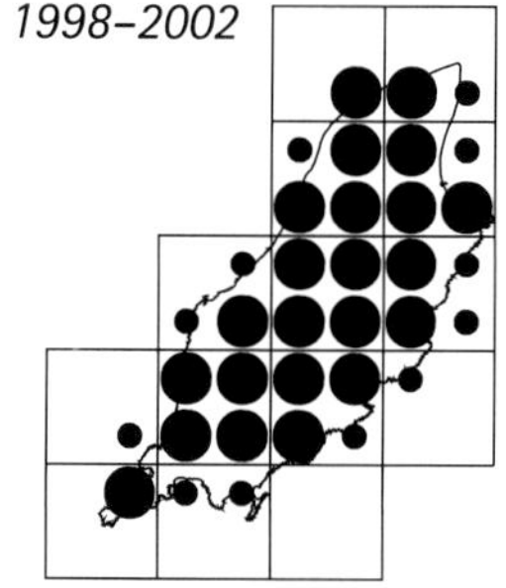

Breeding	Grid squares:	Isle of Man 476 (72%) Britain 2,602 Ireland 927 Total 3,529 (91%)
	Population:	Isle of Man 1,298–1,402 Britain 2,300,000 Ireland 830,000 (8% of European)

Jan Feb Mar Apr May Jun Jul Aug Sep Oct Nov Dec

Corporate Sponsor – The late G W Walker

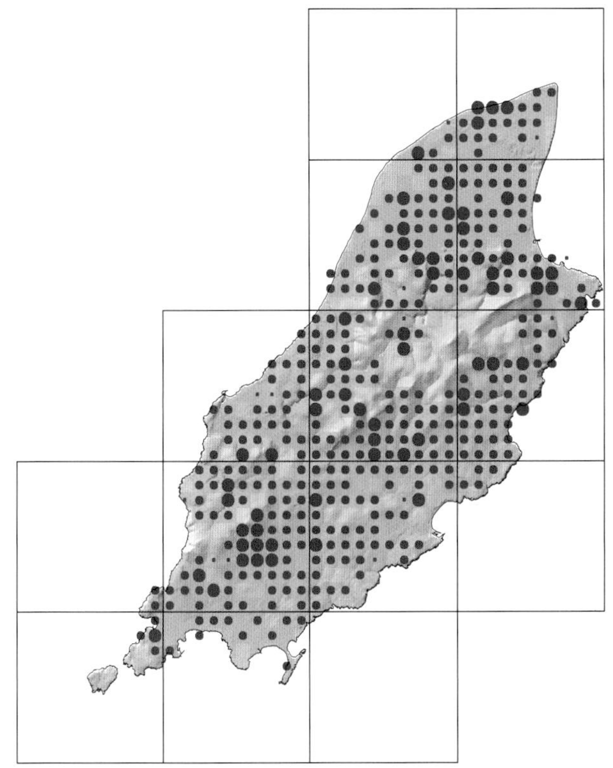

Summer presence and breeding status

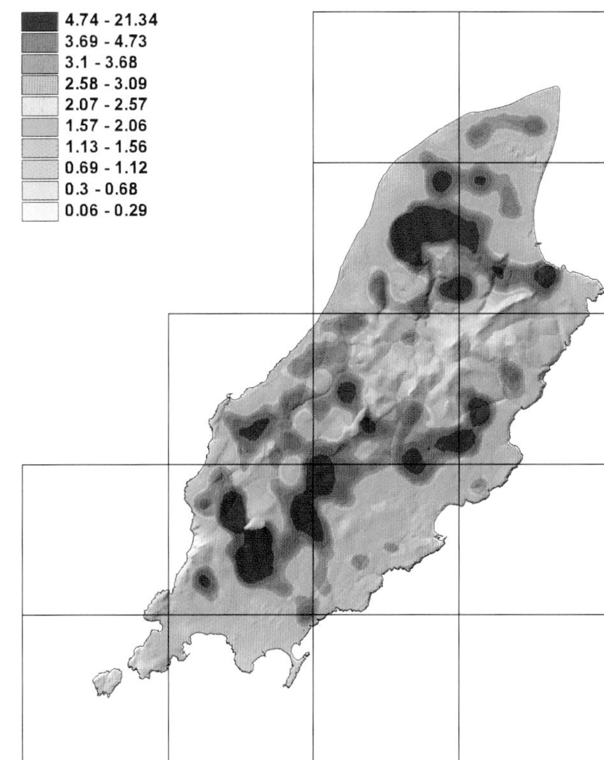

Breeding abundance

Individual Sponsors – Mr. J Davey, Mrs. S Kelly

Goldcrest
Regulus regulus

Manx: *Ushag y fuygh* = Bird of the timber

The Goldcrest is the smallest bird native to the British Isles and is one of the smallest songbirds in the world. As is generally the case with small birds it needs to feed frequently in order to sustain itself; thus Goldcrests are always on the move, flitting through the upper branches of conifers or hanging upside down in the constant search for food, although it is usually the characteristic high-pitched 'zi-zi-zi' calls which first advertise their presence. They will also feed in lower vegetation such as european gorse and are frequently found in mature gardens. It is then that the yellow crest of the female or fiery orange crest of the male is most easily seen.

Dense stands of well-grown conifers of several species are the preferred habitat during the breeding season, though larch and Scots pine are less attractive. Relatively new plantations with trees less than about 2m in height are also used, while parks, large gardens and areas of predominantly broadleaved woodland are favoured, only when suitable conifers are available. Outside the breeding season Goldcrests range freely into deciduous trees and shrubs and out onto open heathlands or even into reedbeds (BWP). They feed primarily on insects and spiders obtained mainly from the tree canopy, but will also take some insects caught by hovering and others may be taken from spiders' webs (BWP).

The breeding range of the Goldcrest extends across much of the Palearctic, from western Europe to central Asia north to the Arctic Circle, with an additional geographically isolated population in China (EBA). Within the British Isles it is one of the more widespread species, being absent only in generally treeless areas, including the most northerly and north-westerly Scottish Isles and the Fens (1988–91 Atlas). On the Isle of Man the Goldcrest is a common resident, summer visitor and passage migrant, with breeding taking place throughout more of the Island than found by C&J. It is largely absent as a breeding species from the northern plain and the uplands, except where suitable plantations exist, and also from some treeless coastal fringes, including Langness, the Mull Peninsula and the Calf of Man. Pockets of high density reflect the distribution of the Island's conifer plantations, though moderate densities are to be found throughout many lowland areas with scattered conifers.

For Goldcrests the main period of autumn migration is from September to November and during this period very many can occur on the Isle of Man and particularly the Calf of Man; the numbers involved being too large to have originated from the Isle of Man alone. These movements probably include birds from the northern parts of the British Isles or northern Europe, heading for southern England or further south into Continental Europe for the winter. Ringing data from the Calf and Britain suggest that many Goldcrests nesting in the British Isles are sedentary, but substantial numbers, mainly young birds, migrate to southern Europe for the winter (1988–91 Atlas, MA). Spring passage occurs during March and April and during this time further large numbers are caught on the Calf, a combination of spring and autumn passage resulting in 4,652 birds being ringed in 1989. During the current survey period an average of 950 birds were ringed annually.

In winter, Goldcrests on the Island have a similar distribution to that for the summer, though they are present through rather more of the northern plain. Areas of high abundance are still apparent in dense conifer plantations, though the winter survey suggests that the species largely abandons the higher areas frequented in summer.

Kermode considered the Goldcrest to be 'resident' and 'generally distributed', but 'less plentiful of late years' and Ralfe thought it 'in winter at least a very abundant species'. Madoc gave no clear estimate of abundance, and C&J considered it a 'common breeding bird, present throughout the year and abundant as passage migrant'. As with many other species, it is, in the absence of detailed numerical data, difficult to assess whether numbers have changed. In Britain there seems to have been little change in recent decades (1988–91 Atlas) and presumably this may also apply on the Island.

1977–81

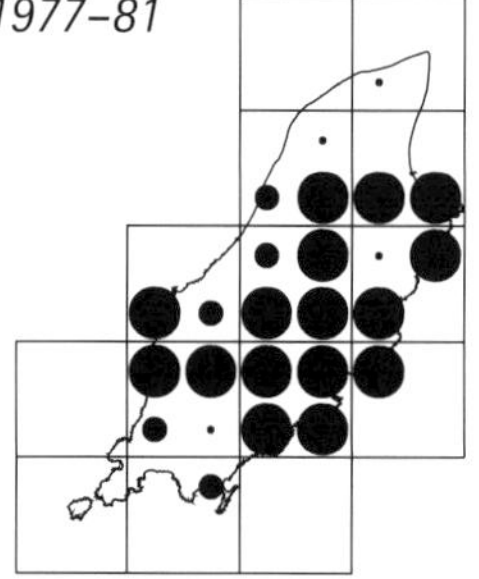

1998–2002

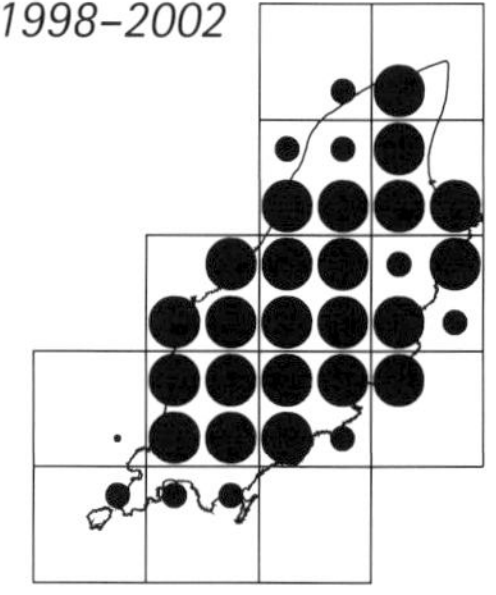

Breeding	Grid squares:	Isle of Man 386 (58%) Britain 2,327 Ireland 852 Total 3,179 (82%)
	Population:	Isle of Man 915–1,262 Britain 560,000 Ireland 300,000 (8% of European)
Wintering	Grid squares:	Isle of Man 347 (52%) Britain and Ireland 3,038 (79%)
	Population:	Isle of Man 3,000+ Britain and Ireland 2–4 million

Jan	Feb	Mar	Apr	May	Jun	Jul	Aug	Sep	Oct	Nov	Dec

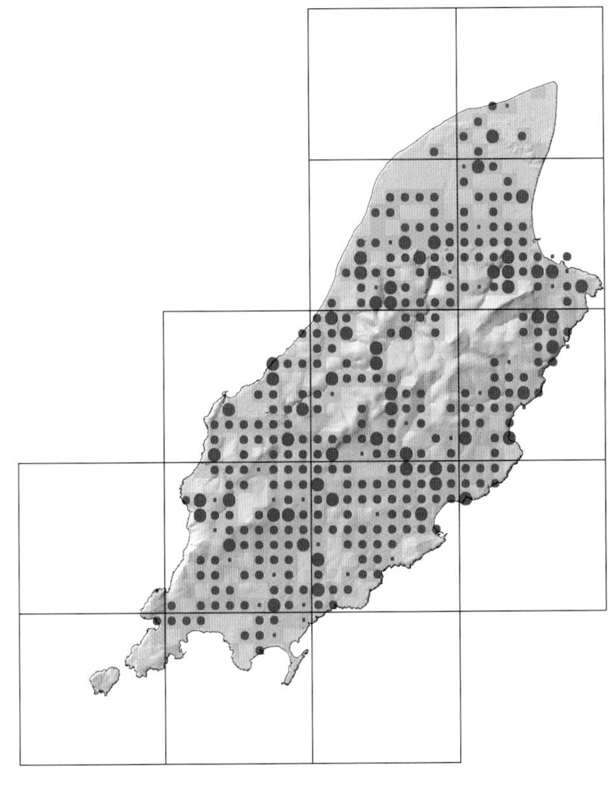

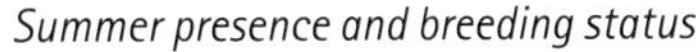

Summer presence and breeding status

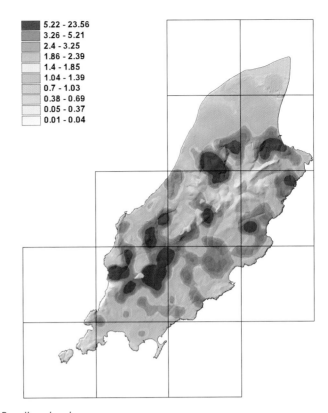

- 5.22 - 23.56
- 3.26 - 5.21
- 2.4 - 3.25
- 1.86 - 2.39
- 1.4 - 1.85
- 1.04 - 1.39
- 0.7 - 1.03
- 0.38 - 0.69
- 0.05 - 0.37
- 0.01 - 0.04

Breeding abundance

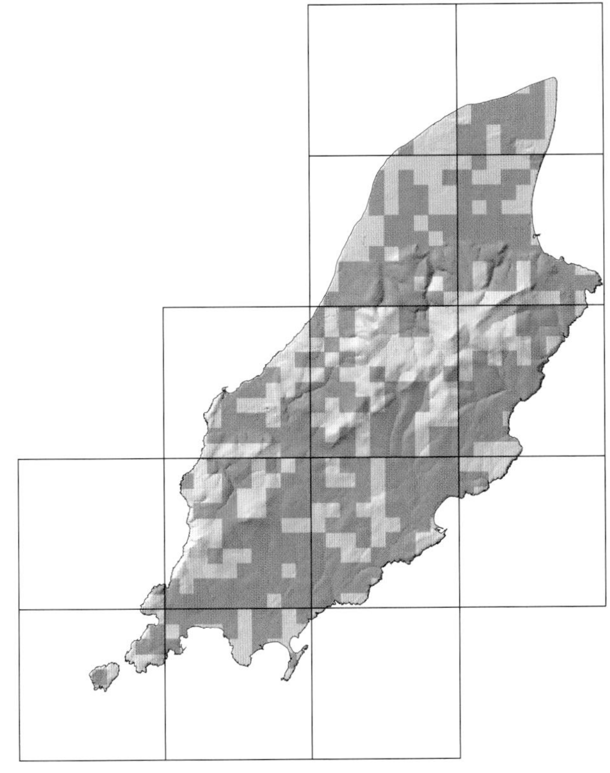

Winter presence

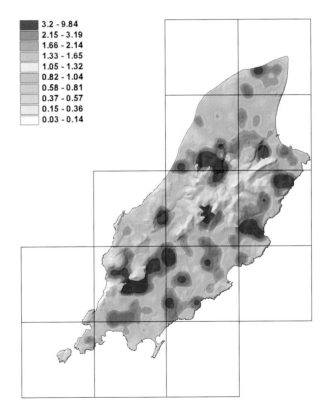

- 3.2 - 9.84
- 2.15 - 3.19
- 1.66 - 2.14
- 1.33 - 1.65
- 1.05 - 1.32
- 0.82 - 1.04
- 0.58 - 0.81
- 0.37 - 0.57
- 0.15 - 0.36
- 0.03 - 0.14

Winter abundance

Individual Sponsors – Mr. B Jones, Mr. A C C Laidlaw, Mrs. I Morris, the late Mrs. M Sharpe, Ms. E Stevenson, Mr. R A Watson, Mrs. G Wheatley

Spotted Flycatcher
Muscicapa striata

Manx: *Skybbyltagh breck*

The Spotted Flycatcher is an unobtrusive species, both in terms of plumage, which lacks any obvious features, and song, which is softly delivered and easily overlooked. Despite, or possibly because of, this the Spotted Flycatcher is always a welcome sight. The first indication of presence is usually when one flies from a branch to catch an insect in mid-air, often returning to the same perching point.

Spotted Flycatchers will breed in almost any sort of habitat that contains trees, though within the British Isles open woodland is preferred, including that found within farmland, parks and large mature gardens. In their wider European range mountain forests and low bushes within steppe habitat are used (EBA). Nest sites are varied and include shallow holes in trees, fallen tree roots and buildings, the species taking well to carefully sited open-fronted nest boxes. The main prey taken is insects, normally caught in flight, though birds will forage among foliage to pick insects off leaves and branches. Especially in autumn berries can be taken, while during incubation females will include calcium-rich food such as woodlice in their diet (1988–91 Atlas).

The species breeds across much of the western and central Palearctic with the subspecies *Muscicapa striata striata* breeding from Ireland and north-west Africa east across to the Urals (MA). In the British Isles Spotted Flycatchers are widely distributed, though population densities are notably lower in northern and western Scotland and in western Ireland (1988–91 Atlas), possibly a result of the cooler and wetter climate in summer in these areas. Over the last 25 years the population of Spotted Flycatchers in the British Isles has declined by more than 50% (Anon 2002). On the Isle of Man the Spotted Flycatcher is a common passage migrant, but breeds only in small numbers. Favoured areas for nesting include wooded parts of the northern plain and the central valley, in the south-east around St Marks and on the western and northern fringes of the northern hills. The low breeding density in the Isle of Man results from the same climate cause as for western Scotland and Ireland.

Spotted Flycatchers are one of the last summer migrants to arrive on the Isle of Man, typically not being seen until the first week of May, with numbers peaking in the middle of the month. On the main Island most reports are of single birds, but on the Calf arrivals of more than 50 birds have been recorded. Return migration, which starts in late July (MA), continues through August, with the last records usually being in late September or, rarely, in early October. Ringing data indicate that British breeding Spotted Flycatchers move south through Europe and winter in west and southern Africa (MA); the Manx population almost certainly does the same.

Kermode knew of only two records of Spotted Flycatchers on the Isle of Man and Ralfe mentioned several records, but clearly regarded the species as uncommon. Madoc considered the species to occur in all parts of the Island and to be getting commoner, and C&J described it as a 'fairly common but locally distributed summer visitor and common passage migrant'. Though the species has probably increased considerably since the time of Kermode and Ralfe it is likely that, on the evidence of fewer 5km squares being occupied during the MBA research than in the time of C&J, it has undergone a decline since the mid-1980s.

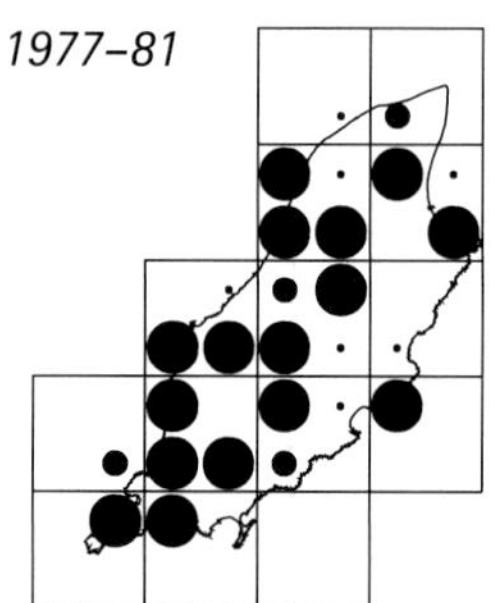

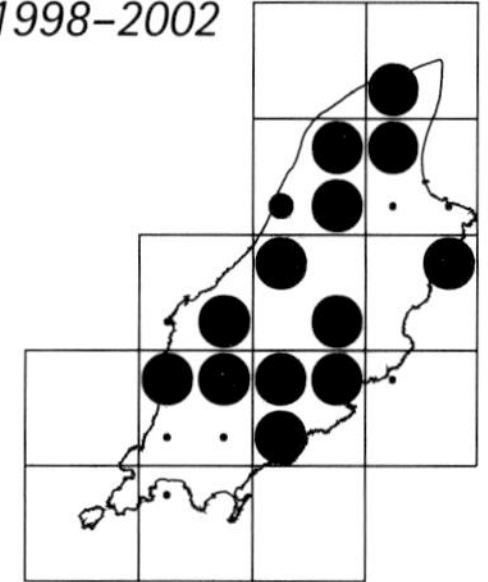

Breeding	Grid squares:	Isle of Man 77 (12%) Britain 2,378 Ireland 728 Total 3,106 (80%)
	Population:	Isle of Man 53-54 Britain 120,000 Ireland 35,000 (2% of European)

Jan Feb Mar Apr May Jun Jul Aug Sep Oct Nov Dec

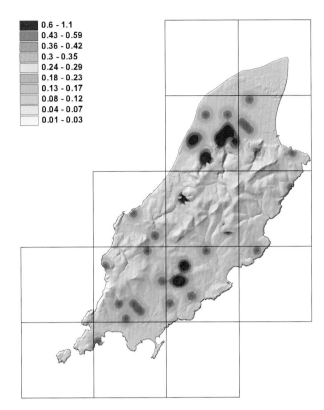

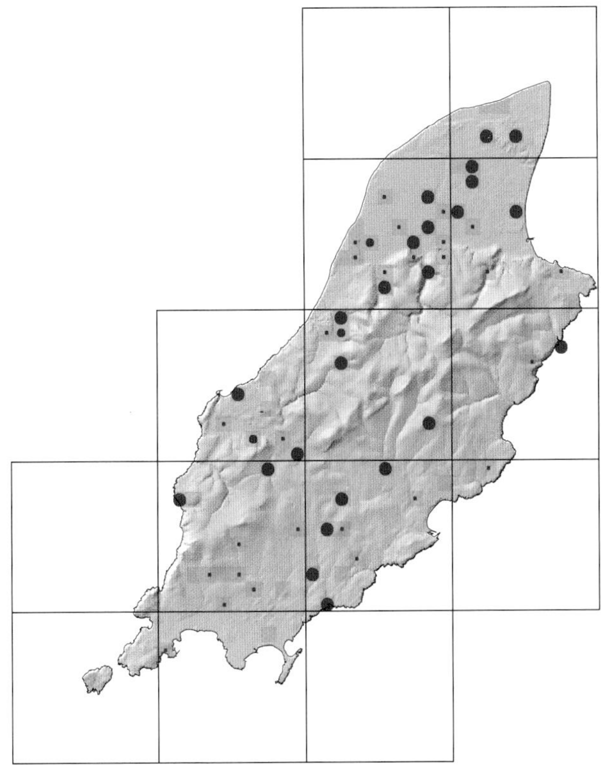

Summer presence and breeding status

0.6 - 1.1
0.43 - 0.59
0.36 - 0.42
0.3 - 0.35
0.24 - 0.29
0.18 - 0.23
0.13 - 0.17
0.08 - 0.12
0.04 - 0.07
0.01 - 0.03

Breeding abundance

Long-tailed Tit
Aegithalos caudatus

Manx: *Caillagh Veg yn Arbyl*

A combination of black, white and pink plumage, together with a remarkably long tail, make the Long-tailed Tit one of our more easily recognised, and also most appealing, small birds. Outside the breeding season they form large family flocks, which are always on the move in the search for food. They stay in contact with each other by noisy high-pitched calls which often give the first indication of their presence.

The Long-tailed Tit's preferred habitat is broad-leaved or mixed woodland with a substantial shrub layer. Edge habitats are favoured, so Long-tailed Tits are also found in scrub, hedgerows and gardens (MA). They feed almost entirely on insects, including the eggs and larvae of moths and butterflies (BWP). The nest is a compact, domed, structure of moss woven with cobwebs, with an outside covering of lichen and over 1,000 feathers used as lining (BWP).

The species has a very large breeding range extending across almost all of Europe, from southern Spain and southern Italy to northern Norway and as far east as China and Japan (BWP, MA). In the British Isles it is more common in the south, but with high ground and large urban areas being poorly populated (1988–91 Atlas). On the Isle of Man the Long-tailed Tit is fairly common as a breeding bird, though it is absent over above 180m, where suitable trees are largely absent, as well as over much of the agricultural northern and southern lowlands where stands of trees can be discontinuous, inhibiting movement of this highly sedentary species. Denser populations are evident along the central and Baldwin valleys and in the area of Ballaugh Curragh, where the mix of willow carr and silver birch with the associated scrub understorey evidently suits the species particularly well.

The British Isles population of Long-tailed Tits is non-migratory, 95% of birds ringed as adults being recovered within 20km, though this distance increases to 60km for birds ringed as immatures. For both adult and immature birds the mean distance is only 2km (MA). It is likely that Long-tailed Tits present in winter on the Isle of Man are all from the local breeding population together with young of the year. It is possible that some might move in from other parts of the British Isles, though the species does not like to cross large expanses of water as it is not a strong flier. As such, records on the Calf of Man are always noteworthy and although flocks in excess of 40 birds have been recorded there, mainly in the autumn, these were all considered to be birds from the main island, probably roaming in search of food.

The range in winter is broadly similar to that for summer, although in wintertime Long-tailed Tits may appear in almost any low-lying area of the Island, where there are trees or bushes. In winter flocks establish foraging territories that are larger than the breeding territories held by pairs during the summer. Such flocks can exceed 50 birds, providing survival advantage as they will roost communally and so be better able to withstand cold weather. Although winter distribution on the Island is largely the same as for the summer, the species is less evident in the central valley, an area where cold air can often lie. During the winters of the MBA research it became clear that Long-tailed Tits frequently visit feeding stations in gardens, presenting a memorable sight, when as many as eight of these quaint little birds might eagerly jostle for position on a nut feeder. Many members of the public reported such events, often providing observers with their first acquaintance with the species. Such behaviour is mentioned by Lack (1986) as occurring in 'very severe' weather conditions. More routine use of garden feeders would therefore appear to be a relatively recent but increasingly widespread event, and may do much to benefit the fortunes of the species on the Island.

Kermode described the Long-tailed Tit as being 'resident in small numbers, which are increased by migrants in winter', and Ralfe considered it 'still uncommon' although 'perhaps increasing, at least as a winter visitor'. Both of these authors provided reports suggesting the species had only recently appeared on the Island (i.e. during the late nineteenth century). Madoc suggested that the species was 'a most uncommon visitor to the Island', but by 1985 C&J considered the Long-tailed Tit to be a fairly common resident and possible winter visitor. The suggestion by previous authors that the Long-tailed Tit is more abundant on the Island in winter, and hence a winter visitor, may be a mistaken impression based on the large flock sizes at this time of year being more likely to draw attention.

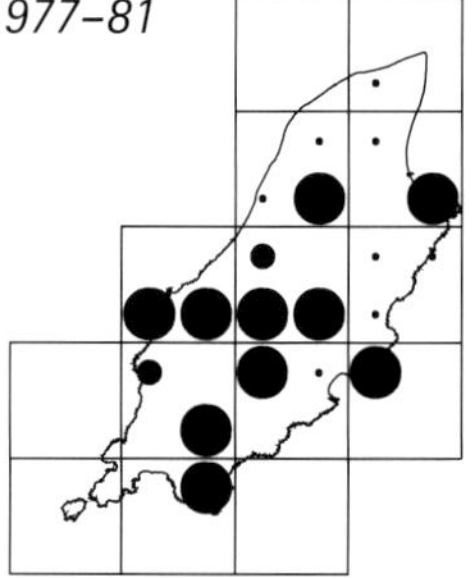

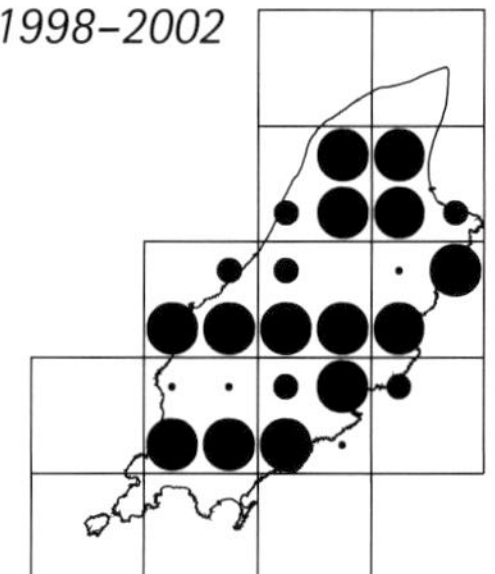

Breeding	Grid squares:	Isle of Man 178 (27%) Britain 2,106 Ireland 546 Total 2,652 (69%)
	Population:	Isle of Man 136–169 Britain 210,000 Ireland 40,000 (8% of European)
Wintering	Grid squares:	Isle of Man 167 (25%) Britain and Ireland 2,575 (67%)
	Population:	Isle of Man <500 Britain and Ireland 96,000

Jan	Feb	Mar	Apr	May	Jun	Jul	Aug	Sep	Oct	Nov	Dec

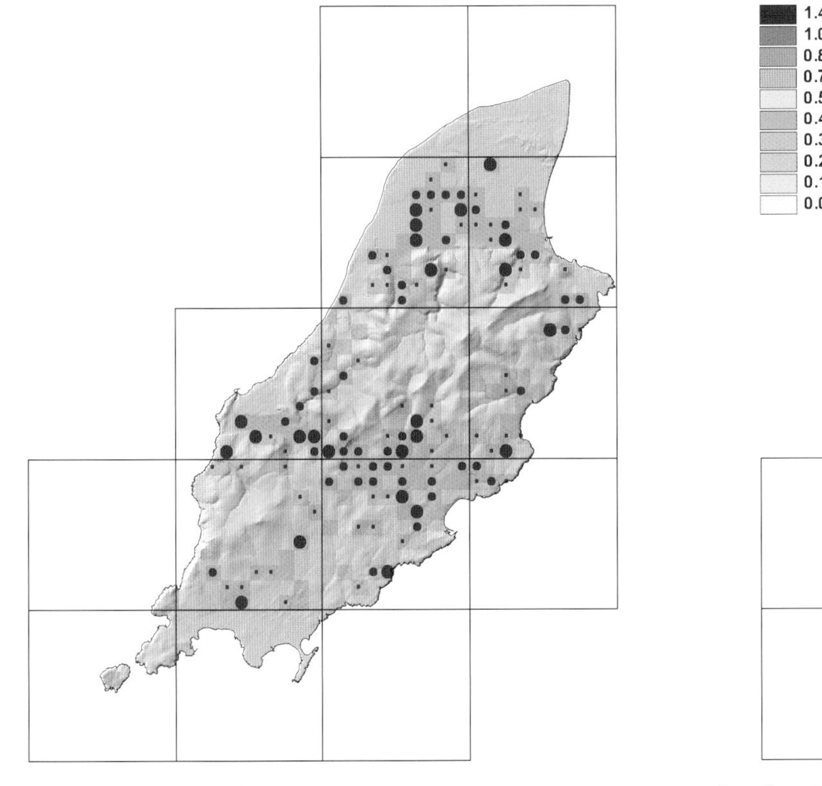

Summer presence and breeding status

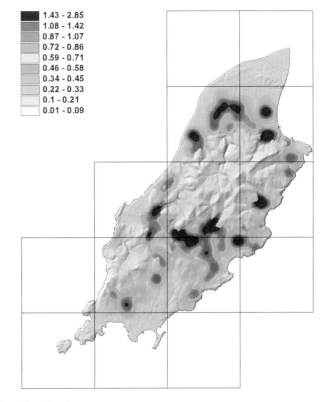

Breeding abundance

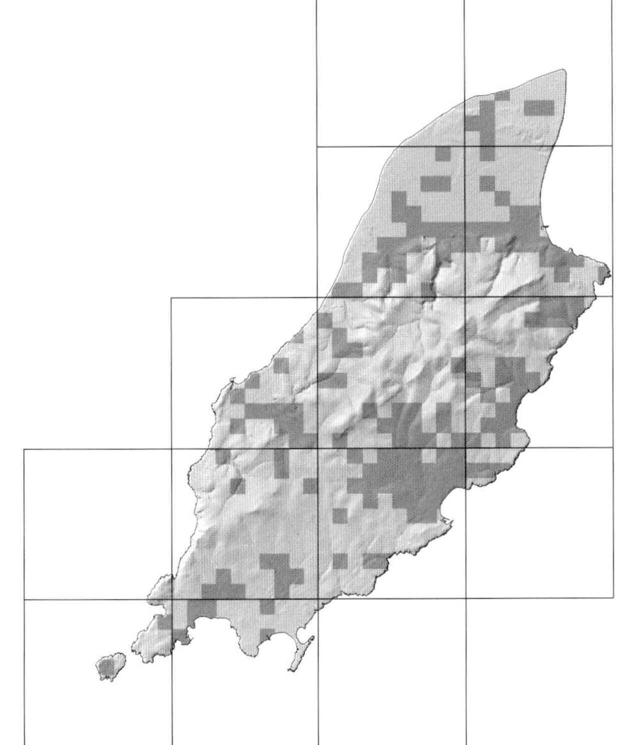

Winter presence

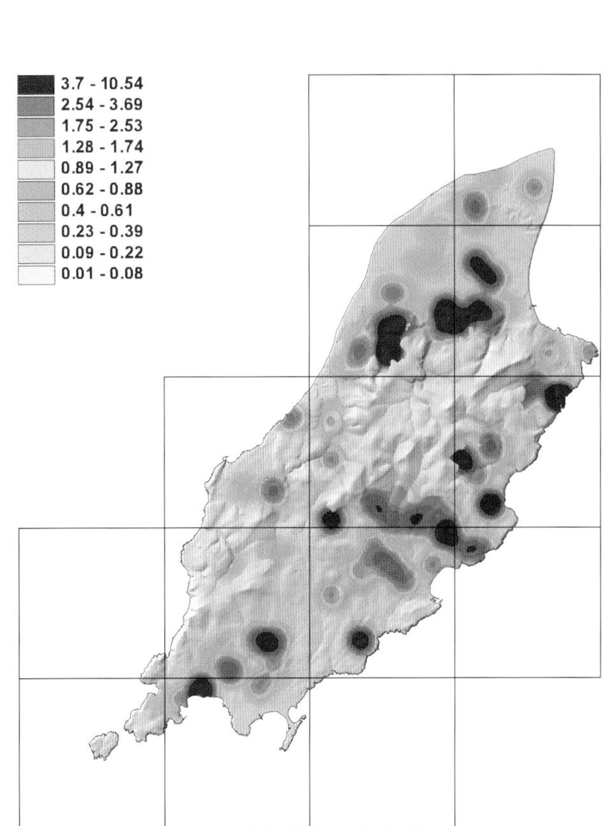

Winter abundance

Individual Sponsors – Mr. M J Brown, Dr. J P Cullen, the late Mr. B Karran, Mr. C Speak

Blue Tit
Cyanistes caeruleus

Manx: *Drean Gorrym*

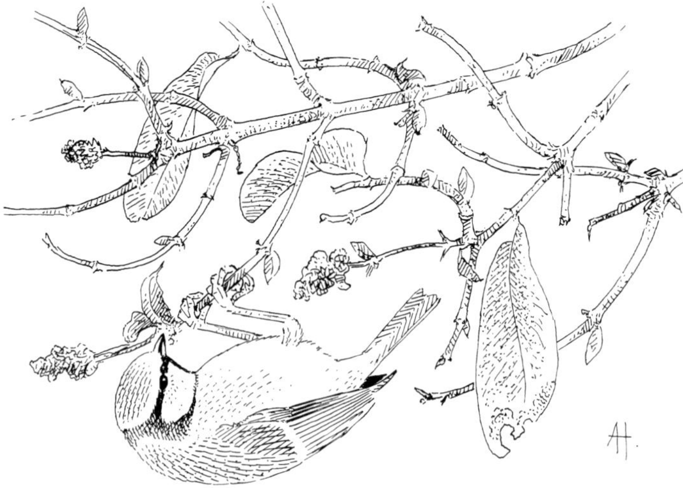

This common and widespread resident is familiar to many. Even in the centre of towns Blue Tits are readily attracted to bird tables and nut feeders, particularly in winter. Their small, round heads are topped with neat blue skull-caps, making their identification relatively straightforward.

Blue Tits occupy a wide range of deciduous, evergreen and mixed woodlands, including parks and gardens. They tend to avoid purely coniferous locations, being primarily adapted to oak woodland (EBA), a habitat that is essentially absent on the Isle of Man. Historically, nests would have been almost exclusively in holes in trees, though now they are also located in holes within man-made structures, such as stone walls and of course, nest boxes, which provide essential nesting opportunities and have doubtless increased the breeding numbers of the species on the Island. Food is mainly insects and spiders, but some fruit and seed are taken outside the breeding season.

Blue Tits have an extensive European breeding range, being missing only from Iceland and Cyprus (EBA). In the British Isles they are absent only from high ground in Scotland, Orkney, Shetland and some of the Hebridean islands, where there is little or no suitable habitat (1988–91 Atlas). Within the Isle of Man, though oak woods are not present, there is much other suitable habitat, thus Blue Tits are widespread, being absent only in treeless areas, such as the uplands, along some coastal areas and the Ayres heath. Areas of high abundance occur along the central valley, across the northern plain and down much of the east coast. It is noticeable that, even in the breeding season, the main towns all have relatively high numbers present.

Blue Tits reared in the British Isles are non-migratory, with analysis of ringing data revealing that 95% of all British and Irish recoveries are within 26km of where they were ringed (MA). Those from northern continental Europe are partial migrants, with some birds likely to reach eastern Britain. As with some other tit species, periodic eruptions occur on the continent, leading to large numbers entering the British Isles in some winters, though there is nothing to suggest that continental birds reach the Isle of Man. On the Calf of Man Blue Tits occur regularly in small numbers in spring and in greater numbers in autumn, but these are likely to be birds from the Isle of Man.

During the winter Blue Tits are less territorial than the related Great Tit, forming mobile flocks that can often attract other species, including other tits, migrant warblers, Long-tailed Tits and Treecreepers (MA). On the Island, winter distribution reflects very closely that for the summer, presence only extending into upland areas where suitable wooded valleys are present, with absences from some exposed, treeless, coastal areas.

Kermode considered Blue Tits to be less common than Great Tits. Ralfe discussed the apparent colonisation of the Isle of Man by the Blue Tit in the late nineteenth century and described the species as 'distributed all over the Island and quickly increasing'. Madoc considered the Blue Tit to be 'immensely common' and C&J describe it as a 'common resident'. From these accounts, and in the absence of numerical data, there is little from which to assess any change in abundance of Manx Blue Tits since Madoc was writing in 1934; they were and remain common. However, as Ralfe pointed out, Wilson (1722) specifically commented on the absence of Blue Tits from the Island and Ralfe also provides evidence of the spread of the species on the Island from the 1870s. It appears therefore that Blue Tits colonised the Isle of Man and spread rapidly in the late nineteenth century and have been common here since that time. In the UK there has been little change in recent years (1988–91 Atlas).

1977–81

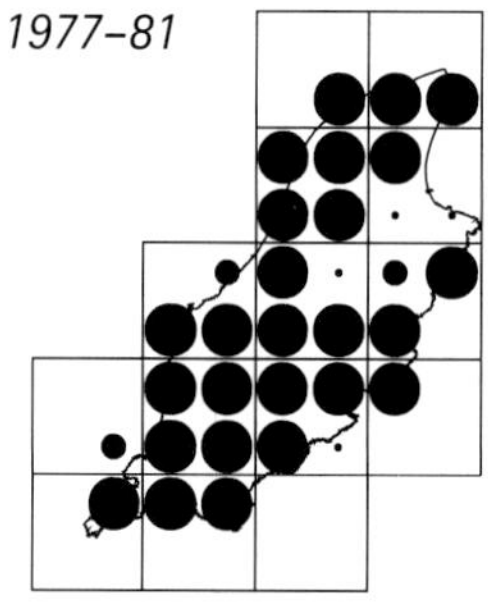

1998–2002

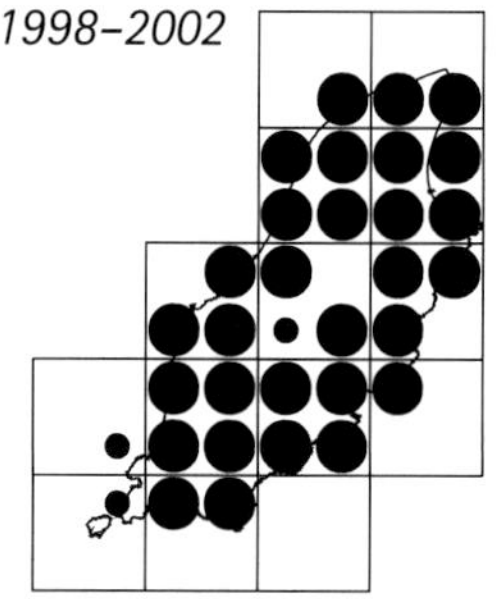

Breeding	Grid squares:	Isle of Man 397 (60%) Britain 2,480 Ireland 930 Total 3,410 (88%)
	Population:	Isle of Man 707–1,122 Britain 3,300,000 Ireland 1,100,000 (25% of European)
Wintering	Grid squares:	Isle of Man 370 (56%) Britain and Ireland 3,395 (88%)
	Population:	Isle of Man 3,000+ Britain and Ireland 15 million

Jan	Feb	Mar	Apr	May	Jun	Jul	Aug	Sep	Oct	Nov	Dec

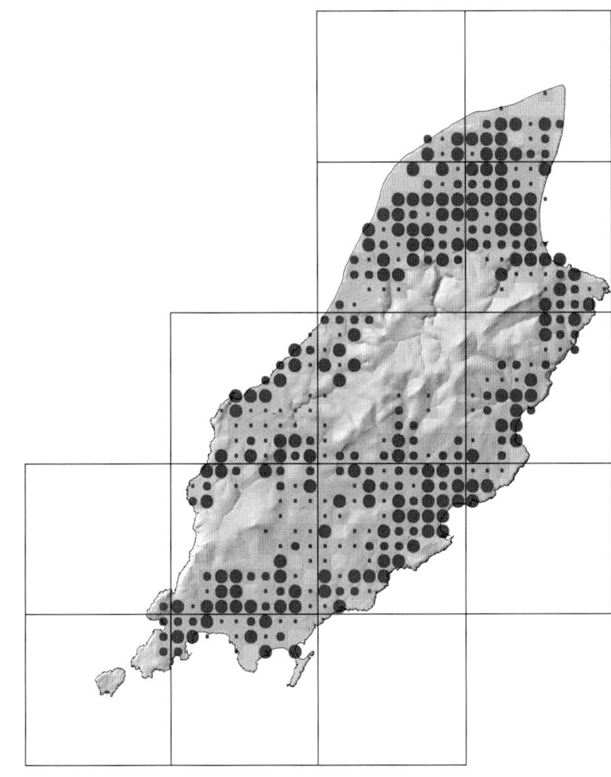

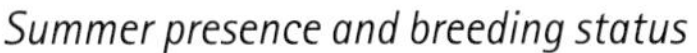
Summer presence and breeding status

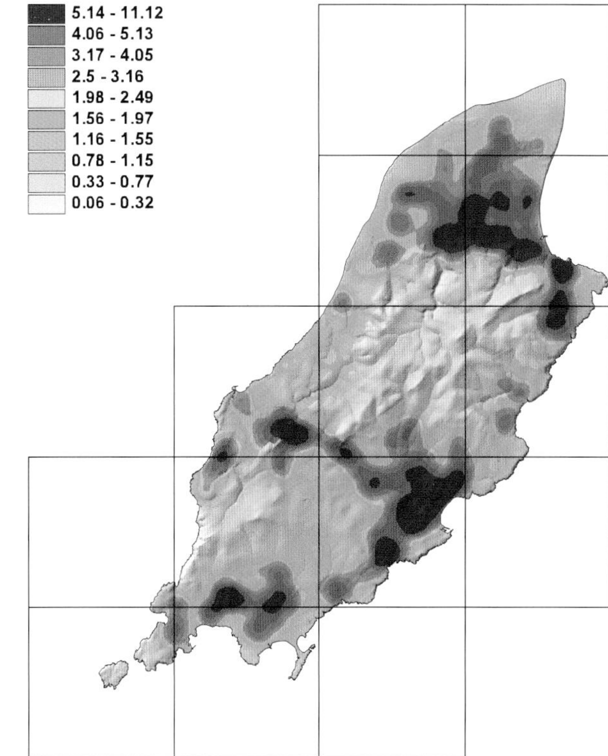

Breeding abundance

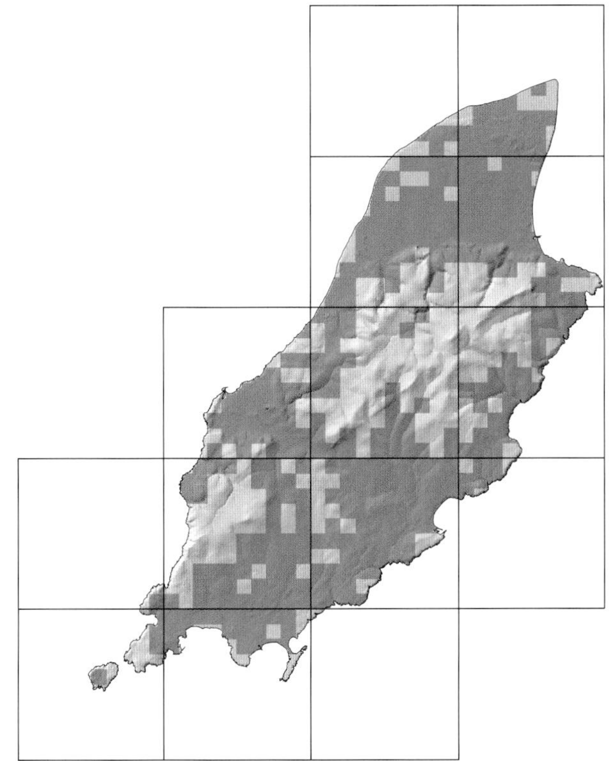

Winter presence

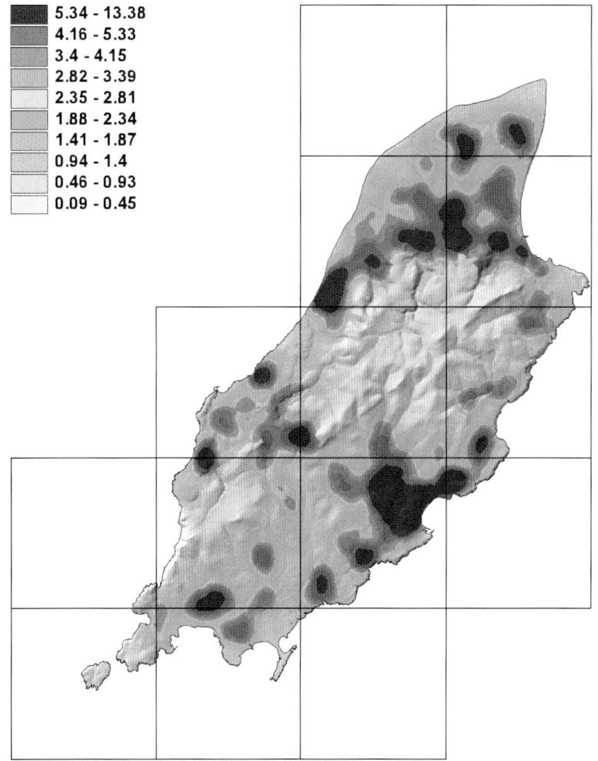

Winter abundance

Individual Sponsors – Mrs. E M Eaton, Ms. M Hudson, Mrs. S M Morrey

Great Tit
Parus major

Manx: *Drean Mooar*

The Great Tit is the largest of the tit family and is very distinctive, with clearly defined white cheek patches and an otherwise black head, the black extending down through the middle of bright yellow underparts. In males the black belly marking is broad and well defined, while in females it is narrow, becoming indistinct by the time it reaches the legs. Like their near relatives the Blue and Coal Tits, Great Tits readily visit gardens to take advantage of human kindness and in doing so they provide good viewing opportunities especially to identify males from females.

Great Tits are a very adaptable species, able to take advantage of a wide range of wooded and semi-wooded habitats including true woodland, scrub, mature gardens, hedgerows and field boundaries. In common with Blue Tits, they nest in natural holes in trees as well as those within stone walls, and take readily to nest boxes. Throughout the year the Great Tit feeds on a wide variety of insects and, when available, berries and fruit. In some parts of its range tree seeds such as beechmast are principal components of the diet (EBA).

The Great Tit has an extensive range, far greater than that of any of the other European tits, and is found almost throughout the Palearctic, from Portugal and Ireland in the west to the easternmost parts of Russia, and also into south-east Asia, including Malaysia and Indonesia (EBA). Breeding distribution in the British Isles is extensive; like the Blue Tit it is absent only from treeless high ground and on Orkney, Shetland and some of the Hebridean islands (1988–91 Atlas). On the Isle of Man the breeding distribution of the Great Tit is very similar to that for the Blue Tit, being absent from higher ground, the largely treeless Ayres heath and a narrow coastal strip. Great Tits did, however, extend further into the uplands via valleys such as Sulby, Glen Helen and East and West Baldwin. The highest altitude at which breeding took place was 360m, compared to 240m for the Blue Tit.

Within the British Isles Great Tits are non-migratory and largely sedentary, though late summer and autumnal dispersal of birds from breeding areas does take place (MA). Breeding birds, especially the males, stay on their territory throughout the year, only leaving if forced to do so to search for food during harsh winters. Information from Great Tits ringed on the Island suggests that none of them travel far. Continental Great Tits can be eruptive and in some winters numbers of them invade Britain, though this is now considered to be occurring less frequently. This behaviour is thought to follow failure of crops of beechmast on the continent (MA). Some of these European birds may occasionally reach the Isle of Man, though this is likely to be a rare event, particularly as there is evidence to suggest that migration of continental birds may be diminishing in response to increased provision of winter food at bird tables (MA). Given their sedentary nature it is hardly surprising that the winter distribution of Great Tits is similar to that in summer, though the upper altitude at which they were found during structured MBA research was 100m lower than during the breeding season.

Kermode considered the Great Tit to be 'resident' and 'plentiful' and Ralfe described it as 'common' and 'well distributed'. Madoc makes it clear that the species was common and very familiar throughout the year and C&J describe it as a 'common resident'. Thus there is no evidence of a change in abundance of Manx Great Tits since Kermode was writing in about 1900. Within the UK Great Tit numbers are thought to have been approximately stable for some decades (1988-91 Atlas), but may have increased recently (EBA).

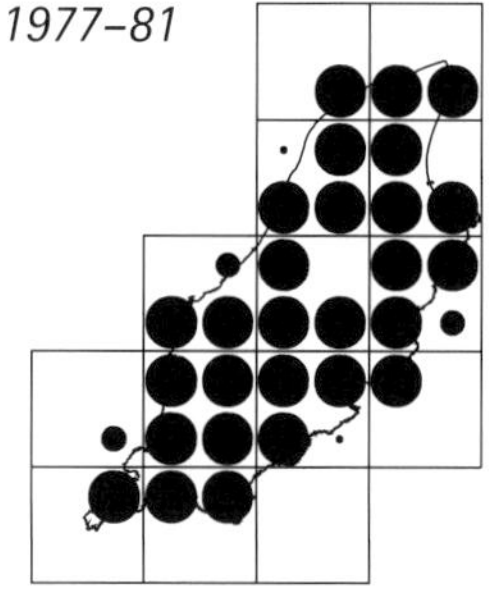

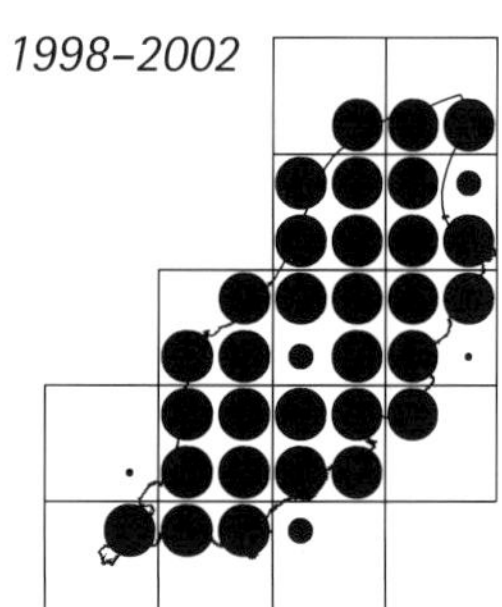

Breeding	Grid squares:	Isle of Man 448 (67%) Britain 2,443 Ireland 883 Total 3,326 (86%)
	Population:	Isle of Man 1,009–1,411 Britain 1,600,000 Ireland 420,000 (5% of European)
Wintering	Grid squares:	Isle of Man 384 (58%) Britain and Ireland 3,256 (84%)
	Population:	Isle of Man 5,000+ Britain and Ireland 10 million

Jan Feb Mar Apr May Jun Jul Aug Sep Oct Nov Dec

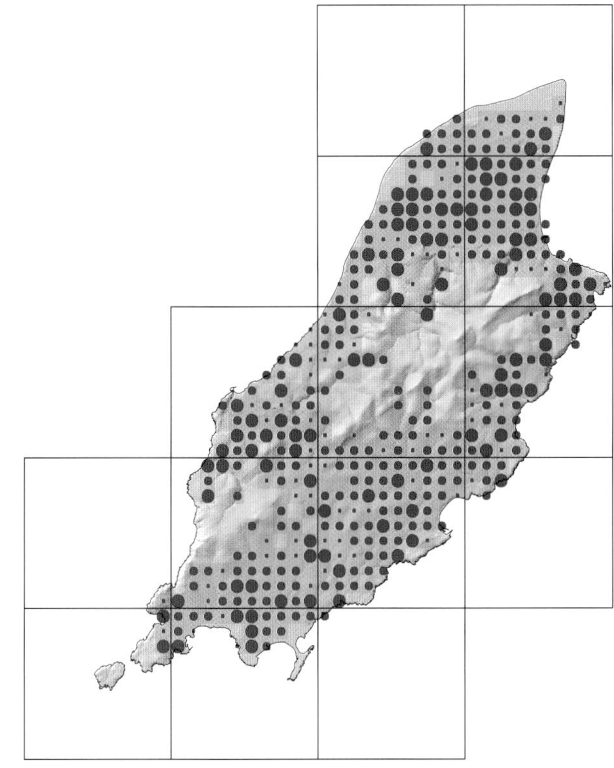

Summer presence and breeding status

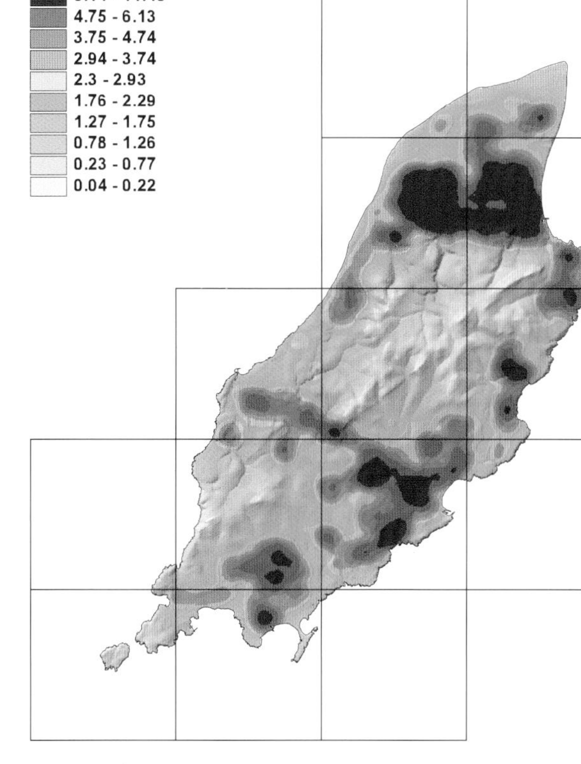

Breeding abundance

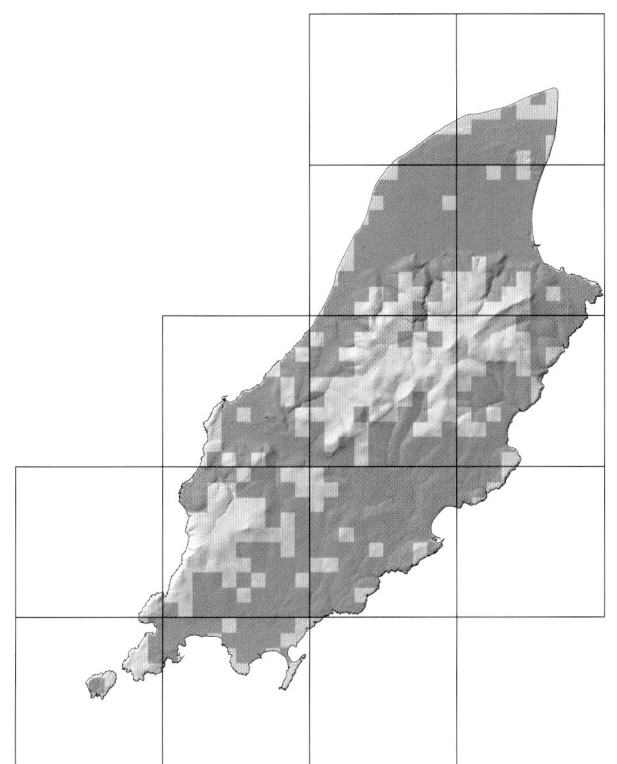

Winter presence

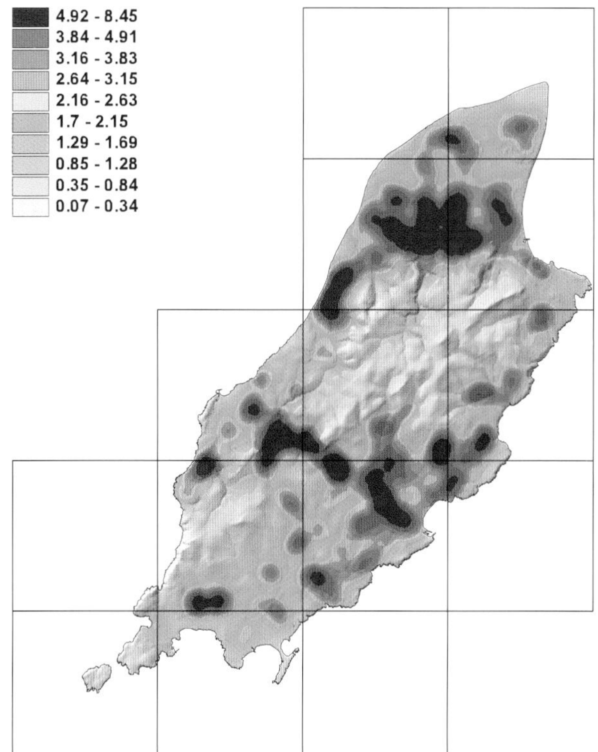

Winter abundance

Individual Sponsor – Mr. D Hudson

Coal Tit
Periparus ater

The Coal Tit is a common resident on the Island, though it may easily go unnoticed by casual observers as this, the smallest of the three species of true tits breeding on the Isle of Man, is less colourful and extrovert than its two close relatives the Great and the Blue Tit. It is similar in size to the Blue Tit and shares the black head and white cheek patch of the Great Tit. The most distinctive feature is the white nape patch which is only visible from behind.

Throughout most of its range the Coal Tit is closely associated with coniferous forest (EBA), the creation of large areas of commercial plantation no doubt aiding expansion of range over time. Even single conifers can prove attractive, further aiding population expansion into parks and gardens in urban and suburban settings. Coal Tits are not entirely reliant on conifers, with breeding also taking place in mixed and broad-leaved woodland (1988–91 Atlas). Nests may be in tree holes, rock crevices, walls or on the ground, ground-nesting probably being a reaction to competition from other hole-nesting species (BWP). Insects and spiders are taken throughout the year, the ability to forage on the underside of snow covered branches being a contributory factor in aiding cold weather survival (1988–91 Atlas). Outside the breeding season Coal Tits will take seasonally available seeds, favouring the spruce. They will readily visit garden food tables, where they will often take nuts and seeds to hoard them, an extension of their treatment of natural seeds and another adaptation to cold weather survival.

Coal Tits are distributed across most of the northern and central Palearctic, from Britain to China and Taiwan (BWP, EBA). Within the British Isles they are widely distributed but absent from Orkney, Shetland, some of the Hebridean islands and areas where trees are largely absent, such as the fens of East Anglia. They are particularly abundant in areas where there are extensive conifer plantations (1988–91 Atlas). Coal Tits are also widely distributed on the Island and, like Blue Tits and Great Tits, are only absent from treeless areas. The locations of pockets of high density differ markedly, however, from the other two species. For Coal Tits, areas of high abundance closely reflect the location of stands of mature plantations, such as Ballaugh, Glen Rushen, South Barrule, Stoney Mountain and Cornaa. It was notable that the relatively new plantations extending from Beary Mountain to Little London supported only low numbers of breeding Coal Tits.

On the Island there is no evidence of migratory behaviour, although small numbers of Coal Tits are seen on the Calf in autumn as well as odd birds in spring. Described as one of the most sedentary species in the UK (1988–91 Atlas), Manx ringing data support this view. Continental Coal Tits can be eruptive in some years, with invasions reaching the British Isles, although no continental birds are known to have reached the Isle of Man.

It is not surprising, given the species' highly sedentary nature, that the distribution and abundance maps for winter are very similar to those for the summer.

Kermode considered the species to have only recently (1896) arrived in the Isle of Man, while Ralfe was of the same view and knew of no records of breeding, but considered the species to be colonising the Island. By 1934 Madoc described the Coal Tit as 'fairly common' and C&J thought it a 'common resident'. It is difficult, in the absence of detailed numerical data, to assess whether numbers have changed greatly in recent decades. It is clear that the species arrived on the Island in the late nineteenth century and increased rapidly during the early twentieth century. In Britain the population probably shows little long-term change (1988–91 Atlas). It is likely, given the extensive areas of conifer plantation on the Island, that the future fortunes of the Coal Tit on the Isle of Man are secure. Future all-Island surveys may well find differences in areas of high density as some plantations mature and others are harvested.

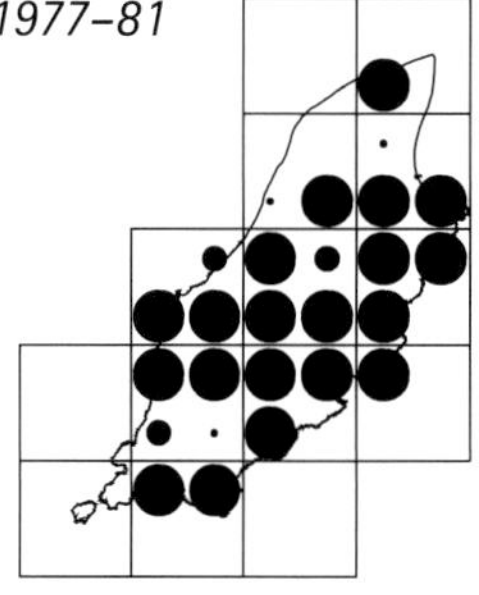

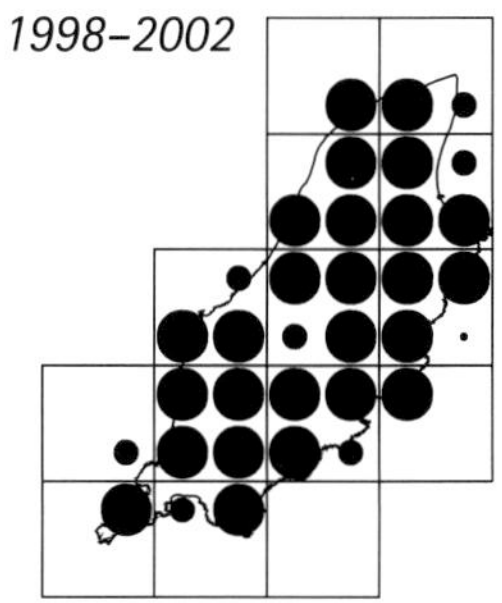

Breeding	Grid squares:	Isle of Man 377 (57%) Britain 2,315 Ireland 854 Total 3,169 (82%)
	Population:	Isle of Man 772–1,030 Britain 610,000 Ireland 270,000 (6% of European)
Wintering	Grid squares:	Isle of Man 339 (51%) Britain and Ireland 3,032 (79%)
	Population:	Isle of Man 3,000 Britain and Ireland 4 million

Jan	Feb	Mar	Apr	May	Jun	Jul	Aug	Sep	Oct	Nov	Dec

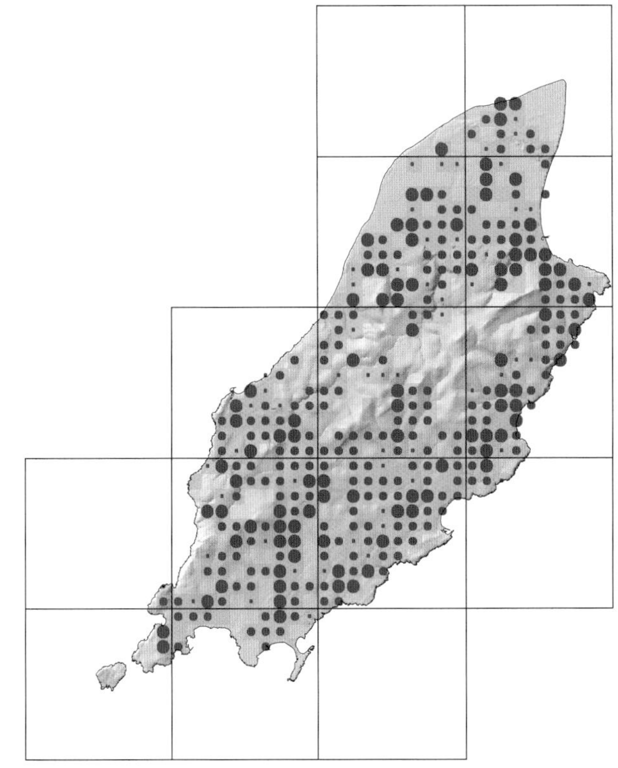

Summer presence and breeding status

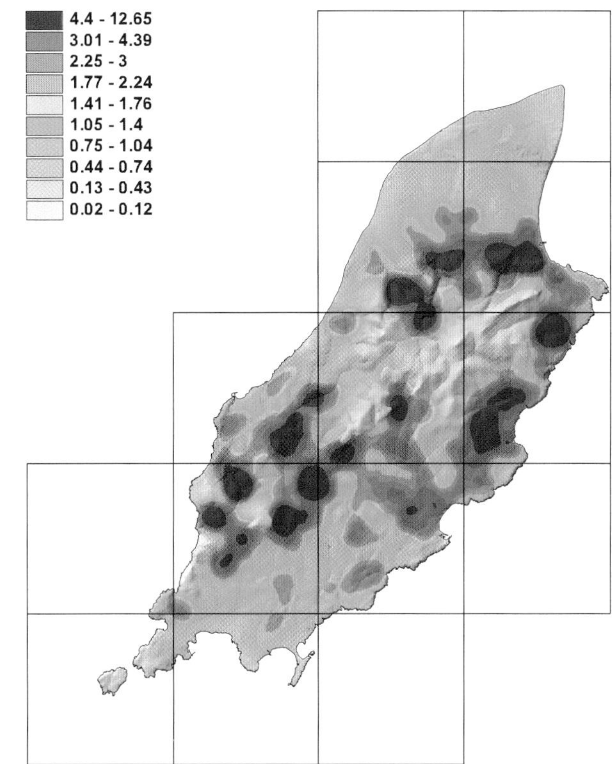

Breeding abundance

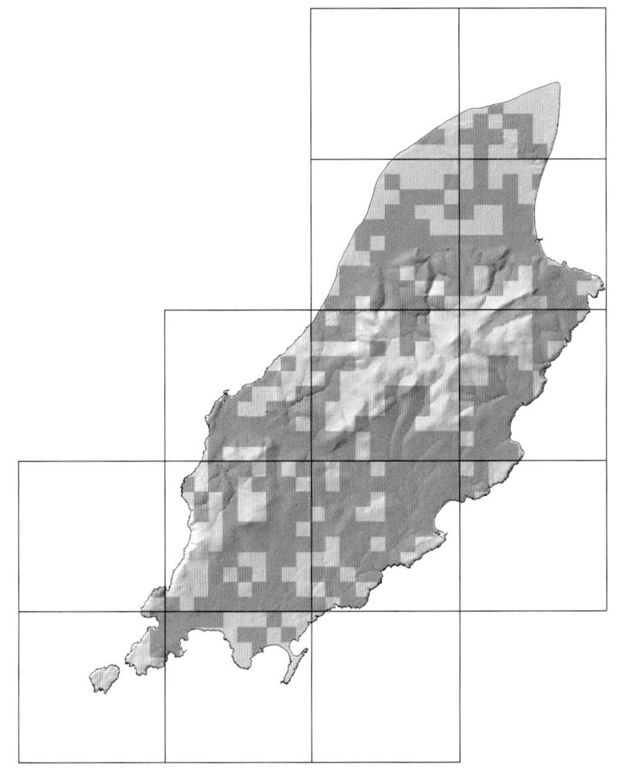
Winter presence

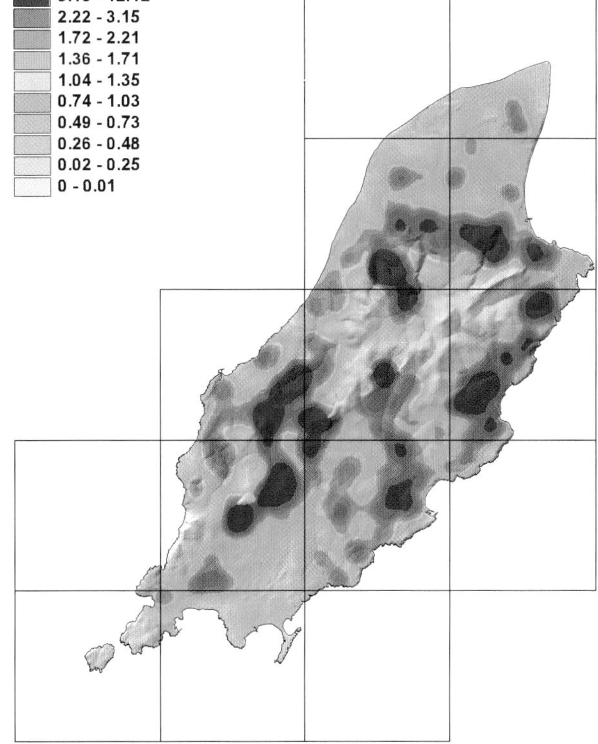

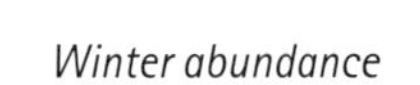
Winter abundance

Individual Sponsors – Ms. I Barker, Mr. D Dentith & Ms. S Corlett

Treecreeper (Eurasian Treecreeper)
Certhia familiaris

Manx: *Snaueyder*

Treecreepers can be seen at any time of year, but these endearing birds are not easy to find. Their cryptic plumage is well suited to a life spent mainly against the trunks of trees and their habit of creeping, in preference to flying, means their white bellies are seldom seen. Often, the first indication of the presence of a Treecreeper is the distinctive call, though even this can easily go unnoticed, as it is both softly delivered and high-pitched.

The Treecreeper is arguably the most arboreal of all the bird species found on the Isle of Man. Trees of practically any species are suitable, provided they have more or less perpendicular trunks and are covered in bark providing crevices to contain invertebrate food organisms. Within Britain the Treecreeper is predominantly found in mature broad-leaved trees, in woodland, parks, large gardens or hedgerows or other farmland timber (BWP), provided trees are not too widely spaced, as Treecreepers do not like to fly across open terrain. Nests are usually on a tree trunk behind a flap of loose bark or in a crevice, though buildings are sometimes used; during MBA research a nest was found between the wall and partially rotted doorframe of an outbuilding. Treecreepers feed almost entirely on insects extracted from crevices in the bark of trees. Their usual *modus operandi* is to alight on the lower part of the trunk of a tree and then to climb slowly upwards in a spiral around the trunk, probing and searching as they go. On reaching the top of the trunk they then fly down to the base of the next tree and repeat the operation.

Treecreepers breed across northern and middle latitudes of the Palearctic, from Britain to China and Japan; there is also a geographically isolated population to the south of the Himalayas (BWP, MA). Within the British Isles Treecreepers are widely distributed, though at relatively low densities, thinnest areas being associated with highlands and open moor (1988–91 Atlas). On the Isle of Man the breeding distribution of Treecreepers reflects areas of mature broad-leaved woodland, particularly those within the numerous glens and valleys. Within conifers only mature plantations appear to suit the species, as relatively young stands of commercially managed conifers may lack suitable nesting opportunity. Stands of isolated deciduous trees are often unoccupied.

Treecreepers in the British Isles are considered to be non-migratory and remarkably sedentary, analysis of ringing data revealing that movements of Treecreepers in excess of 5km are exceptional (MA). Treecreepers from Scandinavia and eastern Europe are occasionally seen in the British Isles, generally in years when there are eruptive movements on the continent (MA), and it is possible that a continental bird may reach as far west as the Isle of Man. Odd birds occur on the Calf and a few have been ringed, providing no evidence of movement beyond the main Island. Winter distribution is broadly similar to summer, minor differences such as that mapped in the south probably being a result of birds being even more difficult to detect in winter than in summer. In winter Treecreepers sometimes move around in mixed species flocks with tits and other small birds.

Treecreepers were apparently unknown on the Island before the late nineteenth century. Kermode considered the Treecreeper to be 'Resident' and recorded that it was first seen in December 1882; he first saw one in 1900. Ralfe gives similar information, recording breeding in 1904 but expresses doubt as to whether the species was new to the Island, or had been previously overlooked. Madoc noted the Treecreeper as 'probably far more common than is thought' and considered that they 'sometimes move in great numbers', while C&J describe it as a 'fairly common resident'. The species continues to be a widespread breeding bird in suitable habitat, and being arboreal and inconspicuous it is probably under-recorded. In Britain the population is thought to be 'increasing slowly and steadily', although Treecreepers may be losing ground in Ireland (1988–91 Atlas). As with several other species it is doubtful whether the apparent rapid colonisation of the Island in the late nineteenth century actually occurred and it is more likely that increased awareness of the species by birdwatchers gave the impression of a population increase. There is little to suggest any recent change of status in the species on the Island, the map comparing MBA research results with that from C&J showing only marginally greater distribution, probably reflecting greater observer effort.

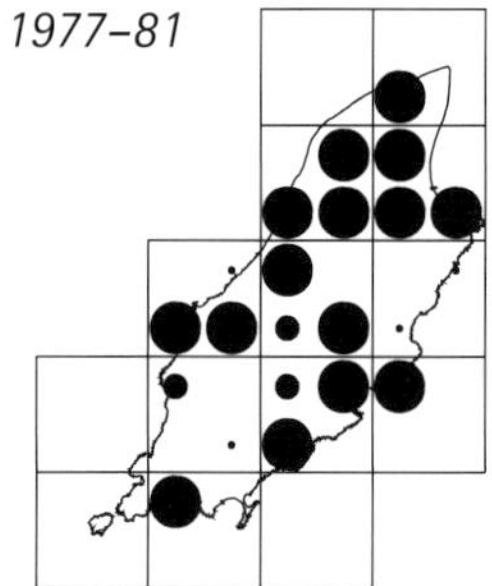

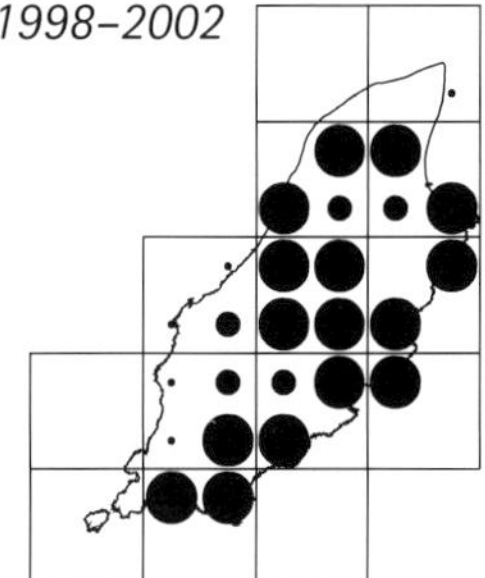

Breeding	Grid squares:	Isle of Man 131 (20%)
		Britain 2,120 Ireland 567 Total 2,687 (70%)
	Population:	Isle of Man 118–149
		Britain 200,000 Ireland 45,000 (8% of European)
Wintering	Grid squares:	Isle of Man 130 (20%)
		Britain and Ireland 2,628 (68%)
	Population:	Isle of Man <500
		Britain and Ireland 1 million

Jan	Feb	Mar	Apr	May	Jun	Jul	Aug	Sep	Oct	Nov	Dec

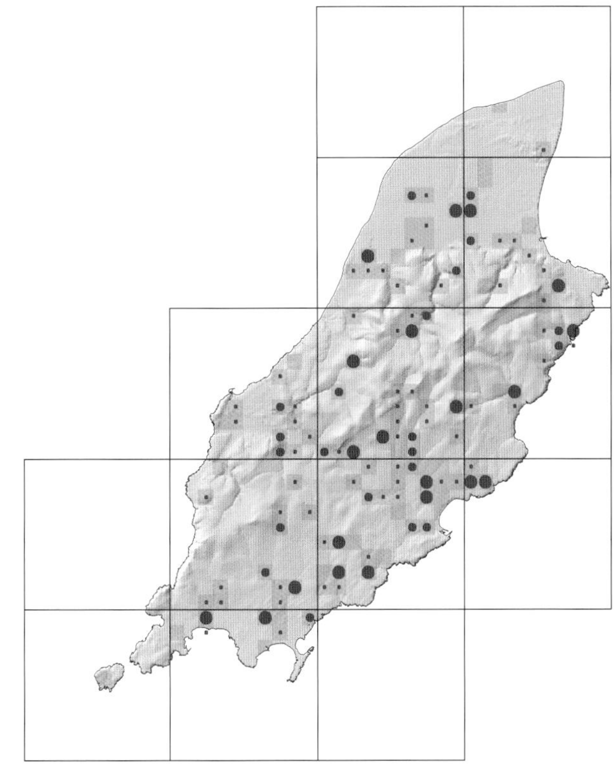
Summer presence and breeding status

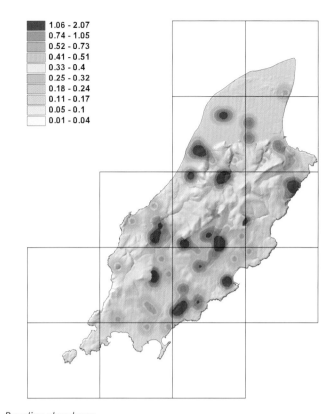

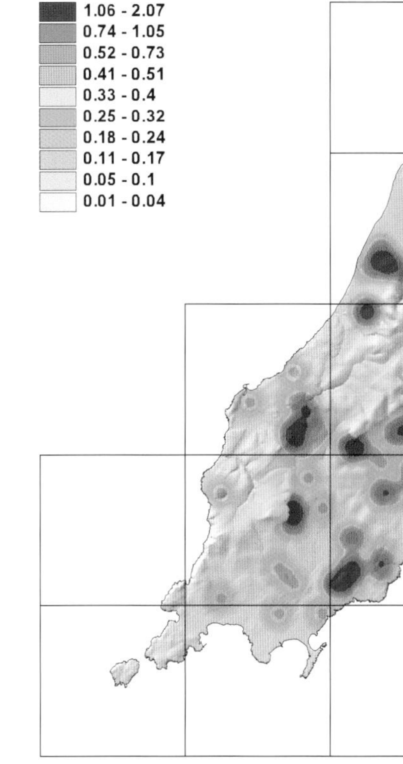

Breeding abundance

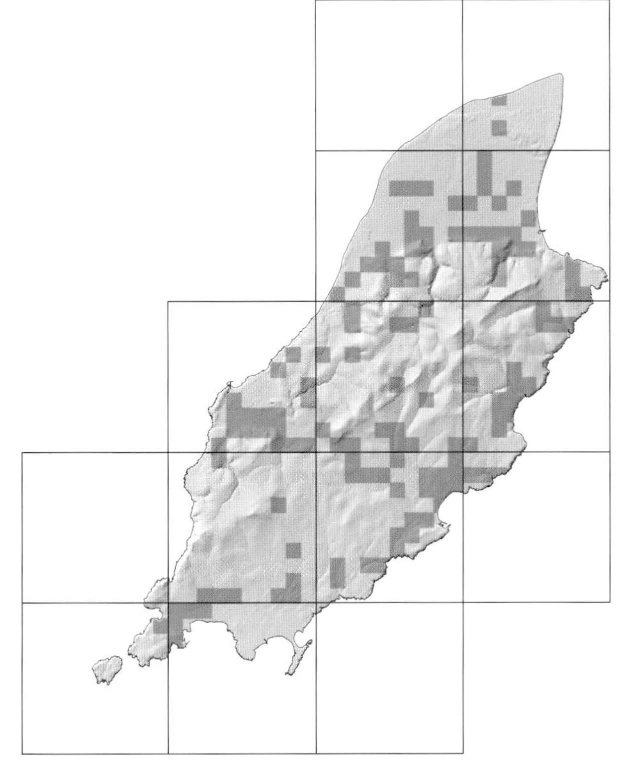
Winter presence

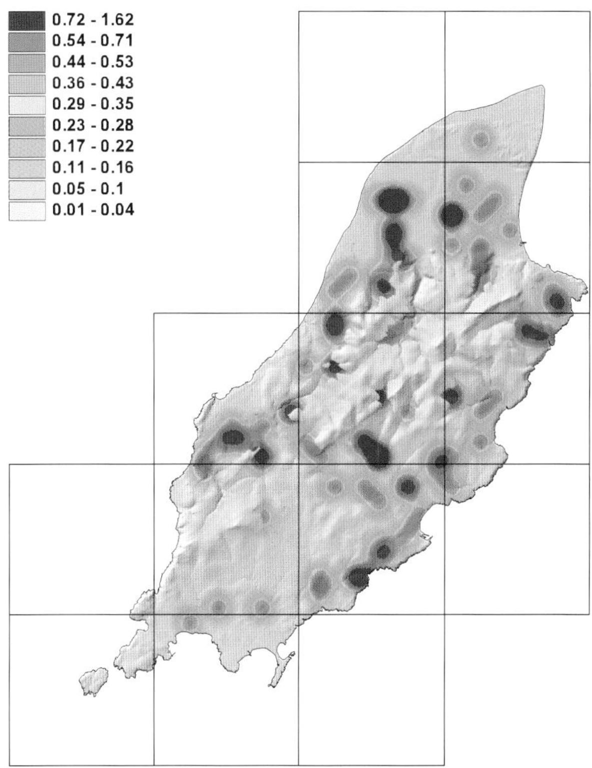

Winter abundance

Individual Sponsors – Mr. J S Cox, Dr. J P Cullen, Mrs. M Halliday, Mr. J A Lister

Magpie (Black-billed Magpie)
Pica pica

Manx: *Pieanat, Piannad*

Handsome, cocky, arrogant, impudent, mischievous – adjectives all equally applicable to the Magpie. Black and white with a long tail glossed with a metallic green sheen, it is one of our most familiar birds.

It is found in a great variety of habitats, especially farmland, parks and gardens, lowland heath and on the coast. It is attracted to man, whose activities provide a ready food supply, but is at the same time remarkably wary and unwilling to allow close approach. It is omnivorous; although most renowned as a marauder of nests, it also feeds on invertebrates, carrion and discarded kitchen scraps.

Present over large parts of the northern hemisphere in both Old and New World, apart from the islands of the Mediterranean and Iceland it is present in every European country. Compared to its distribution in the rest of the British Isles, its Scottish range is quite limited, the population being concentrated mainly in the Clyde/Forth area and to the north-east of a line drawn between Aberdeen and Inverness. On the Isle of Man the Magpie is widely distributed throughout the lowlands. They breed far up the valleys of Sulby, Neb and Glass, but do not extend into the hills. Usually domed and with much mud strengthening the foundations, Magpies' nests are very durable and are often repaired and re-used year after year. Nests are typically built in hedgerow trees, but on the coastal brooghs, are in bramble and blackthorn thickets. During their heyday on the Calf, open nests were built on maritime cliff faces. Building material may be collected as early as the last week in January (Magpies were even carrying sticks at Port Erin and Douglas in October 1991), although in this survey, such activity was not recorded prior to 3 March. Five or six, and occasionally seven, eggs are laid during April and are followed by an incubation period of 18–19 days, surviving chicks fledging after a further month. Family parties of parents with three or four relatively short-tailed youngsters begging noisily are a familiar feature of early summer, and they will remain under parental care for around six weeks (Birkhead 1991).

The Magpie is a particularly sedentary species and this is reflected in the broadly similar maps for both summer and winter. Strangely, of some half dozen ringing recoveries, three showed relatively distant movement of 15, 32 and 46 km.

Magpies were introduced to Ireland in the late seventeenth-century, but their arrival on the Isle of Man (likely through human agency) probably preceded this by several decades. Well established, to the point of being a nuisance, by the early eighteenth-century (Wilson 1722), Magpies increased significantly during the last century, although numbers breeding on the Calf may perhaps reflect a recent reversal of this trend. From two nests in 1959, breeding numbers on the islet had increased to 14 pairs by 1979, but fell away to around seven pairs during the period 1982–92. After four nests in 1995, only one pair has bred annually since. Similarly, if flock size is of any relevance in trying to assess recent changes in the Manx population, then Magpies do appear to be in decline. The winter of 1988 had seen over 100 going to roost at Billown Quarries and, in early November 1990, a record 170 Magpies flew west over the Calf. Flocks in excess of 60 were recorded on the Calf in both 1991 and 1992, since when, and notably during the MBA survey period, Manx flocks have typically been in the 15-30 range. Unfortunately no details are currently available regarding population trends in Britain and Ireland since 1991.

1977–81

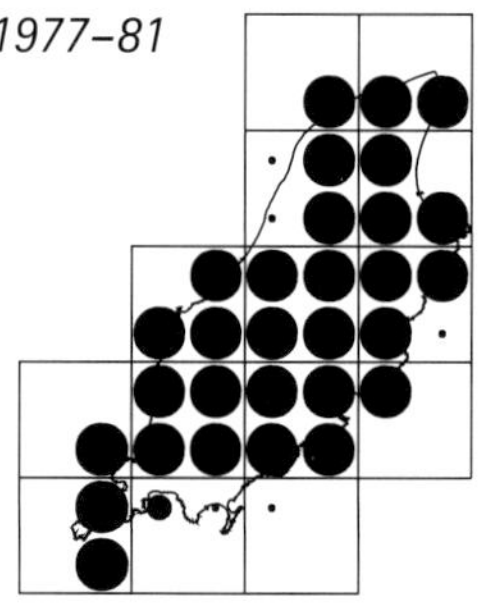

1998–2002

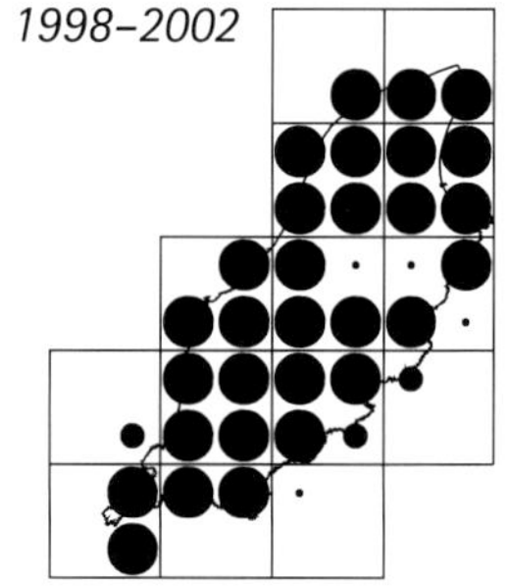

Breeding	Grid squares:	Isle of Man 475 (71%) Britain 1,958 Ireland 962 Total 2,920 (76%)
	Population:	Isle of Man 692–1,078 Britain 590,000 Ireland 320,000 (10% of European)
Wintering	Grid squares:	Isle of Man 412 (62%) Britain and Ireland 2,886 (75%)
	Population:	Isle of Man 2,500 (pairs) Britain and Ireland 250,000–500,000

Jan Feb Mar Apr May Jun Jul Aug Sep Oct Nov Dec

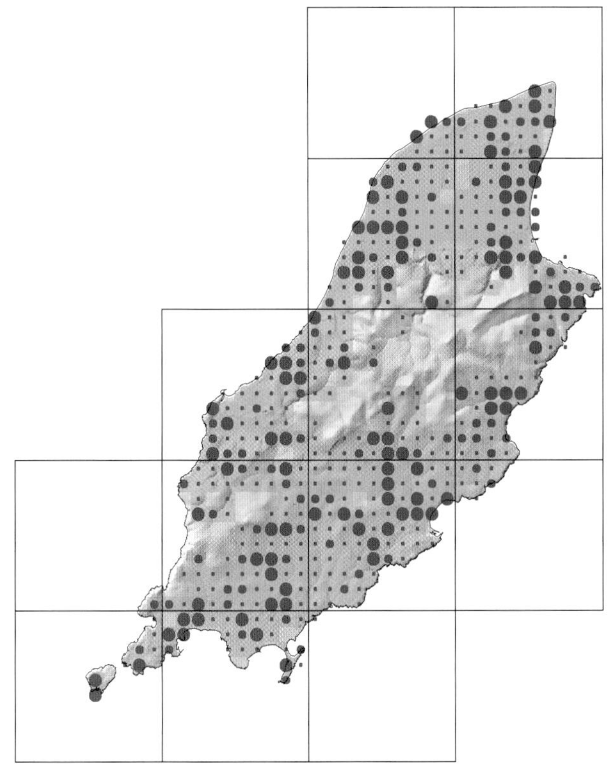
Summer presence and breeding status

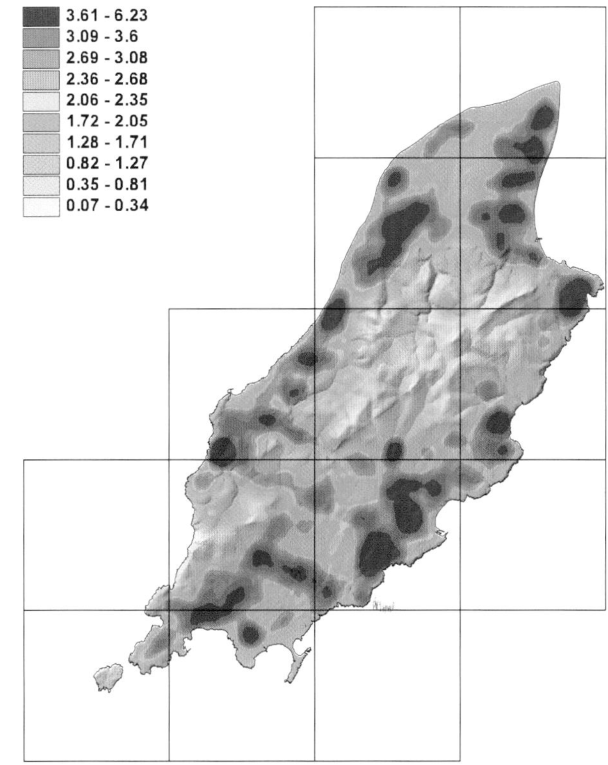

Breeding abundance

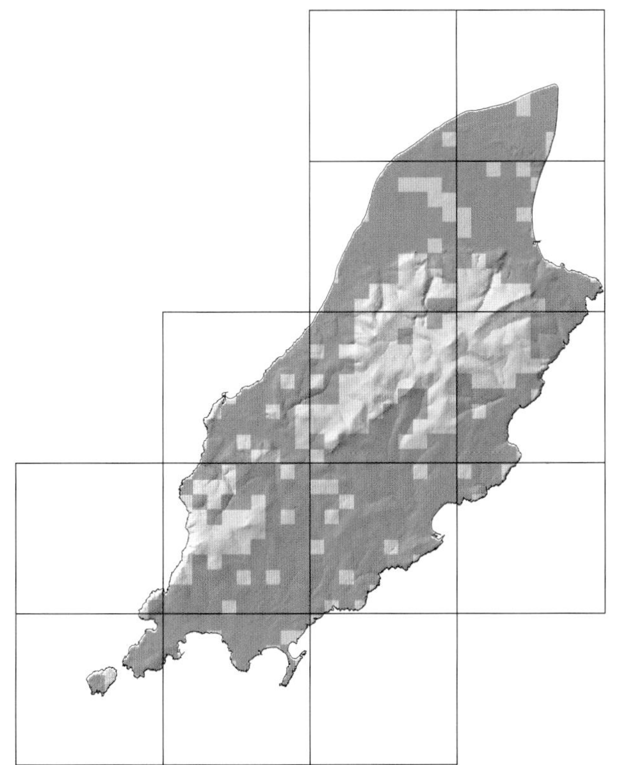
Winter presence

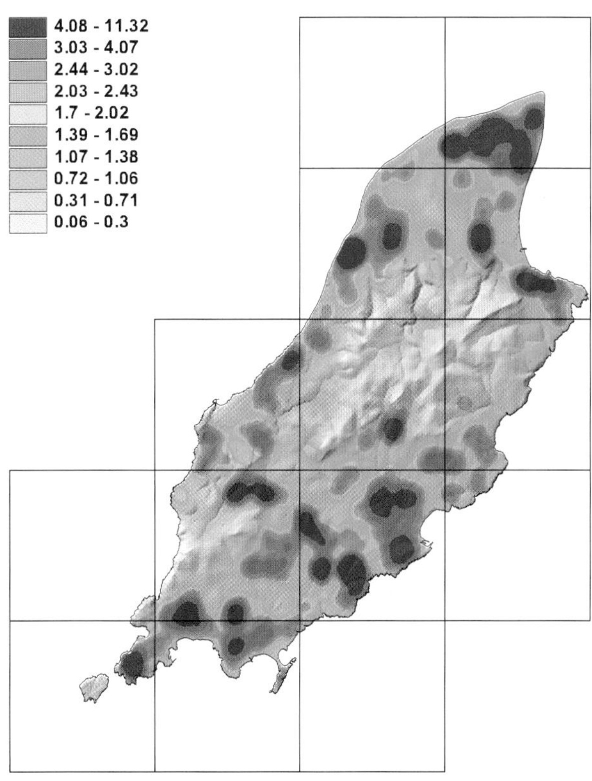

Winter abundance

Individual Sponsor – Mr. W G Gawler

Chough (Red-billed Chough)
Pyrrhocorax pyrrhocorax

Manx: *Caaig*

Writing in the Journal of the Manx Museum in 1943, Cowin and Megaw entitled their paper 'The Red-legged King of the Crows', a very apt description of this most engaging of Manx birds. The red legs are surpassed in colour by the long, decurved, vermilion bill, contrasting with the all-black glossy plumage. The high-pitched calls, so accurately represented by the Manx name *Caaig*, advertising a party of perhaps ten birds, exhibiting great *joie de vivre* as they tumble and dip on broad, fingered, wings in a marvellous display of aerial mastery, never fail to bewitch the observer.

The Chough is essentially an inhabitant of the Island's rocky coastline, where the nest, composed largely of heather stems and lined with wool, is built in crevices and sea caves. Inland, there are perhaps ten sites where Choughs nest in mine and farm buildings, often rather dilapidated and sometimes still being used as animal shelters. Here most nests were at heights of between 190 and 245m AMSL, but this merely reflects the lack of suitable buildings at higher altitudes. The maintenance of short-cropped turf by sheep is an important ingredient of the Chough's prosperity and in this context the dwindling frequency of myxomatosis has allowed that other essential grazer, the rabbit, to prosper. Both excessively dry weather, driving larvae too deep for the Chough's probing bill, and too much rain, can affect breeding success.

Irregularly distributed across temperate areas of Eurasia, the Chough has a patchy range, embracing the more mountainous parts of southern Europe and especially Spain, where the estimated Chough population probably exceeds the aggregate of all the remaining countries of the continent (EBA). In both Spain and France, Choughs are found around their rugged, most north-westerly coasts, aping the western distribution in Britain and Ireland. In 2002, a pair of Choughs nested in Cornwall, marking the return of the species as a breeding bird in England after an absence of 50 years. In Wales, the coast between Pembrokeshire and Anglesey is irregularly tenanted (with an extension into Snowdonia), while in Ireland the distribution follows the Atlantic coast from Waterford round to Rathlin, continuing across the North Channel to Galloway and the Scottish islands of Islay and Colonsay. The Choughs of the British Isles thrive at these most northerly latitudes owing to the warming effect of the Gulf Stream along these coasts.

The Manx Chough population is probably now prospering as never before. Although abundant in the early part of the nineteenth century, there followed a drastic slump, followed by a minor recovery during the final two decades. The period 1900–40 witnessed a reasonable increase in the population, which remained fairly stable for the next forty years. The unequivocal growth in the population is clearly demonstrated in the results of the last three decennial censuses. These show breeding totals of 49–60 (1982), 68–77 (1992) and 128–150 (2002) (Johnstone *et al* 2006). The Chough is a protected species, unfortunately the target of those acting illegally by stealing eggs. Therefore the distribution map shows breeding status at 5km resolution, rather than the 1km used for most other species.

Although the largest flocks are seen mostly between October and March, when breeding pairs and their young join non-breeding flocks, the Calf, in particular, had summer flocks in excess of 60 in four of the five Atlas years, the largest containing 86 birds on 25 June 1999. Other notable summer flocks were 70 near Baldrine and 40 at Little Ness, both in July 2000; otherwise, taking the survey period as a whole, flocks of 40 or more all occurred south of a line between Langness and Eary Cushlin. Shoreline feeding is important during the winter months, and at Sandwick particularly, flocks of 60 or more birds may be seen probing the sand, almost disappearing into the piles of seaweed in search of sandhoppers and the larvae of kelp flies. The largest reported flock involved 120 birds on 29 October 1999. Smaller flocks often frequent the Glen Wyllin area, the Marine Drive and the fields above Clypse and Kerrowdhoo Reservoirs. On 25 December 2000, a party of eight was seen jostling for position around the chimneypots of Clypse Reservoir House. The winter distribution and abundance maps reveal a largely coastal distribution, as for the summer. Ringing recoveries had suggested that Manx Choughs do not leave the island, but in the autumn of 1990 a Calf-ringed bird reached County Down, Northern Ireland, a distance of 71 km.

Skeletal remains of several individuals were identified from the Perwick Bay midden deposit dated at AD90. The first reference to Choughs in the literature did not appear until Jardine (1838-43) wrote of them as 'so common that we once procured nearly thirty specimens in a forenoon'. Despite the mixed fortunes highlighted earlier, the prospects for the Manx Chough appear promising.

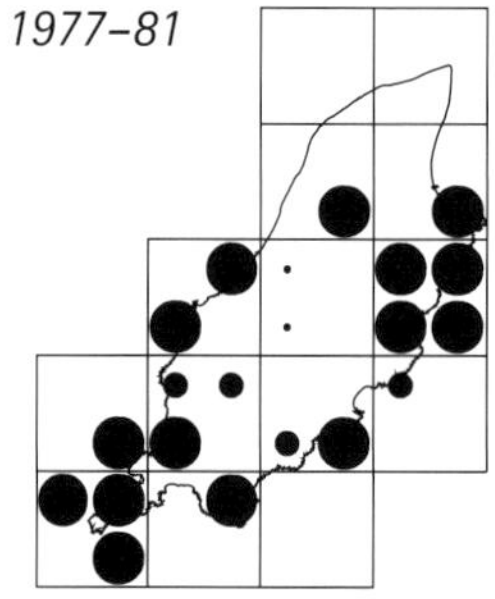

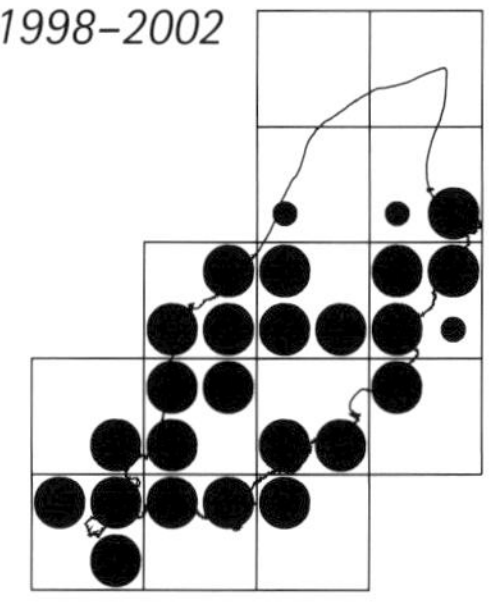

Breeding	Grid squares:	Isle of Man 202 (30%) Britain 88 Ireland 168 Total 256 (7%)
	Population:	Isle of Man 121–150 Britain 340 Ireland 830 (8% of European)
Wintering	Grid squares:	Isle of Man 201 (30%) Britain and Ireland 243 (6%)
	Population:	Isle of Man 500+ Britain and Ireland 3,000–5,000

Jan	Feb	Mar	Apr	May	Jun	Jul	Aug	Sep	Oct	Nov	Dec

Corporate Sponsor – Bank of Bermuda Conservation Sponsor – Manx Chough Project

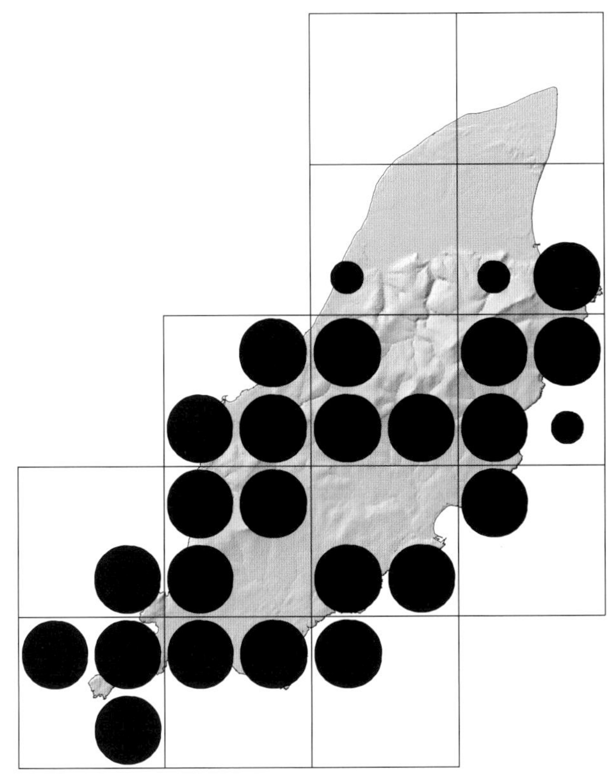
Breeding status

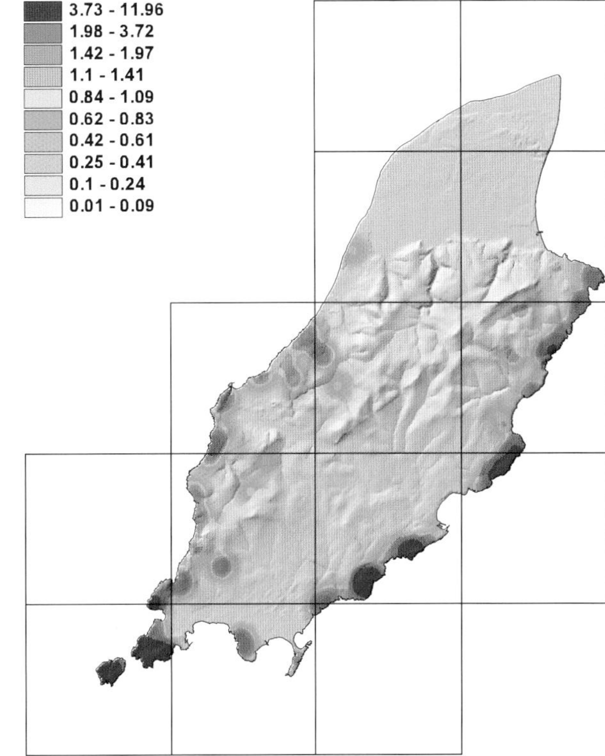

Breeding abundance

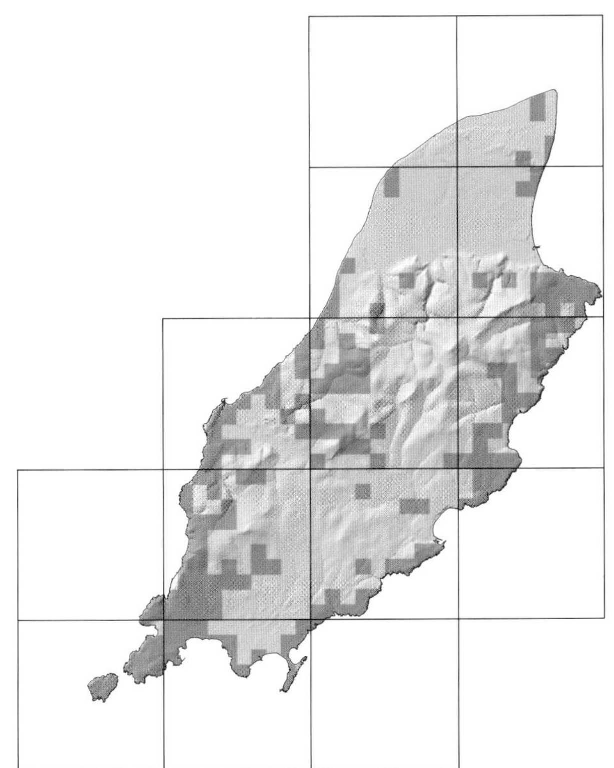
Winter presence

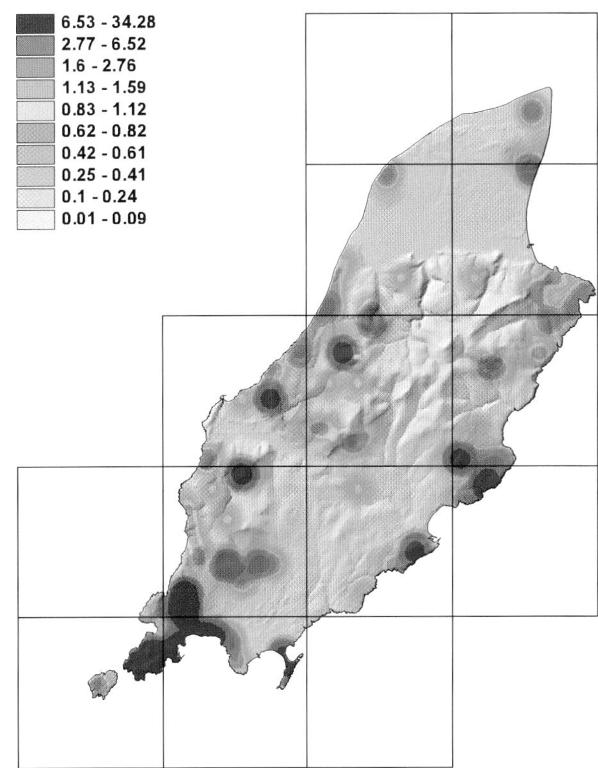

Winter abundance

Individual Sponsors – Dr. R Charles, Mr. J L Cojeen, Mr. G Craine, Ms. S Foster, Mr. H K Larsen, Mrs. J Lever, Mr. N W Park, Mrs. C Shafto

Jackdaw (Eurasian Jackdaw)
Corvus monedula

Manx: *Caaig, Juan teayst* = John Dough

Smallest of the Manx corvids, Jackdaws frequently combine with Rooks in substantial flocks, when feeding and roosting. On the coast confusion with the Chough might arise, but the 'jyaack' call lacks that piercing, high-pitched quality of the larger Chough, and the different flight silhouette and relative lack of agility combine to make separation easy. At rest, the Jackdaw reveals itself as a dark grey bird, with lighter grey neck and nape, and although the eye is greyish white, it can appear pale blue.

Jackdaws are often closely associated with human habitations, nesting in chimneys and other cavities in buildings in towns, villages and isolated farms. They also nest in hollow trees, including those in parks and gardens, and are plentiful along the coasts. Depending on the space available, the nest is founded on a base of sticks and the cup is lined with wool and hair, often taken directly from grazing sheep and cattle. Jackdaws are omnivorous, the diet ranging from invertebrates to fruits, seeds, carrion and scraps. They readily come to suburban gardens, where they will clumsily extract peanuts from suspended feeders.

Jackdaws breed across most of Europe, but have a very limited range in both Portugal and Norway. Further east they are found up to latitude 66°N. Within the British Isles, they are widely distributed with the exception of north-west Scotland, the Outer Hebrides and Shetland. On the Isle of Man they are well distributed over the lowlands and nest up to 300m AMSL at Park Llewellyn, the lack of trees or buildings at higher altitudes being the limiting factor. In these more remote and elevated areas, the chimneys and joist-holes of long-neglected tholtans and mine buildings are used. In towns and villages, predictably, they nest mostly in chimneys, while in more rural situations they also favour the pigeon holes which adorn the gables of so many Manx farms and mills, as well as beams sheltered by a roof, as in the lych-gate at Kirk Braddan, and in church towers. They nest at a number of sites around the coast, especially around Santon, choosing holes and fissures in the rocks. It is a curious fact, never satisfactorily explained, that Jackdaws have never bred on the Calf. Areas of high abundance are evident in most of the towns and villages of the Island and through much of the lowland farming area, where nesting opportunity is plentiful. During the present survey, the earliest date on which nest building was noted was 19 March, which is in keeping with the understanding that laying on the Island begins during the last week in April.

There is little difference between Jackdaws' summer and winter ranges. In winter, they join Rooks in flocks several thousand strong, which go to roost in trees at such sites as the Reservoir House at Baldwin. The areas of high density on the winter abundance map do not reflect Jackdaw flocks at, or going to, roost as the timing of MBA fieldwork sought to record where birds were foraging. A close association between areas of high Jackdaw numbers and agricultural field systems is indicated. Jackdaws appear on or over the Calf to some extent during May and in much greater numbers in the autumn. This is a long-established habit, but was particularly prominent during the period 1987–95, with as many as 2,500 birds being seen on a single day. Strangely this habit virtually ceased in 1996, although over 200 birds visited the islet on two days during October 2002. The ten recoveries of birds ringed on the Isle of Man have shown movement of up to 29km, underlining the largely sedentary nature of the species.

Birds with varying degrees of albinism are frequently reported and there are two records, from Rushen and from Douglas, of birds with entirely fawn plumage. A bird resident in Colby had, by 2000, achieved an age of at least 29.

As with the Chough, Jackdaw bones were identified from the Perwick midden deposit dating from the first century AD, yet, unaware of this, Ralfe suspected that it was a late introduction to the Isle of Man. Townley (1791) found them breeding on Douglas Head in 1789 and Ralfe described them as common in towns and villages and knew of many coastal colonies and others among the rocky margins of Sulby Glen. C&J considered that the population had altered little during the twentieth century. Although never subjected to censusing on the Isle of Man, the apparent abundance of the Jackdaw appears to have altered little during the last century.

1977–81

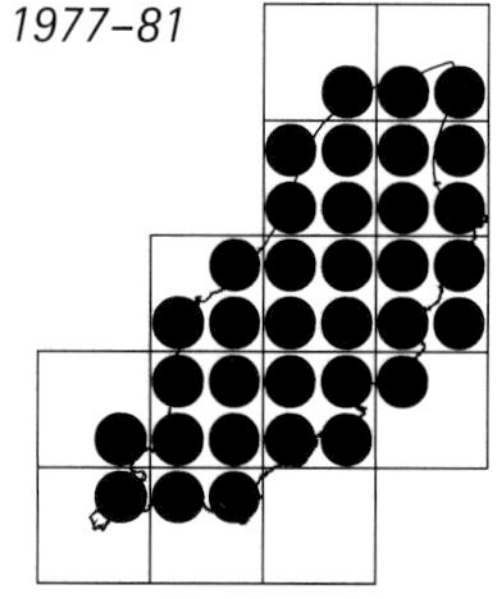

1998–2002

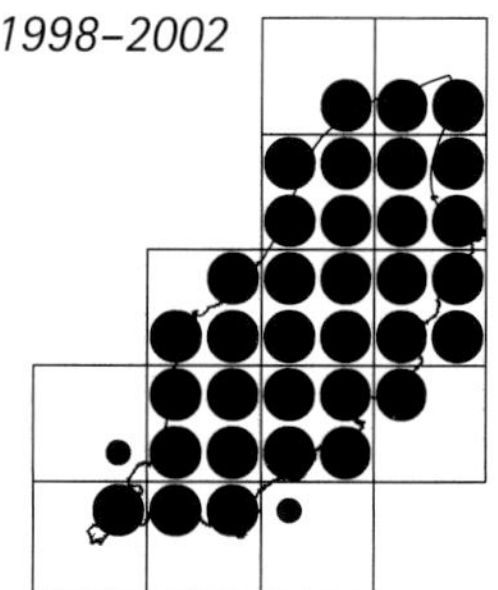

Breeding	Grid squares:	Isle of Man 482 (72%) Britain 2,344 Ireland 944 Total 3,288 (85%)
	Population:	Isle of Man 4,264–8,088 Britain 390,000 Ireland 210,000 (11% of European)
Wintering	Grid squares:	Isle of Man 423 (64%) Britain and Ireland 3,629 (85%)
	Population:	Isle of Man 20,000+ Britain and Ireland 3 million

Jan	Feb	Mar	Apr	May	Jun	Jul	Aug	Sep	Oct	Nov	Dec

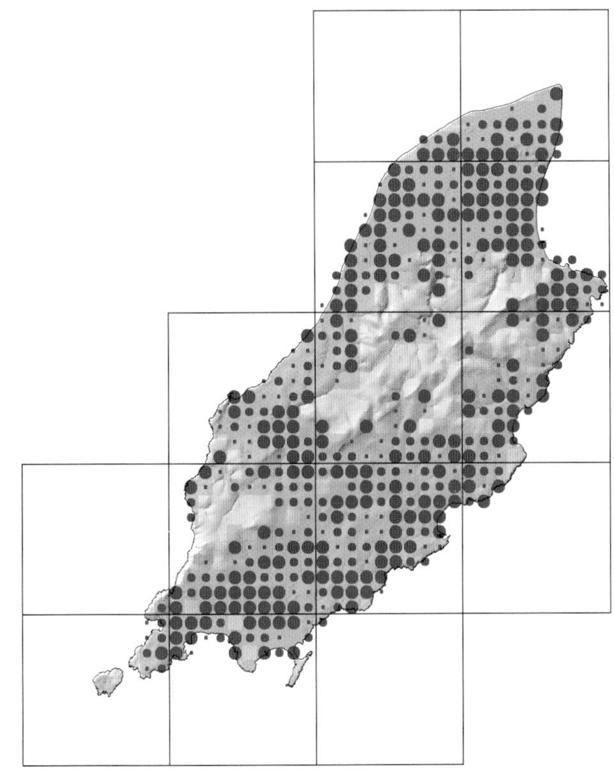

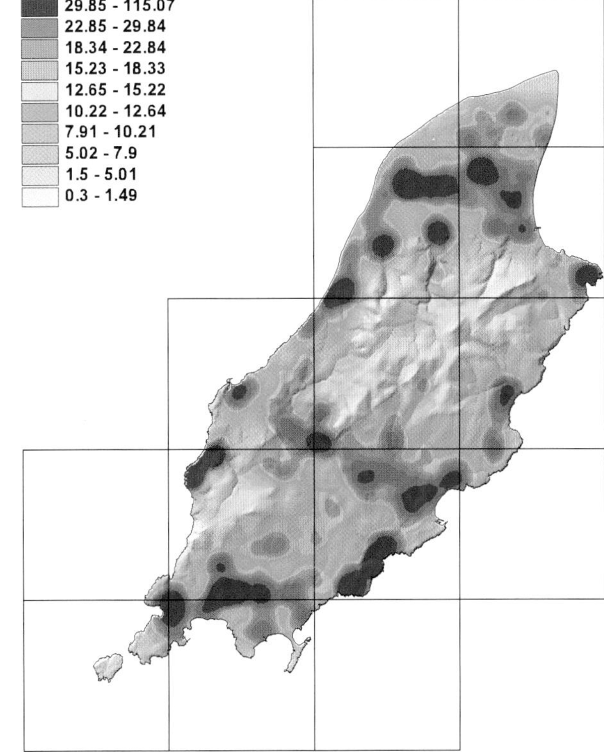

Summer presence and breeding status

Breeding abundance

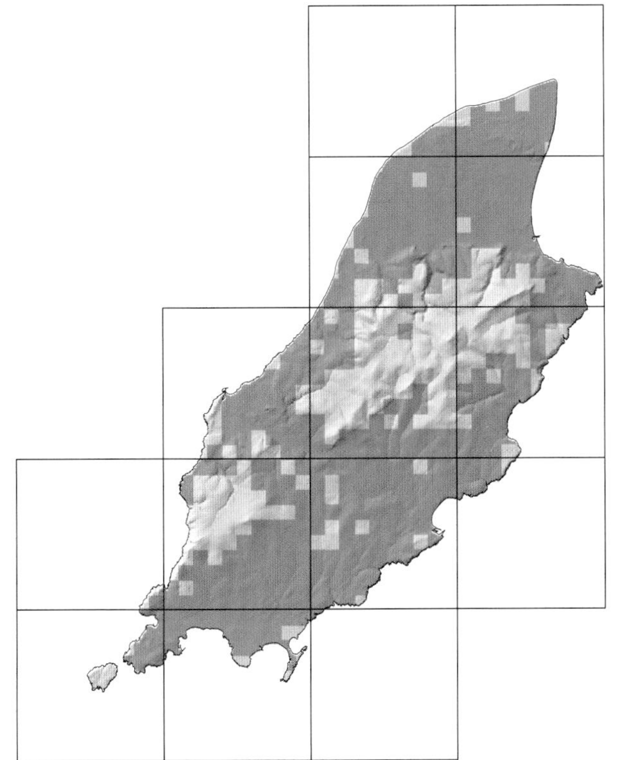

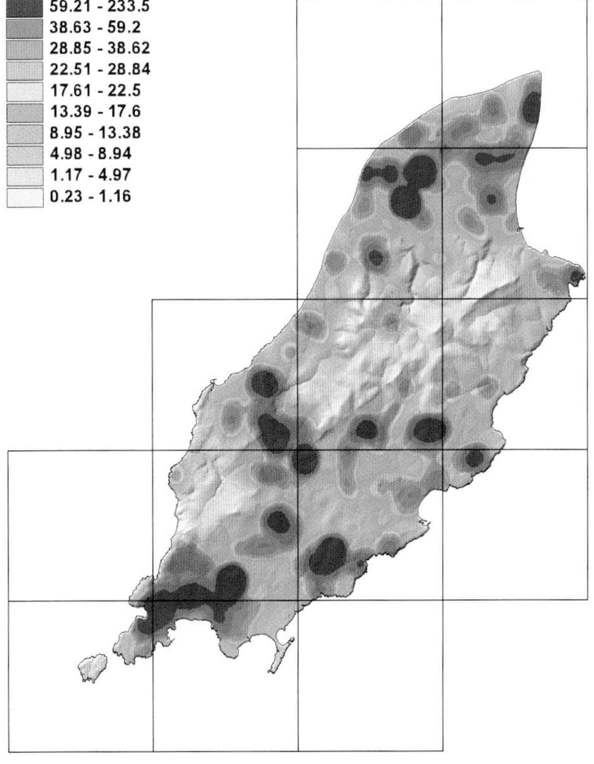

Winter presence

Winter abundance

Individual Sponsors – The late Mrs. E Johnson, Ms. A Looney, Mr. & Mrs. Templeton

Rook
Corvus frugilegus

Manx: *Trogh*

The bare whitish skin around the base of the mature Rook's bill as well as the rather shaggy, trousered look of the belly make identification easy. The juvenile, however, looks very similar to the Carrion Crow, and it is the dagger-shaped, pointed bill that should distinguish it from the similarly sized crow.

Rooks are birds of farmland, nesting colonially near the tops of clumps of trees, often in close association with farms, in churchyards and in villages. They are omnivorous, feeding primarily on invertebrates, some of which are agricultural pests. At the same time they are guilty of taking freshly sown grain, but, although their shooting can earn the marksman a bounty, it has been shown that economically their qualities outweigh their faults.

Rooks are widely, but not consistently, distributed across the temperate and boreal zones of Europe, their range extending eastward across Russia and into northern China. In mainland Europe the main areas of population are in northern France and countries bordering the North Sea and the southern Baltic, with a further concentration embracing the plains of central and eastern Europe (EBA). Britain and Ireland in particular are probably more densely populated than anywhere on the continent, but even so, Rooks are largely absent from the great conurbations, from the more mountainous regions of England and Wales and from most of western Scotland north of the Clyde. There have been fourteen complete censuses of Manx rookeries since 1938, these being at five-yearly intervals since 1975. After the peak count of 6,696 nests in 1941, a low of 4,640 nests was reached in 1975, possibly due to the use of toxic seed dressings. Subsequently there was a steady increase, with a new record of 7,434 nests in 1995, representing a 60% increase on the 1975 figure, although there followed a small reduction to 7,096 in 2000. The following table, which is an extension to that included in C&J, analyses census results from 1938 to 2000.

Nest numbers and nesting density in Manx rookeries 1938–2000

Year	*Total nests*	*Total rookeries*	*Nests per rookery*	*Nests per sq. km.*
1938	5,736	98	58.53	10.00
1940	5,368	101	53.15	9.36
1975	4,640	119	38.99	8.11
1980	5,385	123	43.78	9.39
1985	6,085	122	49.88	10.62
1990	6,538	143	45.72	11.41
1995	7,434	168	44.25	12.97
2000	7,096	145	48.94	12.38

This pattern of decline up to 1975 and subsequent recovery, together with a reduction in rookery size, followed by a slight increase, was also seen in Britain as a whole (Sage and Whittington 1985).

Over half the Manx colonies are less than 50m above sea level and none are at an altitude greater than 230m. The breeding distribution map indicates that Rooks are widely distributed at this time, while the abundance map reveals the areas of highest density to be in the north and along the central valley. Types of tree used in rookeries were recorded in both 1980 and 2000. In both years, conifers accounted for over 30% of all nests, but curiously the use of Beech declined from almost 28% to 21%, while nests in Sycamores increased from 21.5% to almost 30%.

Although the British and Irish populations are almost entirely resident, some dispersal of juveniles, with movement up to 100km, does occur during their first winter (BWP). Flocking, including autumn visits to the Calf, which have recently been in much smaller numbers, together with roosting, closely mirrors that of the Jackdaw. The winter maps indicate a widespread distribution, with birds avoiding high ground and a similar pattern of abundance as that for the summer.

Historically the Island was almost treeless towards the end of the eighteenth century and Rooks were very scarce (Townley 1791, Robertson 1794), but with much tree-planting early in the following century, the Rook population multiplied enormously and towards the end of the nineteenth century Ballachurry (Andreas) held as many as 700 nests. They were shot in large numbers around this time and also during both the First and Second World Wars, yet the number of rookeries listed by Ralfe was virtually the same as that found in 1940. Rooks are subject to periodic fluctuations in population and it has been interesting to see that the dip in numbers seen in the 2000 census had accelerated in the complete survey of 2005.

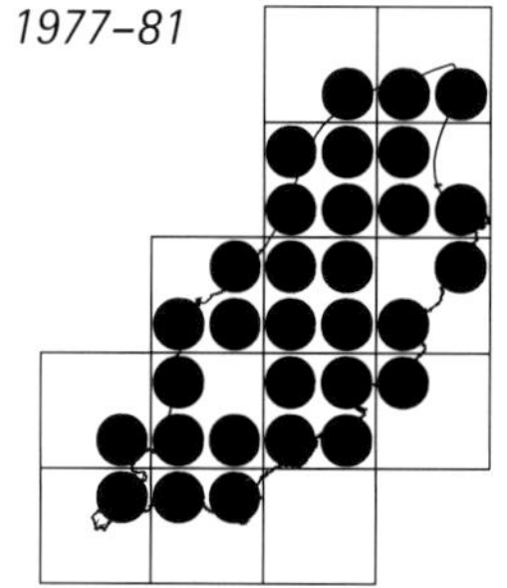

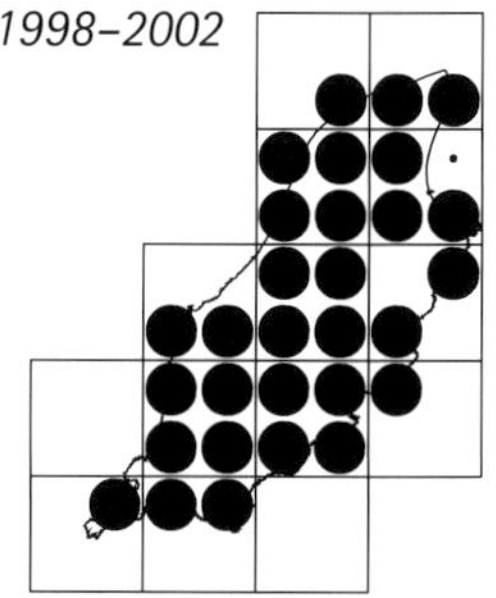

Breeding	Grid squares:	Isle of Man 489 (74%) Britain 2,237 Ireland 919 Total 3,156 (82%)
	Population:	Isle of Man 7,096 Britain 855,000 Ireland 520,000 (39% of European)
Wintering	Grid squares:	Isle of Man 394 (50%) Britain and Ireland 3,320 (83%)
	Population:	Isle of Man 20,000+ Britain and Ireland 4 million+

Jan Feb Mar Apr May Jun Jul Aug Sep Oct Nov Dec

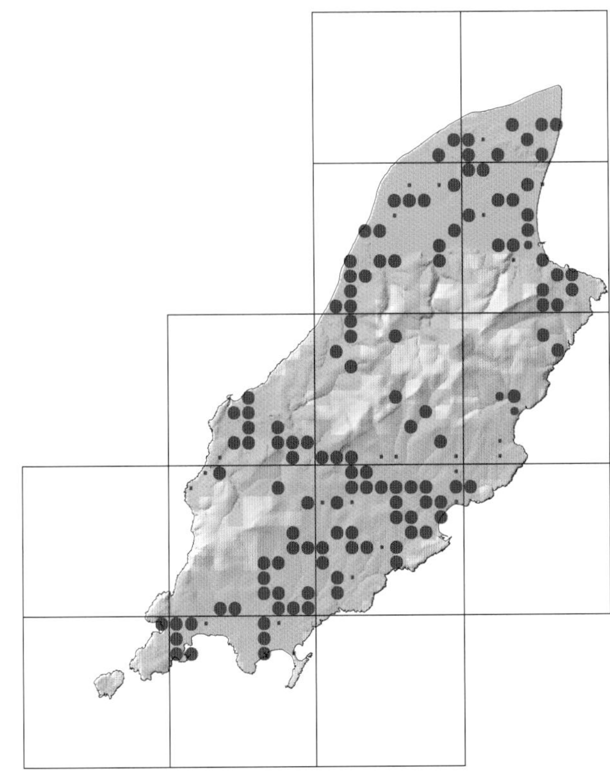

Summer presence and breeding status

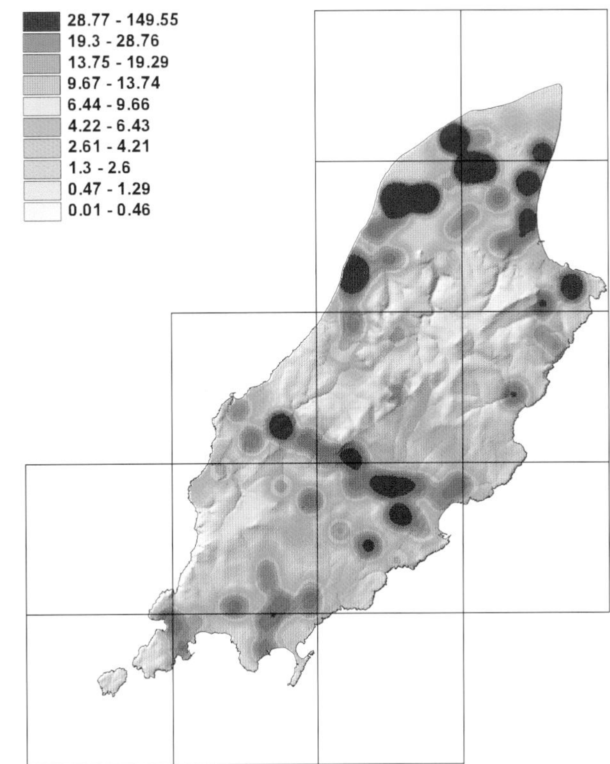

Breeding abundance

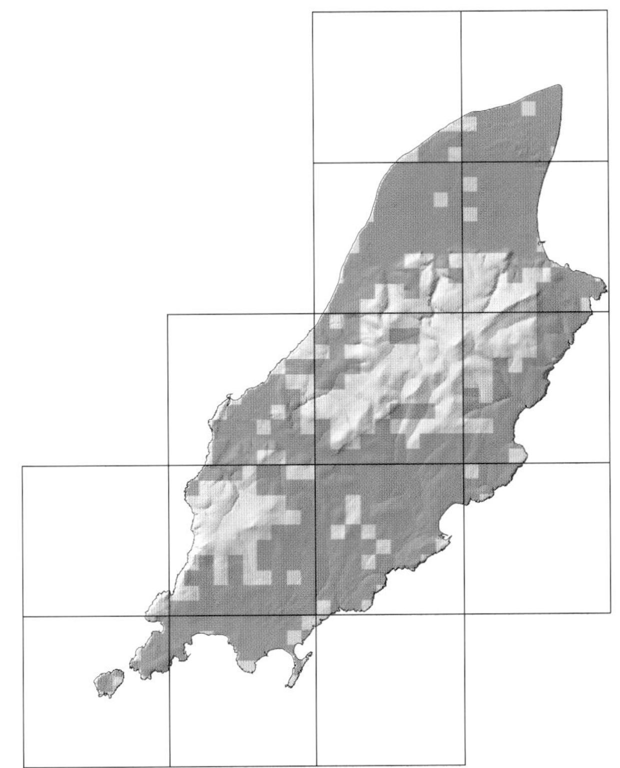

Winter presence

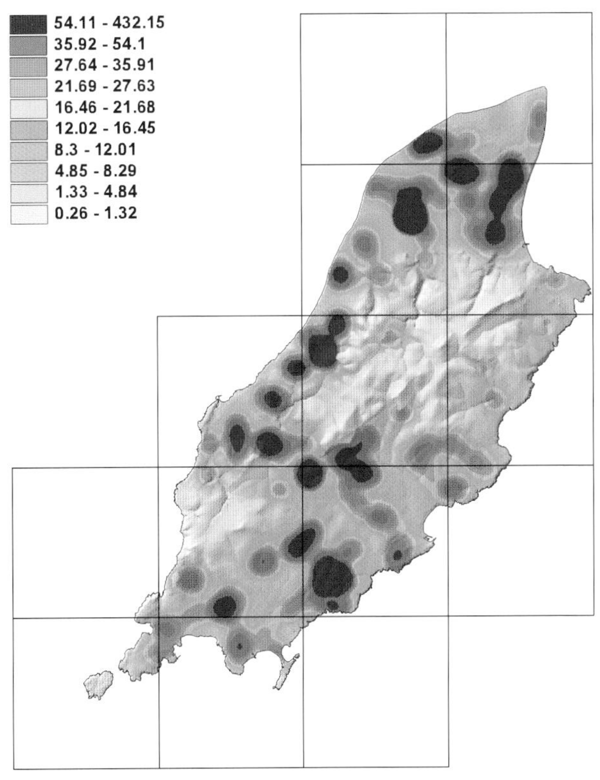

Winter abundance

Individual Sponsors – Mrs. S Bolton, Mrs. S Crellin, Mr. N J Donnithorne, Mr. J D R Kewley, Mrs. H Moore

Carrion Crow
Corvus corone

The all-black Carrion Crow and the grey-backed Hooded Crow were until very recently regarded as conspecific and the two species readily interbreed. The Carrion Crow is black and has a stout bill, with a well curved culmen, which distinguishes it from the juvenile Rook. It is not unlike a small Raven, but the bill is nothing like as powerful and Carrion Crows lack the wedge-shaped tail of the larger bird.

The Carrion Crow is catholic in its choice of habitat, ranging from inner cities, through farmland to high moorland. Most nests at inland sites are built in either isolated trees in hedges or at the edge of woodland. It is also plentiful over a wide range of coastal habitats, nesting in rocky gullies and on high cliffs, such nests being similar to, though smaller than, those of the Raven. Although the main diet consists of invertebrates and grain, the crow is, not surprisingly, always alert to the possibility of carrion, particularly road casualties. Small vertebrates and birds' eggs are also taken.

The European range of the Carrion Crow is quite precise, extending from Iberia through France and the Low Countries to southern Denmark. Further east, it is replaced by the Hooded Crow along a line which roughly follows the old East German border to bisect Austria and follow the southern edge of the Alps to the Mediterranean (EBA). There is a further, eastern Palearctic population ranging through the Himalayas and China. Within the British Isles, a zone of hybridisation with the Hooded Crow pursues an erratic course from the north-eastern tip of mainland Scotland to the Isle of Arran and thence, avoiding the bulge of south-west Scotland, to the Isle of Man. Carrion Crows occupy the country to the south-east and Hooded Crows the north-west. The centre of the hybrid zone was mapped by Meise in 1928, when its northern beginning was in the Fraserburgh area, but by 1974 it had moved north-west, pivoting on Arran (Cook 1975).

The Hooded Crow has always been the typical Manx crow, although Carrion Crows were present (albeit as rarities) in the late eighteenth century. The 1920s saw the first instances of Carrion Crows breeding, but until 1962 the Carrion was invariably mated with a Hoodie. In 1962 a pair of black crows nested on the Calf and there was a further instance near Bulgham Bay in 1981, while since 1980, hybrids have been found paired with both apparently pure Carrions and with Hooded Crows. The plumage of hybrids ranges from almost 'pure' Hooded Crow to almost 'pure' Carrion Crow and at these two extremes the correct assignment to species or hybrid can be difficult.

Based on the situation on Arran, Cook had suggested that there was a measurable tendency for the Carrion Crow to decrease in frequency relative to the Hooded Crow with increasing altitude, and for the latter to predominate on high ground. The Manx Bird Atlas survey has demonstrated that a similar situation obtains on the Isle of Man. No Carrion Crows were found above 270m during MBA research, while Hooded Crows were found at 470m. Carrion Crows and hybrids were more numerous during the breeding season in the north and east than in the south and west. MBA workers found 20 mixed pairs, ten being Hooded and Carrion, four Carrion and hybrid and six Hooded and hybrid.

Carrion Crows are sedentary, but collect in flocks in the autumn and winter, and the winter maps indicate a similar distribution to that for summer. They gather especially on the Ayres heath in increasing numbers. In the early 1980s such flocks barely reached double figures, although there were 17 on the German coast in late December 1983. A flock of 40 with Hoodies was present on the Ayres on 30 September 1993 and in late January 1996 a mixed flock of 122 contained only 30 Hooded Crows. Atlas workers recorded flocks of around 30 Carrion Crows, one such being during the second week of May. Typically, the Calf sees parties of up to six Carrion Crows, so that a flock of 50 near Cregneash in February 1999 was totally unexpected. In other parts of the Island, flocks made up mainly of Hooded Crows may contain up to five Carrion Crows, while on the Ayres between six and eleven hybrids may be included.

While C&J's suggestion of a Carrion Crow breeding population of between ten and 20 individuals seems to be a serious underestimate, there is little doubt that the last twenty years have seen a significant increase in black crows and hybrids.

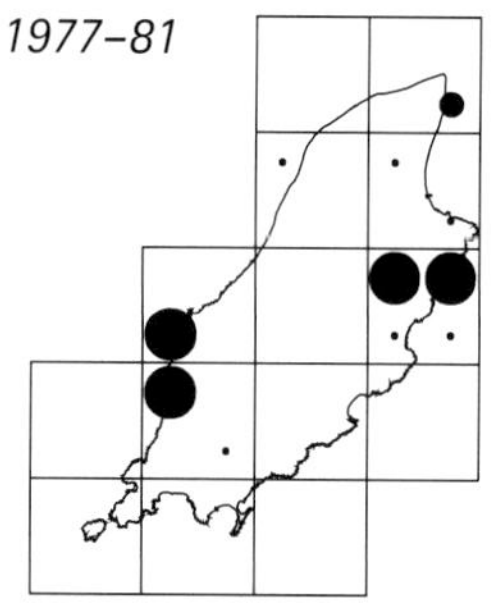

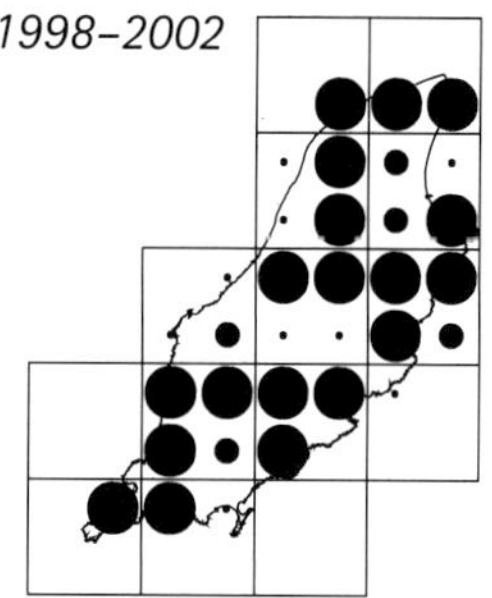

Note: Britain and Ireland grid square figures for breeding, and population figures for both breeding and wintering are those of Carrion Crow and Hooded Crow combined. The wintering grid square figure relates to Carrion Crow only.

Breeding	Grid squares:	Isle of Man 192 (29%) Britain 2,762 Ireland 970 Total 3,732 (97%)
	Population:	Isle of Man 150–189 Britain 970,000 Ireland 290,000 (21% of European)
Wintering	Grid squares:	Isle of Man 115 (17%) Britain and Ireland 2,455 (64%)
	Population:	Isle of Man 500+ Britain and Ireland 3.5 million

Jan	Feb	Mar	Apr	May	Jun	Jul	Aug	Sep	Oct	Nov	Dec

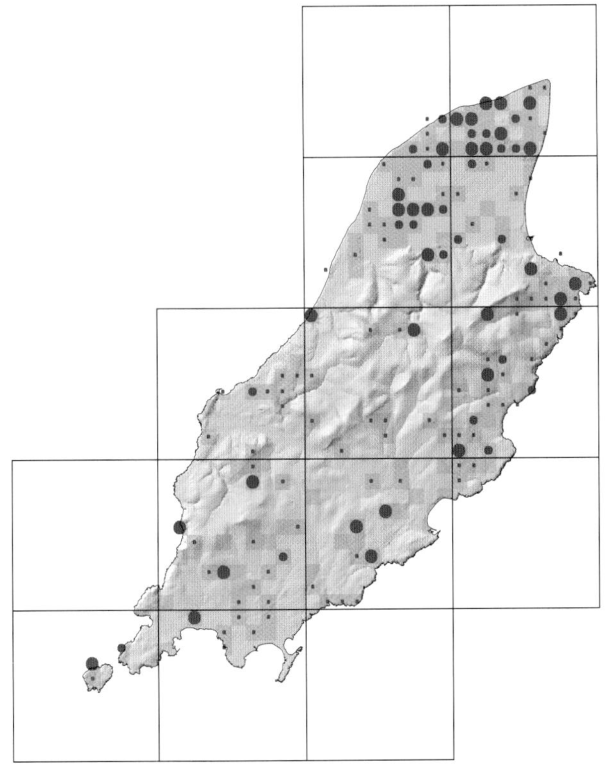
Summer presence and breeding status

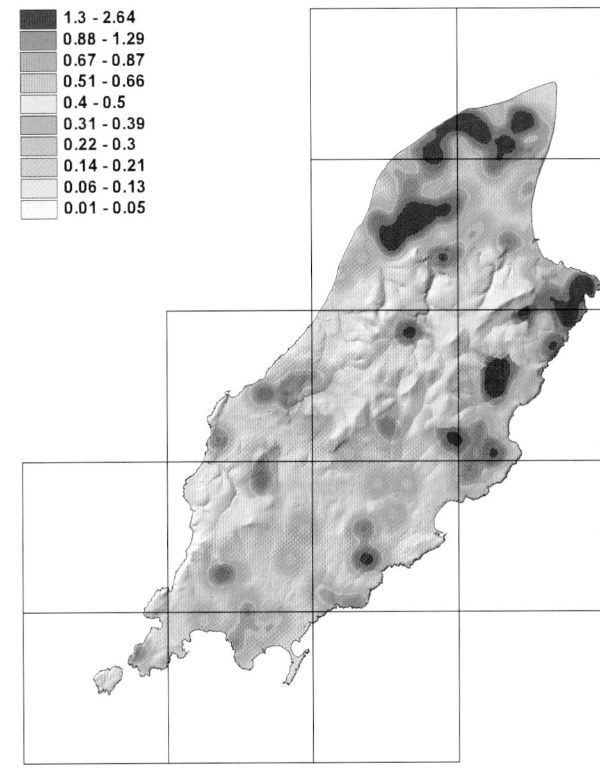

Breeding abundance

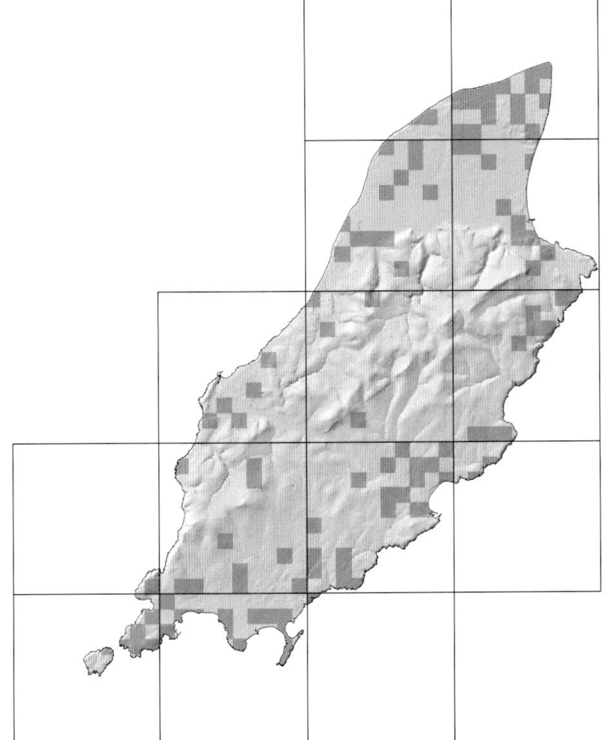
Winter presence

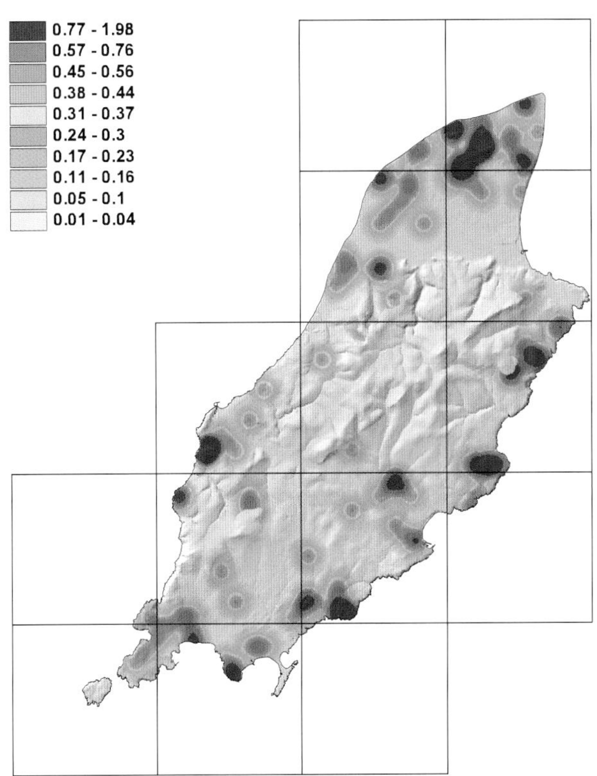

Winter abundance

Hybrid Crow
Corvus corone x *Corvus cornix*

Note: Description of this species is covered under Carrion Crow and Hooded Crow.

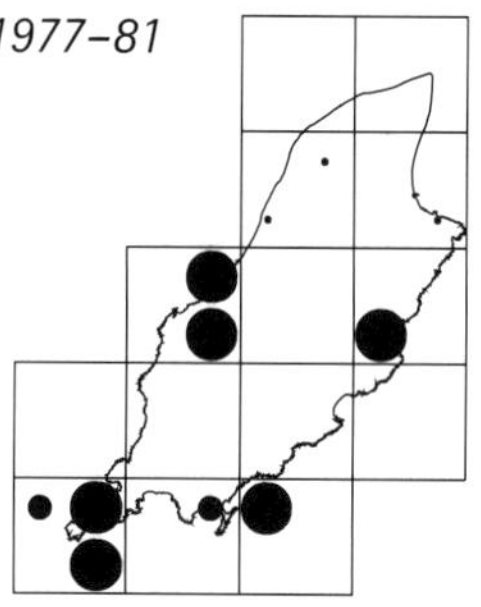

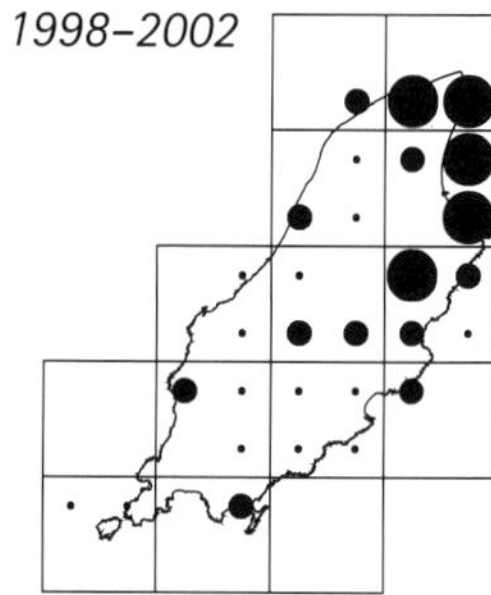

Breeding	Grid squares:	Isle of Man 95 (14%)
	Population:	Isle of Man 71–84
Wintering	Grid squares:	Isle of Man 103 (15%)
	Population:	Isle of Man 2000+

No data available for British and Irish hybrid crows

Jan	Feb	Mar	Apr	May	Jun	Jul	Aug	Sep	Oct	Nov	Dec

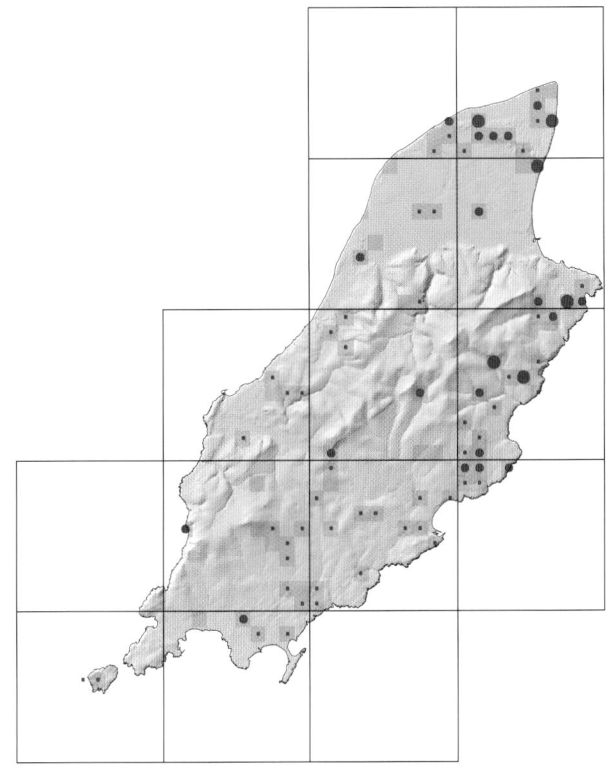

Summer presence and breeding status

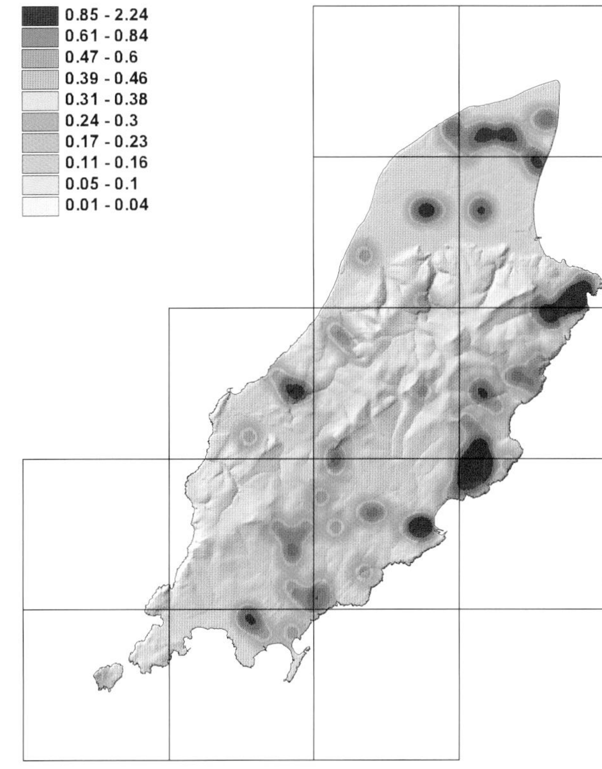

Breeding abundance

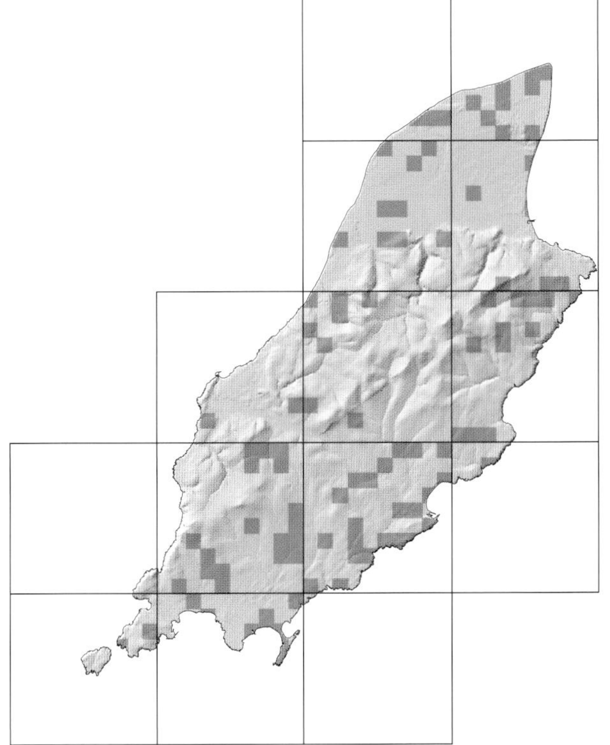

Winter presence

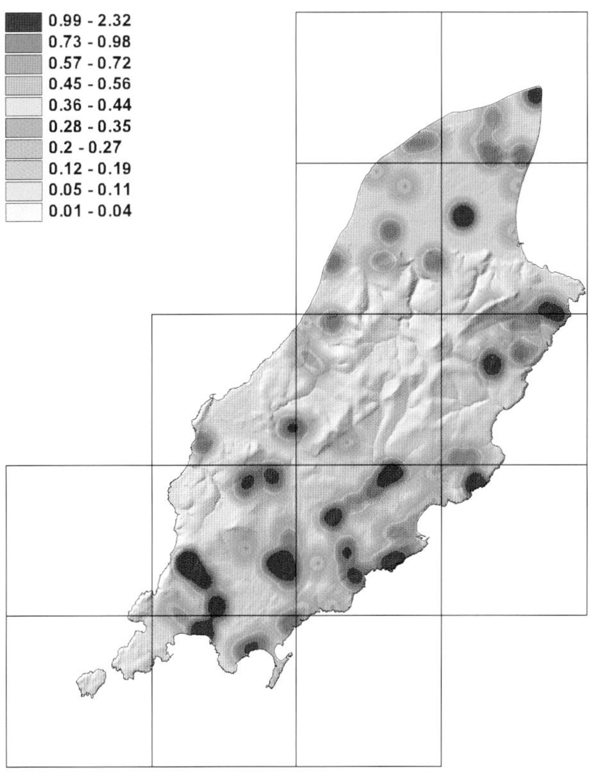

Winter abundance

Hooded Crow
Corvus cornix

Manx: *Fannag Ghlass*

The Hooded Crow, or Grey-back as it is known locally, is identical in size and silhouette to the Carrion Crow, but the dominant colour is grey, with black wings and tail. The head is also black and from it an ink-splash bib extends onto the breast. In its purest form, the grey is a light ash colour, but on the Isle of Man a complete range of darkening reflects the increasing impurity created by hybridisation with the Carrion Crow.

Still very much more common on the Island than the Carrion Crow, but sharing its habitat and food preferences, the Hooded Crow is perceived as a villain by farmers and birdwatchers alike. It is thought to harry lambs, but it is only sick animals that will be persecuted. Its reputation as an egg thief is however entirely justified.

The Hoodie is the crow of Scandinavia and eastern Europe, including Italy and the Balkans and all the Mediterranean islands east of Sardinia. From Norway, its breeding range extends westward to the Faeroes (but not as far as Iceland) and via Orkney and Shetland to that part of Scotland to the north-west of a line roughly linking Nairn and Arran. This line continues in a mainly southerly direction, such that the whole of Ireland is included in the range of the Hooded Crow. Perversely the Isle of Man takes the zone of hybridisation some way to the east of this neat geographical progression. Although Hooded Crows breeding in Britain and Ireland are sedentary, birds from Scandinavia and Denmark move south towards the Low Countries and north-east France, with very few reaching eastern Britain (BWP).

Nest building on the Isle of Man usually starts in late March, coastal nests being typically placed in a gully near the top of a craggy rock face, while most inland nests, in both rural and residential areas, are in trees. Unusual Hooded Crow sites have been on the door runner of a hangar at Ronaldsway Airport and atop a wall of 1.4m height in the Corrany valley. Four is the commonest clutch size, followed by five, while complete clutches of three and six eggs are rare. Most clutches are started in the second half of April, and extreme dates on which nests have been found with four eggs were 5 March (1908) and 19 June (1942) (C&J). Hooded Crows are widespread during the breeding season and some evidence of breeding was found in most 1km squares, though a number of the 'possible' records may relate to birds breeding in the near vicinity. The greatest concentration of breeding was down the east coast.

Outside the breeding season, Hooded Crows form flocks along with Carrion Crows and hybrids. These flocks are often to be found in coastal areas but they are also found on elevated moorland sites, in particular on South Barrule, but also to the north of Glen Helen and above Ballaugh Plantation. During the study period, flocks did not exceed 45 birds, but over 60 are reported from time to time. Ringing has only produced 3 recoveries, all on the Island, but the possibility of some movement to Ireland is suggested by the occurrence of Hybrid Crows in County Down. In winter, as for summer, they are present throughout the Island other than on the highest peaks of the northern and central hills.

The Hooded Crows' unpopularity on the Isle of Man is of long standing, for in 1687 they were regarded as vermin and fetched a bounty of one penny per head. Nevertheless the inference from early writers is that they were not particularly common. Ralfe considered the grey-back to be one of the Island's most characteristic birds, with fair numbers breeding around the rocky coast, although it was sparingly distributed in the highlands and glens. C&J concluded that it had become more common, inferring that nesting in towns was a relatively recent development. While crows as a whole are probably neither more nor less abundant than previously, one's impression is that hybrids are becoming commoner at the expense of the apparently pure grey-back.

1977–81

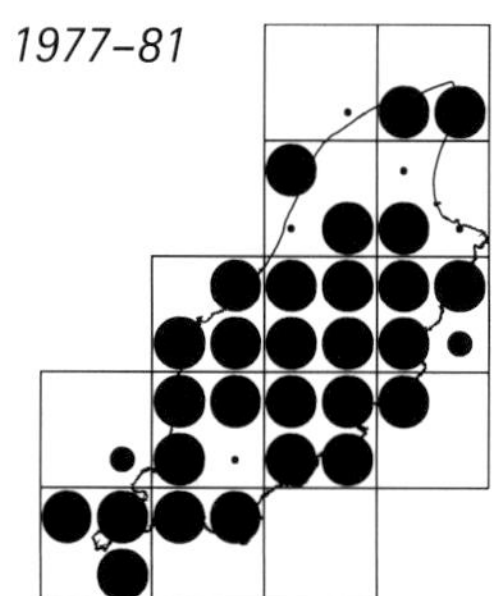

1998–2002

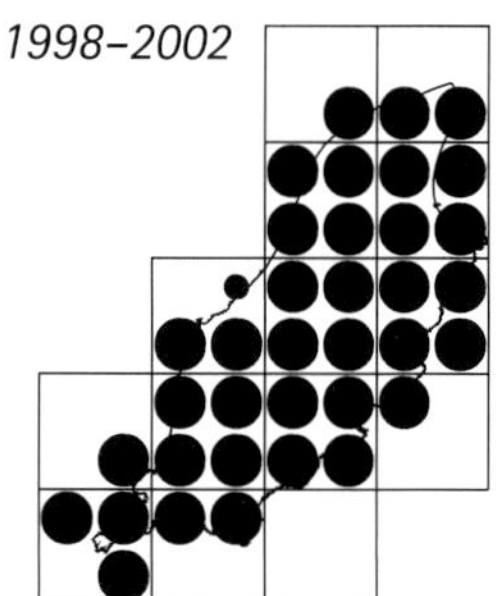

Note: Britain and Ireland grid square figures for breeding, and population figures for both breeding and wintering are those of Carrion Crow and Hooded Crow combined. The wintering grid square figure relates to Hooded Crow only.

Breeding	Grid squares:	Isle of Man 581 (87%) Britain 2,762 Ireland 970 Total 3,732 (97%)
	Population:	Isle of Man 832–1,310 Britain 970,000 Ireland 290,000 (21% of European)
Wintering	Grid squares:	Isle of Man 474 (71%) Britain and Ireland 1,842 (48%)
	Population:	Isle of Man 3,000+ Britain and Ireland 3.5 million

Jan	Feb	Mar	Apr	May	Jun	Jul	Aug	Sep	Oct	Nov	Dec

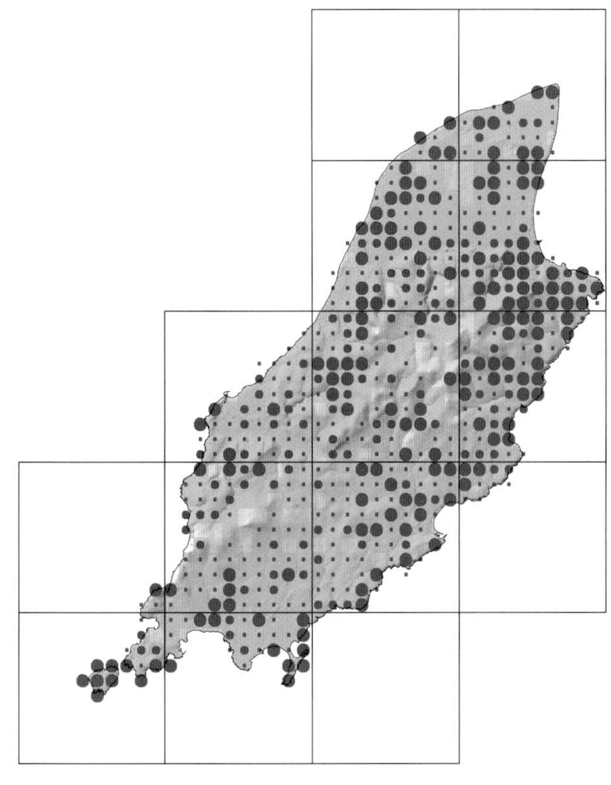

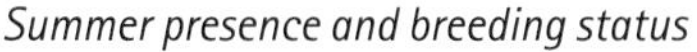

Summer presence and breeding status

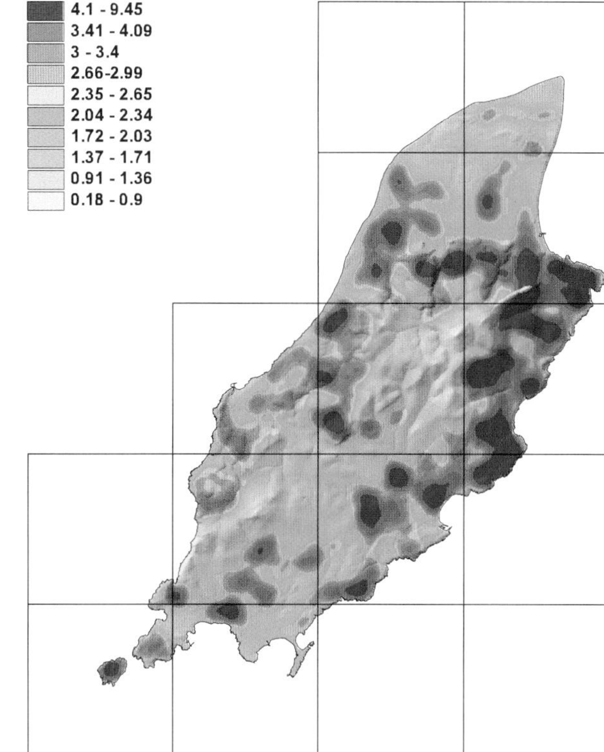

Breeding abundance

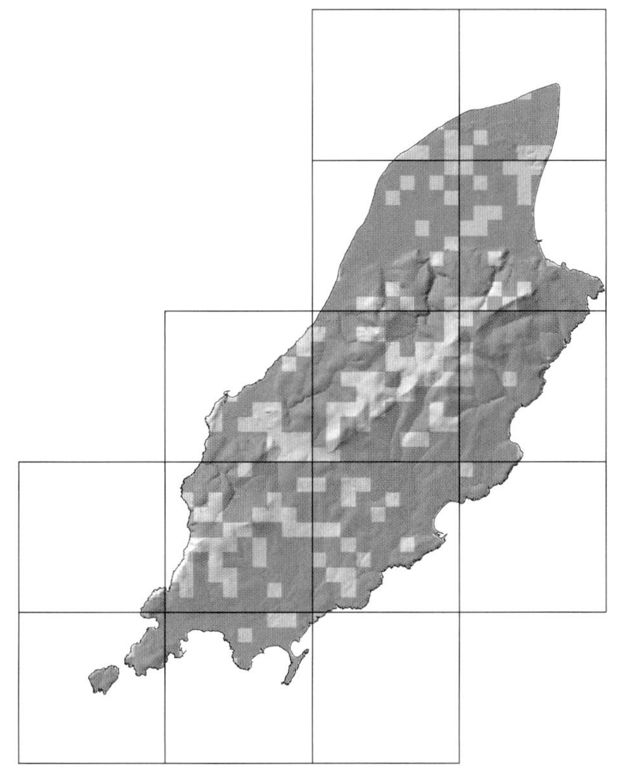

Winter presence

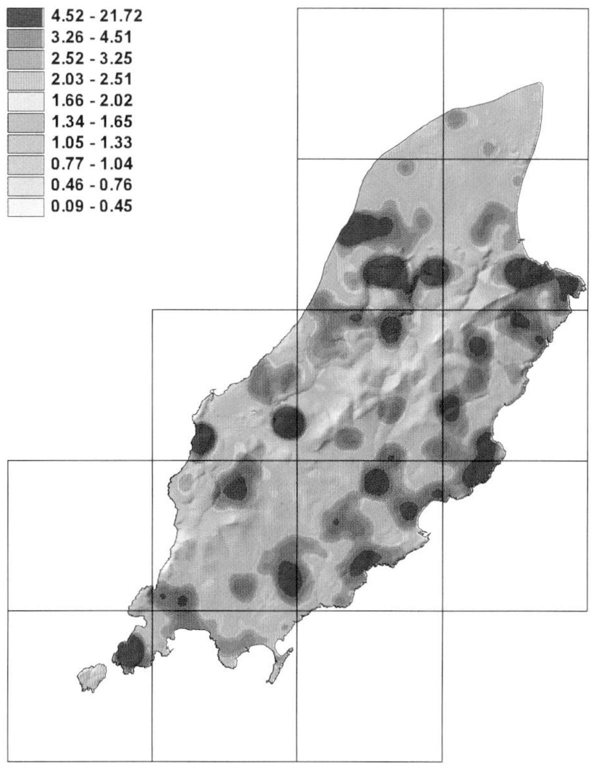

Winter abundance

Individual Sponsor – Mrs. Betty Hopson

Raven (Common Raven)
Corvus corax

Manx: *Feeagh, Feeagh Vooar*

The Raven and the Peregrine are two of the Island's finest and most typical birds, sharing the same habitat and enjoying an antagonistic relationship. Largest of the crow family by a considerable margin, the Raven is easily identified at rest, when the great stout bill and prominent throat feathers are unmistakable. In flight the long wings and wedge-shaped tail also aid recognition. Frequently, it is the call which first advertises the Raven's presence – sometimes a deep, guttural croak, but often a strangely high-pitched triple 'kop-kop-kop' delivered from high in the sky. Early in the year courtship will involve remarkable aerobatics, while, if one trespasses in the vicinity of the nest the pair may hop around clumsily, picking up tufts of grass in their agitation.

The Raven is traditionally perceived as a bird of wild moorland and lonely coastal cliffs, nesting usually on rocky ledges. Increasingly, however, the Manx population is occupying wooded areas, especially those flanking streams, but also trees within the extensive grounds of rural mansions. In winter they may discard their reputation for wariness and visit such populous areas as Douglas Promenade. The Raven is essentially a scavenger, attracted to animal corpses, rubbish tips and the tideline. It will boldly rob the nests of birds as large as a heron and on the moors will identify a sick or dead lamb with vulture-like skill. It is however an omnivore and will readily turn to plant material as well.

The several subspecies are represented over much of the temperate zones of Asia, Europe and North America. The European range is patchy – well represented throughout Fennoscandia, the north-east, the Balkans and, especially, Spain, it is scarce or absent over much of central and northern France, Benelux, western Germany and south-east to western Romania. In the British Isles it is present in the West Country, Wales, the Lake District, the southern uplands of Scotland and the Scottish Highlands and Western Isles. Although plentiful over much of Ireland, it is generally scarce in the central lowlands. It is evenly distributed on the Isle of Man, increasingly nesting in lowland areas in addition to the more traditional coastal and moorland habitats.

Following the MBA protocol, 53 active breeding sites were identified in 1999, but additional sites were found during routine fieldwork and a comprehensive survey was undertaken in 2002, when all historic and recent nest sites were visited, yielding a total of 84 definite breeding pairs with a further four 'probables' and one 'possible'. Of these 84 pairs, 57 were nesting at inland sites, 50 of them in trees (predominantly conifers). Tree nesting on the Island was unknown until 1932, when a pair nested near the heronry at Ballamoar Castle.

Numbers of nests in various sites used by Ravens in selected years 1941–2002.

Year	Coastal rock cliff	Coastal sand cliff	Inland quarry	Inland gorge	Inland cliff	Inland tree	Inland % in trees	Total
1941	17	1	6	5	1	1	8	33*
1977	12	1	6	4	1	6	35	30
1982	11	0	8	4	2	8	36	33
1988	13	1	4	3	2	7	44	30
1992	16	1	3	1	3	6	46	30
1993	13	1	2	2	1	5	50	24
1994	14	1	3	3	2	5	38	28
2002	25	2	5	2	0	50	88	84

* includes two nests in unspecified sites, mentioned as a postscript (Cowin, 1941).

Even allowing for inadequacy of previous censuses, tree nests in particular being easily overlooked, there has been a very notable increase in the population. Thirty-two territories, previously unknown, were identified. Factors which may have aided this population explosion are the virtual cessation of human persecution, the steady increase in the sheep population and the presence of a refuse tip at the Point of Ayre, which might have helped reduce winter mortality rates. Ravens are early nesters and a few clutches will be started in mid-February.

Although flocks of Ravens are seen throughout the year at the Point of Ayre tip, they peak there in winter, when up to 125 birds may gather. The slopes and summit of South Barrule have long been favoured by flocks of up to 50 birds, while smaller flocks turn up on North Barrule and the Michael hills. The winter abundance map reflects these concentrations well, with high densities along the hill ridges and at the (now closed) Point of Ayre tip.

Depicted with Odin on Thorwald's tenth-century cross slab at Kirk Andreas, the Raven receives more attention in historical Manx documents than any other bird. It is also unrivalled in the extent to which it has been studied over the twentieth century. Clearly the more or less stable population in the latter part of the century had increased significantly by 2002. Future monitoring might reveal whether the removal of a convenient winter food supply at the Point of Ayre will have an impact upon breeding levels.

1977–81

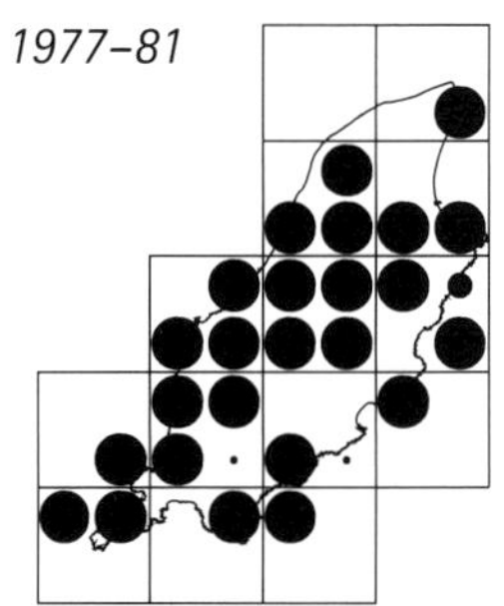

1998–2002

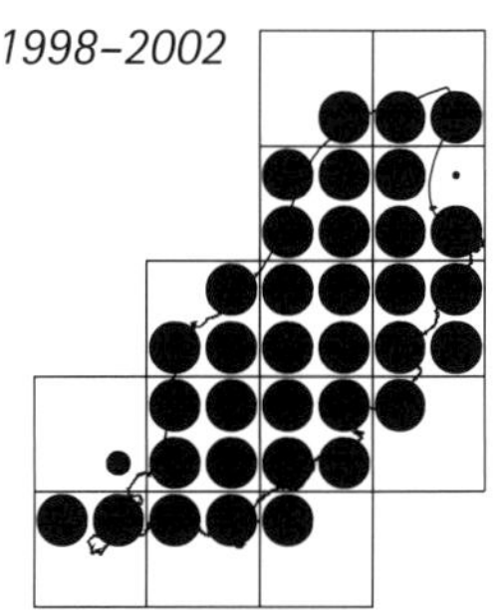

Breeding	Grid squares:	Isle of Man 415 (62%) Britain 1,131 Ireland 686 Total 1,817 (47%)
	Population:	Isle of Man 85–89 Britain 7,000 Ireland 3,500 (1% of European)
Wintering	Grid squares:	Isle of Man 332 (50%) Britain and Ireland 1,712 (44%)
	Population:	Isle of Man 300+ Britain and Ireland 20,000

Jan Feb Mar Apr May Jun Jul Aug Sep Oct Nov Dec

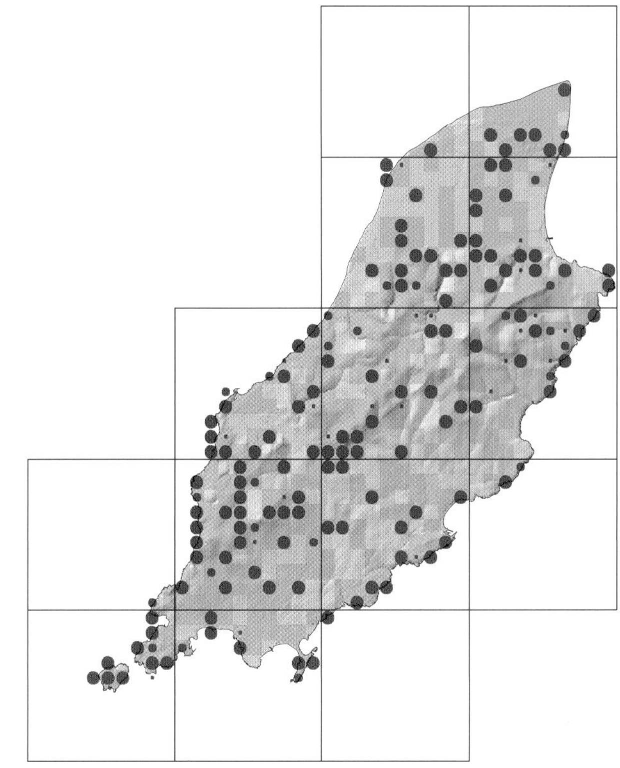

Summer presence and breeding status

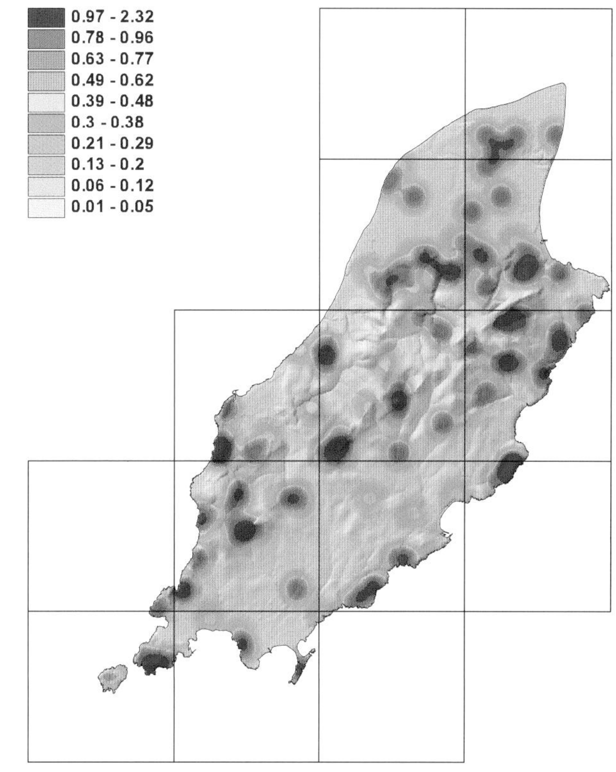

Breeding abundance

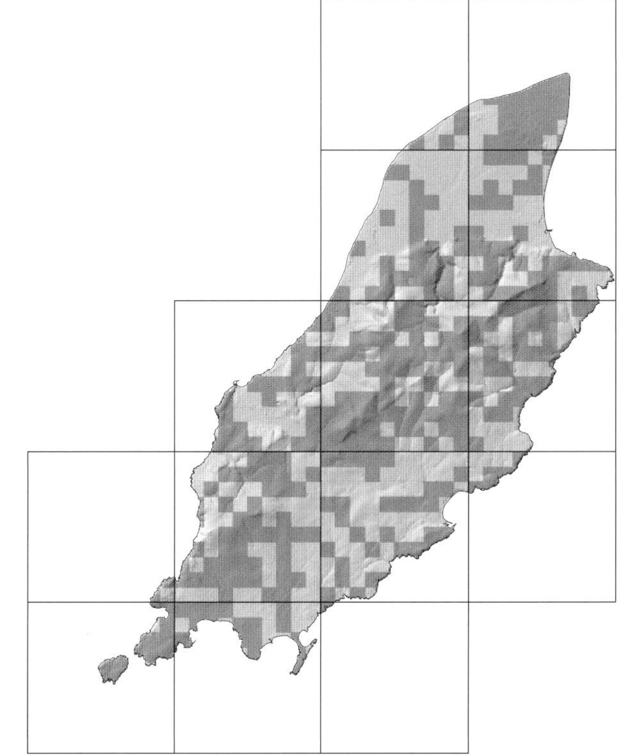

Winter presence

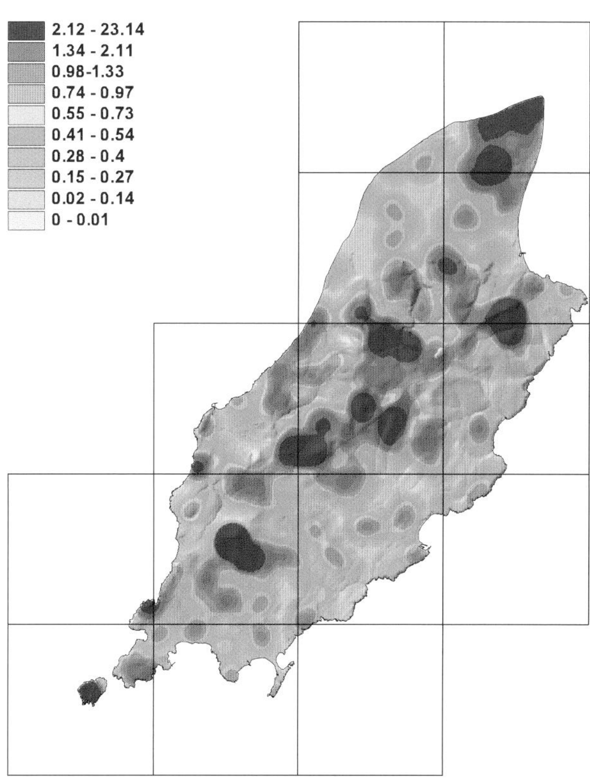

Winter abundance

Individual Sponsors – Mr. R Cullen, Mr. C L Howland, Mr. R & Mrs. M Macleod, Mr. A S Martin, Mr. D J Sharpe, Mr. D P Shearan

Starling (Common Starling)
Sturnus vulgaris

Manx: *Truitlag*

Starlings are one of the best known birds on the Isle of Man, their charismatic presence a welcome addition to gardens as they busily probe for food on the lawn, or squabble over kitchen scraps and bird table offerings. Particularly in summer, their plumage, which appears black at first glance, contains an iridescent sheen that ranges from green through to purple, and is offset by countless white spots. During the breeding season males have a blue-grey base to their yellow bills, providing an easy means of separating the sexes. Females have a pale-pink base – blue for boys, pink for girls.

During the breeding season the choice of nesting habitat is dictated by the availability of suitable holes, either natural (hollows in trees or rock crevices), or artificial (cavities in buildings and stone boundary walls). The species' adaptability in making use of artificial habitats has resulted in its close association with human settlements. Starlings are omnivorous, though generally a greater proportion of invertebrate food is taken in the summer, changing to berries and soft fruit when available in autumn with a larger quantity of seed taken as winter progresses (BWP). Food is mainly taken from the surface or sub-surface of the ground by walking and probing, flocks of Starlings often being observed in long irregular lines, systematically covering fields and parks.

The breeding range of the Starling extends across the Palearctic between about 40°N and 70°N (EBA) and, with help from humans, the species is now also well established in North America, South Africa, Australia and New Zealand. Within the British Isles Starlings have a wide breeding distribution, being absent only from the highlands of Scotland, though densities are generally lower where permanent grassland is not available (1988–91 Atlas). On the Isle of Man they are to be found throughout the lowlands. Though many Manx farms support at least one pair of nesting Starlings, it is in the Island's towns and villages that they most frequently breed. The summer abundance map highlights high densities in the majority of the major towns and villages and the housing and industrial estates at Jurby in the north-west, though comparatively few birds were found in either Laxey or Peel, there being no apparent reason for this.

British ringing data indicate that the breeding population is resident and does not migrate, but significant numbers of Starlings come into the British Isles from across Northern Europe, from Holland to the Baltic States (MA). Manx ringing data support the northern European origin of many Starlings moving through the Island in spring or autumn, or wintering here, birds from, for example, Holland, Denmark, Estonia and Latvia having been found on the Island.

In winter the number of Starlings on the Island increases greatly. The Atlas winter survey data indicate about 5,000 birds, but this may be expected to vary considerably between and within years, depending upon European weather conditions. From late summer through into winter large feeding flocks can be seen on the beaches, particularly in the south in areas like Langness and Strandhall, where insect larvae in rotting seaweed provide an abundant food source. Initially these flocks comprise local breeders and their young, with numbers augmented by migrants with the onset of winter. Starlings are widespread in winter, birds even visiting higher ground in their endless search for food. Sizeable flocks were, however, largely restricted to the north, east and south-east coasts being the result of a combination of available agricultural grassland and plentiful beach foraging opportunities.

In the absence of any historical numerical estimates, it is difficult to compare Starling numbers found during the Atlas work with those present in the past. Kermode considered the Starling to be 'plentiful and apparently increasing' and Ralfe stated that there had been a great increase in numbers and that 'it now nests all over Man'. Both knew the species to be resident, but with greater numbers arriving for the winter. Madoc said that 'it is to be seen everywhere in vast flocks' and C&J describe it as an 'abundant resident, passage migrant and winter visitor'. Thus there is little to suggest any major change in abundance of Manx Starlings, at least up to 1982. In Britain, breeding and wintering numbers of Starlings have dropped greatly in recent years (Feare 1994, Crick *et al.* 1998, MA), as in much of Northern Europe (EBA). It is probable, therefore, that numbers breeding on the Island, as well as numbers arriving for the winter have also declined.

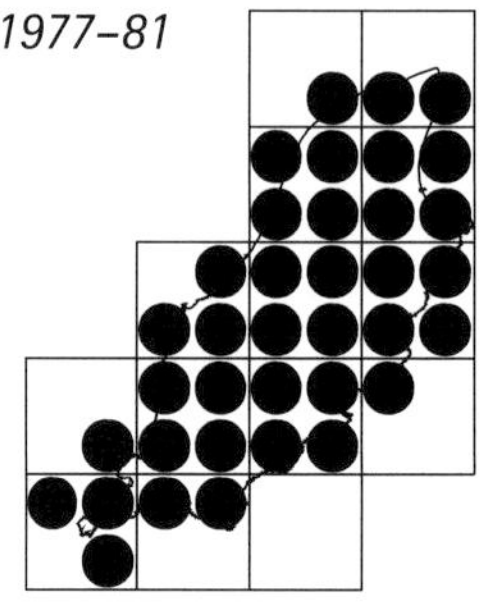

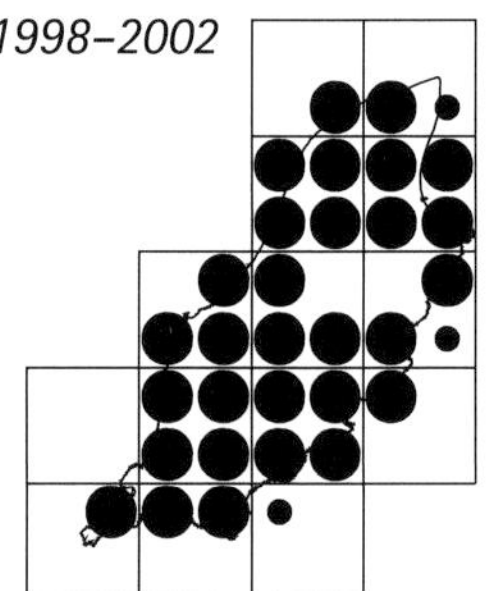

Breeding	Grid squares:	Isle of Man 340 (51%) Britain 2,620 Ireland 957 Total 3,577 (93%)
	Population:	Isle of Man 904–1,609 Britain 1,100,000 Ireland 360,000 (4% of European)
Wintering	Grid squares:	Isle of Man 336 (51%) Britain and Ireland 3,469 (90%)
	Population:	Isle of Man 5,000+ Britain and Ireland 37 million

Jan	Feb	Mar	Apr	May	Jun	Jul	Aug	Sep	Oct	Nov	Dec

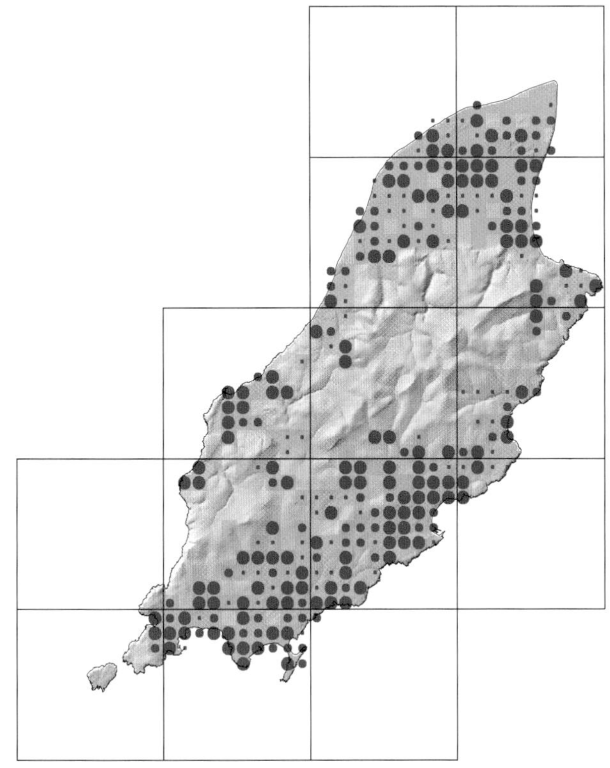

Summer presence and breeding status

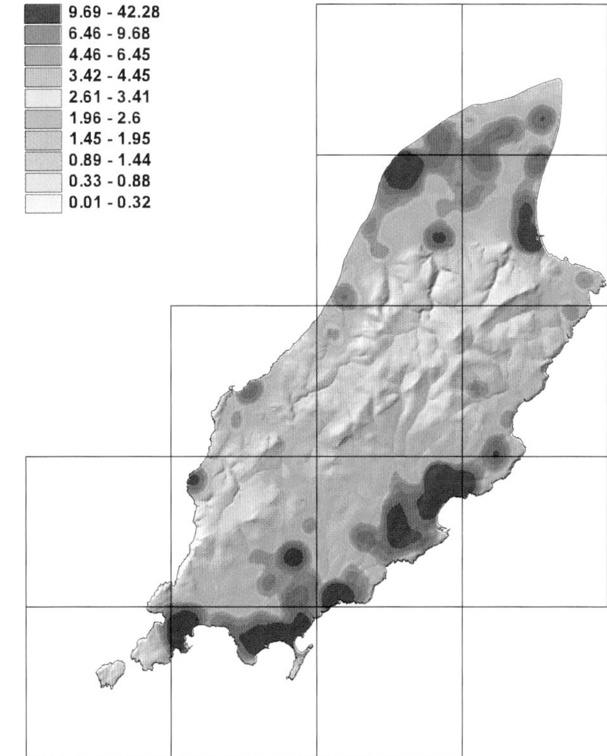

Breeding abundance

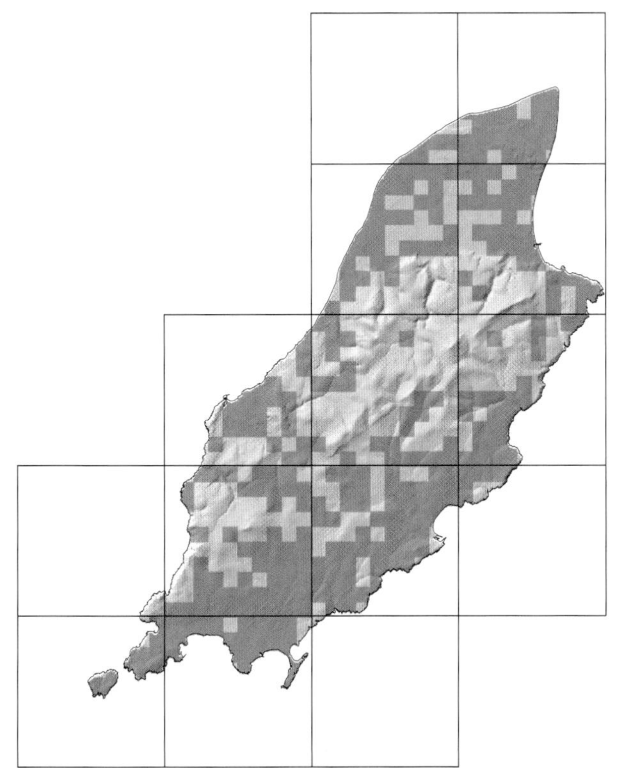

Winter presence

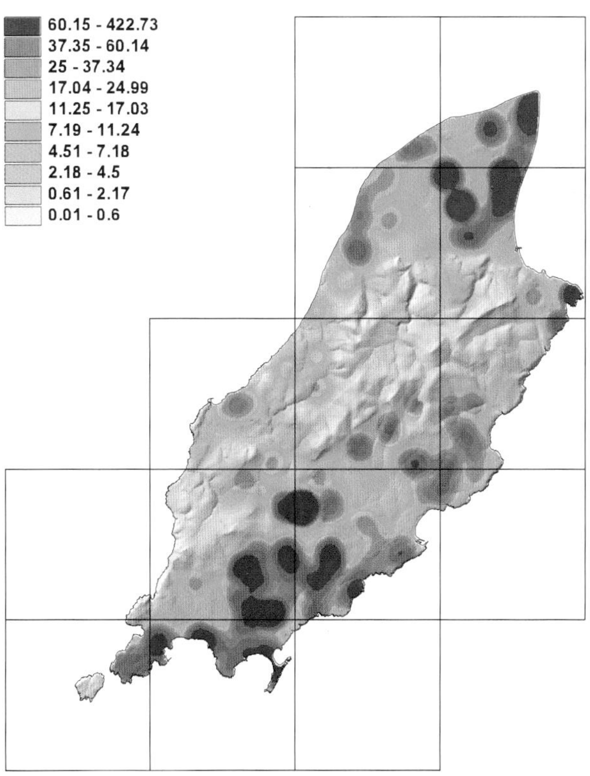

Winter abundance

Individual Sponsor – Mrs. J A Burn

House Sparrow
Passer domesticus

Manx: *Jallyn*

The fact that the House Sparrow is one of the most familiar of birds owes more to its habit of living in close proximity to humans than it does to either a striking plumage or melodious song. Males could possibly be mistaken for the superficially similar, but less common, Tree Sparrow. In breeding plumage, however, the black bib of the male House Sparrow is more extensive than that of its close relative, while at all times the grey crown and off-white/grey cheek patch of the House Sparrow provide the necessary confirmation of identity.

Though House Sparrows are found mainly around houses and other places of human habitation, the most favourable habitat is areas where a combination of buildings provide suitable nesting opportunity and nearby areas of open ground provide suitable feeding locations. They are thus more abundant in suburban areas and at the edges of towns than they are in town centres and cities, unless these contain parkland (1988–91 Atlas). Nests are usually inside buildings, for example under eaves or in holes in walls, though they will also take over nests of House Martins and, less frequently, Swallows, as well as moving readily to nest boxes. Throughout the year adult House Sparrows take mainly seeds, fruit and other plant material, though in the breeding season they are more likely to take invertebrates, while young are fed almost exclusively animal food during the early part of the nestling period (BWP).

The natural breeding range of the House Sparrow extends across Eurasia, north-west Africa and the Nile Valley, reaching above the Arctic Circle in the west and part-way across Siberia. From its association with humans the House Sparrow has also been introduced elsewhere and has spread through most of the Americas from Canada to southern Chile, and also to South and West Africa, Australia, New Zealand and to many oceanic islands (BWP, MA). Within the British Isles House Sparrows are widespread and are missing only from the high ground of the Scottish Highlands. They are more abundant in the east than the west, this perhaps being related to rainfall (1988–91 Atlas). On the Isle of Man the species is widespread, being absent only from high ground and some coastal areas where suitable nest sites are absent. Areas of high abundance reflect centres of human population, with the exception of Laxey on the east coast, which has relatively few House Sparrows. While the reason for this is not known, it may relate to localised high rainfall combined with lower winter temperatures in the steep valley in which most of the village nestles. Away from the towns and villages, House Sparrows are well represented on most farms.

Here, as in mainland Britain, ringing data indicate that House Sparrows are resident and highly sedentary, with few birds moving any distance. In the British Isles the median distance between ringing and recovery is less than 1km, with studies revealing that once birds have bred they remain faithful to the breeding colony for life (MA).

In view of the House Sparrow's sedentary nature, the maps illustrating winter and summer distribution are predictably very similar. Throughout the northern plain there is some indication that they may be more widespread in winter with flocks of foraging birds dispersing to find suitable feeding opportunity.

On the Island there is little to suggest any change of status in the species. Kermode considered the House Sparrow to be 'plentiful' and Ralfe thought it was to be found wherever there were houses. Madoc noted it as numerous and C&J describe it as a 'common resident'. Thus the species continues to be one of our commonest breeding birds. However in parts of Britain and Ireland the population is thought to have declined significantly in recent years, particularly in the countryside and in the centres of large towns (MA), the causes of these decreases being little understood. Locally, the demolition or renovation of old properties in towns and villages, together with improvements to agricultural buildings, are likely to reduce nesting opportunities and might impact on population levels. These losses could be partially offset by erecting nest boxes, while further monitoring should aim to determine whether losses in the wider British Isles are mirrored on the Island.

1977–81

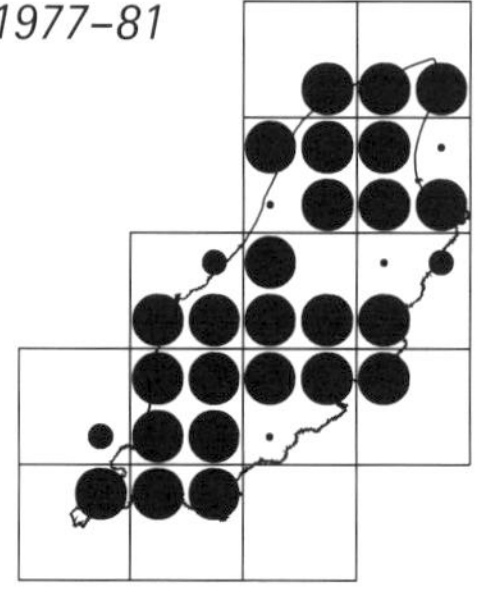

1998–2002

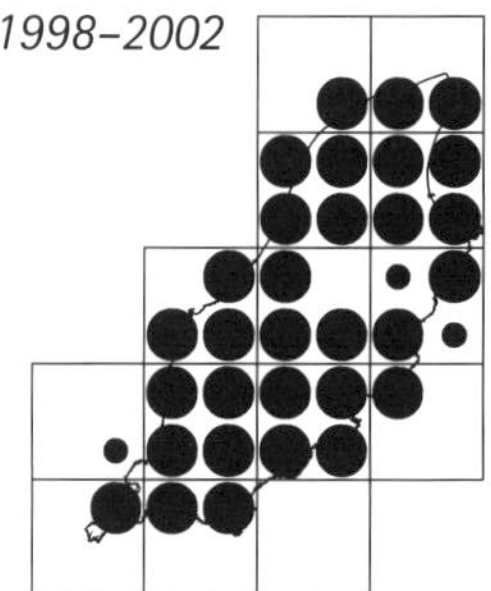

Breeding	Grid squares:	Isle of Man 358 (54%) Britain 2,525 Ireland 901 Total 3,426 (89%)
	Population:	Isle of Man 2,158–3,739 Britain 3,600,000 Ireland 1,100,000 (9% of European)
Wintering	Grid squares:	Isle of Man 294 (44%) Britain and Ireland 3,282 (85%)
	Population:	Isle of Man 10,000+ Britain and Ireland 10-15 million

Jan	Feb	Mar	Apr	May	Jun	Jul	Aug	Sep	Oct	Nov	Dec

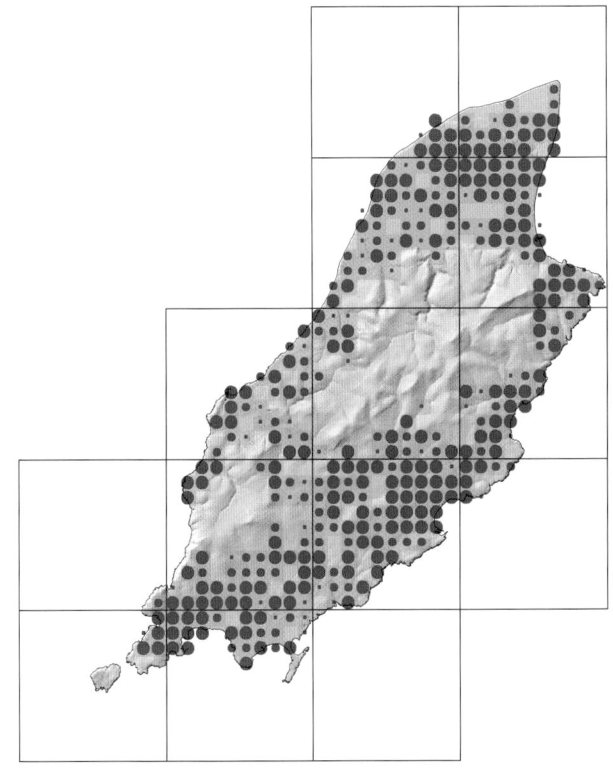

Summer presence and breeding status

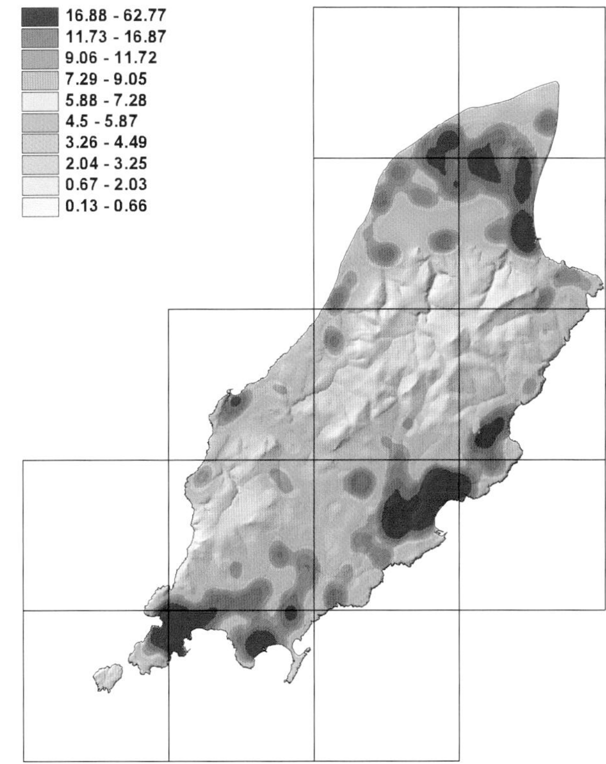

Breeding abundance

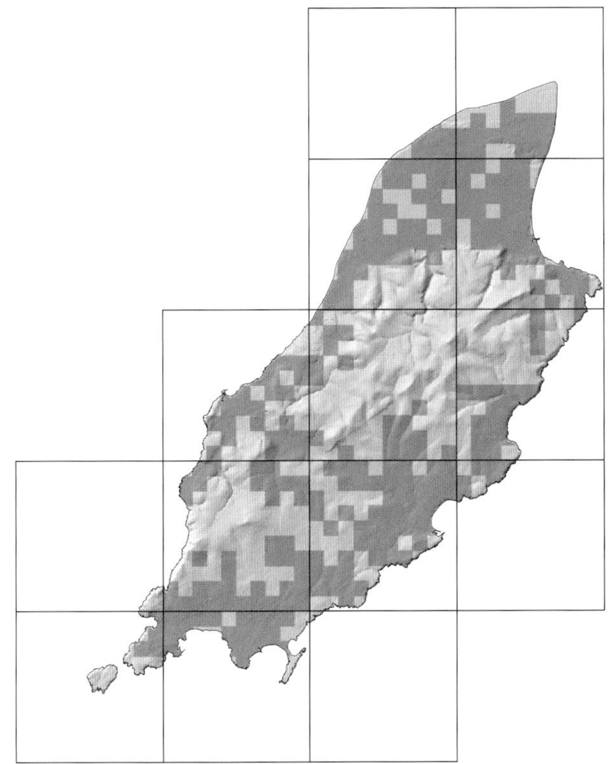

Winter presence

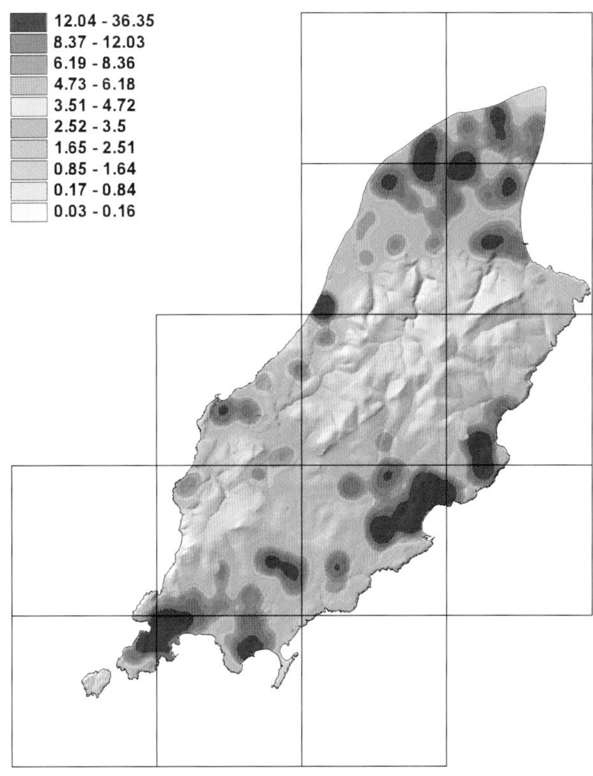

Winter abundance

Individual Sponsors – Mrs. I Bedey, Ms. E Cowin

Tree Sparrow (Eurasian Tree Sparrow)
Passer montanus

Male and female Tree Sparrows have identical plumage, making it impossible to separate the sexes visually. They are slightly smaller than the related House Sparrow and may most easily be distinguished from the male of that species by having an entirely red-brown crown, smaller black bib and a pure white side of the face, broken by a prominent black cheek patch.

Within the British Isles the Tree Sparrow is predominantly a bird of farmland, though further east across Eurasia it becomes more of a bird of built-up areas, being equally at home in towns and villages (MA). The preferred natural nest site is a hole in a tree though, rarely, a free-standing nest may be built in the branches of dense conifers or hawthorn (BWP). During MBA research a number of nests were found in the walls of rural buildings, while nest boxes are adopted as an alternative to natural holes. Both plant and animal food is taken, the proportions varying seasonally. Seeds comprise the main plant matter, usually taken from on the ground (BWP), especially in winter, when flocks of Tree Sparrows often join other seedeaters in stubble fields.

Tree Sparrows have an extensive distribution, ranging across most of the Palearctic into China and Japan and south into Vietnam, Burma and Indonesia. Introduced populations exist in Australia and the United States (BWP, EBA). In the British Isles the Tree Sparrow is essentially a lowland species, most commonly found on farmland and the edge of built-up areas (1988–91 Atlas) and is thus absent or scarce on high ground, many of the treeless Scottish islands and in conurbations. On the Isle of Man breeding distribution is fragmented, being centred on the northern plain, with isolated pockets near Peel in the west and from Port Soderick south to Billown in the south-east. Other scattered sightings, particularly down the east coast, were not thought to represent breeding birds. The importance of the northern agricultural plain is clear on the summer abundance map.

British ringing data indicate that Tree Sparrows are resident and generally highly sedentary; most of those recovered are less than 1km from where they were ringed though a proportion of the British population demonstrates a mostly southerly dispersal during autumn and winter (MA). There is generally no major spring or autumn passage of Tree Sparrows through the Calf of Man and, in some years, none are seen at all. The very few ringed there have yielded no recoveries from elsewhere. Those seen on the Calf in spring may be Manx birds seeking breeding territories while those seen in autumn may be dispersing after breeding.

The winter distribution of Tree Sparrows is broadly as for summer, with a suggestion of some dispersal of the western and southern population, perhaps into suitable feeding areas. The continued presence during winter down the east coast, where there was no evidence of breeding, is puzzling and involves too many sightings from different observers to be explained by misidentification. The apparent higher densities in the winter, compared to the summer, are probably due to the tendency of Tree Sparrows to flock during the winter, giving isolated pockets of high density where such flocks were encountered during surveys. In summer birds were more evenly spread in suitable habitat.

Ralfe describes the Tree Sparrow as being probably widespread, but a few years earlier Kermode had been unaware of the species on the Island. Madoc considered it 'by no means uncommon' and C&J thought the species to be a 'a rather scarce and locally distributed resident, which may also occur as a passage migrant and winter visitor' and suggest the species may have been overlooked before about 1900. Tree Sparrow populations are known to fluctuate greatly in Western Europe (1988–91 Atlas, MA, EBA) and in Britain and Ireland were very high up to about 1980 after which they dropped by about 85%. Presumably similar changes may have occurred on the Island, with the change maps between the time of C&J and MBA research suggesting localised range contraction other than on the northern plain. As regards the future, the continued availability of suitable food, in both summer and winter, will be dependent to some degree on targeted agri-environmental support measures, while the continued availability of nesting sites can be aided by erecting suitable nest boxes near known breeding populations.

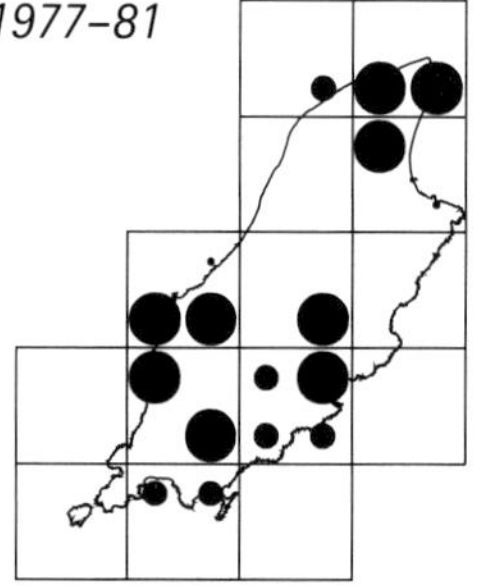

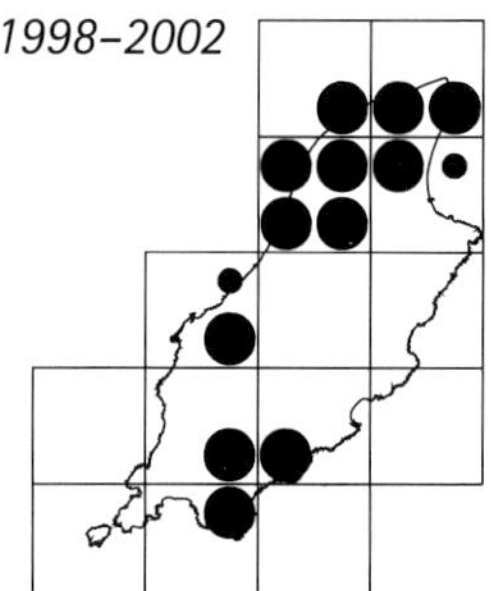

Breeding	Grid squares:	Isle of Man 116 (17%) Britain 1,346 Ireland 130 Total 1,476 (38%)
	Population:	Isle of Man 156–240 Britain 110,000 Ireland 9,000 (1% of European)
Wintering	Grid squares:	Isle of Man 85 (13%) Britain and Ireland 1,537 (40%)
	Population:	Isle of Man <1,000 Britain and Ireland 800,000

Jan	Feb	Mar	Apr	May	Jun	Jul	Aug	Sep	Oct	Nov	Dec

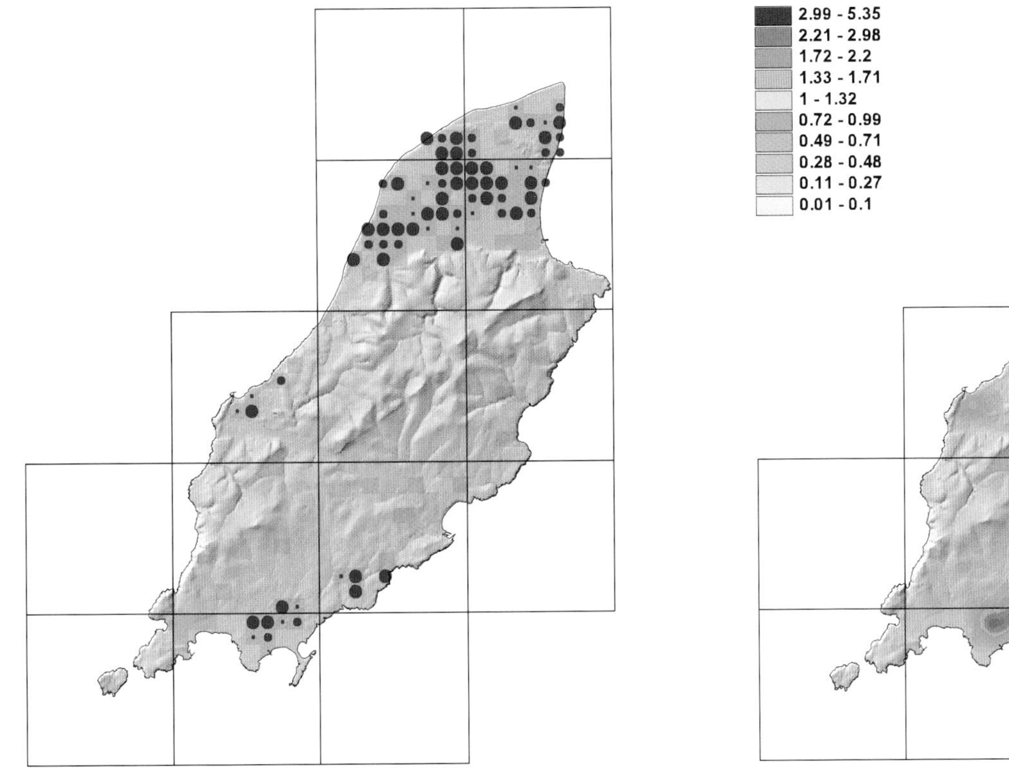

Summer presence and breeding status

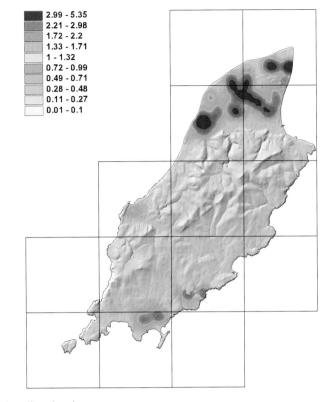

Breeding abundance

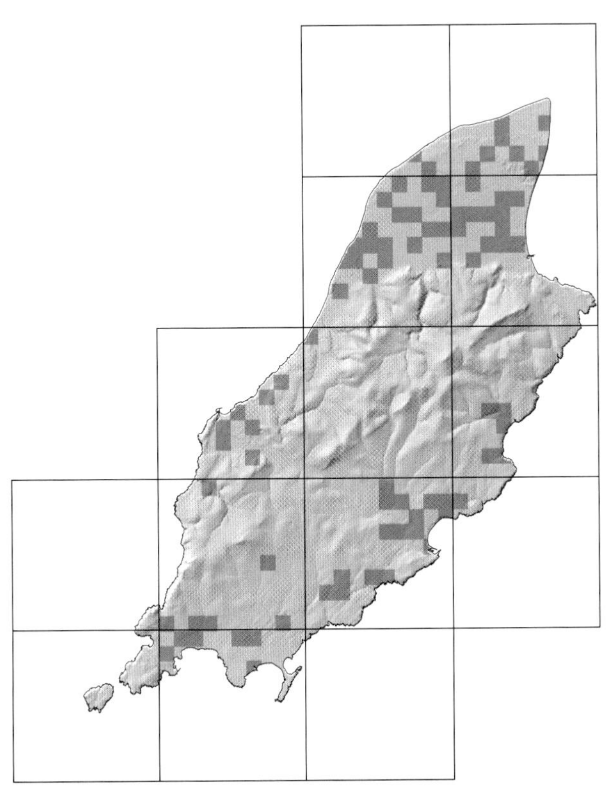

Winter presence

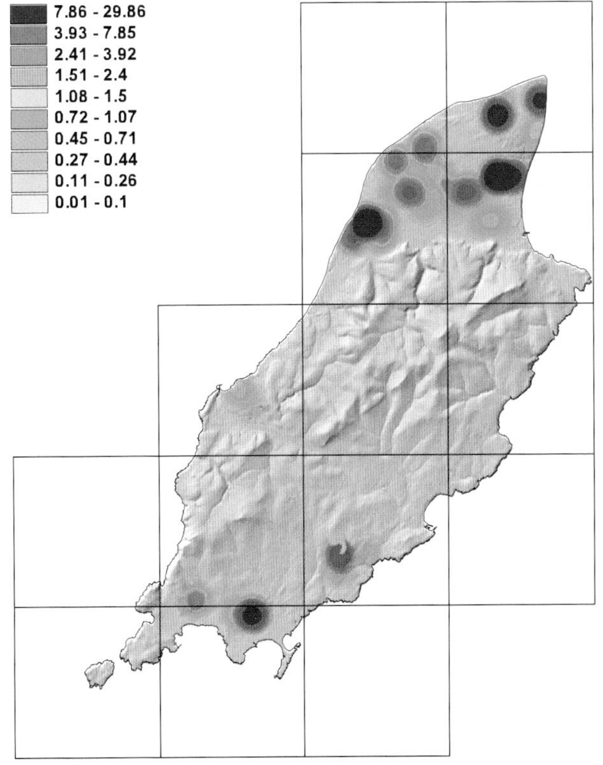

Winter abundance

Individual Sponsors – Mrs. I Bedey, Mr. A Kelly, Mr. P Roper, Mr. I Smith

Chaffinch
Fringilla coelebs

Manx: *Ushag y Choan* = Bird of the valley, *Ushag veg vreck* = Little pied bird

On the Island the Chaffinch has long been, and remains, one of the most abundant breeding birds. Males with their bright rust-red cheeks and breast and blue-grey crown and mantle stand out more readily than the duller females, though in both sexes the distinctive white wing bars and grey-green rump aid identification when birds are seen flying away.

During the breeding season Chaffinches occur in a wide range of wooded habitats, such as broad-leaved, mixed and coniferous woods, farm hedgerows and parks. They are typical garden birds being equally at home in rural, suburban and urban situations (BWP). In winter, Chaffinches also frequent open farmland, where suitable food is available, even if it is some distance from tree cover. In the breeding season invertebrates are mainly taken, usually from within the canopy layer, while at other times seeds and other plant material comprise the bulk of the diet, usually taken on the ground (BWP).

Chaffinches have a breeding distribution extending across the Palearctic from the Azores and Madeira in western Europe to central Siberia and reaching north as far as the limit of the trees (EBA). The distribution in the British Isles is generally governed by the availability of suitable habitat and so the species is largely absent from, for example, the Scottish Highlands and Outer Isles (1988–91 Atlas). As a breeding species Chaffinches are almost ubiquitous throughout the Island below about 400m and are absent only from the higher parts of the northern hills, South Barrule, parts of the coast and parts of the Mull, Scarlett and Langness Peninsulas. Areas of highest abundance largely match areas of optimum habitat with the central valley and the wooded northern foothills and curragh area clearly suiting the species well. Elsewhere, isolated pockets of high abundance were found in the Laxey valleys and in a number of the more mature plantations, such as Ballaugh and Archallagan, which contain well developed rides, clearings and river valleys in which there is a mix of both broad-leaved and coniferous woodland.

Chaffinches breeding in the British Isles are resident (MA), but in winter the population is approximately doubled by a large influx of birds from northern Europe, mainly Fennoscandia (MA, EBA). These arrive in September and October and leave in March. Large numbers of these northern European Chaffinches reach the Island, some remaining as winter visitors, but many as passage migrants en route to Ireland or elsewhere. Of the numerous Chaffinches ringed annually on the Calf, there is a predominance of females. This indicates that these migrants are probably mainly bound for Ireland, as northern females apparently tend to migrate further than the males, leading to an excess of females in Ireland, but an excess of males in England (BWP, MA).

In winter the overall distribution is very similar to that for the summer with birds being absent only from the uplands and some coastal areas. The abundance map reveals a slightly different pattern in winter compared to summer, with areas of higher density in more isolated pockets indicating large flocks scattered throughout generally suitable habitat. Some abandonment of the hill slopes is suggested, with MBA surveys not finding Chaffinches above 340m in winter, compared to 400m in summer.

To Kermode, Ralfe and Madoc the Chaffinch was clearly a very common bird, and it was described by C&J as an abundant resident, passage migrant and winter visitor to the Island, and little seems to have changed since then. This is in keeping with the situation in Britain, where the resident Chaffinch population has probably changed little in recent decades (1988–91 Atlas).

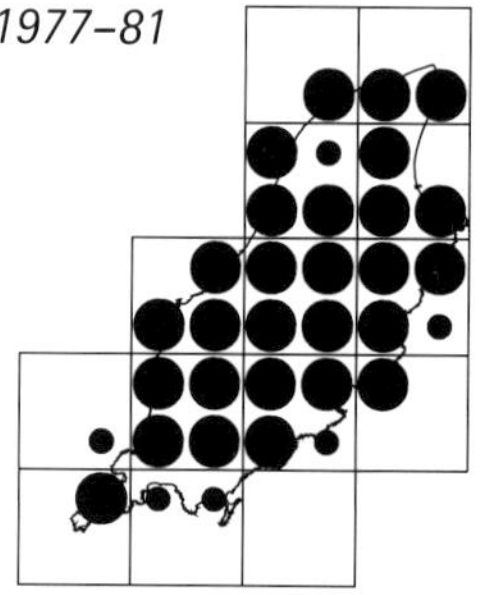

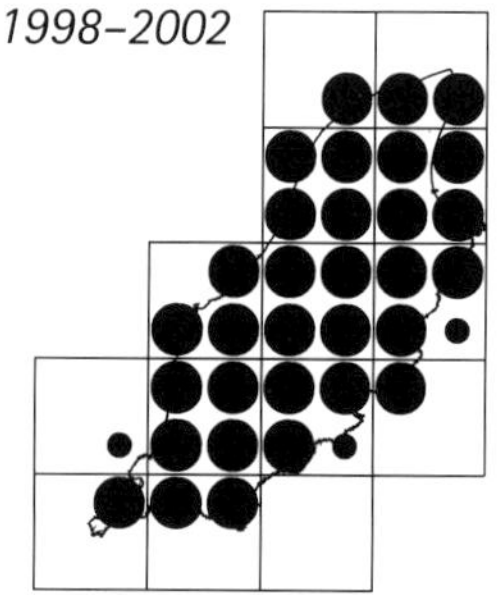

Breeding	Grid squares:	Isle of Man 521 (78%) Britain 2,602 Ireland 950 Total 3,552 (95%)
	Population:	Isle of Man 3,226–4,227 Britain 5,400,000 Ireland 2,100,000 (9% of European)
Wintering	Grid squares:	Isle of Man 457 (69%) Britain and Ireland 3,517 (91%)
	Population:	Isle of Man 20,000+ Britain and Ireland 30 million

Jan	Feb	Mar	Apr	May	Jun	Jul	Aug	Sep	Oct	Nov	Dec

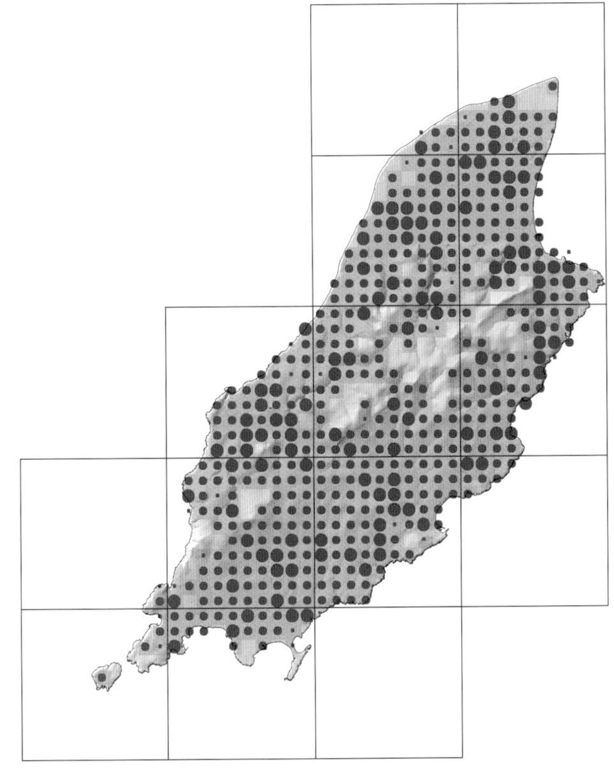

Summer presence and breeding status

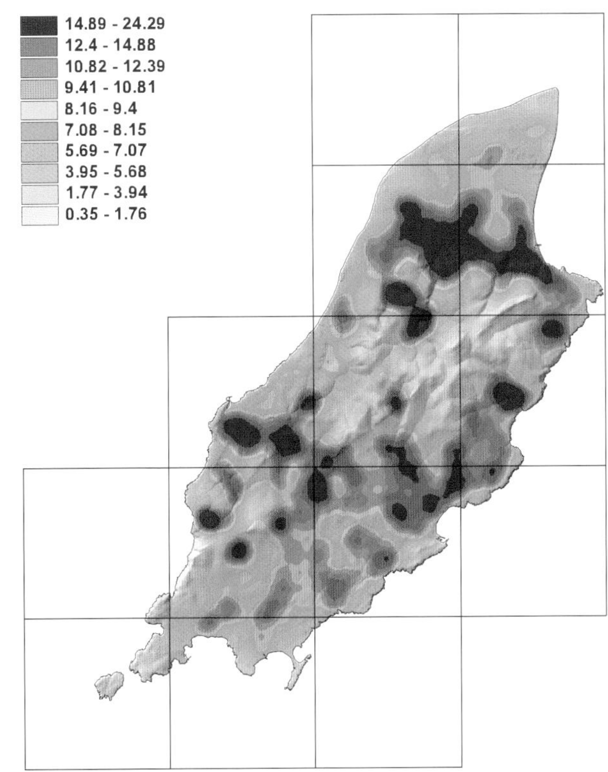

Breeding abundance

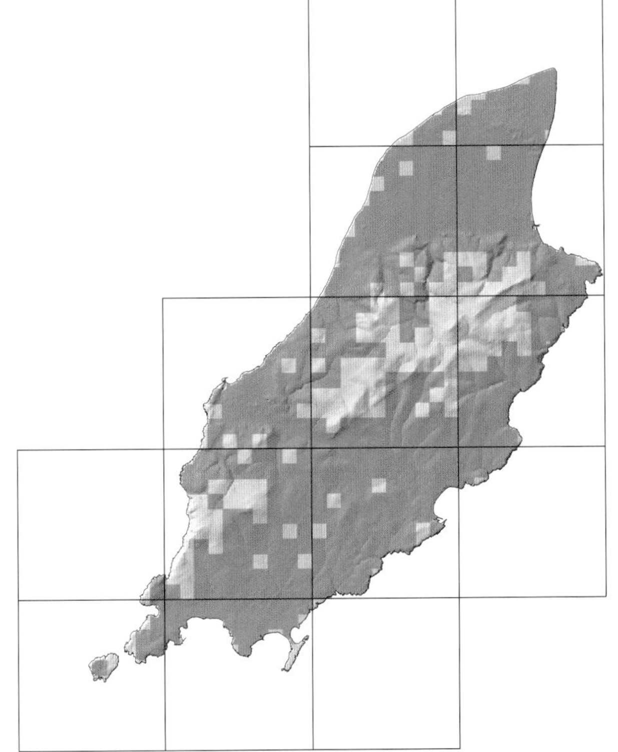

Winter presence

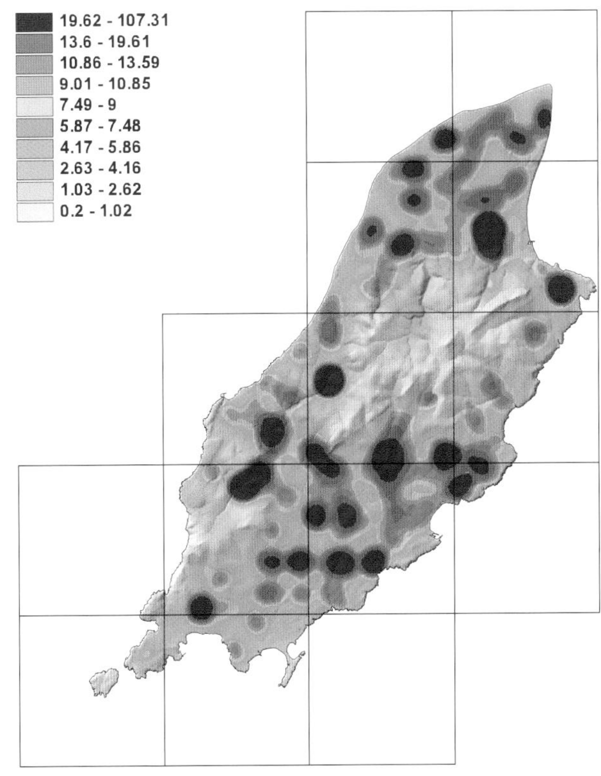

Winter abundance

Individual Sponsors – Mr. E & Mrs. P Edge

Brambling
Fringilla montifringilla

On the Isle of Man the Brambling is a rather scarce, but occasionally abundant, passage migrant and winter visitor. Often Bramblings occur in mixed flocks with Chaffinches and other seed-eating finches and can be overlooked. When flocks take flight, however, Bramblings stand out as they have a prominent white rump, while on the ground the orange chest, more prominent in the dark-headed male, is quite obvious.

Within their breeding range, Bramblings frequent open mixed birch or conifer forests (EBA), at which time they are largely insectivorous. In winter they change to a diet consisting mainly of seeds and this involves a shift to ground feeding, sometimes on farmland or in farmyards. However, their attachment to woodland remains strong, especially where beech mast is plentiful (BWP). Although Bramblings will frequent gardens to take advantage of feeding stations they are less prone to do so than Chaffinches.

Bramblings breed within the northern boreal zone across the Palearctic from Norway to Eastern Siberia (BWP, EBA). They are found well north into subarctic regions and, for breeding, favour northern birch forests in Fennoscandia, but mixed conifer forest in the Siberian taiga (BWP, EBA). Bramblings breed only sporadically in the British Isles, one pair raising three young in the Scottish Highlands in 2002, the second consecutive year of breeding after a gap of seven years (Ogilvie *et al.* 2004). The European breeding population is estimated at about 4,700,000 pairs (EBA).

Bramblings leave their northern breeding areas from early September, with some birds reaching the east coast of Britain from the middle of that month. Migration continues until November, after which there may be further movement from the continent in response to weather conditions (MA).

In the British Isles, Bramblings are widely, but patchily, distributed in winter, with numbers varying greatly between and within winters, depending on conditions elsewhere; large influxes probably follow the exhaustion of food supplies (particularly beechmast), or severe weather in parts of continental Europe (WA, MA). Compared to other parts of the British Isles, Bramblings are scarce in Ireland (WA) and this is also the case on the Isle of Man, where they can be hard to find and are absent in some winters. They do, however, visit the Island during most winters, with the first few birds usually arriving in the first half of October. Most records on the Island are of birds feeding on agricultural land, particularly stubble fields, or visiting rural and peripheral suburban gardens. The largest flock during the MBA research period consisted of at least 50 birds during December 2001, feeding as part of a mixed flock of passerines in a brassica/sunflower fodder field in the north of the Island.

The winter distribution map indicates that Bramblings are sparsely distributed in the north and central areas of the Island; high ground and areas of coast or curragh are mostly avoided.

Kermode thought Bramblings occurred in small numbers, and Ralfe was aware of only a limited number of records. Madoc suggested that they visited the Island only spasmodically and in small numbers. C&J considered the Brambling a regular passage migrant and rather scarce winter visitor. Through the twentieth century the status of the Brambling here may have been much the same as at present, always less than common with considerable variation between years.

Wintering	Grid squares:	Isle of Man 35 (5%)
		Britain & Ireland 1,811 (47%)
	Population:	Isle of Man 0-200+
		Britain and Ireland 50,000–2 million

Jan	Feb	Mar	Apr	May	Jun	Jul	Aug	Sep	Oct	Nov	Dec

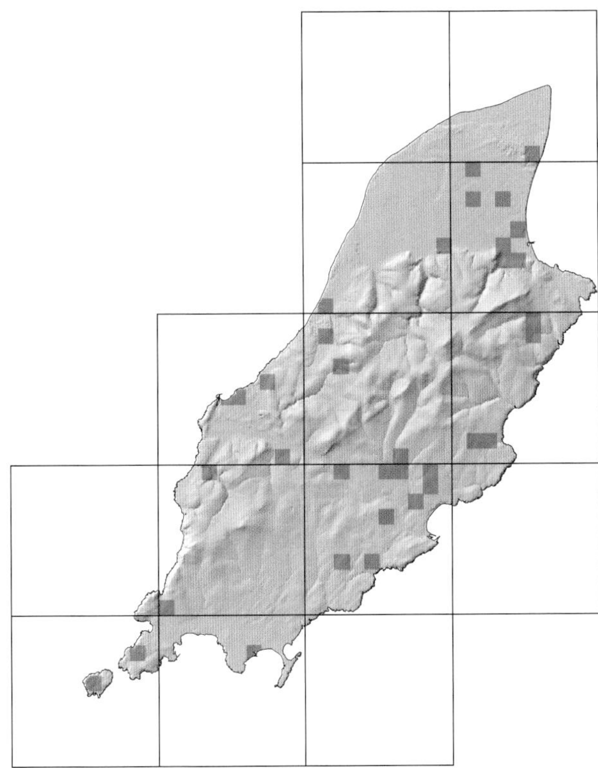

Winter presence

Greenfinch (European Greenfinch)
Carduelis chloris

Manx: *Corkan Keylley glass*

Greenfinches are a familiar sight to almost everyone who puts food out in the garden for the birds. In winter they are gregarious and bullying, trying to monopolise the peanut or seed feeders, giving the impression of spending more energy defending the supply than they might get from feeding. In the summer they become much less obvious, though the song-flight of the male is worth looking out for. Starting from the top of a suitable tree the male commences a lengthy, erratic flight, with deep slow wing beats, which have been likened to those of a bat (BWP), usually returning to the same starting perch.

Their favoured habitat includes woodland fringes, hedgerows, parks and gardens, indeed wherever there are thick bushes for nesting. Outside the breeding season flocks can often be found in open areas with few trees or bushes. Greenfinches are essentially seed-eaters, though some invertebrates are taken, especially during the breeding season. They feed on the seeds of herbs, trees, shrubs and cereals and are particularly fond of rose hips. Food is obtained either while perching or on the ground (BWP).

Greenfinches breed over most of the western Palearctic, extending from Scandinavia south to North Africa, and east into parts of western Asia (EBA). They have also been introduced to various other parts of the world, including both Australia and New Zealand. In the British Isles they are abundant and widespread as a breeding species and are absent only from high ground and other treeless areas such as those found in central Wales, Shetland, and the north-west of both Scotland and Ireland. On the Island Greenfinches are common residents. As can be seen from the maps they breed throughout most of the Island up to about 270m. The summer abundance map indicates high densities in towns and villages such as Ramsey and Laxey and also Douglas, where they breed along the wooded slope of the old sea cliff behind the promenade.

Most Greenfinches that breed in the British Isles, including those on the Isle of Man, are non-migratory and many remain close to or within their breeding territories during the winter. Some do appear to be at least partially migratory, though numbers vary between years, and may include birds dispersing due to low autumn food supplies in their breeding areas, rather than true migrants. A small number of Greenfinches present in Britain during the breeding season or later, move to Ireland (MA) and it is likely that some of these might move only as far as the Isle of Man with others passing over. On the Calf of Man they occur commonly as passage migrants, especially in autumn. In most years some continental, mainly Norwegian, Greenfinches migrate and some of these reach the British Isles though the numbers involved are annually variable. The extent to which continental birds reach the Isle of Man is not known.

As in the summer, Greenfinches are widespread and common on the Island during winter. Again, about 270m is the upper limit of their range. Although they generally occupy the same areas and habitat types in winter as in summer, birds flock together and are more mobile at this time of year. Flocks can be found some distance from stands of trees, with Greenfinches commonly foraging on arable land, especially stubble fields. A flock, sometimes exceeding 60 birds, collects and feeds on weed seed on the Langness saltmarsh and at Sandwick.

It is clear from Kermode and all subsequent writers that Greenfinches have been common here since at least the late nineteenth century. Within the British Isles Greenfinch numbers are thought to have been largely stable for several decades, although there has been some decline (attributed to changing farming practices) in rural areas (1988–91 Atlas). Earlier numerical data are lacking, but on the Island numbers may have changed little in many years, though a comparison of the change maps for MBA research and that of C&J suggest a current distribution wider in the east than was the case in the early 1980s.

1977–81

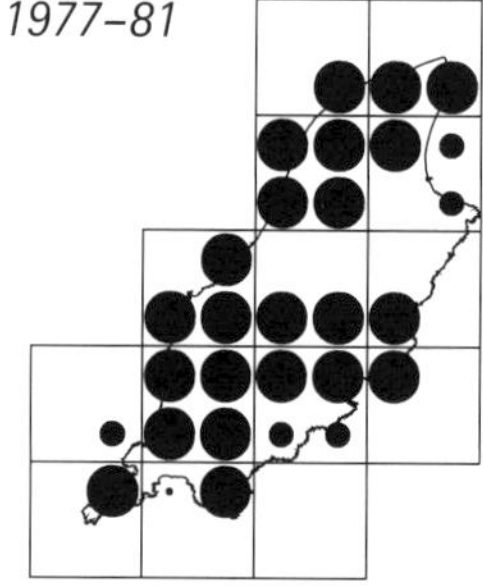

1998–2002

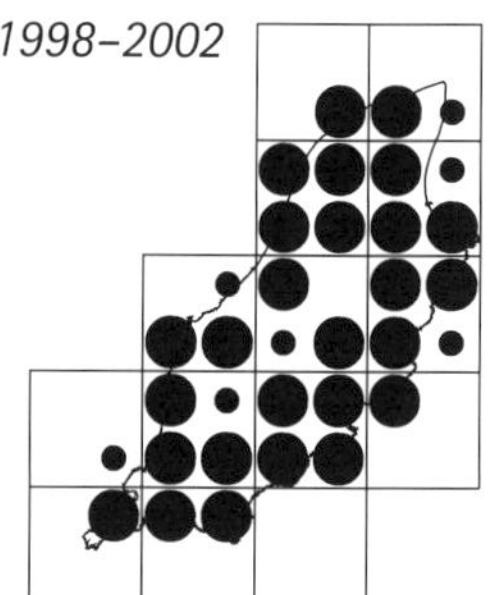

Breeding	Grid squares:	Isle of Man 423 (64%) Britain 2,323 Ireland 813 Total 3,136 (81%)
	Population:	Isle of Man 1,174–1,839 Britain 530,000 Ireland 160,000 (5% of European)
Wintering	Grid squares:	Isle of Man 331 (50%) Britain and Ireland 2,879 (75%)
	Population:	Isle of Man 5,000+ Britain and Ireland 5–6 million

Jan	Feb	Mar	Apr	May	Jun	Jul	Aug	Sep	Oct	Nov	Dec

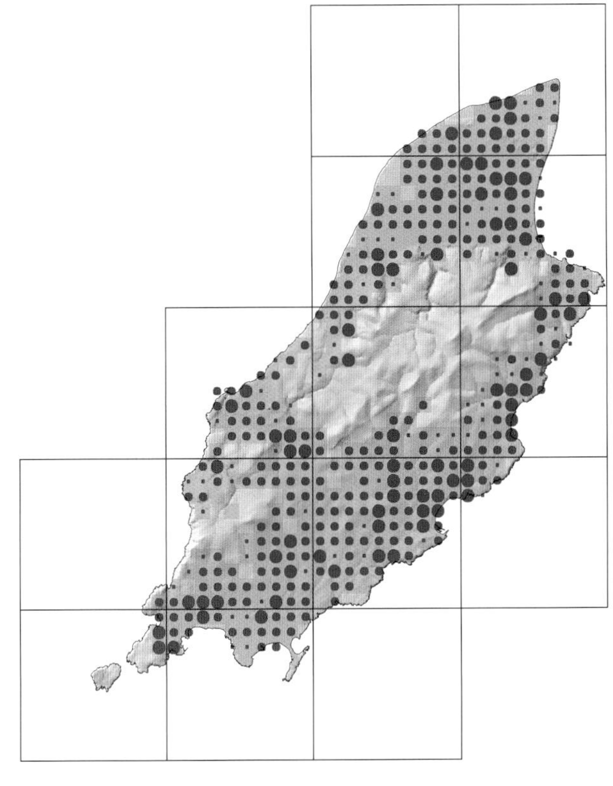

Summer presence and breeding status

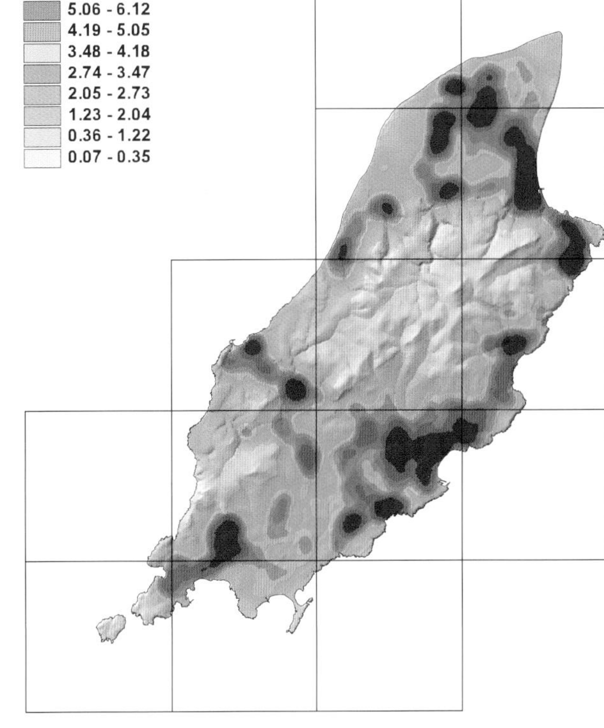

Breeding abundance

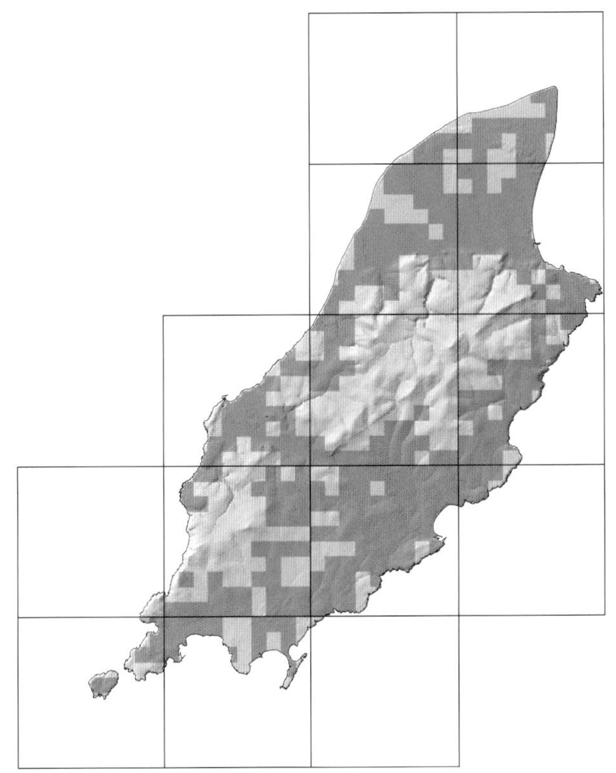

Winter presence

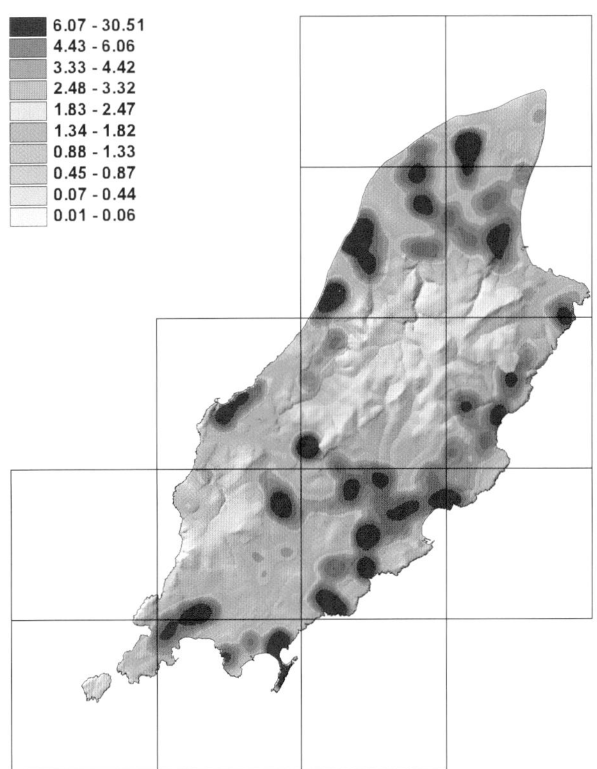

Winter abundance

Individual Sponsor – Mrs. M Skelly

Goldfinch (European Goldfinch)
Carduelis carduelis

Manx: *Lossey ny Keylley* = Flame of the woods, *Kiark my Leydee* = My lady's hen

The Goldfinch is common on the Isle of Man as a resident, summer visitor and passage migrant. Adult Goldfinches, if viewed clearly, are unmistakable, a combination of red face, white cheeks, throat and belly and bold bright yellow wing bars setting them aside from all other finches. Young Goldfinches lack the distinctive head pattern and can cause some identification challenges. This is an endearing species that is admired by all who are fortunate enough to enjoy the sight of a 'charm' (as they are collectively known) visiting garden feeding sites and delivering their very characteristic twittering song.

Goldfinches were originally birds of the forest edge and open woodland, though they now breed throughout cultivated landscapes, often nesting in trees in or near human settlements as well as in riverside woodland and thickets of scrub species such as hawthorn and gorse (EBA, BWP). When feeding, Goldfinches are particularly agile and animated as they skillfully maintain their balance in the search for small seed heads that make up the bulk of their diet. They will readily change host plants throughout the year to take advantage of seasonally available half-ripe seeds, resulting in foraging trips of several kilometres, even during the breeding season (BWP). Particularly in winter, small flocks of Goldfinches can be seen feeding on thistles and other weeds in gardens and on waste ground.

The native range of the Goldfinch extends from the Azores and Ireland in the west, across Europe (but absent from Iceland) and Africa north of the Sahara as far east as the Himalayas. Introduced populations exist in many areas of the world including Australia, New Zealand and Bermuda (EBA). In the British Isles it is widespread, being absent only from mountainous and moorland regions, especially in the north and west of Scotland. On the Isle of Man, Goldfinches are widely distributed in the summer, and are absent only from high ground where suitable nesting habitat is scarce. Areas of high abundance are associated with lowland agricultural land and rural human habitation.

Goldfinches are partial migrants and while many British and Irish birds winter within Britain and Ireland others undertake a predominantly southerly migration through France and into Iberia, but with some birds from Britain also probably over-wintering in Ireland (MA). Passage birds move through the Isle of Man annually in autumn (mainly late September to November), and are likely to include individuals from the Manx population as well as those from further north in England and Scotland. Though it is accepted that some birds from continental Europe pass through the British Isles on migration, it is unknown whether, or to what extent, such birds winter there (MA). It is also not known whether a passage of continental birds occurs through the Island. Return passage in spring can be a protracted affair, occurring from February through to May. During the MBA research many Goldfinches were observed flying over the Island, particularly in April at a time when other Goldfinches had already started to breed. Distinguishing these 'fly-over' birds separately resulted in a number of coastal and upland 1km squares recording species presence, but no breeding.

In winter Goldfinches, though still widespread, were recorded in 50% fewer 1km squares than in the summer. This can probably be partly explained by the greater tendency for the species to flock in winter and thereby occur in fewer areas, coupled with the likelihood of part of the Manx population undertaking migration. Winter abundance suggests a movement to lowland, coastal areas, the generally colder central valley seeming not to suit the species.

Kermode described the Goldfinch to be 'resident ... greatly decreased of late years' and Ralfe also considered it scarce, but formerly common. Madoc described the species as 'very scarce'. However, by 1986, C&J were able to describe it as a fairly common resident and passage migrant. As C&J have pointed out, it appears that there was a great decline of Goldfinches over the late nineteenth and first part of the twentieth century, but the population then recovered to a greater or lesser extent. This decline and recovery were general throughout the British Isles and have been attributed to a rise and subsequent decline in the capture of Goldfinches by professional bird catchers (1988–91 Atlas). In the UK and in Europe populations are now thought to be increasing (1988–91 Atlas, EBA). Judging from the number of records obtained during the MBA research from people seeing Goldfinches in their gardens 'for the first time', Goldfinches are also currently increasing on the Island.

1977–81

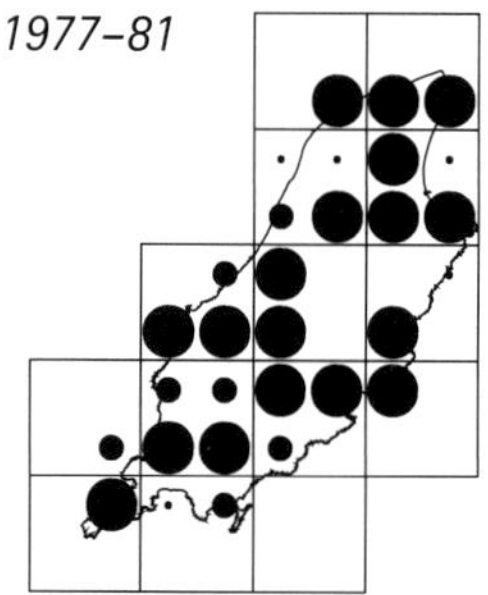

1998–2002

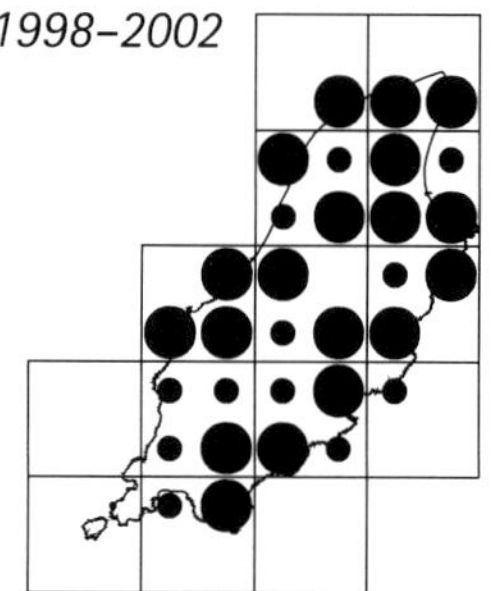

Breeding	Grid squares:	Isle of Man 407 (61%) Britain 2,209 Ireland 749 Total 2,958 (77%)
	Population:	Isle of Man 477–696 Britain 220,000 Ireland 55,000 (3% of European)
Wintering	Grid squares:	Isle of Man 202 (30%) Britain & Ireland 2,614 (68%)
	Population:	Isle of Man 1,000+ Britain and Ireland 100,000

Jan	Feb	Mar	Apr	May	Jun	Jul	Aug	Sep	Oct	Nov	Dec

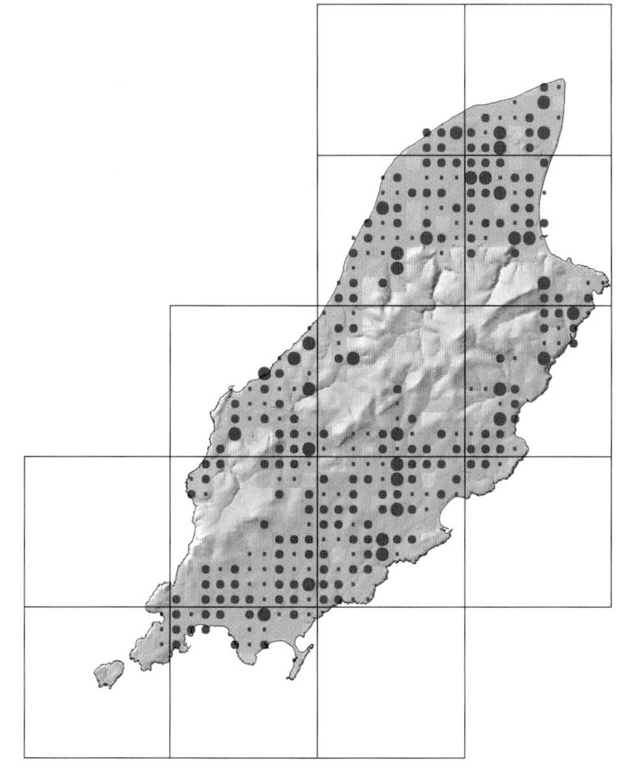
Summer presence and breeding status

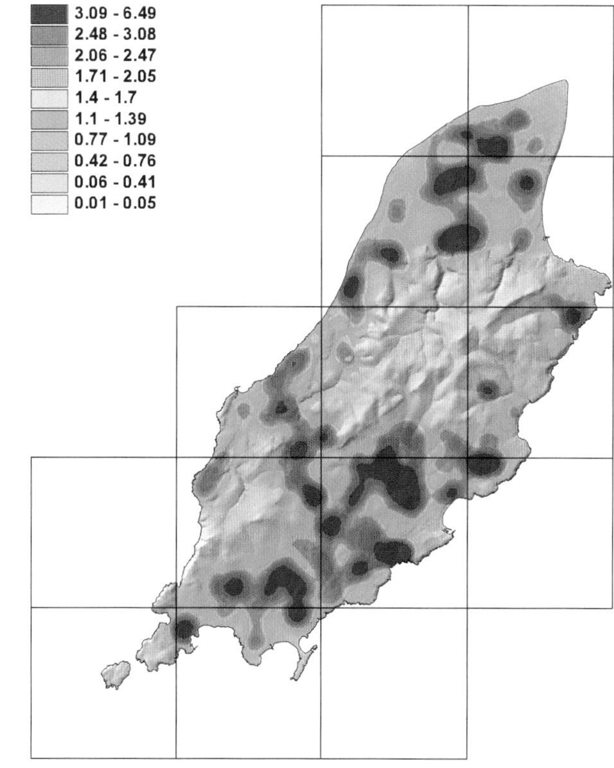

Breeding abundance

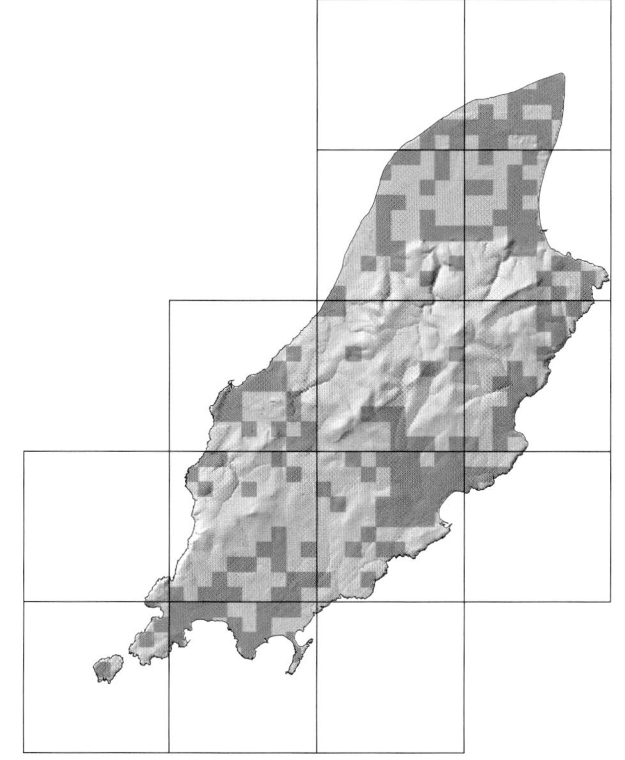
Winter presence

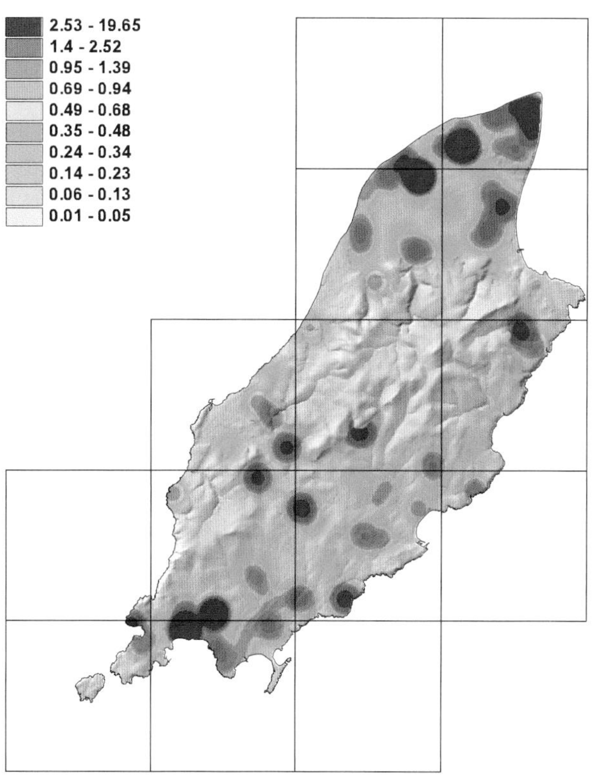

Winter abundance

Individual Sponsors – Mrs. E Clucas, Mr. D Dentith & Ms. S Corlett, Mr. & Mrs. D J Edwards, Miss F Johnson, Mr. D D Sharpe

Siskin (Eurasian Siskin)
Carduelis spinus

In common with several other finch species on the Island, Siskins are now regular visitors to many garden feeding stations from late summer onwards. It is here that they may be seen to full advantage, perching at all angles on peanut and seed feeders. They are surprisingly aggressive for small birds, and readily defend their place in the pecking order by adopting threat postures, which include flicking their wings, highlighting the extensive yellow on wings, rump and tail.

Siskins breed mainly in conifers, particularly spruce, but also fir and pine, especially mature, well-spaced stands of trees. Outside the breeding season streamside locations are preferred, often well away from conifers (BWP). In the breeding season invertebrates form a part of the diet, though at all times of year seeds are mainly taken, especially those of conifers, alders and birches. Feeding Siskins are constantly on the move, flitting through the canopy hanging upside down to examine cones, this agility being reflected in their garden feeding behaviour.

The breeding range of the Siskin extends across the boreal and temperate zones wherever there are suitable conifer forests, from the British Isles to Sakhalin in the Russian Far East, reaching as far north as northern Norway and as far south as the Pyrenees and Balkan mountains (EBA). The main European populations are in Fennoscandia, the Baltic States and Russia. In the British Isles Siskins have undergone a considerable expansion of range since the 1968–72 Atlas, closely linked to maturing conifer plantations (1988–91 Atlas). In keeping with their dependence on conifers, centres of high abundance are to be found in northern and western Britain and Ireland. Likewise on the Isle of Man, breeding evidence of Siskins is to be found in areas where conifers are abundant. They are thus largely absent from the agricultural lowlands, save where these areas are interspersed with glens containing conifers, such as at Port Soderick and Port Grenaugh. It is in mature stands of conifer plantations that the species is most abundant in the summer, hence population centres exist in the wooded valleys and slopes of the northern, central and southern hills.

If food is available some Siskins may remain in breeding areas for the winter, though the majority have abandoned conifer forests by late July in favour of areas of birch and alder. At this time they may also frequent garden feeding stations, sometimes in large numbers following a good breeding season or when pine cone supplies are poor. Such an occasion was witnessed in July 2002 when, in one morning, 67 birds, nearly all young, were caught in a garden in Sulby. Many British and Irish Siskins from northern areas move south to winter in central and southern England, with some of these continuing on their migrations to winter as far south as Iberia and northern Africa (MA). The autumn passage of birds on the Isle of Man is likely to include local birds as well as those from northern parts of Britain. Siskins that do not leave British shores are joined for the winter by birds from continental Europe, the majority probably being from Fennoscandia and the Baltic states. Numbers arriving are likely to vary greatly between years, depending upon breeding success and food supplies. Many of these immigrants arrive by crossing the English Channel, though some move across the North Sea to reach the east coast of Britain (MA). The extent to which continental birds reach the Island is not known.

In winter, Siskins are still widespread on the Island with many records from rural and suburban gardens. The distribution map reveals a change in emphasis for the species at this time of year with many of the plantations in which breeding took place being abandoned in favour of areas where birch, alder and willow occur. The central valley and Ballaugh Curragh support wintering populations that probably comprise breeding birds from adjacent conifer plantations.

Kermode and Ralfe knew of hardly any records, but Madoc considered the Siskin to be a regular winter visitor and thought it overlooked. C&J describe it as a 'regular passage migrant and winter visitor', but thought that Siskins did not breed at that time. It is clear that Siskins are now far more common than they were thought to be and breed in some numbers.

Breeding	Grid squares:	Isle of Man 250 (38%) Britain 1,158 Ireland 284 Total 1,442 (37%)
	Population:	Isle of Man 228–325 Britain 300,000 Ireland 60,000 (13% of European)
Wintering	Grid squares:	Isle of Man 155 (23%) Britain and Ireland 1,915 (50%)
	Population:	Isle of Man 1,000+ Britain and Ireland 150,000

Jan	Feb	Mar	Apr	May	Jun	Jul	Aug	Sep	Oct	Nov	Dec

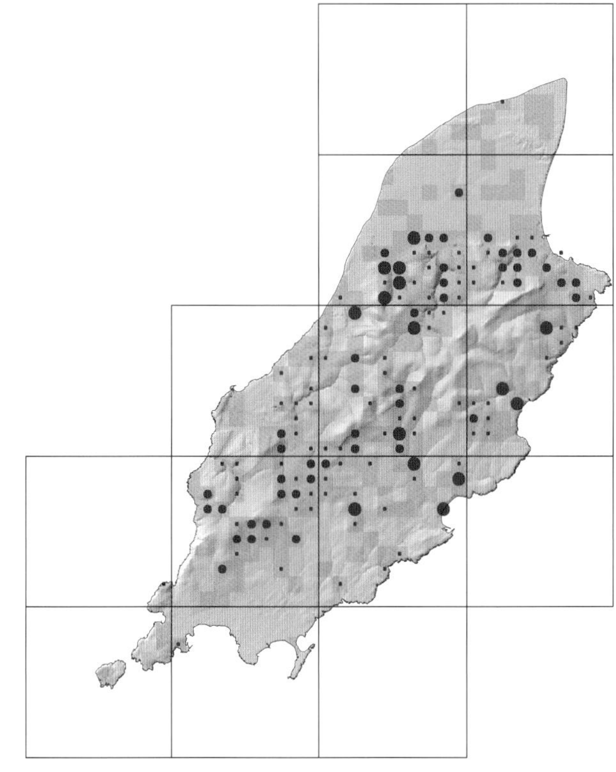

2.49 - 7.42
1.64 - 2.48
1.15 - 1.63
0.79 - 1.14
0.53 - 0.78
0.37 - 0.52
0.26 - 0.36
0.16 - 0.25
0.07 - 0.15
0.01 - 0.06

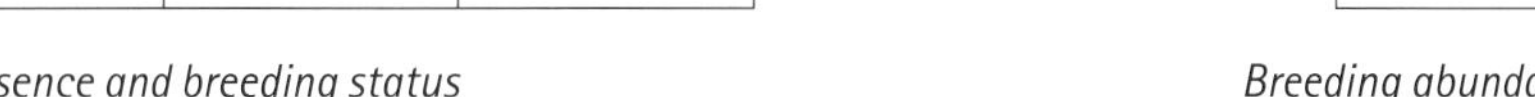

Summer presence and breeding status

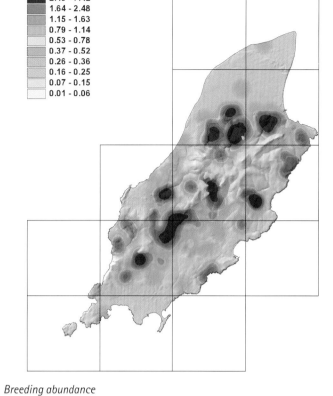

Breeding abundance

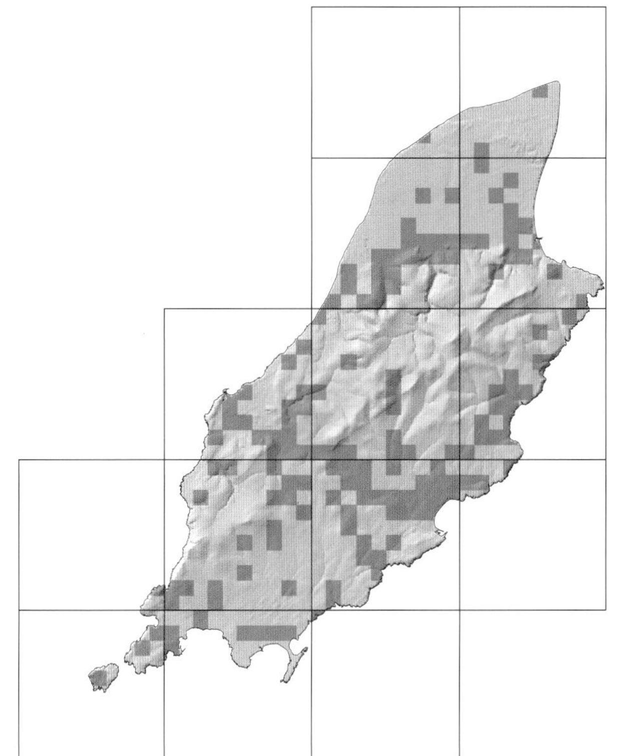

Winter presence

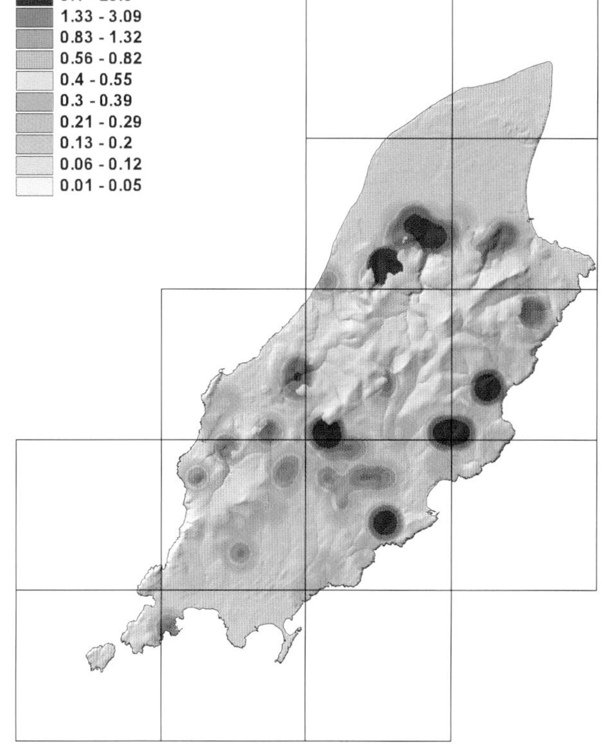

Winter abundance

Individual Sponsors – Dr. J P Cullen, Mr. R Fryer, the late Mrs. J Stigant, Mr. G & Mrs. I Taggart

Linnet (Common Linnet)
Carduelis cannabina

Manx: *Fillip ny Kempey* = Sparrow of the hemp, *Ushag y lieen* = Bird of the flax

Listening to the attractive song of a male Linnet, while admiring his striking red breast and head markings, it is easy to understand why the 'old cock linnet' of music hall fame was formerly such a prized cage bird. Fortunately, the practice of keeping wild song birds is largely a thing of the past and our enjoyment of these birds is now rightly restricted to the countryside.

Linnets prefer scrub and heath vegetation with a dry sunny aspect, including farmland with hedges or low trees, untended forest edges and in some areas, rural or suburban gardens and industrial wasteland. Outside the breeding season they will shift to more open habitats, such as salt marshes, shingle banks and sand-dunes, as well as farmland (BWP). Where suitable habitat exists, Linnets will sometimes nest semi-colonially. They feed on a variety of small seeds and take fewer insects than many other small finches. They are particularly dependent upon weeds in open country and waste ground, including those closely associated with agriculture (BWP).

Linnets are common across much of the Western Palearctic, where they breed in most areas except the far north and Iceland. The breeding range also extends south into parts of north-west Africa and east into central Asia (EBA). In the British Isles they are widespread in the breeding season throughout England, Wales and southern Scotland and have a restricted, mainly coastal, distribution in Ireland and north-east Scotland (1988–91 Atlas). Areas of highest abundance are in the east and south of England and around the coastline. Breeding is widespread on the Isle of Man, birds being present in most 1km squares in the lowlands and absent only from higher ground in the uplands, where suitable habitat is restricted. Throughout the Island much suitable habitat exists, though from the summer abundance map it is clear that Linnets favour areas of scrub or heath near the coast and similar areas inland where field systems give way to upland grass and heather moor.

The species is well known as a partial migrant, with part of the British breeding population migrating to Iberia or France (MA), while the remainder are resident and it is likely that the same is true of the Manx population. Whether Linnets from northern Britain winter on the Island is unclear, although numbers of these will presumably move through on migration. Autumn observations at three coastal sites during the MBA research indicated that peaks of migration occurred during September and early October. Very few Linnets from northern Europe have been recovered in the British Isles (MA), so the British population that remains for the winter is probably not joined by winter visitors from further afield.

The winter maps indicate that, on the Island, the upland areas are largely abandoned, with Linnets not recorded above 240m in winter, compared to up to 340m in the breeding season. This movement away from higher ground in winter is usual for the species in Britain as a whole (WA). Some lowland areas are also vacated during the winter. Many of the pockets of high density in winter relate to single flocks of Linnets, making use of seasonally available seeds within arable farmland. Such pockets are to be found in the hinterland of the northern coast and in the south-east, notably in the Santon area, where arable farming and winter stubble fields persist.

Kermode considered the Linnet to be 'a common resident'. and Ralfe described it as 'common'. Madoc was clearly very familiar with the species, but gave no estimate of abundance, and C&J describe it as common and present throughout the year. However, in Britain, and indeed over much of Europe, numbers of Linnets have declined in recent years (1988–91 Atlas, EBA). The changes are thought to follow intensification of agriculture leading to a reduction in available food in winter. In the absence of prior data it is not possible to evaluate the extent to which changes in agricultural practice on the Island have influenced the fortunes of the Linnet, though it is reasonable to suppose that at least some reduction in numbers will have occurred.

1977–81

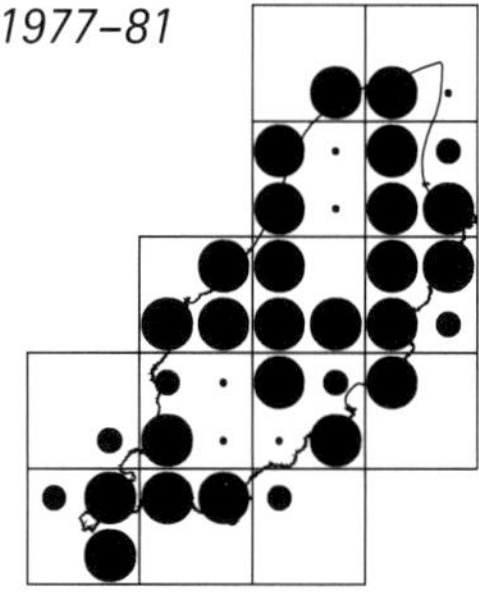

1998–2002

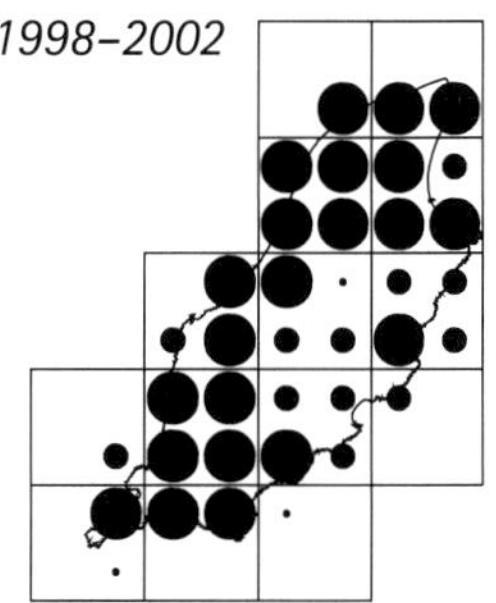

Breeding	Grid squares:	Isle of Man 525 (79%) Britain 2,268 Ireland 783 Total 3,051 (79%)
	Population:	Isle of Man 1,418–2,297 Britain 520,000 Ireland 130,000 (8% of European)
Wintering	Grid squares:	Isle of Man 169 (25%) Britain and Ireland 2,277 (59%)
	Population:	Isle of Man 5,000+ Britain and Ireland 3 million

Jan	Feb	Mar	Apr	May	Jun	Jul	Aug	Sep	Oct	Nov	Dec

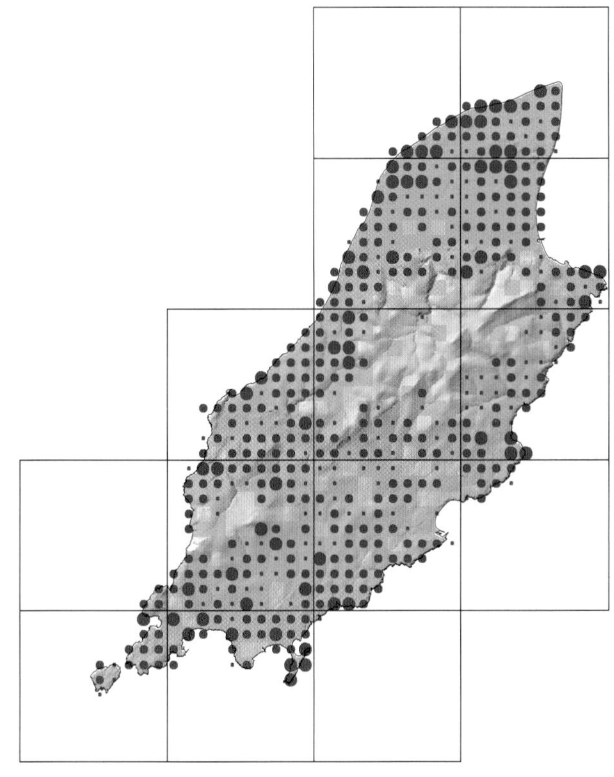

Summer presence and breeding status

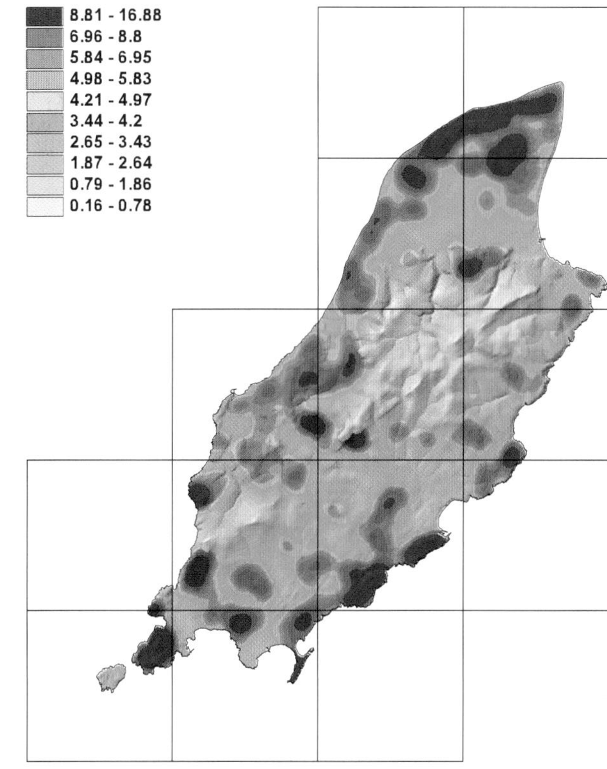

Breeding abundance

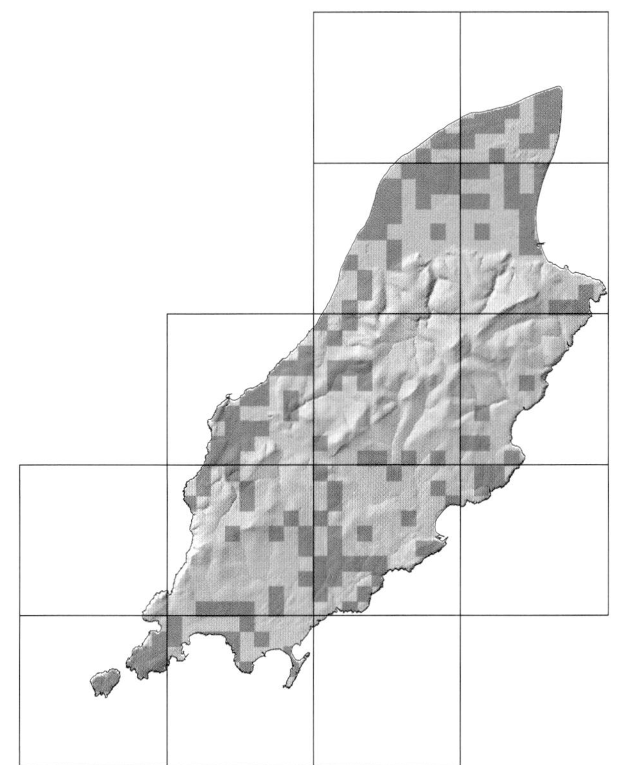

Winter presence

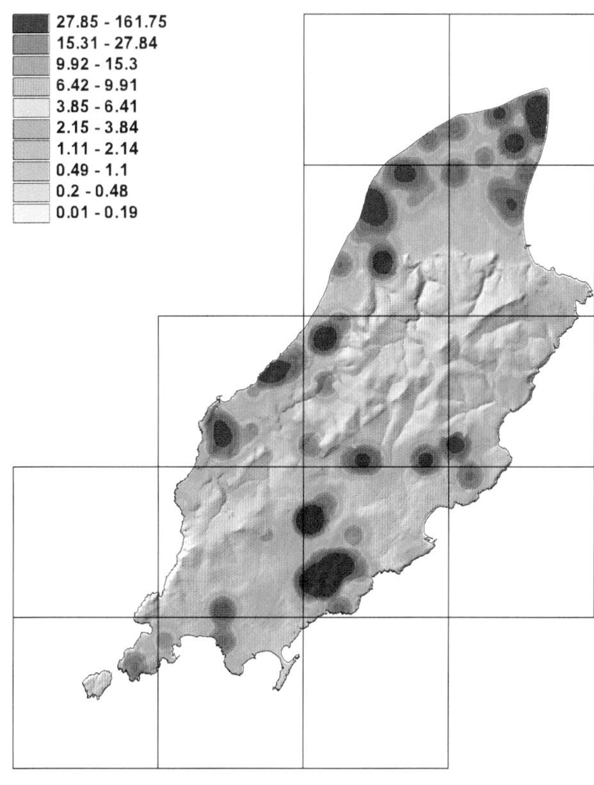

Winter abundance

Individual Sponsor – Mr. C K Maley

Twite
Carduelis flavirostris

The Twite is a regular winter visitor to the Isle of Man, albeit in small numbers. It is a small brown finch, quite similar in appearance to the far more common Linnet. A combination of their inconspicuous plumage and their relative scarcity on the Isle of Man may result in some Twites being overlooked or being misidentified as Linnets. Twites are rather darker than Linnets and during the winter have a yellow or straw-coloured bill. They can also be distinguished in flight by the characteristic twittering call.

For breeding Twites prefer terrain that is more or less free of trees and shrubs, often selecting stony or rocky ground, including sea-cliffs. In Britain and Ireland they favour heather moors, hill farms and upland pasture but avoid mountainous and precipitous areas (BWP). In winter they occur mainly on areas of short turf near the coast and also feed among sparse vegetation at the tops of sandy shores, particularly adjacent to sand dunes. At this time they feed almost entirely on small seeds which they obtain by foraging on the ground or among low herbs. When foraging, flocks creep through the low vegetation, rather like mice, and can be overlooked until they suddenly take flight to move to a new site or wheel round to settle again in the same place. During MBA research flocks of Twites were often seen to feed on lines of seeds deposited round the receding edge of temporary pools within weed-strewn uneven ground.

In Europe breeding is essentially restricted to the British Isles and Norway, but there is also a larger population in central and eastern Asia (EBA). The main British breeding area is in treeless, moorland areas of the Scottish Highlands and northern England along with the crofting lands of north and west Scotland and Ireland (1988–91 Atlas, EBA). No evidence of breeding on the Isle of Man was obtained during the MBA research. Only six records of Twites were obtained during the summer research, all of which were classed as birds on return passage to breeding areas, including that of a male singing on the late date of 1 May 1999 (Cullen 2002).

It is generally accepted that many of the Twites that breed in coastal areas of their British Isles range are sedentary, while many of those from upland areas probably move to lower ground, though some do remain (MA, WA).

Twites are not usually noted on the Isle of Man until late October or into November, with records in September being rare. They were present in all winters of the MBA research, though numbers varied greatly between years, the maximum count being of 216 birds in January 1999 at Wood's Strand, north of Peel. All records during the winter were coastal, the majority being at the Point of Ayre and in the area of Langness and Derbyhaven, where maximum flocks were 80 and 30 respectively. Winter numbers seem to reach their peak during January after which they gradually decline, with, as previously mentioned, only occasional records in the early summer. While the origins of Manx wintering Twites are unknown, it is likely that at least some will be from the breeding population in the Pennines, as some of these birds are thought to winter in north-west England (MA).

Twites were formerly more common on the Isle of Man and used to have the alternative name of 'Manx Linnet' (C&J). Kermode considered the Twite to be 'resident' and Ralfe describes it breeding in small numbers. To Madoc it was a well known resident and familiar breeding species. However, by the time C&J were writing, breeding had long ceased. Thus its status on the Island has apparently changed greatly over the past hundred years. Having become extinct as a breeding species, perhaps as long ago as the 1940s, Twites are now restricted to the status of regular but not very common winter visitor, though the singing bird in May 1999 gave one fortunate observer a flavour of its former status.

Breeding	Grid squares:	Isle of Man 3 (0.5%) Britain 651 Ireland 60 Total 711 (18%)
	Population:	Isle of Man 0 Britain 65,000 Ireland 3,500 (24% of European)
Wintering	Grid squares:	Isle of Man 19 (3%) Britain and Ireland 580 (15%)
	Population:	Isle of Man <200 Britain and Ireland 100,000–150,000

Jan	Feb	Mar	Apr	May	Jun	Jul	Aug	Sep	Oct	Nov	Dec

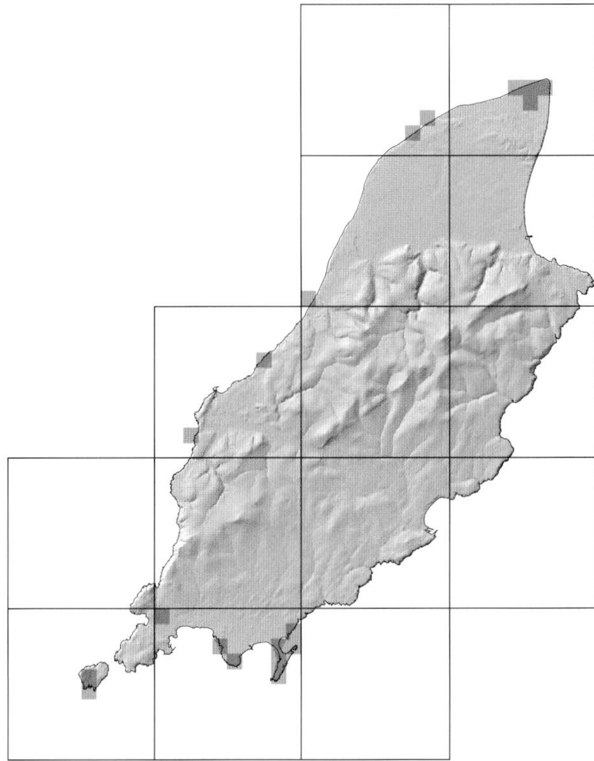

Winter presence

Lesser Redpoll
Carduelis cabaret

Manx: *Bytermmyn dhone, Lossan ruy*

This small brown finch is possibly unfamiliar to many people as, even when perched, the Lesser Redpoll is seldom seen well enough for an observer to note the distinctive identification features of dark-streaked plumage, small yellow bill and inconspicuous black bib. Males are slightly more colourful than females and, in full breeding plumage, have a red fore-crown and a red breast, though both of these features can be variable in extent and colour. As with many woodland birds, it is the song, usually delivered in flight, that first draws the attention. It has a distinctive 'buzzing' drone to it which, coupled with a marked undulating flight display, is usually sufficient to confirm identification. On the Isle of Man the Lesser Redpoll is a fairly common resident and passage migrant.

Formerly, the species 'Lesser Redpoll' was considered to be a subspecies of the 'Common Redpoll'. A further subspecies was known as 'Mealy Redpoll'. Part way through the MBA research period the 'Lesser Redpoll' was separated off and assigned species status in its own right. This account deals only with 'Lesser Redpoll' and the few records of 'Mealy Redpoll' obtained during this research period are summarised in Appendix A dealing with species not featured in the main section of this Atlas.

Lesser Redpolls are found mainly in scrub woodland, including willow carr, and immature conifer plantations (MA). They feed mainly on small seeds, especially birch, but in common with many of the finches they will take invertebrates, especially during the breeding season. Feeding is largely confined to trees, although, through autumn and winter, they will increasingly forage on the ground searching for fallen seeds beneath preferred tree species as well as feeding in more open situations (BWP).

Lesser Redpolls have a restricted breeding range which includes the British Isles, the western fringes of the Low Countries and isolated mountainous areas of western Europe (MA). In the British Isles they have a fairly widespread breeding distribution, though they are generally absent from some of the Scottish isles, the Cheshire plain, some English counties bordering Wales and an area south of a line from the Severn to Beachy Head (1988–91 Atlas). During MBA research, breeding of Lesser Redpolls was largely restricted to areas of curragh and conifer plantations. As indicated on the summer distribution map, the species was also observed in a number of other 1km squares, in which they were assigned a 'non-breeding' status. Many of these records related to birds that were considered to be on spring passage, while others, adjacent to known breeding areas, were of males undertaking a circuitous display flight over habitat unsuitable for breeding. Areas of high abundance closely matched stands of relatively young conifers, such as those at Beary Mountain and Corlea Plantations, although some mature plantings, such as parts of Stoney Mountain, in which there are failed or stunted trees, also supported high numbers.

Lesser Redpolls are partial migrants, many of the birds from more northern parts of their British breeding range moving in a southerly direction to either winter in southern England or, if supplies of favoured birch and alder seeds are low, continuing further to reach western parts of continental Europe (WA). The timing and number of birds involved in this movement will depend to some extent on availability of food in their breeding area, but migration is usually evident through the Isle of Man from late August, continuing into October in some years.

On the Isle of Man the species is present throughout the winter, though it is not known to what extent the population comprises local breeders that have remained, or more northerly birds that have moved here for the winter. A combination of both is likely. During winter, Lesser Redpolls are less obvious than in summer, which may partially account for the comparatively few winter records. It is probable that fewer birds are actually present. Most of the winter records were from within or near to known breeding areas, though some coastal records could represent birds on late migration.

Kermode described the Lesser Redpoll as being 'resident', but gave no further information, and Ralfe considered it 'probably more common than is generally supposed'. Madoc was familiar with the species throughout the year and C&J noted the 'Redpoll' as a locally distributed summer resident and passage migrant, with small numbers remaining through the winter in some years. Lesser Redpolls are thought to have declined over much of the rest of the British Isles since the 1970s (1988–91 Atlas), though the extent to which this has happened locally, if at all, cannot be evaluated.

1977–81

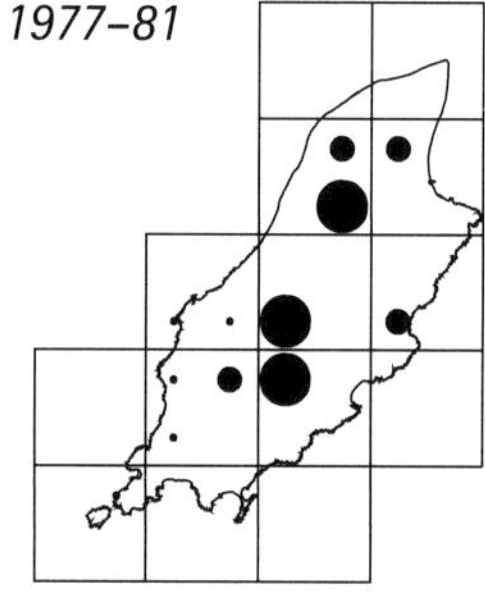

1998–2002

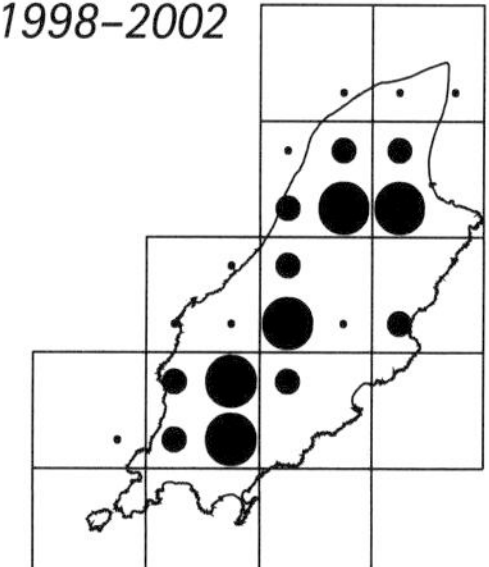

Breeding	Grid squares:	Isle of Man 194 (29%) Britain 1,754 Ireland 538 Total 2,292 (59%)
	Population:	Isle of Man 179–262 Britain 160,000 Ireland 70,000 (15% of European)
Wintering	Grid squares:	Isle of Man 22 (3%) Britain & Ireland 2,006 (52%)
	Population:	Isle of Man <1,000 Britain and Ireland 350,000–850,000

Jan Feb Mar Apr May Jun Jul Aug Sep Oct Nov Dec

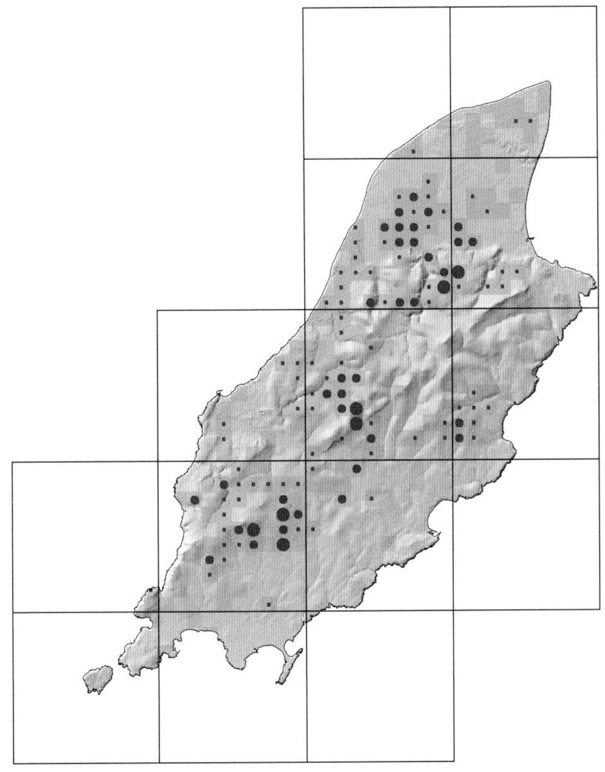

Summer presence and breeding status

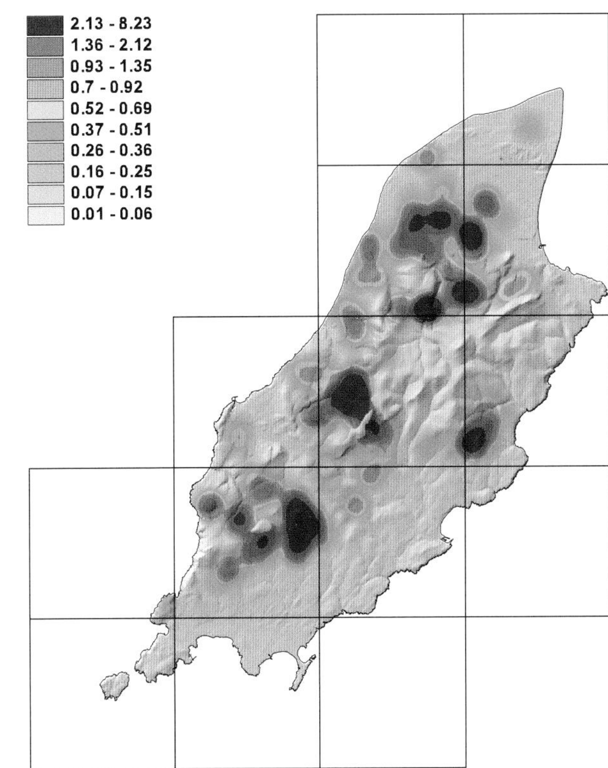

Breeding abundance

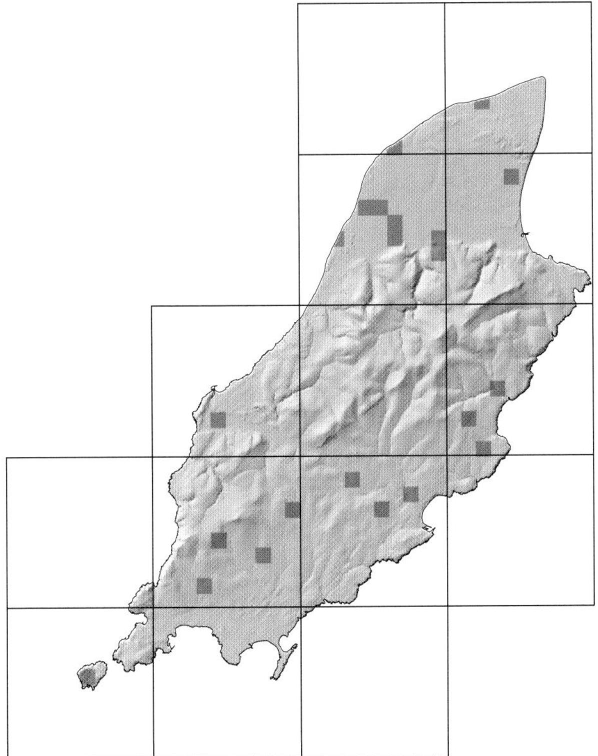

Winter presence

Individual Sponsors – Mrs. S Bolton, Dr. J P Cullen

Crossbill (Common Crossbill)
Loxia curvirostra

Of the four species of Crossbill that breed within northern Europe, only the Common Crossbill, *Loxia curvirostra*, is known to occur on the Isle of Man and is thus the only species being referred to here under the name 'Crossbill'. Provided good views are obtained, the Crossbill is easily identified. It is a large, powerfully built finch with a heavy, crossed bill and a forked tail. Males are essentially orange to red in colour while females and immature birds are grey/green. On the Isle of Man the Crossbill occurs as a migrant and winter visitor which breeds sporadically.

The curious bill structure is a specialised adaptation for extracting seeds from pine cones and these form almost the sole diet, though buds or fruits of other trees, as well as insects, are sometimes taken. Crossbills breed and live almost entirely in conifer forests or plantations (1988–91 Atlas). They are very agile, easily clambering around and hanging upside down from pine cones, often using the bill, parrot-like, to help. Seeds of pine cones are usually removed while the bird hangs from the cone, although the entire cone is sometimes snipped off before being carried to a perch, the seeds then being extracted while the cone is held under the foot (BWP).

The breeding range of Crossbills is extensive and they are found in conifer forests over much of the Northern Hemisphere (MA). The subspecies *Loxia curvirostra curvirostra* breeds in boreal forests across the Palearctic, from Europe to Eastern Siberia and Japan (1988–91 Atlas, MA). The main food of Crossbills is larch and spruce seeds, crops of which are prone to periodic failure, resulting in some years in large-scale irruptions of the species into the British Isles from continental Europe. Many of these birds will stay for only one breeding season, while others may remain for several years, establishing new populations (1988–91 Atlas). During survey work for the 1988–91 Atlas the greatest number of Crossbills was seen in Scotland, but over the four years of research they were also found in many suitable areas of England, Wales and Ireland, though in many of those places, in only one of the four years. During the MBA research Crossbills were seen in several conifer plantations including Ballaugh, Conrhenny, Stoney Mountain, Arrasey and Glen Rushen although they too were often only observed in one of the survey years. Crossbills are known to start breeding as early as November, although locally no evidence of breeding prior to April was found during the current research. In fact, the only definite evidence of breeding was in Slieau Curn plantation, where two agitated males were present in April 1998. From the Atlas survey work, the Manx breeding population is estimated at 27-39 pairs, though this is an aggregate count over the full survey period, and the number breeding in any one year will have been fewer than this. In the past, there have been periods during which, in all probability, no Crossbills were breeding on the Island (C&J).

In winter the Crossbill was observed in only a few locations, but mainly in the same plantations in which they were seen during some summers. As for the summer, the number of birds observed between winters was variable, all but two of the records coming from the winters of 1998-99 and 1999-2000, highlighting the mobile nature of the species.

Kermode described Crossbills as 'occasional' and was aware that some flocks apparently stayed for years and Ralfe also provided several records. Madoc was well aware of the species and wrote vividly of flocks of up to 100 birds, which he saw during the great irruption of 1927. C&J described the Crossbill as 'an irregular visitor in late summer, a few being seen in most irruption years'. They considered that there was no evidence that the species had bred here, but could not dismiss the possibility following invasions in the late nineteenth century. Thus the Atlas data confirming breeding on the Island, albeit on a small scale, are of considerable interest. It is probable that in previous years, when birds have been here, breeding may have sometimes occurred, but gone undetected.

Breeding	Grid squares:	Isle of Man 41 (6%) Britain 763 Ireland 156 Total 919 (24%)
	Population:	Isle of Man 27–39 Britain 10,000 Ireland 1,000 (<1% of European)
Wintering	Grid squares:	Isle of Man 13 (2%) Britain and Ireland 457 (12%)
	Population:	Isle of Man <100 Britain and Ireland 1,000 + irruptions

Jan	Feb	Mar	Apr	May	Jun	Jul	Aug	Sep	Oct	Nov	Dec

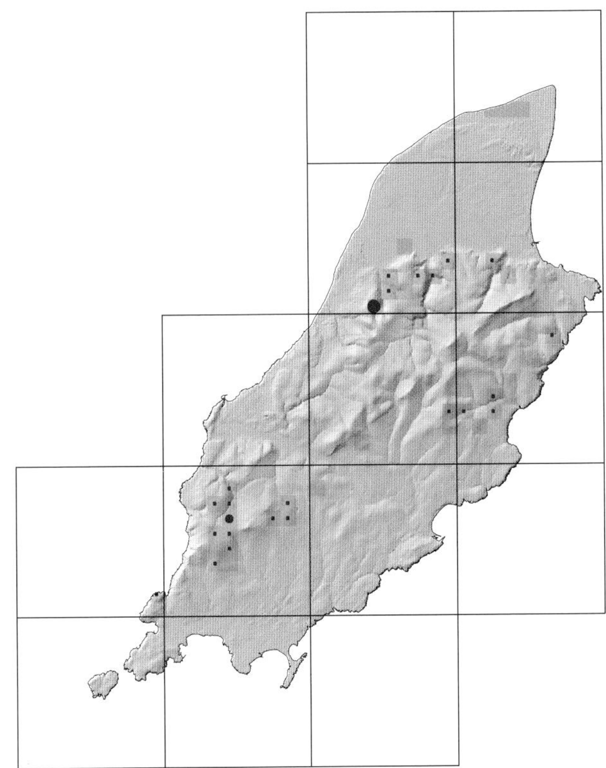

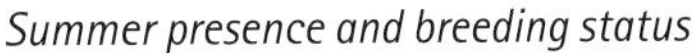

Summer presence and breeding status

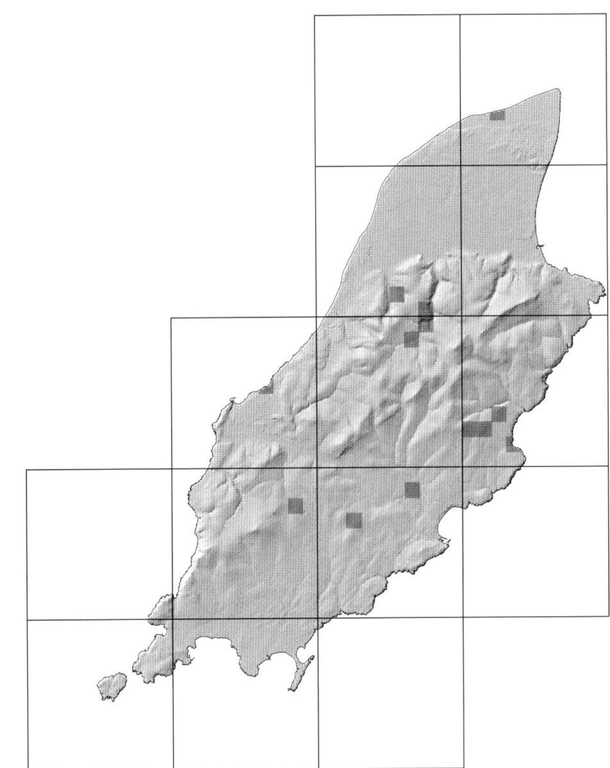

Winter presence

Individual Sponsor – Mr. G F Cory

Snow Bunting
Plectrophenax nivalis

Manx: *Pompee sniaghtee*

If your only goal is to see large numbers of birds, a winter walk over the Manx hills can be an unrewarding experience. Such walks bring with them, however, the chance of seeing a small flock of Snow Buntings, a sight guaranteed to lift the spirits. These large buntings appear very rounded as they forage in the undergrowth with their feathers fluffed to provide insulation. There is much white in the plumage which, in winter, is suffused with a warm buff on the head, back and chest (BWP). In flight they reveal bold white wing panels and extensive white in the tail, though the white in the wing is less pronounced in young birds than in adults. On the Island the Snow Bunting is a scarce winter visitor, but in some winters may be found in reasonable numbers. It is probably also a passage migrant.

Some birds wintering in northern Britain may frequent upland moors, while others favour stubble and turnip fields, with others selecting marram grass behind sandy beaches. In England, wintering birds favour shingle beaches as well as sand dunes and neighbouring stubble fields (BWP). On the Isle of Man, Snow Buntings are found in winter on upland moors, among the vegetation along the shore as well as in stubble fields, reflecting the preferred habitats of both more northerly and more southerly wintering birds. Snow Buntings feed almost entirely on seeds, which are usually picked up off the ground.

The species nests mainly on sparsely vegetated coastal tundra and has the most northerly breeding distribution of any land bird (EBA). It occurs on the fringes of the Arctic Ocean, from Alaska across northern Canada to Greenland, Iceland and northern Scandinavia and across Russia to eastern Siberia (BWP, EBA). There is a small breeding population of about 70-100 pairs in the Scottish Highlands (1988–91 Atlas).

Snow Buntings from the most northerly reaches of their breeding range start to migrate from early September, but birds usually do not reach the British Isles until mid-October (MA), though large numbers can reach the northern isles of Scotland in mid-September. The earliest observation on the Island during MBA research was on 14 October 1999, when six Snow Buntings were seen at Port St Mary. Although many Icelandic birds remain in Iceland for the winter it is estimated that two-thirds of the birds wintering in western Europe are from Iceland, with the remainder probably being from Scandinavia (EBA). Those present on the Isle of Man in winter could therefore be from either breeding population. Numbers arriving in a given winter are variable and, as elsewhere within the British Isles, the species is highly mobile, birds moving around in response to weather and food availability. Snow Buntings may be present in an area for only a short period in each winter before moving to another location either on or off the Island.

In winter, Snow Buntings were seen in scattered locations around the coast, particularly on the Ayres beaches, as well as in the uplands of the northern, central and southern hills. Many of the sightings related to individual birds or small flocks of up to eight, with the majority of the observations during the winters of 1998-99 and 2001-02. Notable counts in 1998-99 included 30 on the slopes of Snaefell in November, 30 at Rue Point in the same month, 40 at Santon Head in December, 20 in stubble with Skylarks at Clay Head in January 1999, and 15 on Slieau Lhean later that month. During the winter of 2001-02 most sightings were of eight or fewer birds, but with one flock of 15 near Sky Hill in December 2001. By March in most years numbers are much reduced. There was only one April record of a bird at Ballaugh Cronk on 3 April 1999.

Kermode considered the Snow Bunting a 'regular winter visitor' and Ralfe endorsed this suggestion. Madoc thought it 'commoner perhaps than may be generally known' and C&J describe the species as a 'regular passage migrant and winter visitor in small numbers', a description that is still appropriate today.

Breeding	Grid squares:	Isle of Man 1 (0.5%) Britain 42 Ireland 0 Total 42 (1%)
	Population:	Isle of Man 0 Britain 85 Ireland 0 (<1% of European)
Wintering	Grid squares:	Isle of Man 29 (4%) Britain and Ireland 705 (18%)
	Population:	Isle of Man 0-50 Britain and Ireland 10,000-15,000

Jan	Feb	Mar	Apr	May	Jun	Jul	Aug	Sep	Oct	Nov	Dec

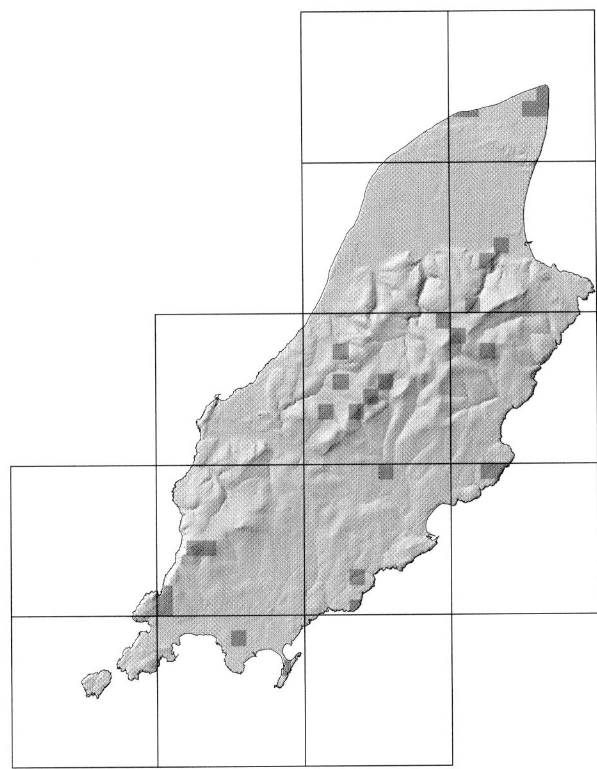

Winter presence

Yellowhammer
Emberiza citrinella

Manx: *Ushag vuigh* = Yellow bird

It is a sad reflection on the fortunes of the Yellowhammer that it is now considered as a noteworthy species, rather than being thought of as commonplace and a routine part of the landscape. Yellowhammers are handsome birds with a lemon-yellow head, more vibrant in males than females, yellow underparts and a chestnut rump. When good views are obtained Yellowhammers are difficult to confuse with any other species. The males' 'little bit of bread and no cheese' song is surprisingly far-reaching, and it can therefore be hard to pinpoint their precise location, especially when the song is delivered from banks of flowering yellow gorse.

Yellowhammers prefer dry sunny habitats with fairly rich and varied vegetation, avoiding dense forest, undrained wetlands, towns or busy inhabited areas (BWP). Locally, they appear to favour well-drained slopes and hedgerows which contain stands of European gorse and scattered hawthorns. Yellowhammers feed mainly on grass seeds, including those cultivated as cereals, though they will take invertebrates throughout the year, especially in the breeding season. During spring and early summer they forage near to nest sites, moving to pasture and arable land, especially stubble fields, with the onset of autumn and through the winter. In winter they may also frequent farmyards or supplementary feeding sites in fields, as well as sometimes visiting rural gardens (BWP).

The breeding range of the species extends from western Europe as far north as the North Cape, and across the temperate Palearctic to central Asia (BWP). Within the British Isles the Yellowhammer is widely distributed across lowland areas, with populations concentrated in the east and the Midlands. Marked declines in populations have been noted in parts of the British range, such declines being linked to increased agricultural specialisation, especially in milder moist areas of western Britain and Ireland, where livestock grazing is most favoured. A switch from spring to autumn cereal sowing generally throughout the British Isles is also likely to have had an adverse impact on a species so closely associated with winter stubbles (1988–91 Atlas). Over most of the rest of Europe the much larger populations are thought to be stable (EBA). On the Island, the breeding distribution of Yellowhammers is restricted to a few locations. This is in marked contrast to the situation in the 1980s when, as shown by the change maps, the species was present throughout most of the Island. Now, the main stronghold lies north of a line from Jurby to Bride, with isolated pockets to the south, at Orrisdale (near Ballaugh) and Regaby. Further south the only significant population lies between Peel and St Johns in the west of the Island, with occasional pairs seen at Santon in the south-east, and in the vicinity of Ballakilpheric in the south.

Continental Yellowhammers are migratory, but throughout the British Isles the species is considered to be entirely sedentary (EBA), and there is no evidence of migration on the Island. The winter maps reveal a largely similar distribution to that for the summer, underlining the sedentary nature of the species. Some localised movement is evident, particularly in the north and east, and this probably relates to birds seeking suitable stubble fields in which to forage.

Kermode considered the Yellowhammer to be 'plentiful' and Ralfe thought it, with the Chaffinch 'the most abundant of small birds'. Madoc described it as 'one of the common birds of the Island' and C&J described it as a 'common resident'. In 1986 C&J considered that the numbers and range of Yellowhammers had declined since the 1960s, but since they were writing the range has contracted much further. Numerical comparisons are not possible because of the lack of earlier data, but the current population of Yellowhammers on the Island may be only a few per cent of that up to about 50 years ago. It is reasonable to suppose that such a drastic decline is attributable to the same influences as in the wider British Isles, namely reduced acreage under cereal production and a move from spring to autumn sowing. Thrower (2002) notes that on the Isle of Man the total acreage under cereals in 2000 was the same as in 1970 (when Yellowhammers were still abundant), though significantly less oats and more barley are now grown. Since 1990, agricultural returns to the Department of Agriculture, Fisheries and Forestry have recorded acreage of winter and spring varieties of barley separately, and in the period from then until 2000, there has been no significant reduction in acreage of spring sown barley (Thrower 2002). The species needs to be carefully monitored to establish which factors are causing decline here and to assess whether the population continues to decrease.

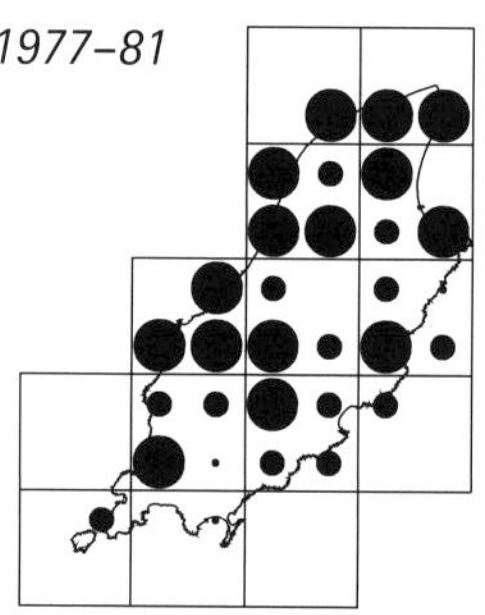

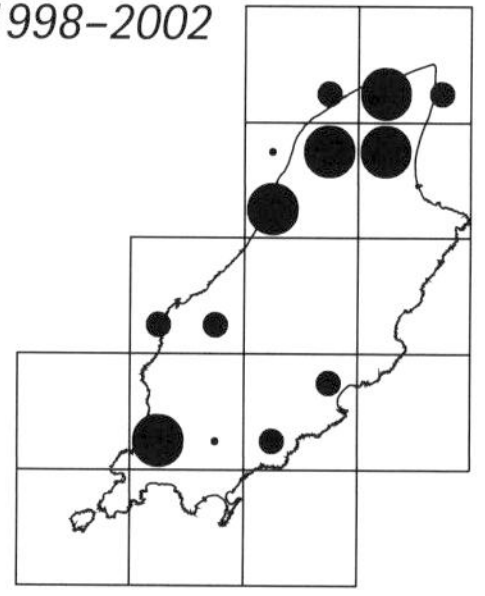

Breeding	Grid squares:	Isle of Man 64 (10%) Britain 2,224 Ireland 587 Total 2,811 (73%)
	Population:	Isle of Man 122–146 Britain 1,200,000 Ireland 200,000 (7% of European)
Wintering	Grid squares:	Isle of Man 36 (5%) Britain and Ireland 2,473 (64%)
	Population:	Isle of Man <500 Britain and Ireland 3,500,000

Jan	Feb	Mar	Apr	May	Jun	Jul	Aug	Sep	Oct	Nov	Dec

Corporate Sponsor – Manx Heritage Foundation

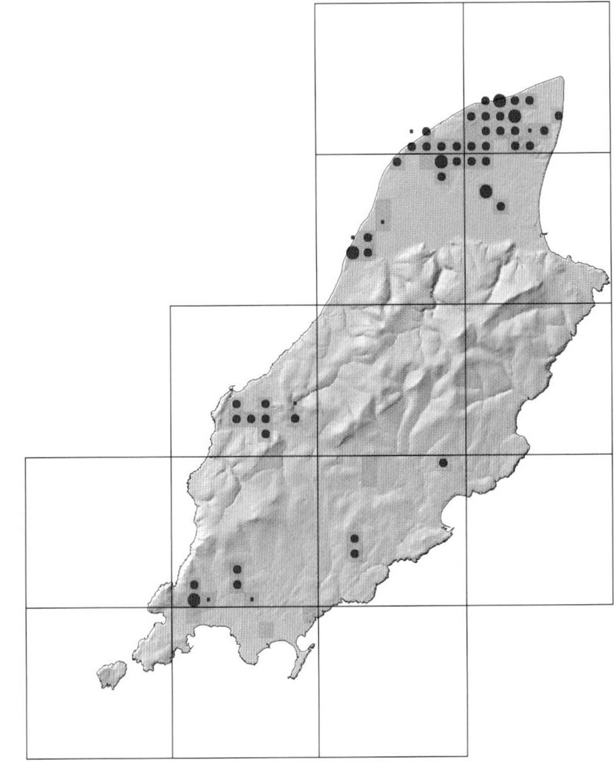

Summer presence and breeding status

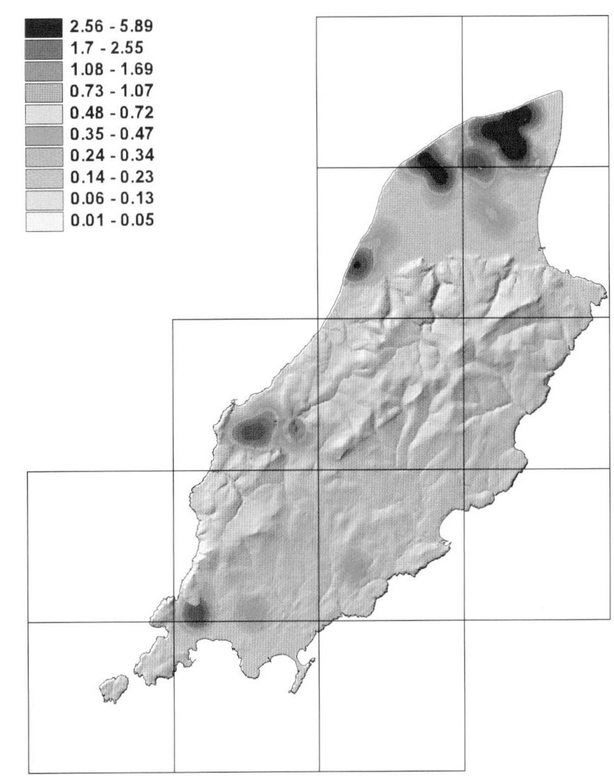

Breeding abundance

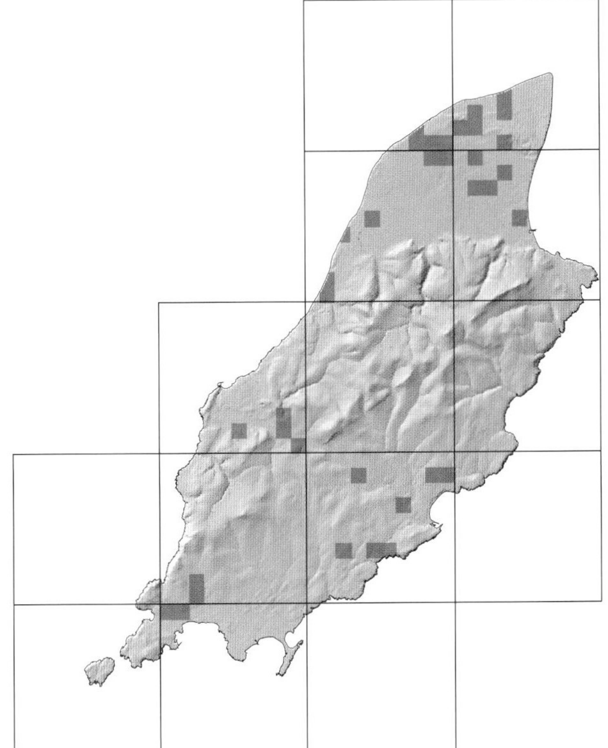

Winter presence

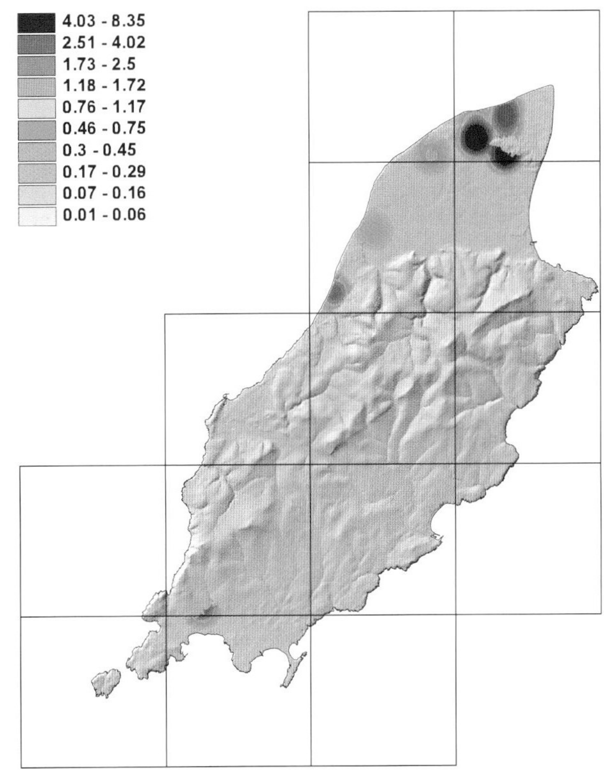

Winter abundance

Individual Sponsors – Mr. G Craine, Mr. I & Mrs. J Kelly, Mr. G Rollins, Mr. D R Sharp, Mrs. M Skelly

Reed Bunting
Emberiza schoeniclus

Manx: *Pompee ny Guirtlagh*

Reed Buntings are common residents on the Isle of Man, but they tend to skulk in dense vegetation and may therefore be unfamiliar to many. The adult male has a rather smart black head and white collar, while the female is largely brown, but Reed Buntings are often detected by their seemingly amateur attempts at squeezing out a rather discordant little song.

During the breeding season Reed Buntings occupy marshes, fens, bogs and riversides, though this apparent attachment to wet areas relates more to their associated vegetation types, such as reedbed, alder and willow, rather than a particular need for water (BWP). Outside the breeding season, Reed Buntings continue to be found in their breeding habitat, but also occur in drier areas, where they often join flocks of mixed seed-eaters to forage in stubble fields. In common with all buntings, Reed Buntings mainly feed on seeds and other plant material, though during the breeding season they are almost entirely insectivorous (MA).

The Reed Bunting is one of the most widely distributed of European buntings and is abundant throughout northern and north-central Europe, though absent from Iceland and from most of the Mediterranean region. Reed Buntings are widespread and common throughout the British Isles, but are generally absent from higher upland areas, and they occur at higher densities in Ireland than elsewhere in the British Isles (1988–91 Atlas).

As can be seen from the breeding distribution map, Reed Buntings have a wide, but patchy, breeding distribution over the Island, largely reflecting the availability of suitable habitat. Areas of curragh or willow carr are favoured, as are well vegetated upland valleys, such as those running off the central hills into Glen Helen. Nearer the coast, including parts of Langness and the Ayres slacks, patches of scrub containing bramble hold scattered breeding pairs.

Within the British Isles the Reed Bunting is essentially sedentary and non-migratory though some short-distance dispersal after the breeding season can occur (MA). Such movements relate to birds leaving higher ground and, more generally, birds dispersing to take advantage of available winter food. A small number of migrants from the continent do reach the British Isles each winter, though these are mainly seen on the east coast and are unlikely to reach the Isle of Man.

In winter, Reed Buntings are much less obvious than in the breeding season, especially as males are less vocal, and they can easily be overlooked. This probably accounts for the more patchy winter distribution suggested by both winter maps. Although Reed Buntings still occurred throughout much of the Island they were much less evident in many of the upland breeding areas, where, presumably, food is in relatively short supply. The winter abundance map reveals areas of relatively high abundance in isolated pockets, reflecting the location of small feeding flocks. During the structured surveys from which the map is derived, many of these flocks were found on winter stubble fields in areas such as Clay Head, Scarlett and parts of the northern plain.

Kermode describes the Reed Bunting merely as resident, while Ralfe considered the species to be scarce and local, but Madoc thought it by no means uncommon. C&J thought the species to be a 'common resident, summer visitor and passage migrant'. Thus there is no evidence of substantial population change on the Isle of Man since Madoc, although numbers may have increased since Ralfe was writing. In the rest of the British Isles the population of Reed Buntings is thought to have declined slightly in recent decades, particularly in northern and western areas (1988–91 Atlas). The reasons for this decline are not known, but may relate to a reduction in available weed seeds around farmland in winter as a result of more intensive use of herbicides (1988–91 Atlas).

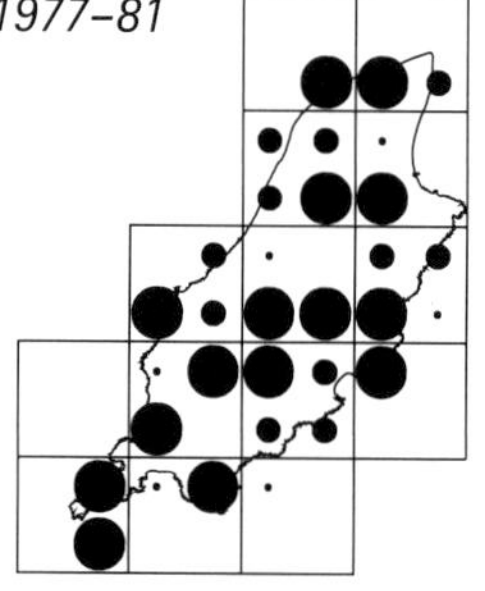

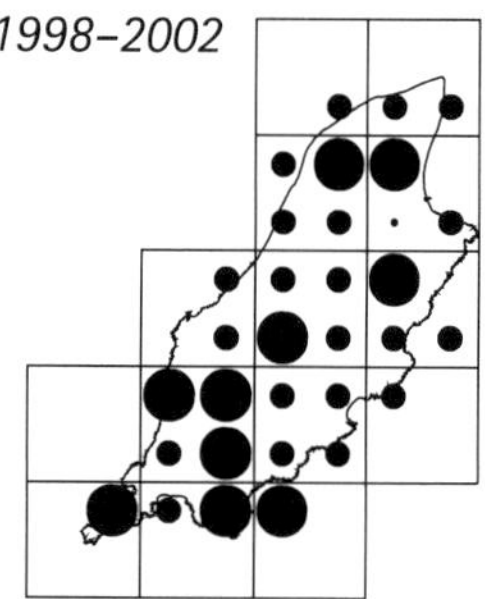

Breeding	Grid squares:	Isle of Man 168 (25%) Britain 2,188 Ireland 831 Total 3,019 (78%)
	Population:	Isle of Man 211–232 Britain 220,000 Ireland 130,000 (10% of European)
Wintering	Grid squares:	Isle of Man 86 (13%) Britain and Ireland 2,491 (65%)
	Population:	Isle of Man <1,000 Britain and Ireland 1,200,000

Jan	Feb	Mar	Apr	May	Jun	Jul	Aug	Sep	Oct	Nov	Dec

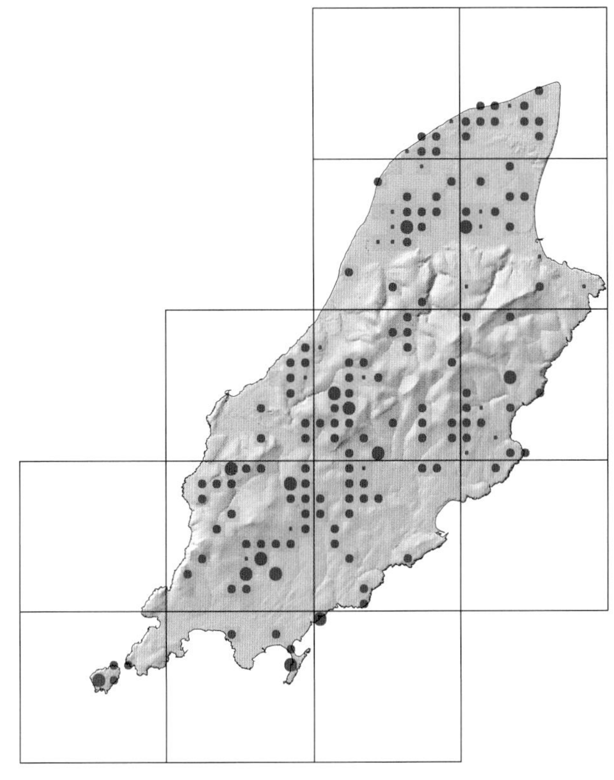

Summer presence and breeding status

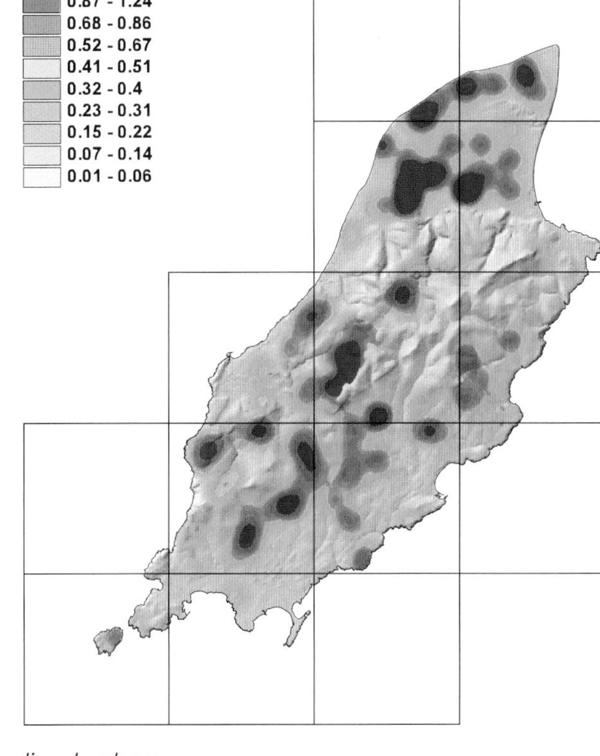

Breeding abundance

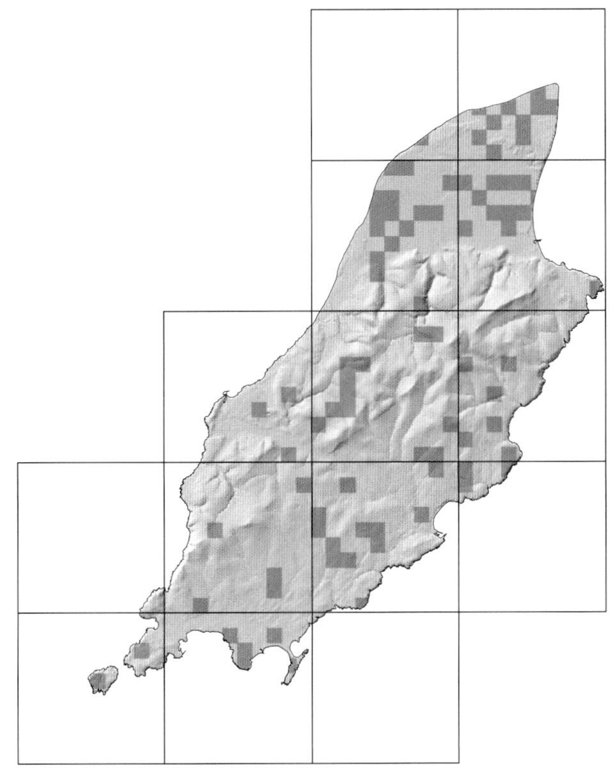

Winter presence

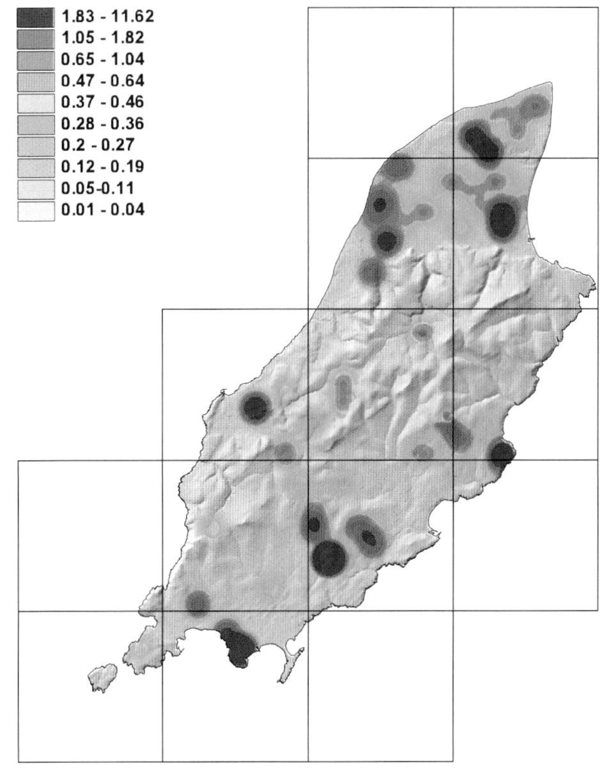

Winter abundance

Individual Sponsors – Mr. H Devitt, Mr. B Haycock

Species richness, avian density and birds of conservation concern

In the species accounts covered in the main body of this Atlas, maps are used to depict the relative abundance of each species during the breeding and winter periods. The generation of abundance maps such as these is only possible if the data from which they are derived have been gathered in a way that removes variation in observer effort. As previously explained, staff of the charity undertook systematic coverage of the Island during the summer and winter, producing data which were standardised for observer effort and thus enabled meaningful abundance maps to be produced.

While a study of individual species abundance lies at the heart of the Atlas research, it is also of interest to use the results of the structured surveying to provide data on such aspects as 'species richness' and 'avian diversity'. The maps in this section demonstrate the results of some of the analyses undertaken, with each set of maps (breeding and wintering) being accompanied by a short explanatory narrative. While the maps are of interest in their own right, their true value will be revealed in the future when the data from further research can be used to evaluate change.

As with the abundance maps for individual species, records of birds with a 'non-breeding' status during the breeding period are excluded from the data from which the following maps are derived. For the winter, records of birds observed 'flying over' and therefore not deemed to be using the tetrad being surveyed are similarly discounted. Within each value range shown, the upper and lower values may by slightly curtailed by smoothing errors in the mapping software.

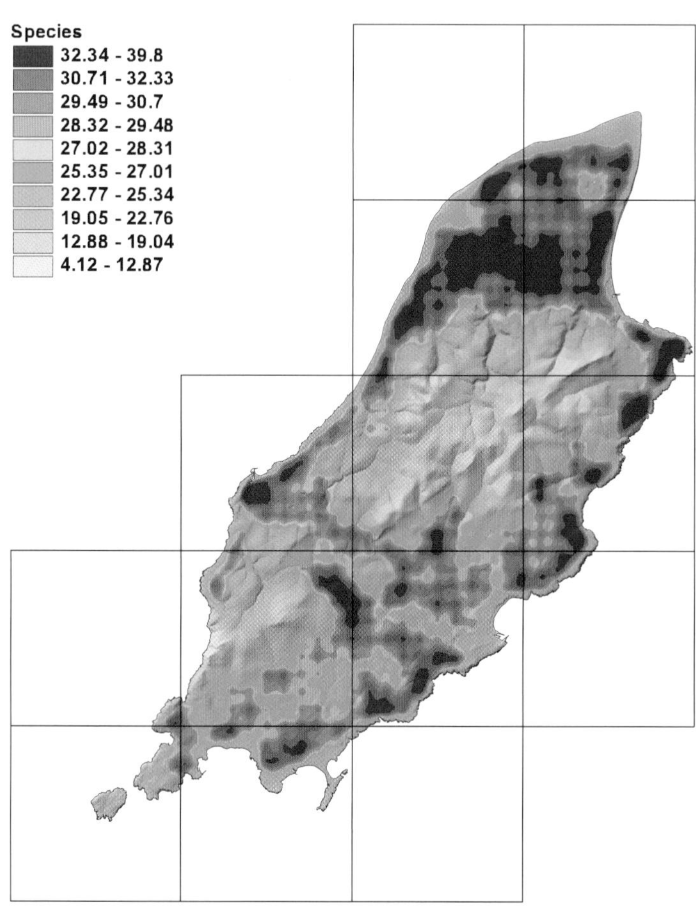

Breeding species richness

Species richness

This is measured as the total number of species observed in each 1km square. At first glance the maps for both summer and winter appear very similar with, as would be expected, higher densities in the lowlands than in the uplands. A few points are, however, worth noting. The winter map reveals how sparsely populated the uplands can be at this time, with an average of fewer than one species per 1km square in some areas, compared to a minimum of four in the breeding season. In summer, high densities are evident across the southern half of the northern plain, particularly in the areas of curragh from Ballaugh to slightly east of St Judes. In winter this area contains fewer species, probably because many of those present in the summer are migratory and therefore absent in winter. Also, a high proportion of the winter visitors are non-passerines and hence might avoid the dense undergrowth of curragh, favouring instead

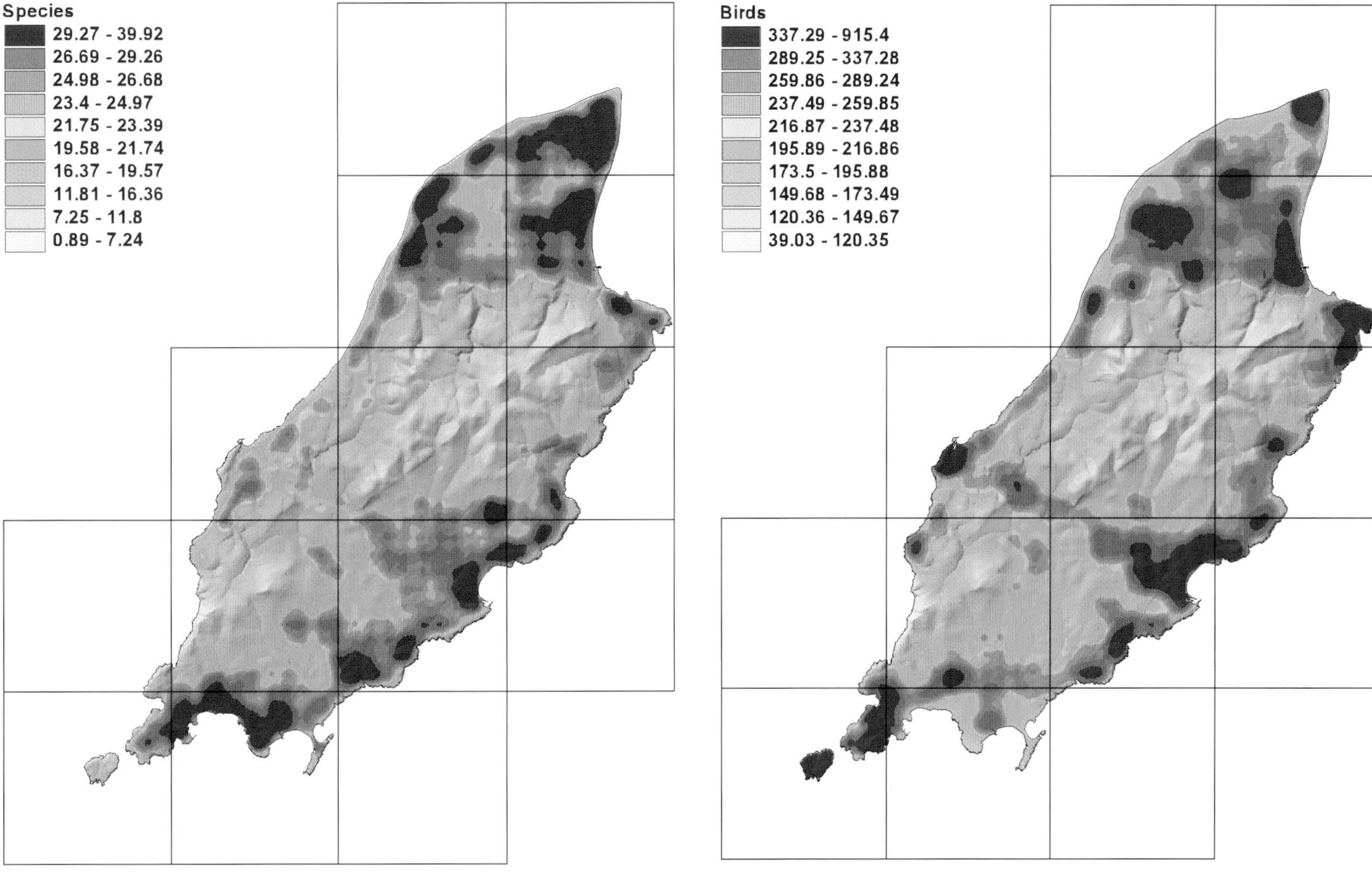

Winter species richness

Avian breeding density

the more open field systems and coastal areas, where areas of high winter abundance are evident. The maps suggest some diminution of numbers in the west of the Island.

Avian density

These maps show the total number of birds seen in each 1km square during both survey periods. As such, the areas of highest density in the summer will be influenced by the presence of species that breed in colonies; on the Island these species are mainly seabirds. In winter areas of high density will be largely dictated by the location of species, such as Jackdaws, Rooks, Herring Gulls, Starlings and many of the wintering wildfowl, which form large flocks in particular areas. In summer high abundance does indeed largely mirror the location of seabird colonies, thus the gull colony at the Ayres and mixed colonies at Maughold Head, the Chasms/Sugar Loaf, Calf of Man and Peel Hill are all highlighted. Other pockets of high density match locations of rookeries or, in the case of the area near St Johns, a large Sand Martin colony within a sand quarry. On the winter map, the extreme north of the Island is dominated by the large flocks of gulls, mainly Herring Gulls, at the Ayres landfill site. These, combined with flocks of wildfowl on the adjacent gravel pits and waders on the Ayres, formed the largest aggregation of wintering birds on the Island. The area of high abundance north of Douglas again mainly relates to Herring Gulls which frequent the Clypse and Kerrowdhoo reservoirs, while concentrations near Santon, to the south of Douglas, comprised mixed flocks of Rooks, Starlings and seed-eating passerines. At Langness, Castletown Bay and Strandhall flocks of waders, wildfowl, gulls and Starlings combine to produce high overall densities of birds.

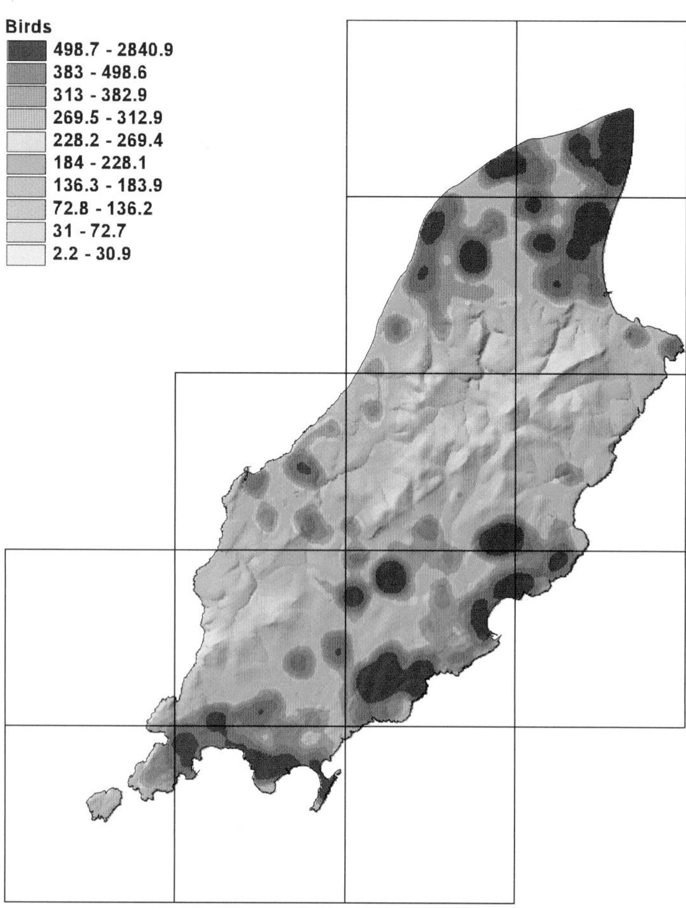

Avian wintering density

Manx Wildlife Act 1990 – Schedule 1 protected species

Under the Wildlife Act 1990 protection is afforded to most bird species. The few exceptions relate to pest species, for which a licence may be obtained to control numbers, and to birds listed as game, though these latter birds are protected during the breeding season. Under the Act a general protection is given to 'non-pest' species, and during the breeding season, their nests, eggs and dependent young are also protected. Penalties exist for those found guilty of deliberately killing or injuring birds, destroying their eggs or nests or disturbing them while they are nesting. In addition, within Schedule 1 of the Act, a number of species are listed for which the above offences attract increased penalties. Species are included on Schedule 1 for a number of reasons, including their susceptibility to illegal persecution or theft of eggs, and a recognition that a species has an unfavourable conservation status either locally or in an international context. Within Appendix D, which lists all species covered in the main species accounts, those species currently included in Schedule 1 are indicated. The abundance map of birds included within Schedule 1 of the Act relates to species, rather than numbers of individuals, and that for the summer shows high concentrations in the north of the Island. Many of the species included in Schedule 1 are closely associated with agricultural land and include Curlews, Tree Sparrows, Yellowhammers and Lapwings; the map serves to underline the importance of the northern plain to these species. In winter the areas of highest density of Schedule 1 species are influenced by the occurrence of flocks of waders and wildfowl such as Curlews, Golden Plovers, Lapwings, Shelducks and geese and hence concentrations are in the northern plain and around the favoured coastal feeding areas in the south.

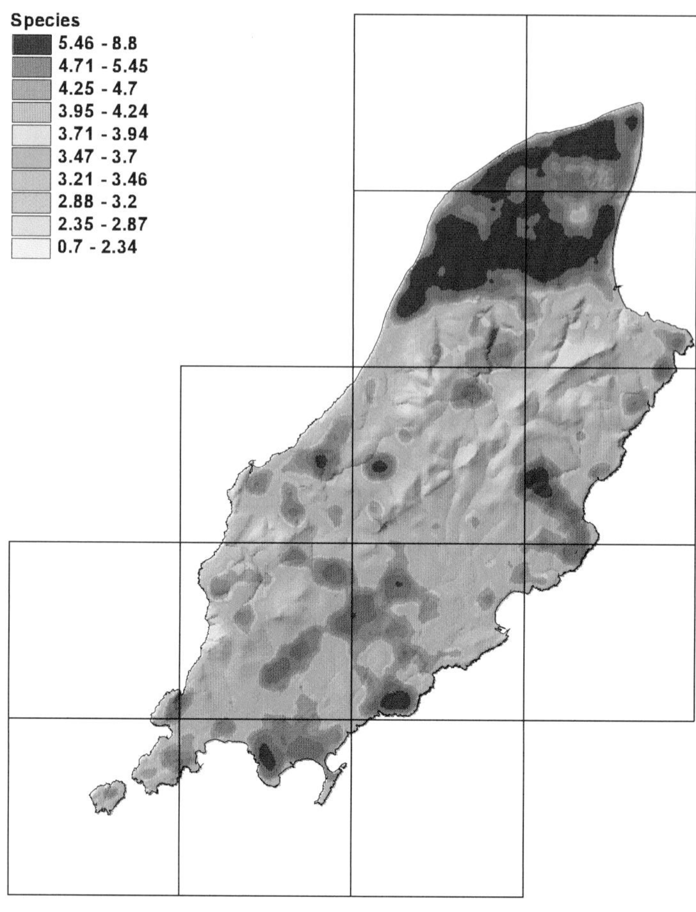

Schedule 1 species: breeding presence

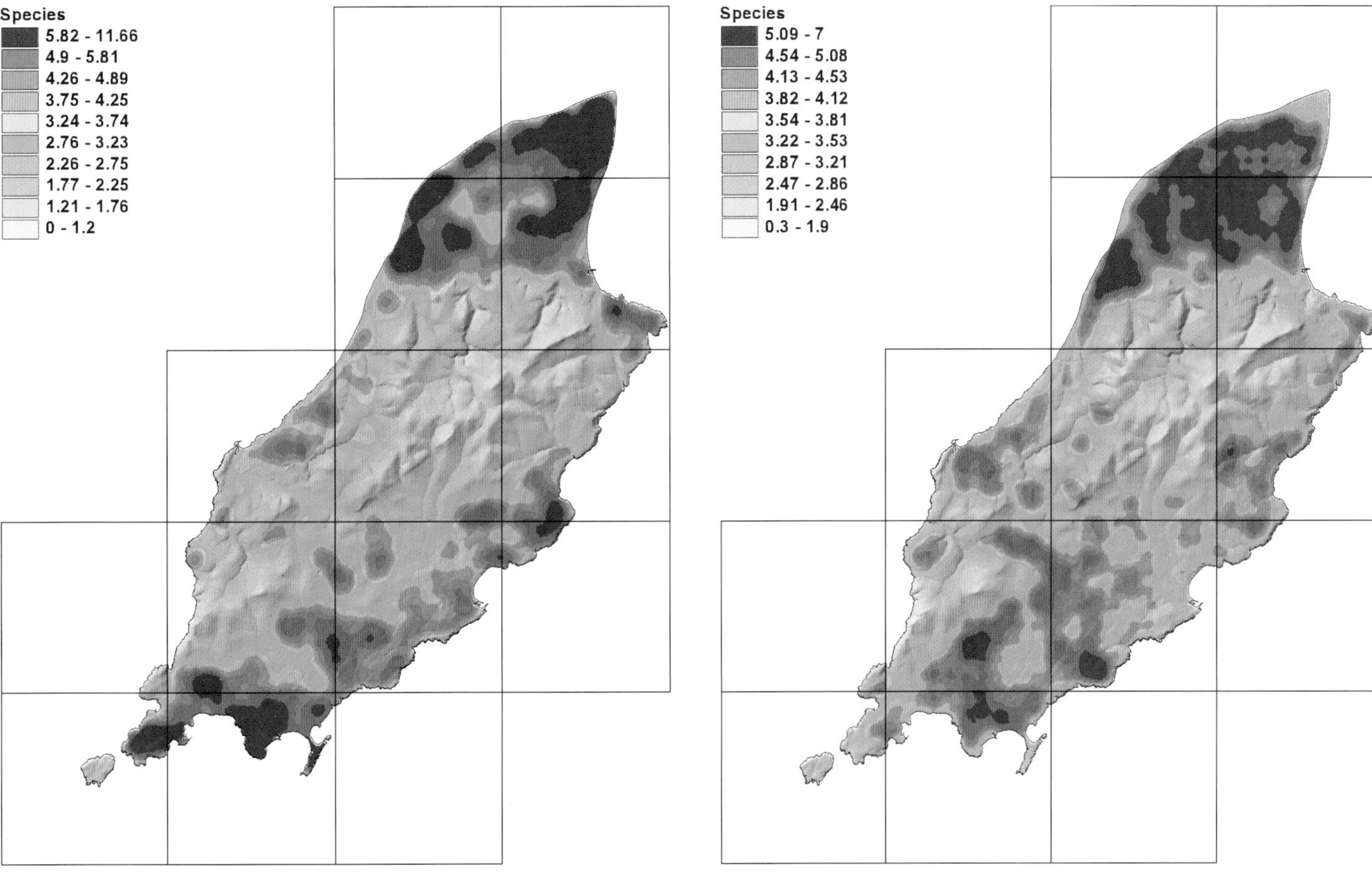

Schedule 1 species: winter presence

Red-listed species: breeding presence

Birds of conservation concern in Britain and Ireland

Every five years, leading governmental and non-governmental conservation organisations in the UK review the population status of birds that regularly occur there, basing their findings upon the most up-to-date information available. Of the 247 species whose status has been reviewed, each has been assigned to one of three lists – red, amber or green, with those on the red list being the species of highest conservation concern. Species are included on the red list if they are globally threatened, their populations have undergone an historical decline (1800-1995), or their UK breeding range or breeding populations have declined by 50% or more in the last 25 years. The amber list includes species of medium conservation concern, namely those with an unfavourable conservation status in Europe; those whose population range or numbers have undergone moderate decline (25-49%) in the last 25 years; rare breeders; those with internationally important or localised populations and those still recovering from historical declines. Species on the green list are those that meet none of the criteria for inclusion on the red or amber lists.

Currently, for the UK, 40 species are red-listed, 121 are amber-listed and 86 are on the green list (Anon 2002). The current lists are valid until 2007. The lists cover the Isle of Man, though, to date, limited information has been available locally to help in the process of compiling or reviewing the lists. It is hoped that the Atlas research will be of use when the lists are next reviewed. In the medium term the Island should perhaps work to produce its own lists. Appendix D indicates those species covered in this Atlas which are included in the red and amber lists for the UK, as well as those included in similar lists for Ireland. Currently, 14 species that are on the UK red list breed in the Isle of Man, while 12 are known to winter here, with amber-listed species numbering 53 in the breeding season and 66 during the winter.

Many of the species on the red list are birds that have a strong association with agriculture, in particular arable production. These species include Grey Partridge, Skylarks, Starlings, Tree Sparrows and Linnets; it is, therefore, unsurprising that the breeding and winter maps that depict red-listed species abundance are a good fit with areas of Manx lowland agriculture, in particular the north and the south-east where most arable production is concentrated.

Many of the species on the amber list are species of coastal and freshwater wetlands, such as many of the gulls, auks, wildfowl and divers. Such an emphasis results in the summer map for amber-listed birds showing a correlation with known concentrations of breeding gulls and auks, with winter concentrations also evident along the coast, where concentrations of gulls, waders and wildfowl are to be found.

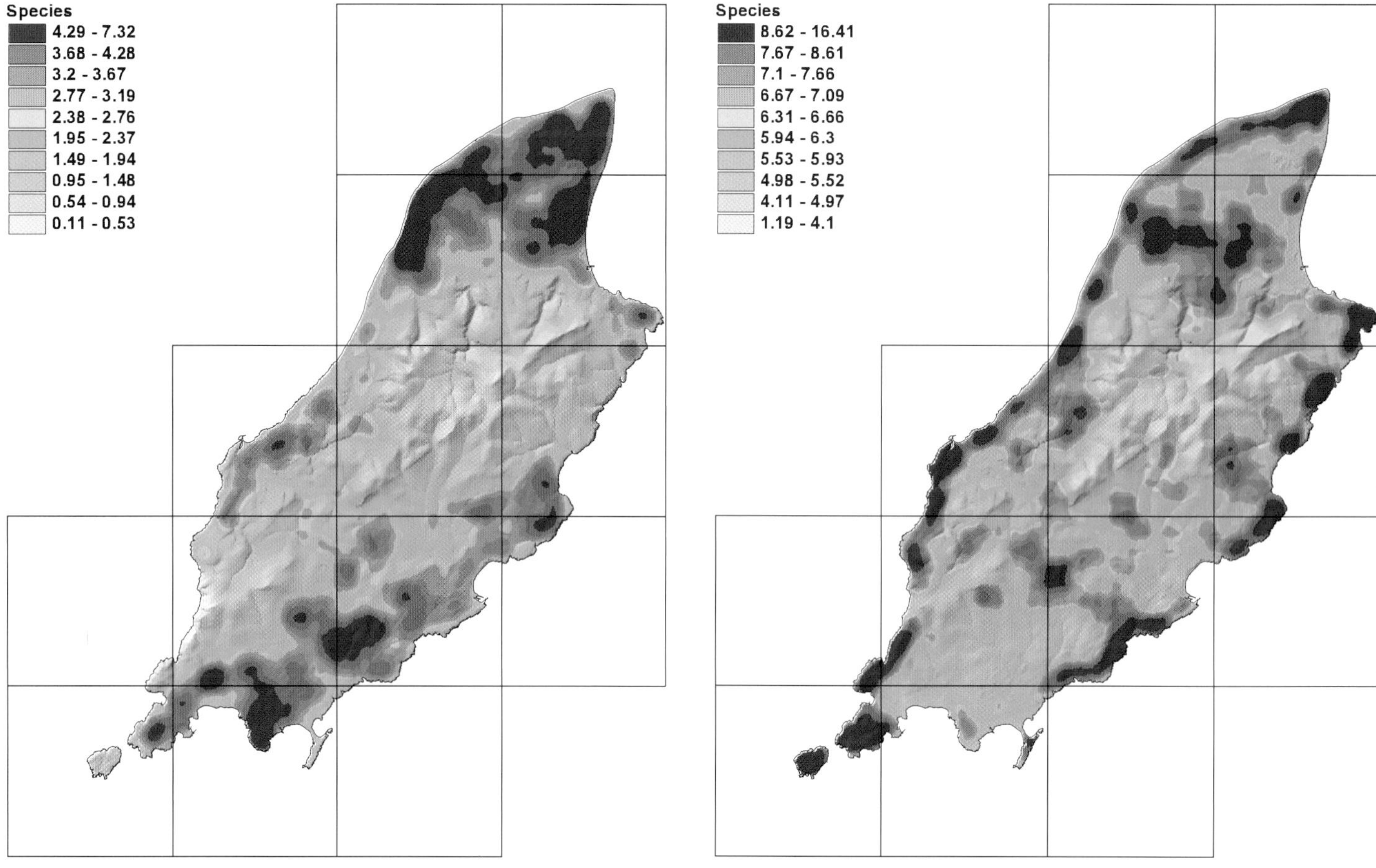

Red-listed species: winter presence

Amber-listed species: breeding presence

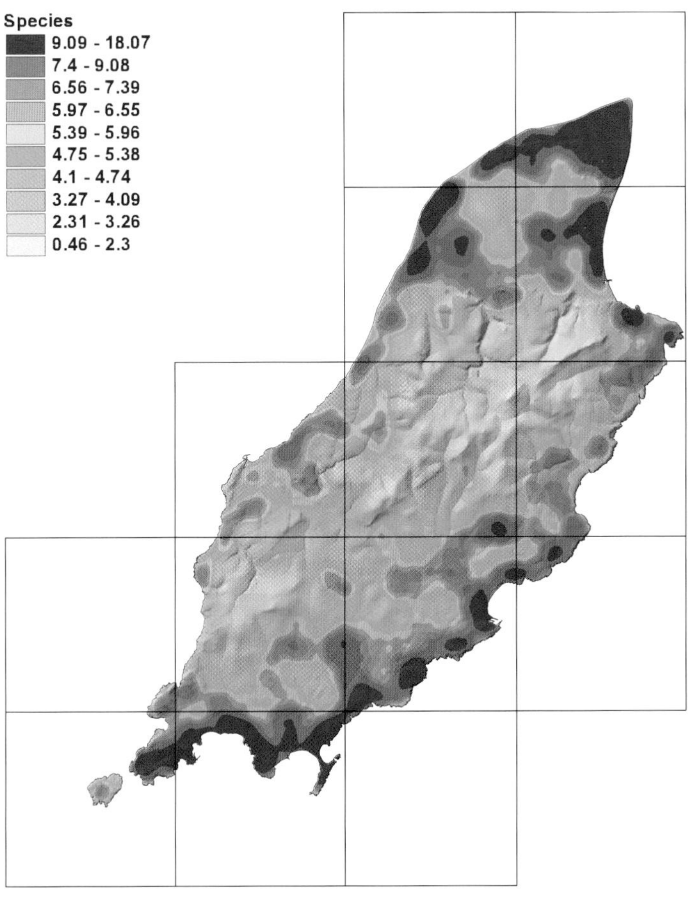

Amber-listed species: winter presence

Appendix A: Other species recorded

The main focus of the atlas research relates to species that bred on the Island during the summers 1998–2002 and those that were considered to be wintering during the winters 1998–99 to 2002–03. Accounts for these are included within the main body of the publication. During the research period a range of other species were noted. Some occurred on only one occasion whereas others, though occurring more frequently, did not breed or were not present frequently enough to justify a full account.

Such species are listed below, some warranting only a brief mention of grid reference and date of observation, others meriting a brief commentary. For some species maps are included indicating where the species was observed. All maps shown in this section include records for the full period April 1998 to March 2003. Appendix B lists each 1km sq on the Island, together with a relevant place name.

Black Swan

Cygnus atratus
Classed as an escape.
SC2067 One in April 1998, in company with Mute Swans

White-fronted Goose (Greater White-fronted Goose)

Anser albifrons
SC4991 Two, 11 December 2001
NX4503 One, 9 September 2002
NX4504 One, 4 January 2003

Bar-headed Goose

Anser indicus
Classed as escaped birds
NX4504 Two, 4 May 2001

Barnacle Goose

Branta leucopsis
NX4504 One, wary bird in October 1999, which was probably wild
SC2168 Three birds flying over on 7 February 2001 were classed as wild

Red-breasted Goose

Branta ruficollis
Classed as an escaped bird
SC1968 One from early September 2000 until at least 27 January 2001

Mandarin Duck

Aix galericulata
All birds classed as escapes or in private collections
SC2669 Up to five birds present through period including one pair
SC3996 A pair present in May 2000
SC3072 A single male in July 2002

Wood Duck

Aix sponsa
Classed as escaped birds
SC2667 Two males and a female present in April 1998, with the last bird reported as present in March 2001, with no evidence of breeding
SC4483 Male present from November 1998 to January 2001

Green-winged Teal

Anas carolinensis
SC2866 One, 6 January 2000

Pintail (Northern Pintail)

Anas acuta

Recorded during each year of the survey period, the majority of the records were obtained during the months of September/October and March/April, indicating autumn and spring passage. On 20 October

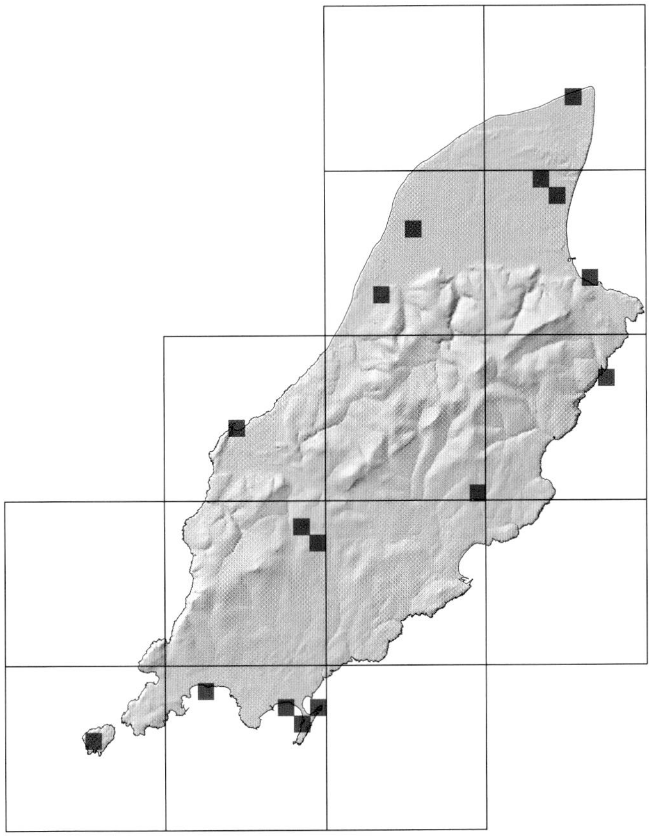

Pintail – all records

2000 a single bird flew south off Peel, with two flying south off the Calf on 7 September 2002. Coastal records were largely confined to shallow bays including Castletown, Langness, Derbyhaven and Port Lewaigue. Inland, records were obtained from frequently watched areas of shallow water and it is likely that the species is under-recorded, especially females, which could be overlooked by the casual observer. No evidence of over-wintering or summering birds was obtained.

Garganey

Anas querquedula
SC1565 One, 21 May 2000

Red-crested Pochard

Netta rufina
Classed as escaped birds
SC2866 One, 12 December 1999
NX4504 One throughout December 2001 and January 2002

King Eider

Somateria spectabilis
NX4003 One, 27 May–1 June 2002. The first Manx record.

Surf Scoter

Melanitta perspicillata
NX3902 One, 14 November 2001. The first Manx record.

Smew

Mergellus albellus
SC3980 One, 29 December 2000 until 21 February 2001

Northern Bobwhite

Colinus virginianus
Classed as an escape
NX4201 A male calling for over a week in July 1998

Golden Pheasant

Chrysolophus pictus
SC3593 One, 5 November 2002

Great Crested Grebe

Podiceps cristatus

The Great Crested Grebe breeds primarily on shallow freshwater bodies, a habitat which is largely absent on the Island. This probably accounts for the lack of breeding records locally, both during the research period and historically. During the period, records of an estimated 27 individual birds were received, mainly of birds on the sea, in the shallow bays of Peel, Ramsey, Castletown and Derbyhaven or in the shallow waters of the Ayres. Exceptions were of a single bird flying over the Ballaugh Curragh in March 2000 and three sightings from recently created gravel pits at the Ayres. As the restoration of these pits proceeds it may be speculated that they could yield the first Manx breeding of this attractive species.

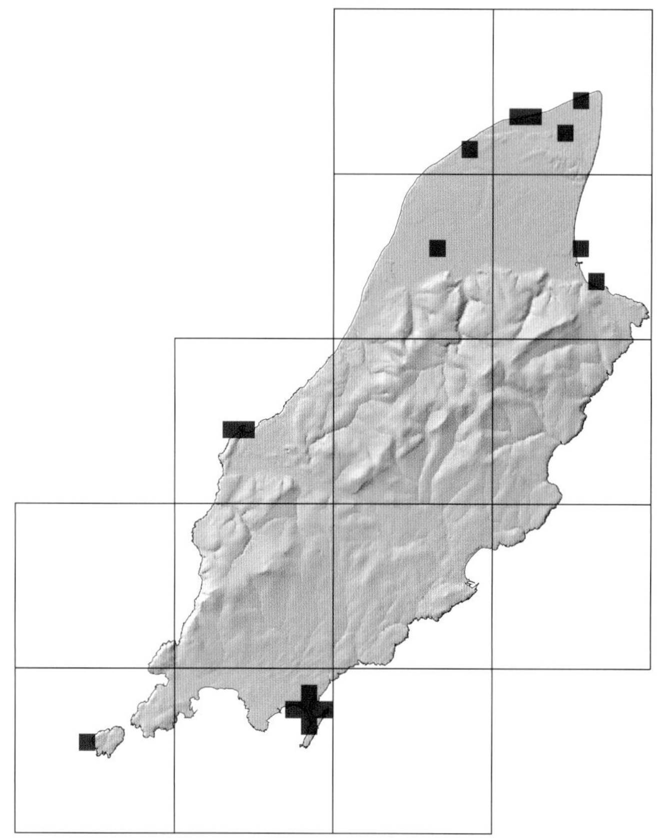

Great Crested Grebe – all records

Red-necked Grebe

Podiceps grisegena

NX3902 One, 20 December 1998

Sooty Shearwater

Puffinus griseus

Jan Feb Mar Apr May Jun Jul Aug Sep Oct Nov Dec

SC1565 Five, 3 August 1998

SC1465 Singles on 16 September, 1 and 2 October 1999

SC2484 One, five miles off Peel 29 July 2001

SC2865 One, 14 August 2001

SC1465 Two, 21 August 2001

SC1565 One, 6 September 2001

SC2484 One, 7 September 2001

NX4605 Two, 9 September 2001

SC2484 One, 30 August 2002

SC1565 Two, 6 September 2002

Balearic Shearwater

Puffinus mauretanicus

Jan Feb Mar Apr May Jun Jul Aug Sep Oct Nov Dec

SC1564 One, 7 May 1998

SC1465 Two, 3 July 1999 and singles 29 August, 9 September and 2 October 1999

SC1465 Two, 13 June 2000

SC2865 One, 31 August 2000

SC1465 One, 21 August 2001

Leach's Petrel

Oceanodroma leucorhoa

Jan Feb Mar Apr May Jun Jul Aug Sep Oct Nov Dec

SC1565 One, 8 September 1998

SC2484 Singles on 12 September and 13 October 1998

SC2484 One, 22 July 1999

SC1465 Singles on 30 August and 3 October 1999

SC1465 Singles on 12 August, 21 September and 24 October 2000

SC2484 One, 25 October 2000

SC2282 One, 29 July 2001

SC1465 Two, 13 August and one 7 September 2001

SC2484 Fourteen, 7 September 2001

NX4605 One, 9 September 2001

SC2484 One, 12 and two 15 September 2001

NX4605 Two, 15 September 2001

SC2484 Three, 3 February 2002

SC1565 One, 6 September 2002

SC2484 One, 7 September 2002

Magnificent Frigatebird

Fregata magnificens
SC2566 A storm-blown bird was found exhausted on the 22 December 1998. Taken into care, where it died some months later. The first Manx record.

Bittern (Great Bittern)

Botaurus stellaris
SC1565 One, 2 September 2001

Little Egret

Egretta garzetta

Jan Feb Mar Apr May Jun Jul Aug Sep Oct Nov Dec

Not recorded as a breeding species in Britain and Ireland in the 1988–91 Atlas, the species has, since then, undergone a significant change in status. First confirmed as breeding in 1992, it is estimated that 146–162 pairs bred in 2002, spread over 22 localities. Though most of these were in the south-west and south-east of England, they included a female in Lancashire and North Merseyside, laying one egg, and a pair on Anglesey fledging four young, with another pair possibly raising one fledgling (Ogilvie 2004).

It is not surprising therefore that on the Island records of Little Egrets have become more frequent in recent years. Having been first recorded in July 1985, the species was absent until 1990, when, during a seven-week period in early spring, a total of 53 sightings of, possibly, three birds were obtained (Hopson & Moore 1991). Further occasional records during the mid-1990s reflected the increasing numbers and range within the British Isles, with the species occurring annually during the 1998–2003 survey period. Other than a single bird seen at the Point of Ayre in December 1998 all the records were of birds in the southern half of the Island. Most birds did not stay long, though one individual was present from 12 January to 17 February 2001, during which time it moved from near St Johns to Colby and Langness, often observed feeding inland among livestock.

Great White Egret (Great Egret)

Ardea alba
SC2866 One, from 18–24 June 2000. The first Manx record.

Purple Heron

Ardea purpurea
SC1564 One, 9 September 1999. The first Manx record.
SC1565 One, 1 May 2001

White Stork

Ciconia ciconia
SC2566 One, 6 June 2000 probably an escape

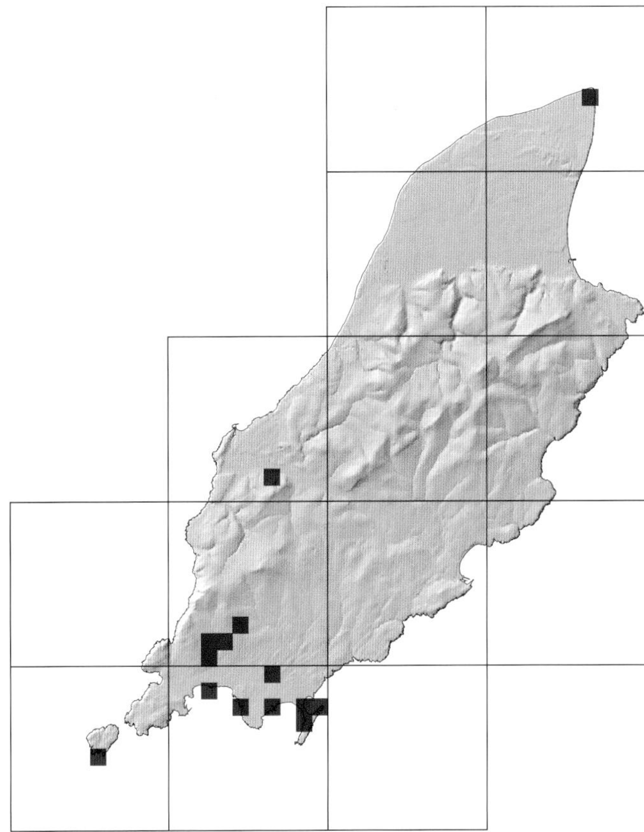

Little Egret – all records

Spoonbill (Eurasian Spoonbill)

Platalea leucorodia
SC2866 One, from 9–22 May 1998

Honey Buzzard (European Honey-buzzard)

Pernis apivorus
SC1565 Singles on 2 October 1998 and 22 September 2000

Red Kite

Milvus milvus
SC1565 Singles on 9 May 1998, 1 May 2000 and 20 September 2002
SC4397 One, 11 November 1998

Marsh Harrier (Eurasian Marsh Harrier)

Circus aeruginosus

Of the 14 birds recorded during the period, ten were observed on the Calf of Man. The species has greatly increased in range and breeding numbers in the British Isles over recent years, with 503 young reared in 2002, compared to 244 young in 1993. Though concentrated in the counties of Lincolnshire, Norfolk and Suffolk, seven young were reared from three nests in Lancashire and North Merseyside in 2002. (Ogilvie 2004) Such an increased population, at least some of which is migratory, probably accounts for the increased numbers seen on the Island, all of which were observed during spring or autumn passage.

Goshawk (Northern Goshawk)

Accipiter gentilis
Occasional escapes reported, but these records deemed to be wild birds

SC4384 One, 1 April 2000
SC2968 One, 21 August 2000
NX4602 One, 23 August 2001
SC3892 One, 25 and 26 March 2002
SC2672 One, 8 April 2002
SC2475 One, 25 April 2002

Common Buzzard

Buteo buteo

Recorded with increasing frequency on the Island, it must only be a matter of time before the species starts to breed locally. Most records were of birds that were seen singly and on only one occasion, however two birds were seen on 4 April 2000 between the Sloc and South Barrule (Cullen 2003). During the winter of 2002–03 there were a number of sightings in the St Judes/Andreas area and it is highly likely that these were of the same individual, the first indication that an individual may have over-wintered.

Rough-legged Buzzard

Buteo lagopus
SC2468 One, 28 March 2002

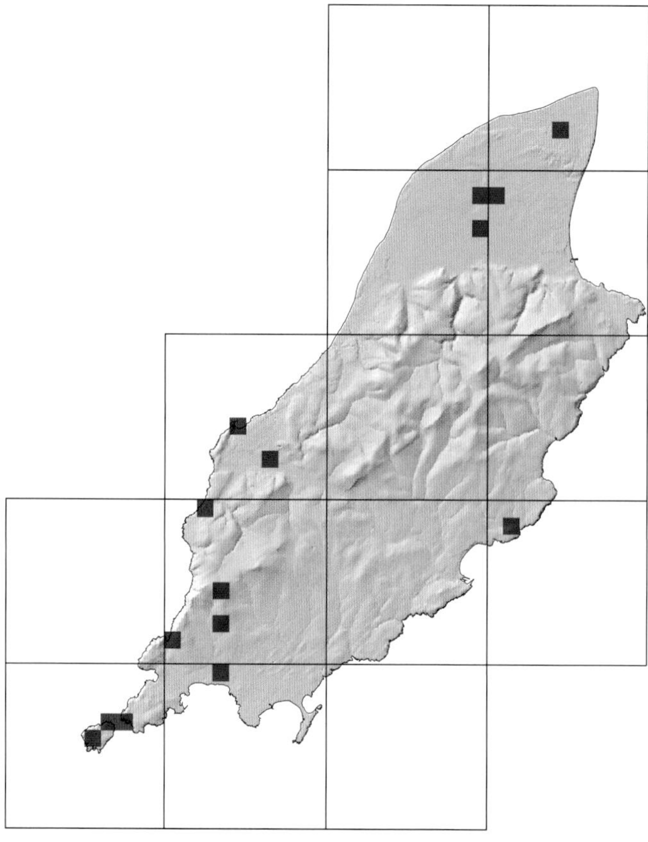

Common Buzzard – all records

Osprey

Pandion haliaetus

Recorded during each of the five years, the spring passage produced slightly more records (17) than that of the autumn (12). Scottish birds are known to winter in West Africa, moving through France, Spain and Portugal en route. Depending upon prevailing winds during migration a variable number will pass through the Island, accounting for the year on year variation in local sightings. In 2002 a satellite-tagged juvenile left its natal area in Nairnshire on 12 September and was recorded as spending the night of 13 September at Bride, in the north of the Island. By 21 September it was at Torrao, Portugal, at one stage during the journey being pushed 800km west of Lisbon by bad weather.

Hobby (Eurasian Hobby)

Falco subbuteo
SC1564 One, 3 September 1998
SC1565 Singles 29 April 1999 and 3–4 September 2001
NX4605 One, 18 May 2002

Crane (Common Crane)

Grus grus

Jan Feb Mar Apr May Jun Jul Aug Sep Oct Nov Dec

All records came from the northern part of the Island

SC3496 One, 20 March–10 April 2000

SC3498 One, 2–12 April 2002

SC3292 A juvenile present from 14 November to 18 December 2002. Present at Orrisdale for November it ranged more widely in December, moving to Glascoe (SC4498) and Cranstal (NX4602), where it was last seen

SC3596 On 2 February 2003 a bird was present near St Judes, ranging as far as Cranstal (NX4502), before last being observed back at St Judes on 23 March

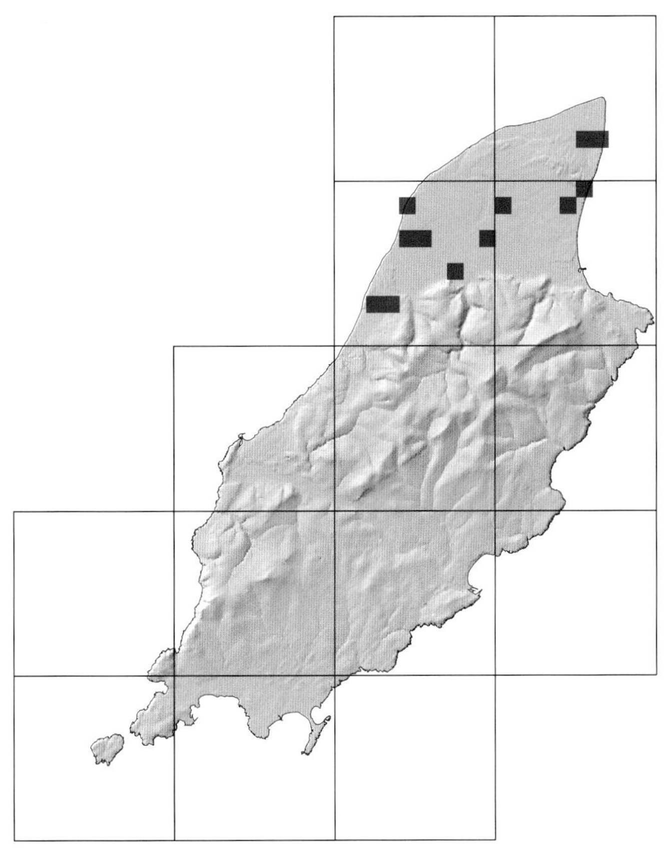

Crane – all records

Avocet (Pied Avocet)

Recurvirostra avosetta

SC2866 One, 18 May 2002. The first Manx record.

Little Ringed Plover (Little Plover)

Charadrius dubius

SC1565 One, 9 May 2002.

Dotterel (Eurasian Dotterel)

Charadrius morinellus

Jan Feb Mar Apr May Jun Jul Aug Sep Oct Nov Dec

An upland breeding species, the British Isles population is confined to Scotland, where an estimated 840–950 pairs breed (1988–91 Atlas). All records during the survey period were of birds on spring migration. Prior to this period only ten sightings had been recorded on the Isle of Man, involving 16 birds. The following seven sightings of 22 birds, spread over only two years, are therefore of particular note.

NX4103 One, 27 April 1998

SC1866 Seven, 28 April 1998

SC2967 Five, 17 April 1999

NX4303 Three, 3 May 1999

SC3282 Two, 3 May 1999

SC4191 Three, on 4 May 1999

SC3387 One, 16 May 1999

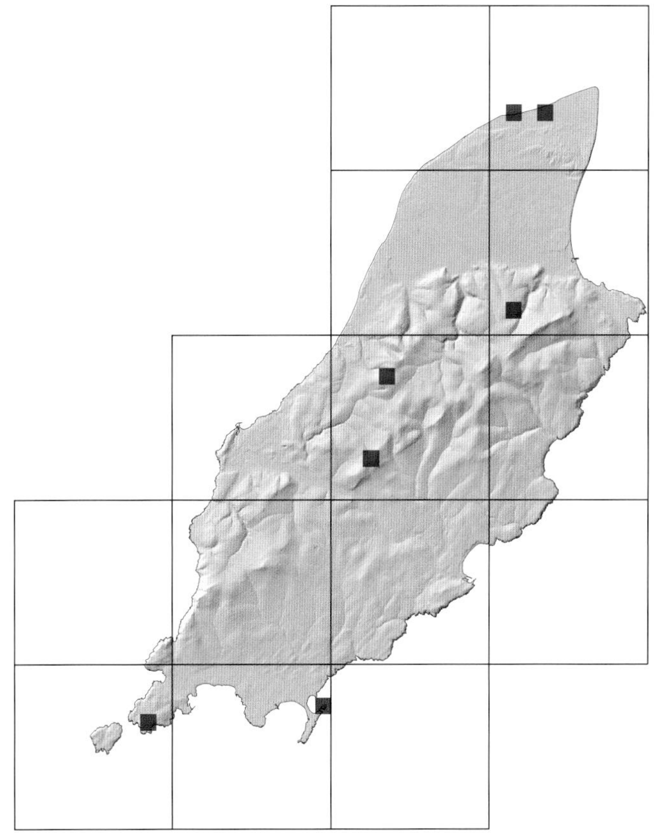

Dotterel – all records

Little Stint

Calidris minuta

NX4103 One, 24 May 1999
SC2866 One, 25 July 2000
NX4103 One, 1 September 2000
SC2866 One, 20 September 2001
SC2867 One, 22 September 2001
SC2868 One, 9 October 2001

Pectoral Sandpiper

Calidris melanotos

SC2866 Up to two birds present from 21–28 September 1999. The first Manx record.

Curlew Sandpiper

Calidris ferruginea

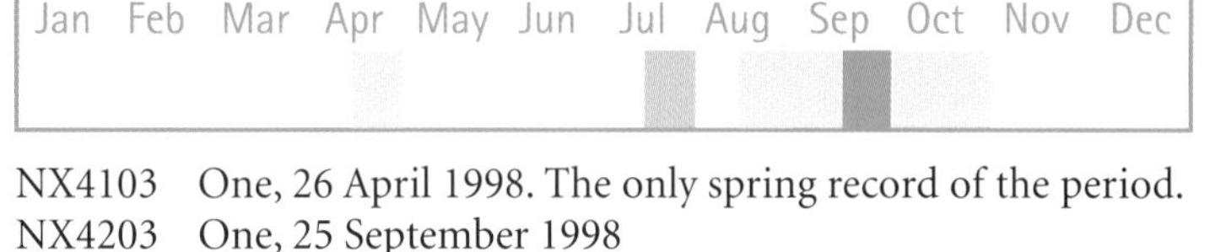

NX4103 One, 26 April 1998. The only spring record of the period.
NX4203 One, 25 September 1998
NX4103 Two, 25 July 1999
SC2866 Up to two birds, 23–25 September 1999
NX4103 Singles, 28 August and 19 September 2000
SC2866/7 Singles, 10 and 14 October 2000
SC2866 One, 17–19 July 2001
SC2866 One, 13 September 2001
SC2867 One, 22 September and two on 26 October 2001

Ruff

Philomachus pugnax

Jan Feb Mar Apr May Jun Jul Aug Sep Oct Nov Dec

SC1666 One, 5 September 1998
SC2866 One, 6 October 1998
SC2866 One, 23 September 1999
SC2866 One, 4 March 2000
SC2666 One, 14 September 2000
NX4103 One, 1 October 2000
SC2484 Two flying south, 2 October 2000
SC2866 One, 6 August 2001
SC2866 One, 22 October 2002
SC2484 Three flying south, 1 December 2002
SC2867 One, 5 January 2003
SC4498 One, 30 March 2003

Black-tailed Godwit

Limosa limosa

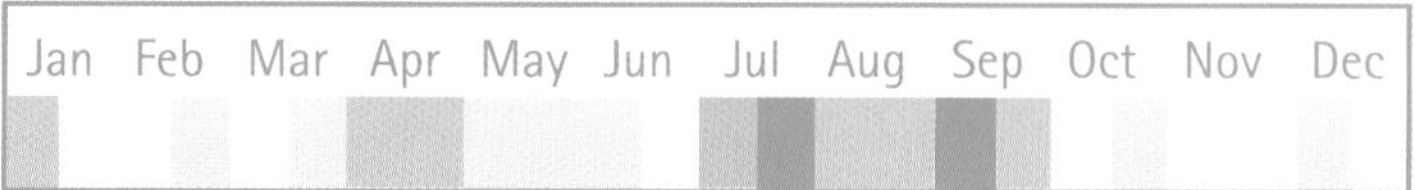

Though not a frequently observed species it is a regular passage migrant and was recorded in every month, except November. During the spring, a very clear peak of movement is evident with a total of 25 birds observed compared to one in March and three in May. During the autumn, return migration appears more protracted, in some years starting in early July and continuing until the latter part of September. Many of the birds wintering in the British Isles are of the race *L.l. islandica* (MA), and, of those observed locally, many display the plumage of that race.

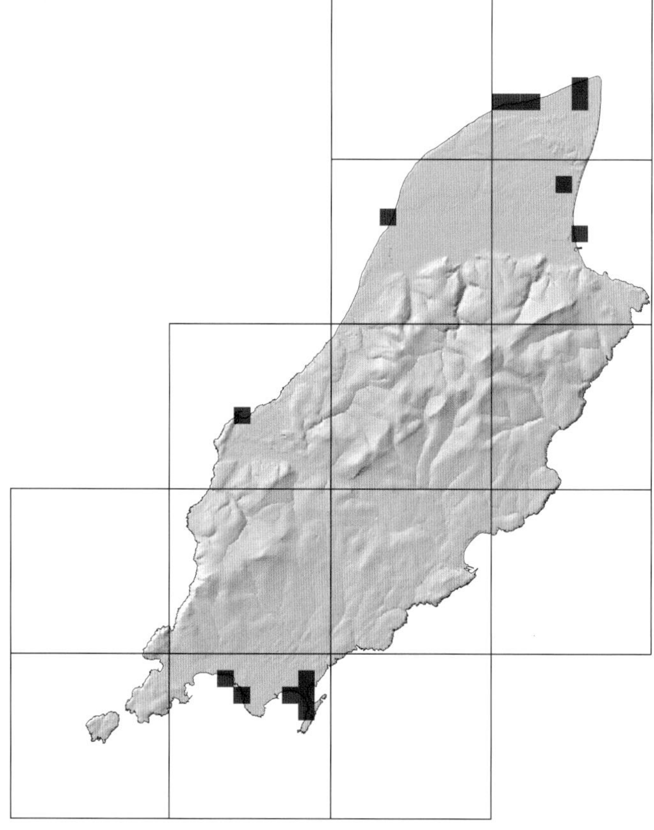

Black-tailed Godwit – all records

Whimbrel

Numenius phaeopus

Though there is a small breeding population of Whimbrels in Shetland and Orkney, the vast majority of birds recorded on passage locally will be from the main breeding grounds of Iceland, the Faeroes, Fennoscandia and north-west Russia (BWP). The main passage is evident in the spring, with the first few birds recorded in April, reaching a peak in May, quickly tailing off in June. The relatively few records in July were probably of failed breeders, starting their return passage to coastal sites of western and southern Africa. Sightings in autumn were fewer than in spring, studies elsewhere indicating that the birds returning south follow a more easterly route than birds heading north in spring (MA). The few inland records shown on the map were of birds heard overhead during nocturnal migration.

Spotted Redshank

Tringa erythropus

SC1565 One, 10 September 1998
SC2866 One, 23 November 1998
SC1666 One, 24 August 2000
SC2866 One, 18 October 2001
SC1564 One, 9 May 2002

Greenshank (Common Greenshank)

Tringa nebularia

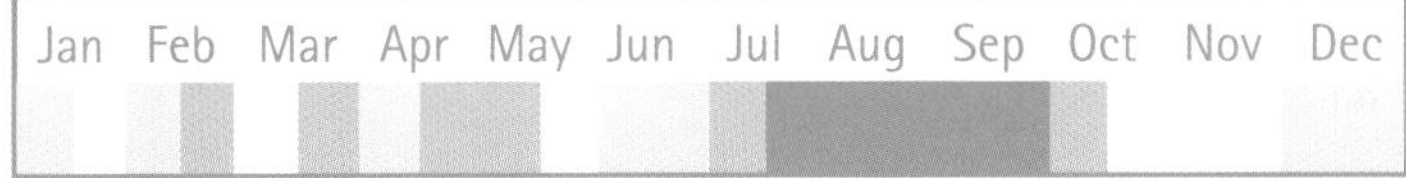

The species has a marked peak of presence on the Island during July to September, when around 75% of the records were obtained. It is largely absent during the winter months, with a spring passage involving fewer birds than the autumn. Individual birds do not usually stay long, using places like Langness and the gravel pits to forage before continuing their migration. Most records relate to single birds, with notable records of four on 15 August 2000 at NX4504 and five on 25 September 2000 at SC2866.

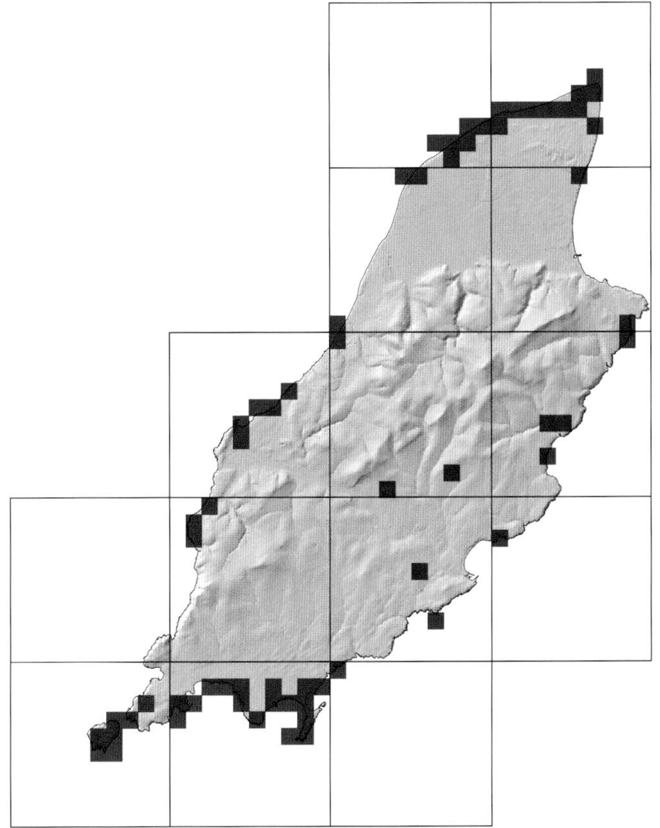

Whimbrel – all records

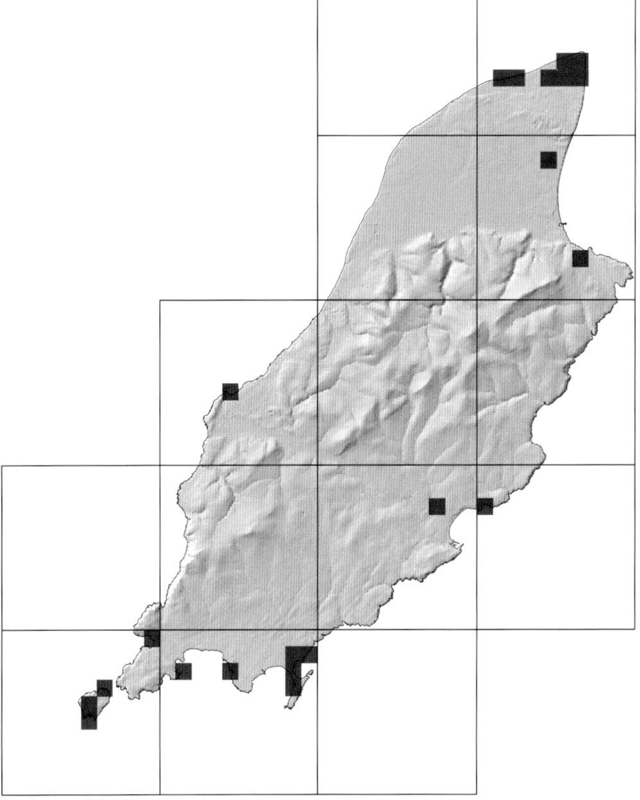

Greenshank – all records

Green Sandpiper

Tringa ochropus

SC2866 One, 25 July 1998
SC2878 One, 3 September 1999
SC2867 One, 29 October 1999
SC3596 One, 21 May 2000
SC2866 One, 21 September 2000
SC1565 One, 25 October 2000
SC2866 One, 3 and 4 February 2001
SC3777 Five, 23 April 2001

Wood Sandpiper

Tringa glareola

NX4504 One, 20 May 2001

Common Sandpiper

Actitis hypoleucos

During the period of the survey no evidence of breeding was found, though historic records do indicate that breeding has sometimes taken place. Two distinct peaks of movement were evident. From early April the first few birds can be expected, though it is not usually until mid-month that the main influx occurs, lasting only a short time, with few records after the third week of May. By June very few birds were observed, but from early July numbers build again, probably initially comprising early returning failed breeders. By early September most birds have passed through, with only one October record during the period. No records were obtained for the period November to March.

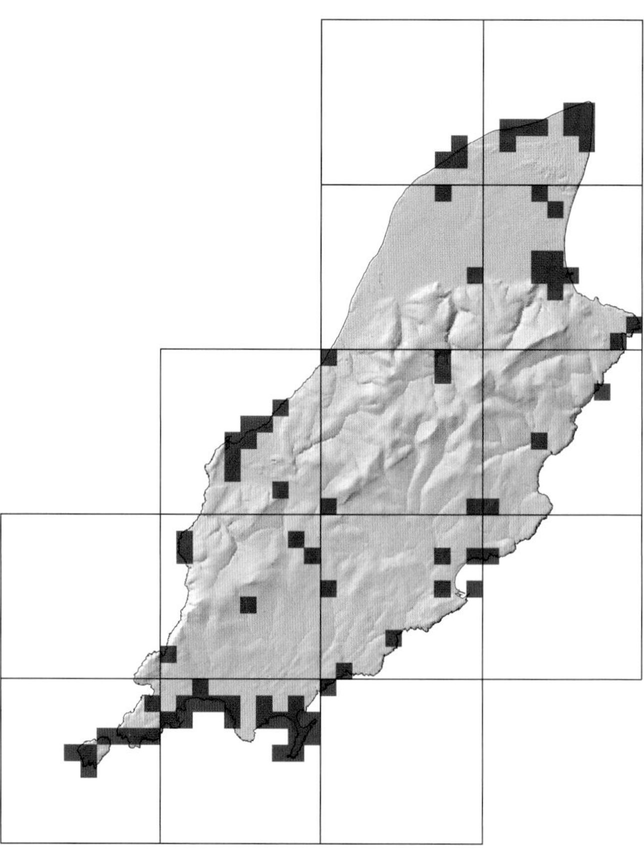

Common Sandpiper – all records

Wilson's Phalarope

Phalaropus tricolor

NX4604 One, 20–21 September 1999. The first Manx record.

Grey Phalarope

Phalaropus fulicarius

SC1766 Two, 10 October 1999
SC2168 One, 15–23 December 2000
SC2867 One, 4 February 2001

Pomarine Skua

Stercorarius pomarinus

Jan Feb Mar Apr May Jun Jul Aug Sep Oct Nov Dec

SC1565 One, 10 October 1998
SC1666 One, 28 September 1999
NX4203 One, 26 August 2000
SC2484 One, 7 July 2001
NX4605 Two, 9 September 2001
SC2484 One, 30 August 2002
SC1565 One, 5 September 2002

Arctic Skua

Stercorarius parasiticus

Most records of Arctic Skuas were of single birds, either passing the Island at one of the regularly watched vantage points of the Calf, Ayres or Peel Castle or occasionally harassing terns for food. Early season records were rare, with only three in April and four in May. The autumn records pick up from mid-July and, in some years, can continue through September into October.

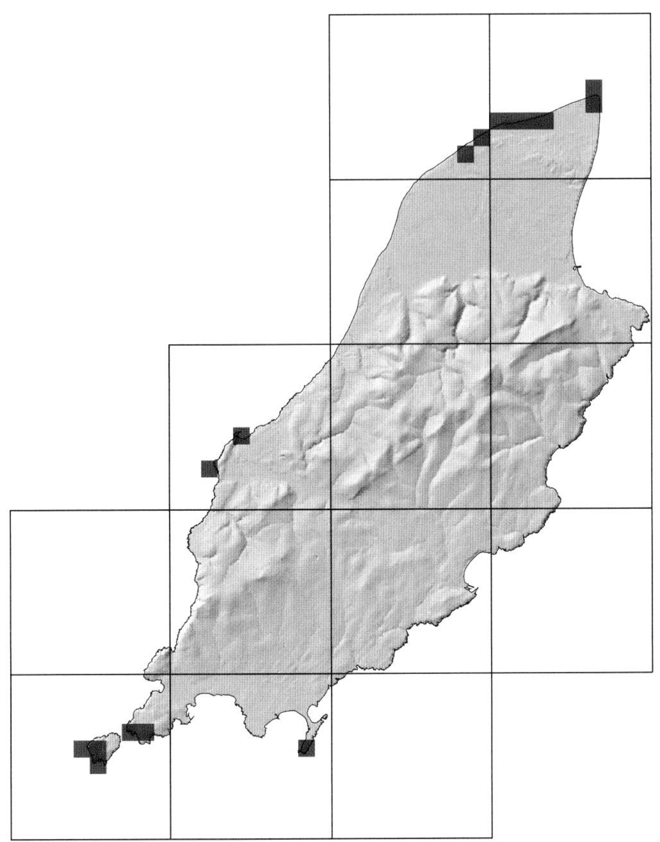

Arctic Skua – all records

Great Skua

Stercorarius skua

Jan Feb Mar Apr May Jun Jul Aug Sep Oct Nov Dec

Only one record was obtained during April, none in May, one in June and only three in July, serving to underline the limited time period during which the species moves past the Island's coast. During August, September and, in some years, October, time spent watching offshore is likely to produce records of Great Skuas, distinctive with its overall dark brown, heavy-set appearance with white wing panels.

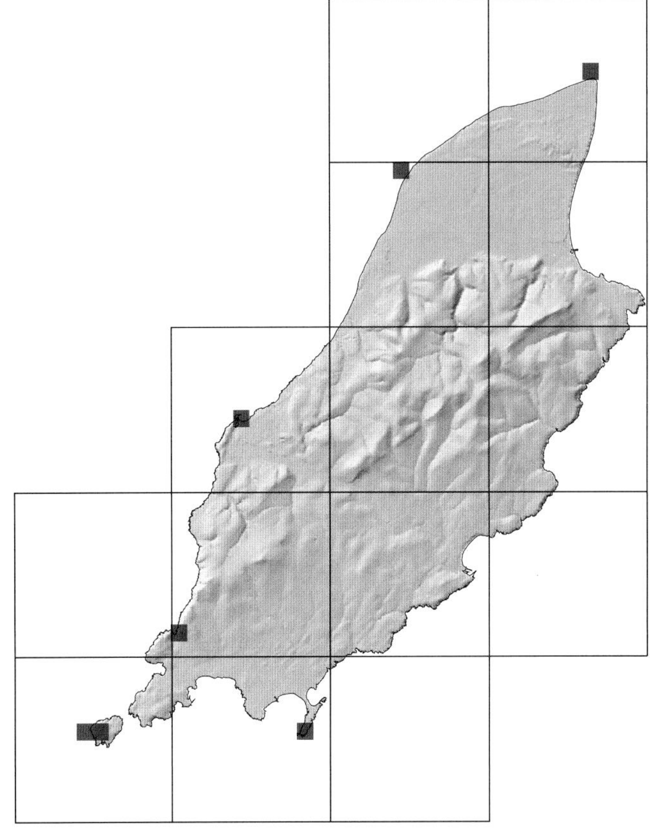

Great Skua – all records

Mediterranean Gull

Larus melanocephalus

SC3090 Two, 16 July 1998
SC1565 One, 30 August 2000
NX3902 One, 17 June 2001

Little Gull

Larus minutus

SC1565 Singles, 10 September and 21 October 1998
SC1564 One, 10 June 1999
NX4103 One, 28 June 1999
SC4596 One, 2 July 1999
SC2866 One, 2–7 February 2002
SC2484 Singles, 10 February and 10 March 2002
NX4003 One, 5 February 2003
SC2484 One, 11 March 2003

Sabine's Gull

Larus sabini

SC1565 Singles, 11, 16 and 29 October 1998
SC1565 One, 2 September 2000
SC1465 One, 4 October 2000
NX4605 Two adults and an immature, 9 September 2001
SC1565 One, 7 September 2002

Ring-billed Gull

Larus delawarensis

SC2786 One, 8 January 2000

Yellow-legged Gull

Larus michahellis

SC1666 One, 30 August 2000
NX4504 One, 6 October 2000
NX4503 One, 16 November 2001

Iceland Gull

Larus glaucoides

SC1666 One, 9 May 1998
SC2484 Singles, 22 January, 29 January and 2 April 2000
SC2268 One, 29 December 2001
SC2167/68 One, 3 January–9 May 2002
NX4604 One, 15 March 2003

Glaucous Gull

Larus hyperboreus

SC2767/2867 One, 7–15 December 2000
SC2484 One, 3 February 2001
SC2866 One, 11 March 2002
SC2484 One, 11 March 2003

Sandwich Tern

Sterna sandvicensis

The Sandwich Tern is a common passage migrant that has been recorded as breeding only once, in 1991, when 26 nests were present in the Point of Ayre Gravel Pits, though all nests failed, probably due to predation. On spring passage the first few birds are usually seen in late March each year, often in one of the Island's larger bays, numbers building through April when some birds will loiter along the Ayres foreshore, before continuing their migration. In some years courtship

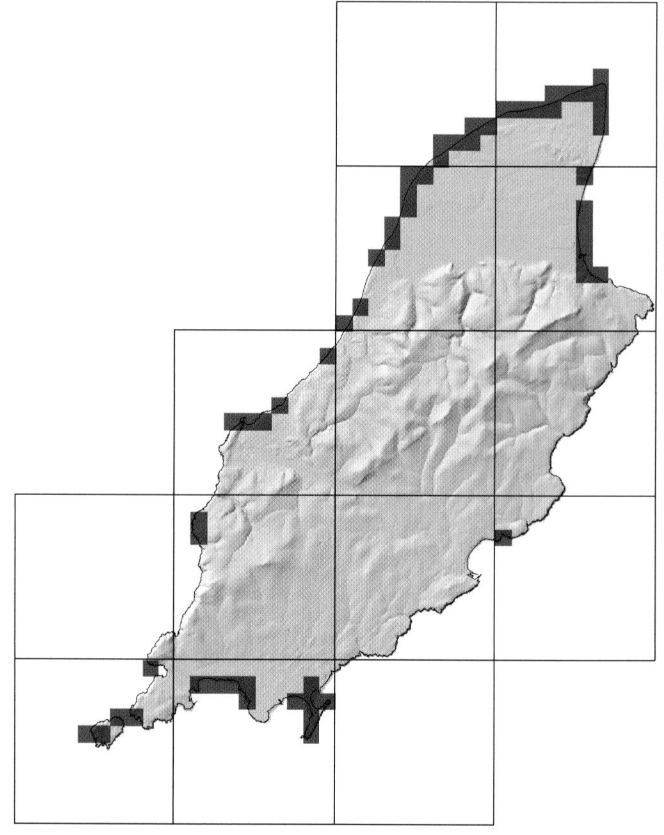

Sandwich Tern – all records

display including mating was observed, but no breeding evidence was obtained. Although observed throughout the summer, numbers in late May and June are smaller than at other times, with a marked increase from mid-July, when family parties arrive on the Ayres beaches, where adults can be seen feeding young birds. Many of these young birds are fitted with rings, with most of those caught proving to be from breeding sites on the islets in Strangford Lough, County Down, the adults bringing them to the rich feeding grounds of the Ayres shore shortly after fledging. Numbers present at this time can often exceed 200 birds, and can remain high until mid-September, though it is unlikely that individual birds remain throughout that period. After mid-September numbers decline, most later records relating to birds seen passing the coast, the latest record during the survey period being on 31 October 2001, in Derbyhaven Bay.

Common Tern

Sterna hirundo

Jan Feb Mar Apr May Jun Jul Aug Sep Oct Nov Dec

Although it formerly bred on the Island, with over 50 pairs at Rue Point and more at Ballaghennie, the species is now seldom seen, with only eleven sightings during the period. Birds were only seen on passage during April/May and August to September, not being recorded in June. The majority of records were of single birds, though on 22 July 1999, twelve were seen flying south off Peel.

Little Auk

Alle alle

Jan Feb Mar Apr May Jun Jul Aug Sep Oct Nov Dec

Recorded in all years during the period this, the smallest of the auk species that occurs locally, is only a winter visitor to the British Isles, with the nearest breeding sites being in Svalbard and Iceland. Annual numbers were variable, possibly caused by factors such as over-population or food supply failure (EBA). The period November 2002 to February 2003 produced a large number of sightings, with up to six present in Derbyhaven Bay in January.

Common Tern – all records

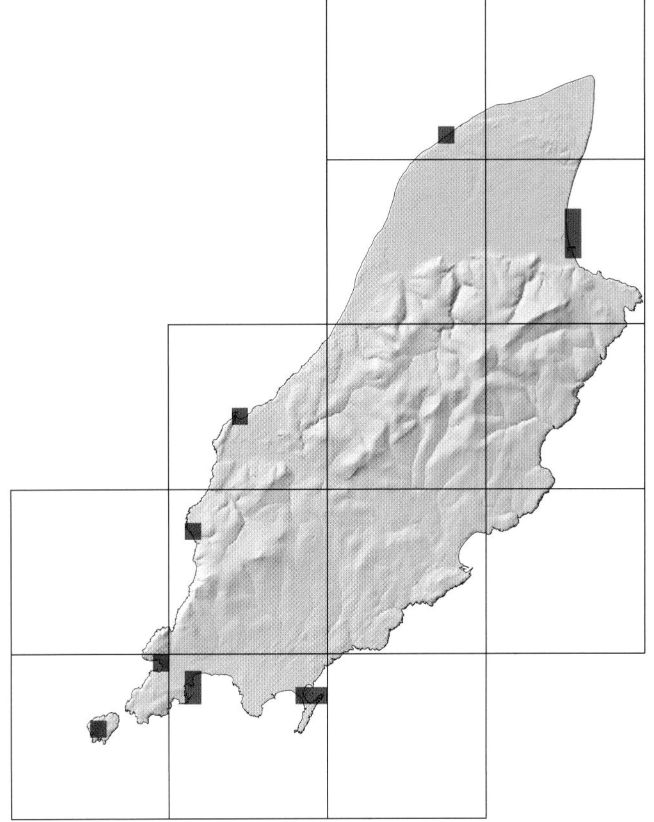

Little Auk – all records

Turtle Dove (European Turtle Dove)

Streptopelia turtur

SC1565 Singles, 9 May and 1 June 1998
SC3998 One, 6 June 1998
SC1565 One, 30 April 2000
SC3978 One, 26 June–9 July 2001
SC1564 One, 3 September 2001
SC4197 One, 12 May 2002
SC2669 One, 13 June 2002

Rose-ringed Parakeet

Psittacula krameri

SC2873 One, 31 May 2002

Nightjar (European Nightjar)

Caprimulgus europaeus

Jan	Feb	Mar	Apr	May	Jun	Jul	Aug	Sep	Oct	Nov	Dec

SC1565 One, 30 April 1998
SC2987 One, 7 August 1998
SC2574 One, 8 September 1999
SC1565 One, 8 May 2002

Bee-eater (European Bee-eater)

Merops apiaster

SC1565 Two, 24 May 2001

Hoopoe

Upupa epops

Jan	Feb	Mar	Apr	May	Jun	Jul	Aug	Sep	Oct	Nov	Dec

During the period a number of records were received of this distinctive and eye-catching bird. A total of eleven individual birds were probably present at some stage, most only being observed on one or two days, many only staying for a short number of hours. Eight birds were seen during spring passage (31 March to 7 May), with only three during autumn (18 September to 14 October). Notably, on 7 May at least two birds were present, one on the Calf and the other near the Lhen, whilst a third sighting, on 1 May at Phildraw, might have been either one of those individuals. Locally, Hoopoes have become an almost annual passage migrant, though the European range and breeding population have undergone recent declines.

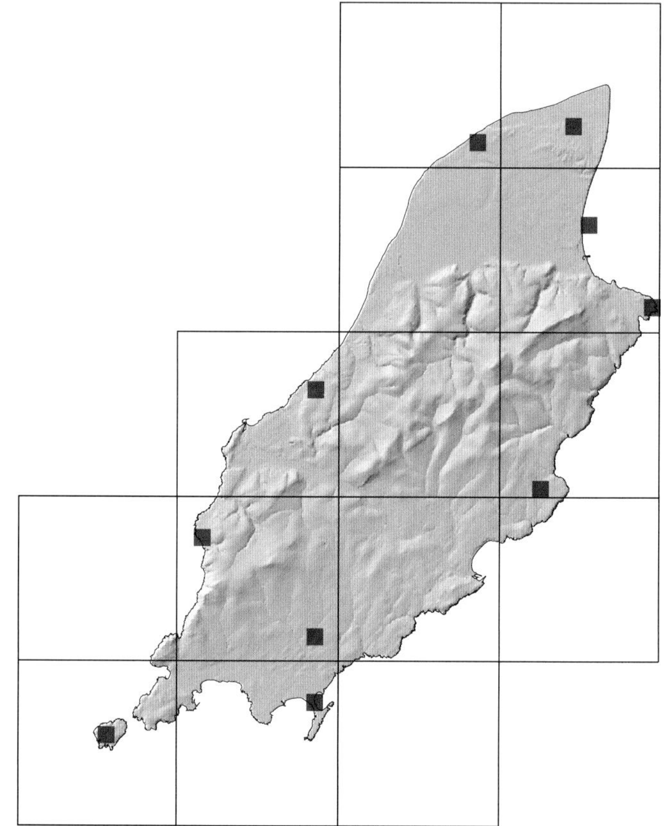

Hoopoe – all records

Wryneck (Eurasian Wryneck)

Jynx torquilla

SC4383 One, 21 April 2000
SC1565 One, 30 April 2000
SC1566 One, 4 September 2000
SC4692 One, 26 August 2001

Green Woodpecker

Picus viridis

SC3187 One, 21 January 2000
SC1565 One, 2 December 2000
SC3788 One, 24 March 2001
SC3481 One, 15 April 2002 – for several weeks around this date
SC1565 One, 2 May 2002

Shore Lark (Horned Lark)

Eremophila alpestris

NX4003 Three, 25 January 2000

Richard's Pipit

Anthus richardi

SC3596 One, 23 December 1998
SC1565 One, 23 April 2000

Tawny Pipit

Anthus campestris

SC2572 One, 13–14 April 1999
SC1565 One, 7–8 September 2001

Olive-backed Pipit

Anthus hodgsoni

SC1564 One, 10 May 2002. The first Manx record.

Water Pipit

Anthus spinoletta

SC2865 One, 6 April 2000

Yellow Wagtail

Motacilla flava

NX4403 One, 9 May 1998
SC1565 Singles, 7 August and 5 September 1998
SC2368 One, 13 November 1999
SC2866 Two, 25 April 2000
SC2866 One, 2 May 2001
SC1565 One, 4 May 2001
SC1564 One, 30 August 2001
NX4605 One, 5 May 2002
NX4604 One, 1 September 2002
SC1565 One, 4 September 2002

Dipper (White-throated Dipper)

Cinclus cinclus

SC1565 One, 10 June 1999

Nightingale (Common Nightingale)

Luscinia megarhynchos

SC3675 One, 30 April 2000
SC1565 Singles, 9 May 2000, 30 April 2001 and 30 July 2002

Redstart (Common Redstart)

Phoenicurus phoenicurus

Not recorded as a breeding species locally since 1971, the Isle of Man is towards the western limit of the Redstart's breeding distribution, with only a few pairs breeding in Ireland. The relative shortage of open broad-leaved woodland, especially oak forest, will also be influential. During the survey period, in common with previous years, most records were received from the Calf of Man, the majority being during spring passage lasting from mid-April to late May. In the autumn passage is from mid-August to the end of September.

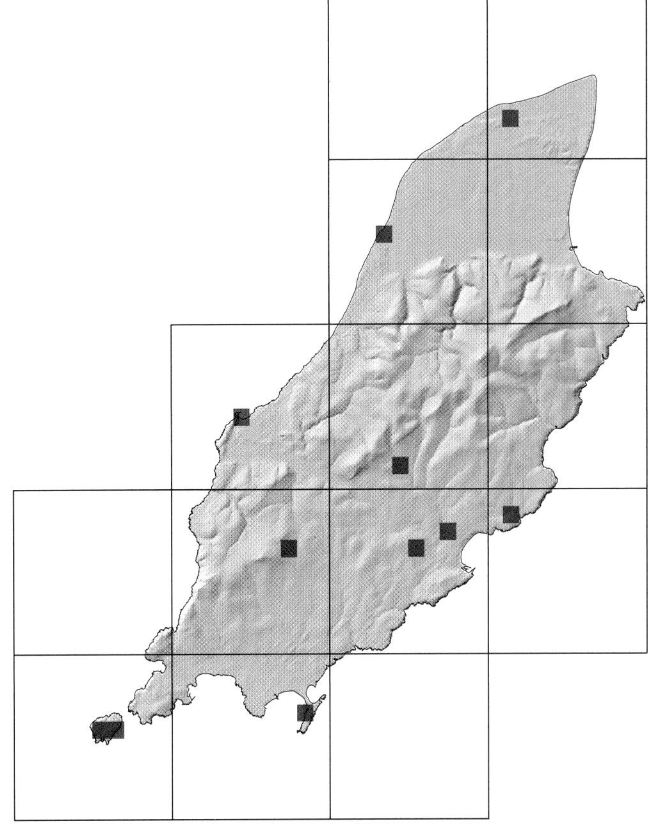

Redstart – all records

Desert Wheatear

Oenanthe deserti

SC2177 One, 6–17 January 2002. The first Manx record.

Ring Ouzel

Turdus torquatus

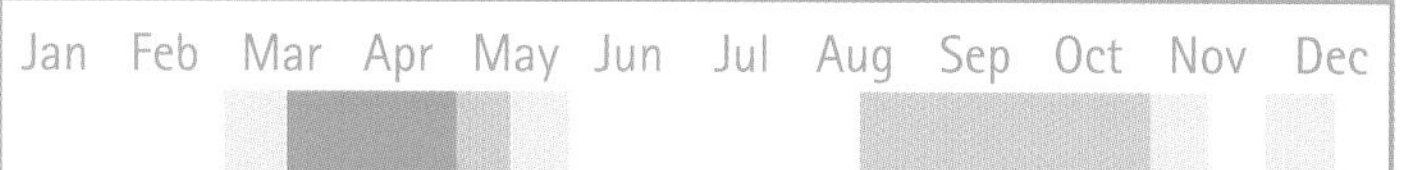

Despite a number of promising early spring records on the main island, no evidence of breeding was found for this upland breeding species, with no records obtained in either June or July. All records were confined to the two main passage periods. Spring migration is largely confined to April, though occasional records were obtained in late March. By early May passage is complete, though a late record of a female at the Ayres on 16 May 2002 was noteworthy. Late August marks the start of autumn migration, which is completed by late October. On a particularly late date of 11 December 2002 a male was seen at Snuff the Wind.

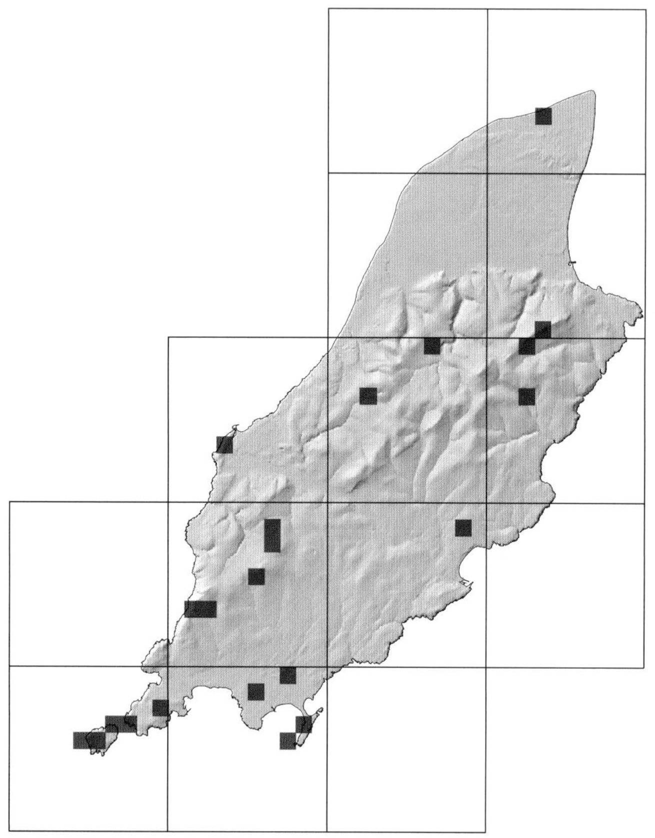

Ring Ouzel – all records

Icterine Warbler

Hippolais icterina

SC1565 One, 13 September 1999

Melodious Warbler

Hippolais polyglotta

SC1565 Singles, 6 May 1998, 12 June 1999, 1 May 2001 and 16 August 2002

Barred Warbler

Sylvia nisoria

SC1565 Singles, 11–12 September 1998, 13 September 1999, 8 September 2000 and 4 September 2002

Yellow-browed Warbler

Phylloscopus inornatus

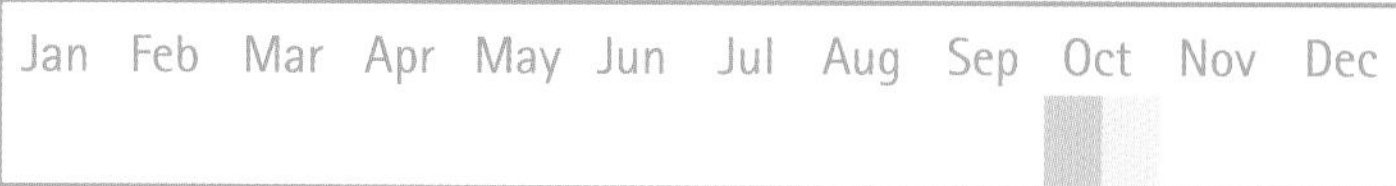

SC1565 Singles, 2 and 31 October 1998 and 1–2 October 2000

Firecrest

Regulus ignicapilla

SC1565 Singles, 26 April, 17 May, 30 October and 2 November 1998

SC1565 Two, on 2–3 October 1998

SC1565 One, 21 October–4 November 2000

SC1565 Singles, 31 August 2002 and 24 March 2003

Red-breasted Flycatcher

Ficedula parva

SC1565 Singles, 30 April and 3–4 September 1999, with a further bird present on the latter date

Pied Flycatcher

Ficedula hypoleuca

Like the Redstart, Pied Flycatchers show a marked preference for oak woodland throughout their British Isles breeding range (1988–91 Atlas). This fact probably accounts for the lack of breeding locally, as suitable habitat is largely absent. Most records were obtained in the autumn, the majority being from the Calf of Man, in fact the species is seldom recorded on the main island. Main movements occur from mid-April to mid-May and again from mid-August to early October.

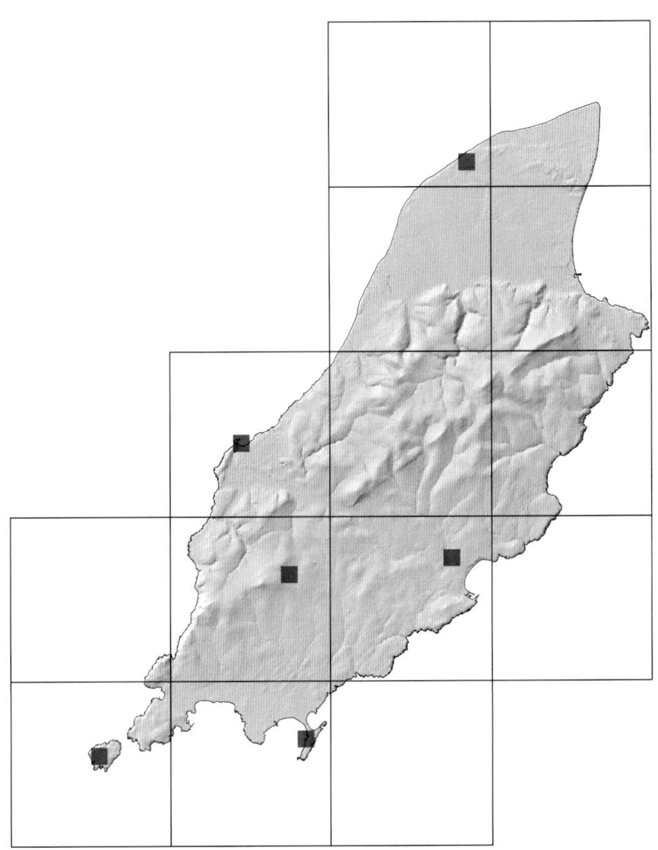

Pied Flycatcher – all records

Nuthatch (Wood Nuthatch)

Sitta europaea
SC3695 One, 2 February 1999
SC2370 One, 3 May 2001

Golden Oriole (Eurasian Golden Oriole)

Oriolus oriolus
SC1565 One, 29 April 2001

Red-backed Shrike

Lanius collurio
SC1565 Singles, 4 May and 1 June 1998

Great Grey Shrike

Lanius excubitor
SC2574 One, 10 November 1998

Woodchat Shrike

Lanius senator
SC4178 One, 11 May 1998

Rose-coloured Starling (Rosy Starling)

Sturnus roseus

Jan Feb Mar Apr May Jun Jul Aug Sep Oct Nov Dec

SC2484 One, 10 October 1999. The first Manx record.
SC3575 One, from 3 September 2000 for several weeks
SC2067 One, 10–16 June 2001
SC3190 One, 27 July 2001
SC2067 One, 9 June 2002
SC4991 One, 29 June 2002
SC2667 One, 20–25 July 2002

Serin (European Serin)

Serinus serinus
SC1565 Singles, 9 September 1999 and 6 May 2000

Common Redpoll

Carduelis flammea

Jan Feb Mar Apr May Jun Jul Aug Sep Oct Nov Dec

SC3898 Three, 8 March 1999
SC3899 Four, 17 February 2000
NX4503 Four, 30 October 2002
NX4603 Two, 18 November 2002
SC2371 Four, 21 February 2003

Common Rosefinch

Carpodacus erythrinus
SC1565 One, 24–25 September 1998
One, 12–14 September 1999
One, 20–21 September 2000
One, 2 June 2002

Bullfinch (Common Bullfinch)

Pyrrhula pyrrhula

Jan Feb Mar Apr May Jun Jul Aug Sep Oct Nov Dec

C&J comment on the lack of breeding Bullfinches on the Island and during the period of this survey no evidence of breeding was found. The species is abundant in Ireland and, though its main breeding densities are in central and southern England, they occur throughout northern England and Scotland, so the lack of Manx breeding is curious. Unlike the data used in compiling C&J, which demonstrated a spring bias in records, the data gathered during this survey show more sightings in October through to December, with no records in March, April or May. It is likely that the majority of birds seen were of Scandinavian origin, British and Irish birds being mainly sedentary.

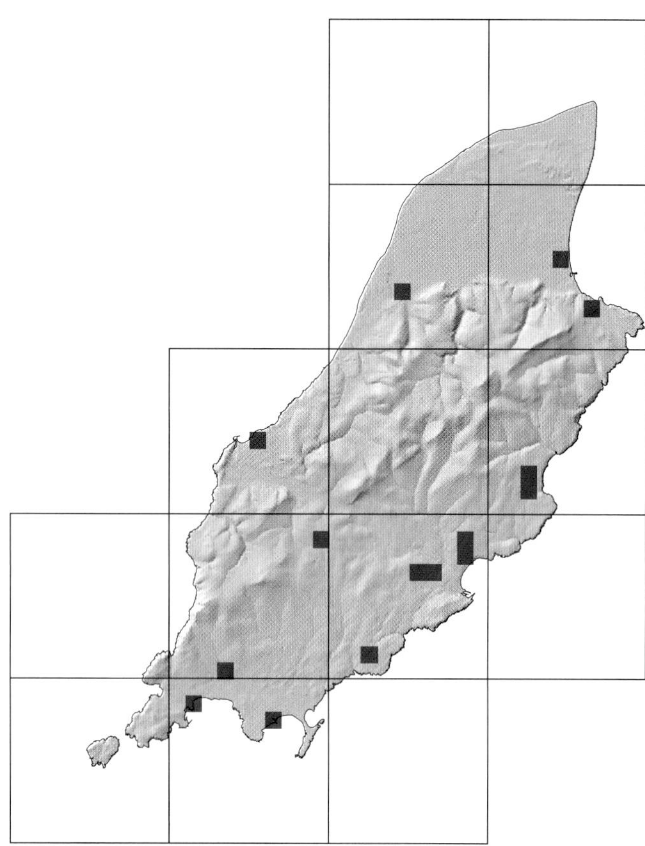

Bullfinch – all records

Hawfinch

Coccothraustes coccothraustes
SC4392 One, 19 December 1999

White-throated Sparrow

Zonotrichia albicollis
SC2685 One, 28 May 1999. The first Manx record.

Lapland Bunting (Lapland Longspur)

Calcarius lapponicus
SC1565 One, 18 October 1998
SC2866 One, 4–5 October 1998
NX4101 One, 9 January 1999
NX4604 One, 28 December 1999
NX4103 One, 22 September 2000
NX4504 One, 6 October 2002

Ortolan Bunting

Emberiza hortulana
SC1566 One, 2 April 2002

Little Bunting

Emberiza pusilla
SC1565 One, 28 April 2001

Red-headed Bunting

Emberiza bruniceps
A probable escape
SC4184 One, 16–17 June and 5 July 2001

Red-winged Laughingthrush

Garrulax formosus

5km square – SC39NE Four documented sightings between June 2000 and January 2003 of up to two birds, including one singing male, with other non-documented sightings from property owners in the area.

The species was formerly kept in captivity at the Wildlife Park which is situated within the 5km square from which the above sightings were obtained. By 1998, all of the original ten birds imported in 1990 had either died or escaped and the first records of birds in the wild were obtained in 1995 (Thorpe and Sharpe 2004). In 1996 adults were seen feeding a young bird, thus confirming wild breeding, and it is likely that the species is still breeding in the wild. The last record during the MBA research was thirteen years after the species was imported and records as late as July 2005 have since been obtained, nine years after the first indication of wild breeding. Though it is possible that the small population that currently exists might prove not to be self-sustaining, it is considered more likely that the species will become established in the long term. The information on sightings has been presented at 5km level at the request of some of the property owners in whose gardens the birds are occasionally seen.

Appendix B: List of 1km squares and associated place names

1km square	Place name
NX3500	Cronk y Cliwe
NX3600	Cronk y Scottey
NX3601	Ballagarraghyn
NX3700	Ballaghaie
NX3701	Cronk y Bing
NX3800	Ballaclucas
NX3801	west of The Lhen
NX3802	west of Blue Point
NX3900	Ballagunnell
NX3901	The Lhen
NX3902	Blue Point
NX4000	Leodest Farm
NX4001	east of The Lhen
NX4002	Knock e Dooney
NX4003	Rue Point (car park)
NX4100	Ballaquane
NX4101	The Dhowin
NX4102	Ballakinnag
NX4103	Rue Point
NX4200	Braust
NX4201	Ballabane (east of Dhowin)
NX4202	south of Ayres plantation
NX4203	The Ayres (plantation)
NX4300	West Kimmeragh
NX4301	Ballagarrett
NX4302	Ballacregga Farm
NX4303	Ballaghennie Ayres
NX4304	north of Ballaghennie Ayres
NX4400	Kimmeragh Farm
NX4401	Bride Village
NX4402	Ballamin Farm
NX4403	east of Ballaghennie Ayres
NX4404	north-east of Ballaghennie Ayres
NX4500	Ballacottier
NX4501	Ballaquark Farm
NX4502	Cranstal
NX4503	north of Cranstal
NX4504	Point of Ayre gravel pit
NX4600	Ballavarkish
NX4601	north of Ballavarkish
NX4602	Phurt
NX4603	north of Phurt
NX4604	Point of Ayre (Lighthouse)
NX4605	Point of Ayre
SC1465	The Stack, Calf of Man
SC1564	The Puddle, Calf of Man
SC1565	Bird Observatory, Calf of Man
SC1566	Gibdale Point, Calf of Man
SC1664	south of Kione ny Halby, Calf of Man
SC1665	Kione ny Halby, Calf of Man
SC1666	Kione Beg, Calf of Man
SC1766	Burroo Ned
SC1767	Aldrick
SC1865	Spanish/Black Head
SC1866	Meayll Peninsula
SC1867	Cregneash
SC1868	Bay Fine
SC1869	Bradda Head (Milner's Tower)
SC1870	Creg Harlot
SC1871	west of Bradda Hill
SC1966	The Chasms
SC1967	The Howe
SC1968	Ballnahow
SC1969	Port Erin
SC1970	Bradda East
SC1971	Bradda Hill
SC2066	south of Perwick Bay
SC2067	Port St Mary
SC2068	Four Roads
SC2069	Ballachurry
SC2070	Ballafesson
SC2071	Fleshwick Bay
SC2072	Eairnyery
SC2073	north of Eairnyery
SC2077	Niarbyl Point
SC2166	south of Kallow Point
SC2167	Port St Mary Bay
SC2168	Gansey Point
SC2169	Ballagawne
SC2170	Ballakillowey
SC2171	Ballarock
SC2172	Kirkill
SC2173	The Sloc
SC2174	Stroin Vuigh
SC2175	Gob yn Ushtey
SC2176	west of Kerrowdhoo plantation
SC2177	Niarbyl
SC2178	Dalby Point
SC2179	north of Dalby Point
SC2268	Kentraugh Black Rocks
SC2269	Croit e Caley
SC2270	Ballacorkish
SC2271	Ballakilpheric
SC2272	Lingague
SC2273	Scard
SC2274	Cronk ny Arrey Laa
SC2275	Eary Cushlin
SC2276	Kerrowdhoo plantation
SC2277	north of Kerrowdhoo plantation
SC2278	Dalby
SC2279	Glen Maye gorge
SC2280	Traie Cronkan
SC2281	Ellan ny Maughol
SC2282	Contrary Head
SC2283	north of Contrary Head
SC2368	Strandhall
SC2369	Cronkmooar
SC2370	Colby
SC2371	south of Earystane
SC2372	Earystane
SC2373	Earystane plantation
SC2374	Cronk Fedjag
SC2375	south of Slieau Mooar plantation
SC2376	Slieau Mooar plantation
SC2377	Dalby Mountain
SC2378	Doarlish-Cashen
SC2379	Glen Maye
SC2380	Raby Moar
SC2381	south of Knockaloe Moar
SC2382	Knockaloe Moar
SC2383	Thistle Head
SC2384	Peel Hill
SC2466	West Scarlett Head
SC2467	Poyllvaaish
SC2468	Balladoole
SC2469	West of Ballabeg Station
SC2470	Ballaclague – Ballabeg
SC2471	Ballafodda
SC2472	Ronague
SC2473	East of Slieau Earystane
SC2474	West of Cringle Reservoir
SC2475	Round Table
SC2476	Glen Rushen Plantation
SC2477	Clagh Bane
SC2478	Creg ny Crock
SC2479	East of Glen Maye
SC2480	Raby Beg – Patrick
SC2481	Shenvalla – Patrick
SC2482	The Raggatt
SC2483	Peel
SC2484	Peel Bay
SC2566	Scarlett
SC2567	Castle Rushen School
SC2568	Ballakaighen + Farm
SC2569	Ballabeg Station
SC2570	East Ballabeg
SC2571	Upper Ballavarkish
SC2572	West of Grenaby
SC2573	Ballarobin
SC2574	Cringle Reservoir
SC2575	South Barrule
SC2576	North of South Barrule
SC2577	Beckwith Mines
SC2578	East Arrasey Plantation
SC2579	Garey – North of Arrasey Plantation
SC2580	East of Slieau Whallian
SC2581	Ballacosnahan
SC2582	Ballawyllin Farm
SC2583	Ballawattleworth Farm

1km square	Place name
SC2584	Peel Headland
SC2585	The Stack – Peel
SC2667	Castletown
SC2668	Great Meadow
SC2669	Billown – Crossroads
SC2670	Billown Lime Quarry
SC2671	Ballatrollag
SC2672	Grenaby
SC2673	Kerrowmoar
SC2674	Glenmoar farm
SC2675	Corlea Plantation
SC2676	South Barrule Quarry
SC2677	Turn off to Beckwith
SC2678	Doarlish Ard
SC2679	Gleneedle
SC2680	Slieau Whallian
SC2681	Ballaspit
SC2682	Sandhouse
SC2683	Poortown Quarry
SC2684	Ballagyr
SC2685	White Strand
SC2686	Will's Strand
SC2765	Langness Point
SC2767	Hango Hill
SC2768	King Williams College
SC2769	Old racecourse – Silverburn
SC2770	Silverdale
SC2771	Silverdale Glen
SC2772	Lower Ballamodha Straight
SC2773	Shebeg Pottery
SC2774	Upper Ballamodha Straight
SC2775	Southern South Barrule Plantation
SC2776	South Barrule Plantation
SC2777	Upper Foxdale
SC2778	Foxdale
SC2779	Lower Foxdale
SC2780	Ballahig
SC2781	St Johns
SC2782	Brack a Broom
SC2783	Southern Switchback
SC2784	East Lhergydhoo (Switchback)
SC2785	Knocksharry
SC2786	Ballanayre Strand
SC2787	West of Gob y Deigan
SC2865	Langness Lighthouse
SC2866	Madoc's Memorial
SC2867	Sandwick – Derbyhaven
SC2868	Ronaldsway Airport
SC2869	Balthane Ind Estate
SC2870	Ballasalla
SC2871	Phildraw
SC2872	Ballanank
SC2873	Ballamodha Mooar
SC2874	East of St Marks
SC2875	South Stoney Mountain Plantation
SC2876	Stoney Mountain Plantation
SC2877	North Stoney Mountain Plantation
SC2878	Kionslieu Reservoir
SC2879	East of Lower Foxdale
SC2880	Kennaa
SC2881	Ballacraine
SC2882	Ballig
SC2883	The Beary
SC2884	Staarvey
SC2885	East of Knocksharry
SC2886	Lynague
SC2887	Gob y Deigan
SC2888	North of Gob y Deigan
SC2966	Langness – South of Fort Island
SC2967	Fort Island
SC2968	East of Ronaldsway Airport
SC2969	Santon Gorge
SC2970	Ballaquaggan (South of Blackboards)
SC2971	Orrisdale
SC2972	Knock e Vriew
SC2973	South of St Marks
SC2974	St Marks
SC2975	Shenvalley – St Marks
SC2976	Tosaby
SC2977	Eairy
SC2978	West Archalligan Plantation
SC2979	Cornelly House
SC2980	West of Greeba
SC2981	Ballagarraghyn
SC2982	North of Ballagarraghyn
SC2983	Eairy Beg Plantation
SC2984	Sarah's Cottage – Glen Helen Pub
SC2985	Manannan's Chair
SC2986	Ballakaighin
SC2987	Skerrisdale Moar
SC2988	Ballaquine
SC2989	North of Ballaquine
SC3069	Port Soldrick
SC3070	Arragon Veg
SC3071	Fairy Bridge
SC3072	Cooil Cam
SC3073	Ballacroak
SC3074	North of Ballacroak
SC3075	South of Ballanicholas
SC3076	Ballanicholas
SC3077	Dreemlang Farm
SC3078	East Archalligan Plantation
SC3079	North east Archalligan Plantation
SC3080	Greeba
SC3081	Greeba Bridge
SC3082	Kerrow Glass
SC3083	West Beary Mountain
SC3084	Glen Helen
SC3085	Cronk y Voddy
SC3086	11th Milestone
SC3087	South of Ballacarnane Beg
SC3088	Ballacarnane Beg
SC3089	Glen Mooar
SC3090	West of Glen Wyllin
SC3170	Port Grenagh
SC3171	Glen Grenaugh
SC3172	Santon Railway Station
SC3173	Ballagick
SC3174	Sulbrick
SC3175	Stuggadhoo
SC3176	Slieau Chairn
SC3177	St Patrick's Chair
SC3178	North of St Patrick's Chair
SC3179	Cooil Ingel
SC3180	The Highlander
SC3181	Greeba Mountain
SC3182	Cooil Slieu
SC3183	Beary Mountain
SC3184	Earyglass
SC3185	Rhenass Farm
SC3186	Handley's Corner
SC3187	Ballaskyr
SC3188	Barregarrow Crossroads
SC3189	Cooil Dharry
SC3190	Kirk Michael
SC3191	North of Kirk Michael
SC3192	Orrisdale Head
SC3193	North of Orrisdale Head
SC3270	Meary Voar
SC3271	Ballaquiggin Farm
SC3272	Oatlands
SC3273	Newtown – Santon
SC3274	Mount Murray Hotel
SC3275	Chibbanagh Plantation
SC3276	Braaid
SC3277	Corvalley Farm
SC3278	Ellerslie Farm
SC3279	Crosby
SC3280	Ballavitchel Farm
SC3281	East Greeba Plantation
SC3282	Slieau Ruy
SC3283	North of Slieau Ruy
SC3284	Plantation East of Blaber River
SC3285	Glion Gill
SC3286	Little London – Eary Farm
SC3287	West Sartfell
SC3288	Ballakilleyclieu Farm
SC3289	Cronk Urleigh
SC3290	East Kirk Michael
SC3291	Rhencullen
SC3292	Bishop's Court
SC3293	Orrisdale – Kirk Michael
SC3294	North of Orrisdale – Kirk Michael
SC3295	North west of Ballacooiley
SC3370	Santon Head
SC3371	Meary Veg
SC3372	Crogga
SC3373	Crogga River
SC3374	Richmond Hill – Transmitter
SC3375	Colooneys
SC3376	Ballabunt
SC3377	Ballacotch Manor
SC3378	Glen Vine
SC3379	Ballawilleykilley
SC3380	Cronk ny Moghlane
SC3381	Cronk Breck
SC3382	East Slieau Ruy
SC3383	Lhargee Ruy
SC3384	West Colden
SC3385	Slieau Maggle
SC3386	Cronkdhoo
SC3387	Sartfell
SC3388	West Freoaghane
SC3389	East of Cronk Urleigh
SC3390	West Slieau Curn
SC3391	North-west Slieau Curn
SC3392	Bishop's Court Glen
SC3393	Standing Stone – Bishop's Court
SC3394	West of Dollagh
SC3395	West of the Cronk
SC3396	North-west of the Cronk
SC3471	Pistol Castle
SC3472	Port Soderick
SC3473	Quines Hill
SC3474	Richmond Hill
SC3475	Ballavagher
SC3476	Cooil
SC3477	North of Cooil
SC3478	Glenlough
SC3479	Upper Ballaclucas
SC3480	Rhyne
SC3481	Ballagrawe
SC3482	South of The Creg – near West Baldwin
SC3483	The Creg – near West Baldwin
SC3484	Colden
SC3485	East of Slieau Maggle
SC3486	Brandywell Cottage
SC3487	South Slieau Freoaghane
SC3488	Slieau Freoaghane
SC3489	West Slieau Dhoo
SC3490	Slieau Curn
SC3491	West Glen Dhoo
SC3492	Ballacurn Mooar – Ballaugh
SC3493	Ballaugh
SC3494	Dollagh
SC3495	The Cronk
SC3496	Crawyn
SC3497	Ballasalla – Jurby
SC3498	Jurby Head
SC3499	Cronk ny Arrey Laa – Jurby
SC3572	Keristal Point
SC3573	Keristal
SC3574	Kewaigue
SC3575	Spring Valley
SC3576	Ballastowell
SC3577	Union Mills
SC3578	Camlork

1km square	Place name	1km square	Place name	1km square	Place name	1km square	Place name
SC3579	Mount Rule	SC3775	Douglas – inc. Leigh Terr + old Hospital	SC3974	Douglas Head	SC4185	Close Mooar Farm – Lonan
SC3580	Renscault Farm	SC3776	Douglas – inc. Qurterbridge Road	SC3975	Douglas Breakwater	SC4186	Laggan Agneash
SC3581	West Baldwin Village	SC3777	Tromode + Cronkbourne	SC3977	Port Jack	SC4187	west Slieau Lhean
SC3582	North West Baldwin Village	SC3778	Ballanard	SC3978	Onchan Village	SC4188	Clagh Ouyr
SC3583	west West Baldwin Reservoir	SC3779	Abbeylands	SC3979	Little Mill – Onchan	SC4189	Mountain Box
SC3584	Colden/Injebreck Plantations	SC3780	Sulby river – north of Abbeylands	SC3980	south Kerrowdhoo Reservoir	SC4190	north of Mountain Box
SC3585	Injebreck Hill	SC3781	Strenaby	SC3981	Creg ny Baa	SC4191	south of Park ne Earkan
SC3586	North Injebreck Hill	SC3782	west Slieau Ree	SC3982	Slieau Meayll	SC4192	Park ne Earkan
SC3587	South West of Druidale	SC3783	Eary Ween	SC3983	Plantation top of Glen Roy	SC4193	Glentramman
SC3588	Montpellier	SC3784	Dhoon – South-east Carraghan	SC3984	Windy Corner	SC4194	Glenduff
SC3589	Slieau Dhoo	SC3785	South-west Beinn y Phott	SC3985	Brandywell	SC4195	Closelake – Sulby
SC3590	Southern Ballaugh Plantation	SC3786	Top of Glen Crammag	SC3986	Bungalow	SC4196	Ballacrebbin – Sulby
SC3591	Ballaugh Plantation	SC3787	Glen Crammag	SC3987	Les Graham Memorial	SC4197	Rye Hill
SC3592	North of Ballaugh Plantation	SC3788	Sulby Reservoir	SC3988	Snaefell	SC4198	Ballavoddan
SC3593	Ballamooar	SC3789	south Tholt y Will Plantation	SC3989	Block Eary	SC4199	Andreas
SC3594	Dollagh Mooar	SC3790	north Tholt y Will Plantation	SC3990	Slieau Managh	SC4277	south of Port Groudle
SC3595	North of Dollagh Mooar (Close Sartfield)	SC3791	Mount Karrin	SC3991	north Slieau Managh	SC4278	Port Groudle
SC3596	West of Lough Dhoo	SC3792	Ballacuberagh Plantation	SC3992	south Ohio Plantation	SC4279	Lonan Old Church
SC3597	Ballacain	SC3793	Ballacaley – Sulby	SC3993	Ohio Plantation	SC4280	Ballamenaugh Beg
SC3598	Jurby West	SC3794	Sulby Straight	SC3994	Cronk Sumark	SC4281	Baldrine
SC3599	Sartfield	SC3795	The Rule – Sulby	SC3995	Close Chairn	SC4282	Ballacannell – Lonan
SC3672	Little Ness	SC3796	Ballamoar Beg Farm	SC3996	St Judes	SC4283	south Axnfell Plantation
SC3673	Wallberry Hill	SC3797	Sandygate	SC3997	Ballacleator – north of St Judes	SC4284	Glen Roy
SC3674	Ellenbrook	SC3798	East of Jurby Airfield	SC3998	The Guilcaugh	SC4285	Laxey Glen
SC3675	Pulrose	SC3799	The Loughan – Jurby	SC3999	Ballachrink – on Lhen Trench	SC4286	west of Agneash village
SC3676	Quarterbridge/Braddan Bridge	SC3874	Marine Drive	SC4077	Onchan Head	SC4287	Slieau Lhean
SC3677	Braddan Cemetery	SC3875	Douglas Harbour	SC4078	Onchan incl. Whitebridge	SC4288	north Slieau Lhean
SC3678	The Strang	SC3876	Douglas – Broadway + Queens Prom	SC4079	Ballakilmartin	SC4289	north-east Clagh Ouyr
SC3679	Ballaoates	SC3877	Douglas – Nobles Park + Victoria Road	SC4080	Top Kerrowdhoo Reservoir + Clypse	SC4290	Mountain Mile
SC3680	Ballamenagh	SC3878	Douglas – Governor's Hill + Signpost	SC4081	Plantation next to Clypse Reservoir	SC4291	top of Glen Auldyn
SC3681	East Baldwin	SC3879	Hillbery + Cronk ny Mona	SC4082	west Conrhenny Plantation	SC4292	Glen Auldyn
SC3682	St Lukes Church	SC3880	Brandish Corner	SC4083	Glen Roy Dam	SC4293	Sky Hill
SC3683	east West Baldwin Reservoir	SC3881	Lanjaghan	SC4084	North of Glen Roy	SC4294	Lezayre Church/ Garey Ford
SC3684	Carraghan	SC3882	Kate's Cottage	SC4085	Mullagh Ouyr	SC4295	Garey – Sulby
SC3685	North Carraghan	SC3883	33rd Milestone	SC4086	Cronk y Vaare	SC4296	Ardonan
SC3686	South-west Glen Crammag	SC3884	west of Windy Corner	SC4087	Snaefell Mines	SC4297	Regaby Beg
SC3687	South of Druidale	SC3885	south-east Beinn y Phott	SC4088	Black Hut	SC4298	Ballaseyre Equestrian Centre
SC3688	Druidale Farm	SC3886	Beinn y Phott	SC4089	east Block Eary	SC4299	Ballaseyre – Andreas Airfield
SC3689	South-west Tholt y Will Plantation	SC3887	Glen – east of Glen Crammag	SC4090	south-east Slieau Managh	SC4378	east of Port Groudle
SC3690	North-west Tholt y Will Plantation	SC3888	east of Sulby Reservoir	SC4091	north-east Slieau Managh	SC4379	Ballakilley Farm – Lonan coast
SC3691	East Ballaugh Plantation	SC3889	east of Tholt y Will pub	SC4092	Top of Narradale	SC4380	Clayhead Farm
SC3692	Bullrenney	SC3890	east of Tholt y Will Plantation	SC4093	Narradale	SC4381	Garwick Bay
SC3693	Gob y Volley	SC3891	Sulby Glen – Ballaimish	SC4094	Kerrowmoar – Sulby	SC4382	Laxey Bay
SC3694	Wildlife Park	SC3892	Ballakerka Plantation	SC4095	Close yn Ellan – Sulby	SC4383	South Cape
SC3695	The Curraghs	SC3893	The Claddagh	SC4096	Ballachurry – Sulby	SC4384	Laxey
SC3696	Lough Dhoo	SC3894	Sulby Village	SC4097	Kerroogarroo	SC4385	Laxey Wheel
SC3697	Ballamoar Castle	SC3895	Kella – back road	SC4098	Ballavarry	SC4386	Agneash Village
SC3698	Jurby Airfield	SC3896	Close e Kewin	SC4099	west Andreas	SC4387	Slieau Ouyr
SC3699	Jurby Ind Estate	SC3897	Summerhill	SC4177	Howstrake	SC4388	north Slieau Ouyr
SC3773	Wallberry	SC3898	Rhendhoo	SC4178	Groudle Glen	SC4389	Cornaa House – Corrany Valley
SC3774	Carnane	SC3899	Jurby East	SC4179	Bibaloe Beg	SC4390	Park Lewellyn
				SC4180	Cooil Roi Mansion House	SC4391	Guthrie's Memorial
				SC4181	Conrhenny	SC4392	Brookdale Plantation
				SC4182	Conrhenny Plantation	SC4393	Glen Auldyn Village
				SC4183	Ballalheanagh Gardens	SC4394	Milntown Cottage
				SC4184	Baldhoon – Glen Roy	SC4395	Whitebridge – Ramsey
						SC4396	Aust

1km square	Place name
SC4397	Regaby
SC4398	Ballacorey – north of Regaby
SC4399	Ballaslig – Andreas
SC4479	The Clett – Clay Head
SC4480	Clay Head
SC4481	Braggan Point – Clay Head
SC4483	Laxey Head
SC4484	Minorca
SC4485	The Clarum – Ballaragh
SC4486	Rhennie Farm – The Dhoon
SC4487	East slope Slieau Ouyr
SC4488	west of Glen Mona
SC4489	The Mines House – Corrany Valley
SC4490	North Barrule
SC4491	north North Barrule
SC4492	Top of Elfin Glen
SC4493	Elfin Glen
SC4494	Ramsey – Poyll Dhooie
SC4495	Ramsey – Grove + Mooragh Lake
SC4496	The Dhoor
SC4497	Curragh Beg – west of Dog Mills
SC4498	Glascoe Farm
SC4499	Ballavair
SC4583	east of Laxey Head
SC4584	Skinscoe
SC4585	Bulgham Bay
SC4586	Dhoon Glen
SC4587	Ballellin – Lonan
SC4588	Glen Mona
SC4589	Corrany
SC4590	Margher e Kew
SC4591	Hibernian
SC4592	Ballure Plantation
SC4593	Albert Tower
SC4594	Ramsey Harbour
SC4595	Mooragh Promenade
SC4596	Grand Island
SC4597	Dog Mills
SC4598	Kionlough
SC4599	Sand Cliffs south of Shellag Point
SC4686	Dhoon Bay
SC4687	Barony Hill
SC4688	Cornaa Plantation
SC4689	Ballaglass Glen
SC4690	Ballvelt south-east of the Hibernian
SC4691	Ballsaig east of the Hibernian
SC4692	Slieau Lewaigue
SC4693	Port Lewaigue
SC4694	end of Ramsey Pier
SC4787	Port Cornaa
SC4788	Traie ny Halsall
SC4789	Ballaskeig Beg
SC4790	Ballajora
SC4791	Dreemskerry
SC4792	Port e Vullen
SC4793	Gob ny Rona
SC4888	south of Traie ny Unaig
SC4889	Gob ny Garvain
SC4890	Port Mooar
SC4891	Ballakilley – Maughold
SC4892	Stack Mooar – Maughold
SC4990	Gob ny Portmooar – Maughold
SC4991	Maughold Head
SC4992	Cor Stack – Maughold

Appendix C: Gazetteer of local place names

Place	Grid Ref
Agneash	431860
Anagh Coar	354755
Andreas	413996
Anvil, The	197662
Archallagan, *Pl.*	302787
Arrasey *Pl.*	250789
Auldyn River	434938
Aust	432969
Awin Ruy	279706
Baldrine	428812
Baldwin	353810
Ballabeg	248705
Ballacain Dubs	359968
Ballachrink (Santon)	312714
Ballachrink	353802
Ballachurry (Andreas)	404966
Ballachurry (Rushen)	208698
Ballacoar	420828
Ballacoine (K Michael)	323885
Ballacorey	434991
Ballacreetch (Onchan)	376795
Ballacross	261838
Balladoole	248685
Ballagarraghyn	292815
Ballaghaie	371002
Ballaghaue	420994
Ballaghennie Ayre	436039
Ballaglass Glen	465898
Ballakillingan	424945
Ballakilpheric	224712
Ballamaddrell (Arbory)	251708
Ballamoar (Jurby)	368979
Ballamoar (Patrick)	250821
Ballamodha	276738
Ballamona Hospital	364782
Ballanayre Strand	276867
Ballanea	310888
Ballanette	431801
Ballasalla	280701
Ballaskeig	473891
Ballaspit	268816
Ballasteen	407991
Ballaugh	348935
Ballaugh Cronk	341959
Ballaugh Curragh	365948
Ballavale	315724
Ballavarrey	406985
Ballure Reservoir	453929
Ballure	461934
Barregarrow	321880
Bay ny Carrickey	226687
Beary Mountain	313832
Beinn y Phott	381860
Billown Farm	263696
Billown House Dams	262695
Billown Mooar	260696
Billown Quarries	269701
Bishop's Dub	335933
Bishopscourt	328924
Black Head	187658
Blue Point	392026
Braaid	320762
Bradda Head	182699
Bradda Hill	193711
Brandywell	390858
Bride	448010
Brough Jairg	339935
Bulgham Bay	457858
Burroo Ned	177664
Calf of Man Bird Observatory	156658
Calf of Man	158656
Carnanes, The	211724
Carraghan	368849
Carrick	384929
Cashtel Mooar	231832
Cass ny Hawin	303694
Castletown	264675
Chapel Bay	211682
Chasms	193663
Chicken Rock	142639
Clagh Ouyr	414889
Clay Head	443805
Close Sartfield reserve	358955
Clypse Reservoir	403808
Colby	231701
Colden *Pl.*	356840
Colden	343843
Congary	248829
Conister Rock	388755
Conrhenny	412816
Contrary Head	227828
Corlea *Pl.*	261749
Cornaa	473878
Corrany	453898
Cow Harbour	166664
Cranstal	462023
Cregneash	189672
Cringle *Pl.*	251749
Cringle Reservoir	252745
Crogga	336728
Cronk Fedjag	237750
Cronk ny Arrey Laa	225747
Cronk y Voddy	301859
Cronkgarroo	401936
Crosby	326795
Dalby	219784
Derby Castle	396773
Derbyhaven	284676
Dhoo River	350777
Dhoon	461863
Dog Mills Lough	449978
Dog Mills	452978
Douglas Bay	385766
Douglas Borough Cemetery	382774
Douglas Harbour	387751
Douglas Head	391747
Druidale	363883
Eairy Dam	297778
Eary Beg *Pl.*	296837
Eary Cushlin	224757
Eary Farm	324864
East Baldwin	369825
East Lhergydhoo	272846
Elfin Glen	448932
Ellerslie	323786
Fenella Beach	241844
Fleshwick	201714
Fort Island	296673
Foss, The	421870
Foxdale	278779
Gansey Point	217679
Gansey sewage works	222690
Gansey	215687
Garey Mooar	242741
Garth, The	320775
Garwick	434814
Ghaw Gortagh	243677
Glascoe Dub	446989
Glass River	368800
Glen Auldyn	433931
Glen Drink	434862
Glen Grenaugh	314712
Glen Helen	302844
Glen Maye	236798
Glen Mooar	302894
Glen Roy	415838
Glen Rushen *Pl.*	240762
Glen Rushen	241767
Glen Truan Golf Course	440030
Glen Vine	335787
Glen Wyllin	314902
Glenfaba	240830
Glion Gill	325841
Gob Lhiack	347718
Grants' Harbour	167662
Great Meadow	265688
Greeba Mountain	317815
Greeba *Pl.*	320812
Groudle	420782
Guilcagh	395981
Herring Tower	285657
Hillberry	385797
Howstrake	405781
Injebreck	355849

Place	Grid Ref
Jurby Airfield	364985
Jurby Head	343983
Jurby	363989
Kallow Point	212671
Kentraugh Black Rocks	225686
Kentraugh	225691
Kerrowdhoo *Pl.*	226765
Kerrowdhoo Reservoir	400803
Killane River mouth	340968
Kionslieau	289782
Kirby	364766
Kirk Braddan	363768
Kirk Michael	317908
Kirkill	217721
Kitterland	171665
Knockrushen	260671
Ladyport	288879
Lagg River	218771
Laggan Agneash	417868
Lanagore	235752
Langness Farm	286664
Langness	287665
Laxey Fire Station	431849
Laxey Flour Mills	431843
Laxey Head	445832
Laxey River	426855
Laxey	433845
Leigh Terrace	376751
Lezayre Church	423941
Lhagagh, The	409014
Lhen Trench	396996
Lhiattee ny Beinnee	211728
Little London	321861
Little Ness	366729
Lonan Old Church	427793
Lough Cranstal	451024
Marine Drive	372735
Maughold Head	499913
Mill Giau	154650
Milntown	437942
Molly Quirk's Glen	402789
Monk's Bridge	279704
Montpelier	354881
Mooragh Lake	449952
Mount Karrin	377919
Mullagh Ouyr	397862
Neb, River	273820
Niarbyl	209775
North Barrule	442909
Nunnery, The	371753
Oatlands	325725
Onchan Harbour	404776
Onchan Head	401771
Onchan	399782
Orrisdale Head	318928
Orrisdale	325930
Park Llewellyn	438900
Park ne Earkan	414927
Patrick	244823
Peel Bay	246846
Peel Breakwater	243846
Peel Castle	241845
Peel Quarry	238834
Peel Hill	233830
Peel Road	367759
Peel	245840
Perwick Bay	203670
Phildraw	282714
Phurt, The	468026
Pistol Castle	339714
Point of Ayre gravel pits	458042
Point of Ayre	467051
Poortown	269831
Port Cranstal	468026
Port Erin	196690
Port Grenaugh	315704
Port Jack	399773
Port Lewaigue	468930
Port Mooar	487910
Port Soderick	347727
Port Soldrick	303696
Port St Mary	209675
Port e Chee Lake	372769
Port e Vullen	473928
Poyll Breinn (Stinking Dub)	285666
Poyll Dhooie	443951
Poyllvaaish	245675
Queen's Promenade (Douglas)	390772
Raggatt	244829
Ramsey Harbour	452945
Ramsey	452943
Regaby	431975
Reservoir House (Baldwin)	358831
Rhenass	313857
Richmond Hill	340746
Ronague	245725
Ronaldsway Airport	282684
Round Table, The	247758
Rue Point	408034
Rule, The (Ballaugh)	372951
Rushen Abbey	278701
Saddlestone	358762
Sandwick	283673
Santon Burn	308734
Santon Gorge	298693
Santon Head	333703
Santon	320731
Sartfell	333871
Sartfield	354993
Scarlett Road	263671
Scarlett	258664
Shellag Point	459998
Shenvalla (Patrick)	243816
Silverburn River	271690
Silverdale	275710
Sir George's Bridge	367793
Skerrip	454842
Sky Hill	431939
Slieau Curn *Pl.*	347912
Slieau Earystane	236732
Slieau Freoghane	341883
Slieau Lhean	426877
Slieau Managh	396910
Slieau Ouyr	437879
Slieau Ruy	328824
Slieau Whallian	264804
Sloc	214734
Snaefell	398881
Snuff the Wind	265777
Sound, The	172664
South Barrule	257759
South Harbour	159648
Spanish Head	179659
St John's	277818
St Judes	395966
St Mark's	296741
St Patrick's Isle	241845
Stoney Mountain	283764
Strandhall	238687
Strang	360781
Sugar Loaf	194662
Sulby Bridge	392947
Sulby Claddagh	386939
Sulby Glen	382915
Sulby Reservoir	372888
Sulby River	384920
Sulby	388947
The Glen – Calf	155654
The Pollies	361950
Tholt y Will *Pl.*	370897
Traie ny Feeyney	488923
Traie Vane	215771
Tromode Dam	372782
Tromode	372777
Upper Lhergydhoo	285849
Vollan, The	451959
Wallberry	370734
West Baldwin Reservoir	362833
West Baldwin	353812
Whing	360731
Whitebridge (Ramsey)	441950
Wildlife Park	366942
Wood's Strand	271863

Appendix D: Summary of breeding and wintering populations

Species	Breeding Pop est	Method	Summer 1km squares – breeding status: Non–breeding	Possible	Probable	Definite	Total 1km sq present	(%)	Winter: Pop est	1km sq present	(%)	Schedule 1 Wildlife Act 1990	Conservation concern: UK/Irish red list	UK/Irish amber list
Mute Swan	11–12	Census	18	2	4	11	35	5	50+	39	6			UK
Whooper Swan	0		5	0	0	0	5	1	60+	33	5	Y		UK + Irish
Pink-footed Goose	0		3	0	0	0	3	0.5	50+	8	1	Y		UK
Greylag Goose	42–55	Analysis	33	3	1	10	47	7	600+	27	4	Y		UK + Irish
Canada Goose	28–29	Analysis	15	8	8	9	40	6	70+	23	3	Y		
Brent Goose	0		7	0	0	0	0	1	6–40	10	2	Y		UK + Irish
Shelduck	105–109	Analysis	19	11	28	29	87	13	100–130	28	4	Y		UK + Irish
Wigeon	0		14	0	0	0	0	2	1000	44	7			UK + Irish
Gadwall	1	Analysis	4	1	1	0	6	1	0–2	5	1	Y		UK + Irish
Teal	10–15	Analysis	27	7	15	1	50	8	1500	66	10	Y		UK + Irish
Mallard	596–688	Analysis	33	96	102	124	355	53	2000+	221	33			
Shoveler	1–2	Analysis	5	2	1	0	8	1	<10	12	2	Y		UK
Pochard	0		7	0	0	0	7	1	<80	18	3			UK + Irish
Tufted Duck	<20	Analysis	8	4	12	10	34	11	<50	25	4			Irish
Scaup	0		1	0	0	0	0	0.5	0–4	8	1	Y		UK + Irish
Eider	<50	Analysis	17	11	21	12	61	9	100	35	5			UK + Irish
Long-tailed Duck	0		1	0	0	0	1	0.5	0–2	8	1			
Common Scoter	0		8	0	0	0	8	1	10–40	15	2		Irish	
Velvet Scoter	0								1–4	7	1			UK
Goldeneye	0		10	0	0	0	10	1	70–80	46	7			UK + Irish
Red-breasted Merganser	0		16	0	0	0	16	2	0–4	22	3			Irish
Goosander	0		1	0	0	0	1	0.5	0–2	11	2			Irish
Ruddy Duck	1		1	0	1	1	3	0.5	0–3	3	0.5			
Red Grouse	52–63	Analysis	2	12	13	8	35	5	<100	26	4		Irish	UK
Red–legged Partridge	116–130	Analysis	5	30	59	14	108	16	400	43	6			
Grey Partridge	49	Analysis	7	14	32	2	55	8	100+	21	3		UK + Irish	
Quail	0–3	Analysis	0	0	3	0	3	0.5				Y	UK + Irish	
Pheasant	1740–2092	Analysis	3	50	376	87	516	77	12000+	399	60			
Red-throated Diver	0		16	0	0	0	16	2	10–100	36	5			UK + Irish
Black-throated Diver	0		8	0	0	0	8	1	0–20	18	3			UK + Irish
Great Northern Diver	0		11	0	0	0	11	2	0–10	33	5			UK
Little Grebe	1–3	Analysis	2	2	1	0	5	1	<10	15	2	Y		
Slavonian Grebe	0								0–2	5	1			UK
Fulmar	2981–3143	Seabird	36	9	61	15	121	18	<8000	66	10			UK
Manx Shearwater	>20	Census	33	3	0	2	38	6		2	0.5	Y		UK + Irish
Storm Petrel	0		16	0	0	0	16	2				Y		UK + Irish
Gannet	0		84	0	0	0	84	13	?	20	3			UK + Irish
Cormorant	134	Seabird	121	5	0	5	131	20	<300	106	16			UK + Irish
Shag	912	Seabird	61	6	0	49	116	17	2000	114	17	Y		UK
Grey Heron	47–49	Census	188	7	0	9	204	31	150	140	21			
Hen Harrier	51	Census	173	83	30	60	346	52	<150	268	40	Y	UK + Irish	
Kestrel	120	Analysis	98	74	12	32	216	32	200	185	28	Y		UK
Sparrowhawk	75–80	Analysis	132	61	4	16	213	32	200+	214	32	Y		
Merlin	0–4	Analysis	30	4	0	0	34	5	<30	72	11	Y		UK + Irish
Peregrine Falcon	25–29	Census	113	38	14	37	202	30	<100	144	22	Y		UK + Irish
Water Rail	36–47	Census	0	18	6	0	24	4	<100	18	3	Y		UK + Irish
Corncrake	<10	Analysis	4	1	3	5	13	2				Y	UK + Irish	
Moorhen	197–268	Analysis	2	79	11	77	169	25	1000+	127	19			
Coot	49–51	Analysis	4	7	4	27	42	6	200	33	5			Irish
Oystercatcher	337–372	Analysis	13	31	27	116	191	29	1500	116	17			UK
Ringed Plover	89–95	Analysis	8	8	8	28	52	8	<500	44	7	Y		UK
Golden Plover	1	Analysis	33	0	0	1	34	5	500–2000	66	10	Y		Irish

Species	Breeding Pop est	Method	Summer: 1km squares – breeding status: Non–breeding	Possible	Probable	Definite	Total 1km sq present	(%)	Winter: Pop est	1km sq present	(%)	Schedule 1 Wildlife Act 1990	Conservation concern: UK/Irish red list	UK/Irish amber list
Grey Plover	0		8	0	0	0	8	1	5–20	19	3			UK + Irish
Lapwing	96–110	Analysis	9	10	14	29	62	9	500–1500	94	14	Y	Irish	UK
Knot	0		11	0	0	0	11	2	0–10	9	1			UK + Irish
Sanderling	0		14	0	0	0	14	2	20–100	15	2			
Purple Sandpiper	0		15	0	0	0	15	2	<100	19	3			UK
Dunlin	0		34	0	0	0	34	5	<500	27	4			UK + Irish
Jack Snipe	0		2	0	0	0	2	0.5	<50	29	4	Y		Irish
Snipe	21–24	Analysis	26	17	1	5	49	7	<500	162	24	Y		UK + Irish
Woodcock	<50	Analysis	2	3	6	2	13	2	100+	109	16	Y		UK + Irish
Bar-tailed Godwit	0		9	0	0	0	9	1	1–10	9	1			UK + Irish
Curlew	399–483	Analysis	97	57	102	92	348	52	<2000	97	15	Y	Irish	UK
Redshank	1	Analysis	32	1	0	1	34	5	200	58	9			UK + Irish
Turnstone	0		31	0	0	0	31	5	300+	41	6			UK
Black-headed Gull	0–6	Seabird	72	0	0	4	76	11	2000+	118	18			UK + Irish
Common Gull	6–10	Seabird	15	0	1	4	20	3	<400	63	10			UK + Irish
Lesser Black-backed Gull	114	Seabird	130	14	5	27	176	26	<100	30	4			UK
Herring Gull	7126	Seabird	459	22	5	129	615	92	20000–30000	468	70			UK
Great Black-backed Gull	405	Seabird	267	19	7	84	377	57	<1000	176	26			
Kittiwake	1045	Seabird	36	0	0	9	45	7	<20	15	2			UK
Sandwich Tern	0	Seabird	46	0	1	0	47	7				Y		UK + Irish
Arctic Tern	15	Seabird	7	6	0	4	17	3				Y		UK + Irish
Little Tern	6–25	Seabird	8	3	0	4	15	3				Y		UK + Irish
Guillemot	4566 – adults	Seabird	14	17	1	2	34	5	0–1500	19	3			UK + Irish
Razorbill	1524 – adults	Seabird	18	26	3	6	53	8	100–200	30	5			UK + Irish
Black Guillemot	602 – adults	Seabird	16	16	20	5	57	9	100–200	37	6			UK + Irish
Puffin	85 – adults	Seabird	4	9	3	1	17	3	<10	1	0.5			UK + Irish
Feral Pigeon	488–907	Analysis	53	72	22	8	155	23	2000+	88	13			
Stock Dove	32–37	Analysis	15	11	19	0	45	7	<10	2	0.5			UK + Irish
Woodpigeon	1363–2402	Analysis	14	93	279	63	449	68	<3000	290	44			
Collared Dove	534–790	Analysis	20	38	175	26	259	39	2000	183	28			
Cuckoo	25	Analysis	48	6	15	4	73	11						UK + Irish
Barn Owl	<40	Analysis	30	9	2	7	48	7	<100	48	7	Y	Irish	UK
Tawny Owl	1	Analysis	3	1	0	0	4	1	<4	1	0.5	Y		
Long-eared Owl	22	Analysis	17	8	0	13	38	6	100	14	2	Y		
Short-eared Owl	0–5	Analysis	20	11	2	5	38	6	10–20	28	4	Y		UK + Irish
Swift	193–222 – adults	Census	126	28	10	6	170	26				Y		
Kingfisher	0–2	Analysis	0	2	0	0	2	0.5	0–4	2	0.5	Y		UK + Irish
Great Spotted Woodpecker	0–2	Analysis	2	2	0	0	4	1	2–4	8	1			
Skylark	787–984	Analysis	6	9	141	48	204	31	1000+	141	21	Y	UK	Irish
Sand Martin	1128 – nest holes	Census	87	4	0	20	111	17				Y		UK + Irish
Swallow	1689–2577	Analysis	125	97	129	188	539	81						UK + Irish
House Martin	1456–1714	Census	84	66	6	149	305	46						UK
Tree Pipit	1	Analysis	10	0	0	1	11	2				Y		UK
Meadow Pipit	3602–6198	Analysis	62	75	103	305	545	82	2000+	384	58			UK
Rock Pipit	207–272	Analysis	2	12	46	43	103	15	500+	66	10			
Grey Wagtail	99–113	Analysis	80	40	28	26	174	26	<300	237	36			UK
Pied Wagtail	579–851	Analysis	44	241	72	136	493	74	2000+	332	50			
Waxwing	0								0–200	27	4			
Wren	9329–9832	Analysis	1	6	288	324	616	93	25000+	599	90			
Dunnock	2344–26177	Analysis	5	6	419	113	543	82	10000	466	70			UK
Robin	4844–5691	Analysis	4	10	214	314	542	82	20000	553	83			

Species	Breeding Pop est	Method	Summer 1km squares – breeding status: Non–breeding	Possible	Probable	Definite	Total 1km sq present	(%)	Winter: Pop est	1km sq present	(%)	Schedule 1 Wildlife Act 1990	Conservation concern: UK/Irish red list	UK/Irish amber list
Black Redstart	0								<5	18	3	Y		UK
Whinchat	59–62	Census	20	3	22	7	52	8				Y		Irish
Stonechat	426–464	Analysis	18	26	42	199	285	43	1000	198	30			UK + Irish
Wheatear	114–132	Analysis	197	29	16	27	269	40						
Blackbird	2122–3217	Analysis	5	76	156	299	536	81	10000+	508	76			
Fieldfare	0		66	0	0	0	66	10	500–1500	243	37			UK
Song Thrush	952–1334	Analysis	6	38	258	160	462	69	5000+	470	71	Y	UK	
Redwing	0		21	0	0	0	21	3	500–1500	272	41			UK
Mistle Thrush	334–463	Analysis	42	85	103	91	321	48	1000+	288	43			UK
Grasshopper Warbler	57	Analysis	58	1	48	2	106	16				Y	UK	Irish
Sedge Warbler	188–220	Analysis	47	10	79	29	165	25						
Reed Warbler	1–2	Analysis	1	0	1	0	2	0.5						Irish
Blackcap	343–349	Analysis	53	3	159	20	235	35	<100	80	12			
Garden Warbler	8	Analysis	16	1	7	0	24	4						
Lesser Whitethroat	7–8	Analysis	7	0	7	0	14	2						Irish
Whitethroat	725–815	Analysis	46	12	222	100	380	57						
Wood Warbler	3	Analysis	4	2	1	0	7	1						UK + Irish
Chiffchaff	183–185	Analysis	71	6	131	4	212	32	<50	23	3			
Willow Warbler	1298–1402	Analysis	74	14	323	65	476	72						UK
Goldcrest	915–1262	Analysis	29	34	263	60	386	58	3000+	347	52			UK
Spotted Flycatcher	53–54	Analysis	23	27	3	24	77	12				Y	UK	Irish
Long-tailed Tit	136–169	Analysis	51	59	44	24	178	27	<500	167	25			
Coal Tit	772–1030	Analysis	24	57	198	98	377	57	3000	339	51			
Blue Tit	707–1122	Analysis	21	122	100	154	397	60	3000+	370	56			
Great Tit	1009–1411	Analysis	23	73	187	165	448	67	5000+	384	58			
Treecreeper	118–149	Analysis	26	63	21	21	131	20	<500	130	20			
Magpie	692–1078	Analysis	23	264	90	98	475	71	2500	412	62			
Chough	121–150	Census	84	8	32	78	202	30	500+	201	30	Y	Irish	UK
Jackdaw	4264–8088	Analysis	31	101	138	212	482	72	20000+	423	64			
Rook	7096	Census	337	24	3	125	489	74	20000+	394	50			
Carrion Crow	150–189	Analysis	49	89	22	32	192	29	500+	115	17			
Hooded Crow	832–1310	Analysis	55	253	112	161	581	87	3000+	474	71			
Hybrid Crow	71–84	Analysis	20	50	19	6	95	14	200+	103	15			
Raven	85–89	Census	252	28	20	115	415	62	300+	332	50			
Starling	904–1609	Analysis	49	81	77	133	340	51	5000+	336	51	Y	UK	
House Sparrow	2158–3739	Analysis	4	49	104	201	358	54	10000+	294	44	Y	UK	
Tree Sparrow	156–240	Census	40	16	23	37	116	17	<1000	85	13	Y	UK	
Chaffinch	3226–4227	Analysis	5	24	328	164	521	78	20000+	457	69			
Brambling	0		8	0	0	0	8	1	0–200+	35	5			
Greenfinch	1174–1839	Analysis	20	73	254	76	423	64	5000+	331	50			
Goldfinch	477–696	Analysis	90	115	168	34	407	61	1000+	202	38			
Siskin	228–325	Analysis	108	83	44	15	250	38	1000+	155	23			
Linnet	1418–2297	Analysis	45	125	292	63	525	79	5000+	169	25		UK	
Twite	0		3	0	0	0	3	0.5	<200	19	3	Y	UK + Irish	
Lesser Redpoll	179–262	Analysis	76	77	34	7	194	29	<1000	22	3			UK + Irish
Crossbill	27–39	Analysis	17	22	1	1	41	6	<100	13	2	Y		
Snow Bunting	0		1	0	0	0	1	0.5	0–50	29	4			UK
Yellowhammer	122–146	Analysis	10	7	41	6	64	10	<500	36	5	Y	UK + Irish	
Reed Bunting	211–232	Analysis	8	22	124	14	168	25	<1000	86	13	Y	UK	
Red-winged Laughingthrush	1+	Analysis	3	0	1	0	4	0.5	<10	1	0.5			

Breeding population estimates were derived in one of three ways:
1 Analysis: An examination of data gathered during timed fieldwork in each 1km square, with additional records from members of the public.
Population estimates derived from analysis of 1km square data represent the minimum numbers likely to be present as no account is taken of birds that may have gone undetected.
2 Census: Island wide survey of the species – undertaken during one of the years of research.
3 Seabird: Survey of all seabirds undertaken during the summer of 1999.

Winter population estimates were derived from an examination of data gathered during structured winter surveys.
These estimates should be viewed as an informed opinion.
For most species, an accurate assessment of wintering numbers is not possible.
Wintering birds tend to range more widely and their numbers vary within seasons to a greater extent than during the breeding season, resulting in a greater probability that numbers present are understated.

Appendix E: Plants mentioned in the text

Common name	Scientific name
Alders	*Alnus* spp.
Beech	*Fagus sylvatica*
Bilberry	*Vaccinium myrtillus*
Birch	*Betula* spp.
Blackthorn	*Prunus spinosa*
Bluebell	*Hyacinthoides non-scriptus*
Bog Myrtle	*Myrica gale*
Bogbean	*Menyanthes trifoliata*
Bracken	*Pteridium aquilinum*
Bramble	*Rubus fruticosus* agg.
Broom	*Cytisus scoparius*
Bulrush	*Scirpus lacustris*
Cowberry	*Vaccinium vitis-idaea*
Crab Apples	*Malus sylvestris sens. lat.*
Dwarf Willow	*Salix herbacea*
Eel-grass	*Zostera marina*
Elder	*Sambucus nigra*
Fern, Royal	*Osmunda regalis*
Gorse	*Ulex* spp.
Gorse, European	*Ulex europaeus*
Hawthorn	*Crataegus monogyna*
Heather, Bell	*Erica cinerea*
Heather, Ling	*Calluna vulgaris*
Horsetails	*Equisetum* spp.
Ivy	*Hedera* spp.
Larch, European	*Larix decidua*
Larch, Japanese	*Larix kaempferi*
Lichens	*Cladonia* spp.
Marram	*Ammophila arenaria*
Oak	*Quercus* spp.
Orchid, Dense-flowered	*Neotinea maculata*
Pine, Corsican	*Pinus nigra*
Pine, Lodgepole	*Pinus contorta*
Pine, Scots	*Pinus sylvestris*
Reed, Common	*Phragmites australis*
Rose, Burnet	*Rosa pimpinellifolia*
Rowan	*Sorbus aucuparia*
Sedges	*Carex* spp.
Silver Birch	*Betula pendula*
Spruce	*Picea* spp.
Spruce, Sitka	*Picea sitchensis*
Sycamore	*Acer pseudoplatanus*
Thyme, Wild	*Thymus polytrichus*
Water Horsetail	*Equisetum fluviatile*
Watercress	*Rorippa nasturtium-aquaticum* agg.
Willow	*Salix* spp.
Willow, Creeping	*Salix repens*

Appendix F: Names of birds mentioned in the text

Arctic Skua	*Stercorarius parasiticus*
Arctic Tern	*Sterna paradisaea*
Avocet (Pied Avocet)	*Recurvirostra avosetta*
Balearic Shearwater	*Puffinus mauretanicus*
Bar-headed Goose	*Anser indicus*
Barn Owl	*Tyto alba*
Barnacle Goose	*Branta leucopsis*
Barred Warbler	*Sylvia nisoria*
Barrow's Goldeneye	*Bucephala islandica*
Bar-tailed Godwit	*Limosa lapponica*
Bee-eater (European Bee-eater)	*Merops apiaster*
Bewick's Swan (Tundra Swan)	*Cygnus columbianus*
Bittern (Great Bittern)	*Botaurus stellaris*
Black Guillemot	*Cepphus grylle*
Black Redstart	*Phoenicurus ochruros*
Black Swan	*Cygnus atratus*
Blackbird (Common Blackbird)	*Turdus merula*
Blackcap	*Sylvia atricapilla*
Black-headed Gull	*Larus ridibundus*
Black-necked Grebe	*Podiceps nigricollis*
Black-tailed Godwit	*Limosa limosa*
Black-throated Diver	*Gavia arctica*
Blue Tit	*Cyanistes caeruleus*
Brambling	*Fringilla montifringilla*
Brent Goose	*Branta bernicla*
Bullfinch (Common Bullfinch)	*Pyrrhula pyrrhula*
Canada Goose (Greater Canada Goose)	*Branta canadensis*
Carrion Crow	*Corvus corone*
Chaffinch	*Fringilla coelebs*
Chiffchaff (Common Chiffchaff)	*Phylloscopus collybita*
Chough (Red-billed Chough)	*Pyrrhocorax pyrrhocorax*
Coal Tit	*Periparus ater*
Collared Dove (Eurasian Collared Dove)	*Streptopelia decaocto*
Common Buzzard	*Buteo buteo*
Common Gull (Mew Gull)	*Larus canus*
Common Redpoll	*Carduelis flammea*
Common Rosefinch	*Carpodacus erythrinus*
Common Sandpiper	*Actitis hypoleucos*
Common Scoter	*Melanitta nigra*
Common Tern	*Sterna hirundo*
Coot (Common Coot)	*Fulica atra*
Cormorant (Great Cormorant)	*Phalacrocorax carbo*
Corncrake (Corn Crake)	*Crex crex*
Crane (Common Crane)	*Grus grus*
Crossbill (Common Crossbill)	*Loxia curvirostra*
Cuckoo (Common Cuckoo)	*Cuculus canorus*
Curlew (Eurasian Curlew)	*Numenius arquata*
Curlew Sandpiper	*Calidris ferruginea*
Desert Wheatear	*Oenanthe deserti*
Dipper (White-throated Dipper)	*Cinclus cinclus*
Dotterel (Eurasian Dotterel)	*Charadrius morinellus*
Dunlin	*Calidris alpina*
Dunnock (Hedge Accentor)	*Prunella modularis*
Eider (Common Eider)	*Somateria mollissima*
Feral Pigeon/Rock Dove (Rock Pigeon)	*Columba livia*
Fieldfare	*Turdus pilaris*
Firecrest	*Regulus ignicapilla*
Fulmar (Northern Fulmar)	*Fulmarus glacialis*
Gadwall	*Anas strepera*
Gannet (Northern Gannet)	*Morus bassanus*
Garden Warbler	*Sylvia borin*
Garganey	*Anas querquedula*
Glaucous Gull	*Larus hyperboreus*
Goldcrest	*Regulus regulus*
Golden Oriole (Eurasian Golden Oriole)	*Oriolus oriolus*
Golden Pheasant	*Chrysolophus pictus*
Golden Plover (European Golden Plover)	*Pluvialis apricaria*
Goldeneye (Common Goldeneye)	*Bucephala clangula*
Goldfinch (European Goldfinch)	*Carduelis carduelis*
Goosander	*Mergus merganser*
Goshawk (Northern Goshawk)	*Accipiter gentilis*
Grasshopper Warbler (Common Grasshopper Warbler)	*Locustella naevia*
Great Black-backed Gull	*Larus marinus*
Great Crested Grebe	*Podiceps cristatus*
Great Grey Shrike	*Lanius excubitor*
Great Northern Diver	*Gavia immer*
Great Skua	*Stercorarius skua*
Great Spotted Woodpecker	*Dendrocopos major*
Great Tit	*Parus major*
Great White Egret (Great Egret)	*Ardea alba*
Green Sandpiper	*Tringa ochropus*

Green Woodpecker	*Picus viridis*
Greenfinch (European Greenfinch)	*Carduelis chloris*
Greenshank (Common Greenshank)	*Tringa nebularia*
Green-winged Teal	*Anas carolinensis*
Grey Heron	*Ardea cinerea*
Grey Partridge	*Perdix perdix*
Grey Phalarope	*Phalaropus fulicarius*
Grey Plover	*Pluvialis squatarola*
Grey Wagtail	*Motacilla cinerea*
Greylag Goose	*Anser anser*
Guillemot (Common Guillemot)	*Uria aalge*
Hawfinch	*Coccothraustes coccothraustes*
Hen Harrier	*Circus cyaneus*
Herring Gull	*Larus argentatus*
Hobby (Eurasian Hobby)	*Falco subbuteo*
Honey Buzzard (European Honey-buzzard)	*Pernis apivorus*
Hooded Crow	*Corvus cornix*
Hoopoe	*Upupa epops*
House Martin	*Delichon urbicum*
House Sparrow	*Passer domesticus*
Hybrid Crow	*Corvus corone* x *Corvus cornix*
Iceland Gull	*Larus glaucoides*
Icterine Warbler	*Hippolais icterina*
Jack Snipe	*Lymnocryptes minimus*
Jackdaw (Eurasian Jackdaw)	*Corvus monedula*
Kestrel (Common Kestrel)	*Falco tinnunculus*
King Eider	*Somateria spectabilis*
Kingfisher (Common Kingfisher)	*Alcedo atthis*
Kittiwake (Black-legged Kittiwake)	*Rissa tridactyla*
Knot (Red Knot)	*Calidris canutus*
Lapland Bunting (Lapland Longspur)	*Calcarius lapponicus*
Lapwing (Northern Lapwing)	*Vanellus vanellus*
Leach's Petrel (Leach's Storm Petrel)	*Oceanodroma leucorhoa*
Lesser Black-backed Gull	*Larus fuscus*
Lesser Redpoll	*Carduelis cabaret*
Lesser Whitethroat	*Sylvia curruca*
Linnet (Common Linnet)	*Carduelis cannabina*
Little Auk	*Alle alle*
Little Bunting	*Emberiza pusilla*
Little Egret	*Egretta garzetta*
Little Grebe	*Tachybaptus ruficollis*
Little Gull	*Larus minutus*
Little Ringed Plover (Little Plover)	*Charadrius dubius*
Little Stint	*Calidris minuta*
Little Tern	*Sternula albifrons*
Long-eared Owl	*Asio otus*
Long-tailed Duck	*Clangula hyemalis*
Long-tailed Tit	*Aegithalos caudatus*
Magnificent Frigatebird	*Fregata magnificens*
Magpie (Black-billed Magpie)	*Pica pica*
Mallard	*Anas platyrhynchos*
Mandarin Duck	*Aix galericulata*
Manx Shearwater	*Puffinus puffinus*
Marsh Harrier (Eurasian Marsh Harrier)	*Circus aeruginosus*
Meadow Pipit	*Anthus pratensis*
Mediterranean Gull	*Larus melanocephalus*
Melodious Warbler	*Hippolais polyglotta*
Merlin	*Falco columbarius*

Mistle Thrush	*Turdus viscivorus*
Moorhen (Common Moorhen)	*Gallinula chloropus*
Mute Swan	*Cygnus olor*
Nightingale (Common Nightingale)	*Luscinia megarhynchos*
Nightjar (European Nightjar)	*Caprimulgus europaeus*
Northern Bobwhite	*Colinus virginianus*
Nuthatch (Wood Nuthatch)	*Sitta europaea*
Olive-backed Pipit	*Anthus hodgsoni*
Ortolan Bunting	*Emberiza hortulana*
Osprey	*Pandion haliaetus*
Oystercatcher (Eurasian Oystercatcher)	*Haematopus ostralegus*
Pectoral Sandpiper	*Calidris melanotos*
Peregrine (Peregrine Falcon)	*Falco peregrinus*
Pheasant (Common Pheasant)	*Phasianus colchicus*
Pied Flycatcher	*Ficedula hypoleuca*
Pied Wagtail	*Motacilla alba*
Pink-footed Goose	*Anser brachyrhynchus*
Pintail (Northern Pintail)	*Anas acuta*
Pochard (Common Pochard)	*Aythya ferina*
Pomarine Skua	*Stercorarius pomarinus*
Puffin (Atlantic Puffin)	*Fratercula arctica*
Purple Heron	*Ardea purpurea*
Purple Sandpiper	*Calidris maritima*
Quail (Common Quail)	*Coturnix coturnix*
Raven (Common Raven)	*Corvus corax*
Razorbill	*Alca torda*
Red Grouse (Willow Ptarmigan)	*Lagopus lagopus*
Red Kite	*Milvus milvus*
Red-backed Shrike	*Lanius collurio*
Red-breasted Flycatcher	*Ficedula parva*
Red-breasted Goose	*Branta ruficollis*
Red-breasted Merganser	*Mergus serrator*
Red-crested Pochard	*Netta rufina*
Red-headed Bunting	*Emberiza bruniceps*
Red-legged Partridge	*Alectoris rufa*
Red-necked Grebe	*Podiceps grisegena*
Redshank (Common Redshank)	*Tringa totanus*
Redstart (Common Redstart)	*Phoenicurus phoenicurus*
Red-throated Diver	*Gavia stellata*
Redwing	*Turdus iliacus*
Red-winged Laughingthrush	*Garrulax formosus*
Reed Bunting	*Emberiza schoeniclus*
Reed Warbler (Eurasian Reed Warbler)	*Acrocephalus scirpaceus*
Richard's Pipit	*Anthus richardi*
Ring Ouzel	*Turdus torquatus*
Ring-billed Gull	*Larus delawarensis*
Ringed Plover	*Charadrius hiaticula*
Robin (European Robin)	*Erithacus rubecula*
Rock Pipit	*Anthus petrosus*
Rook	*Corvus frugilegus*
Rose-coloured Starling (Rosy Starling)	*Sturnus roseus*
Rose-ringed Parakeet	*Psittacula krameri*
Rough-legged Buzzard	*Buteo lagopus*
Ruddy Duck	*Oxyura jamaicensis*
Ruff	*Philomachus pugnax*
Sabine's Gull	*Larus sabini*
Sand Martin	*Riparia riparia*
Sanderling	*Calidris alba*

Sandwich Tern *Sterna sandvicensis*
Scaup (Greater Scaup) *Aythya marila*
Sedge Warbler *Acrocephalus schoenobaenus*
Serin (European Serin) *Serinus serinus*
Shag (European Shag) *Phalacrocorax aristotelis*
Shelduck (Common Shelduck) *Tadorna tadorna*
Shore Lark (Horned Lark) *Eremophila alpestris*
Short-eared Owl *Asio flammeus*
Shoveler (Northern Shoveler) *Anas clypeata*
Siskin (Eurasian Siskin) *Carduelis spinus*
Skylark (Sky Lark) *Alauda arvensis*
Slavonian Grebe *Podiceps auritus*
Smew *Mergellus albellus*
Snipe (Common Snipe) *Gallinago gallinago*
Snow Bunting *Plectrophenax nivalis*
Song Thrush *Turdus philomelos*
Sooty Shearwater *Puffinus griseus*
Sparrowhawk (Eurasian Sparrowhawk) *Accipiter nisus*
Spoonbill (Eurasian Spoonbill) *Platalea leucorodia*
Spotted Flycatcher *Muscicapa striata*
Spotted Redshank *Tringa erythropus*
Starling (Common Starling) *Sturnus vulgaris*
Stock Dove (Stock Pigeon) *Columba oenas*
Stonechat *Saxicola torquata*
Storm Petrel (European Storm-petrel) *Hydrobates pelagicus*
Surf Scoter *Melanitta perspicillata*
Swallow (Barn Swallow) *Hirundo rustica*
Swift (Common Swift) *Apus apus*

Tawny Owl *Strix aluco*
Tawny Pipit *Anthus campestris*
Teal (Eurasian Teal) *Anas crecca*
Tree Pipit *Anthus trivialis*
Tree Sparrow (Eurasian Tree Sparrow) *Passer montanus*
Treecreeper (Eurasian Treecreeper) *Certhia familiaris*
Tufted Duck *Aythya fuligula*
Turnstone (Ruddy Turnstone) *Arenaria interpres*
Turtle Dove (European Turtle Dove) *Streptopelia turtur*
Twite *Carduelis flavirostris*

Velvet Scoter *Melanitta fusca*

Water Pipit *Anthus spinoletta*
Water Rail *Rallus aquaticus*
Waxwing (Bohemian Waxwing) *Bombycilla garrulus*
Wheatear (Northern Wheatear) *Oenanthe oenanthe*
Whimbrel *Numenius phaeopus*
Whinchat *Saxicola rubetra*
White Stork *Ciconia ciconia*
White-fronted Goose (Greater White-fronted Goose) *Anser albifrons*
White-headed Duck *Oxyura leucocephala*
Whitethroat (Common Whitethroat) *Sylvia communis*
White-throated Sparrow *Zonotrichia albicollis*
Whooper Swan *Cygnus cygnus*
Wigeon *Anas penelope*
Willow Warbler *Phylloscopus trochilus*
Wilson's Phalarope *Phalaropus tricolor*
Wood Duck *Aix sponsa*
Wood Sandpiper *Tringa glareola*
Wood Warbler *Phylloscopus sibilatrix*
Woodchat Shrike *Lanius senator*
Woodcock (Eurasian Woodcock) *Scolopax rusticola*
Woodpigeon (Common Wood Pigeon) *Columba palumbus*
Wren (Winter Wren) *Troglodytes troglodytes*
Wryneck (Eurasian Wryneck) *Jynx torquilla*

Yellow Wagtail *Motacilla flava*
Yellow-browed Warbler *Phylloscopus inornatus*
Yellowhammer *Emberiza citrinella*
Yellow-legged Gull *Larus michahellis*

Appendix G: Names of other animals mentioned in the text

Common name	Scientific name
Badger	*Meles meles*
Baltic tellin	*Macoma baltica*
Bat, Natterer's	*Myotis nattereri*
Bats	Chiroptera
Bluebottles	*Calliphora* spp.
Bullhead	*Cottus gobio*
Butterfish	*Pholis gunnellus*
Caddis fly	Trichoptera
Coalfish	*Pollachius virens*
Cod	*Gadus morhua*
Common toad	*Bufo bufo*
Deer	Cervidae
Earthworm	Oligochaeta
Eel	*Anguilla anguilla*
Flounder	*Platichthys flesus*
Fox	*Vulpes vulpes*
Freshwater mussels	Unionidae
Freshwater shrimps	*Gammarus* spp.
Goat, feral	*Capra hircus*
Grasshopper, lesser mottled	*Stenobothrus stigmaticus*
Hare, brown	*Lepus europaeus*
Hare, mountain	*Lepus timidus*
Hedgehog	*Erinaceus europaeus*
Herring	*Clupea harengus*
Hoverflies	Syrphidae
Kelp flies	*Coelopa* spp.
Lugworm	*Arenicola* spp.
Midge	Chironomidae
Mink	*Mustela vison*
Minnow	*Phoxinus phoxinus*
Mole	*Talpa europaea*
Mouse, house	*Mus domesticus*
Mouse, wood	*Apodemus sylvaticus*
Mussels	*Mytilus edulis*
Perch	*Perca fluviatilis*
Polecat-ferret	*Mustela furo*
Rabbit	*Oryctolagus cuniculus*
Rat, brown	*Rattus norvegicus*
Robberflies	Asilidae
Salmon	*Salmo salar*
Sandeels	*Ammodytes* spp.
Sandhopper	Talitridae
Sawfly	*Pontania proxima*
Sea urchin	*Echinus esculentus*
Seal, grey	*Halichoerus grypus*
Sheep, loaghtan	*Ovis aries*
Shrew, common	*Sorex araneus*
Shrew, pygmy	*Sorex minutus*
Snakes	Serpentes
Squirrels	Sciuridae
Stickleback	Gasterosteidae
Stoat	*Mustela erminea*
Trout, brown	*Salmo trutta*
Trout, sea	*Salmo trutta*
Vole, short-tailed	*Microtus agrestis*
Wallaby, red-necked	*Macropus rufogriseus*
Winkles	*Littorina* spp.
Woodlice	Oniscidea
Wrasse	Labridae
Zebra mussel	*Dreissena polymorpha*

Appendix H: The Manx List 2005

This list contains the names of all species ever recorded on the Island and has been reproduced with the permission of the Manx Ornithological Society.

Key:

Species listed in bold type are known to have bred on at least one occasion.

Category A: Species that have been recorded on the Isle of Man in an apparently natural state at least once since 1 January 1950.

Category B: Species that would otherwise be in category A but have not been recorded since 31 December 1949.

Category B2: Extinct

Category C: In the Manx List this is sub-divided as follows:

C applies to species that have established breeding populations derived from introduced stock, that maintain themselves on the Isle of Man without necessary recourse to further introduction.

C* applies to species fulfilling the above requirements in Britain, but do not breed on the Isle of Man and have occurred there naturally as visitors.

Category D: Species that would otherwise appear in categories A or B except that there is reasonable doubt that they have ever occurred in a natural state.

Category E: Species that have been recorded as introductions, transportees or escapes from captivity, and whose breeding populations (if any) are thought not to be self-sustaining.

*** after the popular name indicates that a written description is required by the Rarities Sub-committee of the Manx Ornithological Society.**

**** after the popular name indicates that records of the species are considered by the British Birds Rarities Committee (BBRC)**

A written description should be submitted to the Rarities Sub-committee of the Manx Ornithological Society for any species new to the Manx List.

Common English name	Current BOU name	Scientific name	Category
Mute Swan		***Cygnus olor***	AC
Bewick's Swan	Tundra Swan	*Cygnus columbianus*	A
Whooper Swan		*Cygnus cygnus*	A
Bean Goose*		*Anser fabalis*	B
Pink-footed Goose		*Anser brachyrhynchus*	A
White-fronted Goose*	Greater White-fronted Goose	*Anser albifrons*	A
Greylag Goose		***Anser anser***	AC
Canada Goose		***Branta canadensis***	AC
Barnacle Goose		*Branta leucopsis*	A
Brent Goose		*Branta bernicla*	A
Shelduck	**Common Shelduck**	***Tadorna tadorna***	A
Wigeon	Eurasian Wigeon	*Anas penelope*	A
Gadwall*		*Anas strepera*	AC
Teal	**Eurasian Teal**	*Anas crecca*	A

Common English name	Current BOU name	Scientific name	Category
Green-winged Teal**		*Anas carolinensis*	A
Mallard		***Anas platyrhynchos***	AC
Pintail	Northern Pintail	*Anas acuta*	A
Garganey*		*Anas querquedula*	A
Shoveler	**Northern Shoveler**	***Anas clypeata***	A
Red-crested Pochard*		*Netta rufina*	A
Pochard	Common Pochard	*Aythya ferina*	A
Ring-necked Duck*		*Aythya collaris*	A
Ferruginous Duck**		***Aythya nyroca***	A
Tufted Duck		***Aythya fuligula***	A
Scaup*	Greater Scaup	*Aythya marila*	A
Eider	**Common Eider**	***Somateria mollissima***	A
King Eider*		*Somateria spectabilis*	A
Long-tailed Duck		*Clangula hyemalis*	A
Common Scoter	Black Scoter	*Melanitta nigra*	A
Surf Scoter*		*Melanitta perspicillata*	A
Velvet Scoter*		*Melanitta fusca*	A
Goldeneye	Common Goldeneye	*Bucephala clangula*	A
Smew*		*Mergellus albellus*	A
Red-breasted Merganser		***Mergus serrator***	A
Goosander*		*Mergus merganser*	A
Ruddy Duck		***Oxyura jamaicensis***	C*
Red Grouse	**Willow Ptarmigan**	*Lagopus lagopus*	
Red-legged Partridge		***Alectoris rufa***	C
Grey Partridge		***Perdix perdix***	AC
Quail	**Common Quail**	***Coturnix coturnix***	A
Pheasant	**Common Pheasant**	***Phasianus colchicus***	C
Red-throated Diver		*Gavia stellata*	A
Black-throated Diver		*Gavia arctica*	A
Great Northern Diver		*Gavia immer*	A
Little Grebe		***Tachybaptus ruficollis***	A
Great Crested Grebe		*Podiceps cristatus*	A
Red-necked Grebe*		*Podiceps grisegena*	A
Slavonian Grebe*		*Podiceps auritus*	A
Black-necked Grebe*		*Podiceps nigricollis*	A
Fulmar	**Northern Fulmar**	***Fulmarus glacialis***	A
Cory's Shearwater*		*Calonectris diomedea*	A
Great Shearwater*		*Puffinus gravis*	A
Sooty Shearwater*		*Puffinus griseus*	A
Manx Shearwater		*Puffinus puffinus*	A
Balearic Shearwater*		*Puffinus mauretanicus*	A
Little Shearwater**		*Puffinus assimilis*	A
Storm Petrel	European Storm-petrel	*Hydrobates pelagicus*	A
Leach's Petrel*	Leach's Storm-petrel	*Oceanodroma leucorhoa*	A
Gannet	Northern Gannet	*Morus bassanus*	A
Cormorant	**Great Cormorant**	***Phalacrocorax carbo***	A
Shag	**European Shag**	***Phalacrocorax aristotelis***	A
Magnificent Frigatebird**		*Fregata magnificens*	A
Bittern*	**Great Bittern**	***Botaurus stellaris***	A
Little Bittern**		*Ixobrychus minutus*	A
Night Heron*	Black-crowned Night Heron	*Nycticorax nycticorax*	A
Little Egret*		*Egretta garzetta*	A
Great White Egret**	Great Egret	*Ardea alba*	A
Grey Heron		***Ardea cinerea***	A

Common English name	Current BOU name	Scientific name	Category
Purple Heron*		*Ardea purpurea*	A
Spoonbill*	Eurasian Spoonbill	*Platalea leucorodia*	A
Honey Buzzard*	European Honey Buzzard	*Pernis apivorus*	A
Black Kite**		*Milvus migrans*	A
Red Kite*		*Milvus milvus*	AC*
White-tailed Eagle*		*Haliaeetus albicilla*	B
Marsh Harrier*	Eurasian Marsh Harrier	*Circus aeruginosus*	A
Hen Harrier		***Circus cyaneus***	A
Goshawk*	Northern Goshawk	*Accipiter gentilis*	AC*
Sparrowhawk	**Eurasian Sparrowhawk**	***Accipiter nisus***	A
Buzzard*	Common Buzzard	*Buteo buteo*	A
Rough-legged Buzzard*		*Buteo lagopus*	A
Golden Eagle*		*Aquila chrysaetos*	A
Osprey*		*Pandion haliaetus*	A
Kestrel	**Common Kestrel**	***Falco tinnunculus***	A
Red-footed Falcon**		*Falco vespertinus*	A
Merlin		***Falco columbarius***	A
Hobby*	Eurasian Hobby	*Falco subbuteo*	A
Gyr Falcon**		*Falco rusticolus*	B
Peregrine	**Peregrine Falcon**	***Falco peregrinus***	A
Water Rail		***Rallus aquaticus***	A
Spotted Crake*		*Porzana porzana*	B
Baillon's Crake**		*Porzana pusilla*	B
Corncrake*	**Corn Crake**	***Crex crex***	A
Moorhen	**Common Moorhen**	***Gallinula chloropus***	A
Coot	**Common Coot**	***Fulica atra***	A
Crane*	Common Crane	*Grus grus*	A
Oystercatcher	**Eurasian Oystercatcher**	***Haematopus ostralegus***	A
Avocet*	Pied Avocet	*Recurvirostra avosetta*	A
Stone-curlew*		*Burhinus oedicnemus*	A
Little Ringed Plover*	Little Plover	*Charadrius dubius*	A
Ringed Plover		***Charadrius hiaticula***	A
Kentish Plover*		*Charadrius alexandrinus*	A
Dotterel*	Eurasian Dotterel	*Charadrius morinellus*	A
Golden Plover	**European Golden Plover**	***Pluvialis apricaria***	A
Grey Plover		*Pluvialis squatarola*	A
Lapwing	**Northern Lapwing**	***Vanellus vanellus***	A
Knot	Red Knot	*Calidris canutus*	A
Sanderling		*Calidris alba*	A
Little Stint		*Calidris minuta*	A
Temminck's Stint*		*Calidris temminckii*	A
White-rumped Sandpiper**		*Calidris fuscicollis*	A
Pectoral Sandpiper*		*Calidris melanotos*	A
Curlew Sandpiper		*Calidris ferruginea*	A
Purple Sandpiper		*Calidris maritima*	A
Dunlin		*Calidris alpina*	A
Buff-breasted Sandpiper*		*Tryngites subruficollis*	A
Ruff		*Philomachus pugnax*	A
Jack Snipe		*Lymnocryptes minimus*	A
Snipe	**Common Snipe**	***Gallinago gallinago***	A
Great Snipe		*Gallinago media*	B
Long-billed Dowitcher**		*Limnodromus scolopaceus*	A
Woodcock	**Eurasian Woodcock**	***Scolopax rusticola***	A
Black-tailed Godwit		*Limosa limosa*	A

Common English name	Current BOU name	Scientific name	Category
Bar-tailed Godwit		*Limosa lapponica*	A
Whimbrel		*Numenius phaeopus*	A
Curlew	**Eurasian Curlew**	***Numenius arquata***	A
Spotted Redshank*		*Tringa erythropus*	A
Redshank	**Common Redshank**	***Tringa totanus***	A
Greenshank	Common Greenshank	*Tringa nebularia*	A
Lesser Yellowlegs**		*Tringa flavipes*	B
Green Sandpiper*		*Tringa ochropus*	A
Wood Sandpiper*		*Tringa glareola*	A
Common Sandpiper		***Actitis hypoleucos***	A
Turnstone	Ruddy Turnstone	*Arenaria interpres*	A
Wilson's Phalarope**		*Phalaropus tricolor*	A
Red-necked Phalarope*		*Phalaropus lobatus*	A
Grey Phalarope*		*Phalaropus fulicarius*	A
Pomarine Skua*		*Stercorarius pomarinus*	A
Arctic Skua		*Stercorarius parasiticus*	A
Long-tailed Skua*		*Stercorarius longicaudus*	A
Great Skua		*Stercorarius skua*	A
Mediterranean Gull*		*Larus melanocephalus*	A
Little Gull*		*Larus minutus*	A
Sabine's Gull*		*Larus sabini*	A
Black-headed Gull		***Larus ridibundus***	A
Ring-billed Gull*		*Larus delawarensis*	A
Common Gull	**Mew Gull**	***Larus canus***	A
Lesser Black-backed Gull		***Larus fuscus***	A
Yellow-legged Gull		*Larus michahellis*	A
Herring Gull		***Larus argentatus***	A
Iceland Gull*		*Larus glaucoides*	A
Glaucous Gull*		*Larus hyperboreus*	A
Great Black-backed Gull		***Larus marinus***	A
Kittiwake	**Black-legged Kittiwake**	***Rissa tridactyla***	A
Bridled Tern**		*Onychoprion anaethetus*	A
Little Tern		***Sternula albifrons***	A
Black Tern*		*Chlidonias niger*	A
Sandwich Tern		***Sterna sandvicensis***	A
Common Tern		***Sterna hirundo***	A
Roseate Tern*		*Sterna dougallii*	A
Arctic Tern		***Sterna paradisaea***	A
Guillemot	**Common Guillemot**	***Uria aalge***	A
Razorbill		***Alca torda***	A
Great Auk		*Pinguinus impennis*	B2
Black Guillemot		***Cepphus grylle***	A
Little Auk*		*Alle alle*	A
Puffin	**Atlantic Puffin**	***Fratercula arctica***	A
Pallas's Sandgrouse**		*Syrrhaptes paradoxus*	B
Rock Dove	**Rock Pigeon**	***Columba livia***	A
Stock Dove	**Stock Pigeon**	***Columba oenas***	A
Woodpigeon	**Common Wood Pigeon**	***Columba palumbus***	A
Collared Dove	**Eurasian Collared Dove**	***Streptopelia decaocto***	A
Turtle Dove*	European Turtle Dove	*Streptopelia turtur*	A
Mourning Dove**		*Zenaida macroura*	A
Rose-ringed Parakeet		*Psittacula krameri*	C*
Great Spotted Cuckoo**		*Clamator glandarius*	A
Cuckoo	**Common Cuckoo**	***Cuculus canorus***	A

Common English name	Current BOU name	Scientific name	Category
Yellow-billed Cuckoo**		*Coccyzus americanus*	A
Barn Owl		***Tyto alba***	A
Scops Owl**	Eurasian Scops Owl	*Otus scops*	A
Snowy Owl**		*Bubo scandiacus*	B
Little Owl*		*Athene noctua*	C*
Tawny Owl*		*Strix aluco*	A
Long-eared Owl		***Asio otus***	A
Short-eared Owl		***Asio flammeus***	A
Nightjar*	**European Nightjar**	***Caprimulgus europaeus***	A
Swift	**Common Swift**	***Apus apus***	A
Alpine Swift*		*Apus melba*	A
Kingfisher	**Common Kingfisher**	***Alcedo atthis***	A
Bee-eater*	European Bee-eater	*Merops apiaster*	A
Roller**	European Roller	*Coracias garrulus*	A
Hoopoe		*Upupa epops*	A
Wryneck*	Eurasian Wryneck	*Jynx torquilla*	A
Green Woodpecker*		*Picus viridis*	A
Great Spotted Woodpecker*		*Dendrocopos major*	A
Calandra Lark**		*Melanocorypha calandra*	A
Woodlark*	Wood Lark	*Lullula arborea*	A
Skylark	**Sky Lark**	***Alauda arvensis***	A
Shore Lark*	Horned Lark	*Eremophila alpestris*	A
Sand Martin		***Riparia riparia***	A
Swallow	**Barn Swallow**	***Hirundo rustica***	A
House Martin		***Delichon urbicum***	A
Richard's Pipit*		*Anthus novaeseelandiae*	A
Tawny Pipit*		*Anthus campestris*	A
Olive-backed Pipit**		*Anthus hodgsoni*	A
Tree Pipit*		***Anthus trivialis***	A
Pechora Pipit**		*Anthus gustavi*	A
Meadow Pipit		***Anthus pratensis***	A
Rock Pipit		***Anthus petrosus***	A
Water Pipit*		*Anthus spinoletta*	A
Yellow Wagtail*		*Motacilla flava*	A
Grey Wagtail		***Motacilla cinerea***	A
White/Pied Wagtail		***Motacilla alba***	A
Waxwing*	Bohemian Waxwing	*Bombycilla garrulus*	A
Dipper*	**White-throated Dipper**	***Cinclus cinclus***	A
Wren	**Winter Wren**	***Troglodytes troglodytes***	A
Dunnock	**Hedge Accentor**	***Prunella modularis***	A
Robin	**European Robin**	***Erithacus rubecula***	A
Thrush Nightingale**		*Luscinia luscinia*	A
Nightingale*	Common Nightingale	*Luscinia megarhynchos*	A
Bluethroat*		*Luscinia svecica*	A
White-throated Robin**		*Irania gutturalis*	A
Black Redstart		*Phoenicurus ochruros*	A
Redstart	**Common Redstart**	***Phoenicurus phoenicurus***	A
Whinchat		***Saxicola rubetra***	A
Stonechat		***Saxicola torquata***	A
Wheatear	**Northern Wheatear**	***Oenanthe oenanthe***	A
Black-eared Wheatear**		*Oenanthe hispanica*	A
Desert Wheatear**		*Oenanthe deserti*	A
Ring Ouzel		***Turdus torquatus***	A
Blackbird	**Common Blackbird**	***Turdus merula***	A
Fieldfare		*Turdus pilaris*	A

Common English name	Current BOU name	Scientific name	Category
Song Thrush		***Turdus philomelos***	A
Redwing		*Turdus iliacus*	A
Mistle Thrush		***Turdus viscivorus***	A
Grasshopper Warbler	**Common Grasshopper Warbler**	***Locustella naevia***	A
Aquatic Warbler*		*Acrocephalus paludicola*	A
Sedge Warbler		***Acrocephalus schoenobaenus***	A
Marsh Warbler*		*Acrocephalus palustris*	A
Reed Warbler*	**Eurasian Reed Warbler**	***Acrocephalus scirpaceus***	A
Icterine Warbler*		*Hippolais icterina*	A
Melodious Warbler*		*Hippolais polyglotta*	A
Blackcap		***Sylvia atricapilla***	A
Garden Warbler		***Sylvia borin***	A
Barred Warbler*		*Sylvia nisoria*	A
Lesser Whitethroat*		***Sylvia curruca***	A
Whitethroat	**Common Whitethroat**	***Sylvia communis***	A
Subalpine Warbler**		*Sylvia cantillans*	A
Sardinian Warbler**		*Sylvia melanocephala*	A
Greenish Warbler**		*Phylloscopus trochiloides*	A
Pallas's Warbler*	Pallas's Leaf Warbler	*Phylloscopus proregulus*	A
Yellow-browed Warbler*		*Phylloscopus inornatus*	A
Dusky Warbler**		*Phylloscopus fuscatus*	A
Bonelli's Warbler**	Western Bonelli's Warbler	*Phylloscopus bonelli*	A
Wood Warbler*		***Phylloscopus sibilatrix***	A
Chiffchaff	**Common Chiffchaff**	***Phylloscopus collybita***	A
Willow Warbler		***Phylloscopus trochilus***	A
Goldcrest		***Regulus regulus***	A
Firecrest*		*Regulus ignicapilla*	A
Spotted Flycatcher		***Muscicapa striata***	A
Red-breasted Flycatcher*		*Ficedula parva*	A
Pied Flycatcher*		*Ficedula hypoleuca*	A
Bearded Tit*		*Panurus biarmicus*	A
Long-tailed Tit		***Aegithalos caudatus***	A
Blue Tit		***Cyanistes caeruleus***	A
Great Tit		***Parus major***	A
Coal Tit		***Periparus ater***	A
Marsh Tit*		*Parus palustris*	A
Nuthatch*	Wood Nuthatch	*Sitta europaea*	A
Treecreeper	**Eurasian Treecreeper**	***Certhia familiaris***	A
Golden Oriole*	Eurasian Golden Oriole	*Oriolus oriolus*	A
Red-backed Shrike*		*Lanius collurio*	A
Great Grey Shrike*		*Lanius excubitor*	A
Southern Grey Shrike**		*Lanius meridionalis*	A
Woodchat Shrike*		*Lanius senator*	A
Jay*	Eurasian Jay	*Garrulus glandarius*	A
Magpie	**Black-billed Magpie**	***Pica pica***	A
Chough	**Red-billed Chough**	***Pyrrhocorax pyrrhocorax***	A
Jackdaw	**Eurasian Jackdaw**	***Corvus monedula***	A
Rook		***Corvus frugilegus***	A
Carrion Crow		***Corvus corone***	A
Hooded Crow		***Corvus cornix***	A
Raven	**Common Raven**	***Corvus corax***	A
Starling	**Common Starling**	***Sturnus vulgaris***	A
Rose-coloured Starling*	Rosy Starling	*Sturnus roseus*	A
House Sparrow		***Passer domesticus***	A
Tree Sparrow	**Eurasian Tree Sparrow**	***Passer montanus***	A

Common English name	Current BOU name	Scientific name	Category
Chaffinch		***Fringilla coelebs***	A
Brambling		*Fringilla montifringilla*	A
Serin*	European Serin	*Serinus serinus*	A
Greenfinch	**European Greenfinch**	***Carduelis chloris***	A
Goldfinch	**European Goldfinch**	***Carduelis carduelis***	A
Siskin	**Eurasian Siskin**	***Carduelis spinus***	A
Linnet	**Common Linnet**	***Carduelis cannabina***	A
Twite		***Carduelis flavirostris***	A
Redpoll	**Lesser Redpoll**	***Carduelis cabaret***	A
Mealy Redpoll*	Common Redpoll	*Carduelis flammea*	A
Arctic Redpoll**		*Carduelis hornemanni*	A
Crossbill	Common Crossbill	*Loxia curvirostra*	A
Scarlet Rosefinch*	Common Rosefinch	*Carpodacus erythrinus*	A
Bullfinch*	Common Bullfinch	*Pyrrhula pyrrhula*	A
Hawfinch*		*Coccothraustes coccothraustes*	A
Yellow-rumped Warbler**		*Dendroica coronata*	A
Song Sparrow**		*Melospiza melodia*	A
White-throated Sparrow**		*Zonotrichia albicollis*	A
Lapland Bunting*	Lapland Longspur	*Calcarius lapponicus*	A
Snow Bunting		*Plectrophenax nivalis*	A
Yellowhammer		***Emberiza citrinella***	A
Cirl Bunting*		*Emberiza cirlus*	B
Ortolan Bunting*		*Emberiza hortulana*	A
Rustic Bunting**		*Emberiza rustica*	A
Little Bunting*		*Emberiza pusilla*	A
Reed Bunting		***Emberiza schoeniclus***	A
Black-headed Bunting**		*Emberiza melanocephala*	A
Corn Bunting*		***Emberiza calandra***	A
Baltimore Oriole**		*Icterus galbula*	A

Species belonging to Category D

Red-headed Bunting*	*Emberiza bruniceps*

Species belonging to Category E

Great White Pelican	*Pelecanus onocrotalus*
White Stork	*Ciconia ciconia*
Flamingo sp.	*Phoenicopterus ruber/chilensis*
Black Swan	*Cygnus atratus*
Lesser White-fronted Goose	*Anser erythropus*
Bar-headed Goose	*Anser indicus*
Ross's Goose	*Anser rossii*
Snow Goose	*Anser caerulescens*
Red-breasted Goose	*Branta ruficollis*
Egyptian Goose	*Alopochen aegyptiacus*
Mandarin Duck	*Aix galericulata*
Wood Duck	*Aix sponsa*
Rosy-billed Pochard	*Netta peposaca*
Black Grouse	*Tetrao tetrix*
Common Bobwhite	*Colinus virginianus*
Budgerigar	*Melopsittacus undulatus*
Great Horned Owl	*Bubo virginianus*
Red-winged Laughingthrush	***Garrulax formosus***
Hill Myna	*Gracula religiosa*
Long-tailed Rosefinch	*Uragus sibiricus*
Yellow-billed Grosbeak	*Eophona migratoria*

References

Anon. (2002). *The Population Status of Birds in the UK. Birds of conservation concern*. Bird Life International, Cambridge.

Bagworth, T. (1999). *The Calf of Man Bird Observatory Annual Report for 1998*. Manx National Heritage, Douglas.

Bagworth, T. (2000). *The Calf of Man Bird Observatory Annual Report for 1999*. Manx National Heritage, Douglas.

Banks, A.N., Coombes, R.H. and Crick, H.Q.P. (2003). *The Peregrine Breeding Population of the UK and Isle of Man in 2002*. Norfolk.

Bawden, T.A., Garrad, L.S., Qualtrough, J.K. and Scatchard, W.J. (1972). *Industrial Archaeology of the Isle of Man*. David and Charles, Newton Abbot, Devon.

Birkhead, T.R. (1991). *The Magpies. The Ecology and Behaviour of Black-billed and Yellow-billed Magpies*. T. & A.D. Poyser, London.

Bishop, J.P. & Giovannini P.G. (2000) Breeding of the Golden Plover *Pluvialis apricaria* on the Manx Hills. *Peregrine* **8. 1:** 56–57.

Bunn, D.S., Warburton, A.B. and Wilson, R.D.S. (1982). *The Barn Owl*. T. and A.D. Poyser, Calton, Staffordshire.

Camden, W. (1586). *Brittania*. London.

Campbell, L.H., Cleeves, T.R., Lindley, P. and Stenning, J. (1994). *Survey of Moorland Breeding Birds in the Isle of Man – 1990*. RSPB, Sandy, Bedfordshire.

Challoner, J. (1656). *A Short Treatise of the Isle of Man*. London.

Cook, A. (1975). Changes in the Carrion/Hooded Crow hybrid zone and the possible importance of climate. *Bird Study*, **22:** 165–168.

Cowin, W.S. & Megaw, B.R.S. (1943). The Red-legged 'King of the Crows'. *J. Manx Mus.* **5. 69:** 121–122.

Craine, G.D. and Moore, A.S. (1997). Manx Bird Report for 1994. *Peregrine* **7.4:** 296–356.

Cramp, S. and Perrins, C.M. (eds) (1977–1994). *Handbook of the Birds of Europe, the Middle East and North Africa, Birds of the Western Palearctic*, vols I–IX. Oxford University Press, Oxford.

Crick, H.Q.P. and Ratcliffe, D.A. (1995). The Peregrine Falcon, *Falco peregrinus*, breeding population in the United Kingdom in 1991. *Bird Study*, **42:** 1–19.

Crick, H.Q.P., Bailie, S.R., Balmer, D.E., Bashford, R.I., Beavan, L.P., Dudley, C., Glue, D.E., Gregory, J.H., Marchant, J.H., Peach, W.J. and Wilson, A.M. (1998). *Breeding Birds in the Wider Countryside: their conservation status* (1972–1996). Research Report 198, BTO, Thetford, Norfolk.

Cullen, J.P. (1980). A Review of the Status of Terns in the Isle of Man. *Peregrine*. **5.2:** 68–73.

Cullen, J.P. (1985). The first Manx nest for Red-breasted Merganser. *Peregrine* **6.1:** 35.

Cullen, J.P. (2002). Manx Bird Report for 1999. *Peregrine* **8.2:** 129–154.

Cullen, J.P. (2004). Manx Bird Report for 2002 and 2003. *Peregrine* **8.4:** 254–338.

Cullen, J.P. and Weaver, P. (2003). Manx Bird Report for 2000 and 2001. *Peregrine* **8.3:** 165–226.

Cullen, J.P. and Jennings, P.P. (1986). *Birds of the Isle of Man*. Bridgeen Publications, Douglas, Isle of Man.

Feare, C.J. (1994). Changes in the numbers of common Starling and farming practice in Lincolnshire. *British Birds*, **87:** 200–204.

Foulkes-Roberts, P.R. (1949). Late Breeding of Barn Owls. *Peregrine* **1. 6:** 16.

Garrad, L.S. (1972). Bird remains, including those of a Great Auk, *Alca impennis*, from a midden deposit in a cave at Perwick Bay, Isle of Man. *Ibis*, **2:** 258–259.

Garrad, L.S. (1972). *The Naturalist in The Isle of Man*. David & Charles, Newton Abbot.

Gibbons, D.W., Reid, J.B. and Chapman, R.A. (1993). *The New Atlas of Breeding Birds in Britain and Ireland 1988–1991*. T. and A.D. Poyser, London.

Griffiths, J. and Lamb, J. (1995). The effects of afforestation on water-courses. *Manx Hill-Land Report.*

Hagemeijer, W.J.M. and Blair, M.J. (1997). *The EBCC Atlas of European Breeding Birds*. T. and A.D. Poyser, London.

Hamer K.C., Phillips, R.A., Hill, J.K., Wanless, S. and Wood, A.G. (2001). Contrasting foraging strategies of Gannets, *Morus bassanus*, at two North Atlantic colonies. Marine Ecology Progress Series, **224:** 283–290.

Haycock, R.J. (1975). *Prey taken by Short-eared Owls on the Calf of Man*. In: *The Calf of Man Bird Observatory Annual Report for 1974*. Pp. 68–79. Manx Museum and National Trust, Douglas.

Holloway, S. (1996). *The Historical Atlas of Breeding Birds in Britain and Ireland: 1875–1900*. T. and A.D. Poyser, London.

Hopson, A.J. and Moore, A.S. (1991). Manx Bird Report for 1990. *Peregrine* **7.1**: 3–39.

Hudson, R. (1965). The spread of the Collared Dove in Britain and Ireland. *British Birds*, **58**: 105–139.

Hudson, R. (1972). Collared Doves in Britain and Ireland during 1965–70. *British Birds* **65**: 139–155.

Jardine, Sir W. (1838–43). *Birds of Great Britain and Ireland*.

Johnstone, I.G., Thorpe, R.I., Moore, A.S. and Finney, S.K. (2006). The Breeding Status of Choughs, *Pyrrhocorax pyrrhocorax*, in the UK and Isle of Man in 2002. Bird Study, In press.

Kermode, P.M.C. (1888). List of birds of the Isle of Man. *Transactions of the Isle of Man Natural History and Antiquarian Society*, **1**: 15–23.

Kermode, P.M.C. (1901) *List of Birds of the Isle of Man with notes*. Brown and Sons, Douglas.

Lack, P.C. (1986). *The Atlas of Wintering Birds in Britain and Ireland*. T. and A.D. Poyser, Calton, Staffordshire.

Ladds, E.F. (1948). The first nesting of the Black-headed Gull. *Peregrine*, **1.5**: 22–23.

Lloyd, C.S., Tasker, M.L. and Partridge, K. (1991). *The Status of Seabirds in Britain and Ireland*. T. and A.D. Poyser, Calton, Staffordshire.

Madoc, H.W. (1934). *Bird-life in the Isle of Man*. H.F. and G. Witherby, London.

McCanch, N.V. (1997). Sparrowhawk, *Accipiter nisus*, passage through the Calf of Man 1959–1993. *Ringing and Migration*, **18**: 1–13.

McCanch, N.V. (1999). *Ornithological studies from the Calf of Man*. Unpublished thesis, University of Liverpool, Port Erin, Isle of Man.

McIntyre *et al.* (1978). Nesting of the Hen Harrier on the Isle of Man. *Peregrine*, **4.6**: 283–284.

Mead, C. (2000). *The State of the Nation's Birds*. Whittet Books, Stowmarket, Suffolk.

Mitchell, P.I., Newton, S.F., Ratcliffe, N. and Dunn, T.E. (2004). *Seabird Populations of Britain and Ireland*. T. and A.D. Poyser, London.

Moore, A.S. (1987). The number and distribution of seabirds breeding on the Isle of Man during 1985–86. *Peregrine*, **6.2**: 64–80.

Moore, A. S. 1987. Use of nests of other birds by Fulmars in 1985–6. *Peregrine* **6. 2**: 80.

Moore, A.S. and Thorpe, J.P. (1990). Records of the Fieldfare, *Turdus pilaris*, in Glen Rushen during 1989. *Peregrine*, **6.4**: 50–51.

Nelson, B. (1978). *The Gannet*. T. & A.D. Poyser, Berkhamsted.

Nelson, J.B. (1978). *The Sulidae: Gannets and Boobies*. Oxford University Press.

Nelson, J.B. (2002). *The Atlantic Gannet*. Fenix Books, Norfolk

Ogilvie, M.A. (1975). *Ducks of Britain and Europe*. T. and A.D. Poyser, Berkhamsted, Hertfordshire.

Ogilvie M. *et al.* (2004). Rare breeding birds in the United Kingdom in 2002. *British Birds*, **97**: 492–536.

Parslow, J.L.F. (1973). *Breeding Birds of Britain and Ireland*. Berkhamsted: T. and A.D. Poyser

Pooley, E.J. (1997). Non avian vertebrates and the implications of habitat change. *Proceedings of the Manx hill land seminar*: 39–49. Manx Nature Conservation Trust.

Prater, A.J. (1989). Ringed Plover, *Charadrius hiaticula*, breeding population of the United Kingdom in 1984. *Bird Study*, **36**: 154–159.

Ralfe, P.G. (1905). *The Birds of the Isle of Man*. D. Douglas, Edinburgh.

Ralfe, P.G. (1923). *Supplementary Notes to the Birds of the Isle of Man*. D. Douglas, Edinburgh.

Roberts, D.H. (2004). *The sea level of the northern Irish Sea basin and the Isle of Man*. 'The Severance' seminar, Douglas.

Robertson, D. (1794). *A Tour through the Isle of Man*. London.

Sage, B.L. and Whittington, P.A. (1985). The 1980 sample survey of rookeries. *Bird Study*, **32**: 77–81.

Sharrock, J.T.R. (1976). *The Atlas of Breeding Birds in Britain and Ireland*. T. and A.D. Poyser, Berkhamsted, Hertfordshire.

Sim, I.M.W., Gibbons, D.W., Bainbridge, I.P. and Mattingley, W.A. (2001). Status of the Hen Harrier, *Circus cyaneus*, in the UK and the Isle of Man in 1998. *Bird Study*, **48**: 341–353.

Slinn, D.J. (1971). The numbers of seabirds breeding in the Isle of Man during 1969–70. *Proceedings of the Isle of Man Natural History and Antiquarian Society*, **7**: 419–439.

Stenning, E.H. (1958). *Portrait of the Isle of Man*. Robert Hale, London.

Thorpe, J.P. & Sharpe, C.M. (2004). Occurrence of Red-winged Laughingthrushes *Garrulax formosus* on the Isle of Man. *Peregrine* **8.4**: 348–351

Thrower, L.B. (2002). *Manx Agriculture 1945–2000*. Research Report 10. Centre for Manx Studies, Douglas, Isle of Man.

Townley, (1791). *A Journal kept in the Isle of Man*. Whitehaven, Cumbria.

Vinicombe, K.E. (1982). Breeding and population fluctuations of the Little Grebe. *British Birds* **75**: 204–218

Walsh, P.M., Halley, D.J., Harris, M.P., del Nevo, A., Sim, I.M.W. and Tasker, M.L. (1995). *Seabird Monitoring Handbook for Britain and Ireland*. JNCC, Peterborough, Cambridgeshire.

Wernham, C.V., Toms, M.P., Marchant, J.H., Clark, J.A., Sirwardena, G.M. and Baillie, S.R. (2002). *The Migration Atlas, movements of the birds of Britain and Ireland*. T. and A.D. Poyser, London.

Williams, G. (1989). *Land Use and Birds in the Isle of Man*. Research Report, RSPB, Sandy, Bedfordshire.

Wilson, T. (1722). *History of the Isle of Man*. In: Camden, W. (ed.), *Brittania*, 2nd edn. London.

Williamson, K. (1940). Numbers of Black Redstarts on passage in Man. *British Birds*, **33**: 252–254.

Williamson, K. (1940). The Puffins of the Calf Isle. *Journal of the Manx Museum*, 4: 203–205.

Williamson, K. (1975). Birds and climatic change. *Bird Study*, **22**: 143–164.

Acknowledgements

Since the charity was first formed it has enjoyed a high level of support from members of the public, from companies and businesses both on and off the Island, a range of charitable organisations and our Island's Government. The way in which that support has been reflected has been varied but falls into three main categories: funding and technical support, access to land and public participation.

To help fund our research the charity offered a 'sponsor a species' option at both corporate and individual level, with both options attracting considerable support. Many other companies or individuals chose to donate cash rather than enter into formal sponsorship. Further funding was obtained from a wide range of charitable trusts, including major contributions from the Esmee Fairbairn Foundation and the Gough Ritchie Charitable Trust. The Island's Government also played a major role in facilitating our work, providing some funding to help the research to get started and further funds related to specific areas of research in which it had a particular interest. The mapping system, without which the charity would have been unable to present its results so clearly, was granted under licence by Government, while associated software and licences were donated by ESRI (UK) Ltd and Ordnance Survey. In addition to the names of major funding bodies being reflected in the following list, their corporate logos are shown on the back cover. The names of corporate and individual sponsors are also shown on the pages which discuss the species they sponsored.

In order to survey effectively every part of the Island it was necessary to obtain permission from many landowners, primarily those from within the farming community. During the first year of our work a significant amount of time was spent calling at farms, explaining our research, seeking permission to go on the land and mapping the extent of ownership. It is to the lasting credit of the Island's farming community that only fourteen farmers declined to give permission. Many were content to allow access to the land whenever necessary, while others asked that we contact them the night before a planned visit. While the process of seeking permission was time-consuming the benefits were immeasurable.

As our research progressed, an increasing number of people started to submit details of their sightings to our office. This not only added information on the general distribution and breeding status of many species, but also provided valuable sighting information on some of the Island's less common species. All records from the public were also made available to the Manx Ornithological Society, which produces an annual bird report, in the journal '*Peregrine*'.

Managing the information flow of the increasing volume of records, including those from the public, became a time-consuming but vital task. At the start of the process we were particularly fortunate to secure the voluntary services of Andrew Laidlaw, whose working background was in information technology and who has an interest in birds. Countless hours were spent discussing the methods of survey, how the data would be recorded, how they were to be used and presented and in what format they would best be entered onto computer. This proved to be time well spent, Andrew devising a very workable database that not only met our immediate needs but proved to be capable of amendment and upgrading to suit growing demands and the need for more complex analysis. Many of the changes and improvements that were made as time went by were undertaken by Jason Bishop, one of the three staff who were with the charity from the outset. Jason's aptitude for all things 'IT' and his deep knowledge of birds and of our research were as vital to the process as Andrew's initial work, and the charity would have been lost without either of them.

The final piece in the jigsaw that ensured that the charity fulfilled its aims relates to staff. Thanks are due, in particular, to Jason Bishop and Peter Giovannini, who were with the charity from start to finish, and to Aron Sapsford, without whose enthusiasm and birding expertise the project would not have commenced. Thanks to Paul Collins and Simon Davies, who worked for the charity in the summer of 2002, helping to achieve two seasons' fieldwork in one summer, in order to catch up with a lost season in 2001.

Text and artwork

Staff and Directors of the charity largely wrote the introductory chapters and appendices, with the section on climate written by Brian Rae of the Island's Meteorological Office. Chris Sharpe and Peter Weaver compiled the fact boxes that are included within each species account. Pat Cullen (JPC), Chris Sharpe (CMS), John Thorpe (JPT) and Peter Weaver (PW) wrote the species accounts, as detailed below:

Anseriformes – PW
Galliformes – JPC
Gaviiformes – CMS
Podicipediformes – CMS
Procellariiformes – CMS
Pelecaniformes – CMS
Ciconiiformes – JPC
Accipitriformes – CMS
Falconiformes – CMS
Gruiformes – JPC
Charadriformes
  Waders – PW
  Gulls – CMS
  Terns – CMS
  Auks – CMS
Columbiformes – JPC
Cuculiformes – JPC
Strigiformes – JPC
Apodiformes – JPC
Coraciiformes – JPC
Piciformes – JPC
Passeriformes – Corvidae – JPC
Passeriformes – except Corvidae – JPT and CMS

Thanks are due to local artist Ms. Jenny Kissack who designed the Manx Bird Atlas logo.

The front and back cover artwork, together with the frontispiece were donated by Dr. Jeremy Paul, renowned local wildlife artist. The line drawings in the species accounts were commissioned by the charity, the majority being provided by Alan Harris, illustrator of many field and identification guides. Remaining artists were, wherever possible, invited to illustrate species in which they had a particular interest. All line drawings were approved by a working group prior to inclusion in the Atlas.

Thanks are due to Ted Abraham, Jo Hetherington, Dr. Terry Holt, Nick Johnson, Steve Taggart and Peter Weaver for comments on earlier drafts of text.

While we hope that the following list is all-inclusive, we do recognise that we may have inadvertently omitted the names of a few. To those not included in the list we offer our apologies and invite them to let us know of our error, in order that this may be corrected in any future edition.

A J Millichap Ltd
A S Butler Charitable Trust
Abraham T
Acheson T
The late C H Adams
Adams K
Adamson D
Adlard J
Ainley J & C
Allan L M
Allan R T P
Allanson P & S
Allison D
Allison T
Allsebrook D & H
Allton A H
Almond R J
Anders P
Anderson D
Anderson M
The late R J G Anderson
Andrews F B
Ansfield T
Appleby C M
Armitage J S
Arthurs K
Ashcroft A J
Ashmole M
Ashton J
Ashton J
Ashworth J M
Ashworth R W
Ashworth S
Aspinall B
Astill A D
Astill N
Atherton V
Atkins P F
Atkins V S
Atkinson J M
Atkinson T N

Bagworth T
Baker T
Ball J
Ballard J
Ballavoddan Estate
Bank of Bermuda
Bannan R
Bannister M
Banyard R
Barclays Bank plc
Barfoot R M
Barker E T
Barker I
Barker L
Barnaby Mrs
Barnett A
Barrass J
Barrett Mr
Barrett M K
Barron L
Barry P
Bashford R,
The late B Bass
Batchelor G
Bate R
Bates R
Bayley J
Beaman J H
Beavers Mr
Beckett J
Bedey I
Bee S
Begbie S J
Beggs R
Bell A K
Bell A
Bell D
Bell J E
Bell N
Bell P M
Bell S
Bellamy D
Bellando S
Bell-scott M
Bellwood J
Bennett B
Bennett F
Bennett M J & J H
Bennett Roy & Co
Bennett W L
Beresford S
Bernard B
Berringham D
Berrington T
Berry A
Berry C C
Berry I
Best M
Bethune H
Bibby H H
Biggins A
Bignall E
Billown Lime Quarries
Birchenough C
Bird D P
Birding World
Birdwatching Magazine
Birtles D
Bishop A & B
Bishop J
Black W
Blackwell D & G
Blease J
Blevin E
Bloxsidge R
Bolton A J
Bolton A M
Bolton L
Bolton R
Bolton S
Bolton S
Bonbernard A L A
Booth G
Bottell S
Bottomley E
Bourdiec R
Bourne M
Bowen J M
Boyce A N
Boyd Brothers
Boyd J
Boyd S
Boyden G F
Brackpool P
Bradford D
Bradford P
Bradley S
Brady-Glover C
Brain A
Bramall C
Bray P
Bregazzi J
Brennan J
Brew A
Brew A
Brew B
Brew C
Brew D
Brew L M
Brew M
Brew M
Brew W D
Bridges D
Bridson G H
Bridson J
Bridson W E
Brierley M
Briggs H
British Birds
British Nuclear Group
British Ornithologist's Union
British Trust for Ornithology
Brockbank R S
Bromley J P
Brooks J
Brooks-Burdall
Brown B
Brown B
Brown C
Brown D
Brown D
Brown G
Brown I W

Brown L
Brown M J
Brown M
Brown P
Brown S
Brownsdon D J
Brownsdon M M
Bruce S
Brumby F
Brunswick R
Bryan C
Buckler M
Budd C
Bull M J
Bully B
Bunton D
Burgoyne W
Burn D
Burn J A
Burroughs Stewart
Bushill G
Butt D
Buttery J
Button K
Byrne D

Cain A
Cain B
Cain D
Cain H M & W J
Cain J
Cain L
Cain M
Cain M
Cain S
Cain T W & F C
Cain W E
Caine D
Caine J D
Caine J
Caine L
Caine M
Caine P N
Cain's Advocates
Caithness J
Calbreck Mrs
Caley B
Caley B
Caley C
Caley D E
Caley J
Caley P
Caley T P
Caley W P
Calland P
Callin V
Callister A
Callister D
Callister E
Callister E
Callister J
Callister J
Callister K
Callister M
Callister P
Callister W L
Callow B
Callow B
Callow E
Callow F
Callow J P
Callow J Q
Callow J
Callow J
Callow L
Callow R E
The late S Callow
Calvert M
Campbell A
Canada Life International Limited
Canipa P
Cannan D M
Cannan J R
Cannan P
Cannell J C
Cannell J C
Cannell J
Cannell J
Cannell M J
Cannell P
Cannell T
Cannell W J
The late W Carine
Carling H
Carmichael S
Carnham P
Carroll S
Cartmell B
Casey J M
Cashen T
Cassels F K
Castle A
Celtic Bank Ltd
Centre for Manx Studies
Chadwick M
Chadwick R
Chalmers S
Chamberlin P E
Chandler P
Charles R
Charnley B M
Charter H
Charter L
Christian D F
The late F Christian
Christian N
Christian P
Christian T Q
Christian W & L
Christian W
Chrystal Bros. Stott & Kerruish
Chrystal E
Church P
Chynoweth G
Clackson J
The Clague Family
Clague A
Clague D
Clague E J
Clague J
Clague J
Clague J
Clague M A
Clague M
Clague S
Clague S
Clark F D
Clark G
Clark M
Clarke C
Clarke E
Clarke J
Clayton R
The Cleator Family
Cleator B K
Cleator D F
Cleator R
Cleator S
Clegg H
Clelland W
Clucas C
The late E Clucas
Clucas L
Clucas S D
Cocker K P
Cocker R
Cojeen J L
Cole A & T
Coles D
Colland P
Collings A
Collins P
Collins R & H
Collis Mrs
Collister C
Collister D
Collister E
Collister E
Collister H
The late M A Collister
Collister R
Colquitt D L
Coltin A
Comish A
Comish B
Comish R G
Conn A & R
Constable Mrs
Conway G & J
Cooil A
Cooil R G
Cooil R
Cook D
Cook J
Cook K
Cook S
Cook V
Coole D B
Coole K
Coole M A
Cooper Mr & Mrs
Cooper A M
Cooper E
Cooper G
Cooper P J & J I
Cope R
Corkhill C
Corkhill S
Corkhill T E
Corkill A
Corkill E & J
Corkill J R S
Corkill M
Corkill S
Corkill S
Corkish G
Corkish H
Corkish J W
Corkish J
Corkish R
The late Mr Corlett
Corlett A
Corlett A
Corlett Bolton & Co
Corlett Building Materials Ltd
Corlett E Q
Corlett J C
Corlett J H
Corlett J K
Corlett J
Corlett J
Corlett J
Corlett J
Corlett L A R
Corlett M
Corlett N
Corlett P A
Corlett R A
Corlett S
Corlett S
Corlett S
Corlett S
Corlett S
Corlett S
Corlett W J H
Cormode C
Cormode J W
Cormode R
Corrin A
Corrin E J
Corrin J & J W
Corrin J
Corrin T M
Corris A I
Corteen J
Cory G F
Cory M
Cory P
Costain C
Costain H
Costain H
Costain J E
Costain P E
Costain W
Costello J
Couper D C
Cousins B A
Cousins J A
Cowbourne M
Cowdell M
Cowell H C
Cowell L
Cowell L
Cowell T & W
Cowell W F
Cowin B
Cowin E
Cowin E
Cowin E
Cowin F
Cowin F
Cowin G
Cowin G
Cowin J M
Cowin J
Cowin M
Cowin N
Cowin R
Cowin T
Cowley D
Cowley D
Cowley D
Cowley G
Cowley J H S
The late K Cowley
Cowley M
Cowley P
Cox J S
Cox N
Craggs G
Craine D
Craine G C
Craine G D
Craine M
Craine M
Craine R E
Crane C A
Crawford D
Crawley B
Creer C
Creer D C
Creer D
Creer E
Creer W H
Cregeen R
Crellin B & H
Crellin G F
Crellin I & G
Crellin J C
Crellin J
Crellin J
Crellin J
Crellin M S
Crellin M
Crellin R & H
The late R Crellin
Crellin S
Crellin T
Cretney D
Cretney J
Crichton-Stuart H
Cringle C
Cringle J
Cringle M

Cringle M
Cringle N
The late R H Cringle
Cripps R
Croger R
Croll A L & J H
Cromack D
Crome C
Crookall A B
Crosland C & M
Cross Mrs
Crowe F
Crowe G
Crowe P
Crye Mr
Cubberley P
Cubbon G
Cubbon R M
Cubbon S
Cullen J P
Cullen R
Cummins D
Cunningham G L & V
Curphey B
Curphey J
Curphy J
Curphy M E
Currie S
Curry Mr

Dale M J
Dale P W
Dale V
Daley J
Daniels Dr
Daniels G
Daniels J
Darville A
Davenport G L
Davey J
Davey P
Davidson M
Davies A
Davies I
Davies M
Davies P D
Davies S
Davis J C
Davison M
Davy R
Dawson D W
Day J
Deakin B
Dean P E
DeHaven S
DeHeerdt J
Dell-borg R G
Denard A
Denard B
Denham B
Denning R & M
Dentith D
Department of Agriculture Fisheries & Forestry
Department of Local Government & the Environment
Department of Transport
Department of Tourism & Leisure
Devitt E
Dewhirst E
Diamond Mrs
Dickinson Cruikshank & Co
Dickinson L
Dilworth C
Divers J
Dixon A
Dixon C
Dixon J
Dixon R
Dobrzynski C A R
Dobson Mrs
Docking B H
Dod J
Donnelly N J
Donnithorne N J
Douglas Gas
Downey Mrs
Doyle D
The D'Oyly Carte Charitable Trust
Draper T
Drewry K J
Drinkwater-Buckingham N
Dudley S
Duggan B
Duggan C D
Duggan D
Duke R
Duke S
Dunworth J
Durrant W A
Dyer J

Eales M
Eames C
Easson J
Eaton C
Eaton E M
Edge E & P
Edge M
Edgerton K
Edwards & Hartley
Edwards D J
Edwards M B
Edwards S
Elderfield M
Ellis Brown Partnership
Ellis M & M
Ellis S
Ellison J
Elliston H
Ellis-Watson L
EMAP Active Ltd
English Nature
Enterprise PLC
The Environment Partnership
Environmental Services Limited
Ernst & Young
Errington E K
Esmee Fairbairn Foundation
ESRI (UK) Ltd
Etherton P & K
Evans D J
Evans F
Evans F
Everest S

FaberMaunsell Ltd
Facchino Mr
Fagan M
Fairhurst J
Fallaize L
Faragher B D
Faragher C H
Faragher C
Faragher E
Faragher J A
Faragher J B
Faragher J
Faragher J
Faragher K C
Faragher P A
Faragher R
Faragher W L
Fargher J C
Fargher J R
Farlington Ringing Group
Farrant P
Fathers P
Faulds I C & C
Fayle J
Ferrer W
Field P
Finlay D
Firth D
The Fitzpatrick Family
Flashback Photos
Fletcher P A
Flynn H
Flynn T
Forbes Mr
Formby R
Foster C J
Foster E
Foster S
Fowler M
Fraser B
Fraser-Casey M
Friends of the Glens
Frost B
Fryer J
Fryer R & R

Gail S
Galbraith C
Gale D
Galloway E
Gantlett S
Gardiner G
The late L Garrad
Garratt A
Garratt J H
Garratt W S
Garrett A D
Garrett A M
Garrett A
Garrett D
Garrett K
Gartside D
Gaudet K
Gawler W G
Gawne J
Gawne K J
Gawne S
Gelder I
The late P Gelling
Gelling R H
Gelling S
Gelling V S
Gellion P
Gibbons Mr
Gibbons D W
Gibbons T
Gilbey W A
Giles P
The late Mr Gill
The late P Gillman
Giovannini P
Gittings Mr & Mrs
Glassey N
Gleave D L
Gleave E
Gledhill C
Glynn-Riley P D
Goddard A D
Goddard D & Y
Godfrey M
Goff R
The late E Goldie
Goldie R
Goodall A
Goodway P
Goodwin D M
Goodwin S
Gore V
Gorry M
Gosling F
Gotrel B
Grady G
Graham M
Graham W
Graham-George S
Grainger R
Gray E
Green L
Green P
Green R
Green R
Greenhalgh A S
Greggor A
Gregson S
Griffin B
Griffin D
The late H Grundey
Guard C
Gurney K S
Guthrie J L
Guy B

Habib European Bank Ltd
Hadfield C
Hadfield P
Hadrill P, Peter
Hadwin M
Haley E
Haley J
Hall A
Hall D
Hall J
Hall J
Hall J
Halliday M
Halsall D
Halsall L W
Hamilton M
Hammond W
Hampson B & J
Hampton G
Hampton S C
Hand H
Hankinson I W
Hannan M & H
Hanson H D N
Hardman S
Hargreaves K
Hargreaves P
Hargreaves R
Harker H
Harkin D A
Harland I W
Harper J
Harper R
Harris A
Harris D A
Harris D
Harris G
Harris R
Harris-Mayes Mr
Harrison A J
The late G K Harrison
Harrison J D
Harrison P V
Harrison S
Hartley J W
Hartley M
Harvey J A
Harvey N A
Harvey R E
Harvey S
The late T A Harvey
Hassan C
Hastings B & M
Hatton J
Hawkes M
Hawkins K
Haycock B
Hazzle M Q
Healy G
Hedges J C
Heginbotham E

The Helks Family
Helm D
Helps J
Hempsall E
Henderson B
Henthorn Mrs
Heron & Brearley
The Hetherington Family
Hewitt A
Hezlett H
Higgins C
Higgs Mrs
Hill S
Hilton Hotel & Casino Ltd
Hinchliffe J
Hindley L
Hine W
Hinton B
Hirst R
Hodgett H E
Hodgett J
Hodgson F
Hodson Mrs
Hodson F
Hogarth M
Hoggett F
Holden E
Holden S
Hollick M
Holmes B E
Holt R S
Holt T J
Hopkins R J
Hopps C
Hopps J
Hopson B
Horbury C
Horsthuis P & S
Horton C
Hotchkiss P
Howard J V
The late J Howard
Howard M
Howarth E
Howe S
Howell M
Howland C L
Howland M
Hughes B
Hughes B
Hughes D
Hughes D
Hughes I
Hull N
Hulme P J
Hultgren M
Hultgren U
Hume R
Humphreys L
Hunt G
Hunt J
Hunt P
Hunter D
Huntley G & R

Hurst E
Hurst W
Huxham G L
Huxham R
Huyton E
Hyslop D

Ibanez J
Ibanez M
Ingles C W
Inskip R
IOM Assurance
IOM Steam Packet Co Ltd
Ireton J
Irving B
Irwin M
Island Aggregates Ltd
Isle of Man Bank
Isle of Man Bank (Leasing Ltd)
Isle of Man International Broadcasting Company PLC
Isle of Man Lottery Trust
Isle of Man Milk Marketing Association
Isle of Man Newspapers

J & H Marsh & McLennan (IOM) Ltd
Jackson B
Jackson J
Jackson J
Jackson M C
Jackson M J
Jackson P
Jacques C
James C
James J
James J
James R
Jameson Mr
Jeavons R A
Jelfs C
Jenison P
Jenkins Mrs
Jensen L
Jerry C
Jessop A
Johnson B & V M
Johnson C
The Johnson Family
Johnson H
Johnson K
Johnson M
Johnston T D
Johnstone I
Joint Nature Conservation Committee
Jones Ms
Jones A
Jones A
Jones B
Jones B
Jones B
Jones D

Jones G
Jones H
Jones J
Jones M
The late P Jones
Jones P F
Jordan E J

Kaighin J
Kane D
The late B Karran
Kay G P
Kay H
Kaye A
Kaye R
Kearney N C
Kearsley A
Keates C
Keeling J
Keggin D
Keggin J
Keig N & L
Keig N
Kelly A
Kelly B
Kelly C
Kelly C
Kelly D & P
Kelly E M
Kelly I Q & J
Kelly J H
Kelly J M
Kelly J S
Kelly J
Kelly L
Kelly M
Kelly P E
Kelly R
Kelly S
Kelly W D
Kelly W J C
Kennan A J
Kennan J D
Kennaugh Mr
Kennaugh A
Kennaugh Bros.
Kennaugh H T
Kennaugh J
Kennaugh J
Kennaugh J
Kennaugh L
Kennaugh M
Kennaugh R
Kennish J
Kennish S
Kermeen D
Kermeen T P
Kermeen W H
Kermeen W L
Kermeen W
Kermode C
Kermode E L
Kermode J
Kermode L A
Kermode P & C

Kerr O E
Kerruish E W & S
Kerruish K
Kerruish R
The late Sir C Kerruish
Kershaw P
Kewley Mr
Kewley A
Kewley J D R
Kewley J
Kewley J
Kewley M
Kewley V
Killey E
Killey M
Killey P
Killey R
Killey W M
Killip H
The late W J Killip
Kinley M K
Kinnish I J
Kinrade B
Kinrade D
Kinrade F A
Kinrade K P
Kinrade N
The late P H Kinrade
Kinrade P
Kinrade R
Kinrade T
Kinvig B
Kinvig D
Kinvig G W
Kirkpatrick S
Kirkpatrick W M
Kissack A
Kissack J
Kneale B
Kneale E
Kneale E
Kneale G C
Kneale J L
Kneale J
Kneale L
Kneale M
Kneale P
Kneale R
Kneale S M
Kneale T M
Kneale W C
The late D Kneen
Kneen J & M
Kneen J W
The late Mr Kneen
The late P Kneen
Kneen P
Kneen S
Kneen T
Knight G

Labao C
Lace D Q
Lace J J

Lace J
The late E F Ladds
Laidlaw A C C
Laidlaw A
Lamb G E
Lamden M
Lancaster D
Lancaster G
Lane S
Lang A
Langford-Smith P
Lardner-Burke R
Larkin V
Larrosa J
Larsen H K
Lathbury Mrs
Law Mr
Lawton W
Leach B
Leach C & B
Leary R
Lee A
Lee D
Leece Brothers
Leece E
Leece J
Leesley D
Legat M
Leith C
Lever J
Lewin M
Lewin P W
Liddle T
Lillie S
Lishman C
Lister J A
Little D
Liverpool University Press
Livesey C M
Livingston R
Llewelyn J
Lloyd A
Lloyd B
Lloyd B
Lloyd-Davies P D
Loader H W
Lockington-Marshall W
Lockwood Mrs
Lockwood P
Long N
Long P N
Longside F
Longwith E
Longworth D
Longworth P
Looney A R
Looney A
Lorne House Trust Ltd
Lowe A
Lowery M T
Lowey B
Lowey F
Lucas M
Luck M

Lumsden A
Lynch D
Lynch J

Air Marshal & Mrs I D Macfadyen
MacKay A
MacKay M
Macleod A
MacLeod R
MacMillan Mrs
MacMillan W
The late J R A Macmullen
Madayr T
Maddrell B
Maddrell I
Maddrell J
Magee A
Maggs E
Maggs G J & M
Maginn J
Maitland Trust Company
Makin H
Malam B
Malcolm M J
Maley C K
Mann 2000
Mann E A
Mannin Media Group
Mansell A
Manx Airlines Project 2000
Manx American Marketing
Manx Chough Project
Manx Electricity Authority
Manx Game Preservation Society
Manx Heritage Foundation
Manx National Farmers Union
Manx National Heritage
Manx Ornithological Society
Manx Petroleums Ltd
Manx Radio
Manx Society for the Prevention of Cruelty to Animals
Manx Teletext
Manx Television
Manx Wildlife Trust
Mapes M
Marsden D
The late C M Marshall
Marshall R
Marsland A M
Marston T K
Martin A G
Martin A
Martin B
Martin C T
Martin J W
Martin J
Martin J
Masheter M
Mason Mr
The late D Mason
Mason N
Mason P & H
Masser A
Masson J
Masters M
MATCO Food Services Ltd
Mather J
Mathieson N
Matthews D
Matthews D
Matthews J
Matthews M E
Mawson D E
Maynard K
McCallum C
McCanch N
McCartney J
McCracken W T
McCubbin A M
McDonald A J
McDonald C
McFarlane G
McGaw J E
McGilligan Mrs
McGowan M
McIntosh A
McKeown C
McLean D
McLean J S
McManus C
McTaggart D
Mealin A
Mealin B
Media Sales Management (Anglia) Ltd
Meechan A D
Mellon W R
The Mercers' Company
Messenger J
Micklefield N A
Mickley G
Middleton J R
Millard I J
Miller J
Miller M
Millichap A
Millichap M
Mitchell C
Mitchell D
Mitchell I
Mitchell N
Mitchell R
Mitchell Trust
Moffat T
The Moffett Family
Moffitt J W
Molesworth M
Monro J
Montgomerie F
Moore A G
Moore A S
Moore B
Moore C M
Moore D
Moore D
Moore F B
Moore G A
Moore J D
Moore J F
Moore J H B
Moore J H
Moore J K
Moore J S
Moore J W
Moore J W
Moore J
Moore J
Moore P
Moore Stephens
Moore W A
Moreton I
Morgan G
Morland P
Morrey L
Morrey N
Morrey S M
Morris A
Morris D
Morris I
Morris J K
Morrison D
The Moss Family
Moss J
Moss M
Mousley Mr
Moxham S
Munro A
Murcott P
Murgatroyd's Folly Limited
Murphy H
The late K Murray

Needham D
Neeson L
Nelson B
Nelson D
Newbery P
Newman S
Newton Mrs
Nichols P
Nicholson D
Nicholson E
Nicholson P
Niven J
Noble G
The late J V Norris
Norris M
North D & J
North-west Birding
Nutter J

Oake R & C
Oates E
Oates H
The late K O'Brian
Oldham M
Oldroyd A
O'Leary J
Oliver P
O'Neill J
O'Neill M
Ordnance Survey
Orrell G
Orton D
Osborn A J
Osborn B N
Osborn B
Osborn D
Osbourne G C
Osbourne M A A
Osbourne M A
Overty J
Owen L
Owens K
Owens M A

Padley J R
Page F G
Panetta S
Park M
Park S
Parker I
Parker J
Parker K
Parkes C R
Parkes P
Parkin D
Parkin H
Parnell R
Parrick J
Parrish J
Parry H
Parsons W E
Pateman L
Patient S
Pattison F
Paul & Co
Paul J
Pause G M
PDMS
Peck D
Peet J
Penn J
Penn R & R
Percival T
Peregrine Corporate Services Ltd
Perry J
Phillips C
Phillips D
Phillips D
Phillips J
Phillips J
Pickard E
The late A Pilcher-Clark
Pimm P
Pinder N J
Pirrie W
Pitts G M
PKF (Isle of Man) Limited
Plant P
Platt P M
Podobsta A
Ponton Mr & Mrs
Possan Gaelgagh
Postlethwaite L
Potts A
Potts D
Potts E
Powell D
Powell S
Prater E
Prescott S & J
Preston A
Price B
Price C
Price R
Pridham C
Prince C
Prior A
Progress Shaving
Prosser P
Pugh D
Pugh J
Putnam S J
Pye B L

Quaggan C
Qualtrough B
Qualtrough J W
Qualtrough T
Quane S
Quark J B
Quaye M J
Quayle A
Quayle A
Quayle B
Quayle C
Quayle E H
Quayle F S
Quayle H R
Quayle J & E
Quayle J R
Quayle J
Quayle J
Quayle M
Quayle P & J
Quayle P
Quayle P J
Quayle R
Quayle R
Quayle R
Quayle T R
Quayle T
Quigley W
Quilleash J
Quilleash S
Quilliam A
Quilliam J F
The late A Quillin
Quillin W
Quine Mr
Quine A
Quine J
Quine R D
Quinn J L M
Quirk B
Quirk J & R F
Quirk M
Quirk P
Quirk P

Quirk R
The late R Quirk
Quirk S
Quirk S

R P McAllister Memorial Trust
Radcliffe A D
Radcliffe B
Radcliffe D
Radcliffe E
Radcliffe F
Radcliffe G
Radcliffe J C
Radcliffe J N
Radcliffe R
Rae B
Randall D J
Ratcliffe J
Ratcliffe R & J
Rawcliffe R
Rawling D C
Rawson C
Rawson J
Raynor E
Reeves C
Reid S
Rennie F
Renshaw J
Renton P & D
Reynolds S
Richards D
Richardson D
Richardson I
Richmond M
Richmond N
Riddle T
Rigby L
Riley A
Riley M A
Rimmer M J
Ripamonti R
Roberts C
Roberts R
Robertshaw C
Robinson D
Robinson Q
Robson L
Rockwell M
Roger & Co
Rogers A
Rogers F
The late G Rogers
Rollins G
Ronan J E
Ronan J R
Ronan J
Roper H
Roper M
Roper P & C
Rosevear M
Rowe R B
Rowley J
Rowley J
Royal Society for the Protection of Birds
RSK Environment (IOM) Ltd
Rudge J
Rush A
Rushton A & G
Rusling P
Russell B
Russell C
Russell G
Rydeard S
Rye Meads Ringing Group

Sadler B
Sadler R
Salmon D E
Samson A R G
Samson L
Sanders A
Sapsford A & K
Sargent R
Sargent R
Saunders M
Sayer P A
Sayle J
Sayle S
Sayle T
Sayle V A
Scarffe A
Scarffe C T
Scarlett A
Schofield Mrs
Scott A
Scott B
Scott D
Scott I & D
Scott K & H
Scott R M
Scott R
Scott S
Scowcroft I
Scowcroft J A
SCS Ltd
Scuffil N
Seaward P A
Sefton Hotel
Sellick D
Selman R
Senn P A
Senn P A
Sewell S
Seybold M
Seymour F H
Shafto C
Shaikh A
Shanley D
Shanley J
Sharman S J
Sharp D R
Sharpe A & G
Sharpe D D
Sharpe D J
The late Mrs M Sharpe
Sharpe M F
Sharpe P
Sharples Mrs
Sharrock J T R
Shaw D M
Shaw J P
Shaw M
Shaw S
Shearan D P
Sheeley J
Sheen J
Shelley K
Shepherd T A
Sheppard B
The late J Sherry
Shields I W, & S
Shields J
Shillam C
Shillinglaw J A
Shimmin K
Shimmin N
Shimmin P
Sibbold S
Sign & Design
Simcocks Limited
Simons J
Simpkiss P
Simpson C
Simpson J
Simpson M
Simpson M
Sims M
Skelly M
Skillan D E
Skillen D
Skillicorn A
Skinner S
Slack C
Slater B
Slater S
Slatter S
Sleight I
Slinn J
Sloane K
SLR Consulting Limited
Small A
Smallshaw T
Smith D
Smith G
Smith I
Smith I
Smith J
Smith M
Smith R A
Smith W E & M
Smithy House Garage
Smyth J
Snell R A
Souter D
Souter R
Speak C
Speak P W
Speckter R
Spencer G
Spittal C
St John's Charitable Trust
St John Bates T
Stacey D
Stafford J
Stanley G
Stanley K
Starkey F
Starkey W
Steer T
Stephenson A
Stephenson C
Steriopulos G
Stevenson E
Stewart A
Stewart K
The late J Stigant
Stokes P
Stokoe J
Stone R
Stott A
Stott D
Stott M
Stout N A
Stovold J
Stowell J E
Stratford A
Stringer J
Strivens Mr
Strix Ltd
Stroud D
Stuart L
Stuart Smalley & Co
Sugden C
Sullivan J
Sutcliffe Mr
Sutherland R
Swindlehurst Mrs
Symes M R

The Taggart Family
Taggart Mr
Taggart E
The late Mrs F Taggart
Taggart G
Taggart J W
Taggart J
Taggart S G
Talbert V M
Talbot J
The late S Tarr
Tasker A T
Tasker M
Taubman A
Taylor G
The late J Taylor
Taylor J
Taylor J
Taylor J
Taylor N
Taylor R H
Taylor R
Taylor S
The late A L Teare
Teare B
Teare B
Teare F J
Teare I M
Teare J
Teare L
Teare M
Teare P H
Teare P N
Teare R D
Teare S
Teare V
Teare W J
Teare W R
Tedds J
Teggins J
Templeton Insurance Ltd
Templeton J K
Templeton L
Thacker D A
The Port Erin Gaslight & Aerated Waters Company Ltd
Thomas A
The late R D Thomas
Thomas R
Thompson A
Thompson D E
Thompson J
Thompson K
Thompson S
Thomsett A
Thorne J
Thornley M
Thorp K
Thorpe J P
Thrower S
Thrussell J
Tomlinson B
Tovell C J
Tower Insurance Co Ltd
Travers S
Trebicka I J W
Trimnell P
Trinder B N
Truelove H W
Turley M
Turner A E
Turner J E
Turner P W
Turner P
Turner R
Turvey M A
Turvey W

Uhlenbroek D C

The late D A Vale
van Genuchten E
Vanderplank J A
Velade Mr
Venables C J
Vent M
Veris Secretatial Ltd
Vernon E
Vernon J
Vernon J

Vick P
Vokins A
Vondy N

Wadsworth G R
Waggett T
Waiting B K & Mrs
Walden N
Walker A
Walker B
Walker R
Walker R
Walker Sir J & Lady
Walker Sir M & Lady
Wall G
Wallace M J
Waller A
Walls N
Walmsley J G
Walsh W R
Walters R
Walton I
Walton J & B
Walton T
Ward M
Ward R
Warren T A
Warrier L
Warrilow M I
Watkins V P
Watson M
Watson R A
Watson T
Watterson B A
Watterson C
Watterson C
Watterson D G
Watterson E J
Watterson G
Watterson K
Watterson M A
Watterson M
Weaver P
Webb J
Webb M
Webb N
Webster R
Welsh W H
Wenmar Farms Ltd
Wenn M
West N
Westcott S
Weston N G
Westwell P
Whalley M
Wheatley Mr & Mrs
Whipp M
Whipp M
The late T Whipp
Whipp T
White A R
White C
White J
White K
Wilcox M
Wild A F
Wild C
The Wildfowl & Wetlands Trust
Willaston School
Willers P A
Williams D
Williams G & A
Williams G
Williams J
Williams L
Williams P
Williams-Jones C R
Williamson D A
Williamson E
Williamson T F
Williamson T
Wilson A
Wilson A
Wilson G
Wilson J
Wilson M & I
Wilson M
Wilson M
Wilson S
Wilson-Spratt C
Winskill G & E H
Winterburn Mrs
Wolstencroft J
Wolstencroft J
Wolstenholme S E
Wood A F
Wood D E
Wood J
Wood N
Wood R
Wood R
Woodcock G L
Woodcock R
Woods E
Woodworth R
Woollams M E
Wormell C & K
Worner P
Worrall R
Wozniak P
Wrigall D
Wright & Co
Wright D
Wright J
Wright J
Wright P
Wright S
Wrigley A C
Wrigley R
Wrigley R

Yates B C
The late D Yewdall
Young H
Young S
Young W

Zurich Financial Services (Isle of Man) Group Services Limited

Index of birds mentioned in the the text

Vernacular names are indexed under the last word and scientific names under the generic name.
Principal references for the main species are indicated in bold text.
References are only included for those species mentioned within the main body of the text and for those mentioned within Appendix A.

Jeremy Paul ©